THIRD EDITION

Educational Assessment of Students

ANTHONY J. NITKO

University of Arizona

Merrill
Prentice Hall

Upper Saddle River, New Jersey   Columbus, Ohio

Dedicated to Veronica

Library of Congress Cataloging in Publication Data
Nitko, Anthony J.
    Educational assessment of students / Anthony J. Nitko.--3rd ed.
        p. cm.
    Includes bibliographical references and index.
    ISBN 0-13-013708-1
        1. Educational tests and measurements. I. Title.
    LB3051.N57 2001
    371.26--dc21   00-023012

Vice President and Publisher: Jeffery W. Johnston
Executive Editor: Kevin M. Davis
Editorial Assistant: Christina Kalisch
Development Editor: Heather Doyle Fraser
Production Editor: Julie Peters
Production Coordination: Clarinda Publication Services
Design Coordinator: Diane C. Lorenzo
Cover Designer: Allen Bumpus
Cover Photo: UniPhoto
Production Manager: Laura Messerly
Director of Marketing: Kevin Flanagan
Marketing Manager: Amy June
Marketing Services Manager: Krista Groshong

This book was set in Garamond and Arial Narrow by The Clarinda Company. It was printed
and bound by The Banta Company. The cover was printed by Phoenix Color Corp.

Earlier edition, entitled *Educational Tests and Measurement: An Introduction,* © 1983 by Harcourt
Brace Jovanovich.

Merrill
Prentice Hall

9 8 7 6 5 4 3 2 1
ISBN 0-13-013708-1

Preface

The goal of *Educational Assessment of Students*, Third Edition, is to help teachers and teachers in training to improve instruction through better assessment of students. It focuses directly on the professional practices of elementary and secondary schoolteachers. It is a core text written for a first course in educational testing and constructing classroom assessments. It serves equally as the textbook for an undergraduate course or a first graduate course in educational assessment. No formal course work in statistics or college mathematics is necessary to understand the text.

In preparing this edition, a new effort was made to make it easy for the reader to apply the material to classroom practice through clear explanations, many practical examples and illustrations, checklists, and step-by-step how-to instructions. As with previous editions, I have written the text from the viewpoint that teaching and assessment should blend together. To help students with real-world experiences, Internet website addresses have been added throughout to help students to quickly link to examples and resources outside the text.

The book covers basic concepts as well as a complete treatment of educational assessment—from developing plans that integrate teaching and assessment; to crafting objective, performance, and portfolio assessments; to evaluating students and discussing evaluations with parents; to interpreting state-mandated tests and standardized achievement tests.

It is important in a first course that students receive a balanced treatment of the topics. Thus, both the strengths and limitations of each assessment technique are explained. Research is cited that supports or refutes assessment and teaching practices.

This edition focuses more clearly on classroom assessment than the previous edition. Each chapter was revised with the goal of making the material more relevant to the practical issues teachers face. For example, mandated state programs have placed more emphasis on teachers aligning their classroom practices and assessments with state content and performance standards. In each chapter, I integrate suggestions for how to accomplish this alignment.

The book treats teachers as professionals. It recognizes that teachers' experiences and judgments are necessary for proper and valid use of educational assessment. I do not hesitate to point out teachers' erroneous judgments and assessment abuses, however, where good lessons can be learned from them. To ensure that the text material is in keeping with the competencies and standards held to be important by the profession, each chapter is keyed to the American Federation of Teachers, the National Council on Measurement in Education, and the National Education Association *Standards for Teacher Competence in Educational Assessment of Students* (reproduced in Appendix A).

Organization of the Text

As in the previous edition, this book is organized into three parts. Part One provides the foundation for classroom assessment. Part Two centers on how to plan and craft classroom assessments. Part Three discusses how to interpret and use standardized tests.

Each chapter begins with a list of learning targets that the reader should attain. Each learning target is keyed to the *Standards for Teacher Competence in Educational Assessment of Students*. Following the body of each chapter is a summary in list form to help the reader recall information. Each chapter concludes with a list of important concepts and terms, a set of exercises and discussion questions, and a brief annotated list of additional readings. Many of the exercises at the end of the chapters are performance tasks. These require applying and extending the principles taught in the chapter. Readers are often encouraged to compare their exercise results with those of others in the course to obtain greater insight into a topic. Instructors can use these exercises as a basis for in-class activities.

Part I, The Bases for Assessment in the Classroom, contains five chapters presenting the foundations for educational assessment. Chapter 1 discusses classroom decision making and how assessments help to improve it. It provides a brief overview of the assessment landscape, so the reader can see the broader picture of educational assessment before delving into specifics. Chapter 2 discusses goals and learning targets of classroom instruction. The chapter is simplified in this edition by presenting fewer cognitive taxonomies than the previous edition. New to this edition is a discussion of how state standards can be used to develop classroom learning targets for day-to-day teaching. Chapter 3 discusses the validity of assessment results. The chapter has been simplified to focus exclusively on the current conceptions of validity held by the profession. One part of the chapter focuses exclusively on the validity of the results of teacher-crafted assessments, the other on the validity of other assessment results a teacher and a school will use. Chapter 4 describes reliability. The order of presentation of the topics has been improved to make the material flow better for the reader. Chapter 5 discusses teachers', students', and administrators' ethical responsibilities and uses of assessments. It applies the National Council on Measurement in Education's *Code of Professional Responsibilities in Educational*

Measurement (reproduced in Appendix C) as an organizational framework. Also, this chapter describes legal issues regarding assessment and how assessments can be made to validly accommodate mainstreamed learners.

Part II, Crafting and Using Classroom Assessments, demonstrates how a teacher uses artistry and functionality to produce useful teaching tools. The ten chapters in this part provide complete coverage of how to craft virtually all types of assessments a teacher may need to use. Chapter 6 has been extensively rewritten to show clearly how teaching, assessing, and grading fit together. There are new examples showing how several different methods of assessment can be integrated into lesson plans, be matched with assessment purpose, and provide formative and summative assessment throughout an instructional unit. Chapter 7 discusses completion and true-false items, including multiple true-false items. Chapter 8 discusses how to craft multiple-choice and matching exercises. In this edition, material on alternative formats of objective items, such as masterlist and tabular matching exercises, have been integrated into this chapter. Chapter 9 focuses on crafting and marking essay items. Chapter 10 is devoted to assessing higher-order thinking skills, including problem solving and critical thinking. The presentation is simplified from the previous edition.

Two chapters are devoted to alternative and performance assessments in schools. Chapter 11 describes the basic concepts and major components of authentic and performance assessments. It surveys the many different types of performance assessments and projects that are currently used in schools. New to this edition is classroom assessment using the Multiple Intelligences Theory framework. Chapter 12 focuses exclusively on crafting and evaluating performance assessments and portfolios. The chapter shows how to craft the tasks, scoring rubrics, and rating scales necessary to produce valid results. The chapter applies the Dimensions of Learning Model as a framework for performance assessment design. Different methods of crafting rubrics are discussed. Chapter 13 focuses entirely on format, informal classroom assessment for purposes of diagnosing why a student is having difficulty learning. It shows how six different diagnostic assessment approaches may be integrated into the teaching process. Chapter 14 has been simplified, but is still about administering assessments, helping students do their best on assessments, and improving assessment tasks through item analysis. Item analysis for open-response items is new in this edition.

Chapter 15 has been extensively rewritten. It is organized in five major sections. Section One provides background for grading including grading and continuous assessment, formative and summative student assessment, and how various stakeholders use grades. Section Two presents various options that schools use to report student progress, including report cards, parent-teacher conferences, and—new to this edition—narrative reports. Section

Three focuses on sensible grading practices that result in valid summative grades for students. The chapter provides teachers with the tools for creating a grading philosophy that is logically consistent with both their teaching approach and their purposes for assessing students. The tools integrate all the planning considerations discussed in earlier chapters. As a result, teachers can use a coherent and sensible grading model. Linking grades to teaching and assessment plans; and discussions of special problems in grading, such as using zeros and the unclear meaning of failure, are new to this edition. Section Five shows how to set grade boundaries and combine scores to produce summative grades.

The text concludes with Part III, Interpreting and Using Standardized Tests. Chapter 16 describes different types of standardized achievement tests, how to administer them, and how to use their results. The chapter has been updated to reflect new editions of tests and to include material on how to select a standardized test that complements a state's mandated assessment program. Chapter 17 covers norm-referenced scores and contrasts them with criterion-referenced scores. Various types of scores are explained, emphasizing how a teacher should interpret and explain them to parents. Chapter 18 discusses how to locate and evaluate an appropriate standardized test to use in a school setting. The chapter updates material on how to use the Internet to obtain assessment information. Chapter 19 briefly summarizes the types of scholastic aptitude, vocational interest, and personality assessments a teacher may encounter in student reports. New editions of the tests are included. The chapter includes a discussion of aptitudes and learning, and how the classroom and school environments affect these.

No single introductory course is likely to cover all of these chapters in detail. However, with this text an instructor can choose material to suit the needs of teachers at different levels of professional development and experience. The book provides ample material for both independent study and later reference while teaching.

Supplemental Material

The appendixes are especially important for complete learning of educational assessment concepts and applications. Appendix A reproduces the *Standards for Teacher Competence in Educational Assessment of Students*, to which the learning targets of each chapter are keyed. Appendix B reproduces the *Code of Fair Testing Practices in Education*, which describes the obligations of test developers and test users in straightforward language. Appendix C reproduces the *Code of Professional Responsibilities in Educational Measurement*. Appendix D summarizes and gives examples of using several cognitive, affective, and psychomotor taxonomies of educational learning targets. Appendix E summarizes the general cross-curriculum learning targets derived from the

Dimensions of Learning Model. Appendix F illustrates the assessment of metacognition. Appendix G shows several alternative ways to craft an assessment blueprint for summative evaluation. Appendix H is a brief description of basic statistical concepts such as mean, standard deviation, and correlation. Appendix I shows examples of how to calculate reliability and decision-consisting indexes. Appendix J lists commonly used published tests and cites the volume and page of the *Mental Measurements Yearbooks* in which they are reviewed. Appendix K lists the major test publishers' Internet websites and postal addresses.

An Instructor's Manual provides numerous test items. The test bank is also planned in computerized form.

Acknowledgments

A project of this magnitude requires the help of many persons. I am very much indebted to the reviewers whose critical readings of the chapters in this edition's manuscript contributed greatly to their technical accuracy, readability, and pedagogy: Susan M. Brookhart, Duquesne University; Deborah Brown, West Chester University; Robert Lange, University of Central Florida; Craig Mertler, Bowling Green State University; Susan E. Phillips, Michigan State University; Anthony Truog, University of Wisconsin–Whitewater; Richard Wolf, Teachers College, Columbia University; and Michael J. Young, University of Pittsburgh.

I would also like to thank the reviewers of the second edition: Peter W. Airasian, Boston College; Lawrence M. Aleamoni, University of Arizona; Carol E. Baker, University of Pittsburgh; W. L. Bashaw, University of Georgia; Susan M. Brookhart, Duquesne University; Lee Doebler, University of Montevallo; Betty E. Gridley, Ball State University; Thomas M. Haladyna, Arizona State University; Charles Hughes, Pennsylvania State University; Louise F. Jernigan, Eastern Michigan University; Suzanne Lane, University of Pittsburgh; William P. Moore, University of Kansas; Pamela A. Moss, University of Michigan; Bruce Rogers, University of Northern Iowa; William M. Stallings, Georgia State University; Hoi K. Suen, Pennsylvania State University; James S. Terwilliger, University of Minnesota; Michael S. Trevisan, Washington State University; Kinnard White, University of North Carolina; and David R. Young, SUNY–Cortland.

My students at the School of Education, University of Pittsburgh; the Curriculum Development and Evaluation Centre, Botswana Ministry of Education; Jamaica Ministry of Education; and the Examination Development Center, Indonesia Ministry of Education and Culture used the second edition. They provided insightful feedback and corrections of errors that have greatly improved the usefulness of the text. Francis Amedahe helped classify chapter learning targets and write tests items. Huixing Tang of the Psychological Corporation, Wendy Yen of CTB/McGraw-Hill, Sara Hennings of Houghton Mifflin, James Impara of the Buros Institute of Mental Measure-

ments, and David Frisbie and Robert Forsyth of the Iowa Testing Program were most generous in helping me to locate information about, obtain copies of, and understand many of the standardized test materials described in this book. Kevin Davis, Julie Peters, Holly Jennings, and Christina Kalisch, of Merrill/Prentice Hall, as well as Emily Autumn of Clarinda Publication Services, encouraged and cajoled me at every stage from acquisition through production, and applied their considerable knowledge and skill to producing the book. To all of these persons, and others I have failed to mention, I offer my most sincere thanks and appreciation.

No one deserves more thanks, for this edition as well as past editions, than my best friend and darling wife Veronica. The bulk of the revisions for this edition were made evening and weekends in Dhaka, Bangladesh. Veronica made suggestions for improvement, providing a teacher's perspective. She typed the entire manuscript during the day while I was away on project activities. Her energy, enthusiasm, and constant encouragement sustained me during this revision process. She claims that "this is the last time," but I hope she will continue should there be another edition. To Veronica, then, I lovingly dedicate this book.

DISCOVER THE COMPANION WEBSITE ACCOMPANYING THIS BOOK

The Prentice Hall Companion Website: A Virtual Learning Environment

Technology is a constantly growing and changing aspect of our field that is creating a need for content and resources. To address this emerging need, we have developed an online learning environment for students and professors alike—Companion Websites—to support our textbooks.

In creating a Companion Website, our goal is to build on and enhance what the textbook already offers. For this reason, the content for each user-friendly website is organized by chapter and provides the professor and student with a variety of meaningful resources. Common features of a Companion Website include:

For the Professor—

Every Companion Website integrates **Syllabus Manager™**, an online syllabus creation and management utility.

- **Syllabus Manager™** provides you, the instructor, with an easy, step-by-step process to create and revise syllabi, with direct links into Companion Website and other online content without having to learn HTML.
- Students may logon to your syllabus during any study session. All they need to know is the web address for the Companion Website, and the password you've assigned to your syllabus.

- After you have created a syllabus using **Syllabus Manager™**, students may enter the syllabus for their course section from any point in the Companion Website.
- Class dates are highlighted in white and assignment due dates appear in blue. Clicking on a date, the student is shown the list of activities for the assignment. The activities for each assignment are linked directly to actual content, saving time for students.
- Adding assignments consists of clicking on the desired due date, then filling in the details of the assignment—name of the assignment, instructions, and whether or not it is a one-time or repeating assignment.
- In addition, links to other activities can be created easily. If the activity is online, a URL can be entered in the space provided, and it will be linked automatically in the final syllabus.
- Your completed syllabus is hosted on our servers, allowing convenient updates from any computer on the Internet. Changes you make to your syllabus are immediately available to your students at their next logon.

For the Student—

- **Chapter Objectives**—outline key concepts from the text
- **Interactive Self-quizzes**—complete with hints and automatic grading that provide immediate feedback for students

  After students submit their answers for the interactive self-quizzes, the Companion Website **Results Reporter** computes a percentage grade, provides a graphic representation of how many questions were answered correctly and incorrectly, and gives a question by question analysis of the quiz. Students are given the option to send their quiz to up to four email addresses (professor, teaching assistant, study partner, etc.).
- **Message Board**—serves as a virtual bulletin board to post—or respond to—questions or comments to a national audience
- **Net Searches**—offer links by key terms from each chapter to related Internet content
- **Web Destinations**—links to www sites that relate to chapter content

To take advantage of these and other resources, please visit the *Educational Assessment of Students* Companion Website at

www.prenhall.com/nitko

ABOUT THE AUTHOR

Anthony J. Nitko is an adjunct professor, Department of Educational Psychology, University of Arizona, and professor emeritus and former chairperson of the Department of Psychology in Education at the University of Pittsburgh. His research interests include curriculum-based criterion-referenced testing, integration of testing and instruction, classroom assessment, and the assessment of knowledge and higher-order thinking skills. His publications include the chapter "Designing Tests That Are Integrated with Instruction" in the third edition of *Educational Measurement*. He co-authored (with C. M. Lindvall) *Measuring Pupil Achievement and Aptitude*, (with T-C Hsu) *Pitt Educational Testing Aids* (PETA) (a package of computer programs for classroom teachers), and (with R. Glaser) the chapter "Measurement in Learning and Instruction" in the second edition of *Educational Measurement*.

Dr. Nitko has been the editor of the journal *Educational Measurement: Issues and Practice*, and was also editor of *d'News*, the AERA Division D newsletter. Some of the journals in which his research has appeared include *American Educational Research Journal*, *Applied Measurement in Education*, *Educational Evaluation and Policy Analysis*, *Educational Measurement: Issues and Practice*, *Educational Technology*, *Journal of Educational Measurement*, and *Research in Developmental Disabilities*.

Dr. Nitko has been a member of several committees of the American Educational Research Association, was elected secretary of AERA Division D, served on committees of the National Council on Measurement in Education, and was elected to the board of directors and as president of the latter. He received Fulbright awards to Malawi and Barbados and has served as a consultant to various government and private agencies in the United States, Bangladesh, Barbados, Botswana, Indonesia, Jamaica, Malawi, Namibia, and Singapore.

Brief Contents

Contents

APPENDIXES

The Bases for Assessment in the Classroom

CHAPTER 1

Classroom Decision Making and Using Assessment

Learning Targets[1]

After studying this chapter, you should be able to:

1. Give examples of teaching management decisions you need to make before, during, and after instruction. [4, 1, 2]

2. Give examples of assessment procedures that provide you with useful information for making the decisions you stated in Target 1. [1, 2, 3, 4]

3. Define and explain the relationships among teaching, assessment, testing, measurement, and evaluation. [6, 1]

4. Explain the principles that guide you in the process of selecting, developing, and using educationally meaningful assessments. [1, 3]

5. Describe and explain the wide range of educational decisions for which educators need quality assessments. [1, 6]

6. Distinguish between formative and summative evaluation. [1, 4]

7. Describe the type(s) of information assessments provide for making decisions about diagnostic/remedial actions, feedback to students/parents, feedback to teachers, motivating students, and assigning grades to students. [1, 3, 4]

8. Distinguish among selection decisions, placement decisions, classification decisions, counseling and guidance decisions, and credentialing/certification decisions. [1, 3, 6]

9. Explain criterion-referencing and norm-referencing and how they complement one another in educational decision making. [1, 4, 6]

10. Use technical terminology correctly to describe a given assessment procedure in terms of the kinds of items it uses, how student performance is scored, degree of standardization, administrative conditions, language emphasis of the scoring, emphasis on speed of responding, the basis for interpreting scores, and what attribute is measured. [6, 4, 3]

11. Explain how each of the Standards for Teacher Competence in Educational Assessment of Students is related to your teaching activities before, during, and after instruction. [6, 1, 7]

12. Explain how each of the terms and concepts listed at the end of this chapter apply to educational assessments. [6]

I t is almost impossible for you to have attended school without having been exposed to a wide variety of educational and psychological assessment procedures. The fact that you are reading this book for a testing and measurement course places you not only among test takers, but among the successful test takers. Think for a few minutes: How many ways have

---

[1]The Learning Targets that begin each chapter are cross-referenced to the American Federation of Teachers, National Council on Measurement in Education, and National Education Association (1990), *Standards for Teacher Competence in Educational Assessment of Students* (see Appendix A). The numbers that follow each learning target statement refer to one or more of the standards. The order of the standards represents the closeness of the match to the standards: The closest match is listed first. Francis Amedahe helped to classify the learning targets.

you been assessed in your life? When did your assessment experiences begin? Consider this example:

> Meghan's educational assessment began in kindergarten with an interview and an observation. The state in which she lived had no mandatory kindergarten requirement. On registration day, Meghan and her mother came to school and were briefly interviewed. Meghan's cognitive and social-emotional skills were rated by a teacher. Her development was judged normal, and she attended kindergarten.
>
> During the year she experienced difficulty in paying attention to the teacher and participating in group activities, although she was neither aggressive nor hostile. She was given a "readiness test" at the end of kindergarten and performed as an average child. Her teacher recommended that she continue on to first grade, but her parents balked: They didn't think that she was ready.
>
> They took her to a child guidance clinic and requested further psychological assessment. The clinical psychologist administered an individual intelligence test and a "projective test" in which she was asked to tell a story about what was happening in each of a set of pictures. The psychologist interviewed her, her parents, and her teacher. She was described by the psychologist as normal, both in cognitive ability and in social-emotional development.
>
> Her parents withdrew her from the school she was attending and placed her in another school to repeat kindergarten. Later, they reported that whereas her first experience was difficult for her, her second kindergarten year was a great success. In their view, a teacher who was particularly sensitive to Meghan's needs helped her cognitive development to proceed rapidly. By the end of the year she had also become more confident in herself and regularly participated in group activities.

In the situation just illustrated, assessments provided information. Different persons evaluated the information and reached different conclusions. Decisions needed to be and were made, however. Perhaps different decisions could have been made based on the same information.

This brief anecdote shows assessments being used rather early in the person's life. Most of us recall more easily the assessments applied to us later in our lives, as older children, and as adults. You may not even associate the term *assessment* with Meghan's interviews. Yet, as shall be explained later, the interview is included in the broad definition of assessments, because the basic principles of assessment apply as well to it as to other, more familiar procedures.

Meghan's situation also illustrates that assessment results can contribute to a decision, but the results may not be interpreted in the same way by everyone concerned. Although it may appear that Meghan's parents were right in having her repeat kindergarten, there is no way of ascertaining what would have happened if she had gone straight to first grade, because she didn't.

Decisions involve the use of various kinds of information. Sometimes test scores play a major role; at other times, less formal assessments play a more dominant role. This book examines a variety of decisions for which assessments are used in education, especially in the classroom. Each time, it identifies the basic principles that relate to the evaluation and use of assessment information. It emphasizes basic principles rather than prescriptions to follow blindly, even though you will find some of those too. However, if you understand the basic principles, you should be able to determine when those and other prescriptions are inappropriate.

TEACHERS' CLASSROOM DECISIONS

Teaching and learning require you to constantly gather information and make decisions. Teachers often need to make decisions about students at the rate of one every 2 to 3 minutes (Shavelson & Stern, 1981). Sound teaching decisions require sound information. Sound assessment procedures gather sound information. Researchers estimate that teachers may spend from one third to one half of their time in assessment-related activities (Stiggins, Conklin, & Associates, 1992). A few examples of questions you must answer when making teaching decisions follow. Examples of assessment procedures that may give you useful information for making the decisions are listed in parentheses.

Decisions Before Beginning Teaching

1. What content do I need to cover during the next day, week, month, marking period, etc.? (*Review the curriculum, the syllabus, the textbook, and the formal tests your students will need to pass.*)

2. What abilities (cultural background factors, interests, skills, etc.) of my students do I need to take into account as I plan my teaching activities? (*Informal observation of the students during class; conversations with students' previous teachers; scholastic aptitude test results' previous teachers; scholastic aptitude test results; students' past grades and standardized test results; knowledge of the student's personal family circumstances.*)

3. What materials are appropriate for me to use with this group of students? (*Informal observation of students' motivations, interests, beliefs, and experience with the content you will teach; informal observations about students' attitudes toward learning the topics at hand; results from pretests, previous teacher's evaluations, and standardized achievement tests.*)

4. With what learning activities will my students and I need to be engaged as I teach the lesson (unit, course)? (*Review the types of activities I used previously that stimulated the interests of my students; analyze the sequence of the learning activities students will follow; review the student achievement that resulted when the activities were used with other students.*)

5. What learning targets do I want my students to achieve as a result of my teaching? (*Review statements of goals and learning objectives; review test questions students should be able to answer; review performances and thinking skills students should be able to demonstrate after learning.*)

6. How should I organize and arrange the students in the class for the upcoming lessons and activities? (*Informal observation of students with special learning and social needs; informal observation and recall of students' behavior during previous learning activities; information about what classroom arrangements worked best in the past when my students were learning similar targets.*)

Decisions During Teaching

1. Is my lesson going well? Are students catching on (i.e., learning)? (*Observations of students during learning activities; student responses to questions I have asked them; observing student interactions.*)

2. What should I do to make this lesson (activity) work better? (*Diagnosis of the types of errors students made or erroneous thinking students are using; searching my memory for alternative ways to teach the material; identifying which students are not participating or are acting inappropriately.*)

3. What feedback should I give each student about how well he or she is learning? (*Informal observation and experience on the amount and type of praise different students require; information about the quality of each student's learning of the intended target performance; homework and quiz results; interviewing students.*)

4. Are my students ready to move to the next activity in the learning sequence? (*Informal observation and checking students' completed work; questioning students about their understanding; students' homework, quiz, and test results.*)

Decisions After a Teaching Segment

1. How well are my students achieving the short- and long-term instructional targets? (*Classroom tests, projects, observations, interviews with students, standardized test results.*)

2. What strengths and weaknesses will I report to each student and to his or her guardian or parent? (*Observations of each student's classroom participation; review each student's homework results; review each student's standardized achievement and scholastic aptitude test results; review information about a student's personal family circumstances.*)

3. What grade should I give each student for the lesson or unit, marking period, or course? (*Results from classroom learning activities, quizzes, tests, class projects, papers, labs, etc.; informal observation about how well the student has attained the intended learning targets; knowledge of the possible short- and long-term consequences to the student of reporting a particular grade.*)

4. How effectively did I teach this material to the students? (*Summaries of the class's performance on the important instructional targets; summaries of the class's performance on selected questions on standardized tests; summaries of how well the students liked the activities and lesson materials.*)

5. How effective are the curriculum and materials I used? (*Summaries of informal observations of students' interests and reactions to the learning activities and materials; summaries of the class's achievement on classroom tests that match the curriculum; summaries of several classes' performance on selected areas of standardized tests.*)

These lists of questions are not exhaustive; you may wish to list several others. Later in this chapter we discuss several other educational decisions that need to be made by and for students. However, the preceding examples do illustrate that your teaching decisions require you to use many different types of information. Further, they illustrate that the exact type of information you need varies greatly from one teaching situation to the next. Remember that you cannot expect to make good decisions as you teach unless you have good quality information on which to base these decisions.

DISTINCTIONS AMONG ASSESSMENTS, TESTS, MEASUREMENTS, AND EVALUATIONS

The general public often uses the terms *assessment, test, measurement,* and *evaluation* interchangeably, but it is important for you to distinguish among them. The meanings of the terms, as applied to situations in schools, are explained in the following paragraphs.

Assessments

Assessment is a broad term defined as a process for obtaining information that is used for making decisions about students, curricula and programs, and educational policy (see American Federation of Teachers, National Council on Measurement in Education, and National Education Association, 1990). Decisions about students include managing classroom instruction, placing students into different types of educational programs, assigning them to appropriate categories, guiding and counseling them, selecting them for educational opportunities, and credentialing and certifying their competence. Decisions about curricula and programs include decisions about their effectiveness (summative evaluations) and about ways to improve them (formative evaluations). Decisions about educational policy are made at the local school district level, the state level, and the national level. Figure 1.1 illustrates some of the decisions and subdecisions for which educational assessments provide information.

When we say we are "assessing a student's competence," we mean we are collecting information to help us decide the degree to which the student has achieved the learning targets. A large number of assessment techniques may be used to collect this information. These include formal and informal observations of a student; paper-and-pencil tests; a student's performance on homework, lab work, research papers, projects, and during oral questioning; and analyses of a students' records.

Guidelines for Selecting and Using Classroom Assessments

Although *assessment* is a broad and comprehensive term, you should not think of assessment as simply referring to a collection of techniques. Neither should you think that every information-gathering activity is assessment. Remember that assessment is a process for obtaining information for making a particular educational decision. Because you should focus your assessment activities on the information you need to make particular educational decisions, you need to become competent in selecting and using assessments. Here is a set of guiding principles that you should follow to select and use educational assessments meaningfully.

1. *Be clear about the learning target you want to assess.* Before you can assess a student, you must know the kind(s) of student knowledge, skill(s), and performance(s) about which you need information. The knowledge, skills, and performances you want students to learn are sometimes called *achievement targets*. The more clearly you are able to specify the learning targets, the better you will be able to select the appropriate assessment techniques.

2. *Be sure that the assessment technique(s) you select actually match the learning target.* "Do we want to evaluate students' problem-posing and problem-solving in mathematics? Experimental research in science? Speaking, listening, and facilitating a discussion? Doing document-based historical inquiry? Thoroughly revising a piece of imaginative writing until it 'works' for the reader? Then let our assessment(s) be built out of such exemplary intellectual challenges" (Wiggins, 1990, p. 1). The assessment techniques selected should be as practical and efficient to use as possible, but practicality and efficiency should not be the overriding considerations.

3. *Be sure that the selected assessment techniques serve the needs of the learners.* Proper assessment and evaluation show students concrete examples of what they are expected to do with their learning. Assessment techniques should provide learners with opportunities for determin-

ing specifically what they have achieved and specifically what needs to be done to improve their performance. Therefore, you should select assessment techniques that provide meaningful feedback to the learners about how closely they have approximated the learning targets. Good assessment is good instruction.

4. *Whenever possible, be sure to use multiple indicators of performance for each learning target.* One format of assessment (such as short-answer questions or matching exercises) provides an incomplete picture of what a student has learned. Because one assessment format tends to emphasize only one aspect of a complex learning target, it typically underrepresents that learning target. Using triangulation or multiple modalities of assessment usually enhances the validity of your assessments. Matching exercises, for example, emphasize recall and recognition of factual information; essay questions emphasize organizing ideas and writing skill under the pressure of time limits; and a month-long project emphasizes freely using resources, research, and more thorough analyses of the topic. All three of these assessment techniques may be needed to ascertain the extent to which a student has achieved a given learning target.

5. *Be sure that when you interpret the results of assessments you take their limitations into account.* Although Guiding Principle 2 calls for increasing the authenticity or meaningfulness of the assessment techniques, assessments that occur in schools cannot completely reproduce those things we want students to learn in "real life." The information we obtain, even from multiple assessments, is only a *sample* of a student's attainment of a learning target. Because of this, information from assessment contains *sampling error*. Also, factors such as a student's physical and emotional conditions further limit the extent to which we can obtain truly accurate information. Teachers, and others, must make decisions nevertheless. The decisions, however, must keep these limitations in mind.

Tests

Testing Individuals A **test** is a concept narrower than assessment. It is defined as an instrument or systematic procedure for observing and describing one or more characteristics of a student using either a numerical scale or a classification scheme. In schools, we usually think of a test as a paper-and-pencil instrument with a series of questions that students must answer. These tests are usually scored by adding together the "points" a student earned on each question. Thus, they describe the student using a numerical scale. Similarly, a preschool child's cognitive development could be observed by using the *Wechsler Pre-School and Primary Scale of Intelligence* (see Chapter 19) and described as having a percentile rank of 50 (see Chapter 17). Other systematic observation procedures such as the play

FIGURE 1.1 Examples of types of educational decisions for which assessments may be used.

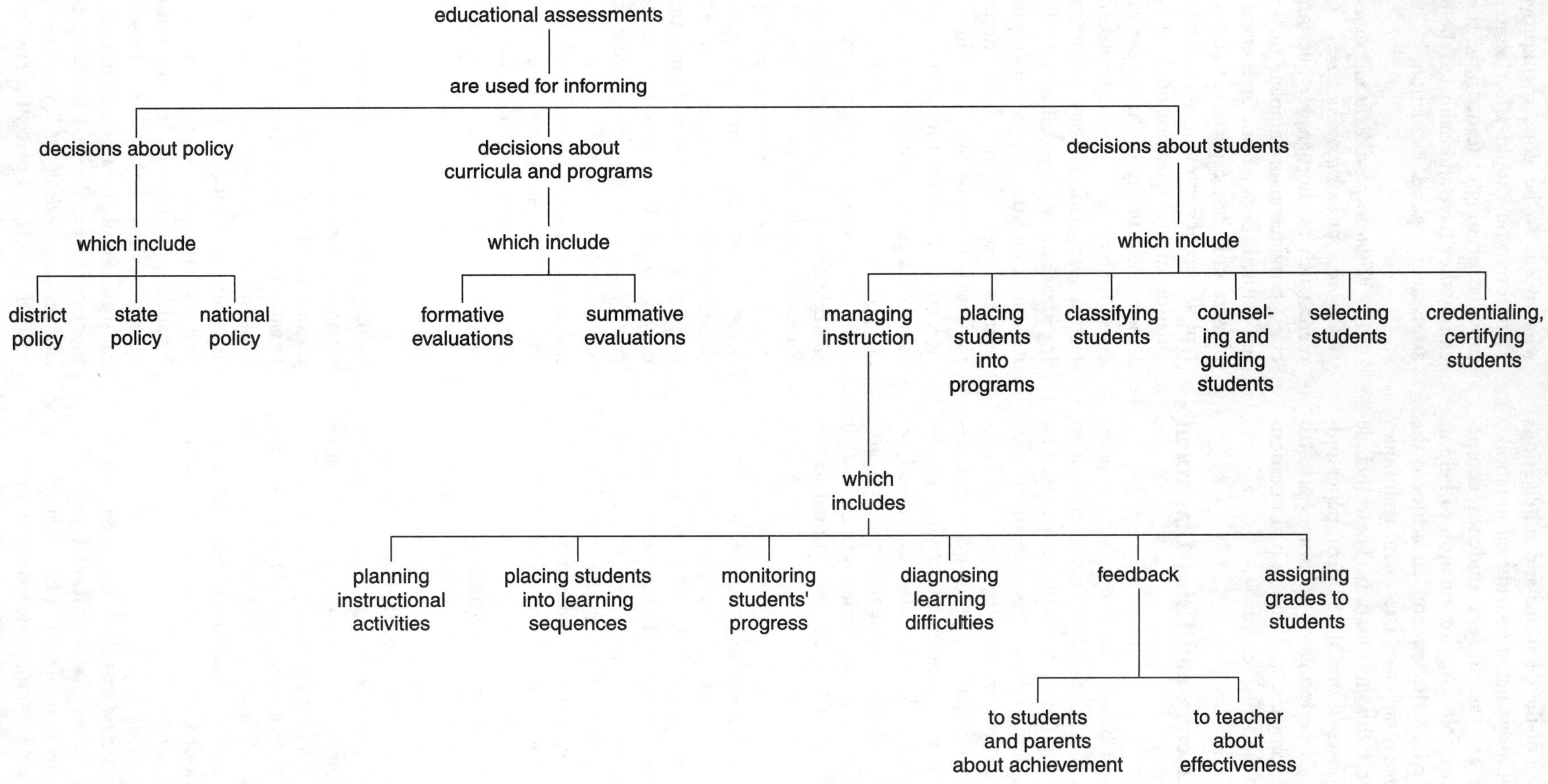

educational assessments

are used for informing

- decisions about policy
  - which include
    - district policy
    - state policy
    - national policy

- decisions about curricula and programs
  - which include
    - formative evaluations
    - summative evaluations

- decisions about students
  - which include
    - managing instruction
      - which includes
        - planning instructional activities
        - placing students into learning sequences
        - monitoring students' progress
        - diagnosing learning difficulties
        - feedback
          - to students and parents about achievement
          - to teacher about effectiveness
    - placing students into programs
    - classifying students
    - counseling and guiding students
    - selecting students
    - credentialing, certifying students
    - assigning grades to students

interview (Murphy, 1956), which is sometimes used by child development specialists with preschoolers, describe the child using a classification scheme. For example, a child may be described as "ego centered" or "drive centered." These categories represent constructs based in Freudian psychological theories.

Survey Testing Programs Although it is natural to assume that tests are designed to provide information about an individual, this is not always true. Some states have testing programs designed to determine whether their schools have attained certain goals or standards. Although these tests are administered to individual students, the focus is on measuring the effectiveness of a school or its programs. In such cases, individual names are not associated with scores, and all students do not need to answer identical questions. The "score" for the school system or for the building at a specific grade level is usually the average score of the students who took the test.

Another example of an assessment program designed to survey the educational system rather than individual students is the National Assessment of Educational Progress (NAEP) (Merwin & Womer, 1969; Mullis, 1991; Tyler, 1966). The NAEP assesses the impact of the nation's educational efforts by describing what students are able to do. (Details are found at http://nces.ed.gov/nationsreportcard). Assessment tasks are assigned to students on a random sampling basis, so that not every student has the same or comparable tasks. Thus, comparisons of individuals are not possible. The idea is to use the assessment to show the progress of education in the entire country. An example of the aspects of reading assessed in the 1992 to 2000 National Assessment is shown in Table 1.1.

Surveys are efficient ways to gather information about the average performance of a group of students, because each student is assessed using very few tasks. This gain in efficiency of assessing the group is at the expense of being able to validly describe the achievement of individual students.

Measurement

Measurement is defined as a procedure for assigning numbers (usually called *scores*) to a specified attribute or characteristic of a person in such a way that the numbers describe the degree to which the person possesses the attribute.

An important feature of the number-assigning procedure in measurement is that the resulting scores maintain the order that exists in the real world among the people being measured. At the *minimum* this would mean, for example, that if you are a better speller than I, a test that measures our spelling ability should result in your score (your measurement) being higher than mine.

For many of the characteristics measured in education and psychology, the number-assigning procedure is to count the correct answers or to sum points earned on a test. Alternately, we may use a scale to rate quality of a student's product (for example, an essay or a response to an open-ended mathematics task) or performance (how well the student carries out chemistry lab procedures). (See Chapter 12 for examples.) There has been considerable debate in the field of psychometrics as to whether such procedures are sufficient to call measurement in psychology and education anything but crude (Campbell, 1928; Johnson, 1928, 1936; McGregor, 1935; Pfanzagl, 1968; Rozeboom, 1966; Stevens, 1951; Suppes & Zinnes, 1963). Although the debate about crudeness of educational measurement surfaces from time to time, most measurement specialists would probably agree that even if a counting or rating procedure is crude, as a practical matter, if scores from assessments are validated by using data from research, they are useful (Jones, 1971; Lord and Novick, 1968; Messick, 1989; Rozeboom, 1966).

You can see from the preceding definitions that an assessment may or may not provide measurements. If a procedure describes a student by qualitative labels or categories, the student is assessed, but not measured in the sense used here. *Assessment* is a broader term than *test* or *measurement*, because not all types of assessments yield measurements.

Evaluation

Evaluation is defined as the process of making a value judgment about the worth of a student's product or performance. For example, you must judge a student's writing as exceptionally good for his grade placement. This evaluation may lead you to encourage the student to enter a national essay competition. In order to make this evaluation, you would have had to assess his writing ability. You may gather information by reviewing the student's journal, comparing his writing to other students and to known quality standards of writing, and so on. Such assessments provide information you may use to judge the quality or worth of the student's writing. A judgment of high quality would lead to a decision to encourage him to enter the competition. Evaluations are the bases for decisions about what course of action should be followed.

Evaluation may or may not be based on measurements or test results. Clearly, evaluation does occur in the absence of tests, measurements, and other objective information. You can—and probably often do—evaluate students on the basis of assessments such as systematic observation and qualitative description, without measuring them. Even if objective information is available and used, evaluators have to integrate it into their own experiences and perspectives to come to decisions. So degrees of subjectivity, inconsistency, and bias influence all evaluations. Testing and measurement, because they are more standardized and objective than other assessment techniques, reduce some of the inconsistency and subjectivity that influence evaluation. To say, however, that using tests and measurements

TABLE 1.1 Illustration of the Reading Literacy Framework for the National Assessment of Educational Progress showing the types of reading abilities assessed.

| | Constructing, Extending, and Examining Meaning | | | |
	Personal Reflection and Response	Demonstrating a Critical Stance	Initial Understanding	Developing Interpretation
	Requires the reader to connect knowledge from the text with his/her own personal background knowledge. The focus here is on how the text relates to personal knowledge.	Requires the reader to stand apart from the text and consider it.	Requires the reader to provide an initial impression or unreflected understanding of what was read.	Requires the reader to go beyond the initial impression to develop a more complete understanding of what was read.
Reading for Literary Experience	How did this character change your idea of _____? Is this story similar to or different from your own experience?	Rewrite this story with _____ as a setting or _____ as a character. How does this author's use of _____ (irony, personification, humor) contribute to _____?	What is the story/plot about? How would you describe the main character?	How did the plot develop? How did this character change from the beginning to the end of the story?
Reading for Information	What current event does this remind you of? Does this description fit what you know about _____? Why?	How useful would this article be for _____? Explain. What could be added to improve the author's argument?	What does this article tell you about _____? What does the author think about this topic?	What caused this event? In what ways are these ideas important to the topic or theme?
Reading to Perform a Task	In order to _____, what information would you need to find that you don't know right now? Describe a situation where you could leave out step X.	Why is this information needed? What would happen if you omitted this?	What is this supposed to help you do? What time can you get a non-stop flight to X? (Search)	What will be the result of this step in the directions? What must you do before this step?

Source: Adapted from Reading Framework for the National Assessment of Educational Progress: 1992–2000 (pp. 18–19) by National Assessment Governing Board, n.d., Washington, DC: U.S. Government.

(or, in general, quantitative information) "greatly improves" evaluation is itself a bias toward the technological.

Not all evaluations are of individual students. You also can evaluate a textbook, a set of instructional materials, an instructional procedure, a curriculum, or an educational program. Each of these things may be evaluated during development as well as after they are completely developed. The terms *formative* and *summative evaluation* are used to distinguish the roles of evaluation during these two periods (Cronbach, 1963; Lindvall & Cox, 1970; Scriven, 1967).

Formative evaluation is judgment about quality or worth made during the design or development of instructional materials, instructional procedures, curricula, or educational programs. The evaluator directs these judgments toward modifying, forming, or otherwise improving the product before it is widely used in schools. A teacher also engages in formative evaluation when revising lessons or learning materials by using information obtained from their previous use. Sometimes we speak of *formative evaluation of students*. This means we are judging the quality of a student's achievement of a learning target while the student is still in the process of learning it. Such judgment can help us guide a student's next learning steps.

Summative evaluation is judgment about the quality or worth of already-completed instructional materials, instructional procedures, curricula, or educational programs. Such evaluation tends to summarize strengths and weaknesses; it describes the extent to which a properly implemented program or procedure has attained its stated goals and objectives. Summative evaluations, more than formative evaluations, inform the consumer whether a particular product "works" and under which conditions or under what degree of implementation. Summative evaluations usually are directed less toward providing the developer with suggestions for improvement than are formative evaluations. Sometimes we speak of *summative evaluation of students*. By this we mean judging the quality or worth of a student's achievement after the instructional process is completed. Giving letter grades on report cards is one example of reporting your summative evaluation of a student's achievement during the preceding marking period.

ASSESSMENT AND EDUCATIONAL DECISIONS ABOUT STUDENTS

As we have discussed, assessment provides information for decisions about students, curricula and programs, and educational policy. In this section we discuss several types of educational decisions that are made about students so you may have a better idea of the purposes for which assessments are used.

Understanding the features of different types of decisions will help you to evaluate various assessment techniques that you may be considering to help you make the decisions. There is no simple answer to the question, "Is this a good assessment procedure?" As you will learn in this course, an assessment procedure may serve some types of decisions very well, but may not serve others well. Understanding the different types of decisions will also help you to explain to parents the purpose(s) for which you used various assessment procedures with their children. Finally, although you may not be required to make all of these types of student decisions yourself, by the time your students have completed their education they will have experienced virtually all of them.

Instructional Management Decisions

Your classroom is a decision-rich environment. You must make many decisions, including planning instructional activities, placing students into learning sequences, monitoring students' progress, diagnosing students' learning difficulties, providing students and parents with feedback about achievements, evaluating teaching effectiveness, and assigning grades to students. We described previously some of the questions that need to be answered to make these decisions.

Instructional Diagnosis and Remediation   Sometimes the instruction you or your school prearranges for an individual student is not effective: The student may need special remedial help or special instruction, relying on alternative methods or materials. Assessments that provide some of the information needed to make this type of decision are called **diagnostic assessments.** Diagnostic decisions center on the question, "What learning activities should I use to best adapt to this student's individual requirements and thereby maximize the student's opportunities to attain the chosen learning target?" Diagnosis implies identifying both the appropriate content and the features of the learning activities in which a student should be engaged to attain the learning target (Glaser & Nitko, 1971; Nitko, 1989; Nitko & Hsu, 1974).

The art of diagnostic assessment is not well developed. One direction toward which diagnostic assessment has turned is the fine-grain analysis of a student's performance. What prerequisite skills are strong or weak? What misinformation or inappropriate thinking processes and associations may interfere with the student's achievement of the learning target? You can craft assessments to answer only some questions such as these. There are at least five approaches to diagnosing a student's learning difficulties. These are described in Chapter 13, along with suggestions for how to craft appropriate assessment techniques.

Feedback to Students   Assessments also provide feedback to students about their learning. Feedback, however, is likely to improve learning only under certain conditions. Simply assessing students and reporting the results to them is not likely to affect their performance. Learners must review both correct and incorrect performance and, in addition, be able to correct their incorrect performance. Therefore, teachers who give students only their grade on a paper or test are not providing enough feedback for them to improve.

Assessments can be used to provide feedback that facilitates learning, provided they are integrated into the instructional process. Feedback from the classroom assessment procedure will not facilitate learning if the students do not have command of the prerequisite learning and/or have comprehended little or nothing of the lesson before the assessment was administered. It is especially important that student errors be corrected—or that the students correct their own errors—before going on to new instruction. Similarly, it is important that feedback, either in the form of assessment results or other information, is provided frequently during the lesson. Additional discussion of feedback appears in Chapter 13.

Feedback to the Teacher Remember that assessments provide feedback to the teacher as well as to students—information about how well students have learned and how well the teacher has taught. Of course, if students have failed to grasp important points, material should be re-taught before proceeding to new material.

Modeling Learning Targets Assessments define for students what you want them to learn. Students can compare their current performance on the learning target with the desired performance. You may teach them to identify the way(s) in which their current performance matches the expected performance and how it is deficient. Your teaching can focus on how to remedy the deficiencies. In these ways, good assessment is good instruction. Also, as students evaluate their own performance, you may teach them the appropriate criteria for judging how well they are learning as well as teaching them what is important to learn.

Motivating Students Assessments may also motivate students to study. Unfortunately, some teachers use this form of accountability as a weapon rather than as a constructive force. Teachers may hope that by using an assessment as a possible threat they can increase the seriousness with which their students study. Sometimes teachers use the "surprise quiz" or "pop quiz" in this manner to encourage more frequent studying and less cramming.

Employing assessments this way cannot be justified through research studies. Further, assessments for accountability ought to be viewed in a more positive light: as roles integral to instruction and as mechanisms for feedback to students (Glaser & Nitko, 1971). Also, teachers or parents who stress test performance as the sole or the major criterion for school success may create undue test anxiety for students. As a result, students may perform poorer in the long run. This point is discussed again in Chapter 14.

Assigning Grades to Students One of the most obvious reasons for giving classroom assessments is to help you to assign grades to students. Although teachers continually assess their students' progress in informal ways, it is necessary for them to "officially" record their evaluations of students' progress through grades. The grades or symbols (A, B, C, etc.) that you report represent your evaluations or judgments about the quality or worth of your students' achievement of the important learning targets. Use a mixture of formats of assessment to provide the information you need to make these evaluations. Although good teaching practice and common sense indicate that scores on tests should not be the only information on which to base a student's grade, many teachers fall back on test scores to justify the grades they assign. Assigning grades involves evaluative decisions, but subjective judgments are often difficult to justify and explain. Tests, especially those of the "objective" variety, give the appearance that judgmental subjectivity is reduced, even though this is not necessarily true. A more complete discussion of grading, including suggestions for assigning grades, is given in Chapter 15.

Selection Decisions

Most people are familiar with **selection decisions:** An institution or organization decides that some persons are acceptable while others are not; those not acceptable are rejected and no longer are the concern of the institution or organization. This feature—rejection and the elimination of those rejected from immediate institutional concern—is central to a selection decision (Cronbach & Gleser, 1965).

An educational institution often uses assessments to provide part of the information on which to base selection decisions. For example, college admissions are often selection decisions: Some candidates are admitted and others are not; those not admitted are no longer the college's concern. Some critics may argue, however, that those rejected are of concern to society generally.

When an institution uses an assessment procedure for selection, it is important for it to show that the candidates' results on these assessments bear a relationship to success in the program or job for which the institution is selecting persons. If the institution's data do not show that these assessment results can distinguish effectively between those candidates likely to succeed and those unlikely to succeed, then these assessment procedures should be improved or eliminated. It may be illegal to continue to use assessment results that bear no relationship to success on the job (United States Supreme Court, 1971; Equal Employment Opportunity Commission, Civil Service Commission, Department of Justice, Department of Labor, & Department of the Treasury, 1979).

Selection decisions need not be perfect, however, and assessment results cannot be expected to have perfect validity for selection decisions (see Chapter 3). The use of imperfect assessments in selection is shown in a simplified way in Figure 1.2. Some applicants would have been suc-

FIGURE 1.2 A simplified illustration of the process of using assessments in a selection situation and the consequences of those decisions. The assessments and the decision rules are evaluated in terms of their consequences.

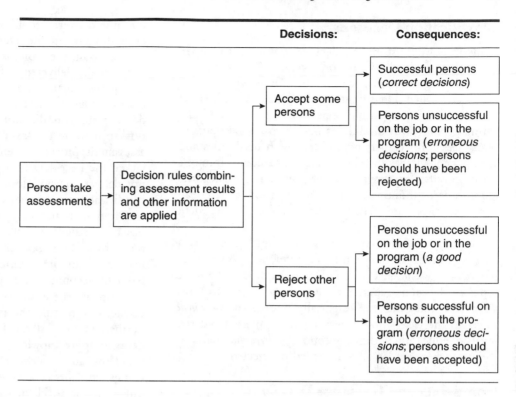

cessful had they been selected instead of rejected; and some, even though they were accepted, turned out to be unsuccessful. Assessments can be evaluated, then, in terms of the consequences of the decisions made when using them. This subject is taken up in Chapter 3.

Placement Decisions

Selecting someone to fill a job opening, or to be admitted to a particular college, is quite different than sectioning a high school class into those receiving different levels of instruction (remedial, regular, honors), forming reading groups in first grade, or dividing a group of kindergartners into those who will or will not receive extra perceptual skills training. The difference is this: In job and college selection situations, rejection is possible; the institution is not concerned about what happens to those rejected. In public school situations, the institutions must make provision for all persons: Unconcerned rejection is not possible. Those students not put into honors sections, upper reading sections, or other special sections, for example, still need to be taught and to be educated to the limits of their ability. Nor can persons be legally excluded from the educational process because of their disabilities (Public Law 94–142, 1975). Thus, instead of selection, we must consider placement.

Placement decisions are characterized as follows: Persons are assigned to different levels of the same general type of instruction, education, or work; no one is rejected, but all remain within the institution to be assigned to some level (Cronbach, 1990; Cronbach & Gleser, 1965).

Those students not enrolled in honors sections, for example, must be placed at other educational levels. Students with low first-grade reading readiness test scores, for example, cannot be sent home. They must be placed into appropriate educational levels and taught to read. You may recognize a decision as a placement decision by noting whether the institution must account for all candidates; the institution's unconcerned rejection of candidates is not possible.

Many, if not most decisions in schools are placement decisions. Oftentimes educators who use the language of selection are, upon closer examination, speaking about placement decisions. For example, when an educator speaks of "screening" students for a gifted and talented program, the decisions are actually placement decisions because their ultimate purpose is to place *all* students into appropriate educational programs. The schools are not free to teach some to read and to reject the rest. If one instructional method is inappropriate for a particular student, then an appropriate alternative method needs to be found. In the end, all students are taught, and most learn to read.

The criteria used to evaluate the quality assessment results used for placement are different from those used to evaluate assessment results used for selection. Assessment results used for educational placement are of high quality if the students who are assigned to the different educational programs on the basis of those results achieve better than they would have if the results were not used for placement. Chapter 3 details how to judge the validity of placement assessment procedures.

Classification Decisions

Sometimes we must make a decision that results in a person being assigned to one of several different but unordered categories, jobs, or programs. These types of decisions are called **classification decisions** (Cronbach & Gleser, 1965). For example, legislation in the area of educating persons with disabilities has given a legal status to many labels for classifying children with disabilities and strongly encourages the classification of students into one (or more) of a few designated categories. These categories are unordered (blindness is not higher or lower than deafness), so these are classification decisions rather than placement decisions.

You may consider *classification* as a more general term that subsumes *selection* and *placement* as special cases (Cronbach & Gleser, 1965). This book considers the three types of decisions separately. *Classification* refers to cases where the categories are essentially unordered, *placement* refers to the case where the categories represent ordered levels of education without rejection, and *selection* refers to the case where students are accepted or rejected.

Counseling and Guidance Decisions

Assessment results are frequently used to assist students in exploring and choosing careers and in directing them to prepare for the careers they select. A single assessment result is not used for making guidance and counseling decisions. Rather, a *series of assessments* is administered, including an interview, an interest inventory, various aptitude tests, a personality questionnaire, and an achievement battery. Information from these assessments, along with additional background information, is discussed with the student during a series of counseling sessions. This facilitates a student's decision-making processes and is an entree to the exploration of different careers. Exploring career options is likely to be an ongoing and changing series of decisions, perhaps occurring throughout a person's life.

Credentialing and Certification Decisions

Credentialing and certification decisions are concerned with assuring that a student has attained certain standards of learning. Student certification decisions may focus on whether a student has attained minimum competence or whether a student has obtained a high standard, depending on the legal mandate. Certification and credentialing may be mandated by a state's legislation or may be voluntary. If a state law mandates that students achieve certain standards of performance, most often students are administered an assessment procedure created at the state level. If they meet the standards, they are awarded a credential (such as a high school diploma).

These certification assessment procedures present special problems for validation. An individual student cannot reasonably be held accountable for instruction that was not delivered to him or that was delivered poorly, even though, on the average, teaching was adequate. A critical point, therefore, is whether the quality of instruction actually delivered to the student corresponds to what is required on the assessment procedure. The closer this correspondence, the fairer the certification is to the student. If students did not have the opportunity to learn how to perform the tasks that appear on the certification assessment procedure, either because a specific school lacked the necessary resources or a particular teacher did not deliver appropriate instruction, the assessment-based certification process seems inherently unjust.

Often, it is not easy to resolve conflicts about what has been taught and what should appear on an assessment procedure. For example, suppose a state had a reading list of "important works" for which students will be held accountable. Suppose one group's teacher did not explain these works directly, but another group's teacher did. Should the first group be held accountable? Further, in some states, high standards may require students to apply knowledge to new situations, to solve new problems, and to exhibit creativity. To assess application to new students, assessments must include tasks that are unfamiliar or novel for students. This is accomplished by deliberately making the assessment materials different from the materials used during teaching (otherwise they would not be "novel"). The validity question is, "Is this fair to students?"

Another example is using assessments for teacher certification. Some states require using paper-and-pencil tests to assess preservice teachers' knowledge. Often there is a battery of tests including basic skills, general knowledge, and professional knowledge. Some tests also include separate assessment of specialty areas such as biology, elementary education, and teaching the hearing impaired. Some states also evaluate a teacher's classroom performance through observation or by assigning a master teacher as a mentor to a beginning teacher.

Some efforts are underway by the National Board for Professional Teaching Standards (NBPTS) to develop assessment procedures to certify experienced teachers who are outstanding in their teaching skills (NBPTS, 1991). Initially, teachers will be assessed in three areas: (1) early adolescent (English, language arts), (2) early adolescent through young adulthood (art), and (3) adolescent and young adulthood (mathematics). Unlike the state-mandated assessments, NBPTS certification is voluntary. Also, the assessment procedures are heavily performance based. That is, teachers may submit portfolios of documents, student work samples, and perhaps videotapes to demonstrate their teaching competence. Their teaching may also be observed, and they may come to an assessment center to participate in simulated teaching activities such as instructional design, group interaction, parent-teacher conferences, peer collaboration, and staff development (Performance Assessment Laboratory, 1992).

NORM-REFERENCED AND CRITERION-REFERENCED INTERPRETATIONS

The "number right" score obtained from an assessment is not very meaningful in and of itself. This score needs to be referenced to something outside the assessment to be interpreted. For example, if I told you that my spelling test score was 49, what would this mean? What kinds of words could I spell? Am I a better speller than you? Two kinds of score-referencing procedures are prominent today, although these don't exhaust all of the possibilities. One is called norm-referencing, the other criterion-referencing.

Norm-Referencing

Norm-referenced interpretations describe assessed performance in terms of a person's position in a reference group that has been administered the assessment. For example, you may report a student's performance on a test as being "better than 80 percent of the class." This report expresses the student's standing in a reference group, but it does not state what the student knows or is able to perform. The reference group is called the **norm group.** Sometimes special norm-referenced scores are developed to express relative position in a reference group. Percentile ranks, grade-equivalent scores, and standard scores are examples of norm-referenced scores. Because these types of scores are used so extensively in education and psychology, Chapter 17 explains them in detail.

Criterion-Referencing

Criterion-referenced interpretations describe assessed performance in terms of the kinds of tasks a person with a given score can do (Glaser & Nitko, 1971). An example of this type of description is, "When applying mathematical rate and ratio concepts to estimate the number of beans in a jar, the student may estimate the number of beans and make a start toward obtaining an accurate solution, but is unable to complete a solution using the instruments and data available." Figure 1.3 illustrates how both criterion-referenced and norm-referenced interpretations may be made from the same assessment task.

It is important to note that both kinds of interpretations are important to understand how well a student is learning. Students who perform poorly relative to their peers (a norm-referenced interpretation) may require special attention or the use of special resources. However, it is what students are able to do (criterion-referenced interpretation) that is most germane to your decision about what to teach a student. For many instructional decisions, you must know such particulars as the kinds of skills a student has already learned, the degree to which skills can be performed, the patterns of errors he habitually makes with respect to performing a task, and the thinking skills he can or cannot use to solve relevant problems. Assessment results referenced only to norms do not provide you with specific information about individuals.

ADDITIONAL WAYS TO DESCRIBE ASSESSMENTS

In the course of reading and studying about assessments, you will encounter many terms describing them. Figure 1.4 is a partial list of terms that appear in this book. The terms are defined in this section.

Kinds of Item Assessments

The questions, exercises, and tasks appearing on an assessment procedure are called **items.** An assessment procedure is often described in terms of the kinds of items it contains. Items can require students to construct or supply their own answers, or they can offer students choices of answers from among two or more alternatives. The latter type of items is called *response-choice items*. They include true-false items, multiple-choice items, and matching exercises. A variety of complex as well as simple performances and thinking can be assessed with response-choice items. Crafting response-choice items is the subject of Chapters 7, 8, and 10.

Some assessment procedures have items requiring the student to supply or construct a response. *Completion items* present an incomplete sentence, and the student is required to supply a word or short phrase that best completes the sentence. Chapter 7 discusses how to craft this kind of item. Completion items are used for personality-adjustment assessment as well as in achievement assessment (Loevinger, Wessler, & Redmore, 1970).

Sometimes an item asks a question, and the student must write a short response. In this type of item, the student usually is not free to express creative and imaginative thoughts. With a corresponding lack of imagination, such items are called *short-answer items*. Essay items and other extended response items assess a student's ability to organize ideas and thoughts and allow for creative verbal expression. Chapters 9, 11, and 12 give suggestions for crafting these types of *constructed-response items*.

Descriptions of the advantages and disadvantages of each of these types of test items come later in the chapters describing how to craft them. Here, however, we want to note that no one type of item has marked superiority over the others for all purposes. In spite of the strong opinions and rhetoric you hear, each item type has its strengths and weaknesses. You must weigh these strengths and weaknesses before you use a type to assess your students. Of principal importance in classroom assessment is identifying the learning targets you want to assess and then using the types of items that permit you to assess the learning targets most directly and accurately.

FIGURE 1.3 Example of two ways to interpret the scores on an assessment task used as a benchmark by the Toronto Board of Education: Criterion-referencing and norm-referencing.

BEANS IN A JAR
Applying Rate and Ratio

In the task for this Benchmark, students were first shown a jar filled with beans and asked to estimate the number of beans. They were then asked to work out the number of beans more accurately using any of the following materials: a calculator, a balance scale and masses, a ruler, a graduated cylinder and a transparent centimetre-squared grid. They were told they could count some but not all of the beans. If the students did not know how to proceed, the evaluators suggested they weigh a small handful of beans. The students were asked to keep an ongoing record of their solutions. After they had solved the problem they were asked to describe the problem and their solutions.

Key Objectives from the Ontario Ministry of Education and Toronto Board Guidelines

- Apply ratio and rate in problem solving
- Consolidate conversions among commonly used metric units
- Collect and organize data
- Consolidate and apply operations with whole numbers and decimals with and without a calculator
- Apply estimation, rounding and reasonableness of results in calculations, in problem solving and in applications
- Develop facility in communication skills involving the use of the language and notation of mathematics
- Develop problem solving abilities

Norm-referenced interpretations	Task Score	Criterion-referenced interpretations
20% of the students scored 5 (80% scored lower than 5)	5	The student understands the problem and immediately begins to search for a strategy, perhaps experimenting with different methods and materials before proceeding. The student monitors the solution as it develops and may check and re-measure. The student uses the materials efficiently and accurately and keeps a good record of the data. All the calculations are performed accurately and a reasonable answer is produced. The student gives a clear explanation of the solution demonstrating sound reasoning with proportions. The student takes ownership of the task and enjoys its challenge.
19% of the students scored 4 (61% scored lower than 4)	4	The student may make some false starts and may be helped by the evaluator to get focussed. The student may use some materials to no purpose or inaccurately, perhaps confusing volume and mass. The student reasons with proportions correctly. Although stuck at various points in the solution, the student perseveres and usually produces a reasonable answer. The student usually gives a clear explanation and enjoys the activity.
20% of the students attained 3 (41% scored lower than 3; the average score is 3.0)	3	There is some confusion in one or more aspects of the solution to the problem. The student may confuse units, make arithmetic errors or perform incorrect operations. The student may have some idea of proportionality but is unable to use it correctly. The student does not use the materials to the best advantage. The student seeks assistance from the evaluator. Although not totally confident, the student may persevere in an attempt to arrive at an answer to the problem.
24% of the students attained 2 (17% scored lower than 2)	2	The student may make a start at solving the problem but is unable to complete a solution. The student may repeatedly switch methods and materials, and be unable to find an effective strategy. There is considerable confusion with units and the interpretation of various measurements. The student usually guesses at the operations which should be performed with the data. The student lacks confidence and seeks a great deal of assistance from the evaluator.
17% of the students attained 1	1	The student may estimate the number of beans but gives no response or very limited response to working out the number more accurately.

Source: Adapted from John L. Clark (1992). The Toronto Board of Education's Benchmarks in Mathematics. *The Arithmetic Teacher: Mathematics Through the Middle Grades, 39*(6), pp. 51–55. Adapted by permission.

FIGURE 1.4 A partial list of terms used to describe and classify assessments.

By kind of item
Choice items (true-false, multiple choice, matching)
Completion items
Short-answer items
Essay items

By how pupil performance is scored
Objective assessments
Subjective assessments

By degree of standardization
Standardized assessments
Nonstandardized assessments

By administrative conditions
Individual assessments
Group assessments

By language emphasis of the scoring
Verbal assessments
Performance assessments

By emphasis on speed of responding
Power assessments
Speed assessments

By the basis for interpreting scores
Norm-referencing
Criterion-referencing

By what attribute is measured
Achievement assessments
   Specific subject assessments
   Survey batteries

Aptitude assessments
   General scholastic aptitude assessments
   Readiness assessments
   Tests of specific aptitudes

Personality and adjustment measures
   Projective techniques
   Structured assessments
   Self-report questionnaires

Interest inventories
   Vocational or career interests
   Other interest inventories

Attitude and values questionnaires

Objective and Subjective Scoring

An assessment can be described in terms of its **objectivity**—the degree to which every observer of a student's performance will give exactly the same report or result (Cronbach, 1990). *Objectivity* and *subjectivity* thus refer to the scoring side of assessment rather than to the type of items or to their content. A true-false and multiple-choice test is said to be objective because once the scoring key is set, nearly everyone who scores a student's responses arrives at the same report. Essay items, portfolios, and performance assessments, on the other hand, have a history of being scored differently by different persons and differently by the same persons on different occasions. Because of this, they are said to be subjective methods of assessment.

Note that objectivity is a matter of degree. Humans who hand-score multiple-choice tests frequently err (Phillips & Weathers, 1958) and, although less frequently, so do scoring machines (Watkins, 1962). Essay and performance tasks can be scored more objectively with a scoring rubric. (See Chapters 9 and 12.)

Degree of Standardization

Standardization can improve the objectivity of assessments as well as the validity of interpreting the results. **Standardization** is the degree to which the observational procedures, administrative procedures, equipment and materials, and scoring rules have been fixed so that, insofar as is possible, the same procedure occurs at different times and places (Cronbach, 1990).

A major reason for standardizing an assessment procedure is to permit fair comparisons of different students' performance or of the same student on different occa-

sions. Exactly what assessment results mean is open to question whenever the procedure, materials, or scoring are not the same from place to place, assessor to assessor, or time to time.

But standardization is an ideal, and so we speak of *degree of standardization*. Even if all directions are specified and production of assessment materials is quality controlled, no two situations can be identical. Examiners vary in personality and rapport; environmental and social conditions change. Many individually administered assessments require the examiner to judge the quality of a student's responses, and no matter how well these quality-judging scoring rules are described, the examiner needs to exercise informed professional judgment. As a consequence, you must use informed professional judgment when interpreting your students' assessment results.

Individual and Group Assessments

Assessment procedures may be administered to one person at a time or simultaneously to a group. Some assessment procedures are especially designed to be administered to one person at a time. These **individual assessment procedures** allow the maximum amount of interaction between the assessor and the student. They are rich in opportunities for clinical observation. In other words, you can observe a student's approach to and performance on the assessment tasks. You also can ask questions that follow up on a student's response to clarify it and to understand it more completely. An individual assessment offers you the opportunity to establish rapport with the student, making the assessment more personalized and perhaps more optimal for the student.

Individual attention and personalized assessment conditions usually require special facilities (such as a private assessment room) and time. If a psychologist, for example, must assess a student's general mental ability, this may require an hour or more per student. Individual assessment is a costly procedure if specialists who are not already on the staff are needed to do the assessing.

Group assessment procedures sacrifice rapport, personalized conditions, and clinical observation for increased efficiency and reduced cost. In the same time it takes to administer and score an individual assessment, an entire class can be assessed. Where large groups need assessing, where finances are tight, and where only coarse information is required, group assessment becomes a more attractive option. Frequently, assessments originated as group assessments can be administered individually; the converse is seldom possible.

Verbal and Performance Assessments

Verbal assessments call for observing the verbal responses of students: for example, how well they can define words, explain their answers, or define similarities or differences between concepts. Most school assessments are verbal because schools emphasize verbal attributes.

Other assessments are crafted to elicit and observe nonverbal responses: assembling objects, completing experiments, performing psychomotor activities, and so on. These are called **performance assessments.** Figure 1.5 shows one performance item from an assessment designed to assess children's motor function.

Although performance assessments emphasize nonverbal responses, verbal ability or language ability are also necessary. Directions to students are usually oral, requiring them to carry a large aural-verbal load. Also, verbal mediation may facilitate learning and performing skills (Adams, 1971; Boucher, 1974).

When assessing school learning targets, performance assessments focus on a student's ability to apply and use knowledge from several areas to make something, produce a report, or give a demonstration. Chapters 11 and 12 describe these performance tasks and how to craft them.

Speed and Power Assessments

Quite frequently your main focus is to assess the amount of knowledge, comprehension, or understanding a student possesses. Usually you are less concerned about how quickly a student responds to questions than about the content of those responses. Accordingly, time limits on such assessments are very generous (sometimes nearly unlimited), allowing all students enough time to consider each question and attempt to answer it. These assessments are called **power assessments.**

In contrast, sometimes it is not the contents of students' responses that are of prime interest. Rather, it is the speed with which students perform tasks or answer questions. Such assessments are called **speeded assessments.**

When your assessment focuses on speed of performance, it is important that you do not confuse the rapidity of a student's performance with the difficulty of the task. For this reason, when you assess speed you craft a procedure that contains questions or tasks that are relatively easy. Students score differently on speed assessments, not because the items are difficult, but because individuals complete the tasks or process information at different speeds.

FIGURE 1.5   Example of a performance item designed to assess certain fine motor movements of the hand. Notice the verbal directions. Would verbal mediation (e.g., counting to oneself) help a child to perform better on this item?

Touching Thumb to Fingertips—Eyes Closed

With eyes closed, the subject touches the thumb of the preferred hand to each of the fingertips on the preferred hand, moving from the little finger to the index finger and then from the index finger to the little finger, as shown in the figure below. The subject is given 90 seconds to complete the task once. The score is recorded as a pass or a fail.

Trials: 1

| 1 | 2 | 3 | 4 |

Administering and Recording

Have the subject sit beside you at a table. Have the subject extend the preferred arm. Then say: You are to touch your thumb to each of the fingertips in order. Then start with your first finger and touch each fingertip again as you move your thumb back to your little finger (demonstrate). Do this with your eyes closed until I tell you to stop. Ready, begin.

The purpose of testing may change over the course of instruction, even though the items on the assessment remain essentially the same. Early in the course of learning, emphasis is usually not on speed of performance; that frequently becomes important after students have mastered the basics of the task. Learning addition facts in first grade is an example. At first, students are permitted to use their fingers and toes and other "manipulatables" when being quizzed. Eventually, speed of response becomes important: A student is marked on the number of addition facts correctly answered within a fixed time limit (or, alternately, the time it takes to complete a fixed number of facts). If the time limits were removed, then practically every student would produce correct answers to all the facts. Similar speed versus power concerns appear in the learning of other academic skills such as reading where, initially, overt and slow phonetic blending is permitted; later, speed of response (i.e., automatic decoding of words) counts more.

For many children, assessments are a mixture of speed and power, even when you intend them to be only power. Such assessments are called *partially speeded assessments*. When constructing assessments, check the time limits carefully to be sure that all students have the opportunity to consider each item before the time is up.

Attributes That Are Assessed

Procedures may be crafted to assess a variety of human attributes. Among them are academic achievement (described in Chapters 6 through 16); a variety of general scholastic and special aptitudes (Chapter 19); and personality, interests, and attitudes (Chapter 19).

Achievement assessments measure the knowledge, abilities, and skills that are the focus of direct instruction in schools. Scholastic aptitude assessments and specific aptitude assessments measure learned behavior also. However, aptitude assessments are crafted to predict students' academic accomplishments in school.

Nonacademic and affective human attributes also may be assessed. In psychological assessment, the procedures for assessing such attributes as emotional adjustment, interpersonal relations, motivation, interests, and attitudes are called *personality assessments* (Anastasi, 1976).

Related to and subsumed under personality attributes are three overlapping categories: interests, attitudes, and values. These are often assessed by questionnaires asking for the student's degree of agreement with various statements. It is sometimes useful to distinguish them in the following way:

Interests are preferences for particular activities. *Example of statement on questionnaire: I would rather repair a clock than write a letter.*
Values concern preferences for "life goals" and "ways of life," in contrast to interests, which concern preferences

for particular activities. *Example: I consider it more important to have people respect me than to like me.*
Attitudes concern feelings about particular social objects—physical objects, types of people, particular persons, social institutions, government policies, and others. *Example: The United Nations is a constructive force in the world today.* (Nunally, 1967, pp. 514–515; bold and italics added)

ACQUIRING THE COMPETENCE TO ASSESS STUDENTS

Assessing students is a very important part of your teaching. Naturally, you want to make good teaching decisions. Good decisions, however, require more than experience and good judgment. They require that you learn the knowledge and the skills you need to obtain and use high-quality information. High-quality information is necessary if your decisions are to be accurate, valid, and fair to students. It is only through high-quality assessments that high-quality information is obtained.

As you teach, you need competence in more than using and interpreting assessment results. You need the competence to select, change, and craft assessment procedures to suit your teaching style, the students you teach, and the school environment in which you work. As you use the assessments you crafted, you also need to be able to explain the results correctly to students, parents, other teachers, and school administrators. Further, as you develop professionally, you may have the opportunity to participate in local and state committees concerned with assessment issues. Educational news emphasizes assessment as a major concern and a newsworthy issue: It is likely to remain so for much of your professional career.

By taking this course in educational assessment, by studying the lessons and practical suggestions taught by your instructor, by studying the material in this book, and by learning from your experience in the classroom, you will acquire the professional attitude and competencies needed to validly assess your students.

To help you assess your present level of competence and to help you focus on important areas of assessment skills, the American Federation of Teachers, the National Council on Measurement in Education, and the National Education Association (1990) published *Standards for Teacher Competence in Educational Assessment of Students*. These standards are reproduced in Appendix A. Each of these seven competencies is addressed throughout this book. I have keyed the learning targets at the beginning of each chapter to the specific competencies to which they refer. Because your assessment competence will continue to grow throughout your professional career, *some* of the competencies listed in Appendix A may be more appropriate for experienced teachers than for beginning teachers.

Summary

- Teaching and learning require the continuous gathering of information for making decisions. Sound assessments are prerequisite to sound educational decisions.
- Assessment is a process for obtaining information that is used for making decisions about students, curricula and programs, and educational policy.
- Assessment techniques include paper-and-pencil tests; formal and informal observation; homework, exercises, and research papers; projects and exhibits; performances; portfolios; oral questioning; and analyses of students' records.
- The selection and use of particular assessment techniques are guided by several important principles, including (1) being clear about the learning target, (2) matching the assessment technique to the learning target, (3) serving the needs of learners, (4) using multiple indicators of achievement, and (5) recognizing the limitations of each technique.
- A test is an instrument or systematic procedure for observing and describing one or more characteristics of a student, using either a numerical scale or a classification scheme.
- Measurement is a procedure for assigning numbers (usually called *scores*) to a specified attribute or characteristic of persons in such a way that the numbers describe the degree to which the person possesses the attribute.
- Evaluation is the process of making a value judgment about the worth of someone or something. Evaluations may or may not be based on information obtained from tests and other assessments.
- Educational policy decisions are made at the district, state, and national levels.
- Decisions about curricula, materials, and programs may be made during their development or after they have been completed.
- Formative evaluations are judgments about the worth of curricula, materials, and programs while they are under development and suggest ways to redesign, refine, or improve them.
- Summative evaluations are judgments about their worth after they are completed and suggest whether they should be adopted or used.
- Decisions about individual students include
  - Managing instruction: planning instructional activities, placing students into learning sequences, monitoring students' progress, diagnosing students' learning difficulties, modeling learning targets, giving feedback to students and parents, deciding on one's own teaching effectiveness, and assigning grades to students.
  - Placing students into programs: assigning students to different levels of learning programs.
  - Classifying students: assigning students to different categories, such as by type of disability.
- Counseling and guidance: assisting students in exploring, choosing, and preparing for different careers; helping them to adjust to home, school, and peer stress, which is part of normal growth and development.
- Selecting students: accepting some students and rejecting others for a job, program, or higher level of education.
- Credentialing and certifying students: deciding whether students meet standards of competence for a diploma or for a certificate that entitles them to apply for employment.
- Assessments may be described and classified in many ways, including by kind of item, degree of scoring objectivity, degree of standardization, administrative conditions, degree of language emphasis of the scoring, degree of emphasis on speed of responding, the basis for interpreting scores, and the type of attributes that are assessed.
- Two fundamental ways of interpreting students' performance on assessments are norm-referencing and criterion-referencing.
- Norm-referenced interpretations describe assessment results in terms of a student's position in a reference group that also has been administered the assessment procedure.
- Criterion-referenced interpretations describe assessment results in terms of the kinds of tasks a student with a given score can do.
- *The Standards for Teacher Competence in Educational Assessment of Students* (American Federation of Teachers et al., 1990) identifies seven standards toward which teachers should strive in order to attain competence in assessing of students. These are reproduced in Appendix A and are keyed to the learning targets of this book that address them.

Important Terms and Concepts

assessment
classification decisions
credentialing
criterion-referenced interpretations
diagnostic assessments
evaluation
formative evaluation
group assessment procedures
individual assessment procedures
items
measurement
norm group
norm-referenced interpretations
objectivity
performance assessments
placement decisions
power assessments
selection decisions
speeded assessments

standardization
summative evaluation
test
verbal assessments

Exercises and Discussion Questions

1. Reflect on a specific lesson you have taught or would like to teach. Make a list of the decisions you made (or need to make) before, during, and after this lesson. Next to each decision, identify how you will obtain the information needed to make the decision. What criterion might you use to judge the quality of each piece of information?

2. Compare and contrast the meaning of *assessment, evaluation, measurement,* and *testing.*

3. Identify a specific assessment procedure you are familiar with or would like to know more about (such as a standardized test of mathematical problem solving or your own technique for assessing a student's competence in your subject area). List each of the five guiding principles for selecting, using, and creating assessment procedures mentioned in the text. For each principle, analyze the procedure you selected and explain the degree to which it meets the principle. Justify your answers. Explain how the assessment might be improved to more nearly meet each principle.

4. Consider the decisions illustrated in Figure 1.1. Which decisions are more important in today's schools? Explain why.

5. Distinguish between summative and formative evaluation in terms of the point at which the evaluation is made and the purpose for which it is made. To evaluate a curriculum or an instructional program, is it necessary to assess students' competence? Explain or discuss.

6. Decide the truth or falsity of each of the following statements. Defend your answer.
   a. To make evaluations, one *must* use measurements.
   b. To measure an important educational attribute of a student, one *must* use a test.
   c. To evaluate a student, one *must* measure that student.
   d. To test a student, one *must* measure that student.
   e. *Any* piece of information a teacher obtains about a student is an assessment.
   f. To evaluate a student, one *must* assess that student.

7. Classify each of these statements as reflecting a selection, classification, placement, career guidance, diagnostic/remediation, or certification decision. Defend your answer.
   a. After students begin kindergarten, they are given a battery of perceptual skills tests to decide which children should receive special perceptual skills training and which should remain in the "regular" program.
   b. A school operates two different third-grade reading programs. At the end of third grade, the standardized reading test results are summarized separately for each program and compared.
   c. A child study team decides whether each child who has been administered a series of screening tests should be included in a particular category of disability (hearing impaired, learning disabled, etc.).
   d. After a school psychologist assesses a student, local education authorities assign the student to the resource room on a daily basis, where the teacher for the learning disabled gives the student special instruction.

   e. Each graduate of this department of education is required to take and pass the state's test before being allowed to teach in the schools.

8. For each statement below, indicate whether norm-referencing or criterion-referencing should be emphasized. Defend your answer.
   a. A reading teacher wants to identify the process a student uses when reading incorrectly.
   b. A mathematics teacher wants to identify the most complex arithmetic problem a student can solve.
   c. A reading teacher wants to know who the top five readers are.
   d. A mathematics teacher wants to know which students are having the most difficulty with arithmetic computations so that further diagnostic assessment can be done.

9. Use one assessment term from each group listed in Figure 1.4 (i.e., eight terms in all) to describe each of the following assessment procedures. Defend each of your choices as the most technically correct term to use.
   a. The examiner meets with one student at a time in a quiet room and tries to establish rapport. Each task the student is to perform is explained by reading a preestablished set of directions. One task consists of touching each finger of one hand to the thumb in sequence, beginning with the little finger, and then reversing the sequence. The student does this with closed eyes. The examiner counts mistakes and records errors according to directions in the manual.
   b. The teacher gives each student a test booklet and an answer sheet. From the examiner's manual, the teacher reads the printed directions that accompany the test. The children are given four choices for each answer and are instructed to make their answers on a separate answer sheet that can be either hand or machine scored. After one hour, the teacher says that time is up and collects both the test booklets and the answer sheets. The children complain because most of them had not finished the test.

10. List each of the seven standards for teacher competence found in Appendix A. Under each standard, describe the kinds of competence you now have and those that you hope to have at the end of this course.

Additional Readings

Brennan, R. L., & Plake, B. S. (1991). Survey of programs and employment in educational measurement. *Educational Measurement: Issues and Practice, 10*(2), 32.

   If you want to know more about employment opportunities in the area of educational testing, this brief article will interest you.

Glaser, R., & Nitko, A. J. (1971). Measurement in learning and instruction. In R. L. Thorndike (Ed.), *Educational measurement* (2nd ed., pp. 625–670). Washington, DC: American Council on Education.

   Analyzes a particular kind of instructional system, types of decisions necessary, and kinds of assessment information required.

Nitko, A. J. (1984). Defining "criterion-referenced test." In R. A. Berk (Ed.), *A guide to criterion-referenced test construction* (pp. 8–28). Baltimore, MD: Johns Hopkins University Press.

Reviews many different types of criterion-referenced assessments, showing the types of information they provide.

Popham, W. J. (1988). *Educational evaluation* (2nd ed.). Englewood Cliffs, NJ: Prentice Hall.

Chapter 2 gives a brief survey of different ideas of how programs should be evaluated. A useful introduction to curriculum and program evaluation if you are not familiar with proposed approaches.

Airasian, P. W. (1991). Perspectives on measurement instruction. *Educational Measurement: Issues and Practice, 10*(1), 13–16.

Brookhart, S. M. (1999). Teaching about communicating assessment results and grading. *Educational Measurement: Issues and Practice, 18*(1), 5–13.

O'Sullivan, R. G., & Chalmick, M. K. (1991). Measurement-related course work requirements for teacher certification and recertification. *Educational Measurement: Issues and Practice, 10*(1), 17–19, and 23.

Sanders, J. R. (1989). Joint Committee for Standards for Teacher Competence in Educational Assessment of Students. *Educational Measurement: Issues and Practice, 8*(2), 25, 30.

Schafer, W. D. (1991). Essential assessment skills in professional education of teachers. *Educational Measurement: Issues and Practice, 10*(1), 3–6.

Stiggins, R. J. (1991). Relevant classroom assessment training for teachers. *Educational Measurement: Issues and Practice, 10*(1), 7–12.

Stiggins, R. J. (1999). Evaluating classroom assessment training in teacher education programs. *Educational Measurement: Issues and Practice, 18*(1), 23–27.

Whittington, D. (1999). Making room for values and fairness: Teaching reliability and validity in the classroom context. *Educational Measurement: Issues and Practice, 18*(1), 14–22, and 27.

This collection of articles describes the state of teacher education in the area of educational assessment of students. Airasian (1991), Schafer (1991), and Stiggins (1991) describe what the courses in educational testing and measurement should cover. The Sanders (1989) article describes how the standards in Appendix A of this book were developed. Brookhart (1999) and Whittington (1999) propose how teachers should be taught about important measurement concepts. Stiggins (1999) proposes a set of criteria that schools of education might use to evaluate how well they are preparing teachers in classroom assessment. After reading some of these articles, you might want to discuss with your classmates and instructor the way you will be taught about educational assessment in this course.

CHAPTER 2

Describing the Goals and Learning Targets of Instruction

Learning Targets

After studying this chapter, you should be able to:

1. Describe how learning targets help to direct the instructional process. [1, 4, 7]
2. List four ways in which learning targets contribute to improved classroom assessment. [1, 4]
3. Distinguish between content and performance standards, general and specific learning targets, and developmental and mastery learning targets. [2, 1]
4. Write specific learning targets for your subject area that meet the three basic criteria for such statements. [2, 1, 4]
5. State the seven criteria that you may use to review and judge the quality of a list of learning targets for a unit or a course. [2, 1, 4]
6. Explain why taxonomies of thinking skills are useful for reviewing learning targets and assessment tasks. [2, 3, 1]
7. Classify learning targets using the Bloom et al. and Marzano et al. classifications of thinking skills. [2, 3, 1]
8. Name and define the major categories of at least one thinking skills taxonomy. [2, 1]
9. Explain why it is desirable to use more than one assessment format to evaluate students on important learning targets. [3, 1, 6]
10. Explain how each of the terms and concepts listed at the end of this chapter may be applied to educational assessment. [6]

IMPORTANCE OF SPECIFYING OBJECTIVES

In Chapter 1, we discussed assessment as a process for obtaining information for making educational decisions. We noted that to select assessment and use results meaningfully you need to be clear about the learning targets you want to teach and be sure the assessment techniques you use actually match the learning targets. We also pointed out that before teaching you must decide the content to cover, the learning activities to use, and the learning targets the students should achieve.

Learning targets is an informal term. Here we use it to emphasize that your teaching involves more than "covering the material" and "keeping students actively engaged." The focus of your teaching should be on student achievements as well as on the learning process. What should students be able to do, value, or feel after you have taught them that they were unable to do, believe, or feel before you taught them? We call these student outcomes *learning* *targets.* A more formal term is *learning objectives.* A **learning objective** specifies what you would like students to be able to do, value, or feel at the completion of an instructional segment.

Learning Targets Help Direct the Instructional Process

Instruction is the process that you use to provide students with the conditions that help them achieve the learning targets. Some planned changes are **cognitive.** For example, you may want students to read a claim made by a political figure and determine whether there is evidence available to support that claim. Other planned changes are not cognitive, such as those relating to values. For example, you may want students to value the right to vote in elections over other activities competing for their time. Still other learning outcomes are **affective.** For example, you may want students to feel comfortable when talking in front of their classmates about how to solve mathematics problems. Yet other learning targets are **psychomotor.** For example, you may want students to set up, focus, and use a microscope properly during a science investigation of pond water.

Deciding the specific learning targets you expect of students is one important step in the teaching process. Instruction may be thought of as involving three fundamental and interrelated activities (Lindvall & Nitko, 1975):

1. Deciding what the student is to learn.
2. Carrying out the actual instruction.
3. Evaluating the learning.

Activity 1 requires you to articulate the learning targets in some way, usually by specifying learning objectives or by providing several concrete examples of the tasks students should be able to do to demonstrate that the learning targets have been reached. Information from Activity 1 informs you and the students about what is expected as a result of teaching and studying. Your understanding of the learning target guides your teaching and provides a criterion for deciding whether students have attained the desired change. Activity 2 is the heart of the teaching process itself. Here you provide the conditions and activities for students to learn. Activity 3, evaluating whether learning has occurred, is central to teaching. Through it you and your students come to know whether they have changed in the desired ways and have reached the learning targets. The more clearly you specify the learning targets, the more directed your instructional efforts and your students' learning efforts can be.

The process is interactive rather than a straight one-two-three process. Setting clear learning targets helps you to plan your teaching efficiently, conduct your instruction effectively, and assess student outcomes validly. Assessment and evaluation of clearly specified learning targets provide you with information about how effective your instruction has been. This information, in turn, may be used to plan the next instructional activities or to better specify the instructional targets themselves.

Additional Reasons for Using Specific Learning Targets

The three activities just presented are a simplified description of the instructional process. They do, however, illustrate that instruction can be easier when a teacher has learning targets clearly in mind. Additional reasons why learning targets should be used in the classroom follow (Gow, 1976).

1. They help teachers and/or curriculum designers make their own educational goals explicit.

2. They communicate the intent of instruction to students, parents, other teachers, school administrators, and the public.

3. They provide the basis for teachers to analyze what they teach and to construct learning exercises.

4. They describe the specific performances against which teachers can evaluate the success of instruction.

5. They can help educators to focus and to clarify discussions of educational goals with parents (and others).

6. They communicate to students the performance they are expected to learn. This may empower them to direct their own learning.

7. They make it easier to individualize instruction.

8. They help teachers evaluate and improve both instructional procedures and learning targets.

Importance of Learning Targets for Classroom Assessment

Obviously, before you can craft your own assessment procedures, you need to know what student outcomes you want to assess. You have to have clearly in mind the students' performances you want to evaluate. If you are not clear on which important learning outcomes you want to evaluate, you may easily fail to assess those outcomes validly. In this chapter, statements of specific learning targets are viewed as having value for at least the following aspects of classroom assessment:

1. *The general planning for an assessment procedure* is made easier by knowing the specific outcomes you wish students to achieve.

2. *Selecting, designing, and crafting assessment procedures* depend on your knowing which specific achievements should be assessed.

3. *Evaluating an existing assessment procedure* you already crafted is easier when you know the specific learning targets.

4. *Properly judging the content relevance of an assessment procedure* requires you to know the specific achievements to be assessed (see Chapter 3).

Educational Goals vs. Specific Learning Targets

Schooling and other organized instruction should help students attain educational goals. One of the many ways to define **educational goals** is that they "are those human activities which contribute to the functioning of a society (including the functioning of an individual *in* society), and which can be acquired through learning" (Gagné, Briggs, & Wagner, 1988, p. 39).

Educational goals are stated in broad terms that give direction and purpose to planning overall educational activities. Examples of statements of broad educational goals appear in reports prepared by state departments of education, local school systems, and associations such as the National Council of Teachers of Mathematics, the American Association for the Advancement of Science, and the Association of American Geographers. Broad goals are organized into subject-matter areas such as mathematics and history. The subject-matter area and content-specific thinking processes may be used as a *curriculum framework* within which you and other educators can define specific learning targets. Some state education agencies take the process further by publishing expected learning outcomes or *standards*. In such cases, you may be held accountable for students' achieving these particular standards.

General Learning Targets vs. Specific Learning Targets

There is an appropriate level of specificity for stating learning targets. If the description of a target is stated too broadly, teachers cannot use it for developing lesson plans and assessment procedures. The following statement, for example, may help to communicate general educational goals, but is too broadly stated to be immediately useful to plan lessons and assessments:

Every student should acquire communication skills of understanding, speaking, reading, and writing.

Some state and local curriculum goals present somewhat more specific statements of expected learning outcomes. These are usually clear enough for general planning of a course but need to be made more specific before

they can become classroom learning targets. The following **general learning target** might be stated for a primary school science unit on measurement in the metric system:

Acquire the skills needed to use common instruments to measure length, volume, and mass in metric units.

When teaching students and assessing their attainment of this general objective, you may need to break it down into two or more **specific learning targets:**

1. Measure the length of objects to the nearest tenth of a meter using a meter stick.
2. Measure the mass of objects to the nearest tenth of a kilogram using a simple beam balance and one set of weights.
3. Measure the volume of liquids to the nearest tenth of a liter using a graduated cylinder.

When learning targets are made more specific, the performance to teach and to assess becomes clear. But beware of overspecificity. Long lists of very narrow "bits" of behavior can fragment the subject to be taught; the students use complex combinations of specific performances to solve everyday problems. A second danger is that lists of specific objectives may become too long and are ignored. Identify a few of the most important learning targets for each instructional unit and focus on these.

It is useful, too, to create learning and assessment situations in which students are required to use combinations of specific skills and knowledge to perform complex tasks and solve real-life problems. Figure 1.3, for example, showed the beans-in-a-jar problem. In solving this problem students were expected to use several specific skills and knowledge (listed at the upper right of the figure) to accurately estimate the number of beans in the jar. A specific statement of objectives for this kind of task is problematic because "beans-in-a-jar" is not the target itself. Rather, it is only one example of many possible benchmark tasks in which the learning target is to apply a combination of proportional reasoning, estimation, measurement, and other skills to solve complex problems. The most important outcomes teachers should assess in this case are the processes and strategies students use to solve these problems. An assessment procedure that focuses exclusively on the degree of correctness of students' *answers* to tasks like this would be invalid because it misses assessing the *processes* that students use.

State Standards vs. Learning Targets

Standards Your state may have mandated that students meet a set of educational standards. Standards are statements about what students are expected to learn. Some states call these statements *essential skills, learning expectations, learning outcomes,* or *achievement expectations.* Often there are two sets of standards. **Content standards** are statements about the subject-matter facts, concepts, principles, procedures, generalizations, theories, etc. that students are expected to learn. **Performance standards** are usually statements about the things students can perform or do once the content standards are learned[1]. You can obtain a copy of your state's standards from your school principal or central administration office. Your state's department of education may also have an Internet web site where its standards may be read and downloaded.

States' standards vary greatly in their quality and degree of specificity. Not all states have done a good job of writing standards. Further, some states have established standards for only some grade levels (e.g., fourth, eighth, tenth, and twelfth grades). Others have specified standards for nearly every grade. Because the establishment of educational standards was a relatively new activity for states in the 1990s, there was no standard way (no pun intended) for standards to be written.

Learning Targets   As you may have gathered from the preceding paragraphs, a state's standards are really a set of learning targets. Once a state's standards are officially adopted, a school is required to make sure all students are taught and achieve those standards. For the most part, state standards are written at a fairly general level. The better-written state performance standards are essentially the same as the general learning targets that we discussed earlier. Some states, however, have written only content standards. In either case, you will need to break down each

standard into two or more specific learning targets in order to teach and assess them. Thus, all of the material in this chapter is applicable to teaching and assessment whether your school and state uses "objectives," "learning targets," or "standards." Table 2.1 compares statements of standards, general learning targets, and specific learning targets for third-grade reading in one school district.

Specific Learning Targets as Mastery Statements

Assessment techniques let you systematically observe and describe what students can do. Assessment focuses on what you are able to observe students doing. From this observation you will *infer* whether they attained the learning targets. For example, a high school biology unit on living cells may have as a general learning target that students should "learn the organizations and functions of cells." But what can the student do to demonstrate learning of this general target? There may be several answers to this question, each phrased as a specific instructional objective and each describing what a student "can do." For example:

1. The student can draw models of various types of cells and label their parts.
2. The student can list the parts of a cell and describe the structures included in each.
3. The student can explain the functions that different cells perform and how these functions are related to one another.

The answers to questions of what students can do as a result of instruction become statements that suggest ways of assessing them. Such statements may be called **mastery learning targets.** Robert Forsyth (1976) has referred to

---

[1]To make matters more confusing, some states define performance standards (or simply "standards") as certain ranges of test scores and then give these labels. For example, a student whose score is between 20 and 40 may be said to have reached the "basic level" of the standards; between 41 and 60 may be at the "proficient level"; and above 60 at the "advanced level." We shall not use the term *standards* in this way in this chapter.

TABLE 2.1 Comparison of a state standard, a general learning target, and specific learning targets for third-grade reading.

Standard

• Students comprehend a variety of reading materials, independently read to learn, and relate readings to other information and experience.

General learning target

• Students set purposes and goals for reading, read a variety of games, and employ appropriate reading comprehension strategies.

Specific learning targets

• Students state what is already known about the topic from their cultural background, travel, experience, and other reading or research.
• Students predict outcomes and content from the title, pictures, and story.
• Students predict content and style from knowledge of the author(s) and illustrations.

Source: Reprinted by permission of Pamela Brown Clarridge and Elizabeth M. Whitaker: *Rolling the Elephant Over: How to Effect Large-Scale Change in the Reporting Process* (Heinemann, A division of Reed Elsevier Inc., Portsmouth, NH, 1997, p. 17, Figure 2–1 and p. 11, Figure 1–4). Paraphrased with permission of the Tucson Unified School District.

them as "can do" statements. They have also been termed *specific learning outcomes* and *behavioral objectives*.

Mastery Learning Targets vs. Developmental Learning Targets

Some skills and abilities are more aptly stated at a somewhat higher level of abstraction than mastery learning targets to communicate that they are continuously developed throughtout life. Consider these:

1. Combine information and ideas from several sources to reach conclusions and solve problems.
2. Analyze and make critical judgments about the viewpoints expressed in passages.
3. Write several paragraphs that explain the author's point of view.
4. Use numerical concepts and measurements to describe real-world objects.
5. Interpret statistical data found in material from a variety of disciplines.
6. Write imaginative and creative stories.
7. Use examples from materials read to support your point of view.
8. Communicate your ideas using visual media such as drawings and figures.

Each of these statements implies a set of skills or abilities that are continuously developed throughout life; hence, these targets may be called *developmental objectives* (Gronlund, 1973) or **developmental learning targets.**

At first glance, it might seem that all one needs to do is to insert a "can do" phrase in front of each of the preceding statements to transform them to mastery learning targets. As Forsyth (1976) points out, however, it is not that simple. First, each statement represents a broad domain of loosely related (not highly correlated) performances. Second, each statement represents skills or abilities typically thought of as developing continuously to higher levels rather than the all-or-none dichotomy implied by the mastery learning targets.

The Problem of a Broad, Heterogeneous Domain To illustrate why it is difficult to make mastery learning targets out of broad, developmental learning targets, consider the following questions. These three questions are taken from the social studies reading subtest of the *Iowa Tests of Educational Development.* Each question requires the student to make an inference based on the information in a particular passage.

1. From his manner and formal training, what opinion might people have formed of John Marshall?   [28%]
2. What do the last two sentences suggest about Patasonian's acceptance of U.S. aid?   [44%]

3. Suppose an uninsured and unemployed motorist damaged someone's car. Which speaker offers a plan that would allow the injured party to collect benefits?   [64%] (Forsyth, 1976, p. 12)

The numbers in brackets indicate the percentage of a statewide sample of Iowa 10th graders answering the question correctly. These (and other data that are not shown) indicate that those who get one question right are not necessarily the same people who get another question right (Forsyth, 1976).

These three questions could be used to assess Developmental Learning Target 2 listed previously. Whether a student has mastered this learning target depends very much on the types of passages, types of viewpoints expressed, the subject matter of the passage, and the types of questions asked. If all of these conditions for performance were specified in a mastery learning target, it would be relatively meaningless because the answer to "mastery of what?" depends on the specific passages, points of view, and subject matter. The following statement includes these factors and achieves a narrowing of the broad, developmental learning target, transforming it into a mastery learning target:

> Johnny can make inferences and draw logical conclusions when given reading material that has no more than 200 words (at least 85% of the words are from the EDL list), that has between 10 and 20 sentences (with a maximum sentence length of 20 words), that is based on the life of John Marshall, and that requires him to answer multiple choice questions using four alternatives. (Forsyth, 1976, p. 14)

Clearly such narrow objectives have little usefulness to teachers in planning and assessing the effects of instruction.

The Issue of Continuous Development of Skill The second concern, the continuous or developmental nature of these learning targets, stems from the fact that "students cannot be expected to fully achieve such objectives. Even the simplest of these . . . is a matter of degree and can be continuously developed throughout life. All we can reasonably expect to do for a particular course or unit of instruction is to identify a sample of specific learning outcomes that represent degrees of progress toward the objectives" (Gronlund, 1973, p. 17). The essential concern here is that the skill(s) represented by these learning targets are complex, the number of tasks that can be used to demonstrate learning is vast, and each represents goals to work toward continuously rather than to master completely (Gronlund, 1973).

Teaching and Assessing Developmental Learning Targets One way to begin designing instruction and to assess progress toward important developmental objectives is to identify for each several specific learning targets that represent the *key* performances expected of a student at a *particular grade or age level*. This is illustrated in the following list, where a broad instructional objective in science is clarified by listing several specific learning targets that support it:

Understands Boyle's Law[2]

1. States a definition of Boyle's Law.
2. States the domain to which Boyle's Law applies.
3. Describes the relation between Boyle's Law and Charles's Law.
4. Uses Boyle's Law to explain an observation in a lab experiment.
5. Appropriately analyzes a new (to the student) situation in terms of Boyle's Law.
6. Solves a new problem or makes an appropriate choice for a course of action, taking into account the implications of Boyle's Law.

Although this list of six specific objectives might be made longer, the given list would likely be considered adequate for describing what is meant by "understanding Boyle's Law" at the end of a first course in high school physics. Specific tasks could then be prepared for assessing achievement of the six specific objectives. Some tasks could assess only one of these learning targets; others could require a student to use several of these learning targets in combination. A student's overall score could be interpreted as indicating the *degree* to which a student has acquired an understanding of Boyle's Law, rather than as a "mastery/nonmastery" description.

TAXONOMIES OF LEARNING TARGETS

Simply writing learning targets "off the top of your head" can be a frustrating experience because there is a seemingly endless number of possible targets. Further, if you are unaccustomed to writing learning targets, you are likely to write first those targets that have a very narrow focus, specify content topics, and represent lower-level cognitive skills. A taxonomy can help you to bring to mind the wide range of important learning targets and thinking skills.

Taxonomies of instructional learning targets are highly organized schemes for classifying learning targets into various levels of complexity. Generally, educational learning targets fall into one of three domains[3]:

1. *Cognitive domain:* Outcomes focus on knowledge and abilities requiring memory, thinking, and reasoning processes.

2. *Affective domain:* Outcomes focus on feelings, interests, attitudes, dispositions, and emotional states.
3. *Psychomotor domain:* Outcomes focus on motor skills and perceptual processes.

Learning targets within each domain may be classified by using a taxonomy for that domain. Because there is more than one way to define a classification scheme, several different taxonomies have been developed for sorting learning targets in a given domain. Only two of these taxonomies for the cognitive domain are described here. Other cognitive domain taxonomies are summarized in Appendixes D (Tables D.2, D.3), E, and F. Chapter 6 will discuss using taxonomies to develop an assessment plan. You may want to look ahead to skim that chapter now. The other chapters in Part Two discuss crafting tasks to assess learning targets at different taxonomy levels.

COGNITIVE DOMAIN TAXONOMIES

Bloom's Taxonomy

When developing a list of learning targets, you may find the *Taxonomy of Educational Objectives, Handbook I: Cognitive Domain* (Bloom, Engelhart, Furst, Hill, & Krathwhol, 1956) to be of considerable value. This taxonomy is a comprehensive outline of a range of cognitive abilities that might be taught in a course. The taxonomy classifies cognitive performances into six major headings arranged from simple to complex (Bloom et al., 1956):

1. **Knowledge** . . . involves the recall of specifics and universals, the recall of methods and processes, or the recall of a pattern, structure, or setting. For measurement purposes, the recall situation involves little more than bringing to mind the appropriate material. (p. 201)

2. **Comprehension** . . . represents the lowest level of understanding. It refers to a type of understanding or apprehension such that the individual knows what is being communicated and can make use of the material or idea being communicated without necessarily relating it to other material or seeing its fullest implications. (p. 204)

3. **Application** . . . The use of abstractions in particular and concrete situations [to solve new or novel problems]. The abstractions may be in the form of general ideas, rules of procedures, or generalized methods. The abstractions may also be technical principles, ideas, and theories, which must be remembered and applied. (p. 205)

4. **Analysis** . . . The breakdown of a communication into its constituent elements or parts such that the relative hierarchy of ideas is made clear and/or the relations between the ideas expressed are made explicit. Such analyses

---

[2]Based on Klopfer (1969).
[3]A single, real-life, complex performance will likely involve components of more than one domain.

are intended to clarify the communication, to indicate how the communication is organized, and the way in which it manages to convey its effects, as well as its basis and arrangements. (p. 205)

5. **Synthesis** . . . The putting together of elements and parts so as to form a whole. This involves the process of working with pieces, parts, elements, etc., and arranging and combining them in such a way as to constitute a pattern or structure not clearly there before. (p. 206)

6. **Evaluation** . . . Judgments about the value of material and methods for given purposes. Quantitative and qualitative judgments about the extent to which materials and methods satisfy criteria. Use of a standard of appraisal. The criteria may be those determined by the student or those which are given to him. (p. 207)

Examples of learning targets and items from each level of this taxonomy are described in detail in Bloom et al. (1956). Table D.1 in Appendix D will give you a further idea of the scope of this taxonomy and may help you identify into which taxonomic categories you may classify various learning targets. The value of such a taxonomy is that it calls your attention to the variety of abilities and skills toward which you can direct instruction and assessment.

It is incorrect to assume that this taxonomy is a teaching hierarchy. Its purpose is to classify various learning targets and assessment tasks. For example, you should not teach "knowledge" first and "comprehension" second.

Note that learning targets classified in the first three categories are more easily assessed with short-answer, true-false, multiple-choice, or matching test items. Learning targets classified in the last three categories might be partially tested by such item formats, but their assessment usually requires a variety of other procedures such as essay questions, homework, class projects, observing performance in labs, and portfolios. Learning targets at more complex thinking levels require students to actually produce or create something, rather than simply to answer questions. Carefully reading the various subcategories of the taxonomy in Table D.1 should make this more apparent.

Table 2.2 is an example of how this taxonomy can help you direct or focus your teaching and assessment strategies. Suppose you are teaching students to understand the elements that authors use when writing short stories. Suppose the selection of short stories you use all concern people's personal problems, and that the ways the characters in the stories handle their personal problems are inappropriate. The questions in Table 2.2 may be used to help you direct your assessment plans. The questions are not assessment tasks themselves, however. We shall show how to craft assessment tasks later in this book. At this point we are studying only the range of thinking skills that should be taught and assessed. Examples of how learning targets in science and social studies may be classified in the Bloom et al. taxonomy are shown in Table 2.3.

Dimensions of Learning Model

A further synthesis of different categories of thinking was developed by Marzano, Pickering, and McTighe (1993) using the Dimensions of Learning Model developed at the McREL Institute in Colorado. In this scheme, many small categories of thinking are organized into seven broader categories. The seven categories and corresponding examples of learning targets are shown in Table 2.4. A more detailed summary, which includes 13 types of complex thinking skills, is given in Appendix E.

The categories of the Dimensions of Learning Model were derived from research and writings on cognitive psychology, higher-order thinking, and critical thinking. The

TABLE 2.2 Examples of how the Bloom et al. taxonomy can be used to focus teaching and assessment on different types of thinking skills in a unit on short stories.

Bloom et al. Category	Examples of Teaching and Assessment Focus
Knowledge	Can students recall the main characters of all the short stories and what they did?
Comprehension	Can students explain in their own words the main ideas and themes of all the stories?
Application	Can students demonstrate how those personal problems of the characters in the stories are similar to the personal problems that real people face?
Analysis	Can students describe the literary devices each of the authors used to convey to the reader the characters' feelings?
Synthesis	Across all of the stories read so far, can students describe the general strategies that result in people failing to resolve their problems successfully?
Evaluation	Can students develop their own set of three or four criteria for judging the quality of a short story? Can they then use these criteria to evaluate several new stories that they did not previously read?

TABLE 2.3 Examples of how different learning outcomes for science and social studies are classified in the Bloom et al. taxonomy.

Bloom et al. Category	Science	Social Studies
Knowledge	• Recall the names of parts of a flower • Identify and label the parts of insects • List the steps in a process	• List known causes of the Civil War • Recall general principles of migration of peoples of Africa
Comprehension	• Find real examples of types of coleoptera • Find real examples of igneous rock and mineral formations • Explain the digestive processes in one's own words	• Explain the meaning of technical concepts in one's own words • Give examples of propaganda usage from current events
Application	• Use scientific principles to make a simple machine • Use a learned process to conduct a new experiment	• Use specified critical thinking skills to explain current events • Carry out a survey and collect data from the field
Analysis	• Show how scientific principles or concepts are applied when designing a refrigerator	• Identify the credible and non-credible claims of an advertisement for clothing • Show the different component parts of a political speech
Synthesis	• Determine what the rule is that underlies the results obtained from several experiments or investigations	• Show the similarities among several schools of social thought • Develop plans for peace among two countries
Evaluation	• Use criteria or standards to evaluate the conclusions drawn from the research findings • Use criteria to evaluate the soundness of a research study	• Use a specific set of criteria to evaluate several political speeches

categories are not meant to be hierarchical. They are, however, meant to be a framework for organizing curriculum and focusing teaching.

Marzano et al. (1993) state that teaching and assessment should require students to perform complex tasks using skills from *several* of the categories shown in Table 2.4. For instance, students may work together as a group to complete a research project. In this project they may interview other students in the school, asking their opinions on the ways to resolve certain local community issues. Your assessment of what students learned from this project should focus on *several* dimensions of learning such as is illustrated in Table 2.5.

The elements in Table 2.5 are not examples of assessment tasks. Rather, they are examples of questions you would use to help you direct or focus your assessment efforts. This example also illustrates that *for complex performance tasks, the traditional one-learning-target-one-taxonomy-category approach to assessment may not be appropriate.* Suggestions for how to craft assessments and scoring rubrics for complex performance tasks are found in Chapter 12.

Problems When Classifying Learning Targets Using a Taxonomy

It is important for you to recognize that (1) thinking skill categories may not be hierarchical, and (2) student performance on complex tasks involves using several thinking skills at the same time. It is possible, therefore, for you to classify a given learning target or assessment task into more than one taxonomy category.

The main purpose for suggesting that you use a taxonomy for assessment is to give you a tool to judge whether you have assessed a wide range of higher- and lower-order thinking skills. A taxonomy may help you find gaps where you have neglected to teach or assess certain levels of thinking; including a wide range of thinking skills in an assessment usually improves its validity.

If this is your first introduction to taxonomies, however, it may be useful for you to begin by classifying the learning target or assessment task into only one category of the taxonomy. This would simplify your organization and analysis of learning targets and assessment tasks, even though this may be somewhat artificial. As you do this, keep in mind that the one category into which you classify a learning target or assessment task is the one representing the thinking skill that is (1) *most prominently used by* or (2) *the main intent of* the learning target or assessment task. Once completed, you should use the classification to decide if some important skills have received too little or too much attention in your teaching and assessment.

Choosing a Taxonomy of Cognitive Learning Targets

We have discussed two different schemes for classifying cognitive learning targets. There are many more taxonomies or schemes that we have not discussed, some of

TABLE 2.4 Categories and examples of learning targets derived from the Dimensions of Learning Model. (See Appendix E also.)

Declarative knowledge—These learning targets tell students what facts, ideas, generalizations, and/or theories you will be assessing.

(*Example learning target:* Describe the characters in the story.)

Procedural knowledge—These learning targets tell students the skills and/or procedures you will be assessing.

(*Example learning target:* Ability to use several different types of maps to plan travel.)

Complex thinking—These learning targets tell students what types of reasoning strategies and ways of applying knowledge you will be assessing.

(*Example learning target:* Ability to use the analysis of a collection of newspaper advertisements to support conclusions about what advertisers think people want from the products they buy.)

Information processing—These learning targets tell students what aspects of information gathering, information synthesizing, information evaluating, and information needs assessment you will be assessing.

(*Example learning target:* Ability to decide what information in newspaper articles is relevant to solving the problem identifying the different views of local government officials on the issue of raising property taxes.)

Effective communication—These learning targets tell students which aspects of ideal communication, audience communication, purposes for communication, and products for communication you will be assessing.

(*Example learning target:* Ability to select the best method for presenting your ideas to your class.)

Collaboration and cooperation—These learning targets tell students what types of work on group goals, interpersonal skills, group maintenance activities, and multiple role activities you will be assessing.

(*Example learning target:* Ability to work together with students more knowledgeable and less knowledgeable than yourself regarding the topic of the performance task.)

Habits of mind—These learning targets tell students the types of self-regulation, critical thinking, and creative thinking performances you will be assessing.

(*Example learning target:* Ability to predict what types of resources are needed to successfully complete each part of the task before beginning.)

Source: Adapted from *Assessing Student Outcomes: Performance Assessment Using the Dimensions of Learning Model* (pp. 16–23) by R. J. Marzano, D. Pickering, and J. McTighe, 1993, Alexandria, VA: Association for Supervision and Curriculum Development. © 1993 by McREL Institute, 2550 South Parker Road, Aurora, CO 80014. Adapted by permission.

which are in Appendixes D (Tables D.2 and D.3) and E of this book (see DeLandsheere, 1988, for a review). Which one should you use? That depends on whether this is a personal decision for use in your classroom only or a more general decision in which the taxonomy will be used throughout the system.

Apply the following practical criteria to judge each taxonomy or classification scheme you are considering. If the decision is a personal one for one classroom, then not all criteria may apply to you.

TABLE 2.5 Example of how several Dimensions of Learning may be assessed through one research project (see text).

Dimension of Learning	Examples of the Assessment Focus
Declarative knowledge	Do students understand the local issues themselves?
Procedural knowledge	Did students conduct the interviews properly?
Complex thinking	Did students support their conclusions with data?
Information processing	Did the students use relevant information from the interviews?
Effective communication	Did students clearly present their report to the class?
Collaboration and communication	Did students work together effectively?
Habits of mind	Did students plan and organize their work?

Practical Criteria for Selecting a Taxonomy of Cognitive Learning Targets

1. *Completeness:* The degree to which the major learning targets can be classified within the taxonomy.

2. *Point of view:* Extent to which the taxonomy can be used as a platform for explaining teaching methods or curriculum characteristics to others.

3. *Reform:* Extent to which the taxonomy helps to evaluate the curriculum or learning targets and lead to revisions of learning targets.

4. *Simplicity:* Ease with which the end users (e.g., teachers, education officials) understand the taxonomy.

5. *Reporting:* Usefulness of the taxonomy as a means of organizing reports of assessment results for individual students, educational officials, government officials, or the public.

SOURCES FOR LOCATING LEARNING TARGETS

You may find lists of learning targets in a variety of sources, including instructional materials and teachers' manuals, local and state curriculum frameworks, state performance standards, reports of the National Assessment of Educational Progress, books on teaching methods, manuals accompanying tests (especially criterion-referenced tests), and reports from educational associations. More than likely you will have to adapt the learning targets found in these sources to your own situation. Statements of learning targets are usually developed for specific purposes. Frequently you will find no consistent form or quality from one developer to another. Nevertheless, these sources and the taxonomies do provide a starting place: *It is much easier to adapt and revise learning target statements than to write them without any assistance.*

Also, a learning target often will cut across several lessons or subject areas. The ability to use library and print resources to obtain information for a report, for example, is likely to be a learning target common to social studies, mathematics, and language arts curricula. A source of learning targets may not list targets that are specific to the content of a particular lesson, and thus the important learning targets you are looking for may not appear. *But you should be aware of such broader, encompassing learning targets and include them in your list for teaching and assessment.* In this regard, the categories provided by the Marzano et al. (1993) learning dimensions and shown in Appendix E were created so that each category would apply across several curricular areas. This appendix may help you plan your assessments for different curricula.

EVALUATING THE LEARNING TARGETS OF A COURSE OR UNIT

It is important to develop a complete or comprehensive list of learning targets. A complete list is not necessarily long, however. Apply the following practical criteria to evaluate your list of learning targets.

Practical Criteria for Evaluating a List of Learning Targets for a Course or Unit

1. Be sure all the learning targets are appropriate for the educational level of the students.

2. Be sure the list of learning targets is limited to only the important outcomes for the course.

3. Be sure all the learning targets are consistent with your state's published learning standards.

4. Be sure all the learning targets are consistent with your local school's philosophy and general goals.

5. Be sure all the learning targets can be defended by currently accepted learning principles.

6. Be sure all the learning targets can be taught in the time limits of the course.

7. Be sure all the learning targets can be taught with teaching resources you have available.

The next section of this chapter discusses ways to phrase or write learning targets so they communicate your instructional intent and help you to craft an assessment plan or "blueprint." This plan, discussed in Chapter 6, will help assure that you develop valid classroom assessments. Validity itself is discussed in the next chapter.

DESIRABLE QUALITIES OF SPECIFIC LEARNING TARGETS

The following **minimum criteria for learning targets** assures their usefulness as a basis for classroom instruction and crafting assessment instruments (Lindvall, 1964, 1967):

1. **Student centered:** Learning targets should focus on the student.

2. **Performance centered:** Learning targets should be worded in terms of what a student can perform after the required learning experiences.

3. **Content centered:** Learning targets should state the specific content to which the student should apply the performance.

Student Centered

Because instruction focuses on changes in student performance, learning targets should describe student performances. However, it is not unusual for some curriculum guides, frameworks, and other materials available to teachers to contain such statements as "to provide for student participation in classroom discussions." The problem with this statement is that it is an activity statement *for teachers* rather than a learning target for students. You may "provide for student participation," yet each student may not participate. Learning targets need to be student centered if they are to be the basis for crafting assessment procedures. Thus, you should say, "A student will participate in classroom discussions." Student-centered learning targets allow you to decide whether the students actually have achieved what you intended from the lesson.

Performance Centered

Not only should a learning target refer to a student, it should state a performance—that is, an observable activity. This can be accomplished by being sure that the statement includes an **action verb** that specifies a student performance.

To help beginners write learning targets that describe students' performances, Table 2.6 lists further examples of various action verbs. These verbs are organized according to categories of Bloom and Krathwohl et al. cognitive and affective taxonomies discussed in Appendix D. When verbs such as these are used in statements of learning targets, the learning targets will usually satisfy the second criterion of expressing observable student performance. A balance is necessary between verbs that are too broad (and thus imply too many nonequivalent performances) and those that are too specific (and which are often just ways of marking answers). Consider this learning target, which is stated too specifically:

> *Poor:* The student is able to put an X on the picture of the correct geometric shape (circle, triangle, rectangle, square, or ellipse) when the name of the shape is given.

The main intent of such an objective is to *select* or *identify* the correct shape, not just to make Xs. *Any* response that indicates the student has correctly identified the required shape is acceptable. Thus, the learning target should be written as:

> *Better:* The student is able to identify a picture of a geometric shape (circle, triangle, rectangle, square, or ellipse) when the name of the shape is given.

Table 2.7 suggests some verbs that maintain this balance and illustrates other verbs that are too specific or too broad to make useful learning target statements.

Content Oriented

When stating a learning target, you should indicate the content to which a student's performance is to apply. A learning target which states, for example, that "the student is able to write definitions of the important terms used in the text" needs to be modified. You need to include a reference to a specific list of "important words" or in some

---

TABLE 2.6 Examples of action verbs to use when writing learning targets. (See Appendix D for additional examples.)

I. **Cognitive domain [Bloom et al., 1956]**
   a. **Knowledge:** define, describe, identify, label, list, match, name, outline, select, state
   b. **Comprehension:** convert, distinguish, estimate, explain, extend, generalize, give examples, infer, paraphrase, predict, rewrite, summarize
   c. **Application:** change, compute, demonstrate, discover, manipulate, modify, operate, predict, prepare, produce, relate, show, solve, use
   d. **Analysis:** break down, diagram, differentiate, discriminate, distinguish, identify, illustrate, infer, outline, point out, relate, select, separate, subdivide
   e. **Synthesis:** categorize, combine, compile, compose, create, design, devise, rewrite, summarize, tell, write
   f. **Evaluation:** appraise, compare, conclude, contrast, criticize, describe, discriminate, explain, justify, interpret, relate, summarize, support

II. **Affective domain [Krathwohl et al., 1964]**
   a. **Receiving:** ask, choose, describe, follow, give, hold, identify, locate, name, point to, reply, select, sit erect, use
   b. **Responding:** answer, assist, comply, conform, discuss, greet, help, label, perform, practice, present, read, report, respond, select, tell, write
   c. **Valuing:** complete, demonstrate, describe, differentiate, explain, follow, form, initiate, invite, join, justify, propose, read, recognize, report, select, share, study, work, write
   d. **Organizing:** adhere, alter, arrange, combine, compare, complete, defend, explain, generalize, identify, integrate, modify, organize, order, prepare, relate, synthesize
   e. **Characterizing by a value or value complex:** act, discriminate, display, influence, listen, modify, perform, practice, propose, qualify, question, revise, serve, solve, use, verify

---

Source: Table adapted from TESTING FOR TEACHERS, Second Edition by Bruce W. Tuckman, copyright © 1988 by Harcourt, Inc. Reproduced by permission of the publisher. (Figure 2.2, p. 17)

TABLE 2.7 Examples of action verbs sometimes used in learning targets.

Specific but acceptable verbs			
add, total	describe	match	rename
alphabetize	divide	measure	rephrase
choose	draw	multiply	select
complete, supply	explain	name	sort, classify
construct, make	identify	order, arrange	state
convert	label	pick out	subtract, take away
count	list	regroup	weigh
delete			

Too broad, unacceptable verbs			
apply	examine	interpret	respond
deduce	generate	observe	test
do	infer	perform	use

Too specific, essentially indicator verbs			
check	draw a line between	put a mark on	underline
circle	draw a ring around	put an X on	write the letter of
color the same as	put a box around	shade	write the number of

Toss-up verbs, requiring further clarification			
answer	contrast	differentiate	give
collect, synthesize	demonstrate	discriminate	locate
compare	determine	distinguish	predict

Source: From "Criteria for Stating IPI Objectives" by C. M. Lindvall, 1976, pp. 214–215. In D. T. Gow (Ed.), *Design and Development of Curricular Materials: Instructional Design Articles* (Volume 2). Pittsburgh, PA: University of Pittsburgh, University Center for International Studies.

other way describe them. If you do not refer to content in your learning target statement, it is not possible for you to know with certainty whether the assessment task is valid for evaluating the student. For example, the assessment may require students to define words that, although in the text, may be unimportant. Without knowing the content, it is difficult for anyone to determine what, if anything, was learned.

MAKING SURE ASSESSMENT TASKS MATCH LEARNING TARGETS

Chapters 6 through 15 discuss the details of crafting high-quality assessment tasks and procedures. Here we wish to point out that the basic purpose of any achievement assessment is to determine the extent to which each student has achieved the stated learning targets. Although this purpose sounds straightforward, it is not always an easy criterion to meet. The quality of your assessment of what each student has learned is evaluated by judging the validity of your assessment results. Validity is the subject of the next chapter; here we discuss validity only in relation to **matching assessment tasks to learning targets.**

Matching Assessments to Mastery Learning Targets

The specific tasks or procedures you use in an assessment should require the student to display the skill or knowl-

edge stated in the learning target. For instance, if your learning target calls for a student to actually build an apparatus, write a poem, or perform a physical skill, your assessment procedure must give the student the opportunity to *perform.* If your assessment procedure required a student *only to list* the parts of an apparatus, to analyze an existing poem, or to describe the sequence of steps needed for performing a physical skill, it would not be valid, because it would not match the learning target's main intent. *A very basic requirement for the validity of classroom assessment procedures is that the procedures should match the intentions of the specific learning targets that you include in your assessment plan.* The methods of developing assessment plans are the subject of Chapter 6.

Matching Assessments to Developmental Learning Targets

As is often the case, developmental learning targets imply a broad domain of performance application. To assure the validity of your classroom assessment, you may need to assess the same learning target in several different ways. For example, assessing spelling achievement might be done both by scoring several samples of students' written assignments and by using a dictated spelling test. The test provides the opportunity to assess a student's spelling of word patterns that might not appear in the natural course of the student's writing, but that may well be part of the learning target. Observing a student's natural writing habits permits you to infer how good the student is likely to spell in typical writing situations. Using both procedures increases the comprehensiveness of your assessment of the students' spelling ability and the validity of your evaluation.

Another reason for using more than one assessment procedure is to obtain more reliable results. Your subjective evaluation of a student's written essay on a topic might be supplemented by a test made up of more objectively scored items. Thus, when the less reliable information about the student's written work (that is, your subjective evaluation) is combined with the more reliable information (the objectively scored test), your overall evaluation result is more reliable. Reliability is discussed in more detail in Chapter 4.

Summary

- Learning targets are important because specifying them helps you to direct your teaching toward the important student achievements that you, the school, and parents have in mind.
- Among the benefits of using specific learning target statements are (1) making educational goals explicit, (2) communicating instructional intent to others, (3) analyzing and sequencing what is to be taught, (4) evaluating instructional procedures, (5) providing focus in discussions with parents, (6) clarifying to students what is expected of them, (7) facilitating individualized instruction, and (8) facilitating the revision of instructional procedures.
- Specifying learning targets has a practical value for your classroom assessments through (1) facilitating your general planning for assessment, (2) clarifying the specific performances for which you should craft or select assessment tasks, (3) facilitating your evaluation of an existing assessment procedure, and (4) facilitating your judgment of the validity of an assessment.
- Statements of general educational goals help to guide the overall educational enterprise, but you must make them more specific before you can implement them in the classroom.
- Specificity is accomplished by organizing goals into subject-matter areas and then developing several general learning targets for each goal. You subsequently define each general learning target by more specific performances that you can teach and assess. You use assessment results from these specific learning targets to infer the degree to which students have attained general learning targets and goals.
- Content standards describe what subject-matter knowledge students are expected to learn. Performance standards describe what students are expected to do with their content knowledge. Standards are often statements of general learning targets. Therefore, teachers need to break standards into more specific learning targets for purposes of teaching and assessment.
- At least two kinds or levels of learning targets useful for classroom instruction can be identified: specific, mastery learning targets, and broader, developmental learning targets.
- Developmental learning targets are never fully achieved by students. However, you can teach and assess the degree of students' achievement at a particular educational level by writing several important, specific learning targets that define appropriate achievement at that level. You use students' performances on this sample of learning targets to estimate the progress students have made in achieving the developmental learning target.
- Developmental learning targets cannot be considered mastery learning targets because: (1) They imply several performances that are not highly related to each other; (2) narrowing their meaning to a single, specific objective destroys the intent of the developmental learning target; and (3) it is reasonable to expect degrees of development or growth in certain achievement areas, rather than complete mastery.
- When writing the learning targets for a lesson or unit and for crafting a classroom assessment, it is important to identify the full range of student performance to be achieved. This is done by (1) referring to taxonomies of cognitive, affective, and/or psychomotor objectives, (2) reviewing instructional materials and teachers' manuals, (3) consulting curriculum frameworks from various sources, (4) reviewing books on methods of teaching the subject, (5) reviewing the criterion-referenced tests of a subject, (6) consulting your state's mandated standards, and (7) reviewing reports from professional organizations.
- The Bloom et al. taxonomy orders levels of cognitive learning targets from simplest to most complex. These are knowledge, comprehension, application, analysis, synthesis, and evaluation. (See Table D.1 of Appendix D for details.)
- The Dimensions of Learning Model approach defines seven broad categories of learning targets: declarative knowledge, procedural knowledge, complex thinking, information processing, effective communication, collaboration and cooperation, and habits of mind. Each of these categories contains a more detailed breakdown of learning targets. (See Appendix E for details.)
- The Dimensions of Learning Model approaches are not hierarchical.
- Taxonomies for the affective and psychomotor domains are presented in Appendix D (Tables D.4 and D.5).
- Criteria for evaluating the quality and importance of the learning targets you select for a unit or a course were listed.
- The minimum criteria for a written statement of a specific learning target are (1) worded in terms of the

student, rather than in terms of a teacher or a school, (2) worded in terms of observable student performance, and (3) worded so the specific content to which a student's performance is applied is clear.

- Specific examples for action verbs that describe student performance are given in Tables 2.6 and 2.7.
- The validity of assessment results increase if the assessment closely matches the intent of the learning targets.
- Sometimes you need to use several different methods of assessing a student's performance before you can validly conclude that the student has met the intent of the learning target.

Important Terms and Concepts

action verb
analysis, application, comprehension, evaluation, knowledge, synthesis
content standards
declarative knowledge, procedural knowledge, complex thinking, information processing, effective communication, collaboration and cooperation, habits of mind
developmental learning targets
educational goals
general learning targets
instruction
learning objective
learning targets
mastery learning targets
matching assessment tasks to learning targets
minimum criteria for learning targets (content centered, performance centered, student centered)
performance standards
specific learning targets
taxonomies of instructional learning targets (affective, cognitive, psychomotor)

Exercises and Discussion Questions

1. What are the advantages of stating teaching goals as specific learning targets?
2. How can statements of specific learning targets help you to plan and organize your teaching? Give an example.
3. State and explain the four reasons why specific learning targets help to improve your classroom assessment procedures.
4. Explain the usefulness of statements of educational goals and of general learning targets to the educational enterprise generally, and to the classroom teacher specifically.
5. Explain the differences and similarities between mastery and developmental learning targets.
6. Explain the meaning of homogeneous domains as used in connection with mastery learning targets.
7. How does a homogeneous domain support the use of mastery learning targets?
8. How does a broad, heterogeneous domain contraindicate the use of mastery learning targets?
9. Write three specific learning targets for a lesson you plan to teach. Explain how each learning target meets the three criteria: student centered, performance centered, and content centered.

10. Here are three learning targets. Decide whether each implies a homogeneous or a heterogeneous domain. Write a brief statement justifying your choice.
    a. When given a Roman numeral, the student is able to write the corresponding Arabic numeral.
    b. Students are able to recognize examples of deductive and inductive reasoning.
    c. Students are able to write a definition of deductive and inductive reasoning.
11. Here are three learning targets. Decide whether each is a mastery learning target or a developmental learning target. Explain the bases for your choices.
    a. The student is able to take the square root of any number using a handheld calculator.
    b. The student is able to determine whether the thesis of the argument is supported adequately.
    c. When given data the student is able to construct a graph to describe the trend in the data.
12. Obtain a list of learning targets for a unit or a course. Evaluate each learning target using the seven criteria stated in the text. Make a two-way grid with the seven criteria on one dimension and the learning targets on the other. In the body of the grid, mark *yes* if the learning target meets the criterion and *no* if it does not. Compare your results with others taking this course. Reconcile any differences between your results and theirs.
13. In what ways are the Bloom et al. and the Dimensions of Learning Model classification schemes similar? Different? Explain your answers by using examples.
14. Make two, two-way grids, one for the Bloom et al. taxonomy and one for the Dimensions of Learning Model taxonomy. On each grid, list the main categories of the respective taxonomy along one dimension. Then list the following specific learning targets along the other. Now, classify each of the learning targets into one thinking skills category in each of the two taxonomies. Record your results in the grid. Compare your results with those of your classmates. Reconcile any differences. Classify these learning targets from a visual art curriculum:
    a. Define *color intensity*.
    b. Define *batik*.
    c. Explain why artists sometimes make sketches before they start a three-dimensional craftwork.
    d. Given several craftworks, rate each according to the degree to which they have effectively used art principles.
    e. Given craftworks such as puppets or masks, describe how each piece depicts "mood."
    f. Given several pieces of different kinds of craftworks, describe how each has used art elements (e.g., curved lines, smooth textures, bright colors, etc.).
15. Extend Exercise 14 to the Gagné, Quellmalz, and Core Thinking Skills classification schemes found in Appendix D (Tables D.2 and D.3) and Appendix E.
16. Decide whether each learning target listed here belongs to the cognitive, affective, or psychomotor domain. Does the performance of each learning target require some use of elements from domains other than the one into which you classified it? Which one(s)? Explain why. Does this mean you should reclassify that learning target? Explain.
    a. The student is able to tune a color television set to get the best color resolution.

b. The student demonstrates knowledge of parliamentary law by conducting a meeting without violating parliamentary procedures.

c. The student contributes to group maintenance when working with classmates on a science project.

d. The student makes 5 baskets out of 10 tries on the basketball court while standing at the foul line.

17. Select a unit of instruction in a subject area you teach (or plan to teach). Write a content outline of the material you would teach in the unit. Using the five practical criteria for selecting a taxonomy, select one of the thinking skills taxonomies. Write one learning target appropriate for this unit in each of the categories of that taxonomy. Be sure each objective meets the three basic criteria for learning target writing.

18. Show your results for Exercise 17 to your classmates. Using the five practical criteria as a basis, explain why you selected the taxonomy. Revise your learning targets if your classmates discover flaws in them.

19. Obtain a copy of your state's (or neighboring state's) standards. Analyze the suitability of these statements for (a) planning units and lessons and (b) for developing assessment exercises. Prepare a criticism of these standards from your point of view as a teacher of a specific grade and subject. In your criticism, be sure to emphasize issues that are concerned with assessment.

Additional Readings

Airasian, P. W. (1991). *Classroom assessment.* New York: McGraw-Hill, Chapter 3, pp. 73–120.

Discusses the instructional planning process and how to use learning targets.

Kendall, J. S. (1997). *Content knowledge: A compendium of standards and benchmarks for K–12 education* (2nd ed.). Alexandria, VA: Association for Supervision and Curriculum Development.

Describes content standards and benchmarks (what should be learned) at each grade.

Marzano, R. J., Brandt, R. S., Hughes, C. S. Jones, B. F., Preseisan, B. Z., Rankin, S. C., & Suhor, C. (1988). *Dimensions of thinking: A framework for curriculum and instruction.* Alexandria, VA: Association for Supervision and Curriculum Development.

Describes a wide range of thinking skills and how they might be taught in school. Explains the Core Thinking Skills in greater detail than this text.

Marzano, R. J., Pickering, D., & McTighe, J. (1993). *Assessing student outcomes: Performance assessment using the Dimensions of Learning Model.* Alexandria, VA: Association for Supervision and Curriculum Development.

Explains the classification reproduced in Appendix E and illustrates how to use it for purposes of performance assessment.

Nitko, A. J. (1989). Designing tests that are integrated with instruction. In R. L. Linn (Ed.), *Educational measurement* (3rd ed., pp. 447–474). New York: Macmillan.

Describes various approaches to diagnostic assessment and points out the limitations of behavioral objectives for these purposes.

Pasch, M., Sparks-Langer, J., Gardner, T. G., Starko, A. J., & Moody, C. D. (1991). *Teaching as decision making: Instructional practices for the successful teacher.* New York: Longman, Chapters 2 and 3.

Gives practical guidelines and practice exercises for identifying, writing, and using learning targets in the classroom.

CHAPTER 3

Validity of Assessment Results

Learning Targets

After studying this chapter, you should be able to:

1. Explain the concept of validity and how it applies to all educational assessment results.   [3, 4, 6]

2. Explain the four principles of validation.   [3, 6, 7]

3. Apply the validity criteria in Table 3.1 to your own classroom assessment results.   [5, 4, 2, 7]

4. Describe each of the eight types of evidence needed to validate interpretations and uses of extra-classroom assessment results.   [6, 3, 7]

5. Describe the relationship among the eight types of validity evidence and the categories of content-related, criterion-related, and construct-related validity evidence.   [6, 3]

6. Explain the concept of correlation and how it is used in validating assessment results.   [6, 3]

7. Explain how scatter diagrams and expectancy tables may be used to interpret relationships between two sets of assessment results.   [3, 6]

8. Explain how various factors affect the magnitude of correlation coefficients.   [6, 3]

9. Explain how to evaluate the criterion measures used in validation studies.   [6, 4, 3]

10. Describe the difference between concurrent and predictive validity evidence.   [6, 4, 3]

11. Explain the special validity problems that arise when extra-classroom assessment instruments are used to evaluate curricula, schools, and educational innovations.   [6, 4, 1]

12. Explain how each of the terms and concepts listed at the end of this chapter apply to the validation of educational assessment results.   [6]

GENERAL NATURE OF VALIDITY

Validity is the soundness of your interpretations and uses of students' assessment results. Validity emphasizes the results you interpret, not the instrument or procedures itself. To validate your interpretations and uses of students' assessment results, you must provide evidence that these interpretations and uses are appropriate. You must also demonstrate that students experience no serious negative consequences when their results are used as you intend. The question "Are these assessment results valid?" has many different answers depending on *how the results are interpreted and used*. For example, your school may have administered the *ABC Reading Test* and wishes to use the scores for one or more of the following: to describe students' growth in reading comprehension; to place students into high, middle, and low reading groups; or to evaluate the school's reading program. The scores from this hypothetical test may have a high degree of validity for one of these purposes but may not have high validity for the others.

When discussing the validity of assessment results, keep in mind the following points:

1. *The concept of validity applies to the ways in which we interpret and use the assessment results and not to the assessment procedure itself.* Thus, we may not say, "Is the *ABC Reading Test* valid?" except as an informal, shorthand way of speaking. Rather, we must ask more specific questions such as, "Is it valid to interpret the scores from the *ABC Reading Test* as measuring reading comprehension?" or "Is it valid to use *ABC Reading Test* scores to place students into reading groups?" and so on.

2. *The assessment results have different degrees of validity for different purposes and for different situations.* The scores from our hypothetical *ABC Reading Test*, for example, may be highly valid when used to evaluate the reading program in your school district because the items on it match the district's reading program objectives quite well. Scores from the same test may have poor validity for evaluating your neighboring district's reading program because the items match that district's reading program objectives poorly.

3. *Judgments about the validity of your interpretations or uses of assessment results should be made only after you have studied and combined several types of validity evidence.* As an example, before you may come to a conclusion about the validity of a proposed interpretation or the use of the *ABC Reading Test*'s scores, you need to collect evidence concerning how well it samples the reading domain. You also need to decide whether the skills assessed represent "authentic" or appropriate reading, whether the scores are unduly influenced by irrelevant factors such as the students' moods or their motivation to be tested, how closely the tested skills match your school district's reading objectives; whether the scores are reliable and so on.

Validity is not the evidence about only one of these areas. Rather, it is a judgment you make after considering evidence from all relevant sources. Until all relevant evidence is collected, reviewed, weighed, and combined, your evaluation of the validity of the results is incomplete. In effect, you validate specific interpretations and uses of assessment results by making a convincing argument that the evidence supports them (Kane, 1992).

Four Principles for Validation

The **four principles for validation** that follow will help you decide the degree to which your assessment results are valid (Messick, 1989b, 1994a). Remember, your validity judgment must be based on all four principles, not just on one of them.

1. The interpretations (meanings) you give to your students' assessment results are valid only to the degree that you can point to evidence that supports their appropriateness and correctness.

2. The uses you may make of your assessment results are valid only to the degree to which you can point to evidence that supports their correctness and appropriateness.

3. The interpretations and uses of your assessment results are valid only when the values implied by them are appropriate.

4. The interpretations and uses you make of your assessment results are valid only when the consequences of these interpretations and uses are consistent with appropriate values.

Appropriate Interpretations Consider, for example, a Lincoln School student, Hiram. Hiram has taken the *ABC Reading Test* each year, but his scores suddenly rose this year. Hiram's suddenly rising scores have several possible interpretations, including these: (1) his reading comprehension has improved, (2) his motivation to do well on reading comprehension tests has improved, and (3) his skill in answering multiple-choice reading comprehension test items has improved. These interpretations are not mutually exclusive. Hiram may have improved in one or more of these areas.

The Lincoln School staff may like to interpret Hiram's assessments to mean that he has improved his reading comprehension. However, before they can assert that such an interpretation has some degree of validity, they need to offer evidence. First they need to show that the *ABC Reading Test* measures reading comprehension in the way comprehension is generally understood by reading specialists. Second, they need evidence to show that Hiram's increased test performance is primarily due to his improved reading, rather than simply reflecting his increased motivation and improved test-taking skills. Third, they need to use other evidence that exists in the school: Hiram's reading teacher and/or classroom teacher can describe his performance in the class and compare his test performance with his classroom reading performance. If, for example, the staff finds contradictory evidence in the assessment research literature that the test scores are easily increased by a student's motivation and test-taking skill, then continuing to interpret Hiram's scores as measuring purely reading comprehension would be unsound or invalid.

Appropriate Uses We distinguish between *interpretations*—which refer to meaning—and *uses*. The Lincoln School staff members might choose several uses of the test. They are (1) to certify that Hiram is reading at an appropriate level for his grade; (2) to diagnose or identify the types of reading comprehension problems Hiram may be experiencing;

(3) to place Hiram into a remedial, regular, or advanced reading group; and (4) to continually monitor Hiram's growth in reading comprehension. The Lincoln School staff may wish to use Hiram's scores for more than one of these purposes. However, the validity of any of Lincoln School's uses of the *ABC Reading Test* scores depends on the evidence they can find to support each use. For example, what evidence can Lincoln School provide to demonstrate that students assigned to remedial reading groups on the basis of their *ABC Reading Test* scores will learn to read better than if they were assigned to the regular reading classes? Evidence should be provided separately for each intended use of assessment results. For published standardized tests, much of this evidence may be available in the test's technical manual so a school may not need to do its own research.

Notice that in examples of Lincoln School's specific uses of the test, we used wording that implied a reading comprehension *interpretation* of the test results. This illustrates an important point about the assessment validation process: *To validate a particular usage of assessment results, you must employ a validated interpretation or meaning of those results.* Thus, if Lincoln School cannot first establish the degree to which the *ABC Reading Test* measures reading comprehension, the school would not be able to validate any further use of the test scores that are *based on the assumption that the test measures reading comprehension.*

Appropriate Values   The interpretations you give to and the uses you make of your students' assessment results arise from your educational and social values. When Lincoln School's staff interpreted Hiram's *ABC Reading Test* scores as measuring reading comprehension and used them to describe and to plan his reading development, the staff's values were implicit in each step.

The very choice of the *ABC Reading Test*, for example, implied that the staff valued the format and content of the test items. Suppose that the *ABC Reading Test* consists of several short passages (less than 500 words each), each followed by several multiple-choice questions. Further, suppose the themes of the reading passages ignore (or are irrelevant to) African American, Hispanic, Native American, and/or other minority cultural experiences. Using and interpreting this test as a measure of reading comprehension implies the staff accepted that such cultural and ethnic experiences are unimportant for assessing a student's reading comprehension.

Using a multiple-choice format for assessing reading comprehension is also a value judgment: Should longer, more "authentic" reading passages and open-ended questions be used instead? Is the cheaper cost of the multiple-choice test valued over the more costly authentic assessment? The staff's use of the test scores to assign students to different reading groups implies that they value homogeneous grouping for reading instruction. Implied, too, is that the benefits received from being taught with others of similar reading ability are more important (valuable) than the benefits received from being taught in a more mixed reading ability group.

Again notice that the discussion of value judgments in the preceding paragraphs uses a reading comprehension interpretation of the test results *and* describes specific ways of using the scores. This illustrates that *you must consider proper interpretations, relevant uses, and appropriate values when asking how valid your assessment results are.*

Appropriate Consequences   Whenever you interpret and use your students' assessment results, intended and unintended consequences result: Every action you take has a consequence. You must consider these consequences when judging whether you are using the assessment results validly. Lincoln School's intended consequence for placing children with low *ABC Reading Test* scores into remedial reading groups was to improve these children's reading ability as rapidly as possible. As the students' reading comprehension improves, the staff believes, so will their other schoolwork and their self-esteem.

But suppose something unintended and unvalued happens instead. Suppose the remedial reading students quickly come to see themselves as incompetent, and their self-esteem is lowered. Suppose, too, that out of frustration their teachers begin drilling them on material they do not understand (instead of building on what they already know). Suppose that eventually the students never leave the remedial reading track. In the face of these unintended and negatively valued consequences, would Lincoln School's use of the *ABC Reading Test* scores to form remedial groups still be highly valid? Even if the test measured reading comprehension, when such negative consequences occur its continued use would be devastating to these children. Interpretations and uses of assessment results must have positively valued consequences (and avoid negatively valued consequences) to have a high degree of validity.

This example uses a reading comprehension interpretation of the test results, describes a specific use of the results (placement into remedial reading groups), and incorporates a positively valued intention (improved student reading and self-esteem). The example shows that the positively valued consequences may not come about for all students. This illustrates that *you must consider appropriate interpretations, appropriate uses, appropriate values, and appropriate consequences when asking how valid your assessment results are.*

VALIDITY OF TEACHER-MADE CLASSROOM ASSESSMENT RESULTS

This section considers criteria for validating the results of classroom assessment methods. Although validity criteria apply to all types of classroom assessments, including brief assignments, long-term assignments, and quizzes, we illustrate the application of these criteria with only one example. The reason for doing this is that judgment of validity depends on knowing the particular interpretation, uses, values, and consequences of the assessment. The one example provides the specific focus we use to illustrate the ideas.

An Example of Assessment Interpretation and Use

The example in this section assumes that a teacher will interpret the classroom assessment results as one summative evaluation of the students' mastery of the material. The assessment purpose includes using the results to assign letter grades to students. It is assumed, also, that the teacher will use the results of this assessment as only one of several important pieces of information in assigning letter grades to students. Finally, it is assumed that the assessment covers a sizable "chunk" of learning, such as a *unit*, a *marking period*, or a *semester*. The criteria we discuss apply to *any* assessment technique used for this purpose; the technique may or may not be a paper-and-pencil test.

Validity Criteria for Improving Classroom Assessments

Several criteria may be used to improve the validity of using your assessment results for grading students. These criteria are summarized in Table 3.1. The table shows the criteria organized into several categories discussed in this section.

Content Representativeness and Relevance

The validity of your classroom assessment results depends very much on how well the assessment samples the learning targets. To create valid assessments, you must (1) clearly identify the important learning targets, and (2) be sure they are well sampled by the assessment procedure.

You must place the learning targets you teach and assess into the appropriate context of your school district and the discipline you are teaching. This means that the tasks included on your assessment should reflect the important content and learning outcomes specified in your school's or state's curriculum framework and content standards. A thinking skills taxonomy is a useful tool in

TABLE 3.1 Criteria for improving the validity of scores from classroom assessments used for assigning grades to students.

Category	Criteria to be attained. Your assessment should:
Content representativeness and relevance	1. Emphasize what you taught 2. Represent school's stated curricular content 3. Represent current thinking about the subject 4. Contain content worth learning
Thinking processes and skills represented	5. Require students to integrate and use several thinking skills 6. Represent thinking processes and skills stated in school's curriculum 7. Contain tasks that cannot be completed without using intended thinking skills 8. Allow enough time for students to use complex skills and processes
Consistency with other classroom assessments	9. Yield pattern of results consistent with your other assessments of the class 10. Contain individual tasks (items) not too easy or too difficult
Reliability and objectivity	11. Use a systematic procedure for every student to assigning quality ratings or marks 12. Provide each student with several opportunities to demonstrate competence for each learning target assessed
Fairness to different types of students	13. Contain tasks that are interpreted appropriately by students with different backgrounds 14. Accommodate students with disabilities or learning difficulties, if necessary 15. Be free of ethnic, racial, and gender bias
Economy, efficiency, practicality, instructional features	16. Require a reasonable amount of time for you to construct and administer 17. Represent appropriate use of students' class time 18. Represent appropriate use of your class time
Multiple assessment usage	19. Be used in conjunction with other assessment results for important decisions

this regard. You should also review each task to assure that from the content perspective it is relevant, important, stated accurately, has an accurate key or scoring rubric, and represents something that is meaningful to learn.

When evaluating your classroom assessment method in relation to representativeness and relevance, you should focus on the following questions:

1. *Does my assessment procedure emphasize what I have taught?* Students have a right to expect to be evaluated on what you have emphasized in class. If you have spent lots of time in one area of the material, that area should be featured prominently in the assessment. A common error teachers make is to uncritically use the tests that come with the curriculum materials or the textbook. Often, the items on these tests are of poor quality, emphasize low-level thinking skills (Center for the Study of Testing, Evaluation, and Educational Policy, 1992), or emphasize different content than was emphasized during teaching.[1] We recall a tragic anecdote in this regard. A teacher used one of these tests without carefully reviewing it. The day of the test, the teacher discovered that 10 of the 40 items covered material that she had not taught. In desperation, the teacher used the first 15 minutes of testing time to try to teach these concepts and then gave the test. Of course, this assessment not only lacked validity but also produced student frustration, and disastrous results. This case is an example, too, of unethical test use on the part of the teacher.

2. *Do my assessment tasks accurately represent the outcomes specified in my school's or state's curriculum framework?* Assessments that you use in grading should reflect the learning targets that the school district and state identify as important. Students' grades will be recorded and eventually be interpreted by persons who have seen the curriculum but who are not familiar with what you taught in the classroom. They will expect the grades to reflect the district's learning targets and the state's content standards. Because grades are based on your assessments, your assessments should reflect these learning outcomes.

3. *Are my assessment tasks in line with the current thinking about what should be taught and how it should be assessed?* What is worth learning is constantly being redefined by educators, philosophers, curriculum theorists, researchers, and others. Professional teachers keep abreast of these developments and implement them in their teaching and assessment practices.

4. *Is the content in my assessment procedure important and worth learning?* The curriculum and content you teach contain many specifics. You must be certain that the as-

sessed content relates directly, rather than tangentially, to important student learning targets. Content included in your assessment should be of great value or significance to a student's further learning or to a student's life skills.

Most worthwhile learning involves students' using combinations of skills and content rather than using isolated skills or bits of content. Assessment tasks, therefore, should also require students to use several aspects of such knowledge, skills, and processes in combination.

Thinking Processes and Skills Represented

Closely related to content representativeness and relevance is whether your assessment method permits you to evaluate students on a sufficiently wide range of thinking skills and processes. Assessment instruments that cover broad areas of learning—a unit, marking period, or semester—should comprehensively assess different types of thinking skills. We stressed using various taxonomies in Chapter 2 because of the importance of this comprehensiveness. Using such taxonomy with a content outline or curriculum framework to write an assessment blueprint helps you to ensure that the important thinking skills and processes are reflected in your assessment procedures. Such comprehensiveness can be accomplished only by consciously planning for it. Chapter 6 discusses how to develop a comprehensive assessment plan.

The following questions will help you judge the validity of your classroom assessment in relation to thinking skills and processes:

5. *Do the tasks on my assessment instrument require students to use important thinking skills and processes?* Every classroom assessment procedure should require students to use a mixture of thinking skills and processes. The issue here, however, is the degree to which your assessment mirrors the important thinking skills used in the discipline you are teaching. The answer is a matter of emphasis and of knowing what curriculum experts have recommended as learning targets for the students at a particular grade level.

The tasks should assess a student's ability to use strategies and processes that reflect how those in the discipline think. For example, mathematics assessment should help you assess whether a student uses good mathematics thinking when solving problems, not only whether the student can obtain the right answer. Assessment in social studies should help you assess how students think critically and apply the material to their daily lives, rather than simply whether they can "compare and contrast" or "list the factors that caused . . . ." Important and worthwhile learning can be applied to real-life situations. Assessment tasks should at least simulate real-life applications at levels appropriate for the students you teach. They should require students to use combinations of several skills and knowledge whenever possible.

---

[1]We believe that you will increase the validity of your classroom-based assessments if you craft your own instruments. The second part of this book is devoted to teaching you how to craft valid classroom-based assessments.

6. *Does my assessment instrument represent the kinds of thinking skills that my school's or state's curriculum framework and performance standards state are important?* Local and state curricula and standards often state, along with content learning, certain types of higher order, critical thinking, and performances as goals of instruction. Your teaching should foster this kind of thinking, and you should assess your students' abilities to use it appropriately.

7. *Do students actually use the types of thinking I expect them to use on the assessment?* If you are going to interpret students' assessment performance as reflecting complex thinking skills, then you should be sure that students are actually using them when completing the assessment. Check this by observing the strategies your students appear to use during the assessment. You may interview a few students, asking them to "think aloud" as they solve assessment tasks. You may also review the tasks on your assessment. Poorly constructed test items will give clues to the correct answers and lower the chances that students will need to use the important thinking skills you want them to use. Similarly, ambiguously worded questions confuse students, interfering with their use of important strategies, and lower the validity of their scores.

8. *Did I allow enough time for students to demonstrate the type of thinking I was trying to assess?* Complex thinking, meaningful problem solving, and creative applications require considerable time for most students to demonstrate. A 40- to 50-minute classroom period is usually too short to permit valid assessment of such thinking. It may be necessary to assess students over a longer time period in order for the results to be validly interpreted as reflecting these types of learning outcomes.

Consistency with Other Classroom Assessments

Over the course of the unit, marking period, or semester, you will have observed the individuals in your class many times. You will have collected much information that is relevant to evaluating each student's attainments. When you administer a test or other assessment for grading, a student's results should be consistent with the student's pattern of performance throughout the time period. Some students may perform higher or lower than you expect, of course, and you should try to determine why. However, the pattern of assessment results for the entire class should not surprise you. If it is a surprise, there may be a validity problem with your assessment procedure. Evaluate this possibility by focusing on these questions:

9. *Is the pattern of results in the class consistent with what I expected based on my other assessments of them?* If the pattern for the class is quite different from what you were expecting, review your assessment procedure in relation to Questions 1–8. Perhaps the emphasis of your assessment did not match the emphasis of your teaching. Perhaps it did not match the content emphasis of the other assessments on which you based your expectations. If these reasons explain the discrepancy, the assessment results may not be able to be interpreted as mastery and may not be used for validly grading the students.

10. *Did I make the assessment tasks too difficult or too easy for my students?* When the tasks are too difficult or too easy, the assessment results are not consistent with your other observations of them. When the assessment is too easy or too difficult, all students will all attain nearly the same result, and you will be unable to distinguish reliable individual differences among them. This may lower the validity of the results for norm-referenced grading. Also, assessments that are too difficult frustrate the students, making them feel as if their study time was wasted. Such a situation is a negative consequence and does not reveal students' best performances. Assessment tasks should be challenging, of course, but not so difficult that only one or two students in the class can perform well on them.

The order of tasks in your assessment instrument is important. The easiest tasks should be placed first. If the more difficult tasks are placed first, students may spend too much time on them. As a result, they may run out of time before attempting the easier tasks that they probably are able to perform. Also, students who are test anxious may experience debilitating anxiety when faced with difficult tasks early in the assessment. Your assessment results have lower validity in these situations because they do not reflect what the students are able to do.

Reliability and Objectivity

Reliability refers to the consistency of the results of assessment. (Reliability is the subject of Chapter 4.) Reliability is affected by the length of your assessment procedure. For example, a single assessment task (e.g., one test question) is but a small sample from a pool of thousands of similar tasks that could have been used. As such, one task is an unreliable basis on which to infer a student's mastery of the learning targets. In general, longer assessments (with more tasks per learning target) are more reliable than shorter assessments.

Another cause of inconsistency in your assessment results is your own day-to-day fluctuations in judgments of the quality of students' performance. However, you can take steps to control unnecessary fluctuations. For instance, you can develop *scoring rubrics* and use them for evaluating students' performance more consistently. (Chapter 12 discusses how to craft scoring rubrics.) Your judgments of a specific student's performance may be inconsistent with those of a knowledgeable teaching colleague. You should reconcile these types of inconsistencies to improve the validity of your assessment results. In general, ratings of oral quizzes, students' performances and products, and essays yield less consistent assessment results than the more objectively scored procedures such as short-answer, multiple-choice, true-false, or matching questions.

The degree of objectivity in your classroom assessment procedure is directly related to the degree that two or more qualified evaluators of a student's performance will agree on what quality rating or score to assign to it. Objectivity and reliability are not all-or-nothing characteristics, of course. They are matters of degree: All assessment results are more or less objective.

This does not mean that the more subjective assessment procedures should be eliminated. As a professional and expert teacher, your judgments are extremely valuable and important to students. It would be unethical for you to refuse to evaluate student performance and achievement simply because such evaluations are subjective. What students seek is consistency and fairness in your professional judgment. Personal flaws that result in unprofessional, idiosyncratic, or erratic behavior should be held in check. Chapter 4 and other chapters will suggest ways of improving the reliability of classroom assessment results.

Unreliable results limit the validity of your interpretations and uses. Therefore, when evaluating your classroom assessment procedures, keep focused on these questions:

11. *Do I use a systematic procedure for obtaining quality ratings or scores from students' performance on the assessment?* Such a procedure may be a scoring key, a scoring rubric, or a rating scale where each rating level is clearly defined. Apply your systematic procedure to every student you are assessing (do not stop using your scoring rubric after the first few students). Your systematic procedure should be crafted well enough that a qualified teaching colleague could use it and obtain the same results as you do.

12. *Does my assessment instrument contain enough tasks relative to the types of learning outcomes I am assessing?* Be sure that your assessment instrument contains several opportunities for students to demonstrate their knowledge and skill for each learning target. If practical constraints do not allow for a more complete assessment in one class period, consider using another class period, a take-home assessment, or combining the results from several assessments administered over the marking period.

Fairness to Different Types of Students

Your assessment procedures should be fair to students from all ethnic and socioeconomic backgrounds, as well as students with disabilities who are mainstreamed in your class. For example, a deaf student may understand the concepts you have taught but not be able to express that understanding on your written or oral assessment. Deaf students' general vocabulary and verbal skills are usually behind their hearing peers. In such cases, a more valid assessment of a student's understanding may be obtained through a special assessment with a lower verbal load (e.g., simplifying or explaining the nontechnical or nonsubject-specific vocabulary) or if the student can use an alternative communication mode (e.g., using a signed language). Chapter 5 discusses assessment accommodation strategies.

Similarly, your assessment should not contain material that is subtly or blatantly offensive to any subgroup of students or that perpetuates **ethnic and gender stereotypes.** For example, you would be perpetuating stereotypes if your assessment materials depict (in words or pictures) only majority race members or males as leaders, technically trained, professional, and so on, or minority race(s) or females as followers, unskilled, or technically backward (see Zoref & Williams, 1980).

As you evaluate your classroom assessment procedure for fairness, focus on the following questions.

13. *Do you word the problems or tasks on your assessment so students with different ethnic and socioeconomic backgrounds will interpret them in appropriate ways?* "Appropriate interpretations" of assessment tasks does not mean that everyone has identical interpretations: There may be several appropriate ways to interpret the same task. Good classroom assessments will permit you to evaluate the richness in the diversity of your students' thinking. You may wish to interview a few students to understand how they interpreted the tasks you set. You should also check whether all students understood the assessment directions and the scoring rules. If students do not understand your directions, they may respond inappropriately through no fault of their own. If this happens, you will not be able to validly use the assessment results for purposes of grading.

14. *Did you modify the wording or the administrative conditions of the assessment tasks to accommodate students with disabilities or special learning problems?* The basic interpretation you wish to make is whether the students have achieved the learning targets you are assessing. If the way that you organize your materials and require students to respond hinders their ability to communicate their understanding, your assessment results are less valid. Some teachers may balk at the types of assessment adaptations implied here. They may claim that such adaptations for a few students make the assessment unstandardized and unfair to the majority of students. But fairness is not a matter of voting for how to obtain information in which the majority wins. Valid assessment results give us a clear picture of what *each* student is capable of doing in relation to the learning targets. This may require using somewhat modified assessment procedures for some students in the class. (See Chapter 5 for details.)

15. *Do the pictures, stories, verbal statements, or other aspects of my assessment procedure perpetuate racial, ethnic, or*

gender stereotypes? Assessments do not have to be free of any reference to race, ethnicity, or gender. Rather, you should eliminate stereotypes and balance the references among various groups. Balanced references represent the diversity of peoples and views in the country.

Economy, Efficiency, Practicality, Instructional Features

Your assessment procedures should be efficient. Although assessing students is a very important part of teaching, you must still teach the students. Assessment activities should not consume all of your time. Assessing students is not the same as teaching them: You can't fatten a calf by weighing it!

The validity of classroom assessment results also depends on whether they can inform and guide your teaching toward important learning goals. When evaluating your assessment procedure, focus on these questions:

16. *Is the assessment relatively easy for me to construct and not too cumbersome to use to evaluate students*? Two practical concerns to keep in mind are how easy it is to create the assessment tasks and how easy it is to obtain quality ratings or scores. It is easier to develop essay questions, for example, than to develop complex problem-solving performance tasks or good multiple-choice items. However, once developed, multiple-choice items are easier to score and may be reused for next year's class. Problem-solving performance tasks set in real-life settings are difficult to construct properly. However, they let you assess more completely whether students can use what they learned to perform complex tasks than do either the typical teacher-crafted multiple-choice items or short-answer questions.

17. *Is the time needed to use this assessment procedure better spent on directly teaching students instead*? Your assessment procedure must be balanced against the best way to use students' time in class. Some procedures, such as interviews and individual observations of students' performance, require a long time to complete. Also, while one student is being interviewed or observed, you need to keep the remainder of the class meaningfully engaged in learning. You administer group tests, on the other hand, to all the students at the same time. You must judge according to the circumstances of your own classroom the appropriate balance between occupying a student's time with assessment activities versus occupying it with other activities.

18. *Does your assessment procedure represent the best use of your time*? Essay tests, term papers, projects, and lengthy written works generally require much student time to complete and much teacher time to grade and evaluate. When using these procedures, you must decide whether they are a wise investment of your time. But remember,

the grading time and student learning time need not be entirely separate. For example, you may be able to evaluate a term paper or a project with the student present. If this can be done in a nonthreatening way and with you "talking through" the reasons for your evaluation with the student, the student has an opportunity to understand the qualities of the work that you are evaluating. This opportunity may also let the student ask questions, clarify the criteria you are using, contribute to the evaluation itself, and otherwise improve her grasp of the learning targets. Such rich interaction is often not possible with multiple-choice testing, which usually yields only one score.

When rich student-teacher interactions do occur, the time you spend assessing is identical with the student's instructional time. Assessment and instruction blend together. Learners can look forward to assessment as feedback about their accomplishments and as opportunities for coaching and guidance toward their chosen goals.

Multiple Assessment Usage

19. *Are the assessment results used in conjunction with other assessment results*? Even though you ask the preceding questions of your assessment technique, you will discover that it does not produce perfectly valid results. The technique will stand up well under the scrutiny of some questions but do poorly under others. Even if you modify your technique to improve its validity, it will not be perfect because a single assessment procedure cannot yield results that are perfectly valid for a given purpose. This means that it is necessary to combine the results from several different types of assessments (such as homework, class performance, quizzes, projects, and tests) to improve the validity of your decisions about a student's attainments. This is called a **multiple-assessment strategy**. Weighing one assessment result too heavily in relation to others (like making the student's semester grade depend almost exclusively on his end-of-semester test performance) results in lowered validity.

VALIDITY OF EXTRA-CLASSROOM ASSESSMENTS

Besides the assessments a teacher crafts and uses in the classroom, many other educational assessments are used in schools. These *extra-classroom assessments* include district- and state-mandated assessments, standardized achievement and aptitude tests, attitude inventories, and individually administered intelligence tests, to name only a few. These and other assessment methods are described in Part Three of this book. In this section we discuss the types of evidence required to support the valid interpretation and use of their results. Knowing these kinds of validity evidence will help you to locate the proper information to evaluate and select an assessment instrument.

Evidence Used to Judge Validity

At least eight types of validity evidence must be considered before you reach a decision about the validity of assessment results for a particular interpretation and use. Each type of evidence does not weigh equally, however, because assessment results are interpreted and used differently in different settings. Each setting requires a somewhat different emphasis on different types of evidence.

Table 3.2 (on page 46) summarizes eight types of evidence that validity theorists (Cronbach, 1988, 1989; Linn, Baker, & Dunbar, 1991; Messick, 1989a, 1989b) have recently identified as important. In addition, the table lists the typical questions each type of evidence addresses and the typical procedures used to gather the evidence.

You will notice the similarity between some of the types of evidence and questions in Table 3.2 and the material presented in the previous section on validating teacher-crafted assessments. This is no coincidence. The validity concerns of teacher-crafted assessment procedures are shared by all educational assessment methods. However, the purposes for using these extra-classroom assessments are usually different from those of teacher-crafted assessments. Therefore, the emphases and mixes of evidence used to judge validity differ also. This section focuses primarily on evidence concerning the validity of extra-classroom assessments.

Before we discuss the details of these types of evidence, you should note the following:

1. *The importance of each type of evidence changes as interpretations and uses of assessment results change.* All of the types of evidence in Table 3.2 apply to nearly every kind of assessment procedure. However, different interpretations and uses of the results of an assessment procedure will require some types of evidence to be stronger than others. For example, the *Scholastic Assessment Test I: Reasoning Test* (SAT I) is intended to predict freshman grade-point averages. Thus, a university or college should weigh more heavily the test's predictive powers and its potential for negative consequences, such as reducing the number of men it selects, than evidence that the test matches curriculum objectives and content. However, evidence about how the SAT I scores are influenced by students' high school performance in academic core curriculum areas should not be entirely ignored.

2. *Providing evidence is the responsibility of both the publisher and the user.* Both the user of assessment results and the publisher of the assessment instrument should provide evidence about validity. Publishers and other agencies that produce assessments are responsible for providing data that support the reliability, validity, and other technical aspects of assessment results. These responsibilities are described in the *Standards for Educational and Psychological Testing* (American Educational Research Association, American Psychological Association, & National Council on Measurement in Education, 1999). The responsibilities of persons who use assessment procedures produced by others are described in a number of resources such as the *Code of Fair Testing Practices in Education*, 1988) and the *Responsibilities of Users of Standardized Tests: RUST Statement Revised* (American Counseling Association, 1989). The *Code* is reproduced in Appendix B.

3. *The fact that you cannot afford to conduct validity studies does not mean that you may ignore concerns about the validity of your assessment results.* Educators at different levels have differing amounts of resources and opportunities for gathering evidence about the validity. Teachers have the smallest resources and fewest opportunities; school district personnel have more; and state-level educators even more. This fact does not relieve those with fewer resources (teachers) from the requirement of validating their interpretations and uses of assessment results. Rather, it means that they must be honest and admit that they do not have the resources to satisfactorily validate the way they use the assessment. Further, in their honesty, they must admit that because they do not have the evidence, their interpretations and uses may have low validity.

CATEGORIES OF VALIDITY EVIDENCE

Measurement specialists now recommend that validity be used as a unitary concept (American Educational Research Association, American Psychological Association, National Council on Measurement in Education, 1999; Messick, 1989b). This book follows this recommendation.[2] Thus, you should think of the following as types of evidence that support an assessment's validity, not as different kinds of validity.

---

[2]Some textbooks and many standardized test manuals still use the traditional view that there are three kinds of validity: content validity, criterion-related validity, and construct validity. Many other terms have been used, including curricular validity, instructional validity, synthetic validity, predictive validity, concurrent validity, convergent validity, factorial validity, nomological validity, and "face" validity. "In general, such terms refer to specific procedures for evaluating validity rather than to new kinds of interpretive inferences from test scores" (American Educational Research Association, American Psychological Association, and National Council on Measurement in Education, 1974, p. 26).

Content Representativeness and Relevance: Content Evidence

The idea of content representativeness and relevance applies to all sorts of assessments: achievement tests, aptitude tests, personality tests, student teacher observation procedures, performance rating scales, and so on. In this section the focus is mostly on extra-classroom achievement tests.

Domain Definition As shown in Table 3.2, this type of evidence comes from judging the content of the tasks or items on the instrument. Judgments of **content representativeness** focus on whether the assessment tasks are a representative sample from a larger domain of performance. One question that arises is *whose* definition of the domain is appropriate: the assessment developer's or the assessment user's? The *ABC Reading Test*, for example, may emphasize paragraph and sentence reading but does not separately measure word attack skills or vocabulary. School personnel selecting a reading test may want these latter areas included in the definition of the reading domain. Here, the test developer and the test user disagree on the definition of the domain and, therefore, on what is or is not to be included in the assessment. Judgments of **content relevance** focus on whether the assessment tasks are included in the test user's domain definition. Making separate judgments about how well the tasks on the assessment represent (1) the de-

veloper's domain and (2) the user's domain will clarify whether the evidence supports a school's intended use of the assessment procedure. See Nitko et al. (1998) for an example of how this can be done.

Table of Specifications A test developer often defines the domain assessed in an accompanying manual or technical publication. Within the manual a typical tool for defining the domain for standardized survey achievement tests is a **table of specifications**. This table contains the major content categories and skills that are assessed. It describes the percent of tasks (items) for each content-skills combination. The percent of tasks per combination is a rough measure of the weight that a combination contributes to the student's total score. Chapter 6 and Appendix G show examples of tables of specifications. Table 1.1 in Chapter 1 describes the NAEP reading assessment framework. This is another way to specify the domain that is assessed. In Table 1.1, the number of tasks or weights is not specified, but that information is given in other technical publications.

Curricular Relevance and Content Domains An assessment method is relevant to a school's definition of the achievement domain to the extent that it matches the school's curriculum learning targets. We call this judgment of the degree of overlap between the curriculum and assessment tasks the **curricular relevance** of the assessment. Studying Figure 3.1 may help to clarify the dis-

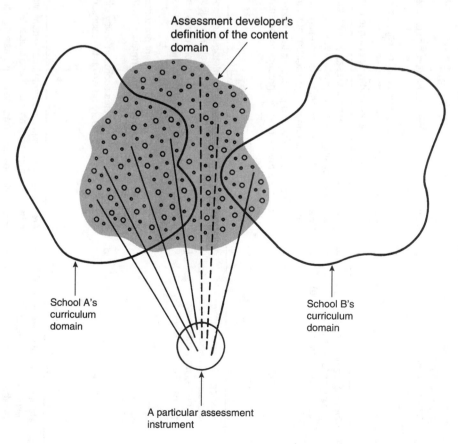

FIGURE 3.1 A schematic illustration of the relationship between an assessment instrument, a developer's content domain, and the curriculum-specific domains of two schools. An assessment may match the developer's domain yet may lack curricular relevance for some schools.

Assessment developer's definition of the content domain

School A's curriculum domain

School B's curriculum domain

A particular assessment instrument

TABLE 3.2 Summary of the different types of validity evidence for educational assessments.

Type of evidence	Examples of questions needing to be answered	Techniques often used to obtain answers
1. Content representativeness and relevance (called *content evidence*)	a. How well do the assessment tasks represent the domain of important content? b. How well do the assessment tasks represent the curriculum as you define it? c. How well do the assessment tasks reflect current thinking about what should be taught and assessed? d. Are the assessment tasks worthy of being learned?	A description of the curriculum and content to be learned is obtained. Each assessment task is checked to see if it matches important content and learning outcomes. Each assessment task is rated for its relevance, importance, accuracy, and meaningfulness. The assessment procedure is viewed as a whole, and judgments are made about representativeness and relevance of the entire collection of tasks.
2. Types of thinking skills and processes required (called *substantive evidence*)	a. How much do the assessment tasks require students to use important thinking skills and processes? b. How well do the assessment tasks represent the types of thinking skills espoused as important curriculum outcomes? c. Are the thinking skills and processes that students actually use to complete the assessment procedure the same ones claimed to be assessed?	The assessment procedure is analyzed to reveal the types of cognitions required to perform the tasks successfully. The relationship between the strategies students are taught to use and those they are required to use during the assessment are determined. Students may be asked to "think aloud" while performing the assessment tasks and the resultant protocols analyzed to identify cognitions the students used. Judgments are made about the assessment procedure as a whole to decide whether desirable, representative, and relevant thinking skills and processes are being assessed.
3. Relationships among the assessment tasks or parts of the assessment (called *internal structure evidence*)	a. Do all the assessment tasks "work together" so that each task contributes positively toward assessing the quality of interest? b. If the different parts of the assessment procedure are supposed to provide unique information, do the results support this uniqueness? c. If the different parts of the assessment procedure are supposed to provide the same or similar information, do the results support this? d. Are the students' responses scored in a way that is consistent with the constructs and theory on which the assessment is based?	a. If students' performance on each task is quantified, correlations of task scores with total scores from the assessment are studied to decide whether all tasks contribute positively. b. Each part of the assessment may be scored separately and these part scores intercorrelated to see whether the desired pattern of relationships emerges. c. Logic, substantive knowledge, and experience are used to generate explanations for high and low performance on the assessment. Not all hypotheses should be consistent with the intended interpretations of how the parts function. d. Empirical studies, both experimental and correlational, are conducted to support or refute the hypotheses generated in (c) above.
4. Relationships of assessment results to the results of other variables (called *external structure evidence*)	a. Are the results of this assessment consistent with the results of other similar assessments for these students? b. How well does performance on this assessment procedure reflect the quality or trait that is measured by other tests? c. How well does performance on this assessment procedure predict current or future performance on other valued tasks or measures (criteria)? d. How well can the assessment results be used to select persons for jobs, schools, etc? What is the magnitude of error? e. How well can the assessment results be used to assign pupils to different types of instruction? Is learning better when pupils are assigned this way?	a. The criterion tasks are identified and analyzed. Assessment of their important characteristics are created. b. Scores from the assessment are compared to scores on the criterion to be predicted. c. Studies of various classification and prediction errors are made. d. Studies show whether the results from this assessment converge with or diverge from results from other assessments in the way expected when the proposed interpretation of the students' performance is used. (Called *convergent and discriminant evidence*.)

5. Reliability over time, assessors, and content domain (called *reliability evidence*)	a. Will the same students obtain nearly the same results if the assessment procedure was applied on another occasion? What is the margin of error expected?	Studies are conducted focusing on the consistency (reliability) of the assessment results. These studies are described in more detail in Chapter 4.
	b. If different persons administered, graded, or scored the assessment results, would the students' outcomes be the same? What is the margin of error?	
	c. If a second, alternate form of the assessment procedure were to be developed, with similar content, would the students' results be very similar? What is the margin of error?	
6. Generalization of interpretations over different types of people, under different conditions, or with special instruction/ intervention (called *generalization evidence*)	a. Does the assessment procedure give significantly different results when it is used with students from different socio-economic and ethnic backgrounds, but of the same ability? If so, is this fair or unbiased?	a. Logic, substantive knowledge, and experience are used to generate explanations (hypotheses) about how the interpretation of the assessment results might change when the procedure is applied to different types of people, under different conditions, or with special instruction (intervention).
	b. Will students' results from the assessment procedure be altered drastically if they are given special incentives or motives? If so, should this change how the assessment results are interpreted?	b. Empirical studies, both experimental and correlational, are conducted to support or refute the hypotheses generated in (a) above.
	c. Will special intervention, changes in instructions, or special coaching significantly alter the results students obtain on the assessment? If so, should this change how the assessment results are interpreted?	
7. Value of the intended and/or unintended consequences (called *consequential evidence*)	a. What do we expect to happen to the students if we interpret and use the assessment results in this particular way? To what degree do these expected consequences happen, and is that good?	a. Studies are conducted to describe the intended outcomes of using the given assessment procedure and to determine the degree to which these outcomes are realized for all students.
	b. What side effects do we anticipate happening to the students if we interpret and use the assessment results in this particular way? To what degree are these anticipated side effects occurring, and are they positive or negative?	b. Studies are conducted to determine whether anticipated or unanticipated side effects have resulted from interpreting and using the given assessment procedure in a certain way.
	c. What unanticipated negative side effects happened to the students for whom we interpreted and used the assessment results in this particular way? Can these negative side effects be avoided by using other assessment procedures/techniques or by altering our interpretations?	c. Logical analyses, substantive knowledge, and value analyses are used to evaluate whether the existing assessment procedure should be continued or replaced by an alternative.
8. Cost, efficiency, practicality, instructional features (called *practicality evidence*)	a. Can the assessment procedure accommodate typical numbers of students?	Logical analyses, cost analyses, reviews by teachers, and field trial data are used to come to decisions about the factors of cost, efficiency, practicality, and usefulness of instructional features.
	b. Is the assessment procedure easy for teachers to use?	
	c. Can the assessment procedure give quick results to guide instruction?	
	d. Do teachers agree that the theoretical concepts behind the assessment procedure reflect the key understandings they are teaching?	
	e. Do the assessment results meaningfully explain individual differences?	
	f. Do the assessment results identify misunderstandings that need to be corrected?	
	g. Would an alternative assessment procedure be more efficient?	

Note: These types of validity evidence have been suggested by Messick (1989b; 1994b) and Linn, Baker, and Dunbar (1991).

tinction between matching the assessment to the developer's achievement domain and the curricular relevance of the assessment. The developer's definition of achievement and the sample of tasks comprising a particular assessment are shown in the center of the figure. The assessment matches the developer's domain if the tasks on it adequately represent the developer's definition. (These tasks are shown by both the solid *and* broken straight lines.) The assessment's curricular relevance is based on how well the tasks on the instrument represent your school's curriculum framework. (In the figure, this is shown by the *solid* straight lines.) As may be seen from the figure, the assessment illustrated has more curriculum relevance for School A than for School B: A considerable proportion of School A's curriculum is *not* assessed.

This is typical: A school's curriculum framework is usually much broader and richer than any single extra-classroom assessment instrument. Thus, even though the assessment instrument illustrated has more curricular relevance for School A than for School B, that degree of relevance still may not be sufficient for the school to use the instrument.

You should keep in mind the questions in Table 3.2 for this area. Curricular relevance is more than a simple proportion of the content that matches the curriculum. The instrument must be reviewed as a whole to judge whether the relative weight or emphases given to different content areas is appropriate to the local curriculum's learning targets. The individual tasks on the assessment must also (1) reflect current thinking of subject-matter experts about what is important to teach and to assess, (2) accurately portray the subject matter, (3) be keyed correctly, and (4) contain meaningful and important content. In addition, the individual assessment tasks must be crafted well. Poorly crafted tasks may "clue" answers to less knowledgeable students or introduce bias and ambiguity, which prevent some students from performing to their best levels.

Thinking Skills and Processes: Substantive Evidence

An assessment should be judged not only in terms of the content it covers but also in terms of the kinds of thinking processes and skills students must use to complete the tasks successfully. As discussed in the section on the validity of classroom assessment results, achievement assessments should require students to use important thinking processes and skill as these are defined by the curriculum framework and by experts in the subject matter being assessed. Such assessment instruments ask students to use combinations of skills and knowledge together to work on "real-life" applications.

To validate a claim that the tasks require students to use higher-order thinking processes and skills, assessment developers should provide you with student-based data to support their claims. This should include (1) a detailed description of the processes and abilities that they claim to be assessing, (2) a clear demonstration of how each type of task or assessment exercise can assess each of these processes and skills, and (3) evidence from research studies that demonstrate that students use the thinking processes and skills that are claimed. The latter may take the form of small studies conducted in cognitive labs. Students are asked to "think aloud" as they work through the tasks on the instrument. Their thinking is organized into "protocols" and analyzed to reveal the types of thinking strategies students say they have used. More rigorous experiments may be reported concerning the strategies students use, but these are rare. These studies should also demonstrate that students do not use inappropriate processes to solve the tasks. For example, suppose a multiple-choice mathematics test developer claims to be assessing students' higher-order problem-solving ability. The developer should provide evidence that students do, in fact, use these higher-order abilities. The developer should also provide evidence that inappropriate question-answering strategies (e.g., working backward from each multiple-choice option) are not used.

Relationships Among Parts of Assessment: Internal Structure Evidence

An assessment procedure should not be only a hodge-podge collection of assessment tasks or test questions. Each task in the procedure should contribute positively to the total result. The interrelationships among the tasks, and the relationship between the tasks and the total results, describe the **internal structure** of the assessment. The internal and external structures of an assessment procedure are important whenever we wish to interpret the assessment results as indicators of a person's standing on an educational or psychological construct. For example, some assessment instruments claim to assess only one student ability, such as arithmetic problem solving. To be certain that our interpretation of the assessment results as measuring only this one student ability is valid, we must locate evidence that supports this claim. The developer should provide evidence that each task on this assessment differentiates students along this single dimension (here, arithmetic problem solving). Often, however, assessment tasks measure more than one dimension. For example, solving an arithmetic problem may depend heavily on reading skill, vocabulary knowledge, computational speed, and general speed of working, as well as arithmetic problem solving. If this happens, you may not validly interpret the results as reflecting only the students' arithmetic problem-solving ability.

On the other hand, some assessment instruments are deliberately crafted to assess two or more dimensions. For example, some scholastic aptitude tests provide measures of verbal ability, quantitative ability, and nonverbal ability. (See Chapter 19 for examples.) If so, then the technical manual should contain evidence that verbal, quantitative, and nonverbal test scores are meaningfully different. Evidence from research studies should demonstrate that, although students' scores on the three parts of the test might be moderately related (because they are aspects of a global or general scholastic aptitude), they are different enough to be interpreted as three different aspects of scholastic aptitude.

The evidence test developers provide to support the validity of these types of interpretations is often in the form of correlation coefficients. These coefficients measure the degree of relationship between two or more sets of assessment scores. The correlation coefficient is discussed later in this chapter.

Relationships of Results to Other Variables: External Structure Evidence

Evidence about the validity of assessment results must go beyond demonstrating how well the tasks sample content and thinking processes or how scores on different tasks correlate with one another. Evidence also comes from how well the assessment results correlate with other variables or criteria. For example, the *Scholastic Assessment Test I* (SAT I) measures both verbal and mathematics abilities. Its validity depends in part on its internal structure—whether the verbal items in fact measure verbal ability, mathematics items measure mathematics ability, and the scores on the two parts of the test are meaningfully different. However, the *primary use* of the SAT I is to add information that helps admissions officers to select applicants who are likely to succeed in college. The most important validity evidence must come, therefore, from studies that establish the correlation of the SAT I scores with an external variable, namely, grades in college. We call the pattern of relationships between assessment results and these types of external variables the **external structure** of the assessment.

The specific evidence you need depends on the particular interpretation and use you want to make from the assessment results. If you want to use the assessment results to help select persons for college, then you need to establish that the assessment results are positively correlated to a college success criterion such as grade point average. Sometimes we want to validate that a new assessment measures the same ability as one that already exists. For example, we may want to validate that a multiple-choice and an oral assessment both measure reading comprehension. If they both measure the same ability, you would expect their scores to be positively correlated: Students with high scores on one should also have high scores on the other. If there is no relationship between the scores on the two assessments, it is likely that they measure different attributes. Additional research would be needed to establish which score, if any, measures reading comprehension. Hypotheses and counterhypotheses about the relationships

of assessment results to external criteria are derived from logical analysis, experience, previous research, and a theory about the nature of the traits or characteristics being assessed.

Notice from these two examples that some evidence is concerned with predicting future performance (such as predicting success in college), and some evidence is concerned with estimating the individuals' current status on a variable. **Predictive validity evidence** refers to the extent to which individuals' future performance on a criterion can be predicted from their prior performance on an assessment instrument. For example, we could collect high school students' grade point averages, wait until they finish one year of college, and collect their college grade point averages. After college grades are collected, we correlate high school grades with them. Prediction over time is the aim. **Concurrent validity evidence** refers to the extent to which individuals' current status on a criterion can be estimated from their current performance on an assessment instrument. For example, we can study students already in college, give them a special aptitude test, and collect their current grade point averages. The relationship between the grades and the test is concurrent validity evidence, because the two measures were collected at the same time. The distinction is important because the time interval between administering the assessment instrument and obtaining criterion results affects the strength of the relationship between the two results: Usually the longer the time interval between the two results, the lower the correlation between them.

Correlation Coefficient

Often, evidence of a relationship between two sets of scores is reported in the form of a correlation coefficient. The **correlation coefficient** is a statistical index that quantifies the degree of relationship between the scores from one assessment and the scores from another. The index is reported on a scale of -1 to $+1$.

An example showing the relationship between the scores from several tests will help explain correlation. Table 3.3 shows the scores of 11 students on each of three tests. The students have been arranged in descending order according to their verbal aptitude scores (V). Look at the first two columns of scores and notice that the verbal scores and the reading scores (R) order the students in about the same way. This is not a perfect ordering, however. Notice, too, that the relationship between the verbal and arithmetic scores (A) is less strong: The order of the students is not as similar on these tests as it is on the verbal and reading tests.

Comparing Students' Rank Orders This correspondence is clearer when we transform each score to a rank, as in the last three columns of Table 3.3. The ranks of the students on verbal aptitude and reading, though not identical in every case, are quite close. The ranks of the students

TABLE 3.3 Hypothetical scores for 11 pupils on a verbal aptitude test, a reading test, and an arithmetic test.

Pupil	Verbal score (V)	Reading score (R)	Arithmetic score (A)	Verbal rank order	Reading rank order	Arithmetic rank order
A	82	59	48	1	1	4
B	77	54	65	2	4	1
C	70	55	43	3	3	7
D	65	58	58	4	2	2
E	59	51	40	5	5	8.5
F	53	44	47	6	6	5
G	45	38	55	7	7	3
H	41	34	44	8	9	6
I	34	35	25	9	8	11
J	30	30	40	10	10	8.5
K	23	26	33	11	11	10

Source: Adapted from *Measuring Pupil Achievement and Aptitude*, 2nd Ed., by C. M. Lindvall and A.J. Nitko, New York: Harcourt, Brace, Jovanovich. © 1975 by C. M. Lindvall and A. J. Nitko.

on verbal aptitude and arithmetic correspond less closely, but the ranks are still similar. There is more shifting in the students' ranks from verbal aptitude to arithmetic than there was from verbal aptitude to reading. Comparing students' rank orders on two assessments is one way of studying how correlated the results are.

Scatter Diagrams   Another way to study the correlation between the scores from assessments is graphically with a **scatter diagram** (sometimes called a **scattergram**). A scatter diagram is a graph on which the *paired scores* are plotted. Figure 3.2 shows these plots for *V* vs. *R* and *V* vs. *A*. When completed, the graph shows the relationship between the paired scores for the entire group of 11 students.

You can obtain considerable insight into how the scores on two assessments are related by making a scatter diagram. In Figure 3.2(A), the plots lie along an almost

straight line from the lower left of the graph to the upper right. In Figure 3.2(B), however, the plots do not come as close to lying along a straight line. However, there is a *trend* in the graph from the lower left of the graph to the upper right.

The tendency for points of a scatter diagram to lie along a straight line is central to the concept of correlation. The higher the degree of correlation between two sets of scores, the closer the points come to lying along a straight line. As the degree of correlation becomes less, the points tend to scatter away from this straight line. The shape of the pattern of the scattering of these points is elliptical. The narrower the elliptical pattern, the higher the degree of correlation. The less the degree of correlation, the wider these elliptical patterns of the scatter diagrams become. When there is no relationship between the two sets of scores, the pattern will widen until it is circular, rather than elliptical.

FIGURE 3.2 Scatter diagram of the verbal aptitude vs. reading test scores and the verbal aptitude vs. arithmetic test scores for the 11 pupils shown in Table 3.3.

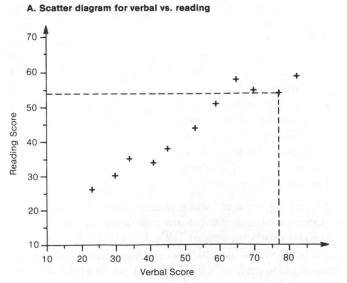

A. Scatter diagram for verbal vs. reading

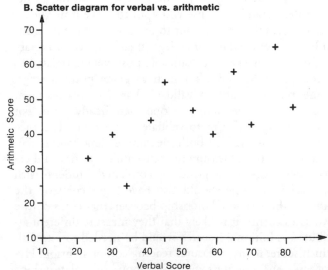

B. Scatter diagram for verbal vs. arithmetic

Pearson Product-Moment Correlation Coefficients Visually comparing rank orders of scores and plotting scatter diagrams are two qualitative ways of studying the correlation between the scores. Most published assessment material uses a quantitative measure of correlation called the **Pearson product-moment correlation coefficient**, which is denoted by r. There are many different types of correlation coefficients, and r is one type. It is the index most commonly used in studying the validity of assessment results, however. For sake of simplicity, I shall refer to r as the *correlation coefficient* in this text.

A correlation coefficient has a possible range of values from $+1.00$ to 0.00 through -1.00. A correlation of 0.00 means that the two sets of scores are unrelated: Students' scores on one assessment cannot be predicted from their scores on the other assessment. A perfect positive relationship would have a correlation coefficient of $+1.00$: A student's score on one assessment can be perfectly predicted from his score on the other assessment. In **positive correlations** high scores on one assessment are associated with high scores on another. A perfect negative relationship would have a correlation coefficient of -1.00. In **negative correlations**, high scores on one assessment are associated with low scores on another. For perfect negative relationships, a student's score from one assessment is perfectly predicted from her score on the other, too; but here we predict that high scores on one are associated with low scores on the other, and low scores on one are associated with high scores on the other. Appendix H illustrates how to calculate the correlation coefficient. In this section we focus on its meaning.

What is the correlation coefficient for the scores in Table 3.3? If you applied the procedure described in Appendix H, you would find that the correlation between the verbal and reading test scores is 0.97 and between the verbal and arithmetic scores is 0.71. You can see that these correlation coefficients are consistent with the impression you had when you compared the rank orders of the scores in the table and studied the scatter diagrams. The number 0.97 reflects a high positive relationship (it is close to 1.00), while 0.71 shows a somewhat lesser degree of relationship.

Degrees of Relationship It is helpful in understanding correlation coefficients to relate them to scatter diagrams. Figure 3.3 shows the scatter diagrams and corresponding correlation coefficients for paired scores that have different degrees of relationships. Each dot represents a pair of scores for a person. The scatter diagrams are arranged to illustrate that positive and negative correlation coefficients having the same absolute numerical value (i.e., the number without the algebraic sign) represent the same strength or degree of relationship.

Compare scatter diagrams A and E, for example. Both show perfect correlation, but diagram A shows a perfect positive correlation, while diagram E shows a perfect negative correlation. The *strength* of the relationship is identical in both cases, but the *direction* of the relationship differs. The negative sign on the correlation coefficient shows that the direction of the relationship is negative. Because the correlation is perfect in both cases, knowing a person's score on one assessment would allow us to predict exactly the score the person obtained on the second assessment: Perfect correlation means perfect prediction.

Perfect correlations are seldom found in practical work with educational and psychological assessment scores. There are many reasons for this, including such things as the assessments containing random error of measurement, the units of measurement being unequal, the distributions of the scores not having identical shapes, and the two assessment results not being related in a simple, linear manner (Carroll, 1961).

Other degrees of relationship are shown in Figure 3.3. In B and F, the correlations are $+0.90$ and -0.90, respectively. Correlations of this magnitude indicate that the assessment results are highly related. Again, the degree of relationship is the same in B and F, but the directions of the relationships are opposite. In both cases, the plotted points in the scatter diagram tend to fall along straight lines, even though they do not fall exactly on the lines as they do in A and E. Although perfect prediction of scores on one assessment from scores on another is not possible when the correlation is $+.90$ or $-.90$, reasonably accurate predictions are possible.

Comparing C with G and B with F, we see that as the correlation between the scores becomes lower, a greater scatter occurs away from a straight line. It is still possible to predict a person's score on Y from knowledge of the person's score on X, but such predictions would have to be made with broader margins of error than in the case when $r = +0.90$ or $r = -0.90$. In D and H the correlations are $+0.40$ and -0.40, respectively. The elliptical patterns are broader still.

Finally, scatter diagram I illustrates a complete lack of correlation between two sets of scores. A person with a high score on Assessment X could have either a high, middle, or low score on Assessment Y. Thus, the scores are said to be unrelated or uncorrelated, and $r = 0.00$. Note the circular pattern of the points in the scatter diagram.

In practical work with assessments, correlations of exactly 0.00, -1.00, and $+1.00$ are rare. These particular numerical values, however, serve as benchmarks: Actual correlation coefficients take on meaning in the context of these limiting values.

Correlation and Causation If the scores from two assessments correlate, this does not necessarily mean that the underlying traits are causally related. For example, there is a positive correlation between shoe size and reading comprehension grade-equivalent score for a population of elementary school children (compare Blommers & Forsyth, 1977). Children with larger feet read better: They are older

FIGURE 3.3 Scatter diagrams for different degrees of correlation.

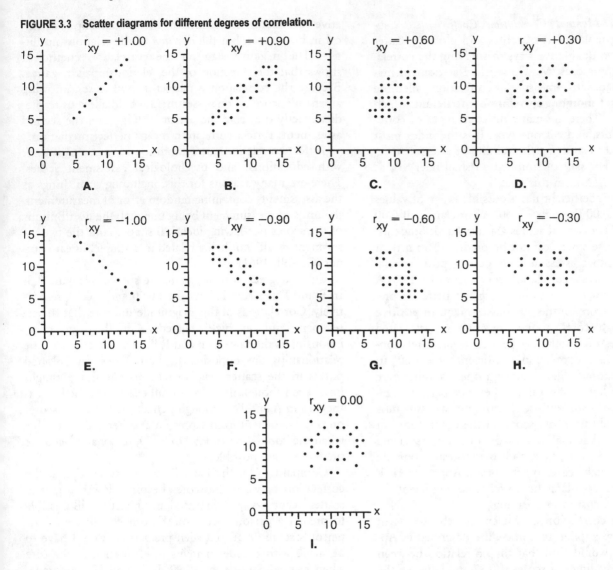

and have had more reading instruction. The larger feet are in eighth grade and, relative to first and second graders, so are the better readers. A third variable, amount of reading instruction, not size of foot, is the most likely "cause" of the correlation between shoe size and reading scores. Of course, we wouldn't recommend a reading readiness program in which we stretched each child's feet. Yet some educators *have* erroneously recommended instructional procedure primarily on the basis of correlations rather than on demonstrations of their effectiveness (Cronbach & Snow, 1977).

Correlation Coefficients and Sample Sizes   The correlation coefficients reported in studies of assessments are based on scores obtained from *samples of persons*, not on the scores of all persons in the population. A correlation computed from a sample only estimates the numerical value of the correlation in the complete population. You should have less confidence in the exact values of correlations computed from smaller samples than you would

from correlations computed from larger samples. In small samples, even one pair of scores can affect the numerical value of the correlation coefficient substantially. Figure 3.4 demonstrates this. The correlation of 0.70 (A) drops to 0.60 (B) when the person with $X = 12$, $Y = 12$ is replaced by another person with $X = 13$, $Y = 7$, even though all the other persons' scores remain the same.

Factors That Raise or Lower Correlation Coefficients   Correlation coefficients appear in test manuals and research reports. When we encounter them, our first tendency is to interpret them as reflecting the true relationship between the characteristics assessed by our instruments. However, the similarity of the characteristics being assessed is only one factor that affects the magnitude of the correlation coefficient reported. In general, higher correlations result (1) when the traits being assessed are alike, (2) when the reliability of the scores on both assessments is high, (3) when the range of scores on both assessments is large, (4) when the shapes of the distributions of the scores on the

FIGURE 3.4 An example of how a change in only one pair of scores can alter the correlation coefficient. In this example, N = 25 pairs of scores.

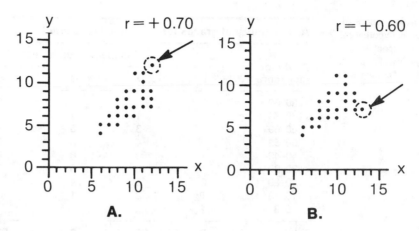

TABLE 3.4 Factors affecting the magnitude of correlation coefficients.

Factor	Effect on correlation coefficient	Example
Similarity of traits assessed	The more similar the traits, the higher the correlation.	Verbal aptitude and reading comprehension test scores will be more highly correlated than verbal aptitude and mathematics aptitude test scores.
Reliability of the scores	Less reliable scores correlate lower than more reliable scores.	Subjective ratings of students' correct English usage from essay examinations correlate lower with reading comprehension test scores than do correct English usage scores from multiple-choice tests.
Range or spread of scores	The larger the range (spread) of scores, the higher the correlation is likely to be.	Algebra aptitude test scores will correlate higher with end of semester mathematics grades when the entire high school freshman class is included in the sample than when only those freshmen in honors mathematics are included.
Similarity of distribution shapes	The more different the shapes of the distribution of scores on the two assessments, the lower the correlation.	Scores from an achievement test that is very difficult and scores from one that is very easy for a particular group of students will correlate less than if the two tests were moderately difficult for this group.
Time interval between assessment administrations	The shorter the time interval between assessment administrations, the higher the correlation is likely to be.	An algebra aptitude test is administered at the beginning of the school year. The correlation between its scores and mathematics grades at the end of the first semester will be higher than with mathematics grades of the same students after two years.

two assessments are alike, and (5) when the time interval between administering the two assessments is short. Table 3.4 summarizes these factors and gives an example of each. Often, more than one of these factors operates at the same time. Read reports of correlational validity evidence carefully, keeping these factors in mind as possible explanations of the numerical correlation values you are interpreting.

Validity Coefficients The usual procedure when studying predictive or concurrent validation evidence is to compute correlations between scores from the assessment instrument and criterion scores. Such a correlation is sometimes referred to as a **validity coefficient**, although, as

you can easily see from Table 3.2, no single number is appropriate to judge the validity of assessment results. In a selection decision situation, the concern is with how large the validity coefficient is.[3] Note that realistically you would expect neither a perfect (error free) prediction nor a correlation of 1.00.

[3]Note that you cannot judge from the correlation coefficient the likely size of the errors that may be made when the assessment results are used to predict criterion scores. For example, if you were predicting college grade point averages, the correlation would not tell you how many GPA units your prediction is likely to be in error. An index that can estimate the likely size of errors of prediction is called the *standard error of estimate*. Its equation is $SD_{Est} = SD_Y \sqrt{1 - r^2}$. The symbol SD_Y denotes a *standard deviation*, which is explained in Appendix H.

TABLE 3.5 The development of an expectancy table for an hypothetical set of 100 pupils. The expectancy table tells the probability of pupils at each predictor test level getting each grade level in the course.

A. Frequency of grades for each predictor score level

Predictor test score	Number of pupils receiving each grade					
	F	D	C	B	A	Totals
80–89			1	3	1	5
70–79		1	4	5	2	12
60–69		3	5	6	1	15
50–59		4	8	5	1	18
40–49	1	5	8	4		18
30–39	1	6	5	3		15
20–29	2	5	4	1		12
10–19	1	2	1			4
0–9	1					1
Totals	6	26	36	27	5	100

B. Expectancy table made by converting frequencies into percents

Predictor test score	Percent of pupils receiving each grade					
	F	D	C	B	A	Totals
80–89			20	60	20	100
70–79		8	33	42	17	100
60–69		20	33	40	7	100
50–59		22	44	28	6	100
40–49	6	28	44	22		100
30–39	7	40	33	20		100
20–29	17	42	33	8		100
10–19	25	50	25			100
0–9	100					100

Expectancy Tables

Another way to display predictive validity data is to make an **expectancy table**. An expectancy table is a grid or two-way table that permits you to say how likely it is for a person with a specific assessment result to attain each criterion score level. Table 3.5 illustrates how an expectancy table is developed to tell the probability that students at particular aptitude score levels will attain each letter grade in a course. (Of course, expectancy tables can be developed to predict other criteria such as supervisors' ratings, amount of sales, success in clinical treatment, and other relevant criteria.)

First a table is constructed, such as Table 3.5(A), in which each cell contains the number of persons with a particular score who attained each course grade (criterion score level). For example, 15 students had aptitude test scores between 60 and 69. This number is shown in the right margin in the 60–69 row. Three of these 15 attained a course grade of "D," five a grade of "C," six a grade of "B," and one a grade of "A."

Second, each cell frequency in Table 3.5(A) is divided by the corresponding row total, converted to a percent, and put into an expectancy table such as Table 3.5(B). These percents may be interpreted as probabilities or chances out of 100 to answer such questions as, "At this

school, what is the probability that a person with an aptitude test score of 65 will succeed in this course?" If we define *succeed* to mean "C" or *better*, then 33% + 40% + 7% = 80% of the students with aptitude scores between 60 and 69 were successful. A person with an aptitude score of 65 is a member of this group. Thus, the answer to the question is, "A person with an aptitude score of 65 has an 80% chance of being successful in this course."

Expectancy tables can help parents and students interpret assessment results, too. For example, suppose an expectancy table is made for a particular college showing how admissions test scores are related to freshmen grade point averages. Persons reading the table can then interpret the admission test results in terms of a student's chances of obtaining various grade point averages. Such interpretations of admissions test scores give more information than scaled scores or percentile ranks (the typical report of results students receive).[4]

If you interpret assessment results using expectancy tables, you should observe common-sense cautions. For example, assessment instruments used to predict success seldom, if ever, measure students' initiative, persistence, or motivation. Thus, they cannot predict with certainty what

[4]Scaled scores and percentile ranks are described in Chapter 17 and Appendix H.

this particular student will do. Rather, the table represents the experience of other students in the past and can offer some guidance only. Therefore, never tell a student that the data in the table "prove" the student can (or cannot) be successful. You must explain how the data show the experience of other students similar to him or her.

The Criterion

Your judgment about whether the assessment developer has provided appropriate validity evidence depends in part on whether the assessment results have been correlated with relevant criteria. It is so difficult to obtain suitable criterion measures to use in validating assessment results that this has been dubbed *the criterion problem* (Thorndike, 1949).

Kinds of Criteria　A variety of criteria is used to provide validity evidence. Personnel classification and selection research in government and industry use four general types: production (quantity and quality of goods, sales), personal data (accidents on the job, length of service, group membership, training course grades), samples of actual or simulated job performance, and judgments by others (checklists, supervisors' ratings) (Lawshe & Balma, 1966). In education, criteria are of three types: achievement test scores; ratings, marks, and other quantified judgments of teachers; and career data. A common example is a reading readiness test given at the beginning of first grade. Scores are often validated by correlating them with scores from a reading achievement test (the criterion) administered at the end of first grade. Using grade point averages in the validation of scores from aptitude and admissions tests was mentioned already. Sometimes teachers' ratings of students' self-concept, sociability, and so on are used as criterion measures. Scores from vocational interest inventories are validated in part by relating them to career data. (See Chapter 19.)

You should note that any single criterion measure is incomplete. Each represents only part of the attainment of the ultimate performance domain that an assessment procedure would like to predict. For this reason, the validation process for a test claiming to be useful in predicting performance should include several studies of the relationship of the test's scores to various criteria. You will need to review all of these studies before coming to a conclusion about the predictive validity of a test.

Judging the Worth of Criteria　The criterion measures used in a validity study are themselves evaluated in four broad areas (Thorndike, 1949): (1) relevance to the long-term or ultimate real-life performance, (2) degree of reliability, (3) extent of bias against individuals or groups, and (4) practical problems of availability and convenience. Most often of interest in a predictive validity study are one or more ultimate real-life performances (Cronbach, 1971; Lindquist, 1951; Messick, 1989b; Thorndike, 1949).

But such ultimate criteria frequently do not occur until many years after the developer initially obtains the assessment results. In such cases, intermediate criteria are used. A developer must present a suitable rationale for using an intermediate criterion before you can accept the data as part of the predictive validity evidence (Cronbach, 1971; Thorndike, 1949).

Low Reliability Limits Validity　Reliability is the topic of Chapter 4. However, here we note that if assessment results have low reliability, their correlations with other measures will be lowered. Frequently, predictor instruments will have good reliability, but the criterion scores with which they are correlated are unreliable. No assessment instrument will be able to predict unreliable criterion scores.

Systematic Errors　Systematic errors in criterion measurement may lead you to the wrong conclusion about the validity of an instrument's scores. For example, a validity study may correlate the instrument's scores with teachers' ratings of students. If these ratings favor boys over girls or students with high verbal skills over those with lower verbal skills, the criterion measures, themselves, may be inappropriate. Systematic biases such as these introduce irrelevant factors into the validation process; they "contaminate" the criterion scores. Thus, before accepting correlation results as evidence for predictive validity, think carefully about the possibility that the scores on the criteria themselves may be biased or invalid.

Practical Considerations　Ideally, it is desirable for scores from an instrument to be validated using data from ultimate real-life criteria. However, practical considerations place a limit on the degree to which a developer can do this. Practicality should not be the sole driving force in a developer's decision to select criterion measures, however. Sometimes a developer could, with very little extra expense and effort, obtain criterion measures that are more appropriate than the surrogates the developer uses in a validation study.

Reliability Over Time, Assessors, and Content Domains: Reliability Evidence

Reliability refers to the consistency of the assessment results. For example, suppose the scores from the *ABC Reading Test* administered today correlated 0.00 with the scores from this test administered next week. This correlation is evidence that the scores have no consistency over this time period. You would question the validity of this test if students' scores had little or no consistency from one week to the next because you believe that reading ability should be stable over a short period. If an assessment instrument produces inconsistent or unstable results, you can have little confidence in those results. Inconsistency means unreliability. Therefore, the reliability of an assessment's results places a limit on its validity. This point is discussed in greater detail in Chapter 4, which is devoted entirely to estimating the reliability of assessment results.

Generalization of Interpretation Over People, Conditions, or Special Instructions and Interventions: Generalization Evidence

This category of validation evidence is concerned with how broadly you may interpret and use assessment results. For example, does the *ABC Reading Test* measure the type of reading comprehension required of students in higher levels of schooling and in real life? Does it measure reading comprehension for nonwhite students in the same way that it measures white students? Is it appropriate to use the scores from this test for remedial reading groups of Spanish-speaking students? Are scores on the *ABC Reading Test* greatly affected by students' moods or motivations at the time the test was administered? If students are given special instruction on what strategies to use to answer the questions on this test (e.g., read the question first, then look for the answer in the text), will this greatly affect their scores?

Answers to questions such as these help us to see the assessment results in a broader perspective. Usually the answers show that our interpretations of assessment results cannot be simplistic. The validity of our interpretations and uses of the results are limited to certain conditions.

Consider the following illustration.[5] Suppose the *ABC Reading Test* had the typical format: a passage of one or two paragraphs followed by several multiple-choice questions. The test directions call for the student to read each passage and to answer the questions that follow it by marking a separate answer sheet. At first glance, it appears that the student needs to read and understand the questions.

Vernon (1962) did a thorough logical analysis of this type of reading comprehension task. That analysis led to hypothesizing several factors, in addition to reading comprehension, which might account for a student's test performance. If these factors alter the student's score, then you cannot interpret the test as a pure measure of reading comprehension. Further, you cannot make decisions about students using scores that depend on such a pure reading comprehension interpretation. Among the factors that may alter a student's score are the following:

1. *Content bias*—A passage may refer to a specific topic, theme, or experience about which some students may have a lot of prior knowledge. For these students, the test is a different kind of task than for students who lack this specific knowledge.

2. *Passage independence*—Students may answer questions without reading the passage because of prior knowledge or poor-quality test items. **Passage dependency** describes the degree to which answers depend on reading and comprehending the passage.

3. *Speededness*—Many tests are timed. If the time limits are not generous enough, the score may depend on reading speed rather than reading comprehension only.

4. *Attitudes and motivation*—If the way the test is presented or administered affects performance, the test will not be a pure measure of reading comprehension. Highly motivated students are likely to score much better than poorly motivated ones.

5. *Sophistication of the students*—Students who are "test-wise" or who have good test-taking strategies are likely to score higher than their peers of equal ability who do not have such skills.

6. *Test directions*—If a student misunderstands test directions, performance probably will be affected adversely.

7. *Ability to mark answers*—Most published multiple-choice tests use separate answer sheets that can be machine scored. Students will differ in the speed and accuracy with which they mark the correct answers. Frequently the type of answer sheet affects the score on the test.

This list is by no means exhaustive. Questions such as these stand as counterhypotheses to the intended interpretation of the scores as measures of reading comprehension. As you raise questions such as these, you should look in the publisher's manual and technical reports for research evidence concerning them. Not all evidence will be included in the publisher's materials, however, especially if it is unfavorable evidence. You may have to review research literature to obtain additional information. *The Mental Measurement Yearbooks* (see Chapter 18) contain reviews of tests and bibliographies of research in which the particular test appeared. You may search ERIC as well.

An example of a research study that sought to determine the effects of motivation on a reading test's scores is given in Figure 3.5. One study cannot provide all the evidence needed to support the validity of assessment interpretations, of course. A series of studies is necessary. Further, you should not assume from the figure that simple incentives, such as "pep talks," prizes, or money, will influence the results of all assessments for all types of students. Nor should you assume that motivation is the only factor that affects students' performance.

[5]This illustration is based in part on an example in Cronbach (1971).

FIGURE 3.5 Can test scores go up if prizes are offered?

Tuinman, Farr, and Blanton (1972) sought to determine the extent to which reading test scores could be increased by offering prizes immediately before giving a posttest which followed an instructional period. Non-problem readers in the seventh and eighth grades were randomly selected and randomly assigned to either an experimental (E) or control (C) group. All students took the *Nelson Reading Test*, Form A (1962) twice; there was a four-week interval between testings. Between the two testing sessions, students took their regular school program.

Directions for retesting the E and C groups were different. The C group was told that the reason they were to be retested was to find out how much they had learned. The E group was shown prizes (6 transistor radios @ $4.95, 9 Indiana University sweatshirts, and large candy bars @ 25¢) and given the following directions (p. 217):

"A few weeks ago you took a test and we have now scored your test. We would like to have you try to beat your first test score. We have some prizes for you if you can do better on this than you did on the last test. We don't care who makes the highest score. We want to see who can make *more points* on this test than on the first test. All you need to do is *raise your own score* by as many points as you can. The students who raise their scores the most will win prizes. *Remember,* it's not the student who scores highest that wins; it's the student who *raises his score the most.*

If you are one of the top six students who gains the most points you will win a transistor radio—NOT the six highest scores but the six who improve the most.

If you are one of the next nine students who raises your score the most points, you will win one of these IU shirts.

And if you raise your score even as little as one point, you get one of these candy bars. So everyone who gets even just one point higher will get a prize.

If you do not score any higher on this test than the first test there are no prizes.

It's not hard, just try to beat your own score. Compete with no one but yourself. All you have to do is work harder and try to do more items and more of them correctly than you did last time. Raise your score and take home one of the prizes."

Some of the results of the study appear here.

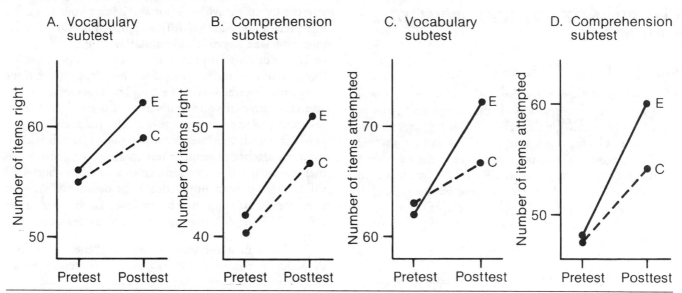

Source: Based on data in "Increases in Test Scores as a Function of Material Rewards" by J. J. Tuinman, R. Farr, and B. E. Blanton, 1972, *Journal of Educational Measurement, 9,* pp. 215–223, Tables 1, 5. Copyright 1972, by the National Council on Measurement in Education, Washington, D.C. Adapted by permission of the publisher.

Intended and Unintended Consequences: Consequential Evidence

As I mentioned in connection with the four principles for validation, the meanings and uses you give to assessment results arise from your educational and social values. We also discussed the consequences and pressures on school curricula when there is a mismatch between the a priori domain sampled by an assessment instrument and the curricular and instructional domains in a local school system. As Moss (1992) notes, "many of the arguments raging today about externally imposed versus classroom-generated assessments or about multiple-choice versus performance assessments are warranted, not in terms of technical validity considerations, but in terms of the consequences for instruction and learning and equity" (p. 236).

Cost, Efficiency, Practicality, and Instructional Features: Practicality Evidence

Assessment results may be technically sound, but practical barriers may exist that impede their proper (and therefore valid) use. For example, if an assessment procedure is too complex for teachers to use, they will not use it properly. If the proper administration of an assessment requires more training than teachers have, the assessment is likely to be administered improperly and yield results of low validity. Further, the validity of an assessment instrument will be enhanced if it is administered and interpreted properly. Some assessment instruments may be accompanied by computerized score reports that help a teacher to identify students needing special help. The availability of these and other auxiliary materials increase the likelihood that the results will be used as they are intended.

Although cost of assessment is not a major consideration for validity, it is a consideration nevertheless. Of concern here is that from among various choices of similar assessment instruments, which one will be most cost effective? Which one will deliver the most valid results under the practical circumstances in a particular school setting?

COMBINING EVIDENCE FOR VALIDITY JUDGMENTS

Multiple Types of Evidence

We have mentioned throughout this chapter that you must be prepared to review and combine several types of evidence before judging the validity of using particular assessment results for a given purpose. This is true whether you are judging a classroom-based assessment procedure or an extra-classroom procedure. Validity is not based on any one piece of evidence, but on the weight of several pieces of evidence concerning the quality of the interpretations and uses you would like to make from the assessment results.

Argument-Based Approach to Validation

Prioritizing Your Validity Evidence Each type of evidence in Table 3.2 has some usefulness for validating the ways you intend to interpret and use assessment results. Confusion can result, however, unless you identify which types of evidence are more important for your particular case. Shepard (1993) suggests that you organize and focus validity evidence to answer questions such as these:

1. What does my assessment practice claim to do?
2. What evidence supports or refutes my claim that my assessment practice achieves what I intend?

3. When I use my assessment practice in an educational setting, what does it do, for good or bad, other than what I claim for it?

The idea is that you prioritize and present the types of evidence described in Table 3.2 in such a way that you can answer these questions. The term **assessment practice** means the way you intend to interpret and use the assessment results in your particular situation. Therefore, these questions may be answered in different ways for the same assessment procedure, depending on how a person intends to interpret and use the results. This reinforces the point we made at the beginning of this chapter, that the question, "Are these assessment results valid?" has many different answers depending on how the results will be interpreted and used.

Argument-Based Validation Kane (1992) suggests that you organize answers to questions such as these as an *argument* to convince others that your interpretations and uses of the assessment results are valid. This approach to validity requires you to (1) state clearly what interpretations and uses you intend to make of the assessment results, (2) present a logically coherent argument to support your claim that the assessment results can be interpreted and used as you intend, and (3) support your logical argument by citing evidence for *and against* your intended interpretation(s) and use(s). This approach is called the **argument-based approach to validation** (Kane, 1992).

The evidence to support your validity argument and refute potential counterarguments comes from the various categories described in Table 3.2. The types of evidence you emphasize in your argument will depend on the assessment practice you want to validate. Kane gives an example in which the assessment practice to be validated is using an algebra placement test to assign students to either a remedial algebra course or to a calculus course. To validate this assessment practice, Kane points out that you need arguments supported by evidence (such as those described in Table 3.2) that the following are reasonable:

1. You can appropriately assess students' success in the calculus course. (That is, a suitable criterion assessment procedure is available.)

2. You can identify the algebra concepts and thinking skills that students will use frequently in the calculus course.

3. The algebra content and thinking skills assessed by the placement test match those that are frequently used in the calculus course.

4. The remedial course to which low-scoring students will be assigned will be successful in teaching the algebra concepts and skills needed in the calculus course.

5. Scores on the placement test are reliable. That is, students' scores are consistent across different samples of test items, different occasions of testing, and different persons scoring the test.

6. It is not helpful for students with high ability in algebra to take the remedial algebra course. That is, students who score high on the placement tests will not significantly improve their chances of success in calculus by first taking this particular remedial algebra course.

7. The placement test scores are not affected by systematic errors that would lower the validity of your interpretation that the placement test measures algebra knowledge and thinking skills.

Summary

- *Validity* refers to the soundness of your interpretations and uses of assessment results, rather than to the assessment instrument itself.
- Assessment results have different degrees of validity, depending on the interpretations and uses made of the results.
- Validity of assessment results may be made only after combining several types of evidence and judging that combination in relation to the particular interpretation and use you wish to make of the results.
- The validity of assessment results depends also on the appropriateness of the values implied by the way you use the assessment results and on the social consequences of that use.
- Classroom-based assessments used for purposes of assigning grades to students should meet the validity criteria in the following categories. The specific criteria are listed in Table 3.1.
  - Content representativeness and relevance
  - Thinking processes and skills
  - Consistency with other classroom assessments
  - Reliability and objectivity
  - Fairness to different students
  - Economy, efficiency, practicality, instructional features
  - Multiple assessment usage
- The validity of results from standardized tests and other extra-classroom assessments should be based on evidence from the following eight categories. Examples of specific questions and validation procedures for each category are summarized in Table 3.2.
  - Content representativeness and relevance (content evidence)
  - Types of thinking skills and processes required (substantive evidence)
  - Relationships among the tasks or parts of the assessment (internal structure evidence)

- Relationships of the assessment results to other variables (external structure evidence)
- Reliability over time, assessors, and content domains (reliability evidence)
- Generalization of interpretation over different types of people, different conditions, or special instructions and interventions (generalization evidence)
- Value of the intended and unintended consequences (consequential evidence)
- Cost, efficiency, practicality, and instructional features (practicality evidence)
- You will need to weigh the evidence from different categories differently depending on the types of interpretations and uses that you wish to make from the results.
- Providing the evidence is the joint responsibility of the publisher of the assessment and the person using the results. Appendix B summarizes many of these joint responsibilities.
- You cannot ignore the need to validate your interpretations and uses of assessment results just because you cannot afford to carry out the necessary validity studies.
- Several types of validity evidence depend on the correlation between two or more sets of assessment scores. *Predictive validity evidence* is concerned with how well scores on the assessment instrument predict future scores on a criterion. *Concurrent validity* evidence concerns the extent to which individuals' current status on a criterion can be estimated from the scores on the assessment instrument. In some cases, correlation coefficients or expectancy tables may provide the validity evidence needed.
- The *criterion problem* arises because it is difficult to obtain measures of criteria suitable for validating assessment results. Criteria are judged by their (1) relevance to ultimate real-life performance, (2) degree of reliability, (3) extent of bias against individuals or groups, and (4) availability and convenience.
- Because most persons interpret a student's assessment performance in a broad way that infers the student's status on an educational or psychological construct like reading comprehension or intelligence, it is necessary to integrate a rather large and diverse amount of information concerning the factors that influence a student's assessment performance. This information comes from all eight categories of Table 3.2.
- Priorities among the eight categories of evidence that are in Table 3.2 need to be made by considering the ways that you intend to interpret and use the assessment results. It is suggested that you prepare a validation argument to address these questions: (1) What does my assessment practice claim to do? (2) What evidence supports or refutes my arguments that my

assessment practice achieves what I claim? (3) When I use my assessment practice in the educational system, what does it do, for good or for bad, other than what I claim for it?

■ Your validation argument must: (1) state clearly what interpretations and uses you intend to make of the assessment results, (2) present a logically coherent argument to support your claim that the results can be interpreted and used as you intend, and (3) support your logical argument by citing evidence for and against your intended interpretation(s) and use(s).

Important Terms and Concepts

argument-based approach to validation
assessment practice
concurrent validity evidence
content relevance
content representativeness
correlation coefficient
curricular relevance
ethnic and gender stereotyping
expectancy table
external structure
four principles for validation
internal structure
multiple-assessment strategy
negative correlation
passage dependency
Pearson product-moment correlation coefficient
positive correlation
predictive validity evidence
scatter diagram (scattergram)
table of specifications
validity
validity coefficient

Exercises and Discussion Questions

1. When speaking of validity, are we speaking of the validity of an assessment instrument or procedure, or of the validity of the results obtained from the instrument or procedure? Explain why such a distinction is important.

2. Identify a particular test and list two or more purposes for which scores from that test have been used. Using evidence categories in Table 3.2, search for evidence to support the validity of each of the purposes of score use you identify. Then, write a brief statement describing the degree to which the test scores are valid for each use and why.

3. Obtain a teacher-made assessment instrument that has been used for assigning students' marks or letter grades for a unit, marking period, or semester. Using the criteria listed in Table 3.1, evaluate the validity of using the assessment results for grading students. Then briefly describe how valid this assessment is for this purpose and why. Finally, using the criteria in Table 3.1, describe how you could improve the validity of this assessment instrument.

4. Obtain a teacher-made assessment instrument (either of your own construction or from someone else). Identify the main or intended interpretations of student results from that assessment instrument. Analyze the assessment logi-

cally. Identify three counterinterpretations (other interpretations that raise questions about the validity of the intended interpretation). Then specify the kind(s) of evidence that could be collected to verify the intended interpretation and invalidate each of the three counterinterpretations. Attach this test to this exercise.

5. A single test cannot be expected to cover all of a school's important learning targets in a subject area. What does this imply about using tests for evaluating a school's (a) curriculum, (b) instructional programs, (c) teachers, and (d) students? Considered strictly from the issue of test validity, should there be fewer or more tests? Explain.

6. What should be the relationship between scores on a standardized achievement test and the amount of time and emphasis a teacher places on certain learning targets? What are the implications of this relationship for a teacher? Should a teacher "teach to the test"? What is the relationship between teaching to the test and the validity of interpreting the test scores as a measure of a student's mastery of the subject matter?

7. What are the implications of the relationship you described in Question 6 for school administrators and school board members?

8. Assume that a new high school science aptitude test is being developed, and in the course of that development several procedures and techniques have been used to provide evidence for its validity. These procedures are listed in the following statements. For each statement, decide which type of evidence in Table 3.2 is directly addressed. Explain why you made the choice you did.
   a. For a sample of 150 tenth graders, scores on the odd-numbered items were correlated with scores on the even-numbered items.
   b. Scores from 300 freshmen obtained from a September administration of the test were correlated with scores of the same freshmen obtained from a February administration.
   c. Scores of 200 freshmen obtained from a September administration of the test were correlated with the general science course grades of these same freshmen obtained from school records in January.
   d. Scores of students who had taken one, two, three, and four science courses were compared to see if they differed on the average.
   e. A section of the test manual describes seven aspects of science aptitude and the number of items measuring each aspect.

9. Each of the following statements is a question that an educator can ask about an assessment procedure. Using Table 3.2, identify for each statement the type(s) of validity evidence that is (are) most important to answering the question directly. Then briefly explain your choice.
   a. "Is this spelling test representative of the type of spelling patterns we teach our sixth graders?"
   b. "Can scores on this reading test help me to assign students to different instructional groups?"
   c. "I'm using this performance assessment to select persons for a special training program. I wonder if the results are significantly influenced by the personality of the person administering the assessment?"
   d. "Does this mathematics performance assessment really assess the mathematics ability of these students?"

e. "We now use a procedure to rate student teachers. Does this procedure permit the student teacher to be observed in the broad range of classroom situations likely to be encountered when teaching in this state?"

10. Read each statement and decide whether it is true or false. Then explain why you marked it the way you did.

a. A verbal reasoning test is given at the start of ninth grade. Scores on this test are correlated with English grades assigned in ninth, tenth, eleventh, and twelfth grades. The correlations between the test scores and the twelfth-grade marks will likely be the lowest of the four correlations.

b. A certain predictor test has perfect reliability (reliability coefficient = 1.00). This means that the predictor test is likely to have very high correlation with just about any criterion measure an investigator wants to use.

c. Another predictor test has zero reliability (reliability coefficient = 0.00). This means that the predictor test will likely correlate zero with just about any criterion measure the investigator wants to use.

11. What kind(s) of evidence would support your claim that the rating given to your teaching by your supervisor or school principal is a valid measurement of your teaching ability?

12. Shepard (1993) states that test validation is analogous to the Federal Drug Administration's standard for approving a new drug: "Do the empirically demonstrated effects weighed against side effects warrant use of the (drug)?" How might this analogy apply to a state's assessment program that seeks to make each school accountable by administering performance-based assessments crafted by the state's department of education?

Additional Readings

American Educational Research Association, American Psychological Association, & National Council on Measurement in Education. (1999). *Standards for educational and psychological testing*. Washington, DC: Author.

Part I discusses the assessment developer's responsibility for the technical aspect of validation; Chapters 11, 13, and 15 describe standards for those who use assessments in schools.

Joint Committee on Testing Practices. (1988). *Code of fair testing practices in education*. Washington, DC: American Psychological Association.

This brief document describes the obligations of both developers and users of extra-classroom educational assessments. It is reproduced in Appendix B.

Linn, R. L. (1994). Performance assessment: Policy, promises, and technical measurement standards. *Educational Researcher, 23*(4), 4–14.

Discusses how the validity concepts in this chapter are relevant to large-scale performance assessment situations.

Messick, S. (1989). Validity. In R. L. Linn (Ed.), *Educational measurement* (3rd ed., pp. 13–103). New York: Macmillan.

A thorough and scholarly treatment of every aspect of validity evidence.

Moss, P. A. (1992). Shifting conceptions of validity in educational measurement: Implications for performance assessment. *Review of Educational Research, 62*, 229–258.

Moss, P. A. (1995). Themes and variations in validity theory. *Educational Measurement: Issues and Practice, 14*(2), 5–13.

Reviews recent developments in validity theory and suggests ways to expand the methods and types of evidence used to validate assessment results. The suggested approaches to validation are useful in the context of performance, portfolio, and traditional assessment procedures.

Nitko, A. J. (1989). Designing tests that are integrated with instruction. In R. L. Linn (Ed.), *Educational measurement* (3rd ed., pp. 447–474). New York: Macmillan.

Discusses ways to match tests to the instructional delivery domain, analyze the validity issues associated with educational diagnostic assessments methods, and discusses validity issues of mandated extra-classroom assessments.

Nitko, A. J., Al-Sararimi, A., Amedahe, F., Wang, S., & Wingert, M. (1998). *How well are the Kentucky Academic Expectations matched to the KIRIS assessments, the CTBS, and the CAT?* Paper presented at the Annual Meeting of the American Educational Research Association, San Diego, CA, April (ERIC/TM ED 420677).

This is an example of how to go about gathering validity evidence concerning how well three tests match a state's curriculum content standards.

Shepard, L. E. (1993). Evaluating test validity. *Review of Research in Education, 19*, 405–450.

Reviews the history of validity and shows how to apply validity concepts to modern educational assessment situations.

Tittle, C. K. (1989). Validity: Whose construct is it in the teaching and learning context? *Educational Measurement: Issues and Practice, 8*(1), 5–13, 34.

Expands the concept of validity to include using teachers' and students' perspectives about the assessment as evidence for validity, instead of limiting evidence to the developers' perspectives as is traditionally done.

CHAPTER 4

Reliability of Assessment Results

Learning Targets

After studying this chapter, you should be able to:

1. Explain the concept of reliability and how it relates to inconsistency in students' assessment results. [3, 6]

2. Explain the relationship between reliability, validity, and the quality of educational decisions. [3, 6]

3. Describe several causes of measurement error and how such error may lead to improper interpretations of students' assessment results. [3, 6, 7]

4. Explain why assessment results might be reliable for some purposes but not for other purposes. [6, 3]

5. Name the different types of reliability coefficients and describe how data are collected for their calculation. [6, 3]

6. Identify the specific reliability coefficient(s) that provide information for answering questions about an instrument's measurement errors. [3, 1, 6, 7]

7. Explain the meaning of decision consistency in relation to using a procedure for assessing mastery. [6, 3, 1]

8. List and give examples of the factors affecting reliability coefficients and standard errors of measurement. [3, 6, 7]

9. Explain the meaning of observed, true, and error scores. [6]

10. Explain the meaning of standard error of measurement, its relationship to reliability, and how it is used to interpret scores. [3, 6, 4]

11. Describe the types of education decisions that require very high levels of assessment reliability and the types for which more moderate levels may be tolerated. [3, 6, 4]

12. Explain how each of the terms and concepts listed at the end of this chapter apply to educational measurement. [6]

GENERAL NATURE OF RELIABILITY

Reliability Defined

Reliability refers to the consistency of assessment results. For example, suppose you asked students today to write an essay explaining the pros and cons of democratic elections. Suppose, further, that you repeated this assignment with the same students a month from now. If the quality of each student's essay is essentially the same on both occasions, the results are consistent over this time period. We say the results are reliable over a month's time.

Now suppose that you marked each student's essay tonight. Then tomorrow, without revealing the marks you assigned, you give the essays to a teaching colleague to mark. If the marks you assigned each student essentially agree with the marks independently assigned by your colleague, we would say that results are reliable with respect to different markers.

To use another example, suppose you rephrased the essay question in a different but equivalent way and asked the students to write essays for both versions. If the qualities of each student's essays were essentially the same on the two versions of the task, we would say that the students' responses are reliable with respect to equivalent versions of the same task.

Reliability, then, is the degree to which students' assessment results are the same when (1) they complete the same task(s) on two different occasions; (2) two or more teachers mark their performance on the same task(s); or (3) they complete different but equivalent tasks on the same or different occasions. As with validity, reliability refers to the assessment *results* or *scores*, not to the assessment instrument itself.

You can see that the reliability is an important concept for you to use when thinking about how much confidence to place in your students' assessment results. Later in this chapter we describe this qualitative concept in more specific ways. This will lead to various indices of the degree of reliability. First, however, we briefly discuss the relationship between reliability and validity.

Reliability Limits Validity

Validity, as we discussed in the last chapter, relates to the confidence we may have in interpreting students' assessment results and in using them to make decisions. Your interpretations and decisions are less valid when your students' assessment results are inconsistent, however. An assessment result's degree of reliability limits its degree of validity.

High Reliability Does Not Guarantee Validity Although high degrees of validity require high degrees of reliability, the converse is not true. *A highly reliable assessment does not guarantee that you can make highly valid interpretations or decisions.* This is because there are many validity criteria in addition to reliability (see Tables 3.1 and 3.2). Reliability is only one important criterion for validity.

As an illustration, consider this example. Ms. Cortez teaches seventh grade arithmetic. She reflects on the kinds of computations that her students will be expected to perform as they go through their daily lives in the local community and lists these skills. She then creates a computation and problem-solving test to assess her students' ability to perform these skills. This paper-and-pencil test has a moderately large number of items, and therefore Ms. Cortez can be confident that the resulting scores will be very reliable.

Knowing that these scores are reliable, however, is not enough to conclude they are valid. Among the questions Ms. Cortez should answer before concluding that she can interpret the results as valid assessments are: Is this test a representative sample of the domain of computations to which she wishes to generalize the results? Are the test items' formats appropriate for assessing the students at this point in their educational development? Are the time limits for the test appropriate? Is performance on the test seriously affected by the students' reading abilities? Will scores on the test help her to plan instruction for these students? Will using these types of test items inadvertently convey to students that computations and problem solving in school are isolated from solving "real-world" or "authentic" mathematics problems? A negative answer to any of these questions means that the validity of the test is low for the types of interpretations she apparently has in mind, even though the scores may be highly reliable.

Reliability Is Necessary for Validity Assessment reliability affects the quality (validity) of decisions. Suppose Ms. Cortez decided that mastering 80% of the target domain of computations is passing. The test is only a sample from the domain, however. If the test scores were of low reliability, it is likely that among all those students who actually mastered 80% or more of the targeted *domain*, some will have test scores below 80%. These students will be erroneously classified as failures. On the other hand, among the students who truly know slightly less than 80% of the targeted *domain*, some are likely to pass the test. These students will be erroneously classified as having sufficient competence.

As another example, a counselor may want to know whether a student's mathematical ability or verbal ability is higher. On a test for each ability, a student's scores on the two tests are not likely to be identical. The validity question is, "Do scores that are different mean that the student is truly different in these two abilities?" In order for the counselor to say that the student is higher in one or the other ability, the counselor needs to know how much scores are likely to fluctuate just because of measurement error. If scores fluctuate widely, the tests' scores are unreliable. Unreliability means that the counselor can have little confidence that differences in the scores indicate the student truly differs in verbal and mathematical ability. Inconsistencies, which are also called *measurement errors*, are of special concern to those needing to validly interpret a student's profile of scores as is done in diagnostic assessment or in vocational counseling assessment.

CAUSES OF MEASUREMENT ERROR OR INCONSISTENCY

Reliability and *error of measurement* are complementary ways of speaking about the same assessment phenomenon. The concept or reliability focuses on the consistency of assessment results; the concept of measurement error focuses on their inconsistencies. Inconsistencies have different causes. Not every cause, however, is equally important to a particular interpretation and use of assessment results.

Consider the following situation. Suppose all of the tasks that might be appropriate for assessing performance in an area could be described. This description of possible tasks is called a *domain*. For example, the domain could be all the open-ended tasks that could be used to assess fifth-grade students' ability to solve mathematical problems involving proportions. The large circle on the left of Figure 4.1 represents this domain.

Now, suppose you wish to determine the percentage of the domain a student knows. Rather than administering the entire domain, an impossible feat, you select from the domain a random sample of 10 tasks and administer them to the student. Clearly, the student's score on this assessment depends on which tasks you happen to sample. A different sample of 10 tasks would be easier or harder than the first sample, resulting in a higher or lower score for the student. Suppose the student's results are 80% right on the first sample and 50% right on the second. What causes this inconsistency? As shown by Figure 4.1, it is a result of using a different content sample (or "form" of the assessment procedure).

Now consider this: Suppose you administer the first sample of 10 tasks on Tuesday, which is a "bad day" for a student, and the student attains 40% right. Perhaps the student had an upsetting encounter on the playground before class, had eaten no breakfast, or his allergies were

acting up and making concentration difficult. For whatever reason, Tuesday is a day on which the student's performance is off. Suppose, now, that the exact same 10 tasks were also administered on Friday. Friday was a very "good day," and the student performed much better than normal, attaining 70%. As shown in Figure 4.1, this type of inconsistency is a result of sampling a different occasion. The identical content sample (i.e., the same 10 tasks) was administered on both Tuesday and Friday, so the source of the inconsistency of the scores cannot be content sampling.

This description considers two of the **factors influencing consistency of assessment performance**: (1) the content or particular sample of tasks appearing on any form of the assessment and (2) the occasion on which the assessment is administered. Solid arrows in the schematic diagram of Figure 4.1 indicate these factors. The figure also shows (via diagonal dashed arrows) the additional possibility that both content and occasion may work together to influence assessment performance.

There are several important conclusions to be drawn from this discussion and Figure 4.1. Your interpretation of assessment results a student obtained on a particular occasion with a particular sample of content and tasks has definite limitations. Obtained assessment results must be reasonably consistent (perfect consistency is not possible) over different samples of content, tasks, and occasions; otherwise, we can have little confidence in them.

Figure 4.1 shows that there are particular kinds of consistencies. Assessment results may be consistent in some ways but not in others. For example, an assessment result

FIGURE 4.1   A schematic diagram illustrating how changes in performance on an assessment relate to content samples and occasions of assessment.

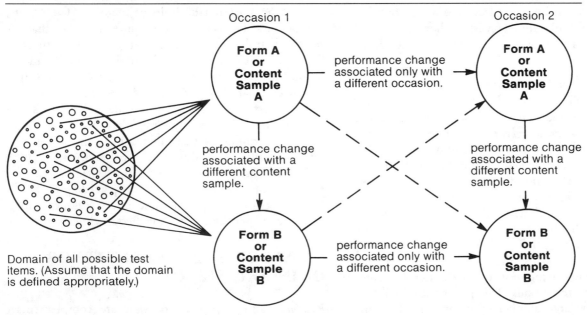

Source: From *Educational and Psychological Measurement and Evaluation* (7th ed.) (p. 130) by K. D. Hopkins, J. C. Stanley, and B. R. Hopkins, 1990, Englewood Cliffs, NJ: Prentice Hall. Reprinted by permission of publisher.

may not be consistent over different samples of tasks but may be very consistent on the same tasks over a short period of time. If you want to generalize a student's performance today to how the student is likely to perform next month or next year, consistency over these longer time periods may be more important than generalizing over tasks. On the other hand, if you know the student is learning rapidly and changing constantly, consistency of performance over time may be less important. If you keep in mind the interpretations and uses you want to make with the particular assessment results, you will be able to better gauge the type of consistency that is important for the assessment results to have.

TYPES OF RELIABILITY COEFFICIENTS

Quantifying the Consistency of Assessment Results

We have just described reliability and errors of measurement in qualitative terms. It also is possible to quantify these concepts and to use statistical methods to provide indices of the degree of reliability and the approximate size of the errors of measurement in the assessment results. Such indices are possible only when an assessment procedure yields quantitative scores or measurements of the students.

The general strategy used to obtain these indices is to administer the assessment procedure to a group of students one or more times and obtain the scores. The scores are examined for consistency in one or both of the following ways. One approach is to correlate the scores from the two administrations. The correlation coefficient is an index of whether the relative standing of the students in the group changes from one administration to the next. This correlation is called a **reliability coefficient**. A second way to evaluate consistency is to estimate the amount by which we can expect a student's score to change from one administration to the next. The index expressing this variation in score consistency is called the **standard error of measurement**. Because both indices are so widely used in describing the quality of tests and other assessment methods, you should understand the basic ideas behind them to properly interpret assessment results. Your understanding of these indices is an important part of your professional development and essential for using assessment results in a responsible way, even if you do not actually calculate them. We first discuss various types of reliability coefficients, then address the standard error of measurement.

Overview of Reliability Coefficients

This section discusses procedures for estimating reliability coefficients. The different reliability coefficients we shall discuss follow the ideas we introduced through Figure 4.1. When questions about educational assessments focus on

the consistency of student results over time (as shown by the horizontal arrows in Figure 4.1), a test-retest reliability coefficient gives the necessary information. If our educational assessment questions focus on consistency of results over both time and changes in assessment content (as shown by the diagonal arrows in Figure 4.1), an alternate forms (different occasions) coefficient is the appropriate index. When questions about educational assessments are concerned with consistency of results from one sample of content to another (the vertical arrows in Figure 4.1), one of several coefficients may be used: alternate forms (same occasion), split-halves, Kuder-Richardson, or coefficient alpha.

This section discusses one other category of coefficients that is not represented by Figure 4.1. Sometimes questions about educational assessments focus on the marking or rating of student responses. In this case interrater reliability coefficients or percent of agreement provides the needed information.

Table 4.1 lists each of the coefficients we discuss, the major questions for which the coefficients provide answers, and the type of measurement error each addresses. As you examine this table and study this section, you will realize that the question "Are these scores reliable?" has many different answers depending on the types of measurement errors about which you are concerned.

Estimating Reliability Over Time

Suppose we ask questions such as: To what extent are scores on identical tasks likely to be different because the occasion is different? or If a student teacher is observed on a Monday, would the same ratings be likely if the observations occur on Wednesday? or If Dr. Adams rates the teacher on Monday and Dr. Meyers rates on Thursday, would such ratings be likely to agree? (Recall Figure 4.1.) Procedures for estimating reliability in situations like these are the subject of this section.

Test-Retest Reliability The first reliability question in the preceding paragraph centers on the *stability of scores* over a time period on a fixed sample of assessment tasks. Studying data obtained from administering the identical tasks to a group of students on two separate occasions will answer this question. Because the same tasks (rather than equivalent tasks) are administered at two different times, the correlation between the scores on the two occasions is known as the **test-retest reliability coefficient**. Sometimes it is also called a **stability coefficient**. This paradigm is shown in Figure 4.2.

You may recall that a correlation of 0.00 represents no relationship between two sets of scores, and a correlation of 1.00 is a perfect positive relationship. Reliability coefficients have a range of 0.00 to 1.00. A completely unreliable (inconsistent) set of scores has a reliability coefficient of 0.00. A perfectly reliable set, containing no errors of measurement, has a reliability coefficient of 1.00. A test-retest

TABLE 4.1 Summary of reliability coefficients.

Type of coefficient	Major question(s) answered	What is counted as measurement error or inconsistency
I. Influence of occasions or time		
Test-retest	a. How are scores on the identical content sample affected by testing on another occasion?	Time or occasion sampling
	b. How stable are scores on this particular test form over time?	
Alternate forms (with time interval)	a. How consistent are the test scores regardless of form used or occasion on which it is administered?	Time or occasion sampling and content sampling
	b. How stable are scores on this trial over time (and content samples)?	
II. Influence of different content samples		
Alternate forms (no time interval)	a. Are scores affected by sampling different content on the same occasion?	Content sampling
	b. Are two carefully matched test forms interchangeable (equivalent, parallel)?	
Split-halves	a. Same as above	Content sampling
	b. What is an estimate of the alternate forms reliability coefficient?	
Kuder-Richardson formulas 20 and 21, coefficient alpha	a. Same as above, except equivalence or parallelism of forms may not concern the investigator.	Content sampling and homogeneity
	b. What is a crude estimate of test homogeneity?	
	c. How consistent are responses from item to item?	
	d. Are scores affected by content sampling on the same occasion?	
III. Influence of different scorers		
Scorer reliability	a. To what extent will the scores be different if different scorers (raters, judges) are used?	Scorer sampling
	b. To what extent is the test objective?	
	c. Are the results from different scorers (observers, raters, judges) interchangeable?	

FIGURE 4.2 Test-retest reliability coefficient.

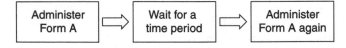

coefficient of 1.00 means that persons' scores on the two occasions have the identical rank order. Test-retest coefficients of 1.00 rarely occur, however. Typically, test-retest coefficients for standardized achievement and aptitude tests are between 0.80 and 0.90 when the interval between testing is between 3 and 6 months.

Of importance when interpreting these test-retest coefficients is the length of time between the two administrations of the assessment and the expected stability of the performance being measured. In general, the longer the time interval between the repeated administrations, the lower the reliability will be. The less stable the performance of

students, the lower the reliability will be. For example, some performances of infants and young children are not consistent from one day to the next. You would expect the test-retest reliability of assessments of these performances to be low, too. On the other hand, traits such as older students' general scholastic aptitude tend to remain stable over a semester or a year. Test-retest reliability of assessments of this trait will be relatively high over a longer time period, and assessments of general scholastic aptitude tend to be useful in predicting future performance over these periods. The validity of assessment results as predictors of future performance is diminished when the results lack stability.

The teacher's concern with whether a student is having an "off day" concentrates on whether the student's performance is consistent over a relatively short time interval. The teacher may not expect the student's performance to stay the same over a longer period, such as a month. Changes in level of performance over a longer time interval would likely reflect actual changes in student ability rather than fluctuations due to the circumstances of a particular occasion or off day. However, such actual changes in ability do reduce the correlation of scores obtained on the two occasions, because different students have different rates of changes or growing.

Alternate-forms Reliability (Different Occasions) Another procedure for estimating reliability is to administer one form of an assessment on one occasion and an alternate form on another occasion. This permits both content and occasion to vary. The correlation between the scores on the two occasions is influenced by differences in both content and in occasion. This paradigm is depicted in Figure 4.3.

This correlation is known as the **delayed alternate-forms reliability coefficient** or the *delayed equivalent-forms reliability coefficient*. The two forms are built to the same specifications of content (i.e., same blueprint) and level of difficulty, but they contain different questions or tasks. When this paradigm is applied, the reliability coefficient reflects both the equivalence of the assessment techniques and the stability of students' performance.

The comments about length of the time interval for the test-retest reliability coefficient also apply to the delayed alternate-forms coefficient. However, because a new sample of tasks is administered (Form B), this eliminates the effects of students' remembering specific assessment questions (but it does not eliminate general practice effects).

Delayed alternate-forms reliability is important when you want to generalize your interpretation of assessment results over both occasions and content samples. You may ask, for example, "How well does this test assess the ability to solve mathematics problems, regardless of test form used or occasion on which I administer the test?" Many interpretations of educational assessment results may be cast into this framework. For example, in estimating the "teaching ability" of a student teacher, a supervisor may want to focus on the consistency of ratings obtained on different occasions and from different raters. Usually, there is less interest in defining teaching ability in terms of only a single occasion (e.g., many supervisors' ratings on Tuesday, October 5) or in terms of only a specific supervisor's ratings over several occasions (Mr. Washington's ratings of teachers throughout the year).

The meaning of *occasions* needs to be carefully specified when interpreting delayed alternate-forms reliability coefficients. For instance, if children are observed while learning a subject they happen to enjoy very much or with an exceptionally enthralling teacher, there may be

very little fluctuation in their attentiveness from day to day. But there might be relatively large fluctuations in attentiveness within the same day as students move from mathematics instruction to language arts to gym. These moment-to-moment or subject-to-subject fluctuations in attentiveness might be larger than day-to-day fluctuations (Goodwin, 1966). Thus, to make subject-to-subject interpretations of the results, you should examine data that studies this subject-to-subject fluctuation.

Rules based strictly on testing and measurement methodology, although often helpful, are not complete foundations for judging the appropriateness of particular reliability coefficients. Deciding the appropriateness of a particular time interval and a particular stability coefficient is a professional judgment. You need to be knowledgeable about (1) the domain of student performance being assessed, (2) the theory and facts concerning which factors influence students' performance in that domain, and (3) the intended interpretation and use of the assessment results. In addition, you need to use your knowledge of the population of students for whom you are interpreting and using the assessment results. You have a wealth of knowledge that is relevant to assessment interpretation. Combining knowledge of reliability and professional experience permits you to evaluate the usefulness of a particular assessment and its accompanying reliability information.

Estimating Reliability on a Single Occasion

Alternate-forms Reliability (Same Occasion) When attempting to interpret students' assessment results, you may wonder whether the results would have been different had you administered a different sample of assessment tasks. Your primary concern is the consistency of two sets of results (one set from each of two comparable forms) obtained on the same occasion.

One way to provide the type of reliability information implied by this question is to administer two forms of an assessment to the same group of students on the same (or nearly the same) occasion and to correlate the scores. This correlation is known as the **alternate-forms reliability coefficient** or the *equivalent-forms reliability coefficient*. This coefficient is most often used with standardized tests having two forms that are to be used interchangeably. Look for alternate-forms reliability coefficients in the publisher's test manual whenever you intend to use a test that has two or more forms. Because teachers usually do not build two forms of a test, this coefficient is seldom used with teacher-crafted tests.

When interpreting this coefficient, remember that only inconsistencies due to fluctuations in content samples are counted as measurement error. Other factors such as practice effects, fatigue, and boredom—all of which may occur on this one occasion—are considered part of the students' true scores.

FIGURE 4.3 Delayed alternate-forms reliability coefficient.

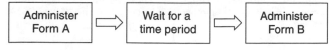

Two forms of an assessment that are made up of tasks carefully matched to the same blueprint are called *parallel forms* (APA, 1974). In this case, the correlation of the scores from the two forms is referred to as a **parallel-forms reliability coefficient**. Ideally, **parallel forms** should (1) have equal observed score means and standard deviations, (2) measure students with equal accuracy (have equal standard errors of measurement), (3) correlate equally with other measurements, and (4) measure the same attribute in precisely the same way. If the two forms of the assessment meet these criteria, it wouldn't matter to the student which form he or she takes: They are interchangeable. Alternate forms that are "built" simply by drawing random samples of tasks from the same domain are not strictly parallel because chance will determine the composition of each form.

Research evidence must be used to justify using two forms interchangeably—that is, to support the professional practice that it doesn't matter which form the student is administered on a given occasion. Any systematic score differences from one form to another are especially important when an individual's results are to be interpreted on their own merits rather than on the basis of the individual's relative standing in a group. For example, when a fixed score is needed for passing or for being certified, decisions about individuals are made on their own merits and not on whether the individuals' scores were larger than the scores of others who took the test along with them. Students are not served well when the different forms of such a certification test lack equivalence. If one form is more difficult than an alternate form, more students than necessary are failed. A less difficult alternate form has an obverse consequence: Many students are certified who may not be qualified. A correlation coefficient of the scores from the two forms won't reveal such consequences because it reflects only rank order rather than the exact values of the scores.

Although in principle many parallel forms of an assessment technique might exist, in practice many assessment procedures have no parallel form. Those procedures that do have parallel forms seldom have more than two or three forms. When any of the following occurs, a developer usually does not create a parallel form of the assessment:

1. The assessment procedure will be used only once with each student. Repeated testings for practical decisions are not anticipated.

2. The very act of taking the assessment may change the student (Thorndike, 1951). For example, if an assessment procedure is crafted to assess the strategies students use to solve unfamiliar problems, completing the assessment tasks themselves may result in the student becoming better at problem-solving strategies.

3. Only one way exists to assess the ability of interest (Thorndike, 1951).

4. It is too costly to build a parallel form of the assessment.

In situations such as the preceding, methods other than alternate-forms reliability are used to evaluate the extent to which content sampling affects observed scores. These methods follow.

Split-Halves Reliability Coefficients   Alternate-forms reliability may be estimated from a single form of an assessment administered on one occasion by a method known as the **split-halves procedure**. In applying the split-halves procedure, the entire test is administered to the students. Then the instrument is split into two equivalent halves. Each half is considered to be a separate (albeit smaller) sample of tasks. For purposes of analysis, every student receives a score for each half of the test. These half-test scores form the basis for estimating the extent of error due to content sampling, much like the alternate-forms method. Of the various possible split-halves procedures (Feldt & Brennan, 1989; Stanley, 1971; Thorndike, 1951), we discuss only one here: the **Spearman-Brown double length formula** (Brown, 1910; Spearman, 1910).[1]

Spearman-Brown Double Length Formula   The Spearman-Brown double length formula (sometimes called the *Spearman-Brown prophecy formula*) is an estimate of the parallel-forms correlation. Students' scores on the halves are correlated, but since this correlation reflects the correspondence of two sets of scores from assessments only half as long as the assessment of interest, this correlation is adjusted or "stepped up" to estimate the reliability of the whole. The Spearman-Brown formula is simple to use:

Whole-test reliability =

$$\frac{2 \times \text{correlation between half-test scores}}{1 + \text{correlation between half-test scores}}$$

[Eq. 4.1]

For example, assume that the correlation between the half-test scores is 0.60. The Spearman-Brown double length reliability estimate for the full-length test is:

$$\text{Whole-test reliability} = \frac{2 \times 0.60}{1 + 0.60} = \frac{1.20}{1.60} = 0.75$$

The double length formula is often used as an estimate of a parallel form's reliability coefficient. To do so properly requires the assessment instrument to be split into

---

[1]Appendix I provides a computing guide for the Spearman-Brown formula as well as for another split-half method, the Rulon (1939) method.

parallel halves, making the halves equivalent in terms of content coverage, difficulty level, and variability in essentially the same manner as when two parallel forms are constructed.

An assessment instrument may be split into halves in many ways,[2] but not all prove satisfactory when applying split-halves procedures. The most commonly used procedure to split an assessment is to let the odd-numbered items (1, 3, 5, 7, . . .) comprise one of the halves and the even-numbered (2, 4, 6, 8, . . .) comprise the other half. This is known as the **odd-even split-halves procedure**. Splitting the assessment and instrument into halves this way works fine as long as (1) the odd half and the even half can be considered parallel samples of content, and (2) the assessment is not speeded. (See Chapter 1 for an explanation of speed vs. power tests.) If an assessment procedure is speeded, agreement among students' scores on the two halves is spuriously high. In general, split-halves procedures should not be used with speeded or partially speeded assessment procedures unless precautions are taken to separately administer and separately time each half. The odd-even split-halves procedure is inappropriate when groups of tasks are linked together, such as when a cluster of items requires answers based on the same reading selection (or on the same data table, figure, graph, etc.), or when items are grouped in homogeneous clusters in a matching exercise (Thorndike, 1951).

Kuder-Richardson Reliability Coefficients Another way to obtain a reliability estimate from a single form of the test is by using one of the Kuder and Richardson (1937) procedures. The two discussed here, **Kuder-Richardson formula 20** (KR20) and **Kuder-Richardson formula 21** (KR21), are used when test items are scored dichotomously (0 or 1). The names of these procedures derive from the numbering scheme Kuder and Richardson used to identify the formulas in their 1937 paper.

The Kuder-Richardson formula 20, like the split-half formula, estimates reliability from a single administration of a test. Unlike the split-half procedure, however, KR20 does not require splitting the test in half. Instead it uses data on the proportion of persons answering each item correctly and the standard deviation of the total scores. The Kuder-Richardson formula 21 procedure is a computationally simpler version of KR20 that uses only the mean and standard deviation of the total scores. Appendix I illustrates the computation of these reliability estimates. The KR20 formula is most often used in published reports of standardized tests and is often provided as output in computer programs that analyze classroom test data.

Kuder-Richardson formulas 20 and 21 are used when the test contains only dichotomously scored items. Not all assessments contain only items scored that way. Some assessments contain a mixture of item types. Items on essay tests are scored more continuously; attitude scales require the student to express agreement with each item on a scale of, say, 1 to 4; and performance assessments may rate a student on a scale from 1 to 5, for example. In these cases, a more general version of KR20 is used. This reliability estimate is known as coefficient alpha (Cronbach, 1951). An example of how to calculate this coefficient is given in Appendix I also. Because **coefficient alpha** is a more general version of KR20, it can be used with either dichotomously or polytomously scored items.

These three procedures are founded on the idea that the consistency with which students respond from one assessment task to the next can provide a basis for estimating the reliability coefficient for the total scores. This focus on task-to-task consistency within an assessment has led to these coefficients being called *internal consistency reliability estimates*. These three procedures are sensitive to the homogeneity of the tasks as well as to their specific content. **Homogeneous tasks** all measure the same trait or attribute. An assessment procedure that contains tasks measuring more than one trait is said to contain *heterogeneous tasks*. If assessment tasks are homogeneous, the KR20 and coefficient alpha procedures will give nearly the same results as the split-halves procedure. When the assessment tasks are heterogeneous, results from the KR20 and coefficient alpha procedures are lower than the split-halves procedure. For this reason, KR20 and coefficient alpha are often called *lower bound estimates of reliability*.

It should be noted that KR20 and coefficient alpha are equal to the average of all possible split-half reliability coefficients that could be computed for the assessment procedure in question (see Cronbach, 1951). All possible split-halves means not just the odd-even split, but all different splits that could divide a test into halves.[3]

Also, the numerical values of KR20 and coefficient alpha are influenced by the length of the test as well as its homogeneity. Longer tests will tend to have higher values of KR20 or coefficient alpha, even though they may be heterogeneous. The KR20, KR21, and alpha coefficients are influenced by speed in the same manner as split-halves coefficients. They should not be used with speeded or partially speeded tests. Finally, as you may notice in Table 4.1, KR20, KR21, coefficient alpha, and the split-half methods do not consider sampling of occasions as a source of measurement error. To estimate the degree of inconsistency attributed to students' day-to-day fluctuations in performance, you must examine test-retest or delayed alternate-forms coefficients.

---

[2]For a 4-item test there are 3 possible ways to split the test into halves. A 6-item test may be split into halves 10 ways; an 8-item test, 35 ways; and a 10-item test, 126 ways. For a general formula see Thorndike (1951, p. 579), Stanley (1971, p. 408), or Feldt and Brennan (1989, p. 120).

[3]See footnote 2.

Estimating Inter-Rater Reliability

Yet another source of measurement error arises from persons (or machines) scoring an assessment. Here concern focuses on questions such as (1) to what extent would a student obtain the same score if a different teacher had scored the paper or rated the performance? (2) to what extent might the assessment procedure be said to be objective? and (3) are the results obtained from different scorers (observers, raters, judges) interchangeable?"

Inter-rater reliability is especially important if you use essay questions, open-ended questions, performance assessments, and portfolio assessment. To improve the reliability of scoring these types of assessments, you should develop and use scoring rubrics. You will learn how to craft scoring rubrics in Chapters 9 and 12. Here we show how to evaluate the reliability of scoring.

Correlating Raters' Scores The most straightforward way to estimate this type of reliability is to have two persons score each student's paper or rate each student's performance. The two scores for each student—one score from each scorer—are then correlated. (Correlation is explained in Chapter 3.) This correlation coefficient is called **scorer reliability** or **inter-rater reliability**. It is an index of the extent to which the scorers were consistent in marking the same students. In this case, *consistency* is defined as similarity of students' rank ordering by the two teachers or judges. The group of four students' ratings in Figure 4.4 illustrates this point in an admittedly exaggerated situation.

The ratings in this example don't "agree" in the absolute sense, but they do agree perfectly in the relative sense because the rankings are in perfect agreement: The correlation coefficient of 1.00 reflects this.

Percent Agreement Agreement in the absolute sense happens when two scorers assign the identical scores or ratings to each student. The extent to which this identical assignment of scorers occurs is sometimes expressed as a **percent of agreement**. (Percent of agreement is calculated in the last section of this chapter.) If scorers always agree in their assignment of scores, there is 100% agreement; if they never agree, the percent of agreement is zero; partial agreement is expressed as a percent falling between these two values.

Percent of agreement is quite a different concept than a correlation coefficient: In general, the numerical values of the two will be different. The choice between a percent of agreement index and a correlation index of inter-rater reliability depends on whether the absolute or the relative score level is important for a particular interpretation and use. Suppose that in Figure 4.4 a rating of 5 or better was needed to "pass." If the scores of Rater A were used, then everyone "failed," but if the scores of Rater B were used, everyone passed. For interpretations of pass and fail, the absolute score level is important. A serious source of error (in this example) is the particular scorer or rater employed. Suppose, on the other hand, that only the rank order of the scores is important, such as when you want to know who in the class is the best, next best, and so on. In this case, the two observers agree perfectly on who the "best" and the "next best" are. In other words, they agree perfectly on their ranking or relative level of accomplishment.

OBTAINED SCORES, TRUE SCORES, AND ERROR SCORES

The scores students receive when you assess them are called **obtained scores**. Obtained scores include ratings from open-ended tasks such as essays, number right scores from multiple-choice or short-answer tests, and standard scores or grade-equivalent scores from norm-referenced standardized tests. You may think of each student's obtained score as really being composed of two parts: a true score and an error score. The sum of these two scores equals the obtained score. Whenever we assess a student, we really want to know the student's true score. However, we are always "stuck" with the obtained score. Our assessment of a procedure is only an *estimate* of the student's true status. Because obtained scores contain errors, we must learn to live with errors of measurement.

If you could quantify the amount of error in a student's obtained score, you would have the **error score**. (Often the error score is referred to as *error of measurement*.) The **true score** is the remaining portion of the observed score and contains no measurement error.

FIGURE 4.4 Ratings and rank order of four students.

Students	Ratings from:		Ratings converted to ranks	
	Rater A	**Rater B**	**Rank from A**	**Rank from B**
Tony	4	8	1	1
Marya	3	7	2	2
Bobby	2	6	3	3
Meghan	1	5	4	4
Mean	**2.5**	**6.5**	$r_{AB} = 1.00$	
SD	**1.12**	**1.12**		

A student's true score is not some hidden property that your assessment procedure seeks to discover or some set of quantities assigned to the student at birth. It is not an "ultimate fact in the book of the recording angel" (Stanley, 1971, p. 361). Rather, a student's true score for a particular assessment procedure is defined as the hypothetical average (mean) of the observed scores the student would obtain if you repeatedly assessed the student under the same conditions (Lord & Novick, 1968).

Because a true score is an average, it is constant for a student from one administration of an assessment procedure to the next. (Different students will have different true scores, however.). For each separate administration of the assessment procedure, a student's error score is different. On any one occasion the student's error score may be either positive, negative, or zero. These errors of measurement result in the student's obtained scores being higher or lower than the student's true score. A consequence of these measurement errors is that scores obtained from any two administrations of an assessment procedure do not rank students in identical rank orders.

As an illustration, suppose you had two students, Suzanne and Georgia. Assume that you gave them the same problem-solving test and that each student scored 52. The score, 52, is their obtained score, the only score you see. You might be tempted to use these results to conclude that Suzanne and Georgia have the same problem-solving ability. Don't yield to this temptation. You cannot conclude these two students have the identical problem-solving ability based solely on the fact they have the identical test score, 52. The score, 52, contains measurement error that needs to be acknowledged.

Let us assume that Suzanne's true score is 50 and that Georgia's true score is 53. If it were possible for you to create a problem-solving test that resulted in scores without measurement error, you would see that Georgia has somewhat more ability than Suzanne. Unfortunately, it is not possible to create such a perfect test. Consequently, both students ended up getting identical obtained scores of 52.

How much measurement error is in their obtained scores? In our example, Georgia's true score is 53. Thus, her error score is $52 - 53 = -1$. Suzanne's true score, on the other hand, is 50, so her error score is $52 - 50 = +2$. This illustrates that errors of measurement may be either positive (e.g., $+2$) or negative (e.g., -1).

Although we illustrated two students having different true scores but the same obtained score, other possibilities exist. Two students may have the *same true score*, but as a result of errors of measurement, they may receive *different obtained scores*. The point is, you need to treat a test score as an imperfect piece of information. To better estimate a student's true score, you need to include more than one test in your evaluation of the student.

STANDARD ERROR OF MEASUREMENT

Meaning of the Standard Error of Measurement

Because no procedure assesses persons with perfect consistency, it is useful to take into account the likely *size* of errors of measurement. One way to describe the inconsistency of assessment scores is to assess a student repeatedly and note the amounts by which scores vary. If you could assess a student many times (without changing the student's ability with respect to the trait you are assessing), you would obtain a collection of the student's obtained scores. Some scores would be higher than others, but most would cluster around an average (mean) value. This average is the true score to which we referred earlier. The standard deviation or spread of this distribution is the **standard error of measurement** (SEM). The SEM estimates the likely distance of a student's obtained scores from their true scores.

In practice it is not possible to repeatedly reassess students without changing them, so the standard error of measurement is not calculated by reassessing students. Instead it is estimated by using the equation

$$\text{SEM} = SD_X \sqrt{1 - \text{reliability coefficient}}$$

[Eq. 4.2]

where SD_X is the standard deviation of the obtained scores of the assessment. (See Appendix H for a description of standard deviation.) The SEM is an estimate of the standard deviation of the errors of measurement. For example, if SD_X was equal to 10 and the reliability coefficient equaled 0.84, then

$$\text{SEM} = 10\sqrt{1 - .84} = 10\sqrt{.16} = 10(.4) = 4$$

The standard error of measurement helps us to understand the *size* of measurement error for a particular assessment procedure. One interpretation is that the numerical value of SEM estimates the amount a student's observed scores are likely to deviate from her true score. Thus, in the preceding examples, SEM = 4.0 may be interpreted to mean that a student's obtained scores are likely to be about 4 points above or below her true score. Because of this likely deviation from true score, you must interpret the obtained score as only an estimate of the student's true score.

Another interpretation of SEM uses a normal distribution. It is assumed that the hypothetical distribution of obtained scores, resulting from repeatedly assessing a student, is normal in form. (See Chapter 17 for normal distribution.) The mean of this distribution is the student's true score, while the standard deviation is the standard error of measurement. Using the relation between standard deviation and percent of cases under a normal curve from Chapter 17, it can be said that 68% of the time the student's obtained score will be within a distance of one SEM from the true score.

The meaning of the SEM is illustrated in Figure 4.5 for a hypothetical student with true score of 52 and SEM of 4.0. Following the normal curve interpretation, one third (32%) of the time that a student is retested, her obtained score will be outside these bounds: It will be greater than 56 (52 + 4) about one sixth (16%) of the time and less than 48 (52 − 4) about one sixth of the time.

Reliability Coefficients and SEMs

As you study Figure 4.5, you may note that if the standard error of measurement became smaller, scores would cluster more closely around the true score. This illustrates what we mean by *consistency*: If the observed assessment scores tend to be very near a student's true score, the scores are consistent. More consistency means smaller measurement errors.

The size of the standard error of measurement, however, depends on both the reliability coefficient and the standard deviation of the obtained scores. In the preceding example, if $SD_X = 5$ instead of 10, then SEM = 2.0. Thus, while the reliability remained at 0.84, SEM be-

comes smaller when SD_X is smaller. This smaller SEM illustrates that the standard deviation of the scores should be taken into account when interpreting the consistency of assessment results. Because different assessment procedures have different units of measurement as well as different standard deviations, it is usually true that the only way to compare the consistency of the scores from *two different assessment methods* is by looking at their reliability coefficients.

The relationship between the SD_X, the reliability coefficient, and the SEM is shown in Table 4.2. For a fixed value for the reliability coefficient, SEM becomes larger as SD_X increases. For a fixed value for the SD_X, SEM becomes smaller as the reliability coefficient becomes larger. If a test manual does not report SEM, Table 4.2 can provide a rough estimate once the SD_X and the reliability coefficient are known.

Using the SEM to Place Confidence Bands

You should not interpret assessment results as if they had great precision. An obtained score is likely to be near, but not exactly equal to, the student's true score. For example, suppose grade-equivalent scores from a standardized achievement test had a reliability coefficient around 0.83 and a standard deviation around 1.0 (on the grade-equivalent scale). The SEM for this test is equal to 0.4. It would be quite likely that, upon retesting, a student's score

FIGURE 4.5 A hypothetical normal distribution of scores resulting from repeated assessment of one student whose "true" score is 52.

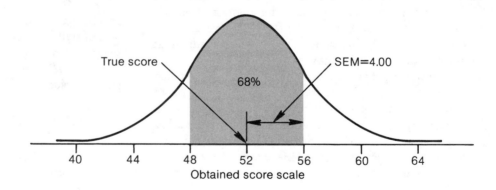

TABLE 4.2 Standard error of measurement for various standard deviations and reliability coefficients.

Reliability coefficient	Standard deviation					
	5	10	15	20	25	30
.98	.7	1.4	2.1	2.8	3.5	4.2
.95	1.1	2.2	3.4	4.5	5.6	6.7
.90	1.6	3.2	4.7	6.2	7.9	9.5
.85	1.9	3.9	5.8	7.7	9.7	11.6
.80	2.2	4.5	6.7	8.9	11.1	13.4
.75	2.5	5.0	7.5	10.0	12.5	15.0
.70	2.7	5.5	8.2	11.0	13.7	16.4
.65	3.0	5.9	8.9	11.8	14.8	17.7
.60	3.2	6.3	9.5	12.6	15.8	19.0
.50	3.5	7.1	10.6	14.1	17.7	21.2
.20	4.5	8.9	13.4	17.9	22.4	26.8
.10	4.7	9.5	14.2	19.0	23.7	28.5

would shift up or down the scale 4 grade-equivalent months (±0.4). Two students with identical true grade-equivalent scores are likely to have observed *differences* in grade-equivalent scores that are larger than 4 months. (See Figure 4.6.)

Although you should be cautious about **overinterpreting** small differences in scores, you should not be so conservative as to err by **underinterpreting** or ignoring meaningful **score differences**. Some measurement specialists recommend, for example, that the value of SEM be added and subtracted from each student's obtained score, thus forming the boundaries of a "score band" or **uncertainty interval** for scores. If such bands are formed for two students, and if these score band boundaries overlap, some specialists interpret the results to mean there is no difference between the true scores. This means that differences that are the size of those observed could arise simply by error of measurement 68% of the time. A similar situation arises if a student is administered two tests, for example, a mathematics test and a science test. Is the student's mathematics ability higher than her science ability? To answer this question, form a score band around the mathematics score and another around the science score. If the bands overlap, you could interpret this to mean that the student's abilities in the two areas are likely to be the same. (See Figure 4.6 for examples.)

But perhaps a more widespread problem than overinterpreting scores is a "do-nothing pattern": failing to interpret score changes or ups and downs of profiles be-

cause of overdemanding criteria of 68%, 90%, or 95% uncertainty bands (Feldt, 1967). To avoid wasting valuable information, corroborate the information obtained from one assessment with information from other sources (such as classroom performance), thereby reducing the probability of errors of overinterpretation (Feldt, 1967).

ADDITIONAL FACTORS AFFECTING RELIABILITY AND SEM

You should keep a number of factors in mind when interpreting reliability and SEM information, especially when comparing such information from two or more assessment procedures.

1. *Longer assessment procedures are more reliable than shorter procedures.* The greater the number of observations (items, judges, occasions of observation, etc.) that enter into the formulation of a score, the more reliable that score will be. This means, for example, that you should put little confidence in a student's performance on only one task from an assessment, or even to responses on clusters of two or three tasks. The relation between lengthening an assessment by adding similar tasks and the reliability of the resultant assessment procedure is given by the *general Spearman-Brown formula*. Appendix I shows a computational example.

FIGURE 4.6   Using the standard error to interpret scores.

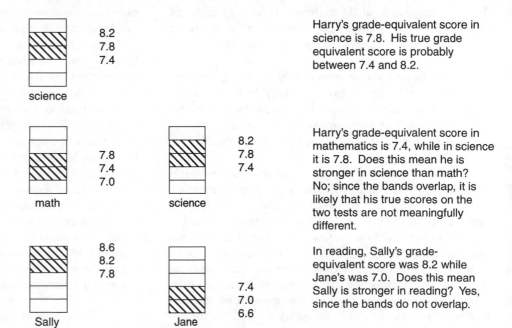

Adding and subtracting the SEM from each student's score provides a range of values that helps prevent overinterpreting scores on a test and differences between scores. In the examples below, SEM = 0.4 and the scores are grade-equivalents.

Harry's grade-equivalent score in science is 7.8. His true grade equivalent score is probably between 7.4 and 8.2.

Harry's grade-equivalent score in mathematics is 7.4, while in science it is 7.8. Does this mean he is stronger in science than math? No; since the bands overlap, it is likely that his true scores on the two tests are not meaningfully different.

In reading, Sally's grade-equivalent score was 8.2 while Jane's was 7.0. Does this mean Sally is stronger in reading? Yes, since the bands do not overlap.

2. *The numerical value computed for a reliability coefficient will fluctuate from one sample of persons to another.* The reliability coefficients reported in a test manual are based on samples of students. These numerical values will fluctuate from one sample to the next, so that any one published number can be considered only as an estimate of what the reliability coefficient would be if the entire population of students were tested. Sampling fluctuations are greater for small samples drawn from the population than from large samples.

3. *The narrower the range of a group's ability, the lower the reliability coefficient tends to be.* It is much easier to distinguish individual differences in ability when students differ widely from one another than when their abilities are very similar. Many educators use assessment results to make decisions about students whose abilities, grade levels, and ages are relatively close together. Therefore, look in test manuals for reliability coefficients calculated on data from students whose abilities are as close together as those with whom you must deal. Put less stock in an assessment's high-reliability coefficients derived by pooling samples from several grades, from groups with wide ranges of ability, and/or from groups spanning many age levels when *you* will be using the assessment to evaluate a group of students whose abilities are rather close together.

4. *Students at different achievement levels may be assessed with different degrees of accuracy.* The SEM, being a single number for an entire assessment test, represents only an average amount of score inconsistency. The consistency of results probably varies with the achievement level of the student assessed. You have to study carefully the manual or technical report of the assessment you are using to determine this. The SEM may be larger in the middle of the score range than at the extremes. If so, very high and very low scoring students are assessed with somewhat more consistency than are middle-range students.

5. *The longer the time interval between testing, the lower will test-retest and alternate-forms reliability coefficients tend to be.* If the same assessment is administered twice, the students' scores will be more similar when the time between the administrations is short than when it is long.

6. *More objectively scored assessment results are more reliable.* You will recall from Chapter 1 that objectivity refers to the degree to which two qualified observers assign the same scores to the same student performances. We called this inter-rater reliability. However, remember that the rule that relates reliability and objectivity applies even to qualitative assessments, such as observing and classifying students. This is why we stress developing formal rating scales and classification schemes for open-ended and performance assessments. (See Chapters 11 and 12 for details.) You should not limit assessment procedures to only multiple-choice, true-false, matching, and short-answer questions. Rather, use a wide variety of assessment methods to improve validity. These alternative assessment methods should be marked as objectively as possible because increasing objectivity increases reliability, and this will have a positive effect on the validity.

7. *Different methods of estimating reliability will not give the same result.* The reliability coefficients differ because they include different sources of error, as described in Table 4.1. Be careful to use the proper coefficient in your interpretation of assessments. Split-halves coefficients, for example, are usually the highest of the reliability coefficients we have discussed in this chapter, because they are calculated with student data collected over no intervening time interval and are influenced by the speededness of the assessment method. Test-retest coefficients may be high when there is no time delay. The longer the time delay between retesting, the lower the coefficient. Most often time delays of one week or more are reported in test manuals. For the same length of time delay between retestings, test-retest coefficients are higher than alternate-forms coefficients because the latter include differences in content as a source of error; the former does not. The Kuder-Richardson formulas give smaller results than the split-half coefficient. (See Appendix I for an example.)

RELIABILITY OF MASTERY DECISIONS

We have been discussing consistency of students' *scores*. This consistency is of concern no matter what type of assessment method you are using. There are certain classroom situations, however, when the consistency of the exact score a student receives is less important than the consistency of the decision made about the student. For example, you may set the passing score on a mastery test as 80% correct. A student who gets 85% receives the same decision (i.e., pass) as does the student who gets 92%. Similarly, two students with 50% and 65%, respectively, receive the same decision—fail.

In this type of assessment interpretation, it makes more sense to speak of the **decision consistency** than of score consistency. For example, suppose you crafted two equivalent forms of a mastery test. You could ask, "Would both tests classify the same students as masters and nonmasters?" Coefficients answering this type of question are called *indices of decision consistency.*

Figure 4.7 illustrates how measurement error may cause an assessment to mask a student's true mastery status. Whenever a student's true status is not revealed by the assessment results, a *decision error* or *error of misclassification* occurs. Several factors influence how often decision errors occur when assessing mastery.

1. *The assessment product may contain tasks that have weak validity for assessing the type of mastery you have in mind.* This may happen, for example, when you use the test

FIGURE 4.7 Relationship between a student's true mastery status and possible errors of classification when you draw conclusions from assessment results.

		True status of a student with respect to the degree of domain proficiency	
		Master	**Nonmaster**
Conclusion the teacher drew about the student from the assessment results	**The assessment results are interpreted as mastery**	*There is no misclassification:* Both the student's true status and the conclusion the teacher drew from the assessment results agree.	*An error of classification:* The student is a nonmaster, but the teacher concluded that the assessment results showed mastery.
	The assessment results are interpreted as nonmastery	*An error of classification:* Student is a master, but the teacher concluded that the assessment results showed nonmastery.	*There is no misclassification:* Both the student's true status and the conclusion the teacher drew from the assessment results agree.

questions that come with the published curriculum materials you use in class. Very often these questions are poorly worded or assess content that you omitted or de-emphasized in your teaching. Weak validity increases decision errors.

2. *Longer assessment methods usually lead to more accurate mastery decisions.* Judging mastery from a short test (i.e., less than 10 response-choice items) or from one project or one performance activity usually raises decision errors to unacceptably high levels. You should use several different pieces of assessment information before finalizing a mastery decision about a student.

3. *Low inter-rater reliability is associated with high rates of mastery decision errors.* More reliable assessments generally lead to more accurate mastery decisions.

4. *The passing score you set for deciding mastery affects the rate of decision errors.* In general, setting the passing score very high (90% or 95%) or very low (20% or 30%) will increase errors of classification.

5. *Students whose true mastery status is very close to the passing score you set are the ones who are most likely to be misclassified.* For example, if you set the passing score at 80%, students whose true mastery status is 70% to 90% will have higher rates of erroneous classification than students outside this range. When student's assessment results are close to the passing score, you should consider additional information (such as performance in class, homework, project performance) before making a final mastery decision.

Percent Agreement

A quantitative index of the degree of decision consistency can be calculated by administering two parallel forms of a mastery test to the same group of students and studying whether students are consistently classified as masters or nonmasters. Two indices may be calculated: percent agreement (P_A) and kappa coefficient (κ) (Cohen, 1960).

Here we show the calculation of P_A. An example of calculating kappa coefficient is shown in Appendix I.

Suppose two forms of an assessment, A and B, were administered to a group of 25 students, and that the mastery criterion on each form was 80%. Table 4.3 summarizes how consistently the two assessment results classified these students. Eleven students were classified as masters by both forms, nine as nonmasters by both forms, and the others as masters by one and nonmasters by the other.

The percent of agreement for the preceding situation may be calculated by the following formula:

$$P_A = \begin{bmatrix} \text{Percent consistent} \\ \text{mastery decisions} \end{bmatrix} + \begin{bmatrix} \text{Percent consistent} \\ \text{nonmastery decisions} \end{bmatrix}$$

[Eq. 4.3]

The result is usually expressed as a decimal fraction. For the example in Table 4.3:

$$P_A = \frac{11}{25} + \frac{9}{25} = \frac{20}{25} = 0.80$$

The value 0.80 is the "total proportion of consistent classification that occurs for whatever reason on the two tests" (Subkoviak, 1980, p. 152).

As illustrated here, percent agreement requires administering two forms of the assessment to the same group of students. Instead of the equivalent-forms paradigm illustrated here, you may also use a test-retest paradigm or two judges of mastery. The latter may be especially important whenever you are using assessments that are not paper-and-pencil tests, such as judging whether a student's product or project meets minimum standards.

The percent agreement need not be limited to the simple, dichotomous case illustrated here: More than two categories could be used for classifying students. One example is the situation in which you assign letter grades of A, B, C, D, and F to students' projects or performances. Formulas for computing percent agreement (and kappa coefficient)

TABLE 4.3 Hypothetical example of how 25 students were classified using the scores from two forms of a mastery test.

		Results from Form A		
		Mastery	Nonmastery	Marginal totals
Results from Form B	Mastery	11	4	15
	Nonmastery	1	9	10
	Marginal totals	12	13	25

for such situations can be found in Cohen (1960) and Swaminathan, Hambleton, & Algina (1974). You may also estimate percent agreement from only one administration of the assessment (see Huynh, 1976; Subkoviak, 1976).

DESIRED LEVELS OF RELIABILITY

Students of educational assessment often ask, "Is thus-and-such reliability coefficient good enough?" You realize by now that perfect reliability is indicated by a coefficient of 1.00. This value is practically unattainable in practice, however, because virtually all assessment results have some degree of inconsistency in every population of students. What can you do to improve the reliability of your assessment results? Figure 4.8 gives nine suggestions.

Different types of assessment instruments have different levels of reliability. Standardized multiple-choice achievement tests typically have reliability coefficients in the .85 to .95 range. Open-ended paper-and-pencil assessments are typically in the .65 to .80 range. Portfolio scoring may have reliability in the .40 to .60 range.

A general rule for estimating "how close to 1.00" a reliability coefficient for a single assessment instrument should be is as follows: *The more important and the less reversible is the decision about an individual from the assessment instrument, the higher the reliability should be.* Decisions such as whether a person is awarded a diploma, admitted to a higher educational program, put into a special education classroom, and given a job are examples of "high-stakes" decisions which, if made erroneously, would have serious consequences for an individual. *The results of a single-assessment instrument should not be used alone to make such decisions.* High reliability coefficients, equal to 0.90 or higher, should be demanded for each instrument used for such decisions. (Another reason for using more than one instrument in these situations is that high validity, as well as high reliability, is needed. A single assessment instrument seldom has sufficient validity to be used alone.)

The classroom is an information-rich environment, and you have many opportunities to assess students. Further, classroom decisions should not be high-stakes decisions. That is, students should have many different opportunities to recover from their learning failures and to

FIGURE 4.8 How to improve the reliability of assessment results.

1. *Lengthen the assessment procedure.* Whenever practical, give more time, use more questions, more observations, and so on.

2. *Broaden the scope of the procedure.* Use procedures that assess all of the essential and important aspects of the target learning performance.

3. *Improve objectivity.* Use a systematic, more formal procedure for scoring student performance (e.g., a scoring schema or rubric).

4. *Use multiple markers.* Whenever possible, have more than one qualified person score each student's essay, term paper, performance, portfolio, or open-ended assessment task. Average the results or confer to reconcile differences.

5. *Combine results from several assessments.* When making important educational decisions, use a combination of the results from several different assessment methods rather than a single assessment result.

6. *Provide sufficient time to students.* Within practical limits, be sure that every student has enough time to complete the assessment procedure.

7. *Teach students how to perform their best.* Provide practice and training to students on how to "put their best foot forward," strategies to use, and so on before using an assessment method.

8. *Match the assessment difficulty to students' ability levels.* Be sure the assessment procedure contains tasks that are not too easy or too difficult for the students. Tailor the assessment to each student's ability level, if possible.

9. *Differentiate among students.* Select assessment tasks that do a good job of differentiating the best students from the least able students.

be retaught. Classroom assessment results typically have moderate reliability levels, but you can (and should) combine assessment results from several procedures before making important classroom decisions (e.g., before assigning marking period grades). Thus, you may tolerate moderate levels of reliability of .70 or higher for any one assessment result as *long as several pieces of information are combined for classroom decisions.*

Summary

- Reliability refers to the consistency of assessment results, rather than to the assessment instrument itself.
- Reliability is a limiting factor for validity. Assessment results that are unreliable cannot be highly valid.
- Reliability is one criterion for validity of assessment results, but not the only criterion. Thus, highly reliable assessment results may not be valid if they do not meet other validity criteria.
- There are several causes of unreliable assessment results. Four were discussed:
  - *Content factors*—Inconsistent results caused by the different content or tasks included in two equivalent assessments.
  - *Time factors*—Inconsistent results caused by the temporary and permanent changes that a student experiences when assessed on different occasions.
  - *Scorer factors*—Inconsistent results caused by the idiosyncrasies of the persons who mark a student's performance.
  - *Combined factors*—Inconsistent results caused by a combination of these (and other) factors.
- Two types of quantitative indicators of inconsistency were discussed: reliability coefficients and the standard errors of measurement.
- A reliability coefficient is more useful when comparing the consistency of results from different assessment procedures. A standard error of measurement is more useful when estimating the size of typical measurement errors on a particular assessment procedure.
- Several types of reliability coefficients were discussed:
  - *Test-retest reliability* measures the stability of scores.
  - *Alternate-forms reliability (different occasions)* measures stability and equivalence of the forms.
  - *Alternate-forms reliability (same occasion)* measures the equivalence of two versions of an assessment instrument.
  - *Spearman-Brown (split-halves) reliability* estimates the equivalence of an assessment instrument using information about the internal consistency of students' responses. This coefficient is not appropriate for speeded assessment instruments.
  - *Kuder-Richardson and coefficient alpha reliability* also estimate the equivalence of an assessment instrument using the internal consistency of students' responses. These formulas also are not to be used when the assessment is speeded.
  - *Inter-rater reliability* measures the consistency with which two judges or evaluators assign ratings to student performance on an assessment instrument.
  - *Percent agreement reliability* measures the consistency of the decisions reached independently, using the results from two equivalent assessment instruments.
- *The standard error of measurement* is a measure of the amount of inconsistency expected for individuals' assessment results.
- The numerical value of the standard error of measurement may be added to and subtracted from a person's score. The result is a "band" or range of scores within which the person's true score is probably located.
- Various *factors affecting the reliability and the standard error of measurement* are described:
  - Longer assessments are more reliable than shorter assessments.
  - Reliability coefficients reported in test manuals are only estimates from samples.
  - Reliability is low when the spread of scores is small.
  - The standard error of measurement may be different at different levels of ability.
  - As the time interval between administering assessments increases, test-retest and alternate-forms reliability coefficients become smaller.
  - The more objective the scoring of assessment performance, the higher the reliability.
- Higher levels of reliability are needed when important and irreversible decisions about individuals are made from assessment results. Moderate levels may be tolerated when decisions are reversible, less important, and based on information from several assessment results.

Important Terms and Concepts

decision consistency
error score, obtained score, true score
factors influencing consistency of assessment performance
homogeneous tasks
inter-rater reliability
parallel forms
percent of agreement
reliability
reliability coefficient
scorer reliability
stability coefficient
standard error of measurement
types of reliability coefficients (alternate forms [same occasion], coefficient alpha, delayed alternate forms, Kuder-Richardson formulas 20 and 21, odd-even split-halves procedure, parallel forms, Spearman-Brown double length formula, split-halves, test-retest)
uncertainty interval (score band)
underinterpreting vs. overinterpreting score differences

Exercises and Discussion Questions

1. Explain why reliability is a property of assessment *results* rather than a property of an *instrument*.
2. Describe three causes of measurement error. Give brief scenarios to illustrate how each type could happen in your classroom. In the scenario, illustrate the negative consequences of each for your students.
3. What are the major ways to estimate reliability? Which coefficients, if any, may be considered equivalent to one another?
4. Which type(s) of reliability coefficient(s), if any, would be a major source of information needed to answer each of the following questions?
   a. A teacher wonders whether her student Meghan's test score could be a result of her having an off day.
   b. An eighth-grade teacher wonders whether the students' aptitude test scores will predict their success in ninth grade.
   c. A tenth-grade English teacher wonders whether the grades he assigns to his student's essays are equivalent to the grades his colleague would assign them.
   d. A twelfth-grade physics teacher wonders whether her final exam this year is equivalent to her final exam last year.
   e. An eighth-grade English teacher has students create portfolios of their work over the semester. Using the portfolios, she classifies the students into three groups: excellent, satisfactory, and unsatisfactory. The teacher wonders whether her classification of students can be made with fewer errors.
5. The correlation between students' scores on the odd and even items of a test is 0.40. The teacher claims that the students would attain the same scores if he used an equivalent test. Is the teacher's claim justifiable? Support your conclusion using an appropriate reliability coefficient.
6. Which of these factors would probably cause a test-retest reliability coefficient to be low? Why or why not?
   a. A test contains items that measure many different skills.
   b. The same teacher scores the test on both occasions.
   c. Different students' moods go up or down from one occasion to the next.
   d. Students' abilities to perform the tasks on the test grow a lot from one testing occasion to the next.
   e. The test is very short.
7. A test-retest reliability coefficient is 0.75 and the test standard deviation is 15. By how many points can we expect individual students' test scores to differ when we test them on two different occasions? (Use Table 4.2 to help you.)
8. Figure 4.6 in the text illustrates the use of the SEM to form confidence bands for students to help us interpret their scores. Suppose that for the students in the figure, the SEM equals 0.2 instead of 0.4. How, if at all, would the interpretations of each of the three illustrations in the box change?
9. A publisher is selling an open-ended mathematics assessment instrument. You are appointed to a committee in your school district to evaluate the instrument and make recommendations about its purpose. The instrument is viewed very favorably by the committee members, but you notice in one of the manuals that accompanied the instrument the following information:
   ■ Correlation between two teachers independently scoring the students' papers is 0.30.
   ■ Correlation between the students' scores when they were reassessed after three weeks is 0.60.
   ■ The standard deviation of the scores is 20, and the standard error of measurement is 17.
   What is your evaluation of the assessment tool in light of these reported results? Explain.
10. For each of the following types of assessment procedures, explain which cause of measurement error is of concern most and why:
   a. Student essays in social studies exams
   b. Science projects
   c. Grades on art projects
   d. True-false tests in science
   e. Portfolios in English courses
   f. Mathematics homework problems
   g. A teacher's marks for students' daily participation in class
   h. A paper-and-pencil test for a unit in social studies consisting of multiple-choice, matching, and short-answer questions

Additional Readings

American Educational Research Association, American Psychological Association, & National Council on Measurement in Education. (1999). *Standards for educational and psychological testing*. Washington, DC: APA.

   The reliability section describes various types of reliability and the kinds of reliability reports that should be included in test manuals.

Anastasi, A. (1988). *Psychological testing* (6th ed.). New York: Macmillan, Chapter 5.

   An alternative explanation of reliability and standard error of measurement.

Feldt, L. S., and Brennan, R. L. (1989). Reliability. In R. L. Linn (Ed.), *Educational measurement* (3rd ed.). New York: Macmillan, Chapter 3.

   A thorough but highly technical explanation of reliability, theory, and the meaning of a great many more reliability coefficients than are presented in textbooks.

Harvill, L. M. (1991). An NCME instructional module on standard error of measurement. *Educational Measurement: Issues and Practice, 10*(2), 33–41.

   Explains the standard error of measurement and how to use it to interpret scores. Contains a self-test and annotated bibliography.

Traub, R. E., & Rowby, G. L. (1991). An NCME instructional module on understanding reliability. *Educational Measurement: Issues and Practice, 10*(1), 37–45.

   A clear explanation of the psychometric theory underlying reliability coefficients. Contains a self-test and an annotated bibliography.

CHAPTER 5

Professional Responsibilities, Ethical Behavior, and Legal Requirements in Educational Assessments

Learning Targets

After studying this chapter, you should be able to:

1. Explain why you have a professional responsibility to use quality assessment information to make classroom decisions. [7]

2. Describe the six areas of professional assessment responsibility for teachers. [7, 6]

3. Identify examples of professionally responsible and irresponsible classroom assessment practices in each of the six areas. [7, 2]

4. Explain specific professional responsibilities when crafting your own classroom assessment procedures and when using published assessment procedures for classroom assessment. [7, 2, 4]

5. Explain several responsibilities you have when scoring your own classroom assessments. [3, 7]

6. Describe students' rights and teachers' responsibilities in relation to assessment. [7, 6]

7. Explain the assessment rights and access to information that students have under the U.S. Constitution and federal legislation. [7, 6]

8. Explain and give examples of ethical and professional responsibility issues surrounding (a) accessing student data for research purposes, (b) purging and correcting students' records, (c) confidentiality of students' achievement records, and (d) informed consent. [7, 6]

9. Describe ways in which classroom assessments may be modified to accommodate students with disabilities. [2, 3]

10. Explain the validity and score-reporting concerns when educational assessment techniques are modified to accommodate students with disabilities. [3, 4, 5]

11. Describe the steps that can be taken to process students' requests for accommodations and make testing accommodation programs legally defensible. [5, 6, 7]

12. Explain and give examples of some of the major psychometric assessment issues presented in court. [7, 6]

13. Explain and give examples of some of the nonpsychometric assessment issues presented in court. [7, 6]

14. Identify and give examples of each of the several definitions of test or assessment bias used in the news media and professional literature. [7, 5, 6]

15. Explain the meaning and educational significance of each of the important terms and concepts listed at the end of this chapter. [6, 7]

A TEACHER'S PROFESSIONAL RESPONSIBILITIES IN ASSESSMENT

Responsibility to Use Quality Information to Make Decisions

Independence Makes You Responsible You have nearly complete control over the assessment processes you use in your classroom. This independence allows you to gather and use information in ways that are especially suited to improving your students' learning. Independence or autonomy also means that you must take **professional responsibility** for gathering and using decision-making information appropriately. You must follow professional standards of practice and ethical principles of behavior to fulfill your responsibilities. These professional responsibilities, ethical principles, and legal requirements are the subjects of this chapter.

Decisions Have Consequences As you teach, you must make hundreds of decisions. Formal and informal assessment tools help you gather useful information for making decisions about your students. If you are as human as the rest of us, not all of your decisions will be correct. Correct or not, each decision you make will have **positive or negative consequences** for your students.

The consequences differ in their degree of seriousness for the students. **Serious consequences of decisions** occur when students benefit or lose something very valuable and cannot easily recover from an incorrect initial decision. For example, your decision to give a student a low final grade in chemistry may lower the student's chances of being admitted as a chemistry major at a particular college. **Less serious consequences of decisions** occur when students benefit or lose something less valuable and can easily recover from an incorrect initial decision. For example, you may decide to reteach a particular chemistry concept to a student, but as you are reteaching you discover that the student already does understand the concept. It is easy for you to readjust your teaching, and the student can easily recover from your incorrect initial decision. The point here is that when the consequences of a decision are serious, you have a responsibility to use the best available information in your decision-making process.

High-Quality Information Leads to Correct Decisions Assessment is the process of gathering appropriate information for making educational decisions. One way to improve your decisions is to use **high-quality information**: Quality information is highly valid and highly reliable for the decisions at hand. Of course, using high-quality information does not guarantee that your decisions will be correct. However, if you base your decisions on poor-quality or erroneous information, you are very likely to make an incorrect decision. This may be harmful to a student. If you cause harm to your students, either deliberately or through negligence, your actions are unprofessional, unethical, and/or illegal.

Code of Professional Responsibility in Educational Measurement

Professional Associations' Ethical Codes Professional associations often develop and enforce codes of ethical behavior for their members. These codes give you guidance on how to act responsibly. Codes of ethics commonly cover such areas as the professional's role in society, integrity, conflicts of interest, diligence and due care, confidentiality, and communication with clients and the public (Schmeiser, 1992). Table 5.1 lists some of the codes that contain statements of professional responsibility when using assessments. Much of the information in this chapter is adapted from the principles described in the National Council on Measurement in Education's (NCME) **Code of Professional Responsibility in Educational Measurement (CPR)**. A copy of the CPR is reproduced in Appendix C. Our focus in this chapter is on ethical, professional, and legal responsibilities of classroom teacher assessment. The CPR, however, offers guidance to a wide range of educational professionals who are involved in assessment activities. These educational professionals include teachers; school and district administrators; professional support staff (supervisors, counselors, school psychologists, etc.); technical, legislative, and policy staff members of research, evaluation, and assessment organizations; test preparation service providers; faculty members, administrators at colleges and universities; and professionals in business who implement educational programs (NCME, 1995).

Related Standards of Conduct The CPR assumes that an informed user of educational assessments will be familiar with and behave in accordance with other assessment-related professional standards. These include the *Code of Fair Testing Practices in Education* (Joint Committee on Testing Practices, 1988) and the *Standards for Educational and Psychological Testing* (AERA, APA, and NCME, 1999). The *Code of Fair Testing Practices* is reproduced in this book as Appendix B. The *Standards* are discussed in Chapter 18 but are not reproduced in this book.

General Principles of Professional Behavior As we discuss your professional responsibilities when using educational assessments, keep in mind that you are expected to uphold the principles of professional conduct. You are expected to:

1. protect the safety, health, and welfare of all examinees;
2. be knowledgeable about, and behave in compliance with, state and federal laws relevant to the conduct of professional activities;

TABLE 5.1 Resources for codes of professional and ethical responsibilities related to using educational assessments.

American Association for Counseling and Development (now American Counseling Association). (1988). *Ethical standards of the American Counseling Association.* Alexandria, Va: Author.

American Association for Counseling and Development (now American Counseling Association) & Association for Measurement and Evaluation in Counseling and Development (now Association for Assessment in Counseling). (1989). *Responsibilities of users of standardized tests: RUST statement revised.* Alexandria, VA: Author.

American Educational Research Association, American Psychological Association, & National Council on Measurement in Education. (1985). *Standards for educational and psychological testing.* Washington, DC: APA.

American Educational Research Association. (1992). Ethical standards of the American Educational Research Association. *Educational Researcher,* 21(7), 23–27.

American Federation of Teachers, National Council on Measurement in Education, & National Educational Association. (1990). *Standards for teacher competence in educational assessment of students.* Washington, DC: NCME.

American Psychological Association. (1992). *Ethical principles of psychologists and code of conduct.* Washington, DC: Author.

American Psychological Association President's Task Force on Psychology in Education. (1992 Draft). *Learner-centered psychological principles: Guidelines for school redesign and reform.* Washington, DC: Author.

Joint Advisory Committee on Testing Practices. (1993). *Principles for fair assessment practices for education in Canada.* Edmonton, Alberta: Author.

Joint Committee on Testing Practices. (1988). *Code of fair testing practices in education.* Washington, DC: APA.

Joint Committee on Standards for Educational Evaluation. (1988). *The personnel evaluation standards: How to assess systems for evaluating educators.* Newbury Park, CA: Sage.

Joint Committee on Standards for Educational Evaluation. (1994). *Standards for evaluations of educational programs.* Washington, DC: Author.

Joint Committee on Standards for Educational Evaluation. (1994). *The program evaluation standards: How to assess evaluations of educational programs.* Thousand Oaks, CA: Sage.

National Association of College Admission Counselors. (1988). *Statement of principles of good practices.* Alexandria, VA: Author.

Source: Adapted from *Code of Professional Responsibilities in Educational Measurement* (p. 7–8) by National Council on Measurement in Education, 1995, Washington, DC.: Author. Copyright 1995 by the National Council on Measurement in Education. Adapted by permission of the publisher.

3. maintain and improve [your] . . . professional competence in educational assessment;

4. provide assessment services only in areas of [your] . . . competence and experience, affording full disclosure of [your] professional qualifications;

5. promote the understanding of sound assessment practices in education;

6. adhere to the highest standards of conduct and promote professionally responsible conduct with educational institutions and agencies that provide educational services; and

7. perform all professional responsibilities with honesty, integrity, due care, and fairness. (NCME, 1995, p. 2)

Six Categories of Responsibility for Teachers

Your teaching involves six categories of assessment-related activities. Each has its own specific professional and ethical concerns:

1. *Crafting assessment procedures*—When you develop your own assessment procedures, you have a responsibility to craft them so they are of a high quality.

2. *Choosing assessment procedures*—When you choose or select assessment procedures that others crafted, you have a responsibility to make sure that they are appropriate for the use you have in mind for them.

3. *Administering assessment procedures*—When you administer assessment procedures, you have a responsibility to assure that your administration process is fair to all students and that it will not result in uninterpretable results.

4. *Scoring assessment results*—When you score the student responses to an assessment, you have a responsibility to evaluate the responses accurately and to report the results to students in a timely manner.

5. *Interpreting and using assessment results*—When you interpret and use assessment results, you have a responsibility to assure that your interpretations are as valid as possible, are used to promote positive student outcomes, and are used to minimize negative student outcomes.

6. *Communicating assessment results*—When you communicate assessment results, you have a responsibility to provide complete, useful, and correct information about students' performance that will promote positive student outcomes and minimize negative student outcomes.

The next sections discuss teachers' professional responsibilities when using assessments in each of these six areas. Although our discussion is influenced by the CPR, it is not the CPR itself; and you should not construe this discussion as being endorsed by the sponsors of the CPR.

Responsibilities When Crafting Assessment Procedures

General Responsibilities   If no appropriate assessment procedure is available, it is your responsibility to craft one. In this case, your professional responsibilities focus on producing an assessment procedure that provides results that (1) are as valid as possible for the interpretations and use you intend to make of them, and (2) are as reliable as is appropriate for the seriousness of the consequences of the decisions you will make. Validity refers to how you intend to interpret and use the results (see Chapter 3). For example, suppose your state's standards require you to evaluate how well a student is able to solve real-life problems using mathematics principles and generalizations. It is your responsibility, not only to teach, but also to craft assessment tasks that require students to actually engage in real-life problem-solving thinking and activities. You would not be acting responsibly if your assessment procedure required students only to recall facts and generalizations, to solve problems that are unlike real life, and to demonstrate general comprehension of mathematics concepts. As important as these learning outcomes may be, they are not real-life problem-solving tasks.

Reliability refers to how consistent the assessment results are (see Chapter 4). Consider the preceding example. Suppose you are deciding what grade to give a student for the term. You would not expect that a student's performance on one question (or on a short test) would be a highly consistent indicator of term-long learning. Therefore, you would be acting irresponsibly if you based a serious decision on only a few questions or a short performance assessment. You may increase the consistency or reliability of the information you use by combining the results from several assessments of the same learning targets such as quizzes, daily class performance, projects, and tests. This "triangulation" of results is likely to give you a more reliable and, hence, more valid picture of the student's achievement and demonstrate a more responsible assessment strategy on your part.

Specific Responsibilities   In addition to this general responsibility to craft valid and reliable assessment procedures, there are more specific responsibilities. As a teacher, you have a professional responsibility to:

1. Apply sound principles of assessment planning, assessment design, task development, item writing, rubric development, and assessment marking to each formal assessment you use.

2. Craft assessment procedures that are free from characteristics irrelevant to assessing the learning target. Assessment procedures should be free of gender, ethnic, race, social class, and religious bias and stereotypes.

3. Accommodate in appropriate ways students in your class with disabilities or special needs.

4. Obtain permission necessary to use copyrighted material used in assessment procedures.

5. Present the crafted assessment procedure in a way that encourages students and others to properly interpret the level of accuracy and the meaning of the results.

6. Assure that assessment materials do not contain errors and inaccuracies in the content, instructions, and scoring key (or rubrics). If errors and inaccuracies are discovered after administering the assessment, you should correct them as soon as possible and rescore the students' responses. Test questions containing errors should not be counted in the total score. You may need to readminister the assessment if rescoring cannot correct the error and if the decision to be made is a serious one.

You can find the knowledge you need to fulfill these responsibilities in several chapters in this textbook as well as in many other texts. Your instructor may provide you with additional knowledge and perhaps some supervised practice. Practice and experience will hone your skills.

Responsibilities When Choosing Assessment Procedures

Choosing Assessments for Classroom Use   Although you will often have to craft your own assessment techniques, you will no doubt also use assessment procedures developed by other persons. Many times these will be assessments that accompany published learning materials: quizzes and tests in the teacher's edition of the book, separate tests and performance tasks sold to accompany instructional units, specimen items and tasks on the Internet and in teachers' magazines and journals, and so on. The main professional obligations in choosing to use these assessments are the same as those you apply when crafting your own: The results from them must (1) be valid for your intended interpretation and use, and (2) have a degree of reliability appropriate to the importance of the decision(s) you will make using the results. In addition, many of the six specific responsibilities listed in the last section also apply to assessments you obtain from other sources.

Responsibility to Use Quality Assessment Materials In some ways, fulfilling your professional responsibilities when using assessment tools made by others is more difficult than crafting your own. Others' assessment tasks often do not match the content, emphasis, vocabulary, or methods you used in teaching. To the degree to which these differences are serious, using them will be unfair to your students and yield invalid results. In short, you violate your professional responsibility by using such assessments without carefully checking and improving their quality. It is often necessary for you to rewrite or recraft others' assessment tools to suit your own classroom circumstances. You should improve a classroom assessment instead of using it "straight out of the box" if it does not match your teaching.

Publication Does Not Guarantee Quality You should be aware, too, that the publication of an assessment task or tool is no guarantee of the accuracy of its content or its quality as an assessment tool. Most of the assessment tasks available through the previously mentioned sources are not prepared or reviewed by professional assessment task developers. Many were not prepared personally by the author(s) of the curriculum materials or textbooks, but by others such as students of these authors. Consequently, there are many poor-quality assessment tasks available to you. It would be irresponsible for you to use these assessment materials without carefully evaluating them, because you are putting your students' assessment results in jeopardy.

Serving on Assessment Selection Committees More experienced teachers sometimes serve on committees at the district or state level to review and select published assessments. Local education authorities should include teachers on assessment selection panels. The CPR states that persons providing such service have a special responsibility "to make sure that the assessments are appropriate for their intended use" (NCME, 1995, p. 5).

If you review the 10 specific professional responsibilities in Section 3 of the CPR (Appendix C), you will see that those engaged in assessment selection activities must have considerable knowledge of both the subject matter to be assessed and the technical principles of educational assessment. Much of this knowledge may be learned by studying the material in this and other textbooks on educational assessment. (Chapters 16 and 18 are devoted to procedures for evaluating published achievement tests.) The *Code of Fair Testing Practice* (Appendix B) contains additional principles and responsibilities for those who select and use published tests.

In addition, the CPR specifies that selectors of assessment procedures have a professional responsibility to consider the potential misuses and misinterpretations of an assessment procedure, as well as its potential for fulfilling the intended purposes. As we discussed in Chapter 3, this relates to the question of validity. You cannot fulfill this professional responsibility if your school experience is narrow, if you have not paid attention to the ways

that other districts and states have used similar assessments, and if you are unaware of unintended consequences that may result. Thus, you should read widely to keep current about assessment and its educational use. Such reading is necessary for professional development if you intend to be involved in evaluating and selecting assessment tools as you fulfill your professional role outside the confines of your classroom. One source for learning about how other districts and states are using and misusing assessments is *Education Week*.

Responsibilities When Administering Assessments

Give Students Sufficient Information The way you administer an assessment affects how well a student performs. Usually, classroom assessments are meant to be opportunities for students to demonstrate their maximum performance. (See Chapter 14 for how to prepare students to do their best.) For students to perform at their maximum, the students need basic information about the assessment, including (1) when it will be given, (2) the conditions under which they are expected to perform, (3) the content and abilities that will be assessed, (4) what the assessment will emphasize, (5) the standard or level of performance expected, (6) how the assessment performance will be scored, and (7) the effect the results of this assessment will have on any decisions (e.g., grades) you will make from the results. The details of these information elements are described in Chapters 6 and 15. However, it is your professional obligation to provide this information to students. If you do not give students the complete information as described in these seven points, you are not acting as a responsible professional.

Conduct the Administration in a Professional Manner A special concern in administering classroom assessments is the assessment conditions you establish. Rushing students unnecessarily or making the assessment tasks too long for the available time creates unfair conditions if the goal is to have the student demonstrate maximum performance. Similarly, if you make students nervous by standing near them or chatting to them as they try to perform the assessment, you create unfair conditions. Sometimes a teacher will be rude, short, or gruff to a student who asks an honest question about the assessment tasks (especially when the teacher did not craft the task or its directions carefully and as a result created some ambiguity). Your professional responsibility is to provide "reasonable opportunities for individuals to ask questions about the assessment procedures or directions prior to and at appropriate times during administration" (NCME, 1995, p. 6).

Accommodate Students with Disabilities If you have students with disabilities in your class, you have a professional and possibly legal responsibility to make reasonable accommodations to assess them properly. Table 5.2 describes some of the **assessment accommodations** that

TABLE 5.2 Examples of types of accommodations that may be appropriate for classroom assessment of students with disabilities.

Type of disability	Examples of possible assessment accommodations
Blindness	Extended time, voice-recorded questions, Braille translation of assessment tasks, raised line drawings, a notetaker/scribe, computer, voice-recorded answers, reader to explain diagrams and read questions, scribe to write answers.
Low vision	Extended time, large print, magnifier for standard print, voice-recorded questions, special lighting, modified format for recording written answers, voice-recorded answers, reader to read questions and explain diagrams, scribe to write answers.
Hearing-impaired	Extended time, notetaker, sign language interpreter, language-simplified questions, modified answer format (e.g., allowing answers to be made in American Sign Language, then having the answer interpreted into standard English).
Physically impaired	Extended time, scribe/notetaker, modified answer format (e.g., allowing oral responses), modified question format, computer, large surface desk.
Learning disabilities	Extended time, environmental controls (e.g., freedom from extraneous noise, distractions), calculator, computer (instead of handwriting the answers), voice-recorded questions or a reader, scribe to write answers, modified answer format.
Health and stress related disabilities	Extended time, environmental controls.

Note: Within a disability category not every student would need every accommodation. There are many students with multiple disabilities, and severity varies widely. Therefore, you have a professional responsibility not to stereotype students but to treat them as individuals.
Source: Adapted from Algozzine (1993), King & Janow (1990), and Roberts (1994).

may be appropriate for students with disabilities. If your school does not have facilities or services for accommodating students, they may be available through your state or county itinerant service provider, a community agency that specializes in assisting persons with disabilities, or the office of services for students with disabilities at a local college or university.

You, your school's administrators, and the school's special-service professionals share professional responsibility in this area. Nevertheless, as the person most in touch with the students on a daily basis, you have a special obligation to identify reasonable accommodations related to classroom assessment activities and to seek the help of the appropriate school personnel. Students with disabilities are often very much aware of what accommodations they may or may not need to be assessed in your class. Whenever possible, consult with the students themselves before imposing on them an inappropriate assessment accommodation. Remember, however, that sometimes a student or a parent may believe that an accommodation will give a higher score. Getting higher scores is not the point. Rather, *valid scores are the primary consideration.* An accommodation should increase the validity of the scores so they reflect students' true achievements. As such, the scores after accommodation may not be higher, yet may be more valid. As a general rule, the accommodations necessary to include students in the classroom learning environment would be appropriate accommodations for administering a classroom assessment. The classroom learning environment accommoda-

tions are described in a student's **individual education plan (IEP)**, and teachers may have a legal responsibility to implement the accommodations.

You have a responsibility to treat each student as an individual rather than as a stereotype of a disability category. For example, not all blind students can read Braille, and not all deaf students can understand a signed language. The severity of students' disabilities varies widely, students' cognitive abilities vary widely, and many students have multiple disabilities. In addition, students may need accommodation for some domains of learning but not for others. The needs for accommodation found in their IEPs may not adequately describe the learning targets (domains) for which students need assessment accommodations (Reschly, 1993). Thus you should not rely on IEPs alone to decide on the type of assessment accommodation a student needs. However, if an accommodation is stated in the IEP, there is a legal mandate to provide it.

Standardized and Mandated Tests **Mandated tests** are those tests you must administer because they are required by school district policy or state law. **Standardized tests** are developed by professional agencies and use the same test materials and same administration procedures for all students. (See Chapter 16.) Your professional responsibilities in this area are similar to those you have in administering your own assessments, except that there are added responsibilities related to (1) fully informing students and parents about the testing and how the results will be used,

(2) carefully following the administration instructions in the test manual, (3) maintaining security, and (4) maintaining testing conditions appropriate for maximum performance. These and other responsibilities are described in Section 4 of the CPR in Appendix C. Chapter 16 describes how to administer standardized tests in more detail.

Preparing Students to Take Standardized Tests   A special concern for teachers is their professional responsibility in preparing students for standardized tests. Teachers feel pressure when they perceive that there will be personal consequences if students do not perform well. It is clearly unethical for you to tell students the answers to questions they are unable to answer, or to change student answers so their scores improve. If you see a colleague engaging in these or other unethical behaviors, you should report him or her to school authorities. A more complete discussion of your responsibilities in preparing students and administering standardized tests is given in Chapter 16 (see Figure 16.6). In Chapter 16, ethical test preparation practices are discussed also, drawing on analyses by Mehrens and Kaminski (1989) and Popham (1991). You should review the appropriate section of Chapter 16 at this time.

Responsibilities When Scoring Assessments

Your Own Classroom Assessments   Your professional obligations are

1. *To score student responses accurately* by using the appropriate tools such as scoring keys, scoring rubrics, checklists, or rating scales. Chapters 9 and 12 explain how to craft and use these accuracy-improving aids.

2. *To score students fairly* by removing from the scoring process anything that would cause scores to be unfairly given. Examples of acting responsibly include using objective items and a scoring key when appropriate, having students place their names on the back of their essay examinations so you are not influenced by the name, scoring all student responses to one question before moving on to another, scoring performance tasks with a scoring rubric, periodically rescoring a sample of student responses as a check against your initial scoring, and having a colleague rescore a sample or all of your papers. Suggestions for improving the fairness of scoring essay and performance assessments are given in Chapters 9 and 12.

3. *To provide students with appropriate feedback.* Your professional responsibility goes beyond simply giving students the score or the letter grade earned on the assessment. You have a professional responsibility to show students what they did incorrectly and what their expected performance level is. A teacher who simply gives the score without even permitting students to see the questions they missed or explaining the correct answer is acting ir-

responsibly. Students must be given the opportunity to learn from the assessment procedure where they need to improve. Chapter 13 discusses how to craft assessments that detect why a student has failed to perform correctly. Final examinations may be problematic in this regard, because students and teachers may leave at the end of the term or the academic year. Nevertheless, if a student requests clarification and information, serious efforts should be made to provide it. Convenience is not the primary criterion here.

4. *To explain to students the rationale for the correct answers and for the scoring rubrics you use.* By explaining how you arrived at the score and what standards and criteria you used, you teach students what is important to learn about the learning target. This clarifies the learning target and teaches students the standards that they are expected to meet.

5. *To give students the opportunity to review their evaluations individually.* Students have a right to know how their responses were marked and evaluated. They have a right to be assured that scoring was done accurately and fairly. You have the professional responsibility to go over your evaluation of a student's response with the student if he requests it.

6. *To correct errors in scoring and make necessary adjustments as quickly as possible.* Because you are human, you will make scoring errors, even if you use multiple-choice tests and a scoring stencil. You should not be threatened by a request from a student or a parent to rescore an assessment. Should you discover a scoring error (even if no one else discovers it), honesty dictates that you correct all errors in scoring and readjust the scores accordingly. This should be done in a timely manner.

7. *To score and return results in a timely manner.* For feedback to be effective, it must be timely. Further, failure to return results as quickly as possible does not allow a student to effectively monitor her progress or permit the student to adjust her study strategy. Slowness in returning assessment results does not allow you or parents to identify a student who is having difficulty in time to provide remediation. As a general rule, you should return students' results within a week or two after the assessment occurs—sooner if possible. You do not act in a professionally responsible manner when you delay returning results for longer periods without good reason.

Standardized and Mandated Tests   Occasionally you may be asked to score standardized tests or other tests mandated by your school district or state. In such cases, ***you have a responsibility to follow the scoring procedures given in the test manual*** or in other materials. Read these materials beforehand and be sure that you understand how to apply the scoring guidelines. Teachers frequently make mistakes in applying scoring keys to multiple-choice items and when looking up norm-referenced scores (e.g., percentile ranks or grade equivalents) in the tables accompanying the test materials. A common error is to use the norm tables for the wrong time of year (e.g., referring to the fall norms table when the test was administered in the spring). *It is your professional responsibility to assure that your scoring is accurate and to check the quality of your work.*

Many times teachers will be required to score open-ended tasks, performance tasks, and portfolios for mandated state assessment programs. *Districts or states requiring teachers to do this have the obligation to provide high-quality scoring rubrics and to train teachers to use them with high degrees of consistency.* As a teacher, *your responsibility is to learn how to use the rubrics and to apply them fairly and consistently.* Using scoring rubrics is discussed in Chapters 9 and 12.

In some states, schools may receive financial rewards or negative sanctions depending on their performance on state assessments. For example, a school may be declared "at risk," its principal replaced, and it may be run by an outside team. In some communities real estate agencies publish neighborhood school assessment results. Pressures are thus put on teachers to raise scores by inappropriate test preparation practices. (See Chapter 16 for details.) It should go without saying that you have a professional responsibility to honestly score and report scores on standardized tests and mandated assessments. Unfortunately, some teachers feel pressured to report the scores as more favorable than they are. It is irresponsible for educational authorities to create a situation in which you are pressured (or perceive you are pressured) into reporting high scores. However, it is still your responsibility not to yield to this pressure, to score students' responses honestly, and to report the actual results. In some communities, the operation of a school may be turned over to a private profit-making organization. Sometimes the organization's profits depend on the students' performance on standardized tests. This "payment by results" situation may increase pressures for teachers and administrators to prepare students inappropriately for the tests or to be less than honest in scoring them. Unfortunate as this pressured situation is, you should not yield to unethical assessment practices.

Responsibilities When Interpreting and Using Assessment Results

Results from Your Own Assessments   Your professional obligations in this area are

1.   *To interpret students' performance on one assessment in the context of the learning targets you taught and emphasized in your teaching.* Students should be held accountable for the learning targets you taught. When you emphasize particular content or a particular learning target, you communicate its importance to students. It would be irresponsible and perhaps a form of deception to base a large part of students' evaluations on their performance in areas that you did not emphasize.

2.   *To interpret students' performance on one assessment in relation to the results from other assessments.* No single assessment procedure is comprehensive enough to cover every important learning target. You should allow students multiple opportunities and modes to express their abilities with respect to the curriculum learning targets. You act irresponsibly if you base your evaluation of a student only on his performance on one assessment.

3.   *To interpret a student's performance in relation to the limitations of the assessment procedure you used.* Not only does a single assessment procedure lack comprehensiveness, it is also not perfectly reliable. If you gave the assessment again tomorrow or next week, or if you used slightly different questions or content, the student's score will likely change. If someone else marked the responses, the grader may come up with different marks. You act irresponsibly, therefore, if you do not consider these limitations when using your own assessment procedure. For example, you act irresponsibly if you tell a student that her grade depends completely on her test performance, or if you do not seriously consider rescoring after an honest query about how you marked a paper.

4.   *To help students and parents properly interpret the assessment results.* Parents and students may not understand the limitations of a single assessment, of paper-and-pencil assessments, of performance tasks, or of scoring reliability. You must communicate these limitations and place results of all the assessments into their proper interpretive context.

5.   *To help students and parents understand the consequences of improperly interpreting the results of your classroom assessments.* Some parents make too much of a test score or the result of a single assessment. Others do not see the pattern of success or failure that develops over time. You act responsibly when you help them understand the negative consequences of their wrong interpretations (e.g., discouraging a student's further learning) and the positive consequences of a correct interpretation (a steady improvement over the course of the marking period).

6.   *To interpret a student's performance in relation to his attainment of learning targets rather than as a weapon for punishing the student or controlling his behavior.* Although assessments may motivate students by providing them the opportunity to have their learning evaluated and possibly

remediated, they are poor weapons for controlling student behavior. You act irresponsibly if you threaten students with tests or try to manipulate them through some assessment procedure.

7. *To keep classroom assessment results confidential and to protect students' rights of privacy.* You act irresponsibly here when you post students' names and assessment results on the classroom wall, or when you tell your students' results to other teachers who have no right to know them. Sometimes a parent will ask how a neighbor's child performed in relation to the parent's own child. You should not honor this request even if it is for the relative comparison instead of the exact score.

Standardized and Mandated Test Results Because external tests do not exactly match the curriculum learning targets and your teaching emphasis, they often are misinterpreted by students, parents, and the public, who are unaware of the impact of school factors on the test results. Further, the test results are often reported as norm-referenced scores (e.g., percentile ranks, grade equivalents), many of which are not easy to interpret properly. Your school administrators and/or state education authorities have serious obligations and responsibilities to properly interpret the results and to see to it that improper interpretations are avoided or at least minimized. Section 6 of the CPR (Appendix C) lists these responsibilities. Many of them apply to the classroom teacher as well. You should review these responsibilities at this time.

Because standardized test results are often sent home through the teacher, teachers are often the first people contacted when parents have questions. For you to fulfill the professional responsibilities listed in Section 6 of the CPR, you need to understand reliability, validity, norm-referencing, criterion-referencing, and standardized tests. Chapters 3, 4, 16, 17, 18, and 19 are devoted to these topics. Studying them will help you fulfill your responsibilities in this area.

Responsibilities When Communicating Assessment Results

Communicating assessment results means communicating the proper interpretations of the results to students, parents, and school authorities. Your responsibility here is to develop proper means of communicating correct interpretations. You must determine the level of understanding of the students, parents, or school officials and tailor your communication to that level. It may involve teaching a student's parent the meaning of certain types of scores or certain assessment concepts. It would not be professionally responsible, for example, to use educational measurement jargon (e.g., percentiles, T-scores, reliability, validity) with parents unless they understood its meaning.

In addition to the level of communication, you have an obligation in relation to the frequency of communication. You have a professional responsibility to establish and follow a regular communication schedule to report student progress to parents. Your school may have a policy on this or may require you to communicate progress to parents when grades are sent home. These policies usually specify minimum communication patterns. You may need more frequent communication depending on the community and the students you teach. However, you should not overdo it: Daily progress reports may not be appropriate for students beyond preschool.

STUDENTS' RIGHTS AS TEST TAKERS

Your school district and state department of education may have policies and procedures related to students' and parents' rights concerning assessment and school records. Federal laws covering these matters, which apply to school districts and states receiving federal funds, include the Family Education Rights and Privacy Act of 1974 (Public Law 93–380), the Education of All Handicapped Children Act of 1975 (Public Law 94–142), the Education of the Handicapped Act Amendments of 1986 (Public Law 99–457), the Individuals with Disabilities Education Amendments Act of 1991 (Public Law 101–476), the Rehabilitation Act of 1973 (Public Law 93–112), and the Americans with Disabilities Act of 1990 (Public Law 101–336). Table 5.3 summarizes some of the student and parental rights under the laws.

Whether or not there is a legal requirement to do so, professional ethics may suggest that some principles underlying the rights summarized in Table 5.3 can apply to classroom assessment practices. You should check with the superintendent of your school district for information on your state's requirements regarding student and family rights. Your school should also have its *own written policy* on (1) maintenance and release of assessment results, (2) release of nonconfidential information, (3) nondiscrimination, and (4) representational consent information.

In addition to legal requirements, professional organizations are working on statements of rights of test takers. The CPR, for example, suggests several areas for which test takers (e.g., students) have rights. The Test-Takers' Rights Working Group (1994) of the Joint Committee on Testing Practices is also drafting **test-takers' rights** statements. Among the areas rights groups are working on are (1) being treated with dignity and respect in the testing process, (2) being tested by a qualified person, (3) being notified about testing schedules and fees, (4) being tested with appropriate accommodations, (5) being informed about the purpose of testing, (6) being informed about how the results will be used, (7) being informed about the quality of the information obtained from the test (e.g., its

TABLE 5.3 Some student and parent testing and school records rights mandated by federal legislation. (Not all of these are absolute rights under the cited legislation. Some exceptions may be granted by the courts.)

I. The Family and Education Rights and Privacy Act of 1974
  A. Right to inspect records
   1. Right to see all of a child's test records that are part of the child's official school record.
   2. Right to have test results explained.
   3. Written requests to see test results must be honored in 45 days.
   4. If a child is over 18, only the child has the right to the record.
  B. Right to privacy: Rights here limit access to the official school records (including test scores) to those who have legitimate educational needs.
  Additional Information: Family Education Rights and Privacy Act (FERPA) Office, U.S. Department of Education, 400 Maryland Avenue, S.W., Washington, DC 20201.

II. The Individuals with Disabilities Education Amendments Act of 1991 and The Rehabilitation Act of 1973
  A. Right to parent involvement
   1. The first time a child is considered for special education placement, the parents must be given written notice in their native language, and their permission must be obtained to test the child.
   2. Right to challenge the accuracy of test scores used to plan the child's program.
   3. Right to file a written request to have the child tested by other than the school staff.
   4. Right to request a hearing if not satisfied with the school's decision as to what are the best services for the child.
  B. Right to fairness in testing
   1. Right of the child to be tested in the language spoken at home.
   2. Tests given for placement cannot discriminate on the basis of race, sex, or socioeconomic status. The tests cannot be culturally biased.
   3. Right to be tested with a test that meets special needs (e.g., in Braille, orally, etc.).
   4. No single test score can be used to make special education decisions. Right to be tested in several different ways.
  Additional Information: National Institute on Disabilities and Rehabilitation, U.S. Department of Education, Switzer Building, Room 3132, 330 C Street, S.W., Washington, DC 20202–2524.

III. The Americans with Disabilities Act of 1990
  A. Right to accommodated testing
   1. Right of a qualified person with disabilities to be tested in a way that they can understand what is being asked and in a way that they can respond.
   2. The test administrator is expected to provide all the necessary test locations, services, aids, or accommodations at no extra charge to the examinee.
  Additional Information: National Institute on Disabilities and Rehabilitation, U.S. Department of Education, Switzer Building, Room 3132, 330 C Street, S.W., Washington, DC 20202–2524. (Also contact your regional ADA Technical Assistance Center.)

Source: Adapted from Fischer (1994), Herndon (1980), and Phillips (1994; personal communication, 1999).

level of reliability and validity), (8) being asked to give informed consent, (9) being given the right to refuse to be tested if legally applicable, (10) being given an understandable explanation of the outcome of the testing, (11) being given an understandable explanation of the consequences and decisions made from the test results, (12) being afforded privacy and confidentiality, and (13) being given the opportunity to review records and appeal interpretations and findings. Although such a "bill of rights for test takers" has not been completed or officially adopted by professional associations, teachers should be aware of these movements and should think carefully about their own assessment practices in relation to these areas of concern. Among the major issues for a classroom teacher are fairness to each student, respecting students, opening up student evaluation processes, and correcting errors in student evaluations as soon as possible.

STUDENTS' RESPONSIBILITIES

The theme of this chapter is your professional responsibilities regarding assessment. We are aware, however, that students, too, have responsibilities in an assessment situation. Students have the responsibility of studying and preparing for tests and examinations in their classes. Students who cheat are dishonest and behave unethically. Plagiarism in the form of copying homework or purchasing papers for projects and other take-home assignments should not be tolerated. Parents, teachers, school administrators, and students should work collaboratively to understand the seriousness of cheating and other forms of intellectual dishonesty. School policies and due-process procedures for handling dishonesty should be written and taught to students before enforcing them. "While teachers must do their part, they also have the right to expect ethical behavior from their students and to not be pressured to lower standards, water down courses, or give high grades for minimal work" (S. E. Phillips, personal communication, May 1999).

SECRECY, ACCESS, PRIVACY, CONFIDENTIALITY, AND THE TEACHER

Secrecy and Access

Secrecy and test security have been the hallmarks of the testing industry since the late 1920s and early 1930s, when large-scale abuse of testing abounded. Withholding test information—either about the items on the test or the exact score(s) a student attained—often was justified on the grounds that **access to assessment results** would do more harm than good. For example:

■ A student might attempt to memorize only specific answers ("a" or "b") rather than focusing on mastery of the general skills the test was designed to measure; this behavior would distort the measurement of knowledge and ability.

■ Tests that measure highly sensitive and personal characteristics may require a high degree of professional training to interpret the scores; examinees lacking this training might cause themselves harm by misinterpreting the results.

■ Releasing test items might result in their being used by unqualified examiners who would misinterpret scores, causing examinees harm.

■ Releasing copies of old forms of a test might require the test developer to spend unreasonable sums of money to develop new forms, assuming that new forms of the test could, in fact, be developed.

In recent years, however, the public has become aware that some test abuses have resulted from such secrecy. For example:

■ Professionals themselves vary in qualifications and have, in fact, misinterpreted tests or abused results.

■ Decisions made about educational placement, ostensibly on the basis of valid and objective test results, have later been discovered to be biased, misinterpreted, or otherwise invalid.

■ Errors in scoring that could not be detected occurred because the tests could not be scrutinized by those having the greatest stake in their accuracy—the students and parents.

■ Although some tests publicly were declared to assess learned skills and abilities, examinees were unable to check their content to decide whether their preparation had been adequate or whether they should seek special remediation or training.

■ Although professionals may have interpreted assessment results properly, records were often open to other persons, who used the results either unprofes-

sionally or in a manner unauthorized by and detrimental to the examinee.

Problems such as these spawned a renewed public interest in the ethics of secrecy and the right of students and parents to know. A number of state and federal laws and court decisions have arisen, mandating greater access for students and parents to assessment results and toward greater participation in the assessment-based decision-making process. Table 5.3 lists some of these access and participation rights under federal legislation. Your own school district should have written policies regarding students' and families' rights regarding access to records and assessment results.

Access to Student Data for Research Purposes

Another point concerns the use of records for research. Usually, obtaining assessment results for research purposes is not considered a violation of privacy provided the identity of the student remains anonymous. The Department of Health and Human Services issued regulations protecting the welfare of human subjects in research projects. Although you are not a researcher, you should be sensitive to **ethical principles** of privacy and confidentiality because you may need to collect data to use on your research projects for graduate courses and degrees, and you may have to protect the rights of students under your care when others (within and outside the school) request student information.

Purging and Correcting School Records

Another issue is the **purging** of outdated files and other student records and correcting erroneous information. Certainly, if you give an incorrect grade you should correct the affected student's record. Sometimes the teacher (or others) will score a standardized test incorrectly, discovering this fact after the information has been entered on the record. This will necessitate changing the record also. Computerized databases are relatively easy to update, despite the often-used excuse by some school officials that it is "too late because the data are in the computer." There is a professional responsibility to correct mistakes in the records. Information such as your anecdotal records should be purged when they are no longer necessary (usually within a year or two). Some schools have policies for the systematic purging of student records. Others may depend on a student's parents to come in and periodically review the records for unnecessary, damaging, or erroneous information.

Privacy, Confidentiality, and the Teacher

An important question is whether a student has the right to expect that certain information be held in confidence. **Privacy** and **confidentiality** affect you in several ways. In the classroom itself, for example, teachers sometimes keep charts or post students' progress. Such a public display may or may not be in the form of grades. This practice raises the question of whether the evaluations should be confidential. Another example is the practice of keeping scores, grades, and anecdotal comments in a student's records. Ethical questions arise about who has authorized access to these files. Teachers and certain other persons have legitimate rights to obtain necessary information from them to help teach a given student. Many schools have forms or other means to keep records of who has used a student's records and for what purposes. Usually a student's test scores and other records cannot be transferred to another institution without that student (or parents') written authorization.

Wagging tongues in teacher's lounges are still another way violations of confidentiality can occur. It is your professional responsibility not to use the teacher's lounge as a place to gossip and spread confidential information about students.

Informed Consent

Privacy is not violated if persons give consent to others to obtain and use personal information. Without going into a detailed ethical analysis of the matter, we shall state that there are at least four levels of consent (McCormick, 1974; O'Donnell, 1974): informed consent, presumed consent, implied consent, and proxy consent. **Informed consent** is obtained directly from the student and presumes that the student, in giving that consent, has received and understands the following information (Boruch, 1971): (1) the exact nature and extent to which personal information will remain anonymous, (2) to what extent participation is voluntary rather than required, (3) who (or what agency) is requesting the information and for what purpose, and (4) what will happen to the information after it is collected (including whether and/or when it will be destroyed).

Obviously, few young students will be able to understand the implications of all of this information, so their consent may not be truly informed. Often consent must come from a *proxy*, such as a parent or a school official. The extent to which school officials can grant permission for collecting and using pupil information will depend, among other things, on the degree to which such consent is *presumed* or *implied* by the fact that students are entrusted to their care. This is sometimes referred to as *representational consent*.

ACCOMMODATIONS FOR STUDENTS WITH DISABILITIES

Issues and Controversies

Standardized test accommodations for students with physical disabilities are less controversial than accommodations for students with cognitive disabilities such as learning disabilities (Phillips, 1994). One concern is the validity of the test result interpretations: If a test was administered under accommodating conditions, do the scores mean the same thing as the scores for students who took the test under standard conditions? Another concern is violation of the privacy rights of students. Should the results for students administered the test under accommodating conditions be identified or flagged in the record or score report?

There are no simple answers to either concern. The validity of interpretations depends on the type of test administered, the purpose of the testing, the type of accommodation, the type of disability the student has, and the nature of the interpretation itself. For example, a student with a severe reading disability (such as dyslexia) may be unable to read the reading comprehension section of a standardized achievement test. If the purpose is to assess the ability to read standard printed English, it would be inappropriate to provide a reader (someone to read the test questions) for the student.

However, suppose the student can read some material if given a longer time to answer. This accommodation violates the standardization conditions, thus invalidating the usual norm-referenced interpretations such as grade equivalents, percentile ranks, and standard scores. Nevertheless, by giving the student more time, you discovered what test material he or she could read when the time element is removed. Your interpretation of the results cannot ignore the accommodations, however; you would need to preface your norm-referenced interpretation with something like: "Here is how Sally compares to other students. The other students took the test under standard conditions and with limited time. However, Sally took the test under nonstandard conditions and with no time limits because [give your rationale]."

A criterion-referenced interpretation (an interpretation of the type of material read and types of questions answered) is often made for test results. However, speed of reading is also part of this interpretation for standardized achievement tests because of the limits imposed by the standardization conditions. Therefore, your criterion-referenced interpretation would need to be stated in a manner that reflects the nonstandard administration, such as, "These are the types of materials and questions Sally was able to read when she took the test under nonstandard conditions and with no time limits." It is sometimes possible to report two results: The student's performance under standard conditions and the student's performance under accommodated conditions.

If the purpose of testing is to assess a student's knowledge and ability in a subject such as social studies or mathematics, then it could be appropriate for a student with a severe reading disability to have a reader. In this case, the concepts, principles, and procedures of the subject are independent of the printed medium in which they are presented on the test. Thus it is logical for you to assess a student's understanding of them through an appropriate accommodation. The problem arises, however, in trying to interpret the results in a norm-referenced framework, because other students took the test under standard conditions in which they had to read the test materials and the questions themselves. Even your criterion-referenced interpretation of the student's results (how well the student understands the concepts, principles, and procedures) needs to be qualified. You do this by stating that the student cannot express or has difficulty expressing his understanding if asked to do so using standard printed English tests.

Those interpretations are likely to be controversial, especially if you extend them to situations in which tests are administered to students with disabilities other than the one used as an example. The intensity of the controversy may increase, too, if the purpose for testing changed from strictly describing a student's achievement to other purposes such as assessing educational progress, assessing general scholastic aptitude, testing for admission to higher education, granting a high school diploma, or selecting for a job. From a strict measurement perspective, in which the validity of the testing program is a primary concern, the following questions might be considered:

1. Will format changes or alterations in testing conditions change the skill being measured?

2. Will the scores of examinees tested under standard conditions have a different meaning than scores for examinees tested with the requested accommodation?

3. Would non-disabled examinees benefit if allowed the same accommodations?

4. Does the disabled examinee have any capacity for adjusting to standard test administration conditions?

5. Is the disability evidence or testing accommodation policy based on procedures with doubtful validity and reliability? (Phillips, 1994, p. 104)

Phillips argues that if you answer yes to any one of these questions, a test accommodation is not appropriate, because the validity of the test results would be reduced. She points out the potential conflict between providing maximum participation in society for persons with disabilities and maintaining test validity. You should be cautious when interpreting yes answers to these five questions. A mean-spirited or a misinformed person could respond yes and be wrong. Further, for answering some of these questions there are no valid research results on which even a well-intentioned and informed person can rely.

Not all would agree, however, with Phillips' conclusions. For example, even though accommodations may change the skill assessed and/or the meaning of the scores (see Questions 1 and 2), such changes may be more, rather than less, valid. Phillips' argument assumes that administering the test under standard conditions is the criterion against which accommodations should be judged. It also assumes that the skill or ability assessed by the test under standard conditions is the relevant skill and ability to be assessed. These assumptions may not be correct. For example, reading short passages and answering questions under timed standard conditions (the typical reading comprehension test) is not the ultimate learning target for education, nor is it a direct assessment of "real-world" reading. Accommodations to the standard test conditions may change both the skill required and the meaning of the results in a more positive direction. This, in turn, may make the accommodated test results more like the ultimate learning targets in the real world. This is more likely to be the case as the Americans with Disabilities Act of 1990 begins to alter the conditions, accommodation patterns, and attitudes in the workplace. The basis for judging the validity of assessment results changes over time as we learn more about the capabilities and contributions of persons with disabilities. For example, for many jobs and real-world situations, reading with accommodations (such as using more time) is permitted and acceptable.

Another serious issue that arises when making accommodations and interpretations is identification. Should we identify in the school record and score reports those students for whom accommodations were made? In effect, this flagging of scores means that you would identify the person as disabled and perhaps even identify the nature of the disability. This information is generally considered to be confidential and private (Phillips, 1994). Persons with disabilities may fear that such disclosure makes them vulnerable to prejudice or misinformed test interpretations by persons who might use the assessment results. Oftentimes, assessment results used for one purpose are later used in different circumstances. Thus, once the scores and flags are on the record, there is little control over how they might be misused in the future. Others might argue that an employer or a postsecondary institution has a right to know whether an accommodation is needed on the job, and therefore flagging the assessment results is necessary and appropriate (Phillips, 1994).

Legally Defensible Assessment Accommodation Policies

As you may have inferred from the preceding discussion, issues of accommodation and inclusion are controversial. They may also result in legal action against a school district or a state. Because the Americans with Disabilities Act requires reasonable accommodations when they are necessary, educational authorities must develop accommodation policies and procedures that preserve assessment validity in the broad sense, are fair and respectful of rights of persons with disabilities, and comply with the law. Educational authorities are urged to seek the advice of their legal counselors and of advocates of persons with disabilities as they draw up accommodation policies. Authorities should keep in mind, however, that because of the large differences in abilities among (and within) disability categories, listening to only one advocacy group is likely to lead to inappropriate policies and practices. For example, the reasonable accommodations required for students with mental retardation are likely to be quite inappropriate for students with hearing losses. You should be aware, too, that while the law may require "reasonable accommodations," exactly what that means is unclear. The teacher, the school officials, and the student (or parents) will need to base accommodations on reasonableness and validity, not on negotiating skill (S. E. Phillips, personal communications, 1999).

The following suggestions are adapted from Phillips (1994), who is both an assessment specialist and a lawyer. Her suggestions help to make the process more legally defensible. You are urged to consult the reference before attempting to implement these suggestions.

1. Prepare a written set of instructions for how a student (parent) should request an assessment accommodation. Protect students' due-process rights by making sure students and parents are aware of these instructions.

2. Prepare a standard form for requesting accommodations, and describe clearly how to return the form and what the deadline is.

3. Require students (parents) requesting accommodations to document their disability. Require:
   a. Verification of the qualifications and disability-related experience of the professional who is describing the disability.
   b. A letter signed by the qualified professional specifying the type(s) of accommodations required.
   c. The professional to provide you with test results and the procedures used to make the diagnosis.
   d. A verification that the professional conducted an in-person evaluation within the past 12 months.
   e. Additional documentation for questionable cases, including documentation of the professional's qualifications and the requesting of student's medical records.

4. Determine if the student's IEP requires a particular accommodation.

5. If you will flag the scores resulting from the accommodated assessment, notify the students and/or the parents of this in writing. Require them to sign statements that they have been notified.

6. Designate a single professional staff member to review and act on all requests. Call in a qualified consultant to handle borderline cases.

7. Develop general guidelines for how to accommodate persons with similar disability patterns, but act only on an individual, case-by-case basis. (You will want to treat similarly situated persons consistently, but because there are so many individual differences within a category, you need to work with students directly.)

8. Designate a professional staff member to collect data that can be used to assess the validity of various accommodations for different types of students. Use this validity data to refine policies and procedures.

9. If you deny an accommodation request, provide for a speedy review of the case. Be sure all information and documentation are available to the reviewer(s) and that the reviewer(s) are qualified to evaluate the decision.

10. Develop a formal appeal procedure and a process for the student whose accommodation is denied. Require the student, parent, or guardian to make a written request to appeal. Allow for new evidence and for representation by legal counsel.

11. Students who are protected by the Individuals with Disabilities Education Act of 1991, Section 504 of the Rehabilitation Act of 1973, and the Americans with Disabilities Act of 1990 probably cannot be asked to pay for additional services and accommodations.

12. Institutionalize or legalize your accommodation policies, so they can be sustained as personnel changes occur over the years. Do not depend on the good will of one person to implement the policies.

The preceding suggestions are written to protect educational authorities and assessment organizations from legal action while assuring due process for students with disabilities. They appear to place a heavy responsibility on the student and his or her legal guardian for documenting disabilities and justifying needed accommodations. They also appear to be set in an adversarial context, rather than a conciliatory or cooperative context.

TESTING CHALLENGED IN COURT

Plaintiffs seeking legal redress for real and/or perceived violations of rights may bring testing programs to the courts. Notable among legal issues are race or gender discrimination, a test's contribution toward segregation in schools and other disparate impact issues, unfairness of particular tests, and the violation of due process—such as failure to give sufficient notice for a test or failure to give opportunities for hearings and appeals. Among the educational testing practices brought to courts are minimum-competency testing programs designed to control graduation, teacher certification tests designed to control who is allowed to teach in a state, and college admissions testing.

Court cases sometimes involve class-action suits in which the plaintiffs represent an entire group of persons, and the judgments handed down by the court apply to all members. This was true, for example, in the *Debra P. et al. v. Turlington* (1979, 1981) case, which challenged Florida's minimum competency test. The court recognized the following classes: "(a) . . . all present and future twelfth grade public school students in the State of Florida who have failed or who hereafter fail the SSAT- II [i.e., the State Student Assessment, Part II]. (b) . . . all present and future twelfth grade African-American public school students in the State of Florida who have failed or who hereafter fail the SSAT-II. (c) . . . all present and future twelfth grade African-American public school students in Hillsborough County, Florida who have failed or who hereafter fail the SSAT-II" (Fisher, 1980, p. 7).

Psychometric Issues Presented in Court

Some issues raised in court focus on the technical aspects of testing. We refer to these as **psychometric issues**. The following aspects of testing have been raised in courts in connection with high-stakes testing such as graduation tests (Fisher, 1980; Langenfeld & Crocker, 1994; Mehrens & Popham, 1992; Phillips, 1994). They appear, however, to be widely applicable in court cases involving other tests.

1. *Test security*. Plaintiffs and special interest groups may want to know the content of the test, sometimes before the test is used. Related to this issue are matters of test security, applicable state and federal "sunshine" laws, and "truth-in-testing" legislation.

2. *AERA, APA, and NCME Standards*. The AERA, APA, and NCME (1999) *Standards* were mentioned earlier in this chapter. The *Uniform Guidelines on Employee Selection and Procedures* (EEOC, CSC, DL, & DJ, 1978) are used also when adverse impact is an issue. These guidelines may not strictly apply to student testing and to teacher certification, because employment is not linked entirely to testing (S.E. Phillips, personal communication, 1999). While not a legal document, the *Standards* do represent a consensus professional opinion and values as to what constitutes good test development practices. Plaintiffs sometimes use these *Standards* as a basis for arguing against the quality or use of a particular test or testing program.

3. *Reliability*. (See Chapter 4.) Plaintiffs may challenge either the magnitude of a test's reliability data or the appropriateness of using particular techniques for ascertaining reliability.

4. *Validity and opportunity to learn*. (See Chapter 3.) With educational tests designed to certify minimum competence, the relation of content present on the test to content taught in the classroom is likely to be challenged. (This is sometimes called *curriculum relevance* or *curricular validity*.)

5. *Test development procedures*. Every stage of test development may be challenged in a particular case: the test plan, the qualifications of the item writers, the correspondence between items and objectives, the readability level, the correct and alternative options to multiple-choice items, the tryout and field procedures, the correctness of the scanning and reporting, and steps taken to reduce or minimize culture, race, gender, and/or regional bias.

6. *Passing scores*. Several methods for setting passing scores exist, all of which plaintiffs may attack. Such attacks may not succeed if a large group, legally empowered to do so, sets the passing score by following acceptable standard-setting practices (see Jaeger, 1989, 1990; Mehrens & Popham, 1992).

7. *Mechanical issues*. Plaintiffs can criticize mechanical aspects of the test, such as the quality of instructions and directions for administering, the color of the ink, the size of the print (some states have laws on this for certain grade levels), and other surface features of the test.

8. *Accommodations for the disabled*. Plaintiffs with mental or physical disabilities can challenge a test if appropriate accommodations are denied. Accommodations include access to the testing room as well as accommodations such as those listed in Table 5.2.

Nonpsychometric Issues Presented in Court

Nonpsychometric issues that are the basis for legal redress in the use of tests include

1. *Legal authority*. Plaintiffs may challenge a test or testing program, not so much on the basis of whether the test is of high quality, but whether the program has been legally authorized or whether individuals making the decisions about testing have the legal authority to do so.

2. *Segregation in the schools*. Here the challenge can be that the tests are biased against the lower-scoring group and/or that they reflect and perpetuate past segregation in the schools, which lowered the quality of education. Thus, the plaintiffs should not be denied access or certification based on test results.

3. *Property interests in a diploma*. The theory is that "the student has the right to expect that a diploma will be forthcoming assuming that all courses were passed, and

any substantive change in the graduation requirements cannot take place without due notice to the student" (Fisher, 1980, p. 4). In a landmark case (*Debra P. et al. v. Turlington*, 1984) concerning the Florida minimum-competency graduation test, the court held that "a diploma is a property right subject to the Fourteenth Amendment protections" (Phillips, 1994, p. 108).

4. *Due process.* This could be either substantive or procedural **due process**. *Substantive due process* concerns the appropriateness of the requirement (e.g., passing the test) and the purpose (e.g., maintaining high-quality teaching). *Procedural due process* focuses on the fairness with which the examinee was treated. Fairness includes notifying the examinee in advance of the requirement, test date, etc.; giving opportunity for hearings and appeals; and making sure that the hearing is conducted fairly.

5. *Stigmatization.* The results of the test may be used to deny a diploma or certificate or to label a person. A plaintiff's challenge may be that such occurrences that result from testing are illegal because they result in stigmatizing a person, especially if the case can be linked to ethnic or gender bias.

Notice that in matters of test use and abuse, the application of particular laws is seldom clear. The resulting legal decision of a court depends on the particular circumstances surrounding a given case, the evidence brought to bear in the case, and the opinion of the judge and jury involved.

BIAS IN EDUCATIONAL ASSESSMENT

Definitions of Bias

One of the concerns surrounding the appropriateness of assessments for various decisions is whether a particular assessment is biased against particular groups. Exactly what is meant by a "biased assessment" is not always clear, because many definitions of **assessment or test bias** exist in the media and the professional literature. Sometimes persons who discuss bias have more than one type of bias in mind, although they may not distinguish between types. The following catalogue of definitions of assessment bias is adapted from Flaugher (1978).

Assessment Bias as Mean Differences

A great many persons use the **bias as mean differences** approach. An assessment is said to be biased against a particular group because the average (mean) score of that group is lower than the average score of another group. (The mean is explained in Appendix H.) Most assessment specialists would not subscribe to this definition of bias because average differences in groups' performances could represent real differences in the level of their attainment, rather than an artificial difference. *Bias* carries with it the idea of "unfair" or "unjust." Thus, *differences as differences* may not represent bias. If one group receives an inferior education or has been socialized away from learning or developing certain skills, a test measuring these things will likely indicate that this group scores lower on the average than a group that has had the opportunity or encouragement to learn.

Although differences in group means do not *necessarily* indicate that an assessment procedure is biased, they should not be dismissed lightly. Such differences may indicate that the groups have been treated unfairly (not given equal opportunity to acquire the abilities assessed), and thus they have developed different ability levels. However, such mean differences in groups may mean that the assessment procedure is biased, too. In other words, several factors can cause a mean difference between groups, including a biased assessment. The problem is that knowing that such differences exist does not in itself explain why they exist.

Assessment Bias as Differential Item Functioning (DIF)

Instead of studying average total score differences among groups, some assessment developers study differences at the individual test item or assessment task level. An individual test question may favor one group over another; but the assessment, as a whole, may not show any difference. The approach here is not to look simply at average difference in an item's performance. Rather, it is to look at whether persons of the same ability performed differently on the item. For example, you would study how boys of low ability compared to girls of low ability, boys of average ability compared to girls of average ability, and boys of high ability compared to girls of high ability. If these comparisons show that students in the two groups who are of the same ability perform differently on the task, this may indicate that the task is biased. However, just as average total test scores do not necessarily confirm a test is biased, so, too, do such item differences not necessarily confirm item bias. In other words, test items may function differently in two groups, but there may be no discernible bias. Because these differences do not prove bias, assessment specialists refer to the differences as **differential item functioning (DIF)** rather than as item bias.

Assessment Bias as Misinterpretation of Scores

Bias as misinterpretation of scores can creep into the interpretations of assessment results when someone who uses the results tries to make inappropriate inferences about students' performances that go beyond the content domain of the assessment (Cole, 1978; Cole & Moss, 1989). It is one thing to say, for example, that a female has difficulty solving two-step arithmetic word problems that involve knowledge of male suburban experiences; it's another to interpret performance on the assessment as an indication that females have lower arithmetic reasoning skills than males. The latter interpretation goes beyond the content domain and demands more than cursory evidence to support a claim that the interpretation is unbiased.

Assessment Bias as Sexist and Racist Content: Facial Bias

Facial bias is the offensive stereotype use of language and pictures in the assessment tasks and materials. Ours has been a white, male-dominated, Anglo-conformity culture. A goal is not to perpetuate this image through the use of language and pictures in assessment (and other) materials. You can judge the content of assessment tasks (and other material) according to whether they represent male or female, white or nonwhite, as well as whether the content depicts certain **role stereotypes**. Table 5.4 shows one set of criteria for such judging. Under the definition of bias described here, an assessment would be biased if its tasks perpetuated undesirable role stereotypes, race stereotypes, or gender stereotypes. This judgment about the offensive nature of assessment content can be called facial bias (Cole & Nitko, 1981). Criteria such as those in Table 5.4 have been applied to the rating of achievement tests and intelligence tests. Special concerns for race and gender facial bias exist in vocational interest inventories. The goal is not to produce a faceless, gender-free, and ethnic-free set of assessment materials. Rather it is to represent gender and ethnic groups in a balanced, inoffensive, and fair way in the assessment materials.

Assessment Bias as Differential Validity

Predictive validity refers to the extent to which a test is able to estimate a person's probable standing on a second measure called a criterion (see Chapter 3). The criterion of interest in assessment bias is usually some measure of job or school success. Under the definition of **bias as differential validity**, an assessment would be biased if it predicted criterion scores better for one group of persons (e.g., whites) than for another (e.g., African Americans) (Cole &

TABLE 5.4 Criteria for judging assessment tasks for racial and sexist content.

Gender representation: the extent to which an item can be characterized as representing a male or female.

1. **Pictorial items.** Which gender does the item picture? Features checked include attire, length of hair, facial characteristics and make-up (e.g., barrettes in a baby's hair mean the illustration presents a female).	2. **Verbal items.** Nouns and pronouns indicate gender: he/she, him/her, John/Jane (e.g., "Marion bought a bell for his bike," describes a male).

Gender role-stereotype: the extent to which an item can be characterized as depicting a male or female stereotyped role. Male role-stereotyped items depict males as intelligent, strong, vigorous, rugged, contributing to history, mechanically apt, professional, famous, etc. Female role-stereotyped items depict females as domestic, passive, generally inactive, crying, physically attractive, and non-intellectual.

1. **Pictorial items.** Does the picture illustrate a gender role-stereotype? (e.g., woman fixing a meal, little girl playing with dolls, man carrying a picnic basket while escorting woman to park, man watching contact sports, or boy being mischievous).	2. **Verbal items.** Does the item contain statements which are gender role-stereotyped? (e.g., question: "Who invented the electric light bulb?" [male role-stereotype] or story theme: brother and sister get a horse, boy rides horse while sister watches and laughs when brother falls in mud [female role-stereotype]). [Bias is implied when nearly all questions represent single-gender, negative sterotypes, rather than a balance of gender accomplishments.]

Race representation: the extent to which an item can be characterized as representing a white or nonwhite person.

1. **Pictorial items.** Are physical features such as skin color eye shape and color, hair color and texture varied?	2. **Verbal items.** Do famous persons to be identified come from various races (e.g., George Washington, Martin Luther King, Jr.)?

Race role-stereotype: the extent to which an item can be characterized as depicting a white or nonwhite role-stereotype. White role-stereotyped items depict whites as wealthy, technically or academically trained, professional, intelligent, and inclined toward academic or intellectual pursuits. Pictures or verbal themes show whites operating instruments such as stethoscopes or surveying transoms. Nonwhite role-stereotyped items depict nonwhites as poor, unskilled, athletic (e.g., boxer, football lineman), culturally primitive, and religiously pagan.

1. **Pictorial items.** Are role-stereotypes depicted (e.g., white male executive, Oriental coolies, native American warriors, and black bellboys)?	2. **Verbal items.** Does the verbal content or story theme represent a role-stereotype (e.g., "Who wrote Hamlet?")?

Source: From "A look at content bias in IQ tests" by L. Zoref and P. Williams, 1980, *Journal of Educational Measurement, 17,* pp. 313–322. Copyright 1980. National Council on Measurement in Education, Washington, DC. Adapted by permission of the publisher.

Moss, 1989). This is called differential validity, meaning that the assessment predicts success better in one group than in another. A "fair" or unbiased assessment would, according to this definition, predict criterion scores with equal accuracy for all groups assessed. There have been a number of empirical studies of differential bias, but the overall conclusion is that few tests exhibit this pattern of differential correlation with educational success criteria. That is, educational selection tests seem to predict educational success equally well (or equally poorly) for most groups.

Assessment Bias as Content and Experience Differential

The definition of **bias as content/experience differential** classifies an assessment as biased if the content of the assessment tasks is radically different from a particular subgroup of students' life experiences but the assessment results are interpreted without taking such differences into proper consideration. For example, consider two high school vocabulary tests, one consisting of word meanings likely to be learned in a white, middle-class suburban high school and the other comprised of slang word meanings likely to be learned only by urban, streetwise, African American youth. Would either or both tests be biased? The answer depends on the use and interpretation of results. Clearly, one would expect African American youth to perform better than white youth on the latter test (Williams, 1975b). However, if the latter test is interpreted as a test of knowledge of this culture-specific vocabulary domain, then it would not be biased against white youth that have not had the experience needed to acquire this learning. On the other hand, if the latter test were interpreted as a broad measure of verbal ability, it might well be biased against white youths, just as the former middle-class suburban vocabulary test might be biased against urban African American youths. But the suburban vocabulary test might validly measure the verbal ability of white suburban youth as developed by their experience, and the African American urban vocabulary test might do the same for African American youth.

When students' experiences and an assessment's content are radically different, it is probably not possible to offer the same construct interpretation (e.g., general verbal ability) for one subgroup's performance as that offered for another subgroup whose experience and assessment content more nearly match. If you restrict your assessment interpretations to the limited domain from which the tasks are sampled (e.g., white middle-class vocabulary knowledge or knowledge of urban African American slang), the issue of content bias is less likely to be raised. Seldom, however, does a teacher, counselor, or other assessment interpreter limit interpretation to the narrow content domain: Most often, even for achievement tests, we use broad-construct interpretations such as math concepts,

listening comprehension, and spelling ability (Cole, 1978).

Assessment Bias as the Statistical Model Used for Selection Decisions

When there are a limited number of openings and a great many applicants, some procedure will be used to select those few applicants who will fill the openings. Most persons in this culture would reject the lottery (random drawing) as a means of selection, because a random process is uncorrelated with the ability to succeed on the job or in school. Most people believe that **selection decisions** should be based on "merits." Combinations of various types of assessments provide information that ranks applicants in order of merit. Among the information-gathering tools are interviews and the application blank itself, as well as a variety of performance assessments and paper-and-pencil tests. All assessments used for selection must show some positive relationship to job or school success. The problem arises when certain subgroups score consistently lower on one or more of the assessments used in the selection process, and when the assessments have slightly different relationships with the measures of the success criterion. The **bias as the statistical model** definition focuses on whether the statistical procedure used for selection is fair to all persons, regardless of group membership.

At least 10 actuarial or statistical models for reducing selection bias have appeared in the literature (Cleary, 1968; Cole, 1973; Cole & Moss, 1989; Darlington, 1971, 1976; Einhorn & Bass, 1971; Gross & Su, 1975; Linn, 1973; Novick & Peterson, 1976; Ravelo & Nitko, 1988; Thorndike, 1971).

Assessment Bias as the Wrong Criterion Measure

Selection tests are used to predict success on a second measure called a *criterion*. But the criterion measure itself may be biased, making the selection process biased, even if the test is unbiased. That is **bias as wrong criterion**. For example, suppose a job did not require reading skills and that on-the-job performance is the relevant criterion. Suppose further that an employer used a paper-and-pencil test of job knowledge as a substitute criterion measure instead of using a measure of actual job performance. Because in this case the paper-and-pencil test would be interpreted erroneously as the "ability to do the job," it would be a biased assessment against those who could not read or who were poor paper-and-pencil test takers but might well be able to perform the job. Some criteria represent traditional cultural values (e.g., supervisors' ratings, grade point average) and may be used as proxies to an ultimate criterion measure such as job performance. Persons able to perform well on the ultimate criterion may not necessarily perform well on these proxy measures.

Bias Stemming from the Atmosphere and Conditions of Assessment

Basic stresses of test taking, such as test anxiety, feeling unwelcomed, or being tested by a member of the opposite gender or another race, can adversely affect the performance of some groups. Others have argued that it is unfair to students and teachers in schools serving the impoverished to use an officially mandated test that serves "to inflict on them periodic, detailed documentation of just how very far away from anything approaching the norm they are" (Flaugher, 1978, p. 677). These would be classified as **bias stemming from testing conditions**.

Summary

- You have professional, ethical, and legal responsibilities concerning the way you craft, use, and report the results of your classroom assessments.
- Professional associations have developed codes of ethics and professional responsibilities. The *Code of Professional Responsibility in Educational Measurement* (Appendix C) is one of them.
- There are six main areas of assessment activities in which you have ethical and professional responsibility: (1) crafting assessments, (2) choosing assessments, (3) administering assessments, (4) scoring assessments, (5) interpreting and using assessment results, and (6) communicating assessment results.
- When crafting assessment procedures, your professional responsibility is to develop a procedure that closely fits the purpose for which you intend to use it and has a degree of reliability appropriate to the seriousness of the decision for which you will use the results.
- Among your assessment-crafting professional responsibilities are assuring that (1) your assessment-crafting process uses the sound and well-known principles of assessment development, (2) your assessments are free from characteristics that are irrelevant to assessing the learning target, (3) you accommodate students with disabilities who are in your class, (4) you obtain necessary permission to use copyrighted material in your assessment, (5) you present the assessment in a way that encourages their proper use, and (6) your assessment materials do not contain errors or inaccuracies.
- When choosing assessment procedures that come with curricular materials or that are separately purchased, you have a professional responsibility to (1) not use them if they do not match your classroom teaching, vocabulary, reading level, or content emphasis, (2) recraft them, if necessary, before using them, and (3) assure that you meet the same six professional responsibilities as you do when you craft your own assessment procedures.
- When serving on a committee to select a standardized test for your school district or for a state assessment program, you have a professional responsibility to be knowledgeable about (1) educational assessment quality characteristics, (2) the AERA, APA, and NCME *Standards* and the *Code of Fair Testing Practices in Education*, (3) the procedures and criteria used to evaluate an educational assessment, and (4) the ways similar assessments have been used in other places and the consequences of such usage.
- When administering assessments to students, you have a professional responsibility to (1) give students sufficient notice of when the assessment will occur, (2) give students complete information about the coverage of the assessment and the conditions under which it will be given, and (3) conduct the assessment in a professional manner that encourages each student to do his or her best.
- You have a professional responsibility to see to it that students with disabilities in your class are provided with appropriate assessment accommodations necessary for them to demonstrate their learning. Table 5.2 shows examples of various types of assessment accommodations.
- In accommodating students with disabilities, you should treat each as an individual rather than stereotyping his or her assessment accommodation needs.
- When administrating standardized or state-mandated tests, you have a professional responsibility to (1) fully inform students about the testing and its purpose, (2) carefully follow the directions for administering the test, (3) maintain the necessary test security, (4) maintain testing conditions appropriate for maximum performance, (5) provide for necessary accommodations for students with disabilities, and (6) avoid cheating, teaching specific answers to test items, and unethical test-preparation practices.
- When scoring your own classroom assessments, you have a professional responsibility to (1) score students' responses accurately, (2) score students fairly, (3) provide students with appropriate feedback, (4) explain to students the rationale for the correct answers and for the scoring rubrics you used, (5) give students the opportunity to review their evaluations individually, (6) correct scoring errors as quickly as possible, and (7) score and return assessment results in a timely manner.
- When scoring standardized and state-mandated assessments, you have a professional responsibility to (1) follow directions in a manual exactly, (2) assure that your scoring is accurate, (3) monitor the quality of your scoring, and (4) learn how to use and to fairly apply the scoring rubrics.
- When using and interpreting assessment results, you have the professional responsibility to interpret students' performance (1) in the context of the learning targets you emphasized in class; (2) in relation to the results from several assessments, not just one; (3) in

relation to the limitations of the assessment procedure; (4) properly to parents; (5) as assessments of learning targets rather than as tools for controlling students; and (6) in ways that protect students' rights of privacy.

■ You have a professional responsibility to learn the meaning of standardized test score-reporting schemes that impact your students (e.g., grade equivalents and standard scores) and to interpret these properly.

■ You have a professional responsibility to (1) communicate correctly and accurately the results of assessments to students, parents, colleagues, and school officials, (2) tailor your communication to each of these groups so they make proper interpretations themselves, (3) communicate in a way that minimizes the likelihood of misinterpretations on the part of the receiver of the information, and (4) establish an appropriate and frequent pattern of communication of assessment results with parents and students.

■ Students have rights as test takers. Some of these are protected by the U.S. Constitution and federal legislation (see Table 5.3). Others follow from your ethical and professional responsibilities. The chapter identifies 13 areas of rights that should be considered.

■ Students have responsibilities as test takers. They have the responsibility to study and prepare for assessments. They have the responsibility not to apply pressure on teachers to lower standards.

■ Students' assessment results and classroom performance are generally considered to be confidential, and you have a professional responsibility to help protect the students' rights to privacy. Responsibilities include requiring researchers to seek permission and informed consent from students or their parents before releasing data.

■ You have a professional responsibility to correct, on the students' records (including computerized records), any errors you make in reporting assessment results or grading students. Your obligation is not lessened if no one but you knows of the error.

■ You have a professional responsibility to limit your posting or display of students' assessment results to protect their rights to privacy. You also have a professional responsibility not to gossip about students to other teachers or to spread confidential information about them.

■ *Informed consent* means that the student understands (1) the nature and extent to which personal information will remain anonymous, (2) the extent to which participation is voluntary, (3) who is requesting information and the purpose of the request, and (4) what will happen to information that is collected.

■ Testing programs have been challenged in courts. Plaintiffs may be individuals or classes of persons. They may challenge the psychometric properties of

tests or nonpsychometric properties. Examples are given in the chapter.

■ There are many different definitions of test bias. Eight are described in the chapter.

Important Terms and Concepts

access to assessment results
assessment accommodations
assessment or test bias
bias as content/experience differential
bias as differential validity
bias as mean differences
bias as misinterpretation of scores
bias as the statistical model
bias as wrong criterion
bias stemming from testing conditions
Code of Fair Testing Practices in Education
Code of Professional Responsibility in Educational Measurement (CPR)
confidentiality
correcting records
differential item functioning (DIF)
due process
ethical principles
facial bias
gender representation
gender stereotype
high-quality information
individual education plan (IEP)
informed consent
mandated tests
positive or negative consequences of decisions
privacy
professional responsibility
psychometric issues
purging records
race representation
race role-stereotype
role stereotype
selection decisions
serious vs. less serious consequences of decisions
standardized tests
test-takers' rights

Exercises and Discussion Questions

1. Write a paper in which you express your personal agreement or disagreement with the professional responsibilities listed in each of the six assessment areas identified at the beginning of this chapter.

   a. For each responsibility with which you disagree, clearly explain the logical basis and reasoning behind your disagreements.

   b. Discuss your paper in class and share it with other class members.

   c. Refine your paper after discussing it in class, and send a copy to the textbook author.

2. Each of these statements describes a situation in which a teacher crafts an assessment procedure. Read each statement and decide whether a violation of professional responsibility

has occurred. After deciding, write an explanation justifying your decision. Discuss your findings with other members of your class.

  a. Mrs. Jones schedules a short quiz in social studies every Friday. She announces this at the beginning of the semester, and every student is aware that this will occur. She jots down the questions on Friday mornings before class and photocopies them to give out during class. She has never taken a course in assessment, nor has she ever read a book on how to improve assessments.

  b. Mr. Smith teaches biology and often uses test items with pictures, graphs, and charts. He often photocopies these from textbooks, magazines, and reference materials that the students do not have. He has not sought permission to use these reproductions from their publishers.

  c. Mr. Roberts teaches science. There is a deaf student in his class. When a test is scheduled, he gives a copy of the test a few days ahead of schedule to the student's sign language interpreter, who simplifies the language of the questions but keeps the technical or scientific terminology. When other students are sitting for the test, the deaf student is in another room being administered the test by the student's sign language interpreter, who interprets the questions to the student.

  d. Ms. Adams teaches literature. She gives an essay test in which students have to interpret the actions of various characters in Shakespeare's plays. When the essays are distributed to students, several ask how they will be marked and whether their own opinions would be counted against them if these opinions were different from Ms. Adams's. Ms. Adams had not thought about scoring the essays, so she tells the students, "Just do your best and don't worry about it."

  e. Mr. Williams teaches history. His tests always have a section in which students have to identify the contributions of several historical persons related to the unit he taught. His questions in this section over the entire term referred exclusively to white males. Women's and minority persons' contributions were mentioned in class, but never appeared on the test.

3. Each of these statements describes a situation in which a teacher chooses or helps to choose an assessment procedure the teacher did not develop. Read each statement and decide whether a violation of professional responsibility has occurred. After deciding, write an explanation justifying your decision. Discuss your findings with other members of your class.

  a. Mr. Smith teaches biology. His teacher's guide comes with a printed multiple-choice test covering the materials in the chapter he just taught. He gives the test to the office secretary for duplication a few days ahead of schedule. On the day he is to give the test, he goes over it to make an answer key. He discovers that out of 40 items, 10 cover material he either did not cover or did not thoroughly teach. He spends the first 15 minutes of class teaching these concepts, then gives the test. All 40 items count toward students' grades.

  b. Mr. Williams teaches history. The authors of the textbook provide multiple-choice unit tests. One of the students brings the test home after the results are returned.

The student's father goes over it and notices that for 5 of the 40 items, his son's answers are correct according to the information in the textbook but were marked wrong by Mr. Williams. He writes a note to Mr. Williams describing the situation and citing the textbook pages to support his claim. Mr. Williams writes back saying the test was written by the textbook authors and is published, so it would be absurd to question the items' correctness. He refuses to reconsider the items or rescore the papers.

  c. Mrs. Harrington teaches mathematics and is very impressed with suggestions in teacher's magazines and journals for using performance tasks. She knows nothing about constructing performance tasks or how to construct scoring rubrics for them. She goes to the library and locates several performance tasks that are suitable for the level of students she teaches. The tasks do not have scoring rubrics, nor are they linked to the school's curriculum guides. Nevertheless, they are interesting activities for the students, and she uses them instead of her usual tests as a basis for grading students. She has no guidelines or scoring rubrics, so she just uses her judgment to mark the students' performances as A, B, C, D, or F.

4. Each of these statements describes a situation in which a teacher administers an assessment. Read each statement and decide whether a violation of professional responsibility has occurred. After deciding, write an explanation justifying your decision. Discuss your findings with other members of your class.

  a. Mrs. Connolly's class is neither well motivated nor attentive. She constantly reminds them, "You better settle down and study. I'm giving you a tough exam, and you will flunk if you don't pay attention."

  b. Mr. Gordon likes to give "pop" quizzes or surprise quizzes to keep his students "on their toes."

  c. Mr. Ortega stands next to students he thinks might cheat while taking the test. He talks while they take the test, saying such things as, "Keep your eyes on your own paper," and "Keep working, don't dawdle."

  d. Mrs. Stravinski believed that the standardized test she was requested to give in reading was too speeded. Consequently she gave the students an extra 10 minutes. She did not report this to anyone.

  e. Mr. Pollak knew that the state assessment was being given to his class in three weeks. He obtained a copy of the specific objectives it covered. He developed sample test items for each objective and drilled his students on these specific objectives and items. As a result his class did well on the assessment, but they did not finish some of the curriculum units the school district wanted taught at that grade level.

  f. Students in Mrs. Courtleigh's class asked her what they should concentrate on for their final exam. Mrs. Courtleigh said, "Well, we covered Chapters 4, 5, and 6 of the book. And we did some independent readings. The exam will cover all those."

  g. During the test, a student asked Mr. Devon to explain the meaning of a question he had put on the test but which the student found ambiguous. "Just do your best and stop asking for hints!" Mr. Devon said, not leaving his desk at the front of the room.

5. Each of these statements describes a situation in which a teacher scores an assessment. Read each statement and decide whether a violation of professional responsibility has occurred. After deciding, write an explanation justifying your decision. Discuss your findings with other members of your class.

a. Mrs. Appleton is an itinerant teacher of the hearing-impaired who assists with the education of mainstreamed students at Mountain View High School. Billy David is a senior deaf student to whom she administers a standardized achievement test battery using an appropriate signed language. She knows that Billy's results will be sent to postsecondary schools for deaf students, and that they will use the results as part of the admission decision. When scoring the test by hand, she noticed that Billy's scores were unexpectedly low. She reviewed the questions he missed and said to herself, "I know he really knows the answers to these." So she changed his answers to about 25 percent of the questions to give him a higher score. She rationalized her actions by thinking, "He really is a good student, and if I simply sent in the scores he got he would not be given the chance I know he deserves."

b. Mr. Pennel gives essay questions and performance tasks as a major part of his assessment. He seldom bothers with developing scoring rubrics because he doesn't know how to do so and they take time to develop. He'd rather spend the time teaching.

c. Three students in Mrs. Carver's class are real troublemakers. They seem to do their best to annoy her. When she marks their papers, she unconsciously marks theirs more stringently than the others.

d. Mrs. Dingle marks the assessments of John and Robert. They both receive the same score, which is right on the borderline between an A and a B. She gives John an A and Robert a B. The boys are friends and they compare papers, discovering the different grades for the same score. John goes to Mrs. Dingle and tells her that Robert deserves the A. Mrs. Dingle says, "John, everyone knows that you are an A student, while Robert is a B student. My grades just reflect this fact so I won't change his grade."

e. Mr. Edwards gave his midterm exam three weeks ago but has not gotten around to marking it and returning the results to the students.

f. Mrs. Faulkner gave a multiple-choice test consisting of 45 items. She had it scored by the school's scanner. She reported the raw score to the students at the next class along with their grades. She refused to give students their answer sheets, to go over the test questions, or to help the students understand what they got wrong.

g. When Blake came to Ms. Porter to complain that he deserved a better mark on his project, Ms. Porter said, "I gave you what you deserved. Don't try to weasel points out of me!" She never went over the paper with him.

h. Professor Markson submitted the final grades for his course and left on his summer vacation the next day. He threw away the exam papers and never told the students how they performed on the final.

i. A student discovered that Mrs. Owens added the semester marks together incorrectly, and that her grade should be a B instead of a C+. She approached Mrs. Owens after the semester reports were sent home to make her aware of her error. Mrs. Owens said, "Well, I'm sorry, but it's too late to change the grade. I submitted it already and it is in the computer system."

6. Each of these statements describes a situation in which a teacher is involved in interpreting and communicating the results of an assessment. Read each statement and decide whether a violation has occurred. After deciding, write an explanation justifying your decision. Discuss your findings with other members of your class.

a. Mr. Carlson said, "Billy, I told you to study! Now you failed this test and it's your own fault."

b. Mrs. Dawson and Mr. Edwards chat in the teachers' lounge about Shannon. They discuss her performance in their respective classes, her personal life at home, and her behavior with Billy in the school cafeteria and corridors. Their conversation does not focus on educational strategies to help Shannon, and several other teachers who happen to be in the lounge at that time overhear it.

c. Mary's mother is concerned about her daughter's standardized test scores and comes to see Mr. Jason. He tells her, "Don't worry! Mary's normalized standard scores show a large differential from her previous performance, and her grade equivalents are well within the range expected by the standard error of measurement of the battery."

d. Mrs. Kenny knows Sandra's parents will punish her when she does poorly on her class assignments and assessments. She makes arrangements to meet with the parents to go over Sandra's work during the last two marking periods. She shows them Sandra's progress and explains how she works hard to achieve. She discusses with the parents their expectations for Sandra and offers suggestions for how their expectations could be met by encouraging and rewarding Sandra's progress to date.

7. What definition(s) of assessment bias is (are) implied by each of the following statements? Justify your classification and share your findings with other members of your class.

a. "This performance assessment is biased because it requires doing work outside of school, and the students from wealthier families have more resources to help them do it well."

b. "This performance task is biased because it requires females to be familiar with automobiles and airplanes, something they are unlikely to be in this community."

c. "This performance assessment is biased because, overall, students from African American families do better on it than students from white families."

d. "This assessment is biased because on Tasks 3 and 7 boys score higher than girls at every ability level."

e. "This assessment is biased because all the pictorial material shows white males in professional roles but females and minorities in passive and subservient roles."

f. "This portfolio assessment is biased because the male teacher favors boys' responses that agree with his positions on controversial matters."

Suggestions for Additional Reading

Fischer, R. J. (1994). The Americans with Disabilities Act: Implications for measurement. *Educational Measurement: Issues and Practice, 13*(4), 17–26, 37.

Phillips, S. E. (1994). High-stakes testing accommodations: Validity versus disabled rights. *Applied Measurement in Education, 1*, 93–120.

Both articles discuss the implications of recent federal legislation for accommodating persons with disabilities in standardized testing programs. Fischer's article limits itself to the Americans with Disabilities Act. Phillips' article is broader discussing implications of other legislation and the results of several court cases (case law).

Langenfeld, T. E., & Crocker, L. M. (1994). The evaluation of validity theory: Public school testing, the courts, and incompatible interpretations. *Educational Assessment, 2*, 149–165.

Mehrens, W. A., & Popham, W. J. (1992). How to evaluate the legal defensibility of high-stakes tests. *Applied Measurement in Education, 5*, 265–283.

These articles review federal legislation and case law in relation to what test developers need to do to assure tests are legally defensible, especially for high-stakes decisions.

Schmeiser, C. B. (1992). Ethical codes in the professions. *Educational Measurement: Issues and Practice, 11*(4), 5–11.

The professional codes of 35 professional organizations are analyzed to identify common areas of ethical responsibility. The author discusses the implications of these common areas for persons developing and using educational measurements.

Willingham, W. W. (1989). Standard testing conditions and standard score meaning for handicapped examinees. *Applied Measurement in Education, 2*, 93–103.

Summarizes a 4-year series of studies on the comparability of SAT and GRE scores administered under nonstandard conditions. The findings show that standard and nonstandard administrations resulted in comparable psychometric properties.

Ysseldyke, J. E., & Thurlow, M. L. (Eds.). (1993). *Views on inclusion and testing accommodations for students with disabilities.* (Synthesis Report 7). Minneapolis: National Center on Educational Outcomes, The College of Education, University of Minnesota.

A collection of seven short papers that discuss whether students with disabilities should participate in large-scale assessments at the state and national levels and how testing conditions could be modified to include them.

PART II

Crafting and Using Classroom Assessments

CHAPTER 6

Planning for Integrating Assessment and Instruction

Learning Targets

After studying this chapter, you should be able to:

1. Describe several ways in which learning to craft assessment tools can improve your teaching. [1, 2]

2. Describe and give examples of common formative and summative uses of assessment results. [4, 1, 3]

3. Craft a formative and summative assessment plan for a marking period and for one instructional unit. [1, 2, 4]

4. Explain how to integrate assessment and instruction through an assessment plan. [1, 2, 4]

5. Use a taxonomy of cognitive learning targets to plan oral questions for lessons. [1, 2, 5]

6. Use a preinstruction framework to craft an instrument for assessing students prior to teaching a unit in your area. [2, 1]

7. Craft a blueprint for a summative assessment instrument for a unit in your area. [2, 1]

8. Explain the major decisions you make when crafting your summative assessment instrument. [2, 1]

9. Apply the validity criteria from Chapter 3 to the classroom assessment instrument described by your blueprint. [2, 1, 3, 7]

10. State the advantages and disadvantages of commonly used formative and summative assessment techniques. [4, 1, 3]

11. Describe the potential validity of using the results from each of the common assessment techniques. [4, 1, 3, 6]

12. Explain why no single assessment technique should be used for all classroom decisions. [1, 3, 6, 7]

13. Explain how each of the terms and concepts found at the end of this chapter may be applied to the creation of plans for assessment and instruction in your classroom. [6]

THE SEAMLESS FABRIC OF ASSESSMENT AND INSTRUCTION

Good Teaching Decisions Are Based on High-Quality Information

You are familiar with the need to develop lesson plans for teaching. You need high-quality information to make such basic lesson-planning decisions as: (1) what content and thinking skills your students should study next, (2) how your students' studies might best be carried out, (3) when a student has mastered specific skills and thinking processes, (4) when students have mastered larger bodies of content and skills (such as those found in one unit or one chapter of a textbook), (5) when students have achieved major learning targets (such as the ability to prepare a certain kind of report, conduct a particular kind of investigation, or achieve a certain level of performance), and (6) when it is necessary for students to review past learning or work on integrating previous knowledge and skill into new knowledge structures and skill complexes (Lindvall & Nitko, 1975).

You can't teach in a vacuum. To make teaching decisions effectively, you must use valid and reliable assessment results. You obtain quality information from carefully crafted assessment procedures. You can see that assessment and teaching are intertwined: They are part of the seamless fabric of instruction and learning.

Valid Interpretation Requires Careful Planning

Using assessment results validly is a challenging professional activity that you should not take for granted. It is easy for you *not* to meet this challenge. All you need to do is avoid assessing students' abilities to solve new problems, to think critically, to organize new information, and to produce new ideas. In fact, several research studies (Fleming & Chambers, 1983; Stiggins, Conklin, & Associates, 1992) demonstrate that *many teacher-made assessments are dominated by tasks requiring students to use only lower-level thinking skills* such as simple recall and literal comprehension. To correct this practice, you need to know the range of thinking skills your students should learn and how to organize your teaching and assessments around them. In Part One of this book, we discussed these thinking skills and their relation to interpreting and using assessment results validly. In this chapter we turn to planning strategies for implementing assessment of thinking skills.

Benefits of Crafting Quality Assessments

Good teaching and good assessment go hand in hand. You can expect the following benefits to your teaching as you improve assessment-crafting skills.

1. *Knowing how to choose or to craft quality assessments increases the quality of your teaching decisions.* By assessing how your students use their knowledge and skills, you are able to monitor and evaluate their progress. This allows you to plan better teaching.

2. *What and how you assess communicates in a powerful way what you really value in your students' learning.* For example, you may tell your students how important it is for them to be independent and critical thinkers, but your words are empty if your assessments consist of only a few matching exercises based on facts from the textbook or handouts. On the other hand, if your assessments require students to integrate their knowledge and skills to solve

"real-life" problems, they learn that you expect integrating and problem-solving abilities.

3. *When you carefully define and craft assessment tasks, you are defining more precisely what you want students to learn.* When you craft assessment tasks, you learn how to create situations in which students can demonstrate their achievement. These skills apply directly to your teaching, because to teach effectively you must have clearly in mind how students should perform their achievement.

4. *You may use your knowledge of how to craft quality assessment tasks when you evaluate assessment materials available from other sources.* Your knowledge of the craft will also help you to evaluate and become a critical consumer of assessment procedures, whether they are part of your curriculum materials or are imposed by or on your school district, such as standardized achievement tests and state-mandated assessments.

5. *Learning to craft assessment tasks increases your freedom to design lessons* (Stiggins, Rubel, & Quellmalz, 1986). Knowing how to assess students validly, especially in relation to higher-order thinking skills, means that you are no longer chained to the assessment procedures already prepared by textbook publishers and others. You can use a wider variety of teaching materials because you are able to craft assessment procedures on your own.

6. *You will improve the validity of your interpretations and uses of assessment results.* Research studies show that teachers who have studied assessment, either through coursework or in-service training, are able to recognize and produce better assessments (Boothroyd, McMorris, & Pruzek, 1992; Plake, Impara, & Fager, 1993).

7. *You will improve your appreciation of the strengths and limitations of each type of assessment procedure.* As a professional, you are required to have the knowledge and skill to independently evaluate proposed assessment approaches. You must evaluate their general educational value *and* their technical ability to make good on the promises implied by their promoters. To fulfill your professional responsibility, you need a solid foundation in the basic principles of assessment development and in the criteria for valid use of the assessment results.

ARE YOU ASSESSING FOR FORMATIVE OR SUMMATIVE PURPOSES?

A major point to keep in mind when planning is whether you are assessing for *formative* or *summative* purposes. We introduced these concepts in Chapter 1. In this chapter we discuss how to apply them to assessment planning. Table 6.1 shows common uses for classroom assessment results. The uses are organized into three groups: formative, summative,

TABLE 6.1 Examples of basic purposes for which classroom assessment results are used.

I. <u>Formative uses</u> help teachers to monitor or guide student learning while it is still in progress.

    A. <u>Sizing-up uses</u> help a teacher to form initial impressions of students' strengths, weaknesses, learning characteristics, and personalities at the beginning of the year or course.

    B. <u>Diagnosing individual students' learning needs</u> helps a teacher to identify what the student has learned and what still needs to be learned, as well as to decide how instruction needs to be adapted to the students.

    C. <u>Diagnosing the group's learning needs</u> helps a teacher to identify how the class as a whole has progressed in its learning, what might need to be reinforced or retaught, and when the group is ready to move on to new learning.

    D. <u>Planning instruction uses</u> help a teacher to design and implement appropriate learning and instruction activities, to decide what content to include or emphasize, and to organize and manage the classroom as a learning environment.

II. <u>Summative uses</u> help a teacher to evaluate student learning after teaching one or more units of a course of study.

    A. <u>Assigning grades for report cards</u> is a way in which a teacher records evaluations of each student's learning progress to communicate evaluations to students, their parents, and responsible educational authorities.

    B. <u>Placing students into remedial and advanced courses</u> are ways in which a teacher attempts to adapt instruction to individuals' needs when teaching is group-based. Students who do poorly in the teacher's class may be placed into remedial classes that provide either alternate or supplemental instruction that is more suitable for the students' current level of educational development. Similarly, students whose educational development in the subject is above that of the rest of the class may be placed into a higher level or more enriched class.

    C. <u>Evaluating one's own teaching</u> requires a teacher to review the learning that students have been able to demonstrate after the lessons are complete, to identify which lessons were successful with which students, and to formulate modifications in teaching strategies that will lead to improved student performance the next time the lessons are taught.

III. <u>Other uses</u> help in teaching generally but may not be directly linked to evaluating individuals.

    A. <u>Using assessment procedures as teaching tools</u> are ways in which a teacher uses the assessment process as a teaching strategy. For example, a teacher may give practice tests or "mock exams" to help students understand the types of tasks used on the assessment, to practice answering and recording answers in the desired way, or to improve the speed at which they respond. In some cases, the performance assessed is identical or nearly identical to the desired learning target so that "practicing the assessment" is akin to teaching the desired learning target.

    B. <u>Controlling students' behavior</u> is a use in which a teacher hopes to motivate students to study and learn by using performance on an assessment instrument as a vehicle for student accountability. The higher the stakes for the student in doing well on the assessment, the greater the incentive to "get a good grade" or "pass" the assessment. Some teachers believe that without such external rewards students will not study and learn the material.

    C. <u>Communicating achievement expectations to students</u> is a use in which a teacher helps to clarify for students exactly what they are expected to be able to perform when their learning is complete. This may be done by showing the actual assessment tasks or by reviewing the various levels or degrees of performance of previous students on specific assessment tasks so that current students may be clear about the level of learning expected of them.

and others. It is important to remember that you will need to plan for *both* formative and summative assessment.

Formative Uses of Assessment Results

Formative uses help you to guide or monitor student learning while it is still in progress. You use a variety of formal and informal assessment results to make formative decisions. In general, formative assessments are less formal. Although you may record the results of these assessments to help your memory, you do not use them to report official letter grades or achievement progress. (As you can see from the table, each of the formative uses helps you to plan what and how to teach.)

Sizing-Up Uses Typically, you use the most informal assessments for sizing-up purposes. **Sizing up** means to form a general impression of a student's strengths, weaknesses, learning characteristics, and personality at the beginning of a course or of the year. The following example illustrates how a teacher pulled together various informally obtained pieces of information to size up Joslyn, a fifth-grade student:

> Joslyn walks into class each day with a worried and tired look on her face. Praising her work, or even the smallest positive action, will crack a smile on her cheeks, though the impact is brief. She is inattentive, even during the exercises we do step by step as a class together. She is shy, but sometimes will ask for help, but before she gives herself a chance, she will put her head down on her desk and close her eyes. I don't know why she lacks motivation so severely. Possibly it's a chemical imbalance or maybe problems at home. She will probably be this way all year. (Airasian, 1991a, p. 37)

You can see that this teacher was using information about Joslyn's cognitive, affective, and psychomotor traits. The teacher's impression of Joslyn helps to form a general strategy for how to teach her and deal with her in class.

Other Formative Uses Typically, you make other formative decisions for which quality information is needed. These include diagnosing individual students' learning needs, diagnosing the group's learning needs, and planning instruction. Chapter 13 discusses diagnosis in detail. These decisions were also described in the first two chapters of this book. We mention them here to emphasize that in order for you to make these decisions correctly, you must use valid assessment information. The validity of your assessment results is increased, of course, when you have carefully planned the assessment.

Summative Uses of Assessment Results

Summative uses help you evaluate your students and your own teaching after you finish teaching one or more units. Often we use summative information about a student's achievement to count toward her grade for a marking period. The grades are used to report to parents and school authorities the progress students have made toward achieving the curriculum framework's learning targets. Often this reporting is done through a home report or a report card. Table 6.1 lists three examples of summative uses for assessment results. Because assigning grades is an important assessment use that all teachers must undertake, we devote Chapter 15 to that topic. However, in Chapter 3 (Table 3.1), we discussed how to improve the validity of results from an assessment you use for assigning grades. You may wish to review that table now. The

validity criteria will be helpful as you study in this chapter ways to select and plan assessments.

Other Uses

Table 6.1 lists three other uses for classroom assessment: as a teaching tool, to control students' behaviors, and to communicate what you expect students to know and perform. We will discuss these uses in Chapters 7 through 15. At this point, however, you should recognize that using assessments to control students' behaviors is a common and sometimes unethical practice. Controlling students through assessments turns a process of information gathering into a process of threatening and punishing. Using assessment results to intimidate or to punish students has negative consequences for their learning and self-esteem.

ASSESSMENT PLANNING FOR A MARKING PERIOD AND FOR ONE INSTRUCTIONAL UNIT

Plans for teaching and assessment should be developed together. The reason is simple: You need to align what and how you teach with what and how you assess. You teach so that students achieve certain learning targets; you assess those same learning targets to see whether students have, in fact, achieved them.

Keeping in mind that you need to plan for both formative and summative assessment, the next thing to consider is the time period for the plan. There are several levels of assessment planning: You may plan for a year, a semester, a marking period, a unit, or a lesson. Your plans for larger segments of your teaching will be less detailed than your plans for smaller segments.

Plans for a year or a semester set out the general approaches and strategies you shall use to teach and to assess. Such a plan contains an outline of the topics you will teach, the general learning targets your students will achieve, and the main strategies you will use to assess students.

Plans for a marking period usually apply to two or three units of instruction. A **unit of instruction** is a teaching sequence covering from one to seven weeks of lessons, depending on the students and topics you are teaching. You use plans for instructional units to break down and organize the larger curriculum into manageable teaching, learning, and assessment sequences. Planning for several units at one time allows for sequencing the units and for keeping your teaching and assessment approaches consistent. It also allows formative and summative assessment to be described.

Plans for only one unit will necessarily be more detailed. You will describe the specific content, concepts, procedures, terminology, and thinking skills your students will learn and use. You also describe your teaching activities and your students' learning activities. You identify the learning targets of the lessons. You also identify the specific formative and summative assessments you will use, and when you will use them.

The shortest term for planning is for one day or one lesson. As you teach, you will begin to reflect on what you have previously taught these students, and how well your students have achieved the unit's learning targets to date. This reflection is an opportunity for you to adjust your unit plan. Your teaching and assessment strategies become more fine-tuned. They become more adaptive to your students' abilities. Each day, you adjust your teaching as you gather new information about your students and your teaching.

This latter point illustrates that your teaching and assessment plans are not set in stone. They are guidelines for teaching and assessing. They are flexible and subject to change as new information about your students' achievement accumulates.

Example of an Assessment Plan for a Marking Period

To stimulate your thinking about assessment planning, let's look at a simple example. Because this is an assessment book we shall emphasize the assessment aspects of planning, but your planning will include instructional ties also. Suppose you were teaching middle-school science. Suppose, further, that you are planning for a nine-week marking period. Perhaps you plan to teach two units: one on the water cycle and one on weather and weather systems. For each unit you would outline the major points of content you will cover, the general sequence and timing of the units, and the learning targets your students will achieve from each unit. Your plan is beginning to take shape.

You need to plan more on the teaching side. You need to answer questions such as the following: What overall approach and strategy will you adopt? The water cycle and weather units are related; how will you make that clear to students? What kinds of learning activities will you need to create and use (e.g., creating a demonstration of condensation, cloud simulation, building a diorama of the water cycle, drawing weather maps, measuring variables related to weather such as wind speed and precipitation, collecting and reading weather maps, or conducting a weather prediction activity)?

How will you evaluate students' achievement of the learning targets? What are your general strategies for formative evaluation? Perhaps you plan for some in-class activities and exercises that will allow you to evaluate how well students are progressing. These also allow you to give students appropriate feedback. Perhaps you plan homework exercises. These allow you to evaluate whether students have mastered the basic concepts. Your thinking

should include planning for how often you assess. At what points in the lessons will homework or quizzes be appropriate, for example?

To provide formative feedback to students, you will have to mark and evaluate their work. Will you do all the marking? Will students' peers evaluate performance? If so, students will need evaluation criteria and scoring rubrics. When you use oral questioning, what levels of the taxonomy will you emphasize most?

Your summative evaluation strategy needs to be planned also. You have many options. You might use a paper-and-pencil test at the end of each unit. You might use a project for one unit and a performance activity for another. For example, students may collect weather data and use them to predict the weather. For some other subjects, term papers, independent investigations, or portfolios might prove useful for summative evaluation. The point is that you need to think ahead, so that you can evaluate students on what you taught them and on the learning targets they should achieve.

Included in the plan is the weighting of each component into the final grade: How much will the tests, homework, projects, etc. each count toward the grade? Will each count equally, or will some weigh more heavily than others? To be fair, you will need to tell students the answers to these questions in advance. (Grading students is an important topic; we devote Chapter 15 entirely to grading.)

Figure 6.1 shows an assessment plan that a hypothetical teacher created when teaching two science units. Although this plan is well organized and neatly typed, your own plan need not be so neat. It may be handwritten, put into your teaching folder, and used as a working document as you teach. The main points are that by planning, (1) you have decided ahead about when and how you will assess, (2) recorded this thinking so that you do not forget, and followed a systematic plan to achieve your assessment needs.

Example of an Assessment Plan for One Unit

Designing an assessment plan for one unit is a bit more detailed. You need to lay out the lesson sequences and the learning targets. Then you need to choose what methods of assessment you will use. Finally, you should identify why you need to use each type, how the assessments are related to the lessons, and what actions you will take once you have information about the students' achievement.

Figure 6.2 shows an example of an assessment plan for one of the science units in Figure 6.1. When you are studying Figure 6.2, keep in mind that I have recorded the thinking a teacher might use when deciding what assessments to conduct. Your own plan might not be so detailed, because the thinking remains in your head. The important points are that you can explain when and why you are using different assessment methods, that you match the assessment

FIGURE 6.1 A long-term plan for a marking period in which two elementary science units will be taught.

General Assessment Plan for a Nine-Week Marking Period

Unit 1. The Water Cycle

General learning target:	Understanding what the water cycle is, how it works, and how it helps living things. Ability to explain the water cycle and apply it to real life.
Time frame:	It will take two weeks to complete.
Formative assessment:	(a) Three homework assignments (taken from Chapter 8) (b) Condensation demonstrations (Group activity; I will ask students to explain what they are doing, how it relates to the water cycle, and how it relates to real life.) (c) Short quiz on the basic concepts at the end of Week 1
Summative assessment:	A written test at the end of the unit (short answers and an essay)
Weights:	(a) Homework 10% (b) Quiz 10% (c) End-of-unit test 80%

Unit 2. Weather Systems and Predicting Weather

General learning target:	Understanding basic weather patterns, their movements, and their influence on local climate. Ability to understand weather maps, weather forecasts; ability to collect weather data and use them to make simple predictions.
Time frame:	It will take seven weeks to complete.
Formative assessment:	(a) Seven homework assignments (taken from Chapter 8 and my own) (b) Seatwork on drawing a simple weather map with symbols (I will circulate among students and ask questions to check their understanding.) (c) Correct use of simple instruments to gather weather-related data. (I will have each student demonstrate each instrument's use and give them feedback when necessary.) (d) Collection of weather maps and forecasts (I will discuss with students what the maps and forecasts mean and be sure they understand them.) (e) Four quizzes on the major concepts and a performance activity (Week 1, Week 3, Week 4, and Week 5)
Summative assessment:	(a) Map drawing (I will provide weather information; students will draw corresponding maps independently. This will be Quiz 4.) (b) End-of-unit test (short answer, matching, map identification, essay question) (c) Independent investigation (Collect weather data for two weeks and make daily two-day weather predictions. I will structure this activity. It will be done toward the end of the unit.)
Weights:	(a) Homework 10% (b) Quizzes 10% (c) Independent investigation 30% (d) Map drawing 20% (e) End-of-unit test 30%

Marking Period Grade

Unit 1 marks count 30%
Unit 2 marks count 70%

methods with the learning target(s) for which they are appropriate, and that you can state what *teaching action* you will take once the information is gathered. *Assessments are useless if you do not take action when you see the results.*

In this example, notice that seven lessons are planned. Directly below each lesson is a brief statement of the lesson's main learning target. The various types or methods of assessment (pretest, observation, homework, quizzes, independent investigations, end-of-unit test) are listed in the leftmost column. Notice that as you go down the column, the purposes of assessment become more summative and the assessment procedure becomes more formal. The most summative purposes require the most formal and most carefully crafted assessments.

FIGURE 6.2 Example of an assessment activity plan for one unit of instruction.

	Assessment Techniques	Description of Assessment Purpose, Activity, and Follow-up Action (Use)						
More Formative in Nature	Pretest	About a week before beginning this unit, I will give a very brief pretest to get a sense of students' attitudes, experiences, knowledge, and belief about weather. (See Figure 6.3.) *Action:* I will use this information to help me develop discussions in class, to develop lessons that overcome students' misconceptions and fears about the weather, and to build on what students already know.						
		Lesson 1 Comprehending basic weather concepts	**Lesson 2** Distinguishing weather patterns and systems	**Lesson 3** Identifying local weather conditions and patterns	**Lesson 4** Using basic tools for measuring weather	**Lesson 5** Understanding and making weather maps	**Lesson 6** Collecting and recording local weather data	**Lesson 7** Using data to predict local weather
	Observation and oral questioning	In every lesson, I will observe students and ask questions during the lesson to assess how well they are responding to the material, how well they seem to understand the daily activities and assignments, and whether they have any misconceptions about the weather concepts we are studying. *Action:* I'll adjust my teaching if most of the class is having difficulty. If only a few are experiencing difficulty, I'll work with them individually, in small groups, or ask another student to teach the concept.						
	Homework	I will assign homework after every lesson. Homework activities will focus on observing and discovering real-world examples of the weather concepts we learn in class. Students will record their observations and write explanations of them using proper scientific language learned in the unit. *Action:* As I read students' homework responses, I will note for each student how accurately and fluently the student uses scientific language to discuss the weather. I will also evaluate their observational and recording skills. I will reteach those materials for which many students experience difficulty. If only a few are having difficulty, I will work with them individually.						
	Quizzes	**Quiz 1** (covers Lesson 1): Short-answer questions testing basic vocabulary *Action:* Students not mastering the basic concepts will be retaught.	**Quiz 2** (covers Lessons 2 and 3): Short-answer questions with some diagrams. Focuses on weather patterns: local, national, and international. *Action:* I will use this quiz to monitor students' understanding of weather patterns and systems. I'll reteach or move on, depending on the outcomes.		**Quiz 3** (covers Lesson 4): This will be a performance activity. I want to be sure each student can use with accuracy the weather-measuring tools and can record data properly. *Action:* I will correct errors on the spot.		**Quiz 4** (covers Lesson 5): I want students to read, interpret, and draw simple weather maps. I will give weather data to the students and ask them to draw an appropriate map using the weather data. I will also give maps already drawn and ask students to interpret them. *Action:* I will reteach if there are problems.	
	Independent investigation (performance assessment)				**Predicting the Weather** (begins after Lesson 4, and includes Lessons 5 and 6): This performance assessment will help me to evaluate whether students can apply the concepts from the lessons to the real world. It will help me to evaluate whether they can synthesize and use criteria to evaluate the data they collect. Students will collect and measure weather data, record it, and use it to predict the local weather for two days in advance. They will repeat the exercise every day for at least two weeks. They will work independently. They will prepare a report describing what they did and evaluating their investigation and its accuracy. *Action:* This is a type of summative evaluation. I will use the exercise to help me decide how well the students have learned the concepts and principles in this unit. I should have a pretty good idea whether students can apply what they learned in class.			
More Summative in Nature	End-of-unit test						**Unit Test** (covers all lessons): This will come at the end of all the lessons. It will be a paper-and-pencil test given in class. (I may give it over two days.) It will be comprehensive, covering most of the important learning targets in the unit.) *Action:* I will use the results of this test along with the results from homework, quizzes, drawing, and the independent investigation to assign a grade to the students for the unit. (Weights are given in Figure 6.1.)	

The statements written in the body of this figure describe the purpose, procedure, and usage of each assessment. Usage is described as **action**, meaning the things the teacher will do to improve students' achievement by using the assessment results. If the statements are spread across the page, that means that the assessment's purpose, procedure, and usage apply to all of the lessons. Statements that appear directly below one or two lessons mean that the assessment applies to only those one or two lessons. The quizzes, independent investigation, and end-of-unit test are of this character. Because the seven lessons are spread out in sequence over time, the plan shows that some assessments occur at different times throughout the unit. Study Figure 6.2 before reading further.

PRETESTING IN ORDER TO PLAN YOUR TEACHING

Notice in Figure 6.2 that the teacher gave a pretest about a week before teaching this unit. The pretest results were not used to evaluate students. Rather, they were used primarily to help the teacher understand the students' attitudes, knowledge, beliefs, and experiences about the weather so that the teacher could better teach the unit.

Importance of Preinstructional Unit Assessment

As you plan instruction for a unit, you must consider more than covering the material. In most subjects, students bring to the unit a complex combination of knowledge, experiences, skills, beliefs, and attitudes that are especially related to the topics to be taught. If you understand your students' thinking before teaching them, you can build your instruction on it.

Often students' beliefs about a topic are contrary to what you will teach. Even after you present the information, students' beliefs may not change. If students do not believe what you are teaching, new concepts are not integrated into their existing ways of thinking, they will be unable to apply that information in the future. For example, youngsters' experiences are that wearing sweaters keeps them warm. When teaching a science unit on insulating properties, you may teach that air has insulating properties. If you ask youngsters what happens to the temperature of a cold bottle of soft drink when you wrap it in a sweater, many may say it gets very warm. If you tell them it will stay cold, many will not believe you because they know sweaters keep them warm. Knowing this, your teaching will have to include learning activities that change students' beliefs by building on their prior experiences and knowledge. Your instruction will have to offer a real demonstration and comprehensive explanation–for example, why a sweater keeps the student warm *and* the soft drink cool–if that instruction is to alter their beliefs.

A Framework for Constructing Instruments

A **preinstruction unit assessment framework** is a plan you use to help you to assess cognitive and affective learning targets and themes of an upcoming unit. Preinstruction assessments should be relatively short, however, so focus your planning on only a few core elements. Do a written assessment so you can summarize the information and make your planning decisions using it. You could also organize a class discussion around the results.

It is especially helpful if you adopt a set framework and use it to generate assessment questions for every unit you teach. This establishes a comprehensive and consistent approach to gathering and using information. The framework in Figure 6.3 is useful to follow for several subject matters. It uses six categories of information. It was originally developed for middle-school science.

	Area Assessed	Example Question
1.	Students' attitudes about the topic.	"I think meteorology is *boring, interesting*, etc."
2.	Students' school experiences with the topics.	"Have you ever studied meteorology or the weather? When?"
3.	Students' knowledge of an explanatory model centrally important in the unit.	"Explain what makes it rain. Include a diagram if you wish."
4.	Students' awareness of common knowledge associated with the topic.	"Imagine you are a TV or radio weather announcer. Write a forecast for what the weather will be tomorrow."
5.	Students' knowledge of technical terms associated with the topic.	"Describe what each of these instruments does or is used for: barometer, thermometer, and weather vane."
6.	Students' personal experiences with some aspect of the topic.	"Describe your most unusual or scary experience involving weather."

FIGURE 6.3 Framework for crafting a written assessment of students' attitudes, knowledge, beliefs, and experiences about a topic.

Source: Adopted from *"Instructional Assessments: Lever for systemic change in science education classrooms."* by B. Gong, R. Venezky, and D. Mioduser, 1992, *Journal of Science Education and Technology, 1*(3), pp. 164–165. Adopted by permission of Plenum Publishing Corporation and the author.

Pretesting for Metacognition Skills

Some teachers have found it useful to pretest students' abilities to monitor and control their own thinking as they perform learning activities during the lessons (Tittle, 1989; Tittle, Hecht, & Moore, 1993). If students are aware that learning one thing is more difficult than another, if they are able to habitually check statements before accepting them as facts, or if they habitually plan their work before beginning it, they are using *metacognitive skills*. You may wish to assess these skills before teaching so you will have a better idea of how well your students are able to monitor and control their thinking about the assignments you will make during the unit. You may wish to integrate teaching some of the metacognitive skills into the unit. The details for doing this are presented in Appendix F.

CRAFTING A PLAN FOR ONE SUMMATIVE ASSESSMENT

This section focuses on one purpose for assessment: assigning grades to students. This is an important responsibility, and you should not base this action on only one test. Chapter 15 will discuss in great detail strategies and techniques for assigning grades. In this section, however, our focus is narrower—*how to develop a plan* for one formal

assessment instrument you will use for this summative purpose.

Organizing a Blueprint

Before crafting an instrument, you need to make a blueprint. The **blueprint** describes both the content the assessment should cover and the performance expected of the student in relation to that content. Some authors call the blueprint a *table of specifications*. The blueprint serves as a basis for setting the number of assessment tasks and for assuring that the assessment will have the desired emphasis and balance. Thus, the **elements of a complete test plan** include (1) content topics to assess, (2) types of thinking skills to assess, (3) specific learning targets to assess, and (4) emphasis (number of tasks or points) for each learning target to be assessed. Figure 6.4 illustrates such a blueprint for a science unit on forces.[1]

The row headings along the left margin list the major topics the assessment will cover. You can use a more detailed outline if you wish. The column headings across the top list the major classifications of Bloom et al. taxonomy of cognitive education objectives. You may use another taxonomy, described in more detail in Appendixes D and

[1]See Appendix G for examples of alternate procedures for test blueprints.

FIGURE 6.4 Example of a blueprint for summative assessment of a science unit.

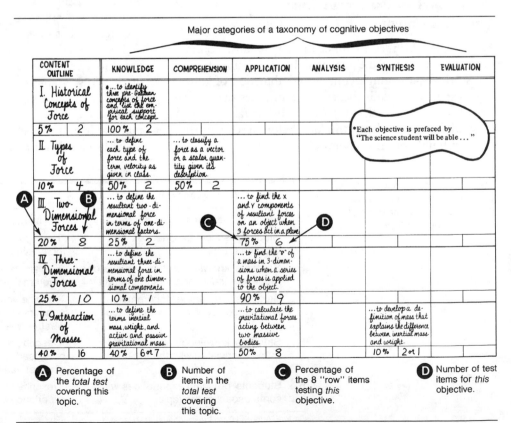

Source: Adapted from *Developing Classroom Tests* (p. 42) by W. J. Kryspin and J. F. Feldhusen, 1974, Minneapolis, MN: Burgess. Adapted by permission of Burgess International Group, Inc., Burgess Publishing, Minneapolis.

E, if you prefer. Notice that there is an increasing complexity from left to right in the types of performances implied by the column headings. Performances that demonstrate knowledge or comprehension, for example, are lower-level cognitive performances. Those reflecting the ability to synthesize or evaluate are higher-level cognitive performances.

The body of the blueprint lists the specific learning targets. The learning targets are thus doubly classified by both a content topic and a level of complexity of the taxonomic category. In this example, most of the learning targets are at the lower and middle levels of the taxonomy. For a different emphasis, you would use the blueprint to identify the cells in which to write other objectives to be assessed.

Rigorous Classification Is Unnecessary

It is difficult to classify learning objectives and items into the categories of some of the taxonomies. This approach to assessment planning is still useful, however. The purpose of formally laying out this two-way grid is not to promote exact or rigorous classification. Rather, it is a tool to help you recall the higher-order cognitive skills that need to be systematically taught and evaluated in the classroom.

Blueprint Specifies Assessment Emphasis

The numbers in the blueprint in Figure 6.4 describe the emphasis of the assessment, both in terms of percentage of the total number of tasks and in terms of the percentage of tasks within each row or content category. You decide how many tasks to include on an assessment after you consider (1) the importance of each learning target, (2) type of tasks, (3) content to be assessed, (4) what you emphasized in your teaching, and (5) amount of time available for assessment.

The following example illustrates how this is done. Suppose the teacher planned to use 40 test items for this unit. The blueprint shows that of these 40, the teacher decided that 20%, or 8 items, should be used to test instructional learning targets that deal with two-dimensional forces. Notice there are only two learning targets for this topic—one at the knowledge level and one at the application level. Of the 8 items, the teacher decided that 2 items (or 25% of 8) should deal with the knowledge-level learning target, and the remaining 6 items (or 75%) with the application-level learning target. Thus, with regard to the topic of two-dimensional forces, this unit assessment emphasizes the application learning target. Notice, too, that 63% (or 25 of the 40) of the *assessment questions* deal with the higher taxonomic levels of application and synthesis, even though there are many *learning targets* at the lower levels of the taxonomy. This example illustrates that the weighting or emphasis of an assessment instrument is related to the number of tasks or points included in a particular category, *not*

the number of learning targets. It reflects that some learning targets are more important for summative student evaluation than others.

Students will expect the various numbers of points on the assessment to correspond to the amount of time devoted to the material in class and to the emphasis they perceive you have placed on that material. If the assessment you are planning does not meet this expectation, it seems fair to notify the students of this fact well in advance of administering it.

This advanced planning for developing a summative classroom assessment allows you to view the assessment as a whole. In this way, you can maintain whatever balance or emphasis of content coverage and whatever complexity of performance you believe is necessary to match your teaching, and the assessment will not be too easy or too hard for your students.

Using the Blueprint to Improve Validity

A blueprint is an important tool to improve the validity of your instrument's results. The criteria for improving the validity of your results are listed in Table 3.1. Review that table at this time, and note that the blueprint is an excellent way to assure that many of the criteria for improving validity are met.

In addition to Table 3.1, you should also consult Table G.1 in Appendix G. This table is a checklist for judging the quality of the blueprint to your craft.

Craft Blueprints Over Time

The assessment-planning procedures described here are a lot of work. Given the many other responsibilities and activities competing for your time, you cannot always utilize them completely. Because the validity of the grading decisions you make is important, however, you need to use some type of systematic plan to develop unit assessments. But, you need not attempt to devise a formal plan for all units in one semester or year. If you develop a blueprint for a few units each year, after a few years most units will have blueprints. As the learning targets change, you can update these blueprints with less work than originally required. Also, several teachers could draft blueprints for different units in a subject and exchange them. Even if a colleague's blueprint has to be modified to suit your particular teaching approach, considerable timesaving is likely. When changes in the blueprints do occur, you should revise and redistribute the blueprints.

Simplified Specifications

The blueprint shown in Figure 6.4 is rather complete. It is possible to create other useful but less complete specifications. Examples of other types of blueprints are given in Appendix G.

BLUEPRINTS FOR STUDENT-CENTERED ASSESSMENT

As you can see, the assessment blueprint is a concise way to explain what is important for students to learn and to decide how much emphasis to give each learning target in students' summative evaluations. Blueprints are useful instructional tools, too, especially with students in junior and senior high school. Therefore, share your assessment blueprints with your students.

Ideally, you should do this sharing when you begin the unit. You should review and discuss the blueprint thoroughly with the students to assure they (1) have no misunderstandings, (2) understand the unit's emphasis, (3) understand what they will be held accountable for performing, and (4) see how the summative assessment is related to their overall grades. In Chapter 5 we discussed your professional responsibility to give students sufficient information when administering assessments. A blueprint is a very good way of proving this information for junior and senior high school students. Older students may offer suggestions for changing the emphasis or manner of assessment, thus more fully engaging in their own learning and evaluation. Students can write test questions for each blueprint cell. Use them for a practice test.

CRITERIA FOR IMPROVING THE VALIDITY OF SUMMATIVE ASSESSMENTS

By now you have an idea of the general process of developing a summative assessment plan. The steps required to move from initial assessment ideas to a draft of the assessment instrument are

1. Define the purpose for assessment at this time.
2. Use the blueprint to specify the performances and processes you wish to observe and assess.
3. Identify the tasks and other techniques you need to use.
4. Develop the initial drafts of these tasks and techniques.

So far, we have discussed the first two steps. The last step, developing the tasks and assessment exercises, is the subject of Chapters 7 through 14.

In this section, we emphasize some of the general criteria for evaluating your own planned assessment. These include (1) matching tasks to learning targets, (2) covering important skills, (3) selecting appropriate assessment task formats, (4) making assessments understandable, (5) satisfying validity criteria, (6) using the appropriate length of the assessment, (7) assuring equivalence, and (8) identifying appropriate complexity and difficulty of tasks.

The discussion in this section necessarily will be general, because we assume that you are not yet familiar with the technical aspects of assessment crafting. This section, however, will show how the knowledge you have already acquired through studying this book is integrated into the initial planning stages of crafting a classroom assessment. Table 6.2 summarizes the main points.

Matching Assessment Tasks to Learning Targets

Your teaching is most effective when your lesson plans, teaching activities, and learning targets are all aligned. All these should also be aligned with your state's curriculum framework and standards (see Chapter 2). Your assessment plans specify the important learning targets to be taught and assessed. It is most important, therefore, that the actual tasks students perform on the assessment match those learning targets. A very basic requirement for the validity of classroom assessment results is that the assessment procedures must be aligned with the learning targets.

The specific tasks must permit students to demonstrate that they have the skill or knowledge stated in the targets. For example, if a learning target calls for a student to actually build a model, write a poem, collect data, or perform a physical skill, the student will need to be administered a performance assessment. If your assessment task requires a student only to list the parts of a model, to analyze an existing poem, to summarize data already collected, or to describe the sequence of steps needed for performing the physical skill, it does not match these learning targets. The validity of your classroom assessment results is seriously reduced when even *some* of the tasks do not match the stated learning targets.

As an example, consider the ninth-grade social studies learning target stated here, and the three assessment tasks that follow it:

Learning target: Students will explain in their own words the meaning of the concept of *culture*.
Task 1. *Name three things that are important to the culture of indigenous Americans.*
Task 2. *Give a short talk to the class comparing three different cultures. In your talk, make sure you describe the similarities and differences among the cultures you have chosen.*
Task 3. *Write a paragraph telling in your own words what is meant by the term* **culture**.

Only Task 3 matches the stated learning target. Consider Task 1: The performance required applies to a specific cultural situation rather than to the general concept of culture as intended by the learning target. Task 1 should not be used for the assessment of this learning target. The performances required in Task 2 are to "compare" and to "describe" ("giving a talk" is only the way the

TABLE 6.2 Criteria and ways to improve the validity of your summative assessments.

Criteria to Use	Ways to Evaluate Your Assessment Plan
Align assessment tasks with curriculum, standards, and instruction	• Be sure you clearly understand the main intent of the learning target to be taught and assessed. • *Think:* What is the main intent of the learning target? Does the assessment task require a student to do exactly as the main intent requires? • Analyze the assessment task to identify which part(s) may not match the learning target. Eliminate or rewrite the non-matching parts.
Assess only important learning targets	• Review the learning targets taught and assessed; prioritize them from most to least important. Eliminate assessments matching low-priority learning targets. • Be sure your state's standards or learning expectations are assessed by one or more of your assessments. • Craft assessments that require students to demonstrate more than one high-priority learning target through the same task.
Use appropriate multiple assessment formats	• Become skilled in crafting many types of assessment formats. • Learn the strengths and limitations of each type of assessment format. • Analyze each learning target. *Think*: What are several different ways I can assess this achievement? How can I use two or more ways? • Analyze the assessment tasks to identify which parts may not match the learning target. Eliminate or rewrite the non-matching parts. • Plan for assessing each important learning target in two or more ways.
Make assessments understandable	• Be sure each assessment procedure has clear directions to the student, and that you have prepared students concerning each assessment. (See "Preparing Students for the Assessment" in Chapter 14.) • Learn to craft assessments well so they will satisfy the criteria and checklists in the tables contained in Chapters 7, 8, 9, 10, 11, 12, and 14. • Learn to craft scoring rubrics well so they will satisfy the criteria and checklists in the tables contained in Chapters 9 and 12.
Follow appropriate validity criteria	• Use the criteria described in Chapter 3, Table 3.1.
Use appropriate length of assessments	• Be sure all students who know the material can finish within the time limits. • Follow the suggestions for improving reliability given in Table 4.8. • Follow the guidelines in Table 6.2 until you have considerable experience with your students.
Assure equivalence across years	• Use blueprints from previous years to guide you in crafting this year's assessment blueprints. • Be sure to make the difficulty and complexity of this year's assessment tasks equivalent to last year's tasks.
Assure appropriate difficulty and complexity of assessment tasks	• Be sure the conditions and tools for students to use during the assessment are appropriate for the learning targets and the students' educational development. • Add appropriate accommodations for students with disabilities (see Table 5.2). • Follow the guidelines in Table 6.4.

student has to indicate she is describing similarities and differences among the cultures). Although these are worthwhile activities, they seem to go beyond the more limited scope and main intent of the learning target. Because this task does not match the learning target, it should not appear on the assessment either.

What should you do if you create or identify a "great" task that does not match the stated learning target? You have only three choices: Disregard the task, modify the task so it matches the learning target, or modify the learning target so it matches the task. Often, by crafting an excellent assessment task we further clarify a learning target: We see the full meaning of the learning target, which was not previously clear from its verbal statement. If this is the case, then you should modify the stated learning target so it more clearly expresses what you intend.

Be careful, however. If you have already communicated the assessment plan to students, you need to be sure that you do not "surprise" them with a more complex or difficult task than the type for which they are preparing themselves. Changing the rules in midstream is often unethical. Usually, it guarantees that you lose the respect of at least some of the students. Rather than completely discarding the task, you could either modify it to suit the stated learning target or save it until the next time you teach the unit. At that time you can more clearly specify the learning target.

Covering Only Important Learning Targets

We want to reinforce here that your summative assessment should cover only the important content and learning targets of the unit. Carefully planning the assessment assures this. Blueprints are the major vehicles for summarizing and evaluating your assessment plans.

Using Appropriate Multiple Assessment Task Formats

Many varieties of assessments are available. In the next section we describe the advantages and disadvantages of each. The most important consideration is the validity of your assessment results. In this section we are focusing on summative evaluation for purposes of grading. (Chapter 13 discusses formative evaluation.)

One of the criteria we discussed in Chapter 3 (Table 3.1) is to present students with multiple ways to demonstrate their competence. It usually improves the validity of your assessment results, therefore, if you use several task formats. Among the many specific **task formats** from which you can choose are

I. Paper-and-pencil formats
  A. Choice formats ("objective" items)
    1. True-false (Chapter 7)
    2. Multiple-choice (Chapters 8 and 10)
    3. Matching exercises (Chapter 8)
    4. Other formats (Chapter 8)
  B. Short-answer and completion format (Chapter 7)
  C. Essay format (Chapter 9)
    1. Restricted response
    2. Extended response
II. Performance formats (Chapters 11 and 12)
  A. Checklists
  B. Rating scales
  C. Sign and category systems
III. Long-term activity formats (Chapters 11 and 12)
  A. Projects
  B. Extended written assignments
  C. Laboratory exercises
  D. Portfolios
IV. Personal communication formats (Chapters 10 and 13)
  A. In-depth interviews, observation
  B. Oral questioning

On your summative instrument, try to use the mixture of formats that *most directly assess the intents* of the stated learning targets.

Making Assessments Understandable to Students

As you plan and craft your assessments, be conscious that you need to make clear to students how and when they will be assessed, what they will be required to do, and when and how they will be evaluated. Chapter 14 has a section called, "Prepare Students for the Assessment," which describes some of the information about your planned assessment that your students need to know. In addition to these, you will want to be sure the directions to students, the assessment tasks themselves (e.g., your test questions), and the scoring rubrics (e.g., criteria for full marks) are understandable to all students. Students who leave constructed-response questions unanswered on the National Assessment of Educational Progress may do so because they "couldn't figure out what the question was asking" (p. 9), "didn't really get the question" (p. 9), "thought it would take too long" (p. 9), or "didn't realize [I]…had to do both parts" (p. 10) (Jakwerth, Stancavage, and Reed, 1999). You can avoid such problems by being clear in how you write and explain your assessments to students and, in turn, being sure students understand before they begin.

Satisfying Appropriate Validity Criteria

The main criteria for judging the quality of your assessment are validity criteria. In Chapter 3, we discussed seven categories of validity criteria for classroom assessments: (1) content representativeness and relevance; (2) thinking processes and skills represented; (3) consistency with other assessments; (4) reliability and objectivity; (5) fairness to different types of students; (6) economy, efficiency, practicality, and instructional features; and (7) multiple assessment usage. The specific criteria are listed in Table 3.1. Review these criteria at this point in your reading, and use them to evaluate your assessment plans and products. Pay special attention during the planning stages using multiple assessment strategies. You will need to allow yourself time to craft these.

Using Appropriate Length of Assessment

As we discussed in Chapter 4, your assessment results should be reliable. The length of your assessment is one of the factors affecting reliability. Three major factors determine how long your assessment should be: (1) the amount of time you have available for assessment, (2) the educational development of the students, and (3) the level of reliability you wish the results to have. Assessments with more tasks are more reliable than shorter assessments. (See Table 4.8 for more suggestions on improving reliability.) Classroom assessments should be power assessments: That is, every student who has learned the material should have enough time to perform each task. Your experience with the subject matter and the students you teach will help you decide on how long to make the assessment.

As practical guidelines, use the time suggestions in Table 6.3 for students in junior and senior high school. In 40 minutes of assessment, for example, you can administer a test with a short essay and 15 to 20 complex multiple-choice items. Remember, however, to modify these time suggestions to suit your students as your experience deepens.

Assuring Equivalence

If the content of the units you are assessing has remained essentially the same since the last time you taught them, your summative assessment instruments on the two occasions should be equivalent. Building this semester's assessment instruments to last semester's blueprints increases the likelihood the two instruments will be equivalent. Using the blueprints will help you to assure that both years' assessments cover the same content and thinking skills and emphasize the same knowledge and skills. Equivalent instruments are fairer to students. **Equivalence** means that students past and present are required to know and perform tasks of similar (but not identical) complexity and difficulty to get the same grade. Of course, if you changed the content or learning targets of the unit, the blueprints and the assessment should change, too. Also, if your past assessments were "lousy," you should not perpetuate *them* from year to year.

Identifying Appropriate Complexity and Difficulty of Tasks

The tasks on your assessment should match the conditions stated in the learning targets. (See Chapter 2.) The complexity of a task is increased by altering the "givens" or conditions under which you expect the students to perform. For example, consider the difference in complexity when students are and are not allowed to use calculators to solve mathematics word problems, or when translating a French passage from memory versus using a dictionary and idiom list. Altering conditions can change the performance from the knowledge level to a higher level of a cognitive level of a taxonomy, such as application. (Review the need for appropriate accommodation in Chapter 5, Table 5.2.)

The percentage of students answering a task correctly is called the **item difficulty level**. The difficulty level is not a property of a task alone, but a function of three things: (1) the complexity of the task, (2) the ability of the students responding to it, and (3) the nature (or quality) of instruction preceding the task administration. The combination of these three factors causes the percentage of students correctly answering a task to be higher or lower. Also, when students *perceive* that an assessment task is too complicated or too difficult, they skip it. As a result, the percentage of students answering it correctly is lower.

When the purpose of an assessment is to make discriminations among the **relative achievement**[2] of students, then somewhat easier tasks are preferred, because difficult tasks tend to result in guesses and random responses on the part of most students. For assessments crafted to measure relative achievement, see the recommended difficulty levels in Table 6.4.

TABLE 6.3 Time requirements for certain assessment tasks.

Type of task	Approximate time per task (item)
True-false items	20–30 seconds
Multiple-choice (factual)	40–60 seconds
One-word fill-in	40–60 seconds
Multiple-choice (complex)	70–90 seconds
Matching (5 stems/6 choices)	2–4 minutes
Short-answer	2–4 minutes
Multiple-choice (w/calculations)	2–5 minutes
Word problems (simple arithmetic)	5–10 minutes
Short essays	15–20 minutes
Data analyses/graphing	15–25 minutes
Drawing models/labeling	20–30 minutes
Extended essays	35–50 minutes

[2]This means distinguishing who is the best, next best, etc. student, rather than deciding how much a given pupil has learned in an absolute sense (see Chapter 14).

TABLE 6.4 Recommended difficulty levels.

Type of Item	Recommended Difficulty Level
True-false	75–85% passing
Three-option multiple-choice	67–77% passing
Four-option multiple-choice	63–74% passing
Five-option multiple-choice	60–69% passing

The recommended difficulty level combines the traditional standards (Ebel, 1979) with Lord's (1953) recommendation. Perhaps the first to suggest that the difficulty level of an item should be above 50% and dependent on the number of choices allowed in an item was Lindquist (1936).

WHAT RANGE OF ASSESSMENT OPTIONS IS AVAILABLE?

Now that you have studied how to plan for assessing students, you realize that your assessment strategies should be chosen wisely. Whether you are assessing for summative or formative purposes, you have a wide range of options at your disposal. Which should you use? Before deciding, you need to know three things: (1) the learning targets students should achieve, (2) the purpose for which you want to use the assessment results, and (3) the advantages of an assessment technique for the specific purpose you have in mind. This section discusses the general advantages and disadvantages of the many assessment options available to you. In the next section, we shall evaluate the validity of each procedure for each classroom use listed in Table 6.1. Keep in mind that Chapters 7 through 14 discuss these assessment techniques in detail; here we present an overview.

Studies of classrooms have shown that teachers use many different sources of information to assess students' achievement (Stiggins et al., 1992). The beginning teacher should consider all assessment methods equally important. However, as you gain experience and teach in particular school settings, you may come to regard some of these methods as yielding more valid results than others when you use them for specific purposes.

The choice of assessment method is not at all a simple matter of "personal preference" or "personal taste." The assessment you use must be the most appropriate for assessing the learning targets you wish students to achieve. You must defend your choice(s) on the basis of the validity and reliability of the results. Part One of this book, and especially Chapters 3 and 4, discussed the criteria that you must apply to evaluate the quality of the results of each technique. These criteria allow you to make informed and appropriate choices among assessment methods. Remember, too, that results from a single assessment are not perfectly valid. Therefore, using several different methods is recommended.

Researchers have identified the most commonly used types of classroom assessment procedures (Airasian, 1991b; Stiggins et al., 1992). These are listed in Table 6.5

along with their advantages, their limitations, and brief suggestions for improved use. The techniques are grouped into two categories: formative assessment techniques and summative assessment techniques.

Formative Assessment Options

You choose from among formative assessment options when you are gathering information to help improve students' achievement of learning targets. This information guides and fine-tunes your thinking. It is information that you use, for the most part, to plan your next teaching activities and to diagnose the causes of students' learning difficulties. You must gather this information while you are still teaching the material and while students are still learning it. As a result, these are **informal assessment techniques**. That is, they occur spontaneously as you need information, and you rarely stop teaching to do the assessment. Table 6.5 summarizes eight categories of formative assessment options. The eight categories may be grouped into three groups, however, as described in the following paragraphs.

Oral Assessment Techniques You may gather information to improve students' learning without creating tests or other paper-and-pencil tasks. *Conversations with teachers* who have taught a student may give you insight into the student's background and which approaches have worked in the past. These conversations may also help as you size up the class at the beginning of the term. *Conversations with students* give you additional insight into their feelings, attitudes, interests, and motivations.

As you teach a lesson, you *question students* about the material. These questions should encourage students to think about the material and to reveal their understandings, including misconceptions. This will help you guide your teaching. Avoid the "recitation" type of questioning in which you seek short answers to your questions. This style of questioning provides little insight into students' thinking and, therefore, provides little formative information. Avoid the tendency to ignore or ask only simple questions of the shy and less verbal students (Brophy & Good, 1999).

A good way to plan your oral questioning is to use a thinking-skills taxonomy. In every lesson, be sure you ask several questions from the higher-order thinking categories of the taxonomy. For example, here are some questions a teacher might ask students who have been studying the short story as a literary form:

Knowledge	"Who was the main character in the last story we read?"
Comprehension	"What were some of the personal problems that the characters in this story had to solve?"
Application	"Are the characters' problems in any way similar to the problems you or

TABLE 6.5 Advantages, limitations, and pitfalls of alternative types of classroom assessment techniques.

Assessment Alternatives	Advantages for Teachers	Disadvantages for Teachers	Suggestions for Improved Use
		Formative Assessment Techniques	
1. Conversations and comments from other teachers	(a) Fast way to obtain certain types of background information about a student. (b) Permit colleagues to share experiences with specific students in other learning contexts, thereby broadening the perspective about the learners. (c) Permit attainment of information about a student's family, siblings, or peer problems that may be affecting the student's learning.	(a) Tend to reinforce stereotypes and biases toward a family or a social class. (b) Students' learning under another teacher or in another context may be quite unlike their learning in the current context. (c) Others' opinions are not objective, often based on incomplete information, personal life view, or personal theory of personality.	(a) Do not believe hearsay, rumors, biases of others. (b) Do not gossip or reveal private and confidential information about students. (c) Keep the conversation on a professional level, focused on facts rather than speculation and confidential so it is not overheard by others.
2. Casual conversations with students	(a) Provide relaxed, informal setting for obtaining information. (b) Students may reveal their attitudes and motivations toward learning that are not exhibited in class.	(a) A student's mind may not be focused on the learning target being assessed. (b) Inadequate sampling of students' knowledge; too few students assessed. (c) Inefficient: students' conversation may be irrelevant to assessing their achievement.	(a) Do not appear as an inquisitor, always probing students. (b) Be careful so as not to misperceive a student's attitude or a student's degree of understanding.
3. Questioning students during instruction	(a) Permits judgments about students' thinking and learning progress during the course of teaching; gives teachers immediate feedback. (b) Permits teachers to ask questions requiring higher-order thinking and elaborated responses. (c) Permits student-to-student interaction to be assessed. (d) Permits assessment of students' ability to discuss issues with others orally and in some depth.	(a) Some students cannot express themselves well in front of other students. (b) Requires education in how to ask proper questions and to plan for asking specific types of questions during the lesson. (c) Information obtained tends to be only a small sample of the learning outcomes and of the students in the class. (d) Some learning targets cannot be assessed by spontaneous and short oral responses; they require longer time frames in which students are free to think, create, and respond. (e) Records of students' responses are kept only in the teacher's mind, which may be unreliable.	(a) Be sure to ask questions of students who are reticent or slow to respond. Avoid focusing on verbally aggressive and pleasant "stars." (b) Wait 5–10 seconds for a student to respond before moving on to another. (c) Avoid limiting questions to those requiring facts or a definite correct answer, thereby narrowing the focus of the assessment inappropriately. (d) Do not punish students for failing to participate in class question sessions or inappropriately reward those verbally aggressive students who participate fully. (e) Remember that students' verbal and nonverbal behavior in class may not indicate their true attitudes/values.
4. Daily homework and seatwork	(a) Provide formative information about how learning is progressing. (b) Allow errors to be diagnosed and corrected. (c) Combine practice, reinforcement, and assessment.	(a) Tend to focus on narrow segments of learning rather than integrating large complexes of skills and knowledge. (b) Sample only a small variety of content and skills on any one assignment. (c) Assignment may not be complete or may be copied from others.	(a) Remember that this method assesses learning that is only in the formative stages. It may be inappropriate to assign summative letter grades from the results. (b) Failure to complete homework or completing it late is no reason to punish students by embarrassing them in front of others or by lowering their overall grade. Learning may be subsequently demonstrated through other assessments. (c) Do not inappropriately attribute poor test performance to the student not doing the homework. (d) Do not overemphasize the homework grade and overuse homework as a teaching strategy (e.g., using it as a primary teaching method).

TABLE 6.5 *(continued)*

	Advantages	Disadvantages	Suggestions
5. Teacher-made quizzes and tests	(a) Although primarily useful for summative evaluation, they may permit diagnosis of errors and faulty thinking. (b) Provide for students' written expression of knowledge.	(a) Require time to craft good tasks useful for diagnosis. (b) Focus exclusively on cognitive learning targets.	(a) Do not overemphasize lower level thinking skills. (b) Use open-ended or constructed response tasks to gain insight into a student's thinking processes and errors. (c) For better diagnosis of a student's thinking, use tasks that require students to apply and use their knowledge to "real-life" situations.
6. In-depth interviews of individual students	(a) Permit in-depth probing of students' understandings, thinking patterns, and problem-solving strategies. (b) Permit follow-up questions tailored to a student's responses and allow a student to elaborate answers. (c) Permit diagnosis of faulty thinking and errors in performances.	(a) Require a lot of time to complete. (b) Require keeping the rest of the class occupied while one student is being interviewed. (c) Require learning skills in effective educational achievement interviewing and diagnosis.	(a) If assessing students' thinking patterns, problem-solving strategies, etc., avoid prompting student toward a prescribed way of problem solving. (b) Some students need their self-confidence bolstered before they feel comfortable revealing their mistakes.
7. Growth and learning progress portfolios	(a) Allows large segments of a student's learning experiences to be reviewed. (b) Allows monitoring a student's growth and progress. (c) Communicates to students that growth and progress are more important than test results. (d) Allows student to participate in selecting and evaluating material to include in the portfolio. (e) Can become a focus of teaching and learning.	(a) Requires a long time to accumulate evidence of growth and progress. (b) Requires special effort to teach students how to use appropriate and realistic self-assessment techniques. (c) Requires high level knowledge of the subject matter to diagnose and guide students. (d) Requires the ability to recognize complex and subtle patterns of growth and progress in the subject. (e) Results tend to be inconsistent from teacher to teacher.	(a) Be very clear about the learning targets toward which you are monitoring progress. (b) Use a conceptual framework or learning progress model to guide your diagnosis and monitoring. (c) Coordinate portfolio development and assessment with other teachers. (d) Develop scoring rubrics to define standards and maintain consistency.
8. Attitude and values questionnaires	(a) Assess affective characteristics of students. (b) Knowing student's attitudes and values in relation to a specific topic or subject-matter may be useful in planning teaching. (c) May provide insights into students' motivations.	(a) The results are sensitive to the way questions are worded. Students may misinterpret, not understand, or react differently than the assessor intended. (b) Can be easily "faked" by older and testwise students.	(a) Remember that the way questions are worded significantly affects how students respond. (b) Remember that attitude questionnaire responses may change drastically from one occasion or context to another. (c) Remember that your personal theory of personality or personal value system may lead to incorrect interpretations of students' responses.

Summative Assessment Techniques

	Advantages	Disadvantages	Suggestions
1. Teacher-made tests and quizzes	(a) Can assess a wide range of content and cognitive skills. (b) Can be aligned with what was actually taught. (c) Use a variety of task formats. (d) Allow for assessment of written expression.	(a) Difficult to assess complex skills or ability to use combinations of skills. (b) Require time to create, edit, and produce good items. (c) Class period is often too short for a complete assessment. (d) Focus exclusively on cognitive outcomes.	(a) Do not overemphasize lower level thinking skills. (b) Do not overuse short-answer and response-choice items. (c) Craft task requiring students to apply knowledge to "real life."
2. Tasks focusing on procedures and processes	(a) Allow assessments of nonverbal as well as verbal responses. (b) Allow students to integrate several simple skills and knowledge to perform a complex, realistic task. (c) Allow for group and cooperative performance and assessment.	(a) Focus on a narrow range of content knowledge and cognitive skills. (b) Require great deal of time to properly formulate, administer, and rate. (c) May have low interrater reliability unless scoring rubrics are used.	(a) Investigate carefully the reason for student's failure to complete the task successfully. (b) Use a scoring rubric to increase the reliability and validity of results. (c) Do not confuse the evaluation of the process a student uses with the need to evaluate the correctness of the answers.

TABLE 6.5 *(continued)*

Assessment Alternatives	Advantages for Teachers	Disadvantages for Teachers	Suggestions for Improved Use
		Summative Assessment Techniques	
	(d) Allow assessment of steps used to complete an assignment.	(d) Results are often specific to the combination of student and task. Students' performance quality is not easily generalized across different content and tasks. (e) Tasks that students perceive as uninteresting, boring, or irrelevant do not elicit the students' best efforts.	(d) Allow sufficient time for students to adequately demonstrate the performance.
3. Projects and tasks focusing on products	(a) Same as 2(a), (b), and (c). (b) Permits several equally valid processes to be used to produce the product or complete the project. (c) Allows assessment of the quality of the product. (d) Allows longer time than class period to complete the tasks.	(a) Same as 2(a), (b), (c), (d), and (e). (b) Students may have unauthorized help outside of class to complete the product or project. (c) All students in the class must have the same opportunity to use all appropriate materials and tools in order for the assessment to be fair.	(a) Same as 2(a), (b), (c), and (d). (b) Give adequate instruction to students on the criteria that will be used to evaluate their work, the standards that will be applied, and how students can use these criteria and standards to monitor their own progress in completing the work. (c) Do not mistake the aesthetic appearance of the product for substance and thoughtfulness. (d) Do not punish tardiness in completing the project or product by lowering the student's grade.
4. Best work portfolios	(a) Allow large segments of a student's learning experience to be assessed. (b) May allow students to participate in the selection of the material to be included in the portfolio. (c) Allow either quantitative or qualitative assessment of the works in the portfolio. (d) Permit a much broader assessment of learning targets than tests.	(a) Require waiting a long time before reporting assessment results. (b) Students must be taught how to select work to include as well as how to present it effectively. (c) Teachers must learn to use a scoring rubric that assesses a wide variety of pieces of work. (d) Interrater reliability is low from teacher to teacher. (e) Requires high levels of subject-matter knowledge to evaluate students' work properly.	(a) Be very clear about the learning targets to be assessed to avoid confusion and invalid portfolio assessment results. (b) Teach a student to use appropriate criteria to choose the work to include. (c) Do not collect too much material to evaluate. (d) Coordinate portfolio development with other teachers. (e) Develop and use scoring rubrics to define standards and maintain consistency.
5. Textbook-supplied tests and quizzes	(a) Allows for assessment of written expression. (b) Already prepared, save teachers time. (c) Matches the content and sequence of the textbook or curricular materials.	(a) Often do not assess complex skills or ability to use combinations of skills. (b) Often do not match the emphases and presentations in class. (c) Focus on cognitive skills. (d) Class period is often too short for a complete assessment.	(a) Be skeptical that the items were made by professionals and are of high quality. (b) Carefully edit or rewrite the item to match what you have taught. (c) Remember that you are personally responsible for using a poor quality test. You must not appeal to the authority of the textbook.
6. Standardized achievement tests	(a) Assess a wide range of cognitive abilities and skills that cover a year's learning. (b) Assess content and skills common to many schools across the country. (c) Items developed and screened by professionals, resulting in only the best items being included. (d) Corroborate what teachers know about pupils; sometimes indicate unexpected results for specific students. (e) Provide norm-referenced information that permits evaluation of students' progress in relation to students nationwide. (f) Provide legitimate comparisons of a student's achievement in two or more curricular areas. (g) Provide growth scales so students' long-term educational development can be monitored. (h) Useful for curriculum evaluation.	(a) Focus exclusively on cognitive outcomes. (b) Often the emphasis on a particular test is different from the emphasis of a particular teacher. (c) Do not provide diagnostic information. (d) Results usually take too long to get back to teachers, so are not directly useful for instructional planning.	(a) Avoid narrowing your instruction to prepare students for these tests when administrators put pressure on teachers. (b) Do not use these tests to evaluate teachers. (c) Do not confuse the quality of the learning that did occur in the classroom with the results on standardized tests when interpreting them. (d) Educate parents about the tests' limited validity for assessing a student's learning potentials.

	someone you know have had? Tell us about that. (Don't use real names if you will embarrass the person.)"
Analysis	"What literary devices, style of writing, or 'writing trick' did the author use to help the reader really understand how the characters were feeling? Explain how this was done."
Synthesis	"So far this semester, we have read eight short stories. In each one, a character (sometimes two characters) wasn't able to solve his or her problem satisfactorily—even though each character tried to do so. Why is that? What do they all have in common that resulted in failure to solve their problems? What general problem-solving approach did all of these characters use that resulted in their failure?"
Evaluation	"What are three or four criteria that we can apply to all of the stories so we can compare and evaluate their literary quality?"

Paper-and-Pencil Assessment Techniques Each day you give students *seatwork* and *homework*. These **paper-and-pencil assessments** let students practice the learning targets and perhaps extend their learning beyond the specific material you taught. You should review the results of seatwork and homework not just for correctness, but for whether the work reveals students' errors or faulty thinking that needs correction. If a student is exhibiting a pattern of errors, the student may have a misconception or may be using a rule consistently but inappropriately. (See Chapter 14, especially Figure 14.1, for an example.)

You also periodically craft and administer short *quizzes* and *tests*. These check on the progress students are making toward achieving learning targets. Tests and exams tend to be somewhat formal and are more useful for summative evaluation of students than for formative evaluation. However, if you use open-ended response items and carefully review students' responses for insights into their thinking, you will be able to derive some diagnostic information from these techniques.

Portfolios and Alternative Techniques Other formative evaluation techniques are somewhat more labor intensive than the ones we have discussed so far. A **growth and learning-progress portfolio** is a selection of a sequence of a student's work that demonstrates a student's progress or development toward achieving the learning target(s). By containing "not-so-good works," "improved works," and "best works," it demonstrates progress and learning during the course.

Typically, both the teacher and the student decide what should be included in a portfolio. Further, students are usually asked to describe the work they included, why they selected it, what it demonstrates about their attaining the learning targets, and their affective reactions to the material and to their learning experiences. Because a portfolio is built up over time, it permits assessments to be more closely integrated with instruction than with some of the other techniques. These attributes are considered advantages of portfolios over "one-shot" assessment techniques because of the richness of information available for the teacher to use.

Growth and learning-progress portfolios are usually evaluated qualitatively, although rating scales are sometimes used. Evaluating the evidence qualitatively requires a significant amount of skill and knowledge about the nature of student learning and of the subject matter. The following excerpt from an evaluation of the language arts portfolio of an eighth-grade student illustrates both the richness of the information in the portfolio and the deep level of teacher knowledge required to evaluate it:

> Our experience is that growth is often manifested in qualitative changes in the writing—changes in the complexity of the problems that students undertake, which may involve losing control over other features of the writing like organization or mechanics. Take Gretchen . . . who included two pieces of expository response to literature in her portfolio. In one sense, the second piece is not as strong as the first—it is not well-organized or coherent—but it is a richer interpretation. Unlike the first piece, which simply compares two groups of characters from *Lord of the Flies* . . ., the second piece, on *Animal Farm*, has a thematic framework about the role of scapegoats that is played out with evidence from Gretchen's own personal experience, from the novel, and from a definition of the term acquired from another resource. A comparison of Gretchen's revisions in the two pieces shows a newly developed awareness of the need for elaboration and for evidence on particular points. (Moss, et al., 1992, p. 13)

You need to acquire knowledge and skill in crafting portfolios before you can use them effectively. There is a temptation for novice portfolio users to include nearly every scrap of a student's work in the portfolio and to omit imposing an organizational framework for the material. This makes the portfolio cumbersome and reduces its usefulness for assessing major trends in educational growth. Portfolios are discussed further in Chapters 11 and 12.

In addition to portfolios, you may conduct *interviews with individual students*. Interviews can give you additional insights into students' thinking and learning difficulties. These interviews are more effective if you organize them around key concepts or specific problem-solving tasks. For example, you could work with the student to create a mental map of the relevant concepts in a unit and discuss with the student how he believes the concepts to be related to one another. Concept map interviews are discussed in detail in Chapter 13. You may also administer a simple questionnaire to your class to gain insight into students' attitudes and values associated with the concepts you are about to teach. We saw this strategy being used in Figure 6.3.

Summative Assessment Options

Summative assessment techniques are used to formally assess whether students have achieved learning targets so you can report to students, parents, and school officials. Usually this results in a home report or a report card grade. Summative assessment techniques are usually more formal than formative assessment techniques. Keep in mind, however, that formative and summative are not always distinct. For example, after you teach a unit, you may give a summative unit test. However, you may find students who have not achieved the learning targets at the level they should. This will usually require you to reteach the students or provide remedial instruction. Because you have used the summative assessment to guide your teaching, it has provided formative assessment information.

Table 6.4 shows six categories of summative assessment options. We may group these into two groups: teacher-crafted techniques and external (extra-classroom) techniques.

Teacher-Crafted Techniques We have already mentioned *tests* and *quizzes*. These paper-and-pencil techniques may include open-ended questions (such as essays and other constructed-response formats), multiple-choice, true-false, and matching exercises. Chapters 7 through 10 discuss how to craft these formats.

But paper-and-pencil techniques are limited primarily to verbal expressions of knowledge. Students must read and respond to the assessment materials using some type of written response, ranging from simple marks and single words to complex and elaborated essays. Students' abilities to carry out actual experiments, to carry out library research, or to build a model, for example, are not assessed directly with paper-and-pencil techniques. Further, it is usually difficult for teachers to craft paper-and-pencil tasks that require students to apply knowledge and skills from several areas to solve real-life or "authentic" problems. Chapter 10 suggests crafting techniques that assess higher-order thinking skills.

Performance assessment techniques require students to physically carry out a complex, extended **process** (e.g., present an argument orally, play a musical piece, or climb a knotted rope) or produce an important **product** (e.g., write a poem, report on an experiment, or create a painting). The performances you assess should (1) be very close to the ultimate learning targets, (2) require students to use combinations of many different abilities and skills, and (3) require students to perform under "realistic conditions" (especially requiring extensive student self-pacing,

self-motivation, and self-evaluation). Some performance assessments require paper-and-pencil as a medium for expression (e.g., writing a research paper or a short story), but the emphasis in these performances is on the complexity of the product, and students are allowed appropriate time limits. This distinguishes such performance assessments from the short answers, decontextualized math problems, or brief (one class period) essay tasks found on typical paper-and-pencil assessments.

Because some performance assessments are very close to the ultimate learning targets of schooling, they may be used as instructional tools. For example, you may instruct a student on presenting arguments orally and require the student to perform the task several times over the course of the term. You might repeat the teaching-performance combination several times until the student has learned the technique to the degree of expertise appropriate to the student's level of educational development.

Principal disadvantages are that a great deal of time is required to craft appropriate tasks, to craft marking schemes or rating scales, to carry out the assessment itself, and to administer several tasks. The last point relates to the validity of interpreting student's results. Seldom may you generalize a student's performance on one task to the student's performance on another. That is, how well a student performs depends on the specific content and task to which the performance is linked (Baker, 1992; Linn, 1994). A student may write a good poem about the people in her neighborhood but an awful poem about the traffic in Los Angeles. How good is the student as a poet in such cases? Quality performance assessment requires you to have a very clear vision of an important learning target and a high level of skill to translate that vision into appropriate tasks and grading criteria (Arter & Stiggins, 1992).

Previously, we discussed the growth and learning-progress portfolio as a formative assessment tool. Portfolios may also be used for summative evaluation. The **best works portfolio** is a representative selection of a student's best products (productions), which provide evidence of the degree to which the student has achieved specified learning targets. In an art course it might be the student's best works in drawing, painting, sculpture, craftwork, and, perhaps, a medium chosen by the student. In mathematics it might include reports on mathematical investigations, examples of how the student applied mathematics to a real problem, writings about mathematics or mathematicians, and examples of how to use mathematics in social studies, English, and science. Best works portfolios focus on summative evaluation. To improve reliability of the evaluations of the portfolio, you need to craft a scoring rubric. You need also to share the rubric with students and to teach them how to select their best work in light of those rubrics. More details on portfolio assessments, including how to craft them, are given in Chapters 11 and 12.

External (Extra-Classroom) Techniques Two other techniques are often used by classroom teachers. One is the *quizzes and tests supplied by textbook publishers*. These are convenient because you don't have to craft them yourself, and they match the book you are using. The problem is that these assessment materials are often of *poor quality*: They do not match local learning targets very well, they tend to focus on low-level thinking skills, and the tasks are not professionally developed (i.e., they tend to be poorly crafted). As we mentioned in Chapter 5, you have a professional responsibility to improve these assessment materials before using them.

Standardized achievement tests also provide summative assessment information. Unlike textbook tests, these materials are usually very well crafted and supported by research on the validity of the scores. The tests consist of a battery of subtests, each covering a different curriculum area. Because the same group of students (norm group) took all subtests, the publisher's percentile norms allow you to compare a student's development in two or more curricular areas; and the publisher's score scales allow you to monitor a student's growth over time. Your own or your school district's tests cannot provide these types of information. A standardized test battery does not match your curriculum or your teaching goals exactly. Therefore, use it to assess broad goals (e.g., reading comprehension) rather than the specific learning targets in your classroom. Chapters 16 through 18 will help you understand this assessment option in more detail.

VALIDITY OF DIFFERENT CLASSROOM ASSESSMENT OPTIONS

Validity Principles to Guide Planning

Your classroom assessment plans must be focused on obtaining the most valid assessment results for your specific interpretations and uses. Because your assessments must match the purposes for which you need information, we summarized the most common classroom purposes in Table 6.1. This section discusses the relationship between these purposes and the validity of the results from assessment options in Table 6.4. This should help you to understand that *different assessment options are not equally valid for all purposes.*

Two important validity principles from Chapter 3 should guide your assessment plans. You should keep these principles to the forefront of your thinking, whether planning for a single assessment or multiple assessments:

1. Assessment results are valid only for specific interpretations and uses, not for all interpretations or uses.
2. Because no single assessment method gives results that are perfectly valid, more than one method should be used to assess the same achievement.

Potential Validity of Assessment Options

Because the validity of assessment results depends on the specific details of how you use them in your classroom, we cannot predict the validity you will actually attain if you use a specific option. However, we can offer some guidance. Table 6.6 shows the assessment uses and the assessment alternatives discussed previously. The table shows, for each combination of use and assessment option, the *potential* validity of using that option for that particular type of decision. For example, the table shows that the results from teacher-made tests and quizzes have the potential of being highly valid for such purposes as planning instruction and assigning grades. The results are moderately valid for sizing up students and placing them into remedial or advanced classes. Finally, the results have low validity for controlling student behavior.

Interpreting Validity Guides

As you develop your assessment plans, you should refer to Tables 6.5 and 6.6 for guidance as to what assessment options are appropriate. When interpreting Table 6.6, you should keep the following points in mind:

1. *Under certain conditions, your assessment results have validity quite different from those shown in the table.* The results in the table are general and can be thought of as estimates of potential validity. You could, for example, craft an exceptionally poor paper-and-pencil test that has very low validity for grading students, even though we show high validity in the table. In this case, your assessment option does not reach its potential.

2. *You must still apply the validity criteria described in Chapter 3 to the specific classroom assessment procedures you use.* Table 6.6 gives *general guidance*, but you still have a professional obligation to develop an argument for the validity of your assessment results yourself. (See Chapters 3 and 5 for further discussion of this point.)

3. *The estimates of potential validity displayed in Table 6.6 are the author's judgments and not the results from scientific experiments.* In making these judgments, I used personal knowledge of the assessment option and my experience of how very good, experienced teachers *typically* craft and use them. I also used my personal experience of the ways in which the purposes are *typically* carried out in classrooms. Finally, I applied to each combination of purpose and assessment method the criteria listed in Table 3.2 to *typical* instruments or procedures of that assessment type. I focused on *classroom use* rather than on external or accountability uses. Perhaps in the future someone will conduct more scientific studies of the validity of classroom assessment results for each decision, but as it stands now, such scientific evidence is weak or lacking. Therefore, I *believe*

TABLE 6.6 Potential validity of various assessment alternatives when they are used by teachers for various purposes.

Assessment alternatives	Various uses for the assessment results									
	Formative uses				Summative uses			Other uses		
	Sizing up	Diagnosing indi-vidual's needs	Diagnosing a group's needs	Planning instruc-tion	Assign-ing grades for report cards	Placing students into reme-dial or advanced classes	Evaluat-ing your own teaching	Assess-ment as a teach-ing tool	Control-ling students' behavior	Commu-nicating achieve-ment expecta-tions to students
Formative Assessment Techniques										
Comments from other teachers	L/M	L	L	L	L	L	L	L	L	L
Casual conversations with students	L	L	L	L	L	L	L	L	L	M/H
Questioning students during instruction	L	M	L	M	L/M	L	M	M	L	H/M
Daily homework and seatwork	M	H	H	H	H	L	L/M	M	L	H
Teacher-made quizzes and tests	H	H	H	H	H	M	H	H	L	L/M
Interviewing students individually	L	H	M	H	M	M	L/M	H	L	H
Growth and learning progress portfolios	L	M/H	L	L/M	L/M	L/M	M	M	L	L
Attitude and values questionnaires	M/H	M/L	L	M	L	L/M	L	L	L	L
Summative Assessment Techniques										
Teacher-made tests and quizzes	M	L/M	L/M	H	H	M	M	M	L	H
Tasks focusing on procedures and processes	L	L/M	L/M	H	H	L/M	M/H	H	L	H
Tasks focusing on products and projects	L	L/M	L/M	H	H	L/M	M/H	H	L	H
Best work portfolios	L	L	L	L/M	M/H	M/H	M	H	L	H
Textbook tests and quizzes	M	M	M	L	L/M	L/M	L/M	L	L	L/M
Standardized tests	M	L/M	M	L/M	L	H	L/M	L	L	L/M

Note: H = results tend to have *high validity* for the indicated purpose
M = results tend to have *moderate validity* for the indicated purpose
L = results tend to have *low validity* for the indicated purpose

125

the validities in Table 6.6 are what you can reasonably expect to attain if you acquire and apply the knowledge and skills outlined in this textbook.

4. *In Table 6.6 "high validity" does not mean perfect validity.* No single assessment instrument or assessment option has perfect validity.

5. *Combining for each student the results from several assessments with low or moderate validity will often result in a higher validity for the combination than for the individual components considered alone.* Although this is generally true, it may not be true in your case. For example, when combining grades from several assessments you may, for some strange reason, weight most heavily the assessment results with the poorest validity. This practice will lower the validity of the combination. Or perhaps each of the component assessment results you have used in your combination is so terrible that even the combined results are not valid for a particular purpose.

Summary

- High-quality assessment and high-quality instruction are part of the seamless fabric of high-quality teaching.
- The ability to craft and to interpret high-quality assessments improves your teaching because it:
  - Increases the validity of the information you use
  - Communicates to students your standards for performance
  - Helps you to more clearly define the learning targets
  - Helps you to evaluate assessment materials acquired from other sources
  - Increases your freedom to design the instruction plans you want
  - Improves the fairness of student assessment
  - Helps you to recognize the limitations of various types of assessment procedures
- Common classroom uses of assessment results are (see also Table 6.1):
  - *Formative uses*—Sizing up, diagnosing individual students' learning needs, diagnosing the group's learning needs, and planning instruction.
  - *Summative uses*—Assigning grades for report cards, placing students into remedial or advanced courses, and evaluating one's own teaching.
  - *Other uses*—Using assessment procedures as teaching tools, controlling students' behavior, and communicating achievement expectations to students.
- Planning for different timeframes was discussed. Examples of planning assessment for a marking period (Figure 6.1) and for an instructional unit (Figure 6.2) were given. These examples illustrated planning for both formative and summative assessment, including a wide range of assessment techniques, matching techniques with appropriate lessons and learning tar-

gets, and the use of assessment results to take action for improving students' learning.
- The importance of obtaining preinstruction assessment information for planning an instructional unit was discussed. A framework for planning and crafting such instruments was discussed. The framework suggests assessing students':
  - Attitudes about the topic
  - School experiences with the topic
  - Knowledge of an explanatory model centrally important in the unit
  - Awareness of common knowledge associated with the topic
  - Knowledge of technical terms associated with the topic
  - Personal experiences with some aspect of the topic
- The chapter described an assessment blueprint (or table of specifications) for a summative assessment:
  - How to organize the blueprint
  - How to use the blueprint to determine the content and skill emphasis of the assessment
  - How to use the blueprint as a teaching tool
- Several types of blueprints were described: two-way grids with learning targets, two-way grids without learning targets, lists of learning targets, and content outlines.
- When crafting your own classroom assessment procedure, you follow these steps:
  - Define the purpose for which you will use the assessment results.
  - Craft a blueprint to specify the learning targets and content you stress.
  - Identify the tasks and assessment options that match the blueprint.
  - Craft initial drafts of the tasks and options.
- General criteria for evaluating your planned assessment are
  - Matching assessment tasks to learning targets
  - Covering only important learning targets
  - Using appropriate multiple-task formats
  - Making assessments understandable to students
  - Satisfying appropriate validity criteria
  - Using appropriate length of the assessment
  - Assuring equivalence
  - Identifying appropriate complexity and difficulty of tasks
- Assessment options were described and the advantages, limitations, and suggestions for using them were discussed (see also Table 6.5):
  - *Formative assessment options*—Conversations and comments from other teachers, casual conversations with students, questioning students during instruction, daily homework and seatwork, teacher-made quizzes and tests, in-depth interviews of individual students, growth and learning-progress portfolios, and attitude and values questionnaires.

- *Summative assessment options*—Teacher-made tests and quizzes, tasks focusing on procedures and processes, tasks focusing on products and projects, best work portfolios, textbook-supplied tests and quizzes, and standardized achievement tests.
- All teachers are urged to learn the advantages and disadvantages of these assessment procedures before planning their assessment strategies.
- The validity results from each of these assessment options, for each of the common classroom purposes, were estimated (see Table 6.6), illustrating that:
  - No technique yields perfectly valid results for any one purpose.
  - Some options yield results with uniformly low validity for virtually all purposes.
  - Some options yield results with low validity for certain purposes and high validity for others.
  - A combination of assessments yields results with more validity.

Important Terms and Concepts

action
assessment planning
best works portfolio
blueprint (table of specifications, assessment plan)
criteria for judging a planned assessment
elements of a complete test plan
equivalence
evaluation skills
formative uses
growth and learning-progress portfolio
informal assessment techniques
item difficulty level
paper-and-pencil assessments
performance assessments
planning skills
preinstruction unit assessment framework
product vs. process assessment
relative achievement
sizing-up uses
summative uses
task (item)
task formats
unit of instruction

Exercises and Discussion Questions

1. List seven reasons why it is important for teachers to learn how to develop assessment tools.
2. Visit a classroom (if you are not an in-service teacher) or use your own teaching experience to answer the following:
   a. Identify one or more specific examples of each classroom assessment purpose described in Table 6.1.
   b. For each example, describe what assessment tools and information the teacher used to make that decision.
   c. Classify each tool or technique into one of the assessment-option categories shown in Table 6.5.
   d. Create a table with row and column headings similar to Table 6.6 to show which assessment tools were used for what purposes.
   e. Evaluate the validity of using the results of assessments for those decisions. Use the criteria listed in Table 3.1 to help your evaluation.
3. Visit a classroom, or look around your own classroom, and list all the instructional resources that provide assessment or assessment-like tools.
   a. Classify each as true-false, multiple-choice, matching, essay, short answer, completion, performance assessments, projects, portfolios, oral questioning strategies, observation strategies, or in-depth interviewing strategies.
   b. Which type(s) are dominant?
   c. Tally the thinking-skill levels each appears to assess. Which levels of thinking do the majority seem to assess?
   d. Judge the quality of each of these materials using the criteria in Table 3.1.
4. Form three to five groups in your testing and measurement course. Divide the assessment techniques and purposes listed in Table 6.5 among the groups. Within each group, use the criteria in Table 3.2 to determine if the group's judgment of the potential validity for each technique-decision combination is the same as that shown in Table 6.6. Discuss your group's results in the full class. Be prepared to justify your agreements and disagreements using validity criteria (from Chapter 3). If you disagree with Table 6.6, write to the author to explain why you disagree and how the table should be altered.
5. Select one or two units in your teaching area. Explain how you could use each of the assessment techniques listed in Table 6.5 to make one or more of the decision types listed in Table 6.1. Explain how you would implement each assessment technique. Use a concrete example in your explanation.
6. What is an assessment blueprint? What are its parts? What is the purpose of each part? How would you indicate on the blueprint the emphasis you would place on each learning target to be assessed?
7. How should you go about deciding: (a) the total number of tasks on the assessment and (b) the number of tasks needed to assess each learning target?
8. Select a unit in your area for which you might craft a summative assessment instrument. Develop a complete blueprint for this assessment, using Figure 6.4 as a model. Describe the kinds of tasks you would include, and explain how you would decide whether the tasks matched the learning targets. Estimate the amount of time it would take students to complete your assessment.
9. Should students be given an assessment blueprint as a learning and assessment preparation tool? Support your position using pedagogical principles.
10. Select a unit in your area for which it is appropriate to craft a preinstructional assessment, as described in Figure 6.3. Craft the assessment tool and share your results with others in the class.
11. Develop an assessment plan for a unit of instruction in your area. Using Figure 6.2 as a model, list lesson learning targets, types of assessment, purpose(s) of assessment, and actions to take using assessment results. Share your results with your classmates.

12. Develop an assessment plan for a marking period or a semester in an area you teach. Using Figure 6.1 as a model, include the time frame for the units, the formative and summative assessment strategies, and the weighting of the assessments within units and across units (i.e., for the entire time periods). Share your results with your classmates.

13. Select a learning activity in the area you teach (or plan to teach). Using the list of metacognitive skills in Appendix F, craft a 20-item questionnaire similar to the format used in Figure F.1. Be sure to include both positive and negative items for each skill area.

14. Explain how you could use the results of the questionnaire created in Question 13 to plan and guide your teaching of the learning activity that is the focus of that assessment.

Additional Readings

Gong, B., Venezky, R., & Mioduser, D. (1992). Instructional assessments: Level for systemic change in science education classrooms. *Journal of Science Education and Technology, 1,* 157–175.

Reports on a comprehensive effort to integrate assessment and instruction in science classes. Explains the use of the preinstruction unit assessment framework illustrated in Figure 6.3.

Marzano, R. J., Brandt, R. S., Hughes, C. S., Jones, B. F., Presseisan, B. Z., Rankin, S. C., & Suhor, C. (1988). *Dimensions of thinking: A framework for curriculum and instruction.* Alexandria, VA: Association for Supervision and Curriculum Development.

Chapter 2 (pp. 9–16) describes metacognition and suggests ways to teach metacognitive skills.

McConney, A., & Ayres, R. R. (1998). Assessing student teachers' assessments. *Journal of Teacher Education, 49,* 140–150.

This article provides six rating scales (rubrics) for evaluating how well student teachers have crafted their assessments. The criteria the authors use are similar to those stated in this chapter under the heading, "Criteria for Improving the Validity of Summative Assessments."

Moss, P. A., Beck, J. S., Ebbs, C., Matson, B., Muchmore, J., Steele, D., Taylor, C., & Herter, R. (1992). Portfolios, accountability, and an interpretive approach to validity. *Educational Measurement: Issues and Practice, 11,* 12–21.

Describes the use of portfolios in language arts instruction. Describes the rich but time-consuming procedures for evaluating portfolios. Illustrates the need for teacher training in the use of portfolio assessment.

Stiggins, R. J., Rubel, E., & Quellmalz, E. (1986). *Measuring thinking skills in the classroom.* Washington, DC: National Education Association.

This brief pamphlet describes the assessment planning chart in detail, gives suggestions for the types of questions to ask at each thinking skill level, and provides examples of charts for science, social studies, and English.

Tittle, C. K. (1989). Validity: Whose construct is it in the teaching and learning context? *Educational Measurement: Issues and Practice, 8*(1), 5–13, 34.

Tittle, C. K., Hecht, D., & Moore, P. (1993). Assessment theory and research for classrooms: From taxonomies to constructing meaning in context. *Educational Measurement: Issues and Practice, 12*(4), 13–19.

These two articles describe a framework for using assessments of metacognitive skills for instructional planning.

CHAPTER 7

Completion, Constructed-Response, and True-False Items

Learning Targets

After studying this chapter, you should be able to:

1. State the three fundamental principles for crafting assessments and explain how they apply to your own classroom situation. [2, 4]

2. Name and give examples of the major variations of short-answer assessment tasks. [2, 1]

3. State the lower- and higher-order abilities that can be assessed by completion items. [2, 1, 3]

4. Explain the strengths and shortcomings of short-answer and completion items as they apply to assessing students in the area(s) you teach. [2, 4, 3]

5. Construct short-answer and completion items in the area(s) you teach that are free from commonly encountered item-writing flaws. [2]

6. Use the checklist for judging the quality of short-answer and completion items to identify and correct flawed items of your own creation and those that are provided with instructional materials. [2, 1]

7. Name and give examples of the six major variations of true-false assessment tasks. [2, 1]

8. State the lower- and higher-order abilities that can be assessed by the varieties of true-false items. [2, 1, 1]

9. Explain the strengths and shortcomings of true-false items as they apply to assessing students in your teaching area(s). [2, 4, 3]

10. Discuss the validity of assessment results obtained from short-answer, completion, and true-false tests and quizzes in your teaching area(s). [3, 4, 5]

11. Explain the roles of blind and informed guessing on true-false tests. [6]

12. List five suggestions for how to begin writing true-false items that are free from the frequently voiced criticisms. [2, 1]

13. Construct various types of true-false items that are free from commonly encountered item-writing flaws. [2]

14. Use the checklist for judging the quality of true-false items to identify and correct flawed items of your own creation and those that are provided with instructional materials in your teaching area(s). [2, 1]

15. Explain the strengths and shortcomings of multiple true-false items as they apply to your teaching area(s). [2, 4, 3]

16. Explain how each of the terms and concepts listed at the end of this chapter apply to educational assessments. [6]

KNOWLEDGE AND SKILLS TO IMPLEMENT ASSESSMENT PLANS

Assessment planning, described in Chapter 6, does not create an assessment procedure: You need to implement your plans effectively. You may have great plans but lack the knowledge and skills needed to create a great assessment. Despite your best intentions, if you lack knowledge and skill you will likely craft assessments that yield results having poor validity.

Beginning with this chapter, we discuss how to craft high-quality assessments. Chapters 7 through 9 focus on the basic principles for crafting items for paper-and-pencil tests and quizzes. In Chapter 10 we consider more advanced forms of assessment: items assessing complex skills, problem solving, and higher-order thinking. We discuss performance and portfolio assessment in Chapters 11 and 12. Informal observation and diagnostic assessment are discussed in Chapter 13.

In this chapter, we discuss simple forms of test items: completion, short-answer, and true-false items. These simple formats are easy to construct and, if you follow the few simple guidelines in this chapter, quite valid for assessing a wide range of lower-order and some higher-order thinking skills.

Before we begin studying the item formats themselves, let's look at the three fundamental assessment-crafting principles. You should commit these basic principles to memory because they are the foundation for the specific suggestions and guidelines in the remainder of this book. These three principles are the key points you should keep in mind no matter what type of assessment—paper-and-pencil or not—you are crafting or evaluating.

THREE FUNDAMENTAL PRINCIPLES FOR CRAFTING ASSESSMENTS

When you craft a classroom assessment, you will want it to follow a few very basic rules: the **three fundamental principles for crafting assessments**. First, you will want the assessment to *focus on the important learning targets*. It is a waste of time to assess whether students have learned trivial performances or minor points of content. Limit the assessment tasks to those that focus on only educationally important learning targets.

A second fundamental principle is that assessment tasks should be crafted so they *elicit from students only the knowledge and performances relevant to the learning target being assessed*. To do this, you need to have a very clear idea of what the learning target is. If a student has achieved the desired degree of learning, the student should complete the relevant task correctly. If, on the other hand, a student has not achieved the desired degree of learning, the deficiency should also be apparent in the assessment results.

Sometimes, however, teachers craft tasks so poorly that the tasks elicit unwanted behaviors from students such as bluffing, fear, wild guessing, craftiness, or test-wise skills. *Test-wiseness* is the ability to use assessment-taking strategies, clues from poorly written items, and experiences in taking assessments to improve one's score beyond what you would otherwise attain from mastery of the subject matter itself. (Test-wiseness is described in more detail in Chapter 14.) These extra, unwanted behaviors may lead you to evaluate a student incorrectly. For example, you may conclude that a truly knowledgeable student did not achieve the learning target; or, conversely, that a poorly prepared student did achieve the target. Many of the suggestions in the next several chapters are specific ways to help you apply the second principle.

A third companion principle is that the tasks that appear on an assessment should *neither prevent nor inhibit a student's ability to demonstrate that he has achieved the learning targets*. Imprecise wording in a question, for example, may make an item so ambiguous that a student who has the knowledge may answer it wrong. Similarly, simple matters such as inappropriate vocabulary, poorly worded directions, or poorly drawn diagrams may lead an otherwise knowledgeable student to respond incorrectly. Even the format or arrangement of an item on the page can inhibit some students from responding correctly. The third principle is amplified and applied to each format discussed in this and the subsequent chapters.

Although not all assessment experts would agree that there are only three basic principles, most are likely to agree that these three are the important and fundamental principles for constructing classroom assessment tasks. We could present a long list of principles common to the development of many types of assessment procedures, but a short list is easier to remember and apply as you craft assessments. These three encompass most of the specific suggestions made over the years for crafting assessment tasks except, perhaps, those practical suggestions for efficient scoring. The three principles are summarized in Table 7.1 so that you can use them as a checklist or rephrase them as questions to review each assessment task you develop.

TABLE 7.1 Three fundamental principles for crafting assessments.

Craft each assessment task to:

1. Focus entirely on an important learning target (content and performance).

2. Elicit from students only the knowledge and performance that are relevant to the learning target.

3. Neither prevent nor inhibit a student's ability to demonstrate attainment of the learning target.

SHORT-ANSWER AND COMPLETION ITEMS[1]

Varieties of Short-Answer Formats

Short-answer items require a student to respond to each item with a word, short phrase, number, or symbol. Three generic types are usually distinguished: question, completion, and association (Odell, 1928; Wesman, 1971). The **question variety** asks a direct question. The **completion variety** requires a student to add words to complete an incomplete statement. The **association variety** consists of a list of terms or a picture for which students have to recall numbers, labels, symbols, or other terms. Figure 7.1 gives some examples.

Usefulness of Short-Answer Items

Abilities Assessed It seems obvious that short-answer items can assess students' performance of lower-order thinking skills such as recall and comprehension of information. The short-answer format also can be used to assess higher-level abilities such as the following (Gronlund, 1976):

1. Ability to make simple interpretations of data and applications of rules (e.g., counting the number of sylla-

[1]Whenever we refer specifically to paper-and-pencil assessment tasks, we shall use the terms *item* and *test item*.

bles in a word, demonstrating knowledge of place value in a number system, identifying the parts of an organism or apparatus in a picture, applying the definition of an isosceles triangle).

2. Ability to solve numerical problems in science and mathematics.

3. Ability to manipulate mathematical symbols and balance mathematical and chemical equations.

Examples of short-answer items are given in Table 7.2. As you will see in other chapters, multiple-choice and other objective items can also assess these abilities.

Strengths and Shortcomings The short-answer and completion formats are popular because they are relatively easy to construct and can be scored objectively. But short-answer items, while frequently scored more objectively than essay items, are not free of subjectivity. You cannot anticipate all possible responses students will make. Therefore, you often have to make subjective judgments as to the correctness of what the students wrote. Spelling errors, grammatical errors, and legibility tend to complicate the scoring process further. For example, to the question, "What is the name of the author of *Alice in Wonderland*?" students may respond Carroll Lewis, Louis Carroll, Charles Dodgson, Lutwidge Dodgson, or Lewis Carroll Dodgson. Which, if any, should be considered correct? Although subjective judgment is proper, it does slow down the scoring process. It also tends to lower the reliability of the obtained scores.

Another advantage of the short-answer format is that students have a low probability of getting the answer correct by random guessing. A student who guesses randomly on a true-false item has a 50-50 chance of guessing correctly; on a four-option multiple-choice item, the student has one chance in four of randomly guessing the correct answer. For most short-answer items, however, the probability of randomly guessing the correct answer is zero. Short-answer items do not prevent students from *attempting* to guess the answer—they only lower the probability of guessing correctly.

In principle, guessing can be distinguished from using one's partial knowledge to help formulate an answer. Partial knowledge can lead a student to select the correct answer to a multiple-choice item, but it is less likely to result in the (exact) correct answer in short-answer items. Teachers, however, often give **partial credit** for responses judged to be partially correct. This is an appropriate practice and can result in more reliable scores if you use a scoring key. A **scoring key** shows the kinds of answers that are to receive each point of partial credit. Using such a scoring key makes your assignment of partial credit more consistent from student to student, improving reliability.

FIGURE 7.1 Sample short-answer items of each variety.

Question Variety

1.	What is the capital city of Pennsylvania?	*(Harrisburg)*
2.	What is the Greek letter commonly used as a symbol for the standard deviation?	*(σ)*
3.	How many microns make up one millimeter?	*(1,000)*

Completion Variety

1.	The capital city of Pennsylvania is	*(Harrisburg)*
2.	$4 + (6 \div 2) =$	*(7)*

Identification or Association Variety

On the blank next to the name of each chemical element, write the symbol used for it.

Element	Symbol
Barium	*(Ba)*
Calcium	*(Ca)*
Chlorine	*(Cl)*
Potassium	*(K)*
Zinc	*(Zn)*

TABLE 7.2 Examples of short-answer items assessing different types of lower-order thinking skills.

	Examples of Generic Questions*	Example of Actual Questions
Knowledge of terminology	What is a ___ ? What does _____ mean? Define the meaning of _____ ?	What is a *level*?
Knowledge of specific facts	Who did _____ ? When did _____ ? Why did _____ happen? Name the causes of _____ .	What is the title of the person who heads the executive branch of government?
Knowledge of conventions	What are _____ usually called? Where are _____ usually found? What is the proper way to _____ ? Who usually _____ ?	What are magnetic poles usually named?
Knowledge of trends and sequences	In what order does _____ happen? Name the stages in _____ . After _____ , what happens next? Over the last _____ years, what has happened to _____ ? List the causes of the _____ .	Write the life cycle stages of the moth in their correct order. 1st _____, 2nd _____, 3rd _____, 4th _____
Knowledge of classifications and categories	To what group do _____ belong? In what category would you classify _____ ? Which _____ does not belong with the others? List the advantages and disadvantages of _____ .	Mars, Earth, Jupiter, and Venus are all _____.
Knowledge of criteria	By what criteria would you judge _____ ? What standards should _____ meet? How do you know if _____ is of high quality?	What is the main criterion against which an organization such as Greenpeace would judge the voting record of a congressman?
Knowledge of methods, principles, techniques	How do you test for _____ ? When ___ increases, what happens to _____ ? What should you do to _____ to get the _____ effect?	Today the sun's rays are more oblique to Centerville than they were 4 months ago. How does Centerville's temperature today compare with its temperature 4 months ago?
Comprehension	Write ___ in your own words. Explain _____ in your own words. Draw a simple diagram to show _____	What do these two lines from Shakespeare's Sonnet XV mean? "When I consider everything that grows, Holds in perfection but a little moment . . . "
Simple interpretations	Identify the _____ in the _____ . How many _____ are shown below? Label _____ . What is the _____ in _____ ?	In the blank, write the adjective in each phrase below. *Phrase* 1. A beautiful girl _____ 2. A mouse is a rodent _____ 3. John found the muddy river _____
Solving numerical problems	(Problem statements or figures to calculate would be placed here.) Use the data above to find the _____ .	Draw a graph to show John's activities between 2:00 p.m. and 2:45 p.m. • John left home at 2:00 p.m. • John ran from 2:00 p.m. to 2:15 p.m. • John walked from 2:15 p.m. to 2:30 p.m. • John sat from 2:30 p.m. to 2:45 p.m.
Manipulating symbols, equations	Balance these equations. Derive the formula for _____ . Show that _____ equals _____ . Factor the expressions below.	Balance this equation ___ Cu + ___ H$_2$SO$_4$ = ___ CuSO$_4$ + ___ H$_2$O + SO$_2$

*The "blanks" in the generic items are for you to fill in. The generic items are simply suggestions to get you started. You generate your own items suitable for testing your students.

Crafting Short-Answer and Completion Items

Short-answer and completion items are easy to construct. You must pay attention, however, to a few simple principles. Table 7.3 summarizes these principles in the form of yes-no questions. Use this table as a checklist to review the items you put on your test. A no answer to any *one* question in Table 7.3 is sufficient reason for you *not* to put the item on the test until you correct the flaw. The principles are really applications of the three fundamental principles for crafting assessments. In the following

TABLE 7.3 A checklist for judging the quality of short-answer and completion items.

1.	Does the item assess an important aspect of the unit's instructional targets?	Yes	No
2.	Does the item match your assessment plan in terms of performance, emphasis, and number of points?	Yes	No
3.	If possible, is the item written in question form?	Yes	No
4.	Is the item worded clearly so the answer is a brief phrase, single word, or single number?	Yes	No
5.	Is the blank or answer space toward the end of the sentence?	Yes	No
6.	Is the statement paraphrased rather than copied verbatim from learning materials?	Yes	No
7.	Is the word omitted in a completion item an important word rather than a trivial word?	Yes	No
8.	Are there only one or two blanks?	Yes	No
9.	Is the blank in this item: (a) the same length as the blanks in other items; (b) if appropriate, arranged in a column?	Yes	No
10.	If appropriate, does the item (or directions) state the degree of detail, specificity, precision, or units you want the answer to have?	Yes	No
11.	Does the item avoid grammatical (and other irrelevant) clues to the correct answer?	Yes	No

Note: Revise any item for which you answered "no" to one or more questions.
Source: Based on ideas from: Ebel, 1951, 1979; Greene, Jorgensen, & Gerberich, 1942; Gronlund, 1976; Hopkins, Stanley, & Hopkins, 1990; Lindvall & Nitko, 1975; Mehrens & Lehmann, 1991; Nitko & Hsu, 1987; Odell, 1928; Sax, 1974; Stalnaker, 1951; Thorndike & Hagen, 1977.

paragraphs, we examine in more detail the principles in Table 7.3.

1 and 2. Importance of what is assessed, and matches to the test blueprint. We have already discussed why you should assess only important performance and content and match tasks to your learning targets and the assessment plan. Even if you perform no other evaluation of your assessment, you should make it a habit to evaluate every test item using these two criteria.

3. Use the question form. Essentially, a completion item asks a question: The student must read the incomplete sentence and mentally convert it to a question before answering. Therefore, *the most straightforward thing to do is ask a direct question* in the first place. If you scrutinize most completion items, you will see that they could be phrased as questions.

Further, the meaning of the items is often clearer if you phrase them as questions instead of incomplete sentences. Consider the examples in Figure 7.2. Because the first version is not written in a question format, many correct answers are possible, including "a story writer," "a mathematician," "an Englishman," and "buried in 1898." The second version phrases the statement as a question, **focusing the item** on the specific knowledge sought.

As with all such rules, this one does have exceptions. Occasionally the question form of the item incorrectly communicates that a longer or more complex answer is required. In this case, the incomplete sentence serves

better. The first version in the examples in Figure 7.3 implies that the teacher wants a paragraph or more. However, the teacher really had a very simple response in mind. This miscommunication is corrected by the second, revised version of the item. Most of the time, however, the question format produces better items. Your first impulse, therefore, should be to *write questions, not incomplete sentences.*

4. Word the items specifically and clearly. Usually, short-answer items require a single correct answer. You should word the question or incomplete sentence so this is clear to the student. Consider the examples in Figure 7.4.

FIGURE 7.2 Sample of improving a completion item by converting it to a direct question.

Poor:	The author of Alice in Wonderland was _____.
Better:	What is the pen name of the author of *Alice in Wonderland*?
	(Lewis Carroll)

FIGURE 7.3 Example of how the question-form of an item may imply a longer than necessary answer.

Poor:	Why are scoring guides recommended for use with essay tests?
Better:	The main reason for using a scoring guide with an essay test is to increase the (*objectivity*) of the scoring.

Several answers are possible to the first version depending on the degree of specificity desired: "Western Pennsylvania," "southwestern corner of Pennsylvania," "Ohio River," "Monongahela and Allegheny Rivers," etc. If you want a specific answer, you must phrase the question in a focused and structured way. If you want to focus on the rivers, for example, the first rephrased version may be used. To focus on the city, use the second rephrased version.

Focusing the item is important because you want a certain answer. Some students who know the desired answer will not give it because they misinterpreted the question. This is especially likely for students at the elementary levels who interpret questions rather literally. For example, in one classroom, fourth graders were given a bar graph to interpret. The teacher then asked the poorly phrased question in Figure 7.5. One hapless student examined the graph and responded, yes. We'll leave the revision of this item to you.

5. *Put the blank toward the end of the sentence.* If blanks are placed at the beginning or in the middle of the sentence, the student has to *mentally rearrange* the item as a question before the student can respond to it. Even a knowledgeable student will have to read the item twice to answer it. Consider the examples in Figure 7.6.

Teachers of elementary-level arithmetic recognize that the skill in solving missing addend problems (e.g., "5 + _____ = 12" or "_____ + 5 = 12") is quite difficult to learn. When blanks are not placed at the end of a sentence, the verbal item functions like these arithmetic problems. Unlike missing addend problems, however, putting blanks at the beginning of a sentence places an *unintended barrier* in the path of a youngster who has command of the relevant knowledge that violates principle 3 of Table 7.1. Elementary students are sometimes observed stopping and puzzling at a blank without reading the entire item: They realize that they should write an answer there, but they lack the experience to read ahead and mentally rearrange the item as a question. If you rephrase the item as a direct question or place the blank at the end, these youngsters are able to display the knowledge they have acquired.

6. *Avoid copying statements verbatim.* When you copy material, you encourage students' rote memorization rather than their comprehension and understanding. Further, textbook statements used as test items are usually quoted out of context. This may lead to item ambiguity or to more than one correct answer. One suggestion is to first think of the answer and then make up a question to which that answer is the only correct response (Ebel, 1979).

7. *Omit important words.* A completion item should require a student to respond to important aspects of knowledge and not to trivial words. Use the item to assess a student's knowledge of an important fact or concept. This means that you should not make the blanks the verbs in the statement unless the item is a language usage item that focuses on the correct verb form (Thorndike, Cunningham, Thorndike, & Hagen, 1991).

8. *One or two blanks.* With more than one or two blanks, a sentence usually becomes unintelligible or ambiguous so that several unintended answers could be considered correct. Figure 7.7 illustrates this point.

9. *Attend to length and arrangement of blanks.* Test-wise students sometimes treat the length of the blank as a clue to the answer. To avoid such unintended clues, keep all blanks the same length. When testing older students, you may save yourself considerable scoring time by using short blanks in the item and by placing spaces for students to record answers at the right or left margin of the paper or on a separate answer sheet. You can lay a **strip key** with the correct answers along the edge of each student's paper and score papers quickly. Typing the items so that all blanks occur in a column accomplishes the same purpose. For example, instead of spreading the items across the page, you can arrange them as in Figure 7.8.

FIGURE 7.4 Example of wording that communicates that a single, specific answer is required.

Poor:	Where is Pittsburgh, Pennsylvania, located? _____
Better:	Pittsburgh, Pennsylvania, is located at the confluence of what two rivers?
	(Allegheny and Monongahela)
	What city is located at the confluence of the Allegheny and Monongahela rivers?
	(Pittsburgh, Pennsylvania)

FIGURE 7.5 Example of an item elementary students easily misinterpret.

Poor:	Was the population greater in 1941 or 1951? _____

FIGURE 7.6 Example of improving an item by putting the blank at end.

Poor:	_____ is the name of the capital city of Illinois.
Better:	The name of the capital city of Illinois is *(Springfield).*

FIGURE 7.7 Example of an item with too many blanks.

Poor:	_____ and _____ are two methods of scoring _____.
Better:	Two different methods of scoring essay tests are the *(analytic)* and *(holistic)* methods.

FIGURE 7.8 Sample placement of blanks.

Poor: Decisions for which rejection of some students is permitted are called _____ decisions.

Decisions for which every student must be assigned to one of several educational programs are called _____.

Better: Which type of decision permits rejection of some students? _____

Which type of decision requires that every student be assigned to one of several educational programs? _____

FIGURE 7.9 Examples of stating the degree of precision expected in the answers.

Poor: If each letter to be mailed weighs $1\frac{1}{8}$ oz., how much will 10 letters weigh? _____

Better: If each letter to be mailed weighs $1\frac{1}{8}$ oz., how much (to the nearest whole oz.) will 10 letters weigh?
(11 oz.)

Better: A kilogram is equal to ___(2.2)___ pounds. (Express your answer to one decimal place.)

FIGURE 7.10 Sample items with and without clues.

Poor: A specialist in urban planning is called an ___(urbanist)___.

Better: A specialist in city planning is called a(n) ___(urbanist)___.

10. *Specify the precision you expect in the answer.* In a short-answer test involving dates or numerical answers, be sure to specify the numerical units you expect the students to use, or how precise or accurate the answers should be. This clarifies the task. It also saves time for those students who continue to work to achieve a degree of precision beyond your intentions. Figure 7.9 includes such specificity. If there are more than one or two numerical items, you can describe the level of precision you expect in the general directions at the beginning of the set of questions, rather than adding words to each item.

11. *Avoid irrelevant clues.* A test item is crafted to assess a specific learning target, but sometimes the wording provides an irrelevant clue. When this happens, a student may answer correctly without having achieved the learning target. The verb in a sentence, for example, may unintentionally clue the student that the answer you want is plural or singular. An indefinite article may be a clue that the answer you want begins with a vowel. Compare the items in Figure 7.10.

The poor version has two clues to the right answer: It uses *urban planning*, which clues *urbanist*, and it uses the indefinite article *an*, which clues the student that the expected answer begins with a vowel sound. The better version corrects these flaws by substituting a synonym (*city planning*) and using *a(n)* for the indefinite article form.

TRUE-FALSE ITEMS

Varieties of True-False Items

A **true-false item** consists of a statement or a **proposition** that a student must judge and mark as either true or false. There are at least six varieties: true-false, yes-no, right-wrong, correction, multiple true-false, and yes-no with explanation. The **true-false** variety presents a proposition that a student judges true or false. The **yes-no** variety asks a direct question, to which a student answers yes or no. The **right-wrong** variety presents a computation, equation, or language sentence that the student judges as correct or incorrect. The **correction** variety requires a student

to judge a proposition, as does the true-false variety, but the student is also required to correct any false statement to make it true. The **multiple true-false** variety looks similar to a multiple-choice item. However, instead of selecting one option as correct, the student treats every option as a separate true-false statement. (More than one choice may be true.) The **yes-no with explanation** variety asks a direct question and requires the student to respond yes or no. In addition, the student must explain why his or her choice is correct. Figure 7.11 gives some examples.

Usefulness of True-False Items

Advantages and Criticisms   Teachers often use true-false items because (1) certain aspects of the subject matter readily lend themselves to verbal propositions that can be judged true or false, (2) they are relatively easy to write, (3) they can be scored easily and objectively, and (4) they can cover a wide range of content within a relatively short period. But some educators have severely criticized true-false items—*especially poorly constructed true-false items.* Among the more frequent criticisms are that poorly constructed true-false items often assess only specific, frequently trivial facts; can be ambiguously worded; can be answered correctly by random guessing; and may encourage students to study and accept only oversimplified statements of truth and factual details. If you follow the suggestions in this chapter for improving true-false items, you will not experience the limitations these criticisms imply.

Assess More Than Simple Recall   Well-written true-false items can assess a student's ability to identify the correctness or appropriateness of a variety of meaningful propositions, including the following (Ebel, 1972):

1. *Generalizations* in a subject area.
2. *Comparisons* among concepts.
3. *Causal or conditional* propositions.

4. *Relationships* between two events, concepts, facts, or principles.

5. *Explanations* for why events or phenomena occurred.

6. *Instances or examples* of a concept or principle.

7. *Evidential* statements.

8. *Predictions* about phenomena or events.

9. *Steps* in a procedure or process.

10. *Computations* (or other kinds of results obtained from applying a procedure).

11. *Evaluations* of events or phenomena.

Examples of items of each of these types are shown in Table 7.4. Some of the key phrases used to construct items in each category appear in the table, too. You may want to refer to Table 7.4 from time to time to glean suggestions for writing true-false items.

Validity of the True-False Item Format

Ebel, perhaps more than any other measurement specialist, defended the use of well-written true-false items for classroom assessment. He offered the following argument for the validity of this format:

1. The essence of educational achievement is the command of useful verbal knowledge.

2. All verbal knowledge can be expressed in propositions.

3. A proposition is any sentence that can be said to be true or false.

4. The extent of a student's command of a particular area of knowledge is indicated by his success in judging the truth or falsity of propositions related to it. (Ebel, 1979, pp. 111–112)

Note that requiring a student to identify the truth or falsity of propositions is not the only means of ascertaining a student's command of knowledge. Assessing a student's command of knowledge is discussed further in the remaining chapters of this book.

Verbal knowledge is an important element of several learning targets, however. Nevertheless, as we saw in Chapters 2 and 6 and will see more of in Chapters 10, 11, and 12, wide ranges of thinking skills and performance outcomes form the learning targets of education. Thus, true-false items can assess some thinking skills and performances beyond simple recall, but you cannot use them exclusively to create valid assessment results. They must be used in combination with other assessment formats to achieve results that can be judged valid by the criteria in Chapter 3.

Guessing on True-False Items: An Ill Wind?

Charles Schulz's "Peanuts" character Linus once observed, "Taking a true-false test is like having the wind at your back." This reflects a common criticism of true-false tests: They are subject to error because students can answer them by using random guessing. It is well known that for a *single* true-false item, there is a 50-50 chance of answering the item correctly if true or false is selected at

FIGURE 7.11   Samples of the six types of true-false items.

True-False Variety

The sum of all the angles inside any four-sided closed figure equals 360 degrees.	T	F

Yes-No Variety

Is it possible for a presidential candidate to become United States president without obtaining a majority of the votes cast on election day?	Yes	No

Right-Wrong (Correct-Incorrect) Variety

Example assessing an arithmetic principle

$5 + 3 \times 2 = 16$	R	W

Example assessing grammatical correctness

Did she know whom it was?	C	I

Correction Variety

Read each statement below and decide if it is correct or incorrect. If it is *incorrect*, change the underlined word or phrase to make the statement correct.

The new student, who we met today, came from Greece.	C	I

Multiple True-False Variety

Under the Bill of Rights, freedom of the press means that newspapers:

1. have the right to print anything they wish without restrictions.	T	F
2. can be stopped from printing criticisms of the government.	T	F
3. have the right to attend any meeting of the executive branch of the federal government.	T	F

Yes-No with Explanation Variety

Situation*: A poll was taken of 500 city Democrats and 500 city Republicans. Each person was asked whether he or she agreed with the statement, "That government is best which governs least." These are the results:

Democratic male:	Agree 12%	Disagree 35%
Democratic female:	Agree 3%	Disagree 14%
Republican male:	Agree 48%	Disagree 12%
Republican female:	Agree 28%	Disagree 7%

I assert that this poll proves that most people want the government to do very little. Am I correct?   Yes   No

If *you* say "no", explain why I am wrong:

Source: *Situation adapted from Sanders, 1966, p. 117.

TABLE 7.4 Types of statements that could form the basis for your true-false items.

Type of Statement	Examples of Introductory Words or Phrases	Examples of True-False Items
Generalization	All . . . Most . . . Many . . .	Most good true-false items are tests of ability to apply information. (T)
Comparative	The difference between . . . is . . . Both . . . and . . . require . . .	The difference between the raw scores corresponding to the 45th and 55th percentiles is likely to be smaller than the difference between the raw scores corresponding to the 5th and 15th percentiles. (T)
Conditional	If . . . (then) . . . When . . .	When one has a normal distribution, the standard deviation and standard error are considered equivalent. (F)
Relational	The larger . . . The higher . . . The lower . . . Making . . . is likely to . . . Increasing . . . tends to . . . How much . . . depends on . . .	Making a test more reliable is likely to make it less valid. (F)
Explanatory	The main reason for . . . The purpose of . . . One of the factors that adversely affect . . . Since . . . Although . . .	One of the factors that adversely affect the reliability of an objective test is the amount of guessing the students do in answering it. (T)
Exemplary	An example of . . . One instance of . . .	An example of a "factual information" question is to ask how horsepower of an engine is calculated. (F)
Evidential	Studies of . . . reveal . . .	Studies of the marking standards and practices of different faculty members reveal that they tend more toward uniformity than toward diversity. (F)
Predictive	One could expect . . . Increasing . . . would result in . . .	One could expect to increase the reliability coefficient of a test from .30 to .60 by doubling its number of items. (F)
Procedural	To find . . . one must . . . In order to . . . one must . . . One method of . . . is to . . . One essential step . . . is to . . . Use . . . of . . . The first step toward . . .	One method of ensuring that scores from a 100-item test and scores from a 25-item test will carry equal weight is to multiply the latter scores by 4. (F)
Computational	(Item includes numerical data and requires computation or estimation.)	The range of the scores 2, 3, 4, and 6 is 5. (T).
Evaluative	A good . . . It is better to . . . than . . . The best . . . is . . . The maximum . . . is . . . The easiest method of . . . is to . . . It is easy to demonstrate that . . . It is difficult to . . . It is possible to . . . It is reasonable to . . . It is necessary to . . . in order to . . . The major drawback to . . . is . . .	It is difficult to obtain reliable scores from a group in which the range of abilities is very wide. (F)

Source: Adapted from *Essentials of Educational Measurement* (pp. 183–185) by R. L. Ebel, 1972, Englewood Cliffs, NJ: Prentice-Hall. Adapted by permission of the copyright holder.

random. This means that persons guessing randomly can expect to get on the average one-half of the true-false items correct.[2] Several points, however, blunt this criticism (Ebel, 1972):

1. Blind (completely random) guessing is quite unlike informed guessing (guessing based on partial knowledge).

2. Well-motivated students (at least at the college level) tend to guess blindly on only a small percentage of the questions on a test.

3. It is very difficult to obtain a "good score" on a test by blind guessing alone.

[2]For example, the average guessing score (called the *expected chance score*) for a true-false test of 50 items is 25; for 10 T-F items it is 5; etc.

4. The fact that a given true-false test has a high reliability coefficient[3] would be evidence that scores on that test are not seriously affected by blind guessing.

Random guessing, of the type that is assumed by the "50-50 chance" statement, is by definition random responding. Random guessing is sometimes called *blind guessing*. But most everyone's experience is that seldom do students respond in this fashion to very many test questions. Rather, students tend to use whatever **partial knowledge** they have about the subject of the questions and/or about the context in which the questions are embedded to make an *informed guess*. Such informed guessers have a higher than 50-50 chance of success on true-false items (but how much higher, we are unable to say). This means that scores from true-false items (as with other item types) are measures of partial knowledge when informed guessing occurs. (Of course, persons who actually know the answer have a 100% chance of answering correctly!)

Although a student who is responding randomly on a single true-false item will have a 50-50 chance of being correct, the laws of chance indicate that the probability of getting a *good* score by random guessing on a test made up of many true-false items is quite small, especially for longer tests. This is illustrated in Table 7.5. Chances are only 2 in 100, for example, that a student who has guessed randomly on *all* the items on a 15-item test will get 80% or more of the items correct. If the test has 20 true-false questions and a student guesses randomly on *all* items, that student has only 2 chances in 1,000 of getting 80% or more items correct. Chances of getting perfect (100% correct) papers are even smaller.

Suggestions for Getting Started Properly

To write good true-false items you must be able to identify propositions that (1) represent important ideas, (2) can be defended by competent critics as true or false, and (3) are not obviously correct to persons with general knowledge or good common sense who have not studied the subject (Ebel, 1972). These propositions are then used as starting points to derive true-false items.

In this regard, Ebel suggested that you should think of a segment of knowledge as being represented by a paragraph; the propositions are the main ideas of that paragraph. You can then use these main ideas as starting points for writing true-false items. Table 7.4 offers suggestions on how to get started in phrasing true-false items from these propositions.

Additional suggestions for getting started are (Frisbie & Becker, 1990):

1. *Create pairs of items, one true and one false, related to the same idea, even though you will use only one.* Creating pairs

of items helps you to check on a statement's ambiguity and whether you need to include qualifications in the wording. Frisbie and Becker suggest that your false item is not worth using if you can only write a true version of it by inserting the word *not*.

2. *If your statement asks students to make evaluative judgments ("The best . . . is . . . ," "The most important . . . is . . . ," etc.), try to rephrase it as a comparative statement ("Compared to . . . , A is better than . . . ").* The comparative statement allows you to put into the item itself the comparisons you want students to make. Usually, when you write "What is the best way of . . . ," for example, you raise in the mind of the student the question, "compared to what?" Thus, if you include your intended comparison in the statement itself, this clears up the ambiguity.

3. *Write false statements that reflect the actual misconceptions held by students who have not achieved the learning targets.* To do this, you have to know your students well and try to think about a proposition the way a misinformed or poorly prepared student thinks about it. As you teach, you may notice these misconceptions. Take notes so you can recall them as you write items.

4. *You may wish to convert a multiple-choice item into two or more true-false items.* Because the foils (or incorrect options) of a multiple-choice item are not correct, they may be used as a basis for writing false statements.

Suggestions for Improving True-False Items

You should review and revise the first drafts of all assessment tasks you craft. I will say this many times in the book: Your first drafts of assessment tasks are not fit for human consumption. Editing assessment tasks is an important step in the assessment development process. Table 7.6 summarizes principles for improving the quality of true-false items. These are written as questions so you can use Table 7.6 as a checklist when you review your item drafts. You should always use the checklist in Table 7.6 to review true-false items that come with your textbook and curriculum materials. These true-false items are notorious for their poor quality. The principles implied by Table 7.6 are explained and illustrated in the following list:

1 and 2. *Importance of what is assessed, and its match to the test blueprint.* As always, the first two criteria that your assessment tasks should meet are importance and match to your assessment plan. Eliminate every item failing to meet these two criteria.

3. *Assess important ideas, rather than trivia, general knowledge, or common sense.* Although this principle applies to all assessment tasks, you need to be especially sensitive

---

[3]See Chapter 4 for an explanation of reliability coefficients.

TABLE 7.5 Chances of a student obtaining various "good scores" by using only random guessing to all items on true-false tests of various lengths.

Number of T-F items on the test	Chances of getting the following percentage of T-F questions right:		
	60% or better	80% or better	100%
5	50 in 100	19 in 100	3 in 100
10	38 in 100	6 in 100	1 in 1,000
15	30 in 100	2 in 100	3 in 100,000
20	25 in 100	6 in 1,000	1 in 1,000,000
25	21 in 100	2 in 1,000	3 in 100,000,000

Note: Computations are based on binomial probability theory.

TABLE 7.6 A checklist for judging the quality of true-false items.

1. Does the item assess an important aspect of the unit's instructional targets?	Yes	No
2. Does the item match your assessment plan in terms of performance, emphasis, and number of points?	Yes	No
3. Does the item assess important ideas, knowledge, or understanding (rather than trivia, general knowledge, or common sense)?	Yes	No
4. Is the statement either definitely true or definitely false without adding further qualifications or conditions?	Yes	No
5. Is the statement paraphrased rather than copied verbatim from learning materials?	Yes	No
6. Are the word-lengths of true statements about the same as those of false statements?	Yes	No
7. Did you avoid presenting items in a repetitive or easily learned pattern (e.g., TTFFTT . . . , TFTFTF . . .)?	Yes	No
8. Is the item free of verbal clues that give away the answer?	Yes	No
9. If the statement represents an opinion, have you stated the source of the opinion?	Yes	No
10. If the statement does not assess knowledge of the relationship between two ideas, does it focus on only one important idea?	Yes	No

Note: Revise any item for which you answered "no" to one or more questions.
Based on ideas from: Ebel, 1951, 1979; Greene, Jorgensen, & Gerberich, 1942; Gronlund, 1976; Hopkins, Stanley, & Hopkins, 1990; Lindquist, 1936; Lindvall, 1967; Nitko & Hsu, 1987; Thorndike & Hagen 1977; Weidemann, 1926; Wesman, 1971.

to this point when writing true-false items. It is easy to write items that assess trivial knowledge. The first item in Figure 7.12 focuses on trivia rather than important information about Washington's role in the early days of the nation. The revised version at least asks a more significant fact about him. The second poor item does not assess anything important. The revised version of this item assesses a student's understanding of an item-writing principle rather than a questionable idiosyncratic fact.

Incidentally, the answer to the second revised item is "false." The practice of taking a textbook sentence and making it false by inserting negative function words (e.g., *not, neither . . . nor*) makes the item you write tricky for students. Tricky items do not belong on your assessment instruments. Even well-prepared students can overlook the negative word (Ebel, 1979). If you follow the suggestions in this chapter for getting started, you are unlikely to create such a flawed item.

4. *Make sure the item is either definitely true or definitely false.* A **proposition** should not be so general that a knowledgeable student can find exceptions that change the intended truth or falsity of the statement. Make sure the item is phrased in a way that makes it unambiguous to the *knowledgeable* student. (Items should, of course, appear ambiguous to the unprepared or unknowledgeable student.) A few suggestions for reducing item ambiguity include the following (Lindvall & Nitko, 1975):

a. *Use short statements where possible.* This makes it easier to identify the idea you want the student to judge true or false. Complex, cumbersome statements make identifying the essential element in the item difficult for even knowledgeable students (Ebel, 1951). If the information you want to describe in the statement is complex, use different sentences to separate the description from the statement students must judge true or false. Frequently, you can shorten a long, complex statement that contains extraneous material by simply editing it (Figure 7.13).[4]

b. *Use exact language.* Frequently, quantitative terms can clarify an otherwise ambiguous statement. For example, instead of saying, "equal to approximately $5.00" or "approximately one-half of . . . ," say "between $4.00 and $6.00" or "between 45 and 55%."

c. *Use positive statements and avoid* **double negatives,** *which many students find especially confusing.* Consider the examples in Figure 7.14. If you must use a negative function word, be sure to underline it or use all capital letters so it is NOT overlooked.

5. *Avoid copying sentences verbatim.* Students often find sentences copied from a text uninterpretable because they have been taken out of context. In addition, such statements are likely to communicate to students that the text's exact (and often idiosyncratic) phrasing is important, rather than their own comprehension. This encourages students to engage in rote learning of textbook sentences. Recall from Table 3.2 that one piece of evidence to support the validity of your assessment is that it does not have such negative consequences.

Copying items from a text is more likely when a teacher is testing for knowledge of verbal concepts (including definitions) and statements of principles (rules). But testing for comprehension demands *paraphrasing* at the minimum, and enhancing a student's comprehension

[4]This suggestion applies to the crafting of all item types, of course.

FIGURE 7.12   Examples of changing items to focus on more important ideas.

Poor:	George Washington had wooden teeth.	T	F
Better:	George Washington actively participated in the Constitutional Convention.	T	F
Poor:	The author of the text provides six suggestions for writing true-false items.	T	F
Better:	A good procedure for developing true-false items is to insert the word *not* into a true proposition taken from a textbook.	T	F

FIGURE 7.13   Examples of editing a true-false item to make it more concise and to the point.

Poor:	Although a single item is generally an unreliable measure, and although it is frequently difficult to write additional items, a test's reliability usually can be improved by making the test longer and thereby increasing the number of times the students' behaviors are observed.	T	F
Better:	Tests containing more items are usually less reliable than shorter tests.	T	F

of concepts and principles seems to be a more important educational goal than encouraging a student to memorize textbook statements word for word. Again, if you follow the earlier-stated suggestions for initially deriving items, you are not likely to copy statements from a textbook.

6. *True and false statements should have approximately the same number of words.* Teachers tend to make true statements more qualified and wordy than false statements. Test-wise students can pick up on this irrelevant clue and get the item right without achieving the learning target. The easiest way to correct this type of flaw is to keep a watchful editorial eye and to rewrite inappropriate statements.

7. *Don't present items in a repetitive or easily learned pattern* (e.g., TFTF . . . , TTFFTT . . . , TFFTFF . . .). Some teachers develop such patterns because they are easy to remember and thus make scoring easier. But if it's easy for a teacher to remember, it will be easy for test-wise students to learn also. Assessment results will then be invalid. You should also avoid a consistent practice of having many more true answers than false, or many more false answers than true. If students notice, for example, that you seldom use a false statement, they will (rightly) avoid choosing false when they are uncertain of the answer. Upper-grade students discover these patterns quickly when a teacher uses lots of true-false items.

Not all educational assessment specialists agree on the proportion of true-to-false answers to include (Frisbie & Becker, 1990). Some specialists (Ebel & Frisbie, 1991; Popham, 1991) recommend having more false items than true ones, because false items have been shown to discriminate[5] better than true items (Barker & Ebel, 1981; Oosterhof & Glasnap, 1974). That is, false items tend to differentiate the most knowledgeable students from the least knowledgeable better than true items. Increased item discrimination improves the reliability of the total test scores.

[5]*Discrimination* is a technical term used in analysis of item response data. See Chapter 14 for an explanation.

FIGURE 7.14   Examples of improving items by avoiding negatives and double negatives.

Poor:	It is not undesirable to use double negatives inadvertently in a true-false item.*	T	F
Poor:	The Monongahela River does not flow northward.	T	F
Better:	The Monongahela River flows southward.	T	F

* Source: Principles of Educational and Psychological Measurement, 3rd edition, by G. Sax. © 1989. Reprinted with permission of Wadsworth Publishing, a division of Thomson Learning. Fax 800 730-2215.

8. *Do not use **verbal clues** (specific determiners) that give away the answer.* A **specific determiner**[6] is a word or phrase in a true-false or multiple-choice item that "over-qualifies" a given statement and gives the student an un-intended clue to the correct answer (Sarnacki, 1979); see Figure 7.15. Words such as *always*, *never*, and *every* tend to make propositions false. Words such as *often*, *usually*, and *frequently* tend to make propositions true. Test-wise students will use these clues to respond correctly even though they do not have command of the requisite knowledge.

You should note that *some* propositions are "always" or "never" true, or "often" or "usually" false. For this reason some assessment specialists suggest that using specific determiners in reverse helps to distinguish the knowledge-able student from the merely test-wise one (Ebel, 1979; Ebel & Frisbie, 1991). I wouldn't recommend using such tactics with elementary school students. Some evidence (Slakter, Koehler, & Hampton, 1970a) indicates that youngsters do not attend to specific determiner clues in multiple-choice items until the ninth grade, even though they do use other types of test-wiseness skills as early as fifth grade. The same seems likely to be valid for true-false items.

9. *Attribute the opinion in a statement to an appropriate source.* If your true-false item expresses an opinion, value, or attitude, you should attribute the statement to an appropriate source. You can use an introductory clause, such as, "According to the text . . ." or "In the opinion of most specialists in this area . . ." or "In Jones' view. . . ." This referencing reduces ambiguity in two ways: (a) it makes clear that the statement is not to be judged in general, but rather in terms of the specific source; and (b) it makes clear that you are not asking for the student's personal opinion.

10. *Focus on one idea.* Have only one idea per item, unless the item is crafted to assess knowledge of the relationship between two ideas. In the poor item in Figure 7.16, a student may respond with the correct answer, F, for an appropriate reason: The student may think (erroneously) that the Monongahela River does not flow north, may be unaware that the confluence of the rivers is at Pittsburgh, or may not know anything about the three rivers. Thus, the student would get the item right without having the knowledge that getting the right answers implies. A separate statement for each idea may be necessary to identify precisely which information the student knows.

Crafting Multiple True-False Items

A multiple true-false item looks like a multiple-choice item in that it has a stem followed by several alternatives.

[6]This term was probably used first in connection with true-false items by C. C. Weidemann (1926).

Unlike when responding to a multiple-choice item, however, the student does not select the single correct or best answer; she responds true or false to every alternative. In turn, each alternative is scored correct or incorrect. Because of this, the item may be crafted to have several correct (true) alternatives instead of only one. The examples in Figure 7.17 illustrate this.

Format   Notice three things about the format of the examples in Figure 7.17. First, unlike multiple-choice items, the *options are numbered* consecutively, and asterisks (or bullets) set off the different clusters' stems. Second, you do not need to have a balance of true or false correct answers within one cluster. Some clusters, like the second one in Figure 7.17, may not have any true or any yes answers. Third, all of the statements within a cluster must relate to the same stem or question. Each statement within

FIGURE 7.15   Examples of items using specific determiners.

Poor:	It is always better to use a longer test than a shorter one.	T	F
Poor:	Frequently, it is better to use a longer test instead of a short test.	T	F

FIGURE 7.16   Example of improving an item by focusing it on only one idea.

Poor:	The Monongahela River flows north to join the Allegheny River at Columbus, where they form the Ohio River.	T	F
Better:	The Monongahela River and the Allegheny River join to form the Ohio River.	T	F

FIGURE 7.17   Sample multiple true-false items.

**	Under current collective bargaining laws, workers have the right to bargain for		
1.	how much workers of each skill level should be paid.	T	F
2.	how much managers should be paid.	T	F
3.	what new products the company should produce.	T	F
4.	which workers should be laid off first.	T	F
**	The following statements are arguments used by some people before the Civil War to justify slavery. Read each statement and decide if it is an argument based on democratic ideas.		
5.	Slavery is right because it existed through most of history.	Yes	No
6.	Slavery is right because it was accepted by the men who wrote the United States Constitution.	Yes	No
7.	Slavery is right because it was supported by the great Greek, Aristotle.	Yes	No

Source: Adapted from Sanders, 1966, pp. 53 & 132.

a cluster is treated as a separate true-false item. Thus, Figure 7.17 contains seven items, not two items.

Advantages   The following advantages are claimed for this item format (Ebel & Frisbie, 1991; Frisbie, 1992): (1) Students can make two or three multiple true-false responses in the same time it takes them to answer one multiple-choice item; (2) a multiple true-false test created from multiple-choice items has a higher reliability than the original multiple-choice test; (3) multiple true-false items can assess the same abilities as straight multiple-choice items that are crafted to assess parallel content; (4) students believe that multiple true-false items do a better job of assessing their knowledge than straight multiple-choice items; (5) students perceive multiple true-false items to be slightly harder than straight multiple-choice items; and (6) multiple true-false items may be easier to write than multiple-choice items because you are not limited to creating only one correct answer.

Limitations   The multiple true-false item format shares many of the same limitations as multiple-choice items. These limitations are discussed in Chapter 8. Some research shows that standard multiple-choice items may be more appropriate than multiple true-false items for assessing higher-order thinking skills and when criterion-related validity evidence is important (Downing et al., 1995).

Summary

- Three fundamental principles guide most recommendations for crafting assessment tasks:
  - Focus only on educationally important learning targets.
  - Elicit only the performances that are relevant to the learning target being assessed.
  - Neither prevent nor inhibit a student's ability to demonstrate that he has obtained the learning target.
- Short-answer items require the student to respond with a word, short phrase, number, or symbol.
- Three types of short-answer items were identified: the question variety, the completion variety, and the association variety.
- Short-answer items assess various abilities, including
  - Simply recalling terminology, facts, symbols, and classifications
  - Applying rules and making simple interpretations of data and other information
  - Solving simple science and mathematics problems
  - Manipulating symbols and balancing mathematical and chemical equations
- Short-answer items are more objective than essay items but are not free of subjectivity in scoring.
- The chances of a student randomly guessing the correct answer on a short-answer item are much less than on a multiple-choice item.
- A checklist for judging the quality of short-answer items is presented in Table 7.3.

- A true-false item consists of a statement or proposition that the student must judge as true or false. Varieties include true-false, yes-no, right-wrong, correction, multiple true-false, and yes-no with explanation.
- True-false items are frequently criticized because they can:
  - Be used to assess specific, trivial facts
  - Be ambiguously worded
  - Be answered correctly by blind guessing
  - Encourage students to study factual details and to accept oversimplified statements of truth
- Carefully constructed true-false questions frequently reach beyond factual details. They are not ambiguously worded, nor do they assess trivial facts. Examples are given in Table 7.4.
- Advantages of true-false items include
  - Ease of construction
  - Objectivity and ease of scoring
  - Increased coverage of content per unit of testing time
- One logical argument for the validity of true-false items concludes that a student's judgments of the truth of propositions in an area of knowledge reflect the student's command or mastery of that area.
- It is possible to guess randomly on true-false items, but it is difficult to get good scores by this process when the test has many items (see Table 7.5).
- A random guess is a completely random response, much like flipping a coin; an informed guess is a response based on partial knowledge and test-wiseness.
- Most well-prepared and well-motivated students are unlikely to use random guessing, but they may use informed guessing.
- Your ability to write good quality true-false items begins with your ability to identify propositions in a subject area that:
  - Reflect important concepts
  - Competent authorities can defend as true
  - Are not obvious or common knowledge
- The chapter describes how to get started in writing quality true-false items.
- As with all assessment tasks, you should carefully review and edit true-false items.
- A checklist for judging the quality of true-false items is presented in Table 7.6.

Important Terms and Concepts

double negatives
focusing the item
partial credit
partial knowledge
proposition
random guessing
scoring key
short-answer varieties (association, completion, question)
strip key

three fundamental principles for crafting assessments
true-false varieties (correction, multiple true-false, right-wrong, true-false, yes-no, yes-no with explanation)
verbal clues (specific determiners)

Exercises and Discussion Questions

1. Write short-answer or completion items in your teaching area(s) that assess each of the lower-order thinking skills listed in Table 7.2.
2. Why are short-answer items not completely objective in scoring?
3. Explain how each of the principles implied by the checklist for short-answer items (Table 7.3) improves the validity of your assessment results.
4. Each of the following completion items contains one or more flaws. For each item, use Table 7.3 to identify the flaw(s), and rewrite the item so it remedies the flaw(s) you identified but creates no new flaws.
   a. _____ is the substance which helps plants turn light energy to food.
   b. The Johnstown Flood occurred during _____.
   c. The _____ is the major reason why _____ and _____ exhibit _____.
   d. San Francisco was named after _____.
   e. A kilogram is equivalent to _____.
   f. Was the population greater in 1941 or 1951? _____.
5. Obtain a teacher's edition of a textbook in your teaching area that contains completion items and true-false items. (These items are sometimes given at the end of a chapter as practice exercises for students.) Select five flawed items of each type, copy them in a list, and, using Tables 7.3 and 7.6, identify the flaws. Then revise each item so there are no flaws. Indicate the source of your items and share your work with others in this course.
6. Obtain a teacher's edition of a textbook (or other curricular materials) that covers the material for the teaching unit you selected for Exercise 8 of Chapter 6. Locate the completion and true-false items presented in the teacher's edition for this unit. Match those items to the learning targets included in the assessment blueprint you crafted for Exercise 8. To what extent do these items match the learning targets and the blueprint? What do your findings suggest about the way you should use the items the textbook gives you? About your need to craft items yourself? Prepare a short report and share your findings with others in this course.
7. Write one true-false item in your teaching area(s) that assesses a student's use of each of the categories of propositions listed in Table 7.4.
8. Summarize Ebel's argument for the validity of the true-false format for assessing educational achievement. Using Table 3.1 as a basis, offer a counterargument that shows that the results of assessments comprised exclusively of true-false items have low validity when used for assigning grades for report cards.
9. What are the chances that a student who guesses randomly on all items in a 20-item true-false test will get a score of 16 or higher? (See Table 7.5.)
10. Each of the following true-false items contains one or more flaws. For each item, use Table 7.6 to identify the flaw(s), and rewrite it, correcting the flaw(s) identified. Be sure your rewritten items do not exhibit new flaws.
    a. The two categories, plants and animals, are all that biologists need to classify every living thing.   T   F
    b. In the United States, it is warm in the winter.   T   F
    c. Editing assessment tasks is an important step in the assessment development process.   T   F
    d. The major problem in the world today is that too many people want more than their "fair share" of the Earth's resources.   T   F
    e. There were more teachers on strike in 1982 than in 1942, even though the employment rate was lower in 1942 than in 1982.   T   F
11. Find or write a paragraph or two in a subject area that represents an important segment of knowledge you would like students to learn.
    a. Summarize the main idea(s) of the paragraph(s) in a sentence or two.
    b. Rephrase the main idea(s) several ways to create true-false items. Write at least one true and one false item for each main idea. These should be written as true-false pairs, as suggested in the text. Be sure to indicate the correct answers.
    c. Put an asterisk next to the item(s) you would include on a test.
    d. Share your work with your classmates in this course.
    e. Revise your items after receiving feedback from your classmates.

Additional Readings

Ebel, R. L., & Frisbie D. A., (1991). *Essentials of educational measurement* (5th ed.). Englewood Cliffs, NJ: Prentice-Hall, Chapter 8.

The authors advocate expanded use of true-false items in achievement testing. They present comprehensive and detailed analysis, offer many suggestions, and give many illustrations of good and poor true-false items.

Frisbie, D. A. (1992). The multiple true-false item format: A status review. *Educational Measurement: Issues and Practice, 11*(4), 21–26.

Reviews the research literature on the reliability and validity of this item format. Identifies 10 areas where further research is needed.

Frisbie, D. A., & Becker, D. F. (1990). An analysis of textbook advice about true-false tests. *Applied Measurement in Education, 4*, 67–83.

This article analyzes the advice given by 17 textbooks on how to write true-false items. It points out contradictions in advice and identifies which of the item-writing "rules" are supported by research.

CHAPTER 8

Multiple-Choice and Matching Exercises

Learning Targets

After studying this chapter, you should be able to:

1. State the basic purpose that any assessment task must serve. [4, 6]
2. Name and describe the function of each part of a multiple-choice item. [2, 6]
3. Describe each of the major varieties of multiple-choice items. [1, 2]
4. State the abilities that can and cannot be directly assessed by multiple-choice items. [1, 2]
5. Describe the situations when you should not use multiple-choice items, even though it appears that they would be applicable. [1]
6. Construct multiple-choice items in the area(s) you teach that are free from commonly encountered item-writing flaws. [2]
7. Name and describe the function of each part of a matching exercise. [2, 6]
8. State the abilities that can and cannot be directly assessed by matching exercises. [1, 2]
9. Construct matching exercises that are free from commonly encountered item-writing flaws. [2]
10. Craft usable items in your teaching area of each of the following types: masterlist (keylist), greater-less-same, best-answer, experiment-interpretation, statement-and-comment, and tabular. [2, 1]
11. Score tabular item sets using the procedures described in this chapter. [3]
12. Explain the value of using the item types listed in Learning Target 10 over traditional true-false, multiple-choice, matching, and short-answer items. [1, 2, 3]
13. Explain the advantages and criticisms of matching exercises. [1, 2, 6]
14. Use the checklist for judging the quality of matching exercises to identify and correct flawed items of your own creation and those provided with instructional materials in your teaching area(s). [2, 1]
15. Describe the types of knowledge, skills, and abilities assessed by each item listed in Learning Target 10. [1, 3, 2]
16. Explain how each of the terms and concepts listed at the end of this chapter apply to the construction of assessment tasks. [6]

This chapter will help improve your multiple-choice and matching item-writing skills. Although these two item formats can be used to assess a wide range of learning targets and thinking skills, in this chapter we are concerned mainly with the very basic item-writing principles. Chapter 10 describes more advanced formats and ways to write items that assess higher-order thinking skills.

We begin the chapter by discussing the usefulness of multiple-choice items: their characteristics, varieties, advantages and criticisms, and when not to use them. Next, we offer suggestions for crafting multiple-choice items in three areas: improving the item stem, improving the alternatives, and wording the correct answer. These suggestions are essentially corollaries of the three fundamental principles for crafting assessments, discussed in Chapter 7. The section is concluded by illustrating alternative varieties of multiple-choice items that assess different types and levels of thinking skills.

After discussing multiple-choice item writing, we discuss crafting matching exercises. This format is rather easy to craft and is popular with many teachers. Suggestions for improving both the exercises you craft and the exercises you adapt from commercial instructional and curricular materials are given. We conclude the chapter by discussing alternative varieties of matching items. These alternatives assess different levels of thinking skills. They may provide useful ways to assess some otherwise difficult-to-assess learning targets.

MULTIPLE-CHOICE ITEM FORMAT

A **multiple-choice item** consists of one or more introductory sentences followed by a list of two or more suggested responses. The student must choose the correct answer from among the responses you list. Figure 8.1 illustrates this format.

Stem

The part of the item that asks the question is called the **stem**. Instead of asking a question, it may set the task a student must perform or state the problem a student must solve. As a general rule, after a student reads the stem, he should understand what you want him to do. That is, you write the stem so that the student understands what task to perform or what question to answer.

Alternatives

Teachers call the list of suggested responses by various names: **alternatives**, **responses**, **choices**, and **options**. The alternatives should always be arranged in a meaningful way (logically, numerically, alphabetically, etc.). The chronological sequence in which events occur and the size of objects (large, medium, small) are examples of logical orders. If no logical or numerical order exists among them, the alternatives should be arranged in alphabetical order. In Figure 8.1, alternatives are in alphabetical order. The reason for this is that you do not want to establish a pattern that can clue the answer for students who do not know it. Secondly, following this rule saves the students' time.

Keyed Alternative and Distractors

Usually, only one of the alternatives is the correct or best answer to the question or problem you pose. This is called the **keyed answer**, **keyed alternative**, or simply the **key**. The remaining incorrect alternatives are called **distractors** or **foils**. The purpose of the latter is to present plausible (but incorrect) answers to the question or solutions to the problem in the stem. These foils should be plausible to those students who do not have the level of knowledge or understanding required by your learning target—those students who haven't learned the material well enough. Conversely, the foils *should not* be plausible

---

FIGURE 8.1 Sample multiple-choice item.[1]

Which of the following, combined with the revolution of the earth around the sun, causes the seasons?

   A The frequency of sunspot occurrences
   B The gravitational pull of the moon
   C The intensity of light emitted by the sun
 *D The tilt of the earth's axis

Source: From *The Geography Learning of High-School Seniors* (p. 44) by R. Allen, N. Bettis, D. Kurfman, W. MacDonald, I. V. S. Mullis, and C. Salter, 1990, Princeton, NJ: National Assessment of Educational Progress, Educational Testing Service. Reprinted by permission.
[1]Correct answers to multiple-choice items will appear with a boldface asterisk (*) throughout this book.

FIGURE 8.2 Sample multiple-choice item with interpretive material.

	Jan	Feb	Mar	Apr	May	June	July	Aug	Sept	Oct	Nov	Dec	Annual
Mean Temperature (in degrees)	79	79	80	81	81	80	81	81	82	82	82	80	80.7
Total Precipitation (in inches)	7	6	6	7	11	12	10	7	3	2	6	11	88

Which of the following regions would have the range of monthly temperature and precipitation shown in the chart above?

   A Savanna
   B Semiarid desert
 *C Tropical rain forest
   D Tundra

Source: Adapted from *The Geography Learning of High-School Seniors* (p. 45) by R. Allen, N. Bettis, D. Kurfman, W. MacDonald, I. V. S. Mullis, and C. Salter, 1990, Princeton, NJ: National Assessment of Educational Progress, Educational Testing Service. Adapted by permission.

to those students who have the degree of knowledge you desire.

Interpretive Material

In some cases, you may need to add information to make a question clearer or more authentic. You may wish to assess a learning target, for example, that requires students to apply their knowledge to data in a table or a graph, to a situation described in a paragraph, to an object, or to an event simulated by a picture. If adding this kind of information makes the stem more than one or two sentences long, then the information is placed in a section that comes *before* the stem. This information is called **interpretive material**, and the item(s) that refer to it are called **context-dependent items**, **interpretive exercises**, or **linked items** (the items are "linked" to the interpretive material). Figure 8.2 illustrates this assessment technique. We give more elaborate suggestions for crafting context-dependent items in Chapter 10.

CONSIDERATIONS BEFORE CRAFTING ITEMS

Multiple Assessments Formats

The **basic purpose of assessment tasks**, which includes the multiple-choice format, is to allow students to demonstrate their knowledge and understanding of your learning targets. You use their responses to infer the extent to which they have achieved those instructional targets. A valid inference requires information about students' performance on several different formats of tasks. (See Chapter 3.)

Adjusting an Item's Difficulty

Students acquire knowledge and successful performance in various degrees. Perfect knowledge or perfect performance, even if it is possible to attain, is seldom a desired educational goal. Think of a student as being located at some point along a **continuum of learning** for a given learning target.[1] You can construct a test item for students at a specific level of this learning continuum. The students who are at this level (or above it) should be able to answer the item correctly; others, lower on the continuum of learning, will not.

Consider Figure 8.3. All three items ask the same question, but the degree of knowledge required to answer that question increases from Item 1 to Item 3. In this example, you can easily see how the *alternatives operate to make the item easy or difficult*: The alternatives require the students to make finer distinctions between the dates. Some research supports the idea that similarity among the alter-

[1]This is not an entirely satisfactory conceptualization from a strictly scientific viewpoint, but it does have pedagogical value.

FIGURE 8.3 Sample items showing that increasing degree of knowledge is needed when alternatives are more similar.

1. In what year did the United States enter World War I?
   - A. 1776
   - B. 1812
   - *C. 1917
   - D. 1981
2. In what year did the United States enter World War I?
   - A. 1901
   - *B. 1917
   - C. 1941
   - D. 1950
3. In what year did the United States enter World War I?
   - A. 1913
   - B. 1915
   - C. 1916
   - *D. 1917

natives increases the difficulty of an item (Green, 1984). Of course, manipulating the alternatives is not the only way to create more difficult items.

For which level of knowledge should an item be written? That depends on several factors—there is no general rule. Factors you need to keep in mind to craft the item so it gives valid results include the type of students, the level of instruction, the purpose for which you will use the assessment results, and the level of knowledge your students need to attain at this point in their educational development. In effect, you need to decide, at least roughly, which level of proficiency is sufficient for each important learning target. Then you construct test items that will allow you to distinguish students who lack sufficient proficiency from those who have acquired it.

Basic Purpose of Assessment Tasks

The preceding statement represents an idealized situation. Seldom will your real assessment tasks separate students this neatly. Some less knowledgeable students probably will answer some tasks correctly, and other, more knowledgeable students will not. In general, though, keep in mind this principle:

> The basic purpose of an assessment task, whether or not it is a multiple-choice item, is to identify those students who have attained a sufficient (or necessary) level of knowledge (skill, ability, or performance) of the learning target being assessed.

Varieties of Multiple-Choice Items

Teachers and professional test developers use several **varieties of multiple-choice items**. Some of these are illustrated in Figure 8.4. As you grow more skilled at evaluating students, you will find that you need to use several of these variations to obtain valid results. Space does not permit us, however, to describe each one in this textbook. If you would like more detail about a particular variety,

FIGURE 8.4 Examples of different varieties of multiple-choice items.

A. The correct-answer variety
Who invented the sewing machine?
- a.   Fulton
- *b. Howe
- c.   Singer
- d.   White
- e.   Whitney

B. The best-answer variety
What was the basic purpose of the Marshall Plan?
- a.   militarily defend Western Europe
- *b. reestablish business and industry in Western Europe
- c.   settle United States differences with Russia
- d.   directly help the hungry and homeless in Europe

C. The multiple-response variety
What factors are principally responsible for the clotting of blood?
- a.   contact of blood with a foreign substance
- *b. contact of blood with injured tissue
- c.   oxidation of hemoglobin
- *d. presence of unchanged prothrombin

D. The incomplete statement variety
Millions of dollars worth of corn, oats, wheat, and rye are destroyed annually in the United States by
- a.   mildews.
- b.   molds.
- c.   rusts.
- *d. smuts.

E. The negative variety
Which of these is *NOT* true of viruses?
- a.   Viruses live only in plants and animals.
- b.   Viruses reproduce themselves.
- *c. Viruses are composed of very large living cells.
- d.   Viruses can cause diseases.

F. The substitution variety
Passage to be read
Surely the forces of education should be fully utilized to acquaint youth with the real nature of the dangers to democracy, *for* no other place

—————
1

offers *as good or better opportunities than* the school

—————
2

for a *rational* consideration of the problems involved.

—————
3

Items to be answered

1. *a. , for
    b.   . For
    c.   —for
    d.   no punctuation needed

2. a.   As good or better opportunities than
    b.   as good opportunities or better than
    c.   as good opportunities as or better than
    *d. better opportunities than

3. *a. rational
    b.   radical
    c.   reasonable
    d.   realistic

G. The incomplete-alternatives variety[a]
An apple that has a sharp, pungent, but not disagreeably sour or bitter, taste is said to be *(4)*

a. p.   b. q   *c. t   d. v   e. w

H. The combined response variety
In what order should these sentences be written in order to make a coherent paragraph?

A. A sharp distinction must be drawn between table manners and sporting manners.

B. This kind of handling of a spoon at the table, however, is likely to produce nothing more than an angry protest against squirting grapefruit juice about.

C. Thus, for example, a fly ball caught by an outfielder in baseball or a completed pass in football is a subject for applause.

D. Similarly, the dexterous handling of a spoon in golf to release a ball from a sand trap may win a championship match.

E. But a biscuit or a muffin tossed and caught at the table produces scorn and reproach.

- a.   A, B, C, D, E
- *b. A, C, E, D, B
- c.   A, E, C, D, B
- d.   B, E, D, C, A

[a]The numeral in parentheses indicates the number of letters in the correct answers (which in this case is "tart"). This convention rules out borderline correct answers.
Source: Adapted from "Writing the Test Item" by R. L. Ebel, in *Educational Measurement* (pp. 194–195) by E. F. Lindquist (Ed.), 1951, Washington, DC: American Council in Education. Also adapted from "Writing the Test Item" by A. G. Wesman, in *Educational Measurement* (2nd ed.) (pp. 91–92) by R. L. Thorndike (Ed.), 1971, Washington, DC: American Council in Education. Adapted by permission.

you should read Ebel (1951) or Wesman (1971), as well as the material listed at the end of this chapter. After we present material about the basics of crafting multiple-choice items, we will discuss the more advanced multiple-choice varieties.

Direct vs. Indirect Assessment

Lindvall (1961) distinguishes between direct and indirect assessment of educational outcomes. A multiple-choice test can be a **direct assessment** of certain abilities. Well-written multiple-choice items, especially those requiring the use of interpretive materials, can help to directly assess a student's ability to discriminate and make correct choices; to comprehend concepts, principles, and generalizations; to make judgments about and choices among various courses of action; to infer and reason; to compute; to interpret new data or new information; and to apply information and knowledge in structural situations.

Multiple-choice items are only **indirect assessments** of other important educational outcomes, such as the ability to recall (as opposed to recognize) information under minimal prompting conditions, to articulate explanations and give examples, to produce and express unique or original ideas, to solve problems that are not well structured, to organize personal thoughts, to display thought processes or patterns of reasoning, to work in groups, and to construct or build things. These are important abilities. Many of them can be assessed directly with paper-and-pencil tasks such as extended written assignments. Others require alternative assessment techniques such as observing a student over an extended period of time working alone or in a group, interviewing a student, or assessing a student's performance, product, or creation. These latter techniques are discussed in Chapters 11, 12, and 13.

ADVANTAGES AND CRITICISMS OF MULTIPLE-CHOICE ITEMS

Advantages

The following are advantages of multiple-choice items:

1. *The multiple-choice format can be used to assess a greater variety of learning targets than other formats of response-choice items.* The various types of abilities have been discussed. It is useful to keep in mind the distinction between direct and indirect assessment of certain learning targets, too.

2. *Multiple-choice items[2] do not require students to write out and elaborate their answers and minimize the opportunity for less knowledgeable students to "bluff" or "dress-up" their answers* (Wood, 1977). This lack of opportunity to write answers is considered a disadvantage to some.[3]

3. *Multiple-choice tests focus on reading and thinking.* They do not require students to use writing processes under examination conditions. You should be aware, however, that "examination writing is far from being the highest form of the art; how could it be when nervous individuals have to write against the clock without a real opportunity to draft and work over their ideas?" (Wood, 1977, p. 196).

4. *There is less of a chance for a student to guess the correct answer to a multiple-choice item than to a true-false item or to a poorly constructed matching exercise.* The probability of a student blindly guessing the correct answer to a three-alternative item is 1/3; to a four-alternative item it is 1/4; etc.

5. *The distractor a student chooses may give you diagnostic insight into difficulties the student is experiencing.* However, for distractors to work this way you must carefully craft them so they are attractive to students who make common errors or who hold common misconceptions. Note, too, that a single item is not a very reliable basis on which to formulate a diagnosis. You will have to follow up to confirm your diagnosis.

Criticisms

Wood (1977) has summarized several criticisms of multiple-choice tests. Of course, most of the criticisms expressed in this section can also be true of any type of assessment procedure. However, in other assessment formats these flaws may show up in the way a teacher sets the task or in the rubrics a teacher uses for scoring students' responses.

1. *Students must choose from among a fixed list of options, rather than creating or expressing their own ideas or solutions.* If you rely exclusively on multiple-choice testing, you will risk giving your students little or no opportunity to write about the topics in the subject they are learning.

2. *Poorly written multiple-choice items can be superficial, trivial, and limited to factual knowledge.* Of course, so can any poorly constructed assessment format. Gaining the knowledge and skill to overcome this criticism is the reason you are taking this course! We will discuss how to craft items requiring more thought later in this chapter and in the next chapter.

3. *Because usually only one option of an item is keyed as correct, brighter students may be penalized for not choosing it.* Brighter students may detect flaws in multiple-choice items due to ambiguities of wording, divergent viewpoints, or additional knowledge of the subject, while the other students may not.

4. *Multiple-choice items tend to be based on "standardized," "vulgarized," or "approved" knowledge.* The problems students solve on multiple-choice items tend to be very structured and closed (having one correct answer). This gives students the impression that there is a single correct answer to all problems in a subject area, which may encourage students to place too much faith in an authority figure's correctness or may misrepresent a subject area as having a fixed and limited knowledge base. Further, if you use multiple-choice tests that do not use items linked to realistic interpretive materials, this results in tests not having a real-world context. This is referred to as **decontextualized knowledge**. As a result, your tests may not assess whether students can use what they have learned in a meaningful and authentic context.

---

[2]These advantages apply to other types of response-choice tasks as well.
[3]You may be surprised to learn that what some persons praise as advantages, others damn with a vengeance!

5. *Exclusive use of multiple-choice testing for important or high-stakes assessments may shape education in undesirable ways.* Those objecting to multiple-choice tests point out that the type of examination you use can shape the content and nature of instruction you deliver to your students. If a high-stakes assessment's multiple-choice items focus on factual knowledge, teachers tend to use drill-and-practice techniques to prepare students for it. If the test contains multiple-choice items that assess using knowledge and applying higher-order thinking skills, drill-and-practice teaching strategies are less effective.

WHEN NOT TO USE MULTIPLE-CHOICE ITEMS

Definite "Nots"

As indicated in previous chapters (especially Chapter 6), tasks must match the student achievements you want them to assess. You would not, for example, substitute multiple-choice questions on English mechanics and grammar for actual samples of writing when your learning target calls for students to write. Nor would you use multiple-choice items when your main learning target requires students to organize their own ideas, develop their own logical arguments, express their own thoughts and feelings, or otherwise demonstrate their abilities of self-expression.

When You Have a Choice

There are times, however, when you have a choice between using completion or short-answer items or using multiple-choice items. Perhaps on the surface, either format seems appropriate. One of these instances is when you are assessing a student's simple recall of information. However, multiple-choice items should *not* be used in classroom assessment when (Lindquist & Mann, 1936):

1. There is *only one* correct answer *and* when that answer is a single word or number.
2. The task calls for a numerical answer, as in computational problems.
3. It is obvious that there are only two possible plausible responses (e.g., yes vs. no, male vs. female, positive vs. negative).
4. Writing the answer doesn't take the student any longer than using an answer sheet or marking the answer to multiple-choice questions.

When these situations exist, it will be difficult for you to write good multiple-choice items requiring students to demonstrate the required degree of recollection and computation. Further, as in Situations 2 and 4, sometimes there is no advantage to the multiple-choice format over the more direct short-answer format.

Exceptions

There are exceptions to these suggestions, of course. When you need to assess a large number of students over large areas of content, and when you have readily available machine scoring, multiple-choice items may be the only practical assessment. Or when you already have a test comprised of many very good multiple-choice items but only one or two of those items fit the four situations previously listed, it is more efficient to go ahead with the multiple-choice assessment.

If your students will be administered a standardized achievement test (either by your school district or by the state), it will be to their advantage to have experience answering multiple-choice items. Therefore, you may wish to use multiple-choice items for some parts of your assessments to give students appropriate practice.

In classroom assessment, it is generally best to use a mixture of assessment formats. You should specifically craft each task to assess learning targets giving the most valid results. The validity of your results, rather than your own convenience, should be your first priority.

Other "Nots" and Exceptions

Some writers recommend that multiple-choice items should not be included when the test will be used only once, or when there are few students. It is easier to formulate short-answer questions than to write good multiple-choice items, and scoring will not be time-consuming when there are few students. However, even when the number of students is small, if you plan to teach the same subject at the same level in subsequent years, it is usually worthwhile to develop a "pool" of multiple-choice items over time. You can then select items from this pool for future tests.

CRAFTING BASIC MULTIPLE-CHOICE ITEMS

Five Basic Skills of the Craft

You will craft useful multiple-choice items if you learn how to do five things: (1) focus items to assess specific learning targets, (2) prepare the stem as a question or problem to be solved, (3) write a concise correct alternative, (4) write distractors that are plausible, and (5) edit the item to remove irrelevant clues to the correct answer. You must remember that when a multiple-choice item first comes out of your thoughts, it is only a crude item. The first draft of any assessment task is unfit for human consumption. It should not be put on a test until it is edited and polished. Dashing off multiple-choice items to put on a test at the last minute is a dead giveaway that you are not living up to your professional responsibilities (see Chapter 5). Editing items is a necessary step, even for the most experienced teachers. This section presents several item-writing guidelines for improving items in this editorial stage.

If you are a beginner, do not be discouraged by the difficulty you experience in writing good multiple-choice items. As is true with other forms of functional writing, crafting high-quality assessment tasks requires practice, frequent rewriting, and editing. This type of writing is unlike freewheeling, expressive writing in which few extrinsic standards apply.

It will be most helpful if you have your items critiqued by your instructor or classmates. Critics should keep in mind, however, that a lot of ego is invested in the creation of an item and that, to the uninitiated, critiquing a person's item is frequently perceived as a personal affront. Nevertheless, criticizing items is a valuable aid to learning skills in item writing.

The suggestions for crafting multiple-choice items are organized into three groups: suggestions for the stem, suggestions for the foils, and suggestions for the correct alternative. Suggestions for improving the quality of the stem portion of multiple-choice items are summarized in Table 8.1 and discussed in more detail in the text that follows.

Crafting the Stem of the Item

Direct Question Asked or Implied　After reading the stem, a student should understand the main intent of the item—what type of response you expect. The stem should ask a direct question or should clearly formulate a problem for the student to solve.

Incomplete sentences sometimes make good stems, but experience and research (Haladyna & Downing, 1989a) indicate that item writers usually produce better items when they phrase the stem as a direct question. The reason is probably that when a teacher does not ask a direct question, the student must *mentally rephrase the stem as a question* appropriate to the alternatives presented. This increases the cognitive complexity of the student's task, perhaps beyond what you may intend. When this happens you are violating the second and third fundamental principles of crafting assessments. When an incomplete sentence is used, a question is implied, of course. Older and brighter students are sometimes able to do this rephrasing without difficulty. However, younger, more average students, and perhaps those experiencing some learning difficulties may find that this "extra process" increases their difficulty in expressing what they know.

A simple way to check for this flaw is to cover the alternatives with your hand. Then, read the stem. *On the basis of that stem alone, can you determine what is expected of the student?* If not, the stem is incomplete and you should rewrite it.

Consider the examples in Figure 8.5. Example 1 is poor because the stem does not set a task or ask a question. (Cover the alternative. What task or problem does the stem set?) The student must read the entire item and infer that the teacher must be trying to find out *something* about W. E. B. DuBois' ideas. The student may very well know DuBois' ideas, but if the student makes the wrong inference about the teacher's intent, the student may answer the item incorrectly. Example 2 is better because the intent of the item is clear after the student reads the stem.

Put Alternatives at the End　If you fail to follow this rule, you will encounter problems similar to those encountered with completion items when the blank is not placed at

TABLE 8.1　Suggestions for improving the quality of the *stems* of multiple-choice items.	To do	To avoid
	1.　If possible, write as a direct question.	1.　Avoid extraneous, superfluous, and non-functioning words and phrases that are mere "window dressing."
	2.　If an incomplete sentence is used, be sure	
	a.　it implies a direct question.	2.　Avoid (or use sparingly) negatively worded items.
	b.　the alternatives come at the end (rather than in the middle) of the sentence.	3.　Avoid phrasing the item so that the personal opinion of the examinee is an option.
	3.　Control the wording so that vocabulary and sentence structure are at a relatively low and non-technical level.	4.　Avoid textbook wording and "textbookish" or stereotyped phraseology.
	4.　In items testing definitions, place the word or term in the stem and use definitions or descriptions as alternatives.	5.　Avoid "cluing" and "linking" items (i.e., having the correct answer to one item be clued or linked to the correctness of the answer to a previous item).

Sources: Ebel, 1951, 1979, Greene, Jorgensen, & Gerberech, 1942, 1943; Gronlund, 1976; Hopkins, Stanley, & Hopkins, 1990; Lindquist & Mann, 1936; Lindvall, 1967; Millman, 1961; Sax, 1974; Thorndike, Cunningham, Thorndike, & Hagen, 1991, Wesman, 1971.

FIGURE 8.5   Example of improving an incomplete stem by rephrasing as a question.

Poor: Incomplete stem

1. W. E. B. DuBois
    *a. actively pressed for complete political participation and full rights for African Americans.
    b. taught that the immediate need was for African Americans to raise their economic status by learning trades and crafts.
    c. emphasized helping African Americans through the National Urban League.
    d. founded the Association for the Study of Negro Life and History.

Better: Asks a question

2. Which of the following comes closest to expressing W. E. B. DuBois' ideas about priorities of the activities of African Americans during the early 20th century?
    a. African Americans should first improve their economic condition before becoming fully involved in politics.
    b. African Americans should postpone the fight for equal access to higher education until their majority acquire salable trade skills.
    c. African Americans should withdraw from white society to form a separate state in which they have complete political and economic control.
    *d. African Americans should become active, seeking out complete citizenship and full political participation immediately.

FIGURE 8.6   Example of improving the stem by listing alternatives at the end.

Poor: Options in middle of stem

1. Before the Civil War, the South's
    *a. emphasis on staple-crop production
    b. lack of a suitable supply of raw materials
    c. short supply of personnel capable of operating the necessary machinery
    was one of the major reasons manufacturing developed more slowly than it did in the North.

Better: Options put at the end

2. Before the Civil War, why did manufacturing develop more slowly in the South than in the North?
    *a. The South emphasized staple-crop production.
    b. The South lacked a suitable supply of raw materials.
    c. The South had a short supply of people capable of operating the necessary machinery.

---

the end of the incomplete sentence (Chapter 7). Consider the examples in Figure 8.6.

Control Vocabulary and Sentence Structure   When testing for subject-matter learning, make sure you phrase the item at a level suitable for the students. You don't want long sentences, difficult vocabulary, and unnecessarily complex sentence structures to interfere with students' being able to answer the item. This complexity may be quite independent of the learning target you are assessing. This

may be especially true when you have students with disabilities mainstreamed in your class. For example, deaf and hard-of-hearing students frequently have relatively large language and vocabulary deficits. These students may very well have acquired the specific knowledge, concept, or principle you are assessing, but the way you phrase an item may interfere with their being able to demonstrate this knowledge (see Suppes, 1974).

Figure 8.7 illustrates how a simple information item can be complicated by uncontrolled language.

Avoid "Window Dressing"   Item 1 in Figure 8.7 demonstrates how extraneous wording can complicate an item unnecessarily. Less obvious is the use of words that tend to "dress up" a stem to make it sound as though it is testing something of practical importance (Ebel, 1965). Often such **window dressing** creeps into an item when you are struggling to measure higher-level cognitive abilities, such as applications. Window dressing makes an item appear to measure applications, when it does not. Figure 8.8 shows that window dressing makes an item more difficult, less discriminating, less reliable, and less valid (Haladyna & Downing, 1989a).

Every word used in an item should have a purpose. Sometimes names, places, and other "facts" about a situation are necessary pieces of information: They can give the student the basis she should use to determine the correct answer. This is illustrated by Figure 8.9.

Avoid Negatively Worded Stems   Phrase items positively if possible. **Negatively worded stems**, such as "which of the following is not . . . ," tend to confuse students, especially the younger or less careful ones. Even well-prepared students often overlook the *not* in an examination question. Positively worded items are easier for students than the corresponding negatively worded items (Haladyna & Downing, 1989a). Figure 8.10 gives an example.

If negatively phrased items *are* used, use the negative word only in the stem or only in an option (not both), and either <u>underline</u> the negative word or place it in CAPITAL LETTERS.

FIGURE 8.7   Examples of improving a stem by making it more concise.

Poor: Unnecessary wordiness and complexity

1. Given the present day utilization of the automobile in urban settings, which of the following represents an important contribution of Garrett A. Morgan's genius?
    a. automobile safety belts
    b. crosswalk markers
    *c. traffic lights
    d. vulcanized rubber tires

Better: More concise

2. Which of the following did Garrett A. Morgan invent?
    a. automobile safety belts
    b. crosswalk markers
    *c. traffic lights
    d. vulcanized rubber tires

FIGURE 8.8 Improving the stem by eliminating window dressing.

Poor: Window dressing

1. There are 10 pre-service teachers in the Department of Education who recently registered for the college-sponsored weight loss program. At the beginning of the program each was weighed, and the 10 had a mean weight of 139.4 pounds. Suppose there were but three men in this group, and their mean weight was 180 pounds. What was the mean weight of the women at the beginning of the program?
   - a. 115.0 pounds
   - *b. 122.0 pounds
   - c. 140.0 pounds
   - d. 159.7 pounds

Better: More concise

2. Ten persons have a mean weight of 139.4 pounds. The mean weight of three of them is 180 pounds. What is the mean weight of the remaining seven persons?
   - a. 115.0 pounds
   - *b. 122.0 pounds
   - c. 140.0 pounds
   - d. 159.7 pounds

FIGURE 8.9 Acceptable inclusion of facts in an item stem.

A company owns a fleet of cars for which it pays all fuel expenses. Three readily available types of gasoline were tested to see which was giving better mileage. The results are shown below in miles per gallon.

	Mean	Median
Type A	19.1	18.5
Type B	18.5	19.1
Type C	18.8	18.9

1. Assuming they all cost the same, which type of gasoline should the company use?
   - *a. Type A
   - b. Type B
   - c. Type C

FIGURE 8.10 Example of improving the stem by using positive wording.

Poor: Negatively phrased stem

1. Sometimes a teacher finds it necessary to use a mild form of punishment. When this occurs, which of the following should not happen?
   - a. Children should not believe all of their behavior is bad.
   - b. Children should understand the reason(s) why they are being punished.
   - *c. Children should understand that the teacher, not them, controls when the punishment will end.

Better: Positively phrased stem

2. Sometimes a teacher finds it necessary to use a mild form of punishment. When this occurs, it is important that the children understand
   - a. that it may be a long time before happy times return to the classroom.
   - *b. the reason(s) why they are being punished.
   - c. that the teacher, not the children, controls when the punishment will end.

Avoid Grading Personal Opinions It is appropriate to ask a student's personal opinion, but do not do it in the context of a multiple-choice test where the student needs to select one option as best or correct. Everyone is entitled to an opinion. If you ask for opinions in a multiple-choice item, every option will be correct (Figure 8.11). Craft essay questions to evaluate the ways in which students use evidence to support their opinions. However, *do not grade the opinions* or the positions taken. Rather, evaluate the way the students use the evidence to support their opinions.

There is no single correct answer to the question in Figure 8.11, because each man's contributions can be judged and evaluated in different ways. The question could form the basis for an extended-response essay or a term paper in which the student supports his opinion with evidence and logical argument.

Avoid Textbook Wording As with true-false items, when you copy sentences verbatim from the text you end up with a poor item because: (1) frequently, a sentence loses its meaning when you take it out of context, (2) you encourage rote memory of textbook material instead of comprehension, (3) you are likely to produce awkwardly worded items with implausible distractors, and (4) learners who have only a superficial understanding of the underlying concept or principle may obtain clues to the correct answer by simply recalling the textbook phrasing. You must use a new, perhaps less familiar, wording of the stem and correct option to test a deeper comprehension of a concept or principle (Lindquist & Mann, 1936). The procedure we discussed earlier in Chapter 7 of stating main ideas of textbook passages in your own words and rephrasing these as questions is a practical one for avoiding **"textbookish" phrasing**.

The poor item in Figure 8.12 is weak because most introductory statistics books associate the term *typical* with *median* and often use income examples to illustrate the application of the median. By knowing these superficial facts, the student can mark "b" without demonstrating an in-depth understanding of this statistical index. The better item, Question 2, assesses a different learning target. It is better because it presents a novel situation and requires an application of the concept.

When testing older students, you may find it helpful to use stereotyped phraseology, certain "pat phrases," and

FIGURE 8.11 The correct answer should not be a matter of personal opinion.

1. Which of the following men contributed most toward the improvement of the self-confidence of African Americans?
   - a. W. E. B. DuBois
   - b. Eugene K. Jones
   - c. Booker T. Washington
   - d. Carter G. Woodson

FIGURE 8.12 Example of improving stems by eliminating textbookish wording.

Poor: Uses textbookish wording

1. The annual incomes of five employees are: $8,000; $8,000; $10,000; $11,000; and $25,000, respectively. Which index should be used to summarize the typical employee's income?
   - a. mean
   - *b. median
   - c. mode

Better: Novel situation for students

A teacher keeps a record of how long it takes students to complete the 50-question final exam. The mean time was 46 minutes and the median time was 20 minutes. The teacher used this information to set the exam's time limit at 20 minutes. The teacher reasoned that these data demonstrate that the typical student could complete the test in that time.

2. In all likelihood, this time limit is
   - a. just about right.
   - *b. too short.
   - c. too long.

FIGURE 8.13 Example of improving an item by not linking the answer to a preceding item.

Preceding item

1. The perimeter of a rectangle is 350 centimeters. The length of the rectangle is 3 centimeters longer than the width. What is the width?
   - a. 18.7
   - *b. 86.0
   - c. 89.0
   - d. 116.7

Poor subsequent item: Linked to Item 1

2. What is the area of the rectangle described in Question 1?
   - a. 1050 sq. cm.
   - b. 7396 sq. cm.
   - *c. 7654 sq. cm.
   - d. 8188 sq. cm.

Better subsequent item: Independent of Item 1

3. The width of a rectangle is 4 centimeters and the length is 3 centimeters. What is the area?
   - a. 9 sq. cm.
   - *b. 12 sq. cm.
   - c. 16 sq. cm.
   - d. 17 sq. cm.

verbal associations *to make distractors plausible* to those students lacking the required degree of knowledge. These phrases may be put into the stem or into the distractors. Item 2 in Figure 8.12, although it is a bit wordy and places a premium on reading, does just this. A student who interprets the correctness of using a particular statistical index only on the basis of the verbal association of *typical* with *median* will not answer the item correctly. Such a student will fail to notice that if the teacher set the time limit for the test at 20 minutes, only half of the class will have enough time to complete it. Surely this is inappropriate for a classroom test.

Create Independent Items With the possible exception of context-dependent items,[4] each item should assess a distinct performance, and the correct answer to an item should not be clued by another item. Two flaws to avoid are linking and clueing. **Linking** means that the answer to one or more items depends on obtaining the correct answer to a previous item. Linked items frequently result in doubly penalizing a student for an incorrect answer, as when a computational result from one item is required to answer a subsequent item. **Clueing** means that a hint to the correct answer to one item is found in the contents of another item in the test.

In Figure 8.13, Questions 1 and 2 illustrate linked items. The preceding item is primarily computational. The poor subsequent item (Item 2) is linked to it. A student could make an incorrect computation in Item 1, obtaining 89.0, for example. Having already made a mistake in Item 1, the student would get Item 2 wrong also, because $89 \times (89 + 3) = 8188$ is keyed as the wrong answer.

One solution to the problem is shown in the better subsequent item: You present a new numerical value for the student to use, which is independent of the preceding item.

Of course, items may provide clues to other items even though they are not linked. You should review all the items in your test to see if any item suggests an answer to other items.

Definitions Go in the Alternatives A common student learning target is knowing the meaning of special terms or other vocabulary. Multiple-choice items often assess students' knowledge of terminology with a definition in the stem. They ask students to select the correct term, phrase, or word from among a list they present as alternatives. The problem with this approach is that it increases the likelihood that students will get the answer correct by only superficial knowledge of the term you wish to assess. Students can obtain the correct answer by knowing only that the words in the definition "look like" (seem similar to) a word in the alternatives (Lindquist & Mann, 1936). To assess whether students have in-depth knowledge of a term, *put the term in the stem* and write various *definitions in the alternatives*. The item can be made easier or harder depending on how similar the alternatives are (Figure 8.14).

Crafting Alternatives or Foils

The alternatives of a multiple-choice item present choices to the students. All of the choices must be appropriate to the stem. If they are not, they may be ambiguous to knowledgeable students and may not be plausible to less knowledgeable ones. When all alternatives are appropriate

[4]Context-dependent items are discussed in Chapter 10.

FIGURE 8.14 Example of improving a definition item by putting the term in the stem and making the alternatives different definitions.

Poor: Definition in the stem

1. The increase in length per unit of length of a metal rod for each degree rise in temperature (Centigrade) is known as the
   - *a. coefficient of linear expansion of the metal.
   - b. elasticity of the metal.
   - c. specific heat of the metal.
   - d. surface tension of the metal.

Better: Definitions in the options

2. What is the *coefficient of linear expansion* of a metal rod?
   - a. the increase in length of the rod when its temperature is raised 1°C
   - *b. the increase in length when the temperature is raised 1°C divided by the total length of the rod at the original temperature
   - c. the ratio of its length at 1 00°C to its length at 0°C
   - d. the rise in temperature (degrees Centigrade) which is necessary to cause the length of the rod to expand 1 per cent

Source: Adapted from "The Construction of Tests" by E. F. Lindquist and C. R. Mann, in *The Construction and Use of Achievement Examinations: A Manual for Secondary School Teachers* (pp. 145–146) by H. E. Hawkes, E. F. Lindquist, and C. R. Mann (Eds.), 1936, Boston: Houghton-Mifflin. Adapted by permission.

to the stem, the item functions better as a complete unit. Suggestions for improving the quality of the alternatives are summarized in Table 8.2 and discussed in more detail in the following text.

Functional and Plausible Alternatives Many of the suggestions that follow are directed toward crafting **plausible distractors**. You should try to base distractors on errors students commonly make such as computational errors, conceptual errors, or errors resulting from faulty common knowledge. In this way, your analysis of students' responses could help you identify their specific difficulties.

Table 8.2 calls for using from three to five **functional alternatives**. *Functional* means that each alternative attracts at least one of the students who do *not* have the degree of knowledge that you expect of all students. An item may have five alternatives. However, if two of them are easily eliminated by even the most superficial learner, only the remaining three are seriously considered plausible answers. In reality, then, the item has only three *functional* alternatives. For practical purposes you may as well delete the two nonfunctional alternatives: they are "**dead-wood**" or **filler alternatives**.

Teachers sometimes ask if each multiple-choice item should have the same number of alternatives and, if so, how many there should be. Assessment specialists have long recognized that there is no virtue in having the same number of alternatives for each item (Ebel, 1965; Lindquist & Mann, 1936). Research supports the rule that you should write as many functional distractors as is feasible; as Haladyna and Downing (1989b) point out, "The key to distractor development is not the *number* of distractors but the *quality* of distractors" (p. 59).

If you can write three to five functional alternatives, then the item is more likely to distinguish those who have the desired degree of knowledge from those who do not. But the more alternatives you try to write, the harder it will be to make them functional. Using two functional alternatives is permissible, but with only two alternatives, guessing is likely to play a major role. As a rule of thumb, strive to write between three and five functional alternatives. Don't waste your time trying to create the same

TABLE 8.2 Suggestions for improving the alternatives of multiple-choice items.

To do	To avoid
1. In general, strive for creating three to five functional alternatives.	1. Avoid overlapping alternatives.
2. All alternatives should be homogeneous and appropriate to the stem.	2. Avoid making the alternatives a collection of true-false items.
3. Put repeated words and phrases in the stem.	3. Avoid using "not given," "none of the above," etc. as an alternative in *best-answer* type of items (use only with *correct-answer* variety).
4. Use consistent and correct punctuation in relation to the stem.	4. Avoid using "all of the above"; limit its use to the *correct-answer* variety.
5. Arrange alternatives in a list format rather than in tandem.	5. Avoid using verbal clues in the alternatives.
6. Arrange alternatives in a logical or meaningful order.	6. Avoid using technical terms, unknown words or names, and "silly" terms or names as distractors.
7. All distractors should be grammatically correct with respect to the stem.	7. Avoid making it harder to eliminate a distractor than to choose the keyed alternative.

Sources: Ebel, 1951, 1979, Greene, Jorgensen, & Gerberech, 1942, 1943; Gronlund, 1976; Hopkins, Stanley, & Hopkins, 1990; Lindquist & Mann, 1936; Lindvall, 1967; Millman, 1961; Sax, 1974; Thorndike, Cunningham, Thorndike, & Hagen, 1991, Wesman, 1971.

number of alternatives for each item if by so doing you are creating fillers or nonfunctional distractors. Give yourself and your students a break! (Incidentally, if a separate answer sheet is used for machine scoring, check to see the maximum spaces allowed per item and adjust the maximum number of alternatives accordingly.)

Homogeneous Alternatives Lack of homogeneity is a primary reason why distractors do not function. Each **homogeneous alternative** should be a member of the same set of "things," *and* each alternative should be appropriate to the stem. For example, if the stem requires students to identify someone's name, then each alternative should be a name and each name should be appropriate to the question. Figure 8.15 should make this point clear.

You may also adjust the degree of homogeneity to control the difficulty of an item. The more alike the distractors are, the more difficult the item is (Green, 1984). This point is illustrated in Figure 8.3. Homogeneity is also a function of the educational development of the students you are assessing. Item 2 in Figure 8.15 could be made more homogeneous (and more difficult) by using the scientific names of several species of grouse, for example. The World War I items in Figure 8.3 illustrate this point, too: The alternatives in Item 1 in that figure may appear homogeneous to less knowledgeable, younger students, but they will likely appear to be quite **heterogeneous alternatives** to knowledgeable, older students.

Put Repeated Words in the Stem In general, it is better to put into the stem words or phrases that are repeated in each alternative. A more complete stem reduces the amount of reading required of the students. To accomplish this, you may find it necessary to rephrase the stem to focus it on the critical point of the learning target (Figure 8.16).

Consistent, Correct Punctuation If the stem asks a question directly (ends in a question mark), the options can be either (1) complete sentences, (2) single words, terms, names, phrases, or (3) other incomplete sentences. Complete sentences begin with a capital letter and end with an

FIGURE 8.15 Example of improving an item by making the options more homogeneous.

Poor: Heterogeneous options

1. What is the official state bird of Pennsylvania?
   a. mountain laurel
   b. Philadelphia
   *c. ruffed grouse
   d. Susquehanna River

Better: Options belong to same category

2. What is the official state bird of Pennsylvania?
   a. goldfinch
   b. robin
   *c. ruffed grouse
   d. wild turkey

FIGURE 8.16 Example of improving an item by eliminating words repeated in each alternative.

Poor: Words repeated in options

1. Which of the following is the best definition of a *seismograph*?
   a. An apparatus for measuring sound waves.
   b. An apparatus for measuring heat waves.
   *c. An apparatus for measuring earthquake waves.
   d. An apparatus for measuring ocean waves.

Better: Stem is more focused

2. What type of waves does a *seismograph* measure?
   *a. earthquake waves
   b. heat waves
   c. ocean waves
   d. sound waves

appropriate punctuation mark; do not use a semicolon or other inappropriate terminal punctuation. If the options are single words or incomplete sentences, do not use terminal punctuation. However, use a consistent rule for capitalizing the initial word in each option: Throughout the test, either capitalize *all* initial words or capitalize *no* initial word (except a proper noun, of course).

With an **incomplete stem**, each option must plausibly complete the sentence. Begin each option, therefore, with a lowercase letter (unless the initial word is a proper noun) and end it with the appropriate terminal punctuation. There are exceptions to these rules, of course, as in Item 1 in Figure 8.17, which is part of a test on using punctuation correctly.

Arrangement of the Alternatives Alternatives are less confusing and easier to read when they are arranged one below the other in list form rather than in **tandem** or beside one another (Figure 8.18).

FIGURE 8.17 Exception to rule of consistent punctuation for alternatives.

1. Julia became very frightened and shouted,
   a. "Please save me."
   b. "Please save me?"
   *c. "Please save me!"

FIGURE 8.18 Poor arrangement of options (tandem).

1. A test-reset reliability coefficient is calculated from test scores separated by a one-week time interval. Which of the following would likely lower the numerical value of this coefficient? **(a)** Differences in the extent to which students have learned the information required to answer the particular items on the test. **(b)** The fact that some students have better command of general test-taking skills than do others. **(c)** The fact that a few students do better on the particular types of items used. ***(d)** Some students became upset during the second test administration. **(e)** All of the above would likely lower the test-reset reliability coefficient for a particular test.

Alternatives should be arranged in a **meaningful order**, such as order of magnitude or size, degree to which they reflect a given quality, chronologically, or alphabetically. This arrangement makes locating the correct answer easier for the knowledgeable student, reduces reading and search time, and lessens the chance that careless errors will be made. Figure 8.19 illustrates this point.

Grammatically Correct Relationship to the Stem   Items that contain grammatical clues to the correct answer are easier and less reliable than items without such clues (Haladyna & Downing, 1989a). Don't clue the correct answer or permit distractors to be eliminated on superficial bases. Examples of inappropriate grammatical clues include lack of subject-verb agreement, inappropriate indefinite article, and singular/plural confusion. Figure 8.20 illustrates some of these problems.

The indefinite article *a* in Item 1 in Figure 8.20, for example, gives the student the clue that alternative (c) is correct. The other two alternatives begin with vowels and thus require the indefinite article *an*. In Item 2, the conjunction *when* is appropriate only to the phrasing of option (b). Item 3, a plural verb form in the stem, clues the student that he should choose more than one definition.

Overlapping Alternatives   Each alternative should be distinct and not a logical subset of another alternative.

FIGURE 8.19   Acceptable arrangement of options.

1. Which of the following is made from the shells of tiny animals?
    *a. chalk
    b. clay
    c. shale

2. A student's percentile rank is 4. What is the corresponding stanine?
    *a. 1
    b. 2
    c. 3
    d. 4

When alternatives include one another, you give the less knowledgeable but test-wise student clues to the correct answer. Several examples of **overlapping alternatives** are shown in Figure 8.21. In Item 1, option (c) overlaps with options (a) and (b). Even if a student didn't know the correct answer, the student is likely to choose option (c). In Item 2, options (a), (b), and (c) essentially say the same thing: A test-wise student, recognizing this overlap, would likely choose option (d) even if the student knew nothing about the need for water in the Lower Colorado River Basin. Similarly, for Item 3, options (b), (c), and (d) all say essentially the same thing, but here "all of the above" is not one of the choices. Therefore, the test-wise student will know that option (a) must be correct.

Avoid a Collection of True-False Alternatives   A frequent cause of this type of flaw is that the teacher did not have in mind a clear problem or question when creating the item. In Item 1 in Figure 8.22, it is difficult to identify any single question to which a student must respond. All options are related only by the fact that they could begin with the phrase, "Reliability is." Options (b), (c), and (d), when used with that phrase, become false statements. This item is unfocused because it really embeds three ideas: how test length affects reliability, how group variability (standard deviation) affects reliability, and the relationship between a reliability coefficient and the standard error of measurement.[5] Only one of these ideas should be selected and used as a basis for a revised item, as is done with Item 2. (To craft *multiple true-false items*, review Chapter 7.)

Avoid "None of the Above"   Research on the phrase **none of the above** as an option in multiple-choice items indicates that it results in less reliable, more difficult items (Haladyna & Downing, 1989b). Therefore, be very cautious when using this phrase as an option. This option

[5]Understanding these reliability concepts is not essential to understanding the point being made here. Reliability is discussed in Chapter 4.

FIGURE 8.20   Examples of improving items by eliminating grammatical clues to the answer.

Poor: Grammatical incorrectness clues the answer	*Better: All options have grammatically correct relations to the stem*

1. A 90° angle is called a
    a. acute angles.
    b. obtuse angles.
    *c. right angle.
	4. What are 90° angles called?
	    a. acute angles.
	    b. obtuse angles.
	    *c. right angles.

2. Green plants may lose their color when
    a. are forming flowers.
    *b. grown in the dark.
    c. are placed in strong light.
    d. temperature drops.
	5. When may green plants lose their color?
	    a. when they form flowers
	    *b. when they are grown in the dark
	    c. when they are placed in strong light
	    d. when the surrounding temperatures drop

3. Which of the following are called scarves?
    a. band of cloth worn around the neck
    b. type of wood joint
    *c. both (a) and (b) are scarves.
	6. What is a *scarf*?
	    a. band of cloth worn around the neck
	    b. type of wood joint
	    *c. both (a) and (b) are scarves

FIGURE 8.21   Examples of improving items by eliminating the overlapping options.

Poor: Overlapping options

1. What is the population of Modesto, CA?
   - a. over 160,000
   - b. over 140,000
   - *c. over 130,000

2. Why is there a shortage of water in the Lower Basin of the Colorado River?
   - a. The hot sun shines almost always.
   - b. There is a wide, hot desert.
   - c. The temperatures are very high.
   - *d. All of the above are reasons why.

3. How long does a *perennial* plant live?
   - *a. It continues to live year after year.
   - b. It lives for only one growing season.
   - c. It needs to be replanted each year.
   - d. It dies after the first year.

Better: Options do not overlap

4. The population of Modesto, CA, is approximately
   - *a. 160,000.
   - b. 140,000.
   - c. 130,000.

5. Why is there a shortage of water in the Lower Basin of the Colorado River?
   - *a. There is low rainfall, and there are only a few tributaries to the Colorado River.
   - b. Water is soaked up quickly by the desert.
   - c. A dam in the Upper Colorado River made the lower part dry up.

6. How long does a *perennial* plant live?
   - *a. It continues to live for several years.
   - b. It lives for only two years.
   - c. It lives for only one year.

FIGURE 8.22   Example of improving an item by eliminating the unfocused collection of T-F options.

Poor: Options are a collection of unfocused T-F statements

1. Reliability is
   - *a. increased by making the test longer.
   - b. decreased by making the test longer.
   - c. unrelated to the test's standard deviation.
   - d. the same as the test's standard error of measurement.

Better: Stem focuses on a problem

2. Which of the following situations will likely result in an increase in a test's reliability coefficient?
   - *a. A 40-question test is lengthened to 50 questions.
   - b. A 50-question test is shortened to 40 questions.
   - c. The coefficient is re-computed using only the highest scoring 27% of the students.

should never be used with the best-answer variety (see Figure 8.4) of multiple-choice items. The very nature of a best-answer question requires that all of the options are to some degree incorrect, but one of them is "best." It seems illogical to require students to choose "none of the above" under these conditions.

It does make sense, however, to use "none of the above" with some correct-answer questions, when students look for one option that is completely correct. In areas such as arithmetic, certain English mechanics, spelling, and the like, a single, completely correct answer can be definitely established and defended. Some assessment experts recommend using "none of the above" only when students are more likely to solve a problem first before looking at the options (as opposed to searching through the distractors before proceeding with the solution to the problem) (Wood, 1977).

Two special problems associated with using "none of the above" are (1) students may not believe that this choice can be correct and, therefore, they do not think it

is plausible; and (2) if this option is correct, students may select it when in fact their answer is incorrect (Ebel, 1951). To avoid the first problem, use "none of these" as the correct answer to a few easy items near the beginning of the test. This conditions students to seriously consider "none of the above" as a possible correct answer for the remainder of the test. It may then be used as either a correct or incorrect answer later in the test. The second problem is handled by using "none of the above" as a correct answer in an item when the distractors encompass most of the wrong answers that can be expected (see Figure 8.23, Item 1), or using it as a distractor for those items in which most of the probable wrong answers cannot be incorporated into the distractors (Ebel, 1951) (see Item 2).

FIGURE 8.23   Acceptable uses of "none of the above."

Acceptable use of "none of the above": As a correct answer

1. What is the difference?

$$\begin{array}{r} 106 \\ -21 \\ \hline ? \end{array}$$

   - a. 81
   - b. 89
   - c. 101
   - *d. None of the above

Acceptable use of "none of the above": As a plausible distractor

2. What is the sum?

$$\begin{array}{r} 46 \\ 47 \\ + 48 \\ \hline ? \end{array}$$

   - a. 161
   - b. 171
   - *c. 141
   - d. None of the above

More than likely, however, items such as 1 and 2 would be better as completion (open-ended) items than as multiple-choice items. If you used completion items, you would be able to check the students' wrong answers to determine why they responded incorrectly; then you can remediate the students.

Two final comments on this point. Avoid using "none of the above" as a filler to increase the number of distractors. Remember that distractors must be plausible. Second, as an option, "none of the above" is probably more confusing to younger students than to older ones.

Avoid "All of the Above" Research on the use of **all of the above** is inconclusive (Haladyna & Downing, 1989b). This option, if used at all, should be limited to correct-answer varieties of multiple-choice items. It cannot be used with best-answer varieties because "all of the options" cannot be simultaneously best. Two further difficulties arise: (1) students who know that one option is correct may simply choose it and inadvertently go on to the next item without reviewing the remaining options, and (2) students who know that two out of four options are correct can choose "all of the above" without having knowledge of the correctness of the third option. The first difficulty can be reduced to some extent by making the first choice in the list read "all of the following are correct." However, this wording can also confuse elementary and junior high students. Generally, the recommendation is to avoid using "all of the above." Rewrite items with multiple answers as two or more items and avoid these problems. Alternately, rewrite the item as a multiple true-false item (see Chapter 7).

Avoid Verbal Clues Failure to follow this rule makes items easier and lowers the reliability of the test (Haladyna & Downing, 1989b). **Verbal clues** in the alternative frequently lead the less knowledgeable but verbally able student to the correct answer. Verbal clues include using overlapping alternatives, silly or absurd distractors, **clang** (i.e., sound-alike words) or other associations between words in the stem and in the correct alternatives, repetition or resemblance between the correct alternative and the stem, and specific determiners. Item 1 in Figure 8.24, for example, uses *agriculture* in both stems and alternative. This creates a "Who is buried in Grant's tomb?" type of question. Similarly, in Item 2, one can easily associate the terms *educational testing* and *educational measurement* to come up with the correct answer without knowing the contents of any of the journals listed.

Specific determiners are words that overqualify a statement so that it is always true or always false. We saw how these operated with true-false items in Chapter 7; they can occur in multiple-choice items. An example is shown in Figure 8.24 as Item 3. Alternatives (a) and (b) can be easily eliminated: No one "invented all" of anything nor would anyone "construct every . . . test published." After these are eliminated, only option (c) remains.

FIGURE 8.24 Sample items with verbal clues.

Poor: Association of stem and answer

1. Which government agency is most concerned with our nation's agricultural policies?
   *a. Department of Agriculture
   b. Department of Education
   c. Department of the Interior
   d. Department of Labor

2. In which journal can you find articles on recent research about educational testing?
   a. *American Psychologist*
   *b. *Journal of Educational Measurement*
   c. *Journal of Abnormal Child Psychology*
   d. *Memory and Cognition*

Poor: Specific-determiners

3. Which of the following was one of E. L. Thorndike's contributions to educational measurement?
   a. He invented all of the types of multiple-choice items now in use.
   b. He constructed every educational test published between 1900 and 1920.
   *c. He helped educational testing to gain scientific respectability.

Avoid Technical and Unfamiliar Wording Teachers writing multiple-choice items sometimes use highly technical or unfamiliar words as distractors. Words beyond the knowledge base of the students may require more ability to reject the wrong answer than to choose the correct answer (Ebel, 1951). Some studies indicate, however, that students view options containing unfamiliar technical words as less plausible, thereby making such alternatives nonfunctional. In one study, when college students were instructed to mark answers to items for which, unknown to them, no real answer existed, students chose options containing familiar, nontechnical words more frequently than options containing either familiar technical words, vaguely familiar technical words, or unfamiliar technical words (Strang, 1977).

Do Not Make a Distractor Too Plausible Incorrect alternatives sometimes may be made so plausible that generally good students get the item wrong, while less able students respond correctly. (Such items are said to be negatively discriminating; see Chapter 14.) The good students' knowledge, though perhaps normally sufficient for selection of the correct answer when embedded in another context, may be insufficient for rejection of all the distractors in a particular item (Lindquist, 1936). The American history item in Figure 8.25 illustrates this. Although an item should be considered a test of a student's ability to eliminate the distractors as well as the ability to select the correct answer, the ability required to eliminate the incorrect answer should not be greater than the ability needed to make a direct choice of the correct answer (Lindquist, 1936).

FIGURE 8.25 Examples of how students' insufficient and wrong learning can result in poorly functioning items.

The Effect of Insufficient Learning or Understanding

The failure of an item to function because of insufficient or wrong learning is something beyond the control of the test constructor. . . .

What was one of the important immediate results of the War of 1812?

a.	The introduction of a period of intense sectionalism	(39%)
b.	The destruction of the United States Bank	(7%)
c.	The defeat of the Jeffersonian Party	(7%)
d.	The final collapse of the Federalist Party	(43%)

(4 per cent omitted the item)

The correct response to this item is (d). Nevertheless, the pupils who selected the first and incorrect response were, on the average, superior in general achievement to those who selected the correct response (d). Again, the pupils selecting the first and incorrect response apparently did so because of positive but insufficient learning. They knew that a period of intense sectionalism did set in before the middle of the century, and therefore chose the first response. Apparently they did not know, or failed to recall, that a short period of intense nationalism was an immediate result of the Second War with Great Britain, and that this war, therefore, could not be considered as "introducing" an era of sectional strife. Other pupils, with less knowledge in general, were able to select the correct response since they were not attracted to the first response by a certain knowledge that intense sectionalism did develop in the nineteenth century. (It should be noted, however, that for an abler group of pupils, capable of making the judgment called for, this same item might have shown a high positive index of discrimination). . . .

The Effect of Wrong Learning

Wrong learning, as well as insufficient learning, on the part of the pupils for whom the test is intended may cause an item in that test to show a negative index of discrimination. . . .

In the second half of the fifteenth century the Portuguese were searching for an all-water route to India because

a.	They wished to rediscover the route traveled by Marco Polo	(4%)
b.	The Turks had closed the old routes	(59%)
c.	The Spanish had proved that it was possible to reach the east by sailing westward	(10%)
d.	An all-water route would make possible greater profits	(26%)

(1 per cent omitted the item)

It will be noted that more than half of the pupils selected response (b). The negative index of discrimination indicates furthermore that the average achievement of the pupils who selected this response was superior to that of the 25 per cent of the pupils who chose the correct response (d). Authoritative historians no longer would accept the second response as a sufficient explanation of Portuguese attempts to round Africa, nor would they deny that response (d) is the best of those given. An analysis of current textbooks in American history, however, will reveal that these lag behind research and that many of them still present the now disproved explanation: "The Turks closed the old routes." It is not surprising, therefore, that the superior pupils are more likely to select this response than those who have made little or no effective attempt to learn the facts contained in their textbooks. This being the case, the inclusion of this item in the test not only contributed nothing to its effectiveness but even detracted from it. There can be little question, however, that the item is free from technical imperfections or ambiguities, and that it does hold the pupil responsible for an established fact of considerable significance in history.

Source: Adapted from *The Construction and Use of Achievement Examinations: A Manual for Secondary School Teachers* (pp. 56–63) by H. E. Hawkes, E. F. Lindquist, and C. R. Mann (Eds.), 1936, Boston: Houghton Mifflin, © 1936 by Houghton Mifflin Company. Adapted by permission of publisher.

Crafting the Correct Alternative

You should word the correct alternative so that those students *without* the requisite knowledge are *not clued* as to the correct answer and those students with the requisite knowledge *are able* to select the correct answer.

1. *In general, there should be only one correct or best answer to a multiple-choice item.* It is possible to write items that have more than one correct alternative (see Figure 8.4). However, such items may not function as you intended, especially with elementary and junior high school students. Students may, for example, mark the first correct alternative they encounter and skip to the next item without considering all of the alternatives. Some beginning item writers attempt to compensate for this behavior by using the combined response variety of multiple-choice items (Figure 8.4) or by using "all of the above." This usually results in poorer quality items.

2. *Be sure that competent authorities can agree that the answer keyed as correct (or best) is in fact correct (or best).* If you violate this rule, you may come into conflict with the more able student (or the student's parent). Further, if you insist there is only one correct answer when students also see another choice as equally logical and correct, students

will likely see you as arbitrary and capricious. To avoid such embarrassment and negative educational effects, have a knowledgeable colleague review the correctness of your keyed answers and the incorrectness of your distractors before you use them.

3. *The correct alternative should be a grammatically correct response to the stem.* The knowledgeable student is faced with a conflict if the content of the keyed response is correct, but the grammar is incorrect.

4. *Check over the entire test to ensure that the correct alternatives do not follow an easily learned pattern.* Use the answer key you develop to tabulate the number of As, Bs, Cs, etc. that are keyed as correct. Sometimes teachers favor one or two positions (e.g., B and C) for the correct answers. Students will quickly catch on to this pattern, which lowers the validity of your assessment. Also, avoid repetitive, easily learned patterns, such as AABBCCDD or ABCDABCD. If you arrange your alternatives in a logical, numerical, or alphabetical order, you should not have any problems. By using a scoring stencil, you can score exams just as quickly without resorting to set patterns of correct answers.

5. *Avoid phrasing the correct alternative in a "textbookish" or stereotyped manner.* To assess comprehension and understanding, you must at least paraphrase textbook statements. Students quickly learn the idiosyncratic or stereotyped way in which you and the textbook phrase certain ideas. If your test items also reflect such idiosyncrasies, you will be encouraging students to select answers that "sound right" to them but which they do not understand. For more mature students, however, stereotyped phrases that have a "ring of truth" in the *distractors* may serve to distinguish those students who have grasped the concept from those with only superficial knowledge (Ebel, 1979). Use this tactic with senior high school and college students, but not with elementary and junior high school students.

6. *The correct alternative should be of the same overall length as the distractors.* Teachers sometimes make the correct option longer than the incorrect options by phrasing it in a more completely explained or more qualified manner. The test-wise student can pick up on this and mark the longest or most complete answer without having the requisite knowledge. Research supports the generalization that if you violate this rule you will make the item easier (Haladyna & Downing, 1989b).

7. *An advantage of a multiple-choice test is that it reduces the amount of time required for writing answers and uses this time to increase the content coverage of the assessment.* Don't defeat this purpose by requiring students to write out their answers. Have the students either mark (circle, check, etc.) the letter of the alternative they choose, write the letter on a blank next to the stem created for that purpose, or use

a separate answer sheet. Separate answer sheets are not recommended for children below fourth or fifth grade (see Aleyideino, 1968; Beck, 1974; Cashen & Ramseyer, 1969; Davis & Trimble, 1978; Gaffney & Maguire, 1971; Moss, Cole, & Trent, 1979; Muller, Calhoun, & Orling, 1972; Ramseyer & Cashen, 1971). However, if your state has a testing program that uses separate answer sheets in the primary grades, use answer sheets with some of your classroom tests to give the children practice.

A CHECKLIST FOR EVALUATING MULTIPLE-CHOICE ITEMS

Practicing the preceding rules will help you to write better multiple-choice items. It is difficult to keep all of the rules in mind, however. Some of the most useful rules appear in a checklist in Table 8.3. You can use this checklist to review the items you have written or those you have found in the quizzes and tests that come with your textbook or teaching materials. As we pointed out earlier, tests that come with textbooks and curricular materials are seldom

TABLE 8.3   A checklist for judging the quality of multiple-choice items.

1. Does the exercise assess an important aspect of the unit's instructional targets?	Yes	No
2. Does the exercise match your assessment plan in terms of performance, emphasis, and number of points?	Yes	No
3. Does the stem of the item ask a direct question or set a specific problem?	Yes	No
4. Is the item based on a paraphrase (rather than lifted directly from a textbook)?	Yes	No
5. Are the vocabulary and sentence structure at a relatively low and nontechnical level?	Yes	No
6. Is each incorrect alternative (foil) plausible so that it cannot be viewed as absurd or silly by a student who lacks knowledge of the correct answer?	Yes	No
7. If possible, is every incorrect alternative (foil) based on a common student error or misconception?	Yes	No
8. Is the correct answer to this item independent of the correct answer to other test items?	Yes	No
9. Are all the alternatives homogeneous and appropriate to the content of the stem?	Yes	No
10. Did you avoid using "all of the above" and "none of the above" as much as possible?	Yes	No
11. Is there only one correct or best answer to the item?	Yes	No

Note: Revise every matching exercise for which you marked "no" for one or more of the questions.
Source: Adapted from *Teacher's Guide to Better Classroom Testing: A Judgmental Approach* (p. 35) by A. J. Nitko and T-C. Hsu, 1987, Pittsburgh, PA: Institute for Practice and Research in Education, School of Education, University of Pittsburgh. Adapted by permission.

written by professional item writers, so the items are usually quite poorly written. Before using them, use the checklist to review each item. Revise every item that does not pass your checklist evaluation before you use it.

CRAFTING ALTERNATIVE VARIETIES OF MULTIPLE-CHOICE ITEMS

This part of the chapter extends your knowledge of multiple-choice item formats. These are usually not taught in traditional assessment courses, but they have considerable usefulness.

The value of these item formats is fourfold. First, some of them will fit your learning targets much more closely than do typical true-false, matching, and multiple-choice formats. It is most important that you craft assessment tasks that closely match the targets you intended students to learn. Second, the formats are objectively scored. As you know, the more objective your scoring, the more likely you are to have reliable scores for evaluating your students. Third, because these tasks take students a relatively short time to complete, your coverage of learning targets is more thorough. That is, since you have only a limited amount of time to assess students, you can assess a wider range of content and learning targets by using one or more of these formats in addition to your traditional assessment formats. Fourth, these formats are relatively easy to craft. In most cases they are easier to craft than traditional multiple-choice and matching items.

The section discusses four item formats: greater-less-same, best-answer, experiment-interpretation, and statement-and-comment. Many of the ideas for this discussion are adapted from Carlson (1985) and Gulliksen (1986). After each format is illustrated, we discuss advantages and criticisms, then offer suggestions for improving the way you craft the items.

GREATER-LESS-SAME ITEMS

Format

The **greater-less-same item** format is used to assess qualitative, quantitative, or temporal relationships between concepts. Figure 8.26 shows several examples. Each greater-less-same item consists of a pair of concepts, phrases, quantities, and so on that have a greater-than, same-as, or less-than relationship. The student's task is to identify the relationship between the concepts and record his answer. You may use before-during-after (Item 7 in Figure 8.26), more-same-less, heavier-same-lighter, or other ordered triads depending on the context of the items. Also, instead of spelling out the words *greater*, *less*, *same*, you can use the letters *G*, *L*, and *S*, respectively. Using letters instead of words may be more appropriate for older students.

Advantages and Criticisms

Advantages The greater-less-same format is especially suited for assessing whether students understand the order between two concepts, events, or outcomes. Orders include greater than vs. less than, more of vs. less of, before vs. after, more correct vs. less correct, more preferred vs. less preferred, heavier vs. lighter, and higher quality vs. lesser quality. When you teach the relationships in class or when students learn the relationships from the textbook, this item assesses recall and recognition. However, the item format need not be limited to recall. You may teach a principle in or a set of criteria and give several examples of its application in class. Then, when assessing the students, *present new examples*. A student can then apply the principle(s) or criteria you taught to deduce the relationship between the concept pairs.

Criticisms The criticisms of greater-less-same items are similar to those for matching and true-false items. That is, teachers often use them to assess rote association and disconnected bits of knowledge. Also, this format limits assessment to relationships among pairs of concepts. If you wish to assess a student's ability to order larger members of events or facts, then use the rank-order item format.

Crafting Suggestions

Begin to craft items by first identifying the learning targets you want to assess. This item format assesses learning targets that include the ability to identify the relationships between two ideas, concepts, or situations. You should make a list of concept pairs that are related; add to this list other paired relationships that your students can deduce from principles or criteria they have learned. Rephrase the members of each pair so they are clearly stated and fit the item format. When arranging the pairs, be sure that you do not have all the "greaters" on one side of the pair.

Write a set of directions for students that explains the basis on which they are to choose greater-same-less (before-during-after, etc.). Normally, the set of items should refer to the same general topic. In Figure 8.26 this is not the case, because we wanted to illustrate items from different subject areas. Therefore, the directions in Figure 8.26 are too general. Your directions should be more focused on the set of items you are using and very clear. Notice, too, that in Figure 8.26, Item 7 does not "fit" the directions. Sample items may be necessary to help students understand what they are to do. Be sure the directions tell the students *which member (i.e., left or right member) of the pairs* in the set they are to use as a referent.

Organize all the items of this format into one section of your assessment. Put the directions and the sample item at the beginning of the set. The numbered items should follow. Be sure that the correct answers do not follow a set pattern. Review the set to be sure the items are

FIGURE 8.26 Examples of greater-less-same item format.

Directions: The numbered items below contain pairs of statements. Compare the two members of each pair. If the thing described on the *left* is greater than the thing described on the right, circle the word "greater"; if the *left* is less than the right, circle "less"; and if the left and right are essentially the same, circle "same."

1. Total area of Lake Erie

   Greater
   Same
   (Less)

   Total area of Lake Huron

2. The meaning of prefix **mono-**

   Greater
   (Same)
   Less

   The meaning of prefix **uni-**

3. Radius of Mars

   Greater
   Same
   (Less)

   Radius of Venus

4. Number of Christians in Africa

   (Greater)
   Same
   Less

   Number of Moslems in Africa

5. Atomic weight of **Ca**

   (Greater)
   Same
   Less

   Atomic weight of **C**

6. $\sqrt{3^2 + 7^2}$

   (Greater)
   Same
   Less

   $\sqrt{3^2} + \sqrt{7^2}$

7. First U.S. passenger railroad opened

   Before
   During
   (After)

   Erie Canal opened

TABLE 8.4 A checklist for judging the quality of greater-less-same item sets.

1. Does each item in the greater-less-same item set assess an important aspect of the unit's instructional targets?	Yes	No
2. Does the greater-less-same item set match your assessment plan in terms of performance, emphasis, and number of points?	Yes	No
3. Do some of the items in the greater-less-same item set require students to apply their knowledge and skill to new situations, examples, or events?	Yes	No
4. Do your directions clearly and completely explain the basis you intend students to use when judging "greater than," "less than," or "same as" for each pair of statements?	Yes	No
5. Do your directions state which pair member (left or right) is the referent?	Yes	No
6. Did you avoid using a pattern (GGSSLLGGSSLL, etc.) for the correct answers?	Yes	No

Note: Revise every greater-less-same item set for which you marked "no" for one or more of the questions.

concisely worded, the task is clear, and that the relationships are not ambiguous.

The suggestions in this section are summarized as a checklist in Table 8.4. Use the checklist to guide you in crafting greater-less-same item sets. Use it, too, to evaluate the item sets you have already crafted.

BEST-ANSWER ITEMS

Format

Best-answer items are multiple-choice items. However, unlike ordinary multiple-choice options, every option is correct to some degree. The student's task is to select the best or most correct option. Figure 8.27 shows two examples of best-answer items. Each distractor contains partial misinterpretations or omissions. The keyed or best answer contains neither misinterpretations nor omissions. A distractor that contains omissions is an incomplete answer to the stem and, therefore, is not as good a choice as the best answer. Only one option can be the "best." Therefore, you should never use "all of the above" or "none of the above" with this format. Neither can some combination of choices (such as "both A and C") be the keyed answer.

Advantages and Criticisms

Advantages   Best-answer items assess students' ability to make relatively fine distinctions among the choices. They must comprehend the question and the criteria used to judge the "best" option. Thus, best-answer items assess relatively high-order verbal reasoning skills.

Criticisms   The best-answer item format is rather difficult to craft. You must know your subject and your students' faulty thinking patterns quite well. You need to create distractors that are partially correct, yet less defensible than the keyed answers. This is unlike typical multiple-choice items for which one option is the only correct one; the others are incorrect. Another criticism is that this format may be unsuitable for some students because their level of educational development is not high enough to make the fine distinctions necessary to select the best answer.

A third criticism is that different teachers may not teach consistently across sections of the same course. Thus, what is legitimately a best answer in one teacher's class (given what students have been taught) is not the best answer in another teacher's class. A fourth criticism is that *best* implies a set of criteria that may not have been taught or understood by students. No answer is

FIGURE 8.27   Examples of best-answer item formats.

1. Which of the following statements best describes why William attacked England?
   A. William felt that his family ties to the kings of England qualified him to take the throne when Edward the Confessor died.
   B. William was asked by the King of Norway, Harold Hardrada, to help him conquer England. William agreed, hoping to dispose of Harold later.
   C. William felt that Edward the Confessor had promised him the throne and Harold, Earl of Wessex, had sworn personal loyalty to him. When the Witan chose Harold to be king, William felt betrayed.
   D. William's cousin, Harold of Wessex, was being held for ransom by Edward the Confessor and William wanted to help release him and then ask him to swear loyalty to William as King of England.

Directions: In the paragraph below is a set of facts about the way two gases, P and Q, react with each other. Following the facts is a hypothesis and brief descriptions of possible experiments to test the hypothesis. In light of the facts, select the experiment that will best test the hypothesis.

Facts: Two gases, P and Q, react quickly when mixed in a glass flask. However, if you heat the flask very hot and then let it cool just before you introduce the gases into it, they do not react. Also, if you use a copper container, the gases do not react at all.

2. **Hypothesis:** Water is necessary in order for the gases to react.
   A. **Experiment:** Before introducing the gases into the flask, you should dry the flask but do not heat it.
   B. **Experiment:** After you introduce the gases into the flask, you should leave the flask open.
   C. **Experiment:** Before you introduce the gases into the flask, you should moisten the walls of the flask with water.
   D. **Experiment:** Before you introduce the gases into the flask, you should heat the flask very hot, let it cool, and then leave it open for several days.
   E. This hypothesis is not tenable or cannot be tested experimentally.

Source: Item 1 is adapted from *Creative Classroom Testing: Ten Designs for Assessment and Instruction* (p. 182) by S. B. Carlson, 1985, Princeton, NJ: Educational Testing Service. Reprinted by permission of Educational Testing Service, the copyright owner. Item 2 is adapted from *Handbook on Formative and Summative Evaluation of Student Learning* (p. 199) by B. S. Bloom, J. T. Hastings, and G. F. Madaus, 1971, New York: McGraw-Hill. Adapted by permission.

unequivocally best unless it is evaluated by applying these criteria. Your students must internalize criteria to apply them. Also, your own knowledge of the subject may be limited. As a result, what you consider the best answer may in fact not be best, because you do not understand other criteria by which the options may be evaluated. A fifth criticism is that a teacher may easily write a "tricky" item—that is, an item in which an option's correctness depends on a trivial fact, an idiosyncratic standard, or an easily overlooked word or phrase.

Crafting Suggestions

As always, first identify the learning targets you want to assess. Those learning targets that require students to choose among several partially correct alternatives may be assessed using this format. Before using this type of item, be sure you have taught your students to use criteria for selecting the best among several partially correct explanations, descriptions, and ideas. These are higher-order thinking skills (often called critical thinking skills) in that students must use criteria (such as "completeness of response" and "no misinformation") to evaluate alternatives.

Draft the question for the stem, then write several ways in which students' responses to that question are typically partially correct. These become the basis for crafting distractors. You could also give your students several open-ended short-answer questions as homework. Then, select from among the students' responses those that represent excellent, good, and poor answers. Edited versions of these could be used as a basis for crafting the options.

(You should not use students' responses verbatim as options. They may be poorly phrased or contain too many other errors to function well as partially correct nonkeyed response options.)

Because the best-answer format is a multiple-choice format, you should follow the basic rules of writing multiple-choice items, discussed earlier. A typical flaw with best-answer items is to make the best or keyed answer the one with the longest wording because it contains the most complete information. Avoid this flaw by being sure the options have approximately equal numbers of words. You should review the checklist in Table 8.3 at this point to be certain you understand what these basic rules are. Table 8.5 is a summary in a checklist format of the suggestions in this section. You should use this checklist to guide you as you craft best-answer items. Use it, too, as an evaluation guide as you review and edit the items you have already crafted.

EXPERIMENT-INTERPRETATION ITEMS

Format

The **experiment-interpretation item** consists of a description of an experiment followed by a multiple-choice item requiring students to recognize the best interpretation of the results from the experiment. Figure 8.28 shows three examples. Items 1 and 2 are for a course in general or physical science; Item 3 is for a social studies unit or a mathematics unit on statistical methods. We use the term *experiment* rather loosely in this section: It means any

TABLE 8.5 A checklist for judging the quality of best-answer items.

1.	Does each best-answer item assess an important aspect of the curriculum's learning targets?	Yes	No
2.	Does each best-answer item match your assessment plan in terms of performance, emphasis, and number of points?	Yes	No
3.	Does each best-answer item require students to apply their knowledge and skill in some manner to new situations, examples, or events?	Yes	No
4.	Do your directions clearly and completely explain the basis you intend students to use when judging "best"? (Have your students been given practice in using the appropriate criteria for judging "best"?)	Yes	No
5.	Are all the options correct to some degree?	Yes	No
6.	Is the keyed answer the only one that can be defended as "the best" by applying the criteria you specify in the directions?	Yes	No
7.	Is each distractor based on an important misconception, misunderstanding, or way of being an incomplete answer? (i.e., did you avoid tricky or trivial ways of making a distractor partially correct or contain misinformation?)	Yes	No
8.	Are all of the options of approximately equal length (within five words of each other)?	Yes	No
9.	Did you avoid (a) having more than one "best" answer and (b) using "all of the above" or "none of the above"?	Yes	No
10.	Did you apply all of the appropriate multiple-choice item-writing guidelines described in the checklist in Table 8.3?	Yes	No

Note: Revise every best answer item for which you marked "no" for one or more of the questions.

FIGURE 8.28 Examples of the experiment-interpretation item format.

Use the following information when answering Question 1.

Billy and Jesse were walking through an empty lot near their home. Billy picked up a whitish rock. "Look," he said, "I found a limestone rock. I know it is limestone because I found a rock last year that has the same color and it was limestone." Jesse said, "Just because it looks the same it doesn't have to be the same."

1. Which of the following explanations best supports *Jesse's* point of view?
   A. During the year the chemical properties of limestone probably changed.
   B. Different minerals have very similar physical properties.
   C. One year is not long enough for the minerals in a rock to change their physical properties.

Use the following information when answering Question 2.

Billy took the rock home and did an experiment with it. He put a piece of the rock in a clear glass and poured vinegar over it. The rock bubbled and foamed. "There!" he said to Jesse, "That proves the rock is limestone." Jesse said, "No! You are wrong. You haven't proved it."

2. Why was *Jesse* correct?
   A. Billy did the experiment only once. He needs to repeat the same type of experiment many times with different bits of the rock. If the mixture bubbles every time, that will prove it.
   B. The experiment was correct but Billy interpreted the results incorrectly. Limestone does not bubble and foam in vinegar.
   C. Billy should do many different kinds of experiments, not just vinegar tests, because many different kinds of substances bubble and foam in vinegar.
   D. Billy should not have used vinegar. He should put the rock into distilled water. If the rock made the water warm, that would prove it was limestone.

Use the following information when answering Question 3.

For a social studies project, a class interviewed all the tenth grade students. They asked how many hours per week students worked at after school jobs. They also asked what their average grades were last term. They found that students with Fs and Ds work about 8 to 10 hours per week, students with Cs and Bs worked 10 to 20 hours per week, and students with As worked 8 to 10 hours per week.

3. Which of the following is the most valid interpretation of these findings?
   A. If you work 10 to 20 hours per week, you will only get Cs and Bs.
   B. Working after school is not related to your grades.
   C. A student who works 10 to 20 hours per week after school is probably not an A-student or an F-student.
   D. The more hours a student works after school, the higher will be that student's grades.

Source: Items 1 and 2 are based on ideas found in Klopfer. 1971.

data-based research study. Scientific or controlled studies are included in the term, but we do not limit its use to only those types of studies. The experiment-interpretation item is similar to the best-answer format, because very often the multiple-choice options will all have some degree of correctness, but only one is the best answer.

A variation is to use a short-answer item along with or instead of the multiple-choice items. For example, you may ask a student to justify her choice on the multiple-choice item. Alternatively, you could use a short-answer question instead of the multiple-choice one. Figure 8.29 shows these variations, based on Item 3 in Figure 8.28.

You should note that the three variations (multiple-choice only, multiple-choice with short-answer, and short-answer only) assess somewhat different abilities. Using multiple-choice only assesses a student's ability to evaluate each of *the interpretations you provide* and to select the best one. Thus you do not know a student's reasoning behind his selection. The multiple-choice *with short-answer* assesses a student's ability to explain or justify her choice from among the interpretations you provide as options. This helps you assess the reasoning behind students' choices. The short-answer *without the multiple-choice items* assesses both a student's ability to interpret the experiment's results and his ability to explain his reasoning. In this latter format there may be multiple correct responses to the open-ended questions.

Advantages and Criticisms

Advantages You may use the experiment-interpretation format to assess a student's ability to evaluate explanations, interpretations, and inferences from data. The multiple-choice-only version allows you to score the items more quickly and more objectively than the other versions. Because students are required only to select the correct answer, their response times are shorter. Therefore, you can use more items and cover more

FIGURE 8.29 Alternative ways of crafting the experiment-interpretation item format.

Use the following information when answering the questions below.

For a social studies project, a class interviewed all the tenth grade students. They asked how many hours per week students worked at after school jobs. They also asked what their average grades were last term. They found that students with Fs and Ds work about 8 to 10 hours per week, students with Cs and Bs worked 10 to 20 hours per week, and students with As worked 8 to 10 hours per week.

Alternative A. Students justify their choice

1. Which of the following is the most valid interpretation of these findings?
   A. If you work 10 to 20 hours per week, you will only get Cs and Bs.
   B. Working after school is not related to your grades.
   C. A student who works 10 to 20 hours per week after school is probably not an A-student or an F-student.
   D. The more hours a student works after school, the higher will be that student's grades.

2. Write a brief explanation of why your answer to Question 1 is the most valid interpretation of these findings.

_____

_____

_____

_____

Alternative B. Students supply their own interpretation and justify it

1. What is the most valid interpretation of the relationship between the number of hours students work and their grades in this study?

_____

_____

_____

2. Explain why your interpretation of these findings is the most valid.

_____

_____

_____

_____

content within a shorter assessment period than with short-answer items.

If the experiments and findings you present in the items are new to the students, your items will assess your students' ability to apply principles and criteria from your subject area. Using experiments and data new to your students in assessment tasks requires you to teach students how to apply criteria and principles to a variety of situations. You will need to give students sufficient practice in applying criteria and principles before assessing them for summative evaluation purposes. This will move your teaching away from teaching facts and results, and toward teaching students to actively apply their knowledge and skill.

If you require students to justify their multiple-choice answers, you will have some information about the reasoning processes that they use. Students often make the correct choice from among the possible interpretations you give them; but they cannot explain why they made the choice, or they give faulty explanations. If you require a student both to supply his interpretation and to justify it, you can assess whether the student can generate and explain his own interpretations of experimental findings.

Criticisms Like the best-answer item format, the experiment-interpretation format is not easy to craft. You must know your subject matter and your students' thinking patterns well enough to craft items that allow you to identify faulty thinking as well as correct answers. Faulty thinking must be reflected in your multiple-choice distractors. This means you must be able to create partially correct interpretations and incorrect interpretations that people typically make.

Criticism is leveled at teachers who use this format to assess whether a student can recall the "correct" interpretations of specific experimental results that the teacher taught. These teachers are not assessing the higher-order thinking ability that this format is capable of assessing. Using this item format to assess recall encourages students to look to the teacher or the text as the source of fixed knowledge. It discourages students from learning skills required to interpret the empirical results of experiments.

Crafting Suggestions

First, identify the learning targets you want to assess. The experiment-interpretation assessment format is appropriate when a learning target requires students to understand and interpret the results of empirical research. Before using this format for summative student evaluation, be sure you have taught and have given practice in interpreting the findings from empirical research studies.

Craft the item to assess the student's ability to apply specific principles. This means that you first identify the principles or rules you want students to apply, then craft the item so it requires students to use the principle in a new situation. For example, in Figure 8.28 the following principles are the ideas around which the items are crafted:

- Different substances may share the same or similar physical properties such as color, texture, and solubility. [Item 1]
- Different substances may share the same or similar chemical properties, such as their reactivity with acids. [Item 2]
- Some patterns of relationships among variables are not strictly increasing or decreasing but are curvilinear. [Item 3]

After identifying the principle(s), you craft the item to require using or applying the principle(s). Usually, this means writing a description of the experiment or research study that results in findings that a student can then interpret using the principle(s). (See the interpretive text that immediately precedes the items in the examples in Figure 8.28.)

Next, draft a stem that asks the student to interpret or explain the experimental findings you describe. You may then list several correct or partially correct interpretations. You may also list incorrect interpretations that result from incomplete or faulty reasoning. Avoid using as distractors in-terpretations that are completely unrelated to the experiment you describe or that are "silly" or "tricky." For example, it would be inappropriate for you to use in Item 1 (Figure 8.28) a distractor that read, "Jesse knows that Billy is a liar."

As with the best-answer item format, distractors should contain interpretations or explanations that are your students' typical misconceptions. Also, you could assign several open-ended questions as homework and select from among the students' responses those that are excellent, good, and poor. Use these selections as a basis for crafting multiple-choice options.

If you use the multiple-choice versions of this format, you should follow the basic rules of writing multiple-choice items that we discussed earlier and that are summarized in Table 8.3. You may wish to review these rules at this time. If you use one of the short-answer versions of this format, you should follow the basic rules of short-answer item writing. We discussed these in Chapter 7 and the rules are summarized in Table 7.3. You may wish to review these at this time also. Table 8.6 is a summary in a checklist format to guide you as you craft experiment-interpretation items and as you evaluate your drafts of these items.

STATEMENT-AND-COMMENT ITEMS

Format

A statement-and-comment item presents a statement about some relevant subject matter and requires the student either to write a comment about the statement or to select the most appropriate comment from among a list you

TABLE 8.6 A checklist for judging the quality of experiment-interpretation items.

	Yes	No
1. Does each experiment-interpretation item assess an important aspect of the unit's learning targets?	Yes	No
2. Does each experiment-interpretation item match your assessment plan in terms of performance, emphasis, and number of points?	Yes	No
3. Is each item focused on requiring students to apply one or more important principles or criteria to new situations, examples, or events?	Yes	No
4. Have you given students practice in applying the appropriate criteria or principles for judging the "best" or "most valid" interpretation?	Yes	No
5. Did you describe an experiment or research study in concise but sufficient detail that a student can use the appropriate criteria or principles to interpret the results?	Yes	No
6. Is the keyed answer the only one that can be defended as "the best" or "most valid" by applying the appropriate criteria or principles?	Yes	No
7. Is each distractor based on an important misconception, misinterpretation, or misapplication of a criterion or principle (i.e., avoid tricky or trivial ways of making a distractor partially correct or contain misinformation)?	Yes	No
8. Did you avoid (a) having more than one "best" or "most valid" answer and (b) using "all of the above" or "none of the above"?	Yes	No
9. Did you apply all of the appropriate multiple-choice item-writing guidelines described in the checklist in Table 8.3?	Yes	No
10. If you used short-answer items, did you apply all the appropriate item-writing guidelines described in the checklist in Table 7.3?	Yes	No

Note: Revise every experiment-interpretation item for which you marked "no" for one or more of the questions.

provide. Figure 8.30 shows examples of statement-and-comment items. The subject-matter area of the items is Shakespeare's play, *Julius Caesar*. The statements are three of the play's themes, which the class discussed. These themes are shown in quotation marks. In the multiple-choice version, a student selects from among several alternate choices the best meaning of the quoted theme. The multiple-choice version is a special case of the best-answer item format. The alternatives should be phrased in language that is not identical to the "pat phrases" learned in class. In the short-answer version, a student must comment directly, writing her own interpretation of the quoted statement.

Advantages and Criticisms

Advantages The statement-and-comment item format assesses a student's ability to evaluate interpretations of a given statement. The multiple-choice version assesses whether students can identify the best interpretation or explanation from among the several that you give them. Explanations should not use the same wording used in class. Rather, they should be comments that are typically made by students when interpreting the quoted statement. In

this way, a student must rely on his comprehension of the quoted phrase instead of his memory of a "set" comment.

The open-ended version assesses a student's ability to recall and write about the meaning of the quoted statement. Although it may be an advantage to have students construct their own comments about the quoted statement, there is a downside. Students may just write an explanation or commentary they memorized from the class discussion or from a textbook. You have some control over what kinds of comments they must evaluate if you present the multiple-choice version.

The short-answer version could assess some higher-order thinking if the quoted statement was from outside the course but can be commented on or evaluated using the knowledge and skills taught in the course. For example, the quote can be from a public official's statement in the newspaper. The task could be to evaluate or criticize the statement using specified principles.

Criticisms The statement-and-comment item format has a rather limited scope of application. You must identify appropriate statements that students should interpret. Although there are many subjects for which such statements

FIGURE 8.30 Examples of two versions of statement-and-comment item formats.

A. Multiple-choice version

Directions: The quote in each numbered statement expresses a theme about the play *Julius Caesar*. Below the quote are several comments about the meaning of the statement in quotes. Choose the one comment that **best** expresses how the quoted theme applies to the play.

1. **"Power corrupts."**
    A. Caesar wanted to be crowned king.
    B. Brutus feared that Rome would be controlled by one man. Therefore, he plotted against Caesar.
    C. Cassius wanted power so much he led a conspiracy against Caesar.

2. **"Cowards die many times before their deaths."**
    A. Caesar ignored the warning he was given because he was not a coward.
    B. Brutus and Cassius ran away because they were afraid of being killed.
    C. Brutus and Cassius led a life of shame and defeat after running away from Rome.

3. **"The evil that men do lives after them."**
    A. Romans would remember Brutus and Cassius for the murders they committed instead of the "noble" motive they had for committing the murder.
    B. Caesar's murderers considered only his bad qualities, not his good qualities.
    C. Anthony remembered only the evil side of Cassius.

B. Short-answer version

Directions: The quote in each numbered statement expresses a theme about the play *Julius Caesar*. Below the quote, write an explanation and your opinion about the meaning of the statement in quotes. Your comments should explain how the quoted theme applies to the play.

4. **"Power corrupts."**

_____

_____

5. **"Cowards die many times before their deaths."**

_____

_____

6. **"The evil that men do lives after them."**

_____

_____

Source: Adapted from *Creative Classroom Testing: Ten Designs for Assessment and Instruction* (pp. 124–125) by S. B. Carlson, 1985, Princeton, NJ: Educational Testing Service. Reprinted by permission of Educational Testing Service, the copyright owner.

exist, the task itself represents a small range of learning targets. The short-answer version of the task does provide an opportunity for students to display their comprehension of the quoted statement. However, students may simply repeat the phrases they learned in class.

Crafting Suggestions

First identify the learning targets you want to assess. This assessment format is appropriate when a learning target requires a student to comprehend statements and themes. For example, a learning target that focuses on a student's understanding of the themes that underlie the play *Julius Caesar* could use this format.

If you give students the short-answer version as a homework exercise, you may use excellent, good, and poor student responses as a basis for creating the alternatives for the multiple-choice version. As with the best-answer variety, of which this may be considered a special case, you usually cannot use students' responses verbatim as multiple-choice options; paraphrase them. Because the multiple-choice version of the statement-and-comment is a type of best-answer item, follow the guidelines suggested in the checklist in Table 8.5.

MATCHING EXERCISE FORMAT

Figure 8.31 is an example of a matching exercise with its various parts labeled. A **matching exercise** presents a student with three things: (1) **directions for matching**, (2) a list of **premises**, and (3) a list of **responses**. The sample

FIGURE 8.31   The parts of a matching exercise.

In the left-hand column below are descriptions of some late-nineteenth century American painters. For each description, choose the name of the person being described from the right-hand column and place the letter identifying it on the line preceding the number of the description. Each name in the right-hand column may be used once, more than once, or not at all.

Instructions for matching

Item numbers

Description of Painter	Name of Painter
(e) 1. A society portraitist, who emphasized depicting a subject's social position rather than a clear-cut characterization of the subject.	a. Mary Cassatt
	b. Thomas Eakins
	c. John LaFarge
	d. Winslow Homer
	e. John Singer Sargent
	f. James A.M. Whistler
(d) 2. A realistic painter of nature, especially known for paintings of the sea.	
(b) 3. A realistic painter of people, who depicted strong characterizations and powerful, unposed forms of the subject.	
(a) 4. An impressionist in the style of Degas, who often painted mother and child themes.	

Responses

Premises

matching exercise requires simple matching based on associations that a student must remember. You may create matching exercises, however, to assess students' comprehension of concepts and principles. Examples of these latter types appear later in the chapter.

Study Figure 8.31. Premises are listed in the left-hand column and responses in the right-hand column.[6] Each premise is numbered because each is a separately scorable item. You can craft matching exercises with more responses than premises, more premises than responses, or an equal number of each. Most assessment specialists consider the last case to be undesirable because it results in **perfect matching**. That is, if a student knows four of the five answers, the student is automatically credited with the fifth (last) choice whether or not he knows the answer. This reduces the validity of the assessment results.

Matching exercises are very much like multiple-choice items. Each premise functions as a separate item. The elements in the list of responses function as alternatives. You could rewrite a matching exercise as a series of multiple-choice items: Each premise would then be a multiple-choice stem, but the same alternatives would be repeated for each of these stems. This leads to an important principle for crafting matching exercises: *Use matching exercises only when you have several multiple-choice items that require repeating the identical set of alternatives (foils).*

ADVANTAGES AND CRITICISMS OF MATCHING EXERCISES

Advantages

A matching exercise can be a space-saving, compact, and objective way to assess a number of important learning targets, such as a student's ability to identify associations or relationships between two sets of things. You can also develop matching exercises using pictorial materials to assess the students' abilities to match words and phrases with pictures of objects or with locations on maps and diagrams. Among the relationships that you may use as a basis for developing matching exercises are those in Table 8.7 (Gronlund, 1976).

Criticisms

Detractors criticize the matching exercise because students can use rote memorization to learn the elements in two lists, *and* because teachers often use matching exercises only to assess such rote associations as names and dates. As a result, critics often see this assessment format as limited to the assessment of memorized factual information.

Thoughtful teachers, however, also use matching exercises to assess aspects of a student's comprehension of concepts, principles, or schemes for classifying objects,

TABLE 8.7   Examples of bases for developing matching exercises.

Possible Premise Sets	Associated Response Sets
Accomplishments	Persons
Noted events	Dates
Definitions	Terms and phrases
Examples, applications	Rules, principles, and classifications
Concepts (ideas, operations, quantities, and qualities)	Symbols and signs
Titles of works	Authors and artists
Foreign words and phrases	English correspondence
Uses and functions	Parts and machines
Names of objects	Pictures of objects

ideas, or events (we will see examples later). *If you want to assess students on these higher-level abilities, craft exercises that present new examples or instances of the concept or principle to the students.* Then require the students to match these examples with the names of appropriate concepts or principles. In this context, *new examples* means instances of concepts that have not been previously taught to or encountered *by the student.* Similarly, a matching task can describe a novel situation to the situation, and the student can decide which of several rules, principles, or classifications is likely to apply.

Figure 8.32 shows an example of this type of matching exercise. The exercise assesses your understanding of five concepts presented in Chapter 1. This type is called a **masterlist variety** of matching exercise. It is also called the **classification** or **keylist variety**. Later in this chapter we present suggestions for crafting this type of matching exercise as well as the double matching exercise or tabular exercise.

A serious practical limitation of matching exercises is the difficulty you often encounter when trying to find **homogeneous premises and responses**. The premises and responses that together form a matching exercise should refer to the same category of things. In Figure 8.32, for example, all premises and responses refer to some type of educational decision. In the example in Figure 8.31, all premises and responses refer to late 19th-century painters. Why should you create matching exercises with homogeneous premises and responses? Because the entire list of responses has to be plausible for *every* premise. If it is not, the students' matching task may be trivial.

Consider the nonhomogeneous, poor-quality matching exercise in Figure 8.33. The responses are not all plausible distractors for *each* premise. As a result, students can answer the items on the basis of general knowledge of a few of the associations and common sense, rather than on any special knowledge learned from the curriculum.

This matching exercise is poor for another, perhaps more important, reason: *The main focus of the exercise seems*

[6]The responses may also be put before the premises. See Figure 8.32.

FIGURE 8.32 Masterlist variety of matching exercise.

Each of the numbered statements below describes a testing situation in which ONE decision is represented. On the blank next to each statement write the letter:

A   if the decision is primarily concerned with *placement*.

B   if the decision is primarily concerned with *selection*.

C   if the decision is primarily concerned with *program improvement*.

D   if the decision is primarily concerned with *theory development*.

E   if the decision is primarily concerned with *motivating students*.

_(A)_ 9. After children are admitted to kindergarten, they are given a perceptual skills screening test to determine which children should be given special training in perceptual skills.

_(A)_ 10. At the end of third grade, all students are given an extensive battery of reading tests, and reading profiles are developed for each child. On the basis of the results, some children are given a special reading program, while the others continue with the regular program.

_(B)_ 11. High school seniors take a national scholastic aptitude test and send their scores to colleges they wish to attend. On the basis of these scores, colleges admit some students and do not admit others.

_(E)_ 12. Students are informed about the learning targets their examination will cover and about how many points each examination question will be worth.

FIGURE 8.33 Example of a poor-quality (nonhomogeneous) matching exercise.

_(d)_	5.	Pennsylvania's official state flower	a. Ruffed grouse
_(a)_	6.	Pennsylvania's official state bird	b. Pittsburgh
_(b)_	7.	Major steel producing city	c. 1,950,098
_(c)_	8.	1970 population of Philadelphia	d. Mountain laurel
			e. Allegheny River

lost. Even if you tried to improve it, your efforts would probably be self-defeating. You may attempt to make the exercise's responses more homogeneous, but this may result in an exercise that does not assess the intended learning target. For example, you could make all the premises refer to different states and all the premises to different official state birds: The task would be to match the birds with the states. Your local curriculum, however, may only require students to identify their own state bird (or other facts and symbols about their own state). Creating a homogeneous exercise, as in this example, may result in a test that does not match the curriculum and, therefore, cannot be used.

Could anything be done to salvage this exercise? Remember the rule mentioned earlier in this chapter: You should reserve the matching exercise for those situations when several multiple-choice items require the same set of responses. Returning to the example in Figure 8.33, note that each premise could be turned into a separate multiple-choice item, each with a *different* set of plausible options. Plausible options for a multiple-choice item on Pennsylvania's official state flower, for example, should all be flowers native to the Pennsylvania region. Similarly, there could be separate multiple-choice items assessing knowledge of the official state bird, names of cities, and size of cities.

CRAFTING BASIC MATCHING EXERCISES

Many of the suggestions for crafting multiple-choice items apply to matching exercises as well. A few maxims, however, apply particularly to matching exercises. If you follow these, your assessment quality will improve. These suggestions are summarized in Table 8.8 and discussed here. Table 8.8 is a checklist to use in reviewing the matching exercises you craft or those that you adapt from teachers' texts or other curricular materials.

1 and 2.   Importance of what is assessed and its match to assessment plan. As always, your assessment tasks should

TABLE 8.8   A checklist for judging the quality of matching exercises.

1. Does the exercise assess an important aspect of the unit's instructional targets?	Yes	No
2. Does the exercise match your assessment plan in terms of performance, emphasis, and number of points?	Yes	No
3. Within this exercise, do the premises and responses all belong to the same category of things?	Yes	No
4. Do your directions clearly and completely explain the basis you intend students to use for matching?	Yes	No
5. Does every element in the response list function as a plausible alternative to every element in the premise list?	Yes	No
6. Are there fewer than 10 responses in this matching exercise?	Yes	No
7. Did you avoid perfect matching?	Yes	No
8. Are the longer statements in the premise list and the shorter statements (names, words, symbols, etc.) in the response list?	Yes	No
9. If possible, are the elements in the response list ordered in a meaningful way (logically, numerically, alphabetically, etc.)?	Yes	No
10. Are the premises numbered and the response elements lettered?	Yes	No

Note: Revise every matching exercise for which you marked "no" for one or more questions.
Source: Based on ideas from: Ebel, 1951, 1979; Greene, Jorgensen, & Gerberich, 1942, 1943; Gronlund, 1976; Hopkins, Stanley, & Hopkins, 1990; Lindquist, 1936; Lindvall, 1967; Nitko & Hsu, 1987; Thorndike, Cunningham, Thorndike, & Hagen, 1991; Wesman, 1971.

meet the dual criteria of importance and match to your assessment plan. Eliminate every item that fails to meet these two criteria.

3. *Make a matching exercise homogeneous.* Although we have discussed this point previously, here we add that often the degree to which students perceive the exercise as homogeneous varies with their maturity and educational development (Gronlund, 1976; Lindquist & Mann, 1936). What may be a homogeneous exercise for primary school-children may be less so for middle-school youngsters and even less so for high schoolers. Consider, for example, the matching exercise in Figure 8.34. The students' task is to match American historical events with their dates. For younger, less experienced students, such a matching task would likely be difficult. It would appear homogeneous, however, because for these children all responses would be plausible options for each premise. High school students would find the task easier—even though they didn't know the exact dates—because they could use partial knowledge to organize the dates into early, middle, and recent history. For them, only (f) and (g) would be plausible options for Item 1.

4. *Explain completely the intended basis for matching.* You must make the directions to a matching exercise clear. Elementary students may need oral explanations and, perhaps, some practice with this format before you assess them. The classification variety of matching exercise usually requires more elaborate directions and may require special oral explanations even for high school students. Avoid long, involved written directions, which place an unnecessary premium on reading skill.

5. *All responses should function as plausible options for each premise.* If you craft homogeneous premises and responses, plausibility problems will be minimized. Also, avoid using specific determiners and grammatical clues. For example, avoid beginning some premises or responses

with *an* and others with *a*, having some plural while others are singular, stating some in the past tense while others are stated in the present or future tense. These clue the answer unnecessarily.

Avoid using incomplete sentences as premises. If you use incomplete sentences for premises, it becomes difficult to make all responses homogeneous and easier for students to respond correctly on the basis of superficial features such as grammatical clues or sentence structure (Lindquist & Mann, 1936). The consequences of not following this maxim are shown in Figure 8.35. The exercise is nonhomogeneous and contains grammatical clues.

6. *Use short lists of responses and premises. For a single matching exercise, put no more than 5 to 20 elements in a response list.* The reasons are that (a) longer lists make it difficult for you to develop homogeneous exercises, (b) longer matching exercises overload a test with one kind of performance, and (c) longer lists require too much student searching time (Ebel, 1951). Finally, (d) some evidence suggests that students attain a lower percentage of correct answers with longer matching exercises than with shorter exercises (Shannon, 1973).

Shorter matching exercises make it easier to keep everything belonging to a single exercise on the same page. For some students, having to turn the page back and forth to answer the exercise may interfere with their ability to show you what they know. For these students, splitting an exercise between two pages increases the likelihood of carelessness, confusion, and short-term memory lapses. In short, a student's ability to answer a test item while flipping pages is an ability irrelevant to the learning target you want to assess.

To fix an exercise that is too long, separate it into two or more shorter exercises. Or you can use each response as a correct answer more than once. When you do this, alert students through either oral or written directions. One standard phrase you may use to do this is "You may

FIGURE 8.34 Homogeneity depends on educational development (see text).

Column A below lists important events in American History. For each event find in Column B the date it happened. Write the letter of the date on the blank to the left of each event. Each date in Column B may be used once, more than once, or not at all.

Column A (events)		Column B (dates)	
(f)	1. United States entered World War I	a.	1492
(d)	2. Lincoln became president	b.	1607
(g)	3. Truman became president	c.	1776
(b)	4. Pilgrims landed at Cape Cod	d.	1861
		e.	1880
		f.	1917
		g.	1945

FIGURE 8.35 Poor matching exercise using incomplete sentences.

(c)	17. Most normally green plants lose their color when	a.	through their stomata
(e)	18. The common characteristic of a flowering plant is	b.	contracts into a rounded mass
(d)	19. Almost all plants which form coal	c.	grown in the dark
(b)	20. When an expanded amoebae is strongly stimulated it	d.	are now extinct
		e.	the formation of a reproductive body

Source: From *The Construction and Use of Achievement Examinations* (p. 69) by H. E. Hawkes, E. F. Lindquist, and C. R. Mann (Eds.), 1936, by American Council on Education. Used by permission. Adapted from an illustration in *Traditional Examinations and New Type Tests*, by C. W. Odell (New York: Century Co., 1928), p. 380.

use each of the [names, dates, etc.] once, more than once, or not at all" (see Figure 8.31).

7. *Avoid "perfect matching."* Perfect matching gives away at least one answer to the student who knows all but one of them. This student's final choice will be automatically correct because it is the only one left, and this reduces the validity of your assessment. You can avoid perfect matching by including one or more responses that *do not match any* of the premises and by using a response as the correct answer for more than one premise.

8. *Longer phrases appear in the premise list; shorter phrases in the response list.* Consider how a student approaches the matching exercise: (a) A student first reads a premise, (b) then searches through the response list for the correct answer, and (c) the response list is reread for each premise. It is, therefore, more efficient and less time-consuming if students read the longer phrases only once. They can reread or scan the shorter phrases (words, symbols) as often as necessary.

9. *Arrange the response list in a logical order.* A student saves time if the response list is arranged in some meaningful order: Dates arranged chronologically, numbers in order of magnitude, words and names alphabetically, and qualitative phrases in a logical sequence. Such arrangements also may contribute to the clarity of the task, reduce student confusion, and lower incidence of student carelessness and oversight.

10. *Identify premises with numbers and responses with letters.* Remember, each premise is a separately scored item. Therefore, premises should carry numbers, which indicate their position in the sequence of items. For example, if the first 10 items are multiple-choice, and these are followed by a five-premise matching exercise, the five premises should be consecutively numbered 11 through 15.

CRAFTING ALTERNATIVE VARIETIES OF MATCHING EXERCISES

This part of the chapter extends your knowledge of matching exercises. Two types of matching exercises—masterlist and tabular—are discussed. These formats may fit some of your learning targets better than the more basic matching exercise. The advantages and disadvantages of each type are described in the sections that follow. As with the alternative varieties of multiple-choice items we discussed previously, these matching formats are objectively scored, do not take students a long time to complete, and are often easier for you to craft than the basic matching format.

MASTERLIST (KEYLIST) ITEMS

Format

A masterlist (or keylist or classification) item set for a 10th-grade civics course is illustrated in Figure 8.36. Notice that a **masterlist item** set has three parts: (1) directions to students, (2) the masterlist of options, and (3) a list or set of stems. To respond to a masterlist item set, a student reads each numbered stem and applies one of the options from the masterlist. Each stem is scored separately. The content learning target for the masterlist item set in Figure 8.36 is the students' ability to relate constitutional *values and principles* to specific modern-day, concrete examples of actions or events. Therefore, in crafting this item you would ensure that each masterlist option (A, B, C, D) is a value or principle expressed by the United States Constitution, rather than a Preamble goal or some other aspect of the Constitution.

Notice that each numbered stem is a brief, realistic, and concrete example of an action or event that illustrates one of the four values in the masterlist. Because the learning target calls for students to relate constitutional principles to concrete examples, each stem must be a concrete example. You would not use textbook abstractions or general descriptions. (For example, you would not word a stem in general language such as, "A law takes effect when the majority of Congress votes to approve it," because this statement describes a general principle rather than a concrete example.) Although the example in Figure 8.36 shows only four stems, you need not limit the stems to four. Use as many stems as are appropriate, as long as each stem is an example of one of the masterlist options. Further, although not the case in this example, each *stem* in a masterlist set may have more than one correct answer from the masterlist.

Advantages and Criticisms

Advantages A masterlist item set is a variation of the matching exercise format, and it has many of the same advantages as that format. It is a space-saving, compact, and objective way to assess learning targets for which you want students to identify associations between two sets of things. However, it is best used to assess a student's understanding of concepts. The masterlist set in Figure 8.36, for example, requires a student to analyze each stem's specific example and to classify it as an illustration of one of the constitutional principles in the masterlist. Each constitutional principle is a different concept. To use this format to assess concept understanding, the examples you give students to classify cannot be the same examples you illustrated in class or which appear in the textbooks or assignments. If your examples are not "new to the students" then the masterlist item set becomes simply an alternate

FIGURE 8.36 Example of a masterlist item set for use in a 10th-grade civics course.

Read each numbered statement and decide which United States constitutional principle it illustrates. Mark your answer:

> **Directions**
>
> Explain the basis for using the masterlist.

A — if the action illustrates the principle of government by the **consent of the governed.**

B — if the action illustrates the principle of government in which the **majority rules.**

C — if the action illustrates the principle of government under a **federal system.**

D — if the action illustrates the principle of government with **limited governmental powers.**

> **Masterlist**
>
> This list of options is applied to each of the stems below.

_____ 1. A Congressman voted for a tax bill that was unpopular in his state. In the next election he was not reelected.

_____ 2. A civil war was taking place in another country. The president of the United States began planning to help to support the antigovernment forces but was warned by cabinet members that he could get in trouble if he attempted to send in the military without going through the proper channels. The president dropped the plan.

_____ 3. A large number of people demonstrated for a ban on nuclear testing. Subsequently, a bill went to Congress asking for such a ban. However, the bill was defeated. The people continued to demonstrate but had to accept further nuclear testing until there was a vote on another bill.

_____ 4. A state in financial trouble decided to establish a system of taxes on goods imported into the state. The law was challenged and found to be in disagreement with a national law. The state had to seek other ways to raise money.

> **Stems**
>
> This list of stems presents situations, actions, or events that need to be classified into one of the categories in the masterlist.

way to assess students' recall and recognition of verbal information. As with matching exercises, you can use pictures, maps, symbols, or diagrams as stems.

The masterlist item also is an efficient way to assess a student's ability to (1) analyze a passage, table, or graph and (2) recognize an appropriate interpretation or conclusion drawn from this interpretative material. Figure 8.37 shows an example of this type of masterlist item set.

Criticisms Because masterlist item sets are "cousins" to matching exercises, they share the same criticisms. Critics point out that teachers often limit using the format to assess rote associations such as names and dates, memorized lists of causes and effects, lists of symbols and definitions, and so on. Although some learning targets do focus on memorization and recall of information, many do not and should not. Therefore, you should craft masterlist item sets to assess students' (1) comprehension of concepts, principles, or schemes for classifying objects, events, and ideas and (2) ability to analyze appropriate interpretations and conclusions. Do this by presenting new examples or new interpretations in the stems, and require students to apply the masterlist.

Crafting Suggestions

To craft your masterlist item set, first identify the learning target you want to assess. For example, this might be "the students' ability to recognize whether data support interpretations about what events occurred." Next write the masterlist of options on which you want to focus. For example, for the item set in Figure 8.36, you would list the four constitutional principles; for the item set in Figure 8.37, you would list *supportive*, *contradictory*, and *neither*. If you will use a table, graph, or other interpretive material, prepare it next.

Select one of the options from the masterlist and write as many stems for it as you can. For example, you might select "consent of the governed" as a principle and write four or five concrete examples that illustrate that principle in a real-world application. Continue selecting options and writing stems until you have several items for each option. Review the stems to be sure that they require students to apply their knowledge and skills to new real-world situations, examples, or events.

Create the directions last: Be sure the directions clearly describe the basis on which the student is to solve the

FIGURE 8.37 Example of a masterlist item set that requires students to recognize proper interpretations of a graph.

Use the graph below to help you answer Questions 1 through 5.

The graph shows that John left his home at 1:00 and arrived at his friend Bill's home at 1:45. The graph shows where John was in the community at different times.

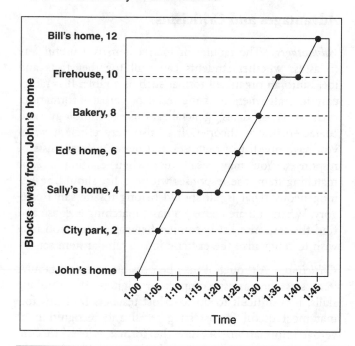

Directions: The numbered statements below tell what different students said about this graph. Read each statement and decide whether the information in the graph is consistent with a student's statement. Mark answer:

A — if the information in the graph **is consistent** with the statement.

B — if the information in the graph **contradicts** the statement.

C — if the information in the graph **neither contradicts nor is consistent** with the statement.

___ 1. John ran or walked very fast between his house and the city park.

___ 2. John stopped at Sally's home on his way to Bill's home.

___ 3. John stopped at Ed's home on his way to Bill's home.

___ 4. John stopped to buy something at the bakery before he got to Bill's home.

___ 5. John traveled faster after he passed by Sally's home than before he reached her home.

TABLE 8.9 A checklist for judging the quality of masterlist item sets.

1. Does each item in the masterlist item set assess an important aspect of the unit's instructional targets?	Yes	No
2. Does the masterlist item set match your assessment plan in terms of performance, emphasis, and number of points?	Yes	No
3. Does the masterlist item set require students to apply their knowledge and skill to new situations, examples, or events?	Yes	No
4. Did you provide enough information so that a knowledgeable student is able to apply the knowledge and skill called for by the item set?	Yes	No
5. Do your directions clearly and completely explain the basis you intend students to use when applying masterlist options to the stems?	Yes	No
6. Within this item set, do the options in the masterlist and the stems all belong to the same category of things?	Yes	No
7. Does every option in the masterlist function as a plausible alternative to every stem?	Yes	No
8. Did you avoid perfect matching?	Yes	No
9. If possible, are the options in the *masterlist* ordered in a meaningful way (logically, numerically, alphabetically, etc.)?	Yes	No
10. Are the stems numbered and the masterlist options lettered?	Yes	No

Note: Revise every masterlist item set for which you marked "no" for one or more of the questions.

masterlist item set. For example, in Figure 8.36, the directions tell students they must read the examples in the statements and decide which constitutional principle each represents. In the example in Figure 8.37, the directions tell the student that the statements are interpretations of the graph and that the student must decide whether the graph supports or contradicts the interpretation. If your masterlist item set refers to interpretive material, your directions should clearly describe the material and how students should use it.

After completing the preceding steps, polish your masterlist item set. Organize the interpretive material, if any, at the beginning of the set. Next, place the masterlist before the stems. Assign *letters to the masterlist options* that the students may use. If you will not use a machine-scorable answer sheet, your letters do not have to be A, B, C, D, or E. For example, in Figure 8.36, you could use C for "consent of the governed," M for "majority rules," and so on. The numbered list of stems follows. If you are not using a separate answer sheet, put a blank *before* the stem number rather than at the end of the stem. You will score the papers much more quickly and accurately if the blank is before the number of the stem. Scramble the stems so that all the stems matching one masterlist option are not together and there is no discernible pattern to the answers (avoid ABCDABCD, etc.). If you have written too many stems, select the best ones and save the others for revision and use at a later date. Edit the stems to make them grammatically correct, clear, and concise. Limit each stem to 40 or fewer words. However, the stems and the other parts of the item set must provide enough information for the student to apply the rule or principle. For example, in Figure 8.36, Stem 2 would not have had sufficient information if it contained only these words:

2.   A civil war was taking place in another country. The president of the U.S. began planning to help support the civil war.

The suggestions in this section are summarized as a checklist in Table 8.9. Use this checklist to guide you in crafting your item set. Use it also to evaluate the draft of your masterlist item set. Remember, if you answer no to one or more questions, you need to revise the item set.

TABULAR (MATRIX) ITEMS

Format

An example of a tabular item format is shown in Figure 8.38. You can see from this figure that the **tabular (or matrix) item** format is a type of matching exercise. Elements from several lists of *responses* (e.g., presidents, political parties, famous firsts, and important events) are matched with elements from a common list of *premises*. The students' task is to select one or more elements from each response list and match the elements with one of the numbered premises. In effect, Figure 8.38 is a quadruple matching exercise: (1) match year and president, (2) match year and president's political party, (3) match year and famous first, and (4) match year and important event. One premise list and several response lists that correspond to it can be efficiently organized into a tabular or matrix item format. Notice that each premise is *numbered*. Thus, each premise is a separate item.

An alternative version is shown in Figure 8.39. In this version there is one premise list (planet descriptions) and

one response list (planet names). Unlike an ordinary match exercise, however, in a tabular item set each premise may apply to more than one response element. For example, in Figure 8.39, all of the planets except Earth are named after Greek or Roman gods. Notice that each premise in the list is numbered.

Advantages and Criticisms

Advantages   The tabular or matrix item is a useful way to assess whether students can pull together facts and ideas into an organized format such as a table. It is rather easy to craft when assessing recall of verbal information, such as facts, dates, generalizations, terminology, and characteristics of theories. It is also very efficient when you have one list of premises and many different lists of responses. You may recall that when crafting a *basic* matching item, the responses within a list should be homogeneous: That is, all should belong to the same category. When you are crafting a basic matching exercise and find the response list becoming heterogeneous, you may wish to reorganize the exercise into a tabular item set.

Criticisms   Although it may be possible to create tabular item sets that assess complex or higher-order thinking skills, it is difficult to do so. Most teachers find this format most useful for assessing recall and recognition of verbal information. Because the format is easy to construct, some teachers overuse it (or its cousin, basic matching) and are therefore subject to criticism of focusing on facts rather than problem-solving, critical thinking, or other higher-order cognitive skills. Also, scoring the set is problematic. We discuss this problem and possible solutions to it later in this section.

Crafting Suggestions

First, identify the learning targets you wish to assess. Targets for which students must cross-classify facts or examples, or for which they must identify several characteristics or properties of dates, events, or objects, are most suitable.

You should first construct a list of premises. For example, in Figure 8.38 the premises were the four-year time spans defining a U.S. president's term of office. In Figure 8.39, the premises were planets' descriptions. Next, create lists of responses organized into homogeneous groups. You need two or more homogeneous response lists. You should add to each list at least one *plausible* response that does not match any of the premises. This will eliminate the perfect-matching flaw we discussed previously. For example, in Figure 8.39, "Eisenhower," "Independent," "First U.S. satellite in space," and "Korean conflict begins" do not match any of the premises (dates).

Create the table or matrix to correspond to your premise and response lists. Be sure to *number the premises*. Label the columns with the same headings you used for

FIGURE 8.38   Example of a tabular or matrix item set.

Directions: Match the names, political parties, famous firsts, and important events in the columns with the dates in the table below. Write the letter in the proper column in the table. You may use a letter once, more than once, or not at all in any cell in the table.

Presidents	Presidents' Political Parties	Famous Firsts	Important Event
A. Coolidge	K. Democrat	N. First airplane fight	U. Atomic bomb on Hiroshima
B. Eisenhower	L. Independent	O. First airplane flight across US	V. Great Depression begins
C. Harding	M. Republican	P. First automobile trip across US	W. NAACP founded
D. Hoover		Q. First telephone talk across US	X. New Deal legislation passed
E. McKinley		R. First transatlantic solo flight	Y. North Pole reached
F. Roosevelt, F.D.		S. First US satellite in space	Z. Panama Canal opened
G. Roosevelt, T.		T. First woman in Cabinet	AA. Panama Canal Treaty signed
H. Taft			BB. Social Security Act passed
I. Truman			CC. United Nations founded
J. Wilson			DD. World War I ends
			EE. Korean Conflict begins

	Year	President	President's Political Party	Famous First	Important Event		Score
1.	1901–1904					1.	_____
2.	1905–1908					2.	_____
3.	1909–1912					3.	_____
4.	1913–1916					4.	_____
5.	1917–1920					5.	_____
6.	1921–1924					6.	_____
7.	1925–1928					7.	_____
8.	1929–1932					8.	_____
9.	1933–1936					9.	_____
10.	1937–1940					10.	_____
11.	1941–1944					11.	_____
12.	1945–1948					12.	_____

FIGURE 8.39   Example of an alternate tabular or matrix item set.

Directions: For each planet description, place an X in the box below the name of the planet that fits the description.

Planets

EARTH   JUPITER   MARS   MERCURY   NEPTUNE   PLUTO   SATURN   URANUS   VENUS

Planet Descriptions

1. has only one moon
2. has no moons
3. larger than Earth
4. has no atmosphere
5. composed mostly of gas
6. can support life
7. has moon with atmosphere
8. named after Roman or Greek god

Source: Adapted from *Creative Classroom Testing: Ten Designs for Assessment and Instruction* (p. 138) by S. B. Carlson, 1985, Princeton, NJ: Educational Testing Service. Reprinted by permission of Educational Testing Service, the copyright owner.

the response lists. For convenience, make a place to record scores at the right of the table.

Directions to students are created next. The directions should clearly tell the students what they are to match, the basis for matching, how they should record their answers, and that a response may be used once, more than once, or not at all.

Craft the exercise in a layout modeled after Figures 8.38 or 8.39 (depending on the type of response required). Put the directions at the top and the lists of responses below the directions and above the table. The exercise is easier to understand with this arrangement than when the response lists follow the table. It is also easier for students to read and keep track of the responses if they appear first. Use letters to identify each response. There are fewer student clerical errors if the lettering continues consecutively across the lists as in Figure 8.38. Finally, place the table and make places to record scores. A grid is easier for students to use and for you to score.

Edit and polish all your work. Check spelling. Alphabetize the elements within each list separately. Keep the response lists side by side (as in Figure 8.38) if at all possible. This makes it easier for students to read the lists. Organize the list of premises into a logical, numerical, or chronological order. Check to be sure that the premises are numbered. If possible, keep the entire exercise on the same page. This reduces the clerical errors and frustrations students experience when they have to flip pages back and forth when answering the items. A word processor or spreadsheet program is helpful in crafting the final version. Use the features of your word processor or spreadsheet program that create tables for both the table itself and for creating the lists of responses.

Table 8.10 summarizes the suggestions in this section in a checklist. Use it as a guideline when crafting the tabular item set and to evaluate your item set when it is complete. Because the tabular item set is closely related to the basic matching exercise, you should review the suggestions for creating basic matching exercises in Table 8.8. Table 8.8 is a checklist for basic matching exercises and is, therefore, a convenient way for you to review the fundamentals of crafting matching exercises.

Scoring

Scoring is a special concern with the tabular or matrix item format. Two options for scoring are available:

1. *You may score each numbered row as completely correct or incorrect* (for example, score each row as a 1 [completely correct] or a 0 [one or more elements are incorrect]).

2. *You may score each row according to how many elements should be placed in its cells.* For example, in Figure 8.39, each row has 9 elements (planets), so scores for a row could range from 0 to 9. Each cell within a row is scored 0 to 1 according to whether an X or a *blank* is properly placed in it. For example, a student who places an X in Row 8 under *Earth* is marked wrong (given a 0 for this cell), because Earth is not named after a Greek or Roman god. Similarly, a student who leaves this cell blank is marked correct (given a 1 for this cell).

Of these two options, I prefer the second: It gives partial credit and yields more reliable scores.

Special problems may arise when (1) the correct answer requires placing more than one response in a cell but a student enters *fewer or more responses* than should be entered and (2) the correct answer is a blank but a student enters *some response(s)* in that cell. In Figure 8.38, for example, both Roosevelt and Truman were president in

TABLE 8.10 A checklist for judging the quality of tabular (matrix) item sets.			
1. Does each item in the tabular item set assess an important aspect of the unit's instructional targets?	Yes	No
2. Does the tabular item set match your assessment plan in terms of performance, emphasis, and number of points?	Yes	No
3. Do your directions clearly explain (a) the basis you intend students to use when matching the responses to the premises, (b) how to mark their answers, and (c) that a response may be used once, more than once, or not at all?	Yes	No
4. Do the responses within each response list all belong to the same category of things?	Yes	No
5. Does every response function as a plausible alternative to every premise?	Yes	No
6. Did you avoid perfect matching?	Yes	No
7. If possible, are the responses within each list ordered in a meaningful way (logically, numerically, alphabetically, etc.)?	Yes	No
8. Are the *premises numbered* and the responses lettered?	Yes	No
9. On the test page are the directions presented first, the response lists second, and the table third?	Yes	No
10. If possible, is the entire exercise printed on one page, rather than split between two pages?	Yes	No

Note: Revise every tabular item set for which you marked "no" for one or more of the questions.

the span 1945–1948: Roosevelt died in office while Truman was the vice president. A student may place an E, an H, or both into the corresponding cell in the "President" column. How should this cell be scored? The correct answer is "E and H," so clearly this should be given full credit or 2 points (1 point for each). Students who mark only E or only H could be given partial credit (1 point), or they could be given no credit (0 points). Giving partial credit would seem to be the fairest thing to do.

Suppose, however, a student responded with both C and H. C is clearly incorrect, but H is correct but incomplete. Some teachers are tempted to punish students by deducting marks for the C. This way of marking seems arbitrary and unfair. I would recommend giving partial credit (1 point) for the correct portion and not subtracting points for the fact that C does not belong in the cell. You could make a note to the student that C is incorrectly placed, however. Arbitrarily subtracting marks makes the exercise difficult for you to score, increasing the likelihood that you will make clerical errors in marking. Also, arbitrarily subtracting points is likely to lead to scores that do not accurately reflect the partial knowledge a student has.

Summary

- The suggestions for writing multiple-choice items represent the clinical lore of experienced item writers, and nearly all of them can be subsumed under the three fundamental principles in Chapter 7.
- A multiple-choice item consists of one or more introductory sentences followed by two or more suggested responses, from which the student chooses the correct answers. Varieties are illustrated in Figure 8.4.
- Each part of a multiple-choice item must work properly before the item as a whole will work:
  - The purpose of the stem is to ask a question, set the task to be performed, or state the problem to be solved.
  - The purpose of the alternatives (responses or options) is to suggest answers to the question or problem specified by the stem. One alternative is usually the correct or best response.
  - The purpose of the distractors (foils) is to appear plausible to students who do not possess sufficient knowledge to select the correct alternative.
- The basic purpose of any assessment task is to identify or distinguish those students who have attained the learning target from those who have not.
- Among the objective types of items, the multiple-choice item is considered to be the most highly valued, applicable, and versatile.
- Multiple-choice items are only indirect procedures for observing such important learning outcomes as the ability to:
  - Recall with minimal prompts.
  - Produce and express unique ideas.
  - Articulate explanations and give examples.
  - Organize personal thoughts.
  - Display thought processes or patterns of reasoning.
- Multiple-choice items can provide opportunities to observe *directly* such important learning outcomes as the ability to:
  - Discriminate and make correct choices.
  - Comprehend concepts, principles, and generalizations.
  - Make judgments about and choices among various courses of action.
  - Infer and reason.
  - Compute.
  - Interpret new information.
  - Apply information and knowledge.
- The *advantages* of multiple-choice items include their:
  - Versatility in assessing a variety of learning targets
  - Reduction of opportunities for the student to bluff or dress up an answer
  - Focus on reading and thinking and thereby not on writing under examination conditions
  - Reduced chances for a student to obtain the correct answer by blind guessing
  - Usefulness in obtaining diagnostic insight when distractors are based on common student errors or misconceptions
- *Criticisms* of multiple-choice items include the following:
  - Such items require students to choose from among fixed options and do not let them express their own ideas.
  - Poorly written items can focus on trivial facts.
  - Brighter students who are forced to choose a single option may be penalized if they have detected ambiguities, recognize divergent viewpoint, or have additional knowledge of the topic.
  - The possibility of getting the item right through blind guessing cannot be eliminated entirely.
  - Multiple-choice items tend to be based on "standardized" conceptions of knowledge, which may lead students to believe that a single, correct answer will be found for every problem in life.
  - Multiple-choice items may shape the content and nature of instruction in undesirable ways, limiting instruction to only those skills measured by the test.
- Among instances in the classroom for which multiple-choice items are *not recommended* (even though they would be appropriate) are
  - Problems or questions requiring a single-word or single-number answer
  - Computational problems in general
  - Questions with only two plausible answers (e.g., yes-no)
  - Items for which writing the answer doesn't take any longer than marking an answer to the multiple-choice item
- As with all types of assessment tasks, multiple-choice items should be carefully edited before being administered.

- Suggestions for crafting the stems of multiple-choice items are summarized by the maxims in Table 8.1. Illustrative examples follow the table.
- Suggestions for crafting the alternatives in multiple-choice items are summarized by the maxims in Table 8.2. Illustrative examples follow the table.
- Special care should be taken to phrase the correct alternative in a way that:
  - Permits those who have the minimum desired degree of knowledge to select the correct alternative
  - Does not permit students who lack the requisite knowledge to select the correct alternative on the basis of test-wiseness or superficial clues
- Suggestions for crafting the correct alternative are discussed.
- Table 8.3 is a checklist for judging the quality of multiple-choice items that you craft or that you obtain from curricular materials.
- The alternative varieties of multiple-choice and matching items in this chapter have the following general advantages: (1) They better match many learning targets; (2) they can be scored objectively; (3) they are efficient, covering more content in a given time span; and (4) they are relatively easy to craft.
- Greater-less-same items may be used to assess students' ability to compare the quantitative, qualitative, or order relationships between pairs of concepts.
- Greater-less-same items may be criticized because teachers use them to assess recall of verbal information rather than to assess application of criteria and principles to new situations. They are also criticized because they assess relationships between only two concepts at a time.
- Suggestions for crafting and evaluating greater-less-same items are presented in Table 8.4.
- Best-answer items may be used to assess students' ability to distinguish between degrees of correctness of various answers or solutions. They assess students' ability to apply criteria to judge qualitatively different answers.
- Best-answer items may be criticized because (1) they are difficult to craft well; (2) they are unsuitable for students with lower levels of educational development; (3) for the same item, different teachers may disagree as to what is the best answer; (4) the criteria for selecting the best-answer choice may not be taught to the students; and (5) some teachers produce options that are tricky for students.
- Suggestions for crafting and evaluating best-answer items are summarized in Table 8.5.
- Experiment-interpretation items may be used to assess students' ability to recognize appropriate interpretations of empirical research study results, appropriate explanations of results, and appropriate inferences from data.
- Open-ended variations of the experiment-interpretation items may be used to assess students' ability to explain and justify their answers.
- Experiment-interpretation items may be criticized because (1) they are rather difficult to craft well, and (2) some teachers use them to assess memorized or "fixed" interpretations.
- Suggestions for crafting and evaluating experiment-interpretation items are summarized in Table 8.6.
- Statement-and-comment items may be used to assess students' ability to evaluate a given set of interpretations of quoted comments using learned criteria. Open-ended versions assess students' ability to recall and write about the meaning of a quoted comment.
- Statement-and-comment items may be criticized because they (1) focus on a relatively narrow set of learning targets and (2) are used by some teachers to assess students' recall of interpretations the teacher presented in class.
- Because the statement-and-comment item format is a special type of best-answer format, you can use Table 8.5 as a guide for crafting and evaluating these items.
- A matching exercise consists of a list of premises, a list of responses, and a set of directions for matching the elements of the two lists.
- Matching exercises are like multiple-choice items in that each premise functions as a separate item. Unlike most multiple-choice items, however, each premise has the same list of options (or responses).
- You should use matching exercises whenever several multiple-choice items would require repetition of the same set of alternatives.
- The *advantages* of the matching exercises include
  - They are compact, space-saving, and objectively scorable.
  - They assess the ability to identify relationships.
  - They assess the ability to classify things.
- A criticism of matching exercises is that teachers frequently use them exclusively for assessing rote associations rather than the abilities to comprehend or classify.
- You can avoid "giving away" answers to matching exercises by crafting homogeneous premises and responses so that each response is a plausible option to each premise. The homogeneity of premises and responses is usually a function of the educational development of the students being assessed as well as of the content of the exercise.
- Suggestions for constructing matching exercises are presented along with illustrative exercises.
- Table 8.8 is a checklist that you can use to judge the quality of the matching exercises you create or that you adapt from curricular materials.
- Masterlist items may be used to assess students' ability to classify new examples into learned classification

frameworks and the ability to apply principles to new situations.

- Masterlist items may be criticized because teachers often use them to assess recall of verbal information rather than to assess application of learning to new situations.
- Suggestions for crafting and evaluating masterlist items are presented in Table 8.36.
- Tabular (matrix) items may be used to assess students' ability to match facts and concepts across several categories of classification and pull together information in a table format.
- The tabular item format may be criticized for the same reasons matching exercises are criticized: Teachers tend to use the format to assess students' ability to recall facts and other bits of verbal information.
- Suggestions for crafting and evaluating tabular items are summarized in Table 8.10.
- Tabular items may present scoring problems. The chapter recommends that each row of the matrix (table) be scored according to how many of the student's entries are correct.

Important Terms and Concepts

"all of the above"
alternatives, choices, options, responses
basic purpose of an assessment task
best-answer item
clueing, linking
context-dependent items, interpretive materials, interpretive exercises, linked items
continuum of learning
correct-answer variety
decontextualized knowledge
direct assessment, indirect assessment
directions for matching
distractors, foils
experiment-interpretation items
filler alternatives, "deadwood" alternatives
greater-less-same items
high-stakes assessment
homogeneous alternatives, heterogeneous alternatives
homogeneous premises and responses
incomplete stem
keyed alternative, keyed answer, key
masterlist items, classification items, keylist items
matching exercise (basic)
multiple-choice items (interpretative material)
meaningfully arranged alternatives
multiple-choice item
negatively worded stem
"none of the above"
overlapping alternatives
perfect matching
plausible distractors, functional alternatives
premises, premise list
responses, response list
specific determiner

statement-and-comment items
stem
tabular (matrix) items
tandem arrangement of options
"textbookish" phrasing
varieties of multiple-choice items
verbal clues, grammatical clues, "clang" associations
"window dressing"

Exercises and Discussion Questions

1. Make a table that compares the advantages and disadvantages of using completion, true-false, multiple-choice, and matching exercises for classroom assessment in a subject that you teach.
2. Consider the eight types of multiple-choice items in Figure 8.4.
   a. Write a brief statement for each type of item, describing the subject matter and grade level for which that type might be especially useful.
   b. Briefly state why you believe this to be the case.
3. What are the advantages and disadvantages of using *indirect* methods for assessing attainment of certain learning targets?
4. Under what circumstances might it be permissible (but not necessarily most desirable) to use indirect assessments? Explain your reasoning.
5. List 10 different circumstances in which multiple-choice items *should not* be used for classroom assessment. Identify those that have not been mentioned in this chapter.
6. For each circumstance in Question 5, explain why you should not use multiple-choice items.
7. For the subject you teach, or one with which you are most familiar, construct one flawless multiple-choice item to assess each of the following abilities. Before writing each item, write a specific learning target that the item will assess. After writing the items, use the checklist in Table 8.3 to evaluate and revise your items. Share your items with the other members of your class.
   a. Ability to discriminate two verbal concepts
   b. Ability to comprehend a principle or rule
   c. Ability to select an appropriate course of action
   d. Ability to interpret new data or new information
8. For the subject you teach, obtain curricular material that has multiple-choice items for teachers and students to use. Select from this material 10 items that would be appropriate for a unit you might teach. Evaluate each item using the checklist in Table 8.3. Identify the flaw(s) in each item, then revise the item to correct the flaw(s). (Be sure to evaluate your revised items so they are flawless.) Discuss your findings with the class.
9. For the subject you teach, obtain curricular material that has matching exercises for teachers and students to use. Select two exercises that would be appropriate for a unit you might teach. Evaluate each exercise using the checklist in Table 8.8. Identify the flaw(s) in each exercise, then revise the exercises to correct the flaw(s). (Be sure to evaluate your revised exercises so they are flawless.) Discuss your findings with the class.
10. Choose two different kinds of relationships from the following list and craft matching exercises for the subject you teach: accomplishments of persons; dates of noted events;

FIGURE 8.40   Use with Exercise 11.

Instructions: Match the two columns

A		B	
1.	chlorophyll	a.	Green plants contain this substance.
2.	igneous	b.	Type of rock formed when melted rock hardens.
3.	photosynthesis	c.	A substance made up of both hydrogen and oxygen.
4.	water	d.	Process by which green plants produce their food.

definitions of terms; examples of applications of principles or rules; symbols for concepts; authors or artists and their specific works: English equivalents of foreign phrases; functions of specific parts of a mechanism; or names of pictured objects. Develop matching exercises for each of the two you chose. Evaluate and revise your exercises using the checklist in Table 8.8 to eliminate all flaws. Present your matching exercises to your class.

11. Evaluate the matching exercise in Figure 8.40 using the checklist in Table 8.8. Prepare a list of the flaws found. For each flaw listed, explain why it is a flaw in this exercise. After completing your analysis, revise the exercise so it has no flaws. Share your findings with your class.

12. Craft one matching exercise that assesses either (a) comprehension of principles or rules or (b) ability to classify new objects. Evaluate and revise your exercise using the checklist in Table 8.8. Share your exercise with the other students in your class.

13. Create a table in which you summarize and give examples from the subject(s) you teach (or plan to teach) of the types of thinking skills and learning targets that can be assessed by each of the six alternative multiple-choice and matching item formats described in this chapter. Use one of the thinking skills taxonomies described in Chapter 2 (or specified by your instructor). Organize your findings into a table as shown in Table 8.11. Share your table with the other students in this course.

14. Prepare a table in which you summarize the advantages and criticisms of each of the six alternative multiple-choice and matching types of item formats described in this chapter. Organize it like Table 8.12.
   a. Discuss the advantages and criticisms with the other persons in this course. Then, revise your table before turning it in to your instructor.
   b. If you discover advantages and criticisms not described in this chapter, send them to the author.

TABLE 8.11   Use with Exercise 13.

Item format	Thinking skills appropriately assessed by the format	Example of learning target or objective for which the format is appropriate

TABLE 8.12   Use with Exercise 14.

Item format	Advantages	Criticisms

15. For each of the six *alternative* multiple-choice and matching item formats described in this chapter, identify one or more learning targets in the subject(s) you teach or plan to teach that may be appropriately assessed by that format. Craft one or more items of each format to assess the learning targets you identified. Evaluate your items using the appropriate checklists (Tables 8.4 through 8.6, and 8.8 through 8.10) before turning them in to your instructor.

16. With the help of your instructor, obtain two other students' item sets from Exercise 15. (Your instructor should remove the students' names and replace them with codes, so you can complete this exercise without knowing who wrote the items. Alternatively, your instructor may use items from students who completed Exercise 15 in previous terms.)
   a. Make photocopies of Tables 8.4 through 8.6, and 8.8 through 8.10. Use the appropriate table to evaluate each item set. Write specific suggestions for improving the items on the item set itself. Attach to each item set containing your suggestions the corresponding checklist table you have completed. Return these to your instructor, who will in turn return them to their author.
   b. When your own evaluated item sets are returned to you, revise them according to the evaluations and suggestions made for improving them. Turn in your revised item sets to your instructor along with the evaluations and comments you received about the original versions.

17. Choose the appropriate checklist for one of the following item formats: masterlist or greater-less-same.
   a. Using the checklist you selected as a guide, create several item sets in which you deliberately violate each of the checklist's suggestions. One item set may violate several checklist suggestions. However, not every checklist suggestion need be violated in the same item set.
   b. Rewrite the item sets so the violations no longer exist. Be sure that you do not create new violations. Turn in both the poorly written and the revised item sets.

18. Select two of the six alternative multiple-choice and matching item formats described in this chapter that you think are best suited for assessing the subject(s) and the students you teach (or plan to teach). Write an essay explaining the value of using these two item formats here over using traditional objective formats (e.g., true-false, matching, multiple-choice, and short-answer). Support your position by using actual examples of items that you create or others have crafted. For example, show a traditional item that was used to assess a particular learning target and a corresponding item set of the type from this chapter. Explain why using the traditional item is not as appropriate for assessing the learning target as using the item of the type from this chapter. In a summary section of your essay, describe the generalizations you have drawn from this analysis.

19. Figure 8.41 shows an answer key and three students' responses to a tabular (matrix) item set. Use them to complete the following exercises.

FIGURE 8.41 Use with Exercise 19.

Answer Key

			Maximum points
A	D, E	I	4
	F	J	3
C	G	K	3
			3
B			3
		L	3
		Total points	19

Student A   Score

A	D	I	
	E, F	J	
C	G		
	H		
B			
		L	
		Total points =	

Student B   Score

	D, E	I	
A			
C	F, G		
B		K	
		L	
	Total points =		

Student C   Score

A	D, E, F	I	
		J	
C	G	K	
B			
		L	
	Total points =		

a. Using the answer key, score each response.

b. Note any difficulty you encountered in scoring a student's response.

c. Compare your scores with those of others in this course. Are there any areas of disagreement? Resolve any differences so that everyone arrives at the same scores.

d. What does your experience in part (c) say about the objectivity of the tabular (matrix) item set?

Additional Readings

Bloom, B. S., Madaus, G. F., & Hastings, J. T. (1981). *Evaluation to improve learning*. New York: McGraw-Hill, Chapters 8–10.

These chapters illustrate how to write multiple-choice items that assess learning targets classified in the higher-order thinking categories of the Bloom et al. taxonomy of educational objectives.

Carlson, S. B. (1985). *Creative classroom testing: Ten designs for assessment and instruction*. Princeton, NJ: Educational Testing Service.

Provides examples for each alternative item format in the subject areas of child psychology, language arts, science, and social studies.

Gulliksen, H. (1986). Perspective on educational measurement. *Applied Psychological Measurement, 10*, 109–132.

Gives a historical perspective and additional rationale for using alternative-object item formats of the type described in this chapter.

Haladyna, T. M., & Downing, S. M. (1989a). A taxonomy of multiple-choice item-writing rules. *Applied Measurement in Education, 2*, 37–50.

Haladyna, T. M., & Downing, S. M. (1989b). Validity of a taxonomy of multiple-choice item-writing rules. *Applied Measurement in Education, 2*, 51–78.

These two articles summarize and compare the item-writing suggestions of more than 43 textbook authors. The second article focuses on the research evidence that does or does not support these authors' suggestions.

Haladyna, T. M. (1997). *Writing test items to evaluate higher-order thinking*. Needham Heights, MA: Allyn and Bacon.

Discusses ways to make multiple-choice items test more than memorization and comprehension.

Haladyna, T. M. (1999). *Developing and validating multiple-choice test items* (2nd ed.). Hillsdale, NJ. Erlbaum.

Provides practical examples of how to construct multiple-choice items of various kinds.

CHAPTER 9

Essay Assessment Tasks

Learning Targets

After studying this chapter, you should be able to:

1. Explain the strengths and weakness of restricted and extended response items. [1, 2]

2. Describe the types of learning targets that you should assess. [1, 2]

3. Explain why you should not use essay items to assess learning targets that are limited to recall and comprehension of verbal information. [1]

4. State the likely influence of using essay items on the study habits of your students. [1, 2, 3, 4]

5. State the types of learning targets for which it is more advantageous to assess using objective items rather than essay items. [1, 2, 3, 4]

6. List the factors that lower the reliability of your students' essay scores and explain how you can improve this reliability. [2, 3]

7. Write good essay questions, free from flaws, that assess a variety of students' thinking skills. [2]

8. Use a checklist of essay-writing criteria to evaluate and improve the quality of your essay questions. [2, 1]

9. Explain why allowing your students a choice of questions to answer on a summative evaluation is generally not a sound assessment practice. [2]

10. Explain the advantages and disadvantages of holistic and analytic scoring rubrics. [2, 1]

11. Create holistic and analytic scoring rubrics for your essay items. [2, 3]

12. List several ways you can improve your essay assessment scoring procedures. [2, 3]

13. List several techniques that will give your students feedback on their responses to your essay questions. [3, 4]

14. Explain how each of the important terms and concepts listed at the end of this chapter are applied to educational assessment. [6]

———

Among paper-and-pencil assessment formats, essay items have the longest history. Teachers have found essay items to be very versatile tools for assessing students' acquisition of learning targets. Despite this versatility, however, teachers may not use them properly or take advantage of their strengths. We shall explore the strengths and limitations of essays in this chapter.

Teachers use essays in two general situations. First, teachers in subject areas such as social studies, mathematics, science, history, and literature use essay items to assess whether their students can explain, communicate, compare, contrast, analyze, synthesize, evaluate, and otherwise express their thinking about several aspects of the subject. Teachers now recognize that students need to write and communicate in all subject areas, not just language-arts subjects. These teachers recognize that essay items are very effective for assessing higher-order thinking but not efficient for assessing students' rote memory. Second, teachers use essay items to assess writing skill per se. Teachers of basic writing skills use essays to assess students' abilities to write standard English, to use appropriate language expressions, to write for different purposes such as exposition or persuasion, and to use writing to communicate with others.

This chapter explores the use of essay items primarily in the first of these important assessment situations. Students' essays and other written work can be used to assess many higher-order thinking skills and problem-solving abilities. This written work can also be part of performance and portfolio assessment activities. Chapter 10, and especially Chapters 11 and 12, describe the more complex uses of written responses. This chapter is more basic: It helps you to learn the fundamentals of crafting quality essay tasks.

VARIETIES OF ESSAY ITEMS

Essay items are usually classified into two groups: restricted response items and extended response items. Both types are useful tools, but for different purposes.

Restricted Response Varieties

Definition **Restricted response essay items** restrict or limit what you will permit the student to answer. The way you phrase a restricted response task requires a student to limit both the content of the answer and the form of the written response. Figure 9.1 offers two examples.

Assessing More than Recall and Comprehension Restricted response items should require students to apply their skills to solve new problems or to analyze novel situations. One way to do this is to focus your tasks on a student's ability to use interpretive material included with the assessment. This material could be, for example, a de-

FIGURE 9.1 Sample restricted response items.

1. Write a brief essay comparing and contrasting the terms *measurement* and *assessment* as they relate to (a) the degree of quantification of students' responses, (b) the process of obtaining information, and (c) the way in which the students' responses are recorded.

2. List five of the suggestions for writing essay questions that your text presented. For each suggestion you list, write a short statement explaining why that suggestion is useful for improving the validity of your essay assessments.

scription of a particular problem or social situation, an extract from a literary work, or a description of a scientific experiment or finding. Essay (and response-choice) items based on this kind of material are called **interpretive exercises** or **context-dependent tasks**. You expect the students to read, listen to, analyze, or otherwise interpret the accompanying material and then to complete one or more tasks based on it. Figure 9.2 illustrates restricted response items and, by way of contrast, an extended response item that requires students to analyze a particular poem in various ways. The items are intended for a high school literature course.

Advantages of Restricted Response This format narrows the focus of your assessment to a specific and well-defined performance. The nature of these items makes it more likely that your students will interpret each question the way you intended. You are in a better position to assess the correctness of student answers when a question is focused and all students interpret it in the same way. When you are clear about what makes up correct answers, your scoring reliability, and hence the scores' validity, improve.

Other Assessment Options As illustrated in Table 9.1, multiple-choice interpretive exercises assess many abilities more reliably than restricted response essays. You are not using restricted response essays properly if you use them only to assess students' recall of factual information. You can assess a student's ability to recall factual information better through completion, true-false, multiple-choice, and matching items. Unfortunately, very often the major difference between a teacher's essays and response-choice items is that the essays require recalling and supplying answers rather than choosing already supplied answers. To assess a learning target that is mainly recognition of an appropriate answer, you should use response-choice items, because they allow for more objective (and therefore more reliable) scoring.

Extended Response Varieties

Definition **Extended response essay items** allow your students to write essays in which they are free to express their own ideas and interrelationships among their ideas and to use their own organization of their answers. Usually no single answer is considered correct. A student is free to choose the way to respond, and degrees of correctness or merit of a student's response can be judged only by a teacher skilled or informed on the subject (Stalnaker, 1951).

Understanding and Writing Ability The two broad uses for the extended response essay format are to assess students' (1) **subject-matter knowledge**, and (2) **general writing ability**. Most of this chapter concerns essays that assess command of a subject rather than general writing ability.

FIGURE 9.2 Examples of restricted response and extended response items based on specified material.

Often restricted response items are directed toward only certain aspects or components of a very complex behavior. The examples below, intended for pupils in secondary schools, all relate to the "analysis" level of the Bloom et al. taxonomy. The restricted response questions ask a few of the many (perhaps 15 or 20) questions a teacher might write to measure a student's ability to perform several components involved in the analysis of the mood of the speaker of a poem. The extended response item attempts to elicit a rather complete and integrated analysis of the poem.

On First Looking Into Chapman's Homer

Much have I traveled in the realms of gold,
And many goodly states and kingdoms seen;
Round many western islands have I been
Which bards in fealty to Apollo hold.
Off of one wide expanse had I been told   5
That deep-browed Homer ruled as his
   demesne;
Yet did I never breathe its pure serene
Till I heard Chapman speak out loud and
   bold;
Then felt I like some watcher of the skies
When a new planet swims into his ken;   10
Or like stout Cortez when with eagle eyes
He stared at the Pacific—and all his men
Looked at each other with a wild surmise—
Silent, upon a peak in Darien.

                           John Keats

Restricted response questions

1. What is the poet's attitude toward literature as it is apparent in lines 1 to 8? What words in these lines make that attitude apparent?

2. Summarize the mood described in lines 9 to 14.

3. What is the relationship between the attitude described in lines 1 to 8 and the mood established in lines 9 to 14?

Extended response question

4. Describe the way in which the structure of the poem reinforces the speaker's mood as it is presented in lines 9 to 14. In your essay show how the attitude in the first part of the poem is related to the mood at the end of the poem.

Source: From "Evaluation of Learning in Literature" by A. C. Purves, in *Handbook on Formative and Summative Evaluation of Student Learning* (pp. 736, 755, 756) by B. S. Bloom, J. T. Hastings, and G. F. Madaus (Eds.), New York: McGraw-Hill 1971. Reprinted by permission.

TABLE 9.1 Examples of varieties of learning outcomes that can be observed using object interpretive exercises and essay items.

Type of test item	Examples of complex learning outcomes that can be measured

Objective interpretive exercises	Ability to—
	   identify cause-effect relationship
	   identify the application of principles
	   identify the relevance of arguments
	   identify tenable hypotheses
	   identify valid conclusions
	   identify unstated assumptions
	   identify the limitations of data
	   identify the adequacy of procedures
	   (and similar outcomes based on the pupil's ability to *select* the answer)

Restricted response essay questions	Ability to—
	   explain cause-effect relationships
	   describe applications of principles
	   present relevant arguments
	   formulate tenable hypotheses
	   formulate valid conclusions
	   state necessary assumptions
	   describe the limitations of data
	   explain methods and procedures
	   (and similar outcomes based on the pupil's ability to *supply* the answer)

Extended response essay questions	Ability to—
	   produce, organize, and express ideas
	   integrate learnings in different areas
	   create original forms (e.g., designing an experiment)
	   evaluate the worth of ideas

Source: Adapted from *Measurement and Evaluation in Teaching* (7th ed.) (p. 224) by R. L. Linn and N. E. Gronlund, 1995, Englewood Cliffs, NJ: Prentice Hall © 1995. Adapted by permission.

Two assessment tasks illustrate the difference between these two categories. Figure 9.3 assesses students' expressive writing skills using a role elaboration situation. In particular, it taps students' skills in expressing their "sensitivity to audience"—a basic communications skill.

You evaluate students' responses to the item in Figure 9.3 in terms of the degree to which their writing skills exhibit role elaboration, expressing the "feelings" and "thoughts" of tennis shoes in an imaginative and unified manner. Because assessing imagination and creative expression is the purpose of this particular exercise, English mechanics and handwriting are not supposed to enter into the evaluations (Klaus et al., 1979).

The essay in Figure 9.4, however, assesses students' competence in reasoning and applying knowledge in the subject of social studies. In the Bloom et al. taxonomy, one aspect of synthesis is the ability to formulate a plan of action for a particular purpose. This essay requires just that.

Advantages Some of your learning targets center around a student's ability to organize ideas, develop a logical argument, discuss evaluations of certain positions or data, communicate thoughts and feelings, or demonstrate original thinking. The restricted response essay format does not lend itself to assessing these types of learning targets. Students need opportunities for more extended responses to demonstrate such skills and abilities. The extended response essay is suited to assessing learning targets that require students to use a combination of skills such as interpreting material, solving a problem, and explaining the problem and its solution in a coherent manner.

Disadvantages One disadvantage of an extended response essay is **scoring reliability**. It is difficult to score an extended response objectively. When the grades or

FIGURE 9.3   Sample essay assessing writing ability.

Sometimes people write just for the fun of it. This is a chance for you to have some fun writing. Pretend that you are a pair of tennis shoes. You've done all kinds of things with your owner in all kinds of weather. Now you are being picked up again by your owner. Tell what you, as the tennis shoes, think about what's going to happen to you. Tell how you feel about your owner. Space is provided below and on the next two pages.

Source: From *Composing Childhood Experience: An Approach to Writing and Learning in Elementary Grades* (Experimental Version) (p. 14) by C. H. Klaus, R. Lloyd-Jones, R. Brown, W. Littlefair, I. Mullis, D. Miller, and D. Verity, 1979, St. Louis: CEMREL. Reprinted by permission.

FIGURE 9.4   Sample essay assessing application of subject-matter knowledge.

Devise a plan to determine whether the Democrats and Republicans are evenly distributed throughout the city, or whether the supporters of each party are concentrated in certain wards.

Source: From *Classroom Questions: What Kinds?* (p. 136) by N. M. Sanders, 1966, New York: Harper & Row. Reprinted by permission.

scores for an assessment are subjective, the validity of the assessment results is lowered. A common problem is evaluating each student's essay using different criteria. If you attend mainly to the quality of ideas in Johnny's paper, to the neatness and grammatical elegance of Sally's, and to the poor spelling in Harry's, then each student is evaluated on a different basis. As a result of your inconsistency, the assessment results are less valid.

A second disadvantage is that scoring these items is often time-consuming. A scoring rubric may improve the reliability (consistency), and hence the validity, of scoring essays. Using a scoring rubric also reduces scoring time. Suggestions for crafting scoring rubrics appear later in this chapter and are explained in detail in Chapter 12.

USEFULNESS OF ESSAY ASSESSMENTS

Abilities and Skills Assessed by Essay Items

The preceding paragraphs described some of the abilities and skills that essays let the student demonstrate. Table 9.1 provides a concise summary of these skills and abilities. Note that the outcomes listed in the table are suggestive, rather than exhaustive (Linn & Gronlund, 1995). Notice from the table that multiple-choice items also can measure some of these same abilities. Suggestions for developing multiple-choice and essay items to measure higher-level abilities are given in Chapters 10, 11, and 12.

What is perhaps unique about the essay format is that it offers students the opportunity to display their abilities to write about, to organize, to express, and to explain interrelationships among ideas. You may assess memory, recall, and comprehension more easily with short-answer and response-choice items. An important point: Select your assessment format to directly assess the learning target you want students to achieve.

Influence on Studying Strategies

One use of assessment tasks is to motivate students to study. It seems reasonable that the type of performance you expect from students will influence their method of study. Some research indicates that when students know that essay questions will be asked, they tend to focus on learning broad concepts and on articulating interrelationships, contrasting, comparing, and so on; those preparing for response-choice questions focus on recalling facts, details, and specific ideas (Douglas & Tallmadge, 1934; Terry, 1933). But because students report that they prepare differently for different types of assessments does not mean that they will in fact perform differently on the different forms. Some studies have found little, if any, difference in performance on essay or response-choice assessments even though students reported different study strategies (Hakstain, 1969; Vallance, 1947).

Where there are state-mandated essay tests, teachers require students to write more, and they report that students' writing skills improve (Evaluation Center, 1995). Outside observers report, however, that although students write more, they do not necessarily write better (Viadero, 1995).

Because both essay and response-choice formats can call for knowledge of specific facts, and both can call for application of complex reasoning skills, the questions' format may not be the key issue in how students plan their study strategies (Ebel, 1979). The kinds of study strategies your students use in preparing for your assessments are likely to be more related to the nature of the thinking skills your assessment tasks will require of them rather than the format (essay or not essay) of the tasks. If two different assessment formats require students to use the same kind of thinking skills, the formats ought to require the same types of study strategies. If your "essays" are really a regurgitation of facts, students' study strategies will focus on remembering and recalling facts. Thus, the advantages of essays and other open-ended response formats will not be realized in your classroom.

If you believe it is important for students to learn to write about ideas in a particular subject-matter area, perhaps the best advice is to be sure you explain and teach those learning targets to students in your class, and assign students a significant number of writing tasks so you can assess these learning targets. Do not limit writing tasks to examinations, of course. Various written assignments such as compositions and term papers can help your students achieve these writing-oriented learning targets. Keep in mind, however, that assessment results are more valid if you use multiple-assessment formats. Your summative assessments should include, therefore, both essay and response-choice items so that a proper range of learning targets is covered.

Depth and Breadth of Content Sampling

Answering essay questions takes a student a long time and limits the breadth of content about which the student can write. If your students can answer one or two response-choice items in one minute, then they can answer 30 to 60 items in a half-hour assessment. Sixty items can cover a very broad area of content and many instructional objectives. In the same 30 minutes, these same students can probably answer only one or two essay questions. Thus, you can assess in-depth learning of a narrower topic using one essay or broad, less in-depth, general coverage using many objective items.

To overcome the shortcoming of an essays' limited content sampling, use a series of compositions, which students write over a longer period of time (Coffman, 1971). You can accumulate these in portfolios. Several out-of-class essays written over a marking period may provide a better assessment of a particular learning target than a single essay written during a brief examination period. You

must remember, too, that writing under the time pressure of an examination may not be the best method to assess a student's maximum ability.

Factors Affecting the Reliability of Essay Scoring

In Chapter 4, we discussed scorer reliability and inter-rater reliability. We spoke of the measurement error introduced into students' marks and grades when teachers are not consistent in their evaluation of students' responses. The essay format is one of the most vulnerable assessment formats for having low inter-rater reliability. You can, however, improve the inter-rater reliability of essay scoring by using scoring rubrics. In addition, you can make a deliberate effort to overcome some of the negative factors that lower the reliability of essay scoring. We discuss these factors in the following paragraphs. By attending to these factors you will reduce the measurement errors in your evaluations of students' work.

Inconsistent Standards A serious problem is the tendency for essay assessment scores to be strongly influenced by factors that lower their reliability. The lack of essay reliability was a major justification for turning to true-false and multiple-choice assessments in education in the early 1900s. Grades assigned to a student's response may vary widely from one reader to the next, both because of the readers' inconsistencies and because of their differences in grading standards. Further, the same reader may mark the same essay differently from one day to the next. All teachers using scoring rubrics can largely overcome this flaw.

Rater Drift Even if scoring criteria are well defined, raters tend either to not pay attention to criteria over time or to interpret them differently as time passes. This tendency to change the way scoring criteria are applied over time occurs slowly is called **rater drift**. The practical application is that you have to periodically stop and determine whether you are applying the scoring standards in the same way to later-scored papers as you did to earlier-scored papers.

Changes in the Topic and Prompt Another factor that causes your assessment results to be inconsistent is the topic (subject) of the essay. A student's scores may vary widely, even when marked by the same reader, depending on the topic, prompt, or questions (Breland, Camp, Jones, Morris, & Rock, 1987; Dunbar, Koretz, & Hoover, 1991). This is a serious problem: If you base your evaluation of a student on one essay question, you will not be able to make general statements about this student's performance on different topics. If your statements about a student are limited to only the one essay a student wrote, the validity of your overall evaluation (e.g., grades) is lowered. This is a strong reason for you to base a student's grade for a marking period on multiple assessments collected over the entire marking period. This means, of course, that you must have an assessment plan for the marking period that identifies what different kinds of assessment formats you will use. (See Chapter 6 for devising assessment plans.)

Reader Biases   Other factors that affect the scores you assign on essay assessments include halo effects, carryover effects, bluffing ability, spelling, penmanship, and grammar. **Halo effect** means that our judgments of one characteristic of a person are influenced by our judgments of other characteristics or by our general impression of that person. Thus, you may tend to grade a particular essay more leniently for a student you admire because you know in your heart that the student has command of the objective or topic. The halo effect works the other way, too: You may mark down a particular essay by a student you do not admire because you "know in your heart" that the student is not very good. One way to correct this flaw is to mark the essays only after concealing the students' names.

A **carryover effect** occurs when your judgment of a student's response to Question 1 affects your judgment of the student's response to Question 2. For example, a student may have a brilliant answer to Question 1 but a mediocre answer to Question 2. The carryover effect occurs when you mark Question 2 right after marking Question 1: You mark Question 2 more favorably because you "carried over" your favorable impression from Question 1. Unless you use the scoring suggestion that follows, the scores you assign to adjacent questions will likely be more similar regardless of the quality of the students' answers than scores on nonadjacent questions. The suggestion is this: Score Question 1 for all students first, then go back and score Question 2 for all, and so on.

Many of the suggestions later in this chapter are directly focused on improving the reliability and validity of scoring essays. Reviews of research studies on these aspects of essay scoring can be found in Coffman (1971); Hopkins, Stanley, and Hopkins (1990); and Stalnaker (1951).

Efficient Use of Teacher Time

Essays and compositions take a long time to properly mark. This time is well spent if these types of tasks are the best ways to assess important learning targets, if performing them is a meaningful student activity, and if the students benefit from your review of their responses. Sometimes, however, because teachers must score large numbers of essays or because they are under the pressures of the day, they score essays carelessly: This is a breach of professional ethics and an abuse of responsibility. Assessing and evaluating students is serious business. Careful planning, including deciding whether the essay format is the most valid method of assessment, can greatly alleviate inappropriate scoring of essay assessments.

Influence of Scoring Criteria and Exemplars

As you will read later in this chapter, it is very important to use well-defined criteria to evaluate students' essay responses. Local school districts and state educational authorities have recognized the importance of developing these criteria. As a result, teachers may be engaged in professional development activities to help define these criteria and to improve their application to students' responses. Much of this effort is focused on defining criteria or rubrics that are used with performance assessment, of which essay assessment can be considered a part. (See Chapters 11 and 12 for details.)

An advantage of the professional development approach is that teachers have gained insight into what constitutes quality responses from students. Through working collaboratively with other teachers, they have crafted criteria that clarify the meaning of statements of state standards and of learning targets in the curriculum.

Similarly, by sharing quality criteria and exemplars of work at different quality levels with students, assessment and instruction have become more integrated. Students learn what the characteristics of quality performance are and, through exemplars, learn what quality performance looks like. Chapters 11 and 12 describe this point in greater detail.

CONSTRUCTING ESSAY ITEMS

Table 9.2 summarizes suggestions for improving essay items. As with previous chapters, the table is a checklist. An answer of no to any one of the checklist questions is sufficient reason not to use that essay item until you correct the flaw. Suggestions are discussed in the paragraphs that follow.

An Example of a Poorly Crafted Essay Item

This section presents a poorly worded essay question and uses the checklist in Table 9.2 to review this essay question. This exercise should help you understand how to evaluate your own essay questions. After we review this essay question, we discuss each of the points in Table 9.2 in more detail.

The Item   Suppose a teacher wanted to assess the following 10th-grade American history learning target:

> Analyze reasons for success of the Colonials during the American War of Independence and explain what alternative actions the British or the Colonials could have taken to alter the outcomes.

The teacher wrote the essay question in Figure 9.5 to assess this learning target. Overall, the teacher's essay item does not assess the learning target very well. Read this item, then we shall evaluate it using the checklist in Table 9.2.

TABLE 9.2 Checklist for judging the quality of essay items.

	Yes	No
1. Does the item test an important aspect of this unit's learning target?	Yes	No
2. Does the item match the specifications of your test plan in terms of required performance, emphasis, and number of points?	Yes	No
3. Does the item require students to apply their knowledge and skill to a new or novel situation?	Yes	No
4. When viewed in relation to other items on the test, does this item contribute to covering the range of content and behavior specified in your test plan?	Yes	No
5. Is the item focused? Does it define a task with specific directions, rather than leave the assignment so broad that virtually any response can satisfy the question?	Yes	No
6. Is the task defined by the item within the level of complexity that is appropriate for the educational maturity of the students?	Yes	No
7. To get a good mark on the item, is the student required to demonstrate more than recall of facts, ideas, lists, definitions, generalization, etc.?	Yes	No
8. Is the item worded in a way that leads all students to interpret the assignment in the way you intended?	Yes	No
9. Does the wording of the item make clear to the students the following:		
a. Magnitude or length of the required writing?	Yes	No
b. Purpose for which they are writing?	Yes	No
c. Amount of time to be devoted to answering this item?	Yes	No
d. Basis on which their answers will be evaluated?	Yes	No
10. If the essay item asks students to state and support their opinions on controversial matters, does the wording of the item make it clear the students' assessment will be based on the logic and evidence supporting their arguments, rather than on the actual position taken or opinion stated?	Yes	No

Note: Revise any essay item for which you answered "No" to one or more of the 10 questions.
Source: From Teacher's Guide to Better Classroom Testing: A Judgmental Approach (p. 31) by A J Nitko and T-C. Hsu, 1987, Pittsburgh, PA: Institute for Practice and Research in Education, School of Education, University of Pittsburgh. Reprinted by permission.

FIGURE 9.5 Example of a poorly crafted essay item.

Analyze the defeat of the British by the Colonials by listing the four factors discussed in class that led to the defeat.

Evaluation Using Table 9.2 Here is a point-by-point analysis using the checklist:

1. Yes, the factors contributing to the success of the Colonials are important learning outcomes of this unit.

2. No, the learning target calls for students to analyze reasons for success and explain alternative possibilities.

3. No, the item requires only listing (recalling) information presented during the class.

4. Yes, this item, in relation to other items (not shown), contributes to the breadth of coverage the teacher had in mind for the unit.

5. Yes, what the student is to do (i.e., list) is clearly stated.

6. No, the learning target implies that the students should be capable of more than the item requires. (The

task, "listing from memory," is within the capability of the students, but it is below the appropriate level of complexity as specified by the learning target.)

7. No, the item requires only recalling verbal information.

8. Questionable; some students may be confused by the word *analyze* but most will probably make a *list*.

9. a. Yes, students should list four reasons.
   b. Perhaps the purpose is simply to repeat what was taught in class, but the purpose isn't stated.
   c. No, a time limit is not stated.
   d. No, but simply being right or wrong seems to be the implied basis for evaluation.

10. Not applicable; no opinion asked.

Revised Item After using the checklist, the teacher rethought the item in relation to the learning target and what he had taught. The teacher recrafted the item to make it more in line with the learning target. This rewritten item is shown in Figure 9.6.

The revised item is more complex and more difficult than the original, but it comes closer to assessing the learning target. Notice that the revised item is expanded

FIGURE 9.6 Example of improving the essay item in Figure 9.5.

A. List four factors that led to the Colonial victory over the British in the War of Independence.   (4 points)

B. For every factor you list, write a short explanation of how that factor helped the Colonists defeat the British.   (4 points)

C. Choose one of these factors that in your opinion the British could have changed or overcome. Explain what actions the British could have taken to change or to overcome this factor.   (4 points)

D. What probably would have happened in the war if the British had taken the actions you stated? Why do you think this would have happened?   (8 points)

Grading   Parts A and B will be marked on how correct your answers are. Parts C and D will be marked on how well you *support* your opinion, but not on what position you take.

Time limit   30 minutes

to include recalling information, explaining the recalled information, *and* using higher-level skills. These higher-level skills require students to explain why they hold logically deduced opinions and to describe probable consequences of actions. The teacher's basis for grading is specified, as is a time limit. Because the class period at this school is 45 minutes long, this essay will probably be the only assessment that the teacher could do that day. To cover other aspects of the unit the teacher would need additional assessments, including quizzes, homework, class discussions, and an objective test over the unit's content.

Discussion of the Suggestions

1 and 2. *Importance of what is assessed and correspondence to the assessment plan.* We cannot stress enough that each of your assessment tasks, no matter what their format, must focus on important learning targets and must match your assessment plan. Learning targets that require essays may be difficult for you to state because the target may be complex and abstract. Further, when assessing these complex learning targets, you may need to use several different types of assessment tasks rather than only one. For example, you may want a student to demonstrate the ability to analyze critically and evaluate passages expressing different points of view about equality of the men and women. This complex learning target will require you to assess the student using several different types of tasks before you conclude the student has attained this objective.

A practical suggestion here is to focus on the type of response you wish the student to make, rather than worrying about how well the learning target is stated. You could, for example, write a specimen answer—an outline of the major points you want the students to make. Or you could state the way(s) you expect the student to approach the problem in an essay question. Then you can refine the essay question so that it will be clear what you wish the student to do.

3. *Essential knowledge applied to new situations.* The essay question format has the potential of assessing a student's command of higher cognitive processes and skills. You do this best when you require a student to apply thinking skills to new or novel problems and situations. If a student is asked to write only information he recalls from the textbook or class discussion, you are assessing only lower cognitive processes. A student's ability to recall verbal information is an important educational goal and reflects general competence, but you can better assess recall of information by using other assessment formats such as completion or short-answer items.

You may find it helpful to study different ways of phrasing questions, so you can craft items that encourage a student to use higher-level cognitive processes and skills. Several authors have attempted to catalogue or classify such "thought" questions (Table 9.3). If you craft questions in a manner similar to those given in the table, you will usually improve their quality. Monroe and Carter (1923), Odell (1928), Curtis (1943), Wesley and Wronski (1958), and Bloom, Hastings, and Madaus (1971) have provided similar classifications.

4. *Covering the range of content and thinking skills.* As you read in Chapter 6, your assessment plan should cover the full range of content and thinking skills that make up your learning targets. Your plan plays a key role in guiding your assessment activities. It helps you to take into account all appropriate learning targets. Review your essay questions in relation to the full range of your learning targets to be sure that they contribute properly to the goal of full coverage and, hence, to the improved validity of your assessments. You should remember that sometimes one essay question may assess several specific learning targets and may be related to more than one thinking-skill category.

Essay items, unlike short objective items, require significant student assessment time. Thus, you have to balance the available assessment time against the range of coverage you have planned. You may need to revise your essay (either by narrowing it or by broadening it) in conjunction with the other assessment formats you could also use. For example, you could make your essay focus more on requiring students to use higher-order thinking than on recall. Given the fixed amount of time in one class period, you may have to reduce the number of non-essay items, or, alternately, carry out essay assessments one day and objective format assessment on another day.

5. *Focus questions; clarify limits and purposes.* You should phrase a question to focus attention on the issues or points on which you want the students to write. If you do not craft the questions carefully, you are likely to find that your students interpret your question in so many different ways it will be impossible to evaluate their responses. Consider the extended response item in Figure 9.2. An unfocused version of this item might read: "Write an essay analyzing the poem." It is unlikely that such an

TABLE 9.3 Ideas for how to phrase essay questions assessing different types of thinking skills.

1. *Concept understanding: Identifying examples, producing examples*
   - Read the newspaper articles attached. Which events illustrate the concept of political compromise?
   - Explain in your own words the meaning of *prejudice.* Give an example of prejudice from your own experience.

2. *Concept understanding: Classifying examples*
   - Read the five mathematics word problems attached. Group these problems into two groups. Explain why the problems belong to these two groups.
   - Study the pictures of the 10 paintings that are attached. Organize these paintings into two or more groups according to their style. Explain the reasons behind your grouping.

3. *Analysis*
   - Look at the family photo attached. Describe the mood or feeling in the photo as well as the body language of the people. Use metaphors or similes to make these descriptions.
   - Read the attached newspaper article. Which statements are opinions? Explain why.

4. *Comparison*
   - Compare Artist A's use of color in her painting with Artist B's use of color in his mask. How are they similar and different? What moods do the colors convey in each piece?
   - Read the attached statements of Senator A and Senator B. In what ways are their points of view similar? Explain the reasons for your conclusions.

5. *Using principles and rules: Inference, prediction*
   - Read the situation above about the Basarwa, a cultural group we did not study. Based on what we did study, what would you predict will happen to them in the next 20 years? Explain the principles you used to make this prediction.
   - Suppose the government of South Africa ordered all of the white citrus fruit farmers to leave the country. Where would you expect them to go? Explain the principles you used to make this prediction.

6. *Inference: Deductions, predictions, generalizations*
   - Compare the information in Table A with the information in Figure A. What conclusions do you draw about how successful rice farming will be in the region to which the data apply? Explain the reasons for your conclusions.
   - Read the attached statements of a scientist, senator, and newspaper editor about the consequences of continuing to use gasoline-powered automobile engines. What generalization can you make about the consequences of continued use of these engines in developed countries?
   - Study the data in the table above. What would you expect to happen to our exports of wheat over the next five years? Explain the assumptions you made in order for your prediction to be valid.

7. *Evaluation*
   - Above are the criteria we use to judge how well an author has used "voice" in writing. Attached is a short piece written by a student in a nearby school. Use the criteria to evaluate the writer's use of voice. Explain why good voice is or is not used by this writer. Use examples from the piece to illustrate your evaluation.
   - Use your daily log and records of your plant's growth to explain the present state of your plant. Explain why your plant is better or worse than your classmates' plants. What could you have done differently? What effect would that have had on your plant's present state?

unfocused item would result in students analyzing the poem's "mood," which is what the teacher had in mind. If an item is not focused, you will find it impossible to distinguish those students who can perform the learning target—but misinterpreted your question—from those who simply cannot apply the skills you taught.

Sometimes, if you find it difficult to clearly state the nature of the task itself, specifying the manner and criteria by which you will evaluate students' responses may increase clarity. For example, sometimes a teacher will give students an extract from a newspaper expressing a point of view and want students to evaluate the extracted statement by applying the strategies and criteria taught in class. However, the teacher's question may simply say, "Do you agree or disagree with this article's position?" There's no telling what kind of responses students would make: Their responses would likely range from a simple yes or no through long-winded polemic entanglements.

The teacher should focus the item more by adding which aspects of the extract the students should address. Also, the teacher should tell the students that their essays will not be evaluated on whether they agree or disagree with the extract, but on how well they frame the argument and the quality of the outside information they bring to the essay to support their positions.

Focusing the question and specifying limits of the intended response do not mean that you need to provide the students with information that gives away the answer. If you want the essay to assess the students' ability to organize a written argument or identify the central issue in a "fuzzy problem," for example, you should not provide students with a particular organization in the question. However, you should tell students that the way they choose to organize the answer is important, and that you will evaluate the paper on how well it is organized.

An important practical suggestion here is to have a colleague or friend review the questions and, if possible, to try the item with a few students. You can then revise the questions if necessary. Following such steps greatly improves the quality of essay questions.

6. *Complexity should be appropriate to educational level.* Because answering an essay requires students to read, think, and write, you must be sure that the item is appropriate to your students' level of educational development. This means avoiding the use of complicated sentence structures and phrasings for elementary students. Avoid phrases that are indirect or that add unnecessary reading to the question. It also means not oversimplifying essays for more advanced students. Essays should challenge students to do their best thinking and use their best writing skills. Because essays require writing, your students must have the level of writing proficiency they need to answer the question. If students do not have enough writing skill to express their knowledge on your essay question, you should consider using another means of assessment.

7. *Require more than recall of verbal information.* Although students must learn various facts, ideas, lists, definitions, and generalizations, you should not use the essay format to assess this type of learning. Use short-answer, completion, true-false, matching, and multiple-choice formats to **assess simple recall** of verbal information. These latter formats are better for *assessing such recall* because they require less time on the part of students and are, therefore, more efficient: You can sample more of a student's verbal information store in a fixed time period with non-essay items than with essays. Using short-answer and response-choice items increases the content coverage of your assessment and adds to the validity of the results for assessing recall.

Do use essays to **assess higher-order thinking**, including comprehension, application, ability to express one's own ideas, and ability to compare, critique, and explain reasons. One assessment strategy is to organize a small group or class discussion about the upcoming essays. The students discuss the problem that is posed in the essay. Through the discussions, the students become familiar with the content covered and discuss various ways to solve the problem stated in the essay. In the following class period, students respond to the essay individually. Another assessment strategy gives students some essay tasks to complete over several days or as take-home assignments. This gives students the opportunity to think, to use prewriting skills, to organize, and to revise their answers. This process is more like the ultimate situations in which your students will be writing.

8. *Make the intention of the essay clear.* This point was discussed in relation to Figure 9.2. You should carefully craft your essay question to be sure it communicates clearly to the students the framework in which they are to respond: the issues their essays are to address; the amount of justification, evidence, and information they are expected to bring to bear in their responses; and the level of detail you expect in their responses.

9. *Clarify response length, purpose, time limits, and evaluation criteria.* You should tell students (a) the approximate length you expect their response to be, (b) the purpose for which they are writing, (c) the goal toward which their essay should aim, and (d) the audience for whom they should target their responses. If you impose time limits, you should clearly announce these to your students. If more than one answer can be correct, your students should be aware of this, too. If you will deduct points for incorrect spelling, poor language usage, or poor penmanship, tell students before they respond. If you do not provide this information for an important summative evaluation of students, you are not acting professionally responsible. (See Chapter 5 for more professional responsibilities.)

10. *Clarify how students' opinions will be evaluated.* Often an essay will require students to state and support their opinions on controversial or nonroutine matters. These essays often provide excellent opportunities to assess students' abilities to analyze, synthesize, and evaluate. In such items, you should make clear that the students' answers will be evaluated on the logic they exhibit and the evidence they use to support their arguments or positions. You should reassure them that their opinions or positions taken will not be marked right or wrong per se.

OPTIONAL QUESTIONS

When the purpose for doing an assessment is summative evaluation, you should require all students to answer the same questions. This is especially important when you grade students based on ranking or comparing them to each other. The validity of your ranking is increased if you compare your students on the same questions.

Some teachers believe that offering students **optional essay questions** (a choice of questions) is fairer because it permits students to "put their best foot forward." Research doesn't bear out this belief, however (Coffman, 1971; Stalnaker, 1951; Wilson, 1976). Some students will choose to answer questions on which they do less well (Cowan, 1972; Meyer, 1939; Stalnaker, 1936; Taylor & Nuttall, 1974). Further, the topics on which questions are based vary in familiarity and difficulty for the students. We have already mentioned how difficult it is to generalize from one essay to the next. In addition, teachers marking essays frequently change their ratings based on their own perceptions of the nature and difficulty of topics. It is extremely difficult, often impossible, to make adjustments fairly to equate tests where students have taken different items (Wang, Wainer, & Thissen, 1995). If all the questions asked on an assessment represent examples of important learning targets, then it seems logical and fair to hold all students accountable for answering all of them (Ebel, 1979).

Perhaps the story would be different if general writing ability is being assessed, rather than subject-matter competence (Coffman, 1971). You could argue that students may demonstrate general writing ability by writing on any one of a number of topics. If you follow this practice, it is advisable to score papers on each topic separately, rather than mixing topics together. This will reduce the topic-to-topic differences that tend to raise or lower your rating of an essay quite apart from its merits. As we pointed out earlier in this chapter, however, the topic and the prompt of the essay questions are very important determinants of how well a student performs. A student can write very well about some topics and very poorly about others. Thus, it does make a difference which topics students choose or are assigned. Even if you are assessing general writing ability, interpret very cautiously students' responses to different topics and prompts. The most important thing for you to do is to use multiple topics and assess students over longer periods of time, rather than base your evaluation on a single essay.

SCORING ESSAY ASSESSMENTS

Our discussion of essay scoring focuses on increasing the objectivity (and, consequently, the reliability) of your marking. There are two general methods for scoring subject-matter essays: the analytic (also called scoring key, point, or trait) method and the holistic (also called global, sorting, or rating) method. In Chapter 12 we discuss more advanced ways to craft scoring rubrics, and our discussion is broader than essay questions. We use scoring rubrics for scoring performance assessments, too.

Analytic Scoring Rubrics

The **analytic scoring rubric** requires you to develop an outline or a list of major elements that students should include in the ideal answer. Next, you decide on the number of points to award to students when they include each element. The analytic scoring rubric works best on a focused, restricted response question. An example of an analytic scoring rubric for a restricted response essay appears in Figure 9.7. The essay question (not shown) asks students to describe why it is important to identify various decision contexts when validating assessments and to compare selection, placement, and classification decision contexts.

In Figure 9.7, the decision to award 2 points or 4 points for certain elements of the answer is based on the teacher's values. In your classroom, you will have to decide which elements are more important to your learning targets and, therefore, for which you should award more points. When assigning the number of points to each element, be sure the total points match the essay's total numerical value in relation to the overall number of points on the assessment.

Usually students' responses will match the scoring rubric to various degrees: A response that is essentially correct receives the full point credit; a completely incorrect answer or an omission receives no points; and a partially correct response receives a partial-credit award. When you assign partial credit in an inconsistent way you increase the unreliability of the scoring process. You retain more reliability if you can specify the number of partial-credit points each type of partially correct answer will receive. Teachers are often inconsistent, too, in assigning partial credit to mathematics word problems that require computation. Figure 9.8 shows one scoring rubric that adds consistency to awarding partial credit for such items.

Crafting partial-credit scoring rubrics may be difficult for a beginning teacher because you are not aware of the types of errors and partial knowledge your students will display to a particular question. After reading a few stu-

FIGURE 9.7   Example of an analytic scoring rubric for the essay on selection, placement, and classification decisions.

1.	Reasons for distinguishing decision contexts	(4 points)
2.	Selection decisions	
	a. Description	(2 points)
	b. Example of selection decision	(2 points)
3.	Placement decisions	
	a. Description	(2 points)
	b. Example of placement decision	(2 points)
4.	Classification decisions	
	a. Description	(2 points)
	b. Example of classification decision	(2 points)
5.	Comparison of the three decision types	
	a. Similarities	(4 points)
	b. Differences	(4 points)

dent papers, however, patterns or errors and misconceptions will emerge. Be alert to these. Then, craft a partial-credit scoring rubric and use it to mark all the papers. Scoring rubrics for higher-order thinking items are covered in Chapters 11 and 12.

Holistic Scoring Rubrics

The **holistic scoring rubric** requires you to make a judgment about the overall quality of each student's response. You do not mark each specific content element that a student included in the answer. Holistic scoring is probably more appropriate for extended response essays involving a student's abilities to synthesize and create and when no definite correct answer can be prespecified. The holistic method is less objective than the analytic method unless you have specified scoring criteria. Two teachers would rate the same student's essay response very differently unless they agreed to use the same scoring criteria and practiced scoring several papers until they reached a reasonable level of scoring agreement.

One way to implement the holistic method is to decide beforehand on the number of quality categories into which you will sort the students' answers. Usually, you can use between three and five categories, such as A, B, C, D, and F; distinguished, proficient, apprentice, and novice; or 4, 3, 2, and 1. A very important point in deciding the categories is to be sure they correspond to your school's grading system. If your school uses A through F, for example, then five categories are needed. Using only three quality levels will make your student evaluations unnecessarily complicated.

After deciding on the categories, you read an essay and determine to which category it will be assigned. After reading and categorizing all of the essays, you should re-examine all the papers *within* a category to be sure they are enough alike in quality to receive the same grade or quality rating. You assign those papers that are dissimilar to a higher or lower category depending on the results of this second reading. You might also compare the papers in one category with those of another to decide whether the distributions between categories are meaningful or whether further reassignments are necessary.

A second and better way of using the holistic method is to craft a holistic scoring rubric, which defines the qualities of the papers that belong in each category. This means, for example, defining what an A paper is, a B paper, and so on. It is best to revise your scoring rubric after you have tried out the draft version on several papers. Trying out the rubric will allow you to identify parts of it that are unclear, and to add qualities of student responses that you may have failed to include in the original draft. Figure 9.9 offers an example. Again, be sure that your rubric has the same number of quality levels as your school's grading system. (See Chapter 15 for more details on grading.)

A third refinement is to select specimen papers, which are good examples of each scoring category. You can then compare the current students' answers to actual specimens of previous students' papers that define each quality level. You then decide into which category to place them.

A fourth way of implementing holistic scoring is to read through the answers and compare one with another to decide which are the best, the next best, and so on. This will result in a rough ranking of all the papers. This approach does not work very well with a large number of papers.

The first three of these four holistic approaches are consistent with a grading philosophy based on criterion-referencing or absolute-quality standards. The fourth is consistent with a norm-referenced or relative-quality standard grading philosophy. (See Chapter 15.)

Advantages and Disadvantages

Analytic and holistic scoring approaches are not interchangeable. They will give you different perspectives on your students' performance. Further, the analytic scoring rubric provides you and your students with much more detail about their strengths and weaknesses. If you use an analytic scoring rubric, take advantage of this added information to enhance your teaching. For example, you could identify which elements or parts of the entire class' answers are weakest and direct your reteaching on that aspect. You will also be able to give your students specific praise for those parts of the answer on which they did well. A summary of the advantages and disadvantages of the two types of rubrics is presented in Table 9.4.

FIGURE 9.8 Example of an analytic scoring rubric for awarding partial credit to the computations arising in mathematics word problems. (The columns at the right show how the partial credits are distributed differently when the total points for the problem change from two to five.)

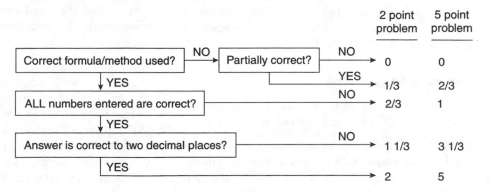

FIGURE 9.9 Example of a holistic scoring rubric for the essay on selection, placement, and classification decisions.

Quality standard	Marks
Level 4	16–20

Makes explicit comparisons among the three types of decisions.

- Includes both similarities and differences in the validity argument needed to support each decision.
- Gives concrete examples of the different decisions.
- Gives examples of the types of validity evidence needed for these specific examples.

Level 3	11–15

- Makes explicit comparisons among the three types of decisions.
- Includes both similarities and differences in the validity evidence needed to support each decision.
- Gives a few concrete examples but does not elaborate on the specifics of how they apply to the validity argument in each case.
- Discusses validity and its necessity but only weakly links it to each decision type.

Level 2	6–10

- Describes the three types of decisions, and implicitly compares them.
- Does not elaborate on their similarities and differences.
- Uses "textbookish" and not very specific descriptions and examples.
- States that validity is important but doesn't link it to different evidence needs for each decision.

Level 1	0–5

- Describes some or all of the three types of decisions but does not describe them correctly and/or does not compare their similarities and differences.
- Examples may be abstract and/or do not match the decision.
- The different type of validity evidence is not discussed properly.

Annotated Holistic Scoring Rubrics

An advantage of using a holistic scoring rubric is the time it saves. It is faster to score a student's essay holistically than analytically. Often the timesaving is considerable, on the order of two or three to one.

Some persons have successfully used a scoring rubric that is a hybrid of the analytic and holistic rubrics. The **annotated holistic rubric** is one such rubric. With this approach, quality levels are defined and the papers are scored holistically. After reaching a holistic judgment, you write on the student's paper very brief comments that point out one or two strengths of the response and one or two weaknesses. You write about only what led you to reach your holistic judgment of the paper. An example of this approach is shown in the portfolio scoring guide in Chapter 11 (Figure 11.10).

More Scoring Suggestions

Some principles apply regardless of which scoring method is used. These principles are summarized in Table 9.5.

Scoring Rubrics Scoring rubrics and model answers were mentioned in connection with analytic and holistic methods. The point of using these tools is to improve the con-

sistency of your scoring so that you apply the same standards from paper to paper. Some states have adopted general rubics that you should use. Check your state's requirements on its Website.

Score One Question at a Time If there is more than one essay question, score all students on the first question before moving on. Then grade all answers to the next question. This method improves the uniformity with which you apply scoring standards to each student. It also allows you to become more familiar with the scoring guide for a given question, and you are less likely to be distracted by responses to other questions (Mehrens & Lehmann, 1991). Finally, using this method helps to reduce the carryover effect discussed earlier. You can reduce carryover effects further by reshuffling the papers after scoring each question.

Score Subject-Matter Correctness Separately Factors other than an answer's content can affect your evaluation. Among such factors are spelling, penmanship, neatness, and language usage. To avoid confounding your judgment of the quality of the ideas or substantive content of a student's answer with these other factors, score the other factors separately—perhaps by using a rating scale (see Chapter 12). Scoring separately for quality of ideas, correctness

TABLE 9.4 Advantages and disadvantages of holistic and analytic scoring rubrics.

I. *Holistic Scoring Rubrics*
  A. *Advantages*
    1. You can score the students' papers a little faster than with analytic rubrics.
    2. It helps you to view the papers as a working whole.
  B. *Disadvantages*
    1. You give a single overall mark and do not point out details to your students that might help them to improve.
    2. Your own bias (e.g., toward neatness or spelling correctly) and errors (paying closer attention to the correctness of a specific element in one student's paper than to another student) can be easily masked by the overall mark.

II. *Analytic Scoring Rubrics*
  A. *Advantages*
    1. By scoring each element separately, you can give students feedback as to their strengths and weaknesses.
    2. By scoring each part separately, you can look over all the papers to see which elements of the answer gave students the most trouble and therefore need to be retaught.
    3. By weighing some elements of the answer more heavily than others, you must face up to your own values (i.e., you must decide which elements you value more than others).
  B. *Disadvantages*
    1. Your scoring will be a little slower with an analytic scoring rubric.
    2. For some essays, you may find it difficult to come up with well-defined elements in the scoring guide.
    3. Beginning teachers may feel a bit frustrated by the amount of time needed to create a useful analytic scoring rubric.

Source: Adapted from *Creating Writers: Linking Assessment and Writing Instruction* 2nd ed (pp. 29–36) by V. Spandel and R. J. Stiggins, 1990, New York: Longman. Copyright 1997, 1990 by Longman Publishers USA. Adapted by permission of Addison-Wesley Educational Publishers Inc.

of content, and other factors also gives you the freedom to weight each factor appropriately. For example, you can weight spelling zero or more heavily, depending on the state policy, school policy, or your classroom practice. But if these factors are to receive a weight of zero, why bother marking them separately? The answer is that you are influenced unknowingly by factors such as penmanship, spelling, and neatness even when you are consciously trying to grade on the basis of ideas or content alone (Marshall, 1967; Marshall & Powers, 1969; Scannell & Marshall, 1966). When such factors are scored separately, their influence on essay grades is lessened, letting you better assess the learning target.

Score Essays Anonymously Anonymous scoring of essays prevents the halo effect mentioned previously. Further, if students know that you score papers anonymously, they are likely to perceive the grading process as fair (Mehrens & Lehmann, 1991). One suggestion for maintaining anonymity is to have students write their names on the back of the answer sheet or exam booklet. Other more elaborate methods, such as using student numbers or other codes, are also effective.

Give Students Feedback An important reason for using essays is the opportunity it gives you to examine the expressive abilities and thought processes students use. You should note strengths and weaknesses in these areas for each student and explain the grade assigned, so that the essay assessment provides an opportunity for further student learning. The following maxims for commenting on student compositions were suggested by Hirsch (1977) to use when the compositions focus on teaching general writing skills. They do, however, seem to be more generally useful for commenting on student responses to essay questions, too.

TABLE 9.5 Summary of principles for scoring responses to subject-matter essay items.

1. Prepare some type of scoring guide (e.g., an outline, a rubric, an "ideal" answer, or "specimen" responses from past administrations).

2. Grade all responses to one question before moving on to the next question.

3. Periodically rescore previously scored papers.

4. Score penmanship, general neatness, spelling, use of prescribed format, and English mechanics separately from subject-matter correctness.

5. Score papers without knowing the name of the pupil writing the response.

6. Provide pupils with feedback on the strengths and weaknesses of their responses.

7. When the grading decision is crucial, have two or more readers score the essays independently.

Source: Coffman, 1971; Ebel, 1979; Greene, Jorgensen, & Gerberich, 1942; Gronlund, 1976; Hopkins, Stanley, & Hopkins, 1990; Lindvall & Nitko, 1975; Mehrens & Lehmann, 1991; Sax, 1989; Stalnaker, 1951; Thorndike, Cunningham, Thorndike, & Hagen, 1991.

1. Comment on just two or three points in any paper. . . .

2. Select those matters for comment which are most important for an individual student at a particular time. . . .

3. Summarize the commentary in usable form.

4. Begin writing comments only after a rapid analysis of the paper as a whole. . . .

5. Choose those comments which will be likely to induce the greatest assessment improvement in the intrinsic effectiveness of the student's next paper. . . .

6. State the comments in an encouraging manner.

7. Do not hesitate to repeat a comment over several papers. . . .

8. Keep track of the comments, so that nothing of great importance for a particular student is omitted during the course. . . .

9. Make clear from the tone of the comments that they deal with a craft to be learned and not with the teacher's personal taste. (pp. 160–161)

Another suggestion for giving feedback is to meet with each student individually to review answers and comments. A brief conference of 10 to 20 minutes with each student is more personal and can provide clearer guidance to the student than written comments in the paper's margin. A short, direct conference with each student may also save you hours of writing copious notes and commentary to clarify a point for the student.

Independent Scoring   The quirks of individual teachers do affect essay scores. The suggestions in Table 9.4 help reduce the impact of your quirks, but they do not entirely eliminate them. The ancient Chinese realized that when important decisions rest on the scores from essays, more than one reader is necessary (Kracke, 1953). Realistically, however, even though everyday grading decisions are important, it is unlikely that you will find the time or consistent cooperation of colleagues to carry out **independent scoring of essays**. Nevertheless, such a practice would improve the consistency of your scoring.

Evaluating Your Scoring Rubrics   You may wish to evaluate the quality of the scoring rubrics you crafted. Use the checklist in Chapter 12 (Table 12.5) to do this.

Summary
- Essay items require the examinee to write a somewhat lengthy response to a question or problem.
- Restricted response essays restrict or limit both the substantive content and the form of the written response.
- Extended response essays permit the student to make fuller use of written verbal reasoning and writing skills, including a full elaboration of the answer to a substantive question.
- The restricted response format:
  - Can be used to measure a variety of complex learning outcomes

- Narrows the focus of the item to more specific content and to well-defined problem situations
  - Can be used as context-dependent or interpretive exercises
  - Is likely to result in nearly all pupils interpreting the intent of the item in basically the same way
  - Is likely to be more reliably scored than the extended response format
- The extended response format:
  - Can be used to measure a more complex variety of learning targets
  - Can be used to assess either the ability to write about the subject matter or the student's general writing ability
  - Has the unique feature of permitting the student to display the abilities needed for written production, organization, and expression of ideas and the interrelationships among these abilities
  - Should not be used to elicit lower-level thinking processes, such as simple recall of information
- Students may study differently when preparing for essay assessments than when preparing for more objective assessments. Study habits are more likely influenced by the substantive nature of the questions and the abilities required to answer them than whether they are essay or objective tasks.
- Essay questions sample a narrower range of content than briefer, objective questions; but they generally require students to show a more in-depth understanding of the content. This is a disadvantage if the learning targets require broad content coverage.
- The subjectivity involved in grading essays presents a serious threat to the reliability and validity of the scores:
  - A given reader may be inconsistent
  - There are often large reader-to-reader differences in the scores of the same students.
  - The type and topic of the question influences a reader's scoring.
  - Halo effects, carryover effects, bluffing, penmanship, spelling, and grammar all influence the scoring.
- To grade fairly and for students to benefit from the reading, you should carefully plan for essay testing.
- Table 9.2 summarizes 10 suggestions for crafting essay assessments.
- Ideas for phrasing essay questions are given in Table 9.3.
- Subject-matter essay questions can be scored analytically or holistically. The approach you should use depends on the nature of the essay question you posed.
- Suggestions for scoring essay questions, which apply to either analytical or holistic scoring, are summarized in Table 9.5.
- Suggestions for commenting on students' essays and compositions are presented.

- You can use either holistic or analytic scoring rubrics to evaluate general writing skill. The advantages and disadvantages of each rubric are summarized in Table 9.4.
- Analytic scoring rubrics help you to assess specific aspects of a student's writing. Therefore, they appear to be useful when you want to diagnose learning needs and to focus your teaching on these needs.
- Any analytic scoring rubric you adopt should contain traits that (1) make good educational sense, (2) apply to a wide range of writing performances, and (3) can be easily taught to students.

Important Terms and Concepts

analytic scoring rubric
annotated holistic rubric
assessing subject-matter knowledge
assessing general writing ability
assessment of simple recall
assessment of higher-order thinking
carryover effect
extended response essay items
halo effect
holistic scoring rubric
independent scoring of essays
interpretive exercises (context-dependent tasks)
optional essay questions
rater drift
restricted response essay items
scoring reliability

Exercises and Discussion Questions

1. For each subject you teach (or plan to teach), identify different types of material that can accompany context-dependent items. For each type, state the educational level of the students for which it is intended.
2. For each thinking-skill category in Table 9.3, craft at least one essay item based on the material you identified in Exercise 1. Use the examples in Table 9.3 as models for phrasing your essays.
3. For each essay item you wrote in Exercise 2, apply the checklist in Table 9.2. Revise any item for which you answered no to a checklist question. Exchange your items with one or more of the students in this course. Review each other's essay items using the checklist. Discuss with your classmates the reasons for assigning a no to an item. Discuss how to improve each item.
4. For each essay item you crafted and revised in Exercises 2 and 3, craft an analytic and a holistic scoring rubric. Exchange scoring rubrics with a classmate. Review each other's work, offering suggestions for improvement. Then administer each of your essays to at least two students. Use your scoring rubrics to evaluate the students' responses. Do your scoring rubrics function well? What problems do you encounter? What does your tryout suggest for revising your scoring rubrics? Report your findings to the others in this course.
5. The chapter discusses several factors affecting the reliability of your students' essay scores. Using the items you developed in Exercises 2 and 3, give an example of how these factors could affect the reliability of your students' scores. For each factor, list one or more suggestions for increasing the consistency of your students' scores for each item.
6. Why should you focus your essay questions so that students attend to the main points you want? Offer some arguments against focusing the questions in the way that the author suggests in the text.
7. Each of these two essay items has one or more flaws. Using Table 9.2, identify the flaw(s), then rewrite each item so it no longer exhibits the flaw(s). Check your rewritten essay item to be sure you have not created another flawed item.
   a. State the two examples of prejudices we discussed in class.
   b. Evaluate the effect of air pollution on the quality of life in the western part of this state.
8. Following are four restricted response essay questions that together constitute a science unit test. After each question is the keyed answer provided by the teacher and Jane Smith's answer. You are to do two things: First, decide the maximum marks (points) of each question. (The entire test has a maximum score of 50 points, so you need to distribute these among the four questions according to what you believe is appropriate.) Second, evaluate Jane Smith's answers with the answer key and award her points according to the degree of correctness of her answer.

Question 1   What is the shape of a quartz crystal?
    Answer key: Hexagonal
    Maximum marks: _____
    Jane's answer: "Six-sided hectogon."
    Jane's score: _____

Question 2   What is a saturated solution?
    Answer key: A solution that contains as much dissolved substance as it can for a particular temperature.
    Maximum marks: _____
    Jane's answer: "Large crystals contain a great deal of substance that has been formed. This process of forming crystals is called crystallization. It occurs both in the laboratory and in nature."
    Jane's score: _____

Question 3   Write a paragraph describing how you can grow very large crystals.
    Answer key: Any answer that says size of crystal is directly related to the rate of crystallization.
    Maximum marks: _____
    Jane's answer: "Large crystals contain a great deal of substance that has been formed. This process of forming crystals is called crystallization. It occurs both in the laboratory and in nature."
    Jane's score: _____

Question 4　Name three major categories of rocks.
　　Answer key: Igneous, sedimentary, and
　　metamorphic
　　Maximum marks: _____
　　Jane's answer:　　　　"The three kinds are
　　fire-formed, settled, and those that have
　　changed their form."
　　Jane's score: _____

9. This exercise should be done during your class.
   a. Compare the maximum marks you assigned to each question in Exercise 8 with those assigned by other persons in this course. (Put the distributions of maximum marks on the chalkboard.) For which questions is there more agreement? For which is there less agreement?
   b. Discuss during class the reasons for agreement and disagreement. Make a list of the factors that seem to affect the maximum value that your classmates assign to each question.
   c. Suggest ways of reducing the variability among persons assigning maximum values to questions. Make sure the suggestions are specific to these four questions.
   d. Compare the scores you gave Jane on each question with the scores given by others in this course. On which items is there more agreement? On which is there less agreement?
   e. Discuss during class the reasons for an agreement and disagreement in marking. Make a list of the factors that seem to affect the score that persons assign to Jane for each question.
   f. Are the questions on which there is more agreement in scoring Jane's responses the same questions on which there is more agreement for maximum marks? Explain.
10. States and the National Assessment of Educational Progress evaluate the essay responses of thousands of students. Some of these large-scale assessment programs use a computer-assisted scoring technology called *imaging* in which students' writings and drawings are scanned into a computer file. Teachers marking these constructed responses do so at a computer screen; then marks are monitored by a supervisor who can see what they are doing via another computer screen. Conduct an investigation into this computer-assisted marking process. Describe the process in detail. Explain its advantages and disadvantages. Share your findings with your classmates.

Additional Readings

Coffman, W. E. (1971). Essay examinations. In R. L. Thorndike (Ed.), *Educational measurement* (2nd ed.). Washington, DC: American Council on Education, Chapter 10, 271–302.
　　Reviews early research on essay items. Gives suggestions for improving the essay examination process.

Gentile, C. (1992). *Exploring new methods for collecting students' school-based writing: NAEP's 1990 portfolio study.* Washington, DC: Education Information Branch, Office of Educational Research and Improvement, U.S. Department of Education, Chapter 2, pp. 18–61.
　　This chapter describes three scoring guides for assessing writing: narrative, informative, and persuasive. Examples of student writing (in student penmanship) are presented to illustrate how each scoring guide is used.

Spandel, V., & Stiggins, R. J. (1990). *Creating writers: Linking assessment and writing instruction.* New York: Longman.
　　Explains the Six Traits analytic scoring rubric in great detail. Gives examples of how to use the rubric to score students' writing and how to integrate writing assessment results into your daily teaching.

Wittrock, M. C., & Baker E. L. (Eds.), (1991) *Testing and cognition.* Englewood Cliffs, NJ: Prentice Hall.
　　A number of chapters relate to issues in using constructed-response tasks to assess cognitive achievement.

CHAPTER 10

Higher-Order Thinking, Problem Solving, and Critical Thinking

Learning Targets

After studying this chapter, you should be able to:

1. Explain why you must use novel material to assess higher-order thinking. [1, 2]

2. Explain the advantages, disadvantages, and layout characteristics of context-dependent item sets. [2, 1]

3. Explain concept learning and how concepts are linked to students' schema. [4, 6, 1]

4. Craft tasks to assess whether a student has learned concrete and defined concepts. [2]

5. Craft performance tasks to assess a student's deeper understanding of concepts. [2]

6. Explain the meaning of rule-governed (principle-governed) thinking and the basic strategies for assessing a student's comprehension of principles and rules. [4, 6, 1]

7. Craft tasks to assess a student's comprehension of principles and rules. [2]

8. Explain the nature of problem solving and the ways students may use general and subject-matter problem-solving abilities, and give examples of problem-solving heuristics. [4]

9. Craft tasks to assess students' ability to perform the following problem-solving abilities: identifying and recognizing problems, defining and representing problems, exploring possible solutions strategies, and acting on and looking back on problem-solution strategies. [2]

10. Explain the meaning of critical thinking and its relation to problem solving. [4, 3]

11. Craft checklists and simple rating scales for assessing students' dispositions toward critical thinking. [2]

12. Craft tasks for assessing the following categories of critical thinking abilities: elementary clarification abilities, basic support abilities, inference abilities, advanced clarification abilities, and strategic and tactical abilities. [2]

13. Explain why it is necessary to assess both students' ability to use problem-solving and critical thinking activities in combination as well as assessing components of these skills separately. [4, 5, 3]

14. Craft tasks to assess students' ability to use reference materials, to read graphs and tables, to read maps, and to read print materials. [2]

15. Craft enhanced multiple-choice items. [2]

16. Explain how each of the terms and concepts listed at the end of this chapter apply to educational assessments. [6]

ASSESSING HIGHER-ORDER THINKING

A basic rule for crafting assessment of higher-order thinking skills is to set tasks requiring a student to use knowledge and skill in new or novel situations. To assess higher-order thinking skills, you should not ask students simply to repeat the reasons, explanations, or interpretations you have stated and they have memorized. If you assess students' ability to simply recall what you say, you will have no assurance that students have understood or can apply the reasons, explanations, and interpretations. In short, you must use **novel materials** to assess higher-order thinking.

As an example, consider teaching the concept *bird.* Suppose that during the lesson you used pictures of three particular birds: a robin, a sparrow, and an eagle. If these same three pictures were used to assess whether the students learned the concept *bird,* you would have no assurance that the students would understand the concept if they encountered penguins and ostriches. The students might have learned only that these particular three pictures were birds.

CONTEXT-DEPENDENT ITEM SETS

Characteristics

Assessing higher-order thinking skills of the type described in this chapter usually requires using introductory material followed by several assessment tasks. You craft the tasks so that a student must think about and process the information in the introductory material to answer the questions, solve the problems, or otherwise complete the assessment tasks. The introductory material, along with the corresponding assessment tasks, is called a **context-dependent item set** or an **interpretive exercise.** The introductory material may be extracts from reading materials, pictures, graphs, drawings, paragraphs, poems, formulas, tables of numbers, lists of words or symbols, specimens, maps, films, and sound recordings.

Figure 10.1 is an example of a context-dependent item set. In this example, the interpretive material is an extract from a dictionary. This extract "simulates" a dictionary page and thus presents a concrete, realistic example. A student has to analyze or process this example to answer the questions.

The example shows multiple-choice items. Context-dependent item sets may be used, however, with any type of item format.

Advantages and Disadvantages

Advantages A context-dependent item set has these advantages: (1) it provides an opportunity to assess students on materials that are relatively close to the real-world or authentic contexts toward which you are guiding your students' learning, (2) it provides, through the introductory material, the same context for all students, (3) its introductory material lessens the burden of memorizing and may moderate the effects of prior experience with the specific content, and (4) it is frequently the only means to test certain intellectual abilities.

FIGURE 10.1 Example of a context-dependent item set.

Below is part of a dictionary. Use it to answer Questions 1, 2, and 3.

ru·bi·ous (roo′bē·əs) *adj.* Of the color of a ruby : RED.
ru·ble (ro͞o′bəl) *n. var. of* ROUBLE.
ru·bric (ro͞o′brĭk) *n.* [ME *rubrike* < OFr. *rubriche* < Lat. *rubrica,* rubric, red chalk < *ruber,* red.] **1.** A part of a manuscript or book, as a heading, title, or initial letter, that appears in decorative red lettering or is otherwise distinguished from the rest of the text. **2.** A title or heading of a statute or chapter in a code of law. **3. a.** A class or category. **b.** A title : name. **4.** A direction in a liturgical book, as a missal or hymnal. **5.** An authoritative direction or rule. **6.** A short commentary or explanation covering a broad subject. **7.** Red ocher. *—adj.,* **1.** Red or reddish. **2.** Written in red. **—ru'bri·cal** *adj.*
ru·bri·cate (ro͞o′brĭ-kāt′) *vt.* **-cat· ed, -cat· ing, -cates.** [Lat. *rubricate, rubricat-,* to color red < *rubrica, rubric.*] **1.** To write, arrange, or print as a rubric. **2.** To provide with rubrics. **3.** To establish rules for. **—ru'bri·ca'tion** *n.* **—ru'bri·ca'tor** *n.*
ru·bri·cian (ro͞o·brĭsh′ən) *n.* One learned in the rubrics of ecclesiastical ritual.
ru·by (ro͞o′bē) *n., pl.* **-bies.** [ME < OFr. *rubi, rubis* < Med. Lat. *rubinus (lapis),* red (stone) < Lat. *rubeus,* red.] **1.** A deep-red translucent corundum highly valued as a precious stone. **2.** Something, as a watch bearing, made from a ruby. 3. A dark or deep red to deep purplish red. *—adj.* Of the color ruby.

Source: Copyright © 1994 by Houghton Mifflin Company. Reproduced by permission from *Webster's II New Riverside University Dictionary.*

1. The u in **rubric** is pronounced like the
   A. u in rubber
   *B. oo in boot
   C. u in lurch
   D. oo in cook

2. Which meaning of **rubric** is used in the following sentence:
   *"Our teacher told us to use the **rubric** when we mark our papers."*
   A. 1
   B. 4
   *C. 5
   D. 6

3. What part of speech is the word **rubrication**?
   A. adjective
   B. adverb
   *C. noun
   D. transitive verb

Disadvantages Some disadvantages of a context-dependent item set are (1) the set may be difficult to construct, (2) you must carefully craft the introductory material to assess higher-order thinking skills, (3) a student's performance on one context-dependent item set may not generalize well to performance on another similar set, (4) the set may require students to use additional abilities (such as reading comprehension and writing skills, which go beyond the major focus of the assessment tasks), and (5) you may need special facilities (such as copying machines and/or drawing skill and equipment) that may not be accessible.

Layout

The way context-dependent material is arranged on the pages of a test booklet is important because a poor arrangement may lead a student to misread or misinterpret the item set. Thus, a poor arrangement can jeopardize the validity of your assessment results.

Figure 10.2 shows one kind of arrangement. Note that a side heading (underlined, in bold, or in capital letters) directs the students to the introductory material and to the particular tasks based on it. Some students may skip over introductory material or become confused about the assessment tasks to which it refers. A side heading helps to avoid this. The introductory material is placed in the center of the page. The items may be placed one under another or as shown in the figure. A drawing should be neat, clear, and, if necessary, labeled. Photographs and magazine pictures may not be

legible when photocopied, so check the reproduction equipment you will use beforehand. If the introductory material is a passage or poem, centering and single spacing are usually all right, but young children and those with certain disabilities may have difficulty with this arrangement. You may need to use enlarged print for some students. Remember to seek permission when using copyrighted material.

Keep the introductory material and all the items that refer to it on the same page, if possible. Otherwise, students will be distracted as they turn pages back and forth while completing the assessment. Some students whose short-term attention and memory are not good may lose their place or make careless errors.

CONCEPTS AND CONCEPT LEARNING

What Are Concepts?

Students' knowledge of concepts forms the basis for their higher-order learning. A **concept** is a class or category of things (objects, people, events, or relations) that are similar. When we speak of the concept *red*, for example, we refer to a category of objects that have a similar color. A student is said to have learned the concept *red* if the student (a) can identify examples or instances of red things (red tricycle, red book, red lipstick, etc.) *and* (b) does not refer to non-red things (green tricycle, purple book, pink lipstick, etc.) as red. Concepts are ideas or abstractions: Only specific examples of a concept exist in the world. The individual members of the concept category are called *instances, examples*, or **exemplars**.

Concrete vs. Defined Concepts

A distinction can be made between concrete concepts and defined concepts (Gagné, 1970). A **concrete concept** refers to a class, the members of which have in common one or more physical, tangible qualities that can be heard, seen, tasted, felt, or smelled. Examples of concrete concepts include *large, triangle, green, house,* and *dog*. A **defined concept** refers to a class, the members of which can be defined in the same way by attributes that are not tangible and which frequently involve relationships among other concepts. Defined concepts are sometimes called *abstract* or **relational concepts** (Gagné, 1970). Defined concepts are usually learned by definitions. Gagné gives an example of the defined concept *diagonal*, which is defined as a line connecting the opposite corners of a quadrilateral figure. The relationship is "connecting." The concepts that are related are "opposite corners," "quadrilateral figure," and "line." Other examples of defined concepts include *beside, friendliness, uncle,* and *mother*. Some concepts are learned initially as concrete concepts and later as defined concepts.

FIGURE 10.2 Arrangement of context-dependent assessment material is important.

Items 1 through 4 refer to the material below

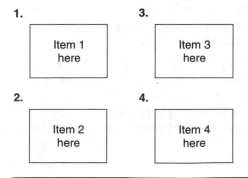

Understanding a Concept

A student's understanding of a concept goes beyond simply identifying examples of it. Concepts are related to each other and linked together in complex ways through schema or networks. A **schema** is the way knowledge is represented in our minds through networks of connected concepts, information, rules, problem-solving strategies, and conditions for actions (Marshall, 1990). For example, Woolfolk (1995) points out that we know counterfeit money is not real, even though it fits the money concept prototype and examples, because we link the money concept to other concepts, such as authority to print, crime, forgery, and so on. You need to help students connect concepts to their existing networks and schema of knowledge before these concepts can be fully understood. Woolfolk (1995) summarized recommended lesson structures for teaching a concept.

ASSESSING CONCRETE CONCEPT LEARNING

Three Assessment Strategies

To assess whether a student has learned a concrete concept, you ask the student to (1) give the name of the concept after you give different exemplars of the same concept, (2) discriminate exemplars from nonexemplars after you give the name of the concept, or (3) produce new exemplars after you give the concept name. Figure 10.3 illustrates these three assessment strategies.

Criticisms of the Three Strategies

Give the Name   In Figure 10.3, Task 1 is usually an unsatisfactory way to assess concept learning. It requires a student to recall the name of the concept and does not require the student to discriminate it from nonexemplars. A student may learn the concept and perhaps can use it without learning the proper name of the concept. The give-the-name assessment strategy does not require a student to discriminate the exemplars from nonexemplars, so you do not know whether the student has **overgeneralized the concept**. For example, the student may confuse circles with ellipses (ovals) and spheres (balls). Finally, this assessment strategy does not require a student to use or apply her understanding of the concept. Thus, even though a student can state the concept name, you do not know whether she has the deeper understanding of the concept necessary to connect it to other concepts and integrate it into her schema.

Discriminate Exemplars from Nonexemplars   Task 2 requires a student to discriminate circles from other shapes. This assessment strategy is preferred over that of Task 1 because it (1) does not require a student to produce the

FIGURE 10.3   Alternate, but not equally appropriate, ways to assess whether a student has learned the shape *circle*.

A. The task requires students to give the concept name after seeing exemplars.

1. What are the shapes in this group called? [Ans.: Circles]

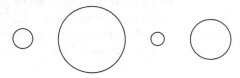

B. The task requires students to discriminate concept exemplars from nonexemplars.

2. Which of these shapes are circles? [Ans.: A, D, G]

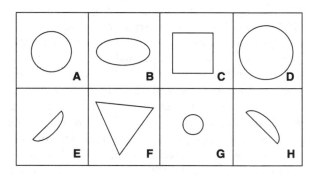

C. The task requires students to produce new exemplars.

3. Draw three circles. Be sure each is different from the others.

concept name to complete the task[1] and (2) allows you to control (a) the degree to which the exemplars and nonexemplars are familiar to the students, (b) the graded membership of the exemplars, (c) the number and type of discriminations between exemplars and nonexemplars, and (d) the total number of exemplars strategy that you must present at least two exemplars for the student to identify; otherwise you do not know whether the student has **undergeneralized the concept**. As with Task 1, this strategy does not require students to use or apply their understanding of the concept. Thus, it does not permit you to assess students' deeper understanding of it.

Produce New Exemplars   Task 3 requires (1) the student to think up examples, (2) you to judge the correctness of the examples, and (3) you to judge whether the student's examples were explicitly taught (whether they are "new"; see Jenkins & Deno, 1971). However, a student's ability to

---

[1]You can separately assess a student's ability to name a concept if you wish.

generate new examples may not be a requirement for learning the concept. Thus, although this strategy may be useful for assessing simple concepts (such as *circle*), it is not preferred for more complex concept assessment because it does not permit you to assess students' deeper understanding of it.

ASSESSING CONCEPT UNDERSTANDING AT A DEEPER LEVEL

Performance Assessment for Several Learning Targets

Understanding a concept goes beyond simply identifying exemplars of it. Students show their understanding when they are able to (1) use the concepts to solve problems, (2) relate the concepts to other concepts, principles, and generalizations they have learned, and (3) learn new material. To assess students' deeper understanding of concepts, you must craft assessment contexts that are more complex and applied than the tasks illustrated in Figure 10.3.

Figure 10.4 shows one way this deeper assessment may be accomplished, even with simple concrete concepts. The figure shows a *performance task* (see Chapters 11 and 12 for a complete discussion of performance assessment) that assesses the following learning:

I. Content targets (in combination)
- A. Understands the importance of shapes in the world
- B. Identifies circles and squares
- C. Discriminates circles and squares from other shapes

II. Complex thinking target (problem solving)
- A. Identifies things that keep you from solving a problem

III. Information processing target
- A. Effectively interprets and synthesizes information

IV. Effective communication target
- A. Communicates ideas effectively

The task in Figure 10.4 takes a relatively long time to administer, probably two or three 40-minute mathematics periods. The main performance is this: Make a drawing of the neighborhood that includes buildings, cars, and people but that does *not* use circles and squares. This drawing presents a problem to be solved: How can you make buildings, cars, and people, yet not use circles and squares? This is a difficult problem for a first grader, because circles and squares are basic shapes comprising much of the student's experience. The student must distinguish between circles, squares, and other shapes to solve the problem. Notice, too, that the assessment requires you to do more than collect the drawings. You must interview or have a conference with each student using the drawing to prompt or draw out from the student information about how well the learning targets have been attained.

Figure 10.5 shows the scoring rubrics. (Rubrics are discussed in Chapters 11 and 12.) There is one rubric for each learning target. However, you do not treat each rubric as a separate test item. You score this assessment task holistically. By reviewing a student's drawing, conferencing with a student, and prompting a student to discuss the mathematical content, you obtain considerable information about the student's attainment of the learning targets. You then holistically rate the quality level of the student's learning of each target.

Advantage of This Strategy

An advantage of assessing concepts through complex performance tasks, such as the one shown in Figure 10.4, is that students use the concepts in realistic situations. These situations activate students' cognitive frameworks and schema. They require students to link the concepts to many others as they complete the task. If you focus on a student's way(s) of using the target concepts while he

FIGURE 10.4 Example of a performance task assessing concept learning in a problem-solving context.

The teacher presents the task orally:

We have been studying two shapes: circles and squares. We will be taking a walk through the school neighborhood to look at the shapes of buildings, people, and cars. Then you will draw a picture of the school neighborhood, your neighborhood, or a city. Your drawing must include buildings, people, and cars. However, you cannot use any circles or squares in your drawing.

As you work, ask a friend to keep checking your picture to see if you have used either of these shapes. If you have, change your drawing so it has no circles and no squares.

When you are finished I will look to see if you have used any circles or squares. While you are working, I will ask you to explain to me, using the words for the shapes we have studied, what you have learned in this assignment about the importance of shapes in our world. I will ask you to explain to me what makes drawing a picture like this without circles and squares so difficult.

Before you begin I will show you some examples of pictures, explain what I will be looking for, and the kinds of answers I will be expecting of you.

Source: Adapted from *Assessing Student Outcomes: Performance Assessment Using the Dimensions of Learning Model*, (pp. 61–62), by R. J. Marzano, D. Pickering, and J. McTighe, 1993, Alexandria, VA: Association for Supervision and Curriculum Development. Reproduced with permission of McREL Institute, 2550 S. Parker Rd., Suite 500, Aurora, CO, 80014. Telephone (303) 337-0990.

FIGURE 10.5 Scoring rubrics for circle and square drawing problem in Figure 10.4.

Identifies circles and squares

4 Always identifies circles and squares with little or no prompting.
3 Identifies circles and squares but needs some prompting.
2 Sometimes confuses circles with ellipses or other curves; sometimes confuses squares with rectangles or other shapes.
1 Demonstrates severe misunderstanding of circles and/or squares.

Understands importance of circles and squares as the basic shapes comprising objects in the world

4 Demonstrates a thorough understanding of how circles and squares are the basic shapes that make up most objects in the world and provides new insights into some aspect of their use.
3 Displays a complete and accurate understanding of how circles and squares are used in the world but doesn't provide new insights into an aspect of their use.
2 Displays an incomplete understanding of how circles and squares are used in the world and has some notable misconceptions about their use.
1 Has severe misconceptions about how circles and squares are used in the world.

Understands that not being able to use circles and squares is an obstacle to depict real world objects accurately

4 Accurately and thoroughly describes that not using circles and squares in the drawing results in distortions or inability to represent objects in drawings. Addresses obstacles or constraints that are not immediately apparent.
3 Accurately identifies the most important constraints or obstacles imposed by not using circles and squares in drawings of objects.
2 Identifies some constraints or obstacles about not using circles and squares that are accurate and some that are not accurate or relevant to the drawing problem.
1 Omits the most significant constraints or obstacles imposed by not being able to use circles and squares to solve the drawing problem.

Effectively interprets and synthesizes information about real-world objects, circles, and squares.

4 Interprets the information about shapes or objects for the drawing problem in an accurate and highly insightful way. Provides a highly creative and unique synthesis of the information.
3 Accurately interprets the information about shapes of objects for the drawing problem and concisely synthesizes it in the drawing.
2 Makes significant errors interpreting the information about the shapes of objects for solving the drawing problem or synthesizes the information imprecisely or awkwardly.
1 Grossly misrepresents the information about the shapes of objects gathered for the drawing problem or fails to synthesize it.

Expresses ideas about circles and squares being basic elements of real-world objects in mathematically correct ways.

4 Clearly and effectively communicates the main ideas about circles and squares with regard to their being basic elements of real-world shapes. Provides support for ideas that contains rich, vivid, and powerful detail. Uses the terminology about shapes in a mathematically correct way.
3 Clearly communicates the main idea that circles and squares are basic shapes comprising real-world objects and provides suitable support.
2 Communicates the basic information about circles, squares, and real-world shapes but not a clear theme or overall structure.
1 Communicates information about circles and squares as isolated pieces of information, perhaps in a random fashion.

engages in problem solving, you assess whether the student has an understanding of the concepts that is deeper than simply naming and identifying them.

ASSESSING DEFINED CONCEPT LEARNING

Four Assessment Strategies

Teachers often use one of three strategies to assess students' learning of abstract or defined concepts. They re-

quire students to (1) produce a correct definition of a concept, (2) produce a new or novel example of a concept, or (3) identify exemplars and nonexemplars of a concept (Jenkins & Deno, 1971). Another strategy is to (4) require students to analyze the defined concept to identify its component concepts and state the relationship among them (Gagné & Briggs, 1979). Sample tasks using each of these strategies are shown in Figure 10.6.

Of the four strategies in Figure 10.6, the strategies requiring students to produce a definition and requiring students to produce new exemplars of the concept are the

FIGURE 10.6 Alternative, but not equally appropriate, strategies to assess whether a student has learned a defined concept.

Tasks Requiring Students to Produce a Definition

1. Define a *prejudice act* in your own words.
2. Tell what is meant by *lonesome*.

Task Requiring Students to Produce Examples

3. Describe two examples of *prejudice actions* that were not discussed in class or in the text but which you witnessed or experienced during the past few weeks.

Tasks Requiring Students to Discriminate Exemplars from Nonexemplars

Directions. Read each numbered statement. In front of the statement mark:

  P — if it is most likely an example of a *prejudice action*.
  NP — if it is most likely *not* an example of a *prejudice action*.

(NP) 4. Sam, a white man, was overcharged by an African American cashier at the company cafeteria. He became upset and refused to speak with the cashier for two weeks afterward.

(P)   5. Ron, a white man, makes it a personal rule never to socialize with his fellow workers who are African American, unless he is forced to do so.

(P)   6. John, an African American manager of a local drug store, is convinced that women are incompetent pharmacists.

(NP) 7. Bill, a professional golfer, stated that in his entire career no woman against whom he competed ever beat him.

8. Which statement *most nearly* describes the concept of **lonesome**?
   a. Ten-year-old Megan decides to play alone today with her dollhouse, even though her friends asked her to play with them.
   b. Each morning Professor Cory closes her office door to be by herself while writing up her research reports.
   *c. Each lunch period 15-year-old Marya stands by herself, not speaking to anyone in the crowded school cafeteria.
   d. Clarese, a cloistered nun, speaks to no one each day and spends many hours alone while praying.

Task Requiring Students to Identify Components and Demonstrate Relationships

[Picture of earth with person on it omitted to save space]

9. In the picture above, draw lines and angle(s) to show the location of the **zenith**. Label the angle(s) and the zenith.

Source: Task 9 prompted by Gagné & Briggs, 1979, p. 227.

weaker strategies and may not be suitable for younger students (Nitko, 1983). The strategies requiring students to discriminate exemplars from nonexemplars and requiring students to identify components and demonstrate relationships are the stronger strategies. Their main advantage is that they require students to recognize new exemplars and thereby provide some assurance that they have not responded with only the chain of words that comprise a definition. The performance (drawing and labeling) aspect of Item 9 has the advantage of not depending solely on highly developed verbal skills. (See Nitko, 1983 for further details.)

Limitations of Verbal Items

Some defined concepts cannot be assessed in the manner illustrated by Figure 10.6. Two of these are (1) relational concepts (e.g., uncle, aunt) and (2) concepts whose exemplars can be described verbally only by repeating the concept name for each exemplar (Anderson, 1972). An *aunt* is a sister of a mother or father. If you tried to write an "instance" of *aunt*, you would need to mention this relation-

ship in the options. Thus, with this type of concept, you cannot completely assess a student's comprehension of the concept using the item types shown in Figure 10.6.

The concept *wings* is an example of the second type of concept (Anderson, 1972). Each exemplar you write would have to include the word *wings* (airplane wings, bird wings, angel wings, etc.), and so a test item would be answerable on the basis of matching a word in the stem with a word in the options. However, a concept such as *tools* can be assessed by the types of items illustrated in Figure 10.6 because instances of tools (screwdriver, wrench, saw) can be written without repeating the term *tool*.

USING RULES IN THINKING

Another important area of learning is rule-governed or principle-governed thinking. We say a student uses rule-governed thinking when she is able to apply a **principle** or rule appropriately in a variety of "new" situations. A student may mimic your classroom demonstration without understanding the rule well enough to know how to apply it in a new situation. Therefore, to assess a student's understanding of a rule or principle, you must ask the student to apply it to a new situation.

Principles students learn in later elementary and high school tend to be abstract. Examples of such principles include

- When performance is followed by a reinforcing event the probability of that performance reoccurring increases.
- Experimental studies allow conclusions regarding functional relations while correlational studies allow only statements of co-occurrence.
- People tend to immigrate to, and find success in, physical environments closely resembling those from which they came.
- The status of a group in a society is positively related to the priorities of that society.
- The rate of increase in law enforcement officials is negatively related to the stability of the society.
- The record of the past is irremediably fragmentary, selective and biased. (Jenkins & Deno, 1971, p. 96)

ASSESSING COMPREHENSION OF RULES AND PRINCIPLES

Basic Strategies for Crafting Tasks

Figure 10.7 shows an example of how to assess students' understanding of a principle. The principle to be understood is: A behavior that is reinforced intermittently (as contrasted with not being reinforced or being reinforced all the time) is highly resistant to extinction.

The question in Figure 10.7 asks what will happen when the reinforcing laughter stops. To answer this question, you need to know the reinforcement conditions that preceded the laughter stopping. If the teacher and the classmates laughed at every joke attempt, the jokester would stop very soon after the laughter stopped. How-

FIGURE 10.7 Sample item assessing comprehension of a principle.

Use the information below when answering Question 1.

A student eager for attention blurts out jokes several times during social studies class. For the first three days, the teacher and the class laugh at some but not all of the jokes. On the fourth day everyone simply ignores the jokes as if they were not occurring. They show no animosity toward the jokester.

1. Assuming that the situation described above remains the same, what is the jokester student most likely to do with regard to his joking behavior?
   A. Become angry at the teacher and/or the class.
   B. Stop telling jokes immediately.
   *C. Continue telling jokes for a long time even though no one laughs.
   D. Tell even more jokes on the fourth and fifth days, but then stop altogether.

ever, because the preceding laughter was intermittent, it is likely that the jokester will continue in the same manner for a rather long time, according to the principle. Although the item in Figure 10.7 is in a multiple-choice format, the task also could be presented as a short-answer, open-ended task.

As Figure 10.7 illustrates, most principles operate under certain conditions and not under others. Further, when a principle does operate, it leads to certain consequences and not to others. This suggests *basic strategies for crafting tasks to assess students' comprehension of principles* (see Anderson, 1972): Either give students (1) the conditions under which the principle can operate and ask for the consequences (as in Figure 10.7) or (2) the consequences and ask for the possible conditions which must exist for the principle to operate. The strategies are diagrammed in Figure 10.8.

Because these items are highly verbal, they are likely to require a good level of reading comprehension. Students with poor reading skills who actually understand the principle may miss the item. You may try reading the item situations to poor readers to see if they will respond better.

Produce or Identify Consequences

Two examples of Strategy A items are shown in Figure 10.9. Students must read and interpret the passage preceding Item 1 before answering it. The principle students are expected to recall and use to answer the question is: In a society the production of tools increases the probability of survival. The purpose of the passage is to describe a situation in which the principle can operate. The question asks students to infer or predict what will happen. They are expected to recall and use the proper principle to make the inference.

For Item 2, students must also read and interpret the passage preceding the item. The principle students are expected to remember and apply is: Correlational studies do not allow conclusions of causes but only of co-occurrence. The passage describes a correlational study. The students are expected to recall and use the principle to evaluate the conclusions listed in the alternatives and to select the most appropriate one.

Produce or Identify Examples

A variation of Strategy A requires students to produce or recall from their experience a new example rather than to select from among choices you provide. Figure 10.10 illustrates how this variation is applied. The principle students are expected to use is: People tend to immigrate to and find success in physical environments most closely resembling those from which they came.

The stem of this constructed response item provides the context in which students are required to (1) recognize

FIGURE 10.8 Diagram of the basic strategies for assessing comprehension of principles.

How a principle works:

	Proper conditions exist and events occur	→	Principle operates	→	Consequences (outcomes) occur
Assessment Strategy A:	Present the student with the proper conditions and events		→		The student produces or identifies consequences (outcomes)
Assessment Strategy B:	The student produces or identifies proper conditions and events		←		Present the student with the consequences (outcomes)

FIGURE 10.9 Examples of items assessing students' ability to identify the consequences of applying a principle.

Use the information below when answering Question 1.

When Thompson explored the South American continent in 1730 he happened upon two small Indian tribes, the Zooloo and the Maylay, who were living in the wilderness. He noted that the Zooloo displayed great physical strength and endurance. They worshipped the sun and seemed very religious. Although the Maylay were not nearly as large or strong as the Zooloo, some compensated by making stone axes and spades. The Maylay appeared less religious than the Zooloo.

1. Which of the following would you predict, based on what we have studied?
   *A. If one tribe is alive it is probably the Maylay.
   B. The Zooloo were probably a better organized society.
   C. The Maylay lived closer to the Amazon than the Zooloo.
   D. The Zooloo were the better gardeners.

Use the information below when answering Question 2.

A researcher drew random samples of children from three socioeconomic levels (SES): upper, middle, and lower. He determined through interviews and observations how frequently children from each level engaged in aggressive behavior (fighting). He found that low SES children were significantly more aggressive than middle and upper SES children, and that middle SES children exhibited significantly more aggressive behavior than upper SES children.

2. On the basis of the results of this study, which of the following conclusions is most valid?
   A. SES influences aggressiveness.
   B. Placing children from a low SES environment into a high SES environment will decrease their aggressive behavior.
   *C. SES is related to aggressiveness.

Source: Adapted from "Assessing Knowledge of Concepts and Principles" by J. R. Jenkins, and S. J. Deno, 1971, *Journal of Educational Measurement, 8*(1), p. 99. Adapted by permission of publisher. © 1979 by the National Council on Measurement in Education.

FIGURE 10.10 Sample item assessing students' ability to produce an example utilizing a principle.

1. Suppose President Smith forced all the grain farmers from the flatlands of the midwest to leave the country. Name two or more geographical locations in the world to which you would expect them to move. Explain your choices.

Source: Adapted from "Assessing Knowledge of Concepts and Principles" by J. R. Jenkins and S. J. Deno, 1971, *Journal of Educational Measurement, 8*(1), p. 100. Adapted by permission of publisher. © 1971 by The National Council on Measurement in Education.

or deduce which principle is applicable and (2) apply that principle to write an appropriate answer. Notice that the item requires students to have knowledge beyond recalling the principle and recognizing its applicability to the situation provided. To answer the item correctly, students have to know geography well enough to state two or more "geographical locations" that resemble the "flatlands of the Midwest." Further, the usual criterion requires that the students use *new* examples.

These requirements make this type of task difficult, especially for younger, inexperienced learners who are not well-read. Further, a student's performance on such tasks may be difficult to interpret. Here are some of the questions you have to answer about a student's response to evaluate it properly:

- Are the student's examples new, or were they presented in the class or in the assigned materials?
- Why can't a student give a good example?
- Is the principle understood?
- Is there weak knowledge of the specific content to which you have asked the principle to be applied?

Write an Explanation Using a Principle

Assessment Strategy B is the reverse of the items in Figures 10.9 and 10.10. Instead of asking students to recognize or produce examples, you give one or more examples. Then you ask the students to state or select an explanation of the example you gave using the appropriate principle (Jenkins & Deno, 1971). In Figure 10.11, the principle the students are expected to use in their explanations is: The rate at which a behavior occurs is influenced by the consequences of that behavior.

The task in Figure 10.11 could be rewritten as a multiple-choice item in which the alternatives are either different explanations of the phenomenon or different principles. When writing such a multiple-choice item, avoid stating the correct answer in textbook wording or in the exact wording you used in class. You want students to think about the example you give and select the correct alternative to show their understanding. A problem occurs with this type of assessment strategy if only one principle was taught in the unit. In this case, the correct alternative may be obvious, even though students do not comprehend it. Make sure that the correct response a student gives reflects comprehension of the principle.

The constructed-response (short-answer) version shown in Figure 10.11 avoids those problems. However, it requires a student to recall the principle without prompting and to articulate it. Students unable to do these two things will not answer correctly. Further, there may be more than one correct explanation for the phenomena stated in your example. This occurs often where the "truth" of the principle or its applicability to various situations is open to question. As discussed earlier, principles usually apply only under certain conditions. These conditions may not be stated properly in your item or its introductory material. This problem, incidentally, may exist in any of the assessment strategies presented in this chapter.

FIGURE 10.11   Sample item assessing students' ability to produce an explanation utilizing a principle.

Use the information below when answering Question 1.

During a recent visit to a classroom, Principal Larson noticed that Mrs. Hewmenist was having difficulty working with one of the children, Dizzy Ordur. Dizzy would work as long as Mrs. Hewmenist remained with him, but as soon as she would leave Dizzy he would "talk out" or leave his seat and she would have to return to him to get him back to work. Mr. Larson observed that this happened once in the first 10 minutes, three times in the second 10 minutes, and four times in the third 10 minutes.

1.   Why do you think Mrs. Hewmenist was having so much trouble with Dizzy Ordur?

Source: Adapted from "Assessing Knowledge of Concepts and Principles" by J. R. Jenkins and S. J. Deno, 1971, *Journal of Educational Measurement,* 8(1), p. 101. Adapted by permission of publisher. © 1971 by the National Council on Measurement in Education.

PROBLEM SOLVING

The Nature of Problem Solving

What Is a Problem?   A student incurs a **problem** when the student wants to reach a specific outcome or goal but does not automatically recognize the proper path or solution to use to reach it. The problem to solve is how to reach the desired goal. Because a student cannot automatically recognize the proper way to get the answer or reach the desired goal, she must use one or more higher-order thinking processes. These thinking processes are called *problem-solving thinking.* For instance, consider the assessment task shown previously in Figure 10.4. Among other things, students are asked to draw a picture of a car without using the circle shape. Attaining this goal is a problem for most kindergarten and first-grade students because some of the common things in their environment are circular. A car, for example, has wheels, a steering wheel, and headlights that are circular. Will a car with noncircular wheels still be a car? Will it move? Most young students do not immediately know the path or solution to this problem: They will need to engage in problem-solving thinking to complete their drawings.

"No-brainers" Are Not Problems   If the procedure for attaining a goal is so well known to a student that he can complete the task without having to reason, he does not have to use problem-solving skills. Older students have a name for these kinds of tasks: They call them no-brainers. They recognize that there is no problem to solve if you do not have to think about the proper solution to use to attain the outcome you desire.

This intuitive concept, no-brainer, should be a useful clue when you set tasks to assess problem-solving ability. If the tasks you set require students to simply repeat a procedure you taught them in a situation that is more or less identical to the one you used in class, you created a no-brainer task and not a problem-solving task. To apply problem-solving skills, a student needs to be given a task that is rather different or new to her. (The task need not be new to the world, just new to the student.)

Well-Structured and Ill-Structured Problems   Most of the problem tasks in teachers' editions of textbooks and in the end-of-chapter exercise set are a few notches above no-brainers. They present tasks that are clearly laid out: All the information students need is given, and there is usually one correct answer that students can attain by applying a procedure you taught in class. These are known as **well-structured problems** (Frederiksen, 1984). Well-structured problems serve a useful purpose in giving students opportunities to rehearse the procedures or algorithms you taught.

However, well-structured problems are unlike the real-life or authentic problems students will eventually have to face. Most authentic problems are **ill-structured** (Simon, 1973). In other words, it is not clear exactly what the problem is. For ill-structured problems, students have to (1) organize the information to understand it; (2) clarify the problem itself; (3) obtain all the information needed, which may not be immediately available; and (4) recognize that there may be several equally correct answers.

A problem with a single correct answer is called a **closed-response task**; a problem with multiple correct answers is called an **open-response task** (see Collis, 1991). Chapter 11 gives several examples of assessing students using both of these types of tasks (e.g., Figures 11.5 and 11.6).

Components of Problem Solving　A task presents a problem to a student if it contains one or more obstacles that the student must overcome to reach the desired outcome. A good problem solver exhibits the following performances in relation to a problem:

- Accurately identifies constraints or obstacles.
- Identifies [creative, plausible] . . . and important alternatives for overcoming the constraints or obstacles.
- Selects and [carries out valid and extensive trials of the] . . . alternatives.
- If [several] . . . alternatives were tried, accurately articulates and supports the reasoning behind the order of their selection, and the extent to which each overcame the obstacles or constraints. (Marzano et al., 1993, p. 79)

Schema-Driven Problem Solving　To complete these performances, a student must engage in a sequence of thinking that leads either to an immediately successful solution strategy or to an appropriate search for a solution strategy. One way to characterize this problem-solving thinking process is shown in Figure 10.12. The figure diagrams a **schema-driven problem solving** process (Gick, 1986). A schema helps us to recognize familiar things about a situation, what we can expect to happen, and how we typically act in a situation. If we recognize a particular problem as part of or very similar to one of our existing schema, we can apply the solution strategy stored in that schema. For example, if we recognize that a mathematics problem is a time problem rather than a cost problem, this activates the "time problem schema" that contains our stored memories of this type of problem and the strategies we typically use to solve these kinds of problems.

How is a schema for a particular problem activated or triggered? One way this is done is by characterizing or representing the problem properly. This is called a **mental model** of the problem. If for some reason you misrepresent a time problem as a cost problem, you will trigger cost-problem solution strategies that, of course, will not work. If a solution strategy you apply does not work, you have to continue looking for other strategies. You might try reconceptualizing the problem—that is, try a different mental model that will trigger an appropriate schema.

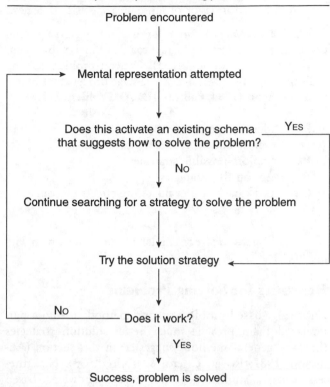

FIGURE 10.12　Steps in the problem-solving process.

Problem encountered

Mental representation attempted

Does this activate an existing schema that suggests how to solve the problem?　Yes

No

Continue searching for a strategy to solve the problem

Try the solution strategy

No　Does it work?

Yes

Success, problem is solved

Source: Paraphrased from "Problem-Solving Strategies" by M. L. Gick, 1986, *Educational Psychologist, 21,* p. 101. Paraphrased by permission of publisher.

Keeping the basic components and processes of problem solving in mind can focus your teaching on what students need to know to become good problem solvers. When you are crafting assessment tasks, be sure they require students to demonstrate command of these problem-solving components and processes.

General vs. Subject-Specific Problem Solving

Power vs. Generalizability　Controversies still exist among cognitive scientists, psychologists, and educators concerning whether we should teach students problem-solving strategies that are general or specific to each curriculum area—strategies specific, for example, to mathematics, history, or art. The curriculum-specific approach is less generalizable across different subjects but more powerful within the specific curriculum; the general approach has some applicability for every curriculum area but has limited power within any specific curriculum (Marzano et al., 1988).

It appears that people actually use *both* general and specific strategies (Alexander, 1992; Perkins & Salomon, 1989; Shuell, 1990). Persons with a great deal of knowledge and expertise in an area use that knowledge and the well-known problem-solving strategies specific to the area. However, if they work outside of their area of expertise, the specific strategies no longer apply: They resort, then, to more general problem-solving strategies. As they develop expertise in an initially unfamiliar area, the general strategies are dropped in favor of more area-specific strategies.

The IDEAL Problem Solver   It is useful to regard a general problem-solving strategy as a broad outline of problem-solving skills (Woolfolk, 1995). General problem-solving skills may be organized into a five-stage process that Bransford and Stein (1984) call the **IDEAL Problem Solver**:

I	Identify the problem
D	Define and represent the problem
E	Explore possible strategies
A	Act on the strategies
L	Look back and evaluate the effects of your activities

These skill areas are very similar to those shown in Figure 10.12.

Heuristics for Solving Problems

Knowledge-based problem-solving methods within a particular domain provide much better solution strategies than the general methods suggested in this section (Anderson, 1987; Royer, Cisero, & Carlo, 1993). Nevertheless, when a student does not have a knowledge-based strategy, a general strategy called a heuristic should be tried. A **heuristic** is a general problem-solving strategy that may help to solve a given problem. The following is a list of 10 problem-solving heuristics (Cyert, 1980; Frederiksen, 1984):

1. Try to see the whole picture; do not focus only on details.

2. Withhold your judgment; do not rush to a solution too quickly.

3. Create a model for a problem using pictures, sketches, diagrams, graphs, equations, or symbols.

4. If one way of modeling or representing the problem does not work, try another way.

5. State the problem as a question; change the question if the original does not suggest a solution.

6. Be flexible: Look for unconventional or new ways to use the available tools; see the conventional in new ways; try responding to the situation from a different angle or point of view; think divergently.

7. Try working backwards by starting with the goal and going backwards to find the solution strategy.

8. Keep track of your partial solutions so you can come back to them and resume where you left off.

9. Use analogical thinking: Ask, "What is this problem like?" "Where have I seen something similar to this?"

10. Talk about and through a problem; keep talking about it until a solution suggests itself.

ASSESSING PROBLEM-SOLVING SKILLS

Seventeen Assessment Strategies

Because the more powerful problem-solving strategies are specific to a domain or subject matter, it is difficult in the amount of space permitted in this book to present detailed examples. Further, the variety of problems within a curriculum area is very large, so even a sample of problems may not do justice to the subject. For example, in junior high school mathematics, you could craft many problems in content areas such as number and operations, patterns, pre-algebra, geometry and measurement, and data analysis (Lane, Parke, & Moskal, 1992).

Within any curriculum content category, you could craft problems and assess the students' answers. However, if you assess only whether an answer is correct or incorrect, you are likely to miss the opportunity to assess a student's thinking skills in general and problem-solving skills in particular. *To assess students' problem-solving skills, you will need to set tasks that allow you to systematically evaluate students' thinking about problem solving.* You will find it necessary to craft different types of tasks to assess the different aspects of problem solving.

The following assessment strategies illustrate the direction your task crafting might take. The assessment strategies are organized using the categories of the IDEAL Problem Solver. The strategy descriptions suggest the general layout or structure of the tasks: You need to apply them specifically to your own teaching area.

Identifying and Recognizing Problems

Assessment Strategy 1. Identifying the Problem   Give students a description of a situation in which persons are inconvenienced or put into unpleasant circumstances. Ask students to identify the real problem or what problem has to be solved. (See Figure 10.13, Item 1.)

Defining and Representing Problems

Assessment Strategy 2. Posing Questions[2]   Give students a statement that contains the problem. Ask students to pose the question(s), using the language and concepts of the

---

[2]Strategies 2, 7, 10, 11, and 12 were adapted from junior high school mathematics performance assessments described by Lane, Parke, and Moskal (1992). I stripped their descriptions of mathematical content to suggest the general structure of the strategy. Using this structure, you should be able to craft tasks specific to your own subject area.

FIGURE 10.13 Example of a context-dependent item set that assesses different aspects of problem solving.

Read the description below, then answer Questions 1 through 5.

A young deaf couple have their first child. The infant needs to be fed and changed whenever it cries in the night, but neither the mother nor the father are able to hear the baby. The couple does not wish to bring the baby into their bed for fear of rolling on it and suffocating it. They also do not wish to put the baby on a strict schedule of changing and feeding at fixed times.

1. Explain the problem that needs to be solved in the above situation.

2. Suggest at least three solutions to the problem. Be very specific in describing your solutions.

3. What assumptions about this couple, their baby, their home life, etc. did you make to come up with the solution to this problem?

4. Which of the solutions you proposed is best? Justify your choice by explaining its advantages and disadvantages.

5. Explain why each of the other solutions is not as good as the one you selected as the best.

subject you are teaching, that need(s) to be answered to solve the problem. (For example, in mathematics, what mathematical question needs to be answered? In social studies, what political question needs to be addressed?)

Assessment Strategy 3. Linguistic Understanding State several problems students should be able to solve. Underline the key phrases and common vocabulary they need to know to comprehend the context of the problem. Ask students to explain in their own words the meaning of these linguistic features of the problem. (The phrase, "makes buckets the fastest," in Figure 10.14 was understood differently by the students than was intended by the task crafter.)

Assessment Strategy 4. Identifying Irrelevancies Give students interpretive materials and a problem statement. Be sure the interpretive material contains information that is both relevant and irrelevant to the problem solution. Ask students to identify all the *irrelevant* information.

Assessment Strategy 5. Sorting Problem Cards Create a collection of several examples of each of several *different types* of problem statements. Put each problem statement on a separate card, but do not specify the type of problem it is. Ask students to sort the problems into categories or groups of *their own choosing*. Then ask students to explain why the problems in a group belong together. Focus your assessment on whether students are attending to only the wording or other surface features of the problem or, more appropriately, to the deeper features of the problem. (For example, students should group together all problems that can be solved using the same mathematical principle, the same scientific law, etc., even though the problems are worded quite differently or are applied to different content.)

Assessment Strategy 6. Identifying Assumptions Give students a problem statement. Ask students for a tentative solution. Ask what assumptions about the current and future problem situation they have made to come up with their solution. (See Figure 10.13, Item 3.)

Assessment Strategy 7. Describing Multiple Strategies Give students a statement of a problem. Ask students to solve the problem in two or more ways. Ask them to show their solutions using pictures, diagrams, or graphs. (See Figure 10.15.)

Assessment Strategy 8. Modeling Problem Give students a statement of a problem. Ask students to draw a diagram or picture showing the problem situation. Focus your assessment on how the students represent the problem rather than on whether the problem is correctly solved.

Assessment Strategy 9. Identifying Obstacles Give students a difficult problem to solve. Perhaps a key piece of information is missing. Ask students to explain why it is difficult to complete the task, what the obstacle(s) are, and/or what additional information they need to overcome the obstacle(s). Focus your assessment on whether students can identify the obstacle to solving the problem. (See Figures 10.4 and 10.5.)

Exploring Possible Solution Strategies

Assessment Strategy 10. Justifying Solutions Give students a problem statement along with two or more possible solutions to the problem. Ask students to select one solution they believe is correct and to justify why it is correct.

Assessment Strategy 11. Justifying Strategies Used Give students a problem statement and two or more strategies for solving the problem. Be certain both strategies yield the correct solution. (For example, the strategies can be ways in which two fictional students have solved the problem.) Ask students to explain why both strategies are correct.

Assessment Strategy 12. Integrating Data Give students several types of introductory material (story, cartoon, graph, data table) and a statement of a problem. Be certain that the problem solution *requires* using some of the information in two or more of the interpretive materials. Ask students to solve the problem and to show and explain the procedure they used to reach a solution.

FIGURE 10.14   Example of a flawed problem-solving task.

The following task was given to sixth grade students.

The Robinson family owns a company which makes cleaning supplies. They need to buy a new machine which makes buckets.

They see the three advertisements below.

The Galaxy Bucket Machine	The Industrial Bucket Machine	The Heavy Duty Bucket Machine

Makes 21 Buckets in just 15 minutes!	Makes 82 Buckets every hour!	Makes 44 Buckets in only 30 minutes!

The family wants to buy the machine which makes buckets the fastest.

A. Which machine do you think they should buy?

Answer: _____

B. Why do you think they should buy this machine?

Many students misinterpreted the phrase, "the machine that makes buckets the fastest." The assessors wanted the "task to assess students' ability to choose the machine that made buckets at the fastest rate (or the largest number for a fixed time period)" (p. 24). However, the students perceived "fastest" in terms of *waiting time*. For example, they thought you had to wait only 15 minutes for the Galaxy Buckets, 60 minutes for the Industrial Buckets, and 30 minutes for the Heavy Duty Buckets. Thus, they chose Galaxy Buckets since the "wait time" was perceived to be the shortest. The students' interpretation is not wrong, but it makes the task a less interesting mathematical problem to solve. As a result, the assessors had to eliminate the task since it did not result in the type of mathematics problem-solving thinking desired.

Source: From *Principles for Developing Performance Assessments* (p. 23) by S. Lane, C. Parke, and B. Moskal, 1992. A paper presented at the Annual Meeting of the American Educational Research Association. Reprinted by permission of authors.

Assessment Strategy 13. Producing Alternate Strategies Give students a problem statement and one strategy that solves the problem. Ask students to show you another way the problem could be solved.

Assessment Strategy 14. Using Analogies Give students a problem statement and a solution strategy for correctly solving the problem. Ask students to describe other problems that could (by analogy) be solved by using this same solution strategy. Ask students to explain how the solution to the problem they generated is like the solution to the problem you gave them. Focus your assessment on the analogical relationship of the students' solution strategy to the solution strategy you gave them. (See Figure 10.16.)

Assessment Strategy 15. Solving Backwards Give students a complex problem situation or a complex (multi-step) task to complete. Ask students to work backwards from the desired outcome to develop a plan or a strategy for completing the task or solving the problem. (For example, develop the steps and timeframe needed to complete a library research paper; develop a plan to gather information to answer the question, "Do students in this school favor curfews for persons under 18 years old?")

FIGURE 10.15 Example of a problem-solving task in which students represent a problem in different ways.

Read the problem below, then answer Question 1.

Mickey has an album of baseball cards. He has six empty pages. Each page holds nine cards. How many baseball cards does Mickey need to fill his six empty album pages?

1. Show two or more ways to answer the question in the above problem. Use numbers, pictures, drawings, or graphs to show how you arrived at your answer.

Some of the students' representations:

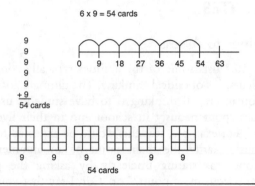

FIGURE 10.16 Problem-solving task that assesses a student's ability to use an analogy heuristic as a way to search for solution strategies.

Question 1 refers to the situation below.

Members of a certain congressional committee frequently talked a lot during committee hearings. Some members talked to explain their own views, some treated a witness as hostile and tried to discredit the witness' testimony some wanted to prevent their opponents on the committee from speaking, and some wanted to prolong the debate and the hearing to postpone or prevent a committee vote. To solve this problem, rules were established to give each committee member a fixed amount of time to speak and to ask questions of a witness. Under these rules, a committee member is allowed to give to another member all or part of his or her allotted time.

1. Describe several other problems in different situations that could be solved by using a set of rules similar to those that the congressional committee used.

2. For each of the problems you listed, explain how the rules might be modified and why this would solve the problem you listed.

Focus your assessment on how well students use backward solution strategies.

Acting on and Looking Back on Problem-Solution Strategies

Assessment Strategy 16. Evaluating the Quality of the Solution
Give students a problem statement and several different strategies for solving the problem. Be certain that not

every strategy works *and* that some strategies work better than others. (For example, some may be more efficient, some may have negative consequences.) Ask students to try to implement each strategy and to thoroughly evaluate it. Ask them to determine the best strategy, explain why some strategies worked better than others, and why some did not work at all. Focus your assessment on the students' ability to justify the hierarchical ordering of the quality of the strategies. (See Figure 10.13, Items 4 and 5.)

Assessment Strategy 17. Systematically Evaluating Strategies
Use the same types of tasks as in Assessment Strategy 16, but focus your assessment on the extent to which a student follows systematic procedures to evaluate each of the solution strategies you proposed.

OTHER PROMISING APPROACHES FOR ASSESSING PROBLEM SOLVING

In the preceding section we suggest that you could assess whether students have the skills associated with each step in the problem-solving process. Other approaches to assessing problem solving show promise, but are still in the experimental and validation states (Royer et al., 1993). Space does not permit our discussion of these methods, however. You may wish follow-up on this topic by checking some of the references listed in the Additional Readings section of this chapter (e.g., Glaser, Lesgold, and Lajoie, 1985; Nitko, 1996). You may wish to review also the assessment of students' knowledge structures in Chapter 13 (Approach 5).

CRITICAL THINKING

Curriculum frameworks frequently state that developing students' abilities for critical thinking is an important educational goal. Critical thinking educational goals focus on developing students who are fair-minded, are objective, reach sound conclusions, and are disposed toward seeking clarity and accuracy (Marzano et al., 1988). What is critical thinking? Psychologists do not agree on all the skills that constitute it (Woolfolk, 1995; Kuhn, 1999). In discussions of critical thinking, we often see many of the same terms used in discussions of problem solving: The two areas are closely related.

In this chapter, we shall adopt the following definition: **"Critical thinking** is reasonable, reflective thinking that is focused on deciding what to believe or do" (Ennis, 1985, p. 54). This definition implies the following (Norris & Ennis, 1989):

1. *Reasonable thinking*—using good reasons
2. *Reflective thinking*—being conscious of looking for and using good reasons
3. *Focused thinking*—thinking for a particular purpose or goal

4. *Deciding what to believe or do*—evaluating both statements (what to believe) and actions (what to do)

5. *Abilities and dispositions*—both cognitive skills (abilities) and tendency to use the abilities (dispositions)

ASSESSING DISPOSITIONS TOWARD CRITICAL THINKING

What Are Dispositions?

Table 10.1 lists critical thinking dispositions. **Dispositions** are **habits of mind** or tendencies to use critical thinking. Although you can assess a student's use of a critical thinking ability or skill on one occasion, *assessment of a student's disposition requires you to focus your assessment on her long-term habits.* Your assessment should report how frequently over a marking period, term, or year a student uses critical thinking in the curriculum subject matter.

Assessing Dispositions

Checklists Dispositions or habits of mind can be assessed through **checklists** and rating scales. Chapter 12 gives specific suggestions for crafting these types of assessment devices. A sample checklist is shown in Figure 10.17. This checklist could help you to keep track of a student's critical thinking actions over the course of a unit. You can see from the checklist that the student exhibited a number of dispositions frequently (e.g., "2. Looks for explanations

TABLE 10.1   Dispositions for critical thinking that could be assessed.

Critical thinkers
1. seek a statement of the thesis or question;
2. seek reasons;
3. try to be well informed;
4. use credible sources and mention them;
5. take into account the total situation;
6. keep their thinking relevant to the main point;
7. keep in mind the original or most basic concern;
8. look for alternatives;
9. are open-minded and
    a. seriously consider points of view other than their own;
    b. reason from starting points with which they disagree without letting the disagreement interfere with their reasoning;
    c. withhold judgment when the evidence and reasons are insufficient;
10. take a position and change a position when the evidence and reasons are sufficient to do so;
11. seek as much precision as the subject permits;
12. deal in an orderly manner with the parts of a complex whole;
13. employ their critical thinking abilities;
14. are sensitive to the feelings, level of knowledge, and degree of sophistication of others.

Source: From *Evaluating Critical Thinking* (p.12) by S. P. Norris and R. H. Ennis, 1989; Pacific Grove, CA: Critical Thinking Books and Software. Reprinted by permission.

and reasons," "6. Open-minded") and others not very frequently (e.g., "5. Looks for alternatives").

Rating Scales Figure 10.18 shows a few items from a simple **rating scale** used to assess the quality level of a student's dispositions toward critical thinking. The anchor points on the items' rating scales were adapted from the Marzano et al. (1993) analysis of habits of mind. Each item's scale shows the degree to which a student is disposed toward using critical thinking. The numerical ratings on the scale are anchored by descriptions of specific and observable categories of performance.

ASSESSING CRITICAL THINKING ABILITIES

Abilities to Assess

Table 10.2 lists some of the abilities typically considered in discussions of critical thinking. The ultimate goal of education in critical thinking is to have students use these abilities spontaneously in school and in their lives after school. For example, students would be expected to spontaneously clarify the main point of an argument that someone was stating unclearly by asking the person, "What is your main point?" or "Can I say that your main point is _____?" As stated in Point 13 of Table 10.1, students should be in the habit of regularly using the abilities listed in Table 10.2.

Critical Thinking in Context

For the most part, critical thinking abilities are best taught and assessed in the context of each subject the student is learning. Ultimately students will apply critical thinking to specific events in their lives, so they must learn to apply these abilities in different contexts. Thus, what constitutes "reasonable reflective thinking" about the quality of visual artistic statements may be quite different from what constitutes "reasonable reflective thinking" about the quality of scientific results of an experiment. Also, different subject matters have their own types of arguments and criteria for verifying truth or credibility. As an example, Table 10.2 shows how middle-school students can use science criteria to critically evaluate their projects.

For these reasons, and for the practical reason of limited space, we cannot illustrate meaningful items in many subject areas for the critical thinking abilities shown in Table 10.2. However, we do show the strategies you could use when crafting assessment tasks for each ability. Some of these are illustrated with sample items. You need to practice applying these strategies to the subject(s) you teach.

The material that follows is organized around the headings in Table 10.2. We explain each of the critical thinking abilities, then describe and illustrate how to assess each ability.

FIGURE 10.17 Example of a checklist to keep track of a student's use of critical thinking dispositions throughout a teaching unit.

Individual Student's Critical Thinking Disposition Record

Student's name: **Class period:**   **Dates:**

Subject/unit: U.S. History/Unit III. Beginning a Government, 1780–1800

Critical thinking dispositions	Assignment/activity				
	Class discussion of the Articles of the Confederation	Essay discussing arguments for and against ratification of the Constitution	Scrapbook collecting and analyzing events reported in the newspaper using concepts from the Constitution	Teams debate the issue, "Have political parties made the United States goverment better?"	Essay evaluating Washington as president
1. Seeks statements of the main point or question	√	—	√	√	NA
2. Looks for explanations and reasons	√	√	√	√	√
3. Uses and cites credible sources	—	√	—	√	—
4. Keeps to the main and relevant point(s)	—	—	NA	√	√
5. Looks for alternatives	—	—	NA	—	NA
6. Open-minded	√	√	√	NA	—
7. Takes a position on an issue		√	—	√	—
8. Changes position on an issue with good reason(s)	NA	—	NA	NA	NA
9. Seeks to be accurate and precise in statements and work	NA	—	√	√	—
10. Sensitive to the feelings, levels of knowledge of others	√	NA	NA	—	NA

FIGURE 10.18 Sample rating scale assessing the quality of some of a student's dispositions toward critical thinking that a teacher might observe as the student completes an assignment.

Rating Scale for Critical Thinking Dispositions

Student's name: Date:

Assignment:

1. Did the student consider different points of view?

0	1	2	3
Acts as if own point of view is accepted by everyone	Aware that own point of view is not accepted by everyone	Shows awareness that others have legitimate points of view that differ from own	Actively looks for and encourages others to express points of view different from or opposing own

2. How did the student treat others' points of view?

0	1	2	3
Acts in a way that avoids or discourages others' points of view	Shows some attention of others' points of view	Makes a serious effort to consider others' points of view, but is not consistently objective or rational	Attends seriously to others' points of view and consistently reviews them objectively and rationally

3. Did the student communicate well with others who had less knowledge or ability?

0	1	2	3
Cannot work or communicate with others who have less knowledge or ability	Attempts to work or communicate with others who have less knowledge or ability, but is less than adequate in doing so	Works and communicates adequately with others who have less knowledge or ability	Works and communicates excellently with others who have less knowledge or ability

4. Was the student sensitive to the feelings of others with less knowledge or ability?

0	1	2	3
Acts apathetically or cruelly toward others who have less knowledge and ability	Does the minimum to help or encourage respect for the feelings of others who have less knowledge and ability	Offers good encouragement and respect for the feelings of others who have less knowledge and ability	Actively seeks to bolster and increase respect for the feelings of others who have less knowledge and ability

TABLE 10.2 Critical thinking abilities that could be assessed.

Elementary Clarification
1. Focusing on a question
2. Analyzing arguments
3. Asking and answering questions that clarify and challenge

Basic Support
4. Judging the credibility of a source
5. Making and judging observations

Inference
6. Making and judging deductions
7. Making and judging inductions
8. Making and judging value judgments

Advanced Clarification
9. Defining terms and judging definitions
10. Identifying assumptions

Strategies and Tactics
11. Deciding on an action
12. Interacting with others

Source: From *Evaluating Critical Thinking* (p. 14) by S. P. Norris and R. H. Ennis, 1989, Pacific Grove, CA: Critical Thinking Books and Software. Reprinted by permission.

Elementary Clarification Abilities

Focusing on a Question   Students possessing the ability to **focus on a question** can critically review an action, a verbal statement, a piece of discourse, a scientific or political argument, or even a cartoon to determine its main point(s) or the essence of the argument. Subskills include (1) formulating or identifying the question or issue being posed, (2) formulating or selecting the proper criteria to use to evaluate the material presented, and (3) keeping the issue and its proper context in mind (Ennis, 1985). When crafting assessment tasks for each ability, use the assessment strategy in Figure 10.19. Figure 10.20, Item 1, shows an example of a multiple-choice item assessing a student's ability to focus on the main issue in a political cartoon.

Analyzing Arguments   Students possessing the ability to **analyze arguments** are able to analyze the *details* of the arguments presented in verbal statements, discussions, scientific or political reports, cartoons, and so on. The subskills include (1) identifying the conclusions in a statement, (2) identifying the stated and unstated reasons behind an argument, (3) seeing similarities and differences among two or more arguments, (4) finding, pointing out, and ignoring (when appropriate) irrelevancies appearing in an argument, (5) representing the logic or structure of

FIGURE 10.19 Strategy for assessing the ability to focus on a question.

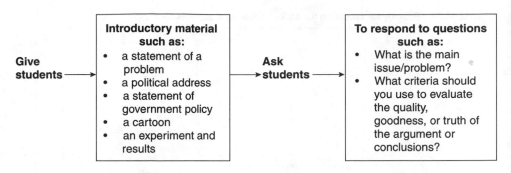

Give students → **Introductory material such as:**
- a statement of a problem
- a political address
- a statement of government policy
- a cartoon
- an experiment and results

Ask students → **To respond to questions such as:**
- What is the main issue/problem?
- What criteria should you use to evaluate the quality, goodness, or truth of the argument or conclusions?

Note: For this and subsequent assessment strategies, you will need to rephrase the questions so they are written at the educational level of your students.

FIGURE 10.20 Example of a context-dependent item set assessing the critical thinking abilities of focusing on the issue by identifying the main question or concern (Item 1) and analyzing arguments by identifying a conclusion to be drawn from them (Item 2).

Questions 1 and 2 refer to the cartoon below.

1. The cartoon illustrates which of the following characteristics of the party system in the United States?

   *a. Strong party discipline is often lacking.
   b. The parties are responsive to the will of the voters.
   c. The parties are often more concerned with politics than with the national welfare.
   d. Bipartisanship often exists in name only.

2. The situation shown in the cartoon is *least* likely to occur at which of the following times?

   a. During the first session of a new Congress
   b. During a political party convention
   c. During a primary election campaign
   *d. During a presidential election campaign

Source: From *Making the Classroom Test: A Guide for Teacher* (No. 4. Evaluation and Advisory Services) (pp. 18–19) by Q. Stodola, 1961, Princeton, NJ: Educational Testing Service. Cartoon courtesy of Army Times Publishing Company. Reprinted by permission of Educational Testing Service, the copyright owner.

an argument, and (6) summarizing an argument (Ennis, 1985). When crafting tasks to assess this ability, use the strategy in Figure 10.21.

Item 2 in Figure 10.20 is an example of drawing a conclusion from the argument presented in cartoon panels. Figure 10.22 shows four social studies items that assess various subskills of the ability to analyze arguments. Note that the items in Figure 10.22 would be preceded by introductory material for students to read before answering the questions.

Questioning to Clarify and Challenge Students possessing the ability to **ask clarifying questions** can do two things: (1) ask appropriate questions of someone who is presenting an argument, and (2) answer critical questions appropriately when making an argument themselves. Among the questions that students should ask and be able to answer are: Why? What would not be an example? How does that apply in this situation? What are the facts that support your position? (Ennis, 1985).

You may find it difficult to assess this ability directly, because you either have to observe a student while he is attending to someone who is presenting an argument or have the student present an argument and ask questions yourself. The first approach is problematic for several reasons: it may be impolite to interrupt a speaker; a student may be shy in asking questions afterward; a speaker's argument may be well presented so that few critical questions are appropriate; or a speaker's presentation may be so poor that students lose interest in it.

Having the student present an argument is less problematic; but it, too, contains elements that threaten the validity of the results. For instance, all students do not have the same degree of knowledge of a topic. Differences in this knowledge will affect the quality of students' presentations and the questions that are appropriate for you to ask. Also, it would be tedious to have 25 or more students present the same or similar arguments to you or to the class. Probably the best way to assess this ability is to collect information about it over a long time period, use a variety of assignments and tasks, and use a systematic procedure for recording your assessments such as a checklist (see Figure 10.17) or a rating scale (Figure 10.18).

FIGURE 10.21 Strategy for assessing the ability to analyze arguments.

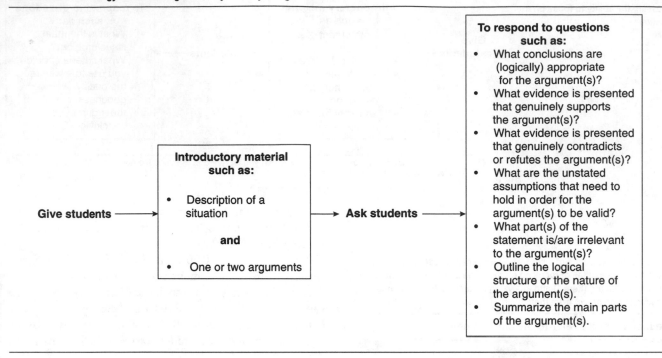

Basic Support of an Argument

Judging the Credibility of a Source Students with this ability are able to evaluate the quality of the evidence someone uses in supporting a position. Standards or criteria a student should be able to use when **judging credibility** include (1) the expertise of the person giving the evidence, (2) whether the person giving the evidence has a conflict of interest, (3) whether different sources of evidence agree, (4) whether the source of evidence has a reputation for being accurate and correct, (5) whether the evidence was obtained by established procedures that give it validity, and (6) whether there are good reasons for using the evidence under the given circumstances (Ennis, 1985). Each discipline will have specific rules of evidence, too.

When crafting tasks to assess this ability, you can use the strategy in Figure 10.23. A number of objective item formats help assess this critical thinking ability. These formats include (1) masterlist, (2) best-answer, (3) experiment-interpretation, (4) statement and comment, and (5) rank order.[3] Formats and sample items for (1) to (4), are given in Chapter 8. Short-answer formats may also be used. An example is shown in Figure 10.24.

To validly assess this ability, you must be careful to include introductory material that was not used as examples in class or the assigned reading, and pose questions that require the students to explain the reasoning behind their evaluations of the credibility of each part of the material. *Assessing students on material you have already analyzed and*

judged for them produces an invalid assessment of the students' ability to judge the credibility of a source for themselves. Also, if you do not ask students to explain why a source is or is not credible, you will not know whether students have used appropriate criteria and critical thinking to arrive at their answer.

Observing and Judging Observation Reports This is the ability of students to evaluate the quality of information obtained from eyewitness or direct observation of an event, phenomenon, or person. Among the standards or criteria students should be able to use when making these judgments are (1) the observer reports observations with minimal referral to others' observations; (2) the time between the event and the report by the observer is short; (3) the observer is not reporting hearsay; (4) records of the observation are kept; (5) the observations reported are corroborated by others; (6) the observer had good access to the event or person so direct observation can be accurate; (7) the observations were recorded properly; and (8) the observer is a credible source (Ennis, 1985). Each discipline may have more specific criteria as well.

Assessing this ability requires you to present students with (1) observation reports, (2) information about the context within which the observations were made, and (3) information about the person making or recording the observations. In other words, students must have access to sufficient information to evaluate, using the criteria just listed. This may be difficult to do without making the task unwieldy and without giving away the answer. Further, to obtain valid assessment results, you must use introductory materials that were not used as examples in class or in assigned reading and require stu-

---

[3]Rank-order items present students with a randomly arranged list and ask students to order the list on the basis of a given criterion. For example, ordering statements according to their degree of credibility.

FIGURE 10.22 Examples of items assessing various subskills of the ability to analyze arguments: Identify assumptions (Item 1), identify the structure of an argument (Item 2), identify similarities among several sources (Item 3), identify differences in two arguments (Item 4).

Items 1 and 2 are based on the reading from Clayton's book.

A reading from Clayton's book

1. What assumption does Clayton's argument make?

 A. Cattle-raising will remain Botswana's most basic economic activity.
 B. The Botswana government should follow a laissez-faire policy for foreign trade.
 C. The economic conditions for ordinary people can be improved by the government helping certain industries.
 D. The Botswana income is not distributed equitably among all people.

2. The fundamental structure of Clayton's argument is that Botswana's people are strongly motivated by their

 A. desire to maximize their individual gains.
 B. desire to place nationalism before their individual gains.
 C. faith that competition in the marketplace will overcome present difficulties.
 D. sincere concern for the general welfare of all the people in the country.

Item 3 is based on the five readings listed below.

Reading A	Reading B	Reading C	Reading D	Reading E

3. Based on your reading of the five articles, list two or three principles on which the government might base its domestic policy.

Item 4 is based on the readings from Clayton's book and Mmualefe's book.

Readings from Clayton's book

Readings from Mmualefe's book

4. What is the most fundamental difference between Clayton and Mmualefe regarding the Botswana economic situation?

 A. They differ on whether a competitive economy is desirable.
 B. They differ in the role that morality plays in economic policy.
 C. They differ in their prediction of whether the government will become corrupt.
 D. They differ in the degree to which government should encourage foreign investment in Botswana.

Note: These items are for illustration only. The readings and persons referred to are fictitious.

dents to explain the reason(s) for their evaluations of the reported observations. *The validity of the assessment results shrinks if you do not include these two elements in your task.*

Newspaper articles in your subject area may be useful sources for introductory material, provided competent reporters write them. A competent reporter usually includes information about the nature of the observation, the background of the observer or reporter (e.g., political affiliation, source of funding for a study), and whether there was corroboration of observations.

You may want to follow the assessment strategy in Figure 10.25 when crafting tasks.

Inferences

Deducing and Judging Deductions Students able to **judge deductions** apply logical thinking when they analyze statements and conclusions. Subskills include (1) using the logic of class inclusion (what elements or members should be logically included in a class or category), (2) using

FIGURE 10.23 Strategy for assessing the ability to judge credibility.

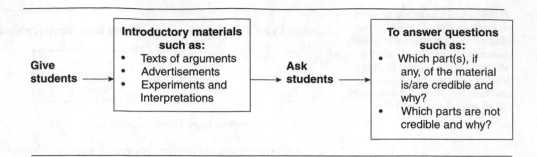

FIGURE 10.24 Example of an item that assesses a student's ability to evaluate the credibility of an argument or a statement.

Question 1 refers to the information below.

The board of directors announced that last year's sales of the XYZ automobile increased by 25% over the previous year. Mr. Hereto, the president of the XYZ Automobile Company, stated that the reason for this increase is that the automobile buyers in this country recognize that the XYZ cars are the best cars available today.

1. Analyze this statement indicating which part(s) of it, if any, are credible and which part(s), if any, are not credible. Give reasons for each of your choices. You may organize your answers in the format below.

Credible part(s):	Reason(s) why:

Part(s) not credible:	Reason(s) why:

FIGURE 10.25 Strategy for assessing the ability to judge observation reports.

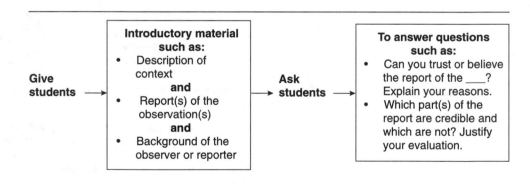

conditional logic (identifying the conditions under which something is true or false), and (3) properly interpreting statements using logical strategies (negatives, double negatives, necessary vs. sufficient conditions, and words such as *if, or, some, not, both*) (Ennis, 1985).

To design an objective task to assess this ability, you can follow one of the strategies in Figure 10.26 (Norris & Ennis, 1989). Figure 10.27 shows two multiple-choice items that follow these strategies.

Inducing and Judging Inductions Students who have the ability to induce can draw valid conclusions by generalizing from given information. Students who have the abil-

ity to **judge inductions** identify the conclusions that best explain the given evidence (Norris & Ennis, 1989). Subskills for generalizing from the data include (1) identifying and using typical features or patterns in the data to make inferences, (2) using appropriate techniques to make inferences from sample data, and (3) using patterns and trends shown in tables and graphs to make inferences (Ennis, 1985). Subskills for identifying the conclusion that best explains the given evidence include (1) understanding and using different types of hypotheses and explanations (recognizing causal claims, recognizing historical claims, etc.), (2) understanding and using valid ways of collecting relevant information (designing empirical re-

FIGURE 10.26 Strategies for assessing the ability to make and judge conclusions.

Strategy A. Comparing different conclusions.

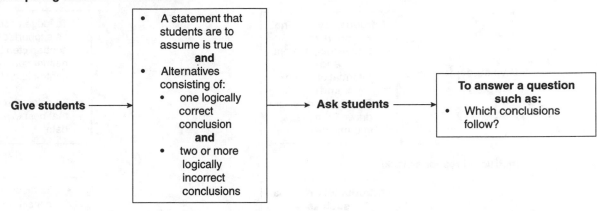

Strategy B. Judging the truth of one conclusion.

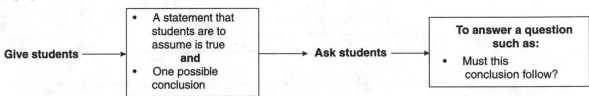

FIGURE 10.27 Examples of items assessing a student's ability to judge logical conclusions.

Questions 1 and 2 are based on the information below.

If this substance is calcium carbonate, then it will bubble when acid is added. But there were no bubbles when I added the acid.

Comparing different conclusions
1. Based on the above information, which of the following is correct?
   A. This substance produces bubbles.
   B. This substance is calcium carbonate.
   C. This substance is not calcium carbonate.
   D. This substance is calcium chloride.

Judging the truth of one conclusion.
2. Based on the above information, is it true that this substance is calcium carbonate?
   A. Yes, it must be true.
   B. No, it cannot be true.
   C. We cannot be certain it is true from the information given.

---

search studies, methods of seeking evidence and counterevidence, etc.), and (c) being able to use criteria to evaluate the extent to which the information (data) supports the conclusion (Ennis, 1985).

Both response-choice and constructed-response tasks can assess students' ability to induce a conclusion. Two assessment strategies are illustrated in Figure 10.28.

Among the formats that are useful to assess this ability are (1) best-answer (see Figure 8.27, Item 2), (2) experiment-interpretation (see Figure 8.28, Items 1–3), (3) experiment-interpretation with written justification supplied by the students (see Figure 8.29, Items 1–4), (4) masterlist (see Figure 8.37, Items 1–5) and (5) short-answer. Suggestions for constructing these task formats are presented in Chapter 8.

You should note that having students justify their answers is an important way to assess whether they can make or judge inductions appropriately. Students may choose the correct conclusion for the wrong reasons or choose an incorrect conclusion because they do not have enough knowledge or background information to correctly interpret the context of the situation you gave them. For example, in Figure 8.37, Items 1–5, students may not comprehend how long a city block is and, therefore, may draw incorrect inferences about the graph. Their critical thinking may be well developed, yet their knowledge base may be lacking in specific areas.

Again, you must present students with situations and information for which you did not already teach the proper conclusion and assess *their* abilities to induce conclusions. You don't want to assess the students' ability to recall the induction *you* made.

Making Value Judgments Not all critical thinking inferences are made using data and syllogisms—some are based on **judging value definitions**. Students with this critical thinking ability are able to identify when inferences have been made on the basis of values, what these values are, and when to use their own values to make inferences. Subskills of this ability include (1) gathering and using appropriate background information before judging, (2) identifying the consequences of the inferences that could be drawn and weighing the consequences before drawing conclusions, (3) identifying alternative actions and their

FIGURE 10.28   Strategies for assessing the ability to judge inductions.

Strategy A. Response-choice tasks.

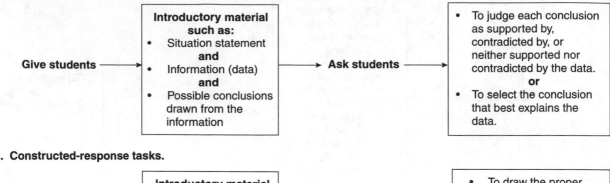

Strategy B. Constructed-response tasks.

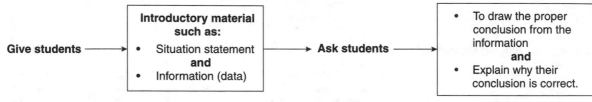

FIGURE 10.29   Strategy for assessing the ability to make value judgments.

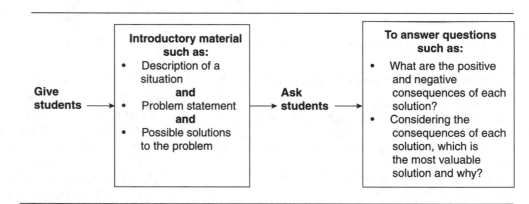

value, and (4) balancing alternatives, weighing consequences, and deciding rationally (Ennis, 1985).

To assess this ability, you must require students to explain the value, worth, or importance behind their inferences. Also, you must assess whether they recognize that different inferences or conclusions imply actions that have different consequences. You want, therefore, to craft an assessment task that requires students to create or judge different courses of action using different values as criteria. For the most part, you would need to ask students to supply their reasons either in writing or orally. You can use the assessment strategy shown in Figure 10.29.

Students' use of consequences and values may appear in assessment tasks that are not originally intended to assess critical thinking. For instance, the arithmetic problem in Figure 10.30 might be used with junior high school students (Silver, Smith, & Nelson, 1995). Teachers reasoned that the correct answer to the problem is the daily payment, because it is the more economical option (3 days × $2 per day + 2 days × $1 per day = $8; this is less than

FIGURE 10.30   Example of an arithmetic task in which students are given the opportunity to explain the value-basis of their answer.

Question 1 refers to the information below.

Juanita must decide whether to buy a weekly bus pass or to pay the fare each day. She must ride the bus to work and back home again on Monday, Tuesday, and Wednesday. She must ride the bus to work on Thursday and Friday, but she receives car rides home from her friends on these two days. Here are the costs of the bus:

    one-way fare $1.00
    weekly pass $9.00

1.   Which option, weekly pass or pay every day, should Juanita choose? Explain your answer.

the $9 weekly pass). However, many students reasoned that the $9 weekly pass was more economical because the weekly pass could be used not only by Juanita, but also in the evenings and on weekends by various family members. Thus, students applied their knowledge of urban life and their values of sharing limited resources with family members to choose an alternative the teachers originally did not consider correct. This example points out the importance of using a wide variety of classroom situations and constructed response tasks to identify how well students are using critical thinking skills.

Advanced Clarification

Defining Terms and Judging Definitions   Students possessing this ability are able to analyze the meanings and definitions of the terms used in the course of arguments, statements, and events to critically evaluate them. Among the subskills of this ability are (1) knowing the various forms that key terms may take and how these forms function in the context of an argument, (2) knowing how different strategies are used to define key terms in arguments, and (3) knowing the validity of the content of the definition itself (Ennis, 1985).

Assessment of this critical thinking ability must go beyond simply asking for definitions or meanings of words in context (although this is related to the ability). The idea is to assess whether a student is skilled at recognizing that words may be defined in certain ways to make a point, distort an argument, or deceive a listener or reader. For example, there may be two or more meanings for a key term. In an argumentative presentation, a writer may shift from one meaning to another (Ennis, 1985). Students skilled in this aspect of critical thinking should be able to detect the shift of meaning and to describe the impact of the shift on the quality of the argument. A strategy for assessing students is illustrated in Figure 10.31.

Identifying Assumptions   Students possessing this ability are able to **identify assumption(s)** that are part of someone's reasoning about what to believe or to do. Norris and Ennis (1989) point out that there are three meanings

of *assumption*, but only one is appropriate in the context of this critical thinking ability:

1. *A tentatively held conclusion* ("I assume you are going to eat, since you got out the plate and dish.")

2. *Pejorative sense of assumption* ("I wouldn't put much faith in her story. Her tale is just an assumption.")

3. *An unstated basis for someone's reasoning* (John said, "Since half the students have baseball cards, at least half the students are males." Sally said, "You are assuming that only male students have baseball cards.")

For purposes of our discussion of critical thinking in this chapter, we use only the third meaning, which is usually intended when educational goals state that identifying implicit assumptions is a critical thinking skill (Norris & Ennis, 1989).

Confusion over the meaning of *assumption* can lead you to set poor-quality assessment tasks. Norris and Ennis point out that short-answer tasks usually result in poor assessment results because students interpret the word *assumption* in its first meaning, when you want them to use the third meaning. As a result, students' responses are likely to consist of tentative conclusions for which they believe there is little support in the introductory material that you gave them. If all students do not interpret the task in the way you intended, the quality of your assessment results would be poor.

A second way you may create poor-quality assessment of this ability is when you use the term *assumption* improperly in an assessment task. A common flaw, as pointed out earlier, is to confuse *assumption* with *conclusion*. Figure 10.32 (Item 1) shows such a flawed item. The problem with this item is that, even though it uses the

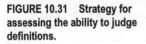

FIGURE 10.31   Strategy for assessing the ability to judge definitions.

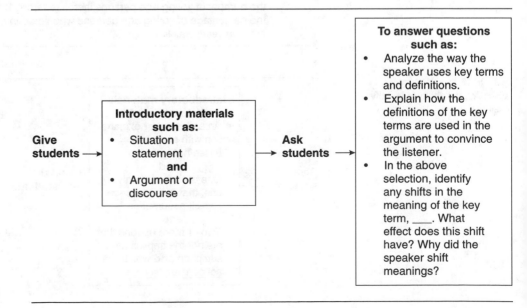

word *assumed*, it actually requires students to draw conclusions from the given data: A student is not required to identify an implicit or unstated assumption that might be the basis for a conclusion. Figure 10.32 (Item 2) shows how the item could be rewritten to focus it on implicit assumptions.

To craft quality tasks that assess students' ability to identify implicit assumptions, you must attend carefully to the concerns described in the preceding paragraphs.

The assessment strategy in Figure 10.33 seems most appropriate (Norris & Ennis, 1989). Figure 10.34 is an example of such an item. (Note: The lengthy passage students must read has been left out of the item.)

Again, do not ask students to identify the same assumption for the same material that you illustrated during the lesson. Also, be sure that the interpretive material you use in fact has an implicit assumption. This means you cannot include passages for which the author makes his or

---

FIGURE 10.32 Poor and better items to assess the ability to identify implicit assumptions.

Poor item: Confuses assumptions with conclusions

Question 1 refers to the information below.

According to the Federal Election Commission, the percents of the voting population who voted in national elections in presidential election years 1932–1988 were:

Year	%	Year	%	Year	%	Year	%
1932	52.4	1948	51.1	1964	61.9	1980	54.0
1936	56.0	1952	61.6	1968	60.9	1984	53.1
1940	58.9	1956	59.3	1972	55.2	1988	50.1
1944	56.0	1960	62.8	1976	53.5		

1. From the above data you can assume that
   A. in 1988 most voters were unhappy with the candidates.
   B. in 1988 voter turn-out was at an all-time low.
   C. voter turn-out declined from 1980 to 1988.
   D. the majority of the voters did not vote.

Better item: Gives conclusion and asks for assumption needed

Question 2 refers to the information below.

FACTS: According to the Federal Election Commission, the percents of the voting population who voted in national elections in presidential election years 1932–1988 were:

Year	%	Year	%	Year	%	Year	%
1932	52.4	1948	51.1	1964	61.9	1980	54.0
1936	56.0	1952	61.6	1968	60.9	1984	53.1
1940	58.9	1956	59.3	1972	55.2	1988	50.1
1944	56.0	1960	62.8	1976	53.5		

CONCLUSION: The number of persons voting in national elections in presidential election years 1932–1988 was at its lowest in 1988.

2. In order for this conclusion to be true, it must be assumed that
   A. the number of voting age persons in 1988 was the same as or less than each of the other presidential election years 1932–1988.
   B. the number of voting age persons increased from 1932–1988.
   C. the percentage of voting age persons who voted in each of the other presidential election years was less than 50.1%

FIGURE 10.33 Strategy for assessing the ability to identify assumptions.

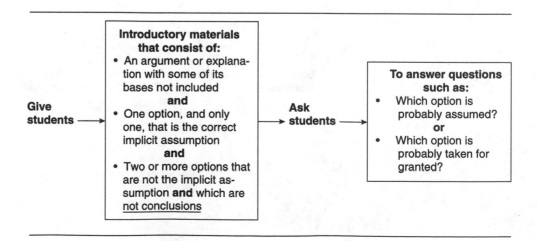

FIGURE 10.34 Example of an item to assess the ability to identify implicit assumptions.

Question 1 refers to the following passage.

(A passage relevant to the subject-matter would appear here)

1. The author bases his argument on the implicit assumption that U.S. citizens are motivated by a very strong desire to
   A. get as much money for themselves as possible.
   B. put the national interests ahead of their own personal interests.
   C. expand the open-market competition.
   D. make the rest of the world just like the United States.

---

her assumptions explicit. It also means you cannot use material for which no assumptions have been made to reach the conclusion. To craft appropriate items, you may have to rewrite some of the passages you select from documents and other sources.

Strategies and Tactics

Deciding on an Action   Students who can **decide on an action** are essentially good problem solvers. The subskills are those we discussed earlier in this chapter on problem solving: defining problems, formulating and evaluating solutions, viewing the total problem and taking action, and evaluating the action taken. The assessment strategies for this ability are the same as those used in assessing problem-solving skills.

Interacting with Others   Students who are good at **interacting with others** are able to identify and use rhetorical devices to persuade, explain, or argue. Among the rhetorical devices the student should be able to identify and use are (1) argumentative verbal tactics (appeal to authority, strawman, etc.), (2) logical strategies, and (3) skillful organization and presentation (Ennis, 1985).

Assessment of this ability may take several forms. One form is to ask students to present argumentative or persuasive work of their own creation. The media and purposes of the presentation may vary widely, depending on the subject matter you are teaching. For example, product or service advertisements are designed to persuade people and may use different media such as printing, still photography, or motion pictures (videos). Debates, on the other hand, are usually more structured.

Assessing student performances requires you to use a scoring rubric, most likely in the form of a rating scale. Without a rating scale you are not likely to be fair or helpful to the student. Using a scoring rubric serves several purposes: (1) it makes clear the criteria you use to evaluate students; (2) you can give the rubric to students, so they can internalize standards for performance; and (3) it greatly improves the consistency (reliability) of your marking. Figure 10.35 shows an example of a rating scale for evaluating an argumentative presentation.

You may also wish to assess whether students can identify the rhetorical mechanisms and tactics that are used in a particular piece of writing, speech, advertisement, or other persuasive material. Two assessment strategies for doing this are described in Figure 10.36 and illustrated in Figure 10.37.

Critical Thinking Skills in Combination

Although it is important to teach and assess students' specific critical thinking skills, you should not lose sight of the ultimate learning target: When faced with real-world applications, the student must spontaneously decide to use these abilities, and use them in selective combinations that fit the circumstances. Students will need instruction and practice in deciding on the appropriate analyses and combined critical thinking skills to use in different circumstances. To assess students' ability to use skills in combination, your assessment tasks themselves must provide realistic situations that require students to use combinations of several critical thinking abilities. Performance tasks, discussed in Chapter 11, offer assessment opportunities for doing this.

Finally, if students are to learn to be disposed toward using critical thinking in their daily activities, you should assess their dispositions continuously throughout the term or year. If some students are not exhibiting a critical thinking disposition, you should alter your teaching of those students so they practice these disposition learning targets.

OTHER SPECIFIC HIGHER-ORDER SKILLS AND ABILITIES

Ability to Use Reference Materials

Undoubtedly it is important to develop the ability to use both general reference materials and special materials for a particular subject area. Among the reference-using skills you may teach and assess are alphabetizing, using tables of contents and indexes, using encyclopedias, using dictionaries, using general reference materials (calendars, maps and globes, textbooks, periodical indexes, atlases, *Who's Who in America*, and magazines), and using a library and its catalogue (Hoover, Hieronymus, Frisbie, & Dunbar, 1993b). The Internet and computer-based CDs are also reference materials. Skills in using these materials should also be taught and assessed. The dictionary items in Figure 10.1 illustrate how to assess a few skills in obtaining information from a dictionary entry: using the guide to pronunciation, locating the meaning in particular usage, and identifying a word's part of speech.

You can use many types of introductory materials to assess abilities related to using reference materials. Introductory materials include a section of an index, a section of a table of contents, a part of an atlas, a list of words to

FIGURE 10.35 Example of a simple rating scale to use as a scoring rubric for assessing the quality of a student's oral or written presentation of an argument.

Student's name: Date:
Topic:

1. Did the student clearly state the thesis or main point?

0	1	2	3
Did not state or imply the main point or thesis	Implied the main point or thesis but did not state it clearly	Stated the main idea or thesis clearly but only matter of factly	Stated the main idea or thesis clearly, enthusiastically, and interestingly for the audience

2. Did the student define the key terms when necessary to do so?

0	1	2	NA
No attempt to define key terms, even when it was necessary to do so	Attempts to define the key terms, but was not effective in doing so	Clearly and effectively defines the necessary key terms	The presentation was such that defining key terms was unnecessary

3. Did the student use sound reasoning to support the main point or thesis?

0	1	2	3
Offered no supporting reasons for the thesis or position taken	Supporting reasons given but they are off-target or they do not lend direct support for the thesis	Gives relevant supporting reasons, but could have given better or more diverse reasons	Gives excellent supporting reasons, good diversity, directly applicable

4. Did the student use relevant facts in appropriate ways to support the thesis?

0	1	2	3
Gave no facts, used completely irrelevant facts, or cited facts from noncredible sources	Gave facts to support the thesis but the generalizations from them were weak, somewhat inappropriate, or incomplete; facts are cited from credible sources	Gives several appropriate facts that support the thesis, generalizations from facts are appropriate, sources for facts are credible	Gives highly appropriate facts, excellent generalizations from facts that support the thesis, sources of facts are credible, facts used well in making the argument

5. Did the student portray and evaluate alternative positions fairly?

0	1	2	3
Alternative positions not mentioned and not evaluated	Alternative positions are mentioned but they are either not portrayed fairly, not evaluated properly, or not relevant to the thesis	Some of the relevant alternative positions are mentioned, they are portrayed properly, and evaluated properly; other important alternative positions are omitted	All relevant and important alternative positions are mentioned, presented fairly, and evaluated properly

6. Did the student rebut the alternative positions well?

0	1	2	3
No attempt was made at rebuttal	Attempts at rebuttal were made but they are ineffective or incomplete	Rebutted adequately, but could have been more effective in explaining the short-comings of the alternatives	Rebutted well, was effective, clear about the inadequacies of the alternatives, convincingly presented

7. Did the student present a well-organized argument?

0	1	2	3
Organization was disconnected, lacked direction, confused the thesis or main point	Organization was clear, but not effective, connections to thesis or main point were not sharp; details were often out of place	Organization was good and contributed to the effectiveness of the argument, but a few details were out of place; sometimes the connections to the main point were weak or out of place	Organization was very clear and enhanced the argument; the presentation kept the audience interest focused on the main issues

FIGURE 10.36   Strategies for assessing the ability to identify the use of rhetorical mechanisms and tactics.

Strategy A. Analyze one piece to identify what is misleading.

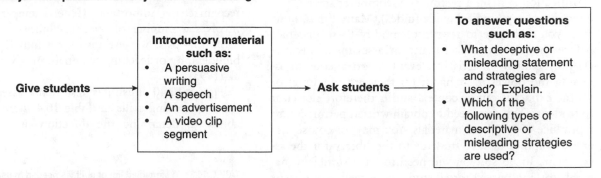

Strategy B. Identify the misleading piece.

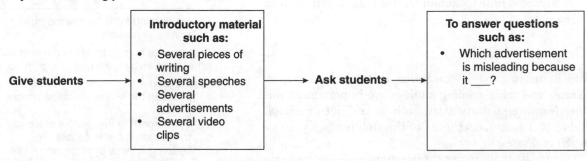

FIGURE 10.37   Examples of items assessing a student's ability to identify misleading approaches in persuasive materials (e.g., advertisements).

Questions 1 and 2 refer to the advertisements below.

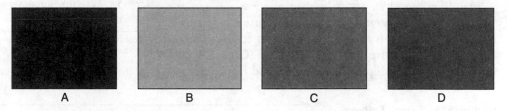

1. Which of the advertisements above should be considered misleading because it inappropriately appeals to scientific authority?

    A. A

    B. B

    C. C

    D. D

2. Which of the advertisements above should be considered misleading because it focuses on the consumer keeping up with the crowd or joining the bandwagon?

    A. A

    B. B

    C. C

    D. D

alphabetize, a reproduction of a library and a catalogue entry card, a section of the Dewey or Library of Congress classification system, a picture of a computer screen, and a section of a periodical guide (index). Many times, however, you will have to rewrite or modify these materials before they are suitable for use in assessment, because (1) they contain material irrelevant or extraneous to assessing the objective at hand; (2) they are too long; or (3) the extract is out of context and is therefore not clear to students. You may need to obtain written permission to reproduce copyrighted materials. You may, of course, use entire volumes or take students to the library for the assessment. To do so, you will need to have sufficient materials (or computers) for all students, as well as sufficient uninterrupted time to administer this type of performance assessment.

Graphs and Tables

Much information is condensed in tables and graphs. **Graph and table reading abilities** are important to further learning in many areas, both in and out of school. Table 10.3 summarizes some of the abilities that you can teach and assess.

Figure 10.38 illustrates the use of multiple-choice items to assess skills in reading tables. Item 1 requires a student to read the table and locate the information in a cell (Capability 3c of Table 10.3) and to compare several values read from the table to determine which is largest (Capability 4A of Table 10.3). Item 2 requires a student to make an inference concerning the likelihood of an event based on understanding the trends and facts presented (Capabilities 6 and 7).

Figure 10.39 illustrates how you might use a graph and multiple-choice items to assess capabilities to draw inference based on the displayed rates or trends (Capability 5), underlying relationships (Capability 6), and facts.

Maps

The ability to read and to learn from maps has long been recognized as important. General **map-reading ability** involves a number of specific abilities, some of which Table 10.4 lists. Suggestions for teaching these skills and a bibliography of teaching materials are given in Hoover et al. (1993).

Figure 10.40 illustrates test items assessing some of the map-reading skills in Table 10.4. Item 1 assesses the ability to determine the direction of places on maps

TABLE 10.3 A simplified list of abilities needed to use graphs and tables.

1. To comprehend from the title the topic on which a graph or table gives information

2. To recognize from subtitles and row or column headings what is shown by each part of a graph or table

3. To read amounts
   a. by using the scale (or scales) on bar, line, and picture graphs
   b. by interpreting the sectors of a circle on circle graphs
   c. by locating a cell in a table
   d. by using special symbols and a key

4. To compare two or more values read from a graph or table
   a. by determining rank
   b. by determining differences between amounts
   c. by determining how many times greater one amount is than another

5. To determine relative rates or trends

6. To determine underlying relationships through correct interpretation of a graph

7. To grasp the outstanding facts portrayed by a graph or table

Source: Copyright © 1971 by The University of Iowa. All rights reserved. Reproduced from the *Iowa Tests of Basic Skills, Teachers Guide to Administration, Interpretation and Use,* Levels Editions, Form 6, p. 46, with permission of The Riverside Publishing Company.

FIGURE 10.38 Examples of items assessing skills in using tables: Locate and compare information (Item 1) and draw inferences based on trends and other information (Item 2).

Use the table below to answer Questions 1 and 2.

	Average Temperature and Rainfall at Windy Hill Town							
	1994		**1995**		**1996**		**1997**	
	Temp	**Rain**	**Temp**	**Rain**	**Temp**	**Rain**	**Temp**	**Rain**
September	64°	0.1 in	63°	0.2 in	66°	0.0 in	64°	0.3 in
October	72°	0.4 in	71°	0.5 in	74°	0.4 in	71°	0.6 in
November	77°	0.9 in	75°	1.0 in	78°	0.8 in	76°	0.7 in
December	81°	2.0 in	80°	2.7 in	85°	1.5 in	80°	2.1 in

1. When did the highest average rainfall occur?
   A. November of 1994
   B. November of 1995
   C. December of 1995
   D. December of 1997

2. Which of the following events is most likely to have occurred between September and December of 1996?
   A. The roads were covered with ice and snow.
   B. The town's water reserves were very low.
   C. The river flowing through town overflowed its banks.

FIGURE 10.39 Examples of items assessing graph-using ability: Inference from the graph (item 1) and interpreting trends underlying the graph (item 2).

Use the information below to answer Questions 1 and 2.

Before the exercise period began, the students' teacher divided the class into two groups. Group 1 was to walk around the track two times. Group 2 was to run around the track one time. All students took their pulses both before and after going around the track. The average pulses for the two groups are shown in the graph below.

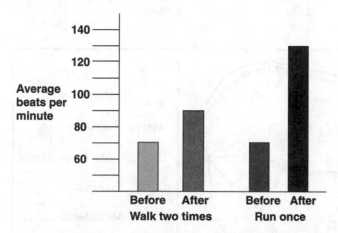

1. According to the graph, which type of exercise made the students' hearts beat faster?

   A. Running

   B. Walking

   C. Neither. They had the same beats with either running or walking.

2. What would be the heart beats about one hour after the exercise period when all the students are reading in the library?

   A. About 70 for both groups.

   B. About 70 for the group that walked twice around and about 130 for the group that ran once around.

   C. About 90 for the group that walked twice around and about 130 for the group that ran once around.

   D. Lower than 60 for both groups.

---

from a given orientation (Capability 1a). Item 2 assesses the ability to visualize landscape features (Capability 7). Item 3 assesses the student's ability to determine distance using a scale of miles (Capability 3b). Item 4 assesses the ability to determine the direction a river flows (Capability 1c).

Reading Skills

Traditional Procedure Having students read material in a subject area and answer questions based on that material is a desirable way to assess reading skills. Although

TABLE 10.4 A simplified list of abilities needed to use maps.

1. Ability to orient map and determine direction
   a. to determine direction from orientation
   b. to determine direction from parallels or meridians
   c. to determine direction of river flow or slope of land
2. Ability to locate and/or describe places on maps and globes
   a. through the use of standard map symbols
   b. through the use of a key
   c. through the use of distance and/or direction
   d. through the use of latitude or longitude
3. Ability to determine distances
   a. determining distance on a road map
   b. determining distance by using a scale of miles
   c. determining distance on a globe
   d. comparing distances
4. Ability to determine or trace routes of travel
5. Ability to understand seasonal variations, sun patterns, and time differences
6. Ability to read and compare facts from one or more pattern maps
7. Ability to visualize landscape features
8. Ability to infer man's activities or way of living
   a. from outline maps
   b. from pattern maps

developing passages followed by questions is not easy, you may need to do so, especially when teaching subjects for which you do not have adequate assessment procedures or study booklets covering these skills. To develop such assessments, the reading materials need to be carefully selected to represent the kind of material students should be able to read. Also, the reading material may need to be rewritten so that the interpretive questions can be answered primarily on the basis of the material presented. Finally, questions need to be phrased in a way that does not require a student to have more background or special information than you deem appropriate for the level of students and subject matter at hand (Ebel, 1951; Wesman, 1971).

The steps for building a set of assessment questions requiring reading and interpreting of a printed passage follow (Ebel, 1951; Wesman, 1971):

1. *Locate a promising passage.* Examine sources (texts, periodicals, reference works, specialized books, and collections and anthologies) until you find a passage for which you can write several interpretive items.

2. *Write initial test items.* Write as many items for the passage as you can. Try to exploit all of the possibilities for interpretation of the passage that fit your original assessment plan.

FIGURE 10.40 Examples of items assessing the ability to read maps.

The map below shows five states. The cities are in alphabetical order beginning at the top. The key at the right tells what the signs on the map mean.

1. Which of these cities is farthest south?
   1. Eton 3. Gull
   2. Follet *4. Hart

2. On which train trip could one see the mountains on one side and the ocean on the other?
   1. Avis to Gull 3. Bison to Darwin
   *2. Bison to Cruz 4. Darwin to Eton

3. About how far is it from Hart to the mainland at the closest point?
   1. 5 miles *3. 50 miles
   2. 15 miles 4. 85 miles

4. Which way does the Ames River flow?
   *1. North 3. East
   2. South 4. West

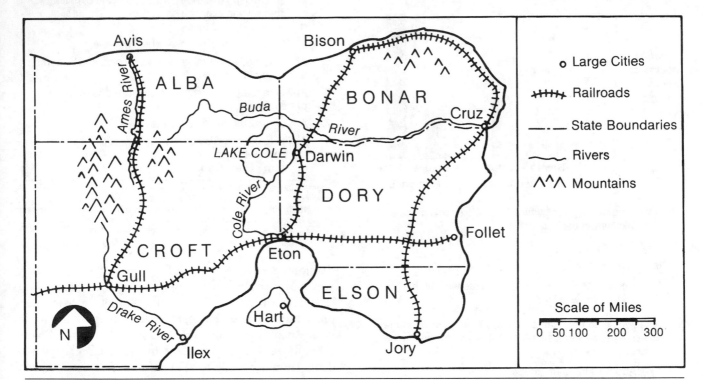

3. *Rewrite the passage.* After you have a tentative set of items, rewrite the passage to eliminate unessential material that does not contribute to the items you have written.

4. *Consider rewriting some of the items.* Changes in the passage may require revising or eliminating some of the items you already wrote. The goal of steps 3 and 4 is to produce a condensed and efficient passage and item set.

5. *Repeat steps 3 and 4 as often as necessary,* until you are satisfied that you have an efficient set of items.

Most commercial survey achievement tests contain reading comprehension subtests. You should consult these for examples of using passages to assess reading comprehension.

Authentic Reading Assessment   If you are most interested in reading comprehension, rather than the students' ability to interpret subject-matter materials, the preceding type of condensation may be undesirable, especially if part of what you want to assess is the ability to read naturally occurring materials and the capacity to distinguish between relevant and extraneous material (Wesman, 1971). Critics of standardized reading comprehension tests argue that the passages and questions created by the traditional five-step procedure are too artificial. The critics would rather use materials that students need to read in the real world or in further schooling. They claim that students exposed to traditional reading comprehension tests come to believe that reading: (1) consists of short passages, (2) requires answering questions whose answers are known by the authorities that set them, and (3) has little to do with interpreting the written word (Resnick, 1989).

Passages are considered authentic if they are drawn from the primary sources of a discipline, age-appropriate books and magazines, newspapers, and textbooks students may encounter. In addition, authentic reading tasks may require students to read longer passages than typically appear on traditional reading comprehension tests. It may also require students to read from several sources to compare points of view or obtain reliable and complete information. For example, a student may read four different accounts of an event or of a procedure and then answer questions about the event or procedure, or about comparisons among the different accounts read.

Alternately, you may want to combine reading, writing, and subject-matter exercises, such as conducting science experiments. For instance, students can individually read several pieces and answer questions about them. Then you can organize students into groups to discuss the pieces they read and to share their insights into interpreting them. Next, students can individually write essays or set up experiments to extend or to synthesize the material they have read and discussed. The purpose of the intermediate discussion is to offer all students the opportunity, through group discussion, to clarify points, obtain information they may have missed through their reading, and "level the playing field" somewhat before the writing phase of the assessment begins.

Longer and more authentic reading tasks use more of your class time for assessment than does the traditional method. An assessment that requires reading several original texts and writing essays after a class discussion may take several class periods to complete. You need to balance your assessment time against your teaching time before deciding which assessment strategy to use. You could try some combination of both. You could use more authentic assessment methods on some occasions and more efficient assessment methods on others. Compare students' performance and the type of information you obtain under the different approaches. This may give you some insight into the validity of the assessment results from each method. (Assessment validity is discussed in Chapter 3.)

The MAZE Item Type Reading comprehension can be assessed through a multiple-choice variety of the **cloze reading exercise** known as **MAZE**. The basic idea is to find an appropriate passage and embed a multiple-choice question in the passage which students can answer only if they comprehend the meaning of the surrounding passage. To better understand this procedure, consider the multiple-choice item in Figure 10.41 (Item A), which requires students to select the word that best completes the sentence, "The baby_____." Notice that all options correctly complete this sentence when it is read outside the context of a reading passage. Now, consider the same item

when it is embedded in a brief passage as shown in Figure 10.41 (Item B). Option B is correct because of the context in which the item is embedded. Item B in Figure 10.41 shows a simple paragraph of a few short sentences; this technique also can be applied to long and complex prose passages.

MAZE items appear to have a considerable advantage over the usual cloze exercises, in which only the blank appears and students must fill in the missing word. They (1) assess whether students can construct meaning from the passages, (2) are objectively scored, (3) do not result in a student filling in blanks with words that leave you wondering whether a student understands the passage, and (4) do not require students to have a great deal of outside knowledge in order for you to assess their ability to read.

The following suggestions for formulating MAZE test items are based on those used for the *Degree of Reading Power* (Touchstone Applied Science Associates, 1995a, 1995b) test.

1. Design the items so that a student needs to read and understand the passage to answer correctly. As in the preceding example, when an item is considered in isolation, each option should make the sentence grammatically and semantically correct. However, once the item is embedded in the text, only one option should be correct.

2. The passage should contain all of the content information a student needs to answer the item correctly. For the item to assess reading ability, a student should not have to depend on recall of special experiences to find the correct answer. This usually means the passages must be especially written for the test.

3. All of the items' options should be common words. All students should recognize and understand the meaning of each option. This assures that when a student misses an item, the fault lies with the student's inability to comprehend the reading passage rather than the student's lack of knowledge about the meaning of the words in the item.

FIGURE 10.41 Example of a MAZE item assessing reading comprehension.

A. Multiple-choice item not embedded in text.
   The baby___*1*___.
1.   A. cried
     B. laughed
     C. slept
     D. walked

B. The same multiple-choice item embedded in text
Mother and her six-month-old baby played for a long time.
The baby___*2*___. She enjoyed being tickled under the arms.
2.   A. cried
     B. laughed
     C. slept
     D. walked

FIGURE 10.42 Examples of enhanced multiple-choice items.

A. Items in language usage

> For a class assignment, Tanya is going to write a report about her work at the recycling center.

> Here is the first part of Tanya's report. Use it to answer questions 6 and 7.
>
> ```
> Our town has a new recycling center.  I work
> (1)                                    (2)
> there every Saturday.  My friend Bob works at
>                                     (3)
> the car wash.  I have learned that our city's
>              (4)
> dump is getting too full.  It is too full to
>                         (5)
> take any more garbage.
> ```

6. Which sentence contains information that does not belong?

   E 2
   F 3
   G 4
   H 5

> Read the next section of Tanya's report and answer question 8. This section has groups of underlined words. The questions ask about them.
>
> ```
> Recycling means reusing things instead of
> (6)
> throwing them away?  People bring things to
>                      (7)
> the center.  Then the center sells these
>              (8)
> things to companies that reuse them.  This
>                                       (9)
> way, natural resources are saved.
> ```

8. In sentence 8, how should Then the center sells be written?

   E Then the Center sells
   F then the center sells
   G Then The Center sells
   H As it is

B. Item in science

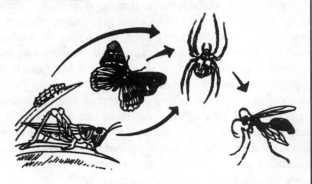

1. **If all of the wasps are killed, which of these will increase first?**

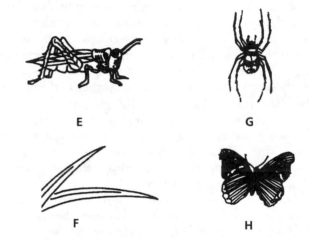

E   G

F   H

B. Item in social studies

HOW COLE EARNED HIS MONEY

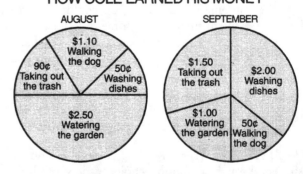

2. **Which statement is true based on these graphs?**

   E Cole earned less money watering the garden in September than in August.
   F Cole earned more money walking the dog in September than in August.
   G Cole washed dishes less often in September than in August.
   H Cole does not take out the trash on school days.

Source: Adapted from *Focus on: Enhanced Multiple Choice Questions* (p. 4, 6, and 7) by the Psychological Corporation, 1992, by Harcourt, Inc. Reprinted by permission.

ENHANCED MULTIPLE-CHOICE ITEMS

Tasks Requiring Combinations of Abilities

A criticism of teacher-made tests is that they often assess skills and knowledge in fragmented "bits." That is, often teachers will assess knowledge that is taken out of the context or application in which it ultimately will be used. A teacher may assess skills one at a time. Or a teacher may focus assessment on outcomes or "correct answers" and not attend to the processes students use to reach their answers. One way to correct these deficiencies is to increase your usage of complex performance tasks in your assessments. Another way is to be sure that each of your objective assessment tasks requires students to use knowledge and skills in meaningful situations. This usually means that you must create tasks that require students to apply more than one skill at a time.

Multiple-Choice Items

Objectively scored items, such as multiple choice, can address many of the preceding criticisms by using enhanced assessment. Enhanced assessment tasks require students to use knowledge and skills in combinations, often through a carefully crafted context-dependent item set. **Enhanced multiple-choice items** differ from simple forms of multiple-choice items in the following ways (Psychological Corporation, 1992a):

1. They require students to use knowledge and skill in a context that is similar to real life or to know how the knowledge and skill will be used in new classroom learning.

2. They assess how well students use the thinking and "doing" processes that are required by the discipline underlying the subject matter.

3. Insofar as possible with paper-and-pencil tasks, they require students to actually perform skills that are the ultimate purpose of a learning target. Some performances are mental activities (decision making, identifying problem solutions, computations, reading, etc.). These cognitive performances can be assessed efficiently with paper-and-pencil tasks.

4. They require students to use processes and knowledge *in combination*, sometimes from different subject matters or from different teaching units of the same subject matter. This allows you to assess "constellations" of skills and abilities rather than only discrete pieces of learning.

Figure 10.42 shows examples of enhanced multiple-choice items from different curriculum areas. More advanced formats for objectively scored items are described in Chapter 8.

Summary

- A basic rule for developing tasks to assess higher-order thinking abilities is that the assessment materials should be new or novel to the student: They should not repeat the specific examples you used during instruction and should be phrased in language that is different from that you used in teaching.
- To assess higher-order thinking abilities, it is often necessary to develop tasks for which the solutions or answers depend on a particular piece(s) of introductory material presented along with them. These are called context-dependent item sets or interpretive exercises.
- A concept is a name that represents a category of things such as persons, objects, events, or relationships.
- A concept is said to have been learned if a student can identify various new exemplars or instances of it and does not refer to noninstances as exemplars. Tasks assessing concept acquisition need to preserve this criterion.
- You may distinguish between concrete concepts and defined concepts:
  - A *concrete concept* refers to a category, the members of which have in common one or more physical, tangible qualities that can be heard, seen, tasted, felt, and/or smelled.
  - A *defined concept* or *relational concept* refers to a class, the members of which have in common some abstract quality or some relational quality.
- Concrete concepts have been assessed by three procedures:
  - Presenting examples to the student and requiring the student to give the concept name or label
  - Presenting a mixture of examples and non-examples of the concept along with the concept name and requiring the student to identify the examples of the concept
  - Giving the name of the concept and requiring the student to produce new examples of the concept
- Assessing concept understanding often requires that the test item call for an indicator performance on the part of the student. You should take care to assure that the indicator behavior is within the repertoire of the student and to avoid confusing the inability to make an indicator response (e.g., stating the concept name) with lack of understanding the concept.
- Considering the appropriateness of an indicator response is very important when testing young children, bilingual learners, students with special learning difficulties, and students with disabilities.
- Defined concepts have been assessed by:
  - Requiring a student to produce a correct definition of a concept
  - Presenting instances and noninstances of the concept and requiring students to identify the instances of the concept

- Giving the name of the concept and requiring a student to produce new instances of the concept
- Requiring students to identify the components of a defined concept and to give an example of the relationship among the components
- A student's deep understanding of a concept is best assessed by using complex performance assessments in which students apply the concept to a new situation and connect it to other concepts and relations. The chapter presents examples of strategies for assessing this understanding.
- A person's behavior is *rule-governed* or *principle-governed* if the person regularly responds to a class of concepts with a class of appropriate relational responses.
- To assess whether a student comprehends a rule, you must be certain that the tasks assess more than the student's ability to verbalize or state the rule. You must require the student to apply the rule to a new or novel situation.
- As with assessments of concept understanding, tasks for assessing whether a student comprehends a principle need to present the student with situations that are different from those you used as examples during instruction and phrased in language that is not identical with what you used during instruction.
- Tasks must not become so dependent on reading comprehension that they interfere with your identifying students who, although they comprehend the rule, cannot read well.
- Two basic strategies for crafting verbal items that assess comprehension of rules or principles are
  - Presenting the student with the antecedent conditions that are specified in the principle and requiring the student to state or select an example of the consequences that would follow if the rule were to be applied
  - Presenting the student with the consequences and requiring the student to state or select the antecedent conditions that would have to exist according to the rule to produce the consequences
- Varieties of tasks similar to the preceding two basic types include
  - Requiring the student to identify inferences or predictions consistent with the application of a principle in a given situation
  - Requiring the student to produce a new example of an inference or the consequence of applying a principle in a given situation
  - Requiring the student to produce a statement of the principle that explains a particular situation or set of events
- *Problem solving* involves identifying obstacles to attaining a desired outcome and using appropriate ways to overcome these obstacles so the goal is attained. Problem solving can be considered from several perspectives, including whether the problems are well structured or ill structured, whether the solutions are schema driven, and whether solution strategies are subject-matter specific or general. Understanding these perspectives is essential to identifying the appropriate assessment strategy.
- Using the *IDEAL Problem Solver* as a framework, the chapter describes and gives examples of tasks you can use to assess specific problem-solving abilities. Strategies are presented for assessing students' ability to identify and recognize problems, define and represent problems, explore and use heuristics and other solution strategies, and look back and evaluate problem solutions.
- *Critical thinking* is the ability to use reasonable, reflective, and effective thinking processes to decide what to do or what to believe. To assess critical thinking, you must assess both the disposition toward using critical thinking and the ability to apply critical thinking skills in appropriate ways.
- *Dispositions* toward critical thinking are the tendencies or habitual uses of critical thinking abilities. Table 10.3 lists these. Illustrations were given of simple checklists and rating scales for assessing these dispositions.
- *Critical thinking abilities* consist of those skills and abilities that enable students to analyze actions and statements to determine their credibility, logical consistency, and value implications so the student knows what to do or to believe. The specific abilities comprising critical thinking are listed in Table 10.2. The chapter provides strategies and examples of tasks for assessing each of these abilities.
- Using a variety of introductory material such as pictures, maps, graphs, drawings, and paragraphs helps in assessing many learning targets. The examples illustrate the use of context-dependent item sets to assess:
  - Ability to use reference materials
  - Ability to use graphs and tables
  - Ability to use maps
- To develop assessment exercises requiring a student to read and interpret a passage of one or more paragraphs, you should follow the five-step process described in the chapter.
- Critics of those who use short passages for assessing reading comprehension suggest that you should give students one (or more), longer passages to read that have not been edited for purposes of assessment. Such passages are said to be more realistic and similar to those students are likely to encounter in the real world.
- *MAZE Items* seem more effective than the usual cloze items for assessing reading comprehension.
- *Enhanced multiple-choice items* assess combinations of skills and knowledge in ways that require students to apply what they know. Examples of the types of items are given in the chapter.

■ The ultimate learning targets are those that require students to use their abilities in applications they encounter after schooling is completed. Students will be expected to use combinations of abilities in relatively ill defined problem situations. Therefore, you should both teach and assess students in ways that foster their growth toward these ultimate learning targets.

Important Terms and Concepts

analyze arguments
ask clarifying questions
checklist
closed-response task
cloze reading exercise
concept
concrete concept
context-dependent item sets
critical thinking
deciding on an action
defined concept
dispositions
enhanced multiple-choice items
exemplar
focus on a question
graph and table reading abilities
habits of mind
heuristic
IDEAL problem solver
identifying assumptions
ill-structured problems
interacting with others
interpretive exercises
judging credibility
judging deductions
judging inductions
judging value definitions
map-reading abilities
MAZE item type
mental model
novel material
open-response task
overgeneralizing a concept
principle
problem
problem-sorting task
rating scale
relational concepts
schema (schemata)
schema-driven problem solving
undergeneralizing a concept
well-structured problems

Exercises and Discussion Questions

1. The author implies that using context-dependent item sets leads to increased validity of classroom tests. Is this contention true? Is it too sweeping? Explain your answer.
2. Explain how concrete concept learning may be applied to arts education in elementary and middle schools. May the children labeled in each of the categories of Table 5.2 be pe-

nalized if a teacher uses inappropriate indicator behaviors to assess their learning of certain art-related concepts? Explain.
3. Is it necessary that students be able to state principles and rules in words? Explain.
4. Explain how each of the following properties is important for crafting tasks that assess understanding of principles: specifying antecedent events, specifying causal conditions, specifying consequences of applying a principle, paraphrasing material presented in the text or class discussion, and presenting material the students have not encountered before.
5. Identify a *defined concept* in a subject you teach (or plan to teach). Then complete each of these tasks:
   a. State the subject and the grade level.
   b. Give the name of the defined concept.
   c. Give the definition of the defined concept.
   d. Give one or more exemplars of the defined concept.
   e. Give one or more nonexemplars of the defined concept.
   f. Prepare one multiple-choice item that assesses a student's ability to discriminate the exemplars of this concept from the nonexemplars. Review your item for flaws using the checklist in Table 8.3.
   g. Prepare one assessment task that requires students to identify the components of the concept and demonstrate their understanding of the relationship(s) among these components.
6. Identify a *concrete concept* in a subject you teach or with which you are familiar. Then complete each of these tasks:
   a. State the subject and the grade level.
   b. Give the name of the concrete concept.
   c. Give two or more exemplars of the concrete concept.
   d. Give two or more nonexemplars of the concrete concept that are very similar to the concept.
   e. Prepare one assessment task that requires students to discriminate the exemplars from the nonexemplars.
   f. Prepare one complex performance task that requires using combinations of skills in which understanding of the defined concept at a deeper level is required of the student.
   g. Develop a scoring rubric for Task f.
7. Identify a *principle* or *rule* in a subject you teach (or plan to teach). Then complete these tasks:
   a. State the subject and the grade level.
   b. State the principle and give its name.
   c. Describe in general terms the conditions under which it is appropriate to use the principle to solve a problem or to explain a phenomenon.
   d. Using general terms, describe the most likely kinds of faulty inferences made or conclusions drawn by those students who misinterpret or misapply the principle.
   e. Using Figure 10.9 as a model for format, prepare one multiple-choice item to assess a student's ability to identify an appropriate conclusion to be made when applying this rule. Use the information in your answer to the previous question as a basis for formulating distractors. Use Table 8.3 to improve your item.
   f. Using Figure 10.10 as a model for format, prepare a constructed response item to assess a student's ability to produce examples of conclusions after applying the principle. This item should assess the same principle that you used for constructing the multiple-choice item just written.

g. Administer both of these items, one at a time, to a student at the appropriate grade level. Administer the constructed response item first, then remove it from the student before administering the multiple-choice item.

h. Compare the results you obtained. What were the similarities and differences in the quality of information you received? Which task is more valid? Why?

i. Share your results with others in this class. How do your results compare with theirs? Were there differences with respect to subject matter and grade level assessed? What conclusions can the class draw from its collective experience?

8. Construct one well-structured and one ill-structured problem for students to solve in the subject you teach or plan to teach. Explain why each is well- or ill-structured. Using the categories of the IDEAL Problem Solver, compare how each type of problem would be solved by a student. Discuss your findings with others in this course.

9. For the subject you teach or plan to teach, develop a notebook with well-crafted tasks that assess different problem-solving abilities. Organize your tasks according to the categories of the IDEAL Problem Solver. Structure your notebook as follows:

a. Craft one assessment task using each of the 17 assessment strategies presented in this chapter.

b. Type one assessment task per page. Label the task with the subject, teaching unit, student grade level, assessment strategy, and category of the IDEAL Problem Solver the task assesses.

c. On a separate page, craft a scoring rubric for the task and write a sample ideal response.

d. Review your work carefully. Be sure that the content of each task and the scoring rubric are accurate and that the tasks are well-crafted.

e. Share your notebook with the other participants in this course.

10. Select a subject and grade level you teach or plan to teach, for which critical thinking is an important learning outcome. Then, complete the following tasks:

a. Identify and briefly describe (in general terms) one or more teaching units in which critical thinking abilities can be taught and practiced.

b. On a large sheet of paper, create a table in which each row heading is one of the 12 critical thinking abilities listed in Table 10.2.

c. Label the columns with the teaching and learning activities in the unit(s) that lend themselves to teaching and practicing critical thinking abilities.

d. For each cell in the body of the table, briefly describe how a student would demonstrate that he or she was engaging in the corresponding critical thinking ability. Not every cell will be filled, because not every ability can be demonstrated with every activity you list. However, in the table as a whole, each ability should be demonstrated at least once. If they are not, then add a unit or an activity to your table.

e. Present your table to the others in this course. Discuss your activities and demonstrations. Revise your table on the basis of the discussion. Then share it with the other class members.

11. For the same subject and grade level you identified in Exercise 10, develop a notebook containing samples of tasks assessing each of the 12 critical thinking abilities in Table 10.2. Structure your notebook around the 12 abilities as follows:

a. Craft one assessment task using each of the critical thinking assessment strategies described in this chapter.

b. Type one assessment task per page. Label the task with the subject, teaching unit, student grade level, assessment strategy, and critical thinking ability the task assesses.

c. On a separate page, craft a scoring rubric for the task and write a sample ideal response.

d. Review your work carefully. Be sure the content of each task and scoring rubric is accurate. Be sure the tasks are well crafted.

e. Share your notebook with the other members of this course.

12. Using the table you created for Exercise 10, craft a checklist and a rating scale to assess a student's dispositions toward using critical thinking skills and abilities.

13. For a subject and grade level you teach or plan to teach, identify a graph and a table (chart) the students should be able to use:

a. Craft a context-dependent item set for the graph assessing the students' ability to use it in a way that goes beyond simply reading values from it. Craft at least two tasks for the set. Review the items using the appropriate checklists from Chapters 7 and 8.

b. Share your context-dependent item sets with the other members of this course.

14. Identify a teaching unit in a subject you teach or plan to teach. Identify the specific skills and learning targets.

a. List the specific skills and learning targets for the unit. Briefly describe the unit in general terms.

b. Craft one enhanced multiple-choice item that assesses students' ability to use combinations of these specific skills in applied and realistic ways.

c. Identify the specific skills you are assessing in combination in *this* item. Explain how this combination of skills must be used to obtain the correct answer.

d. Share your work with the others in your course.

Additional Readings

Bloom, B. S., Hastings, J. T., & Madaus, G. F. (1971). *Handbook on formative and summative evaluation of student learning.* New York: McGraw-Hill.

Gives examples in 11 curriculum areas of items assessing higher-order thinking skills as defined by the Bloom et al. *Taxonomy of Educational Objectives.*

Dossey, J. A., Mullis, I. V. S., & Jones, C. O. (1993). *Can students do mathematical problem solving?* Washington, DC: National Assessment of Educational Process, Office of Educational Research and Improvement, U.S. Department of Education.

Focuses on the constructed response mathematics questions in the 1992 National Assessment of Education Progress. Gives examples of problem-solving tasks, scoring rubrics, and students' responses. Examples cover grades 4, 8, and 12.

Joshua, S., & Dupin, J. J. (1991). In physics class, exercises can cause problems . . . *International Journal of Science Education, 13,* 291–301.

Students were studied over the entire year. Problems "new to the student" presented serious difficulties for average students. Suggestions for teaching are discussed.

Royer, J. M., Cisero, C. A., & Carlo, M. S. (1993). Techniques and procedures for assessing cognitive skills. *Review of Educational Research, 63*, 201–243.

A review of the research literature in cognitive science focusing on the tasks the researchers used to assess thinking skills. The review is organized around the Glaser, Lesgold, and Lajoie developmental framework described in the following reading.

Glaser, R., Lesgold, A., & Lajoie, S.(1985). Toward a cognitive theory for the measurement of achievement. In R.R. Ronning. J. Gloveer, J. C. Conoley, & J.C. Witt (Eds.), *The influence of cognitive psychology on testing and measurement* (pp. 41–85). Hillsdale, NJ: Erlbaum.

This chapter presents a developmental approach to describing problem solving. The authors identify several growth dimensions for problem solving. Then they describe how novice and expert problem solvers differ on each dimension. This framework may be used to assess students' progress in problem-solving development.

Haladyna, T.M. (1997). *Writing test items to evaluate higher-order thinking*. Boston: Allyn and Bacon.

Chapter 2 discusses higher-order thinking skills including problem solving, critical thinking, and creativity. Other chapters give examples of test items and suggestions for crafting them.

Kuhn, D. (1999). A developmental model of critical thinking. *Educational Researcher, 28,* (2), 16–25, 46.

This essay presents a view of critical thinking that is quite different from the one adopted in this chapter. The author views critical thinking as a developmental process that needs guidance and practice from schooling. The author sees metacognition as the overriding thinking process that helps a learner to think critically by being aware of his or her own thinking.

Nitko, A.J. (1996). *Educational assessment of students* (2nd ed.) Englewood Cliffs, NJ: Prentice Hall/Merrill Education.

Chapter 10 gives examples and describes how to craft tasks that assess the following dimensions of problem-solving skill development: knowledge organization and structure, depth of problem representation, quality of mental models, efficiency of procedures, automaticity of performance, and metacognitive skills for learning. The chapter illustrates ways to implement the Glaser, Lesgold, and Lajoie (1985) developmental framework.

Clarke, J. H. (1990). *Patterns of thinking: Integrating learning skills in content thinking.* Boston: Allyn and Bacon.

Fisher, R. (1990). *Teaching children to think.* Oxford, England: Basil Blackwell Ltd.

Halpern, D. F. (1989). *Thought and knowledge: An introduction to critical thinking* (2nd ed.). Hillsdale, NJ: Erlbaum.

Norris, S. P., & Ennis, R. H. (1989). *Evaluating critical thinking.* Pacific Grove, CA: Midwest Publications, Critical Thinking Press.

These volumes contain readable and practical discussions of the various skills and abilities that constitute critical thinking and problem solving. They give suggestions for teaching as well as sample tasks. The Clarke book gives good examples of using concept-mapping tasks (Chapter 8).

CHAPTER 11

Performance, Alternative, and Authentic Assessments

Learning Targets

After studying this chapter, you should be able to:

1. Distinguish performance tasks from other assessment formats.   *[1, 3, 6]*
2. Explain the meaning of authentic assessment and its essential characteristics.   *[1, 6]*
3. Explain the strengths and weaknesses of using performance assessments when teaching from a multiple intelligence perspective.   *[1, 6]*
4. Describe how using performance assessments could improve teaching, learning, and assessment validity.   *[4, 1, 3, 6]*
5. Distinguish classroom performance activities from performance assessment tasks.   *[1, 4]*
6. Explain the major advantages and disadvantages of using performance assessment.   *[1, 6]*
7. List, explain, and give examples of the advantages of the major types of performance assessment.   *[1, 4, 6]*
8. Explain how each of the important terms and concepts listed at the end of this chapter apply to educational assessment.   *[6, 1, 4]*

This chapter gives an introduction to performance assessment. It discusses the meanings and roles of performance assessments in your teaching and for helping students to achieve authentic learning targets. There are many types of and purposes for performance assessments. This chapter provides a map of the landscape. In Chapter 12, we discuss the details of how to craft performance assessments and portfolios for your own assessment needs.

PERFORMANCE ASSESSMENT AND TEACHING

What Is a Performance Assessment?

Definition Whenever a learning target requires students to apply their knowledge and skills from several areas in order to complete an activity or a task, you should use performance assessment. A **performance assessment** (1) presents a hands-on task to a student and (2) uses clearly defined criteria to evaluate how well the student achieved the application specified by the learning target. Unlike traditional test items, performance assessment tasks require students to apply their knowledge and skills from several areas to demonstrate they can perform a learning target. This may require having a student make something (build a bookshelf), produce a report (report on a group project that surveyed parents' attitudes), or give a demonstration (show how to measure mass on a laboratory scale). Figure 11.1 shows a decision-making task that a history teacher constructed. The teacher used the task to assess several types of learning targets derived from the Dimensions of Learning Model (Marzano et al., 1992). (See Appendix E for a summary of these types.)

Balanced Assessment We made the point in Chapter 6 that one must plan assessment by first being clear what learning target you want to assess, and then matching your assessment method to it. Because the curriculum framework is very diverse, not every learning target is a performance activity requiring students to apply their knowledge and skills. Some learning targets, for example, require students to learn a store of declarative knowledge (such as the structure of the nation's government, the main provisions of the Constitution and the Bill of Rights), to comprehend an event or a theory, or to compare two or more concepts. You should use traditional item formats to obtain valid results when assessing these

FIGURE 11.1 Example of a performance task in a high school history course.

Decision-Making Task

President Harry S Truman has requested that you serve on a White House task force. The goal is to decide how to force the unconditional surrender of Japan, yet provide for a secure postwar world.

You are now a member of a committee of four and have reached the point at which you are trying to decide whether to drop the bomb. Identify the alternatives you are considering and the criteria you are using to make the decision. Explain the values that influenced the selection of the criteria and the weights you placed on each. Also explain how your decision has helped you better understand this statement: "War forces people to confront inherent conflicts of values."

Before you begin your task, establish a clear goal and write it down. Then write down a plan for accomplishing your goal. When you are finished with the task, be prepared to describe the changes you had to make in your plan along the way.

As you work on your task, try to use a variety of sources of information: books, magazine articles, newspapers, and people who lived through the war. Keep a list of those sources and be prepared to describe how you determined which information was most relevant and which information was not very useful.

Present your conclusions and findings in at least two of the following ways:

- a written report
- a letter to the president following the completion of the committee meeting
- an article written for *Time* magazine, complete with suggested photos and charts
- a videotape of a dramatization of the committee meeting
- an audio tape
- a newscast
- a mock interview

You will be provided rubrics for and be assessed on each of the following standards:

CONTENT STANDARD
1. Your understanding of the principle that war forces sensitive issues to surface and causes people to confront inherent conflicts of values and beliefs.

INFORMATION PROCESSING STANDARD
2. Your ability to review and evaluate how valuable each source of information is to the parts of your project.

COMPLEX THINKING STANDARDS: DECISION MAKING
3. Your ability to identify important and appropriate alternatives to dropping the bomb.
4. Your ability to identify important and appropriate criteria to evaluate each alternative to be considered.
5. Your ability to accurately evaluate the extent to which each of your alternatives meets each criterion.
6. Your ability to select the alternative(s) that adequately meet the criteria and answer the initial decision question.

HABITS OF THE MIND STANDARD
7. Your ability to effectively define your goal in this assignment and to explain your plan for attaining this goal.

EFFECTIVE COMMUNICATION STANDARD
8. Your ability to communicate your conclusions and findings by using two or more ways of reporting your conclusions and findings.

Source: Adapted from *Assessing Student Outcomes: Performance Assessment Using the Dimensions of Learning Model* (pp. 27–29) by R. J. Marzano, D. Pickering, and J. McTighe, 1993, Alexandria, VA: Association for Supervision and Curriculum Development. Adapted by permission of McREL Institute, 2550 S. Parker Rd., Suite 500, Aurora, CO 80014. Telephone (303)337-0990. © 1993 by McREL Institute. All rights reserved.

types of learning targets. You should use performance tasks, on the other hand, to assess learning targets that require students to do something and to apply their knowledge and skills. As always, you should keep a good perspective about which assessments to use. A good rule of thumb to remember is that simple learning targets require simple assessment formats; complex learning targets require complex assessment (Arter, 1998).

Two Components Needed   A common misconception is that any performance activity used in teaching can be an assessment. Nothing can be further from the truth. Classroom assessment requires that you seriously gather information about how well each student has achieved stated learning targets. This means going beyond doing an activity. It means focusing an activity on defined learning targets and evaluating each student against established criteria. As you study performance assessment techniques, keep in mind that each task has two components: (1) the performance task itself *and* (2) a clearly defined scoring scheme or rubric. For your assessment results to be valid, *both* of these must work together. This means, first of all, that you must *craft and administer the task(s)* so that what a student does is the actual performance that the learning target specifies. For example, if the learning target says the student must weigh chemicals on the laboratory scale, the task should require weighing, not an essay on how to use the scale.

Second, it is not enough for the student to perform the learning target: You must properly *evaluate the quality* of that student's performance. To craft good scoring rubrics, you must be clear about what the standards are for high-quality performance. Using the chemical weighing example, you must craft a procedure that will help you decide *how well* the student weighs chemicals and not simply *that* chemicals were weighed. These two components of performance assessment are discussed further in the paragraphs that follow.

Improving Validity and Reliability   Imagine, for a moment, that you are a judge evaluating Olympic figure skaters. As a judge you do not have the benefit of "instant replays" on television or the commentaries of expert telecasters. The performances are quick, and once they are over they are over—on to the next skater. You can see the need to have criteria to evaluate each skater's performance. Good criteria, expertly applied by you, improve the validity of your ratings. As we discussed in Chapter 4, consistency of rating from one skater to the next can be improved if you apply the quality criteria in the same way across skaters. If you use criteria to evaluate the important and essential aspects of figure skating, and if you apply those criteria expertly and consistently, your ratings will have a high degree of validity (see Chapter 3).

Monitoring Student Learning   Imagine now that you are the skater. Would it be helpful for you to know in advance on what criteria you will be evaluated? Would your skating improve if you knew these criteria early on so you could work toward achieving them? Could you benefit from feedback on how closely your skating matches the criteria? By seeing examples of skating performances that met the criteria and those that did not, could you better understand what you needed to learn to do? I would answer yes to all these questions.

One point of this example is that in performance assessment, criteria should serve the purpose of improving students' understanding of what constitutes high quality application of knowledge and skill. The criteria you use to evaluate students should be taught to them early on so they know what standards of quality are expected of them. A second point is that you should use assessment criteria to continuously monitor and improve the progress of each student. When you are teaching a complex learning target, you are concerned with continuously developing students' progress toward attainment. You should not wait until the end of an instructional unit to evaluate progress, give feedback, and provide further help to students. Your assessment and teaching should not be separated.

Performance Task   A **performance task** is an assessment activity that requires a student to demonstrate her achievement by producing an extended written or spoken answer, by engaging in group or individual activities, or by creating a specific product. Figure 11.1 shows one such activity. When you use a performance task, you require students to demonstrate *directly* their achievement of a learning target. You require only *indirect* demonstration if you ask students simply (1) for a brief answer (e.g., completion items or short answer) or (2) to select an answer from among options you present to them (matching exercises, true-false items, or multiple-choice items).

There are two aspects of a student's performance that can be assessed: the **product** the student produces and the **process** a student uses to complete the product. Depending on the learning target, you may want to evaluate either or both of these aspects. In Chapter 12, you will read more about this distinction and learn how to craft tasks and rubrics that assess product and process. To effectively use the results of performance assessment, you must judge the quality of each student's performance. Most performance tasks have several levels or degrees of the correct response; others may have multiple correct responses. Further, because performance tasks are usually complex, each task offers you an opportunity to assess students on several learning targets or several parts of a performance.

Rubrics for Scoring   To guide your judgments and to ensure that you apply them consistently from one student to the next, you must use a rubric. A **scoring rubric** is a coherent set of rules you use to assess the quality of a student's performance. These rules may be in the form of a rating scale or a checklist. You usually use a scoring rubric to assess one learning target or one part of the performance. Complex performances require that you assess several learning targets or several parts of the performance. To do this, you need several scoring rubrics. You use each to assess different learning targets or parts of a learning target.

A *scale* consists of numerals, such as 0 to 3, or 1 to 4, that reflect the quality levels of performance. The numerals match the order of the quality levels. Thus, numeral 4 means the highest level, 3 the next highest, and so on. To guide you in scoring each student's performance, the quality of the performance at each numbered level is described in the rubric. Thus, each point is *anchored* by a verbal description of each level of quality. Figure 11.2 shows an anchored scoring rubric that is used with the task illustrated in Figure 11.1. The rubric in Figure 11.2 is used to evaluate only the content standard of the task. You would need to craft other rubrics to assess the remaining seven standards. Instead of verbal descriptions, examples or specimens of students' work may anchor each quality level of the rubric's scale. When examples are used as anchors, they serve as concrete illustrations of each quality level.

General and Specific Rubrics   You can assess each learning target in the curriculum with several different but equivalent tasks. Each equivalent task requires students to demonstrate their achievement of the same learning target but in a different way. As students practice and perform many different learning targets throughout the school year, their learning is enhanced if they apply the same general framework of evaluation standards to all of their work. Some research evidence supports this idea, that when students routinely use general, analytic trait criteria in the classroom their achievement improves (Khattri, Reeve, & Adamson, 1997).

The reliability and validity of your scores improves if you use a general scoring rubric as a guideline to craft specific scoring rubrics that you tailored to each task. In this way you are applying the same general framework in a consistent manner to each new performance task. This idea is shown in Figure 11.3.

A **general scoring rubric** is not specific to a particular task. It serves, however, as a general framework for developing the more specific rubrics. A **specific scoring rubric** is a scoring scale that applies the general scoring rubric to a particular task. By carefully applying the general scoring rubric when you craft a specific scoring rubric, you assure that your specific rubric assesses students in a way that is consistent with the general scoring framework. Figure 11.2 shows a general and a specific scoring rubric that a history teacher used to assess students' performance on the decision-making task in Figure 11.1.

Improving Teaching

If you teach your students how to perform tasks, you may improve both your own teaching and the validity of your

---

FIGURE 11.2   General and specific rubrics for a declarative knowledge learning target in history.

Declarative knowledge content standard being assessed: Understands that war forces sensitive issues to the surface and causes people to confront inherent conflicts of values and beliefs.

General rubric for declarative knowledge	Specific rubric adapted for this content
4 Demonstrates a thorough understanding of the generalized concepts and facts specific to the task or situation. Provides new insights into some aspect of that information.	4 Demonstrates a thorough understanding of the generalization that war forces sensitive issues to surface and causes people to confront inherent conflicts of values. Provides new insights into people's behavior during wartime.
3 Displays a complete and accurate understanding of the generalizations, concepts, and facts specific to the task or situation.	3 Displays a complete and accurate understanding of the generalization that war forces sensitive issues to the surface and causes people to confront inherent conflicts of values.
2 Displays an incomplete understanding of the generalizations, concepts, and facts specific to the task or situation and has some notable misconceptions.	2 Displays an incomplete understanding of the generalization that war forces sensitive issues to surface and causes people to confront inherent conflicts of values and has some notable misconceptions about this generalization.
1 Demonstrates severe misconceptions about the generalizations, concepts, and facts specific to the task or situation.	1 Demonstrates severe misconceptions about the generalization that war forces sensitive issues to surface and causes people to confront inherent conflicts of values.

FIGURE 11.3 Relationships between learning targets, tasks, specific scoring rubrics, and general scoring rubrics.

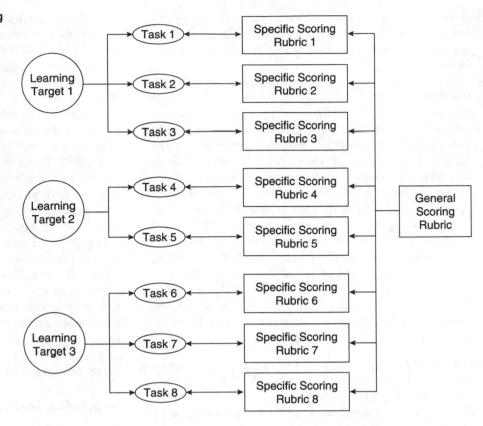

student assessment results. When you require students to complete a well-crafted performance task, you give them the opportunity to apply their learning to a specific realistic situation. The right kind of performance task may help students make connections between the skills and abilities they learned in separate subjects. For example, students must integrate skills and abilities in language arts, mathematics, science, and social studies when they conduct, analyze, and write up a survey of students' opinions in their school. Performance tasks may also help students to realize the connections between "schoolhouse" learning and "real-world" activities. This realization is likely when performance tasks are the same as those people use in real life (planning a trip using a map, using a bus timetable, and making a travel budget) or tasks that involve current events (comparing local politicians' points of view as expressed in speeches, advertisements, and daily newspapers).

As we pointed out previously, however, to improve their performance students must understand the criteria against which the quality of their performance is to be evaluated. As we discussed in Chapter 6 (see Table 6.1), when you share your scoring rubrics with students, you clarify the learning targets for them. The more students understand about the skills and abilities they should demonstrate in the performance, the more able they become in identifying where they should focus their practice and study efforts. Performance assessments in themselves, however, are no guarantee that learning will occur. You need to provide good instruction.

Improving Validity

When part of your evaluation of students is based on performance assessment results, the validity of your evaluations may also be improved. The validity of results depends most heavily on the (1) match of your assessments to the learning targets and (2) extent to which your assessments include the breadth of learning specified in a curriculum.

The first way to improve the validity of your assessment results is to properly craft performance tasks that will require students to use curriculum-specified thinking processes. Once students begin performing these tasks, you can evaluate them. Second, use many different types of assessment procedures (some of which are performance assessments) to begin to sample the breadth of your state's standards and the curriculum's learning targets. If your evaluations are based only on one type of assessment format (e.g., if you rely only on performance tasks), you are likely to have an incomplete picture of each student's learning. *You increase the validity of your assessment results by using information gathered from multiple assessment formats*: short-answer items, objective items, and a variety of long-term and short-term performance tasks.

AUTHENTIC ASSESSMENTS

Performance assessment is sometimes called **alternative assessment** or **authentic assessment**. These terms are not interchangeable, however. The *alternative* in alternative assessment usually means in opposition to standardized achievement tests and to multiple-choice (true-false, matching, completion) item formats. From an educational philosophy perspective, the *authentic* in authentic assessment usually means presenting students with tasks that are directly educationally meaningful instead of indirectly meaningful. For example, reading several long works and using them to compare and contrast different social viewpoints is directly meaningful because it is the kind of thoughtful reading educated citizens do. Reading short paragraphs and answering questions about the "main idea" or about what the characters in the passage did, on the other hand, is indirectly meaningful because it is only one fragment or component of the ultimate learning target of realistic reading. *Realistic* and *meaningful* are terms educators writing about authentic assessment often use. As we shall discuss later, these terms also beg further questions, such as, "Realistic in which context?" and "Meaningful for whom?"

Reviews of the authentic assessment literature (Baron, 1991; Horvath, 1991; Jones, 1994) suggest that you should incorporate the following four features when you craft authentic assessments:

1. *Emphasize applications*: Assess whether a student can *use* his knowledge in addition to assessing what the student *knows*.

2. *Focus on direct assessment*: Assess the stated learning target *directly* as contrasted with indirect assessment.

3. *Use realistic problems*: Frame the tasks in a highly *realistic* way so that the students can recognize them as a part of everyday life.

4. *Encourage open-ended thinking*: Frame the tasks to encourage more than one correct answer, more than one way of expressing the answer, groups of students working together, and taking a relatively long time to complete (e.g., several days, weeks, months).

MULTIPLE-INTELLIGENCES PERSPECTIVE ON PERFORMANCE ASSESSMENTS

Theory of Multiple-Intelligences

In some schools teachers organize their teaching around Howard Gardner's (1983, 1991, 1993) **theory of multiple intelligences**. This theory says that all persons have not one, but eight intelligences, although some persons are stronger in some of these areas than others. These intelligences are briefly described in Table 11.1.

These particular capacities were selected as intelligences because they fit certain criteria. They are (1) necessary for

TABLE 11.1 Summary of the eight intelligences described in Gardner's work.

Intelligence Type	Description
Linguistic intelligence	Capacity to use your own and other languages to express yourself and to understand others.
Logical-mathematical intelligence	Capacity to understand underlying causal principles in ways similar to scientists or logicians, or to use quantitative and mathematical reasoning in ways similar to mathematics.
Spatial intelligence	Capacity to represent the spatial aspects of the world in your mind in ways similar to airplane pilot navigators, chess players, painters, sculptors, or architects.
Bodily kinesthetic intelligence	Capacity to use part or all of your body to solve a problem, make a product, or perform in ways similar to athletes, actors, or dancers.
Musical intelligence	Capacity to mentally process music in a way that recognizes patterns, remembers patterns, and manipulates music to solve problems or to express understanding.
Interpersonal intelligence	Capacity to understand and meaningfully relate to other people. This is accomplished through understanding other persons: what they are able to do, how they approach the world and others, what their reactions are likely to be, what they like, what they avoid, and what they might be feeling.
Intrapersonal intelligence	Capacity to understand yourself, knowing who you are, your strengths and limitations, your goals and aspirations, how you feel, what you should avoid, and how you will react in various situations.
Naturalist intelligence	Capacity to understand nature and the modern world by discriminating among and classifying living and nonliving natural things, as well as among human-made things.

Source: Paraphrased and adapted from Howard Gardner's statements in Checkley (1997). The first seven. . . and the eighth: A conversation with Howard Gardner. *Educational Leadership, 55*(1), 12.

our survival, (2) evolutionary capacities (i.e., existing to some extent in nonhuman animals), and (3) detected by specific brain activities. This theory has inspired an educational philosophy and numerous classroom practices that teach students to (1) be aware that they can be smart in several different ways; (2) appreciate the value of different intelligences in themselves and others; (3) use, practice, and improve all of their intelligences to the best of their ability; and (4) demonstrate their achievement of learning targets by using two or more intelligences (Campbell, 1997).

Using Assessment Menus

It is not my purpose to endorse or even expand on this educational approach. However, the advocates of this approach value using performance assessments. They believe performance assessments have the potential of permitting students' achievements to be demonstrated and evaluated in several different ways. As Gardner says, "The current emphasis on performance assessment is well supported by the theory of multiple intelligences. . . One, let's not look at things through the filter of a short-answer test. Let's look instead at the performance that we value, whether it is linguistic, logical, aesthetic, or social performance; and, two, let's never pin our assessments of understanding on just one particular measure, but let's always allow students to show their understanding in a variety of ways" (Checkley, 1997).

If you wish to assess in a way that is consistent with this educational approach, you would need to hold high standards for students' achievement of learning targets, and at the same time allow students to demonstrate that achievement in multiple ways. Figure 11.4 shows one example of a **multiple-intelligences assessment menu**. Within each type of intelligence the menu contains several suggestions for different performances a student might select to demonstrate her achievement of the learn-

FIGURE 11.4 Example of a multiple-intelligences assessment menu. Students are allowed to demonstrate their achievement of learning targets by choosing an assessment model from one or more of the intelligences categories.

Multiple Intelligences Menus

Linguistic Menu

Use storytelling to explain _____

Conduct a debate on _____

Write a poem, myth, legend, short play, or news article
  about _____

Create a talk show radio program about _____

Conduct an interview of _____ on _____

Logical-Mathematical Menu

Translate a _____ into a mathematical formula

Design and conduct an experiment on _____

Make up syllogisms to demonstrate _____

Make up analogies to explain _____

Describe the patterns or symmetry in _____

Others of your choice _____

Bodily-Kinesthetic Menu

Create a movement or sequence
  of movements to explain _____

Make task or puzzle cards for _____

Build or construct a _____

Plan and attend a field trip that will _____

Bring hands-on materials to demonstrate _____

Visual Menu

Chart, map, cluster, or graph _____

Create a slide show, videotape, or photo album of _____

Create a piece of art that demonstrates _____

Invent a board or card game to demonstrate _____

Illustrate, draw, paint, sketch, or sculpt _____

Musical Menu

Give a presentation with appropriate musical
  accompaniment on _____

Sing a rap or song that explains _____

Indicate the rhythmical patterns in _____

Explain how the music of a song is similar to _____

Make an instrument and use it to demonstrate _____

Interpersonal Menu

Conduct a meeting to address _____

Intentionally use _____ social skills to learn about _____

Participate in a service project to _____

Teach someone about _____

Practice giving and receiving feedback on _____

Use technology to _____

Intrapersonal Menu

Describe qualities you possess that will help you
  successfully complete _____

Set and pursue a goal to _____

Describe one of your personal values about _____

Write a journal entry on _____

Assess your own work in _____

Naturalist Menu

Create observation notebooks of _____

Describe changes in the local or global environment _____

Care for pets, wildlife, gardens, or parks _____

Use binoculars, telescopes, microscopes,
  or magnifiers to _____

Draw or photograph natural objects _____

Source: Campbell, L. (1997). Variations on a theme: How teachers interpret MI theory. *Educational Leadership,* *55*(1), 14–18 (figure on page 18). Educational Leadership, Association for Supervision and Curriculum Development, Alexandria, VA.

ing target. Advocates of the approach would ask students to demonstrate their achievement by using one method from each of two or more intelligences (e.g., Campbell, 1997; Silver, Strong, & Perini, 1997).

Concerns About Validity

You should be aware that although much has been written about this approach to teaching, there is very little sound research to demonstrate the validity of the assessment in the way that validation was described in Chapter 3. If you read the testimonies of the enthusiasts, you will see very useful and interesting performance activities. Students will no doubt enjoy engaging in these activities. Often, however, well-crafted criteria are either not provided or only vaguely described. Often, too, the enthusiast has not described the specific curriculum learning targets for which the activity is specifically designed. Gardner himself advocates that teachers use combinations of intelligences to help students be successful in school-based learning targets, rather than teaching only the intelligences themselves (Checkley, 1997). This point is sometimes lost in discussions of the assessment part of multiple-intelligences teaching.

Other validity issues that have not been addressed are the generalization and meaning of students' assessment results from different menu formats in Figure 11.4. It should be clear to you that each of the entries in the menu is qualitatively different—the activities are not equivalent; they cannot be simply interchanged. Although students *can* use different demonstrations, do the different demonstrations address the same learning target in the same way? Are the modalities of the different formats such that some of them do not assess the main intent of the particular leaning target in which you are interested? It is unclear also whether the same standards and criteria can (or should) apply across modalities. Would the same criteria or same scoring rubric apply, for example, to a student's movement sequence that explains when an airplane should begin its landing descent from 30,000 feet as would singing a rap song for the same explanation? [For further discussion of this point, see the "Response Mode" section on page 272 in Chapter 12.]

Finally, there is the issue of who will craft the scoring rubrics and the tasks themselves. It is one matter to have students select from among several well-crafted tasks that have been carefully prepared to be equivalent demonstrations of a learning target. It is another to expect students to develop their own assessment tasks and scoring rubrics.

Performance Activities vs. Performance Assessment

The area of multiple intelligences is a good one to demonstrate the differences between performance learning experiences on one hand and performance assessment on the other. Assessment is not just the activity. Good assessment requires that criteria and scoring rubrics be well defined and validly applied across students. The assessment describes how well a student has achieved. Learning experiences do not have such requirements. If students and teachers enjoy them, and through engaging in several activities, students learn something, the activities are successful. Appropriate assessment is needed, however, before one can determine specifically how well each student has achieved the learning targets.

Suggestion for Improving Validity

If you wish to use performance assessments in a multiple-intelligences program, you will need to worry about the validity of your assessment results. I suggest that you specify very clearly the particular academic standards and exact learning targets that will be taught by this approach. Use multiple methods of assessment as is consistent and appropriate with the intentions of the approach. However, be very clear about the criteria and scoring rubrics. Perhaps it will be appropriate to use the same scoring rubrics to evaluate the academic learning target for all ways of assessment a student chooses from the menu. You may need to craft the performance tasks for students in order to obtain the information you need to evaluate the student, rather than relying on student-crafted tasks. It may be useful to have a common performance task that all students do and then allow for alternatives after that. Keeping one task common will help you to decide its weakness and the value-added information for a student which comes from the alternatives.

TYPES OF PERFORMANCE ASSESSMENTS

Many types of tasks fit the broad definition we adopted here. Table 11.2 lists most of these. In the paragraphs that follow, we describe them and give some examples.

Structured, On-Demand Tasks

You can assess your students' performance in many different settings, including those in which you exercise control over both the tasks to which and circumstances under which your students must respond. In this case, you are using **structured tasks or exercises**: You decide what and when materials should be used, you specify the instructions for performance, you describe the kinds of outcomes toward which students should work, you tell the students they are being assessed, and you give students opportunities to prepare themselves for the assessment. Such tasks are also called **on-demand** (or controlled) **tasks**.

In opposition to structured, on-demand performances are **naturally occurring performances**. You observe and assess students in natural settings: in typical classroom

TABLE 11.2 Types of performance assessment techniques.

A. Structured, On-Demand Tasks for Individual Students, Groups, or Both

   1. *Paper-and-pencil tasks*

     Examples: Solve this story problem and explain how you solved it; write a story about a typical day in Sally's life after you study the following graph that shows how she uses her time; draw a diagram to illustrate the mathematics ideas in a word problem.

   2. *Tasks requiring equipment and resources beyond paper and pencil*

     Examples: Build as many geometric figures as possible from a set of four triangles; talk on the telephone to ask about a job and request a job application; show how to mix acid and water.

B. Naturally Occurring or Typical Performance Tasks

   Examples: Observe a student's way of dealing with peer conflicts on the playground; summarize the grammatical and spelling errors students make when writing social studies and science assignments; observe whether a student makes change correctly when running the refreshment booth at the school fair.

C. Longer-Term Projects

   1. *Individual student projects*

     Examples: Collect and classify newspaper and magazine advertisements; build a small piece of furniture; build a working model of a camera.

   2. *Group projects*

     Examples: Conduct, analyze, and write up a sample survey of students in the school concerning one or more moral issues; design, plan, and build a model city using a set of geometric forms so that the overall cost of the city stays within the budget assigned.

   3. *Combining group and individual projects*

     Example: The group plans, conducts, and analyzes the survey data as described above, then each student writes an individual report describing how the survey was conducted and offers his or her own interpretation of the results.

D. Portfolios

   1. *Best-work portfolios*

     Example: Select your best writing in each of several categories (such as poems, narrative writing, letters) and describe why each piece was included.

   2. *Growth and learning-progress portfolios*

     Example: Develop a portfolio to show how your writing has developed over the semester; include early drafts, rewrites, your own criticism of earlier work, and your evaluation of how your writing has improved.

---

settings, while on the playground, or while at home. In these settings you are likely to see the way a student typically performs on a learning target, such as cooperating with members of a group to achieve a goal. In natural settings you do not tell students they are being assessed, nor do you control the situation in any way.

Although a naturally occurring setting may let you assess a student's typical performance, this is not always the case. In natural settings you have *to wait for the opportunity to arise* for a particular student to perform the particular activity you would like to assess. This waiting lowers the efficiency of this mode of assessment.

Paper-and-Pencil Tasks　In Chapters 7, 9, and 10 we discussed constructed response and essay items. These formats permit students not only to record their answers but also to give explanations, articulate their reasoning, and express their own approaches toward solving a problem. Sometimes your main focus is on the written *product* itself, such as the poem, report, or drawing a student creates. At other times, you may be more interested in the

process the student uses (for example, when a student records the steps he used to complete an experiment or explains how he solved a problem).

When setting **paper-and-pencil tasks**, you should distinguish between closed-response tasks and open-response tasks (see Collis, 1991). You use a **closed-response task** when you set the question so that you constrain a student's answer to a rather limited set of responses. You set an **open-response task** when students may provide alternative acceptable answers that might be expressed in a variety of ways. Examples are shown in Figures 11.5 and 11.6.

Tasks Requiring Other Equipment and Resources　For many learning targets, performance tasks should not focus on using only paper and pencil. In subjects such as mathematics, science, mechanical drawing, art, first aid and life-saving, home economics, and driver's education, important outcomes require students to do something with equipment and resources rather than write about how to do it. In some academic subjects, performing a **non-paper-**

TABLE 11.2 *(continued)*

E. **Demonstrations**

Example: Demonstrate how to collect, mount, organize, and display insect specimens; perform one or more piano solos to demonstrate your command of the instrument and music selections.

F. **Experiments**

Example: Conduct a series of studies to determine how erosion of soil by water run-off could be controlled; vary the typeface, layout, and color scheme of an advertisement in a study to determine which combinations are most effective in drawing the attention of the reader.

G. **Oral Presentations and Dramatizations**

Example: Two students play roles to argue for and against a local proposition that will come before the voters in the next election; act out the parts of various political leaders to demonstrate how their ideologies differ; act out the planetary system to dramatize rotation, revolution, speed, size, and distance.

H. **Simulations and Contrived Situations**

1. *Actors and "standardized patients"*

Example: An actor is trained to show certain symptoms and act as a patient, and the candidate interviews and examines the actor to diagnose the illness and prescribes treatment; a counselor plays the role of a job interviewer, and each student is "interviewed" for the job, demonstrating competence in handling questions and presenting himself or herself favorably.

2. *Computerized adaptive audio-visual scenarios*

Example: A computer presents a short video describing an experimental situation in a chemistry lab and pauses while the student selects an option as to what the next step in the process should be. Depending on what option is selected, the computer presents a different video sequence showing the consequences of the student's choice, then pauses, offering additional options and courses of action. The process continues until the experiment is complete.

3. *Computerized adaptive text scenarios*

Example: Similar to (2) above except the situation is described by words and displayed on a computer screen.

4. *Computerized audio-visual simulations*

Example: In a flight simulator a pilot must fly and take action in "real-time" under a variety of simulated weather and geographic conditions to assess what decisions the pilot makes. The relationships between the conditions presented, past pilots' actions, and the consequences are known in advance so that the ability of the pilot to avoid air tragedies can be assessed.

---

and-pencil task might be a more direct and preferred option than using a written response, even though either could be done.

For example, in elementary school general science, you would directly assess students' understanding and use of the metric system if you required them to actually measure objects, volume, mass, and so on. You use indirect assessment if you require students only to perform conversions from one system or unit of measurement to another or to answer questions based on pictures of measuring equipment. You could assess students' estimation skills, measuring skills, and systematic thinking skills, for example, by giving students a jar of beans and some simple tools. After giving students suitable directions, you can observe how the students solve the problem of estimating the number of beans in the jar. (See Figure 1.3 for an example.)

You may use non-paper-and-pencil tasks to present problems to be solved by a group, an individual, or some combination of group and individual work. In the latter case, the group may work cooperatively on the task; after

the group solves the problem, individuals describe or write up what the group did and the solution to the problem. Non-paper-and-pencil tasks may also be open response, allowing for alternative correct performances, or closed, allowing only one best or correct answer. An example of an open-response, non-paper-and-pencil performance task is given in Figure 11.7.

Naturally Occurring or Typical Performance Tasks

Instead of creating a task and controlling the assessment situation, you could wait for a performance to occur naturally, assessing it at that point. For example, you could collect all pieces that each student wrote in every subject and analyze them for grammatical, spelling, and syntactic errors to determine a student's typical language usage (at least in school assignments). This technique is very difficult and time-consuming for you, however. Further, it is unlikely to provide you with all the information you need to determine a student's command of even the mechanics

FIGURE 11.5   Sample open-response item.

Question: Why do birds fluff up their feathers in winter?

Student Responses	Comment
"To be bigger." "To frighten away other birds." "To attract a mate."	The responses are not relevant because the students have ignored the important context: "in winter."
"To keep warm." "To keep the cold air away from their bodies." "To make a blanket for themselves."	These responses are better than the first set because the students used one relevant fact as their complete answer.
"The outside air is freezing and the fluffed feathers trap warm air and keep it near their bodies." "Fluffed feathers hold warm air and insulate their bodies from the cold air outside."	These responses are even better because the students used two relevant facts and put them into a logical sequence.
"Birds need to keep their body temperature up and so they have to insulate themselves from the cold environment. Fluffing their feathers enables them to keep air, that is warmed by their bodies, close to them and also insulates them from the cold surroundings. Air is a good insulator. Fluffed feathers act as a blanket."	This response is at a higher level, showing the student can recall several relevant basic facts, relate them, and integrate them into a complete response.
"There is more to this question than what the words say. Birds in tropical climates do not need to fluff their feathers in winter since the air and their body temperatures are very much alike. In northern climates, there is a large difference between the air temperature and the birds' body temperatures. In this case . . ."	This response is more extended and abstract than the others. The student throws some doubt on the generalization implied by the question by citing a case in which that generalization may be untrue. However, the student goes on to complete the answer for birds in "northern climates," citing and integrating several relevant facts as in the previous response.

Source: Adapted from *Assessment of the Learned Structure in Elementary Mathematics and Science* (pp. 7–8) by K. F. Collis, 1991, a paper presented at the Assessment in the Mathematical Sciences Conference, Victoria. Adapted by permission.

FIGURE 11.6   Sample closed-response item.

This is a machine that changes numbers. When you put a number in, it adds that number to itself three times, then it adds 2. So, if you put in 4, it puts out 14.

(Picture of the machine is not shown, but would appear here)

1. If 14 is put out, what number was put in?
2. If you put in a 5, what number will the machine put out?
3. If I got out a 41, what number did I put in?
4. X is the number that comes **out** of the machine. Y is the number that goes **into** the machine. Write a formula that gives the value of Y whenever X is put in.

Comments

1. Question 1 requires simply understanding the problem well enough to find the information.
2. Question 2 requires understanding the problem well enough to follow it like a recipe.
3. Question 3 requires using all the information plus being able to extract the rule and to use it in reverse.
4. Question 4 requires extracting the rule, then expressing it in an abstract form (i.e., as a formula). It requires recognizing that the formula must express the reverse of the rule stated in the stem and so may require solving an equation in one unknown.

Source: Adapted from *Assessment of the Learned Structure in Elementary Mathematics and Science* (pp. 12–13) by K. F. Collis, 1991, a paper presented at the Assessment in the Mathematical Sciences Conference, Victoria. Adapted by permission.

FIGURE 11.7 Example of a science task requiring resources beyond paper and pencil.

Task description: Students must find one or more methods that remove most things from dirty water.

Equipment/resources for each student: 3 clear plastic graduated cups, 2 clear plastic cups, 30 cc of aquarium charcoal, 30 cc of clean aquarium sand, 4 cotton balls, pencils, transparent tape, paper sacks, a student booklet containing an outline and a space for answers.

Equipment/resources for the class: Mixture of $1/4$ cup vinegar, about 30 drops of blue food coloring, and $1/2$ cup of potting soil; one-gallon container to hold the mixture; water to fill the container; wall clock or watches with sweep second hand.

Directions in booklet: The owner of Finny Fishes Pet Store wants to use some water from a pond in the store's aquariums. The water is not very clean. The owner needs your help to find a method that will take the most things out of dirty water. You will need to keep records to show the owner of Finny Fishes Pet Store. [The booklet provides spaces for students to record (a) questions they need to ask to solve the problem, (b) the procedures they use, (c) diagrams and explanatory drawings, (d) the measures they made and data they collected, and (e) a report of the experiment.]

Directions from teacher: The teacher reviews the materials and booklet; demonstrates how to make one type of filter; encourages asking many different questions, making different types of filters, recording observations and data, and experimenting with different ways of solving the problem; and assures students that they are being assessed on how they go about solving the problem rather than on finding a single right answer.

Scoring: Scoring is both holistic and analytic. The analytic scoring includes separate scores for experimenting, collecting data, drawing conclusions, and communicating.

of writing. Not all spelling patterns and forms of sentence structure a student needs to learn, for example, are likely to appear in every student's writings. Thus, you would have no way of thoroughly assessing students' comprehensive use of sentence structures.

This simple example illustrates the difficulty of using naturally occurring events as a major source of assessment tasks. Here are the major shortcomings:

- A lot of your time is consumed by waiting.
- You have little control over what performances will occur and when they will occur.
- You cannot ensure that all students will perform the same task.
- You cannot ensure that all students will perform a task under desirable or even similar conditions.
- Teacher time is used inefficiently.

Longer-Term Projects

Individual Student Projects   An **individual student project** is a long-term student activity that results in a student product: a model, a functional object, a substantial report, or a collection. Craft projects so they require your students to apply and integrate a wide range of abilities and knowledge. When a student writes a library research paper, for example, the student must apply the skills of locating and using reference materials and sources: outlining, organizing, and planning a report; communicating using written language, word processing, and presentation style; and demonstrating his understanding of the topic about which he is writing. She may also engage in critical thinking, creative thinking, and problem solving (see Chapter 10).

Projects often require creativity, originality, and some sense of aesthetics. They require students to present the final product or report in a way that communicates effectively.

Projects are usually worthwhile educational activities. Their usefulness as *assessment tools* for individual students, however, depends on four conditions. You must assure that (1) you and your students are very clear that the project focuses on one or more important curriculum learning targets, (2) each student does his or her own work, (3) each student has equal access to the resources needed to prepare an excellent final product and to achieve an excellent evaluation, (4) you can control your own biases toward certain types of products and fairly evaluate other well-done projects. Middle- and upper-middle-class students with highly educated parents, for example, often have access to more resources than their less fortunate peers. You may tend to evaluate such students' projects more highly because they used these resources and produced very good-looking products. However, by so doing you may be biasing your evaluations toward certain social classes of students.

Similarly, if you are subconsciously predisposed to favor certain types of projects, reports, or formats over others, you may assess some students unfairly. Consider the following true story:

> Veronica, a student, labored long and hard building a working model of a camera for an elementary school science project fair. She learned a great deal about

cameras and could explain very well how a camera worked. As she proudly prepared to bring her model camera to school, her father, who had seven other children attend the same elementary school, called her aside and said, "I know you worked hard, Veronica, and I am proud of what you learned about cameras. However, I don't want you to be disappointed. I want you to realize that the Exploding Volcano Project[1] *always* wins the science project fairs!" And sure enough, it did! [Nitko, personal communication, 1995]

You can overcome these limitations by carefully planning for using them as educational **assessment tasks**, rather than only as **classroom activities**. The following guidelines should help you plan:

1. *Explicitly define the most important learning targets for which the project will provide you with a direct assessment opportunity.*

2. *Identify specific characteristics and qualities of the final project that are most strongly linked to the learning target that you are evaluating.* Evaluate students only on these qualities.

3. *Define a continuum of levels of quality for each characteristic.* Use the student's location on this quality scale as your assessment.

4. *Define the scoring rubric you will use for evaluating each characteristic of each student's project.*

5. *Define the weight you will give each characteristic when you calculate the project grade.*

6. *Limit resources students may use to complete the project if students vary widely in their ability to access resources.*

Group Projects   These projects require two or more students to work together. The major purpose of a **group project** as an *assessment* technique is to evaluate whether students can work together in cooperative and appropriate ways to create a high-quality product. The learning targets on which a group project focuses depend on the subject matter and the level of the students you are assessing. For example, group projects may focus on: *action-oriented learning targets* (creating a newsletter), *student-interest-oriented learning targets* (writing a paper on a topic you're interested in), *subject-matter-oriented learning targets* (understanding how rivers are formed), or *interdisciplinary learning targets* (designing an ideal city) (Harmin, 1994).

Project Management   Because projects usually span several weeks, you must have a plan to manage them. Your classroom project *management goals* should include the fol-

lowing. They are useful for managing both group and individual projects used for assessment purposes:

1. *Monitor individual students to be sure they are making regular progress.*

2. *Mentor students to help them overcome operational problems that may be beyond their control* (e.g., a key person students were to interview for the project has become ill and cannot see them)

3. *Mentor students to keep them focused on completing the project.*

4. *Monitor the procedures and processes the students are using to assure they will be able to address the learning targets set for the project.*

The following suggestions focus on classroom project *management strategies* to help meet the goals:

1. *Clarify the outcome(s) you expect.* Be sure each student thoroughly understands both the purpose(s) of the project (the learning target being assessed) and what you expect the project to look like. Show and discuss examples of high-quality projects you saved from former students.

2. *Put your expectations in writing.* Distribute to and discuss with students a written description of what you expect in the way of a project, processes, and the major purpose of the project.

3. *Clarify the standards you will use to evaluate the project.* Explain and give students copies of the scoring rubrics you will be using to evaluate the project.

4. *Let students participate in setting standards.* Each student should internalize the quality standards and have a sense of ownership of them. Use past projects to help students induce quality dimensions. Help students to describe the quality levels within each dimension.

5. *Clarify deadlines.* Set deadlines that are long enough so students can develop and complete authentic projects. However, make the timeframe short enough to be practical and so that students must keep on task, have no time to waste, and finish on time.

6. *Require progress reports.* For longer projects, specify weekly or biweekly dates for students to report their progress (e.g., every Friday). This helps to keep the students on task and allows you to assess the processes they use and their progress toward completing the project. (We discuss process vs. product assessment in Chapter 12.) It also alerts you to any problems beyond student control that may require your intervention.

[1]In case you have forgotten, the Exploding Volcano consists of a papier mache volcano with a cup of vinegar at the top. Baking soda is added to the vinegar to create an eruption effect.

7. *Minimize plagiarism opportunities.* Each student should do his or her work to the best of their ability. Explain to students what constitutes plagiarism. Explain the seriousness of doing one's own work even though it is not perfect. Avoid using projects and descriptive language that may inadvertently encourage students to plagiarize material. Projects that help to reduce the students' temptation to copy include interviews, comparing opinions, making models, designing ideal projects, locating contrasting views on an issue, producing an object, and creating a dramatization for another group or class (Harmin, 1994).

An example of a group project is shown in Figure 11.8. Students' performance in this project is assessed along several dimensions or categories of standards as described in Table 2.4 and Appendix E. To actually assess students, you must develop scoring rubrics that are specific to the project (or adapt the rubrics from other sources).

Figure 11.9 contains a set of general scoring rubrics for assessing collaboration and cooperation while working with group tasks. Each of these rubrics and anchor points would need to be rewritten so they apply to the specific project at hand—as shown previously in Figure 11.2.

Combining Group and Individual Projects In a **combined group and individual project**, groups of students work on a long-term project together, and after the group activities are completed, individuals prepare their own reports without assistance from the other group members. The combination approach is useful when a project is complex and requires the collaborative talents of several students to complete in a reasonable timeframe, yet the learning target requires that individual students have the ability to prepare final reports, interpret results on their own, and so on. To assess students in this performance setting, you must prepare both group and individual standards and scoring rubrics.

FIGURE 11.8 Example of a group project in an American history course for students in middle school or high school.

Historical Investigation Task

In recent years, controversy has arisen over the status of Christopher Columbus. Was he a hero or villain? As we study Columbus, we will read from a number of resources penned by different historians that will present their views of Columbus.

In cooperative groups, choose at least two resources that describe conflicting reports of events that took place upon Columbus' "discovery" of the New World and during its settlement. Discuss the contradictions you find and try to determine why the historians reported events differently. Using the resources available, develop a clear explanation of the reasons for the contradictions or present a scenario that clears up the contradictions.

Your group will explain to the class *why* historians seem to report the same events differently. In addition, your group will offer to the class its ideas for resolving the contradictions. Your group's presentation to the class may be either a dramatization, panel discussion, or debate.

Your project will be due three weeks from today. Every Friday one member of your group will tell the class the progress you made on the project during the past week, any problems the group had in completing the assignment, and what the group plans to complete during the next week.

Each member of the group will be assessed on the standards that follow. You will be provided rubrics for each of the standards so you may see more clearly what the assessment will be.

Social Studies Content Standards
Your understanding that recorded history is influenced by the perspective of the historian.
1. Your understanding of the events surrounding Columbus' discovery and settlement of the New World.

Complex Thinking Standards: Historical Investigation
1. Your ability to identify and explain the confusion, uncertainty, or contradiction surrounding the past event.
2. Your ability to develop and defend a logical and plausible resolution to the confusion, uncertainty, or contradiction surrounding the past event.

Effective Communication Standards
1. Your ability to communicate for a variety of purposes.
2. Your ability to communicate in a variety of ways.

Collaboration Standards
1. Your ability to work with all the students in your group to complete the project successfully.
2. Your ability to contribute good ideas and resources for presenting the findings to the class.
3. Your ability to do several different kinds of activities to help the group complete the project successfully.

Source: Adapted from *Assessing Student Outcomes: Performance Assessment Using the Dimensions of Learning Model* (p. 60) by R. J. Marzano, D. Pickering, and J. McTighe, 1993, Alexandria, VA: Association for Supervision and Curriculum Development. Adapted by permission of McREL Institute, 2550 S. Parker Rd., Suite 500, Aurora, CO 80014. Telephone (303)337-0990. © 1993 by McREL Institute. All rights reserved.

FIGURE 11.9 Example of general scoring rubrics for four collaboration and cooperation standards.

Rubrics for Collaboration/Cooperation Standards

A. Works toward the achievement of group goals.
4   Actively helps identify group goals and works hard to meet them.
3   Communicates commitment to the group goals and effectively carries out assigned roles.
2   Communicates a commitment to the group goals but does not carry out assigned roles.
1   Does not work toward group goals or actively works against them.

B. Demonstrates effective interpersonal skills.
4   Actively promotes effective group interaction and the expression of ideas and opinions in a way that is sensitive to the feelings and knowledge base of others.
3   Participates in group interaction without prompting. Expresses ideas and opinions in a way that is sensitive to the feelings and knowledge base of others.
2   Participates in group interaction with prompting or expresses ideas and opinions without considering the feelings and knowledge base of others.
1   Does not participate in group interaction, even with prompting, or expresses ideas and opinions in a way that is insensitive to the feelings or knowledge base of others.

C. Contributes to group maintenance.
4   Actively helps the group identify changes or modifications necessary in the group process and works toward carrying out those changes.
3   Helps identify changes or modifications necessary in the group process and works toward carrying out those changes.
2   When prompted, helps identify changes or modifications necessary in the group process, or is only minimally involved in carrying out those changes.
1   Does not attempt to identify changes or modifications necessary in the group process, even when prompted, or refuses to work toward carrying out those changes.

D. Effectively performs a variety of roles within a group.
4   Effectively performs multiple roles within the group.
3   Effectively performs two roles within the group.
2   Makes an attempt to perform more than one role within the group but has little success with secondary roles.
1   Rejects opportunities or requests to perform more than one role in the group.

Source: From *Assessing Student Outcomes: Performance Assessment Using the Dimensions of Learning Model* (pp. 87–88) by R. J. Marzano, D. Pickering, and J. McTighe, 1993, Alexandria, VA: Association for Supervision and Curriculum Development. Reprinted by permission of McREL Institute, 2550 S. Parker Rd., Suite 500, Aurora, CO 80014. Telephone (303)337-0990. © 1993 by McREL Institute, All rights reserved..

Research on cooperative learning indicates that students' achievement is best when the learning setting requires both group goals and individual accountability:

> Two conditions are essential if the achievement effects of cooperative learning are to be realized. First, the cooperating groups must have a *group goal* that is important to them. For example, groups may be working to earn certificates or other recognition, to receive a few minutes extra of recess, or to earn bonus points on their grades (although I am philosophically opposed to having grades largely determined by team performance). . . . Second, the success of the group must depend on the individual learning of all group members. That is, there must be *individual accountability* as well as group accountability. For example, groups might be rewarded based on the average of their members' individual quiz scores. (Slavin, 1988, p. 31)

Assessment in this type of group and individual learning context requires assessing a group's joint success on the project as well as the degree to which individuals attained the learning targets.

Portfolios

For purposes of assessment, a **portfolio** is a limited collection of a student's work that is used to either present the student's best work(s) or demonstrate the student's educational growth over a given time span. A portfolio is not simply a collection of all of a student's work: The work(s) put into a portfolio are limited to those that best serve the portfolio's purpose. A portfolio is neither a scrapbook nor a "dumping ground" for all the student's accomplishments. Items included in a portfolio are carefully and deliberately selected so the collection as a whole accomplishes its purpose. Although there are other purposes for creating a portfolio, this chapter discusses only two *assessment purposes*[2]: presenting best work and demonstrating educational growth.

[2]Three other purposes for portfolios include (1) showcasing, in which the student selects his or her favorite work (Paulson, Paulson, & Meyer, 1991); (2) process documenting, in which the student places commentary and documentation as a long-term project undertaken (Wolf, 1989); and (3) demonstrating the composite achievement of a group of students (Arter & Spandel, 1992). See also Table 12.7.

Best-Work Portfolios   A **best-work portfolio** focuses on presenting for assessment a student's best final products. Examples include art portfolios, writing portfolios, and mathematics problem-solving portfolios. A student may create a best-work portfolio for course evaluation, certification, school or program admission, or placement in a certain level of a program or sequence of courses. Very often the contents of the best-work portfolio are prescribed. For example, to certify a student's accomplishment in art, educational authorities may require a drawing, a painting, a sculpture, a craft product, and one work in any medium of the student's own choosing. In mathematics, an educational authority may require that a student's portfolio contain a table of contents, a letter telling the portfolio evaluator about the entries included, and five to seven best works involving a variety of types of activities, tools, and topics (Kentucky Department of Education, 1993a).

Students need to learn how to create a best-works portfolio to present themselves in the best possible way. Among the portfolio-making skills students need to learn are deciding what they should try to communicate or accomplish through the portfolio; choosing the pieces to include in the portfolio; how best to present the pieces chosen; and matching the qualities of the pieces to the scoring rubrics that will be used. Table 11.3 presents hints to students for preparing a best-work portfolio in mathematics.

As with other forms of performance assessment, you assess best-work portfolios only after you have developed a scoring rubric. Scoring rubrics for portfolios usually apply to the entire portfolio rather than to each piece separately, but there are exceptions. Figure 11.10 shows one example of an **annotated holistic scoring rubric** for scoring the type of portfolio described in Table 11.3.

After reviewing a student's mathematics portfolio, the teacher classifies a student into one of four levels (novice, apprentice, proficient, and distinguished) based on the teacher's overall judgment of the level best supported by the evidence in the portfolio. To assist the teacher in reviewing and analyzing each portfolio, the form contains a

TABLE 11.3 Suggestions given to fourth-grade students on how to prepare their mathematics portfolios.

WHAT WORKS?	CHECK IT OUT!
Here are the types of pieces you should include in your portfolio: • investigations—studying a mathematical topic or doing a mathematical experiment • applications—using mathematics to solve real world problems • non-routine—combining or inventing problem-solving strategies to arrive at solutions or results • projects—completing problems that take several days or longer • interdisciplinary—using mathematics with other subjects • writing—writing about mathematics to explain your thinking or solution These pieces should also show that you can do these things: • understand ways to solve problems and do more with the problem (problem solving) • think by using mathematical ideas and prove your solution is correct by using logical explanations (reasoning) • Explain mathematics to others using mathematical language, symbols, and drawings (mathematical communication) • understand mathematical topics and use mathematics in other subjects and everyday life (understanding/connecting core concepts)	Ask yourself these questions when choosing pieces for your portfolio: • Did I solve the problem in different ways? • Have I done other things with the problem? • Is my answer correct and does it make sense? • Did I use correct mathematical language, symbols, and/or drawings? • Is my mathematics connected to other subjects and everyday life? • Have I listed the mathematical tools (calculators, blocks, beans, etc.) I used? • Did I explain my thinking and show all my work? • Does my explanation show that I understand mathematics? • Have I edited and corrected my work so this is my best effort? • Have I chosen different types of pieces for my portfolio? • Did I show all the mathematical topics (core concepts)? • If I chose a group entry, did I include my own ideas and explanations? • Have I talked with my teacher about the pieces in my portfolio?

Source: From *Portfolios and You* (p. 3) by the Kentucky Department of Education, 1993b, Frankfort, KY: Author. Reprinted by permission.

FIGURE 11.10   Example of an annotated holistic scoring rubric for a best-work portfolio.

KENTUCKY MATHEMATICS PORTFOLIO

HOLISTIC SCORING GUIDE

1993-94

An individual portfolio is likely to be characterized by some, but not all, of the descriptors for a particular level. Therefore, the overall score should be the level at which the appropriate descriptors for a portfolio are clustered.

		NOVICE	APPRENTICE	PROFICIENT	DISTINGUISHED
PROBLEM SOLVING	Understanding/Strategies	• Indicates a basic understanding of problems and uses strategies	• Indicates an understanding of problems and selects appropriate strategies	• Indicates a broad understanding of problems with alternate strategies	• Indicates a comprehensive understanding of problems with efficient, sophisticated strategies
	Execution/Extensions	• Implements strategies with minor mathematical errors in the solution without observations or extensions	• Accurately implements strategies with solutions, with limited observations or extensions	• Accurately and efficiently implements and analyzes strategies with correct solutions, with extensions	• Accurately and efficiently implements and evaluates sophisticated strategies with correct solutions and includes analysis, justifications, and extensions
REASONING		• Uses mathematical reasoning	• Uses appropriate mathematical reasoning	• Uses perceptive mathematical reasoning	• Uses perceptive, creative, and complex mathematical reasoning
MATHEMATICAL COMMUNICATION	Language	• Uses appropriate mathematical language some of the time	• Uses appropriate mathematical language	• Uses precise and appropriate mathematical language most of the time	• Uses sophisticated, precise, and appropriate mathematical language throughout
	Representations	• Uses few mathematical representations	• Uses a variety of mathematical representations accurately and appropriately	• Uses a wide variety of mathematical representations accurately and appropriately; uses multiple representations within some entries	• Uses a wide variety of mathematical representations accurately and appropriately; uses multiple representations within entries and states their connections
UNDERSTANDING/CONNECTING CORE CONCEPTS		• Indicates a basic understanding of core concepts	• Indicates an understanding of core concepts with limited connections	• Indicates a broad understanding of some core concepts with connections	• Indicates a comprehensive understanding of core concepts with connections throughout
TYPES AND TOOLS		• Includes few types; uses few tools	• Includes a variety of types; uses tools appropriately	• Includes a wide variety of types; uses a wide variety of tools appropriately	• Includes all types; uses a wide variety of tools appropriately and insightfully

PORTFOLIO CONTENTS
* Table of Contents
* Letter to Reviewer
* 5–7 Best Entries

BREADTH OF ENTRIES

TYPES
○ INVESTIGATIONS/DISCOVERY
○ APPLICATIONS
○ NON-ROUTINE PROBLEMS
○ PROJECTS
○ INTERDISCIPLINARY
○ WRITING

TOOLS
○ CALCULATORS
○ COMPUTER AND OTHER TECHNOLOGY
○ MODELS/MANIPULATIVES
○ MEASUREMENT INSTRUMENTS
○ OTHERS

○ GROUP ENTRY

WORKSPACE/ANNOTATONS

PERFORMANCE DESCRIPTORS

PROBLEM SOLVING
* Understands the features of a problem (understands the question, restates the problem in own words)
* Explores (draws a diagram, constructs a model and/or chart, records data, looks for patterns)
* Selects an appropriate strategy (guesses and checks, makes an exhaustive list, solves a simpler but similar problem, works backward, estimates a solution)
* Solves (implements a strategy with an accurate solution)
* Reviews, revises, and extends (verifies, explores, analyzes, evaluates strategies/ solutions; formulates a rule)

REASONING
* Observes data, records and recognizes patterns, makes mathematical conjectures (inductive reasoning)
* Validates mathematical conjectures through logical arguments or counter-examples; constructs valid arguments (deductive reasoning)

MATHEMATICAL COMMUNICATION
* Uses appropriate mathematical notation and terminology
* Provides quality explanations for the given task
* Expresses concepts, ideas, and reflections clearly
* Provides various mathematical representations (models, graphs, charts, diagrams, words, pictures, numerals, symbols, equations)

UNDERSTANDING/CONNECTING CORE CONCEPTS
* Demonstrates an understanding of core concepts
* Recognizes, makes, or applies the connections among the mathematical core concepts, to other disciplines, and to the real world

Place an X on each continuum to indicate the degree of understanding demonstrated for each core concept.

DEGREE OF UNDERSTANDING OF CORE CONCEPTS

	Basic			Comprehensive with connections
NUMBER				
MATHEMATICAL PROCEDURES				
SPACE & DIMENSIONALITY				
MEASUREMENT				
CHANGE				
MATHEMATICAL STRUCTURE				
DATA				

Source: From *Teacher's Guide: Kentucky Mathematics Portfolio* (p. 11) by Kentucky Department of Education, 1993c, Frankfort, KY: Office of Assessment and Accountability. Author. Reprinted by permission.

space for notes regarding performance descriptors, to rate the student's degree of understanding of core mathematics concepts, to record the tools the student used, and to record the types of activities included in the portfolio. This latter set of notes, ratings, and recordings is used when the teacher goes over the portfolio to give feedback to a student and to parents.

Growth and Learning-Progress Portfolios   A **growth and learning-progress portfolio** does not focus on the final products a student produces. Instead, you use the portfolio to monitor a student's learning and thinking progress, to diagnose learning and thinking difficulties, and to guide new learning and thinking. The student plays a significant role in deciding what should be included in this portfolio and learns to use the portfolio to understand and evaluate her own progress.

For you to assess a student's progress, the student must place into the portfolio records of intermediate progress. These may include early drafts, records of thinking, and rewrites. The final product is placed into the portfolio, too. A growth and learning-progress portfolio in arts, for example, may include samples of a student's artwork done over a two-year period. By reviewing work done over a long period of time, a student can reflect on changes in his styles, themes, and mastery of artistic technique. Similarly, a growth and learning-progress portfolio in science could include a student's scientific explanations of and thought about natural phenomena. These entries may be made at the beginning, middle, and end of the term. The

student may reflect on how her thinking and scientific understanding has grown over time. As another example, consider Table 11.4. It shows how one school district's language arts teachers organized their students' growth and learning-progress portfolios. Figure 11.11 shows one student's entry into this type of portfolio—the student's self-evaluation of progress.

For a growth and learning-progress portfolio to be effective, it must be carefully crafted. First, be very clear about the learning targets toward which you wish to monitor students' learning progress. The clearer you are, the better your portfolio system will be. Second, you must have a firm understanding of a learning progress theory. The theory you choose to follow will guide you to identify what you should look for when assessing changes in a student's conceptual development or in diagnosing a student's learning difficulties. Third, if several teachers in a school are committed to using growth and learning-progress portfolios, you should collaborate and work cooperatively with them. If teachers coordinate the general approach, contents to be included, and the portfolio organization, the students will not be confused and will receive a consistent message about the nature and purposes of their portfolio activities. Fourth, you must use some type of rubric to define assessment criteria and to help you to be consistent in how you apply these criteria, both across students and with the same student over time.

Growth and learning-progress portfolios, like other assessments, work best when integrated fully into your teaching. Some writers advocate making the portfolio the

TABLE 11.4   Example of how the Bellevue, Washington, teachers organized their students' reading and writing portfolios to assess growth.

Learning Target	What is put into the portfolio	Frequency of entry and assessment
1. Develop a meaningful ownership of one's own learning and work to be evaluated	1. (a) Student selected pieces of work (b) Entry slip explaining why each piece was included	1. Three or more times per year
2. Evaluate one's own progress over time	2. (a) Student reviews his or her own portfolio (b) Student answers questions about his or her development as a reader and writer	2. Two or more times per year
3. Interact with the text to create meaning	3. Entry slip retelling the piece read or explaining its meaning	3. Two or three times per year
4. Choose to read a variety of material	4. Log of books/articles read during a two-week period	4. Two or three times per year
5. Communicate effectively through writing	5. Samples of longer pieces of writing	5. Two or three times per year
6. Student develops as a reader and writer	6. (a) Student drafts, notes, and other work selected by the teacher (b) Teacher's notes and comments about the student's progress	6. Left to the teacher's discretion

Source: Adapted from "Literacy Portfolios for Teaching, Learning, and Accountability: The Bellevue Literacy Assessment Project" by S. W. Valencia and N. A. Place. In *Authentic reading assessment: Practices and possibilities* (pp.139–141) by Sheila W. Valencia, E. H. Hiebert, and Peter P. Afflerbach (Eds.), 1994, Newark, DE: International Reading Association. Adapted by permission of Sheila W. Valencia and the International Reading Association. All rights reserved.

FIGURE 11.11 Example of a middle-school student's portfolio entry after evaluating her own reading and writing progress over the year.

Name _____ Date 5-11-92

Self-Evaluation

Have you changed as a reader? What are your strengths and weaknesses? As I reader I haven't gone through many changes. My only weakness is getting into a book, but once I'm started my strengths take over me. I love to read!!!!

How have you changed as a writer? What are your strengths and weaknesses? As a writer I have relized that it takes many reworkings to come up with a final copy. Spelling is my main weakness and my strengths include sentence structure + punctuation.

Having looked at your work what goals would you set for yourself as a reader and writer? As a reader I plan to widen my spread of books and as a writer I'm going to look more deeply into my work.

Self-Reflection

When you look at your portfolio, how do you feel about yourself as a writer? Tell why you feel that way. I feel great about myself as a writer. I started off rather slow, but have improved 95%, since the start of this year + I plan to keep improving untill the end.

When you look at your portfolio, how do you feel about yourself as a reader? Tell why you feel that way. I feel extra great as a reader. I love reading + I love the feeling that I get when I finish a really good book.

Source: From "Literacy Portfolios for Teaching, Learning, and Accountability: The Bellevue Literacy Assessment Project" by S. W. Valencia and N. A. Place, in *Authentic Reading Assessment: Practice and Possibilities* (p. 146) by Shelia W. Valencia, E. H. Hiebert, and Peter P. Afflerbach (Eds.), 1994, Newark, DE: International Reading Association. Reprinted by permission of Shelia W. Valencia and the International Reading Association. All rights reserved..

center of your instructional planning and activities so you and your students will interact intensively with the portfolio contents. This is called the **portfolio culture model** of conceptual change (Duschl & Gitomer, 1991; Niyogi, 1995). In a portfolio culture, instructional activities and projects are opportunities for students to record their intermediate progress, their progressive understanding of concepts and phenomena, and their interactions with peers and teachers. Duschl and Gitomer suggest the work included must have certain characteristics in order to be useful in a portfolio culture educational setting that focuses on restructuring students' conceptual development. The following characteristics are consistent with their suggestions:

1. *Authentic work.* The work that a student includes in the portfolio must provide direct opportunity for him to actually engage in the types of thinking and abilities typically used by those working in the field or discipline. For example, in a science portfolio a student should work on evaluating evidence, using scientific explanations to account for data, or collecting data to support or refute explanations.

2. *Record conceptual development.* Portfolio entries must record a student's own explanations, understandings, and conceptual frameworks. This record must be updated as the student progresses through a project or a problem solution to show changes in the student's conceptual framework and thinking as the project develops. It is not enough to include only the finished work. For example, a student should periodically record in a science portfolio her current scientific explanation of the events encountered, results observed, and concepts being studied.

3. *Engage in reflective activity.* The student uses the portfolio contents as a basis for discussions with the teacher about his understanding of concepts, principles, and theories that underlie the work. The teacher guides the discussion so that the student uses the thinking strategies and abilities used by workers in the fields or discipline. For example, if the student is working on a scientific problem, she should use the portfolio contents to engage in scientific thinking and activities. The student may record her changes in explanations as new evidence accumulates.

Using these portfolios requires that you have significant knowledge, skill, and ability. Also, you need to be very well versed in the discipline for which you are assessing progress. You should notice, too, that this type of portfolio assessment activity is considerably more spontaneous and less formal than assessing with best-work portfolios. These characteristics are not necessarily weaknesses, because the portfolio is used with interactive instruction and as a formative evaluation tool.

Demonstrations

A **demonstration** is an on-demand performance in which a student shows he can use knowledge and skills to complete a well-defined, complex task. Demonstrations are not as long or as complex as projects. Demonstrations are usually closed-response tasks. The task(s) comprising a demonstration is often well defined and the "right or best way to do it" is often known to both the student and the evaluator. However, individual variations are permitted; style and manner of presentation often count when a student presents a demonstration. The 4-H Clubs often use demonstrations: Boys and girls demonstrate their skills in a variety of agricultural and homemaking areas.

In schools, students may demonstrate their skills in proper techniques of using equipment such as baking equipment or laboratory equipment; in looking up information in a library or on the Internet; or in climbing a rope in physical education classes. For the most part, demonstrations focus on how well a student uses her skills, rather than on how well the student can explain her thinking or articulate the principles underlying a phenomenon. If you use a demonstration for assessment purposes, you should carefully identify the appropriate learning target and use an appropriate scoring rubric.

Experiments

An **experiment** or *investigation* is an on-demand performance in which a student plans, conducts, and interprets the results of an empirical research study. The study focuses on answering specific research questions (e.g., "Do most students in this school support the death-penalty laws of this state?") or on investigating specific research hypotheses ("A brightly colored advertisement will be remembered longer"). As defined here, experiments or investigations include a wide range of research activities that occur in both natural and social science disciplines. They include field and survey research investigations as well as laboratory and control-group experiments and may be conducted as individual or as group activities.

Experiments or investigations let you assess whether students use proper inquiry skills and methods. You can also assess whether students have developed proper conceptual frameworks and theoretical, discipline-based explanations of the phenomena they have investigated. To assess these latter aspects, focus on the quality of students' frames of reference, their mental representations of the problem they are studying, how well they plan or design the research, the quality of the questions or hypotheses they can specify, and the quality of the explanations they offer for why the data relationships exist. To assess these abilities, your experiment or investigation task should require students to:

1. *Make estimates and predictions before they begin collecting data.*
2. *Gather their own data, analyze them, and display the results of the analyses.*
3. *Draw conclusions and support them by citing the appropriate evidence they collected.*
4. *State their assumptions and identify possible sources of error in their methods or data.*
5. *Effectively communicate the findings of the experiment or investigation.* (Barone, 1991)

Oral Presentations and Dramatizations

Oral presentations permit students to verbalize their knowledge and use their oral skills in the form of interviews, speeches, or oral presentations. Decide which learning targets are the focus of the oral presentations. In language and language-arts curricula, for example, many learning targets focus on style and communication skills rather than on the correctness of the content. Fluency is also an important learning target in these curricula. Figure 11.12 shows the major anchor points in the proficiency-level scale suggested for use in an oral proficiency interview.

FIGURE 11.12 Example of a description of competency levels for assessing oral proficiency in a foreign language.

Level	Description
Superior	The Superior level is characterized by the speaker's ability to • participate effectively in most formal and informal conversations on practical, social, professional, and abstract topics; and • support opinions and hypotheses using nature-like discourse strategies
Advanced	The Advanced level is characterized by the speaker's ability to: • converse in a clear, participatory fashion; • initiate, sustain, and bring to closure a wide variety of communicative tasks, including those that require an increased ability to convey meaning with diverse language strategies due to a complication or an unforeseen turn of events; • satisfy the requirements of school and work situations; and • narrate and describe with paragraph-length connected discourse
Intermediate	The Intermediate level is characterized by the speaker's ability to: • create with the language by combining and recombining learned elements, though primarily in a reactive mode; • initiate, minimally sustain, and close in a simple way basic communicative tasks; and • ask and answer questions
Novice	The Novice level is characterized by the ability to communicate minimally with learned material

Source: Adapted from *Oral proficiency interview: Tester training manual* by American Council on the Teaching of Foreign Languages, 1989, Yonkers, NY: Author. Adapted by permission.

Figure 11.13 is an example of a simple scale for assessing the delivery of a classroom speech.

Debates are a special type of oral performance. A debate pits one student against another to logically argue issues. Assessment focuses on the logical and persuasive quality of the argument and the rebuttals. Other forensic activities include poetry reading and oratories.

Dramatizations combine verbalizations, oral and elocution skills, and movement performances. Students may dramatize their understanding of fictional characters or historical persons, for example, by acting a role showing ideological positions and personal characteristics of these persons. Although dramatizations usually involve oral skills, occasionally they may not. For example, after reading about Huck Finn, a teacher could ask the student to pantomime the way Huck Finn might act in the classroom (Armstrong, 1994).

Simulations and Contrived Situations

Actors and "Standardized Patients" **Simulations** are on-demand events that happen under controlled conditions and that attempt to mimic naturally occurring events.

When the performance to be evaluated is the ability to interact with another person, an actor may be trained to play the role of the other person. Originally the **standardized patient format** was used to assess the clinical skills of medical candidates and practicing doctors. The actor is trained to display the symptoms of a particular disorder. Each medical candidate meets and interviews this standardized patient to diagnose the illness and to prescribe treatment. A panel of evaluators observes this interaction and assesses the candidate.

Computerized Adaptive Audiovisual Scenarios The combined technologies of video, CD-ROM, audio, and computers may be used to present realistic situations to students. Students' responses to these presentations are then evaluated by computer. If the situation presented is reasonably structured and the number of possible actions is limited, an **adaptive assessment task** can be built. For example, the technologies present a **scenario** to the student and ask a question or call for a decision. The student responds, and the presentation continues in a way that is dependent on the response of the student. In this way each student receives a somewhat different scenario, depending on his choices of action.

FIGURE 11.13 Example of a simple rating scale for assessing the quality of a student's oral presentation.

Rating Scale for Classroom Speech

Pupil's name _____ Date _____

Speech topic _____

1. Did the speech contain content meaningful to the topic?

1	2	3	4
Most of speech content not truly meaningful	Only about 50 percent of speech relevant	Most content relevant; occasional irrelevant idea	All content obviously and clearly related

2. Was the delivery smooth and unhesitating?

1	2	3	4
Long pauses and groping for words in almost every sentence	Pauses and groping for words in about 50 percent of sentences	Occasional pauses and groping for words	Delivery smooth; no pauses or groping for words

3. Did the speaker use correct grammar?

1	2	3	4
Errors in most sentences	Errors in about 50 percent of sentences	From 1 to 3 errors	No errors

4. Did the speaker look at his audience?

1	2	3	4
Looked away most of the time	Looked at audience only 50 percent of the time	Looked at audience most of the time	Looked continually at audience

Source: From C. M. Lindvall and A. J. Nitko (1975). *Measuring Pupil Achievement and Aptitude* (2nd ed.). New York: Harcourt Brace Jovanovich (p. 220). Reprinted by permission of the authors.

Computerized Adaptive Text Scenarios   This assessed format is similar to the adaptive audiovisual scenario format, except that text displays replace multimedia presentation.

Computerized Audiovisual Simulations   With rapid advances in technology and software, multimedia simulations have become more realistic and complex. In middle-school science, for example, computers can be used to simulate hands-on investigations (Shavelson & Baxter, 1991). In a sow bug investigation, students investigate what the "computer sow bugs" do when simulated light and moisture are varied. Virtual reality technology offers more promise in this area. Flight simulators are examples of how technology combines with a sophisticated knowledge base of the conditions of the live performance and the consequences of different actions.

The advantages of this and the preceding formats are greater economy and consistency compared to real life, and the potential for computerized scoring (Jones, 1994). The further away from actual situations and real people the simulation gets, the less realistic it is and less meaning it has. These are the principal disadvantages of these formats.

ADVANTAGES AND CRITICISMS

Authenticity and Direct Assessment of Learning Targets

Classroom Activities vs. Assessment Tasks   You now have a good idea of the wide range of performance assessment techniques. The proper technique to use depends very much on the learning targets you wish to assess. You should recognize, however, that *not all performance activities are assessment tasks*. When you teach, you craft many learning activities to engage students' interest, to give them experience, and to practice with the learning targets. Many of these activities are useful teaching tools and resemble the performance tasks described in the preceding section.

Performance tasks become assessment tools when you craft the tasks primarily for their value as assessment procedures rather than primarily as opportunities for student practice and enrichment. Assessments must also include criteria and a scoring rubric. This is not to say that performance assessment tasks should be radically different from practices and enrichment activities. However, you use assessment tasks primarily to gather information about students' progress on specific learning targets rather than as student learning activities for those targets. This distinction is similar to the formative and summative student evaluation distinction discussed in Chapter 6. That is, you can use all student activities as occasions for informally gathering formative information about students' progress, but summative evaluation requires more careful

focus on gathering high-quality information from tasks you create specifically for this purpose.

Authentic Characteristics   Performance assessment material you read outside of this textbook makes reference to authentic assessment. This usually means that students are assessed on tasks that are directly educationally meaningful. *Authentic tasks* have the following characteristics (Wiggins, 1990):

- They require students to use their knowledge to do a meaningful task.
- They are complex and require students to use combinations of different knowledge, skills, and abilities.
- They require high-quality polished, complete, and justifiable responses, performances, or products.
- They clearly specify standards and criteria for assessing the possibly multiple correct answers, performances, or products.
- They simulate the ways in which students should use combinations of knowledge, skills, and abilities in the real world.
- They present to students ill-structured "challenges and roles" that are similar to those roles and tasks they are likely to encounter as adults at work and at home.

Your review of the types of performance tasks in Table 11.2 shows that not all performance tasks have all of Wiggins' authenticity characteristics. Further, you should recognize that there are **degrees of authenticity**: tasks will vary in the degree to which they meet any one of the characteristics just described.

Valuable in Their Own Right   Rhetoric surrounding authentic assessment tasks often justifies them by criticizing formats such as multiple-choice, matching, true-false, and short-answer tasks (Hambleton & Murphy, 1992). Such discussions also criticize the use of standardized tests (see Chapter 16 for a summary of these criticisms). Educators who do not distinguish criticisms about how standardized tests are used from criticisms about the merits of using objective assessment tasks mislead and confuse you. Further, such "test bashing" often is unnecessary: Compelling arguments can be made for using performance assessment without putting down either objective tasks or standardized tests.

Advantages of Performance Assessment

Performance assessments have several advantages over other assessments. These advantages (Hambleton & Murphy, 1992; Linn & Gronlund, 1995; Oosterhof, 1994; Rudner & Boston, 1994; Shepard, 1991; Stiggins, 1994; Wiggins, 1990) are summarized here:

1. *Performance tasks clarify the meaning of complex learning targets.* Authentic performance tasks match such complex learning targets to a close degree. When you present

them to students and share them with parents, you make the learning goals clear through actual example.

2. *Performance tasks assess the ability "to do."* An important school outcome is the ability to use knowledge and skill to solve problems and lead a useful life, rather than to simply answer questions about doing.

3. *Performance assessment is consistent with modern learning theory.* Modern learning theory emphasizes that students should use their previous knowledge to build new knowledge structures, be actively involved in exploration and inquiry through task-like activities, and construct meaning for themselves from educational experience. This is called the *constructivist approach* to learning. Most performance assessments engage students and actively involve them with complex tasks. Many performance tasks require exploration and inquiry.

4. *Performance tasks require integration of knowledge, skills, and abilities.* Complex performance tasks, especially those that span longer periods of time, usually require students to use may different skills and abilities. Portfolio assessment, projects, and research reports, for example, require a student to use knowledge from several different subject areas and many different abilities.

5. *Performance assessments may be linked more closely with teaching activities.* When your teaching requires students to be actively involved in inquiry and performance activities, performance assessments are a meaningful component. This is not an advantage of performance assessment if your teaching is primarily teacher directed or uses lecture style.

6. *Performance tasks broaden the approach to student assessment.* Introducing performance assessment along with traditional objective formats broadens the types of learning targets you assess and offers students a variety of ways of expressing their learning.

7. *Performance tasks let teachers assess the processes students use as well as the products they produce.* Many performance tasks offer you the opportunity to watch the way a student goes about solving a problem or completing a task. Appropriate scoring rubrics help you to collect information about the quality of the processes and strategies students use, as well as to assess the quality of the finished product.

Disadvantages of Performance Assessments

Although performance assessments offer several advantages over traditional objective assessment procedures, they have some distinct disadvantages (Hambleton & Murphy, 1992; Linn & Gronlound, 1995; Miller &

Seraphine, 1993; Oosterhof, 1994; Rudner & Boston, 1994):

1. *High-quality performance tasks are difficult to craft.* Good performance assessments match complex learning targets. You will need to learn a significant number of skills to craft high-quality tasks. We discuss how to craft performance tasks in Chapter 12.

2. *High-quality scoring rubrics are difficult to craft.* This is especially true when you want to assess complex reasoning ability or want to permit multiple correct answers and products. Scoring rubric creation is also covered in Chapter 12.

3. *Completing performance tasks takes students a lot of time.* Even short on-demand paper-and-pencil tasks take 10 to 20 minutes per task to complete. Most authentic tasks take days or weeks to complete. If your assessments are not part of your instructional procedures themselves, this means either administering fewer tasks (thereby reducing the reliability of the results) or reducing the amount of instructional time.

4. *Scoring performance task responses takes a lot of time.* The more complex the performance and the product, the more time you can expect to spend on scoring. You can reduce the scoring time by crafting high-quality scoring rubrics. Holistic scoring is quicker than analytic scoring.

5. *Scores from performance tasks may have lower scorer reliability.* With complex tasks, multiple correct answers, and fast-paced performances, scoring depends on your own scoring competence. If two teachers use different frameworks, have different levels of competence, use a different scoring rubric, or use no scoring rubrics at all, they will mark the same student's performance or product quite differently. Inconsistent scoring is not only frustrating to a student, it lowers the reliability and validity of the assessment results. High levels of scorer reliability can be obtained, however, if scorers use the same well-defined rubrics, are well trained, and are monitored so they don't drift away from the standards set in the rubrics (Linn, 1993). Scorer reliability is especially problematic for portfolio assessment (Koretz, Stecher, Klein, and McCaffrey, 1994). This is not to say, however, that portfolio scorer reliability cannot be improved.

6. *Students' performance on one task provides little information about their performance on other tasks.* This results in low reliability from the content-sampling point of view. (See Chapter 4.) The fact that this type of reliability tends to be low for performance assessment is a more serious concern than low scorer reliability. A serious problem with performance assessments is that a student's perfor-

mance on a task very much depends on her prior knowledge, the particular wording and phrasing of the task, the context in which it is administered, and the specific subject-matter content embedded in the task (Shavelson & Baxter, 1991; Lane, Parke, & Moskal, 1992; Linn, 1993). In other words, you may have to use six or seven performance tasks to reliably evaluate a student in a unit of instruction.

The educational importance of these findings is this: *Whenever a learning target implies that a student should be able to perform several quite different tasks under varied conditions and in several contexts* (which is almost always!), *your assessment must include many different tasks, not just one.* The validity of your assessment results is low whenever you use too few tasks.

7. *Performance tasks do not assess all learning targets well.* If a learning target focuses on memorizing and recalling information, rules, generalizations, and theories, then objective format items such as short-answer, multiple-choice, matching, and true-false are better assessment choices. If your learning targets emphasize logical thinking, understanding concepts, or verbal reasoning, objective formats may still be a better choice than performance formats. They allow a much broader coverage of content to be assessed and can assess that broad coverage in a shorter period of time. Further, objective formats are easier to score and the results from them are more reliable. A balanced assessment approach is recommended.

8. *Completing performance tasks may be discouraging to less able students.* Complex tasks that require students to sustain their interest and intensity over a long period of time may discourage less able students. They may see the high standards implied by such tasks as beyond their reach. They may have partial knowledge of the learning target but may fail to complete the task because it does not allow them to use or express this partial knowledge effectively. Group projects may help by permitting peers to share the work, use each other's partial knowledge and differential skills, and motivate one another.

9. *Performance assessments may underrepresent the learning of some cultural groups.* Although performance assessments allow the opportunity for students to use their backgrounds in diverse ways and allow multiple correct solutions, crafting tasks—and especially scoring rubrics—to take advantage of this diversity is difficult. If you are not knowledgeable about how different cultural groups express their higher thinking skills, you may systematically bias your assessments of them. Further, some groups perform better on some types of tasks than others (e.g., word problems vs. computational mathematics).

Performance tasks will not wash away differences among cultural groups: They are likely to make such differences more apparent. Multiple assessment formats may improve this situation somewhat, because they allow knowledge, skills, and ability to be expressed in different formats and media. After reviewing the research literature regarding performance assessments and equity, Baker and O'Neil (1994) drew this conclusion:

> If it is believed that performance-based assessment, if not the only solution, is at least a critical component of integrative educational reform, then attempts must be made to remedy its obvious potential for injury. These remedies include improving the design measures and scoring procedures so that differences in students' world knowledge, specific prior knowledge, perception of meaningfulness, and language facility are considered explicitly. Administration conditions, including climate, setting, and logistical support, must also be comparable. Furthermore, qualifications of raters including their training to avoid ethnic interactions, the models of student performance, and comparable standards of judgment must be made public and subject to independent review. Of course, the real key is that students receive truly comparable and equitable teaching offered in safe environments from qualified teachers with high expectations. Research into all these aspects needs to continue. (p. 24)

10. *Performance assessments may be corruptible.* As you use performance assessments, you will teach your students how to present themselves well on them. This amounts to coaching them how to perform (often called "teaching to the test"). If your coaching amounts to teaching all aspects of your state's standards and your school's curriculum framework's learning targets, you are doing the right thing. However, if you focus primarily on one aspect of the learning targets, you will lower the validity of your results.

For example, a science teacher could teach students how to record and organize their observations in notebooks (Miller & Seraphine, 1993). Thus, if notebooks are the primary products in the performance assessments, students' scores on notebooks may increase. However, the students' ability to do hands-on science may not. In this case, assessment narrows the curriculum from "hands-on science" to "notebook science." In Chapters 2 and 10, we said that a student's use of higher-order thinking is best assessed when the student is faced with performing new or novel tasks. Coaching tends to reduce the novelty of the task or change it from an "application" task to a "following-the-solution-strategy-the-teacher-taught-me" task. These types of coaching reduce the validity of your results, because they do not assess the main intent of learning targets that want students to learn to solve new and ill-structured problems. The quality of a student's education is thereby reduced.

Summary

- Performance assessments require students to demonstrate their ability to complete a task using their knowledge and skills from several areas rather than simply recalling information or saying how to do a task.
- Because curricular areas are very diverse, not all learning targets focus on performance, and thus not all assessments should be performance assessments.
- Performance assessments must be comprised of a task to perform along with a rubric for evaluating the quality of students' performance on the task.
- Scoring rubrics should fit together into a coherent assessment framework that matches the emphasis of the curriculum framework. This usually means creating a general rubric describing the main content and process areas to be assessed and a specific rubric which applies all these areas to the particular task at hand.
- Performance assessments may improve teaching and learning if they are well integrated with instruction, if criteria for performance is clearly stated and understood by all students, if these performance criteria are used appropriately and consistently by the teacher and students, and if students received detailed feedback.
- Performance assessments can improve the validity of classroom assessment results if they are appropriately matched to the curriculum framework's learning targets, match your teaching emphasis, and are included with more objective assessment formats to represent all important learning targets.
- Not all performance assessment tasks are authentic. Authentic performance assessment tasks emphasize applications, focus on direct assessment, use realistic problems, and encourage open-ended thinking.
- A performance assessment task does not have to be authentic to be interesting, challenging, and engaging.
- You can choose from a wide variety of performance task formats. Format choice is guided primarily by its match to the main intent of your curriculum framework's learning targets. A mismatch between task format and learning targets or teaching emphasis will lower the validity of the results, even if authentic performance tasks are used.
- These are the major performance task formats: structured, on-demand tasks (paper-and-pencil and non-paper-and-pencil); naturally occurring or typical performance; longer-term projects (individual, group, and combined); portfolios (best work, and growth and learning progress); demonstrations; experiments or investigations; oral presentations and dramatizations (includes debates); and simulations (standardized patients, computerized adaptive audiovisual scenarios, computerized text scenarios, simulations).
- A portfolio culture model uses growth and learning progress as the focus of instructional activity. This type of portfolio includes entries reflecting authentic work, growth in conceptual development, and focus on reflective activity.
- Although performance types of classroom activities may be very worthwhile teaching techniques, not all such activities lend themselves to high-quality formative and summative assessments. An assessment task—performance or not—needs to be crafted carefully to achieve its purpose.
- Performance assessments can and should be justified in their own right rather than by "bashing'" other assessment tools and formats. Teachers should not be fooled by spurious arguments. They should demand that advocates of any assessment technique justify the technique in its own right.
- Advantages of performance assessments include their potential to clarify learning targets; potential to assess "doing"; consistency with modern learning theory; potential to assess integration of knowledge, skills, and abilities; potential to link with teaching activities; ability to broaden the basis for assessment when combined with other assessment formats; and potential for assessing students' use of processes as well as products.
- Disadvantages of performance assessment techniques include their difficulty to craft and score, requirement for large amounts of assessment time and scoring time, scorer unreliability, low generalization across different task content, tendency to focus on a narrow set of learning targets, tendency to discourage less able students, tendency to underrepresent the learning of some cultural groups, and the possibility they may be corruptible.

Important Terms and Concepts

adaptive assessment task
alternative assessment
annotated holistic scoring rubric
authentic assessment
best-work portfolio
classroom activity vs. assessment task
closed-response task
combined group and individual project
debate
degree of authenticity
demonstration
dramatization
experiment
group project
growth and learning-progress portfolio
individual student project
multiple-intelligences assessment menu
multiple-intelligence theory
naturally occurring performance
non-paper-and-pencil task
on-demand task

open-response task
oral presentation
paper-and-pencil task
performance assessment
performance task
portfolio
portfolio culture model
product vs. process
scenario
scoring rubric (general, specific)
simulation
standardized patient format
structured task (exercise)

Exercises and Discussion Questions

1. Apply the ideas in Table 11.2 to a subject you teach (or plan to teach). For each category and subcategory, describe one performance assessment applicable to your subject. (Do not use the examples given in the table, but you can adapt them.) You do not have to actually create a workable task. Rather, in one or two sentences describe a task that could be created. Which types of tasks are not applicable to your teaching situation? Explain.

2. Do you have any experience with classroom performance activities? Performance assessment? Teaching in a multiple-intelligences framework? Share these experiences with others in your course. Do you agree with the author that performance assessments have potential for improving your teaching? Defend your answer.

3. Make three columns on a sheet of paper. In one column list the four characteristics of authentic performance tasks. Select two performance tasks from either your own experience or from this chapter. Identify each of the other two columns with one of these two tasks. Then, in each cell of the table, evaluate each task against each of the four characteristics: Describe how well each characteristic is exhibited by each task. Share your findings with others in this course.

Suggestions for Additional Readings

Baker, E. L., & O'Neil, H. F. (1994). Performance assessment and equity. *Assessment in Education, 1,* 11–26.

Reviews the literature and the issues concerning equity problems associated with performance assessment.

Hakel, M.D. (1998). *Beyond multiple choice: Evaluating alternatives to traditional testing for selection.* Mahwah, NJ: Lawrence Erlbaum Associates.

A collection of 13 chapters by well-known measurement specialists who critically evaluate alternative assessment methods in the context of selection decisions. A useful set of readings to gain perspective on the issues that go beyond classroom assessment and formative evaluation.

Herman, J. L., Aschbacher, P. R., & Winters, L. (1992). *A practical guide to alternative assessment.* Alexandria, VA: Association for Supervision and Curriculum Development.

Gives a general overview of performance assessment and its relation to educational reform. Contains suggestions for developing performance assessments. Examples come from large-scale assessment programs.

Herman, J. L., & Winters, L. (1994). Portfolio research: A slim collection. *Educational Leadership, 51* (October), 48–55.

A balanced account of the advantages and unresolved issues surrounding portfolios.

Scherer, M. (Ed.) (1997). Teaching for multiple intelligences. (Thematic issue). *Educational Leadership, 55* (1), all.

This issue of *Educational Leadership* is devoted almost entirely to teaching and assessing multiple intelligences. Each author describes how assessment should be accomplished. Performance assessment is highlighted.

Underwood, T. (1998). The consequences of portfolio assessment: A case study. *Educational Assessment, 5,* 147–194.

If you are considering adopting a portfolio system for formative and summative evaluation of students, you should read this article first. It is a rich source of comments by teachers and students alike.

CHAPTER 12

Performance Tasks, Portfolios, Rating Scales, and Scoring Rubrics

After studying this chapter, you should be able to:

1. Describe the stages and steps necessary to craft high-quality performance tasks. [2, 1]
2. Craft performance assessment tasks and their corresponding scoring rubrics. [2]
3. Apply criteria for evaluating the quality of your performance assessment tasks. [2, 1]
4. Describe the major types of scoring rubrics, their advantages, and the process used to develop them. [2, 3, 5]
5. Apply criteria to evaluate the quality of your scoring rubrics. [2, 3, 5]
6. Craft a checklist tool for assessing a student's product or the procedures (process) a student uses to complete a performance. [2, 3]
7. Describe the differences among the advantages, and the disadvantages, of the major types of rating scales. [1, 6]
8. Craft rating scales for assessing student performance. [2, 3, 5]
9. Describe and give examples of the different purposes for which portfolios are used. [1, 6]
10. Explain why different uses of portfolios require different organizations, evaluations, and types or entries. [1, 6, 3]
11. Describe what must be decided in each of the six steps for crafting a portfolio system. [2, 1, 4]
12. Craft a plan for a portfolio system to use with your students. [2, 4, 6]
13. Explain how each of the important terms and concepts listed at the end of this chapter apply to educational assessment. [6, 1, 4]

STAGES IN CRAFTING PERFORMANCE TASKS

It is best to use a systematic approach for crafting performance tasks. The process may be considered to have three stages (Stiggins, 1994): (1) being very clear about the performance you want to assess, (2) crafting the task, and (3) crafting a way to score and record the results. The following sections suggest ways to improve your performance task crafting in each stage. First we present a brief overview of the stages themselves.

Being Clear about What to Assess

As with all assessment procedures, you must first clearly identify the learning targets before you can assess them. Because performance tasks assess complex learning targets, you must be quite clear about what you will assess: for example, the content the task will address, the thinking processes you want the student to use, the type of activities that will allow you to assess both of these, and the quality dimensions or standards against which you will evaluate students' performance. You must know whether the curriculum framework's learning targets you wish to assess are mainly about the process a student uses, the product produced, or both. You must answer these questions:

- Which important learning target will I assess?
- On what content standard will the task focus?
- On what complex thinking skills should I focus this task?
- What are the quality dimensions or criteria along which I shall assess the degree to which a student achieved the content standard and used the thinking skills?
- Does the learning target imply assessing a process, a product, or both?

Crafting the Tasks

When you have a clear understanding of the achievement you want to assess, the next step is to craft the tasks to assess it. Remember that one learning target may be assessed by different tasks (see Figure 11.3). Further, the types of tasks you craft will depend on the learning targets you are assessing. Some targets imply that the tasks should be structured; others require unstructured tasks; tasks can be structured in various ways. The questions you must answer as you craft your tasks include

- What range of tasks are implied by the learning targets?
- Should the overall tasks be structured or unstructured?
- Which parts of the tasks should be structured, and to what degree?
- Does each task require students to perform all the important elements implied by the learning targets?
- Are the tasks crafted to allow me to assess the quality dimensions I need to assess?
- What must I tell students about the task and its scoring to communicate to them what they need to perform?
- Will students with different ethnic and social backgrounds interpret my task appropriately?

Scoring and Recording Results

Your scoring must be consistent, both across different students and for the same student at different times, to be fair and valid. Scoring rubrics not only improve consistency, they also improve validity by making clear the standards of achievement you will use to evaluate your students. Chapter 9 discussed holistic and analytic scoring in connection with essay questions. We shall revisit these scoring approaches in connection with performance tasks.

In addition, you need to decide whether your scoring rubric should be a rating scale or a checklist. Suggestions for making this decision are presented later. Finally, you need to have a way to record your assessment results. As you craft scoring rubrics and ways of recording results, you will need to address questions such as:

- What important criteria and standards do I need to assess?
- What are the levels of development (achievement) for each of these criteria and standards?
- Should I use a holistic or an analytic scoring rubric?
- Do I need to use a rating scale or a checklist as my scoring rubric?
- Should my students be involved in rating their own performance?
- How can I make my scoring efficient and less time-consuming?
- What do I need to record as the result of my assessments?

STAGE ONE: BEING CLEAR ABOUT THE PERFORMANCE TO ASSESS

Select the Learning Target(s) to Assess

When crafting performance assessment, you should be guided by your state's and school's curriculum framework, state and school standards, and specific learning targets in the subject(s) you are teaching. Any performance assessment must be consistent with those guides. You may decide that two or three learning targets can be assessed by the same complex performance assessment. Some learning targets may cut across curricula (e.g., effective communication).

Recall from Chapter 11 that not every learning target can or should be assessed by performance tasks: Select only those that can and should. Recall from Chapter 6 that you should have an assessment plan: The performance assessment you craft should fit into this assessment plan. Finally, recall from Chapter 7 that a fundamental principle of assessment is to focus only on important learning targets: the assessment you craft should assess worthwhile learning targets.

Standards or Dimensions Assessed

Perhaps the most important part of the first stage in performance assessment crafting is specifying the standards or quality dimensions against which you will assess students' performance (see Marzano et al., 1993; Stiggins, 1987). **Standards or quality dimensions** are the knowledge, skills, and abilities that you want students to learn as a result of your teaching. Standards include content or subject-matter-specific standards and lifelong standards. **Content standards** include the specific declarative and procedural outcomes you want students to achieve. Declarative outcomes are the facts, ideas, generalizations, and theories you want a student to learn. Procedural outcomes are the skills and procedures you want a student to learn. **Lifelong standards** include outcomes that cut across curricula or may be useful outside of school, such as complex thinking, information processing, effective communication, cooperation and collaboration, and habits of mind (Marzano et al., 1993). Appendix E shows these categories of standards. Table 2.3 gives examples. You should frame your performance task around them or some other framework that your school district requires you to use.

Limit Dimensions Assessed　You should not try to assess all of the quality dimensions in Appendix E in one performance task, or the task will become unwieldy and confusing. Marzano et al. (1993) suggest that every performance task should assess one quality dimension from each of the following categories: content, complex thinking, information processing, and effective communication. Assessing one quality dimension from each of the other two categories (collaboration/cooperation and habits of mind) is optional. Figures 11.1 and 11.7 illustrate two performance tasks that were developed around the quality dimensions outlined in Appendix E.

Define Quality Levels

Each quality dimension you specify actually represents a continuum of educational growth. Different students will perform with different levels of quality on each dimension. Further, one student may perform with high competence on some dimensions but with less competence on others. Thus, part of crafting your performance task is to define the scale for each dimension. You define this quality scale by spelling out the different degrees of quality performance–from low to high–on each dimension. This continuum forms the basis for crafting scoring rubrics, which we discuss later in this chapter. Figures 11.2 and 11.9 show different continuum levels for a declarative knowledge quality dimension and for several collaboration/cooperation dimensions.

Assessing Student Outcomes: Performance Assessment Using the Dimensions of Learning Model (Marzano et al., 1993) gives general scoring rubrics and quality levels for each of the dimensions shown in Appendix E. You must adapt these general quality dimensions to your own tasks before you can use them. However, the quality levels listed in the book are useful ways to start.

Evaluate Quality Dimensions

You may wonder whether your standards or dimensions are appropriately stated. Table 12.1 provides criteria for evaluating the quality dimensions you specify for each performance task.

Assess Process, Products, or Both

Sometimes a learning target asks the student to demonstrate a **process**. For example, an elementary school learning target may require students to use the "long division" algorithm; a high school chemistry learning target may require students to follow correct safety procedures for handling laboratory chemicals. In some cases, the learning target still focuses on process, even though there may be several correct processes. In a mathematics curriculum, for example, a learning target may ask students to learn several different procedures for division rather than a single correct algorithm.

At other times, even though you teach a specific process, the curriculum framework clearly implies that the major focus is the **product** a student produces. The specific process you teach is only one of several that a student may use. A learning target focuses on the product when the student must write a poem or term paper. There may be several equally good methods for completing such tasks, but the focus is on the result or products. Sometimes *both product and process* are of equal importance, such as obtaining the correct answer with the correct procedure, in performing certain physical skills, or in writing a paper through using a specific procedure.

When to Assess the Process　Focus your assessment on the *process a student uses* if you are able to answer yes to these questions (Highland, 1955):

1. Did you teach students to use a particular procedure? Can you specify those steps?

2. Can you accurately assess the extent to which a student has deviated from the accepted procedure(s)?

3. Is most or all the evidence about a student's achievement of the learning target found in the way the performance is carried out? Is little or none of the evidence you need to evaluate the student present in the product itself?

4. Do you have enough time or assistance to observe, record, and score the procedures a student uses?

When to Assess the Product　Focus your assessment on the *product a student uses* if you can answer yes to the following (Highland, 1955):

1. Can you assess the product accurately and objectively?

2. Is most or all of the evidence about a student's achievement of the learning targets found in the product itself? Is little or none of the evidence you need to evaluate the student found in the procedure a student uses or the way the student performs?

TABLE 12.1 Criteria for judging the quality of the standards or quality dimensions you will use to evaluate students' performance on tasks.

Criterion	Explanation
1. Significance within the broader context of learning targets and real-world applications	Your quality dimensions should only specify the most important performance components; they should include high level content standards and reflect several lifelong or real-world standards, including complex reasoning, information processing, effective communication, and, where appropriate, habits of mind and cooperative standards.
2. Authenticity and fidelity to the way the task should be performed outside of the assessment context	Your quality dimensions should be stated so that you could use them if the performance occurred in its typical setting (e.g., in the real world). They should reflect factors such as resources typically used or available in the real world as well as specify the types of structure and assistance (i.e., scaffolding) a student requires to complete the task.
3. Applies a general quality dimension or standard to the specific performance	Your rubrics, while specific to the performance task you are using, should fit into a general scheme or general rubric framework so that it is easy to see how a student performs across a class or type of parallel tasks, in different contexts, and under different conditions. This type of general framework will make it easier for you and other teachers to apply it consistently with different tasks within the same curriculum.
4. Suitability and fit within a broader framework of competence	Your quality dimensions' continua should be: (a) framed in a sound educationally developmental way so they may be clearly seen as extending from novice to expert performance, (b) limited (bracketed) within the broader framework to performances appropriate for the age and grade level of the students you are assessing, and (c) worded to describe the performance at each level (rather than be worded as value judgments such as "poor").
5. Ease of understanding by students, parents, and teachers	Your quality dimensions should be stated in clear language so they are easily understood by students, parents, other educators, and the community. You may want to have a "plain language" version and a "technical language" version, the former for students and the latter for other teachers in your field.
6. Usefulness for pointing to improvements	Your quality dimensions and their continua should be focused on those features of performance that can be improved. Your standards should be able to communicate to students (and others) what they need to concentrate their learning on to improve.

Source: Based on criteria and ideas in Quellmalz (1991).

3. Are you unable to determine the proper sequence(s) of steps to follow to perform the learning target? Was a specific set of procedures not taught? Although everyone knows the steps, are they difficult to perform?

4. Do you not have enough time or assistance to evaluate the product a student produces?

Tasks Accommodate Students

As you craft an assessment task, you need to be sure that performing the tasks is within the students' ability range. Performance assessments differ depending on the educational level of the students and the mix of general scholastic ability in your class. Further, some students in your class may have disabilities that need to be accommodated before they can participate in the performance assessment. In Chapter 5 we discussed the general principles of assessment accommodation.

Tasks Suit Class Size

The more students you have in your class, the less elaborate will be the performance assessment tasks you can set. The fewer the number in your class, the more time you

have per student for scoring. Your assessment planning should reflect the realities of your classroom.

STAGE TWO: CRAFTING PERFORMANCE TASKS

Create Meaningful Tasks

The tasks you craft should be meaningful to the students. This lets them become personally involved in solving a problem or doing well on the task. The following suggestions (Baron, 1991) will help you identify appropriate ideas around which you can craft your tasks:

1. *Choose a situation or task that is likely to have personal meaning for most of your students.*

2. *Carefully blend the familiar and the novel so students will be challenged by the task.* Do not make the task so demanding or strange that it becomes frustrating for your students.

3. *Choose some situations or tasks that are grounded in the real-world experience of the students you are teaching.*

4. *Choose some situations or tasks that require your students to apply the knowledge and skills they have acquired outside of your class.*

5. *Choose situations or tasks that assess whether students have the ability to transfer their knowledge and skills from classroom activities and examples to similar but new (for them) formats.*

Develop Tasks in Stages

You should not expect to "knock out" a high-quality performance task quickly. Remember that your first drafts are not fit for human consumption. You need to craft tasks through stages. If you proceed along the lines just listed, you first identify the learning targets and dimensions you want to assess and then develop a task around these targets. This ensures that your task lets you evaluate students on these targets. The following steps (Marzano et al., 1993) may be used:

1. *Select a content dimension to build your task around.* This may be either a declarative or procedural knowledge dimension.

2. *Using this content dimension as a guide, select one of the complex thinking dimensions (see Appendix E) that is closely related to the content dimension.* These two dimensions will be the main focus of your task.

3. *Using the content and thinking dimensions, draft your performance task.* Craft the task so that your students know they are required to apply the appropriate thinking skills standard to the content.

4. *Select one appropriate information-processing dimension that is consistent with your content and thinking skills dimensions and with the task you are crafting.* Rewrite the task to include instructions concerning your expectations about applying the information-processing dimension.

5. *(Optional) If your task is a group task, select a collaboration/cooperation dimension to assess in conjunction with the dimensions you already have selected.* You may also wish to assess a "habit of mind standard." (You may wish to do so even if the task is not a group task.)

6. *Rewrite your performance task if you decided to use one or more of the standards described in Step 5.*

7. *Select an effective communication dimension you believe is important to assess with this task.*

8. *Rewrite your performance task to incorporate the effective communication dimension.*

9. *Review and edit the task.* For each dimension, specify several quality levels of performance competence. (This will be the basis for your scoring rubric.)

Figure 12.1 diagrams this process. It implies that you need to develop three or four drafts before the task is well crafted. At this point, refer to Figures 11.1 and 11.8. These performance tasks were developed using the preceding steps.

Importance of Task Tryout

Experience with performance assessments has shown that many of the tasks that seem great on the drawing board are flops as assessment tools. Although a systematic and careful development process can minimize flawed tasks, it does not eliminate them. Flaws become especially noticeable when you try to apply scoring rubrics to many students' responses—this is usually too late to "fix" the task.

Trying out assessment tasks (whether performance or traditional paper-and-pencil) before using them is next to impossible for classroom teachers. You can, however, have your colleagues review and criticize your tasks before you use them. The next best thing to live student tryouts can and should be done: After you use an assessment task, use the information you obtain about flaws in the task or in the rubrics to revise the task or rubric; then reuse the task and rubric next year with a new class of students.

Tasks Vary Along Dimensions

You should be aware of the ways in which tasks assessing the same content learning target can differ from one another. This set of differences makes some tasks useful for

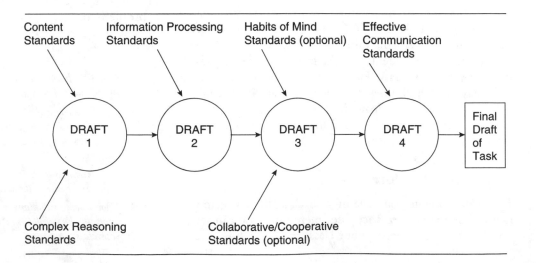

FIGURE 12.1 Process for task development.

assessing different types of lifelong learning targets. Table 12.2 shows five properties that are important in task crafting (some of which we discussed in earlier chapters).

Time Needed to Complete the Work   Some learning targets can be assessed in a relatively short time period of 15 to 40 minutes. For example, the ability to work in groups, write an essay or an explanation, make a graph, or carry out simple experiments can be assessed with **short tasks.** Many learning targets and dimensions, however, imply that students complete **long tasks.** For example, doing a survey and writing it up, building a model town, and developing complex plans for community action require a month or more, and much of the work may need to be done outside of class. Task time limits must match the intent of the learning target and dimensions rather than your own convenience—if your goal is to use the results to make valid interpretations about how well a student has achieved that learning target.

Task Structure   It may be misleading to talk about structured vs. unstructured performance, because you can **structure a task** in various ways (Davey & Rindone, 1990), including the way you define the problem, scaffold the instructions, require alternate strategies, and require alternate solutions. Your task may *define a problem* for a student to solve (structured), or you may require the student himself to identify what the problem is (unstructured or ill-defined).

Scaffolding is the degree of support, guidance, and direction you provide the students when they set out to complete the task. You may suggest how to attack the problem, what books or material to use, and the general nature of the end product you require. These directions and guidance statements add structure to the task. Less scaffolding means less structure. If your task can be performed or solved using only one or two procedures or strategies, it has fewer **alternate solution strategies** and is more structured in this respect. Unstructured alternatives mean that there are a great many equally correct pathways to the correct answer or to producing the correct product. A similar analysis applies to the solution or the product itself: A task is unstructured in this respect

---

TABLE 12.2   Properties of the task that you can vary to better align the students' performance with the requirements of the dimensions and learning targets.

Task Property	Variations in the Task Requirements
Time to complete the task	*Short tasks* can be done in one class period or less. *Long tasks* require a month or more, and work may need to be outside of class.
Task structure provided	Structure may vary in:
	Problem definition: High structure here means you carefully define the problem the student must solve. *Low structure* means the student is free to select and define the problem.
	Scaffolding: High structure here means the student is given lots of guidance or directions in how to begin a solution and what materials to use. *Low structure* here means a student has little or no guidance and must decide for him or herself.
	Alternate strategies: High structure means there are very few correct or appropriate pathways to get to the correct answer. *Low structure* means there are many correct or appropriate approaches to get an acceptable answer.
	Alternate solutions: High structure means there is a correct answer to the task. *Low structure* means there is no single correct answer to this task.
Participation of groups	The task may require:
	Individual work only throughout all phases of performance.
	Mixed individual and group work in which some of the performance occurs in groups and some is strictly individual effort.
	Group work only throughout all phases of performance.
Product and process focus	The task may require:
	Process assessment only in which the student's performance of the steps and procedures and not the outcome are observed and evaluated.
	Both process and product assessment in which both the steps and the concrete outcome (product) are evaluated.
	Product assessment only in which only the concrete product or outcome is evaluated.
Performance modality	The task may require:
	A single modality in which the performance is limited to one mode (e.g., oral, written, wood model, etc.).
	Multiple modality in which the performance must be done in several modes (e.g., do both a written and an oral report).

Source: Based on ideas in Davey & Rindone (1990).

when there are many correct or *acceptable solutions or products*. One task may vary in these elements, as shown in the following examples:

> Assume that students have been asked simply to build a scale model of the solar system. As far as *problem definition* goes, this task has fairly high structure—you have a specified goal to meet. However, there is very little *scaffolding*—students are not told what materials to use, or what proportions to use, or where to get information on the planetary distances and orbits. There are a lot of *alternative pathways* to the solution—consider the fact that no two models will look exactly alike, and will vary in terms of materials used, scale employed, special features included (such as neurons, orbital speeds, etc.), and in a way there's one best solution, a perfectly scaled model of the solar system. (Davey & Rindone, 1990, p. 5)

Participation of Groups　The learning target and the dimensions guide your task construction process. If your learning target calls for cooperative or collaborative learning (or using other group-based skills), you should set a task using, at least in part, group activities. Appendix E, and Figures 11.9 and 12.8 show some of the possible group collaboration dimensions you may choose to assess.

Product and Process　Examples of applications of *product assessment* are given in Figures 11.1, 11.5, 11.6, 11.10, and 12.6. Examples of *applications of process assessment* are given in Figures 11.7, 11.11, 11.12, and 12.4. If you want to assess process, you need to do the assessing while a student is performing. A product, on the other hand, may be taken away and assessed at your convenience. Further, cognitive processes (mental activities) cannot be assessed directly, only *indirectly* through some intermediate or "partial" products. For example, you can ask students to tell you or to write what they were thinking about while they were doing the task. Or you may ask them to record the early drafts they made and ideas they used.

These indirect assessments of a student's mental activities and thinking processes depend on abilities other than those required to complete the task. They depend, for example, on the accuracy of the students' memories, their skill in understanding the thinking processes they used, and their ability to describe these thinking processes orally or in writing. Because cognitive processes are only indirectly assessed, your inferences and judgments about how well a student uses them—that is, the validity of your assessment of cognitive processes—might be weak. Other processes, such as group processes and behavior that occurs in a sequence of steps, are more directly assessed because you can design your tasks to observe them directly.

Response Mode　Some learning targets specify that students should be able to use several ways of expressing their knowledge, solve a problem using several media, or express themselves in a variety of modalities. For example,

the task in Figure 11.1 asks the student to report his or her results in two or more modalities. You should not use multiple response modes on a whim. You need to align the modalities with the learning targets, standards, and curriculum framework. Also, you should use alternate modes as a means to accommodate students with disabilities or cultural differences if the mainstream, single mode is not appropriate for them. Accommodating a student's response mode also has meaning in the context of educational programs following a multiple-intelligences framework (see Chapter 11).

However, tasks for these alternative modalities need to focus on the main intents of learning targets and dimensions. If the main intent of a learning target is focused on communicating through the written word, then singing a song, pantomiming an answer, or drawing a picture will not be appropriate even though these are alternative modalities. But if the learning targets focus on content understanding, thinking skills, and problem solving, a written response is not the only way to express competent performance. Even though most students are expected to express their problem solutions in writing, you may assess some students by permitting alternative performances.

Make the Task Clear to Students

When crafting performance tasks, make sure that students understand what you expect them to do. Explain in writing the learning target, the criteria by which you will evaluate performance, and the instructions for completing the task. Task wording and directions should depend on the educational maturity of your students. Make sure that the time limits and the conditions under which you want the task done are clearly stated. Be sure students understand how long a response you are expecting. Share with students the rubrics you will use to assess their performance. When students misinterpret the task, you cannot validly interpret their assessment results in the same way as with other students who interpreted the task correctly. Students from diverse ethnic, linguistic, or gender groups may not interpret your wording as you expect them to (Lane et al., 1992; Duran, 1989). (See also the discussion of projects in Chapter 11.)

The validity of assessment is problematic for those teachers using multiple intelligences menus (Figure 11.4). Letting students choose different response modes may be popular, but not all response modes are valid for assessing a learning target. The first priority, especially for summative assessment, is to match the assessment format to the main intent of the standards and learning targets.

Number of Tasks

As a general rule, the fewer the number of tasks, the fewer learning targets that you can assess, the lower the reliability of the results, and the lower the validity of your interpretations. The number of performance tasks to include in your assessment depends on several factors. However, some of these factors you cannot control. You need to resolve the following issues to decide on the appropriate number of tasks:

1. *Criticalness of the decisions.* If the decision about a student is not critical, you may use fewer tasks than if it is critical. Certification, awarding diplomas, promotion, and graduation are examples of highly critical decisions. Assessments for critical decisions such as these are called *high-stakes assessments.* They require more tasks and longer assessment times to gather sufficiently reliable information. Neither should they be made using only information from one assessment session. Letter-grade assignments are also critical decisions, especially if you are unwilling or unable to change the grade if a mistake is made. Grading may not be as critical a decision as certification, but grades for a term or a marking period should not be based on a single assessment either. Grading requires a significant sampling of the learning targets. Daily instructional decisions for formative evaluation of learning can be easily changed if wrong decisions are made. These less critical decisions can be based on lower-quality information if need be.

2. *Scope of your assessment.* How much instruction are you covering with this assessment—a unit or only one lesson? The broader the scope of your assessment, the more tasks you will need.

3. *Mixture of assessment formats.* If you mix objective formats with performance tasks, you will be able to cover more aspects of the learning targets, balance your assessment, and broaden your assessment scope. In this case, you may need fewer performance tasks because your assessment scope will be broader than if you used performance tasks alone.

4. *Complexity of the learning target.* A complex learning target requires integration of many skills and abilities and may need to be performed over a long time period. In this case, practicality limits the number of tasks of this type you may give. However, because more time is devoted to one (or at most a few) such tasks, the information may be of high quality (i.e., reliable). Nevertheless, the scope or span of your assessment may not be very broad. This could present a validity problem.

5. *Time needed to complete each task.* As a practical matter, you can administer only a few tasks during a typical class period. Decide how much time one task will take a student to complete, and divide this into the length of the class period to determine the maximum number of tasks possible. Students usually take longer to complete a task than you think, so allow for that.

6. *Time available for the total assessment.* You may be willing to devote more or less than one period to assessment. The number of tasks may shrink or expand depending on the available time.

7. *Diagnostic detail needed.* If you need a lot of detail to diagnose a student's learning or conceptual problems, you need to craft tasks that provide this rich detail. This usually means fewer tasks, more detailed performance, and more detailed scoring of the responses. If you assess many students for diagnostic purposes, practicalities of time for performance and scoring will usually limit you to only a few tasks per student.

8. *Available human resources.* If you have an aide or a parent to help you administer or score the assessments, this may free up some time so that you can give a few more tasks. Students may be taught to score the assessments, and although this is educationally useful, it is unlikely to lead to increasing the number of tasks.

Evaluating Performance Tasks

The more important suggestions for improving performance tasks appear as a checklist in Table 12.3. You can use this table to evaluate individual performance tasks. Use this checklist as you used the checklists for objective items formats that we discussed in earlier chapters: A "no" answer to one question in the checklist is sufficient cause for you to revise the task before administering it to students.

STAGE THREE: RUBRICS AND ASSESSMENT RESULTS

Types of Scoring Rubrics

Throughout this chapter and in Chapters 9 and 10, we describe and illustrate three types of scoring rubrics:

1. **Holistic rubrics.** These rubrics rate or score the product or process as a whole without first scoring parts or components separately. Examples are found in Figure 9.9 and in Figures 11.2, 11.12, and 12.3.

2. **Analytic rubrics.** These rubrics rate or score separate parts or characteristics of the product or process first, then sum these part scores to obtain a total score. Examples are shown in Figures 9.7 and 9.8 and in Figures 11.9 and 11.13.

3. **Annotated holistic rubrics.** Raters use a holistic rating first, then they rate or describe a few characteristics that are strengths and weaknesses to support their holistic ratings. Figure 11.10 offers an example.

TABLE 12.3 A checklist for judging the quality of performance tasks.

1. Does the task focus on an important aspect of the unit's learning targets?	Yes	No
2. Does the task match your assessment plan in terms of performance, emphasis, and number of points (marks)?	Yes	No
3. Does the task require a student to actually *do* something (i.e., a performance) rather than only write about how to do it or simply recall or copy information?	Yes	No
4. Do you allow enough time so all of your students can complete the task under your conditions?	Yes	No
5. *If this is an open-response task,* do your wording and directions make it clear to students that they may use a variety of approaches and strategies, that you will accept more than one answer as correct, and that they need to fully elaborate their response?	Yes	No
6. *If the task is intended to be authentic or realistic,* do you present a situation that your level of students will recognize as coming from the real world?	Yes	No
7. *If the task requires using resources and locating information outside of the classroom,* will all of your students have fair and equal access to the expected resources?	Yes	No
8. Do your directions and other wording:		
a. define the task that is appropriate to the educational maturity of your students?	Yes	No
b. lead all students, including those from diverse cultural and ethnic backgrounds, to interpret the task requirements in the way you intend?	Yes	No
c. make clear the purpose or goal of the task?	Yes	No
d. make clear the length or degree of elaboration of the response you expect?	Yes	No
e. make clear the bases on which you will evaluate the responses to the task?	Yes	No
9. Are the drawings, graphs, diagrams, charts, manipulatives, and other task-materials clearly drawn, properly constructed, appropriate to the intended performance, and in good working order?		
10. Do you need to modify or adapt the task to accommodate students with disabilities?	Yes	No

Note: Revise any task for which you answered "no" to one or more questions.

Table 9.4 summarizes the advantages and disadvantages of holistic and analytic scoring rubrics. Holistic scoring rubrics are easier to use and take less time per student. They permit an overall evaluation, which allows the rater to report a general impression over all aspects of the performance. An analytic scoring rubric is more time-consuming, because the rater has to look for and separately rate each component of a performance. This level of detail is useful when your focus is diagnosis or helping students to understand your expectations for each part of the performance. This may be especially useful to helping students learn, even if it is more time-consuming. Using a *general, analytic trait rubric* (e.g., the type illustrated by Figure 9.8) in a consistent way through the entire year may improve learning if students understand it and if they receive feedback linked to it.

The annotated holistic scoring rubric is a restricted combination of the holistic and analytic rubrics. You first evaluate the performance holistically; then you select one or two points to either describe or rate analytically. The additional analytic ratings are restricted to only a few characteristics, which do not change the initial holistic rating. The advantage is that it allows you to quickly rate the papers and to support your rating with a few salient points. These points can be used to give feedback to students but may not be useful for diagnosis, because all components of the performance are not rated separately.

Finally, you should note that holistic and analytic scoring rubrics may tap into different aspects of a student's performance (Taylor, 1998). You should *not* believe that "it doesn't matter which method I use." Analytic trait scoring may be more valid if it allows you to evaluate several dimensions of performance as well as how the student integrates those dimensions when performing the task.

Creating Scoring Rubrics

Scoring rubrics are necessary for all of the performance assessment methods described in this chapter, including the portfolio. In Stage One of the development process, you identified dimensions of quality and the scale of progress for each dimension, from very low progress to very high progress. To develop a scoring rubric you need to refine these descriptions of performance levels to be sure they are clear. You may associate each level with a numerical value (illustrated in Figures 11.2. and 11.9). Alternately, you may associate each level with a qualitative description such as novice, apprentice, proficient, and distinguished. These qualitative descriptions are illustrated in Figures 11.10 and 11.12. Describe the characteristics of performance that distinguish one quality level from another, because these descriptions anchor the scale at each level. It is important to have as many levels as your school has letter grades. In that way rubrics can support your grades.

A scoring rubric may be crafted by using one of two processes. The first is to begin with a conceptual framework that you can use to evaluate students' performance to develop scoring rubrics; follow these steps:

1. *Adapt or create a conceptual framework of dimensions of quality that describes the content and performance processes that you should assess.*

2. *Develop a detailed outline that arranges the content and process from Step 1 in a way that identifies what you should include in the general rubric.*

3. *Craft a **general scoring rubric** that conforms to this detailed outline and focuses on the important aspects of content and process to be assessed across different tasks. The general rubric will be used to craft specific rubrics.*

4. *Craft a **specific scoring rubric** for a specific performance task.*

5. *Use the specific scoring rubric to assess the performances of several students; use this experience to revise the rubric as necessary.*

Steps 1, 2, and 3 may be difficult to achieve on your own and may require you to work with groups of teachers. A simple assessment framework for elementary and middle-school science is given in Figure 12.2. No rubrics are given for it, however. Figure 12.3 illustrates a mathematics assessment framework that has been developed into a holistic scoring rubric.

To identify a conceptual framework and the important dimensions or criteria to assess, you might try answering the following questions (Herman, Aschbacher, & Winters, 1992):

■ What are the characteristics of good writing, good problem solving, good collaboration, good scientific thinking, etc.? What evidence should I look for to decide if a student has produced an excellent response?

■ What are the important characteristics of the learning target that I should assess?

FIGURE 12.2 Example of scientific criteria used by middle-school students to critically evaluate each others' scientific projects and ideas. It is applied in a group process known as assessment conversations. This example comes from the SEPIA (Science Education through Portfolio Instruction and Assessment) Project.

Relationships
How do these terms go together?
Why do they belong together?
Is there a name we can give to the relationship?
Is there anything that does not belong?
How are things alike?

Clarity
Is it clear?
What does it tell someone?
What makes it clear to someone?
What makes it clear to someone else?

Consistency with Evidence
How is the statement supported by observations?
How is the statement supported by the observations of others?
How is the statement supported by lab data?
How does evidence from nature support the statement?
How well does your statement reflect the data?

Use of Examples
Can you give an example?
Why is it a good example for this purpose?
Is there a better example for this purpose?
Can you think of an original example?

Making Sense
Is this what you expected?
Are there any surprises here?
Is there anything that does not fit?
Does your hypothesis make sense, given what you know?
Can you predict what will be the outcome?

Acknowledging Alternative Explanations
How else can this be explained?
Is your explanation or hypothesis plausible? Can it happen?
What does this explanation say that the other doesn't?

Elaboration of a Theme
How is this term related to something we did before?
Is it familiar? If so, how?
How is it related to anything you did in another class?

Accuracy
Is the statement consistent with other information on the same topic?
How does your model compare with other models?
How does it compare with other representations?

Source: Moupgo, N. S. (1995). *Capturing the power of classroom assessment.* (Focus 28, extract from box on page 20.) Reprinted by permission of Educational Testing Service, the copyright owner.

FIGURE 12.3 Example of a holistic general scoring rubric for mathematics problem-solving tasks.

Score level = 4

Mathematical knowledge

- Shows understanding of the problem's mathematical concepts and principles;
- Uses appropriate mathematical terminology and notations;
- Executes algorithms completely and correctly.

Strategic knowledge

- May use relevant outside information of a formal or informal nature;
- Identifies all the important elements of the problem and shows understanding of the relationships between them;
- Reflects an appropriate and systematic strategy for solving the problem;
- Gives clear evidence of a solution process, and solution process is complete and systematic.

Communication

- Gives a complete response with a clear, unambiguous explanation and/or description;
- May include an appropriate and complete diagram;
- Communicates effectively to the identified audience;
- Presents strong supporting arguments which are logically sound and complete;
- May include examples and counter-examples.

Score level = 3

Mathematical knowledge

- Shows nearly complete understanding of the problem's mathematical concepts and principles;
- Uses nearly correct mathematical terminology and notations;
- Executes algorithms completely. Computations are generally correct but may contain minor errors.

Strategic knowledge

- May use relevant outside information of a formal or informal nature;
- Identifies the most important elements of the problems and shows general understanding of the relationships between them;
- Gives clear evidence of a solution process. Solution process is complete or nearly complete, and systematic.

Communication

- Gives a fairly complete response with reasonably clear explanations or descriptions;
- May include a nearly complete, appropriate diagram;
- Generally communicates effectively to the identified audience;
- Presents supporting arguments which are logically sound but may contain some minor gaps.

Source: From "The Conceptual Framework for the Development of a Mathematics Performance Assessment Instrument" by S. Lane, 1992, *Educational Measurement: Issues and Practice, 12*(2), p. 23. Copyright 1992 by the National Council on Measurement in Education. Reprinted by permission of the publisher.

- What characteristics in task performance distinguish the poor, acceptable, and excellent student?
- Are there samples of student work (excellent and poor) that I can contrast to identify the characteristics that differentiate them?
- Does my school district, state assessment program, a national curriculum panel, or a professional society have examples of rubrics or curriculum frameworks that show standards and criteria?
- Are there any suggestions in teachers' magazines, state teacher's newsletters, professional journals, or textbooks?

Rubrics need a framework-based organization. The rubric in Figure 12.2 is organized around the framework of mathematical knowledge, strategic knowledge, and communication (Lane, 1992). This three-part organization helps to define the specific standards within each level of the rubric. Similarly, Appendix E shows the framework for organizing the general rubrics that are consistent with the Dimensions of Learning Model. An analytic rubric for scoring writing may be organized around ideas and content, organization, voice, word choice, sentence fluency, and conventions (Spandel & Stiggins, 1990). Compare the general rubric you draft with those developed by other districts, state assessment programs, na-

FIGURE 12.3   *(continued)*

Score level = 2
Mathematical knowledge
- Shows understanding of some of the problem's mathematical concepts and principles;
- May contain serious computational errors.

Strategic knowledge
- Identifies some important elements of the problems but shows only limited understanding of the relationships between them;
- Gives some evidence of a solution process, but solution process may be incomplete or somewhat unsystematic.

Communication
- Makes significant progress towards completion of the problem, but the explanation or description may be somewhat ambiguous or unclear;
- May include a diagram which is flawed or unclear;
- Communication may be somewhat vague or difficult to interpret;
- Argumentation may be incomplete or may be based on a logically unsound premise.

Score level = 1
Mathematical knowledge
- Shows very limited understanding of the problem's mathematical concepts and principles;
- May misuse or fail to use mathematical terms;
- May make major computational errors.

Strategic knowledge
- May attempt to use irrelevant outside information;
- Fails to identify important elements or places too much emphasis on unimportant elements;
- May reflect an inappropriate strategy for solving the problem;
- Gives incomplete evidence of a solution process; solution process may be missing, difficult to identify, or completely unsystematic.

Communication
- Has some satisfactory elements but may fail to complete or may omit significant parts of the problem; explanation or description may be missing or difficult to follow;
- May include a diagram which incorrectly represents the problem situation, or diagram may be unclear and difficult to interpret.

Score level = 0
Mathematical knowledge
- Shows no understanding of the problem's mathematical concepts and principles.

Strategic knowledge
- May attempt to use irrelevant outside information;
- Fails to indicate which elements of the problem are appropriate;
- Copies part of the problem, but without attempting a solution.

Communication
- Communicates ineffectively; Words do not reflect the problem;
- May include drawings which completely misrepresent the problem situation.

---

tional curriculum panels, or professional societies. Refine yours to make it clearer and more complete.

If you do not follow Steps 1, 2, and 3 to create a general rubric, your scoring rubrics across all your performance tasks will lack coherence and consistency. The coherence focuses not only your assessment but also your teaching, and it helps your students to understand the standards that their learning should meet.

Regarding Steps 3 and 4, an example of a general rubric and its corresponding specific rubric is shown in Figure 11.2. Regarding Step 5, you should administer a performance task to your students, then apply the specific rubric. If you have difficulty rating a student's performance, you should reexamine your rubric to see where it is unclear. Often you will need to expand the descriptions of each quality level in the rubric to include an example or to describe an aspect of a student's performance you initially forgot to include.

A *second* way to proceed is to begin with students' work. Use examples of different levels of quality to help you identify the dimensions along which students can be assessed. The following steps may be helpful:

1. *Obtain copies of about 10 to 12 students' actual responses to a performance item.* Be sure the responses you select illustrate various qualities of the general ability you are assessing. For example, science understanding, letter writing, critical reasoning, etc.

2. *Read the responses and sort all of them into three groups: high-quality responses, medium-quality responses, and low-quality responses.*

3. *After sorting, carefully study each student's responses within the groups, and write very specific reasons why you put that response into that particular group.* How are the students' responses in one group (e.g., high-quality group) different from the responses in each of the other groups? Be as specific as you can. For example, don't say they write better or have better ideas. Rather, say the student's sentences are more complex, or the student expresses unusual ideas in a very clear way. Write a specific and complete explanation on every student's response as to why it is placed into the group. (Don't be afraid to put a response into a different category if you think you have made an error.)

4. *Look at your comments across all categories and identify the emerging dimensions.* In essence you are creating your own conceptual framework in this step of the process. For example, if the responses are for a mathematics task, you may see computation, complete explanations, logical approach, and good mathematical reasoning as the dimensions.

5. *Separately for each of the three quality levels of each dimension, write a specific student-centered description of what the responses at that level are typically like.* You may have one to six dimensions. Your descriptions become the scoring rubric for marking new responses. Figure 12.2 shows how your final product may look.

The procedure just described has been used extensively by the Northwest Regional Laboratory (1998) to train teachers to develop scoring rubrics. You must recognize, however, that the two methods for creating rubrics will not lead to the same end product. They are not equivalent procedures.

TABLE 12.4   Some useful methods for recording performance assessments.

Recording method	Description	Recommended use	Example of uses
Anecdotal records	You observe the performance and write a description of what the student did.	These are primarily useful for keeping records of unanticipated or naturally occurring performances. Usually you can record only one student at a time.	A student shows unusual insights into current events and you want to keep a record of these to put into his portfolio or to recommend the student for a summer program for leadership.
Behavior tallies	You create a list of specific behaviors of which you want to keep a record for a student. As you observe the performance you tally how many times each behavior occurs. The list is usually limited to only a few behaviors.	These are primarily useful for well-defined lists of behaviors that you can expect to occur frequently. They may be useful to keep track of undesirable behaviors, too.	As a communications arts teacher, you keep track of how often a student uses "uh-h-h" when speaking in front of the class.
Checklists	You create a list of specific steps in a procedure or specific behaviors. You check each behavior that occurs. The list may be long.	These are primarily useful if the behaviors are in a sequence or if all the subtasks that make up the complete performance can be listed.	You are a science teacher and want to be sure that each student performs the steps in setting up a microscope properly. You are an automotive shop teacher and want to be sure that each student properly completes all the tasks necessary to change the oil in a car.
Rating scales	You create standards or criteria for evaluating a performance. Each standard has levels of competence, and you rate students according to how well they performed each standard as they complete the task.	These are especially useful if each standard can be judged according to the level or the degree of quality rather than as simply being present or absent.	You are an art teacher and rate each student's painting as to its composition, texture, theme, and technique. You are a mathematics teacher and rate a student's problem solution according to how well the student demonstrates mathematical knowledge, uses a good strategy to solve the problem, and communicates her explanation of the solution in writing.

Recording the Results

Several useful ways to record your assessments of students' performance are briefly described in Table 12.4. Although each of the ways listed in the table has a special use, checklists and rating scales are the most frequently used with performance tasks. Suggestions for developing checklists and rating scales are given in the next two sections.

Improving Checklists

Usefulness of Checklists   A **checklist** consists of a list of specific behaviors, characteristics, or activities and a place for checking whether each is present or absent. You may also use a checklist to assess a student performing a series of discrete steps in a procedure. Figure 12.4 shows a checklist for evaluating whether a student is able to use a microscope properly. This checklist contains descriptions of possible inappropriate steps (errors) in the sequence as well as appropriate steps (correct). By including possible errors in the checklist, you can review these errors when you remediate students. The numbers recorded on the form represent the sequence that a particular student used to perform the task. Sometimes the major flaw in a student's performance is the order in which he performs the steps. Recording the correct sequence and the student's sequence on the form will help you attend to this aspect of performance.

You can also prepare checklists to evaluate a student's product, such as a drawing, a constructed model, an essay, or a term paper. Another type of checklist consists of a list of discrete behaviors related to a specific area of a student's performance. For example, you may wish to identify the particular difficulties a student is having in the phonological, semantic, and syntactic aspects of spoken language. The checklist might have items such as "uses only simple sentence structure" or "responds without delay to questions."

Students can use a checklist to review and evaluate their own work. The completed checklist could be used as a basis for a student-teacher conference in which you discuss a student's progress. As an example, consider the situation in which a student produces a best-work mathematics portfolio. (The standards for these portfolios were described in Table 11.3 and Figure 11.10.) To create this portfolio, a student has to complete mathematics tasks and decide which of these completed tasks she should include in the portfolio. A checklist can help a student evaluate each entry of the portfolio and can serve as a basis for discussing the entry with peers, parents, or teachers (Kentucky Department of Education, 1993c). Because the checklist focuses on a portfolio entry, it focuses students' attention on the portfolio scoring rubric (Figure 11.10). However, the checklist is phrased in simpler and less formal language than the scoring rubric used by teachers. An adaptation of this checklist is shown in Figure 12.5.

Crafting Checklists   A *procedural checklist* assesses whether a student follows the appropriate steps in a process or procedure. A *product checklist* focuses on the quality of the product a student makes. To create such checklists, you need a thorough understanding of the subject matter as well as the procedure or the product itself. Without this knowledge it is difficult to identify critical performance and steps, critical flaws in the product, and potential student errors. Thus, crafting checklists requires a rather detailed analysis of the procedure you are evaluating or a careful specification of the precise characteristics of the desired student product.

Before crafting a product checklist, you should examine several students' products—especially those products that differ greatly in quality. Careful study of these products will help you identify the characteristics and flaws you want to include in your checklist. When crafting a *procedural checklist*, first observe and study students performing so you can identify all the appropriate steps. You may find the following steps (Linn & Gronlund, 1995) helpful when crafting procedural checklists:

1. *List and describe clearly each specific subperformance or step in the procedure you want the student to follow.*

2. *Add to the list specific errors that students commonly make (avoid unwieldy lists, however).*

3. *Order the correct steps and the errors in the approximate sequence in which they should occur.*

4. *Make sure you include a way either to check the steps as the student performs them or to number the sequence in which the student performs them.*

If several equally correct procedures for accomplishing the learning target are available, developing a checklist this way will not be useful.

Improving Rating Scales

Usefulness of Rating Scales   You are often concerned with more than simply checking whether a given step or particular action is present. When assessing the quality of a student's oral presentation to the class, for example, you would probably identify several dimensions of a "good oral presentation" and then judge the *degree to which* a student demonstrates each of them. A good oral presentation might include such characteristics as the extent to which a student presents material relevant to the topic, speaks in a smooth, unhesitating manner, uses correct grammar and language patterns, and makes visual contact with the audience (Lindvall, 1961). A student achieves each of these dimensions in varying degrees rather than on an all-or-none, present-or-absent basis. To assess a student on these dimensions requires you to record the degree to which a student demonstrates each dimension. A simple rating scale for doing this was shown in Figure 11.13. A scale for

FIGURE 12.4   A checklist for assessing a student's performance in setting up and using a microscope.

	Student's Actions	Sequence of actions				Sequence of actions
a.	Takes slide	1		au.	Asks, "What do you want me to do?"	
b.	Wipes slide with lens paper	2		av.	Asks whether to use high power	
c.	Wipes slide with cloth			aw.	Says, "I'm satisfied"	
d.	Wipes slide with finger			ax.	Says that the mount is all right for his eye	
e.	Moves bottle of culture along the table			ay.	Says he cannot do it	19,24
f.	Places drop or two of culture on slide	3		az.	Told to start to new mount	
g.	Adds more culture			aaa.	Directed to find object under low power	20
h.	Adds few drops of water			aab.	Directed to find object under high power	
i.	Hunts for cover glasses	4				
j.	Wipes cover glass with lens paper	5			**Skills in which student needs further training**	**Sequence of actions**
k.	Wipes cover glass with cloth			a.	In cleaning objective	√
l.	Wipes cover with finger			b.	In cleaning eyepiece	√
m.	Adjusts cover with finger			c.	In focusing low power	√
n.	Wipes off surplus fluid			d.	In focusing high power	√
o.	Places slide on stage	6		e.	In adjusting mirror	√
p.	Looks through eyepiece with right eye			f.	In using diaphragm	√
q.	Looks through eyepiece with left eye	7		g.	In keeping both eyes open	√
r.	Turns to objective of lowest power	9		h.	In protecting slide and objective from breaking by careless focusing	√
s.	Turns to low-power objective					
t.	Turns to high-power objective	21			**Noticeable characteristics of student's behavior**	**Sequence of actions**
u.	Holds one eye closed	8		a.	Awkward in movements	
v.	Looks for light			b.	Obviously dexterous in movements	
w.	Adjusts concave mirror			c.	Slow and deliberate	√
x.	Adjusts plane mirror			d.	Very rapid	
y.	Adjusts diaphragm			e.	Fingers tremble	
z.	Does not touch diaphragm	10		f.	Obviously perturbed	
aa.	With eye at eyepiece turns down coarse adjustment	11		g.	Obviously angry	
ab.	Breaks cover glass	12		h.	Does not take work seriously	
ac.	Breaks slide			i.	Unable to work without specific directions	√
ad.	With eye away from eyepiece turns down coarse adjustment			j.	Obviously satisfied with his unsuccessful efforts	√
ae.	Turns up coarse adjustment a great distance	13,22			**Characterization of the student's mount**	**Sequence of actions**
af.	With eye at eyepiece turns down fine adjustment a great distance	14,23		a.	Poor light	√
ag.	With eye away from eyepiece turns down fine adjustment a great distance	15		b.	Poor focus	
ah.	Turns up fine adjustment screw a great distance			c.	Excellent mount	
ai.	Turns fine adjustment screw a few turns			d.	Good mount	
aj.	Removes slide from stage	16		e.	Fair mount	
ak.	Wipes objective with lens paper			f.	Poor mount	
al.	Wipes objective with cloth			g.	Very poor mount	
am.	Wipes objective with finger	17		h.	Nothing in view but a thread in his eyepiece	
an.	Wipes eyepiece with lens paper			i.	Something on objective	
ao.	Wipes eyepiece with cloth			j.	Smeared lens	√
ap.	Wipes eyepiece with finger	18		k.	Unable to find object	√
aq.	Makes another mount					
ar.	Takes another microscope					
as.	Finds object					
at.	Pauses for an interval					

Source: From "A Test of Skill in Using a Microscope" by R. W. Tyler, 1930, *Educational Research Bulletin 9*, p. 494. Reprinted by permission.

FIGURE 12.5 Example of a checklist which students use to evaluate their own entries for a best-work portfolio.

Mathematics Self-Assessment and Conference Form

Name: _____

Entry title: _____

Conference with:
___ Classmate Date: _____
___ Teacher Date: _____
___ My parent Date: _____

Mathematics Area	Did I ...	Comments about strengths and needs
Problem solving	1. understand the problem? 2. use more than one strategy to solve the problem? 3. solve the problem? 4. review, revise, or expand the problem? 5. show and explain all my work or my thinking?	
Reasoning	6. make predictions by observing data or recognizing patterns? 7. test my predictions by using logical arguments, using my past knowledge, or collecting additional data? 8. explain and justify my solution?	
Mathematics communication	9. use mathematical words, symbols, graphs, manipulatives, etc. to communicate ideas and thinking? 10. communicate my ideas and thinking through written, oral, or other means?	
Understanding and connecting core concepts	11. show that I understood mathematical topics and ideas? 12. recognize and use mathematics in other subjects or in everyday life? 13. recognize connections and relationships with mathematics?	
	Do the following with your teacher	
Type of entry	14. Circle the kind(s) of entry this is: writing investigation/discovery application interdisciplinary nonroutine problem project	
Core concepts & principles I used	15. Circle the mathematical concepts that you used in this entry: change measurement data number mathematical procedures space & dimensionally mathematical structure	
Tools I used	16. Circle the mathematical tools you used in this entry: algebra tiles fraction bars base 10 blocks geoboards beans pattern blocks calculator protractor compass rulers computer scales decimal squares other	
Type of entry	17. Circle the kind of entry this is: individual group	

Do you want to revise, edit, or polish this entry?   Yes   No

Is this entry one that you want to publish in your assessment portfolio?   Yes   No

Possible changes:

Source: Adapted from *Teacher's Guide: Kentucky Mathematics Portfolio* by Kentucky Department of Education, 1993, Frankfort, KY: Author. Reprinted by permission.

rating critical thinking dispositions was shown in Figure 10.17, and for evaluating an oral presentation of an argument in Figure 10.34.

Rating scales can be used for teaching purposes as well as assessment:

1. *The rating scale helps students to understand the learning target and to focus their attention on the important aspects of the performance.* You can give it to students as they prepare for the performance task.

2. *The completed rating scale gives specific feedback to a student concerning the strengths and weaknesses of the performance.* You can give the rating scale to students after you have used it to evaluate their performance.

3. *Students not only learn the standards but also may internalize them.* This means that they will automatically apply the standards to their work. To accomplish this, you must rate the same standards or criteria across several different specific performance tasks throughout the year.

4. *Ratings help you to show each student his growth.* If you keep copies of ratings in a file, you will have a record to help you to monitor and assess each student's progress. To do this effectively, you need to use the same (or similar) rating scale across all tasks. This assures that the information you collect is comparable from occasion to occasion. This comparability will result if you use a general rubric to create specific rubrics and rating scales.

Numerical Rating Scales   Although there are many varieties of rating scales, two varieties—numerical rating scales and graphic rating scales—when used to their full advantage serve the teacher well for most purposes. When using a **numerical rating scale,** you must mentally translate judgments of quality or degree into numbers. One numerical rating scale used in a technical drawing course is shown in Figure 12.6. The teacher lists 10 dimensions (standards) against which he evaluates each drawing. He rates each dimension on a scale of 0 to 10 and then adds up the ratings. If a particular dimension—for example, quality of arcs, circles, and tangents—does not apply to a particular kind of drawing, then it is omitted. The figure also shows the results of using the rating scale to evaluate a ninth grader's drawing. This is an example of using an analytic rubric for rating a product.

Notice from the example that simply providing a student with "numbers" is not sufficient. You need to make verbal comments—both positive and negative—to give a student the feedback necessary to make improvements. In addition, you may give students the list of criteria and ask them to edit their own work before turning in their assignments.

You will enjoy an increase in objectivity and consistency in results from numerical rating scales if you provide a short verbal description of the quality level each number represents (as in Figure 12.3). Alternately, you can associate with each numerical level an example or actual specimen of the products you are rating. You can match a student's performance to either a verbal description or an actual specimen assigning the corresponding number. The *Thorndike Handwriting Scale* illustrated in Figure 12.7 is an example of the latter.

Graphic Rating Scales   With **graphic rating scales,** you use an unbroken line to represent the particular dimension or standard on which you rate a student's performance or product. Different parts of the line are defined by verbal labels describing levels of quality performance. This guides you in expressing the ratings. Figure 12.8 shows a simple graphic rating scale that a teacher might use to rate a student's attainment of cooperative learning targets in a group project. In Figure 12.8, the endpoints of the line are "anchored" by *Never or Almost Never* and *Always or Almost Always; Seldom, Occasionally,* and *Frequently* define intermediate levels of achievement.

When using a graphic rating scale, you can check any point along the line, not just the defined points. Thus, the graphic rating scale does not force your rating into a discrete category or into being a whole number (as does the numerical rating method). In practice, a serious problem with the use of verbal labels such as *usually, seldom,* and *frequently* is that they are undefined; different raters do not agree on what they mean. Defining the levels on the scale with more behavioral descriptions makes your ratings much more consistent and meaningful.

Descriptive Graphic Rating Scale   This is a better format for rating. **Descriptive graphic rating scales** replace the ambiguous single words (e.g., *frequently*) with short behavioral descriptions of the various points along the scale. The oral presentation rating scale in Figure 11.13 is an example of this type. Each degree of success on each dimension is defined by a brief description. Sometimes numbers are also printed along the line, as in Figure 11.13, combining the features of both a numerical and a graphic rating scale. Describing the points of the scale by behavior descriptions leads to increased consistency of ratings across raters and students. Other examples of descriptive graphic rating scales are given in Figures 10.17 and 10.34.

Rating Scale Errors

You should be aware of several common errors that occur when teachers rate students. **Leniency error** occurs when a teacher tends to make almost all ratings toward the high end of the scale, avoiding the low end of the scale. **Severity error** is the opposite of leniency error: A teacher tends to make almost all ratings toward the low end of the scale. **Central tendency error** occurs when a teacher hesitates to use extremes and uses the middle part of the scale only. Central tendency errors sometimes occur when a teacher

FIGURE 12.6 Example of an analytic rubric in the form of a numerical rating scale used to assess a student's technical drawing (i.e., product assessment).

CRITERIA OF DRAWING EVALUATION

___8___ TITLE BLOCK   *take more time*
                               & care on your
___9___ LINE TECHNIQUE   *title block*
                                        lettering.
__10__ CENTERING AND SPACING

___—___ ARCS, CIRCLES, TANGENTS

___—___ SPACING OF DIMENSIONS

___—___ PLACEMENT OF DIMENSIONS

___7___ FRACTIONS, FIGURES, LETTERING

___—___ ARROWHEADS

__9+__ NEATNESS, OVERALL APPEARANCE

__10__ SOLUTION

TOTAL __53__ AVERAGE _____ GRADE __B+__

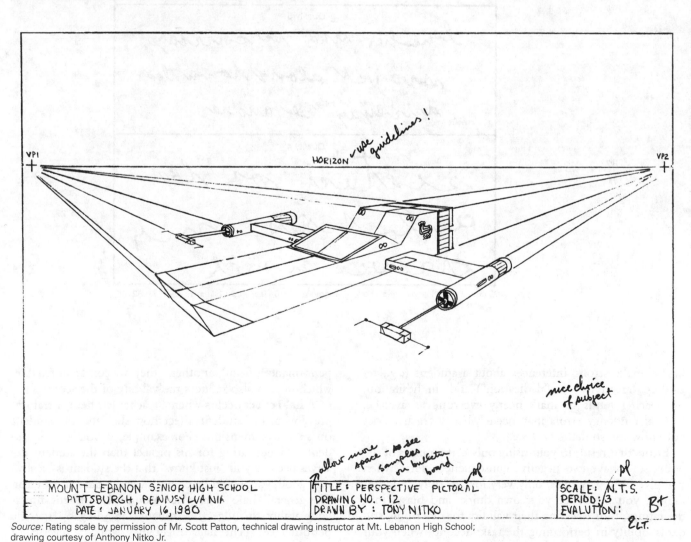

Source: Rating scale by permission of Mr. Scott Patton, technical drawing instructor at Mt. Lebanon High School; drawing courtesy of Anthony Nitko Jr.

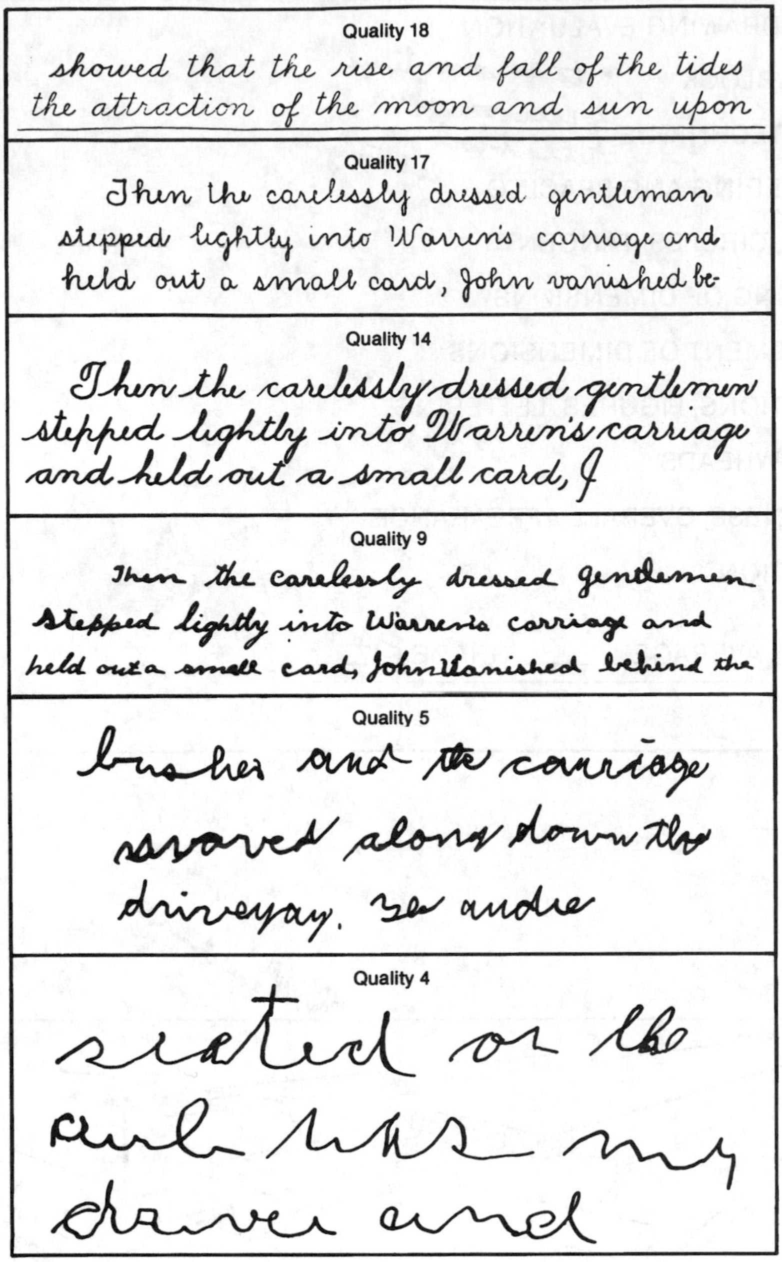

FIGURE 12.7 Thorndike's scale for measuring handwriting. A series of handwriting specimens were scaled on a numerical "quality" scale. To use the scale a student's sample of writing is matched to the quality of one of the specimens and assigned the given numerical value. This figure shows only some of the specimens.

Source: From "Handwriting," by E. L. Thorndike, 1910, *Teachers College Record, 11,* 62, 65, 70, and 73.

has to make strong inferences about a student (e.g., regarding "creativity" or "dedication") and, in hesitation, the teacher tends to mark nearly everyone as average. Central tendency errors may occur when a teacher does not know the students very well.

Errors that result in your using only certain parts of the rating scale have two negative consequences. First, when you give only very high, only very low, or only "middle" ratings, you introduce your own quirks and biases into the ratings, thus lowering their validity for describing students' ability in performing the task. Second, when your ratings bunch up and do not distinguish one student's

performance from another, they become unreliable, which in turn also reduces the validity of the scores.

A **halo effect** occurs when a teacher lets her general impression of the student affect how she rates the student on specific dimensions. For example, if you gave a student a higher rating for his project than the student deserves because you "just know" that the student is "really" very good, you would be committing the halo effect error. The general "halo" you place around the student affects your ability to judge the student's standing on specific performances. (The halo effect may work in reverse, of course: Your general impression of a student as "not very

FIGURE 12.8   A simple graphic scale for assessing cooperative learning targets with a group project.

Form for Rating Collaboration and Cooperation Learning Targets in a Group Project

Student being assessed: Date:

Other group members:

Project description:

Teacher or observer:

Directions: Place a check mark any place along the line to show judgment of the student's performance on that item. If you have not had sufficient opportunity to observe this student, circle N/O.

ACHIEVEMENT OF GROUP GOALS
1. Does the student attend the group meetings?

| Never | Seldom | Occasionally | Frequently | Always | N/O |

2. When attending is the student prepared?

| Never | Seldom | Occasionally | Frequently | Always | N/O |

3. Does the student work actively toward achieving the group's goals?

| Never | Seldom | Occasionally | Frequently | Always | N/O |

4. Does the student work outside of the group meetings on the group project?

| Never | Seldom | Occasionally | Frequently | Always | N/O |

INTERPERSONAL SKILLS
5. Does the student interact appropriately with the group's members?

| Never | Seldom | Occasionally | Frequently | Always | N/O |

6. Is the student sensitive to the others' feelings when expressing own ideas and views?

| Never | Seldom | Occasionally | Frequently | Always | N/O |

7. Is the student's behavior disruptive to others in the group?

| Never | Seldom | Occasionally | Frequently | Always | N/O |

GROUP MAINTENANCE
8. Does the student help the group to decide whether changes in group processes are needed?

| Never | Seldom | Occasionally | Frequently | Always | N/O |

9. Does the student work actively toward helping the group change its processes when necessary?

| Never | Seldom | Occasionally | Frequently | Always | N/O |

COMMENTS:

good" may lead you to lower ratings on specific dimensions more than the student deserves.)

One expression of the halo effect may occur when teachers need to make grading decisions for students whose assessment results put them on the border between two letter-grade categories: The error is that those individuals who favorably impress a teacher are moved into the upper category; those who less favorably impress the teacher are moved into the lower category.

Personal bias occurs when a teacher has a general tendency to use inappropriate or irrelevant stereotypes favoring boys over girls, whites over blacks, or working families over welfare recipients. A teacher's quirks and personal biases may also extend to students from particular families as well as to individual students a teacher may dislike.

A **logical error** occurs when a teacher gives similar ratings on two or more dimensions of performance that the teacher believes are logically related but that are in fact unrelated. For example, a teacher may falsely believe that students with exceptionally high scores on scholastic aptitude tests should be the top students in all subject areas and thus mark the high-scoring aptitude test students in ways that are different from the way the low scorers are marked. Logical errors are a result of a teacher's ignorance and unfounded beliefs about how strongly educational achievements go together, rather than the teacher's personal quirks and biases about individuals or groups of students.

Other errors occur when "outsiders" rate performance assessments. When states and large school districts implement performance assessments, students' work is often rated by someone other than their teacher. In these cases, the raters are trained in and practice using a particular scoring rubric. **Rater drift** occurs when the raters, whose ratings originally agreed, begin to redefine the rubrics for themselves. As a result, the raters no longer produce ratings that agree, even though they were trained on the same rubrics. The remedy for this is to monitor the ratings and to retrain those raters who appear to have drifted away from agreed-upon standards. (See the exercise at the end of Chapter 9.)

A related type of effect is **reliability decay.** Immediately after training, raters apply the rubrics consistently across students and are consistent with one another. However, as time passes, the ratings become less consistent, both across students and across raters. Monitoring and retraining are remedies for this effect, too.

Evaluating Scoring Rubrics and Rating Scales

Throughout this chapter we have discussed how you should craft scoring rubrics and rating scales. This section pulls the major suggestions together so you can use them to evaluate the scoring rubrics you craft.

Evaluation Checklist Table 12.5 is a checklist to evaluate a specific scoring rubric you craft. You will use a specific scoring rubric to assess students' performance on a particular performance task. You evaluate your performance task by applying the criteria in Table 12.3. You evaluate the *scoring rubric* by applying the criteria in Table 12.5. Because many scoring rubrics appear as rating scales, the criteria can be used to evaluate other classroom rating scales, too.

Consistency with Your Grading System

One point in Table 12.5 (point 7) needs special mention here because it has not been discussed previously. Your letter-grade system and your scoring rubrics should have the same number of levels. The meaning of the levels should be consistent, too. Most teachers are expected to report student progress on report cards with letter grades. It will be difficult for you to do so if your scoring rubric isn't aligned to the grading system. One easy way to do this is to be sure that your rubrics have the same number of quality levels as your grading system does. Then as you combine assessment results, they can be more easily related to grades. (Grades are discussed in more detail in Chapter 15.) For example, if your grading system has A, B, C, D, or E, the rubrics should have five levels, not four or six. Consistencies in scales across all assessments are important ways to improve the validity of your assessment results.

Reliability of Ratings The **reliability of ratings** is an important criterion for evaluating performance assessments. We discussed reliability in Chapter 4. The following reliability coefficients are among those appropriate to use with the more continuous scores awarded to students from performance assessments:

Estimating Reliability over Time

■ Test-retest
■ Alternate forms on different occasions

Estimating Reliability on a Single Occasion

■ Alternate forms
■ Coefficient alpha
■ Split-halves coefficient

Estimating Scorer Reliability

■ Correlation of two scorers' results
■ Percent agreement
■ Kappa coefficient

Appendix I shows how to calculate coefficient alpha, split-halves percent agreement, and kappa coefficient. However, the appendix shows percent agreement and kappa calculations only for the special case in which pass-fail or mastery-nonmastery decisions are made. Although these two indices can easily be applied to scores that

TABLE 12.5 A checklist for judging the quality of performance assessment scoring rubrics (including rating scales).

	Yes	No
1. Overall, does the rubric emphasize the most important content and processes of the learning target?	Yes	No
2. Will the scores you get from the *parts* of the rubric (i.e., the standards) match the emphasis you give them in your assessment plan?	Yes	No
3. Do the *total number of marks* obtained from the rubric match the emphasis given this learning target in your assessment plan?	Yes	No
4. Will your students understand the rubric?	Yes	No
5. Are the categories rated with the rubric suitable for giving your students the guidance they need to improve their performance on the learning target?	Yes	No
6. Is the rubric for this particular task a faithful application of the general rubric?	Yes	No
7. Are the levels of the scales for the parts of the rubric (i.e., the levels of the standards) described clearly in terms of performance you can observe students doing?	Yes	No
8. With regard to this specific task, does the rubric allow you to assess the students' use of the appropriate:	Yes	No
a. declarative and procedural content?	Yes	No
b. processes?	Yes	No
9. If the purpose of this task is to assess a student's use of alternate correct answers/products or alternate correct processes/strategies, does the rubric clearly describe how each is to be rated and marked?	Yes	No
10. Does the rubric allow you to distinguish a wide range of students' quality levels of performance on this task rather than putting all students into one or two quality levels?	Yes	No

Note: Revise any rubric for which you answered "no" to one or more of the questions.

TABLE 12.6 Suggestions for improving the reliability of scores from rubrics and rating scales.

1. Organize the items within a scoring rubric into logical groups that match the content and process framework of the curriculum.
2. For each trait or standard, use behavioral descriptions to define each level of performance.
3. Provide specimens or examples of students' work to help define each level of performance with a trait or standard.
4. Have several teachers work together to develop a scoring rubric.
5. Have several teachers review and critique the draft of the scoring rubric.
6. Provide training and supervised practice for all persons who will use a scoring rubric.
7. Have more than one rater rate each student's performance on the task.
8. Monitor raters by periodically sampling their ratings, checking on the accuracy and consistency with which they are applying the scoring rubrics. Retrain those persons whose ratings are inaccurate or inconsistent.

come in more than two categories, that is beyond the scope of this book.

Chapter 4 also discussed how to *improve the reliability* of assessment results. These suggestions were listed in Figure 4.8. Review these suggestions at this time and think about how you should apply them to performance assessment.

In addition, Table 12.6 suggests ways of improving the reliability of ratings from scoring rubrics and rating scales.

CRAFTING PORTFOLIOS

Portfolios are used in many different ways, and what goes into them depends on the purpose you have in mind. Table 12.7 summarizes some of these purposes and the corresponding focus of the portfolios' contents. (See also Table 11.4.) The clearer you are about your portfolio's learning targets and purpose(s), the better you are able to craft it. If the portfolio has to serve more than one purpose, you will need to consider carefully the focus of each portfolio entry, so that each entry serves at least one of your intended purposes.

Organization and Contents

Define the Portfolio's Purpose The organization and contents of a portfolio depend on its purpose(s). You saw an example of a **growth and learning-progress** language arts portfolio in Table 11.4 and Figure 11.11. The organization was decided by a group of teachers working together. Timeframes are spelled out, as are content and who should contribute each entry (both the student and the teacher contribute in this example). You saw an example of a **best-work portfolio** in Table 11.3, Figure 11.10, and

TABLE 12.7   Examples of the many purposes that portfolios may serve in the schools.

General purpose and contents	Examples of specific purposes
Best-Work Portfolios	
Evaluation portfolios: Contents focus on providing convincing evidence that specific types of accomplishments have been attained.	• Evidence of subject-matter mastery and learning. • Evidence of high levels of accomplishment in an area. • Evidence of minimum competence in an area. • Evidence of a school district's accomplishments.
Communication portfolios: Contents focus on providing examples of accomplishments that may be either typical or that may impress others.	• A student's showcase for his or her parents. • Pass on information about a student to the next teacher. • A school district's showcase.
Growth and Learning-Progress Portfolios	
Monitoring progress portfolios: Contents focus on products and work that appear at intermediate stages in the course of a student's learning.	• Teacher and/or students review progress. • Student is able to look over the work and see the "long view" or the "whole picture."
Daily instruction: Contents focus on a student's recently completed correct and incorrect work, on data or recent findings, on a student's conceptual explanations of the work underway, etc.	• Basis for discussions with a student of his or her work and ideas. • Record changes in thinking and conceptual explanations. • Basis for diagnosing learning difficulties.
Self-reflection and self-guidance: Contents focus on work a student has completed at several points separated in time, records of a student's past and present conceptual thinking about the subject-matter, records of a student's past and present evaluations of his or her own work, etc.	• Reflect on one's own progress in knowledge and skill. • Reflect on one's own changes in conceptual thinking. • With other students' portfolios to reflect on one's progress.

Figure 12.5. The portfolio in these examples was part of a state school-accountability system. The state education department mandated portfolio content and organization. Students prepare entries throughout the year. There was no mandated time schedule except the date on which the portfolio is due.

Fit to Curriculum   To be effective, portfolios must be consistent with the goals, standards, and learning targets of the state or school district curriculum framework and your daily teaching activities. Keep in mind the following points as you plan your portfolio organization and contents (Arter & Spandel, 1992):

- Portfolios should emphasize the same standards, curriculum goals, and learning targets emphasized in your daily instruction.
- The criteria used to evaluate students' portfolio entries should be the same as those used in daily instruction.
- The way you organize and use a portfolio should be consistent with the values you convey through your teaching activities (e.g., if your teaching emphasizes students taking responsibility for their own learning, the portfolio procedure you use should be consistent with this approach).

What Counts as Evidence?   The issue here is what should be included in or excluded from the portfolio. If the portfolio is a best-work portfolio and its purpose is to provide evidence of accomplishing the major learning targets, then these learning targets determine what to include. You

will need to decide whether a portfolio is the best method of assessing accomplishments on these learning targets, too. The portfolio, like other performance assessments, should not be used to assess every learning target in curriculum. As students become older and take more responsibility for their own learning, they can decide for themselves what constitutes appropriate evidence of accomplishment. In that case, you will need to give students clear statements of learning targets and of the criteria by which their accomplishments will be judged.

Entry Captions   A portfolio can quickly become a mess of materials and papers that is difficult to assess. Each entry should have an appropriate **portfolio entry sheet** (or **caption**) containing the following information:

- *Name of the student*
- *Date of entry*
- *Title or description of the entry.* For example, "Comparison of the Population Growth of Mexico and the United States."[1]
- *Some indication of the learning target or purpose for including the entry.* For example, "This entry shows that I can use numbers in real-world situations to draw conclusions about how populations grow. I can use growth rates and draw conclusions about when the two populations will be the same."

---

[1]The sample entry is cited in Kentucky Department of Education (1994). The sample quotations are fictitious illustrations based on an actual entry.

■ *Why this particular entry is important or valuable.* For example, "I think this was a good piece to include because it relates to an actual situation in which I had to use mathematics. Population growth is a social studies topic that I applied mathematics to solve. Also, I had to use a computer spreadsheet program to make the calculations many times in order to discover that the two countries will have the same population in about 59 years."

Limits to Portfolio The size of a portfolio is no small matter! A long and many-entried portfolio is difficult to understand and may be confusing to students who can get lost in the mass of materials. Also, evaluating long portfolios is difficult and time-consuming.

The assessment issues of portfolio size are related to validity and reliability. Does the portfolio represent the student's attainment? How many entries and what varieties of entries are needed to assure a representative sample of the student's work? How much less consistently will a long portfolio be scored than a short portfolio?

Self-Reflection on Portfolios For some teaching purposes, a student's review of and self-reflection on the portfolio's contents are the major concerns. Arter and Spandel (1992) suggest asking students the following types of questions to prompt self-reflective activities:

■ What is the process you went through to complete this assignment? Include where you got ideas, how you explored the subject, what problems you encountered, and what revision strategies you used.
■ What were the points made by the group as it reviewed your work? Describe your response to each point—did you agree or disagree? Why? What did you do as the result of their feedback?
■ What makes your most effective piece different from your least effective piece?
■ How does this activity relate to what you have learned before?
■ What are the strengths of your work? What still makes you uneasy? (p. 40)

Although such questions prompt students to review and evaluate their work, the list does not comprise an assessment method per se. Keep in mind that self-reflection is a mental activity. Your assessment of this activity must, therefore, be indirect. Further, although self-reflection appears to be a worthwhile instructional activity, it is not clear educationally that it is either desirable or appropriate to formally assess students' ability to do these self-reflective activities. They may best be handled as informal formative evaluation. In Appendix F, we discuss a related area, metacognition. Figure F.1 illustrates a student self-assessment questionnaire regarding different aspects of metacognition. You may want to adapt this questionnaire to assess portfolio self-reflection.

Special Concerns About Portfolio Contents

If one or two teachers work out a portfolio system for use in one or two classes, the system will likely meet their immediate needs as an informal assessment of students' progress. On the other hand, if a portfolio system is mandated by central educational authorities at the state or local levels, it becomes an "add-on" to already existing classroom activities. As a result, special steps are needed to convince and educate teachers about the usefulness of the mandated portfolio. A portfolio is not well integrated with instruction, for example, if students see one day a week as "portfolio day." They perceive portfolios as a separate subject!

At one time in Kentucky, portfolios were mandated by the commonwealth's department of education as part of the school accountability system. Patterns of portfolio crafting and usage illustrated this lack of integration in the early stages of the mandate. Buren and Lewis (1994) observed the following patterns of portfolio usage for writing.

■ *High-investment portfolios.* These portfolios showed the students were highly invested in the portfolio contents. Each portfolio was highly individual, and the contents were clearly the students' choices. The portfolios generally showed higher writing proficiency than the types described later.
■ *Cookie-cutter portfolios.* All portfolios from the same class look nearly identical. All students write about the same topics and use the same prompts. Students don't choose the contents and there is low student investment. These portfolios typically showed low writing proficiency.
■ *Portfolio-week portfolios.* All portfolios from the same classroom bore the same dates on all pieces. The pieces were not polished or rewritten. Rather, they were completed just before the deadline for submission to the state. The contents do not show high individual student choices or investment. These portfolios typically showed low writing proficiency.
■ *Teacher-generated prompt portfolios.* All portfolios from the same class were based on the same set of prompts. There was little student choice of topics and low student investment. The teacher-generated prompts were inappropriate or limited students' ability to write for different purposes or to different audiences.
■ *Content-limited portfolios.* These portfolios may exhibit any of the foregoing patterns. However, some of the pieces are writings from curriculum areas outside of the language arts area. The content areas are limited, and the portfolios generally show that students' writing outside of language arts classes needs further improvement. The portfolios demonstrate that writing skill is not being applied or integrated across different curriculum areas.

Obviously, you do not want to create a system that produces any of the inappropriate portfolio types. As you follow the steps described in the next section, keep the purpose of your portfolio clearly in mind. Table 12.7 may help to focus your attention on the appropriate assessment purpose for the portfolio.

Six Steps for Crafting a Portfolio System

Because portfolios are used for such a wide range of formative and summative purposes, a single set of design guidelines is difficult to devise. The six steps that follow are general enough, however, to give you overall guidance in the portfolio-crafting process. You should adapt the steps to suit your particular purposes. The steps express an assessment point of view, namely that assessment should be highly aligned to curriculum and teaching.

Following each step is a set of portfolio-crafting questions to sharpen the focus of your development efforts. Notice that after answering the questions in Step 1, you may decide not to develop a portfolio system. Steps 2 through 5 assume that you have completed Step 1 and have decided to use a portfolio system. If you decide to develop a portfolio system, the answers to the questions in Step 1 will set the boundaries and context as you apply the last five steps.

Step 1. Identify Portfolio's Purpose and Focus

- Why do I want a portfolio?
- What learning targets and curriculum goals will it serve?
- Will other methods of assessment serve these learning targets better?
- Should the portfolio focus on best work, growth and learning progress, or both?
- Will the portfolio be used for students' summative evaluation, formative evaluation, or both?
- Who should be involved in defining the purpose, focus, and organization of the portfolio? (e.g., students, teachers, parents)

Step 2. Identify the General Content to Be Assessed

- Do I need to use the same content and thinking processes framework as I do for individual performance tasks?
- Should I focus primarily on how well the student uses the portfolio to reflect on his or her progress or growth?
- What kinds of knowledge, skills, and abilities will be the *major* focus of the portfolio?
- If I want a growth and learning-progress portfolio, what do I want to learn about students' self-reflections?

Step 3. Identify Appropriate Organization

- What types of entries (student products and activity records) will provide assessment information about the content and process dimensions identified in Step 2?
- What should the outline or table of contents for each portfolio contain?
- Define each category or type of entry:
  - Which content and process dimension does it assess?
  - What will the teacher or the student "get out of" each entry?
  - What is the timeframe for each entry being put into the portfolio?
  - When will the entries be evaluated?
  - What are the minimum and maximum numbers of entries per category?
  - How will the entries within a student's portfolio be organized?
  - Will this set of entries fully represent the student's attainment or growth and learning progress?
  - What type of container will I need to hold all of the students' entries, and where will I keep them?

Step 4. Portfolio's Use in Practice

- When will the students work on or use their portfolios? (e.g., 15 minutes of every class period)
- How will the portfolio fit into the classroom routine?
- Will the teacher, student, or both decide what to include in the portfolio?
- Do I need to create a special climate in the classroom to promote the good use of portfolios?
- When will the student and/or the teacher review and evaluate the portfolio?
- How will the portfolio be weighted, if at all, when the time comes to assign letter grades for the marking period?
- Will I schedule a conference to go over the portfolio with the student?
- Will the portfolio be shared with parents? Other teachers? Other students?

Step 5. Evaluation of Portfolio Entries

- Are scoring rubrics already available for each type of entry?
- Does an evaluation framework or general scoring rubric exist for each type of entry?
- Are the general and specific rubrics aligned with the state standards and school district's curriculum framework?
- Will students, teachers, or both evaluate entries? Which ones?
- Will evaluations of every entry count toward a marking-period grade?

Step 6. Evaluation Rubrics

- Given its purpose, is it necessary to have an overall score for the portfolio?
- Should the rubric be holistic, analytic, or annotated holistic?

- Who will score the portfolio? (e.g., student, teacher, outsider)
- How often will the whole portfolio need to be scored? (e.g., each week or each marking period)
- Does an evaluation framework or general scoring rubric exist for evaluating the portfolio as a whole?
- Are scoring rubrics available that are consistent with the purpose of the portfolio? With the way each individual entry was evaluated? With the overall curriculum framework?
- Has the scoring rubric been tried on portfolios from different students? From students with different teachers? With what results?
- Does the scoring rubric give the same results for the same students when applied by different teachers?

Summary

- Performance assessments are developed in three stages: defining and clarifying the performance to be assessed, constructing the performance task, and creating scoring rubrics. In practice, the stages are iterative, not linear.
- The chapter provides numerous suggestions for defining and clarifying the performance to assess. Included are suggestions for using a framework in guiding the definitions of the standards or criteria on which the assessment will focus. Criteria for evaluating standards are given in Table 12.1.
- The chapter provides numerous suggestions for constructing performance tasks: how to identify meaningful tasks, how to develop a task around important content and thinking-process standards, and how to incorporate a variety of task features into the design. A checklist for evaluating performance tasks is given in Table 12.3.
- The number of performance tasks to include on an assessment is critical because such tasks take a long time to complete, and thus there are fewer of them on any one assessment. The chapter reviews the impact of several factors on the decision of how many tasks to use, including criticalness of the decisions, scope of the assessment, mixture of assessment formats, complexity of learning targets, time needed to complete the tasks, time available for assessment, diagnostic detail needed, and available human resources.
- The chapter provides numerous suggestions for crafting scoring rubrics and recording assessment results. Suggestions include developing and using a conceptual framework to organize the rubrics.
- The chapter provides guidelines for crafting checklists and examples of using them for assessing processes and procedures as well as products. A checklist for evaluating scoring rubrics is given in Table 12.5.
- Guidelines for crafting rating scales and examples of their use in implementing scoring rubrics are provided.

- Errors teachers could make when using rating scales as scoring rubrics are described.
- Suggestions are made for improving the reliability of rating scales. These are summarized in Table 12.6.
- Guidelines and suggestions for constructing portfolio systems describe issues surrounding content and purposes of portfolios. The chapter presents a six-step procedure for crafting portfolios.

Important Terms and Concepts

alternate solution strategies
best-work portfolio
central tendency error
checklist
content standard
descriptive graphic rating scale
graphic rating scale
growth and learning-progress portfolio
halo effect
leniency error
lifelong standard
logical error
numerical rating scale
personal bias
portfolio
portfolio entry sheet (caption)
product vs. process
rater drift
reliability decay
reliability of ratings
rubrics (analytic, annotated holistic, holistic)
scaffolding
scoring rubric (general, specific)
severity error
short task vs. long task
stages in crafting performance tasks
standard or quality dimension
structure a task

Exercises and Discussion Questions

1. For a subject you teach (or plan to teach), identify learning targets that would be appropriately assessed with on-demand performance tasks using paper and pencil, and with on-demand performance tasks not using paper and pencil.
   a. Using these results, create one on-demand performance task using paper-and-pencil and one on-demand performance task not using paper and pencil. For both tasks, follow the Marzano et al. (1993) procedure described in the text.
   b. Exchange your tasks with another student in the course. Evaluate each other's task by applying the checklist in Table 12.3. If you select a "no" answer explain why. Revise the tasks where necessary.
   c. Share your results with others in the course.
2. Select one performance task that you created in Exercise 1, or that you obtained from other sources. Following the procedures in this chapter, prepare generic and specific scoring

rubrics. (You may use the framework in Appendix E or another your instructor approves.)

　　a. Write a description of each step in the procedure you used to craft the rubrics.

　　b. Exchange your rubrics with another student in the course. Evaluate each other's specific rubrics using the criteria in Table 12.5. Whenever you check "no" in this checklist, explain why. Revise the rubrics where necessary.

　　c. Share your results with others in your course.

3. Select one performance task and corresponding specific scoring rubric (of your own or others' creation). Justify your selection in terms of appropriate learning targets.

　　a. Administer the performance task to at least five students. Score the task using the scoring rubric.

　　b. Write a short essay describing your scoring experience. Was the scoring rubric adequate? Were there any reliability problems in using it? Why or why not? Make suggestions for improving the scoring rubric based on your experience.

　　c. Prepare a summary of your students' results.

4. This chapter presents suggestions for improving the reliability of the results of using scoring rubrics. Using the rubrics from Exercises 2 and 3, give examples of how you could improve the reliability of the scores.

5. Apply the criteria in Table 12.3 to the following examples from the text in Chapter 11. Write a report of your findings. Be sure to make suggestions on how to improve the tasks. Send a copy of your report to the textbook author.

　　a. "Decision Making" (Figure 11.1)

　　b. "Why do birds fluff up their feathers in winter?" (Figure 11.5)

　　c. "This is a machine that changes numbers" (Figure 11.6)

　　d. "Clean Water" (Figure 11.7)

　　e. "Historical Investigation" (Figure 11.8)

6. "Performance assessments are not worth the trouble it takes to make, administer, and score them." Write an essay either supporting or refuting this statement. Be sure to refer to parts of this chapter to support your argument. Share your views with others in your course.

7. Would you use portfolios as a means of assessment when you teach? Explain why or why not in terms of the purposes for using portfolios given in Table 12.7.

8. Design a best-work portfolio system for assessing students in the subject you teach (or plan to teach). Follow the six-step procedure suggested in the chapter.

　　a. Prepare a report describing the portfolio system you designed. Be sure your report addresses all of the questions listed under each step.

　　b. Discuss your portfolio system in class with other students.

Additional Readings

www.achieve.org

　　This internet site compares standards set by many states for different subjects. It also gives examples of performance tasks that assess the standards.

Glatthorn, A. A., Bragau, K. D., & Parker, J. (1998) *Performance assessment and standards-based curricula: The achievement cycle.* Larchmont, NY: Eye on Education.

　　Practical guide for integrating instruction, standards-based curricula, and performance assessments. Emphasizes planning assessments at the unit level.

Internet resources:

　　http://www.danenet.wicip.org/lms/tnl/steps.htm

　　http://www.teleport.com/~cgrether/resource/oregon/scoring.html

　　http://www.exemplars.com

　　http://www.open.k12.or.us/search/search.html

　　http://mailer.fsu.edu/~jflake/rubrics.html

　　http://www.monroe2boces.org/shared/esp

　　http://www.nwrel.org/eval/index.html

　　http://mcrel.org/resources/

Khattri, N., Reeve, A. L., & Kane, M. B. (1998). *Principles and practices of performance assessment.* Hillsdale, NJ: Erlbaum.

　　Ideas and recommendations based on case studies of 16 schools. Discusses differences in purposes and implementations at state and local levels. Gives insights into all aspects of performance assessments.

Marzano, R., Pickering, D., & McTighe, J. (1993). *Assessing student outcomes: Performance assessment using the Dimensions of Learning Model.* Alexandria, VA: Association for Supervision and Curriculum Development.

　　Describes in detail the standards shown in Appendix E. Gives many examples of performance tasks and scoring rubrics that apply their standards.

Mehrens, W. A., Popham, W. J., & Ryan, J. M. (1998). How to prepare students for performance assessments. *Educational Measurement: Issues and Practice, 17*(1), 18–22.

　　This article give six practical guidelines on how to prepare students to take performance assessments. The focus is on preserving the validity and educational value of performance assessments.

Shaklee, B. D., Barbour, N. E., Ambrose, R., & Hansford, S. (1997). *Designing and using portfolios.* Boston: Allyn & Bacon.

　　Practical guidelines, forms, and examples of using portfolios for instructional purposes. One chapter discusses using portfolios to identify gifted students.

Underwood, T. (1998). The consequences of portfolio assessment: A case study. *Educational Assessment, 5,* 147–194.

　　This article describes a year-long case study of a language arts portfolio system used for report card grades. Read about what students did better as a result of the system, and what teachers liked about it. Learn, too, about "portfolio hell." Find out why the school chose not to adopt the portfolio system, even though it could be documented that students learned more compared to the traditional system.

CHAPTER 13

Formal and Informal Diagnostic Assessments

Learning Targets

After studying this chapter, you should be able to:

1. Explain the dual purpose of diagnostic assessment of learning difficulties.   [*1, 4*]

2. Describe six approaches to diagnostic assessment and give examples of each.   [*1, 4*]

3. Craft diagnostic assessment procedures using each of the six approaches described in this chapter.   [*2, 3, 4*]

4. Explain the strengths and weaknesses of each diagnostic assessment approach.   [*1, 4*]

5. Show through words and/or diagrams how the teaching, diagnosis, and assessment processes may be integrated.   [*4, 3, 1*]

6. Explain how to improve diagnostic assessment interviews of students.   [*2, 4*]

7. Explain the importance to educational assessment of each of the important terms and concepts listed at the end of this chapter.   [*6, 4*]

DIAGNOSTIC ASSESSMENT

Two Purposes of Classroom Diagnostic Assessment

Diagnostic assessment of learning difficulties serves two related purposes: (1) to identify which learning targets a student has not mastered, and (2) to suggest possible causes or reasons why the student has not mastered the learning targets. If you know what specific learning targets a student has not mastered, you can focus your remedial teaching on those specific targets. However, unless you also know or can hypothesize *why* the student cannot perform a learning target, you will likely be at a loss as to how to focus your remedial teaching.

Six Approaches to Diagnosis of Learning Problems

You may use many approaches to diagnosing learning difficulties. The different approaches use different points of view about how students learn and provide different levels of detail about students' **deficits in learning.** They also differ in the degree to which they emphasize the first or second of the purposes of diagnosis described previously. These are the six approaches we shall discuss:

1. The **profiling content areas strengths and weaknesses** approach, in which a deficit is defined as a student's low standing, relative to peers, in a broad learning outcome area

in a subject. For example, a student may have less ability in subtraction and division than in addition and multiplication.

2. The **prerequisite knowledge and skills deficits** approach, in which a deficit is defined as a student's failure to have learned concepts and skills necessary to profit from instruction in a course or a unit.

3. The **mastery of specific objectives** approach, in which a deficit is defined as a student's failure to master one or more end-of-instruction learning targets.

4. The **identifying students' errors in performance** approach, in which a deficit is defined as the type(s) of errors a student makes.

5. The **knowledge structure** approach, in which a deficit is defined as a student's inappropriate or incorrect mental organization of concepts and their interrelationships.

6. The **component competencies of problem solving** approach, in which a deficit is defined as a student's inability to perform one or more of the components necessary to solve a word problem.

Each approach will be described and evaluated in terms of how well it meets the second purpose of diagnostic testing: identifying probable causes of a student's learning difficulty. Figure 13.1 illustrates each of the first four approaches with a specific example and serves as a device for comparing the approaches. The last two approaches, illustrated later, are more in line with cognitively oriented instructional psychology.

FIGURE 13.1 Examples of how different approaches to diagnostic assessment interpret the same student's performance.

Examples of items along with responses of a hypothetical student

(a)	(b)	(c)	(d)	(e)	(f)	(g)	(h)	(i)
17	15	43	337	654	43	63	562	667
−12	−13	−32	−226	−423	−25	−57	−453	−374
5	2	11	111	231	$\sqrt{22}$	$\sqrt{14}$	$\sqrt{111}$	$\sqrt{313}$

Total score for subtraction = 5/9 or 56%. Percentile rank = 18

Approach 1.   Profile of strengths and weaknesses

The score on the subtraction subtest shown above is compared to the scores on other subtests such as addition, multiplication, division, etc. A profile of strengths and weaknesses in arithmetic is created for each student.

Example: The score of 5 correct has a percentile rank of 18 and is lower than other subtest scores.

Interpretation of the results : The student is weak in subtraction.

Approaches 2 and 3. Prerequisite hierarchy combined with mastery of specific objectives

The items above may be derived from a hierarchy of prerequisite arithmetic skills and the mastery of each skill in the hierarchy is assessed. (Skill statements are based on Ferguson [1970].)

Example:	*Hierarchy of Skills*	*Score*
	(4) Subtract 3-digit numbers requiring borrowing from either tens' or hundreds' place. [Items (h) and (i)]	$^0/_2$ or 0 %
	(3) Subtract 2-digit numbers with borrowing from tens' place. [Items (f) and (g)]	$^1/_2$ or 50 %
	(2) Subtract two 2-digit and two 3-digit numbers when borrowing is not needed. [Items (c), (d), and (e)]	$^3/_3$ or 100 %
	(1) Subtract 2-digit numbers when numbers are less than 20. [Items (a) and (b)]	$^2/_2$ or 100 %

Interpretation of the results: The student has mastered the prerequisite Objectives 1 and 2, but has not mastered Objectives 3 and 4. Instruction should begin with Objective 3.

Approach 4. Identifying Errors

The subtraction item(s) that the student answered incorrectly are studied and the student's errors are identified.

Example: The student's responses to Items (f), (g), (h), and (i) are wrong. These are studied to identify the type(s) of errors the student made.

Interpretation of the results: The student is not renaming (regrouping) from tens' to units' place and from hundreds' to tens' place.

INTEGRATING TEACHING, DIAGNOSIS, AND ASSESSMENT

Teaching and diagnosing learning difficulties all flow together. Feedback from assessment of students' learning guides your next steps as you proceed in teaching. The teaching process is complex and cannot be completely captured in simple diagrams. Nevertheless, we use a simplified diagram in Figure 13.2 to show you how the various diagnostic approaches fit into the teaching process. The steps in Figure 13.2 are described here. The sample assumes that you are planning to teach a new unit to the students.

1. *Have the students learned the prerequisites for the next unit?* If not, you will need to identify the deficit prerequisites, then teach them before beginning the new material. Otherwise students will not profit from the new unit.

2. *Teach the next unit.* If students have learned the necessary prerequisites, you can begin to teach the new material.

3. *Students are given practice on the units' learning targets.* Students must practice to master the learning targets.

4. *Have students mastered the units' learning targets?* At this step you can conduct a more formal summative assessment of the students by implementing the assessment plans described in Chapter 6. If students have mastered the material, you can proceed to the next unit. If they have not, you may need to reteach at least some part of the unit.

5. *What learning targets have students not mastered?* Your reteaching should focus on these learning targets. Depending on the content and educational level of your students, simply knowing which targets were not learned sufficiently may be enough information for you to carry out your remedial lesson(s).

6. *What mistakes or errors do students make?* Often you will need to look beyond the learning-target deficits to identify the errors or mistakes a student makes. Your reteaching can focus on correcting the mistakes or errors you identify.

FIGURE 13.2   Example of how the six approaches to diagnosing learning difficulties may be integrated into the teaching process.

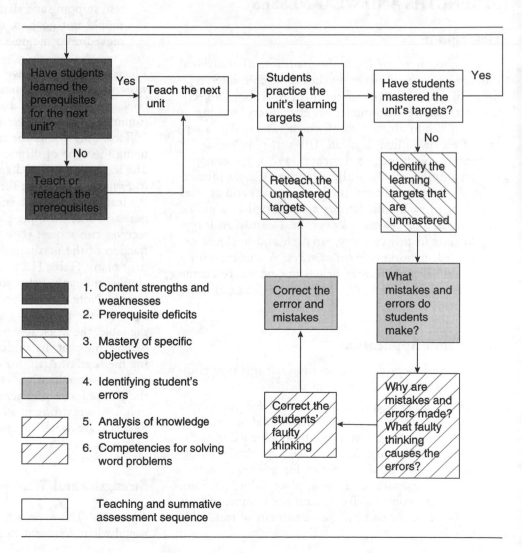

1. Content strengths and weaknesses
2. Prerequisite deficits
3. Mastery of specific objectives
4. Identifying student's errors
5. Analysis of knowledge structures
6. Competencies for solving word problems

Teaching and summative assessment sequence

7. *Why are the mistakes/errors made? What is the faulty thinking that students use when they make mistakes?* Students' errors are very often the result of not understanding concepts, not relating concepts to existing knowledge, applying the wrong rule, or knowing how to do some part of the task but not all of it. If you can identify these deeper thinking errors, you can organize your remedial teaching to help students to correct their thinking. This should reduce their errors and lead to their mastering the learning targets. (See, for example, Approach 4 in Figure 13.1.)

Figure 13.2 describes these steps in a more dynamic way by using a process flowchart. Parts of the diagram are shaded differently to indicate how they are related to the six approaches to diagnostic assessment listed earlier. The following sections discuss each of the six approaches in more detail.

APPROACH 1: PROFILING CONTENT STRENGTHS AND WEAKNESSES

Description

This approach stems from the tradition of individual differences, or trait-factor psychology. Score interpretation emphasizes norm-referencing. A school subject—say, elementary arithmetic or elementary reading—is subdivided into areas, each of which is treated as a separate trait or ability. *KeyMath Diagnostic Arithmetic Test* (Connolly, Nachtman, & Pritchett, 1976), for example, divides primary school arithmetic into 14 areas (numeration, fractions, addition, subtraction, etc.) and assesses a student in each area. Results are reported as a profile of strengths and weaknesses over the 14 areas. As is typical of tests in this category, strength and weakness are interpreted in norm-referenced ways: A student with a "weakness" is significantly below the norm. Percentile ranks are the primary type of norm-referenced score used in this context.

Classroom Application

The following steps describe how to craft this type of diagnostic assessment for classroom use.

1. *Identify two or more content areas over which you want to profile students.* Each content area should be related to the learning targets you will be teaching during the term. For example, you may wish to obtain a diagnostic profile in mathematics for addition, subtraction, multiplication, division, place value, fractions, and word problems. Try to limit the number of areas to two or eight to keep the assessment of reasonable length.

2. *Craft items to span the basic concepts in each content area.* The items should match with the learning targets in each area.
   a. For classroom purposes, it is best to use constructed-response or short-answer items for diagnostic tests of this type. This reduces chances of students answering correctly by blind guessing or because the response-choice items are poorly crafted.
   b. If possible, use 12 to 25 items per content area. This will result in more reliable profiles.
   c. The items should cover the most basic concepts and procedures in each content area. You are trying to identify those few students who are most in need of remediation in an area. The items for each content area should be rather easy for students who have achieved an acceptable level of learning in each area.

3. *Assemble the items into separate **subtests**, with one subtest for each content area.* For example, put all the addition items together, all the subtraction, and so on. Arrange the items within each subtest from easiest to most difficult.

4. *Administer each subtest separately, using separate directions and timing.* All students should work on the same subtest, stopping and starting a subtest together. Students should not go back to a subtest once the class has moved onto the next subtest.

When the students have completed all of the subtests, score each subtest separately. The subtest scores are the ones you interpret diagnostically. The total score (summed over all subtests) has no diagnostic value.

Table 13.1 shows the hypothetical results of administering this type of diagnostic test to a group of students. The test covers French I and would likely be administered to *French II* students at the beginning of the term, so that the teacher would have an idea of the strengths and weaknesses of the incoming class. For each subtest, a student receives two scores: (1) the number right, expressed as a fraction of the maximum possible score, and (2) the student's rank. (Table H.2 in Appendix H explains ranks.) Including the ranks helps you identify the poorest students quickly. Note that the *smaller* the rank, the *better is the student* (i.e., the top-scoring student receives a rank of 1). In the table, the worst scores are circled.

You interpret the students' strengths and weakness using their ranks. Alan, for example, has a weakness in listening comprehension compared to other students in the group. Isaac, who generally did well, is weak in grammar. Leslie is strong in all areas, as is Robert. Miriam and Rebecca are weak in several areas but are average in grammar.

Strengths and Weaknesses

Strengths This approach to diagnostic assessment is most useful when you want to obtain a general idea about stu-

TABLE 13.1 Example of students' strengths and weaknesses profiles resulting from a teacher-made diagnostic test of French I.

	Areas of French I									
	Idioms		Vocab.		Grammar		Para. Reading		Listen. Compre.	
	Correct	Rank	Correct	Rank	Correct	Rank	Correct	Rank	Correct	Rank
Alan	10/12	3.5	11/15	3	11/13	3	9/12	4	3/15	⑤
Isaac	11/12	2	10/15	4.5	3/13	⑥	11/12	2	10/15	3
Leslie	12/12	1	15/15	1	12/13	2	11/12	2	14/15	1
Miriam	3/12	⑥	10/15	4.5	10/13	4.5	2/12	⑥	1/15	⑥
Rebecca	5/12	⑤	3/15	⑥	10/13	4.5	6/12	⑤	4/15	4
Robert	10/12	3.5	14/15	2	13/13	1	11/12	2	12/15	2

dents' performance in subareas of a subject matter. If you know little about an incoming class of students, administering this type of assessment as a pretest at the beginning of the term can help you plan your teaching around the students' profiles. It is easy to craft. It can be scored quickly, which is a benefit if you have a large class or several sections.

Weaknesses For these profiles to be valid, the items you construct must assess the appropriate knowledge and skills, all students must take the same subtests, and the subtests must be reliable. If the subtests each contain only a handful of assessment tasks, the subtest scores probably will be unreliable. Unreliable subtest scores result in an **unreliable profile** over the different subareas. As a result, the students' strengths and weaknesses may be exaggerated or masked by chance errors of measurement.

Diagnosis with such tests is generally rather coarse. The subtest scores used for the students' profiles in the content areas of the subject provide you with only general information about where their problems lie. It is much like saying, "The Holy Grail lies to the north." The information is helpful, but it leaves you with a lot of work to do before the Grail can be found.

A good educational diagnostician will supplement these test results with more detailed testing and observations of students. You use the initial test results to formulate hypotheses concerning students' difficulties. You confirm or reject these hypotheses by following up and gathering additional information. Thus, although the initial profile of strengths and weaknesses is likely to be rather unreliable, the reliability of the final diagnosis will be much higher if it is made by a skilled diagnostician who incorporates into that diagnosis appropriate additional information. This is not to say, however, that the reliability of the profile-generating test should be ignored: High initial reliability helps the initial set of hypotheses to be as focused as possible and assures that

you do not chase a large number of false leads. A test with very low profile reliability wastes the diagnostician's resources.

APPROACH 2: IDENTIFYING PREREQUISITE DEFICITS

Description

This approach explores whether students have fallen behind because they have not acquired the specific knowledge and skills necessary to profit from upcoming instruction. Among the approaches relying upon identification of learning prerequisites is Gagné's **learning hierarchies** (Gagné, 1962, 1968; Gagné, Major, Garstens, & Paradise, 1962; Gagné & Paradise, 1961).

The first step in creating a hierarchy is to analyze one learning target the student must be able to perform. The next steps involve identifying the prerequisite performances a student must learn. For each prerequisite performance identified, you repeat the same analysis, generating a hierarchy of prerequisite performances. This backward analytic procedure identifies critical prior learning, the lack of which could cause students problems in subsequent learning. A number of instructional programs have incorporated such learning hierarchies and used assessments to diagnose students' knowledge of prerequisites within the hierarchical framework. Examples include Primary Education Program (Wang & Resnick, 1978), Individually Prescribed Instruction (Ferguson, 1970; Lindvall & Bolvin, 1967), and Adaptive Learning Environments Program (Wang, Gennari, & Waxman, 1983).

The difference between this approach and the previous one is that you focus on whether each prerequisite was learned rather than on the pattern of profile strengths and weaknesses. Your interpretation of results is criterion-referenced rather than norm-referenced.

Metropolitan Performance Assessment (Nurss, 1994), for example, contains several assessment components to survey prekindergarten and kindergarten students' learning of the basic skills and processes needed for beginning the first grade. One of the assessment components is the *Metropolitan Integrated Performance Tasks*, which assesses readiness skills such as following oral directions, understanding rhyming words, matching uppercase and lowercase letters, copying printed letters, drawing pictures, basic concepts (e.g., top, bottom, middle, under), rote counting, correspondence of number to numerals, counting forward and backward, and reading simple graphs. Information on mastering prerequisites from the *Metropolitan Performance Assessment* is used by preschool and kindergarten teachers to prepare students for first-grade work.

Classroom Application

You can identify prerequisites at the level of a unit of instruction, or for a term. Use the hierarchical approach, or simply identify necessary prerequisites that are not in a teaching order. To develop a learning hierarchy, you should follow the procedure described earlier in relation to the Gagné learning hierarchies. For each learning target, ask yourself, "What must a student be able to do before he is ready to learn this learning target?" Focus on what needs to be learned immediately before. Once you identify that immediately prior (prerequisite) performance,

you ask the same question about it. You may identify one or more performances that are immediately prerequisite. Continue this backward analysis until you have reached the point where you can safely assume that nearly all the incoming students have learned the prerequisites.

Figure 13.3 shows a learning hierarchy for computational subtraction based on an analysis by Ferguson (1970). The final learning target, "subtracting two 3-digit numbers with borrowing from both the tens' and hundreds' place," is at the top. All the other performances are prerequisite to it. Notice that Performance 5 is prerequisite to 4, but that both 2 and 3 are prerequisite to 4. The 2 and 3 performances are not prerequisite to each other, however, so they are shown in parallel branches.

Once you have created the hierarchy, you assess each student with respect to it. To do so, you need to create several items or tasks to assess each of the performances identified. At a minimum, you should use four or five items per performance in the hierarchy. All items for a performance assess only that performance.

If the hierarchy is small, you can start at the bottom and proceed upward, assessing one node at a time. Stop assessing a student when the student reaches a point where she can do none or only one or two of the items at a node. If the hierarchy is very large, you can use an **adaptive testing strategy**. Begin with the performance at the middle of the hierarchy. If a student does well on those items, branch upward to the next performance and

FIGURE 13.3 Prerequisite hierarchy of a subtraction unit.

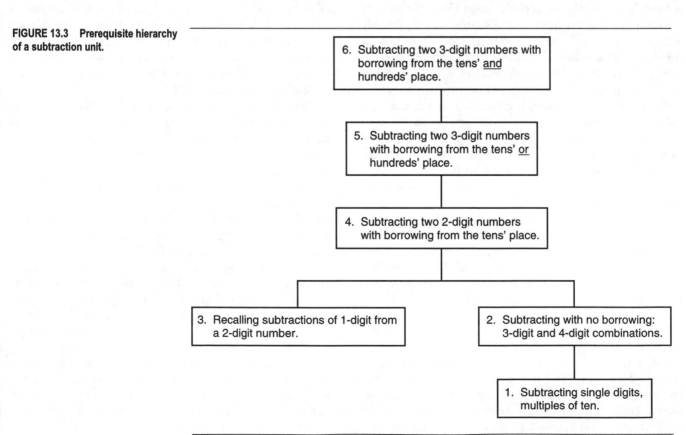

Source: Based on an analysis by Ferguson (1970).

continue assessing until the student reaches a point where it is obvious that he cannot proceed further. Because the performances are in a prerequisite order, the lower performances in the hierarchy are not tested; you assume the student can perform them. If a student does poorly, you can branch downward to the next lower performance, continuing to assess until it is obvious the student knows all the remaining lower nodes. In this case, you assume that the student has learned those performances below that point.

Without a hierarchy, you can still identify the prerequisite learning for the term material or unit you are about to teach. You can identify these prerequisites in a manner similar to the procedure for developing a hierarchy. That is, ask yourself, "What does a student need to know how to do before I can teach the student this learning target?" The answers to such questions should result in a list of prerequisites that students should know before learning the new targets. Once these are identified, you develop four to five assessment tasks for each prerequisite.

Whether or not you use a hierarchy, your ultimate purpose for assessment is to identify for each student the prerequisites that are mastered and those that are not. You then remediate by teaching students the prerequisites they do not know before beginning new instruction.

Strengths and Weaknesses

Strengths This approach very specifically identifies skills that students need to learn before they are ready to be taught new learning targets. A hierarchy suggests the sequence in which the prerequisites are to be taught. Assessments of prerequisite knowledge and skills are most helpful when you know very little about the students, especially when you expect large differences among the students in their mastery of the prerequisites. Once you know each student's command of the prerequisites, you can tailor your teaching to meet individual students' needs.

To be most effective, the prerequisites you identify should be specific to your curriculum and to your teaching approach. Different curricula and different teachers will approach the subject differently. This means that the prerequisites for students you teach may be somewhat different than the prerequisites for students a colleague teaches. (They should not be radically different, however, when both teachers are teaching comparable students the same material.) Further, sometimes the teaching sequence is **spiral**: a topic is taught several times throughout the unit or course with increasing elaboration each time. In this case, a students' level of mastery of the prerequisite skill may not need to be very high because of the repeated reteaching of the topic. A more **linear teaching sequence** may require higher levels of prerequisite mastery, because you don't come back to a topic to reteach and elaborate on it.

Weaknesses This approach is limited by the care and accuracy with which you analyze the learning requirements

of your curriculum. If you do not identify the proper prerequisites, your assessment will lack validity. Further, in a continuous-progress curriculum, the distinction between prerequisites and "regular learning" is rather arbitrary, based more or less on instructional convenience.

The learning theory underlying this approach assumes that learning proceeds best by first teaching the prerequisites. This is a building-block approach, in which prerequisite performances build one on another to facilitate the learning of new targets. It is not clear that this building-block approach to learning is an appropriate teaching strategy for all subjects and for all students.

Prerequisite assessments of the type described provide information about the content (knowledge and skills) students need to learn, but this type of content-based information does not tell you how instruction should be crafted to overcome the prerequisite deficiencies. Prerequisites derived from logical analyses of learning targets have at least two weaknesses that make it difficult to begin remedial instruction: (1) They identify only certain, but not all, types of knowledge and skills necessary to students to learn new material, and (2) they fail to provide you with information about the way students organize or structure their partial knowledge about the content to be learned (see Champagne, Klopfer, & Gunstone, 1982).

Champagne et al. reviewed the instructional implications of the findings of cognitive researchers in the areas of problem solving, recalling meaning, and learning new knowledge, especially as these findings relate to teaching basic principles of mechanics. They found that logical analysis of learning targets failed to identify: (1) the ways in which students entering a physics course mentally organized and understood mechanical principles in their everyday experience, (2) that students need to be taught how to qualitatively analyze problems before attempting to solve them quantitatively (i.e., before applying an equation), and (3) that one goal of instruction is to change students' entering knowledge schemata so that they approach the schemata of experts. (Chapter 10 discusses schema.) As the Champagne et al. review points out, it often is not simply the students' lack of content knowledge that is the primary cause of learning difficulty, but also the conflicts between the students' preconceptions of how the concepts in a subject are related to each other and how the textbook or teacher says the concepts are related. (See the topic of pretesting in Chapter 6.)

APPROACH 3: IDENTIFYING OBJECTIVES NOT MASTERED

Description

This approach begins with a list of the important, specific targets students are expected to learn. The total pool of specific learning targets within a subject area is usually grouped into topical areas (e.g., decoding, work knowledge, comprehension). Short tests then assess each objective. For administrative convenience, objectives close together in the instructional sequence are sometimes assessed in the same test. If each objective is assessed by a separate test, the test is typically five to eight items long. When several objectives are assessed in one test administered in a single sitting, there are usually fewer items, perhaps one to three, per objective. The difference between this approach and the identifying prerequisite deficits approach is that you focus on the objectives that are the *outcomes* of the unit or the course rather than on the prerequisite objectives.

This approach has become the dominant one for diagnosing students' difficulties with a subject. It is often recommended as the method of choice to classroom teachers, as well as to more specialized educational diagnosticians. Despite the many ways and potential uses of criterion-referencing (Nitko, 1980), for many educators the concepts of diagnosis, behavioral objectives, and criterion-referencing are inseparable, as the following extract illustrates:

> Diagnosing and monitoring student learning progress has become an operating feature of programs aimed at adapting instruction to student differences. A key component of such programs is the use of criterion-referenced assessments, that is [assessments] designed to determine the presence or absence of certain specific competencies, providing teachers with the necessary information to determine skills and knowledge already possessed by students so that their appropriate entrance into the learning sequence can be insured. Furthermore, the use of such clear-cut descriptions of the students' capabilities insures that they neither repeat tasks they have already mastered nor work on objectives for which they lack critical prerequisites. (Wang, 1980, p. 5)

The ideal of teaching to specific learning objectives dates back at least to the seminal work of Waples and Tyler (Tyler, 1934; Waples & Tyler, 1930). Teachers in the 1930s and 1940s, however, generally did not write statements of behavior or develop diagnostic assessments based on them.

The current widespread popularity of objectives-based assessment and instruction is principally a result of the commercial availability of integrated sets of objectives and tests. Publishers moved toward such integrated materials in the later 1970s and early 1980s, after educators enthusiastically greeted the concept of criterion-referencing tests (Glaser, 1963; Nitko, 1980). Instructional methods were developed that integrated objectives, learning material, and diagnostic tests. The major prototypes were the mastery learning model (Bloom, 1968; Carroll, 1963), Individually Prescribed Instruction (Glaser, 1968; Lindvall & Bolvin, 1967), Program for Learning in Accordance with Needs (Flanagan, 1967, 1969), Individually Guided Instruction (Klausmeier, 1975), and Personalized System of Instruction (Keller, 1968; Keller & Sherman, 1974).

Classroom Applications

The diagnostic information you want to obtain from this approach is a list of learning targets (objectives) that a student has mastered and not mastered. This means that for each teaching unit you must carefully identify and state the important learning targets. Follow these steps.

1. *Identify and write statements of the learning targets that are the main outcomes of the unit or the course.*

2. *For each learning target, craft four to eight assessment tasks* (items).

3. *If possible, have another teacher review each assessment task and rate how closely it matches the learning targets.* Revise the tasks as necessary to obtain a closer match.

4. *Assemble the tasks into a single instrument if the list of learning targets is relatively short (less than six); otherwise, depending on the students' educational development, you may need to divide the assessment into two or more instruments.* For ease of scoring, keep all the tasks (items) assessing the same objective together in the instrument.

5. *Set a "mastery" or passing score for each learning target.* A frequently used **passing score** is 80% (or as near as you can come to this with the number of items you have for assessing a learning target). There is no educational justification for 80%, however. The important point is not the exact value of the passing score or passing percentage. Rather, it is the minimum level of knowledge a student needs to demonstrate with respect to each learning target to benefit from further instruction. This may vary from one learning target to the next. Use your own judgment, remembering that setting a standard too low or too high results in misclassifying students as masters or nonmasters. (See Figure 4.7 and the related text.)

6. *Administer the assessment to the students.* After administering the assessment, separately score each learning target. Prepare a class list and chart in which the students' scores on each learning target can be recorded. This lets you identify students with similar deficits. Table 13.2 shows an example of such a chart. The scores that are circled in the chart are classified as not mastered. Students should be given remedial instruction on these objectives.

Strengths and Weaknesses

Strengths Diagnostic assessments based on specific objectives are appealing because they (1) focus on specific and limited learning targets to teach, (2) communicate learning targets in an easy-to-understand form, and (3) focus your attention on students' observed performance.

TABLE 13.2 Hypothetical example of diagnosis of specific objectives mastered and not mastered on a teacher-made, objectives-based diagnostic test. Circles mean nonmastery.

Students →	Alan	Isaac	Leslie	Miriam	Rebecca	Robert
Objectives						
1. Names and tells functions of each cell part. [8 items, mastery = 7/8]	7/8	8/8	7/8	(2/8)	(5/8)	(6/8)
2. Lists substances diffused and not diffused through cell membrane. [6 items, mastery = 5/6]	(4/6)	6/6	5/6	5/6	(3/6)	(1/6)
3. Labels parts of animal and plant cells. [6 items, mastery = 5/6]	5/6	5/6	5/6	(4/6)	(2/6)	(4/6)
4. Applies concepts of diffusion, oxidation, fusion, division, chromosomes, and DNA to explain reproduction. [8 items, mastery = 7/8]	(5/8)	7/8	7/8	7/8	(3/8)	(6/8)

These features make assessment easier, instructional decision making simpler, and public accountability clearer.

Weaknesses Objectives-based diagnostic assessments are generally plagued with measurement error, primarily because the assessments tend to have too few items per objective. If you use a diagnostic assessment to decide whether a student has "mastered" an objective, you should evaluate its quality using an index such as percent agreement, rather than a traditional reliability coefficient. Percent agreement is discussed in Chapter 4. A **percent agreement index** estimates how likely students are to be classified in the same category when either the same assessment is readministered or an alternate form of the assessment is administered. (See Appendix I for examples of how to calculate this index.) Consistency of classification (i.e., of mastery or nonmastery) is the main focus, rather than consistency of students' exact scores.

The behavioral objectives approach to diagnostic assessment has other serious limitations. The information obtained is limited to only one aspect of diagnosis: the observable behavior or performance of what is to be learned. This gives you little information about how to remediate the deficits discovered. You know only that a student has not mastered an objective. Like the other approaches we have discussed, behavioral objectives-based assessments are not fully diagnostic.

The behavioral objectives approach can also be criticized for implying an inappropriate theory of how knowledge and skill are acquired. A student's knowledge base is seen as a simple sum of previously learned specific behaviors. Further, critics point out that behavior-based tests fail to assess students' knowledge schemata, problem-solving disabilities, and their abilities to think in new real-world contexts (Haertel & Calfee, 1983). In recent years, instructional and cognitive psychology have stressed the importance of learning a student's internal representation (or schema) of knowledge, the relationships a student makes between knowledge elements, the way students construct meaning from their learning experiences, and the knowledge-processing skills a student commands (Glaser, 1982, 1984; Greeno, 1976).

Finally, focusing on isolated and specific learning targets can make the curriculum seem fragmented. That is, the general themes and the learning targets that express integration of many specific knowledge and skill components are often neglected in favor of the isolated specific objectives.

APPROACH 4: IDENTIFYING STUDENTS' ERRORS

Description

This approach focuses on identifying and classifying a student's errors, rather than simply making a mastery-nonmastery decision about the student's performance on a particular behavioral objective. Examples of errors are: failure to regroup when "borrowing" in subtraction, improper pronunciation of vowels when reading, reversing *i* and *e* when spelling, and producing a sentence fragment when writing. Once you identify and classify a student's errors, you attempt to provide instruction to remediate (eliminate) them (see Figures 13.1 and 13.2).

Related to the error classification approach are methods that analyze complex performance into two or more component performances. If a student cannot perform the entire complex performance, diagnostic assessment identifies which component behaviors are lacking. Resnick and her associates (Resnick, 1975, 1976; Resnick, Wang, & Kaplan, 1973), for example, broke complex preschool mathematics skills into their component skills and identified the sequence in which these subskills should be performed. Burton (1982) identified all the subskills needed for a student to solve a problem correctly. The measurement of each of these less complex subskills in isolation is the basis of diagnosis. Gagné (1970, 1979) proposed a two-stage procedure to assess problem-solving ability. Given that the student failed to solve the problem presented, a second-stage assessment is used to determine which, if any, of the principles the student knows, whether all of the principles are known; and whether the student understands how to combine them.

Classroom Applications

It is not easy to apply this approach because it takes considerable experience and skill to identify students' errors, and there may be more than one cause for an error. Consider the subtraction problems in Figure 13.1, for example. An inexperienced or unskilled teacher may not recognize the possible cause of the student's mistakes. Oftentimes, such teachers will say the student was "not careful" or "made careless errors." However, students' errors are rarely careless or random. Rather, *students' errors are often systematic.* Students may apply a rule or a procedure consistently in both appropriate and inappropriate situations. For instance, in Figure 13.1, the student appears to have consistently applied this rule: "Subtract the smaller digit from the larger digit." This rule works for problems (a) through (e), but does not work for problems (f) through (i). *It is important, therefore, that you consider every error a student makes as having some systematic cause.* Try to identify what caused the error, or what rule the student is using, before you dismiss it as careless or random.

Many student errors are best discovered by interviewing students. You can ask them to explain how they solved a problem, to explain why they responded the way they did, to tell you the rule for solving the problem, or to talk aloud as they go through the solutions to problems. These informal assessment procedures often lead you to the types of errors a student is making.

Chapter 10 discussed higher-order thinking and problem-solving assessment. Those assessment strategies are useful for discovering what types of problem-solving errors a student tends to make.

Strengths and Weaknesses

Strengths The chief advantage of the error classification approach over the behavioral objectives approach is that you discover not only *that* a learning target cannot be performed but also which aspects of the student's performance are flawed. This narrows your search for possible causes of poor performance. A skilled teacher can use this information to quickly identify one or more instructional procedures that have previously worked (remediated the error) with similar students.

Weaknesses Error classification procedures have serious drawbacks, however. There are several practical problems. Students make many different kinds of errors, and these are difficult to classify and to keep in mind while analyzing a student's performance. Frequently students demonstrate the same error for different reasons, so remedial instruction could be misdirected. Also, the amount of individual assessment and interpretation required seems prohibitive, given the amount of instructional time available.

More serious than practical problems of implementation, however, is the problem that, if diagnosis only classifies errors, it still fails to identify the thinking processes a student has used to produce the errors. Just knowing the type of error (failing to borrow in subtraction) does not tell you the appropriate knowledge structures and cognitive processes a student needs to reach the desired outcome. Error enumeration and classification focus on the negative aspects of performance and are insufficient for understanding why students produce errors (Bejar, 1984). Of course, cognitive analyses could be incorporated into error diagnostic procedures. We turn next to this possibility.

APPROACH 5: IDENTIFYING STUDENT KNOWLEDGE STRUCTURES

Description

A shortcoming of the diagnostic assessment approaches already mentioned is their strong ties to the **surface features** of subject-matter information and problem solving. Diagnosis should focus more on how a student perceives the structure or organization of that content (i.e., the student's knowledge structures) and processes information and knowledge to solve problems using that content knowledge. As Sternberg has pointed out in other contexts (Sternberg, 1984; Wagner & Sternberg, 1984), behavioristic and psychometric approaches are not exactly wrong, but they are incomplete. What is needed is an approach that describes a student's mental processes that help to change thinking. Information about knowledge structures and psychological processes may identify why a student is failing to achieve the desired learning targets (Glaser, 1982).

Diagnosis of students before beginning instruction is often as important as diagnosis after instruction. We showed one assessment technique for gathering this information in Table 6.3. Frequently, students' **everyday understandings of terms and phenomena** are at odds with a subject-matter experts' and textbooks' understandings. Further, students' everyday understanding of technical and nontechnical concepts varies from culture to culture, so that instruction geared to certain technical forms of knowledge might need to be adapted to different settings (Urevbu, 1984). These conflicts can interfere with your teaching of technical or specialized knowledge, unless you explicitly address students' knowledge schemata in the course of your teaching (Champagne et al., 1982).

One example of preinstructional assessment is our Chapter 6 discussion of a cold drink and a sweater. If you ask younger students what will happen to the temperature of a bottle of cold soft drink when it is wrapped up in a wool sweater, many will say that the sweater will warm the drink. In their schemata, "sweater" is something that Mother tells you to put on to keep warm. Thus, even though you may explain things clearly, they do not believe that a sweater has insulating properties that will keep a cold drink cold. You must relate the new concepts to their current thinking and schemata. You must help them to reconstruct their knowledge structures. They need to understand how keeping their bodies warm and keeping the soft drink cold are linked together by the concept of insulation. To believe it they need to understand the principles of insulation and how a sweater works as an insulator. You may need to conduct some experiments to further support their new beliefs and understandings.

There is considerable evidence that a person's knowledge structure is important to cognitive performance (Anderson, 1977, 1984; Glaser, 1984; Haertel & Calfee, 1983; Kintsch, 1974; Minstrell & Stimpson, 1990; Prichert & Anderson, 1977; Shank & Ableson, 1977; Shavelson, 1985). This research documents the role of knowledge structures for recalling information, reasoning, acquiring understanding, representing problems, and identifying clues, heuristics, and constraints in solving problems.

Several methods are used for assessing students' knowledge structures. These methods share the common perspective that as individuals become more proficient, their

knowledge becomes more interconnected, more deeply organized, and more accessible. Knowledge organization assessment has a long history, where studies first used free recall and later used word association (Preece, 1976, is one example). Other methods include free sorting of cards (Hambleton & Sheehan, 1977); similarity rating (Johnson, 1967); tree or hierarchical graph building (Fillenbaum & Rapoport, 1971); ordered tree hierarchical recovery (Reitman & Rueter, 1980); modified ordered tree (MOT) hierarchy recovery (Naveh-Benjamin, McKeachie, Lin, & Tucker, 1986); analysis of protocols (Greeno, 1976, 1978; Hewson & Hamlyn, 1984); mapping tests (Surber, 1984; Surber & Smith, 1981); structure formation (SLT) (Ballstaedt & Mandl, 1985); MicoCAM concept mapping (Ju, 1989; Young, 1993); and concept structuring analysis (ConSAT) (Champagne & Klopfer, 1980). These techniques vary in theoretical perspective and the type of knowledge organization they represent. Techniques that make similar assumptions about the theoretical constructs and underlying knowledge structure and how this structure is reflected in what the student records have convergent validity sufficient for classroom assessment purposes (Champagne, Hoz, & Klopfer, 1984; Shavelson & Stanton, 1975).

Classroom Applications

A **concept map** is a graphical way to represent how a student understands the relationships among the major concepts in the subject. Suggestions for capturing a student's concept map are given in Table 13.3. An example of how a student might organize concepts related to a science unit on rocks is shown in Figure 13.4. For this task, the teacher shows a student the list of concepts at the top of Figure 13.4 and works with the student individually, in a manner similar to the procedure described in Table 13.3,

FIGURE 13.4 Hypothetical example of a student's concept map of rocks.

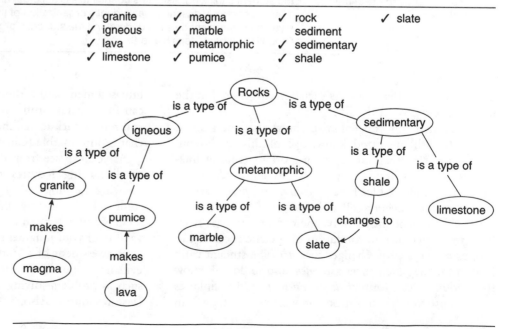

TABLE 13.3 Suggestions for conducting a student interview to create a concept map useful for assessment.

Step	The focus of your interviewing and probing
1. Identify major concepts	Start with giving the student a few of the major concepts in the area you are probing. You could put these on cards. Ask students to tell you about these concepts, what they mean to the student, and some of the other things about which they make the student think. Write every concept the student mentions in a list.
2. Create an arrangement of the concepts to match the student's thinking	Use a large sheet of paper. Review the list created in Step 1 with the student. Ask the student which of the concepts (including the ones you initially showed on the cards) is the major or most important one. Even if the student does not identify one as the major one, ask the student to pick one with which to start. Write this concept in the middle of the page. Ask the student to select another that is most closely related to the one on the page. Write this near the one already on the page. Continue asking for the ones nearest to the central one. Write these around the central concept. Continue with the remaining concepts, asking where they belong. These may be further from the central one and may be near some of the secondary concepts.
3. Establish how the student relates the concepts to one another.	Begin with the central concept, work with the nearest ones to it, one at a time, and take each pair in turn. Ask the student whether the two are related and, if so, why or how they are related. Connect the related concepts with a line. Do not connect the concepts the student says are unrelated, even if you think they should be. Remember, you are trying to picture how the student is thinking. Assure the student frequently that there is no correct answer you are looking for but that you seek to help the student explain how he or she is thinking about these concepts. After connecting the related concepts with a line, write on the line the type of relationship the student tells you. (E.g., "is an example of", "is a", "causes", "is part of", "it makes it go", etc.) If a student just says, "They are related," probe further to understand what the relationship is.
4. Feedback to the student and rearrange the map	Show the student the map so far. Talk about the arrangement. Feedback to the student what the map tells you about the student's thinking and ask if this is correct. Rearrange the map so that it better represents the student's thinking and understanding of the concepts. Talk about each concept and its relationships. Add new concepts if the student mentions them and determine how they are linked to the mapped concepts. Redraw the map if necessary.
5. Elaborate the map to show new concepts, linkages, and examples	Discuss the rearranged map further with the student. Ask the student to tell you more: what else does the student know about these concepts, what are some examples, why are the concepts related, etc. Incorporate this new information into the map and add branches and expansions as necessary to depict the student's thinking.
6. Explore cross-linkages and complex relationships	Go over the map drawn to this point with the student. Ask the student about the pairs of concepts previously unconnected and about the connections of new concepts mentioned in Step 5. Ask the student if he or she thinks three or four concepts should be connected together and why. Record these complex relationships.
7. Feedback to the student and rearrange to make the final map	Show the map to the student and discuss with the student what the map tells you about the student's thinking. Ask the student if this is accurate and rearrange the map to make it more accurately describe the student's organization of the concepts. You may stop here if you have sufficient detail to understand the student's organization of the concepts. Otherwise, repeat Steps 5 and 6.

to create the concept map. As each concept is used in the map, it is crossed off the list.

Notice that this concept map shows that the student has fairly well organized knowledge of this unit's concepts. However, there are some important concept linkages missing. For the most part, the student understands the concepts hierarchically (e.g., *granite* and *pumice* are included in the category called *igneous*, which is a type of *rock*). The student shows only one connection that is related to change or transformation of specific rocks or categories of rocks (*shale* changes to *slate*). The student can't fit into the map the concept *sediment* and so doesn't know that sediment can form *shale* or *limestone*. Other linkages are missing, too: Igneous rocks can weather and transform into sediment and sedimentary rocks; sedimentary rocks can form metamorphic rocks, which in turn can weather and return back to sedimentary rocks; and limestone can change into marble (Champagne & Klopfer, 1980).

As you can see from the example, using this approach to diagnosing requires individually assessing students, knowing the subject very well so you can identify where a student has a missing link, and using considerable judgment when interpreting the resulting concept map. The validity of your judgments is improved if you corroborate your assessment of a student's "missing links" with other evidence about how a student understands the concepts, such as problem-solving tasks and a student's essays and class responses. Also, keep in mind that there may be more than one correct way to relate the information; more than one schema may be correct.

Strengths and Weaknesses

Strengths This diagnostic approach focuses your attention on how a student thinks about the concepts and their interrelationships. It gives you some insight into how the student sees the concepts organized and, perhaps, how they might be related to other concepts and procedures a student has learned. These insights may help you explain why students are making errors, or why they are having difficulty solving problems.

Weaknesses Although assessment of knowledge structures and problem representation may offer you insight into a student's thinking, these clinical procedures are rather experimental. We do not know the degree to which the results are valid, or whether different teachers would reach the same diagnosis for the same student. The way a student reacts to the interviewer (teacher) and the interviewing situation may drastically affect the results. You will need to be cautious, therefore, when you interpret the results.

In large classrooms, these procedures present practical problems. Because you must assess one student at a time, you need to keep the rest of the class occupied. Although some of the procedures listed earlier are group oriented, it is not clear that they lead to the same results as the individual interview methods recommended here. Some authors (Clarke, 1990) recommend teaching students to use concept maps. It is not clear, however, whether the skills students need to create the maps help or hinder their expression of their knowledge organizations. Drawing the concept map and diagramming a model of a problem require spatial skills that all students may not have. Further, it is not clear that all concepts and relationships can be represented spatially. For example, how would you show the relationship spatially between family love, respect for neighbors, and peaceful coexistence in the community?

Some topics can be better represented by other diagrams. For example, when the concepts have a strictly hierarchical relationship, using a table or an outline may better represent them than a concept map. Similarly, if you want to represent a process or a procedure, a flowchart is more appropriate than a concept map.

Especially important to classroom practice, therefore, are the practical and **instructional features of an assessment procedure**. Can the procedure accommodate typical numbers of students? Is it easy for you to use? Can it give quick results to guide your teaching? Will other teachers agree that the theoretical concept of knowledge structure reflects the key understandings they are teaching? Can knowledge structure assessment help explain individual differences among students? Can these assessments identify the most important student misunderstandings that

need to be corrected? Answers to these questions help you build an argument to support the validity of using this assessment technique. (See also Chapter 3.)

APPROACH 6: IDENTIFYING COMPETENCIES FOR SOLVING WORD PROBLEMS

Description

This approach focuses on diagnosing whether students understand the components of word problems. Solving word problems comprises a significant number of learning targets in social studies, mathematics, and science. A word problem is a short verbal account of a more or less realistic situation that requires students to use the given information to answer a question (Marshall, Pribe, & Smith, 1987). Consider the following word problem:

> A bus is carrying 38 passengers. It stops at a bus stop, where 23 passengers get off the bus and 11 other passengers get on. How many passengers are on the bus as it pulls away from this bus stop?

To solve this problem, a student must mentally process it using knowledge from long-term memory in several ways (Mayer, Larkin, & Kadane, 1984):

1. *Translation.* The student must understand each statement in the problem. This requires a student to use factual and **linguistic knowledge**.

    E.g., in the preceding problem, a student must understand the concepts of *bus, carrying passengers, bus stop, get off, and get on the bus, pulling away from the bus stop.* Linguistically, the student has to understand the meaning of the question, "How many passengers are on the bus as it pulls away from this bus stop?"

2. *Understanding.* The student must form an internal representation or model of the problem. In other words, the student must use **schematic knowledge** to recognize how the problem fits into a general framework to identify the type of problem it is. (See Chapter 10 for a discussion of schemata.)

    In the preceding problem, a student must recognize that this is an arithmetic problem involving only addition and subtraction.

3. *Planning.* The student must form a strategy or plan for solving the problem. The student must use **strategic knowledge**. (See Chapter 10 for a discussion of assessing solution strategies.)

    A student must recognize that to know how many passengers are on the bus as it leaves the bus stop, you must subtract from the 38 on the bus those 23 who got off at the stop and add to that remainder the 11 who got on at the stop. Arithmetically, the strategy is: $(38 - 23) + 11$. (Note: For many problems there may be more than one correct strategy.)

4. *Execution.* The student must use an appropriate algorithm (procedure) and carry out the calculations or steps properly. The student must use **algorithmic knowledge**.

> The student must be able to correctly calculate: $(38 - 23) + 11 = 26$ passengers on the bus as it leaves the bus stop.

The diagnosis in this approach is to identify students who are unable to solve word problems, and whether their deficits lie in linguistic and factual knowledge, schematic knowledge, strategic knowledge, or algorithmic knowledge. A student may be unable to solve a problem because the student lacks one or more of these four types of knowledge. Your remedial instruction focuses on teaching students to use the type of knowledge in which they are deficient.

Classroom Applications

You apply this approach by identifying the critical types of linguistic, schematic, strategic, and algorithmic knowledge in each word problem. This means you must analyze each word problem and use the results of your analysis as a basis for asking diagnostic questions. Figure 13.5 is an example, similar to that used by Ismail (1994), of how you could phrase diagnostic items.

1. *To assess linguistic knowledge,* focus your questions on the key terms and key phrases a student must understand to translate the statement into an internal model of the problem. You may need to ask several questions and probe a student's answers to discover his level of understanding of the words and phrases in a problem.

2. *To assess schematic knowledge,* ask students questions to see if they know which rules or principles they need to use to solve the problem. For arithmetic problems, this may mean asking what operations should be used.

3. *To assess strategic knowledge,* focus on the student's ability to identify the proper sequence of steps or the proper processes needed to reach the answer. For arithmetic word problems, this means determining whether the student knows which numbers to use, which operations to use with those numbers, and the proper order of applying the operations. It may be easier to show the student several sequences and ask which is the appropriate one for the given problem (Ismail, 1994). All the numbers in all the alternative solution strategies should relate to the word problem at hand.

4. *To assess algorithmic knowledge,* craft an item that presents the proper sequence and the proper numbers. The focus is on whether the student can follow the algorithm without the context of the word problem. To avoid clueing the student as to the proper schema and strategy, present the algorithmic item after you have completed questioning for linguistic, schematic, and strategic knowledge (Ismail, 1994).

Although it is useful to identify in which of the four types of component knowledge a student is deficient, it is more useful to assess whether a student's deficits have a pattern that persists over several different problems. To identify this pattern, select two word problems in each of several different categories of problems. For each problem, craft diagnostic questions for each of the four types of knowledge previously described. Administer the items in this sequence:

1. Administer all the word problems first.

2. For each word problem, administer the linguistic, schematic, and strategic knowledge items.

3. Administer all the algorithmic knowledge items.

To identify a student's patterns, review the student's answers to the linguistic items across all types of problems. Does the student do consistently well or poorly, or is there difficulty with only one word problem or category of problem? Repeat this review for the schematic items, then the strategic, then the algorithmic. Base your diagnosis on the consistency of a student's responses.

It is possible to craft multiple-choice items that follow this approach (Ismail, 1994). However, it is more informative if you assess students individually with constructed-response items, for which you can probe or follow up to

---

FIGURE 13.5   Diagnostic items for assessing a student's knowledge of the component competencies of word problems.

Word Problem
The weight of an empty cookie tin is 3 ounces. When it is filled with cookies it weighs 1 pound. How many ounces do the cookies inside the tin weigh?

Diagnostic Items for Linguistic Knowledge
1. What is a cookie tin?
2. What do you think the following question means: "How many ounces do the cookies inside the tin weigh?"

Diagnostic Item for Schematic Knowledge
3. What are the arithmetic operations you need to solve this problem?

Diagnostic Item for Strategic Knowledge
4. What steps should you take to solve this problem? (Or, how would you go about solving this problem?)
5. Which of these is a correct way to solve this problem?
    a. $(1 \times 16) - 3$
    b. $(3 - 1) \times 16$
    c. (1×3)
    d. $3 + 1$
    e. $3 - 1$

Diagnostic Item for Algorithmic Knowledge
    $(1 \times 16) - 3 =$

---

clarify a student's answers. You can have a student respond orally, and you can record the answers for the student.

Strengths and Weaknesses

Strengths This approach is most appropriate when you have word problems that are solved by applying a formula or a set of arithmetic operations in an algorithm. These include arithmetic word problems (such as money, time, rate, and cost), word problems in algebra, statistics word problems, social studies word problems involving mathematics, and science word problems. The framework you use to interpret the diagnosis (linguistic, schematic, strategic, and algorithmic knowledge) can be applied consistently across many categories of problems. The framework also suggests how you could remediate a student's deficits.

Weaknesses This approach requires many items per knowledge category before you can be assured of sufficient reliability. Patterns you observe for one type of problem (e.g., money) may not emerge in other problem types (e.g., time). This makes diagnosis less valid if you try to generalize a student's deficits across problem types. Because many items are required, and because individual administration of items is the most appropriate assessment approach, the procedure is time-consuming. The validity of the approach also depends very much on how well you are able to identify key phrases, appropriate schemata, and appropriate strategies for solving the problems. If multiple strategies for problem solving are appropriate, you must be careful to allow students to express these and not confuse the diagnosis by discounting them. Nevertheless, you can use this approach in a very informal way, perhaps asking questions orally, to get some insight into why a student is having difficulty with word problems.

INTERVIEWING STUDENTS

Many of the diagnostic approaches discussed in this chapter require you to work individually with students. Many times you will need to ask students to explain their thinking or ask other questions to follow up on a student's response to gather informal diagnosis information. Here are some suggestions for using an interview for gathering diagnostic information.

1. *Remember that the main purpose of the interview is to gather information about a student's thinking, errors, faulty processes, or faulty approaches to the subject.* You are not looking for a "correct" answer to the questions you pose.

2. *Prepare for an interview as you would prepare for other assessments.* Have in mind the types of information you are seeking, know the general strategy you will use to probe for answers, have necessary materials at hand,

prepare a quiet place for the interview that is free from distractions, make plans to keep the rest of the class occupied, and plan to limit the length of the interview to a few minutes.

3. *Do not intimidate or frighten the student.* Use an informal and friendly conversational manner.

4. *Do not barrage the student with large numbers of rapid-fire questions.*

5. *Wait for the student to respond.* Five- or 10-second waiting time may be a minimum when you are asking students to think or tell you how they process information.

6. *Begin with broader questions and gradually ask more specific and focused questions.* Keep the questions focused on the types of diagnostic information you seek.

7. *Keep notes so you do not have to rely on your memory, and so that you can follow up when planning remedial instruction.*

Summary

- Diagnostic assessment of learning difficulties has two related purposes: (1) identifying which learning targets a student has not mastered, and (2) suggesting possible causes or reasons why a student has not mastered the learning targets.

- The chapter presented six different approaches to diagnosing learning problems: (1) profiling content areas strengths and weaknesses, (2) identifying prerequisite knowledge and skills, (3) identifying nonmastered specific objectives, (4) identifying a student's errors, (5) identifying a student's knowledge structure, and (6) identifying deficits in knowledge components or problem solving.

- Figure 13.2 summarizes how the six diagnostic approaches fit into the teaching process.

- The *profiling content areas strengths and weaknesses approach* presents a student's norm-referenced profile on several topical areas. The approach is useful when you know little about an incoming group of students and want to get a rough idea of their needs. The rough profile of the students provides only general guidance for teaching and must be followed up with more detailed diagnosis. The profile is often unreliable, too. The chapter gives suggestions for crafting and using tests that follow this approach.

- The *identifying deficits in prerequisite knowledge and skills approach* focuses on what a student already needs to know before she can profit from new instruction. The approach uses task analysis to identify entry requirements and may also identify a learning hierarchy of prerequisites. The approach identifies the specific skills that students need to learn before they are ready for learning new material. The approach views learning as cumulative and does not give specific guidance on how to teach the prerequisites. The chapter suggests ways to identify prerequisites and to craft assessment procedures based on them.

■ The *identifying specific objectives that are not mastered approach* focuses on end-of-instruction learning targets. The approach identifies which learning targets are mastered and which are not. The approach is useful because it (1) focuses on specific and limited learning targets to teach, (2) communicates learning targets in an easy-to-understand form, and (3) focuses your attention on student performance. Assessments of the specific objectives are usually short and, therefore, are plagued with measurement error that results in misclassifying some masters as nonmasters and vice versa. The approach focuses only on observable performance and fosters a building-block, fragmented approach to learning. The chapter describes ways to craft assessments consistent with this approach.

■ The *identifying students' errors approach* goes beyond identifying nonmastered objectives to identify and classify the types of errors students make when they do not have mastery of a learning target. The advantage of the approach is that you are able to discover what aspects of a student's performance are flawed. The approach does not identify the causes of the errors or flaws in students' thinking that may make the students' errors consistent rather than random or careless. The chapter suggests ways to implement the approach in classrooms.

■ The *identifying students' knowledge structures approach* focuses on how a student (1) perceives the structure or organization of the concepts and facts of the subject, and (2) processes concepts and facts to solve problems in the subject. The advantage is that this approach requires you to attend to how students think about the interrelated concepts. Attention to this facet of student learning helps you to gather information about why students make errors, or why they have difficulty solving problems. The procedures for obtaining this information are rather experimental, and their degree of validity is not known. The procedures require working intensively with individual students and thus have a degree of impracticality in large classes with only one teacher. The chapter suggests ways to implement this approach with individual students.

■ The *identifying component competencies for solving word problems approach* focuses on word problems in social studies, mathematics, and science. To solve a word problem, students must use linguistic, schematic, strategic, and algorithmic knowledge. Assessment focuses on identifying whether students have sufficient problem-specific knowledge in each of these areas. The approach is most useful for closed-response problems that can be solved by applying appropriate formulas. The framework of types of knowledge can be applied across a wide range of problems and is useful for focusing students' remedial instruction. The approach can be plagued by measurement error if each type of knowledge is assessed by only a few tasks. It is also a time-consuming approach whose validity depends on the quality of your analysis of the word problems. Suggestions for crafting this type of diagnostic assessment are presented in the chapter.

■ Many diagnostic assessment strategies require intensive work with individual students in an interview situation. The chapter provides suggestions for improving diagnostic interviews.

Important Terms and Concepts

adaptive testing strategy
algorithmic knowledge
component competencies of problem solving
concept mapping
deficits in learning
diagnostic assessment
everyday understandings of terms and phenomena
identifying errors in performance
instructional features of an assessment procedure
knowledge structure
learning hierarchy
linear teaching sequence
linguistic knowledge
mastery of specific objectives
passing score
percent agreement index
prerequisite knowledge and skill deficits
profile of strengths and weaknesses
schematic knowledge
spiral teaching sequence
strategic knowledge
subtest
surface feature
unreliable profile

Exercises and Discussion Questions

1. Write an essay that evaluates the usefulness of each of the six diagnostic approaches to the subject(s) you teach or plan to teach. Focus your evaluation on your subject area specifically. Give several reasons and classroom examples to support your choice(s) and rejection(s).

2. Review the categories of validity evidence suggested in Table 3.2. For each of the six diagnostic assessment approaches described in this chapter, identify the specific evidence needed to validate the diagnostic decisions that would be made under the approach. Are there areas of common evidence? Explain.

3. For a subject you teach or plan to teach, craft a diagnostic assessment procedure for Approaches 1, 2, 3, and 4. If there is time, try each approach with students who are experiencing learning difficulties. Revise your assessment procedure based on these student trials. Share the final versions of your assessment procedures with others in your course.

4. Which of the six diagnostic approaches use criterion-referencing schemes for interpreting the results? Explain.

5. Each of these statements describes an instructional decision-making situation. Read each statement and decide the approach(es) to diagnostic assessment that may provide needed information.

   a. A teacher wonders whether Lynn missed several arithmetic story problems because she doesn't know her number facts.

   b. Ray missed several addition computational problems involving mixed decimal fractions. His teacher wonders whether Ray is counting the number of decimal places in each addend and using this count as the basis for placing the decimal point in the final answer.

   c. Lou missed several whole-number arithmetic problems involving carrying (regrouping). His teacher wonders whether Lou has not remembered to add his "carries" to the sum of the digits in the next column.

   d. Janet is a slow reader who frequently misses comprehension questions following a passage. Her teacher wonders whether Janet has reading reversals that cause her to misread some words in the passage.

6. Sometimes students learn an incorrect rule or apply a correct rule at the wrong time. To diagnose a student's learning difficulty in this case, you must identify the rule the student actually used to solve the problem and then decide whether this is an appropriate rule. For example, consider this arithmetic story problem:

   Sally was given 6 pieces of candy. Then she went to the store and bought some candy. Now she has 8 pieces of candy altogether. How many pieces of candy did Sally buy?

   One student gave 14 as the answer to this problem. When the teacher interviewed the student, the teacher discovered that the student was using this erroneous rule: "Whenever you see the word altogether in a story problem, you add the two numbers they give you." Thus, the student added, $6 + 8 = 14$, instead of subtracting, $8 - 6 = 2$.

   a. Consider the subject and the students you teach or plan to teach. Identify two wrong rules you have seen students use. (If you are inexperienced, you may need to work with a few students before proceeding with this exercise.) Below, state the wrong rule, the correct rule, and an example to illustrate each point (as was done in the preceding passage).

   Subject, grade level: _____
      i. Correct rule: _____
      ii. Student's incorrect rule: _____
      iii. Illustrative example: _____
   b. Subject, grade level: _____
      i. Correct rule: _____
      ii. Student's incorrect rule: _____
      iii. Illustrative example: _____
   c. Share and discuss your findings with others in this course.

7. Reconsider the arithmetic story problem given in Exercise 6. Analyze the story problem according to linguistic knowledge, schematic knowledge, strategic knowledge, and algorithmic knowledge.

   a. Describe the specifics of each type of knowledge required to solve this problem.

   b. Using the tasks in Figure 13.5 as a model, craft similar tasks in each knowledge category to diagnose students' level of understanding of each type of knowledge.

   c. If there is time, administer your diagnostic assessment tasks to several students, some of whom did not answer the word problem correctly. Share your findings with others in this course.

8. Obtain a copy of a commercially available diagnostic test, such as the *Stanford Diagnostic Reading Test* or the *KeyMath Diagnostic Arithmetic Test*, which reports results as normative profiles. Evaluate each test in terms of the diagnostic approaches described in this chapter. Describe the strengths of the tests compared to the weaknesses of the five other diagnostic approaches.

9. Apply the teaching diagnosis process chart shown in Figure 13.2 to a unit of content you teach or plan to teach.

   a. Describe the unit and the learning targets (performances) toward which it is directed.

   b. Identify the prerequisites and explain whether you must diagnose students with respect to them.

   c. Identify the learning targets for which you can diagnose mastery or nonmastery at the end of the unit.

   d. Identify the kinds of errors students often made when completing the tasks assessing each learning target.

   e. For each error identified, explain the faulty thinking that is likely to cause each error.

   f. If there is time, teach the unit and collect information about the validity of your assertions for (a) through (e) above.

Additional Readings

Frederiksen, N., Glaser, R., Lesgold, A., & Shafto, M. G. (Eds.) (1990). *Diagnostic monitoring of skill and knowledge acquisition.* Hillside, NJ: Erlbaum.

A collection of 19 papers in which cognitive science findings are applied to diagnostic assessment in the context of computerized instructional systems.

Nitko, A. J. (1989). Designing tests that are integrated with instruction. In R. L. Linn (Ed.), *Educational measurement* (3rd ed.). New York: Macmillan, Chapter 12, pp. 447–474.

This chapter places diagnostic assessment into a broader framework for integrating assessment and instruction.

Nitko, A. J. (1996). *Educational assessment of students* (2nd ed.). Englewood Cliffs, NJ: Prentice Hall/Merrill Education.

Chapter 10 gives more details for assessing knowledge structures, depth of problem representation, and quality of mental models. Those techniques are helpful for diagnosing the way students think about the subject matter and about the problems they are asked to solve.

CHAPTER 14

Preparing Your Students to Be Assessed and Using Students' Results to Improve Your Assessments

Learning Targets

After studying this chapter, you should be able to:

1. Describe how to prepare students for an upcoming assessment, including the minimum information students need to perform their test. [3]

2. Describe necessary test-taking skills and how to teach them to students. [3, 4]

3. Describe test-wiseness and when it might lower the validity of your assessment results. [3, 2]

4. Describe test anxiety, its components, and what you can do to help students who experience it. [4, 3]

5. Explain why the way you assemble and administer an assessment affects the validity of the scores. [3, 4]

6. List the kinds of information that should be included in test directions. [2, 3]

7. List the preparations for scoring you need to make before giving a test. [3]

8. Explain the correction for guessing, and list the factors to consider when deciding whether to use a correction. [4]

9. Describe the important reasons for using item analysis for classroom assessments. [2]

10. Carry out a simple item analysis, including item difficulty and item discrimination. [2, 3]

11. Use item analysis results to improve the quality of true-false, matching, and multiple-choice items. [2]

12. Describe how item analysis data are used to select items for tests having different purposes. [2, 1]

13. Explain how each of the terms and concepts listed at the end of this chapter may be applied to educational assessment. [6]

In Chapter 6, you learned about planning for assessment. Chapters 7 through 13 discussed many different types of assessments, how to craft them, and how to score them. This chapter discusses the final step in the crafting process: actually giving the assessment to students.

In the first section of the chapter you will learn about preparing students so they can do their best on your assessments. To perform well, students need more than subject-matter knowledge. They need to know how to take tests and how to handle anxieties that may arise as a result of the evaluation process. You shouldn't assume that all students will automatically know how to do their best.

The second section of the chapter discusses assembling and preparing for administering your assessment. We discuss practical matters to improve the validity of the assessment results.

In the final section of the chapter you will learn how to use information from students' responses to your assessments to judge how successful the items were. Students' responses can help you to improve your items, to fix what was flawed, and to improve the validity of the results.

SECTION I. GETTING STUDENTS READY

PREPARING STUDENTS FOR THE ASSESSMENT

Maximum vs. Typical Performance Assessment

An achievement assessment assesses maximum performance rather than typical performance (Cronbach, 1990). **Maximum performance assessment** procedures set the conditions so that students are able to earn the best score they can. **Typical performance assessment** procedures gather information about what a student would do under ordinary or typical conditions.

For example, you may have taught students a practical skill such as balancing a checkbook, and your assessment procedure gathers information about whether each student is capable of doing so. This is maximum performance assessment. Some students, on the other hand, may make errors later outside of class when actually using checks while shopping, or they may never reconcile their checking account. Thus, such students may be *capable* of performing the skill you taught, but may *typically not perform* the skill to the high level of their capacity. Because schooling usually attempts to teach learners new abilities at high levels, achievement assessments are carried out under conditions that encourage students to perform to the best of their abilities.

Minimum Information Needed

In Chapter 5 we discussed your professional responsibilities to inform students about an upcoming assessment and about how it will be scored. Here we focus on information that students need. You should review Chapter 5 at this time.

To be assessed under the best conditions, your students need to know at least the following information about an upcoming assessment:

1. When it will be given.
2. Under what conditions it will be given (timed, speeded, take-home test).
3. The general content areas it will cover.
4. The emphasis or weighting of content areas to be included on the assessment (value in points).
5. The types of performance the student will have to demonstrate (the kinds of items on the test, the degree to which memory will be required).
6. How the assessment will be scored and graded (e.g., will partial credit be given?)
7. The importance of the particular assessment result in relation to decisions about the student (e.g., will it count for one-half the marking period grade?)

When an Assessment Will Be Given To do well on an assessment, a student needs to prepare in advance. Students, particularly those taking courses taught by more than one teacher, need to organize their study efforts and set their priorities. They can learn to do this planning when they know the test date in advance. Teachers should coordinate their schedules of assessment so they are spread out. However, the end of the marking period is often problematic.

Pop Quizzes Some teachers advocate "surprise" or "pop" quizzes. Their reasoning is often some vague notion that a good student should always be prepared to perform on command. This seems to be an unrealistic expectation of students. Teachers, for example, make lesson plans and prepare to teach these lessons in advance. They are often resentful (and rightfully so) if asked to teach a class for which they have not had sufficient time to prepare. Most union contracts require teachers to be notified ahead of time if a supervisor, principal, or parent will come to the classroom to observe and/or evaluate them. Good planning requires that a person know in advance what needs to be accomplished. The author recommends giving students at least 48 hours' notice before any assessment.

Some teachers believe that surprise quizzes motivate students. There is no evidence to support this point, but there is some evidence that students will do better if they know in advance that a test is coming (Tyler & Chalmers, 1943). An anecdote reinforces this point: When asked to avoid giving surprise quizzes to a particular child, a teacher became incensed, saying "Why, if I did that, he would get an A on all his quizzes!"

Students with special problems often benefit from knowing about an assessment well in advance. *Test anxiety and fear are likely to be reduced when a student can rationally plan a program of study for a forthcoming assessment* (Mealey & Host, 1992). Children with disabilities mainstreamed in a regular class often have supplemental instruction from an itinerant teacher or tutor who sees them only once or twice a week. Suppose a hearing-handicapped youngster has not understood Wednesday's lesson, and the itinerant teacher regularly comes on Monday. Further, suppose the quiz is "popped" on Friday. How can this youngster be expected to effectively plan and use the resources provided when the regular teacher is unpredictable?

Some teachers use surprise quizzes to threaten or to punish a disobedient class. The author considers this an unethical use of an assessment.

Assessment Conditions You should tell the students the conditions under which they are expected to perform:

How many items will be on the test? How much time will the students be allowed to complete the assessment? Will the assessment be speeded? Will it be open or closed book? Will there be a penalty for guessing? And at what time of day will it be given (if not during a regular period)?

Content to Be Covered Saying that the assessment will cover the first three chapters of the book doesn't help students much. To plan and study effectively, students need more detail. Some teachers prepare lists of study questions to help students focus their efforts. This may be especially helpful for elementary students for whom almost everything in a book seems to be equally important. Study questions also help older students, especially when a large amount of material has been covered during the term.

For high school and college students, an alternative to developing a set of study questions is to give them a copy of the assessment blueprint (see Chapter 6), a list of learning targets, a copy of the scoring criteria (or rubrics), or a detailed content outline indicating the number of items covering each element. (See Appendix G.)

Content Emphasis Weight of the different parts of an assessment should match your teaching emphasis; otherwise, the results will have low validity. You should communicate how the content in an assessment is weighted by telling the students how many items (and how many points) will be devoted to each objective, content element, or blueprint cell. Students can waste hours studying a topic if it will be of little or no importance on the assessment. Assessments must cover the important topics, and the students' study efforts and the learning targets set for students must be in agreement. (See Table 3.1.)

Expected Performance Obviously, students should have the opportunity to practice the kind of performance for which they will be held accountable. Yet, students frequently have to guess at the nature or type of question that will appear on an assessment. A sixth grader we know, for example, was given practice exercises that asked him to identify prepositional phrases in isolation using a given list of words and phrases. The next day, his assessment consisted of finding the subject, predicate, and prepositional phrase in the more authentic context of several paragraphs. Unfortunately, he never had the opportunity to practice the task for which he was held accountable.

The best way to familiarize students with tasks that will appear on an assessment is to give them sample tasks, perhaps an old form of an assessment on which they can practice. This may be particularly effective when the types of tasks to appear on the assessment are complex and/or unfamiliar to the student.

Scoring Knowing how the assessment will be scored helps students prepare, especially for answering open-ended tasks. If you will deduct points for misspelling important terms and proper names, then the students need to practice these spellings in addition to learning the main

ideas and rehearsing how to organize their answers. Students also need to know whether and how you will award marks for less than perfect answers and how much weight (i.e., marks) you will give for each question. Share scoring rubrics with students well in advance of giving a test.

Use of Results Students need to know the importance of the assessment score for any decisions you will make about them, including putting students into groups, placing them in another section of the course, assigning them to remedial instruction, giving them enrichment or advanced work, and assigning grades. Many teachers share their assessment plan with students, telling them at the beginning of the course or marking period the weight they assign to each assignment, quiz, test, and classroom performance activity. Students can then organize their efforts in terms of these priorities.

MINIMUM ASSESSMENT-TAKING SKILLS

Students need to learn the following **minimum assessment-taking skills**, perhaps through direct instruction in the classroom (Ebel & Frisbie, 1991):

1. Paying attention to oral and written directions and finding out the consequences of failing to follow them.

2. Finding out how the assessment will be scored, how the individual tasks will be weighted into the total, and how many points will be deducted for wrong answers, misspellings, or poor grammar.

3. Writing responses or marking answers neatly to avoid lowered scores because of poor penmanship or mismarked answers.

4. Studying throughout the course and in paced reviewing to reduce cramming and fatigue.

5. Using assessment time wisely so that all tasks are completed within the given time.

6. Using partial knowledge and guessing appropriately.

7. Reflecting, outlining, and organizing answers to essays before writing; using an appropriate amount of time for each essay.

8. Checking the marks made on separate answer sheets to avoid mismatching or losing one's place when an item is omitted.

9. Reviewing answers to the tasks and changing answers if there is a better response.

TEST-WISENESS

A Test-Wiseness Quiz

Before reading further, take the following short test. Be sure to mark an answer for every item, even if you are unsure of the answer. There is a correct or best answer for every item. (Items are extracted with slight modification from Diamond and Evans, 1972, p. 147.)

1. The Augustine National Party has its headquarters in
   a. Camden, New Jersey.
   b. St. Augustine, Florida.
   c. Palo Alto, California.
   d. Dallas, Texas.

2. Hermann Klavermann is best known for
   a. developing *all* musical scales used in the western world.
   b. composing *every* sonata during the Romantic Era.
   c. translating *all* Russian classics into English.
   d. inventing the safety pin.

3. The Davis Act of the 20th century
   a. provided more money for schools.
   b. struck down an earlier law.
   c. prohibited the manufacture, sale, transportation, or use of several specific drugs that were being used for illegal purposes.
   d. gave a raise to government employees.

4. Harold Stone's book, *The Last Friendship*, is an example of an
   a. political satire.
   b. autobiography.
   c. science fiction.
   d. biography.

5. The population of Franktown is more than
   a. 50 thousand.
   b. 60 thousand.
   c. 70 thousand.
   d. 80 thousand.

Each item's content is fictitious, but the right answer to each can be determined by using certain clues in the item:

Item 1. An obvious association between a word or phrase in the stem (*Augustine National Party*) and one in an alternative (*St. Augustine*).

Item 2. Specific determiners in the alternatives (*all, every*) result in these being eliminated from consideration.

Item 3. A longer, more qualified answer is keyed as the correct response.

Item 4. A grammatical clue (*an*) is contained in the stem.

Item 5. An alternative overlaps or includes the others.

A Taxonomy of Test-Wiseness Skills

The preceding items illustrate what is often called test-wiseness. **Test-wiseness** is the ability to use assessment-taking strategies, clues from poorly written items, and experience in taking assessments to improve your score beyond what you would otherwise attain from mastery of the subject matter itself. When you write classroom assessments, be aware of how students may take advantage of your idiosyncrasies in item writing or flawed items to improve their scores without attaining the desired level of mastery. Figure 14.1 is an outline or taxonomy of test-wiseness principles.

You should create good-quality assessments that do not permit test-wise students to attain scores that do not validly describe their level of achievement. However, you should also teach students many of the skills listed in Figure 14.1 so they are not at a disadvantage when being assessed with more test-wise peers. Research has demonstrated that test-wiseness is learned, and it improves with grade level, experience in being assessed, maturation, and motivation to do well on the assessment (Sarnacki, 1979; Slakter, Koehler, & Hampton, 1970a).

ADVICE ABOUT CHANGING ANSWERS

Will students benefit if they change their answers once they have been marked on the answer sheet? Despite popular opinion, it *does* pay to change answers if changing them is based on a thoughtful reconsideration of the item. A summary of the research findings (Pike, 1978) on this issue follows.

- Most test takers and many educators believe it does not pay to change answers.
- Most students, however, do in fact change their answers to about 4% of the items.
- Research studies show that it does, in fact, pay to change answers. Typically two out of three answers changed will become correct.
- The payoff for changing answers diminishes as the items become more difficult for the student.
- Lower scoring students benefit less from changing answers than higher scoring students do.

TEST ANXIETY

General Nature of Test Anxiety

Task-Directed and Task-Irrelevant Thoughts Throughout their school careers, students take tests and examinations, sit in recitations, perform in front of their teachers and others, and respond to questions during the lesson. How students perceive these evaluations varies widely. Some students are motivated to perform well; others don't care. Among the students who are motivated to do well, assessments and evaluations are likely to lead to increased emotional tension: **test anxiety**. Students' perceptions of evaluation situations shape their reactions to them. Some well-motivated students may perceive these evaluation situations as challenges, while other equally well motivated students perceive them as threats. A student who

FIGURE 14.1 A taxonomy of test-wiseness principles.

I. Elements independent of test constructor or test purpose.

    A. Time-using strategy.

        1. Begin to work as rapidly as possible with reasonable assurance of accuracy.

        2. Set up a schedule for progress through the test.

        3. Omit or guess at items (see I.C. and II.B.) which resist a quick response.

        4. Mark omitted items, or items which could use further consideration, to assure easy relocation.

        5. Use time remaining after completion of the test to reconsider answers.

    B. Error-avoidance strategy.

        1. Pay careful attention to directions, determining clearly the nature of the task and the intended basis for response.

        2. Pay careful attention to the items, determining clearly the nature of the question.

        3. Ask examiner for clarification when necessary, if it is permitted.

        4. Check all answers.

    C. Guessing strategy.

        1. Always guess if right answers only are scored.

        2. Always guess if the correction for guessing is less severe than a "correction for guessing" formula that gives an expected score of zero for random responding.

        3. Always guess even if the usual correction or a more severe penalty for guessing is employed whenever elimination of options provides sufficient chance of profiting.

    D. Deductive reasoning strategy.

        1. Eliminate options which are known to be incorrect and choose from among the remaining options.

        2. Choose neither or both of two options which imply the correctness of each other.

        3. Choose neither or one (but not both) of two statements, one of which, if correct, would imply the incorrectness of the other.

        4. Restrict choice to those options which encompass all of two or more given statements known to be correct.

        5. Utilize relevant content information in other test items and options.

II. Elements dependent upon the test constructor or purpose.

    A. Intent consideration strategy.

        1. Interpret and answer questions in view of previous idiosyncratic emphases of the test constructor or in view of the test purpose.

        2. Answer items as the test constructor intended.

        3. Adopt the level of sophistication that is expected.

        4. Consider the relevance of specific detail.

    B. Cue-using strategy.

        1. Recognize and make use of any consistent idiosyncrasies of the test constructor which distinguish the correct answer from incorrect options.

            a. He makes it longer (shorter) than the incorrect options.

            b. He qualifies it more carefully, or makes it represent a higher degree of generalization.

            c. He includes more false (true) statements.

            d. He places it in certain physical positions among the options (such as in the middle).

            e. He places it in a certain logical position among an ordered set of options (such as the middle of the sequence).

            f. He includes (does not include) it among similar statements, or makes (does not make) it one of a pair of diametrically opposite statements.

            g. He composes (does not compose) it of familiar or stereotyped phraseology.

            h. He does not make it grammatically inconsistent with the stem.

        2. Consider the relevancy of specific detail when answering a given item.

        3. Recognize and make use of specific determiners.

        4. Recognize and make use of resemblances between the options and an aspect of the stem.

        5. Consider the subject matter and difficulty of neighboring items when interpreting and answering a given item.

Source: From J. Millman, C. H. Bishop, and R. L. Ebel, "An Analyses of Test-Wiseness." *Educational and Psychological Measurement, 25,* pp. 711–713. Copyright © 1965 by Sage Publications. Reprinted by permission of Sage Publications, Inc.

perceives an assessment as threatening may not have the ability to perform the task at hand, not have been taught how to perform the task, or not have properly studied or otherwise prepared for the assessment (Benson, 1989). Not all perceived threats are based upon poor preparation, however.

Students who accept assessments and evaluations as challenges have thoughts that are **task-directed**. Their thoughts and actions are focused on completing the tasks and thereby reduce any tensions that are associated with them (Mandler & Sarason, 1952). Students who perceive assessments and evaluations as threats have **task-irrelevant thoughts**: self-preoccupied, centering on what could happen if they fail, on their own helplessness, and sometimes on a desire to escape from the situation as quickly as possible (Mandler & Sarason, 1952).

Emotionality and Worry Test anxiety very often is considered to have two components: emotionality and worry (Liebert & Morris, 1967). **Emotionality** is the bodily and autonomic arousal that accompanies the test anxiety. **Worry** is part of the cognitive aspect of anxiety: thoughts about the negative consequences of failure and how one's performance will be compared to others.

Research suggests that the emotional reactions to an assessment situation trigger worry, which in turn results in poor performance (Hembree, 1988). Worry may be interpreted as **cognitive interference** (Sarason, 1984). That is, a student's self-preoccupation and worry about doing poorly keeps the student with high test anxiety from focusing attention on doing the task at hand. The more cognitive interference a student experiences, the poorer will be the student's performance on the assessment.

Four Factors in Test Anxiety Student's reactions to assessment situations may be organized into four related factors: tension, worry, test-irrelevant thinking, and bodily reactions (Sarason, 1984). These four factors appear to be appropriate for multinational samples also (Benson & El-Zahhar, 1994). Examples of items that assess each of these factors are given in Figure 14.2. The factors in Figure 14.2 describe test anxiety more specifically than do emotionality and worry. Emotionality is broken down into **bodily reactions** and **tension**; test-irrelevant thinking is seen to be part of test anxiety along with worry.

Three Types of Test-Anxious Students

There are at least three **types of test-anxious students** (Mealey & Host, 1992). Your ability to recognize these differences among students will help you to work with them so they perform their best on your assessments. First are students who do not have good study skills and do not understand how the main ideas of the subject you are

teaching are related and organized. These students become anxious about an upcoming evaluation because they have not learned well (Culler and Holahan, 1980; Naveh-Benjamin, McKeachie, & Lin, 1987). Second are students who do have a good grasp of the material and good study skills but have built up fears of failure associated with assessment and evaluation (Herman, 1990; McKeachie, Pollie, & Spiesman, 1985). Third are students who believe they have good study habits but who do not. They perform poorly on assessments and learn to be anxious about being assessed (Mealey & Host, 1992).

Helping Test-Anxious Students

The following factors were shown to be related to test anxiety (Hembree, 1988) and may be under your control in classroom assessment situations:

1. When students perceive an assessment to be difficult, their test anxiety rises.

2. At-risk students have higher levels of test anxiety than passing students.

3. Students whose teachers gave them item-by-item feedback after the test have lower test anxiety than students who receive no feedback.

4. Tests whose items were arranged from easy to difficult raise test anxiety less than tests with other item arrangements (Tippets & Benson, 1989).

5. More frequent testing of highly test-anxious students seems to improve their performance.

6. High test-anxious students are more easily distracted by auditory and visual activity than low test-anxious students.

7. Giving high test-anxious students instructions to concentrate their attention on the assessment tasks and not to let themselves be distracted from the tasks is more beneficial to their performance than simply reassuring them with "don't worry" or "you'll be fine" statements (Sarason, 1984).

8. Students with low test-taking skills can lower their test anxiety by receiving test-wiseness training.

In addition, Mealey & Host (1992) suggest that you ask your students what you might do to help them feel more relaxed or less nervous before, during, and after you assess them. The researchers' own developmental reading college students reported these suggestions:

1. The teacher should not talk or interrupt while students are working on an assessment.

2. The teacher should review the material with the entire class before the assessment is given.

3. The teacher should not walk around looking over students' shoulders while they are being assessed.

FIGURE 14.2 Samples of items that define Sarason's four factors of test anxiety.

Tension
1. I feel distresssed and uneasy before tests.
2. I feel jittery before tests.
3. I find myself becoming anxious the day of a test.

Worry
1. Before taking a test, I worry about failure.
2. During tests, I wonder how the other people are doing.
3. Before tests, I feel troubled about what is going to happen.

Test-Irrelevant Thinking
1. During tests, I think about past events.
2. Irrelevant bits of information pop into my head during a test.
3. During tests, I find myself thinking of things unrelated to the material being tested.

Bodily Reactions
1. I get a headache during an important test.
2. My stomach gets upset before tests.
3. My heart beats faster when the test begins.

Source: From "Stress, Anxiety, and Cognitive Inferences: Reactions to Tests" by I. G. Sarason, 1984, *Journal of Personality and Social Psychology, 46,* p. 932. Copyright 1984 by the American Psychological Association. Reprinted by permission.

4. The teacher should convey a sense of confidence about students' performance on an upcoming assessment (and avoid such statements as "This is going to be a difficult test").

Further reviews of test anxiety and its treatment can be found in Hembree (1988), Sarason (1980), Tryon (1980), Wine (1971), and Zuckerman and Spielberger (1976).

SECTION II. PUTTING THE ASSESSMENT TOGETHER

ASSESSMENT FORMAT AND APPEARANCE

The final appearance and arrangement of your assessment is important to the validity of the results. An illegible, poorly typed, or illogically arranged assessment annoys the well-prepared student, can cause unnecessary errors, and gives all students the impression that you have not taken your assessment responsibilities seriously. The organization and appearance of an assessment may be especially important for the less able student.

Distribution of Assessment Items

As a rule, you should type (or write neatly) any test that requires students to write answers, and duplicate it so that each student can have a copy. (Obvious exceptions are dictated spelling assessments and assessments of similar aural abilities.) Sometimes a teacher will write the items on the chalkboard or dictate them to the class. Although this procedure saves the teacher time, it may cause problems for students, especially those with visual, listening comprehension, or hearing problems. If you dictate the questions, you use valuable time that your students could otherwise spend in responding to the items. Further, reading a question aloud and requiring students to write their responses places a demand on short-term memory that many students cannot meet (Figure 14.3).

Test Booklet Layout and Design

Organization of Test Items   If there are many objective items, you should arrange them into a test booklet. (The few questions that comprise an essay test may conveniently be presented on a single sheet of paper.) For a large class, you can add a cover page to the test booklet that identifies the course and lists the directions. An example of a cover page is shown in Figure 14.4. The cover page is followed by items grouped together by type or format (e.g., all the true-false items together, all the multiple-choice items together).

FIGURE 14.3   Dictating test questions can be frustrating to students.

Bob was a sixth grade boy of average ability who had difficulty memorizing definitions of science terms. After studying at home for two evenings with the help of his parents, he felt prepared for his classroom test. His teacher decided to dictate the test questions and he got only 4 out of 10 correct. Upon checking his standardized test scores in his permanent record, the teacher found that his listening comprehension skills were far below average in his class; she noted, too, from her own observations that his short-term memory skills were below those of his age group. A retest seemed in order.

FIGURE 14.4   An example of a test booklet with directions to the students.

University of Pittsburgh
Educational Research Methodology   Testing & Meas. In The Classroom
Final Examination: Part I
DIRECTIONS TO STUDENTS

(1)   This is a closed book test. Do not refer to your text or notes.

(2)   Be sure your answer sheet is numbered the same as your test booklet.

(3)   You must use a Number Two graphite pencil.

(4)   Print your NAME on your answer sheet.

(5)   All of the questions in this booklet are in the true-false, matching, or multiple-choice format. You are to choose the best answer or the correct answer to each question and then blacken the corresponding space on your separate answer sheet.

(6)   Attempt to answer each question. Do not spend too much time on any one question. If a given question puzzles you, go on to the next one, which may be easier. You may guess at the right answer. Since there is no penalty for guessing, you should ANSWER EVERY QUESTION.

(7)   As you work on the test, keep your place on the answer sheet. Make certain that the answer you are marking is numbered the same as the item you are answering.

(8)   Do not write in the test booklet except where directed to do so.

A cover page keeps those who receive the booklet first from beginning the test before the rest of the class and before you have answered all clarifying questions. When items are arranged by type of format a student doesn't have to change "mind sets," which reduces errors caused by switching back and forth from one format to another.

Experts usually recommend that items appear in the order of difficulty, with the easiest items placed first. If items are grouped by type of format, arrange them from easiest to most difficult within each format. Most students can go through the easiest items quickly and reserve the remaining test time for the difficult items. Some research shows that the easiest-to-hardest item arrangement reduces anxiety and increases performance (Tippets & Benson, 1989). Another way to arrange items is according to the sequence in which the content was taught or appeared in the textbook. Students can then use this subject-matter organization as a kind of "cognitive map" through which they can retrieve stored information. If you use this sequential arrangement, you should tell students to skip over difficult items and go on to subsequent items, which may be easier. (Always encourage students to return to the omitted items if they have time.) Better yet, within content areas arrange the items from easiest to most difficult. This minimizes test-created anxiety and, in turn, increases validity of your assessment results (Tippets & Benson, 1989).

Directions to Students Assessment directions should contain certain minimum information: the number and format of items; amount of time allowed to complete the assessment, where and how answers should be written; any correction or penalty for guessing; and the general strategy the student should follow when answering questions. (For example, should students guess if they think they know the answer but are unsure? Should they answer all items or should they omit some? Which one? Should they do each item in turn, or should they skip those they are uncertain about, returning to them later if they have time? If the student perceives that the answer to an item requires opinion, whose opinion is being asked?) You would have to supplement the cover page in Figure 14.4 to emphasize these points. However, most written directions need not be elaborate.

Use side headings to signal a change in the general directions that may occur within the test booklet. Some items may require specific directions, as in Figure 14.5.

Duplicating the Test

Duplication Processes More and more schools have photocopying available for teacher use. Whatever equipment you use, be sure the master (or original) is prepared well and the equipment is in good working order. Poor-quality copies may affect student performance. Use the particular duplicating process that best reproduces your items. Pho-

FIGURE 14.5 Examples of side-heading directions.

Read the paragraph below before answering Items 12, 13, 14, and 15.

Paragraph is put here.

Items 9, 10, 11, and 12 are based on the data found in the table below.

Table is placed here.

tocopying is the most versatile technique, permitting drawings and photographs to be reproduced. It may be possible to use different processes for different pages of the test booklet. Whatever process you use, be sure the chemicals do not produce objectionable odors. (A student will have enough problems just trying to figure out the answers!)

Test Security Test security may be a problem if the tests are sent to a central location for duplication and assembly. Be sure to check the security procedures in your school.

PREPARATIONS FOR SCORING THE ASSESSMENT

Prepare for scoring an assessment before you administer it. Prepare and *verify* every answer on the scoring key in advance, so that you can score students' assessments efficiently and accurately, and report results to the students quickly for reinforcement, feedback, and motivation. Advance preparation of the answer key will help you identify errors in the assessment items, too.

Separate answer sheets are not recommended for the first three grades. However, with older elementary and high school students, it may be advisable to use a separate answer sheet for objective items. This greatly facilitates scoring and permits the test booklet to be reused. An answer sheet for completion items might consist of columns with numbered blanks, each number corresponding to an item number. The student writes the answer to an item on the correspondingly numbered blank. If you have essays or extended responses, be sure to provide an answer sheet or examination booklet to record students' responses.

Scannable answer sheets are available in most schools. These can be used for hand-scoring as well as scanning. If you are planning to use scanning, check with the office in your school that does the scanning to be sure that you use the proper answer sheets. Also be sure the students follow the correct answer-marking procedures. You can make your own scoring key by punching out the correct answers on an answer sheet. Lay the punched sheet on top of each student's answer sheet to score it. Chapters 9 and 12 describe the scoring process for essay answer tests and performance assessments. Review those procedures at this point.

CORRECTION FOR GUESSING

Correction for Guessing Formulas

When true-false and/or multiple-choice items are used, **correction for guessing formulas** are sometimes applied to scores by subtracting from the number of right answers a fraction of the number of wrong answers. Here is the usual formula:

$$\text{corrected score} = R - \frac{W}{(n-1)} \quad \text{[Eq. 14.1]}$$

where
  R means the number of items answered correctly,
  W means the number of items marked wrongly, and
  n means the number of options in each item.

If there are two choices per item (e.g., true-false), then

$$\text{corrected score} = R - W$$

If there are four options per item, then

$$\text{corrected score} = R - \frac{W}{3}$$

The correction formula is designed to eliminate the advantage a student might have as a result of guessing correctly. For example, suppose Jim took a 50-question multiple-choice test with four options per item. Further, suppose Jim's test results were 40 items marked correctly, 6 items marked wrongly, and 4 items omitted. Applying the formula, we find:

$$\begin{aligned}\text{corrected score} &= R - \frac{W}{(n-1)} \\ &= 40 - \frac{6}{(4-1)} = 40 - 2 = 38\end{aligned}$$

Notice the number of omitted items is not used in this correction formula; only the number of answers marked wrongly (W) and the number marked correctly (R).

A complementary version of the preceding correction formula does use the number of omitted items: Instead of penalizing a student for responding wrongly, it rewards the student for omitting items (i.e., for refraining from guessing). This formula is

$$\text{Adjusted score} = R + \frac{O}{n} \quad \text{[Eq. 14.2]}$$

where
  R means the number of items answered correctly
  O means the number of items omitted, and
  n means the number of options in each item.

(The term *adjusted* instead of *corrected* distinguishes this formula from the previous one. This is not standard practice. The generic term is *formula scoring*.)

Applying the adjusted formula to Jim's test performance, we obtain

$$\begin{aligned}\text{Adjusted score} &= R + \frac{O}{n} \\ &= 40 + \frac{4}{4} = 41\end{aligned}$$

This formula credits the student with the number of points to be expected if random responses were substituted for the omitted responses. If a student omitted every item, the score would be equal to the average score expected if the student guessed blindly on every item. Thus, the scores obtained by the adjusted score formula will be higher than the same students' scores if they had been obtained from the corrected score formula. However, the scores under the two methods are perfectly correlated (Gulliksen, 1950); that is, the relative ordering of persons is the same regardless of which formula is used.

The uncorrected score (R) is simply the number of items marked correctly. When every student marks every item, the uncorrected scores are perfectly correlated with the corrected or adjusted scores (Gulliksen, 1950) so that here, too, the relative ordering of persons is the same, whether or not the scores are corrected for guessing.

Figure 14.6 lists a few things to keep in mind when deciding whether to use a correction formula.

Current Practices Among Test Publishers

Test publishers disagree about the use of correction for guessing. Most commercial achievement and aptitude batteries simply use the number right score. This is due in part to practical concerns rather than to psychometric considerations: The additional task of correcting for guessing adds one more burden and another possible source of clerical error (Thorndike, 1971). Also, tests using

FIGURE 14.6 Things to consider for correction for guessing.

1. A correction formula does not correct for good luck nor compensate for bad luck.

2. The relative ordering of pupils is usually the same for uncorrected as for corrected scores.

3. The chance of getting a good score by random guessing is very slim.

4. Pupils who want to do well on the test, and who are given enough time to attempt all items, will guess on only a few items.

5. Encouraging pupils to make the best choice they can, even if they are not completely confident in their choice, does not seem to be morally nor educationally wrong.

6. Responding to an item on a rational basis, even when lacking complete certainty of the correctness of the answer, provides useful information on general educational achievement.

7. Using a correction-for-guessing penalty may discourage slower students from guessing blindly on items near the end of a test when time is short.

8. Correction-for-guessing directions do not seem to discourage the test-wise or risk-taking examinee from guessing, but do seem to discourage the reluctant, risk-avoiding, or non-test-wise examinee.

9. A formula score makes the scoring more complicated, offering additional opportunities for the teacher to commit scoring errors.

Source: From *Measuring Educational Achievement*, pp. 251–257, by R. L. Ebel, © 1965 by Allyn and Bacon. Reprinted by permission.

item response theory use mathematic models to take guessing into account when deriving the scores.

When a standardized test is used, the instructions in the manual must be followed exactly. If you fail to apply a correction the publisher intended, apply it when the test publisher didn't intend it to be used, or otherwise alter the instructions to students at the time of testing, you will make the test's norms unusable because the alterations result in new unstandardized test conditions.

SECTION III. USING STUDENTS' RESPONSES TO IMPROVE ASSESSMENTS

ITEM ANALYSIS FOR CLASSROOM ASSESSMENTS

Item analysis refers to the process of collecting, summarizing, and using information from students' responses to make decisions about each assessment task. Standardized test developers, especially developers of norm-referenced tests, try out as many as five times more items than will appear on the final version of a test. Item analysis data from this tryout are used to help select items for the final form. The developers discard items that fail to display proper statistical properties. Your classroom assessments, being more closely linked to the daily teaching-learning process, serve purposes that are somewhat different from published standardized tests. Thus, you will use item analysis data differently than a test publisher.

Classroom Uses for Item Analyses

For teacher-crafted assessments, the following are among the important uses of item analyses.

1. *Determining whether an item functions as you intended.* You can't expect to write perfectly functioning items. To decide whether an item for a classroom assessment is functioning properly, you need to know whether it assesses the intended learning targets, whether it is of the appropriate level of difficulty, whether it distinguishes those who have command of the learning targets from those who do not, whether the keyed answer is correct, and (for response-choice items) whether the distracters are working. A procedure to help you decide whether an item seems to be assessing the intended learning target was described in Chapter 6. The other four elements are discussed in this chapter.

2. *Feedback to students about their performance and as a basis for class discussion.* Students are entitled to know how their performance on each assessment task is marked and the correct answer to each task. Going over a test with students makes instructional common sense: You can correct students' errors, you can clarify for students the level of detail you expect of them, and you can reinforce good (and correct) responses. Also, students lacking test-wiseness skills may learn how a correct answer is formulated or why (in response-choice items) foils are incorrect, and you can alleviate some test anxiety if you teach your students to view your assessments rationally in the context of instruction.

3. *Feedback to the teacher about pupil difficulties.* A simple procedure such as tabulating the percent of students answering an item correctly may provide you with information about areas that need additional instruction and remediation. (Some authorities recommend that you obtain the number of students answering an item correctly by a

show of hands. The author *does not recommend* this practice because it may be upsetting to some students and may violate the privacy of others.) This sort of item analysis can help you focus your teaching on both group and individual needs. Note, however, that a subscore based on a cluster of several items measuring similar learning targets provides more reliable information than does a single item, so use these results cautiously.

You will also find it helpful to identify the nature of students' errors on assessment tasks. With essay, short-answer, and completion items, a **content analysis of the responses** will determine the major types of student errors and how often they occur. You need not conduct a content analysis for every assessment every time you give it, however. You can do one unit each marking period, or colleagues can analyze different units. You can exchange information with others and save the information to use with the next group of students. Over a period of time, you will have available enough information to develop a checklist of student difficulties. Use this list to focus your teaching and to diagnose students' errors.

Many school systems have electronic equipment to scan answer sheets and the capability to tabulate the percent of students answering each response-choice item correctly. As schools acquire microcomputers and as the software for item analysis becomes less costly, these and other tabulations recommended in this chapter will become much easier for you to do routinely. (See Chapter 15 also.)

4. *Areas for curriculum improvement.* If particular kinds of assessment tasks are repeatedly difficult for students, or if certain kinds of errors occur often, perhaps the problem extends beyond you: A more extensive curriculum revision may be needed. Item analysis data help to identify specific problems. But any assessment is likely to represent a school's curriculum objectives incompletely, so you should use caution when attempting to generalize item analysis to the whole of student learning.

5. *Revising the assessment tasks.* Information about students' responses to and perceptions of an assessment task should be used to revise it. Tasks can be reused for future assessments and, if a few are revised each time, the overall quality of the assessment will eventually improve. It is usually less time-consuming to revise an item than to write a new one. Some teachers, especially in the junior and senior high schools (and in colleges), develop an **item file** or **item bank**. They write and try new items, and through item analysis they keep the best items each time, revise some, and discard the rest. Figure 14.7 shows one card in such a file. If you are skilled at using a database program, you can use it to create your item bank. After several years, a file of good items accumulates. Once a file of items is established, equivalent versions of a test can be constructed relatively easily. Equivalent ver-

FIGURE 14.7   An item card with item analysis data for one item. Tabulations were made for Item 3 on the summary record form shown in Table 14.1.

Course: *Testing in the Classroom*   Date(s): *Fall 1995*
                                               Winter 1996
Topic: *Percentile Ranks*   *Spring 1997*

I T E M

Forty-eight scores in a collection of 100 scores are *below* 54. Four scores are *equal* to 54. What is the percentile rank of the score point 54?

    a. 48   *b. 50   c. 52   d. 54

	SUMMARY ITEM DATA		
	Upper Group	Lower Group	Middle Group
A	0	1	
*B	10	7	12
C	0	1	
D	0	1	
omits	0	0	

Difficulty index: *.85*   Number of Students: *34*

Discrimination index: *.30*

sions of tests can be used for makeup tests when persons are absent during the regularly scheduled administration, when a teacher has multiple sections of the same course, or when tests are used in an alternating pattern from year to year.

6. *Improving item-writing skills.* Probably the most effective way to improve your item-writing skills is to analyze the items and the way students respond to them, then use this information to revise items and to try them again with students.

Item Analysis of Response-Choice Tests

The basic bits of data you need to begin an analysis of response-choice items (true-false, matching, or multiple choice) are the responses made by each student to each item. Although this information is easier to use if students have marked their answers on separate answer sheets, such sheets are not necessary. An outline of the steps necessary to organize the information is shown in Figure 14.8.

Although this section is written primarily for conducting analyses of response-choice items, you can use several of the techniques described with any assessment tasks that are **dichotomously scored** (correct/incorrect or pass/fail) such as completion of short-answer items. Item analysis techniques do exist for analyzing tasks scored more continuously, such as essays or performance assessments. We illustrate these techniques in the next section. The complexity of these techniques, however, can render them impractical for teachers who do not have access to computers and/or sophisticated scanning equipment.

FIGURE 14.8 Summary of steps for doing an item analysis.

Step 1. Score each test by marking the correct answers and putting the total number correct on the test (or answer sheet).

Step 2. Sort the papers in numerical order according to the total score.

Step 3. Determine the upper, middle, and lower groups (see text).

Step 4. Summarize the responses to each alternative in the upper and lower groups, and tabulate the number of the middle group which has chosen the correct alternative.

Step 5. Calculate the difficulty index for each item (see text).

Step 6. Calculate the discrimination index for each item (see text).

Step 7. Check each item to search for poor distractors, ambiguous alternatives, miskeying, and indications of blind guessing.

Upper and Lower Scoring Groups

After you have scored the tests, arrange them in numerical order according to the students' total score. Next, form three groups: **upper, middle, and lower scoring groups**. You then contrast the responses of the upper and lower scoring groups in various ways (described later) to determine whether each item is functioning well.

How you form these groups is important. When the total number of students taking your test is between 20 and 40, select the 10 highest-scoring and the 10 lowest-scoring papers (Whitney & Sabers, 1970), but keep the middle-scoring group intact. (When there are 20 students there will be no middle group.) If there are 20 students or fewer than 20 students, the responses of only one or two students may greatly influence the results you will obtain from the procedure described here. If you use item analysis with too few students, you many come to quite incorrect conclusions about how a particular item would function if you were to use it again. Nevertheless, if you want to go ahead with the analysis for groups with very few students in them, separate the test papers into two sets (upper and lower halves) and interpret the results cautiously. For groups larger than 40, testing experts frequently recommend using the upper- and lower-scoring 27% of the group on technical grounds (Kelly, 1939). For purposes of classroom assessment, however, when the group is larger than 40, any percentage between 25 and 33 seems appropriate.

Summarize Responses to Each Item

For each item, record the number of students in the (1) upper group choosing each alternative (and, separately, the number not responding [omitting]); (2) lower group choosing each alternative (and the number omitting the item); and (3) middle-scoring group choosing the correct alternative. Figure 14.7 shows the results of such a tabulation for one item. You also can make a form to record the necessary numbers for several items on a single page, or you can simply write this information in the margin of the teacher's copy of the test.

Without a doubt, the most tedious part of an item analysis is tabulating the students' responses to items. Using an upper and lower group instead of the entire class makes the task easier. One simplifying procedure is to make a form such as shown in Table 14.1. Once you obtain the basic information given in Table 14.1, you can make various summaries. We describe these summaries in this section and explain how to interpret them in subsequent sections of this chapter.

Compute Item Difficulty Index (p)

The fraction of the total group answering the item correctly is called the **item difficulty index** (p). To compute it from the form in Table 14.1, add together the number of students choosing the correct answer in the upper, middle, and lower groups, then divide this sum by the total number of persons who took the test. In Equation 14.3, this is illustrated for Item 3 of Table 14.1. The results are also summarized on the item file card shown in Figure 14.7.

$$p = \left[\frac{\begin{array}{c} \text{number of students} \\ \text{choosing correct alternative} \end{array}}{\begin{array}{c} \text{total number of students} \\ \text{taking the test} \end{array}} \right] \qquad \text{[Eq. 14.3]}$$

$$= \left[\frac{\begin{array}{c} \text{number of students choosing the correct answer} \\ \text{in the upper + middle + lower groups} \end{array}}{\begin{array}{c} \text{total number of students} \\ \text{taking the test} \end{array}} \right]$$

$$= \frac{10 + 7 + 12}{34} = \frac{29}{34} = 0.85$$

As we will discuss later, this fraction can range from 0.00 to 1.00.

Compute Item Discrimination Index (D)

The **item discrimination index** (D) is the difference between the fraction of the upper group answering the item correctly and the fraction of the lower group answering it correctly. The discrimination index describes the extent to which a particular test item is able to differentiate the higher scoring students from the lower scoring students. The following equation is used to compute this index:

$$D = \left[\begin{array}{c} \text{fraction of the upper group} \\ \text{answering the item correctly} \end{array} \right] -$$

$$\left[\begin{array}{c} \text{fraction of the lower group} \\ \text{answering the item correctly} \end{array} \right] \qquad \text{[Eq. 14.4]}$$

TABLE 14.1 Item responses to the first 10 items of a 59-item test taken by a group of 34 college students. It is an example of the basic data needed to do an item analysis. Note that for the middle group you record only the number right and the number of omits.

					Item number:						
		1	2	3	4	5	6	7	8	9	10
Upper group	Doris	A	C	B	B	C	C	B	A	B	D
	Jerry	A	C	B	B	C	C	B	A	B	D
	Robert	A	C	B	B	C	C	E	A	B	D
	Elazar	A	B	B	B	C	C	B	A	B	D
	Marya	A	C	B	B	C	C	B	A	B	D
	Anna	A	C	B	B	C	C	B	A	B	D
	Diana	A	C	B	B	C	C	B	A	B	D
	Harry	A	C	B	B	C	C	B	A	B	D
	Anthony	A	C	B	B	C	C	B	A	B	D
	Carolyn	A	C	B	B	B	C	B	A	B	D
	Key	A	C	B	B	C	C	B	A	B	D
Number choosing each option	A	10	0	0	10	0	0	0	10	0	0
	B	0	1	10	0	1	0	9	0	10	0
	C	0	9	0	—	9	10	0	0	0	0
	D	0	—	0	—	0	0	0	0	0	10
	E	—	—	—	—	—	—	1	—	—	—
	Omits	0	0	0	0	0	0	0	0	0	0
Middle group	No. right	14	12	12	13	12	13	11	11	12	12
	No. omits	0	0	0	0	0	0	0	0	0	0
Lower group	Anita	A	C	B	B	D	C	E	A	A	D
	Larry	A	C	B	B	D	C	D	A	B	D
	Charles	C	B	B	B	C	C	B	A	B	C
	Joel	A	C	B	B	C	C	E	A	B	D
	Leslie	A	C	B	B	C	C	E	A	B	B
	Alida	A	C	B	B	C	C	A	B	B	B
	Marilyn	A	C	D	B	C	C	D	C	D	A
	Wayne	A	B	A	A	C	C	B	B	C	A
	Ina	D	C	C	A	B	B	C	B	A	D
	Donald	C	B	B	B	D	C	E	C	D	D
	Key	A	C	B	B	C	C	B	A	B	D
Number choosing each option	A	7	0	1	2	0	0	1	5	2	2
	B	0	3	7	8	1	1	2	3	5	2
	C	2	7	1	—	6	9	1	2	1	1
	D	1	—	1	—	3	0	2	0	2	5
	E	—	—	—	—	—	—	4	—	—	—
	Omits	0	0	0	0	0	0	0	0	0	0

Note: The dash (—) means that that option was not available for that item.

Here is the discrimination index for the item in Figure 14.7:

$$D = \frac{10}{10} - \frac{7}{10} = 1.0 - 0.7 = 0.3$$

As we will discuss later, this index can range form −1.00 to +1.00. A handheld calculator will facilitate computing the difficulty and discrimination indices.

Item Analysis of Constructed-Response and Performance Assessments

When constructed-response and performance assessments are used, each item is scored in a more continuous way. Instead of scoring 0 or 1, each item is scored on a scale from 0 to 3, 1 to 4, or some other range of scores. Item difficulty and discrimination can be computed for these items as well. There are many ways to compute these, but we shall limit our discussion to simple ways appropriate for classroom assessment.

Computing the Item Difficulty Index (p^*)

The item difficulty for a constructed-response and performance item is simply the average score for the group for that item[1]. For example, if Item 1 was an essay item, scored on a scale of 1 to 6, and if the average score on this item was 4.2, then the difficulty of the item is 4.2.

In order to keep this item difficult on the same scale as the p-value of Equation 14.3, we should divide this average by its possible score range. This will give us a value between .00 and 1.00, the same range as the values resulting from Equation 14.3. This is illustrated here:

$$p^* = \left[\frac{\begin{array}{c}\text{average score for}\\\text{an item}\end{array}}{\begin{array}{c}\text{possible item}\\\text{score range}\end{array}}\right] \quad \text{[Eq. 14.5]}$$

$$= \left[\frac{\begin{array}{c}\text{average score}\\\text{for an item}\end{array}}{\begin{array}{cc}\text{maximum} & \text{minimum}\\\text{possible} - \text{possible}\\\text{item score} & \text{item score}\end{array}}\right]$$

$$= \frac{4.2}{6-1} = \frac{4.2}{5} = 0.84$$

We need to divide the average score by the possible score range to make its interpretation clear. In Equation 14.5, $p^* = 0.84$ means that on average, students received 84% of the maximum possible score range for this item. (This is a pretty easy item.) Suppose, however, that this item was scored on a scale from 0 to 10. The difficulty index then would be:

$$p^* = \frac{4.2}{10-0} = \frac{4.2}{10} = .42$$

An average that is 42% of the full range of marks is quite low. So you see, *you cannot fully interpret the average score of a performance item unless you know the range of the possible marks.*

Incidentally, to distinguish Equation 14.3 from 14.5, I used an * along with p. This is not standard.

Computing the Item Discrimination Index (D^*)

The discrimination index for constructed-response and performance items is simply the difference between the average score on the item for the upper group and the corresponding average for the lower group. The upper and

lower groups are defined in the same way as described previously; that is, based on their ranking in the total assessment.

Suppose the upper group's average for an item is 5.3, and the lower group's corresponding average is 2.8, and the item is scored from 1 to 6. The discrimination for the item is $5.3 - 2.8 = 2.5$.

To keep the item discrimination index on the same scale as the D-value of Equation 14.4, we should divide this difference by the possible score range. This gives us a value between -1.00 and $+1.00$, just as with Equation 14.4. This is illustrated in Equation 14.6.

$$D^* = \frac{\left[\begin{array}{c}\text{average score of}\\\text{the upper group}\\\text{on the item}\end{array}\right] - \left[\begin{array}{c}\text{average score of}\\\text{the lower group}\\\text{on the item}\end{array}\right]}{\text{range of possible item scores}}$$

$$= \frac{\left[\begin{array}{c}\text{difference between the upper}\\\text{and the lower groups' average item score}\end{array}\right]}{\left[\begin{array}{cc}\text{maximum} & \text{minimum}\\\text{possible} - \text{possible}\\\text{item score} & \text{item score}\end{array}\right]} \quad \text{[Eq. 14.6]}$$

$$= \frac{5.3 - 2.8}{6-1} = \frac{2.5}{5} = .5$$

Because we divide by the possible item score range, we can interpret this value to mean that the difference between the average scores of the upper and lower groups for this item is 50% of the possible item score range. (This item discriminates fairly well.) As with the previously discussed discrimination index (Equation 14.4), the index here can show negative values, zero, or positive values. If the value is negative, this means that the lower group scored higher on the average than the upper group. We would generally consider such a result to mean that the item is not good. (We discuss this further in the following sections.)

ITEM DIFFICULTY INDEX

Effect on Test Score Distribution

Shape of the Distribution   The difficulty of test items affects the shape of the distribution of total test scores. Very difficult tests, containing items with $ps < 0.25$, will tend to be positively skewed, whereas easy tests, containing items with $ps > 0.80$, will tend to be negatively skewed. (See Figure H.2 for an explanation of distribution shapes.) The shapes of total score distributions for other kinds of assessments are not so easily deduced.

Average or Mean Test Score   The difficulty of items affects the average or mean test score: The average test score

---

[1]If you have a mathematics background you will note that the average score for an item scored 0 or 1 is the p-value given by Equation 14.3. Thus, it will come as no surprise that we defined item difficulty for a more continuously scored item as the average score for that item.

(M) is equal to the sum of the difficulties of the items. The relationship is given here:

$$M = \Sigma p \qquad \text{[Eq. 14.7]}$$

The mean (M) test score is equal to the sum of the difficulty (p) values of the items comprising the test. When the assessment contains only performance or constructed-response items, the mean is simply the sum of the item means, not the sum of the p^* values from Equation 14.5.

Spread of Scores   The spread of item difficulties and the spread of test scores are related. A test with all p-values clustered around 0.50 has the largest spread of test scores, while tests with difficulties more spread out between .10 and .90 have smaller score spreads.

Item difficulties (p-values) are not the sole factor contributing to the spread of test scores. Another factor is the correlation (Appendix H) among the items: The higher these intercorrelations, the larger the standard deviation. However, the correlations among items may be affected by the p-values: Items for which $p = 0.00$ or 1.00 have correlations of 0.00.

Uses of Item Difficulty Information

Table 14.2 summarizes some of the ways in which teachers and school officials can use p-values in assessment and instruction. For the teacher, perhaps identifying concepts to be retaught and giving students feedback about their learning are the more important uses of item difficulty data. Uses such as obtaining information about curriculum strengths or suspected item bias require district-wide cooperation. Such analysis tends to be employed only with state-mandated and standardized tests, because test publishers make this information readily available. You may find yourself involved in interpreting state-mandated or standardized test data if you serve on school committees

TABLE 14.2 Examples of ways in which item difficulty indices can be used in testing and instruction.

Purpose	Procedure	Comments
Identifying concepts that need to be retaught	Find items with small p-values. These items may point to objectives needing to be retaught.	a. Poor test performance may not reflect poor teaching: Poor performance may reflect poorly written items, incorrect prior learning, or poor motivation on tests. b. A score based on several similar items is more reliable than performance on a single item.
Clues to possible strengths and weaknesses in school curricula	Calculate p-values for clusters of similar items for a school building or district. Compare these to p-values of the same items from the publisher's national norm-group. Note areas of strength and weakness.	a. See a and b above. b. This procedure applies to standardized tests only. c. Items must correspond to local curriculum objectives and instruction. d. No published test will cover all the objectives of a school district.
Giving feedback to students	Report p-value of each item to student along with ID number of the items missed.	a. Such reporting is more useful for high school and college students.
Clues to possible item bias	Separate test papers into groups to be contrasted (e.g., males vs. females, blacks vs. whites). Compute p-values for each item separately for each group. Items for which p-value differences are unusually large are studied further to see if they may be biased.	a. This is only a crude method and not a scientifically satisfactory method (Lord, 1977). b. This procedure is not very useful in small samples of examinees because of sampling fluctuations.
Building tests that have certain statistical properties	See Table 14.3	

or if you are promoted to administrative positions. Procedures for using p-values to build special-purpose tests are described later in this chapter.

ITEM DISCRIMINATION INDEX

Step 6 in Figure 14.8 states that a discrimination index should be computed for each item. Following Equation 14.4, we saw an example of how to compute it. This computation can be summarized by the following formula:

$$D = p_U - p_L \qquad \text{[Eq. 14.8]}$$

where

D stands for the numerical value of the discrimination index,

p_U stands for the fraction of the upper scoring group answering the item correctly, and

p_L stands for the fraction of the lower scoring group answering the item correctly.

This index is sometimes referred to as the *net D index of discrimination*. Net D is seldom used today by commercial test developers; they now use a correlation coefficient as a discrimination index or other indices based on mathematical modeling of item responses. Net D is probably the most useful discrimination index available for use with teacher-made assessments, however. Equation 14.6 is the comparable equation for constructed-response and performance items.

Importance of Item Discrimination

Absolute vs. Relative Achievement **Absolute achievement** assessment focuses mainly on accurately determining the content or behavior each student has learned. **Relative achievement** assessment, on the other hand, focuses mainly on accurately determining the relative rank ordering among students with respect to the content or learning targets learned. When you are gathering information mainly about the rank order of students, you should revise or remove from the test those items that do not contribute information about ordering students or that provide inconsistent, confusing information about this ordering.

Suppose you wanted to order a class of students from high to low using a 30-item unit test. Suppose, further, that when doing an item analysis, you divide the class in half based on the total test score (as usual, higher scorers in the upper group, lower scorers in the lower group). Finally, suppose that for one of the items, you discover that all of the lower group students answered the item correctly, and the entire upper group answered it incorrectly. In this case, the item difficulty index is $p = 0.50$, but the item discrimination index is $D = 0 - 1.00 = -1.00$. This **negatively discriminating item** is poor, because it works in the opposite way from most of the other items. That is,

high-scoring students answer it wrong and low-scoring students answer it correctly. If you were to put such negatively discriminating items on a test, they would work to arrange students in an order that is quite inconsistent with the arrangement made by the positively discriminating items on the assessment.

Only the discrimination index is able to detect the type of malfunctioning item just described. The difficulty index gives the proportion of the class that answers an item correctly, but it does not indicate whether more higher- or lower-scoring students answered correctly. *For this reason, you should give more weight to an item's discrimination index than its difficulty index when deciding whether the item should appear on a test.*

Numerical Limits of D For each item, the discrimination index ranges from -1 to $+1$. If all the discriminations made by an item are *correct discriminations* (everyone in the upper group answers the item right, while everyone in the lower group answers it wrong), net D would equal $+1$. Such an item is said to be a perfect **positively discriminating item**. If the number of correct discriminations equals the number of *incorrect discriminations* (an equal number of upper and lower group students answer the item right), then $D = 0$. Such an item is said to be a **nondiscriminating item**. Finally, if all discriminations were incorrect ones (everyone in the upper group answers the item wrong while everyone in the lower group answers it right), the D would equal -1. Such an item is said to be a perfect negatively discriminating item.

The values $+1$ and -1 are seldom obtained in practice. $D = 0$ is obtained most often for very easy or very hard items. The values -1, 0, and $+1$ serve as benchmarks when interpreting D.

D Can Signal Items Needing Revision Interpret a negative value of D as a warning that you should carefully study the item and either revise or eliminate it. If you cannot find a technical flaw in the item, it might be that students in the upper-scoring group learned the material either incompletely or entirely incorrectly (Lindquist, 1936). (See Figure 8.25 for examples.) Barring any rational explanation to the contrary, all of your assessment's items should be positively discriminating; otherwise, the total score on the assessment won't provide usable information.

Spread of Scores Intuitively, you know that if none of the items discriminated ($D = 0$ for all items), everyone would be bunched together: If individual items can't distinguish students, then the collection of items won't be able to do so either. The larger the assessment's average level of item discrimination, the more spread out the assessment scores will be.

Score Reliability and Item Discrimination Power A more reliable assessment will be made up of tasks with high, positive discrimination indices. Thus, if the primary purpose of using an assessment is to interpret differences in achievement between students, the assessment procedure must be comprised of tasks with high discriminating power. (A more complete discussion of reliability is presented in Chapter 4.)

IMPROVING MULTIPLE-CHOICE ITEM QUALITY

Poorly Functioning Distractors

Response Patterns for Distractors   The main purpose of the distractors or foils in a multiple-choice item is to appear plausible to those students lacking sufficient knowledge to choose the correct answer. Item analysis data of the type summarized in Table 14.1 identifies item distractors for which this purpose may not be fulfilled. The general rule is this: *Every distractor should have at least one lower group student choosing it, and more lower group students than upper group students should choose it.* The following data from the item presented in Figure 14.7 illustrates these points.

Alternative	Upper Group	Lower Group
A	0	1
•B	10	7
C	0	1
D	0	1

Each distractor (A, C, and D) has been chosen by at least one lower group person; no student in the upper group chose a distractor. (Note: Because of fluctuations in responses from one small group of students to another, you must use the rules of thumb in this section carefully.)

The rationale for this rule is as follows: Students scoring lowest on the test are, on the whole, least able (in a relative, not absolute, sense) regarding the performance being assessed. (If they are not, then the test on which they scored lowest must lack validity.) For every item, it is among these lower-scoring students that you should expect to find an item answered incorrectly. Thus, if an item is working properly, one or more lower-scoring students should choose each distractor, and more lower-scoring than upper-scoring students should choose distractors.

Notice that not every lower-scoring person lacks knowledge about every item: In the preceding example, seven out of ten lower-scoring persons knew the answer. Neither is it the case that every higher-scoring person always chooses the correct answer (see, for example, Items 2, 5, and 7 in Table 14.1).

If no student in the lower group chooses a particular distractor, the distractor *may* be functioning poorly. You should review the item and speculate why this occurred. Perhaps the particular alternative contains one of the technical flaws described in Chapter 8. If all students recognize a particular option as obviously incorrect, then you will want to either eliminate the alternative entirely (thus reducing the number of options in the item), substitute an entirely new alternative, or revise the existing alternative.

Subject Matter Has Precedence   It isn't always true that an alternative is flawed if no one in the lower group chooses it. Here's where your knowledge of the subject matter, of the students, and of the instruction students received prior to taking the assessment come into play: Perhaps in this year's group, even the lowest-scoring students have enough knowledge to eliminate a particular distractor, yet they do not have enough knowledge to select the correct answer. Perhaps in other groups a concept will not be learned as well, and this particular distractor will be plausible. Eliminating the alternative would make identifying those few individuals who lack this learning impossible. In other words, use your own expertise along with the data to decide whether to eliminate a distractor that isn't working.

Finally, note that even though it seems reasonable to *expect* a larger number of lower-scoring students than higher-scoring students to choose a particular distractor, this may not always happen. Technical flaws may cause higher-scoring students to be deceived, such as when they know a great deal about the subject and thus are able to give a plausible reason why an unkeyed alternative is at least as correct as the keyed one. In such cases, the alternative definitely should be revised.

But sometimes there is neither a technical flaw nor a subject-matter deficiency in an incorrect alternative, yet higher-scoring students choose it in greater numbers than lower-scoring ones. In these cases, students may have incomplete or wrong learning. Examples of these two cases are shown in Figure 8.25. You should review these examples at this point.

Ambiguous Alternatives

Student responses can provide leads to **ambiguous alternatives**. In this context, alternatives are ambiguous if upper group students are unable to distinguish between the keyed answer and one or more of the distractors (Sax, 1989). When this happens, the upper group tends to choose a distractor with about the same frequency as the keyed response, as illustrated in Figure 14.9.

FIGURE 14.9   Sample distractor response pattern for ambiguous alternatives.

The city of Pittsburgh, Pennsylvania is located on which river?

	Upper group	Lower group
A. Delaware River	0	3
B. Ohio River	5	3
C. Monongahela River	4	1
D. Susquehanna River	1	3

The confluence of the Allegheny and Monongahela Rivers forms the Ohio River at Pittsburgh. The upper group in Figure 14.9 chose B and C with approximately equal frequency, thus reflecting the students' ambiguity in selecting only one of these two alternatives as a correct answer. This item should be revised so that only one answer is clearly correct or best.

You might notice that very often the lower group is equally divided among two or more alternatives. This is usually *not* an indication that you must revise the item. Rather, it means that students with less knowledge will find many alternatives equally plausible, and so the task becomes an ambiguous one for them. The cause of these students' ambiguity is likely to be insufficient knowledge.

Before concluding that you need to revise an item, however, you must study the item in relation to the students taking it and judge whether the ambiguity stems from the students' lack of knowledge rather than from a poorly written item (Sax, 1974). Consider Figure 14.10. Here students are required to apply arithmetic operations in a certain order: multiplication first, then addition. Option B reflects this order, while option C is the answer obtained by adding first and then multiplying. Apparently half the upper group followed this erroneous procedure and chose C. The item is not technically flawed, but from the students' responses the teacher should realize that a number of the students need to learn this principle. (The entire group's responses to this item should be checked.)

Miskeyed Items

If a larger number of upper group students selects a particular wrong response, check to be sure that the answer key is correct. In Figure 14.11, C is the correct answer, but the *teacher* inadvertently used D as the answer key. The response pattern in the figure is typical of such a **miskeyed item**.

Again, be sure to check the item content. The numbers from the item analysis only warn of possible miskeying—perhaps there is no miskeying and the upper group simply lacks the required knowledge.

Blind Guessing

If many of the alternatives are equally plausible to the upper-scoring group, either the item is flawed or the stu-

FIGURE 14.10 Incomplete learning may cause alternatives to appear ambiguous.

$3 + 5 \times 2 = ?$		Upper group	Lower group
A.	10	0	2
*B.	13	5	3
C.	16	5	3
D.	30	0	2

FIGURE 14.11 Sample distractor response pattern for a miskeyed item.

Who was the fourth president of the United States?

		Upper group	Lower group
A.	John Quincy Adams	0	3
B.	Thomas Jefferson	1	4
C.	James Madison	9	3
*D.	James Monroe	0	3

FIGURE 14.12 Blind-guessing distractor response pattern by upper group students signals confusion.

In what year did the United States enter World War I?

		Upper group	Lower group
A.	1913	2	3
B.	1915	2	2
C.	1916	3	3
*D.	1917	3	2

dents have not learned the material the item is assessing. In such situations, students tend to either omit the item or try **blind guessing**. If the upper group students guess blindly, each option tends to be chosen an approximately equal number of times, as illustrated in Figure 14.12.

Remember to look at the pattern of responses of the upper group, not the lower group, to find items on which many students may be guessing. Guessing among the most knowledgeable students may signal widespread confusion in the class. Lower-scoring students may in fact be guessing on the more difficult items too, but this indicates you need to reteach them rather than simply revise the test item. Blind guessing adds errors of measurement to the scores, thereby reducing reliability and validity.

SELECTING TEST ITEMS

Another Purpose for Item Analysis

Most teachers using item analysis procedures will do so for one or more of the following reasons: (1) to check whether the items are functioning as intended, (2) to give students feedback on their assessment performance, (3) to acquire feedback for themselves about students' difficulties, (4) to identify areas of the curriculum that may need improvement, and (5) to obtain objective data that signal the need for revising their items. There is another use for item analysis: selecting some items and culling others from a pool of items.

Purpose of Assessment Helps Select Items

No statistical item selection rule is helpful if it is inconsistent with your purpose for conducting assessments.

Further, any procedure you use for selecting some items over others changes the definition of the domain of performance. Those performances represented by items you eliminate are never assessed.

Relative vs. Absolute Student Attainment   Careful selection of items results in shorter, more efficient, and more reliable assessments. In the classroom, *statistically-based item selection* seems to be most applicable when you are concerned primarily with the relative achievement of students rather than their absolute achievement. You focus on assessing relative achievement when your priority is to accurately rank students with respect to what they have learned. You focus on assessing absolute achievement when your priority is to accurately determine the precise content (or performance) each student has learned.

As an example, consider the need to assess students' learning of the 100 simple addition facts typically taught in first and second grades. If you want to know only the relative achievement of the students (which student knows the most, next most, and so on), you could use a relatively short test, made up of only those addition facts that best discriminate among the students. This test would probably be made up of mostly the middle and upper parts of the addition table. Addition facts that almost everyone knows (such as $1 + 1 = 2$) would not be included on such a test, because these items would not discriminate ($D = 0$) and thus would not provide information about ranking the students. However, excluding certain addition facts from the assessment because they do not discriminate well means that you will be unable to observe a student's performance on all 100 addition facts.

On the other hand, suppose your purpose for assessment is to identify the particular addition combinations with which a student has difficulty. In this case, finding out the absolute level of achievement would be your main assessment focus. You may find it necessary to use a longer, less efficient test, perhaps assessing all 100 facts over a period of several days.

Absolute, rather than relative, achievement is more important for diagnostic assessments intended to identify such things as whether a student has acquired particular reading skills, learned a certain percentage of facts in some specified domain, or has the ability to solve certain types of problems. Relative achievement is more important when you are assessing a student's general educational development in a subject area.

Complete vs. Partial Ordering   For some educational decisions, you may need to accurately rank all students on their test performance, this is called a **complete ordering of students**. On the other hand, you may want to separate students only into five ordered categories so you can assign grades (A, B, C, D, and F). In so doing, you may not wish to make precise distinctions among the students within each category. Similarly, you may wish to divide the class into two groups: For example,

mastery/nonmastery or faster/slower readers. When the categories themselves are ordered, but there is *no ordering of individuals within a category*, this is called a **partial ordering**. Categorizing students by their grades, or into fail-pass groups, are examples of partial ordering.

When you focus your assessment on either partial or complete ordering, it is inefficient to include items that do not contribute to ordering and distinguishing students. Such items therefore are culled from the pool. To cull, you try out items with students *before* creating the final version of the test (or you use items from past administrations of the test). You calculate item statistics (p and D). You select and assemble into the final test those items with high, positive discrimination indices, generally of middle difficulty.

Realities, Content Coverage, and Compromise

In practice, you must include test items with less than ideal statistical properties so a test can match its blueprint. Actual assessment construction tends to be a compromise between considerations of subject-matter coverage and psychometric properties (Henrysson, 1971). The general principle is: *Select the best available items that cover the important areas of content as defined by the blueprint, even though the discrimination and difficulty indices of these items have values that are less than ideal.*

Rules of Thumb for Selecting Test Items

Table 14.3 summarizes guidelines for selecting items for classroom tests, keeping in mind our discussion of the differences between building a test to measure relative achievement and building one to measure absolute achievement. Note that coverage of content and learning targets has primacy over statistical indices when selecting test items by the procedures recommended here. The guidelines shown in the table require you to understand whether the prospective test should assess only one ability or characteristic of a student, or a combination of several abilities. A **homogeneous test** will measure one ability, while a **heterogeneous test** will assess a combination of abilities. If your test contains items for which students can get the right answer by blind guessing (such as with multiple-choice items), then the items you select should be approximately 5% easier than shown in the table.

When crafting a test of relative achievement, remember that in choosing between two items assessing the same learning target, good item discrimination takes precedence over obtaining the ideal item difficulty level. That is, if two items assess the same learning target and are of approximately the same level of difficulty, use the one that discriminates better.

When you design a criterion-referenced classroom test, item statistics play a lesser role for selecting and culling items. You should still calculate item statistics to obtain

TABLE 14.3   Guidelines for selecting items.

| | Relative achievement is the focus | | Absolute achievement is the focus |
	Complete ordering	Partial ordering (two groups)	
General concerns	Ranking all the pupils in terms of their relative attainment in a subject area.	Dividing pupils into two groups on the basis of their relative attainment. Pupils within each group will be treated alike.	Assess the absolute status (achievement) of the pupil with respect to a well-defined domain of instructionally relevant tasks.
Specific focus of test	Seek to accurately describe differences in relative achievement between individual pupils.	Seek to accurately classify persons into two categories.	Seek to accurately estimate the percentage of the domain each pupil can perform successfully.
Attention to the test's blueprint	Be sure that items cover all important topics and objectives within the blueprint.	Be sure that items cover all important topics and objectives within the blueprint.	Be sure items are a representative, random sample from the defined domain which the blueprint operationalizes.
How the difficulty index (p) is used	Within each topical area of the blueprint, select those items with: (1) p between 0.16 and 0.84 if performance on the test represents a single ability. (2) p between 0.40 and 0.60 if performance on the test represents several different abilities. Note: Items should be easier than described above if guessing is a factor.	Within each topical area of the blueprint, select those items with p-values slightly larger than the percentage of persons to be classified in the upper group [e.g., if the class is to be divided in half (0.50) then items with p-values of about 0.60 should be selected; if the division is lower 75% vs. upper 25%, items should have $p = 0.35$ (approximately)]. Note: The above suggestion assumes the test measures a single ability.	Don't select items on the basis of their p-values, but study each p to see if it is signaling a poorly written item.
How the discrimination index (D) is used	Within each topical area of the blueprint, select items with D greater than or equal to +0.30.	Within each topical area of the blueprint, select items with D greater than or equal to +0.30.	All items should have D greater than or equal to 0.00. Unless there is a rational explanation to the contrary, revise those items not possessing this property.

data on how the items might be improved, however. Items exhibiting zero or negative discrimination frequently contain technical flaws that you may not notice unless you do an item analysis.

USING COMPUTERS FOR TEST ASSEMBLY AND ITEM ANALYSES

The calculations and tabulations illustrated in this chapter can be done with a handheld calculator. They can also be done using a computer program. In some schools, students' responses on scannable answer sheets can be scanned directly into a program that does all the item analyses illustrated in this chapter. In other schools the scanner creates a computer file, but you must use your own program to analyze the data. You can accomplish much the same analyses as specialized programs by using a standard spreadsheet program that comes with office suite programs.

Vendors have also created software that allows test items to be banked or stored in a computer file. The software then allows you to select items from the bank, assemble tests, and print them for duplication. Some software permits tests to be administered via intranet or Internet. Other software products offer even more organization: You can align your assignments with your state's standards and school's curriculum objectives, then monitor each student's progress against these standards and objectives.

Software, hardware, and related products vary greatly, not only in their quality, cost, and user friendliness but also in how well they match your teaching and school's instructional goals. Some programs can be run right out of the box, while others require considerable training. We are not able to review the products here. One place you may want to begin is with the article, "Trends: New Products Streamline Testing and Assessment" (Carmona, 1997). This article gives you an overview of the types of scanners, test analyses, and test assembly software that are available. You can follow up to identify the latest versions of the products and their costs. You could also visit the web page of *T.H.E. Journal* (www.thejournal.com) or the web page of firms that produce assessment and item-analysis software (e.g., Assessment Systems Corporation at www.assess.com).

Summary

- Students should demonstrate their maximum performance on classroom assessments.
- If you handle your classroom assessments properly, you can help students demonstrate their maximum capability.
- Before an upcoming assessment, you should tell students the number and kind of items, the assessment's time limits, how you expect them to answer questions, the penalty, if any, you will impose for guessing, and whether there is a general strategy they should follow when responding to the items.
- Give students at least 48 hours' notice before assessing them in a subject. Surprise quizzes do not seem to have the motivating effects frequently attributed to them, and students sometimes view them as unfair.
- Nine test-taking skills are presented. These are the minimum skills your students will need, beyond subject-matter knowledge, to display maximum capabilities on your assessment. Teach all of these skills.
- Test-wiseness refers to a student's ability to use the characteristics of both the assessment materials and the assessment situation to attain a higher score.
- Test-wiseness skills and knowledge can be classified into two broad areas: those that students can use regardless of the purpose for taking the assessment or who developed the assessment procedure, and those that students can use with assessments developed for certain purposes or by certain persons. These skills and knowledge are outlined in Figure 14.1.
- Students' test-wiseness and general test-taking skills become more sophisticated as they progress through the grades, but students' abilities vary greatly. Those with few skills and little test-wiseness are usually at a disadvantage when they take tests with more skilled and test-wise peers.
- Correction for guessing formulas attempt to discourage students from guessing blindly on multiple-choice and true-false items, but only a few of the many explanations of why a student marked or didn't mark an answer appear to fit the rationales needed for using a correction formula. Further, correction for guessing neither corrects for students' good luck nor compensates for bad luck.
- Things to consider before deciding whether to use a correction for guessing formula on a classroom test are listed in Figure 14.6.

- Your assessment's directions to students should clearly indicate whether you will apply a correction and the students' best strategy when responding to the assessment tasks.
- You should teach the important skills and knowledge that will appear on an assessment, but it is unethical to teach students only the answers to those specific items that will appear on the assessment.
- Anxiety associated with taking a test is thought to elicit in examinees task-relevant responses, which facilitate performance on the test, and task-irrelevant responses, which interfere with test performance.
- Task-irrelevant thoughts can debilitate highly test-anxious persons who are preoccupied with their own inadequacy, helplessness, and possible failure.
- Test anxiety consists of a cognitive, worry component and an emotionality component. Alternately, four components may be identified: (1) tension, (2) worry, (3) task-irrelevant thinking, and (4) bodily reactions.
- Three groups of highly test-anxious students are (1) students with poor study habits who have not learned the material assessed, (2) students with good study skills who have built up fears of being assessed, and (3) students who incorrectly believe they have good study skills but do poorly on assessments.
- Suggestions for helping test-anxious students are provided.
- You begin to facilitate students' maximum assessment performance by attending carefully to the assessment materials, including their overall appearance, the arrangement of the assessment tasks, and the way you present the assessment to your students.
- When crafting the format and procedures for a formal assessment, you should be sensitive to the visual and auditory characteristics of your students and how these characteristics may affect their assessment performance.
- Arrange the tasks in an assessment to help students do their best.
- You should prepare the procedures for marking and a scoring key (or marking guide) before you administer the assessment to your students.
- Item analysis refers to the process of collecting, summarizing, and using information about students' responses to each assessment task.
- Important uses of item analyses of classroom assessments are (1) indicating whether the assessment tasks function as you intend, (2) giving students feedback on their performance and creating a basis for class discussion, (3) providing you feedback about the students' learning deficits, (4) suggesting areas for teaching improvement, (5) suggesting how the assessment tasks may be revised, and (6) helping you to improve your skills in setting assessment tasks.

- You can identify poorly functioning distractors on multiple-choice items by tabulating the number of students choosing each alternative. The tabulation is done separately for an upper-scoring and a lower-scoring group. As a general rule, every incorrect alternative should have at least one lower group student choosing it, and more lower group than upper group students should choose each incorrect alternative.

- Alternatives are ambiguous if higher-scoring students are unable to distinguish between the correct answer and one or more of the incorrect alternatives. Either a poorly written item or a lack of knowledge on the part of students may create ambiguity.

- You should check an item for inadvertent miskeying if a large number of higher-scoring students choose a particular wrong response.

- You should suspect that students are engaging in considerable blind guessing if an approximately equal number of higher-scoring students are choosing each alternative.

- A measure of an item's difficulty is p, the fraction of the total group responding correctly to the item. The most difficult items have p close to 0.00, and the easiest items have p close to 1.00.

- A measure of an item's discrimination power is D, the difference between the fraction of the upper extreme group answering the item correctly and the fraction of the lower extreme group answering it correctly. This index ranges from -1.00 to $+1.00$. Items that do not discriminate have D-values near zero. Many test developers strive to have items with $D > +0.30$.

- The shape of your assessment score distribution, its mean, and its spread of scores are affected by the p-values of the items on the assessment.

- Factors affecting an assessment task's difficulty include the effectiveness of your teaching, the assessment task's technical quality, the students' background and previous learning, and the students' motivation when taking the assessment.

- The magnitude of the item discrimination indices in an assessment affects the spread of assessment scores, is limited by the difficulty of the items, and affects the reliability of the assessment scores.

- The assessment of relative achievement focuses mainly on the ranking of students with respect to what they have learned (who has learned most, next most, and so on). Assessment of absolute achievement focuses mainly on accurately describing the content or performance each student has learned. Absolute achievement is of more concern when attempting to diagnose student learning deficits; relative achievement is of more concern in ascertaining a student's general educational development in an area.

- The p and D indices can be used together with the assessment blueprint to select from a larger pool of items that will best measure relative achievement. Rules of thumb for item selections are summarized in Table 14.3.

- The p and D indices generally play a lesser role in selecting items when the focus of the assessment is on absolute achievement.

Important Terms and Concepts

ambiguous alternatives
blind guessing
bodily reactions to anxiety
cognitive interference
complete vs. partial ordering of students
content analysis of the responses
correction for guessing formulas
dichotomous item scoring
emotionality
homogeneous vs. heterogeneous test
item analysis
item bank
item difficulty index (p and p^*)
item discrimination index (D and D^*)
item file
maximum performance assessment
minimum assessment-taking skills
miskeyed items
negatively discriminating item
nondiscriminating item
poorly functioning distractor
positively discriminating item
relative vs. absolute achievement
task-directed vs. task-irrelevant thoughts
tension
test anxiety
test-wiseness
types of test-anxious students
typical performance assessment
upper, middle, and lower scoring groups
worry

Exercises and Discussion Questions

1. In what way(s) might a teacher help a learning disabled student to do her best on an assessment by careful attention to the design and production of assessment materials?

2. Why are surprise or pop quizzes not recommended for use with typical students? For use with students with disabilities?

3. The author considers it unethical for a teacher to use a test or quiz to threaten, punish, or "get back at" students. Might there be circumstances under which the author's position is untenable? Explain your position in this matter. Send your essay to the author.

4. Locate two or more item-writing suggestions from Chapters 7, 8, 9, and 11 that are directed toward helping to overcome the influence of students' test-wiseness (or lack thereof) on

test scores. Share your findings with the members of your class.

5. **a.** What are the components of test anxiety?
   b. How does test anxiety interfere with a student's test performance?
   c. List several ways you might reduce the test anxiety of your students.
   d. List ways you might raise their test anxiety.

6. The author suggests several test-taking skills that all students need. For each skill, describe how you might:
   a. Assess whether a student has acquired it.
   b. Teach it to your students.

7. The following statements are cognitions that students might have during an assessment situation. Read each statement and decide whether it is a task relevant statement (TRS) or a task-irrelevant statement (TIS).
   a. "I have to be very careful in answering this problem. My teacher takes points off for computational errors."
   b. "I am really dumb. I just can't do it!"
   c. "If I don't pass this test, Dad will kill me!"
   d. "I *know* I don't know the answer to this question. It's no use trying to fool Mr. Jones. He'll just think I'm dumber than I am."
   e. "Oops! I forgot to study the material this question is asking. Oh well, I better write *something* down. I usually am able to get a few points from Mr. Jones!"

8. What test-wise strategies are represented by the following statements?
   a. "When Mr. Jones gives a true-false test, I mark *true* when in doubt because he always has more true than false items on his tests."
   b. "When writing essays for a philosophy course I always use words such as *ergo, being,* and *thing.* This makes my answer sound more philosophical."
   c. "The first thing I do is mark B in all the answer spaces. Then I go back and read the questions. If B was wrong, I change it to the correct answer. At least I have a mark on every answer before time is called."

9. **a.** State six important uses of item analysis for teacher-made tests.
   b. State four criteria you may use to judge whether an item is working well.

10. **a.** Describe several ways in which students and teachers benefit from reviewing the test items in class.
    b. What are some reasons why some teachers seldom go over tests with students?
    c. Explain whether each reason in (a) and (b) is educationally sound.

11. How can you adapt the procedure for summarizing multiple-choice items for use with completion and short-answer items?

12. Explain the meaning of each of the following values of D.
    a. +1.00
    b. +0.50
    c. 0.00
    d. −0.50
    e. −1.00

13. Think about how you would use information about students' learning during teaching. Which type of information—relative or absolute—do you believe is used more often? Explain why you believe this emphasis is appropriate or inappropriate.

14. The following statements are questions a teacher might ask about a test. Read each question and decide which type of information is needed to answer the question. You may need more than one type of information to answer a question. Explain reason(s) for your choice(s) in each case.

Questions	*Information*
(1) Is this item too difficult for the students I teach?	**a.** A teacher's judgment.
(2) Are there concepts that my students haven't learned well and that I need to reteach?	**b.** The item difficulty index.
(3) Does this item help me to distinguish those students who know the material well from those who do not know it very well?	**c.** An item discrimination index.
(4) Are these alternatives so similar that they become confusing to my better students?	**d.** An analysis of the response to each distractor.
(5) Does this item assess the skill and ability I want it to assess?	

15. Table 14.4 shows a summary of item analysis data for five multiple-choice items for a class of 30 students. There are 11 students in the upper group and 11 students in the lower group. The keyed answer to each item is marked with an asterisk. For each item, calculate the difficulty index (p) and the discrimination index (D), then decide whether the item has poor distractors, the item is possibly miskeyed, the upper group is possibly guessing, or two options seem to be ambiguous.

16. The following questions refer to your analysis of the item data in Exercise 15.
    a. Which item is a negative discriminator?
    b. Which item is the easiest?
    c. Which item is the most difficult?
    d. For which items do more upper-group students than lower-group students choose a distractor?
    e. Which item has the highest discrimination index?
    f. Which item has the lowest discrimination index?
    g. What is the average (mean) score on this five-item test for the 30 students who took it?

17. Ms. Jones says, "I grade students based on how they perform compared to their classmates." Mr. Smith says, "I grade students based on the percentage of test questions they get right, regardless of how they compare to their classmates." Consider the purposes for testing implied by these two teachers' statements. For each teacher, decide on the properties of the test items to be included on their tests if you were to follow the rules of thumb in Table 14.3.

Ms. Jones	*Mr. Smith*
a. Focus of the test.	**a.** Focus of the test.
b. Attention to the blueprint.	**b.** Attention to the blueprint.

TABLE 14.4 Item analysis summary for use with Exercise 15.

Item Number	Groups	Options A	B	C	D	Faulty distractors	Miskeying	Ambiguous	Guessing
1.	Upper	0	2	*9	0	_____	_____	_____	_____
	Middle			*5					
	Lower	1	2	*4	4	$p =$ _____	$D =$ _____		
2.	Upper	2	*7	0	2	_____	_____	_____	_____
	Middle		*4						
	Lower	0	*9	1	1	$p =$ _____	$D =$ _____		
3.	Upper	9	*1	1	0	_____	_____	_____	_____
	Middle		*1						
	Lower	6	*2	2	1	$p =$ _____	$D =$ _____		
4.	Upper	*5	5	0	1	_____	_____	_____	_____
	Middle	*8							
	Lower	*3	3	3	2	$p =$ _____	$D =$ _____		
5.	Upper	3	2	3	*3	_____	_____	_____	_____
	Middle				*4				
	Lower	3	2	3	*3	$p =$ _____	$D =$ _____		

Note: The idea for this exercise came from Sax, 1980, pp. 109–112.

c. Level of difficulty of the items to be included.

d. Values of the discrimination indices of the items to be included.

c. Level of difficulty of the items to be included.

d. Values of the discrimination indices of the items to be included.

18. Table 14.5 shows student scores for a three-task performance assessment. There were 30 students. Analyze the student data in order to answer the following questions.
   a. Which task is the easiest?
   b. Which task is the most difficult?
   c. Which item is a negative discriminator?
   d. Which item has the highest discrimination index?
   e. What is the average (mean) score on this three-item assessment for the 30 students who took it?

Additional Readings

Benson, J (1998). Developing a strong program of construct validation: A test anxiety example. *Educational Measurement: Issues and Practice, 17*(1), 10–12, 22.

This article describes how the assessment of test anxiety can be researched and validated. Reading this article will help you integrate ideas from this chapter and Chapter 3.

Carey, L. M. (1994). *Measuring and evaluating school learning* (2nd ed.). Boston: Allyn & Bacon, Chapter 7, pp. 201–252.

A more detailed treatment of item analysis for teacher-made tests than included in this book. Introduces more complex discrimination analysis.

Helmke, A. (1988). The role of classroom context factors for the achievement-impairing effects of test anxiety. *Anxiety Research, 1,* 37–52.

This research studied classroom and teacher characteristics related to test anxiety and reduced achievement in mathematics in 39 classrooms. The study demonstrated that specific teacher and classroom practices affect test anxiety that reduced achievement.

Hembree, R. (1988). Correlates causes, effects, and treatment of test anxiety. *Review of Educational Research, 58,* 47–77.

An extensive review and meta-analysis of the research on test anxiety.

TABLE 14.5 Item data for use with Exercise 18.

Item	Group	Scores
Item 1 (possible scores 0 to 6)	Upper	4, 6, 5, 5, 4, 4, 3, 6, 6, 5
	Middle	5, 3, 4, 4, 3, 3, 4, 3, 3, 4
	Lower	0, 4, 3, 2, 2, 1, 1, 4, 2, 3
Item 2 (possible scores 1–6)	Upper	4, 4, 3, 3, 3, 5, 4, 4, 3, 5
	Middle	4, 5, 4, 3, 2, 5, 5, 2, 5, 1
	Lower	4, 5, 6, 3, 5, 5, 6, 6, 6, 5
Item 3 (possible scores 0–3)	Upper	3, 3, 3, 3, 3, 3, 3, 3, 3, 3
	Middle	2, 3, 3, 3, 2, 3, 3, 3, 3, 3
	Lower	2, 2, 3, 3, 3, 3, 2, 2, 2, 2

Millman, J., & Green, J. (1989). The specification and development of tests of achievement and ability. In R. L. Linn (Ed.), *Educational measurement* (3rd ed.). New York: Macmillan, pp. 335–366.

Describes how to develop large-scale educational tests. You will find it useful to compare the procedures described in that chapter with the teacher-oriented approach in this book.

Tobias, S. (1992). The impact of test anxiety on cognition in school learning. In K. A. Hagtvet & T. Backer Johnsen (Eds.), *Advances in test anxiety research* (pp. 18–31). Amsterdam: Swets and Zeitlinger.

Reviews test anxiety research and shows how this research is related to school learning, including cognitions and meta-cognitions. Proposes a model that suggests that anxiety influences learning only indirectly by interfering with the intellectual processes responsible for learning.

CHAPTER 15

Evaluating and Grading Student Progress

Learning Targets

After studying this chapter, you should be able to:

1. Explain why grading students is an important teacher responsibility. [5, 6]
2. Explain the different decisions made from grades and how different stakeholders use grades differently. [5, 4, 6, 7]
3. Explain the arguments for and against using grades to motivate students. [5, 7, 4]
4. Defend your grading system against various criticisms. [6, 7, 4]
5. Describe the different methods for reporting student progress and their advantages and disadvantages. [4, 6, 5]
6. Plan a parent-teacher conference that is effective and educationally productive. [5, 3]
7. Describe the components of a multiple-marking-system report card. [5, 6, 4]
8. Differentiate among assessment variables, reporting variables, and grading variables. [5]
9. Develop your own grading philosophy that is consistent with your teaching approach, is effective for formative and summative purposes, and is valid for reporting students' achievement of standards and learning targets. [5, 6]
10. Explain the advantages and disadvantages of using the three major grade-referencing frameworks: criterion-referencing (absolute standards), norm-referencing (relative standards), and self-referencing (growth standards). [5, 4, 6]
11. Explain how lowering grades for late assignments and giving zero marks for not turning in assignments result in lowering the validity of grades. [5, 4, 6]
12. Grade students using each of the following methods of grading: (a) grading on the curve, (b) the standard deviation method, (c) adjusting for the class's ability level, (d) transforming scores to *SS*-scores, (e) the total points method, (f) the fixed percentage method, (g) the content-based or quality level method, and (h) weighting components for absolute standard systems. [5]
13. Applying the following factors to the components of grading to decide how much weight to give each component: (a) representatives and relevance, (b) emphasis on what you taught, (c) thinking processes and skills required, (d) overlap among the components, (e) fairness to all students, and (f) reliability and objectivity of the assessment results. [5]
14. Explain why using grades to punish students, to control them, and so on violates your ethical obligations to them. [1, 4, 3]
15. Explain how each of the terms and concepts listed at the end of this chapter apply to educational assessment. [6]

This chapter discusses in detail how to use grades to evaluate students. But before doing so, we need to have some background information.

SECTION I. BACKGROUND

WHAT ARE YOUR ATTITUDES TOWARD MARKS AND GRADES?

Before starting this chapter, consider how you feel about assigning grades and marks. Read each of the statements in Figure 15.1. Next to each one, check A if you agree, D if you disagree, and U if you are undecided. Compare your answers with those of your classmates and your in-

structor. Keep these attitudes in mind as you study this chapter and think about how to apply the concepts to your own teaching.

CONTINUOUS ASSESSMENT AND GRADING

Formative and Summative Assessment

Formative Assessment **Continuous assessment** is the daily process by which you gather information about students' progress in achieving the curriculum's learning targets (Nitko, 1995). Continuous assessment has both formative and summative aspects. You use formative

---

FIGURE 15.1   What are your feelings about marks and grades?

	A U D		A U D
1. When academic marks are used, more than three marking categories are desirable.	__ __ __	13. Most current criticisms of marks refer to the act of marking per se and not the specific marking practices.	__ __ __
2. There are justifiable reasons why the marks of some teachers, courses, and departments average consistently higher than others.	__ __ __	14. Absolute standards are more desirable than relative standards in evaluating and marking students in academic areas.	__ __ __
3. If a student fails a course but subsequently passes it, the initial failing mark should remain on his permanent record.	__ __ __	15. In the absence of an institutional marking policy, marks should not be used in determining eligibility for athletics and other extraclass activities.	__ __ __
4. College students should have a substantial role in the evaluation and marking of their own individual achievements in academic areas.	__ __ __	16. "Pass/fail" or "credit/no credit" are more desirable than marking systems with three or more categories for academic classes.	__ __ __
5. Academic marks should be based more on achievement status than on growth or progress.	__ __ __	17. Allowing students to contract for their own marks is preferable to marking on a relative basis.	__ __ __
6. If academic marks are used, they should be numerals, not letters.	__ __ __	18. The majority of teachers rely too much on their subjective judgments in evaluating their students.	__ __ __
7. Students' academic marks should be determined solely by their academic achievements and not by attendance, citizenship, effort, and attitudes.	__ __ __	19. Some type of numerical or letter marking system is essential to good educational practice.	__ __ __
8. Schools that use marks should adopt and enforce a clearly defined institutional marking policy.	__ __ __	20. Typical marking practices create too much undesirable competition among students.	__ __ __
9. If academic marks are assigned to students, they should be viewed as measurements, not evaluations.	__ __ __	21. Final course marks should be based on achievement status at the end and not on the average achievement throughout the course.	__ __ __
10. About the same proportion of high marks should be given to classes of slow learners as to classes of rapid learners.	__ __ __	22. Factors like attitudes and interests should be used deliberately in determining students' marks.	__ __ __
11. Most teachers use too few appropriate statistical techniques in evaluating and marking their students.	__ __ __	23. "If something exists, it exists in some amount, and therefore can be measured."	__ __ __
12. In the absence of an institutional marking policy, marks should not be used in determining students' eligibility for academic courses and programs.	__ __ __	24. Teachers should attempt to evaluate and mark students in such areas as interests, attitudes, and motivation.	__ __ __

Source: From "Agreement Among NCME Members on Selected Issues in Educational Measurement" by W. S. Harris, 1973, *Journal of Educational Measurement, 10,* pp. 67–70. Washington, DC.: NCME. Copyright 1973 by the National Council on Measurement in Education. Reprinted by permission of the publisher.

continuous assessment to make decisions about daily lesson planning and how well your day's lesson is going. You do not formally record formative evaluations on a report card or a permanent record card. Many are reported directly to the student. (For example, "Meghan, I want you to pay special attention to the lesson today," or "Bob, Monday we are going to learn how to do word problems. Please review the number facts with your Dad this weekend.") Other formative evaluations are discussed with parents in a personal conference, by telephone, or in a letter or note to the home.

Summative Assessment   This chapter emphasizes how to use grades to report your summative continuous assessments of students' achievement of the curriculum's major learning targets. **Grading** (or marking) refers primarily to the process of using a system of symbols (usually letters) for reporting various types of students' progress. **Grading for summative purposes** lets you provide yourself, other teachers, school officials, students, parents, postsecondary educational institutions, and potential employers with a report about how well a student has achieved the curriculum learning targets. The grades you give students are reported to the school administration on a permanent record card or folder. In the later years of schooling, they become part of the student's transcript, which may be shared with postsecondary educational institutions and potential employers. The school reports grades to students and parents through various means such as report cards, conferences, or letters.

Validity Is Required   Grades serving official summative evaluation purposes must be based on well-crafted, formal, continuous assessments that are aligned with your school's standards, official curriculum's learning targets, and educational psychology. As one fourth-grade teacher said (cited in Azwell and Schmar, 1995, pp. 7–9):

> I don't know how other teachers feel, but anytime I send out an official report with my name on it, it is the equivalent of a legal document. The information in that report declares itself to be the best and latest educational information on a child. This may sound overly dramatic, but parents are expecting that report to tell them about an important chunk of their child's life. It is supposed to be true, and it is official.

Because many **stakeholders** will use your summative grades for many different purposes, they must be based on valid assessments. Assessments contributing to grades come from several sources: curriculum materials, quizzes and tests, performance tasks you create, projects and other long-term tasks, products students produce, portfolios you and your students assemble, and tasks set by groups of teachers working together.

It seems unfair to base a student's final grade on a single examination (or other assessment). This "big bang" approach to evaluation ignores several important factors

about assessing students: (1) only a limited amount of time is available during one teaching period for assessing; (2) in a limited amount of time, only a small sample of tasks can be administered to students; (3) a student may know much more than what appeared on the "one shot" assessment; (4) student illness or family problems can interfere with the student's ability to demonstrate the required achievement; (5) a student can demonstrate acquisition of the learning target in several different modes other than the way you decided to assess it; and (6) some important learning targets are best assessed through longer-term projects, papers, or out-of-school assignments.

Why Teachers Dislike Grading

Grading for many teachers is one of the most difficult and troublesome aspects of teaching. This has been so for many generations. Why is this? Among the reasons are these (Ebel, 1979):

1. *Educational achievements are difficult to evaluate properly.*
2. *Differing educational opinions and philosophies imply different methods for assessing, evaluating, and reporting students' progress.*
3. *Grading requires teachers to judge students, and many of these judgments are difficult and/or unpleasant to make.*

HOW PEOPLE PERCEIVE AND USE GRADES

Validity, Decisions, and Stakeholders

Table 15.1 gives examples of information frequently found on formal student progress reports and various kinds of decisions that may be based on such information. Study these decisions to become familiar with the ways in which others will use the grades you assign.

Keep in mind that different persons will use grades in different ways. Table 15.2 shows several different types of stakeholders and the ways they use grades. This table illustrates that grades have serious meaning beyond your classroom. The grades you assign must be clear in order to judge whether any of these uses are valid.

Although assessment specialists generally recommend that you keep the meaning of grades clear by basing them only on a student's achievement of your course's learning targets, we know that many teachers do not follow this advice (Brookhart, 1991; Stiggins, Frisbie, & Griswold, 1989; Waltman & Frisbie, 1994). Brookhart states the issue clearly:

> The adjustments teachers make to compensate for grade use and misuse, however, are not uniform and are not necessarily valid either. A hodgepodge grade of attitude, effort, and achievement, created in an attempt to provide positive feedback to the student, is not the answer. Such a

TABLE 15.1 Examples of the types of information found on report cards and the types of decisions made from that information.

Information in report	Decisions that can be made			
	Selection	Placement, remediation	Guidance, counselling	Course improvement
1. Content or objectives learned	Promotion, probation, graduation, admissions	Selection of courses to take, remedial help needed	Next courses to take, additional schooling needed, career-related choices	Where instruction can be improved
2. Comparison of performance in different subjects	Admission	Selection of advanced and/or remedial courses	Pattern of a pupil's strengths and weaknesses	Areas which are strong points of school
3. Performance relative to other people	Scholarships, prizes, admission	Estimating likely success, eligibility for special programs	Estimating likely success in certain areas	
4. Social behavior		Matching personal characteristics to course and teacher placement	Need for adjustment, likes/dislikes, ability to get along with others	Identify problems with a course or with a teacher

hodgepodge grade also falls down under a validity check; it does not possess the characteristic of interpretability. What teachers seem to intend when they add nonachievement factors to grades is to mitigate negative social consequences, but grades are not the appropriate tool for social engineering. Teachers' intuition about social consequences, however, is useful because it points us to the other half of the validity issue: what happens when grades are used for decisions and actions. (p. 36)

Parents' vs. Teachers' Understanding

Communicating to parents is especially challenging. Some research shows that parents' and teachers' understanding of what report card grades mean are often far apart (Waltman & Frisbie, 1994).

Grades Communicate Your Values

Grades communicate more than achievement information about a student. A student's grades communicate your (and your school's) values. If obedience to your classroom rules is rewarded by an A or "performing satisfactorily" in *reading*, but "fooling around" during class means the *reading grade* is lowered, in spite of successful reading performance, you have communicated that obedience is valued more than reading well. The teacher who gives an unsatisfactory grade to the student whose academic performance is satisfactory and then says, "I warned you about passing notes during class!" is perhaps communicating vindictiveness. You may value both social behavior (e.g., conformity) and achievement, but if the grade you report intertwines the two, you are communicating poorly and are

encouraging confusion. To clarify matters, you must separate your evaluations of achievement from your evaluations of noncognitive student characteristics.

Grades as Motivators

Can and should grades be used to motivate students? Educational assessment experts are divided on whether it is appropriate to use the traditional marking system (A, B, C, . . .) to motivate students. Some (such as Ebel, 1979) have held that grades are important motivators for students. To serve this function, many assessment specialists believe that grades must validly and accurately reflect only achievement–students who attain the performance standards to the highest degree should receive the highest grades (Ebel & Frisbie, 1991; Hills, 1990; Linn & Gronlund, 1995; Oosterhof, 1994; Stiggins, Frisbie, & Griswold, 1989; Terwilliger, 1989).

Others offer another view of the motivating effects of grades. Cronbach (1977), for example, gives four principles of motivation: (1) there should be learning targets that students want to achieve, (2) students should believe they can achieve these learning targets, (3) students should understand how near they are to achieving these learning targets, and (4) achieving classroom learning targets should lead students to apply their learning in authentic settings. Cronbach's analysis of traditional A, B, C grading in terms of these principles stated that: (1) grades can serve as goals that at least some students seek to attain; (2) grades do not motivate students who feel high grades are out of reach–a condition likely to exist when grades reflect only a student's final level of attainment,

TABLE 15.2 Various uses to which grades are put by different stakeholders.

	Stakeholder likely to use the grades in the way indicated						
Usage for grades	Student	Parents	Teacher	Guidance counselor	School administrators	Postsecondary educational institutions	Employers
1. Reaffirm what is already known about classroom achievement	✓		✓				
2. Documentation for educational progress and course completion	✓	✓	✓	✓	✓	✓	✓
3. Obtain extrinsic rewards/punishments	✓	✓					
4. Obtain social attention or teacher attention	✓						
5. Request new educational placement		✓	✓	✓	✓		
6. Judge a teacher's competence or fairness		✓			✓		
7. Indicate school problems for a student		✓	✓	✓	✓		
8. Support vocational or career guidance explorations	✓	✓		✓			
9. Limit or exclude student's participation in extracurricular activities		✓	✓		✓		
10. Promotion or retention			✓		✓		
11. Granting graduation/diploma					✓		
12. Determining whether student has necessary prerequisite for a higher level course		✓	✓	✓	✓		
13. Selecting for postsecondary education						✓	
14. Deciding whether an individual has basic skills needed for a particular job							✓

rather than progress in a course that takes initial readiness into account; (3) whether grades can be used by students to judge their progress depends on whether the teacher continually gives students the results of assessments (and whether the teacher clearly explains what the final performance should look like); and (4) grades tend to be holistic judgments rather than descriptions of strengths and weaknesses and thus do not tell students what they need to do better so that their current performance more closely resembles the desired final performance.

CRITICISMS OF GRADES AND MARKS

Types of Criticisms

Educators have voiced a number of criticisms of grades over the years. You need to be aware of these criticisms to explain the rationale for your own grading policy to parents and other educators. Many of these criticisms can be summarized under the four headings in Figure 15.2.

Responses to Criticism

The following comments are offered in response to these criticisms (Ebel, 1974):

1. *Grades are essentially meaningless.* There is some truth in each of the criticisms under this heading. However, in the figure, Criticisms 1, 2, 4, and 5 can be used as arguments for supporting the need to improve and strengthen grading practices rather than for eliminating them. Criticism 3 attributes to grades more than they were ever intended to convey. Summative grades were never intended to substitute for the complex details of achievement needed for daily instructional planning. Grades are summary reports of a student's general level of achievement.

2. *Grades are educationally unimportant.* Criticisms here are a mixture of value statements and unnecessary comparisons. Certainly grades are symbols, but it doesn't follow that symbols are unimportant. Some persons work for concrete, tangible rewards; others work with and for symbolic rewards. To value intangible outcomes exclusively would be to hold that nothing of any value in education can be observed or assessed. This seems untenable. To pit a teacher's grades against a student's self-evaluations implies that only one or the other can be used. There is reason to believe, however, that both should be used. Further, evaluations by teachers help individuals to realistically evaluate themselves. Grades do predict subsequent academic achievement (i.e., subsequent grades), and they do predict some types of out-of-class accomplishments. Grades cannot be expected to be perfect or near-perfect predictors. Much goes into subsequent accomplishment including opportunity, effort, quality of instruction, and luck. Further, valid grades should reflect

FIGURE 15.2 Commonly expressed criticisms of grades.

A. Grades are essentially meaningless
1. There is great diversity among institutions and teachers in grading practices.
2. Many schools lack definite grading policies.
3. A single symbol cannot possibly report adequately the complex details of an educational achievement.
4. Teachers are often casual or even careless in grading.
5. Grades are frequently used to punish or to enforce discipline rather than to report achievement accurately.

B. Grades are educationally unimportant
6. Grades are only symbols.
7. The most important outcomes are intangible and hence cannot be assessed or graded.
8. A teacher's grades are less important to a pupil than his own self-evaluations.
9. Grades do not predict later achievement correctly.
10. What should be evaluated is the educational program, not the pupils.

C. Grades are unnecessary
11. Grades are ineffective motivators of real achievement in education.
12. When students learn mastery, as they should, no differential levels of achievement remain to be graded.
13. Grades have persisted in schools mainly because teachers cling to traditional practices.

D. Grades are harmful
14. Low grades may discourage the less able pupils from efforts to learn.
15. Grading makes failure inevitable for some pupils.
16. Parents sometimes punish pupils for low grades, and reward high grades inappropriately.
17. Grades set universal standards for all pupils despite their great individual differences.
18. Grading emphasizes common goals for all pupils and discourages individuality in learning.
19. Grading rewards conformity and penalizes creativity.
20. Grading fosters competition rather than cooperation.
21. Pressure to get high grades leads some pupils to cheat.
22. Grading is more compatible with subject-centered education than with humanistic, child-centered education.

Source: From "Shall We Get Rid of Grades?" by R. L. Ebel, 1974, *Measurement in Education,* 5(4), pp. 1–2. Washington, DC: NCME. Copyright 1974 by the National Council on Measurement in Education. Reprinted with permission of the publisher.

what students were taught. If the curriculum learning targets do not match the skills, abilities, and attitudes necessary for job success, then you would expect grades to predict job performance poorly, even if they were perfectly valid reflections of what students have learned.

3. *Grades are unnecessary.* The preceding points show that, although not necessary for all evaluative functions, grades cannot be entirely eliminated. Some type of summary report is needed for guidance and counseling and for purposes of accountability—both of the students to the school and the school to students and parents. Human information processing is such that masses of data need to be summarized before they are understood. Thus, imperfect as they are, grades serve summary and record-keeping functions. Parents need to know, for example, how their

children are doing in arithmetic, on the whole, as well as the specific kinds of arithmetic competence the student possesses. Overly detailed reports, however, will be incomprehensible. A high school student, for example, may want to know whether to register for advanced placement calculus or regular calculus. The counselor reaches for this semester's precalculus course grade, not a list of specific mathematics concepts acquired in the last nine weeks. As another example, a student may want to know whether she is progressing satisfactorily. The school is obliged to offer its judgment, possibly summarized in a grade, not simply a description of placement in a curriculum.

4. *Grades are harmful.* Some teachers use grades punitively and vindictively, as weapons rather than as tools. Some parents overstress the importance of grades, putting undesirable pressure on their children to achieve at all costs. But to what extent this pressure is occurring is not clear. For example, are one or two or ten parents per classroom overly ambitious for their children? Are one in twenty teachers vindictive? No one knows for sure.

A real concern among elementary teachers is the discouraging effect of low grades. Cronbach's analysis of the motivating effects of grades suggests some ways in which teacher evaluations can be improved to avoid discouragement. Even though grades may only report learning failure, and cannot be entirely to blame for this failure, it is still important to consider the effects such reports can have on children. As Brookhart (1991) put it, "What do we say when we define an important indicator [of a student's school success] in a way that is guaranteed to defeat some children?" (p. 35).

SECTION II. OFFICIAL REPORTS OF STUDENT PROGRESS

STUDENT PROGRESS REPORTING METHODS

Advantages and Disadvantages

Table 15.3 summarizes the advantages and disadvantages of different **student progress reporting methods**. Your school district may use more than one method of reporting student progress, because different methods may serve different purposes and different audiences. You can find useful summaries of the practical pros and cons of various student-reporting methods in the additional readings listed at the end of this chapter. When evaluating your school district's reporting methods, keep the following points in mind.

1. *Teachers use some methods of reporting student progress more frequently at certain grade levels.* Letter grades, for ex-

ample, are used with high frequency in the upper elementary, junior high, and senior high school levels. Parent-teacher conferences do not occur often in junior and senior high schools.

2. *Often schools use combinations of methods on the same report card.* For example, letter grades may report a student's subject-matter achievement; rating scales may report the student's attitudes and deportment. A parent-teacher conference may convey information on achievement, effort, attitudes, and behavior. Schools may use a combination of nearly all methods.

3. *Conflicts may arise between methods.* School administrators need a concise summary of each student's progress for accountability and record keeping. Parents and teachers may need slightly more detailed explanations of the content taught, the standards mastered, and how a student's educational development compares with members of a peer group.[1] The most detailed methods of reporting identified in the table are the checklist and the narrative.

Checklists

A checklist contains statements of many specific behaviors, which a teacher checks off or rates as a student performs each during the year. Figure 15.3 shows part of a checklist one test publisher offers for assessing high school students' progress in speaking.

Narrative Reports

Advantages **Narrative reports** are detailed, written reports about what each student has learned in relation to the school's curriculum framework and the student's effort in class. The hope is that narrative reports will replace the shortcomings of letter grades, because the latter tend to condense too much information into a single symbol. The concept of providing a rich description of a student's learning and educational development is laudable. When done well, these descriptions can mean much more to parents and students than the simple summaries that grades provide. This would be useful for describing elementary students' learning, especially if a state or school has defined a continuum of learning targets and performance standards over several grades, with benchmarks defined for each grade.

Limitations Narrative reports can be poorly or insensitively written, of course. In such cases they communicate

---

[1]Note that parents may seek norm-referenced information because they have had little experience with students of a given age or grade. After five years of teaching, for example, a teacher may have experienced hundreds of students of a given grade. After 20 years of parenting, parents have experienced only their own children and a few children of friends, relatives, and neighbors.

TABLE 15.3 Advantages and disadvantages of some commonly used methods of reporting student progress.

Name	Type of code used	Advantages	Disadvantages
Letter grades	A, B, C, etc., also "+" and "−" may be added.	a. Administratively easy to use b. Believed to be easy to interpret c. Concisely summarize overall performance	a. Meaning of a grade varies widely with subject, teacher, school b. Do not describe strength and weaknesses c. Kindergarten and primary school children may feel defeated by them
Number or percentage grade	Integers (5, 4, 3 ...) or percentages (99, 98,...)	a. Same as (a), (b), (c) above b. More continuous than letter grades c. May be used along with letter grades	a. Same as (a), (b), (c) above b. Meaning not immediately apparent unless explanation accompanies them
Two-category grade	Pass-fail, satisfactory-unsatisfactory, credit-entry	a. Less devastating to younger students b. Can encourage older students to take courses normally neglected because of fear of lowered GPA	a. Less reliable than more continuous system b. Does not communicate enough information about pupil's performance for others to judge progress
Checklist and rating scales	Checks (√) next to objectives mastered or numerical ratings of degree of mastery	a. Gives the details of what the pupil achieved b. May be combined with letter grades or with group-referenced data	a. May become too detailed for parents to comprehend b. Administratively cumbersome for record keeping
Narrative Report	None, but may refer to one or more of the above; however, usually does not refer to grades	a. Allows teacher the opportunity to describe a student's educational development b. Shows a student's progress in terms of standards, indicators of achievement, learning targets, or a continuum of educational growth c. Provides opportunity to open dialogue and other types of communication with parents and students	a. Very time-consuming b. Requires excellent writing skill and effective communication skills on the teacher's part c. May require translation into language read by parents, with possible loss of meaning in the translation d. Parents who are not skilled readers may not understand it or may be put off e. Parents may be overwhelmed and not respond f. Often modified to include checklist-like list of indicators with short teacher comments
Pupil-teacher conference	Usually none, but any of the above may be discussed	a. Offers opportunity to discuss progress personally b. Can be an ongoing process that is integrated into instruction	a. Teacher needs skill in offering positive as well as negative comments b. Can be time-consuming c. Can be threatening to some pupils d. Doesn't offer the institution the kind of summary record desired
Parent-teacher conference	None, but often one or more of the above may be discussed	a. Allows parents and teachers to discuss concerns and clarify misunderstandings b. Teachers can show samples of students' work and explain basis for judgments made c. May lead to improved home-school relations	a. Time consuming b. Requires teacher to prepare ahead of time c. May provoke too much anxiety for some teachers and parents d. Inadequate means of reporting large amounts of information e. May be inconvenient for parent to attend
Letter to parents	None, but may refer to one or more of the above	a. Useful supplement to other progress-reporting methods	a. Short letters inadequately communicate pupil progress b. Requires exceptional writing skill and much teacher time

FIGURE 15.3 Example of a portion of a checklist to report high school students' speaking behavior.

Speaking Behavior DATES ▶				
Speaks clearly and audibly				
Speaks fluently in home language				
Expresses thoughts in complete sentences				
Uses appropriate phrasing and sentence patterns				
Chooses appropriate topic for presentation				
Organizes material				
▲ Presents both introductory and concluding statements				
▲ Uses notes or note cards				
▲ Uses appropriate visual aids or other support material				
▲				
▲				
Establishes and maintains eye contact to ensure listener attention				
Varies tone, stress, and volume to convey meaning				
Displays good posture while speaking				
Demonstrates poise and confidence				
Uses appropriate gestures and body language to convey meaning				
Uses appropriate language for the form of communication				
Emphasizes main idea(s)				
Uses persuasive devices (e.g., glad names, bad names, bandwagon, testimonial)				
Conveys intended purpose when speaking				

Source: From *Listening and Speaking Checklist, Grades 9–12: California Achievement Test, 5th Edition,* (p. 4) by CTB Macmillan/McGraw Hill, 1992, Monterey, CA: Author. Reprinted by permission of the McGraw-Hill Companies, Inc.

the teacher's incompetence. They may confuse or overwhelm parents, who may be asked to read five to ten pages of narrative to understand what their children are learning. Using narrative reports should not be undertaken without considerable teacher development and input. A mean teacher can be just as mean in narrative writing as in letter grading. One mean teacher wrote, "Johnny thinks like a chicken!" Sensitivity and constructive comments are necessary. It would be important to base teacher development on the successful experience of teachers in schools outside of one's own district to gain perspective and practical advice. Lots of guided practice is needed in writing nonthreatening and nonblaming comments.

Modified Narrative Reports Because meaningful long narrative reports are very time-consuming for teachers to prepare, some schools have modified the reporting process. This is done by combining the checklist or rating-scale procedure with short written comments about each student. Figure 15.4 shows one section of a primary-school pupil narrative report. The full report is four pages and includes a few pages showing the school's educational developmental continuum (Egawa & Azwell, 1995). You can see from Figure 15.4 that the indicators function in a way similar to checklists (even if you do not actually tick them) and provide a kind of framework for interpreting the teacher's brief comments. The presence of the indicators

FIGURE 15.4 Example of a section of a primary-level narrative student progress report using indicators and teacher comments.

Primary Progress Report

Name _____   Class _____

Parents _____   Teacher _____

Reporting Period _____   Phone _____

Days Present _____ Absent _____ Tardies _____

Note to parents: *Under each area of curriculum I have listed indicators which I look for when assessing and evaluating students. Student should be demonstrating or working toward these goals. These indicators are on the left hand side of the report. Specific comments about your child are on to right of the indicators. ** These items will be emphasized in the spring.*

Learning & Social Skills
The members of our school community focus on the following:
- doing their personal best
- being trustworthy
- being truthful
- actively listening to others
- not "putting down" others

- contributes to the learning of other class members
- settles down quickly in appropriate area
- works cooperatively with others
- actively participates in discussions and projects
- takes responsibility for learning
- cleans up before starting the next activity
- respects classroom materials and the property of others
- pays attention when others are speaking

Personal comments are added here for each child:

Reading and the Language Arts
Activities of the curriculum included in this category include: classroom newspaper, dialogue journals, personal notebook and sketchpad, author's folders, literature study, literacy strategies and the arts (drama, music, art)

Classroom Newspaper
- volunteers stories to the weekly news
- contributes conventions (punctuation, spelling, calendar information, temperature, etc.) at teacher request
- joins in the re-reading or shared reading of the dictated news of classmates
- contributes his or her own writing to the second page*
- actively participates and pays attention while others share
- stays in place/seat
- illustrates his/her own news

Parent Comments:

The newspaper is created daily on a plastic overlay that is projected on a large screen. The students contribute information as the teacher writes. *Personal comments are added here for each child:*

Source: "Primary Progress Report" reprinted by permission of Kathy Egawa and Tara Azwell. In *Report on Report Cards: Alternatives to Consider* edited by Tara Azwell and Elizabeth Schmar. (Heinemann, A division of Reed Elsevier Inc., Portsmouth, NH, 1995.)

reduces the need for a teacher to explain for every student what curricular activities were used and evaluated.

Along the same lines is the *standards-based report card*, developed in the Tucson Unified School System (Clarridge & Whitaker, 1997). For each curriculum area, standards were written for Grades 1–2 and 3–6. Each standard was adopted from the state's standards and written to match the district's core curriculum. In that way, standards were linked to specific learning targets. (See Chapter 2 for an example.) The state's standards represent a quality level of 4. Teachers then prepared descriptions of

levels 3, 2, and 1 for each standard to describe lesser levels of achievement, much in the same way one would develop general scoring rubrics. (See Chapter 12 for information on scoring rubrics.) All this was computerized using a database program. For each marking period, the teacher enters a student's name and numeral from 1 to 4 in each curriculum area. The computer prepares a report by automatically printing the words describing the level of achievement the numeral represents. Teachers' own brief comments can be printed, too. Each marking period, progress along the learning continuum (i.e., the levels of the "rubric" for each standard) is the basis for marking. Thus, this is a criterion-referenced reporting system. The use of technology relieves much of the burden for teachers (Clarridge & Whitaker, 1997). Student-learner qualities (self-direction, collaboration/cooperation, problem solving, citizenship, and quality of work produced) were also reported using the same standards and rubric-based procedure. Figure 15.5 shows an excerpt from the form.

Parent-Teacher Conferences

Conducting Conferences Parent-teacher conferences are one of the best ways to build strong connections with parents, to provide them with an understanding of their children's learning strengths and needs, and to help them to be involved in their children's learning. However, you need to conduct them carefully and skillfully if they are to be successful. Figure 15.6 lists some of the things to do before, during, and after the conference to keep it on target. Additional suggestions are given in Shalaway's (1998) *Learning to Teach . . . Not Just for Beginners.*

Limitations of Conferences Parent-teacher conferences have their drawbacks, however. They are time-consuming for the teacher, both in preparation time and in actual contact time. Schools frequently schedule one or two days to hold conferences during school hours; some schedule evening hours for the convenience of working parents. Sometimes schools neglect to give teachers time to plan and prepare for the conferences, however, assuming that teachers either need little or no planning time, or that they will do the necessary preparation after hours. In ad-

dition, parent-teacher conferences can be frustrating and produce anxiety for both teacher and parent, especially if the parties lack confidence in each other.

Attendance may also be a problem. Not all parents will come to conferences. Parents may be unwilling to attend, working, ill, embarrassed about their poor English or their poverty, or otherwise unable to come. Some parents are courteous and will notify you that they cannot attend, but you should not expect most parents to do this.

Finally, teachers and/or parents may have too much information, too many issues, or too many concerns to discuss in the brief time allotted to the conference. Also, some parents (and teachers) talk too much and use up more than their share of time. Scheduling another conference with the parents may be necessary.

Privacy Parent conferences should be private and between one teacher and the parent(s) of one student. The school principal should provide facilities so that discussions are confidential. Avoid holding a conference where other teachers, other students, or other parents can overhear what is being said. This protects the rights of all involved. It may be difficult to limit the conference to one teacher and the parent(s), especially in schools where students have different teachers for different subjects.

Multiple Marking Systems

A Report Card Example When a school uses more than one method to report students' progress, such as a report card with several kinds of marks or symbols, this is called a **multiple marking system**. Figure 15.7 shows a **report**

FIGURE 15.5 Example of a section of a computer-assisted narrative student progress report using a standards- and rubric-based procedure along with teacher comments. The report is for first marking period (4 = the highest rating).

	Semester			
	1st	2nd	3rd	4th
Self-Directed Learner	3			
Student often sets achievable goals, considers risks, and makes some choices about what to do and in what order to do them, usually reviews progress, and often takes responsibility for own actions.	Comments:			
Collaborative Worker	2			
Student is developing the abililty to work in groups, has positive relationships with other students, and is learning to work toward group goals.	Comments:			
Problem Solver	4			
Student reasons, makes decisions, and solves complex problems in many situations, and uses these skills regularly, independently, and efficiently.	Comments:			

Source: Reprinted by permission of Pamela Brown Clarridge and Elizabeth M. Whitaker: *Rolling the Elephant Over: How to Effect Large-Scale Change in the Reporting Process.* (Heinemann, A division of Reed Elsevier, Inc., Portsmouth, NH, 1997).

FIGURE 15.6 Suggestions for organizing and conducting a parent conference.

Planning the Conference

1. Decide the goals you'd like to achieve.
2. Prepare an agenda you share with parents ahead of time.
3. Send home a page that invites parents, states the conference purpose, and lists possible times for an appointment.
4. Plan questions to ask, points to make, suggestions to offer, strategies to use.
5. Anticipate parents' questions to you.
6. Ask parents to bring a list of the student's strengths and needs.
7. Prepare a portfolio of examples of student's work to support your points.
8. Schedule enough time for questions and discussion of issues.

Create the Right Setting

1. Put parents at ease, create comfortable setting, use adult chairs.
2. Greet parents at the door; sit with them; face them.
3. Prepare a table with take-away materials for parents (e.g., grading policy, directory of the school personnel, PTA activities schedule, etc.).
4. Post a list of conferences for the day; keep everyone on schedule.

Conducting the Conference

1. Start by reviewing the agenda; communicate your specific information.
2. Listen to parents' questions, answer their questions directly, explain your points clearly, ask parent to confirm your impressions.
3. Work with parents to jointly set goals for the student.
4. Conclude conference by recommending specific steps parents should take.
5. Invite parents to keep in touch by any means: note, phone, or stopping in.

After the Conference

1. Write the essence of what was said; keep in a folder.
2. List any decisions and commitments you or the parents made.
3. Follow up via phone or note where necessary.
4. List what you have learned that will help you teach the student.
5. Evaluate your own performance; list ways to improve the next conference.

Cautions and Considerations

1. Be sympathetic to parents' mistrust or anger; it shows they care about the student.
2. Recognize that your evaluation of the student may reflect on the parents' self-esteem.
3. Involve students in preparing for the conference (e.g., selecting topics, selecting work examples, etc.).
4. Do not use the conference as the only means to alert parents of student's learning difficulties; send home notes, call, send home work, etc.
5. Be flexible in scheduling to allow for working parents.
6. Recognize changes in family structure; divorced or separated parents may want separate conferences.
7. Review proper interpretations of test scores when preparing (see Chapter 19); confer with principal or school psychologist if uncertain.
8. Explain to parents that standardized tests are only one source of information. Help them interpret test results in the total context of school and home.
9. Be cautious when reporting information given by others (e.g., school psychologist, nurse, other teachers, etc.). Always give the source.
10. Make it a point to explain your grading policy in detail.

Source: Adapted from "Perfecting Parent Conferences" by L. Shalaway, 1993, *Instructor, 103* (1) pp. 58-60, and 64. Adapted by permission of author.

card employing a multiple marking system for grades 4 through 6 in one school district. There are four **marking periods**, each approximately nine weeks long. For each marking period, the teacher uses a checkmark for reporting the student's achievement in each curriculum area. Words (*experiencing difficulty, performing successfully,* and *commendable*) define levels of accomplishment and serve as a rating scale for other areas. A dash (–) and an "I" are used to communicate also. In this report card, the curriculum areas are divided into two to four subareas, which contain the major learning targets of the curriculum in this school district. Reporting progress on them provides both parents and the following year's teacher with more specific information about what a student has achieved in the curriculum.

Progress in nonacademic areas is reported on the right-hand side of the report card. Most schools rate citizenship, behavior, etc. separately from achievement, but this provision varies with the grade level (Kunder & Porwoll, 1977). For kindergarten, primary, and upper elementary grades, most schools provide this separation; somewhat fewer schools do so at the junior high school and senior

high levels. Notice that in the example report card, the nonacademic areas are defined by specific, observable student performances. Thus, instead of asking teachers to rate general traits such as "personality" or "deportment," the school district asks the teacher to focus on specific student performances that can be observed and assessed.

Permanent Record Cards   A **permanent record card** is the official record of a student's school performance. Not all information needs to appear on a student's permanent record card. Putting elementary students' letter grades in a permanent record card is controversial. Many educators (and some professional associations) argue that reporting or recording grades at the elementary level is inappropriate. However, students and parents may become upset if, for the first time in junior high, a student receives a C (or lower) in a subject, when previously the student has received only "performing satisfactorily" checks on the elementary report card or a narrative report.

Some intermediate policy may help a student with this transition from the elementary school marking code to a new marking code at the junior high. A school may

FIGURE 15.7 Example of a multiple marking system report card for grades 4, 5, and 6.

KEY

A dash (—) indicates that performance was not measured during the report period.

(i) indicates improved performance.

The evaluations in this section refer to personal interaction and task-related skill development as viewed by your child's regular subject teacher(s). Special subject teachers may use these numerals to explain improvement needed in their respective areas.

YOUR CHILD IN SCHOOL

Personal Interaction Skills

1 Is courteous in speech and actions
2 Shows respect for others
3 Responds positively to help and correction
4 Respects property of the school and others
5 Takes care of personal belongings
6 Demonstrates self-control
7 Observes rules and regulations

Task-related skills

8 Follows directions
9 Utilizes time effectively
10 Listens attentively
11 Works independently when necessary
12 Starts and finishes work on time
13 Completes assigned work
14 Contributes to class discussion
15 Observes standards of neatness
16 Works quietly
17 Brings necessary material to class

ESTHETIC DEVELOPMENT

Vocal Music

Develops basic performing skills
Comprehends and interprets musical elements
Participates appropriately in activities
Performs commendably

Art

Manipulates a variety of materials
Applies principles of design in projects
Participates appropriately in activities
Uses constructive imagination in art projects
Performs commendably

PHYSICAL DEVELOPMENT

Physical Education

Displays good sportsmanship
Participates in activities
Maintains minimal fitness level
Behaves appropriately
Performs commendably

Health

Demonstrates knowledge of health concepts
Behaves appropriately

Days Absent
Times Tardy
Times Excused Early
Absences affecting progress

REPORT PERIOD

	1st		2nd		3rd		4th	
	Performing Successfully	Experiencing Difficulty	Performing Successfully	Experiencing Difficulty	Performing Successfully	Experiencing Difficulty	Performing Successfully	Experiencing Difficulty

EXPLANATION OF MARKING

Experiencing Difficulty — Basic skills have not been acquired; the student has not reached the performance level set for his or her group or set for the child individually.

Performing Successfully — The student has attained the performance level set for his or her group or set for the child individually. Knowledge and skills have developed satisfactorily.

Commendable — Knowledge and skills are well developed. The student has exceeded the expectations set for him or her individually or for the group. Performance is praiseworthy.

THE LANGUAGE ARTS

Reading

Reads with understanding
Recognizes and applies vocabulary
Uses study and reference skills
Understands elements of literature

Spelling

Spells assigned words accurately
Spells accurately in written communication

Language

Recognizes parts of speech
Applies correct sentence structure
Uses conventional punctuation
Expresses ideas clearly

Handwriting

Writes legibly

MATHEMATICS

Understands concepts
Recalls basic facts (+, −, ×, ÷)
Works accurately
Uses reasoning in solving word problems
Applies principles of measurement and geometry

SOCIAL STUDIES

Understands basic concepts
Uses research skills

SCIENCE

Understands basic concepts
Uses process skills.

REPORT PERIOD

	1st			2nd			3rd			4th		
	Commendable	Performing Successfully	Experiencing Difficulty	Commendable	Performing Successfully	Experiencing Difficulty	Commendable	Performing Successfully	Experiencing Difficulty	Commendable	Performing Successfully	Experiencing Difficulty

Lower Int.	Middle Int.	Upper Int.	Grade 7
Book 4	Book 5	Book 6	Book 7

Intermediate basal reading materials used to date

*A check mark indicates the performance level in the basal reading program which has been covered.

347

decide, for example, to have teachers prepare letter grades for fifth and sixth graders, but not to report them on report cards or on permanent record cards. Parents, however, are apprised of these grades. Thus, a "performing satisfactorily" can mean a C for some students and a B for others. At the end of the year, the letter-grades records are destroyed.

CRAFTING A MULTIPLE REPORTING SYSTEM

No matter which type of system you adopt, you first need to put progress reports into a grading framework so everyone can clearly interpret information about students. Basic grading frameworks include norm-referencing (relative standards), criterion-referencing (absolute standards), and self-referencing (growth standards).[2] Each way of referencing provides a different perspective on a student. Their advantages and disadvantages are explained in Section III of this chapter.

Suggestions for developing a multiple-code report are shown in Figure 15.8. The problem is to design a single system of reporting information to parents, students, teachers, school administrators, and other possible stakeholders. No solid research evidence suggests that the ideas and suggestions in this section will solve student progress reporting problems. Schools will have to evaluate a variety of creative approaches. A school district will frequently form committees of teachers, school administrators, and parents to review, critique, and/or redesign a school district's reporting system. As you may know already, it takes

---

[2]Norm-referencing is sometimes called group-referencing, while criterion-referencing is sometimes called absolute marking, objectives-referencing, or task-referencing.

FIGURE 15.8 Guidelines for developing a multiple marking and reporting system.

1. Be clear about the purposes for which the report will be used and include all information needed for those purposes.

2. Work cooperatively with parents, teachers, and administrators.

3. Organize the marking and reporting system around the school district's curriculum framework and major educational objectives for the various grade levels and courses.

4. Include in the report only those student achievements and characteristics that can be documented by assessment results that have a reasonable degree of objectivity, reliability, and validity.

5. Balance the need for detailed diagnostic information with the needs to be practical and concise.

6. Supplement, rather than replace, the reporting system with parent-teacher conferences.

Source: Adapted and paraphrased from ideas in Linn & Gronlund (1995).

about 15 minutes of the first committee meeting to discover that everyone has a different idea concerning the particular information that is "most important" to report and the "best way" of reporting that information. Perhaps little is to be gained by either closing off one channel of communication, limiting the kinds of information to that which only one party feels is appropriate, or forcing all parties to conform to a particular medium or method of communication. There are no prescriptions; there is no one best system.

SECTION III. CHOOSING A GRADING MODEL

Overview of Section III

Your grades will be meaningless unless you (a) adopt a conceptual framework for assigning them and (b) use that framework in a way that is consistent with your teaching approach. Grades must also be consistent with (a) the reasons why you want to assign them and (b) your school district's educational philosophy and "grading culture." You may not have as much freedom as you might think in adopting a framework. Because grading students is serious business, you will not be professionally responsible if you do not choose and use a grading framework responsibly. You must be able to explain your **grading framework** to students, parents, and school officials. This expectation is explained in Standard 5 of the *Standards for Teacher Competence in Educational Assessment of Students* (AFT, NCME, & NEA, 1990) that is reproduced in Appendix A.

In this section we focus on what you need to learn in order to make a professional decision about which conceptual framework to use. We organize the discussion in the following way. First, we discuss two basic teaching approaches or educational philosophies. One of these approaches may be very close to your own. Next we briefly describe five basic purposes for assigning grades in the classroom. Three of the purposes are for formative evaluation of students; two are for summative evaluation. After studying this material, we hope you will begin to think about your teaching and the role student evaluation plays in it.

Third, we discuss three basic conceptual frameworks for assigning grades. We refer to these as criterion-referenced, norm-referenced, and self-referenced. Because this is an assessment book, we shall discuss and illustrate these frameworks in some detail to be sure you have a good understanding of the concepts.

Fourth, we show the relationships among the teaching approaches, the purposes for grading, and the grading frameworks. We will discuss how some grading frameworks cannot logically be used with some teaching approaches or with some purposes for grading. Through this discussion, we hope that you will be more informed about the need to match grading frameworks with educational purpose and philosophy. Once you choose a teaching approach, you limit the grading options available (assuming you wish to be logically consistent). Although your teaching approaches and purposes may not be identical to the examples in this section, the strategy we use to attack the problem of grading should be applicable to you. From it you will learn how to improve your grading practices.

BASIC CONCEPTS OF GRADING FRAMEWORKS FOR CLASSROOM EVALUATION

Basic Teaching Approaches

There are many teaching methods and educational philosophies. However, most have a great deal in common. In their simplest forms you may group into two broad categories based on what their major focus is.

Focus on Defined Learning Targets Educational approaches in this category have as a major point of view that teaching should focus on having students attain high achievement by meeting high standards and achieving worthwhile learning targets. Their focus is on defining standards and learning targets clearly, and channeling all efforts to achieving them. These approaches have several variations including standards-based (or standards-driven) instruction, performance-based instruction, and learning-objectives-based instruction. Teachers using these approaches believe that a student's self-esteem comes from an internal belief and motivation that she can meet the standards or learning targets. Teaching and instruction provide the conditions for students to learn how to perform the standards.

Focus on Outperforming One's Peers Other educational approaches have as a major point of view that teaching should focus on having students attain high achievement by outperforming their peers. The philosophy is that education should make one competitive; that the "cream comes to the top"; that all students are not capable of achieving high standards. Teachers believe that a student's self-esteem comes from being able to compare herself to her peers and recognizing that she is better than others.

Formative Evaluation Purposes for Classroom Grades

Although in this chapter we focus on summative purposes for grading, these are not the only purposes. The first three we discuss are formative evaluation purposes. If you do not keep in mind the distinction between formative and summative evaluation, you cannot be logically consistent when grading.

Feedback on Progress from a Starting Point One formative evaluation purpose is to communicate to students the progress they have made from the point at which they began. We know that students enter our classrooms with different levels of educational development and different commands of the skills and competencies to be learned. We would like to praise and encourage students who entered the year at a low level but made great strides, even though they have not yet reached high achievement levels. We would also like to encourage students with less ability by showing them how much they have progressed. We say "Look how far you have come from where you began." We hope that such feedback on progress will not discourage students but will encourage greater (or sustained) student effort.

Feedback on Nearness to Achieving Standards Another formative evaluation purpose is to communicate how close students are to achieving the high standards and learning targets. Here we say, "Here is the high standard and here is where you are in relation to it. Look at how near you are to achieving the standard." We believe that when a student understands what a high-quality performance looks like, and how his status differs from that high quality, he will be encouraged to put forth greater (or sustained) effort to achieve the standard.

Feedback on How One Stands in Relation to Classmates A third formative evaluation purpose is to communicate how well a student is performing relative to her classmates or peers at various intermediate points during the year. Here we say, "Here is how you are doing compared to others." We hope that by a student knowing how well she compares to others, she will be encouraged to continue to work hard to keep up or keep ahead of others. Encouragement comes from knowing that she has not fallen behind others or has progressed at the same pace as others. One is not discouraged if one knows that others are also experiencing difficulty learning difficult material.

Summative Evaluation Purposes for Classroom Grades

Level of Achievement in Relation to Standards This summative purpose evaluates how well a student has achieved the specific learning targets or the high standards. In summative evaluation, we are not focusing on where the student is in relation to where he began, nor are we focusing on how much further the student has yet to go before attaining the standards. While these are worthwhile purposes, they are formative, not summative purposes. Here we seek to sum up how much of the standards or learning targets a student has achieved, or the quality level a student has attained.

Standing Relative to Peers Another summative purpose evaluates a student's achievement compared with other students' achievement: Where does a student rank in his class or in the school? We sum up achievement by communicating a student's success compared to other students.

Three Conceptual Frameworks for Grading

There are three basic conceptual frameworks that give meaning to your grades. Shortly we shall discuss how to choose the right one(s) for you, but at this point we discuss what they are. You will need a clear understanding of all three in order to make a professionally responsible choice among them.

The three basic frameworks are *criterion-referencing* (absolute standards), *norm-referencing* (relative standards), and *self-referencing* (growth or improvement standards). Table 15.4 illustrates that grades can reflect the quality of a student's performance in relation to (1) a specific set of quality levels describing performance in relation to learning targets or standards, (2) the performance of others in a specific group (such as classmates), or (3) the student's starting point or overall ability. At this point, however, you may wish to review Figure 1.3 and the related text in Chapter 1 that discusses the distinction between norm-referenced and criterion-referenced interpretations. Before

TABLE 15.4   Examples of the definitions of grades under three different referencing frameworks.

	Absolute Scale: Task-Referenced, Criterion-Referenced	Relative Scale: Group-Referenced, Norm-Referenced	Growth Scale: Self-Referenced, Change Scale
Grade	Relative to the learning targets specified in the curriculum, the student has:	Relative to the other students in the class, the student is:	Relative to the ability and knowledge this student brought to the learning situation, the student:
A	• Excellent command of concepts, principles, strategies implied by the learning targets • High level of performance of the learning targets and skills • Excellent preparation for more advanced learning	• Far above the class average	• Made very significant gains • Performed significantly above what the teacher expected
B	• Solid, beyond the minimum, but not an excellent, command of the concepts, principles, strategies implied by the learning targets • Advanced level of performance of the learning targets and of most skills • Prepared well for more advanced learning	• Above the class average	• Made very good gains • Performed somewhat higher than what the teacher expected
C	• Minimum command of concepts, principles, strategies implied by the learning targets • Demonstrated minimum ability to perform the learning targets and to use basic skills • Deficiencies in a few prerequisites needed for later learning	• At or very near the class average	• Made good gains • Met the performance level the teacher expected
D	• Not learned some of the *essential* concepts, principles, and strategies implied by the learning targets • Not demonstrated ability to perform some *very essential* learning targets and basic skills • Deficiencies in many, but not all, of the prerequisites needed for later learning	• Below the class average	• Made some good gains • Did not quite meet the level of performance the teacher expected
F	• Not learned *most* of the basic concepts, principles, and strategies implied by the learning targets • Most of the *very essential* learning targets and basic skills are not learned • Not acquired most of the prerequisites needed for later learning	• Far below the class average	• Made insignificant or no gains • Performed far below what the teacher expected

Note: This figure is an adaptation of some of the ideas in Frisbie and Waltman (1992).

discussing which of these frameworks to use, we shall discuss each one separately.

Criterion Referencing: Absolute Standards **Criterion-referenced grading** is also referred to as using **absolute standards grading** or **task-referenced grading**. You assign grades by comparing a student's performance to a defined set of standards to be achieved, targets to be learned, or knowledge to be acquired: Students who complete the tasks, achieve the standards completely, or learn the targets are given the better grades, regardless of how well other students perform or whether they have worked up to their potential. Thus, it is possible that you may give all students As and Bs if they all meet the absolute standards specified by the learning targets. Similarly, when you use this framework you must be prepared to assign all students Fs and Ds if none of them meet the standards set by the learning targets.

You should note that learning targets and standards need to be realistic. For example, suppose the students are typical for the grade you teach, and you teach well. Further, suppose the learning target specifies that the students should be able to create meaningful mathematics word problems that mirror real-life situations. If all or most of your students cannot perform this learning target, it may be misplaced in the curriculum. If you are using a criterion-referenced grading framework, you might be tempted to give low grades to all students. However, common sense requires you to discuss the placement of the learning target with other teachers and the curriculum coordinator. Failing students when they are not ready to learn the tasks is inappropriate. (Of course, you must be sure that the standards are in fact inappropriate and that you have in fact taught well. If you taught poorly or used a poor-quality assessment procedure, then you should reteach or assess properly.) This also means that absolute standards must be set using norm-referenced information: What is appropriate or typical for the population of students you are teaching? You will recall that we mentioned early in Chapter 1 that both norm-referencing and criterion-referencing are necessary to properly interpret assessment results.

Criterion-referenced grading is meaningful when you have a well-defined domain of performance for students to learn. The recent educational movement to set standards at the state level has put pressure on school districts to use these standards to set specific learning targets at the classroom level. It is often left to the teachers in a school district to align the specific learning targets with the standards. The aligned learning targets serve as the well-defined domain of performance students are expected to learn. Achievement of these learning targets becomes the basis for assigning grades.

Arguments both for and against criterion-referencing, in general, center on whether it is of value to know exactly what the student has learned independently of the student's own capability and the learning of others. Bellanca and Kirschenbaum (1976) summarize these arguments.

Norm-Referencing: Relative Standards **Norm-referencing** is also called **grading with relative standards** or **group-referenced grading**. To use this approach, you assign grades on the basis of how a student's performance compared with others in the class: Students performing better than most classmates receive the higher grades. Persons advocating group-referencing center their arguments on the necessity of competition in life, the value of knowing one's standing in relation to peers, and the idea that relative achievement is more important than absolute achievement. Arguments against norm-referenced grading center on the ill effects of competition, that the knowledge of standing in a peer group does not describe what a student has learned, and that ascertaining the absolute level of achievement is more important than ascertaining relative achievement. Bellanca and Kirschenbaum (1976) offer a more detailed summary of these arguments.

When you use group-referenced grading, you must define the reference group against which you compare a student. Is the reference group the other students in this section of the course, in all sections taking the course this year, or all students taking the course during the past five years? Just as the criterion-referenced framework requires defining learning targets clearly in order for your grades to be meaningful, so too does a group-referenced framework require defining the reference group clearly.

A grade based purely on a student's relative standing in a group does not convey to parents and school officials what the student is capable of doing relative to the curriculum's learning targets. Further, to act consistently within this framework, you should give good grades to the "top" students, even though they may not possess the level of competence specified by standards or the curriculum's learning targets. Similarly, you should give poor grades to the low-ranking students even though they may have met the minimum level of competence that the curriculum's learning targets specify.

Just as the criterion-referenced framework needs to be grounded in the standards appropriate for the grade level you are teaching, so too must the group-referenced framework be adjusted. Your responsibility as a teacher includes making sure the students learn the curriculum's specified learning targets. It would be irresponsible to give As, Bs, and Cs to students who have not met the standards even though they may be the top students. Those who use the grades you assign will count on you to make the grades reflect these learning targets. Thus, we return to the earlier principle that both norm-referenced and criterion-referenced information is needed to properly interpret the grades.

Don't waffle and retrofit. You may start out wanting to grade using criterion-referencing and standards, but then discover that your students have done poorly. Being afraid to give poor grades, you may then waffle and start to "grade on the curve" (i.e., use norm-referencing). This retrofitting of a norm-referenced framework simply does not fit either approach and is not good educational practice. If the standards you set are grade appropriate and if students performed poorly, then you must determine why. Perhaps your assessment instruments were poorly crafted (e.g., you may have used poor-quality testing materials that came with your curriculum). If so, then your assessments are invalid and no amount of norm-referencing can make them more valid. Perhaps your teaching was inadequate. Then reteaching is in order. Or perhaps the standards are simply not grade appropriate or are not appropriate for the educational development of the students you teach. This is a matter that needs to be addressed by your principal or by the curriculum coordinator. In this case you need to adjust the standards, and then reteach: Grading on the curve in this instance distorts the real educational problem and is, therefore, not acting in a professionally responsible way.

Self-Referencing: Growth Standards **Self-referencing** is also called **growth-based grading** or **change-based grading**. You assign grades by comparing a student's performance with your perceptions of his capability: Students performing at or above the level at which you believe them capable of performing receive the better grades, regardless of their absolute levels of attainment or their relative standing in the group. A student who came to the class with very little previous knowledge but who has made great strides may be given the same grade as a student who has learned more but who initially came to the class with a great deal more of previous learning. A variation of this approach is grading on the basis of improvement, growth, or change.

Arguments in favor of self-referenced grading center on the possibility of reducing competition among students and the concept that grades can be adjusted to motivate, to encourage, and to meet the needs of students. Arguments against the system center on the unreliable nature of teachers' judgments of capability, the need for parents and students to know standing relative to peers, the idea that this procedure tends to be applied mostly to lower ability students, and the possibility that this system may eventually lead to grading based solely on effort (Dunbar, Float, & Lyman, 1980). Additionally, students may not achieve the state's standards set for the grade.

From a statistical viewpoint, grading purely on growth or change may result in a negative correlation between the students' initial level of achievement and their gain of growth: Students coming into class with the highest levels of achievement tend to have the smallest amount of measurable improvement or change, even though their final absolute levels of achievement remain the highest.

(Terwilliger, 1971, illustrates how this can happen.) This presents an irony: Those students knowing most when they come into the course will tend to get the lowest grades because, even though in an absolute sense they may know more than most other students at the end of the course, they have shown a smaller amount of growth or change.

CHOOSING YOUR GRADING MODEL

Integrating Teaching Approach, Evaluation, Purpose, and Grading Framework

Now that you are familiar with the frameworks for grading, and have thought about your teaching approach and the formative and summative purposes for grading, you must consider how to put these together in a logically consistent manner. Which framework should you use? Or should you use more than one framework?

Table 15.5 offers some guidance. The table shows how the different grading approaches match teaching approaches and purposes for grading. *Self-referenced grading,* for example, is consistent with a teaching approach that focuses on standards or learning targets, but *only* when the purpose of grading is for formative evaluation that gives a student feedback on how well he has progressed from his starting point or within the limits of his ability. This combination of purpose and teaching approach is the only one that is consistent with using self-referenced grading.

Criterion-referenced grading, on the other hand, is not consistent with a teaching approach that emphasizes competition among classmates. As shown in the table, criterion-referenced grading is consistent with teaching that focuses on standards or learning targets, but is not consistent with all of the purposes for grading within that teaching approach. Criterion-referenced grading is appropriate for giving students feedback on how close they are to achieving learning targets or to meeting standards. This is a formative evaluation purpose. This grading framework is also appropriate for summative evaluation when the intent is to officially report students' levels of accomplishment in relation to learning targets or performance standards. The following quote from two experienced teachers in the Tucson Unified School District (Clarridge & Whitaker, 1997) reinforces this point:

> If you support the use of performance assessments and portfolios, or if there are state or district mandates in that direction, you will most likely find the rubric [i.e., criterion-referenced] system of grading easier to explain, use, and integrate with your approach to assessment. Be sure to consider the assessment requirements and initiatives of your district before developing a reporting system. (p. 20)

Norm-referenced grading is not appropriate for use in a standards-based or learning-target-based teaching ap-

TABLE 15.5 Recommendations for choosing a grading framework that is consistent with teaching approaches.

	Teaching approaches, philosophies	
Purposes of grading	**Approach Type A.** Standards-based, performance-based, focused on learning targets, focused on learning objectives. High achievement means meeting the standards achieving the learning targets. Self-esteem comes from intrinsic or internal motivation that results from meeting goals and standards.	**Approach Type B.** High achievement means achieving more than one's peers. Education should make one competitive. Self-esteem is achieved by being better than one's peers.
Formative evaluation *(Feedback to students and teachers; monitoring learners' progress)*		
1. Feedback on how much a student has progressed from his/her own starting point or within the limits of his/her capacity.	• *Self-referenced (growth) grading* is consistent with this purpose and teaching approach. It is assumed that knowing one's progress in relation to one's ability will stimulate more effort to learn and be less discouraging to students.	• Achievement as progress or change from where one begins is of less interest to this teaching approach than is the ultimate or final standing at the end of the marking period. Attainment of specific learning targets and standards are less of an interest to this teaching approach.
2. Feedback on how close a student is to achieving the learning targets or to meeting the standards.	• *Criterion-referenced (task-referenced) grading* is consistent with this purpose and teaching approach. It is assumed that understanding what quality learning looks like and what one's own status in relation to that level of learning is will motivate further learning and effort to meet the high standards.	• Achievement of specific learning targets and standards is not emphasized by this approach. Of more interest is outdoing one's peers.
3. Feedback on how a student is achieving relative to peers at this point in instruction.	• Comparisons of achievement among students are not emphasized by this teaching approach. Of more interest is meeting standards and achievement of learning targets.	• *Norm-referenced (group-referenced) grading* is consistent with this purpose and teaching approach. It is assumed that knowing one's current rank in class will motivate one to work harder to achieve more.
Summative evaluation *(Official recording of achievement at end of marking period or end of term; official report of achievement)*		
4. Reporting a student's level of performance in relation to learning targets and to standards.	• *Criterion-referenced (task referenced) grading* is consistent with this purpose and teaching approach.	• Achievement of specific levels of learning in relation to standards is not emphasized by this reading approach.
5. Reporting a student's standing relative to classmates and peers.	• Comparisons of achievement are not emphasized by this teaching approach.	• *Norm-referenced (group-referenced) grading* is consistent with this purpose and teaching approach.

proach. It is consistent with a teaching approach that emphasizes comparisons among peers or classmates. With this teaching approach, the only formative purpose served by norm-referenced grading is giving students feedback on how they compare or rank relative to each other. The only summative purpose norm-referenced grading serves is to officially report students' standing relative to their peers.

It should be clear from Table 15.5 that one grading framework cannot serve all teaching philosophies and all purposes for wanting to assign grades. You may find that your own teaching does not have a clear philosophy or approach: If so, it will be difficult for you to approach grading in a consistent way. The point of Table 15.5 is that if you are to select one or more appropriate grading

frameworks, you need to work within a clear teaching approach and understand that some grading frameworks are more appropriate for certain formative and summative purposes but not for others.

School District Policy and Local Grading Culture

Important factors in selecting a grading framework are the grading policy and a grading culture of your school district. Not every school district has a clearly written grading policy. If your school district has a grading policy, you will be required to work within its guidelines. If it is a poor or inconsistent policy, you may wish to suggest ways to improve it. If you are a new teacher, your suggestions may not be taken seriously until the administration has confidence in your ability to teach. Press on with your reforms after you have taught for a year or two: Begin by working out your ideas with your most valued teaching colleagues. Don't ever give up on improving education for your students.

Grades for Report Cards

A school probably finds some merit in each of the systems of referencing because each addresses a somewhat different aspect of a student's performance: the curriculum, other students, and self. Thus, in the long run, a report card may need to contain all three types of information. A given school district will likely emphasize one of the referencing frameworks at some grade levels and other frameworks at other grade levels.

SECTION IV. SENSIBLE GRADING PRACTICES

We focus in more detail in this section on using the assessment plan for summative grading. Your implementation of summative grading must address a number of important issues so that your grades are valid. First, you will need to consider what types of student behavior you should consider. We distinguish three categories of student behavior: those assessed, those reported, and those graded. Second, we consider the issue of making your marking scales consistent across different assessments throughout the marking period. This has both a practical and a validity side to it. Third, we discuss the components making up the grade and their weighting in relation to the final grade. Again, we shall emphasize the validity of the grades. Fourth, we shall consider the standards or boundaries for each letter grade: How are they set and are they meaningful? Fifth, there is the issue of borderline cases: What do you do with students who are just at the border between two letter grades? Sixth, the issue of failures (Fs) is raised. What does failure mean? Finally, we discuss the practice of assigning zero for a mark on one or more components going into a grade: What is the impact of this practice? When should zero not be given?

TYPES OF BEHAVIOR TO ASSESS

Link Your Grading to Your Assessment Plan

In Chapter 6 we discussed how to craft an assessment plan. Your assessment plan describes what component assessments will make up the summative assessment for each instructional unit and for the marking period. In addition, you specify the weights the components will carry in the grade for each unit as well as the units' weights in calculating the final grade for the marking period. Figure 6.1 showed an example of this type of assessment plan. The assessment plan becomes critical to assigning grades. Without a plan, you will be unable to meaningfully integrate all the assessment components into a valid grade. You will also be unable to explain your grading to students, parents, and school administrators.

What to Assess, Report, and Grade

Assessment Variables   In Chapter 6 we discussed the types of student information you need when teaching, including sizing up the class, diagnoses of students' needs, prerequisite student achievements, students' attitudes, students' work habits, students' study skills, and students' motivation and effort in school. The complete set of these characteristics about which you gather information are called **assessment variables** (sometimes called **evaluation variables** [Frisbie & Waltman, 1992]). However, not all variables you assess need to be recorded and reported. Clearly, you will use some of the information to plan and guide your own teaching. This information is primarily formative in nature. It should not make its way into a grade. A grade is a summative evaluation of a student's achievement.

Reporting Variables   From among all the assessment variables, your school district will expect you to report a subset of them to parents and for official purposes. These are called **reporting variables** (Frisbie & Waltman, 1992). They often include the students' achievement in the subject, study skills, social behavior and interpersonal skills, motivation and study efforts in class, leadership skills, and aesthetic talents.

Grading Variables   Reporting variables represent important school outcomes, and therefore should be appropriately reported to parents and others. They should not be confused, however, with grades for course achievement. That is, from among all the reporting variables, you need to select a more limited subset on which you may base your grades. The variables in this limited subset are called **grading variables** (Frisbie & Waltman, 1992). You use the grading variables to describe a student's accomplishments in the subject. You assess these achievements by crafting more formal procedures such as performance tasks, portfolios, projects, tests, and quizzes. They are the most valid and reasonable bases on which you assign grades.

Eliminate Mixing   It is easy to mix together variables so that your grades' meaning is confusing and invalid. For example, if you punish a student by lowering her grade for failing to turn in an assignment or for turning it in late, then you have confused the student's achievement with the student's deportment. Similarly, if you lower a science or social studies grade because of poor language usage or poor appearance, your grade is a less valid assessment of the student's attainment of the curriculum learning target. Consider the following:

If the social studies essay scores of some students are reduced because of deficiencies in writing mechanics, how well do those scores describe achievement? If a teacher assigns an A to a group project, what does this mean for a member of the group who made little contribution to planning, conducting, or summarizing the project activities? If the grade on a paper is dropped a full letter grade each day it is late, what does the final grade on the paper indicate about achievement in language arts? If a student has an unexcused absence on the day of a test, what does an F grade for that test do to a quarter grade that is supposed to describe achievement? . . . Tainted component scores cause tainted composites. Tainted composites lead to misinterpretation. (Frisbie & Waltman, 1992, pp. 37–38)

The preceding paragraph does not mean that language usage or turning in work on time is irrelevant to a student's school experience. Rather, the intention is clarity of meaning for *grades*. Some schools, for example, use a "writing across the curriculum" approach. This means that social studies, history, mathematics, and science work is evaluated for both the subject-matter correctness and language usage. The language usage evaluation becomes part of the language grade, while the subject-matter evaluation becomes part of the subject grade. Similarly, tardiness, failure to complete work, etc. can be reported separately from achievement and may be used to explain a student's total school accomplishments.

Eliminate Formative Evaluation Components Not all achievement variables should be included as grading variables (Frisbie & Waltman, 1992). Many achievement variables are formative in nature. Homework, quizzes, and oral responses to classroom activities, for example, may be mostly formative to help you decide whether individual students need more reinforcement or whether your lessons are going well. These formative achievement assessments should not be included in the subject grade for the marking period. Not all out-of-class assignments are formative, of course. Some homework, most projects, and most research papers can be used for summative evaluation. The general rule, then, is to *include in the grade the assessments that you establish as useful for summative evaluation and exclude all assessments established primarily for formative evaluation.*

CONSISTENT GRADING THROUGHOUT THE MARKING PERIOD

Craft Marking Scales to Be Consistent Across Different Assessments

Incompatibility of Scales You need to think ahead to make your assessment scales compatible across all the components that go into the summative grade. The assessment plan for the weather unit in Figure 6.1, for example,

shows five components entering into the summative grade for the unit: homework, quizzes, independent investigation, map drawing, and the end-of-unit test. Suppose each of these is marked on a different scale as follows:

Component	Scale
Homework	1–10
Quizzes	1–5
Independent investigation	1–20
Map drawing	1–4
End-of-unit test	1–100

If you simply add students' marks from each of these components using these scales, you will have difficulty because they are incompatible. The map-drawing scale, for example, may be based on a rubric with four levels of quality while the end-of-unit test is based on a percentage scale from 0% to 100%. Such incompatibilities make a simple sum of the marks an invalid basis for a grade. You will need to mark each assessment in a way that makes scales compatible.

It is at the planning stages where you should prevent this situation. You may use one of several options, which we shall discuss later in this chapter. Solving this problem is not that complicated but is best solved beforehand. The following anecdote illustrates this point:

In a school district I work with, eighth-grade teachers were faced with the task of combining percentage-correct scores from conventional language arts tests and writing performances scored on a 4-point rubric into five levels for report card grades (A, B, C, D, F). Several of the teachers did not have the quantitative reasoning background to understand why or how scale conversions could be made, and it had not occurred to any one of the several people who adopted the 4-point writing rubric that it would not be very helpful for assigning five levels of grades. This is a more complicated problem to solve after the fact than to solve at the design stage, when it would be appropriate to choose rubrics and construct decision rules. (Brookhart, 1999, p. 8)

Losing Precision The most reliable scores are those that are able to distinguish small differences in the quality of students' learning. A scale that allows you to demonstrate that Sally's command of a learning target is slightly better than Johnny's is more reliable than a scale that cannot tell the difference between their learning levels. In order to allow small differences between students to be reliably detected, a score scale needs many gradations or "points." A scale that shows Sally at 89 and Johnny at 82 displays their learning quality better than a scale that shows them both receiving the same rating.

You lose precision when you transform scores from a fine-grained scale (e.g., percentage correct scale) to a coarse-grained one (e.g., letter grades). If a B is a score from 80–89, then both Sally and Johnny would receive the same grade, B. Because they both receive the same grade, their true difference cannot be distinguished with the grade scale. By transforming the 89 and 82 both to a B, you have lost reliability.

You should not think that all percentage scales are fine grained. For example, if you have five test questions, each worth one point, then the only possible percentages are 0, 20, 40, 60, 80, and 100. Thus, only six possible percentage values are used, not the 100 values you usually associate with a percentage scale. In this example, the percentage scale is just as coarse as the letter-grade scale. A test of ten questions, each worth one point, is similarly not very fine grained. Keep in mind that scales reporting fine differences among students must use many numerical values that reflect actual differences among students if they are to be reliable. If you use only a few of the many possible values of a scale, then you lose precision.

Although you lose precision when you move from a fine-grained scale to a coarse-grained scale, you do not gain precision by moving from a coarse-grained to a fine one. If we have only the coarse scores initially, no transformation will make them more precise. A scoring rubric may evaluate a student's writing as a 3 on a scale of 1 to 4. You could transform the 3 to a percentage: 3 out of 4 points is 75%. You have not gained any precision in distinguishing among students, however: All students who received 3s will receive 75%. Similarly there are only 4 points on the scale after the transformation (25%, 50%, 75%, and 100%), the same as before the transformation; only the labels changed.

The impact of scale precision, positive or negative, is in addition to the positive impact made by using well-crafted assessment instruments. It will pay you, therefore, to craft your scoring scales as carefully as you craft your assessment instruments themselves.

COMPONENTS OF A GRADE

Weighting the Components

You should not weight every achievement assessment equally when grading. How much weight to assign to home assignments, tests, quizzes, term papers, etc. is decided in relation to their importance to evaluating achievement of the learning targets. You need to make a list of all the components you want to use for evaluating achievement of the grade, decide how these components relate to the learning objectives, and determine how important each is (and thus how heavily each will weigh) in relation to the overall summative grade.

You should consider at least six factors when deciding how much to weight each component:

1. *Components that assess more of the important learning targets and content and should be weighted more heavily than those that focus only on one or a few targets.*

2. *Components that focus on what you spent the most time teaching the students should receive the most weight in determining the grade.*

3. *Components that require students to integrate and apply their learning should receive more weight than those that require students to simply parrot what was taught.*

4. *When two components assess some of the same learning targets, each should be given less weight individually than other components that assess an equal number of unique learning targets (i.e., non-overlapping components)* (Frisbie & Waltman, 1992).

5. *If you know that one of the components you want to count toward the grade has some degree of unfairness to certain groups of students, you should be very cautious in using it for grading. If you decide that on the whole it is still appropriate to use it, you should weight it less, especially the students for whom it is less fair.* For example, you may find that a timed, written test does not adequately assess students with certain disabilities. In such cases, it would be appropriate to weight this procedure less for these students and to give other, more appropriate procedures more weight in determining their grades.

6. *Components that are less reliable and less objective should be weighted less heavily than those that are more reliable and objective.* However, this is not to say that you should avoid using less objectively scored assessments such as essays and portfolios for assigning grades. Rather, you should use scoring rubrics for marking them so the marks are more reliable. (See Chapter 12.)

GRADE BOUNDARIES

Standards or Boundaries Between Grades

An important consideration is how to establish boundaries between the grades. What constitutes an A, B, etc? The answer will depend on (a) which framework you are using and (b) your school district's policy. The procedure for setting norm-referenced grading boundaries is very different from the procedure for setting criterion-referenced grading boundaries. You will need to follow the boundary-setting method that is consistent with your teaching approach. We discuss the details of these boundary-setting procedures later in this chapter.

It is important at this point, however, to recognize that your grade boundaries must have the same meaning across all assessments that will make up the grade. This doesn't mean that you need to use the same number of marks (points) for each assessment. It does mean, however, that an A on one assessment should be of approximately the same standard across all assessments. For example, if each assessment is marked as percentage correct, then the same percentage range (e.g., 90–100%) should be used for an A across all assessments.

Borderline Cases

You will always have **borderline cases**—students whose composite marks come near or put them right on the boundary between two grades. What do you do? How close to the boundary for a grade does a student have to be before you adjust the student's letter grade upward or downward? Many teachers are comfortable reviewing students and raising grades for those who are just under the borderline, but do not consider lowering the grades of those just above the borderline (Brookhart, 1993). Nevertheless, lowering borderline grades is just as valid as raising them when additional achievement evidence justifies it.

As you have learned in Chapter 4, assessment results contain errors of measurement, so students whose scores are on or near the border are likely to have true scores that are different from their observed scores. This argues against being "hard-nosed" and telling a student that she missed the next higher grade by one or two points. You should think of scores near the grade boundary as in an "uncertainty band" much like the one discussed in Chapter 4. You should use additional achievement information about the student to help you decide whether the student's true score is above or below the boundary. Using additional *achievement* information to help make boundary decisions is *more valid than using information about how much effort a student put forth in studying* (Brookhart, 1999). If you are still in doubt, it is better educationally to give the next higher grade than to give the lower grade.

FAILURE GRADES

The Meaning of Failure

As Frisbie and Waltman (1992) point out, the grade F carries a lot of emotion with it, because there are usually negative consequences to students who receive it. What should an F mean? Your answer should be consistent with your grading framework. The least confusing way to use a **failing grade (F)** is to set reasonable minimum standards regarding performance on the curriculum learning targets. Students who *consistently* perform below these minimum performance standards are assigned an F.

Let's get to the practical side of using the failure (F) grade. Billy does not turn in an important assignment, even though he knew the deadline and you made several announcements in class. You decide to give Billy a zero. James, on the other hand, turns in the assignment on time; but the work is so poor, you must give it a 55, which is in the F range. Both James and Billy receive Fs. The question is, do these Fs mean the same thing? If not, how meaningful (i.e., valid) is using an F? We will address this issue momentarily, but first another example.

Many scoring rubrics for performance assessments and constructed-response items use a scoring scale from 1 to 4. Our concern is with the meaning of the lowest category, 1. Usually, the rubric describes 1 as very poor quality work, amounting to failure. However, the 1 is often assigned to students who did nothing, failed to turn in the work, or wrote gibberish. Does a score of 1 mean the same for every student? If not, how valid is it? This issue is not necessarily resolved by using a scoring rubric that goes from 0 to 4. If the zero is given to students who failed to turn in an assignment, as well as to those who turned it in but wrote poorly, the zero has two different meanings. This lowers the validity.

One way to frame this issue is to consider two categories of student performance (Brookhart, 1999): (1) doing work that is of very poor quality, i.e., **failing work** and (2) not doing the work at all, i.e., **failing to try**. The first category is descriptive of the students' achievement: the students' status compared to the standards or learning targets. The meaning of failure marks or grades for such students is reasonably clear.

The second category is descriptive of students' motivation (and perhaps attitudes and personality characteristics, such as lack of self-confidence, test anxiety, rebelliousness, etc.). Billy's not turning in an assignment might be a signal to you that he has not understood what you taught. Billy may not have done the assignment because he didn't know how. This calls for working with Billy and his parent(s) to see that he receives the help he needs. Billy may be insecure and afraid to admit his failure to learn: Not every failure to try is malicious. In "failure-to-try" cases, giving a failure grade (or lowering a grade) is invalid because the resulting grade does not accurately describe a student's achievement. This does not mean that you should not report failure to try; it does mean that describing these two types of student responses with the same mark (0 or 1) or with the same grade (F) is not valid.

A closely related question is, "Should I lower a student's grade when the assignment is turned in late?" Some teachers, for example, mark assignments that are turned in late, but deduct points from the mark or otherwise limit the highest mark possible for this assignment. Again, such a practice lowers the validity of the marks and the resulting grades because it mixes up their meaning: Do not use the same grade to describe only achievement for some students but a mixture of achievement, attitudes, and personality evaluations for other students.

Abhorrent grading practices like these are practiced because teachers face difficult teaching conditions. They seek to use grades (and student evaluations, in general) to control students' behavior. As we discussed in Chapter 5, you act irresponsibly when you threaten, punish, or otherwise try to manipulate students by lowering achievement grades for performance that is unrelated to achievement. The issue of what to do with missing and late assignments is a real one that you must struggle with, but it is not a measurement problem per se. It is a result of the conditions of teaching, school policies, and assumptions people make about the way one should educate (Brookhart, 1999).

A school district's policy needs to address how to handle students who do not turn in assignments or who turn them in late. A culture for punctuality and completing assigned work on time needs to be developed. A policy needs to be legal, fair, valid, and meet criteria for sound educational philosophy. Those parts of the policy that require punishing, threatening, or manipulating students should be eliminated.

From a strictly measurement point of view, assigning an "incomplete" when assignments are never turned in seems reasonable. Students who complete the work beyond the deadline may be given full credit from a measurement perspective. The report card could contain a notation that some of the work on which the grade is based was completed after the due date. Repeated notations of this type describe tardiness but do not detract from describing achievement.

These measurement "solutions," however, do not address all the concerns of teachers. You can raise questions such as: Is it fair to students who habitually complete their work on time to allow other students not to complete on time? Are there circumstances under which late work is allowed (without penalty or commentary) or is appropriate (e.g., illness, personal tragedy)? Will a flexible policy on when to turn in work result in classroom chaos? Is the assignment of an invalid grade or a grade with low validity more ethical than addressing the issues of why students do not behave properly or do not turn in assignments? You may have fun discussing these issues with your instructor and teaching colleagues.

The Deadly Zero

Do you recognize how much a zero can impact a composite score? Suppose Ashley is a good student, capable of B work. What happens to her average marks if she fails to turn in one assignment and you give her a zero for it? Are you surprised to learn that her average grade could drop from a B to a D?

The impact of a zero, of course, depends on the component marks a student receives, how many marks enter into the composite grade, the weights assigned to the component, and the mark the student "would have received" had the student turned in the assignment. Figure 15.9 shows a simple example so you may better understand the impact of zero.

In this example, there are five assignments. To keep things simple, let us assume they are equally weighted. As a point of reference, suppose Ashley's "true performance," what she would have received had she completed all her assignments, is shown in Panel A. Ashley is a B student.

Panel B shows what will happen to Ashley if she fails to turn in one assignment *and* if you were to give her zero for that assignment. The impact on her grades is dramatic: One missing assignment results in her dropping *two* whole grades: from a B to a D. This happens no matter which assignment she does not turn in.

Using a zero means that you have given Ashley the lowest possible failing mark as a substitute for her missing assignment. Instead, you could give her the highest possible failing mark. In this example, the F range is from 0–59, so 59 is the highest possible failing mark. Panel C shows what happens to Ashley's grade if you follow this

---

FIGURE 15.9 Hypothetical example of the impact of substituting zero or 59 for one assignment a student did not turn in. Substituted values are shown in parentheses. (Assume: A = 90–100, B = 80–89, C = 70–79, D = 60–69, F = 0–59.)

	1	2	3	4	5	Avg	Grd
A. True Performance	80	70	85	75	90	80	B
B. Strategy 1—Substitute zero for the missing assessment							
Case 1	(0)	70	85	75	90	64	D
Case 2	80	(0)	85	75	90	66	D
Case 3	80	70	(0)	75	90	63	D
Case 4	80	70	85	(0)	90	65	D
Case 5	80	70	85	75	(0)	62	D
C. Strategy 2—Substitute the highest possible failing mark (i.e., 59) for the missing assessment							
Case 1	(59)	70	85	75	90	76	C
Case 2	80	(59)	85	75	90	76	C
Case 3	80	70	(59)	75	90	75	C
Case 4	80	70	85	(59)	90	75	C
Case 5	80	70	85	75	(59)	74	C
D. Strategy 3—Base the grade on only those assignments that were turned in							
Case 1	—	70	85	75	90	80	B
Case 2	80	—	85	75	90	83	B
Case 3	80	70	—	75	90	79	C
Case 4	80	70	85	—	90	81	B
Case 5	80	70	85	75	—	76	C

strategy. Ashley goes from a B average (Panel A) to a C average (Panel C). Still, one missing assignment has resulted in her average dropping *one* whole grade.

Other strategies could be used. One is shown in Panel D. Here you simply ignore the missing assignment, basing your grade on the remaining four. As shown in Panel D, the impact on her grade depends on which assignment she failed to turn in. If she failed to turn in one of the two on which she could have scored the highest (Case 3, where Assignment 3 was 85, or Case 5, where assignment 5 was 90), her grade would drop a whole grade; in the other cases it would remain at B. Other strategies (not shown) could be used (Brookhart, 1999). For example, use the median grade, use 50 instead of 59, or substitute the average of the four completed assignments for the missing assignment. In Ashley's case these other approaches give the same letter-grade results as shown in Figure 15.9, Panel D.

From the measurement perspective, Strategy 3 (basing the grade on only those assignments turned in) would be the best of the three when (a) assignments are of approximately equal difficulty for the students, (b) assignments are weighted equally (or are worth the same number of points), and (c) there are several assignments and only one or two are missing. This recommendation does not consider other factors, such as whether (a) the "missing assignment" is the most important one to complete (e.g., a project or a final examination), (b) a student didn't turn in an assignment because of illness or personal tragedy, (c) a student didn't complete the assignment because she didn't understand how to do the work, and (d) a student has made a habit of not turning in work on time. As we stated previously, these are not measurement issues per se but matters of educational practice, classroom management, and school policy.

SECTION V. TECHNIQUES FOR SETTING GRADE BOUNDARIES AND COMBINING SCORES

ASSIGNING NORM-REFERENCED LETTER GRADES

There are several methods of assigning grades using relative or norm-referenced standards.[3] One method, called **grading on the curve**, ranks the students' marks: Students' marks are ordered from highest to lowest, and grades (A, B, C, etc.) are assigned on the basis of this ranking. Another method uses the **standard deviation** (see Appendix H) as a unit: A teacher computes the standard deviation of the scores and uses this number to mark off segments on the number line that defines the scale for

the students' marks. These segments become the basis for grade assignment. The two methods do not necessarily give the same results. We explain how to use the methods next.

Grading a Single Test or Assessment

Grading on the Curve   To use the grading on the curve method to assign letter grades, you decide on the percentage of As, Bs, Cs, etc. to award. For example, you may decide:

top 20% of the students get A
next 30% get B
next 30% get C
next 15% get D
lowest 5% get F

There are no rules on how you would select the percentages to use. They are chosen arbitrarily based on your experience as to what is realistic in your school for a distribution of letter grades. This approach *does not* require using a normal or bell curve.

Another way to set the percentages is to divide the range of a *normal* curve (see Chapter 17) into five equal-length intervals. After doing this, you have the following percentages in each interval (see Figure 17.6 for percentages under a normal curve):

top 3.6% of the students get A
next 23.8% get B
next 45.2% get C
next 23.8% get D
lowest 3.6% get F

This set of percentages assumes that the true amount of achievement in the group of students in your class is normally distributed, an assumption which, in the author's view, is hard for you or any teacher to justify. Notice that (1) the percentages are completely arbitrary, (2) the assessment scores must be valid measures of the desired achievement, and (3) there is no reference to the learning targets, skills, or competence the letter grades represent (except that higher-ranked students have more competence than lower-ranked students). If you do decide to grade on the curve, then you must provide a convincing and educationally sound rationale to justify the particular percentages that you use; otherwise, your grades are likely to be unsound.

Standard Deviation Method   To use the **standard deviation method**, you first decide how many multiples of a standard deviation the lower limit of A will lie above the median ($PR = 50$) of the group (Ebel, 1965; Ebel & Stuit, 1954). You then mark off the score scale into four more[4] segments, with each of these four segments a standard de-

---

[3]Your instructor may ask you to postpone studying this section until you have studied Chapter 17.

[4]This assumes an A, B, C, D, F scale. If there are six grades, the intervals will be narrower; if three letter grades, wider, and so on.

viation wide, beginning at the lower limit of A and going downward. (Appendix H explains the standard deviation and how to calculate it.) The steps for doing this, along with an example, are shown in Figure 15.10.

Rather than use the same percentage of As, Bs, Cs, etc. for every class, it seems reasonable to change the percentages as the ability of the class changes. For example, if the class is very bright, then you would expect to give more As and fewer Ds than if the class were average. The method Ebel outlines in Figure 15.10 adjusts the distribution of letter grades to suit the general level of scholastic ability of the group of students in your class. Thus, the first step is to estimate the ability level of the group (poor to exceptional) using either students' previous grade point averages or scores on a common ability test all students have taken. With this method, the choice interval width and the lower limit for A are arbitrary, just as the choice percentages for grading on the curve were arbitrary. Further, as with the grading on the curve method, reference is made only to the person's relative achievement, rather than to an absolute description of the competence the students may possess.

The method assumes that for "average" ability students, the underlying achievement follows a normal distribution, even though the distribution on the test or other assessment being graded does not. The assumptions

FIGURE 15.10   Ebel-Stuit method of grading.

Letter Mark Distribution Statistics for Classes at Seven Levels of Ability

Class Ability Level	Lower limit of A's	Percent of marks					Ability measures	
		A	B	C	D	F	GPA	Percentile
Exceptional	0.7	24	38	29	8	1	2.80	79
Superior	0.9	18	36	32	12	2	2.60	73
Good	1.1	14	32	36	15	3	2.40	66
Fair	1.3	10	29	37	20	4	2.20	68
Average	1.5	7	24	38	24	7	2.00	50
Weak	1.7	4	20	37	29	10	1.80	42
Poor	1.9	3	15	36	32	14	1.60	34

Four steps are involved in this process of assigning marks.

1. Select from [the above table]...a distribution of marks appropriate to the level of ability of the class being graded.
2. Calculate the median and the standard deviation of the scores on which the marks are to be based.
3. Determine the lower score limits of the A, B, C, and D mark intervals, using the median, the standard deviation, and the appropriate lower limit factor from [the table].
4. Assign the designated marks to the students whose scores fall in intervals determined for each mark.

Sample Problem in Letter Mark Assignment

A. Data for the problem

    1. Class ability levels measures:

        a. Mean GPA on previous years' courses: 2.17

        b. Mean percentile on aptitude test: 56.3

        c. Appropriate grade distribution [from above table]: *fair*

    2. Achievement scores (number of students = 38)

112	100	93	84	78	72	66	51
109	97	91	83	75	71	62	47
106	97	90	82	75	70	59	44
105	95	89	81	75	69	59	
104	95	84	80	74	68	58	

B. Calculations from the data

    1. Median = 80.5   2. Standard deviation = 17.6

Marks	Lower Limits			Intervals	Number	Percent
A	$80.5 + (1.3 \times$	$17.6) =$	103.4	103–112	5	13
B		$103.4 - 17.6 =$	85.8	86–102	9	24
C		$85.8 - 17.6 =$	68.2	68–85	16	42
D		$68.2 - 17.6 =$	50.6	51–67	6	16
F				44–50	2	5
					38	100

Source: From R. Ebel, *Essentials of Educational Measurement,* 3rd ed., (pp. 248–251). Copyright 1979 by Allyn and Bacon. Adapted by permission.

about the distribution of achievement for above- and below-average students are represented by the "percentage of marks" in the rows of tables in Figure 15.10. A decided advantage is that this approach helps to make grades more comparable among all teachers who use it.

Grading a Composite of Several Scores

This section discusses how to combine the scores from several grading components into a single (composite) mark. The procedure will be consistent with the norm-referenced grading framework. Later we discuss combining marks from components in a way that is consistent with the criterion-referenced grading framework. Usually a grade on the report card is based on a student's performance on several assessments such as assignments, quizzes, reports, and perhaps an examination. We discussed previously the factors you need to consider when assigning weights to each component of the grade. There is no agreement as to exactly what weights are proper for each grading component.

Weighting Guidelines   When norm-referenced grading is adopted, the component that contributes the most to the final *rankings* of the students in the group carries the most weight. This principle is likely to be violated if you simply multiply the component scores by some arbitrary weights and then add the weighted scores to form a composite. The reason is that the rank of a composite score is influenced by the standard deviations of the components making up the composite (and by the intercorrelations among components).

To illustrate this, consider this small example. Suppose that the final grades are based on the sum of the marks from one exam and one project. Suppose further, that the *project* is intended to weigh twice as much as the exam. In an attempt to accomplish this, the teacher decides to give twice as many points to the project as to the exam: 100 points for the project and 50 points for the exam. Remember that in a norm-referenced grading framework, those who rank highest receive the highest grades. Here are the marks of five students.

	EXAM (50 POINTS)		PROJECT (100 POINTS)		TOTAL	
Student	Marks	Ranks	Marks	Ranks	Marks	Ranks
Anthony	43	1	77	5	120	1
Ashley	33	2	78	4	111	2
Billy	26	3	79	3	105	3
Chad	22	4	80	2	102	4
Vanessa	15	5	81	1	96	5

Notice that the project ranks students exactly opposite from the exam. However, the final order is exactly the same as the *exam*, even though the teacher weighted the project more. This is because the ranking of the students on the total marks depends on the spread of scores rather than on the teacher's intended weighting. The spread of

scores is measured by the standard deviation. (See Appendix H.) The standard deviation of the project scores is small, while the standard deviation of the exam is large. Thus, the students' exam ranking dominates their final total ranking in spite of the teacher's intention to make the project the dominant component. In general, when norm-referenced grading is being used, the larger the standard deviation of a component, the more that component influences the final ranking of students when a composite is formed.

SS-Scores   To preserve the desired influence (weights) of the components comprising a composite in a norm-referenced system, you should first adjust the values of the standard deviations of the components. After adjusting, you may then apply the weights you desire. One way to do this is with the **SS-score method**. First change all of the scores on each component into *SS*-scores (see Chapter 17). This makes all of the standard deviations equal. Second, multiply the components' *SS*-scores by the weights you want. Finally, add these products to form the composite mark for each student. The following formula summarizes these steps.

$$\text{Composite score} = \Sigma(\text{weight} \times SS) \quad \text{[Eq. 15.1]}$$

where
weight = weight you want the component to have
SS = the linear *SS*-score for the component
$= 10 (X - M)/SD + 50$

The procedure is illustrated in Figure 15.11. Note that these composite scores are not themselves *SS*-scores. However, these composite scores do provide you with a basis on which to rank students, so that the weightings you specify will have the desired influence on the students' final standings.

To appreciate the influence of the *SS*-score method on the students' ranking in the final composite, recall our earlier example in which the teacher's attempt to make the project dominate the ranking of the students was not successful. This time, let's apply the *SS* method to the same marks as shown here:

	Exam (Weighted = 1)			Project (Weighted 2)			Total (Weighted Final)	
Student	Marks	SS	Ranks	Marks	SS	Ranks	Composite	Ranks
Anthony	43	66	1	77	36	5	138	5
Ashley	33	55	2	78	43	4	141	4
Billy	26	48	3	27	50	3	148	3
Chad	22	44	4	80	57	2	158	2
Vanessa	15	37	5	81	64	1	165	1

Compare the final rankings in this example with the preceding final rankings. Now the project dominates the rankings based on the composite instead of the exam. This result is what the teacher initially intended. Transforming

FIGURE 15.11　Example of calculating composite marks using SS-scores.

	Components Entering into the Grade			
	Quizzes	**Homework**	**Term paper**	**Exam**
Mean (M)	70	85	75	65
Standard Deviation (SD)	5	8	15	20
Teacher's weight	20%	10%	20%	50%
Calculation for SS[a]	$SS = 10(\text{Mark} - 70)/5 + 50$	$SS = 10(\text{Mark} - 85)/8 + 50$	$SS = 10(\text{Mark} - 75)/15 + 50$	$SS = 10(\text{Mark} - 65)/20 + 50$

[a]SS-scores are calculated by subtracting the component mean from a student's raw score, dividing the difference by the standard deviation, multiplying by 10, and adding 50 to the product. The results for each student are shown below. For example:

The quizzes SS-score for Bob　　$= 10(87 - 70)/5 + 50 = 84$
The quizzes SS-score for Chad　　$= 10(85 - 70)/5 + 50 = 80$
The quizzes SS-score for Susan　$= 10(75 - 70)/5 + 50 = 60$
The quizzes SS-score for Theresa $= 10(70 - 70)/5 + 50 = 50$

	Raw Scores on Components				SS-Scores on Components				
Students	**Quizzes**	**Home-work**	**Term paper**	**Exam**	**Quizzes**	**Home-work**	**Term paper**	**Exam**	**Weighted Composite**
Bob	87	85	70	80	84	50	47	58	60
Chad	85	80	80	70	80	44	53	53	58
Susan	75	82	85	60	60	46	57	48	51
Theresa	70	78	75	65	50	41	50	50	49

Composite scores are calculated by multiplying the component SS-score by the corresponding teacher's component weights and summing the products. For example:

Composite score for Bob　　　$= .2(84) + .1(50) + .2(47) + .5(58) = 60$
Composite score for Chad　　 $= .2(80) + .1(44) + .2(53) + .5(53) = 58$
Composite score for Susan　　$= .2(60) + .1(46) + .2(57) + .5(48) = 51$
Composite score for Theresa　$= .2(50) + .1(41) + .2(50) + .5(50) = 49$

the marks to SS-scores first made the exam-and-project-marks standard deviations equal.[5] Then when the weight of 2 was applied, the composite better matched the teacher's intent.

ASSIGNING CRITERION-REFERENCED LETTER GRADES

There are several methods for **grading using the criterion-referencing grading framework**. In this book we shall discuss only three. One method is known as the **fixed percent method**: The scores on each component entering into the composite are first converted to percent correct (or percent of total points); then the percentages are translated to grades. For each component, you must use the same percentage to define the letter-grade boundaries.

A second method is called the **total points method**: Each component included in the final composite grade is

given maximum point value (e.g., quizzes may count 10 points, exams may count a maximum of 50 points each, and projects may count a maximum of 40 points each); the letter grades are assigned on the basis of the number of total points a student accumulated over the marking period.

A third method is the **quality level method** or the **rubric method**. It is sometimes called the **content-based method** (Frisbie & Waltman, 1992). In this method, you describe the quality level of performance a student must demonstrate for each letter grade—what types of performance will constitute an A, B, C, etc. (An example of these definitions of quality is shown in Table 15.4 in column one.) Given these definitions, you evaluate the student's work on each component, decide what is the quality level of work, and then assign the corresponding grade. This method is very similar to using scoring rubrics for performance tasks (see Chapters 11 and 12 for details about scoring rubrics). When you develop rubrics for a component, you must be sure the number of quality levels corresponds to the number of letter-grade levels.

[5]As an exercise, verify this example using the standard deviation formula in Appendix H.

Grading a Single Test or Assessment

Fixed Percent Method Teachers frequently use percents as bases for marking and grading papers. The relationship between percent correct and letter grade is rather arbitrary. In some schools, 80% is an A; in others, 85% is an A. In still others, 90% is an A. A few school boards have a policy on this matter. The following is an example of one such set of percentages that define letter grades:

90–100% = A
80–89% = B
70–79% = C
60–69% = D
0–59% = F

Note that a percent begs the question, "percentage of what?" Often, the only answer that you can defend is that the score represents the percent of the maximum points on the test or the assignment. This answer ignores the broader concern: The test should be a representative sample from a well-defined domain of performance implied by the curriculum learning targets. If you have not defined this domain and have not built the assessment to sample the domain, then you cannot use the percent grade to accurately estimate the student's status on a broader domain. Such tests (or assessments), and consequently such percentages, cannot be considered criterion-referenced.

The percentage that defines each grade should take into account a teacher's experience with the kinds of students being taught and the difficulty of the tests the teacher develops. Thus, norm-referenced information helps establish a criterion-referenced grading system. If the school district does not have a defined set of percentages for each letter grade, it may take you several years to work out a percent grading scheme that is both fair to the students and represents reasonable standards of scholarship. If you are a new teacher, you should check with colleagues to be sure that your grading scheme is reasonable and not unnecessarily "out of line" with the rest of the teachers.

This method uses the same fixed percentages for A, B, etc. for every component. One limitation of this fixed percentage method stems from the fact that every assessment you create has a different level of difficulty, which you may not know in advance. Thus, if you create a test that is too difficult for your class, you may end up giving too many low grades based on the percentages you fixed in advance. This will be frustrating for students and may put you into a position where you have to change the grading system (for example, you may want to grade on the curve to adjust the number of low grades). A second limitation is that this method encourages you to focus more strongly on the difficulty level of the assessment than on the learning targets it should assess. For example,

if you fix the percentages, you will be looking for ways to make the assessment easy enough or difficult enough so that you get a reasonable distribution of letter grades for your class. This seems to go against the principles of absolute or criterion-referenced grading.

Total Points Method To use this method, you must decide in advance all the components that will enter into the end-of-a-marking-period grade. Then, also in advance, you assign the maximum number of points each component is "worth." Your assessment plan should do this. The number of points each component is worth mirrors the weight you assign to each component. If you want the unit test(s) to count more toward the grade, for example, you would assign the unit tests more of the total points. Finally, you sum all the maximum points for components and set letter-grade boundaries *using this total of points.* Notice that, unlike for the fixed percentage method, you do not assign letter grades for each component, but only for the total summed over all components.

As an example, suppose you used the same four components that were used in Figure 15.11: quizzes, homework, a term paper, and an exam. Suppose further that you assigned the following points to each component:

Component	Maximum Points	"Weighting" Expressed as a Percent
Quizzes	40	20%
Homework	20	10%
Term paper	40	20%
Exam	100	50%
Total Points	200	100%

Having decided on the components and their maximum point values, you then set the boundaries for assigning letter grades to the total points that students accumulate in the marking period. For example,

Total Points	Grade
180–200	A
160–179	B
140–159	C
120–139	D
0–119	F

Notice that these total point *boundaries* correspond to percentages of 90%, 80%, 70%, and 60% for A, B, C, and D, respectively. You may use other percentages to define the letter-grade boundaries. Adjust the total point boundaries accordingly.

One limitation of the total points method is that it makes it too easy for you to give "extra credit" assignments to boost the total points of low-scoring students. Extra credit assignments tend to distort the meaning of the grades, especially when these assignments do not properly assess the same learning targets as the original set of components. For example, if a student did poorly on the term paper, you may be tempted to have the student read and summarize a current events magazine article to boost the student's score instead of writing another term paper. The meaning of the total points for this student would be distorted relative to other students. As a result, your grades are less valid.

Another limitation of this method is that by defining the maximum number of points before creating the assessments, you may be faced with an unacceptable choice when you do create an assessment tool. Consider this situation:

> Suppose I need a 50-point test to fit my [total points] grading scheme, but find that I need 32 multiple-choice items to sample the content domain thoroughly. I find this unsatisfactory (or inconvenient) because 32 does not divide into 50 very nicely. (It's 1.56!) To make life simpler, I could drop 7 items and use a 25-item test with 2 points per item. If I did that, my points total would be in fine shape, but my test would be an incomplete measure of the important unit objectives. The fact that I had to commit to 50 points prematurely dealt a serious blow to obtaining meaningful assessment results. (Frisbie & Waltman, 1992, p. 41)

Grading a Composite of Several Scores

This section discusses how to combine scores from several components into a single composite mark. The discussion is consistent with the criterion-referenced grading framework. As with norm-referenced grading, when using a criterion-referenced framework, you must be careful when assigning weights to components. If weights are not assigned properly, the composite results will not maintain the importance you seek for each component.

Fixed Percentage Method   If you use a fixed percentage grading method, you will have a percentage score for each student for each component. Then, you multiply each component percentage by its corresponding weight, add these products together, and divide the sum of products by the sum of the weights. This procedure may be summarized by the following formula:

Composite
percentage = Σ(weight $\times$ percentage score)
(weighted) $\div$ Σ(weight)   [Eq. 15.2]

where

Σ = sum of
weight = weight you give to a component
percent score = the percentage you gave the student on the component

To illustrate, consider the student scores shown in Figure 15.11. Suppose further that these scores are percentages. Finally, suppose that you want to use the same weight for the components as shown as "teacher's weight" in Figure 15.11. Then you calculate the composite percentages as illustrated in Table 15.6.

Composite scores are calculated by multiplying the percentage score on each component by the corresponding teacher's weight, summing these products, and dividing by the sum of the weights. For example:

Composite
percentage = [20(87) + 10(85) + 20(70) + 50(80)]
for Bob $\div$ [100] = 80%

Composite
percentage = [20(85) + 10(80) + 20(80) + 50(70)]
for Chad $\div$ [100] = 75%

Composite
percentage = [20(75) + 10(82) + 20(85) + 50(60)]
for Susan $\div$ [100] = 65%

Composite
percentage = [20(70) + 10(78) + 20(75) + 50(65)]
for Theresa $\div$ [100] = 69%

If you did not use the weights, each component would count equally toward the composite. This procedure should not be used with norm-referenced grading, because the weights assigned here do not reflect the standard deviations of the components.

Total Points Method   The way we described the total points method in the previous section automatically grades composites. The composite score for a student is the total of the points the student accumulates. However, make sure that the points you assign for each component are proportional to the weight you want each component to contribute to the total composite. For example, if the

TABLE 15.6   Percent scores on components.

Student	Quizzes (wt = 20%)	Home work (wt = 10%)	Term paper (wt = 20%)	Exam (wt = 50%)	Weighted composite percentage
Bob	87	85	70	80	80
Chad	85	80	80	70	75
Susan	75	82	85	60	65
Theresa	70	78	75	65	69

weights you want for the components are quizzes 20%, homework 10%, term paper 20%, and exam 50%, then each component should reflect these percentages of the total maximum points. Thus, if the maximum total points is 200, then all of the quizzes are worth a maximum of 40 points (= 20% of 200), all of the homework a maximum of 20 points, term paper 40 points, and exam a maximum of 100 points.

GRADEBOOK COMPUTER PROGRAMS

A number of the procedures described for calculating composite grades are somewhat complex and involve some tedious multiplication and addition. All these calculations can be made with the help of a handheld calculator, of course. If you have a personal computer, you may also want to use a simple spreadsheet program to make the calculations. There are also several **gradebook programs** in the marketplace to help you. The advantage is that a gradebook program provides you with a spreadsheet already set up for recording and reporting grades. The better programs combine spreadsheets and database functions. These will allow you to choose from a variety of grading frameworks, keep a class roster, keep attendance, record comments about students' assignments, obtain class summaries, and print reports for the total class or for one student to take home.

Figure 15.12 shows a computer screen window for one gradebook program. Notice the "Result Column" at the far right. This column is constantly updated as you enter assessment results for each student. This particular program (*Excelsior 2 Grade for Windows*) allows you to print many different reports, including class grades report, class final grades (six weeks and quarters), class objectives summary, class statistics, period mastery for individuals, class rank roster, period assignments report, individual grades or objectives report, and attendance reports. The program can be networked as well.

Not all gradebook programs are of high quality, however. Some are of limited value, very difficult to use, or very inflexible. Be sure to read reviews of the programs in teachers' magazines or educational technology magazines, and try a program before you purchase it. The web site www.thejournal.com may be helpful. Evaluations of gradebook programs may be obtained from Professor Arlen Gullickson of the Evaluation Center, Western Michigan University.

Summary

- Although good teaching requires continuous assessment, not all assessment results should become part of a student's grade. Only summative assessments of achievement should be part of a student's grade.

- Grades are important summaries of a student's achievements, which are used by students, parents, other teachers, guidance counselors, school officials, postsecondary educational institutions, and employers. Therefore, you must assign grades with utmost care and maintain their validity.

- Marks and grades are difficult for many teachers to assign because educational achievement is difficult to measure, marking systems are frequently controversial, and grading may require difficult or unpleasant decisions about students.

FIGURE 15.12 Example of a computer screen for entering student assessment results into a gradebook program.

Name (Last, First)	1	2	3	4	5	6	7	Homework
Adams, Todd	100	89	78	87	96	97	100	93.1 A
Allen, Crystal	90	78	67	100	90	90	100	88.6 B
Bailey, Linda	87	68	88	100	80	80	98	87.1 B
Boone, Daniel	86	90	90	95			90	87.9 B
Chen, Allison	100	89	67		70	70	88	88.5 B
Cortez, Martin	89	56	89	X			79	83.8 B
Davis, Leigh	90	78	92	67	87	89	50	76.7 C
Durbin, Drew	97	45	95	95	90	90	100	90.9 A
Erickson, Neil	89	34	99	80			88	84.8 B
Espinoza, Anne	100	88	89	X	87	89	72	85.9 B
Fedora, Charles	87	99	87	90	75	75	88	86.1 B
Franklin, Beth	90	89	67		90	90	80	85.1 B
Garcia, William	100	78	58	87	93	93	85	86.9 B
Griffith, Stephanie	98	81	88	98	88	88	100	92.8 A

Title Bar

Menu Bar — American History: American History/First Semester/First Six Weeks

File Edit View Select Define Utilities Options Windows Help

Status Line — 4. Homework: Jamestown   Max: 100

Result Column

Student Index

Information Line — C:\AHISTORY.G2W

Assessment Columns

Source: From *Excelsior 2 Grade for Windows: Self-Paced Learning Modules* (p. 3) by Excelsior Software, Inc., 1991, Greeley, CO: Author. Reprinted by permission.

- The ways you and your school district assign grades communicate your own values and attitudes as well as student progress information.
- Measurement specialists are divided on the issue of whether traditional grades are effective motivators of academic performance. One analysis indicates that traditional grades (1) can serve as goals for some students, (2) reduce motivation when they are perceived by a student as being out of reach, (3) seldom provide continuous information the student can use to judge progress, and (4) provide little information the student can use to improve learning. If conditions 2, 3, and 4 exist, then grades are less likely to be effective motivators of student learning.
- Grades have been criticized on many different grounds. These are summarized in Figure 15.2.
- Among the methods of reporting student progress in the United States, the most popular are letter grades, numbers or percentages, two-category systems, checklists and rating scales, narrative reports, student-teacher conferences, parent-teacher conferences, and letters to parents. Advantages and disadvantages of the various methods are shown in Table 15.3.
- Schools often use more than one method of reporting student progress, and different methods are used at different educational levels.
- Suggestions for conducting parent-teacher conferences are summarized in Figure 15.6.
- Multiple marking systems are needed when a school reports several kinds of symbols and marks students on several kinds of objectives. Suggestions for developing multiple marking systems are given in Figure 15.8.
- It is unlikely that one best system for reporting student progress exists. Schools might consider the total informational needs of different students and parents and design multiple reporting systems tailored to community circumstances.
- Letter grades are assigned within certain grade-referencing frameworks: norm-referencing (relative standards), criterion-referencing (absolute standards), and self-referencing (growth standards).
- Before you can assign valid grades, you need to choose a grading framework that matches your (a) teaching approach and (b) formative and summative information purposes. Depending on these factors you can choose from three grade-referencing frameworks.
- A norm-referenced approach assigns grades to students on the basis of how well their performances compare with one another.
- A self-referenced approach assigns grades on the basis of the teacher's perception of the student's capability and subsequent educational growth.
- A criterion-referenced approach assigns grades on the basis of a comparison of a student's performance

with a defined set of standards, performances to learn, or knowledge to acquire. This approach can be considered criterion-referenced only if you use a well-defined domain of tasks and draw representative samples from the domain on which to observe and assess students. Most teachers do not do this.
- Your grading plan must be based on your assessment plan (see Chapter 6).
- To make your summative grades sensible, you need to:
  - Focus only on grading variables.
  - Eliminate mixing nongrading variables into a grade.
  - Make your marking scales consistent across all components.
  - Assign weights to the components rationally.
  - Use additional achievement assessment information to evaluate students near the grade boundaries.
  - Set grade boundaries using techniques that match your grade-referencing framework.
  - Use F to represent low achievement rather than "failing to try" or "failing to turn in assignments."
  - Avoid giving zeros for failing to turn in assignments or as punishment.
- Grading variables are a subset of reporting variables, and reporting variables are a subset of assessment variables. Grading variables are limited to those assessment variables that reflect summative student achievement of the curriculum's learning targets, which you must report on official school records.
- You should weight each of the categories of assessment components comprising grades differently. Among the factors you should consider in weighting the components are representatives and relevance, emphasis on what you taught, thinking processes and skills required, overlap among the components, fairness to all students, and reliability and objectivity of the assessment results.
- The chapter explained several techniques for assigning grades, including grading on the curve, the standard deviation method, adjusting for the class's ability level, transforming scores to SS-scores, the total points method, the fixed percentage method, the rubrics or quality-level method, and weight components for absolute standards systems.
- Computerized gradebook programs that allow you to use complex grading procedures rather easily are available. They also allow you to easily prepare a number of useful summaries of your grades and reports to submit to students, parents, and school officials.

Important Terms and Concepts

assessment variables (evaluation variables)
borderline cases

continuous assessment

criterion-referenced grading framework (absolute standards, task referenced)

failing grade

failing work vs. failing to try

fixed-percent method for grading

grading

gradebook program

grading for summative purposes

grading on the curve

grading framework

grading variables

marking period

multiple marking system

narrative report

norm-referenced grading framework (group-referenced, relative standards)

permanent record card

quality level method for grading (content-based method, rubric method)

report card

reporting variables

self-referenced grading framework (change based, growth standards)

SS-score method for making composites

stakeholders

standard deviation method of grading

student progress reporting method (checklist, letter grades, letter to parents, narrative reports, numbers, parent-teacher conferences, percentages, pupil-teacher conferences, rating scale, two-category)

total points method for grading

Exercises and Discussion Questions

1. All the students in your assessment course should complete the questionnaire in Figure 15.1. (You may wish to have other teachers complete it as well.) Compare your own responses with those of others in your class (and with any other groups who have completed it).

   a. What are the areas of agreement and disagreement?

   b. What are the reasons you and your classmates offer for agreement? Disagreement?

   c. Are there areas for which different subgroups of teachers (e.g., secondary vs. elementary; math vs. science vs. language arts vs. social studies) differ or agree more strongly?

2. Consider the possibility of using factors other than achievement when assigning student grades.

   a. Should a student's grade in a subject reflect that student's conformity to the teacher's rules and deportment in class as well as achievement? Explain and defend your answer.

   b. Should you lower a student's grade or give the student a zero if that student does not turn in several practice exercise assignments or turns them in late? Under what conditions? Explain and defend your answer.

   c. If the grades you assign your students are lowered because of conformity, deportment, or failure to turn in assignments, what would you tell the postsecondary institution or a potential employer about your student's achievement in the subject area?

   d. Should you raise (lower) the grades of borderline students to the next higher (lower) level? Under what circumstances? What information do you need to take into account? Explain.

3. Do you side with Ebel, Cronbach, or both on the motivating effects of grades? Explain and defend your answer.

4. Which criticisms of grades are most important to your current or future teaching situation? How have you handled (or how do you plan to handle) these criticisms when they are raised against you?

5. Prepare a brief paper explaining the grading system you use (or plan to use). In a separate section explain the educational rationale for using this system, including an explanation of how your system has improved (or will improve) your students' educational development. In your paper, show how you used Table 15.5 to frame your thinking. Discuss your grading point of view with others in your class. In your paper, prepare at least one paragraph explaining each of the following:

   a. The meaning of your grade symbols

   b. The meaning of failure in your class

   c. How you distinguish between "failure" and "failure to try"

   d. How you handle late work or work not handed in

   e. How you avoid the "deadly zero"

   f. What student performances count toward grades you assign your student

   g. The number of each letter (or other symbol) grade you typically assign (or will assign) in your class

   h. What components go (or will go) into the end-of-term grade for your students

   i. How much weight each component in Item h should receive

   j. What boundaries you use (or would use) for each grade

   k. How you handle students who are on the borderline between grades

   l. Any other factors you take into account

6. Talk with school administrators and teachers at several grade levels in the school district in which you live or work.

   a. What method(s) of student progress reporting is (are) used?

   b. Is the district satisfied with the method(s) it uses?

   c. Which of the advantages and disadvantages listed in Table 15.3 has the school district experienced? Explain.

   d. Obtain copies of the district's report card(s). Share all your findings with the other members of your class.

   e. Summarize the similarities and differences among the district represented in your class and offer suggestions for improving student progress reporting.

7. Which of the suggestions for preparing for parent-teacher conferences in each category of Figure 15.6 do you believe is most important for your teaching situation? Explain.

   a. State several disadvantages of the parent-teacher conference method of reporting student progress.

   b. Which disadvantage is most serious for your current or future teaching situation? Why?

   c. What can be done to lessen the impact of these disadvantages?

8. Identify a unit that you have taught or will teach.

   a. In the context of your teaching situation and this unit, identify the assessment variables, the reporting variables, and the grading variables.

b. Prepare a three-column table listing these variables and describing how you have assessed (or will assess) each one.

c. Share your findings with the others in your class.

9. Consider the different grading frameworks in relation to your own teaching situation.

a. What are the principal advantages and disadvantages of the criterion-referencing, norm-referencing, and self-referencing grading frameworks?

b. For which teaching approaches and summative and formative purposes might each of the referencing schemes just mentioned be most appropriate?

10. Name several kinds of student performances (homework, class participation, performance tasks, tests, etc.) that you believe should be included in each of the following levels: primary, middle school, or high school.

a. For each type of performance, state what weight should be assigned to each. Explain the reasons for these weights by discussing each of the six factors stated in the chapter in relation to each kind of performance.

b. Would the weights vary with different grade levels or with different subjects? Explain.

11. Discuss with your classmates the ethical obligations you have when assigning grades to students. Keep in mind such concepts as fairness, meanness, due process, academic integrity, desire to be popular, pressure from your principal, and student self-esteem.

a. List these ethical obligations on the chalkboard and organize them into categories, eliminating redundancies.

b. Copy the list so that each class member has his or her own copy.

12. Is it ethical for a principal to change the final grade you assigned to a student? Under which conditions is it an ethical practice? An unethical practice?

13. Table 15.7 contains information about the performance of a class of 10 students. (Hint: Average the marks within categories—e.g., within homework—before applying the teacher's weight.)

a. Determine an overall report card grade for each student using the following methods: (i) self-referencing; (ii) criterion-referencing, fixed percentage; (iii) criterion-referencing, total points; (iv) norm-referencing, grading on the curve; (v) norm-referencing, standard deviation method; and (vi) norm-referencing, Ebel-Stuit method.

b. Prepare a table with the students' names as the row headings and the four different methods as the column headings. Enter the students' grades under each method and compare the results.

c. Share your results with the others in your class. Where is there most agreement and most disagreement?

d. List the reasons for agreements and disagreements for each method.

Additional Readings

Azwell, T., & Schmar, E. (Eds.) (1995). *Report card on report cards: Alternatives to consider.* Portsmouth, NH: Heinemann.

A collection of articles about innovative ways school districts have used for reporting pupil progress that differ from the traditional letter grades. Some articles describe how to manage the change process.

Brookhart, S.M. (1999). Teaching about communicating assessment results and grading. *Educational Measurement: Issues and Practice, 18*(1), 5–13.

Describes what aspiring teachers need to know about grading and communicating about students' achievement. Points out how teaching aspiring teachers about educational assessment may be different than teaching aspiring psychometricians.

Brookhart, S.M. (1993). Teachers' grading practices: Meaning and values. *Journal of Educational Measurement, 30*, 123–142.

A research study that tests a model for how teachers come to assign grades.

Clarridge, P.B., & Whitaker, E.M. (1997). *Rolling the elephant over: How to effect large-scale change in the reporting process.* Portsmouth, NH: Heinemann.

TABLE 15.7 List students and the marks they received on each component during one marking period. Use this table for Exercise 13.

Pupil	Last year's grade average	Teacher's judgment of ability	Deportment	Homework 1	2	3	Project	Quizzes 1	2	Test score
A	B	Average	Very good	10	3	8	12	8	4	25
B	C	Average	Very good	9	2	7	15	7	4	20
C	A	Very high	Poor	10	0	9	15	10	5	29
D	A	Above average	Excellent	10	4	10	15	6	5	28
E	D	Average	Poor	0	2	5	0	5	3	10
F	B	Average	Good	10	1	2	10	5	3	18
G	C	Below average	Good	10	3	9	8	6	2	15
H	C	Above average	Poor	10	1	4	15	8	4	12
I	C	Above average	Excellent	10	1	3	13	8	3	21
J	C	Above average	Very good	10	1	5	10	8	2	23
Maximum possible score:				10	10	10	15	10	5	30
Mean				8.9	1.8	6.2	11.3	7.1	3.5	20.1
Standard deviation:				3.0	1.2	2.6	4.5	1.5	1.0	6.1
Teacher's weights:				5%	5%	5%	15%	10%	10%	50%

A detailed case study of what was done in the Tucson Unified School District to change to a criterion-referenced grading and reporting system. The authors discuss both the positive and negative aspects of the change process.

Hills, J. R. (1993). Hills' handy hints: Regression effects in educational measurement. *Educational Measurement: Issues and Practice, 12*(3), 31–34.

Gives scenarios of practical situations in which grading on the basis of growth or change leads to misunderstanding of students' actual achievements.

Mt. Lebanon School District. (1992). *Secondary grading philosophy and principles.* Mt. Lebanon, PA: Author.

If your school district does not have a written grading policy, you may wish to obtain this one. Although limited to the secondary level, it covers a wide range of policy issues, including criteria, reporting, exceptions, and responsibilities. (zip code: 15228)

Munk, D.D, & Bursuck, W.D. (1998). Can grades be helpful *and* fair? *Educational Leadership, 55* (4), 44–47.

Discusses whether grades should be different for students with disabilities who are mainstreamed. Explains common grading adaptations. Describes survey research on students' and teachers' views concerning adaptation of grading. Makes suggestions for school district grading policy.

Shalaway, L. (1993). Perfecting parent conferences. *Instructor, 103*(1), 58–66, 64.

Gives suggestions for working with parents to improve communication through parent-teacher conferences.

Stiggins, R.J., Frisbie, D.A., & Griswold, P.A. (1989). Inside high school grading practices: Building a research agenda. *Educational Measurement: Issues and Practice, 8*(2), 5–14.

Reports research on teacher grading practices and how these practices compare to the recommendations made in textbooks by assessment specialists.

Terwilliger, J.S. (1989). Classroom standard-setting and grading practices. *Educational Measurement: Issues and Practice, 8*(2), 15–19.

Presents a way you can combine the absolute and relative standards grading frameworks in situations where some learning targets can be classified as basic skills.

PART III

Interpreting and Using Standardized Tests

CHAPTER 16

Standardized Achievement Tests

Learning Targets

After studying this chapter, you should be able to:

1. Name and describe the major categories of educational achievement tests. *[4, 6, 1]*

2. Explain the advantages of each type of educational achievement test. *[4, 3, 1]*

3. Explain the benefits to a school of using educational survey tests that have been standardized and developed using empirical research. *[4, 3, 1]*

4. Describe the features that standardized achievement batteries have in common. *[1, 6, 7]*

5. Describe the major dimensions along which the standardized achievement batteries differ. *[1, 6, 7]*

6. Explain what you gain and lose when you use the tests that come with your curriculum materials. *[1, 4]*

7. Describe the advantages and disadvantages of teacher-made assessments over published assessments. *[1, 4]*

8. Describe and illustrate the appropriate uses of standardized achievement tests for within-classroom decisions. *[3, 1, 4]*

9. Describe and illustrate the appropriate uses of standardized achievement tests for decisions external to the classroom. *[3, 4, 6]*

10. Describe and illustrate the common misuses of standardized achievement tests in schools. *[7, 3]*

11. Identify the factors that a school must keep in mind when selecting a standardized achievement test for elementary and secondary schools. *[1, 7, 6]*

12. Describe what you need to do before and during the administration of a standardized assessment procedure. *[3]*

13. Identify ethical and unethical practices a teacher could undertake when preparing students for standardized assessments. *[6, 3, 4]*

14. Apply the two principles for judging the ethics of a teacher's standardized-assessment-preparation practices. *[6, 3, 4]*

15. Explain how each of the terms and concepts listed at the end of this chapter apply to educational assessment. *[6]*

I n this chapter we discuss different types of published achievement tests, the ways they differ from each other, and how they differ from teacher-made tests. In Chapter 18 we shall discuss how a published test is developed and evaluated.

TYPES OF TESTS

Overview

There are a great many published achievement tests. These tests vary in their purpose, usefulness, and quality. To appreciate their variety, you may find it helpful to classify them. Here is one classifying scheme:

I. *Published achievement tests*

   A. *Standardized, empirically documented tests* have a high degree of standardization. **Standardized tests** follow the development procedures outlined in Chapter 18, especially the steps that require using **empirically documented** data on their effectiveness. The following types are in this group:

      1. *Multilevel survey batteries* are the familiar, annually administered tests that survey students' general educational growth or basic skill development in each of several curricular areas. *Multilevel* means that the test content spans several grade levels; *battery* means that several curricular areas are assessed by different subtests.

      2. *Multilevel criterion-referenced tests for a single curricular area* provide detailed information about students' status for a well-defined domain of performance in a single subject area (e.g., mathematics).

      3. *Other multilevel tests for a single curricular area* are non-criterion-referenced tests that assess students in a broader way than do subtests in a survey battery.

      4. *Single-level standardized tests for one course or subject* are developed for assessing achievement at only one educational level or for one course (e.g., Algebra I). Usually, they are stand-alone tests, not coordinated with tests from other courses, and are not normed on the same students as other tests.

   B. *Nonstandardized, not empirically documented tests* make little or no attempt to standardize and do not follow all the development procedures outlined in Chapter 18. Publishers do not spend the time and money to empirically document their effectiveness or their quality.

      1. *Some criterion-referenced tests* estimate students' status with respect to a well-defined domain of performance (usually specified by specific behavioral objectives), but they lack standardization and empirical documentation of worth.

      2. *Textbook or curricular accompaniments* are tests or test items found in teacher's editions, at the end of textbook chapters, at the back of the book, or built into instructional materials. They are called different names, such as pretests, posttests, placement tests, progress checks, unit tests, review tests, or curriculum-embedded tests. They lack standardization and empirical documentation. As a teacher, you must keep in mind that these tests are seldom the products of professional item writers, usually measure low-level cognitive skills, and very often have several incorrectly keyed answers.

II. *Teacher-made tests* are crafted by you to measure the specific learning targets your curriculum framework emphasizes. These tests help you in making day-to-day instructional decisions.

The focus of this chapter is limited to standardized, empirically documented achievement tests. The full range of tests in the classification is not discussed.

Multilevel Survey Batteries

The workhorse of standardized achievement testing is the **multilevel survey battery**. Each publisher's test battery emphasizes different details of content and skill. However, the batteries are organized similarly.

Organization of Batteries Each battery is group administered, each contains several subtests, each subtest assesses achievement in a specific curricular area, and each subtest is made up of a coordinated series of **test levels** that span the grades. For example, a subtest may be organized into four levels: one level for grades 1 and 2, another for grades 3 and 4, another for 5 and 6, and a fourth for 7 and 8. It is not unusual for a publisher to have adjacent levels with overlapping grades, for example, one level covering grades 3–4–5 and the next level covering grades 5–6–7.

A **subtest** covers one area, such as reading, mathematics, listening skills, English usage (mechanics), writing, spelling (recognition), vocabulary (word meaning), or skills in using library and reference materials. Not all questions on these subtests are multiple choice: In recent years, publishers have added performance tasks to several subtests. Separate scores are given for each subtest. Usually, a battery assesses six to eight curriculum areas. Different publishers may have different names for an area. Table 16.1 shows the curriculum areas, subtests, and grade levels covered by some of the more popular standardized achievement tests.

Although different publishers' survey batteries are similar in their surface features, they are not interchangeable, even though subtest names may sound similar. The specific content emphasized, the cognitive skills students are required to use to complete the tasks, and the way the norms and scales are developed will be very different from publisher to publisher.

Tests vary in how well they match any school district's curriculum. In some curricula, such as reading and perhaps mathematics, the curricula differ very little from one school district to another within a state. The tests and these curricula may match closely. In other curricula such

TABLE 16.1   Examples of curriculum areas and grade levels assessed by survey batteries.

Curriculum area/subarea [a]	Stanford Achievement Test (9th edition)	Metropolitan Achievement Test (7th edition)	Iowa Tests of Basic Skills (Forms K and L)	Iowa Tests of Educational Development (Forms K and L)	Comprehensive Tests of Basic Skills (5th edition) Complete Battery Plus
Reading multiple-choice					
Alphabet knowledge	K.0– 1.5	K.0– K.5			
Word/sentence reading	K.0– 2.5	1.5– 3.5	K.8– 3.5		1.6– 4.2
Phonetic/structural analysis	1.5– 3.5	K.0– 1.5	K.0– 3.5		1.6– 4.2
Decoding skills	K.0– 1.5	K.0– 1.5			1.6– 4.2
Vocabulary	2.5–13.0	1.5–12.9	K.0– 8.9	9.0–12.9	1.6–12.9
Comprehension	1.5–13.0	1.5–12.9	K.8– 8.9	9.0–12.9	K.0–12.9
Reading performance assessment	1.5–13.0[b]	1.5–12.9[b]	3.0– 8.9[b]	9.0–12.9[b]	1.6–12.9[c]
Language multiple-choice					
Punctuation	1.5–13.0	1.5–12.9	1.7– 8.5	9.0–12.9	1.6–12.9
Capitalization	1.5–13.0	1.5–12.9	1.7– 8.9	9.0–12.9	1.6–12.9
Usage	1.5–13.0	1.5–12.9	1.7– 8.9	9.0–12.9	1.6–12.9
Listening	K.0– 9.9	K.0– 3.5	K.0– 8.9		K.6– 2.6
Sentence/paragraph organization	1.5–13.0	3.0– 8.9		9.0–12.9	1.6–12.9
Language/writing performance assessment	3.5–13.0[b]	1.5–12.9[b]	3.0– 8.9[b]	9.0–12.9[b]	1.6–12.9[c]
Spelling multiple-choice	1.5–13.0	1.5–12.9	3.0– 8.9	9.0–12.9	2.0–12.9
Spelling performance assessment					
Mathematics multiple-choice					
Computation	K.0–13.0	K.5– 9.5	K.0– 8.9		1.6–12.9
Concepts	K.0–13.0	K.5–12.9	K.0– 8.9	9.0–12.9	K.0–12.9
Problem solving	K.5–13.0	1.5–12.9	K.0– 8.9	9.0–12.9	K.6–12.9
Mathematics performance assessment	1.5–13.0[b]	1.5–12.9[b]	K.0– 8.9[b]	9.0–12.9[b]	1.6–12.9[c]
Study skills multiple-choice					
Maps, graphs, tables	4.5–13.0	3.5–12.9	1.7– 8.9	9.0–12.9	1.6–12.9
Library/reference materials	4.5–13.0	3.5–12.9	1.7– 8.9	9.0–12.9	1.6–12.9
Study skills performance assessment		K.0– 8.9[b]		9.0–12.9[b]	1.6–12.9
Science multiple-choice	K.0–13.0	1.5–12.9	1.7– 8.9	9.0–12.9	1.6–12.9
Science performance assessment	1.5–13.0[b]	1.5–12.9[b]	K.0– 8.9[b]	9.0–12.9[b]	1.6–12.9[c]
Social studies multiple-choice	3.5–13.0	1.5–12.9	1.7– 8.9	9.0–12.9	1.6–12.9
Social studies performance assessment	1.5–13.0[b]	1.5–12.9[b]	K.0– 8.9[b]	9.0–12.9[b]	1.6–12.9[c]

Notes: [a]Publishers may have somewhat different names for these areas than those used here. Separate scores are not provided for every area.
[b]Assessments in these areas are available as supplements or additional purchase components that are not part of the battery itself.
[c]Part of the *Multiple Assessments Edition.*

as science and social studies, especially in the elementary schools, there are much larger variations between school districts. For the teacher this means that the different subtests in the battery have less value in assessing the specifics of what a teacher taught during the year. However, such subtests can assess general information and general ability to apply knowledge and skill.

These differences make it necessary for school officials to actually inspect the test items before they adopt a battery, matching their local curriculum to the battery's content and thinking emphasis. If there is a wide gap between your local curriculum's learning targets and the battery's tasks, do not adopt the survey battery.

Publishers think of each subtest (e.g., reading comprehension) as assessing a continuous dimension that grows

or develops over a range of grades. Because each subtest is a graded series of assessments, the publisher can use empirical data to link the levels together and to place the scores of students from every grade on one numerical scale that spans all the grades. The scale allows achievement to be expressed quantitatively. This makes it possible for you to use a multi-level subtest to measure a student's year-to-year educational development and growth in a curricular area. Different types of educational development scales are explained in Chapter 17.

Each publisher norms and standardizes its tests on different samples of students, so the samples and the resulting norm-referenced scores are not comparable. However, all the subtests in one publisher's survey battery are administered to the same national sample of students. The major advantage is that all the different subtest results can be referenced to the same norm group. You can then compare a student's relative strengths and weaknesses across the different curricular areas. You can assess strengths and weaknesses, however, only by comparing a student's percentile rank in one curricular area to that student's percentile rank in another. The kind of comparison you make follows:

> Shanna is better in mathematics than she is in social studies because her score in mathematics is higher than 98% of the students at her grade level, whereas her score in social studies is higher than only 60% of students at her grade level.

Survey batteries report grade-equivalent scores, too, but you should not use them to compare a student's achievement in two curricular areas. Percentile ranks and grade-equivalent scores are explained in Chapter 17.

Common Learning Targets   It is important to keep in mind that virtually all published standardized tests cover content and learning targets judged to be common to many schools rather than one specific school district. Therefore, standardized achievement tests are not focused on the teaching emphasis of one teacher, one school, one text, or one set of curricular materials. This is an advantage, because it gives you an "external" or "objective" view of what your students have learned. It is also a disadvantage, because the cognitive skills and knowledge assessed by the test may not have been taught to the students before they were tested. Therefore, it is imperative that a school district carefully compares a test's content, item by item, to the state's standards and the school district's curriculum framework before deciding to adopt it. Also, a teacher must develop and use his or her own assessment procedures for day-to-day instructional decisions (e.g., whether a student has mastered a specific concept).

Auxiliary Materials   Most publishers of standardized, empirically documented tests provide auxiliary materials to help you interpret and use the assessment results. Teacher's manuals describe in considerable detail the intended purpose and uses of the results, often suggesting ways to improve students' skills by using assessment results for instructional planning. Some publishers provide separate manuals for curriculum coordinators and school administrators to help them use assessment results in curriculum evaluation and reports to the school board. Most publishers provide score reports that the school district may use both within the school and with students and parents.

Multilevel Criterion-Referenced Tests

Multilevel criterion-referenced tests provide information about a student's status with respect to the specific learning targets in a domain. Although some survey batteries also provide this information, most surveys assess very broadly or globally defined educational development. Multilevel criterion-referenced tests tend to focus on a more narrowly defined set of learning targets.

Other Multilevel Tests

Other types of multilevel tests are stand-alone products that cover one curricular area such as reading or mathematics, across several grades. These assessments provide a deeper and broader sampling of content than a corresponding subtest of a survey battery. Thus, more time is devoted to assessing students in a single curricular area than when you use a survey battery subtest. However, if the same sample of students was not used to norm a stand-alone multilevel test concurrently with tests from other curricular areas, you cannot use the stand-alone tests to compare a student's relative strengths and weaknesses across curricular areas. For example, you could not say a student is better in reading than in mathematics.

Single-Level Standardized Tests

If you do not want to measure growth or development, a **single-level test** may be useful. Rather than cover several grade or age levels, such tests are directed toward one level or a particular course. Usually these assessments are built for high school and college courses. There are, for example, tests for Algebra 1, first-year college chemistry, and first-year college French.

Each test is a stand-alone product and is not coordinated with other tests. Thus, these test results cannot be used to compare a student's relative standing in several subjects. Scores from this group of achievement tests are most often interpreted using norm-referencing schemes such as percentile ranks and standard scores.

STANDARDIZED SURVEY BATTERIES

Benefits of Standardized Tests

As discussed in Chapter 1, standardizing is necessary if you want the results to be comparable from time to time, place to place, and person to person. If an assessment procedure is standardized, you are better able to properly interpret students' scores on it. The quality of any assessment procedure is demonstrated by using empirical data to document its validity and effectiveness. These data provide the test developers with a basis for (1) improving and selecting tasks, (2) establishing reliability and validity, (3) describing how well the assessment works in the target population of students, (4) creating scales to measure growth, (5) equating scores (making scores comparable from grade to grade and from one form of the assessment to another), and (6) developing a variety of norm-referenced scores.

Common Features

Most group-administered survey batteries have the following features in common (Iwanicki, 1980).

1. *Test development features.* Manuals and other materials provide the following test development information for each subtest: (a) content and learning targets covered, (b) types of norms and how they were developed, (c) type of criterion-referencing provided, (d) reliability data, and (e) techniques used to screen items for offensiveness and possible sex, ethnic, and racial bias.

2. *Test administration features.* Tests generally (a) have two equivalent forms; (b) require a total administration time of 2 to 3 hours, spread among several testing sessions over several school days (although tests vary widely in length and administration time); (c) provide practice booklets for students to use before being tested; (d) have separate, machine-scorable answer sheets for upper grades (students in lower grades mark answers directly on the machine-scorable test booklets), and (e) permit both **in-level** and **out-of-level testing**.[1]

3. *Test norming features.* Tests generally use broadly representative national sampling for norms development and provide both fall and spring individual student norms. Sometimes **special norms** such as the following are provided: (a) large-city norms, (b) norms for students in special government entitlement programs, (c) norms for high-income communities, (d) norms for nonpublic schools, (e) regional norms, and (f) norms for school-building averages.

4. *Test score features.* Tests provide raw scores for each subtest and the following norm-referenced scores: percentile ranks, normal curve equivalents, stanines, extended normalized standard scores, and grade equivalents (or some similar grade-level indicator score). Attitudes toward using grade equivalents vary. Some tests provide instructional reading-level scores that are keyed to commonly used basal readers.

5. *Test score reporting and interpretation features.* Tests generally have interpretive manuals for teachers, school administrators, and/or counselors. Most group tests provide **computer-prepared narrative reports**. Reports include (a) **item analysis** of class performance on clusters of items (Figure 16.1); (b) a **building report** for one grade

level on all subtests (Figure 16.2); and (c) a **profile report**, especially tailored to an individual student, that interprets the test results to the teacher or parent (Figure 16.3). Some tests have narrative reports that interpret the results for each grade level or for each school building. Such reports are not free, of course.

Differences

Although survey batteries share common features, they are definitely not interchangeable. Scores obtained from different batteries, even on subtests with similar-sounding titles, will be different and cannot be compared directly. Among the features that are different and that seriously affect comparability of scores are the following:

1. *Emphasis within content areas.* Subtest scores on batteries from different test publishers have different meanings. For example, a study of the mathematics subtests of four standardized survey batteries for the fourth-grade level indicated that the percentage of items covering a topic such as fractions varied widely among tests—from 5.4% to 14.4% (Freeman et al., 1982). This factor would affect pupils' scores significantly. Because each test publisher chooses to emphasize each subtopic somewhat differently, there may be a serious mismatch between what a given battery calls "reading comprehension" or "social studies" and what a given school and/or teacher emphasizes in class. These mismatches result in subtest scores (e.g., grade equivalents in a subject area) that may not represent a student's current level of functioning. The overlap of a test and a school's instructional program is an extremely important consideration in choosing among test batteries.

2. *Quality of developmental scales' articulation between grade levels.* One use of a standardized test is to measure students' growth on a continuous scale. If the scale is constructed properly, it is possible to track students' educational growth over the various grade levels. But different test developers use different technical methods for creating developmental scales, even when the scales have the same name. Some publishers use a complex technology called item response theory; others do not. A chief consideration in the practical use of test results concerns the amount of grade-to-grade overlap in the development scores (Peterson, Kolen, & Hoover, 1989). For example, a fourth-grader may have a grade equivalent of 6.0 on the fourth-grade mathematics subtest and a grade equivalent of 4.9 on the sixth-grade counterpart of the same subtest. Different techniques for constructing grade equivalents will create differing amounts of overlap. If this happens, the result will be scores that show a spuriously erratic pattern of growth for youngsters as they progress through the grades.

3. *Quality of services offered to schools.* Test publishers differ in the extent of their technical support and

---

[1]Test booklets are organized by level; each level is designed for use with a few grades. A student is said to be tested in-level if the test booklet level corresponds to the student's actual grade placement. If a student's level of academic functioning is either above or below the actual grade placement, the school may administer the test level that more nearly corresponds to the student's functioning level. This is called out-of-level testing. A student is measured best when a test is tailored to the student's functioning level.

FIGURE 16.1 Example of a report that analyzes your class's performance on clusters of items. This report is for mathematics subtests. It reports the percent correct (%C) for each item and for clusters of items. Comparisons are made for your class, the district at your grade level, and the nation at your grade level. This type of report helps you to see where in the mathematics area your class is strong and weak.

Iowa Tests of Basic Skills

Service 6:
Group Item Analysis
Class Report: Diff=Class Minus National
All Diff's Are Printed

Class/Group:	NESS		
Building:	WEBER	Grade:	4
Building Code:	304	Level:	10
System:	DALEN COMMUNITY	Form:	K
Norms:	SPRING 1992	Test Date:	03/93
Order No.:	000-A33-76044-00-001	Page:	128

Item No.	MATH CONCEPTS & ESTIMATION	Item Count	Class Avg %C N=24	Building Avg %C N=116	System Avg %C N=238	Nat'l Avg %C	Diff Class Minus Nat'l
	NUMERATION & OPERATIONS	8	87	79	76	73	+14
1	Place value & write numbers		100	92	89	85	+15
4	Properties		96	83	79	75	+21
5	Performing operations		87	76	76	82	+5
10	Compare & order		88	90	85	85	+3
12	Place value & write numbers		92	84	85	73	+19
14	Classify by divisibility		88	75	71	65	+23
20	Place value & write numbers		79	63	59	49	+30
22	Compare & order		63	65	67	59	+4
	GEOMETRIC OPERATIONS & PROCEDURES	5	94	78	77	70	+24
2	Geometric shapes		83	72	73	64	+19
9	Perimeter, area, and volume		100	85	87	86	+14
11	Properties, patterns & relationships		100	89	82	71	+29
16	Perimeter, area, and volume		96	75	73	61	+35
18	Geometric shapes		92	69	71	67	+25
	MEASUREMENT	3	82	76	72	64	+18
3	Appropriate unit of measurement		100	89	85	83	+17
21	Time		92	85	83	64	+28
24	Estimate measurement		54	55	48	46	+8
	FRACTIONS, DECIMALS & PERCENTS	3	65	69	68	65	0
7	Create & interpret representations		67	70	69	68	-1
13	Compare & order		79	81	78	71	+8
23	Create & interpret representations		50	55	57	56	-6
	PROBABILITY & STATISTICS	1	88	71	68	61	+27
19	Explain meaning of chance		88	71	68	61	+27
	EQUATIONS, INEQUALITIES & NUMBER SENTENCES	4	94	85	82	75	+19
6	Solve equations		100	93	93	91	+9
8	Use variables & number sentences		96	89	85	80	+16
15	Solve equations		96	85	83	70	+26
17	Use & interpret symbols		83	71	68	59	+24
	ESTIMATE USING STANDARD ROUNDING	7	72	66	64	60	+12
25	In context		79	69	65	61	+18
27	In context		79	72	69	68	+11
30	In context		83	74	75	66	+17
32	In context		58	55	52	51	+7
33	In context		75	68	61	63	+12
34	Without context		67	69	71	62	+5
38	In context		63	55	53	49	+14
	ESTIMATE USING ORDER OF MAGNITUDE	4	66	62	63	64	+2
26	Without context		88	81	83	80	+8
28	Without context		67	65	64	65	+2
35	In context		67	59	65	63	+4
36	Without context		42	44	40	47	-5

Difference (Class Minus Nat'l) -20 0 +20

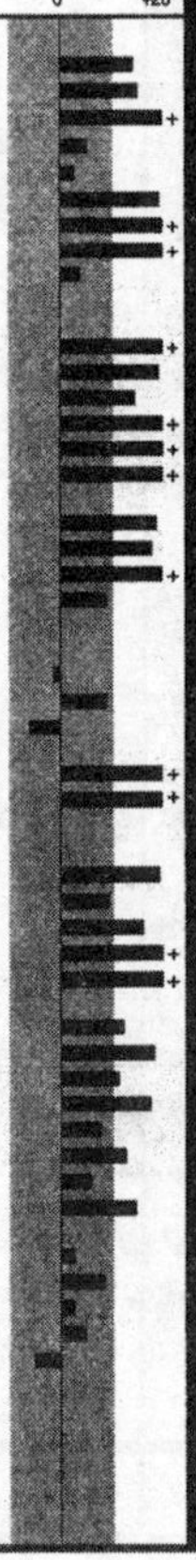

Item No.	MATH CONCEPTS & ESTIMATION (CONTINUED)	Item Count	Class Avg %C N=24	Building Avg %C N=116	System Avg %C N=238	Nat'l Avg %C	Diff Class Minus Nat'l
	OTHER ESTIMATION METHODS	5	38	38	39	37	+1
29	Without context		67	70	68	65	+2
31	Without context		29	30	32	31	-2
37	Without context		38	40	39	36	+2
39	Without context		29	27	31	28	+1
40	In context		25	22	26	26	-1
	MATHEMATICS PROBLEM SOLVING & DATA INTERPRETATION						
	SINGLE-STEP w/: +/-	5	93	87	83	76	+17
1	Whole numbers		96	92	85	84	+12
2	Whole numbers		100	89	81	84	+16
7	Whole numbers		92	87	85	72	+20
10	Whole numbers		92	85	86	70	+22
13	Whole numbers		83	84	79	70	+13
	SINGLE-STEP w/: x/÷	3	65	59	57	62	+3
4	Whole numbers		92	84	80	85	+7
8	Fractions		50	39	41	42	+8
12	Whole numbers		54	55	51	59	-5
	MULTIPLE-STEP	4	63	62	60	58	+5
5	Whole numbers		79	82	79	74	+5
6	Whole numbers		79	75	73	68	+11
14	Whole numbers		67	64	65	66	+1
15	Whole numbers		25	26	24	25	0
	PROBLEM-SOLVING STRATEGIES	4	85	71	69	65	+20
3	Insufficient information		92	80	75	84	+8
9	Insufficient information		96	77	77	71	+25
11	Method of solution		63	56	53	44	+19
16	Insufficient information		88	72	69	61	+27
	READ AMOUNTS	3	81	64	62	65	+16
19	Bar and line graphs		63	42	45	44	+19
21	Circle graph		96	82	77	80	+16
24	Bar and line graphs		83	69	65	70	+13
	COMPARE QUANTITIES	6	53	46	47	48	+5
17	Ranks		63	54	51	51	+12
18	Sums and differences		67	61	63	64	+3
22	Ratios		63	56	58	62	+1
25	Sums and differences		58	42	45	46	+12
26	Sums and differences		42	37	35	38	+4
27	Ratios		25	27	31	29	-4
	INTERPRET RELATIONSHIPS	2	56	48	45	49	+7
20	Conclusions		42	35	25	30	+12
23	Underlying relationships		71	61	65	68	+3

Difference (Class Minus Nat'l) -20 0 +20

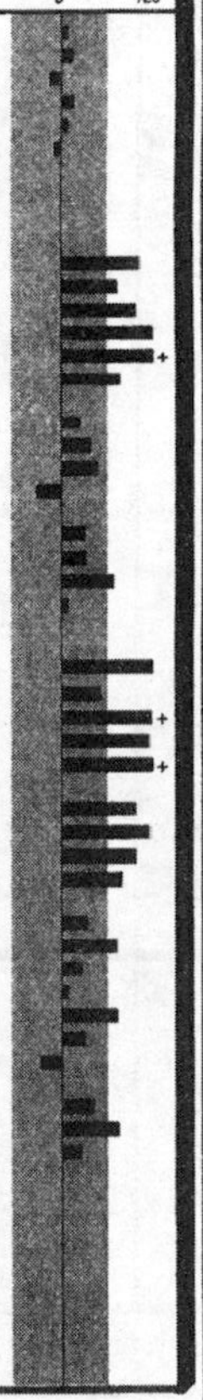

THE RIVERSIDE PUBLISHING COMPANY
a Houghton Mifflin company

Source: H. D. Hoover, A. N. Hieronymus, D. A. Frisbie, and S. Dunbar, 1993b. Copyright © 1993 by The University of Iowa. All rights reserved. Reproduced from the *Iowa Tests of Basic Skills, Interpretive Guide for Teachers and Counselors,* Levels 9–14, p. 60, with permission of The Riverside Publishing Company.

FIGURE 16.2 Example of a building report showing the performance of a school's grade 4 students on each subtest. This report shows (a) how the local 90th, 75th, 50th, 25th, and 10th percentile students performed relative to the national norm group; (b) how the local quarters of the 4th graders performed relative to the national norm group; (c) how many local students were in each quarter of the national norm group, and (d) what percentage of the local students were in each quarter of the national norm group.

TerraNova

MULTIPLE ASSESSMENTS

Evaluation Summary Report

School: WINFIELD

Grade 4

Purpose

This page gives administrators numeric information to evaluate the overall effectiveness of the educational program. This page displays a comprehensive numeric description of your students' achievement. This page is for those who prefer to analyze the data in tabular form.

Simulated Data

No. of Students: 89

Form/Level: A-14
Test Date: 11/01/99   Scoring: PATTERN (IRT)
QM: 08   Norms Date: 1996

District: Winfield USD

City/State: Metropolis, CA

CTB McGraw-Hill   Page 4

	Reading	Lang.	Math	Total Score*	Science	Social Studies
Number of Students	86	87	89	86	88	88
Mean Scores & Standard Deviations						
Grade Mean Equivalent	4.6	5.0	4.5	4.8	4.6	4.3
Standard Deviation	1.5	2.0	1.9	1.3	1.7	1.8
Mean Normal Curve Equiv.	48.0	52.0	49.5	51.4	49.9	47.0
Standard Deviation	13.9	14.9	19.3	15.7	18.2	18.1
NP of the Mean NCE	46	54	49	53	50	44
Mean Scale Scores	696.7	715.3	694.4	696.7	700.5	696.1
Standard Deviation	35.2	33.2	45.4	31.0	40.5	48.3
Local Percentiles/Quartiles						
90th Local Percentile						
National Percentile	84.3	91.2	89.0	88.3	88.9	86.1
Grade Equivalent	8.5	9.9	7.8	7.4	8.2	9.0
Normal Curve Equiv.	71.2	78.3	76.4	75.4	76.2	73.0
Scale Score	748.1	765.3	754.4	744.2	756.6	758.5
75th Local Percentile Q3						
National Percentile	62.8	75.4	72.3	70.2	74.3	65.6
Grade Equivalent	5.4	6.8	5.8	5.5	5.8	5.4
Normal Curve Equiv.	56.9	64.4	62.7	61.0	63.9	58.7
Scale Score	719.8	741.5	725.3	719.7	731.3	726.6
50th Percentile (median) Q2						
National Percentile	41.8	53.3	54.0	52.7	56.7	49.8
Grade Equivalent	4.3	4.8	4.8	4.6	4.9	4.6
Normal Curve Equiv.	45.9	52.0	52.0	50.2	53.3	50.6
Scale Score	695.3	719.3	704.0	699.7	711.3	707.8
25th Local Percentile Q1						
National Percentile	30.0	36.1	24.8	30.1	26.0	29.0
Grade Equivalent	3.6	3.5	3.3	3.7	3.4	3.5
Normal Curve Equiv.	39.0	42.4	35.5	38.9	36.5	38.5
Scale Score	678.0	698.2	665.5	678.0	647.0	679.0
10th Local Percentile						
National Percentile	12.1	15.5	10.9	13.2	11.0	12.3
Grade Equivalent	2.6	2.7	2.9	2.9	2.6	2.7
Normal Curve Equiv.	25.2	29.0	24.3	26.1	24.1	25.6
Scale Score	635.3	661.0	639.7	646.9	647.0	644.3
National Quarters						
Local/Number Per Quarter 76-99	10	22	19	16	20	13
51-75	24	25	26	30	27	30
26-50	38	26	21	25	20	26
01-25	14	14	23	15	21	19
Local/Percent Per Quarter 76-99	11.6	25.3	21.3	18.6	22.7	14.8
51-75	27.9	28.7	29.2	34.9	30.7	34.1
26-50	44.2	29.9	23.6	29.1	22.7	29.5
01-25	16.3	16.1	25.8	17.4	23.9	21.6

*Total Score consists of Reading, Language, and Mathematics.

Source: From *Information systems: Score reports for TerraNova, including CTBS, Multiple Assessments, and SUPERA,* p. 31. Monterey, CA: CTB/McGraw-Hill, 1997. Reproduced with permission of McGraw-Hill Companies, Inc.

FIGURE 16.3 Example of a computer-prepared narrative report on an individual student's standardized test performance. The report is meant to be sent home to parents.

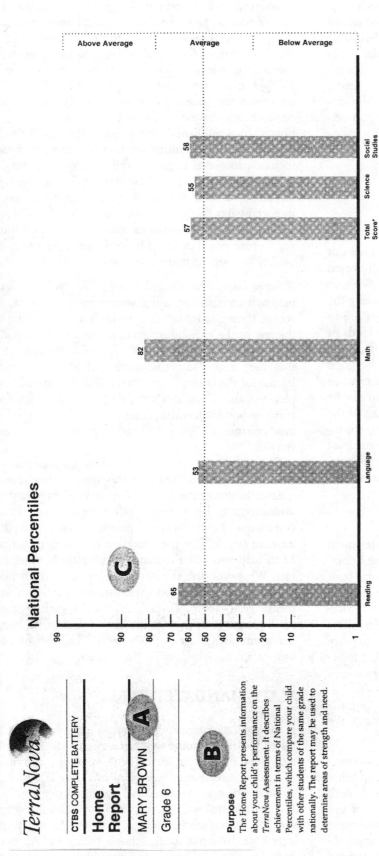

TerraNova

CTBS COMPLETE BATTERY

Home Report

MARY BROWN 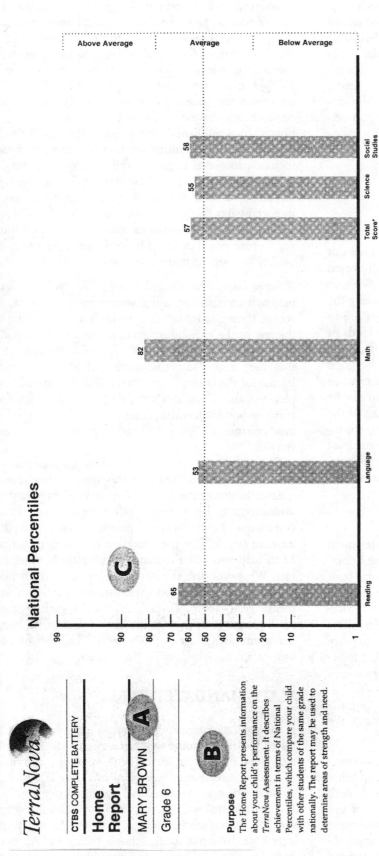A

Grade 6

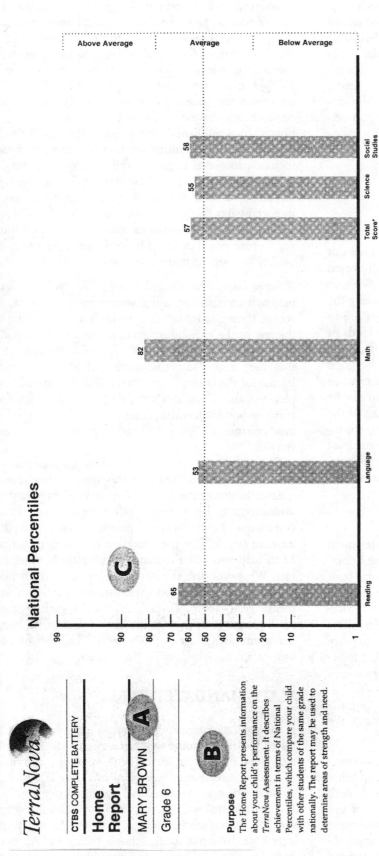B

Purpose

The Home Report presents information about your child's performance on the *TerraNova* Assessment. It describes achievement in terms of National Percentiles, which compare your child with other students of the same grade nationally. The report may be used to determine areas of strength and need.

National Percentiles

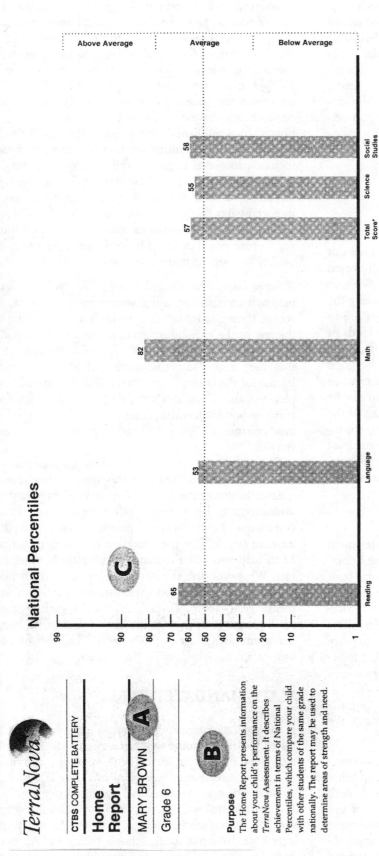C

*Total Score consists of Reading, Language, and Math.

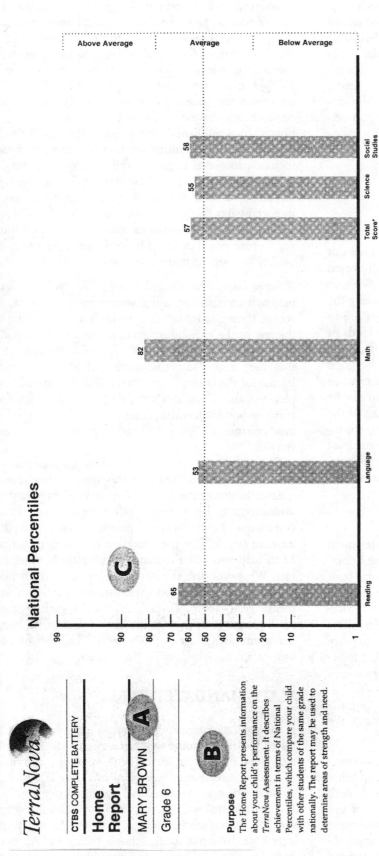D

Observations

The height of each bar shows your child's National Percentile score on each test. The percentile scale is shown on the left. The graph shows that your child achieved a National Percentile of 65 in Reading. This means your child scored higher than approximately 65 percent of the students in the nation.

The scale on the right side of the graph shows score ranges that represent average, above average, and below average

in terms of National Percentiles. Average is defined as the middle 50 percent of students nationally. Your child has five out of six National Percentile scores in the average range. One score is above the average range and no scores are below the average range.

See the reverse side for more detailed information about your child's strengths and needs.

Simulated Data

A

Birthdate: 02/08/85
Special Codes:
A B C D E F G H I J K L M N O P Q R S T
3 5 9 7 3 2   1 1 1
Form/Level: A-16
Test Date: 04/01/97   Scoring: IRT (Pattern)
QM: 08   Norms Date: 1996
Class:
School:
District:

City/State:

Source: From *Teacher's guide to TerraNova*, Figure 3, p. 150. Monterey, CA: CTB/McGraw-Hill, 1997. Reprinted with permission of McGraw-Hill Companies, Inc.

interpretative services for schools using their products. Some publishers sell the product and certain standard services (such as computer printouts summarizing test results for a school district) but do not provide knowledgeable consultants who can advise a school on particular problems or even on how to interpret their results in general. A school official who is planning to purchase a survey battery should explore fully with the publisher's sales representative the nature and cost of technical support services that will come with the test battery.

NONSTANDARDIZED ACHIEVEMENT TESTS

Disadvantages

If a test is not standardized, a publisher has not tried out the assessment materials and has not collected student-based data concerning how well the test is functioning. Without empirical data there is little hope for either improving the assessment or verifying that its intended purposes are in fact being accomplished. A great many of these kinds of assessments, however, are purchased and used by teachers.

These nonempirically documented tests *may* be good tests, but because there is no documentation, you can't be certain. As you read in Chapter 3, validity should not be an article of faith: It should be judged on the basis of the support given by a variety of empirical data. Unfortunately, many school officials are ignorant of the principles of assessment validation and purchase such assessments, so these publishers stay in business while children suffer.

Textbook-Based Tests

Appeal   Teacher's editions of texts often have assessment tasks at the end of chapters or at the back of the books. Some curriculum materials have assessment tasks built into the learning materials; others have separate tests for photocopying or duplicating. These assessment procedures appeal to a teacher for two reasons: (1) If you follow the textbook closely, the tests' topics appear to very closely match what you teach; and (2) they appear to relieve you of the responsibility for creating quality assessments. From a publisher's perspective, adding tests to curriculum materials is usually a marketing tool: Making the curriculum materials appealing to teachers increases the likelihood of adoption.

Disadvantages   The quality of assessments that come with curriculum materials varies widely. The publisher rarely uses trial data to improve these assessment materials. Trying out assessment materials for purposes of improvement is especially important when the assessment tasks are performance tasks, because wording strongly influences how students interpret the tasks, and scoring rubrics need to be refined using them with actual student responses. Also, a text-series author is seldom proficient in assessment development. The publisher's editorial staff do not edit the tasks for their technical assessment merits using checklists such as those found in Tables 12.3 and 12.5. Sometimes the keyed answers to the questions are incorrect or contradict what is in the curriculum materials. (When this latter error was pointed out for two items on a unit test, one teacher we know insisted that such contradictions were impossible because the test was printed by a publisher! Don't follow this teacher's example.) Often the questions on these assessment materials focus on low-level cognitive skills such as recalling facts and definitions. Despite these flaws, many teachers place unwarranted faith in these tests and use them to make important day-to-day decisions about students' learning progress. Chapter 5 explains why you are not fulfilling your professional responsibility if you use these poor-quality assessment materials.

What to Do   What should you do when your curriculum materials contain appealing assessment tasks? First, don't accept their quality on face value, no matter how good the rest of the curriculum materials are. Look carefully at the embedded or "homework" type of exercises to be sure that they assess something worthwhile for students to learn, that the answers are correct, and that the tasks completely match your state's standards and your school district's important learning targets. Second, be prepared for disappointment: You may need to rewrite these exercises yourself.

Third, review carefully any tests or quizzes that come with the materials. You use the scores from tests and quizzes to determine students' grades, so you want these assessments to be of high quality. Review each item for correctness, importance, and match to standards and your learning targets. Use the checklists in Chapters 7 through 12 to help you edit the items, revising them when necessary. When you use the items in class, use your students' responses to them to help you discover flaws and correct them (see Chapter 14). Teachers should work together in small groups to review and improve assessment materials that come with curriculum materials. This can be done a little at a time, over two or three years.

STATE-MANDATED TESTS

It has become common for states to require students to sit for official **state-mandated assessments**. State-mandated tests vary greatly in their focus, makeup, and quality. Most state assessments have accountability as a focus. Accountability may be at the school district, school building, or student level. At the district or school level there may be serious consequences if scores do not improve over time. In some states, schools failing to improve can be "taken over" by a team appointed by the state. In some states, teachers may be rewarded or financial assistance may be given to help remediate poorly performing students. When the school district or building is held accountable, testing occurs at only certain grade levels: 4, 8, and 11; or 3, 5, 10; etc. In such programs individual students often do not receive their results; or if they do, little is done with them because the results are not of high reliability for individuals. Thus, the test may be a high-stakes test for a school, but a low-stakes test for a student.

In some states, individual student accountability is in place. This is usually in the form of a graduation test. The test may cover basic skills or be more challenging, depending on the state. Often a basic skills graduation test is given in grade 9 or 10, so that students with low scores may be forewarned and placed into remedial programs to improve their skills. Graduation tests are high stakes for students.

State assessments are usually based on a state's curriculum framework or standards. A national movement, Goals 2000, has increased the pressure on states to develop or adopt standards with corresponding assessments.[2] The trend had been to make standards that are challenging to students rather than to limit them to minimum competencies or basic skills.

State assessments are usually built and marked by a proprietary agency under a state contact. Several arrangements have been tried by different states. Some states have simply adopted one of the standardized tests we have just discussed. Test publishers tender bids in response to a state's request for proposals. Usually, the publisher winning the bid uses a secure form of the survey battery (it is parallel to the unsecured form) and supplements the batttery with additional test items that match those state standards not covered by the original battery.

Other states contract with a test publisher to develop a custom test to match its standards. The contractor may be asked to develop either basic skills or more challenging assessments. States have experimented with large-scale performance assessments and portfolios, with mixed success. The latter are costly to develop; time-consuming to administer; costly to score; and difficult to craft to high technical standards of reliability, validity, and year-to-year comparability. Some states have persisted, and done well; but many returned to either multiple-choice testing or a mixture of multiple-choice testing with a small portion of performance assessment and writing assessments.

State assessment programs are often spawned and killed by state legislatures and governors. Authentic and performance assessments are often seen as radical reforms requiring students to express their opinions, values, and personal creativity. Conservative persons may view these as inappropriate for students. They may wish to assure that students be held accountable for challenging standards that do not require students to learn "liberal" values and ideas. Politically liberal persons may wish students to think beyond what is conventional, to read and evaluate materials that challenge traditional values—or that question government, authority, or established religion. Assessments may be seen by this side as an opportunity for reforming educational practice as well as the curriculum. You can read about state assessment programs and their controversies in a weekly periodical called *Education Week* (www.educationweek.com).

As a teacher, you will no doubt find yourself working in a controversial state assessment environment. Legislators tend to blame teachers for what is wrong with the educational system (but seldom give them credit for what is right with it). You will be required to implement and participate in your state's assessment program.

The principles you have learned in this book can be applied to state assessments. You may be required to defend your state's assessments using these principles. You may also wish to offer constructive criticism using them. The principles in Appendices A, B, and C should be applied as well.

You can usually find out about your state's assessment program through its education department's Internet web site. You can locate information about a state's assessment program through the web site of the state's department of education. The links to each state's education department are found through the U.S. Department of Education's National Center on Educational Statistics (www.ed.gov/Programs/bastmp/SEA.htm). The web sites of individual schools can be located by searching www.gsn.org/hotlist/index.html.

The consensus is that state assessment programs wanting to change classroom practices must place great emphasis on teacher development, because assessment programs alone do not improve schools (Linn & Baker, 1997; McDonnell, 1997; Smith, 1997). In addition, compromises due to financial constraints, time pressures, technology limitations, and political pressures usually mean that the original plans for state assessment need to be scaled back. This may result in failing to implement key components such as improving classroom assessment practices, using performance assessments, or failing to implement appropriate teacher development programs.

USING STANDARDIZED TEST RESULTS

Appropriate Uses of Test Results

Within-Classroom Uses How can you use standardized test results? Here are some suggestions (Hieronymus, 1976) of **within-classroom use of test results**:

1. *Describe the educational developmental levels of each student.* Use this information about the differences among your students to modify or adapt instruction to accommodate individual students' needs.

---

[2]For more information about the National Education Goals Panel go to *www.negp.gov*.

2. *Describe specific qualitative strengths and weaknesses in students.* These strengths vary from one curriculum area to another. Use this information to remediate deficiencies and capitalize on strengths.

3. *Describe the extent to which a student has attained the prerequisites needed to go on to new or advanced learning.* Combine these results with a student's classroom performance to make recommendations for placement.

4. *Describe commonalties among students.* Use this information to group students for more efficient instruction.

5. *Students' performances on clusters of items help you to describe students' performances with respect to specific instructional targets.* Use this information to make immediate instructional decisions.

6. *Provide students with operational descriptions of what kinds and levels of performances are expected of them.* Discuss these expectations with students and how you can work with them to fulfill them.

7. *Provide students and parents with feedback about students' progress toward learning goals.* Use this information to establish a plan for home and school to work together.

Survey tests measure broad, long-term educational goals rather than immediate learning outcomes. It may take all year for a student to learn to read well enough, for example, to show some sign of improvement on a survey test. Meanwhile, however, the student may learn many specific skills and reading strategies. The student may perform well on your classroom assessments of these immediate learning targets.

Norm-referenced survey information is not likely to give you the fine-grain details you need to design an individual student's daily or weekly instructional plans. Assessment procedures that you craft yourself provide information about a student's performance in more delimited areas. They are likely to be more useful to you for daily or weekly instructional planning than are ordinary survey tests.

Standardized tests are often administered in the fall, after you have organized the class, and the answer sheets are sent away for scoring. By the time you receive students' results, several weeks of schooling have already passed. Such circumstances work against the possibility of using standardized tests for immediate instructional decisions. This is not to say, however, that you should disregard the results and refuse to modify your teaching plans if the results indicate otherwise.

Another use of standardized test results is to confirm or corroborate your judgment about a student's general educational development. It is important to realize that no single source of information about a student is entirely valid—be that source your own observations, results from assessments you developed, or results on standardized tests. Standardized tests can provide additional informa-

tion that may alert you to the need to consider a particular student further.

Extra-Classroom Uses Standardized survey tests are also useful for extra-classroom purposes. Among these **external uses of test results** are (Hieronymus, 1976) the following:

1. *The average scores of a group (class, building, or school system) help school officials to make decisions about curriculum or instructional changes.* The results provide one important piece of information if the tasks they present are judged by school officials to be relevant and important to the goals of the local community.

2. *Help educational evaluators to describe the relative effectiveness of alternate methods of instruction and some of the factors moderating their effectiveness.*

3. *Help educational researchers to describe the relative effectiveness of innovations or experiments in education.*

4. *Help school superintendents to describe to school boards and other stakeholders the relative effectiveness of the local educational enterprise.* However, school board members should realize that no single instrument can account for all the factors that affect the learning of students in a particular community.

All of these purposes relate in some way to accountability. But accountability purposes are not served well if the assessment instrument used does not correspond to what is happening in the classroom. Further, when your school officials overemphasize standardized tests, pressures may intrude into your classroom practices. As a result, you may believe that having the students "pass the test" is more important than teaching them the important abilities defined in the broader curriculum framework. This unfortunate attitude ultimately leads to a narrowing of the curriculum in undesirable ways, such as teaching only those things that will appear on the test and not teaching those things that will not appear on the test.

Inappropriate Uses of Test Results

Criticisms Criticisms of norm-referenced standardized achievement tests are very common. For some critics, the very idea of a commercial, external, norm-referenced, summative, and/or quantitative device for measuring educational outcomes is repugnant and incredible. Of course, any assessment procedure—standardized or not, normreferenced or criterion-referenced, formative or summative, external or teacher-made, qualitative and quantitative—can be misused. Much of this misuse, moreover, comes not from characteristics inherent in a particular procedure, but from the invalid claims that persons make for some assessments and the unscrupulous way(s) in which an assessment might be used. Throughout this text, we discuss appropriate uses and emphasize the need to validate claims made for assessments. You must use professional judgment in administering and interpreting all assessment procedures. The *Code of Professional Responsibilities in Educational Measurement* (Appendix C) and the *Code of Fair Testing Practices in Education* (Appendix B) describe your responsibilities with regard to standardized achievement tests.

Figure 16.4 summarizes some of the many criticisms of standardized survey achievement batteries. As the figure shows, criticisms may focus on some intrinsic characteristic of a test, such as its content coverage; something which is not part of a test, such as its failure to test certain student characteristics; or the effects of using a test, such as inappropriately classifying or labeling a student.

Airasian (1979) discussed several things about these three domains of criticisms:

1. *Critics often describe perceived misuses of tests using arguments from more than one of the three domains.* For example, they may say that tests (a) measure only a small portion of what is taught in the classroom (intrinsic characteristic), (b) do not measure the real goals of an educational program (characteristics not measured), and (c) foster undesirable changes in school curricula or teacher emphasis (effects of testing).

FIGURE 16.4 Examples of three categories of criticisms of standardized, norm-referenced, and survey achievement tests.

A. Criticisms directed toward an intrinsic test characteristic:
1. Tests assume that everyone values the skills tested.
2. Tests assume a homogenous culture and/or a common curriculum.
3. Tests are biased, favoring white, middle class pupils.
4. Tests assume that approximately half the pupils are below average.
5. Tests are too impersonal, vague, undemocratic, and/or irrelevant.
6. Tests cover only a small fraction of what schools try to accomplish.
7. Tests are invalid measures of behaviors specifically learned in schools.

B. Criticisms directed toward a characteristic not measured by a test:
1. Tests are not diagnostic.
2. Tests do not measure the objectives of innovative instructional programs.
3. Tests do not measure creativity, interest, initiative, and/or values.
4. Tests compare students rather than measure an individual's learning.

C. Criticisms directed toward the effects of using a test:
1. Children are "labeled" (or "mislabeled").
2. Test use alters the school curriculum by encouraging teaching toward the test.
3. Tests result in competition among learners.
4. Tests cause fear.

Source: Adapted from "A Perspective on the Uses and Misuses of Standardized Achievement Tests" by P. W. Airasian, 1979, *Measurement in Education, 10*(3). Copyright 1980 by the National Council on Measurement in Education. Reprinted by permission of the publisher.

2. *Some criticisms are contradictory.* The same test may be criticized by some persons because its focus is too narrow and by others because its scores are influenced by too broad a range of human characteristics.

3. *Many of the criticisms can be overcome.* You may overcome many problems by either using the test in the way it was intended to be used or by choosing another, more appropriate test.

4. *A single test cannot be expected to measure the "whole person."* Human characteristics are too rich and too diverse to be assessed by any one assessment. It is an open question, furthermore, whether some human characteristics (interest, attitudes, values, emotional states, etc.) ought to be assessed regularly by a school district.

5. *A criticism of a test may or may not be the same thing as a misuse of a test.* Educators can criticize a test for not measuring a certain student characteristic (e.g., feelings toward someone), but such a failure may not be a misuse. Sometimes, measuring that characteristic (feelings toward someone) may be the misuse (by violating a student's privacy). (See Chapter 5 and Appendix C for professional responsibilities toward assessment.)

Misuses You should always strive to use the results of achievement assessments—survey batteries, performance assessments, or authentic tasks—in valid and professional ways. One of the "fatal errors" you will be tempted to make in your career is to use a single assessment result to make an important decision about a student. For example, you may be tempted to base a student's grade exclusively on the student's examination score, ignoring daily classroom performance or the student's personal situation when the student took the test. Similar misuses are made by teachers and school administrators regarding standardized test results. *Inappropriate* uses of a survey achievement battery are listed here. You should also note that using a state's assessment in these ways is also inappropriate (Hoover et al., 1993b).

1. *Placing a student in a special instructional program solely on the results from a standardized achievement test.* Special programs include remedial programs as well as programs for the gifted and talented. School officials can overcome this misuse by using many pieces of information when making these decisions. They should include students' daily classroom performance, teacher's assessments, and results from other assessments in addition to the survey achievement battery.

2. *Retaining a student in a grade solely on the results from a standardized test.* First, you should recognize that retaining students is very much an open educational question, and the common practice of retention in the early grades

often does not help students (Karweit & Wasik, 1992). Second, your daily observation, teaching, and evaluation of a student are the most relevant types of information that a school official should use when making this decision. Third, parents have information about a child that school officials and teachers do not. Although standardized achievement test scores may have some bearing on this type of decision, their importance should have little weight in the final decision.

3. *Judging an entire school program's quality solely on the basis of the results from a standardized achievement test.* School programs are complex. They teach many things other than those assessed by standardized tests. You know, too, that even within a curriculum area assessed by a test, there is no perfect match between what is assessed and all the instructional targets in the curriculum framework. Table 18.1 lists many of the school and community factors that should be considered when using survey battery scores for curriculum evaluation. School officials can overcome misuse by aggressively placing program evaluation decisions in a broader context of the full curriculum framework and the full context of school and community factors.

4. *Using a survey achievement battery to prescribe specific content teachers should teach at certain grade levels.* You know that a test only samples the many tasks that the students could be asked to perform. Although test tasks are important, each task is not an end in itself. Because the tasks are a sample from this larger domain, they allow you to generalize beyond them to estimate a student's performance on the domain. If school officials manipulate the sample or try to limit the curriculum domain primarily to the sample appearing on a test, they destroy the ability to generalize. School officials may overcome this misuse by developing curriculum frameworks using appropriate principles drawn from educational development, child development, learning, and the subject-matter disciplines. They should then select the test that best matches the important curriculum learning targets, rather than vice versa.

5. *Attributing a student's poor assessment results to only one cause.* Sometimes a teacher or school administrator interprets a student's assessment result as though it were entirely the result of the student's own shortcomings rather than the result of several interacting conditions. A student's poor assessment result may very well reflect the quality of previous teaching, the nature of the student's home environment, or other personal experiences.

6. *School officials or parents trying to blame the teacher if the class does poorly on a standardized test.* Before a person can attribute the rise (or fall) of a class's test scores solely to a particular teacher, that person would have to consider the influence on the scores of each of several factors: Did the content of the test match the breadth and emphasis of what was taught in the classroom? Did the students in this year's class have, on the whole, better or worse general school aptitude than classes in the past (or classes assigned to other teachers)? Were students in this (or another) class taught the answers to the items or otherwise given unfair advantage? Did last year's teacher do an exceptionally good (or poor) job of teaching, and did this influence carry over to this year? What home factors related to the students' successes (or lack thereof)? Did the school principal (or other instructional leader) facilitate or inhibit the teacher's teaching or the students' learning? You can probably name other factors to consider when trying to find the reasons for a class's test results. Unlike an automobile manufacturer or an owner of a pizzeria, schools and teachers have relatively little control over their raw materials and the conditions under which they must operate (Feldt, 1976).

MULTILEVEL SURVEY BATTERIES

A great many achievement survey batteries are available in the marketplace. (Each edition of the *Mental Measurements Yearbook* lists dozens of different tests.) Here, in alphabetical order, are the most widely used batteries. The grade ranges they cover are noted in parentheses.

> *California Achievement Tests* (K–12)
> *Comprehensive Assessment Program Achievement Series* (K–12)
> *Comprehensive Tests of Basic Skills TerraNova* (K–12)
> *Iowa Tests of Basic Skills* (K–9)
> *Iowa Tests of Educational Development* (9–12)
> *Metropolitan Achievement Test* (K–12)
> *Peabody Individual Achievement Test* (K–adult)
> *Sequential Test of Educational Progress* (K–12)
> *SRA Achievement Series* (K–12)
> *Stanford Achievement Test Series* (K–12)
> *STS Educational Development Series* (2–12)
> *Tests of Achievement and Proficiency* (9–12)
> *The 3-R's Test* (K–12)
> *Wide Range Achievement Test* (K–adult)

These are all group-administered tests, except for the *Peabody* and the *Wide Range*, which are individually administered. Publishers are listed in Appendices J and K. Details about each battery can be obtained from the publishers' catalogues. Critical reviews are found in the *Mental Measurements Yearbooks*, *Test Critiques*, and other sources identified in Chapter 18.

Group-Administered Survey Batteries

Group-administered survey batteries have several subtests, each assessing a different curricular area. Although each multilevel survey battery is quite different in the content and skills it emphasizes, Table 16.1 shows areas typically measured by each of several batteries. Separate scores are provided for several (usually six to eight) areas; different publishers may have different names for an area.

Individually Administered Surveys

Individually administered achievement batteries are commonly used for students with special needs, such as students with disabilities who otherwise would have difficulty taking assessments in group settings. Students who cannot be assessed in group settings often can be validly assessed in individual sessions where the assessment administrator can provide the special accommodations they need and can establish greater rapport than is possible in a group.

Sometimes individual achievement batteries are used as "screening" tests to identify students with learning difficulties, or as part of a broader series of individual assessments when a school psychologist conducts a general psychological evaluation. A school district may use individual achievement survey batteries to assess the general educational development of a newly transferred student, or as a double-check on a previously administered group survey test when the results are being questioned for a particular student. Because both the content and norms of an individual assessment are different from the group test, you should proceed very cautiously when double-checking. You can expect a student's results from the two types of tests to correspond only very roughly.

Two commonly administered individual survey achievement tests are the *Wide Range Achievement Test* (WRAT) and the *Peabody Individual Achievement Test* (PIAT). These single instruments contain items that span many ages or grades (essentially ages 5 to adult). Thus, by their very nature, they contain very few items specifically associated with a given age or grade level. Such tests do not have as much in-depth coverage as group survey tests that have separate levels for each age or grade level. This comment is not necessarily a criticism of these tests. The purpose of such wide-range tests is obtaining a quick assessment of a student's strengths in several basic curricular areas. This quickly obtained assessment is used to direct the teacher to the appropriate relatively weak areas for a more in-depth diagnostic follow-up.

The PIAT is administered using an easel format. The student does not write responses to the multiple-choice items; they must only say or point to the option. Within each subtest the items are arranged in order of difficulty. A student does not take each item; a starting point (called a *basal level*) and an ending point (called a *ceiling level*) are established, based on the student's pattern of correct answers and errors.

Using Results to Plan Instruction

Suggestions for using survey battery information in planning classroom instruction are outlined in Figure 16.5.

Other procedures for reviewing test scores appear in Chapter 17. You should review these at this time.

CHOOSING STANDARDIZED TESTS

Survey Achievement Battery Selection

As mentioned, you must examine and review each test individually to decide whether it is appropriate for your school. School officials should keep the following advice in mind before selecting an *elementary school survey battery* (Gronlund, 1976):

1. Survey batteries measure only part of the outcomes desired for elementary schools. Use additional assessment procedures to evaluate the other outcomes.
2. Specific content in subjects such as social studies and science may become dated quickly. Tests designed to measure broad cognitive skills or levels of educational development become dated less quickly.
3. Tests measuring broad cognitive skills or levels of educational development need to be supplemented by teacher-made or standardized tests of specific content.
4. Each battery has a different mix and emphasis of content and behavior; each is accompanied by various kinds of interpretive aids. Examine a test battery carefully before deciding to purchase it.

Because so much variation exists in high school curricula, choosing a survey battery for this educational level is difficult. Choosing a test at this level requires a rather complete knowledge of the major curriculum emphasis and philosophy of a school. School officials should keep the following points in mind before selecting a high school test battery (Gronlund, 1976):

1. Survey batteries that emphasize basic skills (reading, mathematics, language) may be more useful as measures of high school readiness than as measures of high school outcomes (unless a high school program were especially directed toward basic skills development).
2. Some tests are more oriented toward testing specific content than educational development broadly defined. If you want a content-oriented test, review each item on the test carefully to see if the test measures what the school intends.
3. Tests stressing the measurement of levels of educational development that cut across several subject areas rather than measure knowledge and specific content tend to measure more complex skills and global processes.
4. The variety of course offerings at the high school level makes it more necessary than at the elementary level to carefully examine the content of each survey battery.
5. You may find it necessary to supplement a high school survey battery with assessments measuring content knowledge of specific subjects.

FIGURE 16.5   A systematic procedure for using the results of a standardized achievement test to plan instruction for a class.

Step 1. Review the class report to determine weaknesses
Use a report that summarizes performance on clusters of items for all students in your class. Within each curriculum area, identify on which clusters your students need improvement most.

Use your knowledge of the subject and of your students to verify the areas of greatest need. Don't be afraid to contradict the picture given by the test if you have good evidence that supports the fact that the students know more than they have shown on the test.

Step 2. Establish instructional priorities
Review your list of instructional needs. Put them into an order for instruction. Be sure to teach prerequisite needs first. Concentrate on the most important areas—those that will help students in their further understanding of concepts and principles in the subject.

Step 3. Organize the class for instruction
The test information may help you to form small groups of students who have similar instructional needs. Alternately, you could form small groups that have students at different levels of learning so that those who already know the material can help instruct those who have not yet mastered it. You will need to use your own resources to organize your class, as the test cannot do that directly.

Step 4. Plan your instruction before you begin
Be clear about your instructional targets. Look at the test items to get an idea of the types of tasks you want students to learn to do, but remember that you are trying to teach generalizable skills and abilities. The tasks on the test are only a small sample of the domain of tasks implied by the curriculum.

Look to the curriculum to see where the areas of need fit into the larger scheme. Teach within this larger framework, rather than narrowing your teaching to the test items.

Create your own assessment instrument for each of the areas of need so you can clarify what you will expect students to do at the end of the lessons. Organize your teaching activities to accomplish these ends.

Step 5. Assess students' progress toward your instructional targets
Monitor students' progress through both informal and formal assessments. Observe students as they complete the assignments you give them to see if they are making progress toward your learning targets. Use performance and paper-and-pencil assessments to monitor their progress in more formal ways.

Adjust your teaching for those students who are not making appropriate progress. Give feedback to students by showing them what they are expected to do (i.e., the learning target), explaining to them what their performance is like now, how it is different from the target performance, and what they have yet to learn to accomplish the target performance.

Step 6. Carry out summative assessment
Use a variety of assessment techniques to assess each student so that you are certain that the student has learned the target and can apply the concepts and principles to appropriate realistic situations. Use performance assessments, extended responses, and objective items in appropriate combinations. Do not limit your assessment to only one format.

---

6. A practical consideration is the continuity of measurement from elementary to secondary levels. This often means purchasing a high school battery from the same publisher as the elementary school battery used.

Complementing Your State Assessment

If your state mandates its own assessment, you will need to take its coverage into account before choosing a published standardized test. Most state assessments have accountability as their main purpose. This is not the case for a published standardized test, which is used primarily to measure individual students' educational growth. Keep the following points in mind if you are trying to select a standardized multilevel achievement test when you are also faced with a state-mandated assessment.

1. *All things being equal, choose a standardized test that requires students to demonstrate learning that is very consistent with your state's standards or curriculum framework.*

2. *If your community does not like the focus of your state-mandated assessment, choose a multilevel achievement test that reflects the community's concerns.* For example, your community may not wish to limit assessment to the

higher-order thinking and complex problem solving on which the state assessment focuses. The community may wish to know whether basic skills such as computation, reading comprehension, English writing mechanics, and spelling are being learned.

3. *Plan to use the chosen test over a period of at least 5 years, so that you can track changes in your school district.*

4. *Test at those grade levels not tested by the state-mandated assessment in order not to overburden students and teachers.*

Uses for Single-Subject Tests

If you are teaching in a single subject area, such as Algebra I or 19th-Century English Literature, you may be interested in assessing how well students are performing in just that subject. Multilevel tests are often inappropriate for such courses, because they span several grades with relatively few items and thus lack content relevance for a particular course. *For most purposes, a teacher-made test for a subject is most appropriate: It is closest to the course content and contains the emphasis you desire.*

Single-subject or course tests have been found most useful, however, for such purposes as pretesting to determine the general background of students coming into a course, advanced placement in college courses, exemption from required or introductory courses, contests and scholarship programs directed toward general knowledge of a particular subject, and granting college credit for knowledge acquired by independent study, work experience, or other types of nontraditional education. Many tests for specific subjects are listed in the *Mental Measurements Yearbooks*.

ADMINISTERING STANDARDIZED TESTS

Standard Administration Procedures

It is certain that you will be required to administer a standardized assessment to your students, most likely one or more per year. These assessments may be standardized achievement tests, performance assessments, or assessments mandated by your state department of education. Part of the validity of your students' results will depend on how well you follow the standardization procedure specified in the teacher's administration manual.

There are two important areas of assessment administration that you directly control and that directly affect the validity of your students' results. One area is how you prepare yourself and the students for the assessment. Standardized assessments, regardless of whether they are performance or multiple-choice formats, require students to be aware of (1) the fact that they will be assessed, (2) on what they will be assessed, (3) the reasons for the assessment, and (4) how their results will be used. Students should be prepared to do their best. You must also be prepared to administer, and perhaps to mark, the assessments. In this regard you must be familiar with the assessment procedures and materials, prepare the assessment environment so that a valid assessment can be done, understand how to administer the assessment, including what you are permitted to say to the students, and know how to prepare the students for the assessment.

A second area in which you need to perform well is in actually administering the assessment. Valid assessment results will depend on how well you carry out your responsibilities during the administration phase. You need to follow the stated procedures exactly for the assessment result to be comparable across students and for the norms, if any, to be usable. Also, you need to monitor students to be sure they are following directions, marking their answers in the proper manner, and otherwise attending to the tasks. Figure 16.6 is a checklist of performances necessary to administer a standardized assessment procedure without lowering its validity.

Student Practice for Standardized Assessments

The question of what type of practice to give students before they take a standardized assessment is an important one for you to answer. There is some controversy among

FIGURE 16.6 A checklist for administering a standardized assessment procedure to your students.

Before the assessment date
1. Prepare a schedule for assessment, including dates and times for each component you need to administer.
2. Discuss the upcoming assessments with the students.
    a. Explain the purpose of the assessment.
    b. Explain what they will be doing.
    c. Explain when and how they will receive the results.
    d. Explain how the results will be used.
3. Become familiar with the assessment procedure and the directions for administering it. (Practice taking the assessment yourself.)
4. If proctors are necessary, schedule and train them.
5. Be sure that all the assessment materials are available, that students have pencils and other necessary tools, and that scratch paper and other materials are available.
6. Make any necessary physical adjustments to the room.
7. Make a sign that reads, "Assessing. Please do not disturb us!" Use the sign during the assessment sessions.

During the assessment
1. Follow the directions exactly as given in the directions manual.
2. Monitor students to be sure they are working on the correct pages and activities and are recording their responses properly.
3. Supervise the work of any proctors that are present.
4. Make notes describing any irregularities, either for individual students or for the entire group.

Source: H. D. Hoover, A. N. Hieronymus, D. A. Frisbie, and S. B. Dunbar, 1993a. Copyright © 1993 by The University of Iowa. All rights reserved. Adapted from the Iowa Tests of Basic Skills, Directions for Administration, Forms K and L, Levels 9–14, p. 15, with permission of The Riverside Publishing Company.

educators concerning what is appropriate (Cohen & Hyman, 1991; Mehrens, 1991; Mehrens & Kaminski, 1989; Popham, 1991). The issue centers on **ethical test preparation practices**. The validity of the student's assessment results after a teacher has prepared the students in certain ways for taking a particular assessment is sometimes questioned. Do certain preassessment activities give your students unwarranted advantages that are not available to other students? If your students receive certain types of practice, can you or others still validly interpret their scores? If you teach your students certain responses or answers, can you generalize their assessment results properly?

One aspect of assessment validity is **generalization of assessment results**. (See Table 3.27.) That is, you infer a student's performance on the entire curriculum domain from the specific items the student took. For example, suppose there are 100 key concepts in a particular area of social studies. Further, suppose that instead of teaching students strategies for understanding and organizing these course concepts and principles, you picked only the four concepts that will appear on a standardized social studies test and only taught answers to questions about those four concepts. Assuming you are a good teacher, your students would do very well on the test questions related to these concepts, and their test scores would be higher. However, your students would most likely not understand the broader social studies framework and would not have a way of understanding and integrating the full set of concepts the course was supposed to teach. In other words, by narrowing your teaching to only those few tasks that appear on a specific test, you have failed to provide your students with empowering strategies to organize social studies concepts and principles. Further, you cannot interpret their test results as reflecting their general knowledge of the course concepts and principles. By teaching only those four concepts, you invalidated the student's test results.

When you assess a student, you want to generalize from the performance the student provides on this assessment to the larger and broader domain of abilities and knowledge that the curriculum framework is supposed to foster. The responses on a particular test or assessment are only signs or pointers to the student's possible performance in the larger domain implied by the learning targets of the curriculum framework. However, if you give specific practice only on the questions or tasks on the assessment, you focus a student's learning only on these few tasks. It is very unlikely that such narrowly focused instruction and learning can generalize to the broader learning targets that are the real goals of education.

There is a range of practice activities that you can provide your students to improve their performance on an assessment. Which of these is appropriate? The following is an ordered list of assessment preparation activities, ranging from the most legitimate to the least legitimate (Mehrens & Kaminski, 1989):

1. Teaching the learning targets in the curriculum without narrowing your teaching to those targets that appear on a standardized assessment.

2. Teaching general test-taking strategies, such as those discussed in Chapter 14.

3. Teaching all those learning targets derived by a commercial organization after an analysis of several widely used standardized tests, including the one your students will take.

4. Teaching only those learning targets that specifically match the targets that will appear on the standardized assessment your students will take.

5. Teaching only those learning targets that specifically match the targets that will appear on the standardized assessment your students will take and giving practice using the same types of task formats that will appear on the assessment.

6. Giving your students practice on a published parallel form of the assessment they will take.

7. Giving your students practice on the same questions and tasks that they will take later.

Most educators would agree that the first activity is always ethical, because it is the teacher's job to teach the official curriculum. The sixth and seventh activities would always be considered unethical, because they narrow instruction to only the specific assessment procedures that your students will be administered and practically eliminate your ability to generalize from the assessment results to the performance domain specified by the curriculum. Most educators would also agree that the second activity, teaching students how to take tests and do their best on them, is not unethical.

Thus, Mehrens and Kaminski indicate that the boundary between ethical and unethical test preparation practices is somewhere between activities 3 and 5. They indicate that the deciding factor lies in the degree to which a school wishes to generalize the test results. The closer the activity is to the fifth one, the less able are school officials to generalize students' assessment results to the official curriculum—unless, of course, the official curriculum is identical to the assessment instrument. School officials must realize that the goal of education is to improve such things as a students' competence, knowledge, cultural awareness, and thinking skills—not to improve test scores.

Popham (1991) provides two ethical standards that summarize the principles illustrated in the preceding discussion. You may use them to judge whether you or others in your school are preparing students appropriately for standardized assessments:

- **Professional ethics**: No test-preparation practice should violate the ethical standards of the education profession (p. 13).
- **Educational defensibility**: No test-preparation practice should increase student's test scores without simultaneously increasing student mastery of the content domain tested (p. 13).

Summary

- There is a variety of published achievement tests in the marketplace. The chapter distinguished two broad groups: standardized, empirically documented tests and nonstandardized, not empirically documented tests.
- Standardized, empirically documented tests include multilevel tests designed to span several grade levels or age levels and single-level tests designed for only one grade level or course.
- Multilevel tests include achievement survey batteries and criterion-referenced and/or norm-referenced tests in particular curricular areas such as mathematics or reading.
- Single-level tests measure achievement in a particular subject or course such as Algebra I or French II.
- Nonstandardized, not empirically documented tests do not employ empirical data from samples of subjects to improve and refine tests and to document their degree of reliability and validity.
- Standardized achievement tests can be used for a variety of within-classroom and extra-classroom purposes.

The usefulness of a particular standardized achievement test for any of these purposes depends on its curricular relevance to a given school.

■ Criticisms of standardized achievement batteries have been directed toward their intrinsic properties, missing properties, and effects on students and school curricula. Proper test selection and use can overcome many criticisms.

■ Among the misuses of achievement test scores are (1) failing to consider the possibility of measurement error, (2) using a single score as the only criterion for important decisions, (3) uncritically accepting a score as a pure measure of a characteristic, and (4) failing to recognize that students' test performances are caused by a complex set of antecedent conditions.

■ The features of group-administered and individually administered multilevel achievement tests were described and illustrated along with suggestions for interpreting scores and using test results for instructional planning. Specific tests are listed in Appendix J.

■ It is important that you prepare yourself and your students for taking a standardized assessment, whether this assessment is a paper-and-pencil test or a performance test. The chapter offers suggestions for appropriate ways to undertake these preparations.

■ There are also inappropriate or unethical ways to prepare students to take assessments. The chapter describes a continuum of assessment-preparation activities from most legitimate to most illegitimate, so that you can judge your own behavior using this continuum.

Important Terms and Concepts

Code of Fair Testing Practices in Education
Code of Professional Responsibilities in Educational Measurement
computer-prepared narrative reports (building report, item analysis report, profile report)
empirically documented
ethical test preparation practices
external uses of test results
generalizability of assessment results
in-level vs. out-of-level testing
multilevel survey battery vs. single-level test
Professional Ethics Principle and Educational Defensibility Principle
special norms
standardized test
state-mandated assessment
subtest
test level
within-classroom uses of test results

Exercises and Discussion Questions

1. Using test publishers' catalogues, the *Mental Measurements Yearbooks*, and other resources, identify one published test that fits into each category of the author's scheme for classifying published achievement tests. Share your findings with your classmates.

2. The text lists several within-classroom purposes that may be served by standardized achievement tests. For each of the purposes listed, discuss the usefulness of (a) standardized, norm-referenced achievement survey batteries; (b) standardized criterion-referenced tests; (c) standardized performance assessments; and (d) teacher-made tests.

3. Explain the makeup of multilevel survey achievement batteries. Describe scores that provide information about (a) students' educational growth and (b) students' strengths and weaknesses in different subjects.

4. Most published assessments—whether they are survey batteries, performance assessments, or single-subject tests—cover content and objectives common to many schools rather than specifically focus on one school.
   a. Would this present problems for the school in which you teach (or plan to teach)?
   b. Describe these problems.
   c. Give two suggestions for a teacher and/or school administrator to help minimize these problems.

5. Discuss the pros and cons of using standardized achievement tests (norm-referenced or criterion-referenced) for purposes of accountability of schools to the public.

6. Describe five features that most group-administered standardized achievement batteries have in common.
   a. Does this commonality imply that each test exhibits these features in quality equal to that of the others? Explain.
   b. Why can't the results on one publisher's survey battery be interchanged with those of another?

7. The content of the assessment tasks that accompany textbooks, teacher's editions, and curriculum materials is generally closely matched with what you have taught your students. However, if you use these assessments uncritically, you may be doing yourself and your students a disservice. Explain why this is so, and describe what you should do to improve this situation.

8. What are the advantages of teacher-made tests over published tests? What are the advantages of published tests over teacher-made tests?

9. a. Distinguish between achievement tests that emphasize (i) content, (ii) basic skills, and (iii) general educational development.
   b. What does each assess?
   c. What does each imply about the need for additional assessments to supplement it?

10. Describe the students, their community, and subject(s) that you teach (or plan to teach). Give specific examples of how you may *misuse* achievement test results in this context in each of the following ways. Share your findings with the others in your course.
   a. Failing to consider measurement error when interpreting a student's scores
   b. Using only the test results for making a decision about a student
   c. Uncritically interpreting a student's score as measuring a pure trait
   d. Failing to consider the complex nature of the causes of a particular student's test performance

11. Evaluate the appropriateness of each of the following standardized-test-preparation practices using Popham's two ethical principles.

TABLE 16.2 Comparisons of the characteristics of various kinds of published tests with teacher-made tests.

Characteristic	Published tests in the marketplace							Teacher-made tests
	Standardized, empirically documented					Not standardized, not empirically documented		
	Multilevel		Other single area tests	Single-level		Criterion-referenced tests	Textbook accompaniments	
	Survey batteries	Criterion-referenced tests		Single-course tests				
Content/ objectives covered 1. Common to many schools 2. Specific to one teacher/ school 3. Specific to one text or set of materials								
Intended to measure 1. Growth over time 2. Status on each specific objective in domain 3. Profile of strengths and weaknesses								
Norm-referencing provided 1. Several types of scores 2. Several types of norm groups 3. Spans several grades								
Criterion-referencing provided 1. Many items per objective 2. Diagnosis possible								
Provides materials for interpreting scores to 1. Students 2. Parents 3. Teachers 4. Administrators								
Technical quality 1. Professionally written items 2. Empirical data on reliability and validity								

a. The school uses the latest version of a certain test. A teacher uses a version of the test that is no longer being administered in the school to give students special practice.

b. A teacher copies items from a test that is currently being used in the school and gives these to students for practice.

c. A teacher teaches students general rules and strategies for taking standardized tests, such as how to eliminate options and "guess" when they are not certain, and how to plan their testing time wisely.

d. The curriculum framework calls for learning the grammar rules covered by the test the school uses. The teacher teaches the students how to use these rules to answer the same format of questions that will appear on the test, but does not provide practice in more natural contexts of writing sentences and paragraphs.

e. The curriculum framework calls for learning the grammar rules covered by the test the school uses. The teacher teaches the students how to use these rules to answer the same format of question that will appear on the test, but also teaches them how to apply the rules in their own writing of sentences and paragraphs.

f. A deaf student who is mainstreamed in an inclusive program plans to go to a special postsecondary school for the deaf. For admission, the postsecondary school requires the student to submit results from standardized reading and mathematics tests. The teacher gives the tests to the student to read a few days ahead of time and answers any clarifying questions the student has about the vocabulary and the type of strategies that should be used when answering the questions. Then the teacher administers the tests to the student under standardized conditions but with the help of an interpreter for the deaf.

12. Table 16.2 lists various types of tests across the top and various characteristics as row headings. For each characteristic, describe the extent to which it is found in each type of test. In the cells in the body of the table, mark:

a. + + if most tests in that category exhibit this characteristic.

b. + if a few tests in that category exhibit this characteristic.

c. 0 if it is very rare that tests in that category exhibit this characteristic.

13. Using www.ed.gov/Programs/bastmp/SEA.htm, locate three states' education departments and descriptions of their state assessment program. If your state has an assessment program, be sure to include it as one of the three. Compare the assessment programs in terms of student vs. school accountability; objective vs. constructed-response assessment; use of standards, teacher development and capacity building; and general objectives and purposes. Share your findings with others in this course.

Additional Readings

Anastasi, A., & Urbina, S. (1997). *Psychological testing* (7th ed.). New York: Prentice Hall.

Discusses and illustrates a number of achievement tests, including diagnostic and preschool tests.

Bauernfeind, R.H. (1989). Article on test taking problematic. *Educational Measurement: Issues and Practice, 8*(4), 28.

Cohen, S.A., & Hyman, J. S. (1991). Can fantasies become facts? *Educational Measurement: Issues and Practice, 10*(1), 20–23.

Hills, J.R. (1990). Response to two letters: Grading practices and improving standardized test scores. *Educational Measurement: Issues and Practice, 9*(3), 33.

McDonnell, L. (1997). *The politics of state testing; Implementing new student assessments.* CSE Technical Report 424. Los Angeles: National Center for Research on Evaluation, Standards, and Student Testing, UCLA.

Studies and compares the innovative assessment programs in California, Kentucky, and North Carolina. Emphasis is on what made the programs work or not work.

Mehrens, W.A. (1991). Facts about samples, fantasies about domains. *Educational Measurement: Issues and Practice, 10*(2), 23–25.

Mehrens, W.A., & Kaminski, J. (1989). Methods for improving standardized test scores: Fruitful, fruitless, or fraudulent? *Educational Measurement: Issues and Practice, 8*(1), 14–22.

Mehrens, W.A., & Lehmann, I.J. (1991). *Measurement and evaluation in education and psychology* (4th ed.). Chicago: Holt, Rinehart, & Winston, Chapter 16.

Discusses and illustrates several standardized achievement tests including group and individually administered tests.

Popham, W.J. (1991). Appropriateness of teachers' test-preparation practices. *Educational Measurement: Issues and Practice, 10*(4), 12–15.

This set of articles and letters to the editor addresses the debate over the appropriateness of the ethical continuum of test-preparation practices advocated by Mehrens and Kaminski. The discussion is worthwhile in understanding the assessment issues behind the recommendations. It would be best to read the articles in chronological order.

Smith, M.L. (1997). *Reforming schools by reforming assessment: Consequences of the Arizona Student Assessment Program (ASAP): Equity and teacher capacity building.* CSE Technical Report 425. Los Angeles: National Center for Research on Evaluation, Standards, and Student Testing, UCLA.

Looks in depth at the Arizona state assessment efforts, to identify why the program experienced so much difficulty.

CHAPTER 17

Interpreting Norm-Referenced Scores

Learning Targets

After studying this chapter, you should be able to:

1. Explain why it is necessary to use both norm-referencing and criterion-referencing frameworks to properly understand a student's assessment performance. *[3, 6, 4]*

2. Explain the purposes and usefulness of local, national, and special norm-group comparisons. *[3, 4]*

3. Apply criteria of relevance, representativeness, and recency to evaluate the quality of norm data. *[3, 4]*

4. Explain the advantages and disadvantages of various types of criterion-referenced scores. *[3, 4, 6]*

5. Explain the advantages and disadvantages of norm-referenced scores. *[3, 4, 6]*

6. Accurately look up students' norm-referenced scores in standardized test publishers' norm tables. *[3]*

7. Correctly explain to parents the meaning of the norm-referenced scores their children obtained on standardized tests. *[6, 4]*

8. State the most common misconceptions that some teachers and school administrators hold about normal distributions of aptitudes, intelligences, and achievements of students. *[6, 4, 7]*

9. State the seven most common misconceptions that some teachers and school administrators hold about grade-equivalent scores. *[6, 4, 7]*

10. Use standardized test reports of the students in your class to confirm your own observations about them, identify their patterns of strengths, find possible weaknesses needing remediation, and understand how the group performed as a whole. *[3, 4]*

11. Explain how each of the terms and concepts listed at the end of this chapter apply to interpreting educational assessment results. *[6]*

Suppose that you took a spelling test and your score was 45, found by giving one point for each word that was spelled correctly. How well have you performed? Knowing only that your task was "a spelling test" and that your score was 45 leaves you unable to interpret your performance.

Raw scores are the number of points (marks) you assign to a student's performance on an assessment. You may assign these marks by adding the number of correct answers, the ratings for each task, or the number of points awarded to separate parts of the assessment. Like the preceding spelling score example, a raw score tells a student "what he or she got," but tells very little about the *meaning of the scores*.

TWO REFERENCING FRAMEWORKS

Practically all educational and psychological assessments require you to use some type of referencing framework to interpret students' performance. A *referencing framework* is a structure you use to compare a student's performance to something external to the assessment itself. You enhance your interpretation of a student's assessment results when you use an external framework.

Norm-Referencing Framework

Norm-Referencing You use a **norm-referencing** framework to interpret a student's assessment performance by comparing it to the performance of a well-defined group of other students who have also taken the same assessment. The well-defined group of other students is called the **norm group**. To make valid norm-referenced interpretations, all persons in the norm group must have been given the same assessment as your students and under the same conditions (same time limits, same directions, same equipment and materials, etc.). This is why you must follow administration instructions exactly when administering a standardized achievement test whose results you later will want to interpret through a norm-referenced framework.

To understand a norm-referenced interpretation, let's return to your score on the spelling test. Suppose your raw score of 45 means that your percentile rank (*PR*) is 99—that is, 99% of the persons who took the spelling assessment have scored lower than 45. Before you congratulate yourself, however, you should determine who is in the norm group to which your raw score is being referenced. You would interpret your performance differently if you knew the norm group was comprised of third graders than if the norm group was comprised of adults.

Validity of Norm-Referenced Interpretations Your norm-referenced interpretations are less valid when the norm group is not well defined. The more you know about who is in the norm group, the better able you are to interpret a student's performance in a norm-referenced framework. Consider the difference in interpreting your performance on the spelling assessment, for example, when the norm group is adults in general as compared to the norm group being adults who have won prizes in national spelling contests.

Norm-Referenced Scores Norm-referenced interpretations are made easier by using *derived scores*. A more or less standard set of derived scores is now rather routinely reported for most published tests in education:

1. *Percentile rank* tells the percentage of persons in a norm group scoring lower than a particular raw score.

2. *Linear standard score* tells the location of a particular raw score in relation to the mean and standard deviation of a norm group.

3. *Normalized standard score* tells the location of a particular raw score in relation to a normal distribution fitted to a norm group.

4. *Grade-equivalent score* tells the grade placement for which a particular raw score is the average for a norm group.

Criterion-Referencing Framework

Beyond Norm-Referencing Norm-referencing is not enough to fully interpret your score: You may be a better speller than other people—whoever they happen to be—but *what* can you spell? At a minimum, you would need to know the kinds of words in the pool from which those on the spelling test were selected, the number of words selected, and the process used to select the words. Were they really words, or were they nonsense syllables? Were they English words? Were they selected from a list of the most difficult (or easiest) English words? Were there 45 words or 500 words on the test? Were the words on the test representative of some larger class or domain? Did spelling the words require you to use certain mental processes or to apply certain spelling rules?

These questions are especially important when you need to make absolute interpretations of students' assessment performance—for example, when you need to know which specific learning target your students are having trouble mastering. Norm-referencing provides information helpful for your relative interpretations of scores, but frequently these are not enough. Scores that reflect relative achievement such as rank order, for example, may be helpful in picking the best readers, or in sectioning a class into better, good, and poor readers. However, to plan appropriate instruction, eventually you need to know the kinds of reading performances each student can do and the particular types of difficulties each student is experiencing. When your diagnosis and prescription are based on students' error patterns or on your analysis of their faulty reasoning or thinking processes, as described in Chapter 13, you must put aside the norm-referencing framework and use a criterion-referencing framework.

Criterion-Referencing You use a **criterion-referencing** framework to infer the kinds of performances the student can do in a domain, rather than the student's relative standing in a norm group. This domain of performance to which you reference a student's assessment results is called the *criterion*. When you use the criterion-referencing framework, you infer a student's status in a targeted domain, not in relation to how well other students performed. When you teach, the criterion that is of most interest is the domain of performance implied by your state's standards, your curriculum framework, and your lessons' learning targets.

Validity of Criterion-Referenced Interpretations Your criterion-referenced assessment interpretations lose validity when the domain of performances to which you wish to infer your students' status is not well defined, or when your assessment is a poor sample from that domain. The more you know about the domain from which the tasks on your assessment were sampled, the more validly you can interpret their results. For example, if you did not construct your assessment using clearly defined statements of learning targets, or if your assessment only poorly represents the wide range of performance implied by a clearly defined set of learning targets, then you have only a weak basis for making criterion-referenced interpretations.

You can easily see why by reviewing the spelling example again. Suppose you knew that the spelling domain was the 10,000 most frequently misspelled English words, and that the assessment had been constructed as a sample of 100 words representative of the spelling patterns in this domain. In this case you may interpret your score of 45 on a 100-word assessment as an estimate of the proportion of those 10,000 words you know how to spell. You can see that if there were only 50 words on the assessment, your estimate would be less accurate than when there are 100. A sample of 10 words is even less accurate. Further, if the 100 words did not sample the domain representatively, your estimate would be less accurate also, even though there were 100 words. For example, the 100 words may contain only regular spelling patterns and ignore others. Thus, both the number of items on the assessment and their representativeness of the domain contribute to how valid your criterion-referenced interpretation is.

Criterion-Referenced Scores Criterion-referenced assessments do not have well-developed, derived score systems like norm-referenced assessments. Nevertheless, certain types of scores are often used with these assessments:

1. *Percentage*—a number telling the percent of the maximum points earned by the student (percent correct, percent of objectives mastered, etc.).

2. *Speed of performance*—the amount of time a student takes to complete a task, or the number of tasks completed in a fixed amount of time (typing 40 words per minute, running a mile in 5 minutes, completing 25 number facts correctly in 1 minute, etc.).

3. *Quality ratings*—the quality level at which a student performs ("Excellent," rating of "5," "mastery," etc.).

4. *Precision of performance*—the degree of accuracy with which a student completes a task (measuring accurately to the nearest tenth of a meter, weighing accurately to the nearest gram, fewer than 10 typing errors, etc.).

USING NORMS

Importance of Norms

Norm-referencing involves finding out how one student's performance compares to the performances of other students. You should realize, however, that simply comparing students with one another is not a very good reason for assessing them (Hoover et al., 1993b). Here are the major reasons for assessing students:

1. To describe, within each subject area, the performances a student has achieved

2. To describe, within each subject area, student deficiencies that need further improvement

3. To describe, across the curriculum, which subjects are the student's strengths and weaknesses

4. To describe, within each subject area, the amount of educational development (progress) a student has made over the course of one or more years

The first two purposes are best served within a criterion-referencing framework. In essence, this requires you to look carefully at a student's performance, item by item, and to compare this performance to your learning targets.

The second two purposes are best served within a norm-referencing framework. A student's relative strength in reading and mathematics, for example, cannot be described on purely a criterion-referenced basis. It is possible to describe what a student can do in each area, but a norm basis is required in order to conclude whether these are relative strengths or weaknesses. A teacher may say, for example, that a student is able to solve routine linear and quadratic equations in mathematics and is able to read with comprehension age-appropriate stories. However, which is the stronger area? Teachers must use normative information to determine this.

Standardized tests describe students' relative strengths and weaknesses in different curricular areas because of the normative information they provide. The same group of students at the same grade level (the norm group) is administered tests covering several curricular areas. Thus, if fourth grader Blake ranks at the top of the norm group in mathematics but in the middle of the norm group in reading, we know that of the two subjects, Blake is stronger in mathematics.

The fourth purpose given earlier, measuring educational growth and development, also requires norm-referencing. Norm groups provide the basis for defining an educational development scale (such as the grade-equivalent scale) across different grade levels. If assessment procedures for different grades are linked to this scale, then it is possible to measure a student's growth. We assess a student once every year or two, each time referencing the student's results to this developmental scale. Growth is measured by the student's progress along this scale.

The remainder of this chapter discusses the various norm-referenced scores and scales used in educational assessment. As a teacher, you will not be required to create growth scales or calculate scale scores. However, you will be required to interpret and to use such scales and scores with your students. In addition, you will be expected to explain the meaning of reports of these scores to your students and their parents.

Types of Norm Groups

Test manuals report the performance of large representative samples of students, or the norm group. The performance of a norm group on a particular assessment represents the present, average status of that group of students on that particular assessment. A group's current average does not represent a standard, however, nor does it establish what your school or your students should attain. What students should achieve is established by your state's content and performance standards and your curriculum's learning targets. Comparing your students and school to norm groups can help you, however, decide the general range of performance to expect from your students, provided your students are similar to those in the norm group. As you will see, test publishers may provide information on several different groups when reporting norm-referenced scores.

Multiple Norm-Group Comparisons Ordinarily, a student is a member of more than one group. For example, a 14-year-old, eighth-grade boy with a hearing impairment took a standardized mathematics concepts assessment and obtained a raw score of 32. This may represent a percentile rank of:

- 99 in a national group of deaf eighth graders
- 94 in the test publishers' national eighth-grade standardization sample
- 89 in the group of eighth graders in his local community
- 80 in the group of eighth graders currently enrolled with him in an advanced mathematics course

Depending on the decisions you must make, referencing a student's score to more than one norm group may be in order. Vocational counseling decisions, for example, may require that you compare a student's profile of abilities and achievements to each of several occupational or vocational groups about which the student is seeking career information. Comparing the person only to "students in general" may offer less information for career exploration.

Local Norms For many of your norm-referenced interpretations, the most appropriate group with which you should compare a student is the **local norm group**: the group of students in the same grade in the same school district. It is this group with which you and the students will interact the most. Local percentile ranks or standard scores are easy to compile for a school's testing program, and your director of testing should provide them to you every time a standardized test is administered. Publishers also offer this service for their customers—frequently at extra cost, however.

National Norms Most norm-referenced, standardized achievement and aptitude batteries have what are called **national norms**. In principle, the national norm groups are supposed to be representative of the country in some way, and some publishers expend a great deal of effort to assure representativeness. But each publisher will use a somewhat different definition of what constitutes a truly representative national sample and will conduct the sampling processes somewhat differently. The result is that the norms from different publishers are not comparable. You should note, however, that no publisher's norming sample exactly mirrors the nation's schools. A school's participation in a publisher's norming sample is voluntary. Sometimes this creates a self-selection bias in a given publisher's norms that may distort the norms in favor of those schools that have used that publisher's tests in the past (Baglin, 1981). A more detailed description of how publishers obtain norming samples is given in Chapter 18.

National norms need not be composed simply of students in general at a grade level. A publisher may provide separate male/female norms or may provide separate norms for minorities. Sometimes **modal-age norms** are provided. Modal-age norms include, from among all students at a particular grade level, only those near the most typical chronological age for that grade.

Special Norm Groups For some tests **special norm groups** are formed. Examples include students with deafness or blindness, students with mental retardation, students enrolled in a certain course of study or curriculum, and students attending regional schools. A student may be a member of more than one special group, of course.

School Averages Norms If your school principal wants to know how the school's third-grade average score compares with that of other school buildings, then the principal needs to use school averages norms. For individual student's norms, a distribution of individual students' scores is made and used as the basis for norm-referencing. But individual students vary widely in their scores, so much so that comparing a school's average to that group may lead to misinterpretations.

School averages norms consist of a tabulation of the average (mean) score from each school building in a national sample of schools and provide information on the relative ordering of these averages (means). This distribution of averages is *much less variable* than the distribution of individual student scores. Figure 17.1 illustrates this difference in variability for one publisher's reading test.

To get some idea of what your school district may gain from using school averages norms, suppose that in your school building the average spring fifth-grade developmental standard score on the *Iowa Test of Basic Skills* (Reading Comprehension subtest) is 250. (Refer to Figure 17.1.) A principal who looks up this number in the individual student norm erroneously concludes that the school ranks higher than 85% (*PR* = 85 for individuals) of the schools. (In Figure 17.1, look at the row labeled "NPR of Avg. SS: Student Norms".) Actually, the school is much better, ranking at the top 1% (*PR* = 99 for school averages). In general, if someone uses individual scores norms erroneously and their school is above average, the results will underestimate their standing among other schools; those whose schools are below average will overestimate their standing among other schools. You can verify this principle by checking several developmental standard score values and percentile ranks in Figure 17.1.

Using Publishers' Norms

Know When the Assessment Was Normed   You obtain the most accurate estimate of a student's standing in a norm group when the student is tested on a date nearest the time of year the publisher established the norms. Publishers commonly interpolate and extrapolate to develop norm tables: They may provide spring norm tables, for example, even though no tests were actually administered to the norm group in the spring. Each publisher's empirical norming dates are different, but the publisher should state the dates in the test manual or technical report. To be accurate, your school should administer a standardized test within two or three weeks on either side of the midpoint date of the publisher's empirical norming period.

Criteria for Evaluating Norms   It is generally accepted (APA, AERA, & NCME, 1974) that published norms data should satisfy three Rs: **relevance, representativeness, and recency**. First, the norm group(s) a publisher provides should be relevant: They should be the group(s) to which you will want to compare your students. Second, the norm sample must be representative: The manual should tell you clearly that the norm data was based on a carefully planned sample and should provide you with information about the subclassifications (sex, age, socioeconomic level, etc.) used to assure representativeness. Remember that the size of the sample is not as crucial as its representativeness is. (Of course, a representative sample will necessarily have to be rather large for a very large population.)

Third, the norms must be based on recent data. As the curriculum, schooling, and social and economic factors change, so will the performance of students on assessments. Further, if your school uses the same form of a test year after year, the students' scores will generally increase,

FIGURE 17.1   Comparison of the distributions of student scores and school averages for the Reading Comprehension Subtest of the Iowa Tests of Basic Skills, grade 5, spring norms.

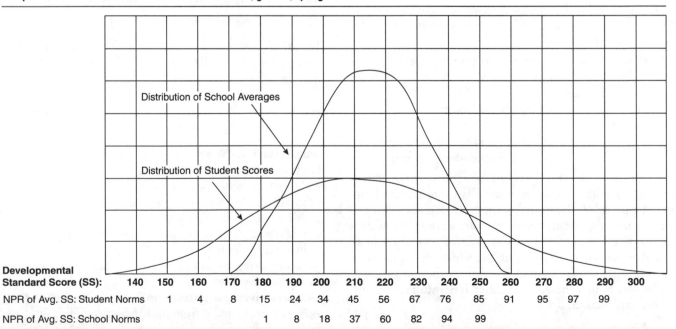

Developmental Standard Score (SS):	140	150	160	170	180	190	200	210	220	230	240	250	260	270	280	290	300
NPR of Avg. SS: Student Norms	1	4	8	15	24	34	45	56	67	76		85	91	95	97	99	
NPR of Avg. SS: School Norms				1	8	18	37	60	82	94	99						

Note: NPR = national percentile rank
Source: From H. D. Hoover, A. N. Hieronymus, D. A. Frisbie, and S. B. Dunbar, 1993d. Copyright © 1993 by The University of Iowa. All rights reserved. Adapted from the Iowa Tests of Basic Skills, Norms and Score Conversions, Complete and Core Batteries, (Form K, Levels 5–14) p. 10, with permission of The Riverside Publishing Company.

because the students become familiar with the format and teachers tend to prepare students specifically for that test (Linn, Graue, & Sanders, 1990; Shepard, 1990; Wiser & Lenke, 1987). If the norms are not recent, they will mislead, conveying the impression that your students are learning better than they really are.

OVERVIEW OF NORM-REFERENCED SCORES

Norm-referenced scores are derived from the raw scores of an assessment. You should be aware that many types of norm-referenced scores exist. Space permits discussion of only the ones you will most often encounter, which are represented in Figure 17.2. If you are interested in pursuing the study of norm-referenced scores in greater detail, consult the very readable book, *Test Scores and What They Mean* (Lyman, 1998).

Using Norms Tables

Test manuals contain tables—called *norms tables*—for converting raw scores to different kinds of norm-referenced scores. No computation is required: You need "only" look up the score. *Only* is in quotes because, as trivial a task as it may seem, looking up scores in a table and copying them into a student's record is something teachers seem to have a hard time doing correctly. Studies of the kinds of errors found in federal program evaluations indicate that using the wrong norms table and misreading a table

are common problems (Crane & Bellis, 1978; Finley, 1977; Johnson & Thomas, 1979; Moyer, 1979). Specimen tables (Tables 17.1, 17.7, and 17.9) are shown in this chapter, along with a discussion of the particular scores, so that you can practice using the tables.

Percentile Ranks

Perhaps the most useful and easily understood norm-referenced score is the percentile rank. The **percentile rank** tells *the percentage of the students in a norm group that have scored lower than the raw score in question*. Table 17.1 is an example of a percentile rank norms table. The raw score obtained from the assessment is located in the correct column in the body of the table, and the corresponding percentile rank is read out. For example, suppose a seventh grader named Veronica takes the *Differential Aptitude Tests* (DAT) on October 23, and she scores 48 in Mechanical Reasoning. Her percentile rank from Table 17.1 is 98. She is above average in the norm group of seventh-grade females in mathematics; her raw score exceeds 98% of the females in the standardization group.

Notice there are three sets of percentile ranks in Table 17.1—one for the seventh-grade boys, one for the seventh-grade girls, and one for the combined group. This is common practice for norm-referenced assessments in which there are large differences between males and females.

A raw score of 48 has a percentile rank of 90 for boys. This lower percentile rank for boys for the same raw score reflects that seventh-grade boys do much better as a group on this Mechanical Reasoning test. As a result, 48 does

FIGURE 17.2 The organization of major score-referencing schemes.

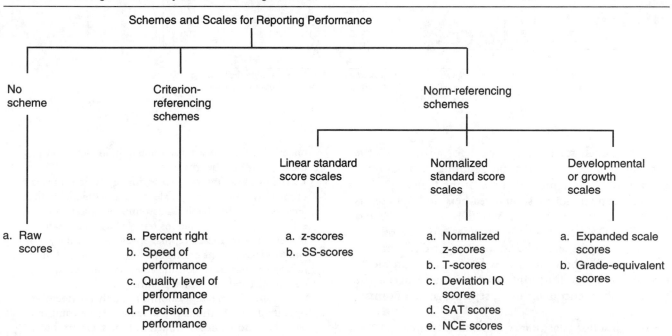

TABLE 17.1 Example of a percentile norms table: *Differential Aptitude Tests*, Level 1, Form C.

MECHANICAL REASONING

MALE				FEMALE				COMBINED			
Raw Score	%-ile Rank	Sta-nine	Scaled Score	Raw Score	%-ile Rank	Sta-nine	Scaled Score	Raw Score	%-ile Rank	Sta-nine	Scaled Score
60	99	9	343	60	99	9	343	60	99	9	343
59	99	9	330	59	99	9	330	59	99	9	330
58	99	9	316	58	99	9	316	58	99	9	316
57	99	9	307	57	99	9	307	57	99	9	307
56	99	9	301	56	99	9	301	56	99	9	301
55	99	9	296	55	99	9	296	55	99	9	296
54	99	9	292	54	99	9	292	54	99	9	292
53	98	9	288	53	99	9	288	53	99	9	288
52	97	9	285	52	99	9	285	52	99	9	285
51	95	8	282	51	99	9	282	51	98	9	282
50	94	8	279	50	99	9	279	50	97	9	279
49	92	8	277	49	99	9	277	49	97	9	277
48	90	8	274	48	98	9	274	48	95	8	274
47	88	7	272	47	98	9	272	47			
46	85	7	270	46		9	270				
45	82	7	268	45			268				234
44	79		266	23	15		266	24	14	3	232
				22	14			22	13	3	231
				21	13	2		21	10	2	229
20			227	20	12	2	227	20	8	2	227
19	6	2	226	19	10	2	226	19	7	2	226
18	5	2	224	18	9	2	224	18	5	2	224
17	4	2	222	17	7	2	222	17	4	2	222
16	3	1	220	16	6	2	220	16	3	1	220
15	2	1	218	15	4	1	218	15	3	1	218
14	2	1	216	14	3	1	216	14	2	1	216
13	1	1	214	13	2	1	214	13	2	1	214
12	1	1	212	12	2	1	212	12	1	1	212
11	1	1	209	11	1	1	209	11	1	1	209
10	1	1	207	10	1	1	207	10	1	1	207
9	1	1	204	9	1	1	204	9	1	1	204
8	1	1	201	8	1	1	201	8	1	1	201
7	1	1	198	7	1	1	198	7	1	1	198
6	1	1	194	6	1	1	194	6	1	1	194
5	1	1	190	5	1	1	190	5	1	1	190
4	1	1	185	4	1	1	185	4	1	1	185
3	1	1	178	3	1	1	178	3	1	1	178
2	1	1	169	2	1	1	169	2	1	1	169
1	1	1	155	1	1	1	155	1	1	1	155

Source: From *Differential Aptitude Tests: Fifth Edition, Fall Norms Booklet* (p. 66) by The Psychological Corporation,1991, San Antonio: Author. Copyright © 1990 by The Psychological Corporation. Reprinted by permission. All rights reserved.

not rank as high for boys as it does for girls. When the boys and girls are combined, the resulting distribution is shown in the "Combined" column of the table.

Which gender norms should teachers and counselors use? The answer depends on how they will use the test scores. The DAT, for example, provides a profile of each student's strengths and weaknesses in eight different cognitive areas. Teachers and counselors use this profile to help a student plan for further schooling and careers. The DAT publishers encourage using separate-gender norms:

Although at first glance it may appear that reporting norms for females and males separately represents an undesirable form of sex discrimination; in fact, exactly the opposite may be true.

The two sexes typically score differently on some tests of the DAT. In particular, males tend to score higher than females on the Mechanical Reasoning test and to a lesser extent on the Space Relations test, while females earn higher scores on the Perceptual Speed and Accuracy test and to a lesser extent on the Spelling test. Some of these differences may be of considerable consequence in educational and vocational planning. . . .

The use of separate-sex norms not only provides the opportunity for both males and females to be compared with the performance of students of the same sex, but also with students of the opposite sex. . . .

In spite of the recent changes in the job world, there are still many career fields dominated by one sex or the other. Thus, in counseling a female who wishes to enter a mechanical field, her scores on the Mechanical Reasoning test should be compared with those of males at the same grade level. On the other hand, in counseling a male who wishes to enter a clerical or an editorial field, his score on the Perceptual Speed and Accuracy test, as well as Spelling, should be compared with those of females at the same grade level. . . .

Because females and males tend to perform about the same on many of the tests of the DAT, it is entirely possible that, with the increasing changes in the job market, the sex differences . . . will diminish over time. (Psychological Corporation, 1991, pp. 31–33)

Be sure to use the norms table that corresponds to the time of year during which the student takes the assessment. In our example, a raw score of 48 in the fall of the year corresponds to a percentile rank of 99. If you looked up a raw score of 48 in the spring norms table, it would have a slightly lower percentile rank. This lower percentile rank reflects that students learn or improve during the year.

As with all scores, you should not interpret percentile ranks too precisely. For example, a student with a percentile rank 44 and a student with a percentile rank 46 differ little. Therefore, for many educational decisions you should interpret these scores as essentially equivalent. Some publishers, to reflect that all scores contain measurement error, report percentile bands or uncertainty intervals instead of a single percentile rank. These percentile bands are based on the assessment's standard error of measurement (see Chapter 4). The advantages and limitations of percentile ranks are summarized in Table 17.2.

Because percentile ranks are easy to understand, your school district will most likely report them. Percentile ranks are also easy to calculate. Figure 17.3 shows the procedure. The same procedure can be used for results from your classroom or for your entire district.

Remember that percentile ranks are specific to the group being referenced. After your students take a standardized test, the publisher will probably report both the local percentile ranks and the national percentile ranks. Your student Robert, for example, may have a national percentile rank of 40 and a local percentile rank of 30. Local percentile ranks are lower than national percentile ranks only when the students in a local school system score higher, on the average, than the national standardization sample. You must keep in mind the reference group when you interpret percentile ranks.

Linear Standard Scores

A **linear standard score** tells *how far a raw score is from the mean of the norm group, the distance being expressed using standard deviation units.*[1] In general, linear standard scores have the same-shaped distribution as the raw scores from which they are derived (this is not true of percentile ranks and nonlinear standard scores) and can be used to make two distributions more comparable by placing them on the same numerical scale. Linear standard scores are called linear because if you plot each raw score against its corresponding linear standard score in a graph and then connect these points, you will always have a straight line.

z-Scores The fundamental linear standard score is the **z-score** which tells *the number of standard deviation units a raw score is above (or below) the mean of a given distribution.* Other linear standard scores are computed from z-scores. Equation 17.1 explains.

$$z = \frac{X - M}{SD} \qquad \text{[Eq. 17.1]}$$

where

X represents the raw score
M represents the mean (average) raw score of the group
SD represents the standard deviation of the raw scores for that group

[1]The standard deviation is an index that measures the spread of scores in a distribution. The standard deviation, denoted as SD in this book, is explained in Appendix H.

TABLE 17.2 Summary of the advantages and limitations of percentile ranks.

Advantages	Limitations
1. Easily understood by pupils, parents, teachers, and others	1. Can be confused with percentage correct scores
2. Clearly reflect the norm-referenced character of the interpretation	2. Can be confused with some other type of two-digit derived scores
3. Permit a person's performance to be compared to a variety of norm-groups	3. Differences between *PR's* in the middle of the scale tend to be overinterpreted. Differences of the same magnitude near the tails of a distribution tend to be underinterpreted
4. Can be used to compare a pupil's relative standing in each of several achievement or ability areas	

FIGURE 17.3   Example of calculating percentile rank norms.

Raw	Tally	Frequency	Cumulative frequency	$PR = \dfrac{\frac{1}{2}\left[\begin{array}{c}\text{number of persons}\\ \text{having the score}\end{array}\right] + \left[\begin{array}{c}\text{number of persons}\\ \text{below the score}\end{array}\right]}{\text{total number of persons}} \times 100$
36	/	1	25	$98 = \dfrac{.5 + 24}{25} \times 100$
35		0	24	96
34		0	24	96
33		0	24	$96 = \dfrac{0 + 24}{25} \times 100$
32	/	1	24	$94 = \dfrac{.5 + 23}{25} \times 100$
31	/	1	23	$90 = \dfrac{.5 + 22}{25} \times 100$
30		0	22	$88 = \dfrac{0 + 22}{25} \times 100$
29	//	2	22	$84 = \dfrac{1 + 20}{25} \times 100$
28	////	4	20	$72 = \dfrac{2 + 16}{25} \times 100$
27	⁄⁄⁄⁄	5	16	$54 = \dfrac{2.5 + 11}{25} \times 100$
26	⁄⁄⁄⁄	6	11	$32 = \dfrac{3 + 5}{25} \times 100$
25	//	2	5	$16 = \dfrac{1 + 3}{25} \times 100$
24	/	1	3	$10 = \dfrac{.5 + 2}{25} \times 100$
23		0	2	8
22		0	2	$8 = \dfrac{0 + 2}{25} \times 100$
21	/	1	2	$6 = \dfrac{.5 + 1}{25} \times 100$
20		0	1	4
19		0	1	4
18		0	1	4
17		0	1	4
16		0	1	4
15		0	1	$4 = \dfrac{0 + 1}{25} \times 100$
14	/	1	1	$2 = \dfrac{.5 + 0}{25} \times 100$
		N = 25		

Step-By-Step

1. List the possible scores in descending order (Column 1). (You may group the scores into intervals if you wish.)
2. Tally the number of students attaining each score (Column 2).
3. Sum the number of students attaining each score (Column 3).
4. Add the frequencies consecutively, starting at the bottom of the column with the lowest score. Place each consecutive sum in the cumulative frequency column (Column 4). E.g., $0 + 1 = 1, \ldots, 2 + 1 = 3, 3 + 2 = 5$, etc.
5. Calculate the percentile rank of each score (Column 5). Below is an example for the score 27.
   (a) Calculate one-half of the frequency of the score ($1/2 \times 5 = 2.5$).
   (b) Add the result in (a) to the cumulative frequency just below the score ($2.5 + 11 = 13.5$).
   (c) Divide the result in (b) by the total number of scores ($13.5 \div 25 = .54$).
   (d) Multiply the result in (c) by 100 ($.54 \times 100 = 54$).

As an example, suppose a student's raw score was 38 on Test A. Suppose further that the test mean is 44 and the standard deviation is 4. The corresponding z-score is calculated as follows:

$$z = \frac{38 - 44}{4} = \frac{-6}{4} = -1.5$$

The z-score tells the number of standard deviations a raw score is above or below the mean. A compact way of saying this is that a student's test score, for example, is located below the mean a distance equal to one and one-half times the standard deviation of the group. The student's z-score in this example equals −1.50. A z-score is negative when the raw score is below the mean, positive when the raw score is above the mean, and equal to zero when the raw score is exactly equal to the mean.

An advantage of using z-scores is that they communicate students'· norm-referenced achievement. In many groups, the majority of students' scores cluster near the mean, usually within a distance equal to one standard deviation on either side of the mean. A distance of one standard deviation above the mean is $z = +1.0$; a distance of one standard deviation below the mean is $z = -1.0$. Thus, you would interpret a student whose z-score is between +1.0 and −1.0 as having rather typical or average attainment. (Remember, this is a norm-referenced framework, not a criterion-referenced framework. That is, the interpretation is relative to others and not an absolute interpretation.) Similarly, you would interpret a student with $z = -1.5$ or less as having atypically low attainment because few students have z-scores of −1.5 or less. You interpret a student with $z = +1.5$ or greater as having atypically high attainment because relatively few students attain z-scores of +1.50 or greater.

Another advantage of using z-scores is to put raw scores with different metrics on the same norm-referenced scale. Consider the example in Table 17.3, in which the same students are measured in both pounds and kilograms. Notice what happens when each student's measurements are transformed to z-scores.

Even though the pounds mean and standard deviation are different from the kilograms mean and standard deviation, the students' relative positions in the distributions are the same. This is expressed by the z-scores (which are identical for pounds and kilograms), not by the pounds and kilograms raw scores.

The z-score has several practical disadvantages. It is difficult to explain to students and parents: Understanding it requires an understanding of the mean and standard deviation. Another practical disadvantage is that plus and minus signs are used. Transcription errors, resulting in omitted or interchanged algebraic signs, are frequent. Further, you will find it difficult to explain to students (or parents) why assessment performances are reported as negative and/or fractional numbers. For example, a student may say, "I got 15 of the 45 questions right. How could my score be −1.34?" Likewise, the decimal point is subject to frequent transcription error.

These practical problems are easily overcome, however, by transforming the z-score to other types of scores. These additional transformations maintain the conceptual norm-referenced advantage of z-scores while overcoming their practical limitations.

SS-scores To remedy some of the disadvantages of z-scores, some publishers apply a modification (transformation) to eliminate both the negative scores and the fractional portion of the z-scores. I shall refer to these as **SS-scores**. An SS-score tells *the location of a raw score in a distribution having a mean of 50 and a standard deviation of 10*. The SS-score is expressed in an equation as:

$$SS = 10z + 50$$
$$= (10 \text{ times the z-score}) + 50 \quad \text{[Eq. 17.2]}$$

First z-scores are computed; then, each z-score is transformed to an SS-score: The z is multiplied by 10, and the product rounded to the nearest whole number, and finally 50 is added. Multiplying by 10 and rounding eliminates the z-score's decimal. Adding 50 eliminates the z-score's negative value.

As an example, suppose Ashley's z-score was computed to be −1.37. To convert this to an SS-score, multiply it by 10 and add 50 to the result. Thus,

$$SS = 10(-1.37) + 50$$
$$= -13.7 + 50 = -14 + 50$$
$$= 36$$

The result of applying this conversion to the z-scores is that the distribution of SS-scores will have a mean of 50 and a standard deviation of 10. Once you know this fact, you can interpret anyone's SS-score, essentially by doing a mental conversion back to a z-score. For example, Ashley's SS-score was 36; a score of 36 is 14 points or 1.4 standard deviations below the mean. Thus, Ashley's z-score is −1.4.

SS-scores have the advantages of not changing the shape of the original raw score distribution, always having a mean

TABLE 17.3 Student's z-scores remain the same even though the measurement scale changes.

Student	Weight in kilograms		Weight in pounds	
	X	z	X	z
A	48	−1.52	105.2	−1.52
B	52	−0.17	114.4	−0.17
C	54	0.51	118.8	0.51
D	56	1.18	123.2	1.18

TABLE 17.4 Comparision of SS- and z-scores.

Raw score in a group with $M = 41$ and $SD = 3$	Corresponding linear standard score on	
	z-score scale	SS-score scale
32	−3.00	20
35	−2.00	30
38	−1.00	40
41	0.00	50
44	+1.00	60
47	+2.00	70
50	+3.00	80

of 50 and a standard deviation of 10, and being interpretable in terms of standard deviation units while avoiding negative numbers and decimal fractions. A disadvantage is that a person needs to understand the concepts of standard deviation and linear transformation to interpret them.

Comparison of Linear Standard Scores   It may help you understand these scores if we display the relationship between them. Because all linear standard score systems reflect essentially the same information, interpreting their meaning is easy once you know the multiplier and the added constant. Table 17.4 shows how each type of score is related to the other and to the raw scores.[2]

[2]The values of M and SD have been set arbitrarily.

NORMAL DISTRIBUTIONS

Definition

Assessment developers have found it advantageous to transform the scores to a common distributional form: a normal distribution. A **normal distribution**, sometimes called a *normal curve*, is a mathematical model, invented in 1733 by Abraham deMoivre (Pearson, 1924). It is defined by a particular equation that depends on two specific numbers: the mean and the standard deviation, signifying that many normal distributions exist and each has a different mean and/or standard deviation. Figure 17.4 shows several different normal curves. Each of these was obtained by using the normal equation and plotting points on a graph. In Figure 17.4A, each normal distribution has the same mean but a different standard deviation. Although each is centered on the same point on the X-scale, some appear flatter and more spread out because their standard deviation is larger. Figure 17.4B shows three normal curves, each with the same standard deviation but each with a different mean. The degree of spread is the same for each, but each is centered on a different point on the score scale.

Every normal curve is smooth and continuous; each has a symmetrical, bell-shaped form. In theory, a normal curve never touches the baseline (horizontal axis) but is asymptotic to it, extending out to infinity in either direction from the mean. Graphs of actual raw-score distributions are nonsymmetrical and jagged. For actual raw-score

FIGURE 17.4 Illustrations of different normal distributions.

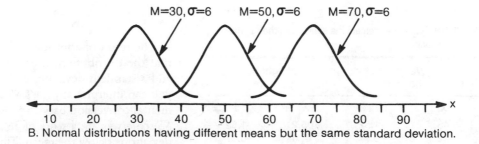

A. Normal distributions having the same mean but different standard deviations.

B. Normal distributions having different means but the same standard deviation.

Source: From *Measuring Pupil Achievement and Aptitude* (2nd ed.) (p. 87) by C. M. Lindvall and A. J. Nitko, 1975, New York: Harcourt Brace Jovanovich. Reprinted by permission of the authors.

distributions, the lowest possible score is 0 and the highest possible score is equal to the total number of items on the assessment. An idea of how an actual distribution compares to the mathematically defined normal curve may be obtained from Figure 17.5. Both distributions have the same mean and the same standard deviation. This normal curve approximates the actual distribution but does not match it exactly.

Natural Law vs. Normal Distributions

Early users of normal curves believed that somehow natural laws dictated that nearly all human characteristics

FIGURE 17.5 Illustration of the actual distribution (histogram) of creativity test scores for 55 twelfth-grade students and a normal curve (smooth curve) that has the same mean and standard deviation.

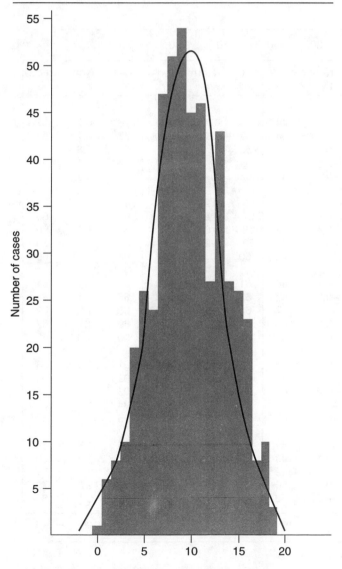

Source: From *Measuring Pupil Achievement and Aptitude* (2nd ed.) (p. 88) by C. M. Lindvall and A. J. Nitko, 1975, New York: Harcourt Brace Jovanovich. Reprinted by permission of the authors. Histogram based on data from *Introduction to Statistical Procedures: With Computer Exercises* (pp. 248–252) by P. R. Lohnes and W. W. Cooley, Copyright © 1968, New York: John Wiley & Sons. Reprinted by permission of John Wiley & Sons, Inc.

were distributed in a random or chance fashion around a mean or average value. This view of the applicability of the normal curve was, perhaps, begun by deMoivre (1756), but it was adamantly held to be true for intellectual and moral qualities by Quetelet (1748) (Dudycha & Dudycha, 1972; Landau & Lazarsfeld, 1968).

This thought—that somehow the distributions of human characteristics are by nature normal distributions—has carried over to mental measurement. It is frequently held, too, that because assessment scores have a bell-shaped distribution, this indicates that not just the scores but also the human abilities underlying the scores are normally distributed. This converse statement is, of course, not true. The assessment's score of distribution depends not only on the *underlying* abilities of the persons tested but also on the properties of the assessment procedure itself. An assessment developer can, by judicious selection of tasks, make the score distribution have any shape: rectangular, skewed bimodal, symmetrical, and so on (Lord, 1953). (See Appendix H for shapes of distributions.) These nonnormal score distribution shapes could appear in the data, for example, even though the underlying ability of the group is normal in form.

From your own experience, you know that you can control the shape of a test score distribution. For example, if all items on a test are easy, there will be a lot of high scores and few low scores. A very difficult test will have many low scores and few high scores. The point is, the normal distribution is a convenient model, but you should not believe it is a natural representation of educational achievement outcomes.

Percentile Ranks and z-scores in a Normal Distribution

If we cut up a normal distribution into sections one standard deviation wide, each section will have a fixed percentage of cases (see Figure 17.6) or **area under the normal curve**. For example, a section that is one standard deviation wide and located just above the mean contains approximately 34% of the area. The comparable section just below the mean contains, by symmetry, 34% as well. Together those two sections contain 68% of the area. About two-thirds of the area in a normal distribution will be within one standard deviation of the mean; 95% are within two standard deviations; and 99.7% of the area is within three standard deviations. Thus, if a distribution is normal, nearly all of the scores will span a range equivalent to six standard deviations.

You can use these facts about the percentage of cases in various segments to determine the correspondence between percentile ranks and z-scores in a normal distribution. This correspondence, the same for all normal distributions, permits an easy interpretation of standard scores in normal distributions. For example, look at the drawing in Figure 17.6 and the two scales below the drawing. The

FIGURE 17.6 Relationship between percentile ranks, z-scores, and T-scores in a normal distribution.

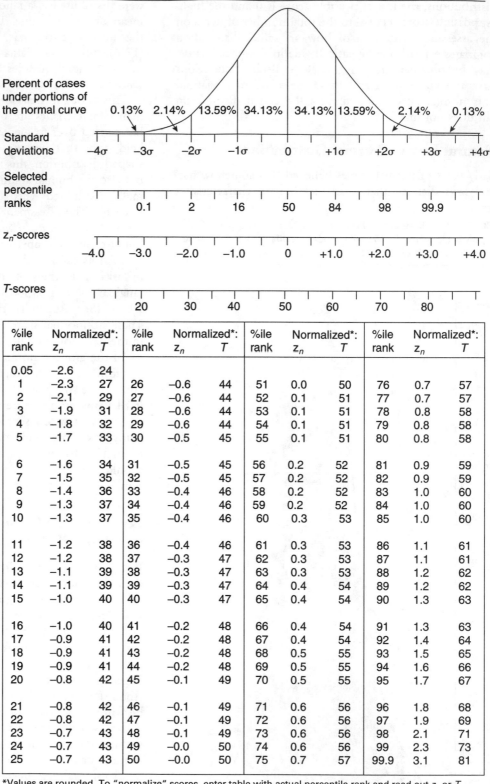

%ile rank	Normalized*: z_n	T	%ile rank	Normalized*: z_n	T	%ile rank	Normalized*: z_n	T	%ile rank	Normalized*: z_n	T
0.05	−2.6	24									
1	−2.3	27	26	−0.6	44	51	0.0	50	76	0.7	57
2	−2.1	29	27	−0.6	44	52	0.1	51	77	0.7	57
3	−1.9	31	28	−0.6	44	53	0.1	51	78	0.8	58
4	−1.8	32	29	−0.6	44	54	0.1	51	79	0.8	58
5	−1.7	33	30	−0.5	45	55	0.1	51	80	0.8	58
6	−1.6	34	31	−0.5	45	56	0.2	52	81	0.9	59
7	−1.5	35	32	−0.5	45	57	0.2	52	82	0.9	59
8	−1.4	36	33	−0.4	46	58	0.2	52	83	1.0	60
9	−1.3	37	34	−0.4	46	59	0.2	52	84	1.0	60
10	−1.3	37	35	−0.4	46	60	0.3	53	85	1.0	60
11	−1.2	38	36	−0.4	46	61	0.3	53	86	1.1	61
12	−1.2	38	37	−0.3	47	62	0.3	53	87	1.1	61
13	−1.1	39	38	−0.3	47	63	0.3	53	88	1.2	62
14	−1.1	39	39	−0.3	47	64	0.4	54	89	1.2	62
15	−1.0	40	40	−0.3	47	65	0.4	54	90	1.3	63
16	−1.0	40	41	−0.2	48	66	0.4	54	91	1.3	63
17	−0.9	41	42	−0.2	48	67	0.4	54	92	1.4	64
18	−0.9	41	43	−0.2	48	68	0.5	55	93	1.5	65
19	−0.9	41	44	−0.2	48	69	0.5	55	94	1.6	66
20	−0.8	42	45	−0.1	49	70	0.5	55	95	1.7	67
21	−0.8	42	46	−0.1	49	71	0.6	56	96	1.8	68
22	−0.8	42	47	−0.1	49	72	0.6	56	97	1.9	69
23	−0.7	43	48	−0.1	49	73	0.6	56	98	2.1	71
24	−0.7	43	49	−0.0	50	74	0.6	56	99	2.3	73
25	−0.7	43	50	−0.0	50	75	0.7	57	99.9	3.1	81

*Values are rounded. To "normalize" scores, enter table with actual percentile rank and read out z_n or T.

percentage of cases below $z_n = -2.00$ is 2.27% (= 0.13 + 2.14). To emphasize that we are speaking only of a normal distribution, Figure 17.6 denotes the z-scores as z_n. (Figure 17.6 also shows T-scores, which we will explain later in this chapter.) Thus, in a normal distribution the percentile rank corresponding to $z_n = -2.00$ is (rounded) 2. Other z-scores' percentile ranks can be computed similarly from Figure 17.6, as shown in Table 17.5. The chart under the

TABLE 17.5 Relationship between z_n-scores and percentile ranks in a normal distribution.

z_n	PR (rounded)	How computed			
–3.0	0.1 =	0.13			
–2.0	2 =	0.13 +	2.14		
–1.0	16 =	0.13 +	2.14 +	13.59	
0.0	50 =	0.13 +	2.14 +	13.59 +	34.13
+1.0	84 =	50 +	34.13		
+2.0	98 =	50 +	34.13 +	13.59	
+3.0	99.9 =	50 +	34.13 +	13.59 +	2.14

drawing in Figure 17.6 provides more complete information on percentile rank correspondences between z_n-scores and normal curves.

NORMALIZED STANDARD SCORES

Test publishers may transform raw scores to a new set of scores that is distributed normally (or nearly so). Such transformation changes the shape of the original distribution, squeezing and stretching the scale to make it conform to a normal distribution. Once this is accomplished, various types of standard scores can be derived, and each can have an appropriate normal curve interpretation. The derived scores publishers obtain by such a transformation are called **normalized standard scores**. These are also termed *area transformations*, as opposed to linear transformation. This section reviews a few of the common varieties reported in test manuals.

Normalized z-scores (z_n)

When the z-scores have percentile ranks corresponding to what we would expect in a normal distribution, they are called **normalized z-scores** and the following symbol is used:

z_n = the z-score corresponding to a given percentile rank in a normal distribution

If a distribution of raw scores is *not normal* in form, the percentile ranks of its z-scores will not correspond to what would be expected in a norm distribution. You may be surprised to learn, however, that one can create a set of "normalized" z-scores for any nonnormal distribution. After making this transformation, the new set of scores is more nearly like a normal distribution. **"Normalizing" a set of scores** is done in the following way: (1) determine the percentile rank of each score in the norm group, (2) look up each percentile rank in a normal curve table (e.g., the chart in Figure 17.6), and (3) read out the z_n-value that corresponds to each. The resulting z_n-values are "normalized." That is, they are the z-scores that *would have been attained if the distribution had been normal in form.*

To show you how the process works, and to illustrate the difference between z and z_n, consider Table 17.6, based on the test scores of the class of 25 students in Figure 17.3. In Figure 17.3, percentile ranks were calculated. Next, you look up each percentile rank in Figure 17.3 and in Figure 17.6, and read out the corresponding z_n. The results appear in Table 17.6. For the sake of comparison, the actual, *linear* z-scores are computed via Equation 17.1, using $M = 26.75$ and $SD = 3.8$. The difference between the normalized and linear z-scores represents the "stretching and squeezing" necessary to make the original distribution correspond more nearly to a normal distribution.

Normalized T-scores (McCall's T)

A **normalized T-score** tells *the location of a raw score in a normal distribution having a mean of 50 and a standard deviation of 10*. The normalized T-score is the counterpart to the linear SS-score. Thus,

$$T = 10z_n + 50 \qquad \text{[Eq. 17.3]}$$

The difference between this equation and Equation 17.2 ($SS = 10z + 50$) is that z_n is a normalized z-score instead of a linear z-score.

Normalized T-scores have the same advantages over normalized z-scores as SS-scores have over linear z-scores, with the additional advantage that T-scores have the percentile rank interpretations of a normal curve. For example, if Joey's T-score is 40, he is one standard deviation below the mean of the norm group, and his percentile rank is approximately 16. If Betty's percentile rank is 84, her

TABLE 17.6 Illustration of normalized z-scores and (actual) linear z-scores for the distribution of test scores in Figure 17.3.

Raw score	%ile rank	Normalized[a] z-score (z_n)	Linear[b] z-score (z)
36	98	2.05	2.43
33	96	1.75	1.64
32	94	1.55	1.38
31	90	1.28	1.12
30	88	1.18	0.86
29	84	0.99	0.59
28	72	0.58	0.33
27	54	0.10	0.07
26	32	–0.47	–0.20
25	16	–0.99	–0.46
24	10	–1.28	–0.72
22	8	–1.41	–1.25
21	6	–1.55	–1.51
15	4	–1.75	–3.09
14	2	–2.05	–3.36

[a]z_n-values obtained by looking up the percentile ranks in Figure 17.6
[b]z-values based on the actual distribution and using the equation:
$z = \dfrac{X - M}{SD}$ where $M = 26.75$ and $SD = 3.80$.

T-score is 60, and she is a distance of one standard deviation above the norm-group mean. Figure 17.6 shows the correspondence between percentile ranks, *T*-scores, and z_n scores in a normal distribution. That figure can help you convert percentile ranks directly to *T*-scores without using Equation 17.3.

Deviation IQ Scores (DIQ)

One type of normalized standard score is the **deviation IQ score (DIQ)** used with certain assessments of mental ability. The norm group is usually made up of all those students with the same chronological age, regardless of grade placement. A deviation IQ score tells the location of a raw score in a normal distribution having a mean of 100 and a standard deviation of 15 or 16. For example, if the test developer sets the standard deviation at 16, *DIQ*s are given by

$$DIQ = 16z_n + 100 \qquad \text{[Eq. 17.4]}$$

These *DIQ*s are interpreted in a way similar to *T*-scores. If Meghan has *DIQ* = 116, this means she has scored one standard deviation above the mean of her age group and has a percentile rank of 84. Usually, assessment manuals provide tables that permit you to directly convert raw scores to *DIQ*s.

Stanines

A **stanine score** tells *the location of a raw score in a specific segment of a normal distribution.* Figure 17.7 illustrates the meaning of a stanine score. A normal distribution is divided into nine segments, numbered from a low of 1 through a high of 9. Scores falling within the boundaries of these segments are assigned one of these nine numbers (hence, the term *stanine* from "standard nine"). Each segment is one-half a standard deviation wide, except for stanines 1 and 9. The percentage of the cases in a normal curve falling within each segment is shown in Figure 17.7, along with the range of percentile ranks associated with each.

All persons with scores falling within an interval are assigned the stanine of that interval. For example, all persons with scores having percentile ranks from 11 through 22 are assigned a stanine of 3; all from 23 through 29 a stanine of 4; and so on. Twelve percent of the persons in the norm group would be assigned a stanine of 3 and 17% a stanine of 4.

Publishers frequently recommend using **national stanines** for norm-referenced interpretation of achievement and aptitude assessments. Table 17.1 shows stanines and percentile ranks for the DAT Mechanical Reasoning Test. Advantages claimed for stanines include that they are single-digit numbers only, have approximately equal units all along the score scale, and do not imply an exactness greater than that warranted by the assessment. When raw scores from normal distributions are converted to stanines, the stanines have a mean of 5 and a standard deviation equal to 2.

Not all assessment experts agree with using stanines for norm-referenced interpretations. Some hold that stanines present more difficult interpretative problems than percentile ranks, especially for reliable assessments, because stanines reflect rather coarse groupings of scores (Hoover et al., 1993b).

FIGURE 17.7   Illustration of a normal distribution showing stanines, percentile rank intervals, and percentage of cases having each stanine.

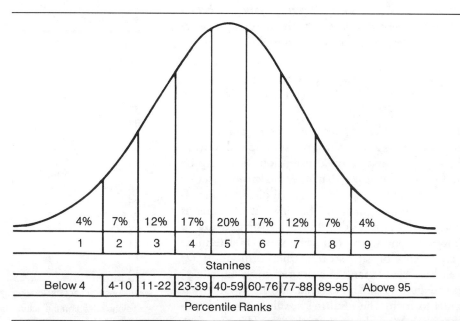

As with percentile ranks, stanines are specific to the reference group on which they are calculated. Some test publishers report both local and national stanines. For a specific student, these two stanines may be different, depending on how the student ranks in each reference group.

Figure 17.8 shows the details of transforming scores to stanines.

SAT Scores

The *Scholastic Assessment Test I* (SAT I) results are reported on a normalized standard score scale. The **SAT-score scale** is based on a reference group of 1,052,000 students who graduated from high school in 1990 and who took the SAT in either their junior or senior year of high school (Dorans, 1994). The scores of this reference group were normalized, the mean set to 500, and the standard deviation set to 100. This is shown in Equation 17.5.

$$SAT\text{-score} = 100z_n + 500 \qquad [\text{Eq. 17.5}]$$

Tests given after 1990 are statistically equated to the performance of the 1990 reference group. This assures that the scores have the same meaning from year to year. Thus, an SAT-score tells *the location of a score in the 1990 normal distribution that has a mean of 500 and a standard deviation of 100*. Percentile ranks corresponding to each current year's scores are provided to test users to facilitate interpretation for the current year.

Normal Curve Equivalents (NCE)

The **normal curve equivalent** is a *normalized standard score with a mean of 50 and a standard deviation of 21.06*. It was developed primarily for use with federal program evaluation efforts (Tallmadge & Wood, 1976). Its primary value is evaluating gains from various educational programs that use different publishers' tests. Although some publishers present norm tables for *NCE*s in their assessment manuals, using these scores for reporting individual student results is not recommended because they are too easily confused with percentile ranks. *NCE*-values are found by the

FIGURE 17.8 How to transform raw scores to stanines.

You may transform any set of scores to stanines by applying the normal curve percentage relationship implied by Figure 17.7. These theoretical percentages are:

Stanine	Percent of scores	Stanine	Percent of scores
9	top 4%	4	next 17%
8	next 7%	3	next 12%
7	next 12%	2	next 7%
6	next 17%	1	bottom 4%
5	middle 20%		

The preferred procedure is to begin assigning stanines at the middle of the score distribution (i.e., assigning stanine = 5 first) and then work toward each end. This procedure helps to make the resulting distribution of stanines more symmetric than if you started at the top or bottom. I illustrate the procedure below using the 25 students' scores shown in Figure 17.3.

Step-by-step	Results from Figure 17.3	Comments
1. Make a frequency distribution or list the scores in order from high to low.	See Figure 17.3, first and third columns.	
2. Locate the median or middle score.[a]	25 scores × ½ = 12.5 scores. Therefore, the middle score is 27.	Round the median to a whole number.
3. Use the theoretical percentages to determine how many scores should be assigned a stanine of 5.	20% of 25 = 5 scores.	
4. Assign stanines of 5 to the number of scores calculated in Step 3. (You should include scores just above and below the median if necessary to come as close as possible to the desired number.)	It so happens that in Figure 17.3 exactly 5 persons had a score of 27, so that we do not need to look to adjacent values. (See below.)	Remember that *all* equal scores must have the same stanine assigned to them.
5. Working up from the scores assigned stanine 5, use the theoretical percentages to assign scores to stanine categories of 6, 7, 8, and 9. Come as near to the theoretical percentages as possible.		
6. Repeat the procedure for the scores that are below those assigned stanine 5.		
7. It is important that you assign all equal scores the same stanine.		

Scores	Stanines	Actual number	Theoretical number
36	9	1	1
32 – 35	8	1	2
29 – 31	7	3	3
28	6	4	4
27	5	5	5
26	4	6	4
24 – 25	3	3	3
15 – 23	2	1	2
14	1	1	1

[a]The median is explained in Appendix H.

following formula. Their highest possible value is 99 and their lowest possible value is 1.

$$NCE = 21.06z_n + 50 \qquad \text{[Eq. 17.6]}$$

As stated previously, *NCE*-scores have a mean of 50 and a standard deviation of 21.06. By comparison, *T*-scores have a mean of 50 and a standard deviation of 10. Why choose a standard deviation of 21.06? This choice of standard deviation was made so the *NCE*-scores would span the range 1 to 99.

Table 17.7 shows the relationship between selected percentile ranks, *NCE*-scores, and stanines. As you can determine from the table, percentile ranks of 1, 50, and 99 are identical in value to *NCE*-scores. At other points, however, percentile ranks and *NCE*-scores differ: *NCE*-scores are less spread out than percentile ranks in the middle of the distribution and more spread out than percentile ranks at the lower and upper extremes. Notice the *NCE*-scores look very similar to percentile ranks. For this reason they are often confused with percentile ranks. Although some publishers present *NCE* norms tables in their standardized test manuals, we do not recommend *NCE*-scores for reporting individual student results because of this percentile rank confusion.

You may notice the relationship of the *NCE*-score to stanines. If you move the *NCE* decimal point to the left one digit and round to the nearest whole number, you will roughly have the stanine. For example, an *NCE* = 72 has a stanine equivalent of 7; *NCE* = 58 a stanine equivalent of 6; and so on. This rough correspondence stems from the fact that both *NCE*-scores and stanines are

based on a normal distribution, and *NCE*-scores and percentile ranks have the same range.

EXTENDED NORMALIZED STANDARD SCORE SCALES

The normalized standard score scales discussed so far are specific to a particular grade level or age group. You would find it useful, however, if your students' educational growth were reported on a scale that spanned the school years. Survey achievement batteries, for example, usually span several grades; say second through eighth, or ninth through twelfth. If the score scale of such batteries did not link the assessments from several grade levels to the same developmental score scale, you could not measure your students' growth over those years.

An example shows why percentile ranks cannot reflect growth per se. Suppose a student tested at the 84th percentile in grade 5, grade 6, and grade 7. Although this student would be growing in skills and knowledge, the student's percentile rank (84) has stayed the same. The number, 84, by reflecting only location in the current grade's norm group, does not communicate the student's growth. Similarly, a student's *T*-score determined separately for each grade's norm group could remain nearly the same from year to year, say about 60, while the student in fact exhibited educational growth each year.

An **extended normalized standard score** tells *the location of a raw score on a scale of numbers that is anchored to a lower grade reference group.* Educators find that a "ruler" or achievement continuum on which a student's progress can be measured over a wide range of grades–is very useful. On this continuum, low scores represent the lowest levels of educational development and high scores the highest level of educational development. Publishers refer to this type of scale with a variety of names, for example: obtained scale score (*California Achievement Tests*), scale score (*Comprehensive Tests of Basic Skills*), extended standard score (*Gates-MacGinite Reading Tests*), standard score (*Iowa Tests of Basic Skills*; *Metropolitan Achievement Tests*), or growth-scale values (*Iowa Tests of Educational Development*).

Although each assessment developer prepares expanded scales somewhat differently,[3] and the numbers obtained are not comparable from publisher to publisher, expanded scaled scores share the same goals and the same general method of development: (1) a base or anchor group is chosen and normalized *z*-scores are developed that extend beyond the range of scores for this anchor group; (2) a series of assessments is administered with common items given to adjoining groups (e.g., second and third graders take a common set of items, then third and fourth graders, and so on); (3) distributions of scores

TABLE 17.7 Correspondence between selected percentile ranks, *NCE*-scores, and stanines in a normal distribution.

Percentile rank	NCE	Stanine
1	1	1
5	15	2
10	23	2
20	32	3
25	36	4
30	39	4
35	42	4
40	45	5
45	47	5
50	50	5
55	53	5
60	55	6
65	58	6
70	61	6
75	64	6
80	68	7
85	72	7
90	77	8
95	85	8
99	99	9

[3]Some publishers use more complex procedures that employ technology based on item response theory (IRT). This use of IRT is beyond the scope of this book.

are tabulated and normalized for each grade; and (4) through these overlapping items, all of the groups are placed on the extended *z*-score scale of the anchor group. This extended *z*-scale becomes the ruler or growth scale spanning the several grades. The expanded *z*-scale is then transformed again to a scale that removes the unpleasant properties (such as negative numbers and decimals) of the *z*-scores. The new scale may range from 00 to 99, from 000 to 999, or any other set of numbers, depending on the publisher; there are no standards for what this range should be. Figure 17.9 illustrates how a publisher establishes such scales in a hypothetical case. The scaled scores reported in Table 17.1 are examples of expanded standard scores reported in an actual test manual.

Recent technical advances have resulted in some publishers offering schools two methods of calculating expanded standard scores. One method uses the traditional raw score for students (i.e., number right score) as a beginning step for calculating. A second method uses **item response theory (IRT)** in which a mathematical equation is fit to the publisher's norm sample of students' item responses. The results are then used to derive a score scale. According to this method, a student's score depends on the pattern of her right or wrong answers. **IRT pattern scoring** considers whether a student answered an easy or difficult item correctly, and how sharply that item distinguishes students of different achievement levels. This means, for example, that two students who answer correctly the same *number* of items may get different scaled scores if the correctly answered items were very different for the two students. The advantage is that the resultant expanded standard scores can have lower measurement error and greater reliability than traditional number-right scores. The disadvantages are (1) the direct link between the number correct and the expanded scale score is broken (when certain equations are used), and (2) the method does not work well for every type of test and every population of students.

Although program evaluators and school researchers generally prefer to use expanded standard scores, their meaning is not immediately apparent to teachers, parents, and students. Some educators consider this an advantage because it lessens the chance of over-interpreting scores. On the other hand, if no one knows what they mean, they will not be used, and therefore the scores will be underutilized.

Note that expanded standard scores show different standard deviations between subjects and progressively increasing standard deviations from grade to grade. Thus, you cannot compare a student's expanded assessment score from one subject area to another. In this respect, they share a common property with grade-equivalent scores, discussed next.

GRADE-EQUIVALENT SCORES

Basic Idea of Grade-Equivalent Scores

A **grade-equivalent score (GE)** tells *the grade placement at which a raw score is average.* GEs are educational development scores often used with achievement tests at the elementary school level. The grade-equivalent score is reported as a decimal

FIGURE 17.9 A hypothetical example of how scores on a series of achievement tests are converted to a common extended score scale. The successive groups are located on the scale by linking together the overlapping tests in a special administration.

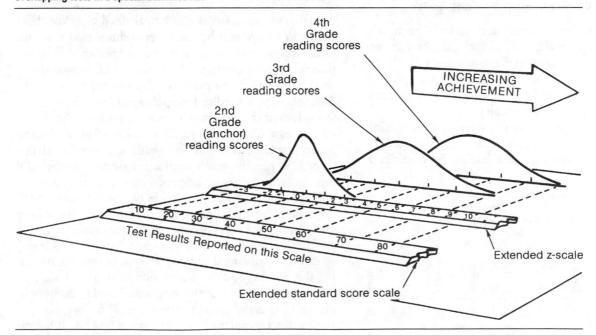

fraction, such as 3.4 or 7.9. The whole number part of the score refers to a grade level, and the decimal part refers to a month of the school year within that grade level. For example, you read a grade-equivalent score of 3.4 as "third grade, fourth month"; similarly, you read 7.9 as "seventh grade, ninth month." Suppose the grade-equivalent score corresponding to the raw score 31 is 6.3. This means that the average in the norm group during the third month of sixth grade was 31.

Grade-equivalent scores are useful for reporting a pupil's educational development. If a standardized test is administered periodically throughout a student's school years, the resulting grade-equivalent scores can help to monitor the student's educational progress using a grade-based educational development scale. To a lesser extent, grade equivalents can be used to monitor a student's grade placement. *The problem with grade placement interpretations of GE scores is that they depend on the closeness of the match between what is on the test and what was taught to the students up to the point at which the test was administered. The poorer this match, the less valid are grade placement interpretations.*

Grade-equivalent scores cannot be used to identify a student's strengths and weaknesses across different subject matters. Nor can they be used to determine a student's rank among his or her peers. An explanation of these limitations follows in the remainder of this section.

When using these scores, you assume that the time between June and September (i.e., the summer months) represents an increment of one-tenth (or one month) on the grade-equivalent scale (Figure 17.10). As a result of this way of defining the grade-equivalent scale, the *average* of the scores shows 10 month's growth every year. (However, you should not expect every student to show one month's growth each summer.)

Development of Grade-Equivalent Scores

Administrators, teachers, parents, and students frequently misinterpret grade equivalents. Understanding how the assessment publisher obtains grade equivalents will help you to prevent misinterpretation. There is no need, of course, for you to compute them because test manuals provide the needed conversion tables.

The development process is illustrated with a reading test, but the same process applies to all subject areas. Suppose a publisher wishes to assess reading from grades 1

through 8 and to develop grade equivalents. The publisher creates a series of overlapping tests that span the desired grades: one test for first and second grades, one for third and fourth, and so on. Each test is appropriate for specific grade levels. The publisher administers the appropriate tests to a large national sample at each grade level. Usually, the publisher does this once or twice during the year (fall and/or spring), because it is impossible to administer them continuously throughout the year. The dates on which tests are administered are called **empirical norming dates**. These overlapping tests are then linked together using an expanded score scale. This allows the different tests to be placed on a reading ability scale. The process is called *vertical linking* or *vertical equating*.

On this common scale, large differences in reading ability exist in the norm group at each grade level. Therefore, at each grade level there is a spread of reading scores. These distributions of reading scores are shown in Figure 17.11. In this illustration, the publisher administered the assessments only once during the year—in February (month = 0.5), so the figure graphs the distributions directly above 1.5, 2.5, 3.5, etc.

The publisher's first step is to locate and plot on a graph the median score (the mean score is used sometimes instead) in each grade's norm group. For instance, in the figure first graders in the norm group taking the test in February have an average (median) score of 10. The grade equivalent corresponding to the raw score 10 because the grade placement of this median is 1.5. Norm-group second graders in February have an average score of 15, and their corresponding grade equivalent is 2.5. Grade equivalents for grades four and five are similarly plotted in Figure 17.11.

Interpolation and Extrapolation

Actual grade equivalents can be obtained only for those points in time when the publisher administered the tests. Grade equivalents for other points are obtained by interpolation or extrapolation. In Figure 17.11, notice that a solid line connects the medians of the actual distributions. This solid line is used to **interpolate** and thereby estimate the values of the in-between grade equivalents. For example, the raw score 13 is not an actual median of a norm-group distribution. However, we draw a horizontal line from 13 across the graph until it intersects with the solid line and then drop a perpendicular line down to the grade-placement scale. The grade placement corresponding to this vertical line (2.1) becomes the interpolated grade equivalent that corresponds to a raw score of 13.

Consider a raw score of 8. A grade equivalent for this score can be obtained only by **extrapolation**: by extending the line beyond the norm groups actually tested according to the trend of the medians. The dashed lines in Figure 17.11 represent this extension. Thus, the extrapolated grade equivalent of the raw score 8 is 1.1. If the extrapolation is incorrect, so will be the grade equivalent.

FIGURE 17.10 Grade-equivalent score scale.

Month of school year									
September	October	November	December	January	February	March	April	May	June
.0	.1	.2	.3	.4	.5	.6	.7	.8	.9

Decimal portion of the grade equivalent

FIGURE 17.11 Hypothetical example of data used to obtain grade-equivalent scores.

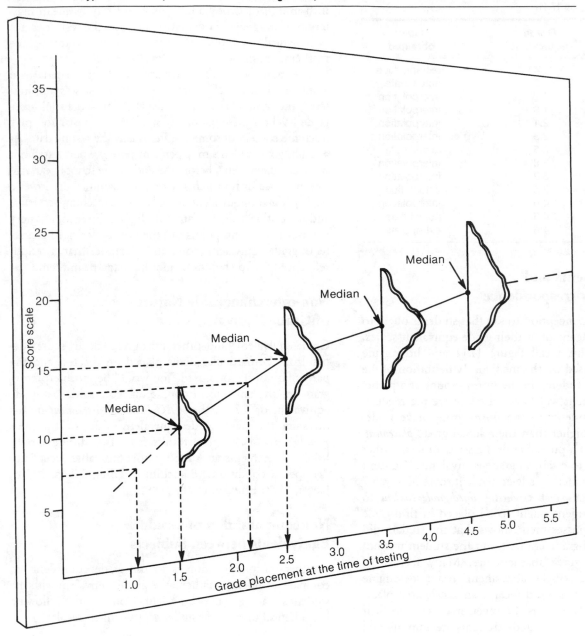

Table 17.8 summarizes what has been said so far about extrapolation and interpolation. An actual conversion table from a published test is shown in Table 17.9. You will use this type of conversion table when you consult a publisher's norms booklet to convert your students' raw scores to grade equivalents.

Spring-to-Fall Drops: Summer Losses

One special concern in the process of interpreting grade equivalents is the phenomenon of summer achievement losses. In some subject areas—arithmetic, for example—students' performance loses some of its edge over the summer months (Beggs & Hieronymus, 1968; DeVito & Long, 1977; Tallmadge, 1973; Tallmadge & Horst, 1974; Tallmadge & Wood, 1976). A performance drop over the summer months has several meanings: (1) the assumption of an over-the-summer growth of one month is not true in every subject area, (2) educational growth is not regular and uniform for many children, and (3) using fall-to-spring gains in grade-equivalent scores to evaluate an instructional program may lead to wrong conclusions. The third point is less problematic when the test publisher has separate fall and spring norms and when a school system tests on dates very close to the dates on which the publisher's norms were established.

TABLE 17.8   Raw-score to grade-equivalent conversion table for the hypothetical data in Figure 17.11.

Raw score	Grade equivalent	How obtained
9	1.4	extrapolation
10	1.5	actual data
11	1.7	interpolation
12	1.9	interpolation
13	2.1	interpolation
14	2.3	interpolation
15	2.5	actual data
16	2.8	interpolation
17	3.2	interpolation
18	3.5	actual data
19	4.0	interpolation
20	4.5	actual data
21	4.6	extrapolation

Grade Equivalents and Curriculum Correspondence

It would be a misconception to say that students ought to have the same placement as their grade-equivalent scores. To understand why, recall Figure 17.11 and how grade equivalents are based on the median. By definition of the median, half the students in the norm groups at a particular grade placement will have scores above the median. Thus, half the students in the norm group have grade-equivalent *scores* higher than their actual grade *placement*. Second, recall that a publisher uses a series of tests, rather than a single test, to establish grade equivalents. You can't interpret a third grader's grade-equivalent score of, say, 5.7 on an mathematics test covering *third-grade content* to mean that this student ought to be placed in fifth-grade mathematics. The assessment shows that the student did very well on third-grade content, but the student was not assessed on fifth-grade mathematics. Many factors, of course, besides a single assessment result determine whether the student should receive an accelerated placement. Some test publishers, however, may develop their test batteries so that third-grade students are administered fifth-grade content for purposes of developing a grade-equivalent scale. In such cases, it may be appropriate to say cautiously that the third graders with a grade equivalent of 5.7 do know some fifth-grade content (Hoover et al., 1993b).

Grade Equivalents and Mastery

Sometimes teachers, parents, and school administrators misinterpret grade equivalents to mean mastery of a particular fraction of a curricular area. For example, a parent may erroneously think that a student's grade equivalent of 3.5 in mathematics means the student has mastered five-tenths of the local school's third-grade mathematics curriculum. The most that can be said about this student, however, is that on this test the student's score is equal to the average score of the norm group when it was in the fifth month of *third* grade. This is unlikely to mean mastery of third-grade mathematics, because the test does not systematically sample the entire domain of third-grade mathematics in the student's local curriculum.

The more closely the test items match the material you emphasized in the classroom before the test was administered, the more likely your students are to score well *above* grade level on these nationally standardized tests. You may teach the content of some test items *after* the testing date. As a result, your students may perform poorly when tested but will learn the material before the end of the school year. Answering three or four items wrong will significantly lower a student's grade-equivalent score. If your teaching sequence and the testing sequence are not aligned, inferring mastery is problematic. This points out the norm-referenced character of grade-equivalent scores and illustrates that criterion-referenced interpretations cannot be made from them.

Non-interchangeable Nature of Grade Equivalents

Grade-equivalent (and other norm-referenced) scores depend on the particular items placed on the test and the particular norm group used. You would be misinterpreting grade equivalents, for example, if you said, "A grade equivalent of 3.7 on the *ABC Reading Assessment* means the same thing as a grade equivalent of 3.7 on the *DEF Reading Assessment*." The results from two different publishers' assessments are simply noncomparable except under special conditions (Bianchini & Loret, 1974a, 1974b; Jaeger, 1973; Peterson et al., 1989).

Noncomparability of Grade Equivalents between Subjects

Another misinterpretation is to use grade equivalents to compare a student's mathematics grade equivalent with the student's reading grade equivalent. Consider the following hypothetical third-grade students' assessment results.

		Survey subtest	
		Reading	Mathematics
John	GE	4.9	4.9
	PR	78	90
Howard	GE	4.9	4.3
	PR	78	78
Susan	GE	4.9	4.6
	PR	78	84

Notice that John has two identical grade equivalents, but their corresponding percentile ranks are *different*. Howard has two different grade equivalents but has *identical* percentile ranks. Finally, Susan has one grade equivalent higher than another, yet her higher grade equivalent has a *lower* percentile rank than her lower grade equivalent.

TABLE 17.9 Part of a grade-equivalent table for the *Metropolitan Achievement Tests* (7th edition), *Forms S/T, Fall norms*. Notice that you enter the table with the (expanded) scaled score and read the grade-equivalent scores in the margins. Expanded scaled scores are obtained first from another table (not shown here), which you enter with raw scores.

Grade Equiv.	Word Recognition	Reading Vocabulary	Reading Comprehension	Prereading/ Total Reading	Concepts & Problem Solving	Procedures	Grade Equiv.
7.9	665	661	656	659	644	650	7.9
7.8	663–664	660	654–655	657–658	642–643	648–649	7.8
7.7	661–662	659	–	655–656	641	647	7.7
7.6	660	658	653	654	640	–	7.6
7.5	–	657	–	–	639	646	7.5
7.4	–	656	–	–	638	645	7.4
7.3	659	655	652	653	637	–	7.3
7.2	–	654	–	–	636	644	7.2
7.1	658	653	651	652	635	643	7.1
7.0	657	651–652	650	651	634	642	7.0
6.9	656	650	649	650	633	641	6.9
6.8	653–655	648–649	647–648	647–649	632	639–640	6.8
6.7	651–652	646–647	645–646	645–646	630–631	638	6.7
6.6	649–650	644–645	643–644	643–644	628–629	636–637	6.6
6.5	647–648	642–643	642	641–642	626–627	634–635	6.5
6.4	646	640–641	640–641	640	624–625	632–633	6.4
6.3	644–645	638–639	639	638–639	622–623	629–631	6.3
6.2	642–643	636–637	637–638	636–637	620–621	626–628	6.2
6.1	641	634–635	635–636	635	618–619	623–625	6.1
6.0	639–640	632–633	633–634	633–634	616–617	621–622	6.0
5.9	637–638	630–631	631–632	631–632	614–615	618–620	5.9
5.8	634–636	628–629	630	628–630	613	616–617	5.8
5.7	632–633	626–627	628–629	626–627	611–612	614–615	5.7
5.6	630–631	624–625	626–627	625	610	611–613	5.6
5.5	628–629	622–623	624–625	623–624	609	608–610	5.5
5.4	626–627	620–621	623	621–622	608	606–607	5.4
5.3	624–625	618–619	622	619–620	607	604–605	5.3
5.2	622–623	616–617	621	618	606	602–603	5.2
5.1	620–621	614–615	620	617	605	600–601	5.1
5.0	618–619	612–613	618–619	616	603–604	597–599	5.0
4.9	616–617	610–611	617	615	601–602	595–596	4.9
4.8	613–615	607–609	615–616	613–614	599–600	592–594	4.8
4.7	611–612	604–606	613–614	610–612	597–598	590–591	4.7
4.6	608–610	601–603	610–612	607–609	595–596	587–589	4.6
4.5	605–607	598–600	607–609	603–606	592–594	584–586	4.5
4.4	602–604	595–597	604–606	600–602	590–591	581–583	4.4
4.3	599–601	592–594	601–603	598–599	587–589	577–580	4.3
4.2	596–598	589–591	598–600	596–597	585–586	573–576	4.2
4.1	593–595	586–588	596–597	594–595	582–584	569–572	4.1
4.0	589–592	583–585	594–595	591–593	580–581	566–568	4.0

Source: From Multilevel norms book: *The Metropolitan Achievement Tests: Seventh Edition,* (p. 171). Copyright © 1993 by Harcourt, Inc. Reproduced by permission. All rights reserved.

The reason for the phenomena is that scores for one subject area are more spread out than those of another, resulting in different patterns of interpolation when grade equivalents are prepared. Expanded standard scores cannot be used to compare a student's performance in different areas, either.

What should you use to describe a student's relative strengths and weaknesses in different subject areas? If all students in the norm group took the same tests in all subjects, then we recommend using percentile ranks. Thus, in

the preceding illustration, John is somewhat better in mathematics and in reading, Howard is about the same in both subjects, and Susan is slightly better in mathematics than in reading. Because these are norm-referenced interpretations, "better" implies "compared with other persons."

"Normal" Growth

Sometimes teachers and school administrators use grade equivalents to answer questions of what educational growth they should expect of a student. The results of doing this often are not satisfactory. One view of **normal growth** is this: "A student ought to exhibit a growth of 1.0 grade-equivalent units from one grade to the next." Under this view, a student taking the test in second grade and scoring 1.3, for example, would need to score 2.3 in third grade, 4.3 in fifth, and so on to show "normal" or expected growth.

This view of normal grade-equivalent growth cannot be supported. Table 17.10 illustrates what will happen to three hypothetical students on the mathematics subtest of two published tests if this view is adopted. The students have these characteristics: Student A is one year behind in terms of grade equivalents, Student B is at grade level, and Student C is one year ahead. Each year, the students' grade equivalents show a one-year "growth" over the preceding year. But look at the percentile ranks corresponding to their scores: Student A, who starts out one year behind, has to *exceed more persons* in the norm group to maintain a one-year-behind grade equivalent. Being one year behind in second grade means being at the 16th or 17th percentile. However, one year behind in grade 8 means being around the *41st or 42nd percentile*. One has to move from the bottom of the group toward the middle. An opposite phenomenon occurs for Student C, who begins one grade ahead at around the *86th or 92nd percentile*. In this case, the student can fall behind more and more students and still be "one year ahead." Students who are at grade level (Student B) have raw scores equal to the average. By definition, the average at a grade is assigned one year's growth from the preceding year. Thus, only students who are exactly at the average year will maintain their percentile rank from year to year.

An alternate norm-referenced definition of normal growth is: "A student shows normal growth if that student maintains the same position (i.e., percentile rank) in the norm from year to year." Table 17.11 shows what happens to a student's grade-equivalent score if that student's *percentile rank* stays the same each year. Lower-scoring students (such as Students A and D)—even though they do not change their position in the norm group—have grade equivalents indicating they are further and further behind. (An opposite trend occurs for initially high-scoring students.) The exact magnitude of this falling-behind phenomenon will vary from one publisher's test to another's and depends on the student's percentile rank. The grade-equivalent scales of some tests are created in such a way that the falling-behind effect is held to a minimum. Students close to the 50th percentile will exhibit less of the falling-behind effect than will those further from the center of the distribution. The reasons for this effect are two: (1) the line connecting the medians of the distributions at each grade level (see Figure 17.11) tends to flatten out at higher grades rather than being a diagonal line, and (2) scores at upper grades become more spread out, spanning a larger range than scores at lower grades.

Unequal Units

You should be aware that the grade-equivalent ruler does not have a one-to-one correspondence with the number of questions a student answers correctly on a test. This means, for example, that students in the middle of the distribution who get one more item correct are likely to raise their grade-equivalent scores by only one-tenth (i.e., one "month"). For students in the upper part of the distribution, however, one additional correct item may result in an increment of several tenths (several "months" of growth). As a result of these unequal units, calculating averages using grade equivalents becomes problematic.

TABLE 17.10 Changes in percentile ranks for three hypothetical students as each "gains" one year in grade-equivalent units from second through eighth grade.

| Grade placement at the time of testing | Metropolitan Achievement Tests, Total Mathematics | | | | | | Iowa Tests of Basic Skills, Total Mathematics | | | | | |
| | Student A: "Below grade level" | | Student B: "On grade level" | | Student C: "Above grade level" | | Student A: "Below grade level" | | Student B: "On grade level" | | Student C: "Above grade level" | |
	GE	PR	GE	PR	GE	PR	GE	PR	GE	PR	GE	PR
2.3	1.3	16	2.3	63	3.3	86	1.3	18	2.3	54	3.3	92
3.3	2.3	29	3.3	64	4.3	85	2.3	18	3.3	55	4.3	85
4.3	3.3	34	4.3	63	5.3	80	3.3	28	4.3	56	5.3	77
5.3	4.3	37	5.3	61	6.3	77	4.3	34	5.3	54	6.3	71
6.3	5.3	36	6.3	57	7.3	73	5.3	34	6.3	52	7.3	66
7.3	6.3	39	7.3	60	8.3	70	6.3	38	7.3	52	8.3	65
8.3	7.3	42	8.3	55	9.3	60	7.3	41	8.3	53	9.3	64

TABLE 17.11 Year-to-year changes in grade-equivalent scores for four hypothetical students as each student's percentile rank remains the same.

Grade placement at the time of testing	Metropolitan Achievement Tests, Total Mathematics				Iowa Tests of Basic Skills, Total Mathematics			
	Student A: "Below grade level" (PR = 16 each year)		Student B: "Above grade level" (PR = 84 each year)		Student C: "Below grade level" (PR = 16 each year)		Student D: "Above grade level" (PR = 84 each year)	
	GE	"Grades behind"	GE	"Grades ahead"	GE	"Grades behind"	GE	"Grades ahead"
3.3	2.1	1.2	4.8	1.5	2.1	1.2	4.7	1.4
4.3	2.6	1.7	6.3	2.0	2.8	1.5	5.9	1.6
5.3	3.1	2.2	7.7	2.4	3.3	2.0	7.3	2.0
6.3	3.9	2.4	9.0	2.7	4.0	2.3	8.8	2.5
7.3	4.5	2.8	10.1	2.8	4.7	2.6	10.3	3.0
8.3	5.1	3.2	10.6	2.3	5.1	3.2	11.9	3.6

Source: Some data are reproduced from The Psychological Corporation (1993a). *The Metropolitan Achievement Tests* (7th ed.), *Forms S/T*, Fall. Copyright © 1993 by Harcourt, Inc. Reproduced by permission. All rights reserved. Other data are adapted from Hoover, Hieronymus, Frisbie, & Dunbar (1993c). *Iowa Tests of Basic Skills: Norms and score conversions, complete and core batteries, Form K.* Copyright © 1993 by The University of Iowa. All rights reserved. Reproduced by permission of The Riverside Publishing Company.

Grade Mean Equivalents

Because it is problematic to average grade-equivalent scores, some publishers (e.g., CTB/McGraw-Hill) have tried other ways to give schools information on how well their students performed on the average. One technique is to report the **grade mean equivalent** that tells *the grade placement of a group's average expanded scale score.* Instead of averaging grade-equivalent scores directly, you first average the expanded scale scores. Second, you look up the grade equivalent that corresponds to this average expanded scale score. For example, if a fourth-grader class's average (mean) reading expanded scale score on the *Terra-Nova* assessment was 641, this would convert to a grade equivalent of 4.9. This means that 641 is the national average for all norm group students who have completed the ninth month of Grade 4 (CTB/McGraw-Hill, 1997).

Recommendations

In light of the problems with grade equivalents, you may wonder why they are used at all. Indeed, many assessment specialists feel they should be eliminated. Yet such scores are popular with teachers and administrators who are generally unaware of the complex criticisms. Teachers and school administrators have a real need for at least some crude measure of educational development or growth that they can relate to years of schooling. Despite the technical difficulties in doing so, grade equivalents seem intuitively to be a "natural metric." Some assessment specialists recommend extended standard scores as measures of growth, but they possess many of the same interpretive problems as grade equivalents. Further, because extended standard scores are not referenced to grade levels, their interpretation can be confusing.

You should use grade equivalents only as coarse indicators of educational development or growth and then only when you

report them with their corresponding percentile ranks. Grade equivalents are norm-referenced growth indicators. If you want information about the content of a student's learning, you need to look carefully at the kinds of performances the student can do. To do that, you need to review for each student the kinds of test items the student answered correctly. When you do this, of course, you are making criterion-referenced interpretations.

Summary of Grade Equivalents

As a summary of grade-equivalent scores, consider the situation in which a school administered a published, norm-referenced achievement test to third graders in May. Further, assume that the school's teachers have judged the assessment to validly match the curriculum and to be an appropriate way to assess the students. Finally, assume that the publisher's norms are appropriate. Then, even under all these nice assumptions, each of the following statements—except the first—*is false.*

1. Pat's Reading Subtest grade-equivalent score is 3.8. This suggests that she is an average third-grade reader.

2. Ramon's Arithmetic Subtest grade equivalent is 4.6. This means that he knows arithmetic as well as the typical fourth grader who is at the end of the sixth month of school.

3. Melba's Arithmetic Subtest grade equivalent is 6.7. This suggests that next year she ought to take arithmetic with the sixth graders.

4. Debbie's Reading Subtest grade equivalent is 2.3. This means she has mastered three-tenths of the second-grade reading skills.

5. John's grade-equivalent profile is Vocabulary = 6.2, Reading = 7.1, Language = 7.1, Work-Study Skills =

7.2, Arithmetic = 6.7. This means that his weak areas are vocabulary and arithmetic.

6. Two of Sally's grade equivalents are Language = 4.5 and Arithmetic = 4.5. Because her language and arithmetic grade equivalents are the same, we conclude that her language and arithmetic ability are about equal.

7. Half of this school's third graders have grade equivalents below grade level. This means that instructional quality is generally poor.

8. This year Mrs. Murray was assigned all of the students whose assessment scores were in the bottom quarter. The average of her class's grade equivalents this May was further below grade level than the class's average last year. This means that Mrs. Murray's instruction has been ineffective for the class as a whole.

[Statements 1 through 6 are from Lindvall and Nitko (1975, p. 98). Statements 7 and 8 have been adapted from Hills (1976, pp. 87–88).]

COMPARISON OF VARIOUS NORM-REFERENCED SCORES

Table 17.12 summarizes the various norm-referenced scores discussed in this chapter. Although each type of score describes the student's location in a norm group, each does so in a somewhat different way. The easiest type of score to explain to parents and students is a percentile rank. Various types of linear standard scores require an understanding of the mean and standard deviation for their meaning to become clear. Usually you will need to interpret normalized standard scores in conjunction with

TABLE 17.12 How to interpret different types of norm-referenced scores.

Type of Score	Interpretation	Score	Examples of Interpretations
Percentile rank	Percentage of scores in a distribution below this point.	$PR = 60$	"60% of the raw scores are lower than this score."
Linear standard score (z-score)	Number of standard deviation units a score is above (or below) the mean of a given distribution.	$z = +1.5$	"This raw score is located 1.5 standard deviations *above* the mean."
		$z = -1.2$	"This raw score is located 1.2 standard deviations *below* the mean."
Linear standard score (SS-score or 50 ± 10 system)	Location of score in a distribution having a mean of 50 and a standard deviation of 10. (Note: For other systems, substitute in these statements that system's mean and standard deviation.)	$SS = 65$	"This raw score is located 1.5 standard deviations *above* the mean in a distribution whose mean is 50 and whose standard deviation is 10."
		$SS = 38$	"This raw score is located 1.2 standard deviations *below* the mean in a distribution whose mean is 50 and whose standard deviation is 10."
Stanine	Location of a score in a specific segment of a normal distribution of scores.	Stanine = 5	"This raw score is located in the middle 20% of a normal distribution of scores."
		Stanine = 9	"This raw score is located in the top 4% of a normal distribution of scores."
Normalized standard score (T-score or normalized 50 ± 10 system)	Location of score in a normal distribution having a mean of 50 and a standard deviation of 10. (Note: For other systems, substitute in these statements that system's mean and standard deviation [e.g. *DIQs* have a mean of 100 and a standard deviation of 16: this is a 100 ± 16 System].)	$T = 65$	"This raw score is located 1.5 standard deviations above the mean in a normal distribution whose mean is 50 and whose standard deviation is 10. This score has a percentile rank of 84."
		$T = 38$	"This raw score is located 1.2 standard deviations below the mean in a normal distribution whose mean is 50 and whose standard deviation is 10. This score has a percentile rank of 12."
Expanded standard score	Location of a score on an arbitrary scale of numbers that is anchored to some reference group.		(No interpretation is offered here because the systems are so arbitrary and unalike.)
Grade-equivalent score	The grade placement at which the raw score is average.	$GE = 4.5$	"This raw score is the obtained or estimated average for all pupils whose grade placement is at the fifth month of the fourth grade."

Source: Adapted from *Measuring Student Achievement and Aptitude* (2nd Ed.) (p. 99) by C. M. Lindvall and A. J. Nitko, 1975, New York: Harcourt Brace Jovanovich. Reproduced by permission of the authors.

percentile ranks. From test to test, normalized standard scores will have the same percentage of cases associated with them. Consequently, their meaning remains fairly constant as long as a normal distribution can be assumed. Grade equivalents and expanded standard scores provide scores along an educational growth continuum, but because of their inherent technical complexities, teachers and school administrators frequently misinterpret them. Limit using grade equivalents to gross estimates of yearly student growth. Use them only when you accompany them with percentile ranks. Use percentile ranks to compare an individual student's performance in different curriculum areas.

GENERAL GUIDELINES FOR SCORE INTERPRETATION

Teachers and school administrators should consider the following points when interpreting student scores on norm-referenced assessments (Prescott, Balow, Hogan, & Farr, 1978):

1. *Look for unexpected patterns of scores.* An assessment should confirm what a teacher knows from daily interactions with a student; unusually high or low scores for a student should be a signal for exploring instructional implications.

2. *Seek an explanation for patterns.* Ask why a student is higher in one subject than another. Check for motivation, special interests, special difficulties, etc.

3. *Don't expect surprises for every student.* Most students' assessment results should be as you expect from their performance in class. A valid assessment should confirm your observations.

4. *Small differences in subtest scores should be viewed as chance fluctuations.* Use the standard error of measurement (Chapter 4) to help decide whether differences are large enough to have instructional significance.

5. *Use information from various assessments and observation to explain performance on other assessments.* Students low in reading comprehension may perform poorly on the social studies subtest, for example.

FIGURE 17.12   Parent's copy of a score report along with computerized interpretations.

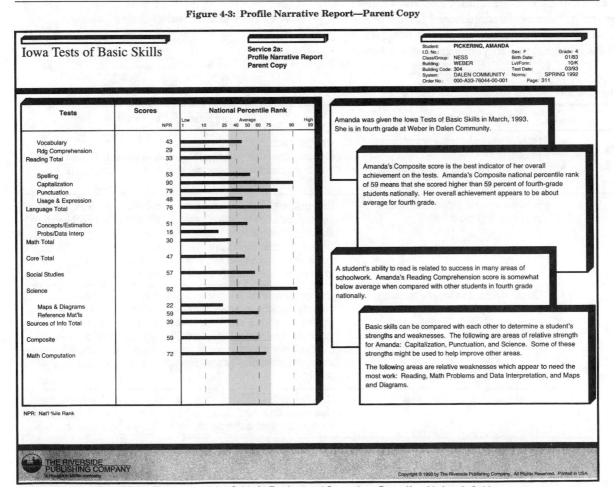

Source: From *Iowa Test of Basic Skills, Interpretive Guide for Teachers and Counselors, Forms K and L. Levels 9–14,* (p. 52) by H. D. Hoover, A. N. Hieronymus, D. A. Frisbie, and S. B. Dunbar, 1993b, Chicago: Riverside Publishing Company. Copyright © 1993 by The University of Iowa. Adapted with permission of The Riverside Publishing Company.

You may wish to try your hand at implementing these general guidelines by reviewing the case presented in Figure 17.12. Your interpretation of Amanda Pickering's report may be different from that of the computer.

INTERPRETING SCORES TO PARENTS

A teacher has the most direct contact with parents regarding norm-referenced score reports. You must be prepared, therefore, to explain students' norm-referenced test results to their parents. Studying the concepts and principles in this chapter is a prerequisite for effectively communicating to parents.

Types of Questions and Answers

Table 17.13 contains examples of many of the questions parents ask when they receive standardized test results from a school. The questions are organized into five categories: standing, growth, improvement needed, strengths, and intelligence. You should be prepared to answer questions in these categories. The table contains suggestions for answering each category of questions. Note that we indicate which type of norm-referenced score to use. Although other scores might be used, we believe the ones suggested will be most helpful to your explanation. No-

tice, too, that we suggest always using a student's classroom performance to complement and explain the student's standardized test results. Because in the majority of cases students' standardized test performance will be very consistent with their classroom performance, using students' classroom performance to illustrate their standardized test performance will help you to reinforce to the parents your assessment of the students.

Parent Misunderstandings

Parents also have misunderstandings about what norm-referenced test scores mean. We have discussed already many of the misconceptions and limitations in this chapter. The following list *summarizes common parent misunderstandings* about which you need to be clear before you can help parents correct them:

1. The grade-equivalent score tells which grade the student should be in. . . .
2. The percentile rank and percent-correct scores mean the same thing. . . .
3. The percentile rank norm group consists of only the students in a particular classroom. . . .
4. "Average" is the standard to beat. . . .
5. Small changes in percentile ranks over time are meaningful. . . .

TABLE 17.13   How to answer parents' questions about standardized test results.

Category	Examples of questions	Suggestions for answering
Standing	• How is my child doing compared to others? • Is my child's progress normal for his or her grade?	Use percentile ranks to describe standing. Explain that a standardized test gives partial information only. Use information from classroom performance to explain progress.
Growth	• Has my child's growth been as much as it should be?	Use grade-equivalent scores to show progress from previous years. Use composite scores (i.e., all subjects combined) to show general growth; use scores from each subject to explain growth in particular curricular areas. Obtain past performance information from the child's cumulative folder. Use information from classroom performance to explain growth.
Improvement needed	• Does my child have any learning weaknesses? • How can I help to improve my child's learning?	Use percentile ranks to identify relative weaknesses. Use information about a student's performance on clusters of similar questions to pinpoint weaknesses. Use information from class performance to explain specific weaknesses. Don't overemphasize weaknesses. Explain a student's relative strengths, too; give specific suggestions as to how parents can help.
Strengths	• What does my child do well?	Use percentile ranks to pick out areas of relative strengths. Use class information to illustrate the point. Make suggestions for how parents can help improve these areas even more.
Intelligence	• How smart is my child? Is my child gifted?	Explain that an achievement test is not an intelligence test. Explain that an achievement test is very sensitive to what was taught in class and that high scores may only reflect specific opportunities to learn. Use class information to illustrate your points.

Source: This table is based on suggestions in Hoover, Hieronymus, Frisbie, & Dunbar, 1993b.

6. Percent-correct scores below 70 are failing. . . .

7. If you get a perfect score, your percentile rank must be 99. . . . (Hoover et al., 1993b, pp. 103–105)

Summary

- By themselves, raw scores on educational and psychological tests are difficult to interpret: You need to reference them to a well-defined norm group and to a well-defined domain of performances.

- Norm-referencing frameworks compare a student's performance with well-defined groups of other students who took the same test. Norm-referencing answers the question, "How did this student do compared to other students?"

- Criterion-referencing frameworks compare a student's performance against the domain of performances the assessment samples. Criterion-referencing answers the question, "How much of the targeted learning did this student achieve?" For many of your daily teaching decisions, criterion-referencing frameworks are most useful.

- There are many groups to which a student may be compared. These are called norm groups, and they include local, national, and special norms.

- The average score in a school building should be compared only to school averages norms.

- Three criteria you may use for judging the quality of norm data are relevance to your school, representativeness of the publisher's sampling plan, and recency of the norm-group test administration.

- The most common criterion-referenced scores are percentage correct, speed of performance, quality ratings, and precision of performance.

- The most common norm-referenced scores are percentile ranks, linear standard scores, normalized standard scores, and grade-equivalent scores. These are found in test publishers' norms tables.

- Linear standard scores include z-scores, SS-scores, and SAT-scores. Normalized standard scores include z_n-scores, T-scores, stanine scores, DIQ scores, and extended-scale scores.

- A normal curve helps you interpret the relationship between normalized standard scores and percentile ranks. You should not believe, however, that students' aptitudes, intelligences, or achievements are naturally normally distributed. A normal curve is not a law of nature for educational assessments. It is a tool to help you interpret test results.

- Grade-equivalent scores help you to interpret a student's standardized test performance by providing a grade-based scale of educational development. Grade equivalents are not criteria or standards, however.

- Among the *misconceptions* that teachers and school administrators sometimes have about grade equivalents are (1) growth over the summer is the same in each subject, (2) students are expected to have the same placement as their grade-equivalent scores, (3) students should have grade-equivalent scores equal to or higher than their grade placement, (4) grade equivalents tell what fraction of the curriculum a student has mastered, (5) a student's grade equivalents for one curriculum subject can be compared to those of other subjects, (6) grade-equivalent scores from different publisher's tests mean the same thing, and (7) a student should gain one year in grade-equivalent scores for each year in school. Remember that these are misconceptions: If you believe any one of these seven statements, you are *wrong*.

- When interpreting or explaining to others a student's grade-equivalent scores, you should include the student's percentile rank in the explanation.

- Table 17.12 summarizes and compares the various norm-referenced scores.

- You should review a student's profile of scores on a standardized test (1) to identify unusually high or low scores, (2) with a questioning attitude as to why the student obtained a particular score, (3) with an expectation of confirming what you already know about the student rather than of "surprises," (4) without overemphasizing small differences in scores, and (5) in light of the other knowledge you have about the student's performance on other assessments and in your classroom.

- You should be prepared to use norm-referenced scores and classroom performance to answer parents' questions about their children's standing, growth, needed improvement, strengths, and intelligence. Suggestions for doing so are given in Table 17.13.

Important Terms and Concepts

area under the normal curve
empirical norming dates
extended normalized standard score
grade-equivalent scores (GE)
grade mean equivalent
interpolation vs. extrapolation
IRT pattern scoring
item response theory (IRT)
linear standard scores (z, SS)
modal-age norms
normal curve equivalent (NCE)
normal distributions
normal growth
normalized standard scores (z_n, T, DIQ, NCE, SAT)
"normalizing" a set of scores
norm groups (local, national, special)
norm-referencing vs. criterion-referencing
percentile ranks (local and national)
relevance, representativeness, and recency of norm data
SAT-score scale
school averages norms
stanine scores (national stanine)

Exercises and Discussion Questions

1. Consider how score meaning is obtained from an assessment-referencing framework.
   a. When is each most helpful? Least helpful?
   b. Illustrate the usefulness of each framework by finding examples of two criterion-referenced and two norm-referenced scores of your students, and interpreting them in these frameworks.
2. Why should teachers and school administrators use local norm-group comparisons to interpret students' assessment results?
3. Why should school administrators schedule standardized test administration at the time of the year nearest to the test publisher's empirical norming dates?
4. A student takes a test during the middle of the school year. By mistake, the student's teacher uses the norms tables published for the end of the school year to look up the student's percentile rank. What effect does this error have on the percentile ranks the teacher reports? What would be the effect in this case if the teacher used the norms tables from the beginning of the year?
5. Read each of these statements and decide to which norm-referenced score(s) each mainly refers. Justify your choice(s) to your classmates.
   a. In this skewed distribution, John's score places him one standard deviation below the mean.
   b. Bob's test score is the same as the average score of students tested in the fourth month of fifth grade.
   c. Because Bill's score increased this year, I know that his general educational development has increased, even though his position in the norm group remained the same.
   d. Nancy's score is 5 because it is located in the middle 20% of a normal distribution.
6. Judge each of the following statements true or false. Explain the basis for your judgment in each case.
   a. A person's percentile rank is 45. This means that the person's raw score was the same as 45% of the group assessed.
   b. Sally's arithmetic assessment score is 40. The class's mean score is 45, and its standard deviation is 10. Therefore, Sally is located one standard deviation below the mean.
   c. The norm tables show that the distribution of deviation IQ scores on a school ability test is approximately normal in form. This means that for the people in the norm groups, the intellectual ability that naturally underlies the scores is normally distributed.
7. Explain why Statements 2 through 8 under "Summary of Grade Equivalents" in this chapter are false.
8. Table 17.14 shows several types of normalized scores. Use the relationships between the scores to complete the table and thereby show how various scores are related to one another. The first two are completed for you. You may use Figure 17.6 for assistance.
9. Table 17.15 shows part of a norms table that might appear in a manual of a standardized achievement test. The table shows selected raw scores, grade-equivalent scores, and percentile ranks for the publisher's standardization sample (i.e., norm group). Assume that (1) the local school system has judged the test's content to be a good match to its curriculum, (2) the norm data were collected during the seventh month of the fourth grade, (3) the norms are appropriate for use with the local school system, (4) the publisher has computed grade equivalents and percentile ranks in the usual way and with no errors, and (5) the school tested the students in April.

Use the table and your knowledge of norm-referenced frameworks to judge each of the following statements as true or false. Explain and justify your judgment in each case.

   a. James is a fourth-grade student with a grade-equivalent profile of V = 6.2, R = 5.6, L = 5.6, W = 5.6, A = 6.2. Decide whether each of the following conclusions is true or false, and explain the basis for your judgment.
      i. James should be in fifth grade.
      ii. James is strongest in vocabulary and arithmetic.
      iii. James' scores are above average for his grade.
   b. Fourth grader Sue's raw score on Reading is 50, and on Language it is 30. Decide whether each of the following conclusions is true or false, and explain the basis of your judgment.
      i. Sue is more able in reading because her raw score in reading is higher.
      ii. Because Sue's grade-equivalent scores are equal, she is equally able in reading and vocabulary (relative to the norm group).
      iii. Sue is more able in language than reading (relative to the norm group) because her percentile rank in language is higher.
10. Obtain copies of the norms tables for two standardized survey achievement test batteries. Locate the tables reporting grade equivalent scores. On a sheet of paper make two columns. At the top of each column, write the name of the test battery and grade level(s) of the norms tables. Answer the following questions for each test.
    a. With what kind of score do you enter each table? For example, can you enter the table directly with the raw score?
    b. Is there one table for each grade level, or are there several tables for each grade (e.g., fall, midyear, and spring)? Specify the months of the year for which the tables are appropriate.
    c. For each test, choose one subtest (e.g., reading) and one grade (e.g., fifth). Use the same subtest and grade for both tests. Look up the grade-equivalent scores corresponding to each of the following percentile ranks and for each time of the year (e.g., fall, midyear, and spring): PR = 2, 16, 25, 50, 75, and 95.

TABLE 17.14   Use with Exercise 8.

Percentile Rank	Stanine	z_n	DIQ (SD=15)	T-score
99.9	9	+3.00		
98				
84				
50				
16				
2				
0.1				

TABLE 17.15 Use with Exercise 9.

Raw Score	Vocabulary (V) GE	PR	Reading (R) GE	PR	Language (L) GE	PR	Work-study (W) GE	PR	Arithmetic (A) GE	PR
5	1.8	1	1.6	1	1.9	1	2.3	1	2.5	1
20	4.1	34	3.3	17	4.4	41	5.6	74	5.5	65
30	5.1	61	4.2	36	5.6	75	7.0	96	6.2	74
40	6.2	74	4.8	52	6.4	86	7.6	99	6.9	97
50	7.0	96	5.6	74	7.9	99	8.0	99	7.7	99
70			8.1	99						

d. For the same subtest, grade, and percentile ranks as (c), compare the two tests' grade-equivalent scores for comparable times of the year. Are they identical from test to test for the same time during the year? Are they closer for some percentile ranks than for others? Which ones?

e. Summarize your findings resulting from the comparison in (d). Share your results with the others in this course.

f. Discuss why there are differences and similarities among the tests reviewed.

g. Discuss the mistakes that teachers and school administrators may make if they erroneously believe that different publisher's grade equivalents are interchangeable.

Additional Readings

Hoover, H.D., Hieronymus, A.N., Frisbie, D.A., & Dunbar, S. (1993b). *Interpretive guide for teachers and counselors: Iowa Tests of Basic Skills, Levels 9–14, Forms K and L.* Chicago: Riverside Publishing.

This manual describes the scores discussed in this chapter in relation to interpreting a specific standardized achievement test battery.

Lyman H.B. (1998). *Test scores and what they mean* (6th ed). Boston: Allyn & Bacon.

This small book explains a wide variety of test scores and how to interpret them. It also discusses administering standardized tests and interpreting score reports.

Peterson, N.S., Kolen, M.J., & Hoover, H.D. (1989). Scaling, norming, and equating. In R. L. Linn (Ed.), *Educational measurement* (3rd ed.). Phoenix: Oryx Press, Chapter 6, pp. 221–262.

This chapter discusses how scores and norms are developed. The focus is on the technical aspects of development and theoretical strengths and limitations of each technique.

Rudner, L.M., Conoley, J.C., & Plake, B.S. (1989). *Understanding achievement tests: A guide for school administrators.* Washington, DC: The ERIC Clearinghouse on Tests, Measurements, and Evaluation, pages 9–44.

These pages provide a simple discussion of various types of scores from standardized tests and suggest ways these scores may be used by school administrators.

Internet resources for learning more about norm-referenced scores.

www.ctb.com

www.ericae.net

www.hemweb.com

www.riverpub.com

CHAPTER 18

Finding and Evaluating Published Assessments

Learning Targets

After studying this chapter, you should be able to:

1. Name the major print and nonprint sources of information about published assessments. [1, 3, 6]

2. Describe the kinds of sources you would seek in locating an assessment instrument to use for a specific purpose, professional reviews of assessment instruments, names and addresses of assessment publishers, technical information about an assessment, and assessment specialists who could answer your questions about a particular assessment instrument. [1, 3, 6]

3. Identify the steps necessary to locate and evaluate specific published assessment instruments. [1, 3]

4. Explain the local school district factors to be considered before looking for a published assessment. [1, 3, 4]

5. Name several nontest factors that must be reported along with assessment results when evaluating a school's or district's effectiveness. [4, 7, 6]

6. State what materials you need to obtain from the publisher to review an assessment procedure properly. [1, 3]

7. Identify and explain the major categories of information you should evaluate before purchasing a published assessment instrument. [1, 3]

8. Explain the major research and development steps for developing a standardized test. [1, 3]

9. Explain your responsibilities and the assessment developers' responsibilities for using a test properly. [1, 3, 4, 7]

10. Explain how each of the terms and concepts listed at the end of this chapter apply to educational assessment. [6]

As your career as an educator develops, you will be increasingly involved with tests and other assessment procedures that are not of your own making. School districts frequently administer achievement test batteries to assess students' progress in general educational development and to evaluate the district's programs. As a professional, it is important that you become involved not only in interpreting your students' scores on these assessments, but also in providing input for selecting them in the first place.

There are literally hundreds of achievement and aptitude tests in the marketplace. Most tests do not meet the high standards of quality set by professional associations and measurement specialists. To contribute significantly to the selection of proper assessments, you will need to use test locator resources and the evaluations of testing specialists regarding an instrument under consideration for adoption. After you locate information, you must organize and use it for proper evaluation. Studying the topics in this chapter should help you achieve these goals.

INFORMATION ABOUT STANDARDIZED TESTS

You can consult a number of sources to find information about specific tests. Some of these are described in this section; you can find most in a college library, a testing and measurement office of a college campus, or in a school's testing office.

Buros Institute of Mental Measurements Publications

Among the most useful resources for locating information on tests are the publications of the Buros Institute of Mental Measurements (located at the University of Nebraska at Lincoln, Lincoln, Nebraska 68588-0348). The late Oscar K. Buros founded the Institute and began a series of test bibliographies and *Mental Measurements Yearbooks* (MMY).

The *Mental Measurements Yearbooks* (Buros, 1938 through present) (Z5814 P8M46) are a series of volumes that critically evaluate most of the currently available published tests in English. Each volume supplements rather than replaces the earlier editions, so it is occasionally necessary to consult earlier volumes to obtain complete coverage of a test. One or more experts review tests especially for the MMYs, and each volume gives excerpted journal reviews as well. Each *Mental Measurements Yearbook* contains original reviews of hundreds of tests. Each test entry contains test title, age or grade levels, publication dates, special comments, number and type of part scores, authors, publishers, references, and bibliographic information. Each entry is cross-referenced to previous reviews in earlier MMYs. Names and addresses of hundreds of test publishers are listed in each MMY. A disadvantage of the printed MMYs is that because of the publication lag, editions of tests reviewed may not correspond to publishers' new editions.

Tests In Print V (Murphy, Conoley, & Impara, 1998) contains information on over 4,000 commercially available instruments. You can use this source to identify appropriate tests, locate reviews of tests, and find publishers' addresses. To appear as an entry in *Tests in Print V*, a test must be currently available commercially and must be published in English. Each entry includes the following information about a test: a description of the test and its purpose, information on population and scoring, references in professional journals relevant to the test, test

editions available and their price, name of the publisher, and location of the test's review in the *Mental Measurements Yearbook*.

Test Corporation of America Publications

Test Critiques (Sweetland & Keyser, 1985–1987) (BF176 T419) is a series of volumes that reviews the most frequently used tests in business, education, and psychology. Each test is reviewed by a testing specialist. Entries cover an introduction to the test, practical uses and applications, technical aspects, and an overall evaluation of the test.

Tests: A Comprehensive Reference for Assessments in Psychology, Education, and Business (Sweetland & Keyser, 1986) is a reference guide listing and describing thousands of tests, but giving no evaluations of them. Each listing describes the purpose of the test, for whom it is intended, costs, and publisher. The organization of the indexes makes locating tests easy.

The Test Corporation of America is located at 4050 Pennsylvania, Suite 310, Kansas City, Missouri 64112.

Educational Testing Service Publications

Tests in Microfiche contains over 800 unpublished tests used in education, business, and psychology. It is available in many college and university libraries in their microforms collections.

Educational Testing Service File is an online index of the more than 15,000 published and unpublished tests in the ETS Test Collection. The file may be accessed through the Bibliographic Retrieval Service. The entries include title, date, availability, persons for whom the test is intended, and an abstract. No reviews are included. The print equivalent is the *Collection Catalog, Volume I: Achievement Tests and Measurement Devices* (Educational Testing Service, 1986) (LB3051). Volume 2 (Educational Testing Service, 1987) lists vocational measures. Some of the tests themselves are in the *Tests in Microfiche* collection. *News in Tests* is a periodic newsletter describing the new additions to the test collection and related services offered to clients. Educational Testing Services is located in Princeton, New Jersey 08541.

Professional Journals

Professional journals in a field often review tests that have potential application in a particular area, such as reading, mathematics, child development, or learning disabilities. Specialized testing and measurement journals review tests that have a wide appeal to school practitioners and psychologists. Among the journals frequently reporting test reviews (Buros, 1978) are *Developmental Medicine and Child Neurology; Journal of Educational Measurement; Journal of Learning Disabilities; Journal of Personality Assessment; Journal of Reading; Journal of School Psychology; Journal of Special*

Education; Measurement and Evaluation in Guidance; Modern Language Journal; Psychological Reports; Psychology in the Schools; and *Reading Teacher.*

Bibliographic information about these and other journals (including those which review testing books) appears at the back of each *Mental Measurement Yearbook.* Journal references are indexed in such sources as the *Education Index, Dissertation Abstracts, Research Studies in Education, Psychological Abstracts,* and *Research in Education* (ERIC).

Test Publisher's Catalogue and Technical Manuals

An important way to get information about a test is directly from the test publisher. (See Appendix K for a partial list of publishers and their websites.) Most test publishers have catalogues that describe the tests they publish in detail. A publisher's catalogue is especially helpful for finding out about current editions of tests along with information about scoring services, costs, and how to obtain specimen sets, test manuals, and technical reports. Current information of this sort is seldom found in other print sources. Your school's testing office and the testing and measurement office of a college or university usually maintain collections of recent catalogues. The publisher's catalogue will list any restrictions on test purchasing: This sale of certain tests, especially individually administered intelligence and personality tests, is restricted to qualified psychologists. The catalogues provide prices and ordering information also. It goes without saying that a publisher's catalogue will not provide negative critical reviews of a test.

Technical information about a test is not found in a publisher's catalogue. Information about how the test was developed, reliability coefficients, standard errors of measurement, correlational and validity studies, equating methods, item analyses procedures, and norming-sample data are found in a test's **technical manual**. Technical manuals must be ordered separately from the tests. Although school testing directors should have copies of the technical manuals for the tests the school uses, too often they do not. Some colleges and universities that maintain test collections for their faculty and students may have technical manuals. Usually, you will need to order the technical manual directly from the test's publishers.

Textbooks on Testing and Measurement

A number of textbooks list, describe, and/or review selected tests. If you are looking for a test in a specific area, looking in the index of a textbook in the area may be a useful way to see which tests are frequently used. (Appendix I in this book lists a selection of published tests in several areas.) A textbook, however, is not a comprehensive source for information about tests because (1) tests are often selected for inclusion primarily for their merits in illustrating an author's point, (2) space permits only a few tests being mentioned, (3) often only the most popular or easily available tests are mentioned or illustrated, and (4) no single author is aware of all available tests.

Professional Contacts and Organizations

Your professional contacts may help you locate a test. The director of your school testing office or the school psychologist are frequently useful resources. Testing and measurement professors at colleges and universities usually work in departments of educational research, educational psychology, measurement and statistics, counseling and guidance, or psychology. Many larger colleges and universities have testing offices designed to help their faculties and students with testing problems, and such offices are usually available to answer questions from the public, as well.

Figure 18.1 lists organizations that may be helpful to you. Larger testing companies and agencies usually have an information and/or advisory office to answer questions over their toll-free telephone numbers. Professional organizations, such as the National Council on Measurement in Education (located in Washington, D.C.), can sometimes help by referring you to a member in your local area who can be of assistance. Some professional associations whose focus is not on assessment per se may have special interest groups that are interested in specific assessment issues such as performance assessment, assessing critical thinking, or classroom assessment. In some areas, federally funded research and development centers and regional laboratories have technical assistance offices that can help with testing problems. In some states, county-based school agencies, state-related school agencies, or technical assistance centers are specially organized to offer assistance in reviewing and using tests.

Test *Standards* and the *Code*

A useful publication for evaluating educational and psychological tests is the ***Standards for Educational and Psychological Testing***. This is a set of standards for publishers and users of tests prepared jointly by the American Educational Research Association, the American Psychological Association, and the National Council on Measurement in Education. The *Standards* describe various kinds of information that a publisher might provide in a test manual and accompanying materials. A new edition of the *Standards* was published in 1999. Further information can be obtained by calling the National Council on Measurement in Education (202-223-9318).

The ideas and concepts in the *Standards* are directed to the professional tester rather than to measurement students and the public. However, the Joint Committee on Testing Practices (1988) prepared a set of major obligations of professionals (like yourself) who use professionally

FIGURE 18.1 Example of organizations that provide information on educational assessment.

Professional associations prepare periodicals and other publications related to educational assessment, work toward improved assessment usage, and may be contacted to identify members who are experts in certain areas of educational assessment.
1. American Educational Research Association (Washington, DC) [www.aera.net]
2. Association for Assessment in Counseling (Arlington, VA) [www.ddc.uc.edu/acc]
3. International Reading Association (IRA) (Newark, DE) [www.reading.org]
4. National Association of Test Directors (NATD) [www.natd.org]
5. National Council on Measurement in Education (NCME) (Washington, DC) [www.ncme.org]

Clearinghouses collect documents on assessment, abstract them, and make them available through the Educational Research Information Center (ERIC). Online services are provided.
1. ERIC Clearinghouse on Assessment and Evaluation (ERIC/AE) (University of Maryland, College Park, MD) [www.ericae.net]

Research centers and regional laboratories invest in research on technical or policy issues in educational assessment. They have catalogues of these publications and sometimes answer inquiries about specific assessment issues.
1. Buros Institute of Mental Measurements (University of Nebraska) [www.unl.edu/buros]
2. Center for the Study of Testing, Evaluation, and Educational Policy (Boston College) [www.csteep.bc.edu]
3. Center for Research on Evaluations, Standards, and Student Testing (CRESST) (UCLA) [www.cse.ucla.edu]
4. Northwest Regional Educational Laboratory (NREL) (Portland, OR) [www.nwrel.org]
5. Comprehensive Regional Assistance Centers [www.ed.gov/EdRes/EdFed/EdTechCtrs.html]
6. Mid-continent Regional Educational Laboratory (Mcrel)(Aurora, CO) [www.mcrel.org]

Nonprofit testing corporations offer a wide range of assessment services, conduct assessment research, and disseminate assessment information.
1. American College Testing Program (ACT) (Iowa City, IA) [www.act.org]
2. Educational Testing Service (ETS) (Princeton, NJ) [www.ets.org]

Nonprofit advocacy and public interest groups research matters of legality, individual rights, and public policy related to assessment.
1. National Center for Fair and Open Testing (Fair Test) (Cambridge, MA) [www.fairtest.org]

Source: Adapted and updated from *Organizations That Provide Test Information, Digest No. 109* by R. T. Boyd, 1989, Washington, DC: ERIC Clearinghouse on Tests, Measurement, and Evaluation.

developed tests in formal testing programs in education. These obligations, called the *Code of Fair Testing Practices in Education*, are included in Appendix B. The *Code* will be especially useful to you as you evaluate a test or evaluate your school's testing program. The *Code* lists separate obligations for test users and for test developers. The *Code of Professional Responsibilities in Educational Measurement* (National Council on Measurement in Education, 1995) also describes professional obligations and is reproduced in Appendix C. (See also Chapter 5.)

Online Services through Internet

Now you can use **online services** to research tests. More and more schools are linking to the Internet, and many colleges and universities have gateways to the Internet. Many state education departments have gateways that permit libraries, teachers, and school administrators access to the Internet. In addition, there are several commercial electronic service providers.

One of the most useful comprehensive assessment locators is provided by **ERIC/AE** (see Figure 18.1) at www.ericae.net (800-464-3742). The Test Locator provides descriptions of over 11,500 tests and survey instruments.

This site allows you to search and read the following (Doolittle, 1994):

1. *Code of Fair Testing Practices in Education*
2. *Test Evaluation* (an essay on how to evaluate a test)
3. *ETS/ERIC Test File* (the ETS test database)
4. *CEEE/ERIC Test Database* (a database of descriptions of tests commonly used with Limited English Proficiency students)
5. *Test Review Locator* (a database of test review citations in the MMYs and in ProEd directories)
6. *Buros/ERIC Test Publisher Locator* (names and links to over 10,000 assessment instruments and test publishers)

You may also access the ERIC/AE web site through the ERIC system web page at www.aspensys/eric.org.

In addition, ERIC/AE participates in the AskERIC program. Using e-mail on the Internet, you send a message to AskERIC listing your questions and other information you need about assessment. Someone at ERIC/AE will search ERIC for you and within a few days send you ERIC listings of the documents that will help answer your questions. You can access this service by sending an e-mail message to ericae@cua.edu. or askeric@askeric.org.

Web sites are also operated by CRESST (see Figure 18.1) and the National Council on Measurement in Education (NCME). Among the files available through the CRESST site is the *Alternative Assessments in Practice Database*, which lists alternative and performance assessments from hundreds of sources. You can access the CRESST site directly at www.cse.ucla.edu or indirectly through the ERIC/AE. The NCME site can be accessed at www.ncme.org.

You can connect to the ERIC Clearinghouse on Assessment and Evaluation via the Internet. You will find assessment news; "full text resources including books, essays, and newsletters on assessment and evaluation; test schedules of major standardized tests; the Test Locator; places to search ERIC databases; descriptions of major testing projects; materials pertaining to Goals 2000 and world class standards; and pointers to other web sites containing assessment and evaluation information" (Drake, Rudner, & Pierce, 1995). The adjunct Test Collection Clearinghouse is at www.ericae.net. The home page has hot links to many World Wide Web sites, and list servers dealing with educational assessment. Among the hot links are Buros Institute of Mental Measurements (www.unl.edu/buros/), Educational Testing Service (www.ets.org), and CRESST. The National Center for Fair and Open Testing is accessed at www.fairtest.org.

EVALUATING AND SELECTING A TEST

Because tests play important roles in the educational system, school officials should select them carefully. Before your district adopts a test, it should carefully examine and evaluate it. This section describes a systematic procedure. The author recommends that a school district appoint a committee of teachers, school administrators, and citizens to review and decide whether to adopt a test. It is part of your professional responsibility as a teacher to participate and offer informed judgments when serving on such test selection committees. School administrators who select tests without the informed judgment of teachers run the risk of egregious errors. Because no test can perfectly match a school district's needs, comparing the merits of one test with another is an important step in choosing the better product.

Clarify Your Purpose

You look for an assessment procedure because you perceive the need for a specific kind of information. The first step, then, is to pinpoint the specific purpose(s) for obtaining student information and to find out who will be using the information to make decisions. The clearer you are about the purposes and conditions under which assessment information will be used, the better you will be able to select the appropriate procedure. At this point, re-read

Chapter 3 which discusses test score validity. Things you need to keep clearly in mind as you begin your selection include

1. *The general school setting in which the assessment will be used*: type of community, ages or grades of students, persons who will be helped by an appropriate assessment, and persons who will be in charge of using the assessment results.

2. *The specific decisions, purposes, and/or uses intended for the assessment results*, such as identifying specific reading skills needing remediation, appraising a student's emotional needs or areas of anxiety as a prelude to counseling, appraising a student's aptitude for mechanical activities that a counselor will discuss during guidance sessions, or surveying general levels of reading and mathematics achievement to report curriculum evaluation information to the school board.

3. *The way you believe that using test scores or other assessment information will help to improve the decision, serve the purpose, or solve the problem.* The better you can articulate, from the outset, what you expect to accomplish by using an assessment procedure, the better you will be able to evaluate the many options open to you and to choose the most satisfactory one.

4. *The need to strike a balance between the strengths and limitations of performance tasks relative to multiple-choice tests.* You need to have in mind a balance between such factors as time, cost, in-depth assessment of narrow curricular areas, and less in-depth assessment of broad areas of the curriculum. The assessment procedure you select will be the result of compromises on several dimensions, so it is helpful to think about these early in the process.

Put the New Assessment Plans into Local Context

Before you set out to select a new assessment procedure, you should take stock of the assessments already being used in the district. For example, what type of assessments do teachers already do, of what quality are these assessments, and do they serve the perceived need?

We can distinguish between externally imposed and internally crafted assessments. *Externally imposed assessments* do not match a local curriculum framework exactly. Thus, you will need a perspective on what an external assessment contributes beyond the internal assessments currently being used by teachers. You may decide, for example, that it will be wiser and have more instructional payoff to improve teacher-crafted assessment procedures than to purchase an **external assessment procedure** such as a standardized test. In general, you should rely on teacher-crafted assessments for 90% to 95% of your assessment needs.

In many states, a state assessment program is mandated. This may be a basic skills assessment, an accountability program, or a more complex assessment. To reduce redundancy, the assessment you purchase should supplement this mandated assessment and serve other, nonduplicating purposes. There is likely to be an increase in mandated state assessments if the federal Goals 2000 legislation becomes operational. Content and performance standards will be defined, and states will be required to attend to these to participate in federal funding. Chapter 16 gave a set of guidelines for selecting a standardized achievement test that is compatible with your state-mandated assessment.

As discussed in Chapter 16, standardized assessments with norms and educational development scales are most helpful to (1) assess students' relative strengths and weaknesses across curricular areas, (2) assess students' growth within a specific curricular area, and (3) provide an "independent, external" assessment of student's accomplishments relative to a standardization sample. These purposes should be weighed against teacher-based assessments using instructional benefit to students as a criterion.

Another consideration is the qualifications of a school district's staff in relation to the assessment procedure proposed. For example, specially trained professionals are needed to administer and interpret individual intelligence and personality tests. If such professionals are in short supply in a district, you will want to use other assessment procedures. Similarly, using performance assessments and portfolios requires educating teachers about scoring and interpreting these procedures. This will cost time and money that a district may not have. Sometimes partial implementation may be helpful, such as assessing students at some grades and not others.

Sometimes a school district wishes to use an external assessment, such as a standardized test, to evaluate itself. School officials should be aware that not only do single tests provide an especially poor foundation on which to evaluate teachers and curricula, but program evaluation itself is a technical area requiring well-prepared professional evaluators. Very often, qualified program evaluation personnel are not on a district's payroll. Being unaware of the need for a professional program evaluator, school officials often assign the task to persons professionally trained in other areas, such as school psychologists or guidance counselors. Superintendents wanting to use assessments for program evaluation may wish to consult curriculum evaluation experts before designing these evaluation strategies. One suggestion is to contact the American Educational Research Association [www.aera.net] and ask about contacting a member of Division H who lives near your school district. Table 18.1 summarizes some factors affecting the difficulty of the school's educational task. Information about these factors should be used along with test results to help interpret a school's effectiveness.

Review Assessment Materials

If you have done your homework as just described, you will be in a good position to locate assessments and to begin reviewing them. The information sources described earlier in this chapter will help you identify assessments that approximate your needs. Of particular help in identifying tests and obtaining descriptions of them are the following:

Tests in Print V
Mental Measurements Yearbooks
Tests
ETS Test Collection File
ERIC/AE Test Locator Service
Test publishers' catalogues

The following sources are helpful for locating reviews of tests:

Mental Measurements Yearbooks
Test Critiques
ERIC/AE Test Locator Service
Professional journals

After narrowing your choices to a few assessment procedures that appear to suit your needs, you should obtain copies of the assessment materials and tasks; detailed descriptions of the assessment content and rationale behind its selection; materials related to scoring, reporting, and interpreting assessment results; information about the cost of the assessment materials and scoring service; and technical information about the assessment.

Much of this material is bundled together in a **specimen set**, which is designed as a marketing tool as well as for critical review of materials. As a result, not all materials you will need to intelligently review a test are included. For example, some publisher's specimen sets do not include complete copies of the assessment booklets or scoring guidelines. You will need to order these separately. Also, technical manuals are not typically included in specimen sets and must be ordered separately, as well. The publisher's catalogue lists the cost of specimen sets and other related materials.

Once you obtain the materials, you and/or your committee can review them. Be sure to compare similar assessments against the purposes you had in mind for using the assessments. It might be helpful for the committee to obtain input from noncommittee members for certain parts of the assessment: for example, mathematics teachers for the mathematics section, reading teachers for the reading assessment, etc. You could also call upon a college or university faculty member to help: For example, a testing and measurement faculty member may be helpful in reviewing and/or explaining technical material. Contact the National Council of Educational Measurement (www.ncme.org) for the names of specialists who live near your school district.

It is important to match each test item with your state's standards, and state or local curriculum. You do

TABLE 18.1   Facts to be reported in addition to standardized test results when evaluating school effectiveness.

Attendance	Includes absences of staff and students from school and parents from participation in parent-teacher organizations.
Holding power	Includes graduation and dropout rates.
Parent involvement	Includes parent-teacher organizations, volunteers, and parent-staffed programs.
Diversity	Includes staff and student gender, ethnicity, and home language and staff responsibilities.
Economic conditions	Includes parent income levels and students receiving free or reduced-cost lunches.
Stability	Includes percent of staff and students new to a school district.
Experience	Incudes years teaching experience and years of education beyond the initial qualifications.
Staff development	Includes inservice programs, peer mentoring, collaboration with businesses or colleges, and courses taken.
Programs for students	Includes study skills, counseling, dropout and at-risk prevention, reentry, cross-age tutoring, extra-curricular, and summer school.
Achievement	Includes performance of students at the next higher educational level, longitudinal patterns of achievement test results, student awards and honors, per-student library loans, National Merit scholars, college entrance test results, and out-of-class student accomplishments.
School environment	Includes incidents of vandalism and violence, gang-related activities, types of disciplinary actions, special services, extra-curricular activities, and library facilities.
Instructional variables	Includes length of day, year, and class periods; amount of time per subject per week; number of students using extended day academic program; homework actually assigned; and percent of school days devoted exclusively to academic learning.
Fiscal	Includes average teacher, staff, and administrator salaries; expenditures per student.

Source: Adapted from "Putting Test Scores in Perspective: Communicating a Complete Report Card for Your Schools" by K. K. Matter, *Understanding Achievement Tests: A Guide for School Administrators* (pp. 121–129) by L. M. Rudner, J. C. Conoley and B. S. Plake (Eds.), 1989, Washington, DC: ERIC Clearinghouse on Tests, Measurements, and Evaluation.

this by obtaining the complete list of standards or learning targets, organized by grade level. Two persons independently read each test item and record which standard or learning target it matches. When all items have been matched, the persons compare their results and reconcile the differences. The findings are summarized in a table that lists each standard and the I.D. number of the test items matching each. The number of nonmatching items is also recorded. This should be done separately for each grade, because a test's items may appear at a grade level that is different than the grade at which the corresponding learning target is taught. If there are a lot of these grade-sequence mismatches, the test will not be suitable for your school district. Be sure to note especially the match between the kinds of thinking and performance activities implied by the standards and the test items. Often the content matches, but the thinking processes and performances required do not. An example of how to do this is found in Nitko, Al-Sarimi, Amedahe, Wang, & Wingert (1998). Finally, find out the month of the school year during which the test is planned to be administered. Then, determine what proportion of the test's items con-

tain content that will have been taught before testing begins. (See Chapter 17 for futher discussion of this point in connection with grade-equivalent scores.)

If possible, you might administer the assessment to a few students to get a feel for how students might respond. This would be especially important if writing tasks or performance tasks are included. It may be that for some otherwise appealing performance tasks, student time limits or instructions are not sufficient and confusion results. This is less likely if the assessment was professionally developed and standardized on a national sample.

Summarize Your Review Systematically

It will help your review if you systematically organize relevant information in one or two pages. You may want to develop a form for this purpose, or simply follow the same outline for every assessment procedure you review. The form is a concise way of sharing information among committee members or with others who may help make decisions about the choice. Figure 18.2 suggests what information to record for your review.

FIGURE 18.2 A suggested outline for recording relevant information for reviewing and evaluating an assessment procedure.

Identifying information
1. Title, publisher, copyright date
2. Purpose of the test as described by the publisher
3. Grade level(s), subject(s), administrative time
4. Cost per student, service costs
5. Types of scores and norms provided

Content and curricular evaluation
1. Publisher's description and rationale for specific types of tasks
2. Quality and clarity of the tasks themselves
3. Currency of the content and match to recent curricular trends
4. Match of the tasks to each of the school district's curricula
5. Inclusion of ethnic and gender diversity in the task content

Instructional use evaluation
1. Publisher's description and rationale for how the assessment results may be used by teachers to improve instruction
2. Local teachers' evaluations of how the assessment results could be used for improving their instruction
3. Overlap of assessment with the existing teacher-based assessment procedures.

Technical evaluation
1. Representativeness, recency, and local relevance of the national norms
2. Types of reliability coefficients and their values (use average values if necessary)
3. Summary of the evidence regarding the validity of the assessment for the purpose(s) you have in mind for using it
4. Quality of the criterion-referenced information the assessment provides
5. Likelihood that the assessment will have adverse affects on students with disabilities, minority students, and female students

Practical evaluation
1. Quality of the manual and teacher-oriented materials
2. Ease of administration and scoring
3. Cost and usefulness of the scoring services
4. Estimated annual costs (time and money) if the assessment procedure is adopted for the district
5. Likely public reaction to using the assessment procedure

Overall evaluation
1. Comments of reviewers (e.g., *MMY* or *Test Critiques*)
2. Conclusions about the positive aspects of the assessment
3. Conclusions about the negative aspects of the assessment
4. Summary and recommendation about adoption

List of references and sources used

1. Preliminary ideas.
2. Evaluate proposal (approve/reject).
3. Make formal arrangement (sign contract if publication is approved).
4. Prepare test specifications.
5. Write items.
6. Conduct item tryout.
   a. Prepare tryout sample specifications.
   b. Prepare participants.
   c. Prepare tryout materials.
   d. Administer tryout items.
   e. Analyze tryout data.
7. Assemble final test form(s).
8. Conduct national standardization.
   a. Prepare standardization sample specifications.
   b. Obtain participants.
   c. Prepare standardization materials.
   d. Administer tests.
   e. Analyze data.
   f. Develop norms tables.
9. Prepare final materials.
   a. Establish publication schedule.
   b. Write manual.
   c. Prepare test books and answer forms.
   d. Manufacture/produce/print materials.
10. Prepare marketing plan.
    a. Initiate direct mail promotion.
    b. Initiate space advertising.
    c. Train sales staff.
    d. Attend professional meetings and conventions.
11. Publish.

As a consumer of assessments, you should be aware of the activities involved in each of these steps. Information on how well the assessment publisher carried out each step should be part of your judgment of the quality of an assessment procedure. The activities involved in each step are briefly described in Robertson (1990).

Note, however, that many assessments available in the marketplace do *not* follow all steps, because they are quite costly and time-consuming. Unfortunately, if an assessment publisher omits steps during the developmental process, the publisher will probably omit those concerned with collecting and analyzing *data* used to improve the quality of the test and/or to support the validity of the claims made for the test. Shortcutting assessment development steps usually means lowering validity, so beware of poorly developed assessments.

HOW A STANDARDIZED TEST IS DEVELOPED

A standardized test should be the product of a carefully conducted program of research and development. Such a program involves the work of many persons and includes the following steps (Robertson, 1990, pp. 62–63).

QUALIFICATIONS FOR TEST PURCHASE

Assessments are ordered through a publisher's catalogue. In an effort to guard against assessment abuse, some publishers restrict the sale of test materials. The previously mentioned *Standards for Educational and Psychological Testing* gives the test publisher the responsibility for telling the user what qualifications are needed to interpret test results properly. However, the *Standards* (AERA, APA, & NCME, 1985) states, "A test user should know his own qualifications and how well they match the qualifications required for use of specific tests" (p. 58).

Sales restrictions vary with the publisher, each implementing a somewhat different policy on establishing a purchaser's qualifications and selling tests. Some publishers are very explicit about stating the professional qualifications a customer needs before being permitted to purchase an assessment, and such statements appear in their catalogues. Most publisher's catalogues of psychological tests contain statements about the need for purchasers to be qualified for administering and interpreting a test. The test user must be sure to acquire the requisite training and experience before purchasing a test. A form needs to be completed, signed, and submitted to the publisher for approval before a person can purchase.

Summary

- There are numerous sources you may use to locate information about assessment procedures. These include publications of:
  - Buros Institute of Mental Measurements
  - Test Corporation of America
  - Educational Testing Service
  - Professional associations
  - Test publishers
- Other test information sources include
  - Testing and measurement textbooks
  - Professional contacts and organizations
  - Test *Standards*
  - Online services through Internet
- Before searching for and selecting a published assessment instrument, you should:
  - Clearly identify the purposes for which you want to use the results.
  - Think about new assessments in your local educational context, including the type of nontest information you need to report (see Table 18.1).
  - Identify the sources likely to have the information you need.
  - Obtain specimen sets, administration manuals, and technical manuals for all assessments you are evaluating.
  - Summarize information from your review of each assessment procedure using an outline similar to that in Figure 18.2.
- One aspect of evaluating a published assessment is judging how carefully it was built.
- A professionally developed assessment should have gone through several research and development steps before being made available to consumers.
- Qualifications for assessment purchase were discussed. Although a publisher is obliged to tell you and other prospective users what qualifications are

necessary to use and interpret an assessment, you bear the ultimate responsibility of knowing your own qualifications and whether they match those required for using the assessment properly.

Important Terms and Concepts

Educational Testing Service File
ERIC/AE
external assessment procedure
Mental Measurements Yearbooks (MMY)
online services
specimen set
Standards for Educational and Psychological Testing
technical manual
Test Critiques
Tests in Microfiche

Exercise and Discussion Questions

1. Describe the types of assessment information you would find in each of the following sources:
   a. *Mental Measurements Yearbook*
   b. *Tests In Print*
   c. *Tests*
   d. *Test Critiques*
   e. *ETS Test Collection File*
   f. *News on Tests*
   g. *Standards for Educational and Psychological Tests*
   h. www.ericae.net
   i. a test publisher's catalogue
   j. www.ncme.org
2. Describe how each of the following professional organizations may help you obtain test information:
   a. Association for Measurement and Evaluation in Counseling and Development
   b. International Reading Association
   c. National Association of Test Directors
   d. National Council on Measurement in Education
3. Explain how an educator should go about locating and selecting an educational achievement test for use in a school system.
4. Read each of these statements and identify the one source that would most likely contain the information the speaker is requesting.
   a. "I want to know what kinds of instruments are available to assess attitudes of female students toward work, home, marriage, and family life."
   b. "I want to know what professionals in the field think of this criterion-referenced test."
   c. "What services does a publisher provide for interpreting assessment results, and what are the charges?"
   d. "I want to know the newest instruments developed for assessing perceptual-motor development of primary school students."
5. Suppose you have already located a particular test and you want the specific information about it implied by the following statements. What source would you consult first for each statement?
   a. "What are the reliability coefficients for their test?"
   b. "What kind of norms does the publisher provide?"

c. "How do test specialists view the quality of the procedures the publisher followed when developing the test?"

d. "What research studies and reports have used this assessment instrument?"

6. Using the procedures described in this chapter, locate a specific standardized assessment instrument you believe can serve a purpose you have identified.

a. Then, following the procedures described in this chapter, review and evaluate this assessment instrument in relation to your stated purpose. Write your review and evaluation using the outline given in Figure 18.2, using headings and subheadings appropriately.

b. Share your evaluation with others in this course.

7. Some test publishers check carefully on the qualifications of persons who order tests and other assessments. Some customers are refused purchase.

a. Should a publisher verify the qualifications of persons wishing to purchase a test? Why or why not?

b. What responsibility does a test user have in ascertaining whether he or she is qualified to use a test?

c. Is there an ethical consideration here? Explain.

8. Why is it important for teachers and school administrators to be aware of the steps in the development of a standardized test?

9. Commercial assessment developers may perform a market analysis to decide whether it is profitable to develop and sell a particular kind of assessment procedure. Discuss the pros and cons of this profit motive for the assessment consumer.

10. Visit a school district.

a. Obtain as many bits of information as you can in the categories described in Table 18.1. Also obtain the district's standardized test score reports for a recent year.

b. Compare your findings for this school district with the findings reported by others in this course.

c. Discuss what impact the variables in Table 18.1 have on the districts' average test scores.

Additional Readings

American Educational Research Association, American Psychological Association, & National Council on Measurement in Education. (1999) *Standards for educational and psychological testing*. Washington, DC: Author.

Contains technical standards that assessment developers and users should meet. A useful tool against which to evaluate the assessment instruments your school district uses.

Crosby-Muilenburg, C. (1988). *Psychological and educational tests: A selected annotated guide*. (TM 011 545) Washington, DC: ERIC/AE.

A guide developed for the Humbolt State University Library. References are listed within specific disciplines such as counseling, early childhood, and special education.

Drake, L., Rudner, L., & Pierce, J. (1995). *Assessment and Evaluation on the Internet*. Washington, DC: ERIC Clearinghouse on Assessment and Evaluation, Catholic University of America.

Identifies more than 17 World Wide Web and Gopher sites and 15 list servers that provide information on educational assessment. When accessed online, this document has hot links to connect you directly to all sites and list servers mentioned in the document.

Keyser, D.J., & Sweetland, R.C. (Eds.). (1985–present). *Test critiques*. Kansas City, MO: Test Corporation of America.

Test reviews emphasize the practical aspects of administration.

Keyser, D.J., & Sweetland, R.C. (Eds.). (1986–present). *Tests: A comprehensive reference for assessment in psychology, education, and business*. Kansas City, MO: Test Corporation of America.

Presents concise descriptions of thousands of instruments but does not provide evaluative reviews.

Nitko, A.J. (1997). *The Kentucky Institute for Educational Research Guide to tests in Kentucky: A description and comparison of the CAT, CTBS, TerraNova, and the Kentucky Instructional System Assessments*. Frankfort, KY: Kentucky Institute for Educational Research.

An easy-to-read explanation of how standardized achievement tests and state assessments differ as well as complement one another. Useful examples to use with parents, school board members, and legislators.

Nitko, A. J., Al-Sarimi, A., Amedahe, F .K., Wang, S., & Wingert, M. (1998). *How well are the Kentucky Academic Expectations matched to the KIRIS assessments, the CTBS, and the CAT?* Paper presented at the annual meeting of the American Educational Research Association, San Diego, April. (ED420677)

This is an example of how to review the content of standardized tests to see how well they match the state standards and the state's own assessment.

Impara, J.C., & Plake, B.S. (Eds.) (1998). *The thirteenth mental measurements yearbook*. Lincoln, NE: The Buros Institute of Mental Measurements.

Contains over 690 candidly critical reviews of hundreds of educational and psychological tests published in the English language.

CHAPTER 19

Scholastic Aptitude, Career Interests, Attitudes, and Personality Tests

Learning Targets

After studying this chapter, you should be able to:

1. Explain why it is important to assess and use information about students' general intellectual skills and aptitudes in teaching. [4, 1]

2. Explain why aptitude tests do not describe a student's future capacity to learn or to succeed. [4, 1]

3. Distinguish between aptitude and achievement test. [4, 7, 3]

4. Explain how the fixed conditions under which most students must learn increase the ability of aptitude tests to predict their success. [4, 3]

5. Explain the factors that keep students' aptitude test scores stable or consistent over time. [4, 3]

6. Explain the factors that tend to cause students' scholastic aptitude test scores to change over time. [4, 3]

7. Explain the advantages and disadvantages of using omnibus, two-score, and multiple-factor aptitude tests for educational decisions. [3]

8. Describe some of the popular group-administered tests of scholastic aptitude, including some of the types of scores teachers are likely to receive with reports about students. [6, 3]

9. Explain the advantages of using group tests of specific aptitudes in education. [6, 7, 3]

10. Explain the advantages of using individually administered tests of general scholastic aptitude in assessing students. [4, 3, 6, 7]

11. Describe the popular individually administered tests of general scholastic aptitude in terms of their content, the ages of students for whom they are used, and the types of scores they report. [4, 6, 7]

12. Explain why it is necessary to systematically assess a low-functioning student's adaptive behavior. [4, 6]

13. Explain the usefulness of using information from vocational interest inventories in addition to achievement and aptitude information when counseling a student on further schooling and career choices. [4, 6, 7]

14. Distinguish between the concepts *achievement*, *aptitude*, *attitude*, *interests*, and *values*. [4, 1]

15. Explain the two major approaches to building career interest inventories. [4, 6]

16. Describe the content, organization, and types of scoring of a career interest inventory. [4, 6]

17. Distinguish between expressed, manifested, tested, and inventoried tests. [4, 6]

18. Explain the factors you should keep in mind when using the results of attitude assessments with your students. [4, 6, 7]

19. Explain the two major approaches to assessing personality characteristics. [4]

20. Discuss the usefulness of students' personality assessment results for a classroom teacher. [4]

21. Explain how each of the terms and concepts listed at the end of this chapter apply to educational assessment. [6]

This chapter discusses four types of standardized tests that assess a variety of student traits other than curriculum-based achievement. The first category of tests is used to assess general scholastic aptitude.[1] You may be required to administer and interpret some of these tests for students in your classroom. Others are administered and interpreted only by qualified persons such as a school psychologist. You need to be familiar with these tests, nevertheless, because you may be required to read and interpret the psychologist's report or participate in an individual educational planning team.

A second category of tests is used to assess career and job interests. As students mature, they begin to focus on lifelong goals and the world of work. You provide some of the information they need through your classroom discussions and student interactions. Information from tests of general scholastic aptitude help students understand their strengths in relation to further schooling. Career interest inventories further complete the picture for students. They help students to identify and organize their current pattern of interests compared to men and women who have been successful in different types of jobs. Teachers and guidance counselors can assist students in reviewing and interpreting these test results and in guiding the students' career explorations.

A third category of tests is used to assess students' attitudes. Students' attitudes reflect their disposition toward school, family, and other institutions. Most school districts profess that positive attitudes toward school, family, community, work, and further learning are important learning targets. Tests in this category help you to assess students' progress in these attitudinal areas.

The fourth category of tests is used to assess personality characteristics. These assessment procedures should be administered and interpreted by a qualified psychologist. Nevertheless, you may be required to read and interpret a psychologist's report for some of your students. You should thus have some awareness of them.

APTITUDES FOR LEARNING

General vs. Specific Intellectual Skills

Assessments of the kind discussed in this chapter describe a learner's **general intellectual skills**, rather than describing the **specific intellectual skills** a learner needs in, say, next week's geometry lessons. When the knowledge or skills a student needs for an upcoming lesson are specific and narrow, the student's learning success is best predicted by the student's present level of knowledge and skills. For most of these specific, day-to-day instructional decisions, you will have to develop your own procedures for assessment.

General Intellectual Skills and Aptitudes Measurement

A student's specific past performance in a course is not very helpful in establishing expectations for learning new material whenever the student must face these conditions: (1) learning to perform in ways that are quite different from those learned in the past, (2) the student's past performance has been very erratic, (3) previous test scores or school grades are known to be very unreliable or invalid, or (4) the student's record of past performance is not available.

Consider a high school freshman, for example, who wants to study Spanish for the first time, having had no previous foreign language training or experience. For such a student, a test of Spanish language knowledge provides no information about the student's chances of succeeding in an upcoming Spanish course. In such cases, an assessment of more general intellectual skills and abilities *related to language learning* will better predict success. Usually such tests assess English language skills and concepts, acquired auditory learning skills, and applied memory skills. Similarly, a student transferring from another school system or moving from one educational level to the next may have complete records, but the meaning of these records may be unclear. To clarify them, a school may test the student with an instrument assessing broad intellectual skills or scholastic aptitude.

There are any number of ways school officials can predict a student's likely success in an educational program. Three examples are the student's: (1) level of past achievement of the same specific type of performance as the new performance the student needs to learn, (2) level of general scholastic ability, and (3) ability in several specific aptitudes related to the new performance to be learned. The validity of these predictors is related to the specificity of the performance the school wants to predict. If the student's performance that a school wants to predict is very specific (for example, solving quadratic equations), then: (1) a student's prior achievement of a very similar kind is

---

[1]We discussed multiple intelligences theory and its assessment implications in Chapter 11. Further, because the creator of that theory is opposed to creating tests to separately measure students' intelligences (Gardner in Checkley, 1997), we have chosen not to discuss such tests in this chapter.

the best predictor, (2) a student's general scholastic aptitude is the next best predictor, and (3) assessment of specific aptitudes is least preferred. If the student performance the school wants to predict is very general (such as general school performance as measured by freshman grade point average), then the preferred order of predictors is (1) general scholastic aptitude assessment, (2) then assessments of prior specific achievement, and (3) last, assessments of specific abilities (Snow, 1980).

Aptitude Tests Measure Learned Behavior

Capacity Is Not Fixed Tests assessing aptitude or intellectual skills reflect only past learning. They do not directly assess innate ability or "capacity." Further, because we cannot obtain a sample of performance from the future, they cannot directly assess future ability. We have to be content to use past and present learning to predict future learning. It is important for you to recognize that a student's "aptitude for learning" applies a specific type of instructional approach. If you change the instructional approach, the student's aptitude for learning changes also. A student's aptitude is influenced also by a number of facts of development (including biological makeup), experience in the environment (including interactions with other persons), and a complex interaction of the two.

The very idea of "capacity" places some upper limit on a student's ability to learn. This limitation is likely to be true in only a very specific way. For example, a student's capacity to do algebra may depend on the way a teacher currently teaches it, on the mathematics concepts the student learned previously, and on the motivational level a teacher stimulates in the student, as well as on some kind of native endowment. It seems reasonable to conclude that both developmental (life history) and instructional conditions affect the particular potentials realized by a person: "So long as a way is open to invent better conditions of development, no one knows the limit of human potentialities" (Cronbach, 1977, p. 274).

Aptitude-Achievement Distinctions It sometimes troubles teachers to see assessment instruments bearing titles such as readiness, intelligence, general mental ability, and "aptitude for X"–but containing items closely resembling items found on achievement tests. The troublesome aspect appears to be related in part to a teacher's failure to distinguish between the *abstract concepts* of **aptitude** and **achievement** and the *observations we make to infer the state* of a person's aptitude and achievement. We can define *an aptitude for X as the present state of a person that indicates the person's expected future performance in X if the conditions of the past and present continue into the future* (see Carroll, 1974). A student's present aptitude (or state) could be indicated in many ways.

Thus: [An] "aptitude test" is only one indicant of aptitude. Other indicants of aptitude could include scores on achievement tests, data on prior performance in activities similar to those for which we wish to predict success, and information derived from procedures for assessing personality, interest, attitude, physical prowess, physiological state, etc. (Carroll, 1974, p. 287)

Aptitude tests deliberately set out to assess a student's reasoning rather than the student's recall of factual knowledge or ability to use well-learned rules on problems practiced in school. These tests differ from traditional standardized achievement tests in at least three ways:

First, tests of reasoning ability, especially mathematical reasoning, require a relatively small declarative knowledge base. The . . . amount of mathematical knowledge required by the typical SAT [for example] is rarely beyond that taught in a first year high school algebra course and an introductory semester of geometry. . . . [The SAT places heavy demands, however, on] procedural knowledge or, more precisely, the procedural use of declarative knowledge. . . .

A second way in which reasoning tests differ from subject matter tests is in the quite deliberate way in which they were constructed to not depend upon specific subject-matter content. The verbal reasoning skills measured by the SAT-V, for example, have no specific secondary school course sequence on which they can be referred.

A final way in which verbal and mathematical reason tests differ from at least some achievement tests is in degree of problem-solving and reasoning, as distinct from simple memory. Tests in subject matters such as geography, foreign languages, and history make primary demands on memory but minimal demands on problem-solving skills and reasoning. (Bond, 1989, pp. 429–430)

Teaching Conditions for Aptitude Development

Nonadaptive Teaching An important part of the definition of aptitude given earlier concerns the continuance of past learning conditions into the future. One thing that makes aptitude tests useful predictors of future school success is that schools are generally not very adaptive to individual learners. Thus, the conditions under which students learn this year are usually quite similar to last year's learning conditions.

Underemphasizing Adaptive Teaching When a student must learn under the same conditions from year to year, there is a danger that teachers will believe that the results of the student's scholastic aptitude testing determine what the student is able to accomplish. That is, once they see a student's present aptitude level, they will do little to modify learning conditions to improve the student's aptitude. Past psychological conceptions of the learner have led some educators to *overemphasize* the (1) consistency of the general scholastic ability of learners, (2) passivity of learners as receivers of information, and (3) categorical placement of learners into educational tracks with narrow ranges of instructional options. They have *underemphasized* the (1) adaptivity and plasticity of learners, (2) learners' ability to actively construct information during problem solving, and (3) responsibility of educational systems to adapt to learners' initial performance levels (Glaser, 1977).

Invalidity for Instructional Placement   Unfortunately, the aptitude tests described in this chapter have not been validated for use in assigning students to different kinds of instructional methods. Rather, they have been built to predict how well students will perform when they must adapt to the fixed type of instruction. You should view the tests' helpfulness for decision making in that light.

Scholastic Aptitude Test Score Stability

Importance of Score Stability   An important school concern is whether a student's scholastic aptitude remains constant or stable over a period of time. If a student's scholastic aptitude test score changed erratically every year, you would have no confidence that it assessed a useful characteristic. Although on a student-by-student basis scores may systematically rise or decline, a definite tendency exists for a student to maintain similar, but not identical, ranking in the student's age group throughout his school years. In general, change in students' rankings on general scholastic aptitude tests tend to be greater (1) as the time interval between the two testings becomes longer and (2) the younger the students were at the time of the initial testing. Although groups of students tend to maintain their relative position in the distribution of aptitude scores, important changes in individual students do occur. Therefore, if a school wants to use a student's scholastic aptitude score for guidance or placement decisions, it should bear in mind that there are sufficient differences in individual students' patterns of score change to justify reassessment each time a decision is made (Sattler, 1988).

Factors for Score Stability   Among the factors that work to keep students' rankings on aptitude tests about the same over time are (Anastasi, 1988; Ausubel, Novak, & Hanesian, 1978; Sattler, 1988):

1. The genetic makeup of students remains stable.

2. If a student's socioeconomic level, family configuration, and sociocultural influences remain stable over a long period, these contribute to aptitude stability.

3. Development and prerequisite learning is rarely reversible, so earlier development and learning continues to exert similar impact on new development and learning.

4. If the content assessment by different scholastic aptitude tests is similar, students' scores will be similar from one testing to the next.

Reasons for Score Changes   Among the factors that work to change student's rankings on aptitude tests from one testing to another are the following:

1. *Errors of measurement*—Even if the person's "true score" were to stay the same, the obtained score is likely to be different due to a test's unreliability (see Chapter 4).

2. *Test differences*—The content of tests produced by different publishers will vary. Also, the content of the same publisher's test may vary with the age level of the student taking the test. Tests designed for young children are somewhat more concrete and perceptual; those designed for older children are more abstract and verbal.

3. *Norm-group differences*—The norms of different publishers' tests are not comparable. Because mental ability scores are norm-referenced, differences in scores may be due to differences in norms.

4. *Special interventions and enriched environments*—If a person's environment dramatically and persistently becomes more intellectually nurturing over a period of time, that person's scores on a scholastic aptitude test are likely to increase. Conversely, if the person becomes physically or emotionally ill or deprived in a way that interferes with intellectual development, then aptitude scores may decrease.

GROUP TESTS OF SCHOLASTIC APTITUDE

Types of Group Aptitude Tests

Advantage   The principal advantage of group testing over individual testing is the efficiency and cost savings gained by testing many persons at the same time. The ease with which group tests can be administered and scored has contributed greatly to schools adopting them.

Number of Aptitudes Reported   There are different types of group aptitude tests. The **omnibus test** contains items assessing different abilities that comprise general scholastic aptitude, but it provides only a single score. A *two-score test* also assesses several different kinds of specific abilities, but reports only two scores, usually verbal/quantitative or verbal/nonverbal. The items on the verbal section of the test, for example, may assess several kinds of specific verbal abilities, but only one verbal ability score is reported.

Some school ability tests report *three scores*, such as verbal, quantitative, and nonverbal. **Nonverbal tests** assess how well students process symbols and content that have no specific verbal labels, such as discerning spatial patterns and relations or classifying patterns and figures. **Multiple-aptitude tests** assess several different abilities separately and provide an ability score for each. Multiple-aptitude tests, for example, may provide separate scores for verbal reasoning, verbal comprehension, numerical reasoning, and figural reasoning.

Type of Test to Use The type of group scholastic aptitude test a school should use depends on the decisions the staff will make with the scores. Multiple-aptitude tests are most useful when a student wants information about her profile of strengths and weaknesses to make better decisions about further schooling or planning a career. Omnibus tests are most useful when a school wants an estimate of a student's general level of school ability for purposes of predicting the student's future success under standard classroom conditions. Examples of a two-score and multiple-score aptitude test are given in the following sections. Others are listed in Appendix J.

Two-Score Test: Otis-Lennon School Ability Test

Test Content The *Otis-Lennon School Ability Test* (OLSAT) provides verbal and nonverbal part scores as well as a total score. The identification of a test item as verbal vs. nonverbal depends on whether the student must understand the English language to answer the item. For example, "numeric inference . . . is classified as nonverbal because facility with the English language is not necessary to successful performance on the items. That is, given that the directions are understood, an examinee could answer the questions without knowing English. Arithmetic Reasoning, on the other hand, is classified as verbal because it consists of word problems and is therefore dependent on understanding English" (Otis & Lennon, 1990, p. 15). Table 19.1 describes the clusters and types of items the OLSAT contains. (A seventh edition of the OLSAT is in preparation at the time of this writing.)

Test Organization The *OLSAT* is organized into seven levels according to grades: Level A (kindergarten), Level B (grade 1), Level C (grade 2), Level D (grade 3), Level E (grades 4 and 5), Level F (grades 6, 7, and 8), and Level G (grades 9, 10, 11, and 12). Not all of the different types of items are given at every grade. Items at the lower grade levels are pictorial, do not require reading, and are teacher-paced. Items at the upper levels are self-administered: Students read the directions and answer the items without teacher-pacing, In Grades K through 3, the test items are

TABLE 19.1 Description of the kinds of items on the OLSAT.

		Cluster description	Types of items
Verbal Clusters		**Verbal Comprehension** is dependent on the ability to perceive the relational aspects of words and word combinations, to derive meaning from types of words, to understand subtle differences among similar words and phrases, and to manipulate words to produce meaning.	Following Directions Antonyms Sentence Completion Sentence Arrangement
		Verbal Reasoning is dependent on the ability to infer relationships among words, to apply inferences to new situations, to evaluate conditions in order to determine necessary versus optional, and to perceive similarities and differences.	Aural Reasoning Arithmetic Reasoning Logical Selection Word/Letter Matrix Verbal Analogies Verbal Classification Inference
Nonverbal Clusters		**Pictorial Reasoning** assesses the ability in young children to reason using pictorial representations. These items assess the ability to infer relationships among objects, to evaluate objects for similarities and differences, and to determine progressions and predict the next step in those progressions.	Picture Classification Picture Analogies Picture Series
		Figural Reasoning items assess the ability to use geometric figures to infer relationships, to perceive progressions and predict the next step in those progressions, to generalize from one set of figures to another and from dissimilar sets of figures, and to manipulate spatially.	Figural Classification Figural Analogies Pattern Matrix Figural Series
		Quantitative Reasoning items assess the ability to use numbers to infer relationships, derive computational rules, and predict outcomes according to computational rules.	Number Series Numerical Inference Number Matrix

Source: Adapted from *Resources for Measuring Educational Performance* (pp. 98–99) by the Psychological Corporation, 1994, San Antonio: Author. Copyright © 1989 by Harcourt, Inc. Reproduced by permission. All rights reserved.

organized into three sections, each section containing distinct item types. However, in Grades 4 through 12, similar types of items are not grouped together into subtests, but are arranged into a **spiral format**, similar to that shown in Figure 19.1. One item of each type is presented; then the sequence is repeated, but with more difficult items.

Norm-Referencing Scheme The publisher of the OLSAT uses several norm-referencing schemes to report the verbal, nonverbal, and total test results. These are illustrated on the individual student report shown in Figure 19.2. These types of scores are described in the following list. The letters in this description correspond to the letters in Figure 19.2. (You should review norm-referencing schemes in Table 17.2 if you are uncertain of the terminology.)

A. **Age-based scores** compare this student with norm-group students who are the same age, regardless of grade placement. In addition to raw scores, OLSAT re-ports (1) *School Ability Index* (SAI), a normalized standard score with mean 100 and standard deviation of 16; (2) *National Percentile Rank* (PR); (3) *National Stanine* (S); and (4) *Normal Curve Equivalent* (NCE).

B. **Grade-based scores** compare this student with norm-group students who have the same grade placement, regardless of their age. The scores reported in this section are: (1) *Scaled Score*, an expanded scaled score that allows you to track growth in scholastic aptitude over several years since the scale spans all grades; (2) *National Percentile Rank* (PR), (3) *National Stanine* (S), (4) *Local Percentile Rank* (PR), (5) *Local Stanine* (S), and (5) *Local Normal Curve Equivalent* (NCE).

C. *Percentile bands* show the uncertainty interval for the student's scores that are reported in Sections A and B of Figure 19.2. Uncertainty bands are formed by adding and subtracting one SEM to the student's score. (See the discussion of SEM in Chapter 4.)

FIGURE 19.1 Examples of some of the type of items on the *Otis-Lennon School Ability Test* (7th ed.).

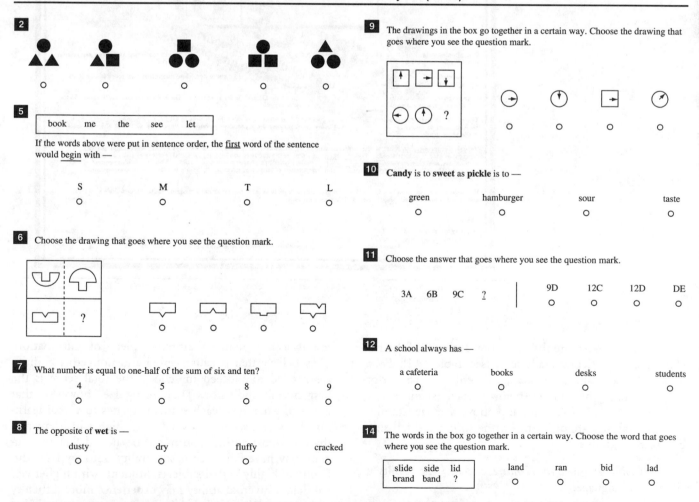

FIGURE 19.2 An individual student's report showing the type of scores reported for the *Otis-Lennon School Ability Test*. (Note: Scores are simulated results.)

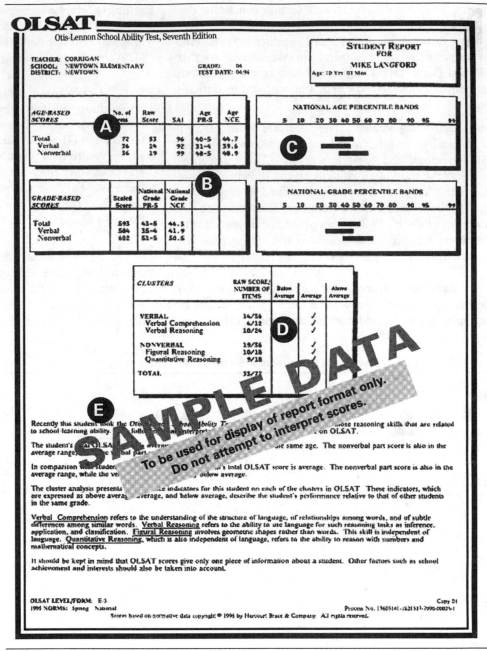

D. *Cluster scores* are the raw scores for each of the five clusters at a particular grade level (see Table 19.1). *Below average, average,* and *above average* describe cluster performance in terms of stanines: below average (stanines 1, 2, 3), average (stanines 4, 5, 6), and above average (stanines 7, 8, 9). Stanines are different for the spring and fall standardization groups.

E. *Computer-generated narrative* explains the results in simplified language.

Interpretation of Results Although the OLSAT is a two-score test, its authors encourage you to use the total test results as the main interpretive piece of information. They believe that because verbal and nonverbal abilities are needed to succeed in school, the total score is the best overall indicator. They recognize, however, that much of what you teach students relates to verbal learning. Thus, if a student is very much higher in nonverbal than in verbal ability, you might be alerted that the student may have good scholastic ability but may have difficulty in highly verbal subjects. Students with higher verbal than nonverbal ability may experience more difficulty with quantitative subjects. The authors recommend that you consider score differences larger than two stanines as meaningful. You should interpret smaller differences much more cautiously, because they may represent only measurement error.

Other possible causes for a verbal-nonverbal difference include bilingualism, reading problems, learning disability, hearing impairment, visual impairment, anxiety, illness, or irregularities in test administration. You should request a readministration of the OLSAT if a student has a large verbal-nonverbal difference. If retesting verifies a difference and you want further diagnostic information, then you should request assessment with an individual test such as the *Wechsler Intelligence Scale for Children*, Third Edition (described later in this chapter).

Achievement/Ability Comparisons   If you administer the OLSAT along with either the *Stanford Achievement Test* or the *Metropolitan Achievement Tests*, a score called the Achievement/Ability Comparison (AAC) is reported on a student's test report. The AAC describes, for each achievement survey battery subtest, how this student's achievement compares relative to norm-group students who have the same OLSAT total score.

To do this, students in the grade-base OLSAT norm group are first sorted into stanines. Second, the students within each OLSAT stanine are then sorted into stanines for the achievement test subtest (e.g., reading comprehension stanines for all students whose OLSAT stanine is 5). Third, within each achievement subtest group from step two, students are clustered into high (stanines 7, 8, 9), middle (stanines 4, 5, 6), and low (stanines 1, 2, 3) groups. This third grouping is reported alone with each achievement subtest score.

For example, Don's OLSAT stanine is 5. Don also took the *Stanford Achievement Test* and scored stanines of 4, 5, and 6 in Total Reading, Total Mathematics, and Spelling respectively. Compared to the entire norm group for the achievement test, these stanines are in the middle of the distribution. However, if we look only at those students who attained an OLSAT stanine of 5, Don will be in the low AAC range in Total Reading, in the middle AAC range in Total Mathematics, and in the high AAC range in Spelling. These AAC results tell us that compared to other students with the same scholastic aptitude as Don, he is below average in Total Reading, average in Total Mathematics, and above average in Spelling.

Multiple-Aptitude Test: Differential Aptitude Tests

Purpose   The battery of *Differential Aptitude Tests (DAT)* was originally developed in 1947 to satisfy the needs of guidance counselors and consulting psychologists working in schools, social agencies, and industry (Bennett, Seashore, & Wesman, 1974). The tests were revised in 1962, 1972, 1982, and 1990. An individualized computer-administered version is also available: *DAT Adaptive Edi-*

tion. The computer, using item response theory methodology, selects the items most appropriate for each examinee. This reduces the test length by one-half in most cases.

The primary purpose of the tests is to provide information about a student's profiles with respect to different cognitive abilities. This information is used for guiding and counseling students in junior and senior high schools (grades 7 through 12) as they prepare for career decisions. There are two levels: Level 1 (grades 7–9) and Level 2 (grades 10–12). The DAT are also used with adults for vocational and educational counseling and as part of a battery of tests for job selection.

Test Content   The *Differential Aptitude Tests* report scores for each of the eight subtests shown in Figure 19.3. An additional ninth score, Scholastic Aptitude, which is a combination of the Verbal Reasoning and Numerical Reasoning scores, is reported: This score is used to assess general scholastic aptitude. Figure 19.3 also shows examples of items from each subtest.

Gender-Specific Norms   The DAT have separate male and female norms, as well as combined norms. Separate norms allow comparisons of a student with his or her own gender, as well as with members of the opposite gender. Cross-gender comparisons may help a student consider an occupation or educational program that he or she would have overlooked. This may surprise you and may seem like a form of gender discrimination. However, because the tests are used for guidance and counseling, this purpose is better served by these separate norms, given the realities of the current job market. This issue was discussed in Chapter 17 in connection with Table 17.1.

Advantage of Test   An advantage of using a multiple-aptitude battery such as the DAT instead of an omnibus or two-score aptitude test is the opportunity it provides for finding some aptitude for which a student has a relative strength. For example, a student may have low general scholastic ability (Verbal Reasoning and Numerical Reasoning) but have high Perceptual Speed and Accuracy or high Mechanical Reasoning. This provides the counselor with some information on aptitude that can be used to encourage a student.

Combining Aptitude with Interest Assessment   The DAT come with an optional Career Interest Inventory. Using the results of this instrument along with aptitude scores, achievement scores, and school grades can help a student make realistic career or further education decisions. The interest inventory presents sentences describing activities in various types of work and school situations. Students indicate their degree of agreement with the sentences. (Interest inventories are described in greater detail in this chapter.)

FIGURE 19.3 Brief descriptions, time limits, number of items, and a sample item from each subtest of the *Differential Aptitude Tests* (5th ed.).

Verbal Reasoning (25 min., 40 items)

Measures the ability to see relationships among words; may be useful in predicting success in business, law, education, journalism, and the sciences.

SAMPLE ITEM

Which answer contains the missing words to complete this sentence?

. . . . . is to fin as bird is to . . . . .

A water — — feather
B shark — — nest
*C fish — — wing
D flipper — — fly
E fish — — sky

Numerical Reasoning (30 min., 40 items)

Measures the ability to perform mathematical reasoning tasks; important in jobs such as bookkeeping, lab work, carpentry, and toolmaking.

SAMPLE ITEM

What number should replace R in this correct addition example?

$$\begin{array}{r} 7R \\ + \underline{R} \\ 88 \end{array}$$

*A 9
B 6
C 4
D 3
E None of these

Abstract Reasoning (20 min., 40 items)

A nonverbal measure of the ability to reason using geometric shapes or designs; important in fields such as computer programming, drafting, and vehicle repair.

SAMPLE ITEM

Choose the Answer Figure that should be the next figure (or fifth one) in the series.

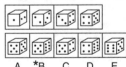

A *B C D E

Perceptual Speed and Accuracy (6 min., 200 items)

Measures the ability to compare and mark written lists quickly and accurately; helps predict success in performing routine clerical tasks.

SAMPLE ITEM

Look at the underlined combination of letters or numbers and find the same one on the answer sheet. Then fill in the circle under it.

1 XY Xy XX <u>YX</u> Yy
2 6g <u>6G</u> G6 Gg g6
3 <u>nm</u> mn mm nn nv
4 Db <u>BD</u> Bd Bb BB

Xy Yy YX XX XY
○ ○ ● ○ ○
nn mn nv nm mm
○ ○ ○ ● ○
g6 Gg 6g G6 6G
○ ○ ○ ● ○
BD BB Bd Db Bb
● ○ ○ ○ ○

Mechanical Reasoning (25 min., 60 items)

Understanding basic mechanical principles of machinery, tools, and motion is important for occupations such as carpentry, mechanics, engineering, and machine operation.

SAMPLE ITEM

Which load will be easier to pull through soft sand?

A B C

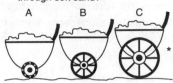

Space Relations (25 min., 50 items)

Measures the ability to visualize a three-dimensional object from a two-dimensional pattern, and to visualize how this object would look if rotated in space; important in drafting, architecture, design, carpentry, and dentistry.

SAMPLE ITEM

Choose the one figure that can be made from the pattern.

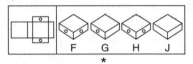

F G H J
*

Spelling (10 min., 40 items)

Measures one's ability to spell common English words; a useful skill in many academic and vocational pursuits.

SAMPLE ITEM

Decide which word is not spelled correctly in the group below.

*A paragraf
B dramatic
C circular
D audience

Language Usage (15 min., 40 items)

Measures the ability to detect errors in grammar, punctuation, and capitalization; needed in most jobs requiring a college degree.

SAMPLE ITEM

Decide which of the four parts of the sentence below contains an error. If there is no error, mark the space on your answer sheet for the letter next to No Error.

Jane and Tom/ is going/ to the office/ this morning.

A   *B   C   D

E No Error

GROUP TESTS OF SPECIFIC APTITUDES

The kinds of general scholastic aptitude tests illustrated earlier are widely used in schools, but other types used for special decisions should be mentioned, too. Among these are readiness tests, high school and college admissions tests, and tests of aptitude for specific subjects.

Readiness Testing

Schools often use **readiness tests** as supplemental information to make instructional decisions for the first-grade pupils. Often such tests are used to supplement a kindergarten teacher's judgment about a youngster's general developmental and readiness level for first-grade work, especially reading, where grouping by readiness level is a common practice. Because readiness tests measure a child's acquired learning skills, they are frequently classified as achievement tests rather than aptitude tests. (The discussion at the beginning of this chapter described the distinction between aptitude and achievement used in this book.)

Teachers frequently use readiness tests to help form instructional groups (for example, for reading instruction). When used in this way, they should be considered placement tests. Since teachers use readiness tests to implicitly predict a pupil's likely success in instruction, we have classified them as aptitude tests in this book, although they also may be classified as achievement tests.

You should keep in mind the test author's point of view when selecting a readiness test. The author's viewpoint of what constitutes "readiness to learn" will determine the test content (as does an author's viewpoint for every test, of course). If you want to use the scores on a readiness test to make a statement about whether a student has mastered specific prerequisites, you must carefully examine the actual test items to see if they measure the kinds of skills and abilities you expect each student to have acquired before entering the new instruction.

Admissions Testing

Multiple-Assessment for Admission Test scores, previous grades, letters of recommendation, interviews, and biographical information on out-of-school accomplishments are among kinds of information used by colleges and selective high schools to make admissions decisions. Some private and parochial high schools, for example, use a battery of achievement and aptitude tests to screen applicants. Testing sessions are usually held at the local high school, and the tests are generally administered by its staff.

College Admissions Tests Two widely used college admissions testing programs are the College Entrance Examination Board's *Scholastic Assessment Test Program*[2] and the

American College Testing Assessment Program. Both programs administer secure tests. Both administer the tests through local testing centers (usually high schools and colleges) at pre-established dates during the year. Although the tests are secure prior to their administration, students can obtain copies of their test booklets and answers after they have taken them. For both programs, test booklets and answer sheets are returned to their respective publishers for scoring, recording, and processing results to the colleges the students designate.

Scholastic Assessment Test I: Reasoning Test The College Entrance Examination Board (CEEB), currently located in New York City, was formed around 1899 to help selective colleges in the northeastern United States coordinate their admissions testing requirements. The tests developed out of that effort around 1926 and were created by Carl Brigham, associate secretary for the CEEB (Donlon & Angoff, 1971). Educational Testing Service in Princeton, New Jersey, currently develops the test for the CEEB.

The program includes *SAT I: Reasoning Test* and *SAT II: Subject Tests.* Students generally take one or both types during their senior year of high school. The SAT I may be considered an aptitude test; the SAT II is an achievement test. Only the SAT I is discussed in this chapter. The SAT I reports a Verbal and a Mathematics score. The Verbal subtest emphasizes critical reading, word knowledge, and reasoning with words. Three types of items are used: analogies, sentence completion, and critical reading. The Mathematics subtest emphasizes quantitative thinking using arithmetic, algebra, and geometry knowledge. Three types of items are used: standard multiple-choice, quantitative comparison, and student-produced response. In student-produced response items, an examinee's numerical answer is "bubbled in" on a special answer sheet. The test booklets and answer sheets are sent to the Educational Testing Service for scoring, recording, and processing to the colleges the student designates.

The American College Test The *American College Testing* (ACT) Assessment Program was formed in 1959, with the ideas and help of E. F. Lindquist, among others. This admissions testing program is of a different character than the SAT I program. Whereas initially CEEB was concerned primarily with the private selective colleges of the northeast, the ACT program initially sought to serve midwestern public colleges and universities. What these colleges needed was help in (1) eliminating the few incapable students who were applying, (2) providing guidance services for those admitted, and (3) measuring broad educational development rather than narrower verbal and quantitative aptitudes (Lindquist in Feister & Whitney, 1968). Today the ACT program in Iowa City is as active a research and test development enterprise, as is the Educational Testing Service.

The *ACT Assessment* has four subtests: English, Mathematics, Reading, and Science Reasoning. All test items are

---

[2]Before 1994, this test was called the *Scholastic Aptitude Test* (SAT).

multiple choice. The English Test emphasizes standard written English conventions and rhetorical skills. The Mathematics Test emphasizes quantitative reasoning and problem solving using pre-algebra, algebra, geometry, and trigonometry knowledge. The Reading Test contains passages representative of topics in social studies, natural sciences, fiction, and humanities. The items focus on using inference and reasoning for reading comprehension.

The Science Reasoning Test contains several sets of related data tables, diagrams, and verbal descriptions drawn from biology, chemistry, physics, and earth/space science. The items focus on interpreting data, interpreting experimental results, and reasoning with respect to alternative viewpoints. The developers view the test items as "work samples"—simulations of the kinds of learning activities typically required of the college freshman.

In addition to these tests, students taking the SAT I or *ACT Assessment* are asked to report information about themselves, including recent grades, high school activities, out-of-class accomplishments, planned college major, and demographic information. Among other purposes, this questionnaire permits the student to indicate any special talents and accomplishments not reflected in course grades (such as winning a state debate). In addition, the *ACT Assessment* includes the *ACT Interest Inventory*. This consists of a list of activities, and students indicate whether they would like, dislike, or are indifferent about doing each activity on the list. The interest inventory helps students get a better idea of how their career interests fit into the mainstream of various major areas of college.

INDIVIDUALLY ADMINISTERED TESTS OF GENERAL SCHOLASTIC APTITUDE

Stanford-Binet Intelligence Scale

History   The *Stanford-Binet Intelligence Scale* is a widely used, individually administered test of general scholastic aptitude. First prepared in 1916 by Lewis M. Terman as a translation and revision of the Binet-Simon Scale, the test was revised in 1937 (with Maud A. Merrill), revised again in 1960, renormed in 1972, and revised and renormed in 1986.

Content   The *Stanford-Binet* is used with a wide range of ages: from 2 years old through adults. You can gain an idea of the nature and content of this assessment instrument by studying Figure 19.4. The figure shows that the subtests may be clustered into four areas: verbal reasoning, abstract/visual reasoning, quantitative reasoning, and short-term memory. The subtests are numbered in the order in which they are administered. However, not every subtest is administered at every age. Figure 19.5 shows the age range for which each subtest is appropriate.

Not all items in each subtest are administered, because within each subtest items are arranged in order of increasing difficulty. The psychologist administering the test first needs to determine a **basal level**, the highest level where four items are passed. The lowest level where three or four (or all four) items are failed is called the **ceiling level**. It is assumed that, because the items are arranged in order of increasing difficulty, the person would pass all items below the basal level, so they are not administered. Similarly, it is assumed that the person would fail all items above the ceiling level. The vocabulary subtest is given first and is used as a *routing test*. The student's performance on this test, along with the student's age, tells the psychologist the difficulty level on the other tests at which he or she should begin testing the student.

Not all subtests appropriate for an age range need to be administered. Sattler (1988) recommends that either 8, 10, or 12 subtests be administered, depending on the student's age.

Scores   A student's raw score on each subtest is converted to a normalized standard score called a **standard age score (SAS)** for the subtest. The SASs for subtests have a mean of 50 and standard deviation of 8 in the norm group having the same age as the student being tested. Within each of the four clusters shown in Figure 19.4, a student's subtest SASs are added, and the sum is converted to an *Area SAS* (mean = 100, standard deviation = 16). The score on the entire assessment is found by adding all the areas SASs and converting this sum to a *Stanford-Binet Composite Score* (mean = 100, standard deviation = 16). Thus, the Composite Score is a deviation IQ *(DIQ)*, as explained in Chapter 17, Equation 17.4.

The concepts of **mental age** and intelligence quotient (IQ) are no longer used with tests such as the *Stanford-Binet* (4th ed.). Thus, the ratio IQ (100 times mental age divided by chronological age) has been replaced by the *DIQ*.

Norm-Referenced Character   Tests of scholastic aptitude describe a student's ability as the student's location in a norm group having the same age as the student. If the student's intellectual development does not keep pace with others in the norm group, the student will receive a lower *DIQ*. Norms become outdated and from time to time a test will have to be renormed.

Wechsler Intelligence Scales

Another widely used set of individual tests is the *Wechsler Intelligence Scales*. This set consists of three different intelligence tests, each designed for use with a different age level: (1) *Wechsler Preschool and Primary Scale of Intelligence–Revised* (WPPSI-R), 3 years to 7 years, 3 months; (2) *Wechsler Intelligence Scale for Children–Third Edition* (WISC-III), 6 to 16 years, 11 months; and (3) *Wechsler Adult Intelligence Scale–Revised* (WAIS-R), 16 to 74 years.

FIGURE 19.4 Description of the subtests on the *Stanford-Binet* (4th ed.).

Order Administered	Verbal Reasoning Subtests
1.	**Vocabulary** (14 pictures and 32 words) The first 14 items are pictures, which the examinee names. The next 32 items are words, which the examinee defines.
6.	**Comprehension** (42 items) Lower level items relate to naming body parts in a picture; higher level items ask social comprehension questions.
7.	**Absurdities** (32 items) Examinee identifies what is funny or foolish in the pictures.
14.	**Verbal Relations** (18 items) Examinee is presented with four concept names and asked to describe how the first three are alike but different from the fourth.

Abstract/Visual Reasoning Subtests

5.	**Pattern Analysis** (6 items for form board, 36 items for blocks) Lower level items require putting shapes into holes; higher level items require modeling patterns using cubes.
9.	**Copying** (12 items blocks, 16 items copying) At lower levels, examinee copies pattern built by examiner. At higher levels examinee copies geometric patterns using pencil and paper.
11.	**Matrices** (26 items) Examinee is given a matrix and selects the object, letter, or pattern that completes the relationship shown in the matrix.
13.	**Paper Folding and Cutting** (18 items) Examiner folds and cuts paper in several ways. Examinee selects the option that shows what the paper would look like if it were unfolded.

Quantitative Reasoning Subtests

3.	**Quantitative** (40 items) Examinee answers arithmetic questions.
12.	**Number Series** (29 items) Examinee is shown a series of numbers and must induce the pattern and state what two numbers come next.
15.	**Equation Building** (18 items) Examinee is given a set of numbers, one or more arithmetic operators, and an equal sign. Examinee must use these to make a true equation.

Short-Term Memory Subtests

2.	**Bead Memory** (42 items) Examinee reproduces bead patterns shown in pictures.
4.	**Memory for Sentences** (42 items) Examinee repeats sentences read by examiner. Sentences get longer as the items progress.
8.	**Memory for Digits** (26 items) Examinee repeats the sequence of digits read by the examiner. The sequences are 3–9 digits long when repeating forward is required, and 3–7 digits long when repeating backward.
10.	**Memory for Objects** (14 items) Examinee is presented with 2–8 pictured objects individually in a sequence. Then the examinee is shown another picture containing all of the objects plus others not in the presented sequence. The examinee must point to the individual objects in the sequence they were presented.

General Design All the Wechsler tests have the same general design, although the items are not identical. The subtests are organized into two groups: Verbal and Performance. The items within a subtest are similar in content but differ in difficulty. (The subtests on the different scales—WPPSI, WISC, and WAIS—contain different types of items, however.) All examinees are administered all subtests, but since the items are arranged in order of increasing difficulty, as with the *Stanford-Binet*, not all items within a subtest need to be administered. All the Wechsler scales report subtest results as normalized, standard scores (mean = 10, standard deviation = 3). All of the scales report Performance IQ, Verbal IQ, and the total or Full Scale IQ. These three are *DIQ* scores (mean = 100, standard

FIGURE 19.5 Age spans for which various *Stanford-Binet* (4th ed.) subtests are used.

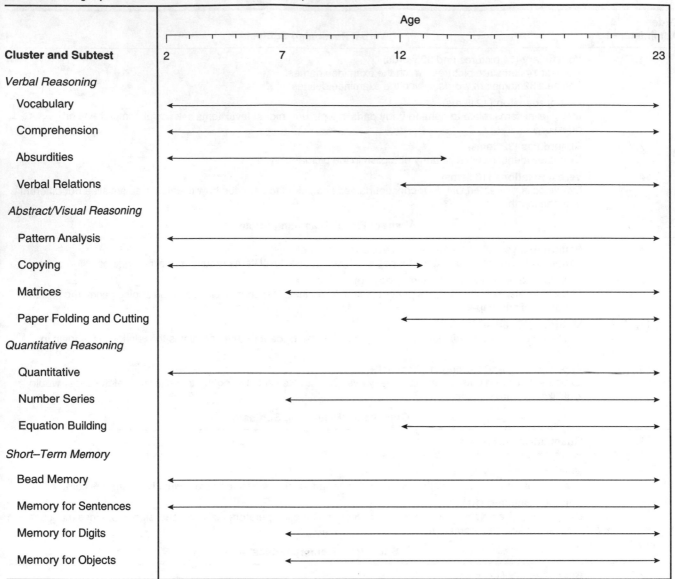

deviation = 15). The norm group to which a student is referenced is the group of students with the same age.

WAIS-R The *Wechsler Adult Intelligence Scale–Revised* is used with ages 16 to 74 years. It overlaps with the WISC–III for age 16. It contains 11 subtests: 6 Verbal and 5 Performance. The subtests in the Verbal category are Information, Similarities, Arithmetic, Vocabulary, Comprehension, and Digit Span. Performance category subtests are Picture Completion, Picture Arrangement, Block Design, Object Assembly, and Digit Symbol.

The WAIS-R is generally considered to be a reasonably valid and reliable tool for assessing general cognitive ability. Following are some of its limitations (Sattler, 1988): (1) it does not provide low enough scores for persons with severe mental retardation, (2) it does not provide high enough scores for persons with extremely gifted mental ability, and (3) the range of subtest scaled scores is restricted for some age groups.

WISC-III The *Wechsler Intelligence Scale for Children–Third Edition* is used with children ages 6 years through 16 years, 11 months. It contains 10 core and 3 supplemental subtests. In the Verbal category are Information, Similarities, Arithmetic, Vocabulary, and Comprehension (Digit Span is a supplemental Verbal subtest). In the Performance category are Picture Completion, Coding, Picture Arrangement, Block Design, and Object Assembly (Symbol Search and Mazes are supplemental Performance subtests).

The WISC-III was standardized with the *Wechsler Individual Achievement Test* (WIAT), an individually administered basic skills achievement test. This makes it possible to compare mental ability results from the WISC-III with the WIAT, a comparison often made for students experiencing learning difficulties in school. This assists in the process of establishing individual education plans (IEPs).

The WISC-III is generally considered to be a good test of general mental ability. Among its strengths (Sattler, 1992) are its (1) high-quality norms; (2) good reliability and validity; (3) usefulness in diagnosing cognitive abilities of most students; (4) good features of the materials, administration, and scoring; and (5) extensive research literature. Among its limitations (Sattler, 1992) are its (1) lack of usefulness of extremely low and high ability children, (2) restriction of the range of scores for certain subtests and age levels, (3) lack of appropriate norms when a subtest is substituted, (4) susceptibility to large practice effects on the Performance Scale, and (5) potential for penalizing students who do not place a premium on speed of responding.

WPPSI-R The *Wechsler Preschool and Primary Scale of Intelligence–Revised* is used with children aged 3 years through 7 years, 3 months. It overlaps with the WISC-III for ages 6 years through 7 years, 3 months. For this overlapping age range, the WISC-III is recommended (Sattler, 1992). The WPPSI-R contains 10 subtests and 2 supplemental subtests. In the Verbal category are Information, Vocabulary, Arithmetic, Similarities, and Comprehension (Sentences is a Supplemental Verbal subtest). In the Performance category are Animal Pegs, Picture Completion, Mazes, Geometric Design, and Block Design (Object Assembly is a supplemental Performance subtest). The WPPSI-R has many of the same strengths and limitations as the WISC-III (Sattler, 1992).

Kaufman Assessment Battery for Children

General Description The *Kaufman Assessment Battery for Children* (K-ABC) is an individually administered test of both intelligence and achievement (Kaufman & Kaufman, 1983). It is used with children aged 6 years, 3 months through 12 years, 5 months. The K-ABC differs in several ways from other approaches to measuring scholastic aptitude described thus far: (1) the intelligence scales focus on the process used to solve a problem rather than on the content processes (verbal comprehension), (2) the subtests were derived from psychological and neuropsychological theory, (3) mental processing ("intelligence") is tested separately from learning of school-related material ("achievement"), (4) both verbal and nonverbal achievement are assessed, (5) norms include both normal and exceptional children, and (6) the mental processing and achievement scales were normed on the same group of children. This simultaneous norming allows scores in the two areas to be compared and is helpful when professionals are developing IEPs for students.

Content The K-ABC has 16 subtests: 10 associated with the mental processing (intelligence scale) and 6 associated with the achievement scale. Not all subtests are administered to all students: Younger students take 7, and older students take 13. The scales and their subtests are organized as follows:

- *Sequential Processing Scale* requires students to solve tasks by mentally arranging the stimuli in a sequential or serial order (3 subtests): Hand Movements, Number Recall, Word Order.
- *Simultaneous Processing Scale* requires students to solve spatial and analogic tasks by mentally integrating and processing many stimuli at once (7 subtests): Magic Window, Face Recognition, Gestalt Closure, Triangles, Matrix Analogies, Spatial Memory, Photo Series.
- *Achievement Scale* requires students to solve tasks using factual knowledge and skills learned in and out of school (6 subtests): Expressive Vocabulary, Faces and Places, Arithmetic, Riddles, Reading/Decoding, Reading/Understanding.
- *Nonverbal Scale* is not a separate set of subtests. Rather, it consists of those subtests from the Sequential and Simultaneous Scales that do not require word understanding: Hand Movements, Face Recognition, Triangles, Matrix Analogies, Spatial Memory, Photo Series.

Figure 19.6 describes these subtests and states the ages for which they are intended.

Scores The K-ABC provides *DIQ* scores (mean = 100, standard deviation = 15) for each of the global scales: Sequential Processing, Simultaneous Processing, Mental Processing Composite, Achievement, and Nonverbal. The Mental Processing Composite is obtained from the scores. The Mental Processing Composite is obtained from the scores on the Sequential Processing and Simultaneous Processing subtests only. The mental processing subtests results are reported as normalized standard scores (mean = 10, standard deviation = 3). Each of the achievement subtests results is reported as a *DIQ* (mean = 100, standard deviation = 15) and, for reading and arithmetic, as grade equivalents.

Usefulness of the K-ABC Approach Although the authors suggest that organizing assessment information into three scales (Sequential Processing, Simultaneous Processing, and Achievement) provides a better way to understand students with learning disabilities and with mental retardation, not all assessment specialists agree. Sattler (1988) summarizes much of the criticism of the K-ABC: (1) it is misleading to call some subtests mental processing and others achievement, because many of the achievement subtests require considerable mental processing and many of the mental processing subtests are heavily influenced by specific achievements; (2) simultaneous processing and sequential processing are ambiguous and not well distinguished; and (3) it is not recommended for classifying students with mental retardation or students with gifted intelligence at certain ages.

FIGURE 19.6 Description of the subtests and age levels for the K-ABC.

Sequential Processing Scale

Hand Movements ($2\frac{1}{2}$–$12\frac{1}{2}$) Child performs series of hand movements in same sequence as the examiner performed them.

Number Recall ($2\frac{1}{2}$–$12\frac{1}{2}$) Repeating digits in same sequence as presented by the examiner.

Word Order (4–$12\frac{1}{2}$) Child touches silhouettes of common objects in same sequence as examiner orally names them.

Simultaneous Processing Scale

Magic Window ($2\frac{1}{2}$–4 yrs. 11 mo.) Child identifies a picture that is partially exposed when the examiner moves it behind a narrow window.

Face Recognition ($2\frac{1}{2}$–4 yrs. 11 mo.) One or two faces are exposed briefly, and child has to find them when a group photograph is presented.

Gestalt Closure ($2\frac{1}{2}$–$12\frac{1}{2}$) Naming the object or picture in a partially completed drawing.

Triangles (4–$12\frac{1}{2}$) Arranging identical triangles to match a pattern in a given model.

Matrix Analogies (5–$12\frac{1}{2}$) Selecting the picture that best completes a visual analogy.

Simultaneous Processing Scale *(cont.)*

Spatial Memory (5–$12\frac{1}{2}$) Recalling location of pictures on a page that was briefly exposed.

Photo Series (6–$12\frac{1}{2}$) Arranging photographs in chronological order.

Achievement Scales

Expressive Vocabulary ($2\frac{1}{2}$–4 yrs. 11 mo.) Stating the name of an object in a photograph.

Faces and Places ($2\frac{1}{2}$–$12\frac{1}{2}$) Naming the well-known person, place, or thing in a photograph.

Arithmetic (3–$12\frac{1}{2}$) Knowing school-related arithmetic concepts and skills.

Riddles (3–$12\frac{1}{2}$) Naming a concrete or abstract concept after being presented with a list of its characteristics.

Reading/Decoding (5–$12\frac{1}{2}$) Naming letters; reading words.

Reading/Understanding (7–$12\frac{1}{2}$) Reading sentences and following the commands presented in them.

Source: Kaufman Assessment Battery for Children (K-ABC) by Alan and Nadeen Kaufman © 1995 American Guidance Service, Inc., 4201 Woodland Road, Circle Pines, MN 55014-1796. Adapted for catalog copy with permission of publisher. All rights reserved.

ASSESSING ADAPTIVE BEHAVIOR

Meaning of Adaptive Behavior

Tests such as the *Stanford-Binet,* the WISC-R, and the K-ABC measure general scholastic ability. A school setting is not, of course, the only environment in which persons are expected to cope. Some students may appear to teachers and other school personnel to suffer from mental retardation, but their families, neighbors, and peers accept the students and consider the students normal in all other facets of life (Mercer, 1973). It is recommended, therefore, that before labeling a student as having mental retardation, the student's ability to cope with the demands of his or her environment outside of classroom learning be assessed (Grossman, 1983).

Adaptive behavior assessment focuses on how independently students can care for themselves and how well they can cope with the demands placed on them by the immediate culture in which they are living. Thus, these types of assessments focus on a student's success as a family member, consumer, wage earner, member of a nonacademic peer group, person interacting with adults, and person caring for his or her health and physical needs. A psychological report for a student often includes assessment of the student's adaptive behavior as well as his or her general scholastic aptitude. This section presents one example.

Vineland Adaptive Behavior Scales (VABS)

The *Vineland Adaptive Behavior Scales* (VABS), authored by Sara S. Sparrow, David A. Balls, and Domenic V. Cicchetti in 1984, is a developmental checklist that assesses adaptive behavior in five areas: Communication (expressive, receptive, and written), Daily Living Skills (domestic tasks, personal habits, behavior outside the home), Socialization (interacting with others during play and other free time), Motor Skills (gross and fine motor), and Maladaptive Behavior (inappropriate and undesirable behavior). The first three areas are assessed for children from birth through 19 years (and low-functioning adults). Motor Skills assessment is limited to children younger than 9 years and the Maladaptive Behavior area to children 5 years and older. A child's parent or caregiver is interviewed by a trained interviewer, who completes the assessment.

The VABS has three editions: Interview Edition, Survey Form, which provides standard scores for each of the five areas as well as a total adaptive behavior score; Interview Edition, Expanded Form, which in addition to the standard scores provides specific, detailed information for preparing educational and habilitation programs; and Classroom Edition, for ages 3 to 13, which a teacher completes as a questionnaire and which provides standard scores for four adaptive behavior areas as well as a total adaptive behavior score. A qualified professional is needed to interpret the scores. The VABS provides national norms for all three editions. For the two Interview Editions, special supplemental norms are available for adults with mental retardation (residential and nonresidential), children with hearing impairments, children with visual impairments, and children with emotional disturbances (the latter three groups in residential settings).

ASSESSING VOCATIONAL AND CAREER INTERESTS

What Are Interests?

Attitudes, Interests, and Values In Chapter 1, we discussed three characteristics of students that were closely related: attitudes, interests, and values. These student characteristics are very often assessed by using some type of questionnaire. The questionnaires appear similar because, when responding to the questionnaire, a student reads several statements and expresses his or her degree of agreement with the statements. You must remember, however, that in spite of their similarity, the three concepts are not identical.

To interpret the assessment results properly, you must distinguish between these three concepts. An **attitude** is a positive or negative feeling about a physical object, a type of people, a particular person, a government or other social institution's policy, ideas, or the like. For example, when a student expresses agreement with the statement, "My mathematics class helps me to become a better person," the student is expressing his or her attitude toward the mathematics class.

Interests, on the other hand, are a person's preferences for specific types of activities when a person is not under external pressure. For example, when a student expresses agreement with the statement, "I enjoy working on the mathematics problems my teacher assigns," the student is expressing his or her interest in a mathematics activity. **Values**, unlike attitudes and interests, are a person's long-lasting beliefs of the importance of certain life goals, a life style, a way of acting, or a way of life. For example, when a student expresses agreement with the statement, "I consider it more important to be one of the best students in mathematics than to be one of the best players in a football game," the student is expressing his or her valuing of mathematics success over football (athletic) success.

When studying about ways of assessing attitudes, interests, and values, you should keep in mind that the methods you use for assessing them are "highly susceptible to faking, require frank responses from the subject, and are

therefore able to assess only the characteristics that the individual is able to, or wishes to, reveal" (Mehrens & Lehmann, 1991, p. 405).

Focus on Career Interests This cluster of students' interests is important as students begin to prepare themselves for further schooling and for the world of work. No single piece of information is sufficient for a student to use in making vocational decisions, of course. However, the student's interest in various activities associated with specific types of work or work environments is an important consideration. Besides knowing the duty requirements of the job market, and his or her own abilities and aptitudes, a student should also understand his or her own interests regarding work-related activities. Thus, the types of career interest inventories described next can provide one source of information to help a student make educational and vocational choices.

Expressed, Manifested, Tested, and Inventoried Interests

Interest inventories of the type described in this section are limited to only vocational interests or career interests. Even career interests are narrowed even further. You may find it useful to distinguish between expressed, manifested, tested, and inventoried interests (Super, 1947, 1949).

Expressed Interests **Expressed interests** are obtained when you ask students directly about their interests. The interests a student verbally professes when you ask the student directly may not express the student's true preferences: A youngster may express an interest in being a doctor, for example, because it is perceived to be something parents expect of the child. Or a teenager may say she wants to be a mortician just to see the reaction of her parents.

Manifested Interests **Manifested interests** are deduced from what a student actually does, or the activities in which the student actually participates. When you attempt to deduce students' interests from their activities, you may be in error, also. For example, you may conclude a girl is interested in athletics because she participates in the junior high track team, but you later find out she only wants to be with her friends after school.

Tested Interests **Tested interests** are those you infer from the results of an assessment of a student's information and knowledge of a particular subject matter. For example, you may hypothesize that a student who has a lot of scientific knowledge and information has more interest in science than a student who knows little about science. Such knowledge assessments are not used very often in current vocational counseling practice.

Inventoried Interests **Inventoried interests** are identified through various paper-and-pencil tests or interest inventories. A limitation here is that the interests you discover through a particular interest inventory do not represent all interests or even all career interests. Further, as with other forms of educational and psychological assessment, you should not assume that the interest patterns identified with one publisher's interest inventory are the same ones that could be identified with others. When counseling students, keep in mind that you should use all three interests—expressed, manifested, and inventoried—to assess a student's interest pattern (Davis, 1980).

Vocational Interest Inventories

Vocational interest inventories are formal paper-and-pencil questionnaires that help students express their likes and dislikes about a very wide range of work and other activities. A student's pattern of interests is then determined from the student's responses. This profile or pattern of interests becomes one source of information a student can use for career exploration, career counseling, and career decision making.

Building Interest Inventories   The traditional view of describing a person's inventoried interests is a variation on the "birds of a feather flock together" theme (Darley & Hagenah, 1955). This rationale has been called the **people-similarity rationale** (Cole & Hanson, 1975, p. 6):

> *Rationale 1.* If a person likes the same things that people in a particular job like, the person will be satisfied with the job.

Certain parts of the *Kuder Occupational Interest Survey* (KOIS) and the *Strong Vocational Interest Blank of the Strong Interest Inventory* (SVIB-SII) follow this rationale. Both the KOIS and the Occupational Scales of the SVIB-SII, for example, are **empirically keyed scales**, made up of items especially selected because research has shown that persons' responses to these items clearly differentiate between the persons who are currently and happily employed in a particular occupation and people in general.

A second rationale has been called the **activity-similarity rationale** (Cole & Hanson, 1975, p. 6):

> *Rationale 2.* If people like activities similar to the activities required by a job, they will like those job activities and consequently be satisfied with their job.

Inventories built using this rationale present the students with lists of activities that are similar to those required of persons working in certain jobs or studying certain subjects. The developers assume that if a person has an identifiable pattern of likes and dislikes common to a particular job, that person will be satisfied with that job. Among the inventories developed using this rationale are the *ACT Interest Inventory* and the *Ohio Vocational Interest Survey, Second Edition* (OVIS-II).

Formats of Interest Items   Figure 19.7 shows sample items from three vocational interest inventories. Notice that the items from the first two inventories, ACT and SVIB-SII, ask students to rate each activity or statement on a like/dislike continuum. The last inventory, KOIS, presents activities in sets of three (triads). These latter items ask the student to mark the one activity in the triad that the student most ("M") likes and the one activity the student least ("L") likes. This is equivalent to asking a student to rank the three activities from most liked to least liked. This approach, called a **forced-choice item format**, was designed to overcome the tendency for some students to have very high personal standards for "like," while others have very low standards. When this difference in standards occurs, two students who may in fact have the *same order* of likes or dislikes for an activity may mark their answer sheets differently. Measurement experts have criticized the forced-choice format, however, because using it results in a statistical artifact that causes a negative correlation among the scales of the inventory.

Item Content   The pioneers of the interest inventory technique used a variety of content to survey interests, including asking examinees likes and dislikes of job titles,

FIGURE 19.7   Examples of items on three interest inventories.

The ACT Interest Inventory

I would *dislike* doing this activity . . . . .D
I am *indifferent* (don't care one way
    or the other) I
I would *like* doing this activity .L

1. Explore a science museum
2. Play jazz in a combo
3. Help settle an argument between friends

SVIB–SII

*1.	L	I	D	Actor/Actress
2.	L	I	D	Advertising executive
3.	L	I	D	Architect

Kuder Occupational Interest Survey, Form DD

** 1.	Visit an art gallery . . . . M	L
	Browse in a library. . . . . M	L
	Visit a museum . . . . M	L
2.	Collect autographs . . . . M	L
	Collect coins . . . . M	L
	Collect stones . . . . M	L

---

* L = like, I = indifferent, D = dislike
** M = most liked, L = least liked

Sources: The test items from the *ACT Interest Inventory*, p. 10 in Registering for the ACT Assessment. Copyright by ACT, Inc. Reproduced by permission of the publisher.
SVIB-SCII items modified and reproduced by special permission of the publisher, Consulting Psychologists Press, Inc., Palo Alto, CA 94303 from *Strong Interest Inventory® of the Strong Vocational Interest Blanks®, Form T317.* Copyright 1994 by the Board of Trustees of the Leland Stanford Junior University. All rights reserved. Printed under license from Stanford University Press, Stanford, CA 94303. Further reproduction is prohibited without the Publisher's written consent. The test items from the *Kuder Occupational Interest Survey, Form DD* are reproduced by permission. Published by National Career Assessment Services Inc.™, PO Box 277, Adel, Iowa 50003. 800-314-8972 / www.kuder.com. Copyright by National Career Assessment Services, Inc.™. All rights reserved.

school subject matter, hobbies, leisure activities, work activities, types of persons, and type of reading material, and assessing examinees' personal characteristics (Davis, 1980). Over time, however, the concept of interests narrowed to the world of work and careers. Today the content of most inventories is limited exclusively to lists of activities, and most are concerned with work activities. An exception is the SVIB-SII, which uses a large variety of content. The 317 items on the SVIB-SII measure a person's interest in 109 careers.

Interest Inventory Use   Among the uses made of scores on vocational interest inventories are these: (1) to reassure people about tentative choices, (2) to give people a structure for understanding the world of work, (3) to help people resolve conflicting alternatives, (4) to help people plan their personal development, (5) to call attention to desirable alternatives that the average person usually does not know about or overlooks, (6) to help people understand their job dissatisfaction, (7) to help employers select people who will be better workers, (8) to help people plan their career advancement, (9) to aid in the scientific study of the world of work and to link this research to other research in the social sciences (Holland, 1975, p. 22).

Strong Vocational Interest Blanks—Strong Interest Inventory

A number of vocational interest inventories are listed in Appendix J. One of the inventories, the *Strong Vocation Interest Blank–Strong Interest Inventory* (SVIB-SII), is briefly described here.

Organization   The 1994 revision, which is used with students 14 years old and older, is composed of 317 items. A student is presented with occupations, school subjects, activities, amusements, and types of people and rates each item as *like*, *dislike*, or *indifferent*. The student is also presented with pairs of activities and chooses which, if any, is preferred. Also, the student states if each of the list of characteristics describes him or her. The responses are then scored via a computer (tests can't be scored locally) and reported as standard scores on various scales. The results of the SII are reported to the examinee in three ways: (1) 6 General Occupational Themes, which describe a person's overall pattern of occupational interests, (2) 25 Basic Interest Scales, which describe the somewhat narrower categories of activities a person likes, (3) 211 Occupational Scales, which describe the extent to which a persons' likes and dislikes are similar to persons in specific occupations, and (4) 4 Personality Style Scales.

General Occupational Themes   The student receives a score on each of six personality types, which were adapted from Holland (1973). These are Realistic, Investigative, Artistic, Social, Enterprising, and Conventional. A counselor can use the student's profile regarding these types of personalities to help a student understand his or her overall or general pattern of interests and how he or she appears to be oriented to the world of work. A normalized standard score (*T*-score) is reported for each of the six themes.

Basic Interest Scales   The 25 scales are grouped in clusters under each of the six themes according to their relationship to the theme. For example, five of the basic interest scales–Teaching, Social Service, Athletics, Domestic Arts, Religious Activities–are clustered under the general occupational theme of Social. The basic interest scales intermediate between the general occupational themes and the more specific occupational scales (described next). The basic interest scales describe the clusters of activities a student likes. These activity areas may be common to several specific occupations (for example, there are many types of teachers).

Occupational Scales   Farmer, air force trainer, school administrator, fine artist, and science teacher are some of the 211 occupations listed. A student receives a standard score for each occupation. This score describes how similar the student's pattern of likes and dislikes is to persons who are experienced and satisfied in each occupation.

Special Scales   Two nonoccupational scales are used: the Academic Comfort Scale and the Introversion-Extroversion Scale. The first is an assessment of the extent to which a student likes intellectual activities. The second assesses the extent to which a student likes to interact and work with other people as contrasted with being content working alone. In addition to these scales, there are special administrative indexes. These are used to assess whether the student's responses can be interpreted with some confidence.

The Total Response Index checks whether the student answered enough items to make a useful interpretation of the SVIB-SII results. If a student omitted 15 or more items, the results may not be valid. The Infrequent Response Index checks on whether the student's responses are marked incorrectly. It compares the student's responses to those in a general norm group. A third index assesses like, dislike, and indifference percentages. This is used to assess whether a student's response patterns indicate improper scoring, misunderstood directions, or marking the answer sheet improperly. The administrative indexes help a counselor to decide whether the student responded well enough to make the results meaningful.

Male-Female Differences   Although the SVIB-SII has a single booklet for both males and females, there are separate norms for each gender. The authors have kept the norms separate, because (1) there are large differences in the strength of interests in the two genders in many areas and (2) combined-sex (unisex) scales appear less valid for many occupations. Students may understand their interests better if they can compare them to both like-gender and opposite-gender norms. This may be especially helpful to students who are thinking of entering occupations dominated by the gender opposite of their own.

MEASURING ATTITUDE

Attitudes and Their Characteristics

Attitudes are characteristics of persons that describe their positive and negative feelings toward particular objects, situations, institutions, persons, or ideas. When discussing attitudes and using the results of attitude inventories, you should keep in mind the following points (Mehrens & Lehmann, 1991):

1. A student learns attitudes, and once learned they direct or guide the students' actions.

2. You cannot observe a student's attitudes directly; you must infer them from the student's actions or from responses to an attitude questionnaire.

3. Different ways of constructing attitude scales include Thurstone, Guttman, Liker, Semantic Differential, and Item Response Theory. These methods are not interchangeable.

4. Because it is difficult to construct an attitude scale, you may need to look seriously into the validity and reliability of the results before you use one.

5. Because students can fake their responses to attitude questionnaires, you should interpret the results very cautiously.

6. When interpreting student's attitudes, keep in mind that they differ in both **direction** and **intensity**. Two students may hold the same positive attitude (direction), but the students may differ greatly regarding the strength of feeling (intensity) they attach to that attitude.

7. Students will also differ in the **affective saliency** or emotionality with which they hold particular attitudes. Two students may have the same positive attitude, but one may become much more emotional than the other regarding it.

8. The attitudes of older students and adults are changeable, but it is much easier to change the attitudes of younger students.

School Attitude Measure The *School Attitude Measure* (SAM) (Wick et al., 1989) assesses students' attitudes and self-concept in five areas. There are five levels of the questionnaire: one each for grades 1–2, grades 3–4, grades 5–6, grades 7–8, and grades 9–12. The five areas assessed are described here.

Scale 1: Motivation for Schooling Assesses students' positive and negative feelings about schooling.

Scale 2: Academic Self-Concept—Performance Based Assesses students' self-confidence in their ability to learn and perform in school.

Scale 3: Academic Self-Concept—Preference Based Assesses students' perception of what others (family, peers, teachers) think about the student's ability to learn and perform in school.

Scale 4: Student's Sense of Control Over Performance Assesses whether the students feel a sense of control over what happens to them in school and can accept responsibility for what happens.

Scale 5: Student's Instructional Mastery Asks students to report their beliefs about the level of their actual school performance.

Students respond to each item by marking whether they "never agree," "sometimes agree," "usually agree," or "always agree" for each statement. (Students in grades 1 and 2 simply respond yes or no.) The statements comprising the items are balanced to reflect both positive and negative attitudes and feelings. Thus, when an item is phrased positively (e.g., "the best students in class think I do good school work"), students marking "always agree" receive an item score of 4, while those marking "never agree" receive a score of 1. When an item is phrased negatively (e.g., "there is no way that a student like me will get good grades in school") students marking "always agree" receive an item score of 1, while those marking "never agree" receive a score of 4. In this way, all the items receive a positive scoring, and the higher the raw score on the questionnaire is, the more positive is a student's attitude.

Teachers receive class reports listing each student's total score and the score on each scale (except for grades 1–2, where only the total score is reported). Scores include the raw score, national percentile, local percentile, national stanine, local stanine, and normal curve equivalent for each scale.

ASSESSING PERSONALITY DIMENSIONS

A variety of techniques have been developed to measure various aspects of personality. Personality tests and vocational tests are the two most numerous varieties of tests. A person using a personality test must be trained in psychological interpretation of the results. This usually requires extensive graduate work in counseling or school psychology and a rather lengthy supervised internship. Thus, for the most part, teacher-training programs leave teachers unqualified to administer and interpret personality tests. *Teachers will encounter the results of such tests*, however, if they are part of a child study team or if they read psychological reports of students. Thus, some familiarity with a few basic concepts of personality measurement is in order.

Assessment Approaches

The kind of personality tests a counselor or psychologist uses depends primarily on the psychological orientation of the particular professional. Currently, there is no standard model or conception of personality, nor do counselors and psychologists agree on which particular aspects of personality are most important to assess. The implication of this diversity is that the kind(s) of personality tests used in psychological reports a teacher may encounter depend(s) on the background and training of the psychologist assigned to a given student's case.

Projective Techniques

Projective Hypothesis Two broad categories of methods for assessing personality dimensions are projective techniques and structured techniques. **Projective techniques** present the examinee with ambiguous stimuli and ask the examinee to respond to them. The proponents of this technique assume that an examinee's interpretations of these vague stimuli will reveal the examinee's innermost needs, feelings, and conflicts, even though the examinee is unaware of what he or she is revealing. This assumption is known as the **projective hypothesis** (Frank, 1939). A trained examiner is needed to interpret an examinee's responses. Examples of projective personality tests are the *Rorschach Test*, the *Thematic Apperception Test* (TAT), word association tests, various sentence completion tests, certain picture arrangements tests, and various figure drawing tests.

Rorschach The *Rorschach Test*, for example, presents to the examinee one at a time several cards on which inkblots are printed. The examinee is asked to tell what each inkblot means or to describe the things seen in the inkblot. Because the examinee's responses are based on associations, the Rorschach is classified as an **association test**. The psychologist analyzes the content of the responses as well as the process and manner in which the subject responds. As a result of this analysis, the psychologist generates hypotheses about the subject's personality dynamics that the psychologist can explore with the client and can confirm or reject during subsequent interview sessions.

Thematic Apperception Test TAT pictures are more structured than the Rorschach inkblots. They show surrealistic pictures of scenes involving one or more persons. The examinee is asked to tell a story about the picture: What happened before the event pictured? What is happening at the moment? Who are the characters? What are their feelings? How will the story end? Because examinees must construct stories, the TAT is sometimes classified as a **construction test**. The psychologist analyzes the content of the story in terms of H. A. Murray's (1938) personality theory of "needs" and "press," generating hypotheses about the examinee's personality for further exploration during interviews.

Sentence Completion Assessments Sentence **completion tests of personality** ask the examinee to complete sentences related to various aspects of self and of interpersonal relations (e.g., "Compared with most families, mine . . ."). The results of content analyses are used similarly to generate hypotheses about a subject's personality.

Structured Techniques

Definition **Structured personality assessment techniques** follow very specific rules for administering, scoring, and interpreting the tests. Usually they follow a response-choice format: yes-no, true-false, or multiple-choice. Examples of structured personality tests are the *Guilford-Zimmerman Temperament Survey*, the *Minnesota Multiphasic Personality Inventory*–Second Edition, the *California Psychological Inventory*, the *Sixteen Personality Factors Questionnaire*, and the *Personality Inventory for Children*.

Self-Report Characteristic Each test is sometimes referred to as a **self-report personality inventory**, because it requires the examinee to respond to the items in a way that describes his or her personal feelings. For instance, examinees may be asked whether the statement, "I usually express my personal opinions to others," is true of themselves.

Dimensions of Personality Another characteristic of structured personality inventories is that the items are related to various scales or personality dimensions. The *Guilford-Zimmerman Temperament Survey*, for example, reports an examinee's profile with respect to 10 scales: general activity, restraint, ascendance (leadership), sociability, emotional stability, objectivity, friendliness, thoughtfulness, personal relations, and masculinity.[3]

Usefulness of Tests for the Teacher

Self-report personality inventories require persons to (Thorndike et al., 1991): (1) read and comprehend each item, (2) be able to understand their own actions enough to know whether a given statement is true of them, and (3) be willing to respond honestly and frankly. Reading in the context of personality testing requires that students understand the items well enough to be able to decide the degree to which the statements apply to their own lives. To decide whether a statement applies, a student must view that behavior objectively, which may not be within the repertoire of an unsatisfactorily adjusted student. Finally, if a student is not able or willing to respond frankly to the items, a distorted personality description

---

[3] *Masculinity* is the term these authors use.

may result. This lack of frankness may occur more often when testing children who feel vulnerable or threatened if they reveal their feelings to the teacher or, more generally, to the school.

Considering the shortcomings of self-report personality and adjustment inventories, some measurement experts answer the questions of whether to use them in the following way: "these instruments have limited role in education and should be used in educational settings only when the results are to benefit the examinee and will be interpreted by a person with adequate clinical training and experience" (Thorndike et al., 1991, p. 416).

Summary

- Tests of general scholastic ability or intelligence describe a learner's general intellectual skill rather than the specific abilities needed to learn a particular lesson or task.
- Information about general intellectual skills becomes important when trying to forecast a pupil's future academic performance in general and when the conditions for future learning are expected to remain similar to the past learning conditions.
- General scholastic ability test scores are less valid when predicting very specific kinds of academic learning, but more valid when predicting more global kinds of academic accomplishments.
- A person's capacity to learn is a function of biological makeup, experience in the environment, and a complex interaction of the two. The capacity of a person to learn something new will depend on previous learning, the way the new material is taught, the pupil's motivation, and a host of other factors, as well as the pupil's native endowment.
- Both achievement tests and aptitude tests can reflect a person's present aptitude level. Test items that best predict future attainment, however, would tend to be found on aptitude tests.
- All predictions made from aptitude test scores assume that the same learning conditions that existed in the past will extend into the future.
- This chapter discusses three general types of group-administered scholastic aptitude tests: an omnibus test, a two-score test, and a multiple-aptitude test. Suggestions for using these test scores appear.
- School readiness tests are also described.
- High school and college admissions tests are designed to predict success at the next higher level of schooling. The chapter describes two college admissions tests.
- As a group, pupils' scholastic aptitude test scores tend to be stable over time.
- In general, test-retest correlations for scholastic ability tests (1) tend to become lower (less stability) as the time interval between the testings becomes longer, and (2) for a fixed interval between testings, tend to be lower for younger children than for older children.
- Some factors that contribute to the relative stability of persons' aptitude scores are (1) the cumulative nature of intellectual skills, (2) the stable environment that persons experience, and (3) the generative nature of earlier acquired prerequisite skills.
- Some factors that contribute to changes in a person's aptitude scores are (1) errors of measurement, (2) test and norm differences, and (3) special interventions and enriched environments.
- Growth in intellectual skills in the early years seems to be associated with an environment that is emotionally supportive and accepting and in which there are many opportunities for experiencing and reinforcing a person's cognitive successes.
- The Stanford-Binet Intelligence Scale, the Wechsler Intelligence Scales, and the Kaufman Assessment Battery for Children are examples of individually administered tests of general scholastic aptitude. The text describes each and the similarities and differences among them.
- Behavior checklists help psychologists assess whether a student has acquired normal, age-appropriate adaptive behaviors. These behaviors indicate a child can cope with the social and physical environment, especially outside the context. In a comprehensive assessment of a pupil, ascertaining level of the pupil's adaptive behavior (as well as the level of general academic skills) is necessary.
- Vocational interest inventories are paper-and-pencil questionnaires that help individuals express their likes and dislikes about certain work-related activities. Individuals' patterns of likes and dislikes are used to help them in career exploration and career decision making.
- Interest inventories contain one of two item formats: (1) a rating format in which persons rate the degree to which they like the activities presented to them, or (2) a forced-choice ranking format in which the persons must rank the activities presented from best liked to least liked.
- Nearly all vocational interest inventories limit the activities in the items to work-related activities. The Strong Vocational Interest Bank of the Strong Interest Inventory is an exception because of the diversity of item content it includes (e.g., occupational titles, school subjects, amusements, work- and nonwork-related activities, types of people, and personal characteristics).
- Attitudes describe a person's feelings toward particular objects, situations, institutions, persons, or ideas.
- Several factors to consider before you use the results of an attitude questionnaire are presented.
- The choice of the particular kind of personality test often depends on the training and orientation of the psychologist examining the person. Projective tests of personality present ambiguous stimuli and assume

that the examinee's responses reflect the person's underlying psychological needs and personality dispositions. Structured personality tests usually use a response-choice format. Examinees either rank or rate statements in terms of how well the statements describe themselves. Structured personality test scores describe a person's normative standing on each of several dimensions or aspects of personality.

■ Teachers probably should not administer and interpret personality tests because (1) the tests are subject to distortion by pupils, (2) such tests have limited predictive validity when used alone, (3) paper-and-pencil inventories depend on the examinee's reading ability and insight into his or her own behavior, (4) teachers generally do not have the requisite coursework and supervised training necessary to interpret them, and (5) teachers seldom have the time needed to explore the meaning of a test score with an individual pupil.

Important Terms and Concepts

abstract/visual reasoning subtests
adaptive behavior
affective saliency
age-based scores vs. grade-based scores
aptitude (vs. achievement)
association test of personality
attitudes
basal level, ceiling level
completion test of personality
construction test of personality
direction and intensity of attitude
empirically keyed scales
figural reasoning
forced-choice item format
general vs. specific intellectual skills
interests
inventoried interests, manifested interests, tested interests, expressed interests
mental age
multiple-aptitude tests
nonverbal tests
omnibus test
people-similarity rationale vs. activity-similarity rationale
pictorial reasoning
projective hypothesis
projective personality test techniques
quantitative reasoning
quantitative reasoning subtests
readiness test
short-term memory subtests
spiral format
standard age score (SAS)
structured (self-report) personality assessment techniques
values
verbal comprehension
verbal reasoning
verbal reasoning subtests
vocational interest inventories

Exercises and Discussion Questions

1. Describe several school situations in which knowing a student's level of specific skill development is less helpful than knowing a student's general intellectual skill development in setting expectations for learning new material.

2. Describe in a general way how the predictive validity of past achievement scores, general school ability test scores, and specific aptitude test scores is related to learning specific learning targets and learning general intellectual skills.

3. Why is the concept that each student has a fixed capacity to learn unsatisfactory?

4. **a.** What are the principal advantages of group aptitude tests over individual aptitude tests?
   b. What are the principal advantages of individual scholastic aptitude tests over group scholastic aptitude tests?

5. Distinguish between the following tests: OLSAT, DAT, SAT-I, ACT, SB-IV, WISC-III, and K-ABC. Name at least one advantage of each of these over the others.

6. **a.** What characteristics of a student's background lead to the student's general scholastic aptitude test score remaining more or less stable over a long period of time?
   b. What characteristics of a student's background lead to the student's general scholastic aptitude test score changing greatly over a long period of time?
   c. Explain this statement: "Present aptitude tests predict how well a learner can adapt to a fixed instructional setting."
   d. What can you do in your teaching to adapt to learners with different patterns and levels of scholastic aptitudes?

7. Explain how each of the eight aspects of validity in Table 3.2 specifically applies to the following tests. Give examples of how you would rephrase the questions in Table 3.2 for each test and what kinds of validity evidence you would need to answer these questions for each test.
   a. OLSAT
   b. DAT
   c. SAT-I
   d. ACT
   e. SB-IV
   f. WISC-III
   g. K-ABC

8. For each test in Question 7, state which aspect of validity in Table 3.2 is most important. Explain why you believe this aspect to be most important.

9. Read each of the following statements of educational needs. For each statement choose the type of test that *possibly* could meet the stated need. Next to each type of test you selected for a need, put a plus sign (+) if you believe the need can actually be met by the type of test you selected, and a minus sign (−) if you believe that the need cannot actually be met by the test. Defend your choices. Choose from among the tests in this set to respond to this exercise: OLSAT, DAT, readiness tests, SAT-I, ACT, aptitude tests for a specific subject, SB-IV, WISC-III, K-ABC.
   a. "In addition to finding out a student's verbal and quantitative aptitudes, I would like to know how well the student processes symbols and other nonverbal material."
   b. "I'd like to give all ninth graders a test that would provide information helpful to them in making career decisions."
   c. "I would like to know which of my fifth-grade students could learn computer programming quickly and well."

d. "I need a general ability test for a student who recently arrived from Cuba."

e. "I need a college admissions test that gives me information that I can use in guidance and counseling activities as well as in admissions."

10. What kinds of information do paper-and-pencil vocational interest inventories use to discern a student's pattern of interests?

11. Describe the similarities and differences between a people-similarity rationale and an activity-similarity rationale for interest inventory development.

12. Both the DAT and SVIB-SII report results on separate general norms. Explain why they do so, and discuss whether this practice is helpful to the career and further schooling planning of females.

13. **a.** What are the nine uses of interest inventories scores cited by Holland (1975)?

b. Visit your school's guidance department and determine whether its counselors use interest inventories scores in any of these ways.

c. Share your findings with your classmates.

14. **a.** Explain how each of the eight aspects of validity in Table 3.2 would apply to the SVIB-SII.

b. Give examples of how you would rephrase the questions in Table 3.2 for this assessment and what kinds of validity evidence you would need to answer these questions for the SVIB-SII.

15. Distinguish between achievements, aptitudes, attitudes, interests, and values as these are applied in educational assessment.

16. Read the following statements. Each statement expresses a student's status with respect to achievement, aptitude, attitude, interest, or values. Classify each statement into one of the five categories.

a. "I am in control of my learning in this class at all times."

b. "I like science fiction stories better than biographies."

c. "I think my math class is boring."

d. "It is more important for me to be in personal control of my working hours than to earn a high salary."

e. "I am constantly striving to be the best student in this school."

17. Distinguish between projective techniques and structured techniques for assessing personality aspects. What are the advantages and disadvantages of each technique?

18. Do you agree with this statement: "Little useful purpose is served by making personality test results available to teachers"? Explain your position, and compare your position with others in your class.

Additional Readings

Armstrong, T. (1996). *Multiple intelligences in the classroom.* Alexandria, VA: Association for Supervision and Curriculum Development.

Discusses Howard Gardner's theory of seven types of intelligence, activities you can do in the classroom to strengthen each type of intelligence, and simple checklist techniques you can use to assess students' behavior in each area.

Cropley, A.J. (Ed.). (1993). Giftedness in the school: New issues and challenges. *Special issue of International Journal of Educational Research, 19*(1).

Six short chapters review research and theory on giftedness, as seen by scholars from several countries.

Gregory, R.J. (1992). *Psychological testing: History, principles, and applications.* Boston: Allyn & Bacon, Chapters 5–12.

Discusses many different tests of general mental ability, interests, and personality. Discusses research findings with each.

Sattler, J.M. (1992). *Assessment of children* (3rd ed.). San Diego: Author.

Sattler, J.M. (1992). *Assessment of children: WISC-III and WPPSI-R supplement.* San Diego: Author.

Comprehensive descriptions of individual general mental ability test, adaptive behavior inventories, and other related instruments. Summarizes the research on each instrument and gives suggestions for administering and interpreting their results.

Snow, R.E., & Lohman, D.F. (1989). Implications of cognitive psychology for educational measurement. In R. L. Linn (Ed.), *Educational measurement* (3rd ed.) (pp. 263–331). New York: Macmillan.

Summarizes research from the cognitive psychology and information processing literature in terms of its implications for testing.

APPENDIX A

Standards for Teacher Competence in Educational Assessment of Students

Developed by the American Federation of Teachers
National Council on Measurement in Education
National Education Association

The standards are intended for use as:
- a guide for teacher educators as they design and approve programs for teacher preparation
- a self-assessment guide for teachers in identifying their needs for professional development in student assessment
- a guide for workshop instructors as they design professional development experiences for in-service teachers
- an impetus for educational measurement specialists and teacher trainers to conceptualize student assessment and teacher training in student assessment more broadly than has been the case in the past

1. Teachers Should be Skilled in *Choosing* Assessment Methods Appropriate for Instructional Decisions.

Skills in choosing appropriate, useful, administratively convenient, technically adequate, and fair assessment methods are prerequisite to good use of information to support instructional decisions. Teachers need to be well-acquainted with the kinds of information provided by a broad range of assessment alternatives and their strengths and weaknesses. In particular, they should be familiar with criteria for evaluating and selecting assessment methods in light of instructional plans.

Teachers who meet this standard will have the conceptual and application skills that follow. They will be able to use the concepts of assessment error and validity when developing or selecting their approaches to classroom assessment of students. They will understand how valid assessment data can support instructional activities such as providing appropriate feedback to students, diagnosing group and individual learning needs, planning for individualized educational programs, motivating students, and evaluating instructional procedures. They will understand how invalid information can affect instructional decisions about students. They will also be able to use and evaluate assessment options available to them, considering among other things the cultural, social, economic, and language backgrounds of students. They will be aware that different assessment approaches can be incompatible with certain instructional goals and may impact quite differently on their teaching.

Teachers will know, for each assessment approach they use, its appropriateness for making decisions about their pupils. Moreover, teachers will know where to find information about and/or reviews of various assessment methods. Assessment options are diverse and include text- and curriculum-embedded questions and tests, standardized criterion-referenced and norm-referenced tests, oral questioning, spontaneous and structured performance assessments, portfolios, exhibitions, demonstrations, rating scales, writing samples, paper-and-pencil tests, seatwork and homework, peer- and self-assessments, student records, observations, questionnaires, interviews, projects, products, and others' opinions.

2. Teachers Should be Skilled in *Developing* Assessment Methods Appropriate for Instructional Decisions.

While teachers often use published or other external assessment tools, the bulk of the assessment information they use for decision-making comes from approaches they create and implement. Indeed, the assessment demands of the classroom go well beyond readily available instruments.

Teachers who meet this standard will have the conceptual and application skills that follow. Teachers will be skilled in planning the collection of information that facilitates the decisions they will make. They will know and follow appropriate principles for developing and using assessment methods in their teaching, avoiding common pitfalls in student assessment. Such techniques may include several of the options listed at the end of the first standard. The teacher will select the techniques which are appropriate to the intent of the teacher's instruction.

Teachers meeting this standard will also be skilled in using student data to analyze the quality of each assessment technique they use. Since most teachers do not have access to assessment specialists, they must be prepared to do these analyses themselves.

3. Teachers Should be Skilled in Administering, Scoring and Interpreting the Results of both Externally-produced and Teacher-produced Assessment Methods.

It is not enough that teachers are able to select and develop good assessment methods; they must also be able to apply them properly. Teachers should be skilled in administering, scoring, and interpreting results from diverse assessment methods.

Teachers who meet this standard will have the conceptual and application skills that follow. They will be skilled in interpreting informal and formal teacher-produced assessment results, including pupils' performances in class and on homework assignments. Teachers will be able to use guides for scoring essay questions and projects, stencils for scoring response-choice questions, and scales for rating performance assessments. They will be able to use these in ways that produce consistent results.

Source: From *Standards for Teacher Competence in Educational Assessment of Students* (pp. 1–4) by American Federation of Teachers, National Council on Measurement in Education, and National Education Association, 1990, Washington, DC: National Council on Measurement in Education. Copyright 1990 by the National Council on Measurement in Education. Reprinted by permission of the publisher.

Teachers will be able to administer standardized achievement tests and be able to interpret the commonly reported scores: percentile ranks, percentile band scores, standard scores, and grade equivalents. They will have a conceptual understanding of the summary indexes commonly reported with assessment results: measures of central tendency, dispersion, relationships, reliability, and errors of measurement.

Teachers will be able to apply these concepts of score and summary indices in ways that enhance their use of the assessments that they develop. They will be able to analyze assessment results to identify pupils' strengths and errors. If they get inconsistent results, they will seek other explanations for the discrepancy or other data to attempt to resolve the uncertainty before arriving at a decision. They will be able to use assessment methods in ways that encourage students' educational development and that do not inappropriately increase students' anxiety levels.

4. Teachers Should be Skilled in Using Assessment Results when Making Decisions about Individual Students, Planning Teaching, Developing Curriculum, and School Improvement.

Assessment results are used to make educational decisions at several levels: in the classroom about students, in the community about a school and a school district, and in society, generally, about the purposes and outcomes of the educational enterprise. Teachers play a vital role when participating in decision-making at each of these levels and must be able to use assessment results effectively.

Teachers who meet this standard will have the conceptual and application skills that follow. They will be able to use accumulated assessment information to organize a sound instructional plan for facilitating students' educational development. When using assessment results to plan and/or evaluate instruction and curriculum, teachers will interpret the results correctly and avoid common misinterpretations, such as basing decisions on scores that lack curriculum validity. They will be informed about the results of local, regional, state, and national assessments and about their appropriate use for pupil, classroom, school, district, state, and national educational improvement.

5. Teachers Should be Skilled in Developing Valid Pupil Grading Procedures which Use Pupil Assessments.

Grading students is an important part of professional practice for teachers. Grading is defined as indicating both a student's level of performance and a teacher's valuing of that performance. The principles for using assessments to obtain valid grades are known and teachers should employ them.

Teachers who meet this standard will have the conceptual and application skills that follow. They will be able to devise, implement, and explain a procedure for developing grades composed of marks from various assignments, projects, in-class activities, quizzes, tests, and/or other assessments that they may use. Teachers will understand and be able to articulate why the grades they assign are rational, justified, and fair, acknowledging that such grades reflect their preferences and judgments. Teachers will be able to recognize and to avoid faulty grading procedures such as using grades as punishment. They will be able to evaluate and to modify their grading procedures in order to improve the validity of the interpretations made from them about students' attainments.

6. Teachers Should be Skilled in Communicating Assessment Results to Students, Parents, Other Lay Audiences, and Other Educators.

Teachers must routinely report assessment results to students and to parents or guardians. In addition, they are frequently asked to report or to discuss assessment results with other educators and with diverse lay audiences. If the results are not communicated effectively, they may be misused or not used. To communicate effectively with others on matters of student assessment, teachers must be able to use assessment terminology appropriately and must be able to articulate the meaning, limitations, and implications of assessment results. Furthermore, teachers will sometimes be in a position that will require them to defend their own assessment procedures and their interpretations of them. At other times, teachers may need to help the public to interpret assessment results appropriately.

Teachers who meet this standard will have the conceptual and application skills that follow. Teachers will understand and be able to give appropriate explanations of how the interpretation of student assessments must be moderated by the student's socio-economic, cultural, language, and other background factors. Teachers will be able to explain that assessment results do not imply that such background factors limit a student's ultimate educational development. They will be able to communicate to students and to their parents or guardians how they may assess the student's educational progress. Teachers will understand and be able to explain the importance of taking measurement errors into account when using assessments to make decisions about individual students. Teachers will be able to explain the limitations of different informal and formal assessment methods. They will be able to explain printed reports of the results of pupil assessments at the classroom, school district, state, and national levels.

APPENDIX B
Code of Fair Testing Practices in Education

Prepared by the Joint Committee on Testing Practices

The Code of Fair Testing Practices in Education states the major obligations to test takers of professionals who develop or use educational tests. The Code is meant to apply broadly to the use of tests in education (admissions, educational assessment, educational diagnosis, and student placement). The Code is not designed to cover employment testing, licensure or certification testing, or other types of testing. Although the Code has relevance to many types of educational tests, it is directed primarily at professionally developed tests such as those sold by commercial test publishers or used in formally administered testing programs. The Code is not intended to cover tests made by individual teachers for use in their own classrooms.

The Code addresses the roles of test developers and test users separately. Test users are people who select tests, commission test development services, or make decisions on the basis of test scores. Test developers are people who actually construct tests as well as those who set policies for particular testing programs.

The roles may, of course, overlap as when a state education agency commissions test development services, sets policies that control the test development process, and makes decisions on the basis of the test scores.

The Code presents standards for educational test developers and users in four areas:

A. Developing/Selecting Tests **C.** Striving for Fairness
B. Interpreting Scores **D.** Informing Test Takers

Organizations, institutions, and individual professionals who endorse the Code commit themselves to safeguarding the rights of test takers by following the principles listed. The Code is intended to be consistent with the relevant parts of the *Standards for Educational and Psychological Testing* (AERA, APA, NCME, 1985). However, the Code differs from the Standards in both audience and purpose. The Code is meant to be understood by the general public; it is limited to educational tests; and the primary focus is on those issues that affect the proper use of tests. The Code is not meant to add new principles over and above those in the Standards or to change the meaning of the Standards. The goal is rather to represent the spirit of a selected portion of the Standards in a way that is meaningful to test takers and/or their parents or guardians. It is the hope of the Joint Committee that the Code will also be judged to be consistent with existing codes of conduct and standards of other professional groups who use educational tests.

A. Developing/Selecting Appropriate Tests*

Test developers should provide the information that test users need to select appropriate tests.

Test Developers Should:

1. Define what each test measures and what the test should be used for. Describe the population(s) for which the test is appropriate.
2. Accurately represent the characteristics, usefulness, and limitations of tests for their intended purposes.

3. Explain relevant measurement concepts as necessary for clarity at the level of detail that is appropriate for the intended audience(s).
4. Describe the process of test development. Explain how the content and skills to be tested were selected.
5. Provide evidence that the test meets its intended purpose(s).
6. Provide either representative samples or complete copies of test questions, directions, answer sheets, manuals, and score reports to qualified users.
7. Indicate the nature of the evidence obtained concerning the appropriateness of each test for groups of different racial, ethnic, or linguistic backgrounds that are likely to be tested.
8. Identify and publish any specialized skills needed to administer each test and to interpret scores correctly.

Test users should select tests that meet the purpose for which they are to be used and that are appropriate for the intended test-taking populations.

Test Users Should:

1. First define the purpose for testing and the population to be tested. Then, select a test for that purpose and that population based on a thorough review of the available information.
2. Investigate potentially useful sources of information, in addition to test scores, to corroborate the information provided by tests.
3. Read the materials provided by test developers and avoid using tests for which unclear or incomplete information is provided.
4. Become familiar with how and when the test was developed and tried out.
5. Read independent evaluations of a test and of possible alternative measures. Look for evidence required to support the claims of test developers.
6. Examine specimen sets, disclosed tests or samples of questions, directions, answer sheets, manuals, and score reports before selecting a test.
7. Ascertain whether the test content and norms group(s) or comparison group(s) are appropriate for the intended test takers.

The Code has been developed by the Joint Committee on Testing Practices, a cooperative effort of several professional organizations, that has as its aim the advancement, in the public interest, of the quality of testing practices. The Joint Committee was initiated by the American Educational Research Association, the American Psychological Association, and the National Council on Measurement in Education. In addition to these three groups, the American Association for Counseling and Development/Association for Measurement and Evaluation in Counseling and Development, and the American Speech-Language-Hearing Association are now also sponsors of the Joint Committee.

This is not copyrighted material. Reproduction and dissemination are encouraged. Please cite this document as follows:

Code of Fair Testing Practices in Education. (1988). Washington, D.C.: Joint Committee on Testing Practices. (Mailing Address: Joint Committee on Testing Practices, American Psychological Association, 1200 17th Street, NW, Washington, D.C. 20036.

*Many of the statements in the Code refer to the selection of existing tests. However, in customized testing programs test developers are engaged to construct new tests. In those situations, the test development process should be designed to help ensure that the completed tests will be in compliance with the Code.

8. Select and use only those tests for which the skills needed to administer the test and interpret scores correctly are available.

B. Interpreting Scores

Test developers should help users interpret scores correctly.

Test Developers Should:

9. Provide timely and easily understood score reports that describe test performance clearly and accurately. Also explain the meaning and limitations of reported scores.
10. Describe the population(s) represented by any norms or comparison group(s), the dates the data were gathered, and the process used to select the samples of test takers.
11. Warn users to avoid specific, reasonably anticipated misuses of test scores.
12. Provide information that will help users follow reasonable procedures for setting passing scores when it is appropriate to use such scores with the test.
13. Provide information that will help users gather evidence to show that the test is meeting its intended purpose(s).

Test users should interpret scores correctly.

Test Users Should:

9. Obtain information about the scale used for reporting scores, the characteristics of any norms or comparison group(s), and the limitations of the scores.
10. Interpret scores taking into account any major differences between the norms or comparison groups and the actual test takers. Also take into account any differences in test administration practices or familiarity with the specific questions in the test.
11. Avoid using tests for purposes not specifically recommended by the test developer unless evidence is obtained to support the intended use.
12. Explain how any passing scores were set and gather evidence to support the appropriateness of the scores.
13. Obtain evidence to help show that the test is meeting its intended purpose(s).

C. Striving for Fairness

Test developers should strive to make tests that are as fair as possible for test takers of different races, gender, ethnic backgrounds, or handicapping conditions.

Test Developers Should:

14. Review and revise test questions and related materials to avoid potentially insensitive content or language.
15. Investigate the performance of test takers of different races, gender, and ethnic backgrounds when samples of sufficient size are available. Enact procedures that help to ensure that differences in performance are related primarily to the skills under assessment rather than to irrelevant factors.
16. When feasible, make appropriately modified forms of tests or administration procedures available for test takers with handicapping conditions. Warn test users of potential problems in using standard norms with modified tests or administration procedures that result in non-comparable scores.

Test users should select tests that have been developed in ways that attempt to make them as fair as possible for test takers of different races, gender, ethnic backgrounds, or handicapping conditions.

Test Users Should:

14. Evaluate the procedures used by test developers to avoid potentially insensitive content or language.
15. Review the performance of test takers of different races, gender, and ethnic backgrounds when samples of sufficient size are available. Evaluate the extent to which performance differences may have been caused by inappropriate characteristics of the test.
16. When necessary and feasible, use appropriately modified forms of tests or administration procedures for test takers with handicapping conditions. Interpret standard norms with care in the light of the modifications that were made.

D. Informing Test Takers

Under some circumstances, test developers have direct communication with test takers. Under other circumstances, test users communicate directly with test takers. Whichever group communicates directly with test takers should provide the information described below.

Test Developers or Test Users Should:

17. When a test is optional, provide test takers or their parents/guardians with information to help them judge whether the test should be taken, or if an available alternative to the test should be used.
18. Provide test takers the information they need to be familiar with the coverage of the test, the types of question formats, the directions, and appropriate test-taking strategies. Strive to make such information equally available to all test takers.

Under some circumstances, test developers have direct control of tests and test scores. Under other circumstances, test users have such control. Whichever group has direct control of tests and test scores should take the steps described below.

Test Developers or Test Users Should:

19. Provide test takers or their parents/guardians with information about rights test takers may have to obtain copies of tests and completed answer sheets, retake tests, have tests rescored, or cancel scores.
20. Tell test takers or their parents/guardians how long scores will be kept on file and indicate to whom and under what circumstances test scores will or will not be released.
21. Describe the procedures that test takers or their parents/guardians may use to register complaints and have problems resolved.

Note: The membership of the Working Group that developed the Code of Fair Testing Practices in Education and of the Joint Committee on Testing Practices that guided the Working Group was as follows:

Theodore P. Bartell
John R. Bergan
Esther E. Diamond
Richard P. Duran
Lorraine D. Eyde
Raymond D. Fowler
John J. Fremer
    (Co-chair, JCTP and Chair,
    Code Working Group)
Edmund W. Gordon
Jo-Ida C. Hansen
James B. Lingwall
George F. Madaus
    (Co-chair, JCTP)

Kevin L. Moreland
Jo-Ellen V. Perez
Robert J. Solomon
John T. Stewart
Carol Kehr Tittle
    (Co-chair, JCTP)
Nicholas A. Vacc
Michael J. Zieky
Debra Boltas and Wayne
    Camara of the American
    Psychological Association
    served as staff liaisons

Additional copies of the Code may be obtained from the National Council on Measurement in Education, 1230 Seventeenth Street, NW, Washington, D.C. 20036. Single copies are free.

APPENDIX C

Code of Professional Responsibilities in Educational Measurement

Prepared by the NCME Ad Hoc Committee on the Development of a Code of Ethics:
Cynthia B Schmeiser, ACT—Chair
Kurt F. Geisinger, State University of New York
Sharon Johnson-Lewis, Detroit Public Schools
Edward D. Roeber, Council of Chief State School Officers
William D. Schafer, University of Maryland

Preamble and General Responsibilities

As an organization dedicated to the improvement of measurement and evaluation practice in education, the National Council on Measurement in Education (NCME) has adopted this Code to promote professionally responsible practice in educational measurement. Professionally responsible practice is conduct that arises from either the professional standards of the field, general ethical principles, or both.

The purpose of the Code of Professional Responsibilities in Educational Measurement, hereinafter referred to as the Code, is to guide the conduct of NCME members who are involved in any type of assessment activity in education. NCME is also providing this Code as a public service for all individuals who are engaged in educational assessment activities in the hope that these activities will be conducted in a professionally responsible manner. Persons who engage in these activities include local educators such as classroom teachers, principals, and superintendents; professionals such as school psychologists and counselors; state and national technical, legislative, and policy staff in education; staff of research, evaluation, and testing organizations; providers of test preparation services; college and university faculty and administrators; and professionals in business and industry who design and implement educational and training programs.

This Code applies to any type of assessment that occurs as part of the educational process, including formal and informal, traditional and alternative techniques for gathering information used in making educational decisions at all levels. These techniques include, but are not limited to, large-scale assessments at the school, district, state, national, and international levels; standardized tests; observational measures; teacher-conducted assessments; assessment support materials; and other achievement, aptitude, interest, and personality measures used in and for education.

Although NCME is promulgating this Code for its members, it strongly encourages other organizations and individuals who engage in educational assessment activities to endorse and abide by the responsibilities relevant to their professions. Because the Code pertains only to uses of assessment in education, it is recognized that uses of assessments outside of educational contexts, such as for employment, certification, or licensure, may involve additional professional responsibilities beyond those detailed in this Code.

The Code is intended to serve an educational function: to inform and remind those involved in educational assessment of their obligations to uphold the integrity of the manner in which assessments are developed, used, evaluated, and marketed. Moreover, it is expected that the Code will stimulate thoughtful discussion of what constitutes professionally responsible assessment practice at all levels in education.

Section 1: Responsibilities of Those Who Develop Assessment Products and Services

Those who develop assessment products and services, such as classroom teachers and other assessment specialists, have a professional responsibility to strive to produce assessments that are of the highest quality. Persons who develop assessments have a professional responsibility to:

1.1 ensure that assessment products and services are developed to meet applicable professional, technical, and legal standards.

1.2 develop assessment products and services that are as free as possible from bias due to characteristics irrelevant to the construct being measured, such as gender, ethnicity, race, socioeconomic status, disability, religion, age, or national origin.

1.3 plan accommodations for groups of test takers with disabilities and other special needs when developing assessments.

1.4 disclose to appropriate parties any actual or potential conflicts of interest that might influence the developers' judgment or performance.

1.5 use copyrighted materials in assessment products and services in accordance with state and federal law.

1.6 make information available to appropriate persons about the steps taken to develop and score the assessment, including up-to-date information used to support the reliability, validity, scoring and reporting processes, and other relevant characteristics of the assessment.

1.7 protect the rights to privacy of those who are assessed as part of the assessment development process.

1.8 caution users, in clear and prominent language, against the most likely misinterpretations and misuses of data that arise out of the assessment development process.

1.9 avoid false or unsubstantiated claims in test preparation and program support materials and services about an assessment or its use and interpretation.

1.10 correct any substantive inaccuracies in assessments or their support materials as soon as feasible.

1.11 develop score reports and support materials that promote the understanding of assessment results.

Section 2: Responsibilities of Those Who Market and Sell Assessment Products and Services

The marketing of assessment products and services, such as tests and other instruments, scoring services, test preparation services, consulting, and test interpretive services, should be based on information that is accurate, complete, and relevant to those considering their use. Persons who market and sell assessment products and services have a professional responsibility to:

2.1 provide accurate information to potential purchasers about assessment products and services and their recommended uses and limitations.

2.2 not knowingly withhold relevant information about assessment products and services that might affect an appropriate selection decision.

2.3 base all claims about assessment products and services on valid interpretations of publicly available information.

2.4 allow qualified users equal opportunity to purchase assessment products and services.

2.5 establish reasonable fees for assessment products and services.

2.6 communicate to potential users, in advance of any purchase or use, all applicable fees associated with assessment products and services.

2.7 strive to ensure that no individuals are denied access to opportunities because of their inability to pay the fees for assessment products and services.

2.8 establish criteria for the sale of assessment products and services, such as limiting the sale of assessment products and services to those individuals who are qualified for recommended uses and from whom proper uses and interpretations are anticipated.

2.9 inform potential users of known inappropriate uses of assessment products and services and provide recommendations about how to avoid such misuses.

2.10 maintain a current understanding about assessment products and services and their appropriate uses in education.

2.11 release information implying endorsement by users of assessment products and services only with the users' permission.

2.12 avoid making claims that assessment products and services have been endorsed by another organization unless an official endorsement has been obtained.

2.13 avoid marketing test preparation products and services that may cause individuals to receive scores that misrepresent their actual levels of attainment.

Section 3: Responsibilities of Those Who Select Assessment Products and Services

Those who select assessment products and services for use in educational settings, or help others do so, have important professional responsibilities to make sure that the assessments are appropriate for their intended use. Persons who select assessment products and services have a professional responsibility to:

3.1 conduct a thorough review and evaluation of available assessment strategies and instruments that might be valid for the intended uses.

3.2 recommend and/or select assessments based on publicly available documented evidence of their technical quality and utility rather than on unsubstantiated claims or statements.

3.3 disclose any associations or affiliations that they have with the authors, test publishers, or others involved with the assessments under consideration for purchase and refrain from participation if such associations might affect the objectivity of the selection process.

3.4 inform decision makers and prospective users of the appropriateness of the assessment for the intended uses, likely consequences of use, protection of examinee rights, relative costs, materials and services needed to conduct or use the assessment, and known limitations of the assessment, including potential misuses and misinterpretations of assessment information.

3.5 recommend against the use of any prospective assessment that is likely to be administered, scored, and used in an invalid manner for members of various groups in our society for reasons of race, ethnicity, gender, age, disability, language background, socioeconomic status, religion, or national origin.

3.6 comply with all security precautions that may accompany assessments being reviewed.

3.7 immediately disclose any attempts by others to exert undue influence on the assessment selection process.

3.8 avoid recommending, purchasing, or using test preparation products and services that may cause individuals to receive scores that misrepresent their actual levels of attainment.

Section 4: Responsibilities of Those Who Administer Assessments

Those who prepare individuals to take assessments and those who are directly or indirectly involved in the administration of assessments as part of the educational process, including teachers, administrators, and assessment personnel, have an important role in making sure that the assessments are administered in a fair and accurate manner. Persons who prepare others for, and those who administer, assessments have a professional responsibility to:

4.1 inform the examinees about the assessment prior to its administration, including its purposes, uses, and consequences; how the assessment information will be judged or scored; how the results will be kept on file; who will have access to the results; how the results will be distributed; and examinees' rights before, during, and after the assessment.

4.2 administer only those assessments for which they are qualified by education, training, licensure, or certification.

4.3 take appropriate security precautions before, during, and after the administration of the assessment.

4.4 understand the procedures needed to administer the assessment prior to administration.

4.5 administer standardized assessments according to prescribed procedures and conditions and notify appropriate persons if any nonstandard or delimiting conditions occur.

4.6 not exclude any eligible student from the assessment.

4.7 avoid any conditions in the conduct of the assessment that might invalidate the results.

4.8 provide for and document all reasonable and allowable accommodations for the administration of the assessment to persons with disabilities or special needs.

4.9 provide reasonable opportunities for individuals to ask questions about the assessment procedures or directions prior to and at prescribed times during the administration of the assessment.

4.10 protect the rights to privacy and due process of those who are assessed.

4.11 avoid actions or conditions that would permit or encourage individuals or groups to receive scores that misrepresent their actual levels of attainment.

Section 5: Responsibilities of Those Who Score Assessments

The scoring of educational assessments should be conducted properly and efficiently so that the results are reported accurately and in a timely manner. Persons who score and prepare reports of assessments have a professional responsibility to:

5.1 provide complete and accurate information to users about how the assessment is scored, such as the reporting schedule, scoring process to be used, rationale for the scoring approach, technical characteristics, quality control procedures, reporting formats, and the fees, if any, for these services.

5.2 ensure the accuracy of the assessment results by conducting reasonable quality control procedures before, during, and after scoring.

5.3 minimize the effect on scoring of factors irrelevant to the purposes of the assessment.

5.4 inform users promptly of any deviation in the planned scoring and reporting service or schedule and negotiate a solution with users.

5.5 provide corrected score results to the examinee or the client as quickly as practicable should errors be found that may affect the inferences made on the basis of the scores.

5.6 protect the confidentiality of information that identifies individuals as prescribed by state and federal law.

5.7 release summary results of the assessment only to those persons entitled to such information by state or federal law or those who are designated by the party contracting for the scoring services.

5.8 establish, where feasible, a fair and reasonable process for appeal and rescoring the assessment.

Section 6: Responsibilities of Those Who Interpret, Use, and Communicate Assessment Results

The interpretation, use, and communication of assessment results should promote valid inferences and minimize invalid ones. Persons who interpret, use, and communicate assessment results have a professional responsibility to:

6.1 conduct these activities in an informed, objective, and fair manner within the context of the assessment's limitations and with an understanding of the potential consequences of use.

6.2 provide to those who receive assessment results information about the assessment, its purposes, its limitations, and its uses necessary for the proper interpretation of the results.

6.3 provide to those who receive score reports an understandable written description of all reported scores, including proper interpretations and likely misinterpretations.

6.4 communicate to appropriate audiences the results of the assessment in an understandable and timely manner, including proper interpretations and likely misinterpretations.

6.5 evaluate and communicate the adequacy and appropriateness of any norms or standards used in the interpretation of assessment results.

6.6 inform parties involved in the assessment process how assessment results may affect them.

6.7 use multiple sources and types of relevant information about persons or programs whenever possible in making educational decisions.

6.8 avoid making, and actively discourage others from making, inaccurate reports, unsubstantiated claims, inappropriate interpretations, or otherwise false and misleading statements about assessment results.

6.9 disclose to examinees and others whether and how long the results of the assessment will be kept on file, procedures for appeal and rescoring, rights examinees and others have to the assessment information, and how those rights may be exercised.

6.10 report any apparent misuses of assessment information to those responsible for the assessment process.

6.11 protect the rights to privacy of individuals and institutions involved in the assessment process.

Section 7: Responsibilities of Those Who Educate Others About Assessment

The process of educating others about educational assessment, whether as part of higher education, professional development, public policy discussions, or job training, should prepare individuals to understand and engage in sound measurement practice and to become discerning users of tests and test results. Persons who educate or inform others about assessment have a professional responsibility to:

7.1 remain competent and current in the areas in which they teach and reflect that in their instruction.

7.2 provide fair and balanced perspectives when teaching about assessment.

7.3 differentiate clearly between expressions of opinion and substantiated knowledge when educating others about any specific assessment method, product, or service.

7.4 disclose any financial interests that might be perceived to influence the evaluation of a particular assessment product or service that is the subject of instruction.

7.5 avoid administering any assessment that is not part of the evaluation of student performance in a course if the administration of that assessment is likely to harm any student.

7.6 avoid using or reporting the results of any assessment that is not part of the evaluation of student performance in a course if the use or reporting of results is likely to harm any student.

7.7 protect all secure assessments and materials used in the instructional process.

7.8 model responsible assessment practice and help those receiving instruction to learn about their professional responsibilities in educational measurement.

7.9 provide fair and balanced perspectives on assessment issues being discussed by policymakers, parents, and other citizens.

Section 8: Responsibilities of Those Who Evaluate Educational Programs and Conduct Research on Assessments

Conducting research on or about assessments or educational programs is a key activity in helping to improve the understanding and use of assessments and educational programs. Persons who engage in the evaluation of educational programs or conduct research on assessments have a professional responsibility to:

8.1 conduct evaluation and research activities in an informed, objective, and fair manner.

8.2 disclose any associations that they have with authors, test publishers, or others involved with the assessment and refrain from participation if such associations might affect the objectivity of the research or evaluation.

8.3 preserve the security of all assessments throughout the research process as appropriate.

8.4 take appropriate steps to minimize potential sources of invalidity in the research and disclose known factors that may bias the results of the study.

8.5 present the results of research, both intended and unintended, in a fair, complete, and objective manner.

8.6 attribute completely and appropriately the work and ideas of others.

8.7 qualify the conclusions of the research within the limitations of the study.

8.8 use multiple sources of relevant information in conducting evaluation and research activities whenever possible.

8.9 comply with applicable standards for protecting the rights of participants in an evaluation or research study, including the rights to privacy and informed consent.

Afterword

As stated at the outset, the purpose of the *Code of Professional Responsibilities in Educational Measurement* is to serve as a guide to the conduct of NCME members who are engaged in any type of assessment activity in education. Given the broad scope of the field of educational assessment as well as the variety of activities in which professionals may engage, it is unlikely that any code will cover the professional responsibilities involved in every situation or activity in which assessment is used in education. Ultimately, it is hoped that this Code will serve as the basis for ongoing discussions about what constitutes professionally responsible practice. Moreover, these discussions will undoubtedly identify areas of practice that need further analysis and clarification in subsequent editions of the Code. To the extent that these discussions occur, the Code will have served its purpose.

To assist in the ongoing refinement of the Code, comments on this document are most welcome. Please send your comments and inquiries to:

Dr. William J. Russell
Executive Officer
National Council on
Measurement in Education
1230 Seventeenth Street, NW
Washington, DC 20036-3078

Summaries of Taxonomies of Educational Objectives: Cognitive, Affective, and Psychomotor Domains

TABLE D.1
Categories and subcategories of the Bloom et al. taxonomy of cognitive objectives.

1.00 Knowledge
- **1.10 Knowledge of Specifics**
  - **1.11 Knowledge of Terminology** Knowledge of the referents for specific symbols (verbal and nonverbal). . . .
  - **1.12 Knowledge of Specific Facts** Knowledge of dates, events, persons, places, etc.
- **1.20 Knowledge of Ways and Means of Dealing with Specifics**
  - **1.21 Knowledge of Conventions** Knowledge of characteristic ways of treating and presenting ideas and phenomena.
  - **1.22 Knowledge of Trends and Sequences** Knowledge of the processes, directions, and movements of phenomena with respect to time.
  - **1.23 Knowledge of Classifications and Categories** Knowledge of the classes, sets, divisions, and arrangements that are regarded as fundamental for a given subject field, purpose, argument, or problem.
  - **1.24 Knowledge of Criteria** Knowledge of the criteria by which facts, principles, and conduct are tested or judged.
  - **1.25 Knowledge of Methodology** Knowledge of the methods of inquiry, techniques, and procedures employed in a particular subject field as well as those employed in investigating particular problems and phenomena.

2.00 Comprehension
- **2.10 Translation** Comprehension as evidenced by the care and accuracy with which the communication is paraphrased or rendered from one language or form of communication to another.
- **2.20 Interpretation** The explanation or summarization of a communication.
- **2.30 Extrapolation** The extension of trends or tendencies beyond the given data to determine implications, consequences, corollaries, effects, etc., that are in accordance with the conditions described in the original communication.

3.00 Application The use of abstractions in particular and concrete situations. The abstractions may be in the form of general ideas, rules of procedures, or generalized methods.

4.00 Analysis
- **4.10 Analysis of Elements** Identification of the elements included in a communication.
- **4.20 Analysis of Relationships** The connections and interactions between elements and parts of a communication.
- **4.30 Analysis of Organized Principles** The organization, systematic arrangement, and structure that hold the communication together.

5.00 Synthesis
- **5.10 Production of a Unique Communication** The development of a communication in which the writer or speaker attempts to convey ideas, feelings, and/or experiences to others.
- **5.20 Production of a Plan or Proposed Set of Operations** The development of a plan of work or the proposal of a plan of operations.
- **5.30 Derivation of a Set of Abstract Relations** The development of a set of abstract relations either to classify or to explain particular data or phenomena, or the deduction of propositions and relations from a set of basic propositions or symbolic representations.

6.00 Evaluation
- **6.10 Judgments in Terms of Internal Evidence** Evaluation of the accuracy of a communication from such evidence as logical accuracy, consistency, and other internal criteria.
- **6.20 Judgments in Terms of External Criteria** Evaluation of material with reference to selected or remembered criteria.

TABLE D.2
Gagné's levels of complexity in human skills, characteristics of responses to tasks assessing these capacities, and examples of specific objectives written for each capacity.

Type of ability or capacity	Characteristics of responses to assessment tasks	Example of a specific learning target
1. **Discrimination:** ability to respond appropriately to stimuli that differ. The stimuli can differ in one or more physical attributes such as size, shape, or tone. (capacity verb: *discriminates*)	The learner's response must indicate that the learner has distinguished between the different stimuli. The learner may do this by indicating "same" or "different."	Given two cardboard cutouts, one a triangle shape and the other a square shape, the learner can point to the one that is a "square."
2. **Concrete concept:** ability to identify a stimulus as belonging to a particular class or category. The members of the class have one or more physical properties in common. (capacity verb: *identifies*)	The learner's response must indicate that two or more members of the class have been identified.	Given several differently shaped figures of various colors and shapes, half of which have triangular shapes, the learner can point to all the "triangles."
3. **Defined concept:** ability to demonstrate what is meant by a defined class of objects, events, or relations—that is, demonstrate an understanding of a concept. (capacity verb: *classifies*)	The learner's response must go beyond memorization to identify specific instances of the defined concept and to show how these instances are related to each other (and are thereby members of the same concept or category).	Given descriptions and brief biographies of each of several different persons not born in this country, the learner is able to identify all the persons who are immigrants and state their relationship to each other.
4. **Rule:** ability to make responses that indicate a rule is being applied in a variety of different situations. (capacity verb: *demonstrates*)	The learner's response must indicate that a particular rule is being applied in one or more concrete instances, but the learner need not be able to state the rule.	Given a "story" problem of the type presented in class involving two single-digit addends, the pupil is able to add the digits correctly.
5. **Higher-order rule** (problem solving): ability to form a new (for the learner) rule to solve a problem, by combining two or more previously learned rules. (capacity verb: *generates*)	The learner's response must indicate that a new complex rule has been "invented" and applied to solve a problem that is new or novel for the learner. Once the rule is invented, the learner should be able to apply it to other situations (transfer of learning).	Given an announcement about a specific job opening for which the learner is qualified, the learner is able to generate and write an appropriate letter of application for that job.
6. **Cognitive strategies:** ability to use internal processes to choose and change ways to focus attention, learn, remember, and/or think. (capacity verb: *adopts*)	The learner's responses provide only a way of inferring that internal cognitive strategies were used. Among the cognitive strategies a learner may use are rehearsing (practicing), elaborating, organizing information, and metacognition. It is sometimes necessary to ask a learner to "think aloud" while performing a task in order to discover the cognitive processes the learner is using.	Given the task of learning a list of new Spanish vocabulary words, the learner is able to associate an English word with an "acoustical link" to help memorize the Spanish words' definitions.

Source: Table and excerpts adapted from *Principles of Instructional Design* (3rd ed.) (pp. 12, 57–68) by Robert M. Gagné, Walter W. Wager and Leslie J. Briggs, copyright © 1988, by Holt, Rinehart and Winston, Inc. Reprinted by permission of the publisher.

TABLE D.3
Summary of the Quellmalz Taxonomy.

Classification	Definition	Illustration	Relation to Bloom Taxonomy
Recall	Most tasks require that students recognize or remember key facts, definitions, concepts, rules, and principles. Recall questions require students to repeat verbatim or to paraphrase given information. To recall information, students need most often to rehearse or practice it, and then to associate it with other, related concepts. The Bloom taxonomy levels of knowledge and comprehension are subsumed here, since verbatim repetition and translation into the student's own words represent acceptable evidence of learning and understanding.	Who was the main character in the story?	Recall Comprehension
Analysis	In this operation, students divide a whole into component elements. Generally, the different part/whole relationships and the parts of cause/effect relationships that characterize knowledge within subject domains are essential components of more complex tasks. The components can be the distinctive characteristics of objects or ideas, or the basic actions of procedures or events. This definition of analysis is the same as that in the Bloom taxonomy.	What are the different story parts?	Analysis
Comparison	These tasks require students to recognize or explain similarities and differences. Simple comparisons require attention to one or a few very obvious attributes or component processes, while complex comparisons require identification of the differentiation among many attributes or component actions. This category relates to some of the skills in the Bloom level of analysis. The separate comparison category emphasizes the distinct information processing required when students go beyond breaking the whole into parts in order to compare similarities and differences. This is akin to the Bloom level of synthesis.	How was this story like the last one?	Analysis
Inference	Both deductive and inductive reasoning fall into this category. In deductive tasks, students are given a generalization and are required to recognize or explain the evidence that relates to it. Applications of rules and "if then" relationships require inference. In inductive tasks, students are given the evidence or details and are required to come up with the generalization. Hypothesizing, predicting, concluding, and synthesizing all require students to relate and integrate information. Inductive and deductive reasoning relate to the Bloom levels of application and synthesis. Application of a rule is one kind of deductive reasoning; synthesis, putting parts together to form a generalization, occurs in both inductive and deductive reasoning.	What might be a good title for this story?	Application Synthesis
Evaluation	These tasks require students to judge quality, credibility, worth, or practicality. Generally, we expect students to use established criteria and explain how these criteria are or are not met. The criteria might be established rules of evidence, logic, or shared values. Bloom's levels of synthesis and evaluation are involved in this category. To evaluate, students must *assemble* and *explain* the interrelationship of evidence and reasons in support of their conclusion (synthesis). Explanation of criteria for reaching a conclusion is unique to evaluative reasoning.	Is this a good story? Why or why not?	Synthesis Evaluation

Source: Adapted from *Measuring Thinking Skills in the Classroom* (Table 1, pp. 8 and 19), revised edition, by R. J. Stiggins, E. Rubel, and E. Quellmalz. Copyright 1988. Washington, DC: National Educational Association. Adapted by permission of the NEA Professional Library.

TABLE D.4
Categories and subcategories of the Krathwohl et al. taxonomy of affective objectives with illustrative statements of objectives.

Category	Definition	Learning Targets
1.0 Receiving (attending)		
1.1 Awareness	Be conscious of something . . . take into account a situation, phenomenon, object, or state of affairs. . . .	Develops awareness of aesthetic factors in dress, furnishings, architecture, city design, good art, and the like.
1.2 Willingness to Receive	Being willing to tolerate a given stimulus, not to avoid it. . . . Willing to take notice of the phenomenon and give it . . . attention. . . .	Appreciation (tolerance) of cultural patterns exhibited by individuals from other groups—religious, social, economic, national, etc.
1.3 Controlled or Selected Attention	The control of attention, so that when certain stimuli are presented they will be attended to. . . . The favored stimulus is selected and attended to despite competing and detracting stimuli. . . .	Alertness toward human values and judgments on life as they are recorded in literature.
2.0 Responding		
2.1 Acquiescence in Responding	"Obedience" or "compliance." . . . There is a passiveness so far as the initiation of behavior is concerned. . . .	Follows school rules on the playground.
2.2 Willingness to Respond	The learner is sufficiently committed to exhibiting the behavior that he does so not just because of fear . . . but "on his own" or voluntarily. . . .	Volunteers to help classmates who are having difficulty with the science project.
2.3 Satisfaction in Response	The behavior is accompanied by a feeling of satisfaction, an emotional response, generally of pleasure, zest, or enjoyment.	Finds pleasure in reading for recreation.
3.0 Valuing		
3.1 Acceptance of a Value	The emotional acceptance of a proposition or doctrine upon what one considers adequate ground. . . .	Continuing desire to develop the ability to speak and write effectively.
3.2 Preference for a Value	The individual is sufficiently committed to a value to pursue it, to seek it out, to want it. . . .	Assumes responsibility for drawing reticent members of a group into conversation.
3.3 Commitment	"Conviction" and "certainty beyond a doubt." . . . Acts to further the thing valued . . . , to extend the possibility of . . . developing it, to deepen . . . involvement with it.	Devotion to those ideas and ideals that are the foundation of democracy.
4.0 Organization		
4.1 Conceptualization of a Value	The quality of abstraction or conceptualization is added [to the value or belief which permits seeing] . . . how the value relates to those he already holds or to new ones. . . .	Forms judgments as to the responsibility of society for conserving human and material resources.
4.2 Organization of a Value System	To bring together a complex of values . . . into an ordered relationship with one another. . . .	Weighs alternative social policies and practices against the standards of the public welfare rather than the advantage of . . . narrow interest groups.
5.0 Characterization by a Value or Value Complex		
5.1 Generalized Set	Gives an internal consistency to the system of attitudes and values. . . . Enables the individual to reduce and order the complex world . . . and to act consistently and effectively in it.	Judges problems and issues in terms of situations, issues, purposes, and consequences involved rather than in terms of fixed, dogmatic precepts or emotional wishful thinking.
5.2 Characterization	One's view of the universe, one's philosophy of life, one's *Weltanschauug*. . . .	Develops for regulation of one's personal and civic life a code of behavior based on ethical principles consistent with democratic ideals.

Source: Adapted from *Taxonomy of Educational Objectives: Book 2: Affective Domain* (pp. 176–185) by David R. Krathwohl, Benjamin S. Bloom, and Bertram B. Masia, 1964, White Plains, NY: Longman. Copyright © 1964 by Longman Publishing Group. Adapted by permission of Addison-Wesley Educational Publishers, Inc.

TABLE D.5
Categories and subcategories of the Harrow taxonomy of psychomotor and perceptual objectives.

Classification Levels and Subcategories	Definitions	Learning Targets

1.00 Reflex Movements
  1.10 Segmental Reflexes
  1.20 Intersegmental Reflexes
  1.30 Suprasegmental Reflexes
	Actions elicited without conscious volition in response to some stimuli.	Flexion, extension, stretch, postural adjustments.

2.00 Basic-Fundamental Movements
  2.10 Locomotor Movements
  2.20 Non-Locomotor Movements
  2.30 Manipulative Movements
	Inherent movement patterns which are formed from a combining of reflex movements and are the basis for complex skilled movement.	Walking, running, jumping, sliding, hopping, rolling, climbing, pushing, pulling, swaying, swinging, stooping, stretching, bending, twisting, handling, manipulating, gripping, grasping finger movements.

3.00 Perceptual Abilities
  3.10 Kinesthetic Discrimination
  3.20 Visual Discrimination
  3.30 Auditory Discrimination
  3.40 Tactile Discrimination
  3.50 Coordinated Abilities
	Interpretation of stimuli from various modalities providing data for the learner to make adjustments to his environment.	The *outcomes* of perceptual abilities are observable in *all purposeful* movement.
		Examples:
		Auditory—following verbal instructions.
		Coordinated—jumping rope, punting, catching.

4.00 Physical Abilities
  4.10 Endurance
  4.20 Strength
  4.30 Flexibility
  4.40 Agility
	Functional characteristics of organic vigor which are essential to the development of highly skilled movement.	Distance running, distance swimming, weight lifting, wrestling, touching toes, back bend, ballet exercises, shuttle run, typing, dodgeball.

5.00 Skilled Movements
  5.10 Simple Adaptive Skill
  5.20 Compound Adaptive Skill
  5.30 Complex Adaptive Skill
	A degree of efficiency when performing complex movement tasks which are based upon inherent movement patterns.	All skilled activities which build upon the inherent locomotor and manipulative movement patterns of classification level two.

6.00 Non-Discursive Communication
  6.10 Expressive Movement
  6.20 Interpretive Movement
	Communication through bodily movements ranging from facial expressions through sophisticated choreographies.	Body postures, gestures, facial expressions, all efficiently executed skilled dance movements and choreographies.

Source: Adapted from *A Taxonomy of the Psychomotor Domain: A Guide for Developing Behavioral Objectives* (pp. 104–106) by A. J. Harrow, 1972, White Plains, NY: Longman. Reprinted by permission of the author.

Categories of Learning Targets Derived from the Dimensions of Learning Model

Declarative Knowledge
Procedural Knowledge
Complex Thinking

A. Effectively translates issues and situations into meaningful tasks that have a clear purpose.
B. Effectively uses a variety of complex reasoning strategies.

REASONING STRATEGY 1: COMPARISON Comparison involves describing the similarities and differences between two or more items. The process includes three components that can be assessed:

a. Selects appropriate items to compare.
b. Selects appropriate characteristics on which to base the comparison.
c. Accurately identifies the similarities and differences among the items, using the identified characteristics.

REASONING STRATEGY 2: CLASSIFICATION Classification involves organizing items into categories based on specific characteristics. The process includes four components that can be assessed:

a. Selects significant items to classify.
b. Specifies useful categories for the items.
c. Specifies accurate and comprehensive rules for category membership.
d. Accurately sorts the identified items into the categories.

REASONING STRATEGY 3: INDUCTION Induction involves creating a generalization from implicit or explicit information and then describing the reasoning behind the generalization. The process includes three components that can be assessed:

a. Identifies elements (specific pieces of information or observations) from which to make inductions.
b. Interprets the information from which inductions are made.
c. Makes and articulates accurate conclusions (inductions) from the selected information or observations.

REASONING STRATEGY 4: DEDUCTION Deduction involves identifying implicit or explicit generalizations or principles (premises) and then describing their logical consequences. The process includes three components that can be assessed:

a. Identifies and articulates a deduction based on important and useful generalizations or principles implicit or explicit in the information.
b. Accurately interprets the generalizations or principles.
c. Identifies and articulates logical consequences implied by the identified generalizations or principles.

REASONING STRATEGY 5: ERROR ANALYSIS Error analysis involves identifying and describing specific types of errors in information or processes. It includes three components that can be assessed:

a. Identifies and articulates significant errors in information or in process.
b. Accurately describes the effects of the errors on the information or process.
c. Accurately describes how to correct the errors.

REASONING STRATEGY 6: CONSTRUCTING SUPPORT Constructing support involves developing a well-articulated argument for or against a claim. The process includes three components that can be assessed:

a. Accurately identifies a claim that requires support rather than a fact that does not require support.
b. Provides sufficient or appropriate evidence for the claim.
c. Adequately qualifies or restricts the claim.

REASONING STRATEGY 7: ABSTRACTING Abstracting involves identifying and explaining how the abstract pattern in one situation or set of information is similar to or different from the abstract pattern in another situation or set of information. The process includes three components that can be assessed:

a. Identifies a significant situation or meaningful information that is a useful subject for the abstracting process.
b. Identifies a representative general or abstract pattern for the situation or information.
c. Accurately articulates the relationship between the general or abstract pattern and another situation or set of information.

REASONING STRATEGY 8: ANALYZING PERSPECTIVES Analyzing perspectives involves considering one perspective on an issue and the reasoning behind it as well as an opposing perspective and the reasoning behind it. The process includes three components that can be assessed:

a. Identifies an issue on which there is disagreement.
b. Identifies one position on the issue and the reasoning behind it.
c. Identifies an opposing position and the reasoning behind it.

REASONING STRATEGY 9: DECISION MAKING Decision making involves selecting among apparently equal alternatives. It includes four components that can be assessed:

a. Identifies important and appropriate alternatives to be considered.
b. Identifies important and appropriate criteria for assessing the alternatives.
c. Accurately identifies the extent to which each alternative possesses each criteria.

d. Makes a selection that adequately meets the decision criteria and answers the initial decision question.

REASONING STRATEGY 10: INVESTIGATION Investigation is a process involving close examination and systematic inquiry. There are basic types of investigation:

- *Definitional Investigation*: Constructing a definition or detailed description concept for which such a definition or description is not readily available or accepted.
- *Historical Investigation*: Constructing an explanation for some past event for an explanation is not readily available or accepted.
- *Projective Investigation*: Constructing a scenario for some future event or hypothetical past event for which a scenario is not readily available or accepted.

Each type of investigation includes three components that can be assessed:

a. Accurately identifies what is already known or agreed upon about the concept (definitional investigation), the past event (historical investigation), or the future event (projective investigation).
b. Identifies and explains the confusions, uncertainties, or contradictions about the concept (definitional investigation), the past event (historical investigation), or the future event (projective investigation).
c. Develops and defends a logical and plausible resolution to the confusions, uncertainties, or contradictions about the concept (definitional investigation), the past event (historical investigation), or the future event (projective investigation).

REASONING STRATEGY 11: PROBLEM SOLVING Problem solving involves developing and testing a method or product for overcoming obstacles or constraints to reach a desired outcome. It includes four components that can be assessed:

a. Accurately identifies constraints or obstacles.
b. Identifies viable and important alternatives for overcoming the constraints or obstacles.
c. Selects and adequately tries out alternatives.
d. If other alternatives were tried, accurately articulates and supports the reasoning behind the order of their selection, and the extent to which each overcame the obstacles or constraints.

REASONING STRATEGY 12: EXPERIMENTAL INQUIRY Experimental inquiry involves testing hypotheses that have been generated to explain phenomenon. It includes four components that can be assessed:

a. Accurately explains the phenomenon initially observed using appropriate and accepted facts, concepts, or principles.
b. Makes a logical prediction based on the facts, concepts, or principles underlying the explanation.
c. Sets up and carries out an activity or experiment that effectively tests the prediction.

d. Effectively evaluates the outcome of the activity or experiment in terms of the original explanation.

REASONING STRATEGY 13: INVENTION Invention involves developing something unique or making unique improvements to a process to satisfy an unmet need. It includes four components that can be assessed:

a. Identifies a process or product to develop or improve to satisfy an unmet need.
b. Identifies rigorous and important standards or criteria the invention will meet.
c. Makes detailed and important revisions in the initial process or product.
d. Continually revises and polishes the process or product until it reaches a level of completeness consistent with the criteria or standards identified earlier.

Information Processing

A. Effectively interprets and synthesizes information.
B. Effectively uses a variety of information-gathering techniques and resources.
C. Accurately assesses the value of information.
D. Recognizes where and how projects would benefit from additional information.

Effective Communication

A. Expresses ideas clearly.
B. Effectively communicates with diverse audiences.
C. Effectively communicates in a variety of ways.
D. Effectively communicates for a variety of purposes.
E. Creates quality products.

Collaboration/Cooperation

A. Works toward the achievement of group goals.
B. Demonstrates effective interpersonal skills.
C. Contributes to group maintenance.
D. Effectively performs a variety of roles within a group.

Habits of Mind

A. Is aware of own thinking.
B. Makes effective plans.
C. Is aware of and uses necessary resources.
D. Evaluates the effectiveness of own actions.
E. Is sensitive to feedback.
F. Is accurate and seeks accuracy.
G. Is clear and seeks clarity.
H. Is open-minded.
I. Restrains impulsivity.
J. Takes a position when the situation warrants it.
K. Is sensitive to the feelings and level of knowledge of others.
L. Engages intensively in tasks even when answers or solutions are not immediately apparent.
M. Pushes the limits of own knowledge and ability.
N. Generates, trusts, and maintains own standards of evaluation.
O. Generates new ways of viewing a situation outside the boundaries of standard convention.

Source: Adapted from *Assessing Student Outcomes: Performance Assessment Using the Dimensions of Learning Model* (pp. 65–93) by R. J. Marzano, D. Pickering, and J. McTighe, 1993, Alexandria, VA: Association for Supervision and Curriculum Development. (Copyright by McREL Institute, 2550 South Parker Road, Aurora, CO 80014.) Adapted by permission.

APPENDIX F
Assessment of Metacognition

Definition of Metacognition

There are many facets to teaching students to use thinking skills. In Chapter 2 we discussed several frameworks for identifying thinking skills that should be incorporated into your teaching and assessment practices. One broad area of thinking that has received considerable attention in recent years from researchers and curriculum specialists is students' abilities to monitor and control their own thinking in relation to the cognitive tasks they are performing. Monitoring and controlling one's own thinking processes are complex skills themselves. The cluster of such related skills is known as metacognitive skills.

Metacognition is defined as "one's knowledge concerning one's own cognitive processes and products or anything related to them. . . . For example, I am engaging in metacognition . . . if I notice that I am having more trouble learning A than B; if it strikes me that I should double check C before accepting it as a fact. . . . Metacognition refers, among other things, to the active monitoring and consequent regulation and orchestration of these processes . . . usually in the service of some concrete goal or objective." (Flavell, 1976, p. 232)

As can be surmised, students engage in metacognitive thinking when they are aware of their thoughts as they perform specific learning activities and then use this awareness to control what they are doing (Marzano et al., 1988).

Types of Metacognitive Skills

The metacognitive cluster of skills can be organized in several ways. The Marzano et al. (1988) organization gives a brief overview of this domain of learning targets.

I. **Self-regulation skills** are used by students when they are aware that they can control their commitment, attitudes, and attention toward academic tasks.
   A. *Commitment to an academic task* is a student's conscious decision to choose to do the task, whether or not it is fun for the student.
   B. *Positive attitude toward an academic task* is a student's belief that she can perform the task and that the main determiner of success on it is her own efforts, to luck, natural talent, or help from others.
   C. *Controlling attention to the requirements of an academic task* occurs when a student recognizes that he must control the level and focus of his attention to match the requirements of the task to be performed.

II. *Types of knowledge* used by students must be appropriate for performing the academic task at hand.
   A. **Declarative knowledge** is exhibited when a student knows what needs to be done, knows factual information, or knows that something is to be done.
   B. **Procedural knowledge** is exhibited when a student is able to perform a task or to apply strategies to complete tasks.

   C. **Conditional knowledge** is exhibited when a student is aware of why certain procedures or strategies are used or in what circumstances one procedure or strategy is preferred over another.

III. **Executive control skills** are used by students when they evaluate, plan, and check their own progress in completing an academic task.
   A. **Evaluation skills** are used when a student assesses her current state of knowledge before, during, and at the completion of an academic task; identifies available and still-needed resources for completing the academic task; and identifies the goals and subgoals of the academic task.
   B. **Planning skills** are used by a student before and during the completion of an academic task when the student deliberately chooses procedures and strategies to do the task.
   C. **Regulating processes skills** are used by a student while completing an academic task when the student monitors his progress toward completing the task successfully.

These categories of skills are not hierarchical and, in practice, students usually use them in combination to complete academic tasks.

Assessing Metacognition with Paper-and-Pencil Instruments

Suggestions for how to model and teach these skills are found in other sources (Good & Brophy, 1999; Marzano et al., 1988). Here we give some examples of simple ways to assess students' perceptions of whether they use these skills.

Teachers have found this type of assessment information useful for planning instruction (Tittle, 1989; Tittle, Hecht, & Moore, 1993). To create an instrument, you need to identify a specific instructional activity on which to focus the items. For example, you may wish to focus on students' metacognitions during class, while working with others, while doing homework or other assignments and projects, or when they complete tests or other assessment activities used for summative evaluation (Tittle et al., 1993). Then, using the subcategories of metacognitive skills, write statements describing a student's thoughts, beliefs, or awareness about the specific type of activity. Write both positive and negative statements (i.e., "good" and "poor" metacognitions) for each category. Give each student a copy of the list and ask him or her to indicate how often he or she does the things in each statement.

Figure F.1 shows some examples of statements related to various metacognitions that may occur when students work on a social studies research paper. Students are asked to identify how often they engage in the thoughts, actions, or beliefs listed. The statements are arranged to follow the outline of metacognitive skills discussed earlier. The statements are in pairs: The odd-numbered member of the pair is a positive statement, and the even-numbered one is a negative statement. The codes in the brackets identify the skill in the outline and whether the statement is positively or negatively worded. Remember that Figure F.1 is just a list of examples, not a sample instrument per se. In an actual instrument you would scramble the order of positive and negative statements so as not to have a pattern, omit the codes, and have more than two statements per category. Also, you might not assess some categories because of the nature of the particular activity on which you are focusing. Note that such an instrument may be inappropriate for primary children, whose reading skills may not be sufficient to understand it.

FIGURE F.1

Examples of positively and negatively phrased items that assess how students report using metacognitions when preparing a social studies research paper. (Codes in brackets refer to outline in the text.)

Directions to students: These questions ask about how often you do some things when you write a research paper in social studies. Circle the number that tells how often you do each thing.

Never or almost never	Sometimes	Often	Always or almost always	Don't Know
1	2	3	4	DK

Item	1	2	3	4	DK
1. When the paper is not a lot of fun, I work very hard to do a good job on it. [I.A,+]	1	2	3	4	DK
2. When the paper is not a lot of fun, I do not work very hard on it. [I.A,–]	1	2	3	4	DK
3. I do a good job on the paper even though I am less talented than other students. [I.B,+]	1	2	3	4	DK
4. I have to get really lucky to do a good job on the paper. [I.B,–]	1	2	3	4	DK
5. When I read articles related to my paper, I read only those parts related to my topic. [I.C,+]	1	2	3	4	DK
6. When reading articles about the topic of my paper, I give equal attention to everything in the article. [I.C,–]	1	2	3	4	DK
7. My research papers have an introductory section that tells why the topic is important. [II,A,+]	1	2	3	4	DK
8. My research papers list the facts about the topic but do not give my interpretation of the meaning of the facts. [II.A,–]	1	2	3	4	DK
9. I make tables in my research papers to compare information on the topic. [II.B,+]	1	2	3	4	DK
10. I do not use note cards when preparing my research paper. [II.B,–]	1	2	3	4	DK
11. Before I decide to use a graph or a chart I ask myself which idea in the paper it supports. [II.C,+]	1	2	3	4	DK
12. I use lots of graphs or charts in my research reports. [II.C,–]	1	2	3	4	DK
13. One of the first things I do when I start my paper assignment is to make a list of what I already know about the topic. [III.A,+]	1	2	3	4	DK
14. Before I do anything else on the paper I go to the library to find all the books and articles about my topic. [III.B,–]	1	2	3	4	DK
15. After I complete my research paper I ask myself what I learned about the topic. [III.A,+]	1	2	3	4	DK
16. After I complete my research paper, I do not think about the topic anymore. [III.A,–]	1	2	3	4	DK
17. When I am ready to begin collecting information, I ask myself what sources would be best to use first. [III.B,+]	1	2	3	4	DK
18. No matter what the topic of my paper, I go first to the encyclopedia to look up the topic. [III.B,–]	1	2	3	4	DK
19. While I am writing the paper I think about whether it meets the criteria for a good research report. [III.C,+]	1	2	3	4	DK
20. As soon as I have a little information on the topic, I begin writing the paper [III.C,–]	1	2	3	4	DK

APPENDIX G

Examples of Alternative Blueprints for a Summative Unit Assessment

TABLE G.1
A checklist for judging the quality of a teacher's plan for a summative unit assessment.

1.	Does your plan clarify the purpose(s) of the assessment and what you expect it to tell you about each student?	Yes	No
2.	Does your plan indicate the main subject-matter topics and performances you want to assess?	Yes	No
3.	Will your plan help you to judge whether the assessment tasks match the major content topics and learning targets you have specified?	Yes	No
4.	Have you clearly identified the elements of knowledge and performance that *all* students need to know?	Yes	No
5.	Does your plan give the most important learning targets the heaviest weights in the total score? Are the least important learning targets given the least weight? (You may wish to give certain tasks more weight than others.)	Yes	No
6.	Do you know what kind(s) of assessment tasks should be used to assess each content-thinking skill combination? Are these tasks the best ways to assess the combination?	Yes	No
7.	Have you estimated the amount of time students need to complete this assessment? Is this estimated time realistic?	Yes	No
8.	Have you estimated the amount of time you will need to evaluate the students' responses? (Consider how this time might be shortened, without reducing the validity of the results, by changing some of the tasks, rearranging tasks on a page, or using the capabilities of a micro-computer or other scoring device.)	Yes	No

Note: Revise your assessment plan if you answered no to one or more of the questions in the checklist.
Source: Adapted from *Teacher's Guide to Better Classroom Testing: A Judgmental Approach* (p. 26) by A. J. Nitko and T-C. Hsu, 1987, Pittsburgh, PA: Institute for Practice and Research in Education, School of Education, University of Pittsburgh. Adapted by permission.

TABLE G.2
Complete specifications with modified taxonomy headings.

Content Outline	Recalling information taught or read	Applying knowledge in situations very similar to those taught	Applying knowledge in a new or novel context

I. Basic Parts of Cell
   A. Nucleus
   B. Cytoplasm
   C. Cell membrane
	1. Names and tells functions of each part of cell	8. Labels parts of cell shown on a line drawing	11. Given photographs of actual plant and animal cells, labels the parts

_40_ % of Total = _8_ pts	_37_ % of Row = _3_ pts	_37_ % of Row = _3_ pts	_26_ % of Row = _2_ pts

II. Plant vs Animal cells
   A. Similarities
   B. Differences
      1. cell wall vs membrane
      2. food manufacture
	2. Explains differences between plant and animal cells
	3. Describes the cell wall and cell membrane		

_10_ % of Total = _2_ pts	_100_ % of Row = _2_ pts	___ % of Row = ___ pts	___ % of Row = ___ pts

III. Cell Membrane
   A. Living nature of
   B. Diffusion
   C. Substances diffused by cells
	4. Lists substances diffused and not diffused by cell membranes
	5. Gives definition of diffusion
		9. Distinguishes between diffusion and oxidation	

_20_ % of Total = _4_ pts	_75_ % of Row = _3_ pts	_25_ % of Row = _1_ pts	___ % of Row = ___ pts

IV. Division of Cells
   A. Phases in division
   B. Chromosomes and DNA
   C. Plant vs Animal cell division
	6. Gives definitions of division, chromosomes, and DNA
	7. States differences between plant and animal cell division
		10. Given the numbers of chromosomes in a cell before division, states the number in each cell after division	

_30_ % of Total = _6_ pts	_67_ % of Row = _4_ pts	_33_ % of Row = _2_ pts	___ % of Row = ___ pts

Source: Adapted from *Teacher's Guide to Better Classroom Testing: A Judgmental Approach* (p. 4) by A. J. Nitko and T-C. Hsu, 1987, Pittsburgh, PA: Institute for Practice and Research in Education, School of Education, University of Pittsburgh. Adapted by permission.

TABLE G.3
Blueprint without objectives stated.

Content Outline	Recalling information taught or read	Applying knowledge in situations very similar to those taught	Applying knowledge in a new or novel context
I. Basic Parts of Cell A. Nucleus B. Cytoplasm C. Cell membrane	1 item, scored 0–3 (short-answer)	1 item, scored 0–3 (label parts of cell drawing)	2 items, each scored 0–1 (label parts of cell photographs)
__40__ % of Total = __8__ pts	__37__ % of Row = __3__ pts	__37__ % of Row = __3__ pts	__26__ % of Row = __2__ pts

II. Plant vs Animal cells
A. Similarities
B. Differences
  1. cell wall vs membrane
  2. food manufacture
	2 items, each scored 0–1 (short-answer)		

__10__ % of Total = __2__ pts	__100__ % of Row = __2__ pts	_____ % of Row = _____ pts	_____ % of Row = _____ pts
III. Cell Membrane A. Living nature of B. Diffusion C. Substances diffused by cells	2 items, one scored 0–2, the other scored 0–1 (short-answer)	2 items, each scored 0–1 (multiple-choice)	
__20__ % of Total = __40__ pts	__75__ % of Row = __3__ pts	__25__ % of Row = __1__ pts	_____ % of Row = _____ pts
IV. Division of Cells A. Phases in division B. Chromosomes and DNA C. Plant vs Animal cell division	4 items, each scored 0–1 (definitions, short-answer)	1 item, scored 0–1 (short-answer)	
__30__ % of Total = __6__ pts	__67__ % of Row = __4__ pts	__33__ % of Row = __2__ pts	_____ % of Row = _____ pts

Source: Adapted from *Teacher's Guide to Better Classroom Testing: A Judgmental Approach* (p. 4) by A. J. Nitko and T-C. Hsu, 1987, Pittsburgh, PA: Institute for Practice and Research in Education, School of Education, University of Pittsburgh. Adapted by permission.

TABLE G.4
Blueprint using only a list of learning targets.

Objectives of the unit	Number of items	Number of points
1. Names and tells functions of each cell part.	1	3
2. Explains differences between plant and animal cells.	1	1
3. Describes the cell wall and cell membrane.	1	1
4. Lists substances diffused and not diffused through cell membrane.	1	2
5. Gives definition of diffusion.	1	1
6. Gives definition of division, chromosomes, and DNA.	3	3
7. States differences between plant and animal cell division.	1	1
8. Labels parts of a cell when shown a line drawing.	3	3
9. Distinguishes between diffusion, oxidation, and fission.	2	2
10. Given the number of chromosomes in a cell before division, states the number in each cell after division.	1	1
11. Given photographs of plant and animal cells, identifies parts of cells without using prompts.	2	2
	Total points = 17	Total points = 20

Source: From *Teacher's Guide to Better Classroom Testing: A Judgmental Approach* (p. 39) by A. J. Nitko and T-C. Hsu, 1993, Pittsburgh, PA: Institute for Practice and Research in Education, School of Education, University of Pittsburgh. Reprinted by permission.

TABLE G.5
Blueprint using only a content listing.

Major Topics of Unit	Number of items	Number of points per item	Total number of points
I. Basic Parts of a Cell			
A. Nucleus	2	2	4
B. Cytoplasm	3	1	3
C. Cell membrane	1	1	1
	subtotal = 6		subtotal = 8
II. Plant vs. Animal Cells			
A. Similarities	1	1	1
B. Differences			
1. cell wall vs. cell membrane	1	1	1
2. food manufacture	0		0
	subtotal = 2		subtotal = 2
III. Cell Membrane			
A. Living nature of	0		0
B. Diffusion	2	1	2
C. Examples of different substances	1	2	2
	subtotal = 3		subtotal = 4
IV. Division of Cells			
A. Phases in division	2	1	2
B. Role of chromosomes and DNA	2	1	2
C. Plant vs. animal cell division	2	1	2
	subtotal = 6		subtotal = 6
	Total test items = 17		Total test points = 20

Source: From *Teacher's Guide to Better Classroom Testing: A Judgmental Approach* (p. 38) by A. J. Nitko and T-C. Hsu, 1993, Pittsburgh, PA: Institute for Practice and Research in Education, School of Education, University of Pittsburgh. Reprinted by permission.

APPENDIX H
Basic Statistical Concepts

It is necessary for you to have an understanding of a few basic statistical concepts to bettter understand the results of your classroom assessments, to better summarize assessment results when you grade students, to interpret your students' norm-referenced test scores, to understand the basic data in published test manuals, and to understand assessment summary reports provided by your school district or state. This appendix focuses on concepts rather than on computations. However, the computations of certain statisical indices are illusrated so you will understand the origin of their numerical values.

Although you may believe that mathematics or computations are your weak suit, you should not shy away from learning the few techniques shown in this appendix. With the availability of inexpensive calculators, computations become simple and accurate with only a little practice. Some computerized gradebook programs will make a few calculations, also. You should buy an inexpensive scientific calculator that has a "correlation" or "r" function. Such a calculator will allow you to enter the scores from your assessments and painlessly carry out calculations for all of the statistical indices in this appendix.

Statistical methods are techniques to summarize scores so that you may better understand how a group of students has performed and how well an individual student has performed relative to others in the group. A *statistical index* (or *statistic*) is a summary number that concisely captures a specific feature of a group of scores. For example, measures of central tendency focus on an average or typical score for a group. Measures of variability focus on quantifying the extent to which students' scores differ from one another. This appendix presents four categories of statistical methods that you will find most useful in understanding test scores and other assessment results: (1) distribution of scores, (2) typical or average score, (3) variability of scores, and (4) degree to which two sets of scores are correlated.

Describing Distributions of Test Scores

Suppose the scores shown in Table H.1 are scores of our students on two tests you gave. The arrangement of the scores in the table is similar to how they might be arranged in your gradebook: Students' names are arranged alphabetically with their mark next to their names. This arrangement does not make it easy to answer such questions as:

1. How many students in the class have similar scores?
2. What scores do most students obtain?
3. Are the scores widely scattered along the score scale, or do they bunch together?
4. Does the pattern of scores in the class appear unusual in some way? Or are they as expected?
5. Does any student score unusually higher or lower than his or her classmates?

TABLE H.1
List of students in a class and their scores on two tests.

Name	Test 1	Test 2
1. Anthony	89	94
2. Ashley	75	68
3. Blake	74	72
4. Chad	84	77
5. Donald	56	66
6. Edward	80	68
7. Festina	66	68
8. George	86	73
9. Harriet	68	73
10. Irene	98	86
11. Jesse	65	78
12. Katherine	44	60
13. Lorraine	45	53
14. Marya	61	75
15. Nancy	75	76
16. Oprah	68	54
17. Peter	55	53
18. Quincy	70	68
19. Robert	69	65
20. Sally	60	47
21. Tina	73	74
22. Ula	75	88
23. Veronica	71	73
24. Wallace	43	61
25. William	83	87
26. Xavier	95	83
27. Yvonne	96	85
28. Zena	75	70

Ranking Scores

One simple way to begin answering questions such as these is to rank the scores. Most people know how to do this already. To rank the scores, *order them from largest to smallest*. The largest score is assigned a rank of 1; the next largest, a rank of 2; and so on, down to the smallest score. In this way all of the raw scores (marks) are transformed into ranks.

Table H.2 demonstrates the procedure for scores from Test 1. Notice what is done when students have the same score. In this case they are tied for the ranks. The tie is resolved by awarding each of the persons whose scores are tied the average of the ranks for which they are tied. For example, four students have a score of 75 and thus are tied for ranks 9, 10, 11, and 12. Rather than arbitrarily awarding one person a rank of 9, and another a rank of 10, and so on, each person is awarded the average of the tied ranks, that is:

$$\frac{9 + 10 + 11 + 12}{4} = 10.5$$

TABLE H.2
Rank order of students from Table H.1 according to their scores on Test 1.

Name	Test 1	Rank	
Irene	98	1	
Yvonne	96	2	
Xavier	95	3	
Anthony	89	4	
George	86	5	
Chad	84	6	
William	83	7	
Edward	80	8	
Zena	75	10.5	
Ula	75	10.5	Four scores
Nancy	75	10.5	tied for ranks
Ashley	75	10.5	9, 10, 11, and 12
Blake	74	13	
Tina	73	14	
Veronica	71	15	
Quincy	70	16	
Robert	69	17	
Oprah	68	18.5	Two scores tied
Harriet	68	18.5	for ranks 18 and 19
Festina	66	20	
Jesse	65	21	
Marya	61	22	
Sally	60	23	
Donald	56	24	
Peter	55	25	
Lorraine	45	26	
Katherine	44	27	
Wallace	43	28	

A simple ranked list of scores helps you answer some basic questions about how well your class performed on a test. The list shows quickly the highest and lowest scores. It shows how the scores are spread out and which scores occur most often. This ranked list may be all you need to understand how your students performed on a test. However, ranked lists are not easily understood if the number of students is very large: for example, the score of all fourth graders in the school district or in the state. A better way to organize the scores in such cases is discussed later.

Interpretations of simple ranks of this sort depend on the number of students in the group. For example, suppose I told you that of all the classes in testing and measurement I have taught, your class ranked second. You might be proud as a group until I also told you that I have taught only one other class. Adding another 13 classes might result in your class's rank dropping, say, from second to 15th: Although the class's rank has changed from second to 15th, its relative position—dead last—has not changed. The point is that a student's rank cannot be fully interpreted without knowing the number of other students being ranked. This problem is largely overcome by using *percentile ranks* (see Chapter 17).

Stem-and-Leaf Displays

A simple way to organize a large group of scores is to prepare a stem-and-leaf display. Table H.3 illustrates the procedure for the scores of the 28 students in Table H.1 for each of the two tests. The "stem" is the tens' digit and the "leaves" are the ones' digits of the score. For example, consider the scores 80, 83, 84, 86, and 89 from Test 1. The tens' digit is 8 and is written in the stem column. The ones' digits 0, 3, 4, 6, and 9 are the leaves and are written in the row to the right of the 8.

The stem-and-leaf display has the advantage of showing how the entire group of scores is distributed along the score scale when they are grouped together by intervals of 10. That is, it organizes the scores into the groupings of 40s, 50s, 60s, 70s, 80s, and 90s. With the ones' digits displayed, you can easily "reconstitute" individual values of the scores. This is useful if you need to make future calculations. In the "Frequency" column, the number of scores is written in each row.

Notice that tens' digits in the stem column (0, 1, 2, etc.) are ordered from lowest to highest. When you turn the page on its side, the display is a type of graph: The length of the "leaves" row is proportional to the frequency of the scores.

The scores in Table H.3 are grouped into interval widths of 10. You could also group the scores into narrower intervals, say five digits wide, as shown in Table H.4. In the table the stem 4 represents the scores 40, 41, 42, 43, and 44; the stem 4* represents the scores 45, 46, 47, 48, and 49. Tables H.3 and H.4 contain the same information, but are organized slightly differently. Notice, too, that you can easily construct a ranked list from a stem-and-leaf display, because the individual score values are easily recovered from the display.

TABLE H.3
Stem-and-leaf display of the distribution of the students' scores from Table H.1.

	Test 1			Test 2	
Stem	Leaves	Frequency	Stem	Leaves	Frequency
0			0		
1			1		
2			2		
3			3		
4	3 4 5	3	4	7	1
5	5 6	2	5	3 3 4	3
6	0 1 5 6 8 8 9	7	6	0 1 5 6 8 8 8 8	8
7	0 1 3 4 5 5 5 5	8	7	0 2 3 3 3 4 5 6 7 8	10
8	0 3 4 6 9	5	8	3 5 6 7 8	5
9	5 6 8	3	9	4	1
		N=28			N=28

TABLE H.4
Stem-and-leaf display of the scores from Table H.1 when the interval width equals 5.

	Test 1				Test 2		
Stem	Leaves		Frequency	Stem	Leaves		Frequency
0				0			
0*				0*			
1				1			
1*				1*			
2				2			
2*				2*			
3				3			
3*				3*			
4	3 4		2	4			
4*	5		1	4*	7		1
5			0	5	3 3 4		3
5*	5 6		2	5*			0
6	0 1		2	6	0 1		2
6*	5 6 8 8 9		5	6*	5 6 8 8 8 8		6
7	0 1 3 4		4	7	0 2 3 3 3 4		6
7*	5 5 5 5		4	7*	5 6 7 8		4
8	0 3 4		3	8	3		1
8*	6 9		2	8*	5 6 7 8		4
9			0	9	4		1
9*	5 6 8		3	9*			0
			N = 28				N = 28

Frequency Distributions

When the number of scores to be organized is very large, ranked lists and stem-and-leaf displays are cumbersome. In such cases, the collection of scores is organized into a table called a *frequency distribution*. This table shows the number of persons obtaining various scores. Table H.5 shows frequency distributions for the two tests.

Notice that the table shows scores grouped into intervals of five points on the score scale: 95–99, 90–94, 85–89, and so on. Grouping scores into intervals is a common practice when the students' scores span a wide range of values. The advantage is that the table shows the distribution of scores in a more compact space. The number of intervals is set at some convenient value, say 10 or 12. A common practice is to make the width of the interval an odd number, because then the midpoint of the interval is a whole number. Whole-number midpoints are desirable when the information in the table is to be used to construct a graph or for later calculations. The midpoints of each interval are shown in Table H.5. Often the midpoints are not presented when the table can be interpreted without that information. Similarly, the "Tally" column is seldom shown in a finished table. Its only purpose is to make it easier and more accurate to count the scores in each interval. At the bottom of the frequency column you should record the sum of the frequencies. This is N, the total number of scores in the collection.

You can calculate the width of the interval to use as follows. Subtract the lowest score in the group from the highest score. Divide this difference by 12. The interval width to use is the nearest odd number to this quotient. For example, for Test 1, the highest score is 98 and the lowest is 43. Thus, $(98 - 43) \div 12$ is 4.56, and the nearest odd number is 5. For Test 2, this calculation is 3.91 and the nearest odd number is 3. However, if you want to compare the distributions of Tests 1 and 2, it is best to use the same interval width. Thus, we have used a width of 5 for

TABLE H.5
Frequency distributions of the scores in Table H.1. (Interval widths equal 5.)

	Test 1				Test 2		
Interval	Tally	Midpoint	Frequency	Interval	Tally	Midpoint	Frequency
95–99	///	97	3	95–99		97	0
90–94		92	0	90–94	/	92	1
85–89	//	87	2	85–89	////	87	4
80–84	///	82	3	80–84	/	82	1
75–79	////	77	4	75–79	////	77	4
70–74	////	72	4	70–74	ҬҤ /	72	6
65–69	ҬҤ	67	5	65–69	ҬҤ /	67	6
60–64	//	62	2	60–64	//	62	2
55–59	//	57	2	55–59		57	0
50–54		52	0	50–54	///	52	3
45–49	/	47	1	45–49	/	47	1
40–44	//	42	2	40–44		42	0
			28				28

each test distribution. This illustrates that there are no hard and fast rules for fixing interval widths.

To make the table, it is best to make the lower limit of the interval a multiple of the interval width. This makes it easier to construct the table. Thus, the lower limit of the highest interval in Table H.5 is 95, the next is 90, next is 85, and so on. Be sure that the highest interval contains the highest score. You need not continue the intervals below the interval containing the lowest score. Thus, the lowest interval in Table H.5 is 40–44.

The *grouped frequency distribution*, as Table H.5 is called, provides the same convenient summary of the distribution of scores as the stem-and-leaf display. However, unlike the stem-and-leaf display, information about the specific numerical values of the scores in each interval is lost: Only the frequency of the scores falling into the interval is recorded. Unlike the stem-and-leaf display, however, the frequency distribution table can summarize large collections of scores in a compact, easy-to-interpret format.

Frequency Polygons and Histograms

Frequency distributions are often graphed because graphs permit an increased understanding of the distribution of scores. Two common types of graphs of frequency distributions are the histogram and frequency polygon. For both, a scale of score values is marked off on a horizontal axis. The *histogram* (sometimes called a *bar graph*) represents the frequency of each score by a rectangle. The height of each rectangle is made equal to (or proportional to) the frequency of the corresponding score. Figure H.1A shows a histogram for the Test 1 scores of Table H.5. A *frequency polygon* for these same scores is shown in Figure H.1B. A dot is made directly above the score-value to indicate the frequency. (If no one has obtained a particular score-value, the dot is made at 0.) The dots are then connected with straight lines to make the polygon.

A graph communicates in an easy manner the shape or form of a frequency distribution. Using the names of these shapes is a compact way of describing how the scores are distributed.

Figure H.2 shows a variety of distributional forms, their corresponding names, and examples of measurement situations that might give rise to them.

Frequency Distributions and Graphs

The illustrations of Figure H.2 are idealized and do not represent actual distributions. Nevertheless, it is helpful to have a mental picture of these distributional forms because, in practice, actual test score distributions resemble the ideal forms at least roughly. Test manuals and school and state reports often describe score distributions using the terms.

Score distribution shape depends on both the test-takers and the test. The shape of a score distribution reflects the characteristics of the test as well as the ability of the group being tested. There is no single "natural" or "normal" shape toward which the test scores of a given group of students tends. A test composed of items that are not too difficult and not too easy for a particular group is likely to result in distributions of scores similar to those illustrated by A, B, or C of Figure H.2. This same group, with the same ability, could take a test in the same subject made up of items that few persons could answer correctly or a test made up of "easy" items. In these latter cases, skewed distributions (F or G) might result. It is not accurate, therefore, to come to a conclusion about the *underlying ability* distribution of a group of

FIGURE H.1
Histogram and frequency polygon for the scores of Test 1 from Table H.5.

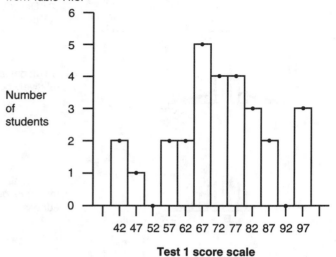

Test 1 score scale

A. Histogram

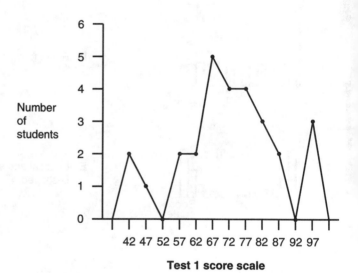

Test 1 score scale

B. Frequency polygon

students by examining only the shape of the distribution of observed test scores. The characteristics of the test the group took also need to be made a part of the decision.

Choice between Histogram or Polygon For many classroom purposes, you could use either a polygon or a histogram; the choice between them is rather arbitrary. The polygon emphasizes the continuous nature of the attribute that underlies the scores you see on the test; the histogram emphasizes the discrete nature. Although observed test *scores* usually are discrete whole numbers (0, 1, 2, . . .), the underlying characteristic a test is designed to measure is often thought of as continuous rather than discrete.

FIGURE H.2
Histograms showing various forms of frequency distributions.

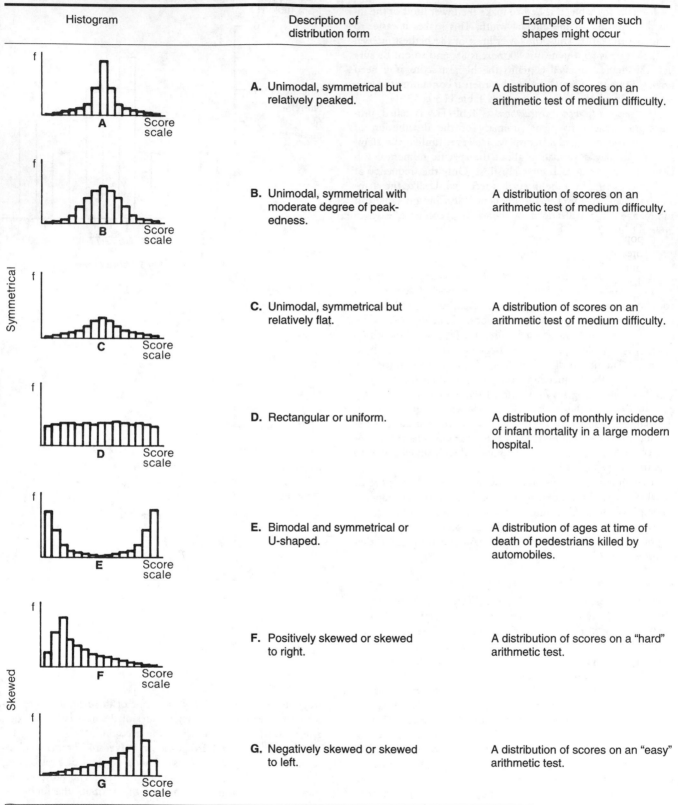

Histogram	Description of distribution form	Examples of when such shapes might occur
A	**A.** Unimodal, symmetrical but relatively peaked.	A distribution of scores on an arithmetic test of medium difficulty.
B	**B.** Unimodal, symmetrical with moderate degree of peak-edness.	A distribution of scores on an arithmetic test of medium difficulty.
C	**C.** Unimodal, symmetrical but relatively flat.	A distribution of scores on an arithmetic test of medium difficulty.
D	**D.** Rectangular or uniform.	A distribution of monthly incidence of infant mortality in a large modern hospital.
E	**E.** Bimodal and symmetrical or U-shaped.	A distribution of ages at time of death of pedestrians killed by automobiles.
F	**F.** Positively skewed or skewed to right.	A distribution of scores on a "hard" arithmetic test.
G	**G.** Negatively skewed or skewed to left.	A distribution of scores on an "easy" arithmetic test.

Source: Adapted from *Elementary Statistical Methods in Psychology and Education* (2nd ed.) (pp. 30–31) by P. J. Blommers and R. A. Forsyth, 1977, Boston: Houghton-Mifflin. Adapted by permission of the author.

Comparing Two Distributions It is sometimes useful to compare two or more frequency distributions by graphing on the same axes using polygons, rather than histograms. A graph could compare, for example, a class of students before and after instruction, or it could compare two different classes of students. Such a graph would display the forms of the distributions, the variability or disbursement of scores, and the place(s) along the score scale where the scores tend to cluster.

Measures of Central Tendency

It is quite common when interpreting assessment results to speak of the "average score," as we speak of the "average student," "being above average in spelling," or "of average intelligence."

There are many ways to define averages, but we describe only three: *mode, mean,* and *median.* The *mode* is the score that occurs most frequently in relation to other scores in the collection. Thus, the modal score is average in the sense of being most popular or most probable in the group. The *mean,* or more precisely the *arithmetic mean,* is found by summing the scores and dividing by their number. Thus, the mean is the average that takes into account all of the scores and is the "center of gravity" of the collection. The *median* is the score point that divides the score scale so 50% of the scores in the collection are above it and 50% are below it. This makes the median a typical score in the sense of coming nearest in the aggregate to all the scores.

Mode

You find the mode by listing the scores and identifying the most frequently occurring. In Table H.6, the mode of the Test 1 distribution is 75, and the mode of the Test 2 distribution is 68. You could identify the mode from either a stem-and-leaf display or a frequency distribution.

If in one distribution two scores occur with approximately equal frequency, there are two modes. Such a distribution is said to be *bimodal.* A distribution with one mode is *unimodal.*

The mode is the point on the score scale where a large number of scores in a distribution are located. If there is more than one mode, there are concentrations of scores at more than one score level. You should note that a distribution may not have a mode. For example, the uniform distribution in Figure H.2D does not have a mode.

Mean

To calculate the mean, add the scores and divide by their number. The formula is

$$M = \frac{Sum\ of\ all\ the\ scores}{Total\ number\ of\ scores}$$
$$= \frac{\Sigma X}{N}$$

where M represents the mean, N represents the total number of scores involved, and Σ represents "sum of." The means of the Test 1 and Test 2 scores in Table H.6 are 71.4 and 71.3, respectively.

An important property of the mean is that its value is affected by every one of the scores in the collection, because the sum on which it is based includes every score. When you want an average that focuses on the total rather than the typical or most frequent, choose the mean. The mean reflects the highest

TABLE H.6
Scores on Test 1 and Test 2 ranked separately and showing measures of central tendency.

Test 1	Test 2
98	94
96	88
95	87
89	86
86	85
84	83
83	78
80	77
75 ⎫	76
75 ⎪ Mode = 75	75
75 ⎬	74
75 ⎪	73
74 ⎭	73
73	73
71 ← Median = 72	72 ← Median = 72.5
70	70
69	68 ⎫
68	68 ⎪ Mode = 68
68	68 ⎬
66	68 ⎭
65	66
61	65
60	61
56	60
55	54
45	53
44	53
43	47
$\Sigma X = 1{,}999$	$\Sigma X = 1{,}995$
$M = (1{,}999) \div 28 = 71.4$	$M = (1{,}995) \div 28 = 71.3$

and lowest scores, whereas the mode reflects only the most frequent. This influence of extremely high or low scores may be undesirable because such scores are not typical scores for the distribution. The median is preferred when you want an average to focus on typical performance and to be uninfluenced by extremely high or extremely low scores.

Median

A simple way to calculate the median is to arrange the scores by rank, and then count to the point on the score scale that has the same number of scores above it as below it. If there is an even number of scores in the collection, the median is halfway between the two middle scores. If there is an odd number of scores, the median is the middle score.

In Table H.6, the median for Test 1 is 72; the median for Test 2 is 72.5. Notice that the median does not have to be a score that any person has attained. This is so because the median is a point on the score scale that divides the distribution into halves. The mean also need not be a score anyone attained; however, the mode must be a score that many persons attained.

Because the median separates the distribution into two halves, it is also the *50th percentile.* Further, it does not sum up all of the scores. As a result, its value is not affected by extremely high or low scores (as the mean is). The median is the average to use when you do not want an average that is sensitive to such extreme scores.

Measures of Variability

Although averages summarize the central tendency of a group of scores, they do not summarize how the scores spread out over the score scale. For example, the mean reading test scores of two seventh-grade classes may be 75. However, in one class the scores may range widely from 55 to 95, while in the other the scores may range only from 70 to 80. Obviously, the students in the latter class are more nearly alike in their reading achievement than the students in the former class. You will need to cater to more widely different reading levels when teaching the former class than when teaching the latter.

This section describes three measures of the spread or variability of a set of scores: the *range*, the *interquartile range*, and the *standard deviation*.

Range (R)

The range is a simple index of spread. It is the difference between the highest and lowest scores in the set. For the two tests in Table H.6, the range is 55 for Test 1 ($98 - 43 = 55$) and 47 for Test 2 ($94 - 47 = 47$). Although for either test the range is relatively large, it is smaller for Test 2, showing the scores are spread over a smaller part of the score scale. The procedure may be summarized as follows:

$$R = highest\ score - lowest\ score$$

A weakness of the range as an index of variability is that it is based on only two scores. It ignores the scores between the highest and lowest scores. Another problem with the range is that a change in either the highest or lowest score in the set can radically alter its value.

Interquartile Range (IR)

The interquartile range describes the spread of the middle 50% of the scores. It is the difference between the third and the first quartiles. *Quartiles* are points that divide the group of scores into quarters. The first quartile (Q_1) is the point *below which* the lowest 25% of the students score. The third quartile (Q_3) is the point *above which* the highest 25% of the students score. The second quartile (Q_2) is the median.

To obtain the interquartile range, you first order the scores and proceed similarly to calculating the median. That is, count down from the highest score 25% of the scores to locate Q_3 and up from the lowest score 25% to calculate Q_1. The interquartile range is the difference between these two values:[1]

$$IR = Q_3 - Q_1$$

In Table H.6, $Q_3 = 83$ and $Q_1 = 61$ for Test 1. That is, for Test 1 the 75th percentile is 83 and the 25th percentile is 61. The $IR = [83 - 61] = 22$ for this test. Thus, the middle 50% of the scores on Test 1 have a 22-point spread. For Test 2, $Q_3 = 73$, $Q_1 = 65$, and $IR = [73 - 65] = 8$. The middle 50% of the students have only an 8-point spread on Test 2.

Standard Deviation (SD)

The most frequently used index of variability is the standard deviation. Large numerical values of this index indicate that the scores are spread out away from the mean. Small values indicate that the scores tend to cluster near the mean. The standard deviation is the average amount by which the scores differ from the mean score.[2] In some test reports the squared standard deviation (SD^2), or *variance*, is used.

The definitional formula for the standard deviation is:

$$SD = \sqrt{\frac{\Sigma (X - M)^2}{N}}$$

$$= \sqrt{\frac{sum\ of\ the\ squared\ deviations\ from\ the\ mean}{total\ number\ of\ scores}}$$

Many inexpensive scientific calculators and microcomputer programs have procedures for calculating the standard deviation. You should use one of these to calculate SD. If you want to calculate the standard deviation using a calculator that does not have this procedure built in, follow these steps:

1. First arrange the scores into a frequency distribution, as in Table H.5 and reproduced in Table H.7.

2. Apply a computational formula such as the one shown here. (You can find other computational formulas in an applied statistics text.)

$$SD = \sqrt{\frac{\Sigma f(X^2)}{N} - M^2}$$

$$= \sqrt{\frac{sum\ of\ the\ products\ of\ the\ square\ of\ each\ score\ and\ its\ frequency}{total\ number} - [square\ of\ the\ mean]}$$

This is not as hard to compute as it looks:

Steps	Symbols
1. Square each interval midpoint.	1. X^2
2. Multiply each square by its frequency.	2. $f(X^2)$
3. Add together all of these products.	3. $\Sigma f(X^2)$
4. Divide by the total number.	4. $\dfrac{\Sigma f(X^2)}{N}$
5. Square the mean. (If the mean has not been computed already, you need to compute it.)	5. M^2
6. Subtract the square of the mean from the result found in Step 4. (Stop here if you want only the variance.)	6. $\dfrac{\Sigma f(X^2)}{N} - M^2$
7. Take the square root of the difference. This is the standard deviation.	7. $\sqrt{\dfrac{\Sigma f(X^2)}{N} - M^2}$

Table H.7 illustrates these calculations for Test 1. (Note that in this example, the result obtained from Table H.7 is not the same result you would obtain if you did not group the scores into intervals. Grouping scores results in some error. However, the result is still useful.)

---

[1]Some books divide the interquartile range by 2 to obtain the *semi-interquartile range (SIR)*. This value indicates the approximate distance you would need to move on the score scale above and below the median to encompass the middle 50% of the scores.

[2]This is not strictly correct, but as a practical matter little interpretive harm regarding assessment results is done by thinking of the standard deviation in this way.

The Correlation Coefficient

Calculating the correlation coefficient requires using a calculator or a computer. Some scientific calculators have this capability already built in as a statistical function, so all you need to do is enter the paired scores of students. However, this section illustrates the calculation for those with calculators that do not have the correlation coefficient function built in.

For practical work, you can use the following computational formula:

$$r = \frac{N(\Sigma XY) - (\Sigma X)(\Sigma Y)}{\sqrt{[N(\Sigma X^2) - (\Sigma X)^2][N(\Sigma Y^2) - (\Sigma Y)^2]}}$$

This formula is illustrated in Table H.8 with the scores from the two tests in Table H.1. In this example, Test 1 is symbolized X and Test 2 is symbolized Y. Table H.9 shows the calculation.

If you have already computed the standard deviations and means of each variable, then the following formula (which is equivalent to the previous equation) will save you some computational labor.

$$r_{xy} = \frac{\dfrac{\Sigma XY}{N} - M_x M_y}{(SD_x)(SD_y)}$$

To illustrate with the data in Table H.9, for which

$$M_x = 71.39, \; M_y = 71.25$$
$$SD_x = 14.81, \; SD_y = 11.57$$

we have:

$$r = \frac{\dfrac{145{,}902}{28} - (71.39)(71.25)}{(14.81)(11.57)} = .75$$

(The slight difference you obtain from these two equations is due to rounding error.)

TABLE H.7
Computing the standard deviation of Test 1 scores after they are organized into a frequency distribution.

Score interval	Midpoint	Frequency (f)	Step 1 (X_2)	Step 2 $f(X_2)$
95–99	97	3	9,409	28,227
90–94	92	0	8,464	0
85–89	87	2	7,569	15,138
80–84	82	3	6,724	20,172
75–79	77	4	5,929	23,716
70–74	72	4	5,184	20,736
65–69	67	5	4,489	22,445
60–64	62	2	3,844	7,688
55–59	57	2	3,249	6,498
50–54	52	0	2,704	0
45–49	47	1	2,209	2,209
40–44	42	2	1,764	3,528
		n = 28		150,357

The formula is:

$$SD = \sqrt{\frac{\Sigma f(X^2) - M^2}{N}}$$

(Note that using the grouped data above, M = 71.8)

Putting the numbers into the formula:

$$SD = \sqrt{\frac{150{,}357}{28} - (71.8)^2}$$

After Steps 4 and 5:

$$SD = \sqrt{5{,}369.89 - 5{,}155.24}$$

Then Step 6:

$$SD = \sqrt{214.65}$$

Step 7 gives the final result: $SD = 14.65$

TABLE H.8
Example calculating a correlation coefficient.

Steps	Symbols	Examples
1. List everyone's pair of scores.	1. X, Y	1. *Blake: X* $= 74, Y = 72$
2. Square each score.	2. $X^2\ Y^2$	2. *Blake:* $X^2 = (74)^2 = 5{,}476$ $Y^2 = (72)^2 = 5{,}184$
3. Multiply the scores in each pair.	3. XY	3. *Blake:* $XY = 74 \times 72$ $= 5{,}328$
4. Sum the X, Y, X^2, Y^2, and XY columns.	4. $\Sigma X, \Sigma Y$ $\Sigma X^2\ \Sigma Y^2$ ΣXY	4. $\Sigma X = 1{,}999, \Sigma X^2 = 148{,}635$ $\Sigma Y = 1{,}995, \Sigma Y^2 = 145{,}761$ $\Sigma XY = 145{,}902$
5. Put the sums into equation.		

$$r = \frac{28\,(145{,}902) - (1{,}999)\,(1{,}995)}{\sqrt{[28\,(148{,}635) - (1{,}999)^2]\,[28\,(145{,}761) - (1{,}995)^2]}}$$

$$= \frac{4{,}085{,}256 - 3{,}988{,}005}{\sqrt{(4{,}161{,}780 - 3{,}996{,}001)\,(4{,}081{,}308 - 3{,}980{,}025)}}$$

$$= \frac{97{,}251}{\sqrt{(165{,}779)\,(101{,}283)}} = \frac{97{,}251}{129{,}578.53} = .75$$

TABLE H.9
Computing a correlation coefficient between the scores in Table H.1.

Names	Test 1 X	Test 1 X^2	Test 2 Y	Test 2 Y^2	Cross Products XY
Anthony	89	7,921	94	8,836	8,366
Ashley	75	7,625	68	4,624	5,100
Blake	74	5,476	72	5,184	5,328
Chad	84	7,056	77	5,929	6,468
Donald	56	3,136	66	4,356	3,696
Edward	80	6,400	68	4,624	5,440
Festina	66	4,356	68	4,624	4,488
George	86	7,396	73	5,329	6,278
Harriet	68	4,624	73	5,329	4,964
Irene	98	9,604	86	7,396	8,428
Jesse	65	4,225	78	6,084	5,070
Katherine	44	1,936	60	3,600	2,640
Lorraine	45	2,025	53	2,809	2,385
Marya	61	3,721	75	5,625	4,575
Nancy	75	5,625	76	5,776	5,700
Oprah	68	4,624	54	2,916	3,672
Peter	55	3,025	53	2,809	2,915
Quincy	70	4,900	68	4,624	4,760
Robert	69	4,761	65	4,225	4,485
Sally	60	3,600	47	2,209	2,820
Tina	73	5,329	74	5,476	5,402
Ula	75	5,625	88	7,744	6,600
Veronica	71	5,041	73	5,329	5,183
Wallace	43	1,849	61	3,721	2,623
William	83	6,889	87	7,569	7,221
Xavier	95	9,025	83	6,889	7,885
Yvonne	96	9,216	85	7,225	8,160
Zena	75	7,625	70	4,900	5,250
	1,999	148,635	1,995	145,761	145,902

APPENDIX I

Computational Procedures for Various Reliability Coefficients

TABLE I.1
Example of how to compute the Spearman-Brown double length and the Rulon split-halves reliability estimates.

A. Pupil's item scores and total test scores[a]

Pupils	Items on test 1	2	3	4	Total score (X)
Alan	1	0	0	0	1
Issac	1	1	0	0	2
Leslie	0	0	1	1	2
Miriam	0	0	0	0	0
Rebecca	1	1	0	1	3
Robert	1	1	1	1	4

$$M = \frac{\sum X}{N} = \frac{12}{6} = 2; \quad (SD_x)^2 = \frac{\sum (X-M)^2}{N} = \frac{10}{6} = 1.67$$

[a]An item is scored 1 if it is answered correctly; 0 otherwise.

B. Computation for Spearman-Brown formula

Pupils	Half-test scores odd items (1 + 3)	even items (2 + 4)	z-scores for: odd	even	Product ($z_o \cdot z_e$)
Alan	1	0	0	−1.22	0
Issac	1	1	0	0	0
Leslie	1	1	0	0	0
Miriam	0	0	−1.72	−1.22	2.10
Rebecca	1	2	0	+1.22	0
Robert	2	2	+1.72	+1.22	2.10
Means	1.0	1.0			
SDs	0.58	0.82			

Computing correlation between halves[b]

$$r_{nn} = \frac{\sum z_o z_e}{n} = \frac{4.2}{6} = 0.70$$

Spearman-Brown double length

$$\text{reliability estimate} = \frac{2r_{nn}}{1 + r_{nn}} = \frac{(2)(.70)}{1 + .70} = 0.82$$

[b]Other procedures may be used for computing the correlation coefficient (see Table H.8).

C. Computation for Rulon formula

Pupils	Half-test scores[c] odd items (1 + 3)	even items (2 + 4)	Difference between half-test scores
Alan	1	0	1
Issac	1	1	0
Leslie	1	1	0
Miriam	0	0	0
Rebecca	1	2	−1
Robert	2	2	0

TABLE I.1 (continued)

Variance of differences = $(SD_{diff})^2 = 0.33$

Variance of total scores = $(SD_x)^2 = 1.67$

Rulon split-halves
reliability estimate

$$= 1 - \frac{(SD_{diff})^2}{(SD_x)^2}$$

$$= 1 - \frac{0.33}{1.67} = 0.80$$

[c]Neither the Spearman-Brown nor the Rulon formula is restricted to an odd-even split. Other splits may be used (see text).

TABLE I.2
Example of how to compute the Kuder-Richardson Formula 20 (KR20) and the Kuder-Richardson Formula 21 (KR21) reliability estimates.

A.   Computing KR20

Pupils	Items on test[a]				Total score[b](X)
	1	**2**	**3**	**4**	
Alan	1	0	0	0	1
Issac	1	1	0	0	2
Leslie	0	0	1	1	2
Miriam	0	0	0	0	0
Rebecca	1	1	0	1	3
Robert	1	1	1	1	4
Fraction passing each item (p-values)	0.67	0.50	0.33	0.50	$M = 2.0$ $(SD_x)^2 = 1.667$
(1-p)	0.33	0.50	0.67	0.50	
p(1-p)	0.222	0.250	0.222	0.250	$\Sigma p(1-p) = 0.944$

$$KR20 = \left[\frac{k}{k-1}\right]\left[1 - \frac{\Sigma p(1-p)}{(SD_x)^2}\right] = \left[\frac{4}{4-1}\right]\left[1 - \frac{0.944}{1.667}\right]$$

$$= (1.333)(1 - .566) = (1.333)(.434) = 0.58$$

[a]An item is scored 1 if it is answered correctly; 0 otherwise.
[b]The mean and variance are computed in Appendix H.

B.   Computing KR21

Pupils	Total score[a] (X)
Alan	1
Isaac	2
Leslie	2
Miriam	0
Rebecca	3
Robert	4

$M = 2.0$; $(SD_x)^2 = 1.667$

$$KR21 = \left[\frac{k}{k-1}\right]\left[1 - \frac{M(k-M)}{k(SD_x)^2}\right]$$

$$= \left[\frac{4}{4-1}\right]\left[1 - \frac{2(4-2)}{4(1.667)}\right]$$

$$= (1.333)\left[1 - \frac{4}{6.668}\right]$$

$$= (1.333)(1 - .600)$$

$$= 0.53$$

[a]The mean and variance are computed in Appendix H.

C.   Comparing the values of various reliability estimates for the same test[a]

Estimating procedure	Numerical value
Spearman-Brown	0.82[b]
Rulon	0.80[b]
KR20	0.58
KR21	0.53

[a]See Appendix H also.
[b]Based on an odd-even split.

TABLE I.3
Example of how to compute a coefficient alpha reliability estimate for a set of essay questions or judges' ratings.

Persons	Questions or Judges I	II	III	IV	Total score (X)
Aaron	4	3	4	4	15
Dorcas	2	5	5	5	17
Katherine	3	5	5	3	16
Kenneth	1	3	1	1	6
Lee	5	5	5	4	19
Peter	4	3	4	4	15
$(SD_i)^2$ values	1.81	1.00	2.00	1.58	$(SD_x)^2 = 16.89$

$$\Sigma(SD_i)^2 = 1.81 + 1.00 + 2.00 + 1.58 = 6.39$$

$$\alpha = \left[\frac{k}{k-1}\right]\left[1 - \frac{\Sigma(SD_i)^2}{(SD_x)^2}\right] = \left[\frac{4}{4-1}\right]\left[1 - \frac{6.39}{16.89}\right] = (1.33)(1-.38) = (1.33)(.62) = 0.82$$

TABLE I.4
Example of computing the general Spearman-Brown reliability estimate.

A. Formula

$$r_{nn} = \frac{nr_{11}}{1 + (n-1)r_{11}}$$

B. Example

Q. A teacher has a 10-item test with reliability coefficient equal to 0.40. What would be the reliability if the teacher added 15 new items similar to those currently on the test?

A. Here $r_{11} = 0.40$ and $n = \dfrac{25}{10} = 2.5$. (The new test would be 25 items long and, hence, 2.5 times as long as the original test.) Thus, the new test reliability is:

$$r_{nn} = \frac{(2.5)(0.40)}{1 + (2.5-1)(0.40)}$$

$$= \frac{1.00}{1+0.6} = \frac{1.0}{1.6} = 0.625$$

C. Results of applying the formula to various values of r_{11} and n.

Original reliability	Number of times original test is lengthened (n) 2	3	4	5	6
.10	.18	.25	.31	.36	.40
.20	.33	.43	.50	.56	.60
.30	.46	.56	.63	.68	.72
.40	.57	.67	.73	.77	.80
.50	.67	.75	.80	.83	.86
.60	.75	.82	.86	.88	.90
.70	.82	.88	.90	.92	.93
.80	.89	.92	.94	.95	.96
.90	.95	.96	.97	.98	.98

TABLE I.5

Example of how to compute percent agreement and the kappa coefficient. The kappa coefficient adjusts the percent agreement for chance agreement that is not related to the assessment procedure.

A. General layout of the data

		Results from Test 1		
		Mastery	Non-Mastery	Marginal totals
Results from Test 2	Mastery	a	b	$a + b$
	Non-Mastery	c	d	$c + d$
	Marginal Totals	$a + c$	$b + d$	$N = a + b + c + d$

B. Formulas

P_A = total percent agreement in table

$$= \frac{a}{N} + \frac{d}{N} = \frac{a + d}{N}$$

P_c = percent agreement expected because of the composition of the group.

$$= \left[\frac{a + b}{N} \times \frac{a + c}{N} \right] + \left[\frac{c + d}{N} \times \frac{b + d}{N} \right]$$

$$\kappa = \frac{P_A - P_C}{1 - P_C}$$

C. Numerical example

		Results from Test 1		
		Mastery	Non-Mastery	Marginal totals
Results from Test 2	Mastery	11	4	15
	Non-Mastery	1	9	10
	Marginal Totals	12	13	25

$$P_A = \frac{11}{25} + \frac{9}{25} = \frac{11 + 9}{25} = \frac{20}{25} = 0.80$$

$$P_c = \left(\frac{15}{25} \times \frac{12}{25} \right) + \left(\frac{10}{25} \times \frac{13}{25} \right) = \frac{180}{625} + \frac{130}{625} = \frac{310}{625} = 0.50$$

$$\kappa = \frac{0.80 - 0.50}{1 - 0.50} = \frac{0.30}{0.50} = 0.60$$

A Limited List of Published Tests

Title	Age/Grade Level	Publisher[1]	Review[2]
Multilevel survey achievement batteries (group)			
• California Achievement Tests, 5th Ed	K–12	CTBMH	**13**:40
• California Achievement Tests Written Assessment System	K–12	CTBMH	**11**:51
• Comprehensive Tests of Basic Skills	K–12	CTBMH	**11**:81, **14**
• Iowa Tests of Basic Skills, Form J	K–9	RP	**11**:184
• Iowa Tests of Educational Development, 8th Ed.	Gr. 9–12	RP	**10**:156
• Metropolitan Achievement Tests, 7th Ed.	Gr. 1–11	HEM	**12**:232
• Sequential Test of Educational Progress, III	K–12	CTBMH	**9**:1115
• SRA Achievement Series	K–12	CTBMH	**11**:376
• Stanford Early School Achievement Test	K–1.5	HEM	**11**:378
• Stanford Achievement Test, 9th Ed.	Gr. 2–12	HEM	**11**:377, **12**:371
• Tests of Achievement and Proficiency, Form J	Gr. 9–12	RP	**11**:455
• Wide Range Achievement Test—3	K–12	JA	**10**:389, **12**:414
Multi-level survey achievement batteries (individual)			
• Peabody Individual Achievement Test—R	K–Adult	AGS	**11**:280
Multi-level criterion-referenced achievement tests			
• Degrees of Reading Power	Pre-K–6	TASA	**12**:101
• Key Math—Revised	K–9	AGS	**11**:191
• New Standards	4, 8, 10	HEM	
Reading survey tests			
• Gates–MacGinite Reading Tests, 3rd Ed.	K–12	RP	**11**:146
Reading diagnostic tests			
• Diagnostic Reading Scales	Gr. 1–8	CTBMH	**9**:338
• Stanford Diagnostic Reading Test, 3rd Ed.	Gr. 1–13	HEM	**9**:1178, **13**:294
• Woodcock Diagnostic Reading Battery	K–16.9	RP	**10**:391
Adaptive behavior inventories			
• Vineland Adaptive Behavior Scales	3–19 yrs.	AGS	**10**:381
Individual general ability/scholastic aptitude tests			
• Bayley Scales of Infant Development, 2nd Ed.	1–42 mo.	HEM	**10**:26, **13**:29
• Columbia Mental Maturity Scale	3–11 yrs.	HEM	**8**:210
• Draw A Person	5–17 yrs.	AGS	**11**:114
• Kaufman Assessment Battery for Children	2–12 yrs.	AGS	**9**:562
• McCarthy Scales of Children's Abilities	1–8 yrs.	HEM	**9**:671
• Peabody Picture Vocabulary Test—Revised	2–Adult	AGS	**9**:926
• Porteus Maze Test	3–Adult	PC	**9**:965
• Raven Progressive Matrices	5–Adult	PC	**9**:1007
• Stanford-Binet Intelligence Scale, 4th Ed.	2–Adult	RP	**10**:342
• System of Multicultural Pluralistic Assessment	5–11 yrs.	PC	**9**:1222
• Wechsler Adult Intelligence Scale—Revised	16–74 yrs.	PC	**9**:1350
• Wechsler Intelligence Scale for Children, 3rd Ed.	6–16 yrs.	HEM	**12**:412
• Wechsler PreSchool & Primary Scale of Intelligence—R	4–6 yrs.	PC	**11**:466
Group-administered tests of scholastic aptitude			
• Enhanced ACT Assessment	Gr. 12	ACT	**12**:139
• Closed High School Placement Test	Gr. 8–9	STS	**8**:26
• Cognitive Abilities Test—Form 4	K–12	RP	**10**:66
• Cooperative School and College Ability Test	Gr. 3–13	CTBMH	**9**:1075
• Kuhlman Anderson Tests	Gr. K–12	STS	**9**:579
• Otis-Lennon School Ability Test, 7th Ed.	Gr. K–12	PC	**11**:274
• College Board SAT Reasoning Test	Gr. 12+	ETS	**9**:244
• Short Form of Academic Aptitude	Gr. 1–12	CTBMH	**8**:202

[1]See Appendix K for names and addresses of publishers.
[2]The boldface number is the number of the *MMY* volume; the number after the colon is the entry number. If the entry number is missing, it was not available at the time of publication.

A Limited List of Published Tests, *continued*

Title	Age/Grade Level	Publisher[1]	Review[2]
Multiple aptitude batteries			
• Differential Aptitude Test	Gr. 7–12	PC	**12**:118
• Flanagan Aptitude Classification Test	Gr. 9–12	SRA	**7**:675
• USES Nonreading Aptitude Test	Gr. 9–12 Adult	USGPO	**9**:1305
Vocational interest inventories			
• ACT Career Planning Program	Gr. 12+	RP	**8**:989
• Hall Occupational Orientation Inventory	Gr. 3–Adult	STS	**12**:175
• Harrington-O'Shea Career Decision-Making System	Gr. 8–Adult	AGS	**12**:178
• Jackson Vocational Interest Survey	Gr. 9–Adult	SAS	**10**:158
• Kuder Occupational Interest Survey—R, Form DD	Gr. 10–12	CTBMH	**10**:167
• Kuder Form C Preference Record: Vocational	Gr. 9–Adult	CTBMH	**8**:1011
• Kuder General Interest Survey, Form E	Gr. 6–12	CTBMH	**12**:209
• Ohio Vocational Interest Survey, 2nd Ed.	Gr. 7–college	PC	**9**:896
• Self-Directed Search, Form E—1990 Revision	Gr. 9–Adult	PAR	**13**
• Strong Interest Inventory, 4th Ed.	16 yrs.–Adult	CPP	**12**:374

APPENDIX K
List of Test Publishers and Their Web Sites

See current *MMY*, The Buros Institute of Mental Measurements (www.unl.edu/buros), The ERIC Clearinghouse on Assessment and Evaluation test locator (www.ericae.net), or the index of test publishers (www.testpublishers.org/aboutatp.htm) for additional names and addresses.

Addison-Wesley Publishing Co. (AW)
2725 Sand Hill Road
Menlo Park, CA 94025
www.awl.com

American College Testing Program
 (ACT)
2201 N. Dodge Street
PO Box 168
Iowa City, IA 52243
www.act.org

American Council on Education (ACE)
Suite 800
1 Dupont Circle
Washington, DC 20036
www.acenet.edu/calec/ged/home.html

American Guidance Services (AGS)
4201 Woodland Road
P.O. Box 99
Circle Pines, MN 55014-1796
www.agsnet.com/index.asp

CTB/McGraw Hill (CTBMH)
 Publishers Test Service
20 Ryan Ranch Road
Monterey, CA 93940-5703
www.ctb.com

Center for Applied Linguistics (CAL)
1118 22nd Street N.W.
Washington, DC 20037
www.cal.org

College Entrance Examination Board
 (CEEB)
45 Columbus Avenue
New York, NY 10023-6992
www.collegeboard.org

Consulting Psychologist Press (CPP)
3803 East Bayshore Road
P.O. Box 10096
Palo Alto, CA 94303
www.cpp-db.com

Educational and Industrial Testing Service
 (EDITS)
P.O. Box 7234
San Diego, CA 93167
www.edits.net/noframes/home.htm

Educational Records Bureau, Inc. (ERB)
P.O. Box 6650
Princeton, NJ 08541-6650
www.erbtest.org

Educational Testing Service (ETS)
P.O. Box 6736
Princeton, NJ 08541-6736
www.ets.org

Institute for Personality and Ability
 Testing (IPAT)
P.O. Box 1188
Champaign, IL 61824-1188
www.ipat.org

Harcourt Educational Measurement (HEM)
555 Academic Court
San Antonio, TX 78204-2498
www.hemweb.com

Pro-Ed (PE)
8700 Shoal Creek Boulevard
Austin, TX 78757-9965
www.proedinc.com

The Psychological Corporation (PC)
555 Academic Court
San Antonio, TX 78204-2498
www.harcourt.com/assessment

Riverside Publishing Co. (RP)
425 Spring Lake Drive
Itasca, IL 60143-2079
www.riverpub.com

Scholastic Testing Service, Inc. (STS)
480 Meyer Road
P.O. Box 1056
Bensenville, IL 60106
www.ststesting.com

Scott, Foresman (SF)
1900 East Lake Avenue
Glenview, IL 60025-2055
www.scottforesman.com

Sigma Assessment Systems (SAS)
P.O. Box 610984
Port Huron, MI 48061-0984
www.sigmaassessmentsystems.com

Slosson Educational Publishers, Inc.
P.O. Box 280
East Aurora, NY 14052-0280
www.slosson.com

Touchstone Applied Science Associates,
 Inc.
4 Hardscrabble Heights
P.O. Box 382
Brewster, NY 10509-0382
www.tasa.com

United States Government Printing Office
 (USGPO)
Washington, DC 20402
www.gpo.ucop.edu/search/

Western Psychological Services (WPS)
12031 Wilshire Boulevard
Los Angeles, CA 90025-1251
www.wpspublish.com

REFERENCES

Adams, J. A. (1971). A closed-loop theory of motor learning. *Journal of Motor Behavior, 3,* 111–149.

Airasian, P. W. (1979). A perspective of uses and misuses of standardized achievement tests. *NCME, Measurement in Education, 10*(3), 1–12.

Airasian, P. W. (1991a). *Classroom assessment.* New York: McGraw-Hill.

Airasian, P. W. (1991b). Perspective on measurement instruction. *Educational Measurement: Issues and Practice, 10*(1), 13–16.

Alexander, P. A. (1992). Domain knowledge: Evaluating themes and emerging concerns. *Educational Psychologist, 27,* 33–51.

Aleyideino, S. C. (1968). The effects of response methods and item types upon working time scores and grade-equivalent scores of pupils differing in levels of achievement. *Dissertation Abstracts International, 29,* 1774A–1775A. (University Microfilms No. 68–16, 773).

Algozzine, R. (1993). Including students with disabilities in systemic efforts to measure outcomes: Why ask why? In J. E. Ysseldyke & M. L. Thurlow (Eds.), *Views on inclusion and testing accommodations for students with disabilities* (pp. 5–18). Minneapolis: National Center on Educational Outcomes, University of Minnesota.

Allen, R., Bettis, N., Kurfman, N., MacDonald, W., Mullis, I. V. S., & Salter, C. (1990). *The geography learning of high school seniors.* Princeton, NJ: National Assessment of Educational Progress, Educational Testing Service.

American College Testing Program. (1994). *ACT Interest Inventory.* Princeton, NJ: Author.

American Council on the Teaching of Foreign Languages. (1989). *Oral proficiency interview: Tester training manual.* Yonkers, NY: Author.

American Counseling Association. (1988). *Ethical standards of the American Counseling Association.* Alexandria, VA: Author.

American Counseling Association & Association for Assessment in Counseling. (1989). *Responsibilities of users of standardized tests: RUST statement revised.* Alexandria, VA: Author.

American Educational Research Association. (1992). *Ethical standards of the American Educational Research Association. Educational Researcher, 2*(21), 23–27.

American Educational Research Association, American Psychological Association, & National Council on Measurement in Education. (1985). *Standards for educational and psychological testing.* Washington, DC: APA.

American Educational Research Association, American Psychological Association, & National Council on Measurement in Education. (1999). *Standards for educational and psychological testing.* Washington, DC: Author.

American Federation of Teachers, National Council on Measurement in Education, & National Education Association. (1990). *Standards for teacher competence in educational assessment of students.* Washington, DC: National Council on Measurement in Education.

American Psychological Association. (1992). *Ethical principles of psychologists and code of conduct.* Washington, DC: Author.

American Psychological Association, American Educational Research Association, & National Council on Measurement in Education. (1974). *Standards for educational and psychological tests.* Washington, DC: American Psychological Association.

American Psychological Association, President's Task Force on Psychology in Education. (in press). *Learner-centered psychological principles: Guidelines for school redesign and reform.* Washington, DC: Author.

Anastasi, A. (1976). *Psychological testing* (4th ed.). Englewood Cliffs, NJ: Merrill/Prentice Hall.

Anastasi, A. (1988). *Psychological testing* (6th ed.). Englewood Cliffs, NJ: Merrill/Prentice Hall.

Anderson, J. R. (1987). Skill acquisition: Compilation of weak-method problem solutions. *Psychological Review, 94,* 199–210.

Anderson, R. C. (1972). How to construct achievement tests to assess comprehension. *Review of Educational Research, 42,* 145–170.

Anderson, R. C. (1977). The notion of schemata and educational enterprise: General discussion of the conference. In R. C. Anderson, R. J. Spiro, & W. E. Montague (Eds.), *Schooling and acquisition of knowledge.* Hillsdale, NJ: Lawrence Erlbaum.

Anderson, R. C. (1984). Some reflections on the acquisition of knowledge. *Educational Researcher, 13,* 5–10.

Armstrong, T. (1996). *Multiple intelligences in the classroom.* Alexandria, VA: Association for Supervision and Curriculum Development.

Arter, J. A, (1998, April). *Teaching about performance assessment.* Paper presented at the annual meeting of the National Council on Measurement in Education, San Diego, CA.

Arter, J. A., & Spandel, V. (1992). NCME instructional module: Using portfolios of student work in instruction and assessment. *Educational Measurement: Issues and Practice, 11*(1), 36–44.

Arter, J. A., & Stiggins, R. J. (1992, April). *Performance assessment in education.* Paper presented at the annual meeting of the American Educational Research Association, San Francisco, CA.

Ausubel, D. P., Novak, J. D., & Hanesian, H. (1978). *Educational psychology: A cognitive view* (2nd ed.). New York: Holt, Rinehart & Winston.

Azwell, T., & Schmar, E. (Eds.). *Report on report cards: Alternatives to consider.* Portsmouth, NH: Heinemann.

Baglin, R. F. (1981). Does "nationally" normed really mean nationally? *Journal of Educational Measurement, 18,* 92–107.

Baker, E. L. (1992). Issues in policy, assessment, and equity. In *Proceedings of the National Research Symposium on Limited English Proficiency Student Issues: Vol. 1 and 2: Focus on Evaluation and Measurement.* Washington, DC.

Baker, E. L., & O'Neil, H. F., Jr. (1993). Policy and validity prospects for performance-based assessment. *American Psychologist, 48,* 1210–1218.

Baker, E. L., & O'Neil, H. F., Jr. (1994). Performance assessment and equity: A view from the USA. *Assessment in Education, 1,* 11–26.

Ballstaedt, S. P., & Mandl, H. (1986). *Diagnosis of knowledge structure in text learning.* (Technical Report 37). Turbingen: University of Turbingen, Deutsches Institut für Fernstudien.

Barker, K., & Ebel, R. L. (1981). A comparison of difficulty and discrimination values of selected true-false item types. *Contemporary Educational Psychology, 7,* 35–40.

Barone, J. B. (1991). Strategies for the development of effective performance exercises. *Applied Measurement in Education, 4,* 305–318.

Beck, M. D. (1974). Achievement test reliability as a function of pupil-response procedures. *Journal of Educational Measurement, 11,* 109–114.

Beggs, D. L., & Hieronymus, A. N. (1968). Uniformity of growth in the basic skills throughout the school year and during the summer. *Journal of Educational Measurement, 5,* 91–97.

Bejar, I. I. (1984). Educational diagnostic assessment. *Journal of Educational Measurement, 21,* 175–189.

Bellanca, J. A., & Kirschenbaum, H. (1976). An overview of grading alternatives. In S. B. Simon & J. A. Bellanca (Eds.), *Degrading the grading myths: A primer of alternatives to grades and marks.* Washington, DC: Association for Supervision and Curriculum Development.

Bennett, G. K., Seashore, H. G., & Wesman, A. G. (1974). *Fifth edition manual for the Differential Aptitude Tests. (Forms S and T).* New York: Psychological Corporation.

Benson, J. (1989). Structural components of statistical test anxiety in adults: An exploratory model. *Journal of Experimental Psychology, 57,* 247–261.

Benson, J. (1998). Developing a strong program of construct validation: A test anxiety example. *Educational Measurement: Issues and Practice, 17*(1), 10–17, 22.

Benson, J. & El-Zahhar, N. E. (1994). Further refinement and validation of the Revised

Test Anxiety Scale. *Structured Equation Modeling, 1*, 203–221.

Bianchini, J. C., & Loret, P. G. (1974a). *Anchor test study. Final project report.* (Vol. 1). (ERIC Document Reproduction Service No. ED 092 601).

Bianchini, J. C., & Loret, P. G. (1974b). *Anchor test study supplement. Final report.* (Vol. 31). (ERIC Document Reproduction Service No. ED 092 632).

Blommers, P. J., & Forsyth, R. A. (1977). *Elementary statistical methods in psychology and education* (2nd ed.). Boston: Houghton-Mifflin.

Bloom, B. S. (1968). Learning for mastery. *Evaluation Comment, 1*, 1–12.

Bloom, B. S., Englehart, M. D., Furst, E. J., Hill, W. H., & Krathwohl, D. R. (1956). *Taxonomy of educational objectives: The classification of educational goals. Handbook I: Cognitive domain.* White Plains, NY: Longman.

Bloom, B. S., Hastings, J. T., & Madaus, G. F. (1971). *Handbook on formative and summative evaluation of student learning.* New York: McGraw-Hill.

Bond, L. (1989). The effects of special preparation on measures of scholastic ability. In R. L. Linn (Ed.), *Educational measurement* (3rd ed., pp. 429–444). Englewood Cliffs, NJ: Merrill/Prentice Hall.

Boothroyd, R. A., McMorris, R. F., & Pruzek R. (1992, April). *What do teachers know about testing and how did they find out?* Paper presented at the annual meeting of the National Council on Measurement in Education, San Francisco, CA.

Boruch, F. R. (1971). Maintaining confidentiality of data in educational research: A systemic analysis. *American Psychologist, 26*, 413–430.

Boucher, J. L. (1974). Higher processes in motor learning. *Journal of Motor Behavior, 6*, 131–138.

Boyd, R.T. (1989). Organizations that provide test information. *Digest, no. 109.* Washington, DC: ERIC Clearinghouse on Tests, Measurements, and Evaluation.

Bransford, J. D., & Stein, B. S. (1984). *The IDEAL problem solver.* New York: W. H. Freeman.

Brelend, H. M., Camp, R., Jones, R. J., Morris, M. M., & Rock, D. A. (1987). *Assessing writing skill.* (Research Monograph no. 11.). New York, NY: College Entrance Examination Board.

Brennan, R. L., & Plake, B. S. (1991). Survey of programs and employment in educational measurement. *Educational Measurement: Issues and Practice, 10*(2), 32.

Brookhart, S. (1991). Letter: Grading practices and validity. *Educational Measurement: Issues and Practice, 10*(1), 35–36.

Brookhart, S. M. (1993). Teachers' grading practices: Meaning and values. *Journal of Educational Measurement, 30*, 123–142.

Brookhart, S. M. (1999). Teaching about communicating assessment results and grading. *Educational Measurement: Issues and Practice, 18*(1), 5–13.

Brophy, J. E., & Good, T. L. (1999). *Looking in Classrooms.* Glenview, IL: Addison Wesley Longman.

Brown, (1910). Some experimental results in the correlation of mental abilities. *British Journal of Psychology, 3*, 296–322.

Bruininks, R. H. (1978). *Examiner's manual: Bruininks-Oseretsky test of motor proficiency.* Circle Pines, MN: American Guidance Service.

Buren, A., & Lewis, S. (1994). *Regional writing portfolio audit meetings: Final Report.* Frankfort, KY: Kentucky Department of Education.

Buros, O. K. (1938). *The nineteen thirty-eight mental measurements yearbook.* New Brunswick, NJ: Rutgers University Press.

Buros, O. K. (Ed.). (1978). *The eighth mental measurements yearbook.* Highland Park, NJ: Gryphon Press.

Burton, R. R. (1982). Diagnosing bugs in a simple procedural skill. In D. Sleeman & J. S. Brown (Eds.), *Intelligent tutoring systems* (pp. 157–183). New York, Academic Press.

Campbell, L. (1997). Variations on a theme: How teachers interpret MI theory. *Educational Leadership, 55*(1), 14–18.

Campbell, R. N. (1928). *An account of the principles of measurement and calculations.* London: Longmans, Green.

Carey, L. M. (1994). *Measuring and evaluating school learning.* (2nd ed.) Boston: Allyn and Bacon.

Carlson, S. B. (1985). *Creative classroom testing: Ten designs for assessment and instruction.* Princeton, NJ: Educational Testing Service.

Carmona, J. (1997, November). New products streamline testing and assessment. *T.H.E. Journal*, pp. 18, 20, 22, 24.

Carroll, J. B. (1961). The nature of the data or how to choose a correlation coefficient. *Psychometrika, 26*, 347–372.

Carroll, J. B. (1963). A model of school learning. *Teachers College Record, 64*, 723–733.

Carroll, J. B. (1974). The aptitude-achievement distinction: The case of foreign language aptitude and proficiency. In D. R. Green (Ed.), *The aptitude-achievement distinction: Proceedings of the Second CTB/McGraw-Hill Conference on Issues in Educational Measurement.* Monterey, CA: CTB/McGraw-Hill, Inc.

Cashen, V. M., & Ramseyer, G. C. (1969). The use of separate answer sheets by primary age children. *Journal of Educational Measurement, 6*, 155–158.

Champagne, A. B., Hoz, R., & Klopfer, L. E. (1984). *Construct validation of the cognitive structure of physics concepts.* Paper presented at the annual meeting of the American Educational Research Association, New Orleans.

Champagne, A. B., & Klopfer, L. E. (1980). *Using the ConSAT: A memo to teachers.* (LRDC Reports to Educators RTE/4). Pittsburgh, PA: University of Pittsburgh, Learning Research and Development Center.

Champagne, A. B., Klopfer, L. E. (no date). *Research in science education: The cognitive perspective.* Unpublished manuscript, University of Pittsburgh, Pittsburgh, PA.

Champagne, A. B., Klopfer, L. E., & Gunstone, R. F. (1982). Cognitive research and the design of science instruction. *Educational Psychologist, 17*, 31–53.

Checkley, K. (1997). The first seven . . . and the eighth: A conversation with Howard Gardner. *Educational Leadership, 55*(1), 8–13.

Clark, J. L. (1992). The Toronto Board of Education's Benchmarks in Mathematics. *The Arithmetic Teacher: Mathematics Education Through the Middle Grades, 39*(6), 51–55.

Clarke, J. H. (1990). *Patterns of thinking: Integrating learning skills in content thinking.* Boston: Allyn & Bacon.

Clarridge, P. B., & Whitaker, E. M. (1997). *Rolling the elephant over: How to effect large-scale change in the reporting process.* Portsmouth, NH: Heinemann.

Cleary, T. A. (1968). Test bias: Prediction of grades of negro and white students in integrated colleges. *Journal of Educational Measurement, 5*, 115–124.

Coffman, W. E. (1971). Essay examinations. In R. L. Thorndike (Ed.), *Educational measurement* (2nd ed.). Washington, DC: American Council on Education.

Cohen, J. (1960). A coefficient of agreement for nominal scales. *Educational and Psychological Measurement, 20*, 37–46.

Cohen, S. A., & Hyman, J. S. (1991). Can fantasies become facts? *Educational Measurement: Issues and Practice, 10*(1), 20–23.

Cole, N. S. (1973). Bias in selection. *Journal of Educational Measurement, 10*, 237–255.

Cole, N. S. (1978, March). *Approaches to examining bias in achievement test items.* Paper presented at the annual meeting of the American Personnel and Guidance Association, Washington, DC.

Cole, N. S., & Hanson, G. R. (1975). Impact of interest inventories on career choice. In E. E. Diamond (Ed.), *Issues of sex bias and sex fairness in career interest measurement.* Washington, DC: Career Education Program, National Institute of Education, Department of Health, Education, and Welfare.

Cole, N. S., & Nitko, A. J. (1981). Instrumentation and bias: Issues in selecting measures for educational evaluations. In R. A. Berk (Ed.), *Educational evaluation methodology: The state of the art.* Baltimore: Johns Hopkins University Press.

Cole, N. S., & Moss, P. A. (1989). Bias in test use. In R. L. Linn (Ed.), *Educational measurement* (3rd ed., pp. 201–219). Englewood Cliffs, NJ: Merrill/Prentice Hall.

Collis, K. F. (1991). *Assessment of the learned structure in elementary mathematics and science.* Paper presented at the Assessment in the Mathematical Sciences Conference, Victoria, Australia.

Connolly, A. J., Nachtman, W., & Pritchett, E. M. (1976). *Manual: KeyMath diagnostic arithmetic test.* Circle Pines, MN: American Guidance Service.

Consulting Psychologists Press, Inc. (1994). *Strong interest inventory.* Palo Alto, CA: Author.

Cowan, J. (1972). Is freedom of choice in examinations such an advantage? *The Technical Journal*, February.

Crane, L., & Bellis, D. (1978). *Preliminary results of Illinois pilot district edits.* Unpublished memorandum to Technical Assistance Center Directors. October 16, no city.

Cronbach, L. J. (1951). Coefficient alpha and the internal structure of tests. *Psychometrika, 16*, 297–334.

Cronbach, L. J. (1963). Course improvement through evaluation. *Teachers College Report* (Publication no. 64), 672–683.

Cronbach, L. J. (1971). Test validation. In R. L. Thorndike (Ed.), *Educational measurement* (2nd ed.). Washington, DC: American Council on Education.

Cronbach, L. J. (1977). *Educational psychology* (3rd ed.). New York: Harcourt Brace Jovanovich.

Cronbach, L. J. (1988). Five perspectives on validity argument. In H. Wainer (Ed.), *Test validity* (pp. 3–17). Hillsdale, NJ: Erlbaum.

Cronbach, L. J. (1989). Construct validation after thirty years. In R. L. Linn (Ed.), *Intelligence: Measurement, theory, and public policy* (pp. 147–171). Urbana: University of Illinois Press.

Cronbach, L. J. (1990). *Essentials of psychological testing* (5th ed.). New York: Harper & Row.

Cronbach, L. J., & Gleser, G. C. (1965). *Psychological tests and personnel decisions* (2nd ed.). Urbana: University of Illinois Press.

Cronbach, L. J., & Snow, R. E. (1977). *Aptitudes and instructional methods: A handbook for research on interactions.* New York: Irvington.

CTB Macmillan/McGraw-Hill (1992). *Listening and speaking checklist, Grades 9–12: California Achievement Tests* (5th ed.). Monterey, CA: Author.

CTB/McGraw-Hill. (1985). *Kuder occupational interest survey, Form DD.* Monterey, CA: Author.

CTB/McGraw-Hill. (1993). *California achievement tests, Class management guide* (5th ed.). Monterey, CA: Author.

CTB/McGraw-Hill. (1994). *Catalogue of CTB/McGraw-Hill.* Monterey, CA: Author.

CTB/McGraw-Hill (1997). *Winter norms book: TerraNova.* Monterey, CA: Author.

Culler, R. E., & Holahan, C. J. (1980). Test anxiety and academic performance: The effects of study-related behaviors. *Journal of Educational Psychology, 72,* 16–20.

Curtis, F. D. (1943). Types of thought questions in textbooks of science. *Science Education, 27,* 60–67.

Cyert, R. M. (1980). Problem solving and educational policy. In D. T. Tuma & F. Reif (Eds.), *Problem solving and education: Issues in teaching and research.* Hillsdale, NJ: Erlbaum.

Darley, J. G., & Hagenah, T. (1955). *Vocational interest measurement.* Minneapolis: University of Minnesota Press.

Darlington, R. B. (1971). Another look at "cultural fairness." *Journal of Educational Measurement, 8,* 71–82.

Darlington, R. B. (1976). A defense of "rational" personnel selection, and two new methods. *Journal of Educational Measurement, 13,* 43–52.

Davey, B., & Rindone, D. A. (1990, April). *Anatomy of a performance task.* Paper presented at the annual meeting of the American Educational Research Association, Boston.

Davis, B. G., & Trimble, C. S. (1978). *Consumable booklets vs. single answer sheets with nonconsumable booklets.* Frankfort: Kentucky State Department of Education. (ERIC Document Reproduction Service No. ED 160–656).

Davis, R. V. (1980). Measuring interests. In D. A. Payne (Ed.), *New directions for testing and measurement: Recent developments in affective measurement* (no. 7). San Francisco: Jossey-Bass.

DeLandsheere, V. (1988). Taxonomies of educational objectives. In J. P. Keeves (Ed.), *Educational research, methodology, and measurement: An international handbook* (pp. 345–354). Oxford: Pergamon Press.

DeVito, P. J., & Long, J. V. (1977, April). *The effects of spring-spring vs. fall-spring testing upon the evaluation of compensatory educational programs.* Paper presented at the annual convention of the American Educational Research Association, New York City.

Diamond, J. J., & Evans, W. J. (1972). An investigation of the cognitive correlates of test-wiseness. *Journal of Educational Measurement, 9,* 145–150.

Donlon, T. F., & Angoff, W. H. (1971). The Scholastic Aptitude Test. In W. H. Angoff (Ed.), *The College Board Admissions Testing Program: A technical report on research and development activities relating to the Scholastic Aptitude Test and Achievement Tests.* New York: College Entrance Examination Board.

Doolittle, P. (1994). *ERIC/AE Test Locator Service.* Washington, DC: ERIC/AE.

Dorans, N. J. (1994, May). *Choosing and evaluating a scale transformation: Centering and realigning SAT score distributions.* Princeton, NJ: Educational Testing Service.

Douglas, H. R., & Tallmadge, M. (1934). How university students prepare for new type of examinations. *School and Society, 39,* 318–320.

Downing, S. M., Baranowski, R. A., Grosso, L. J., & Norcini, J. J. (1995). Stem type and cognitive ability measured: The validity evidence for multiple true-false items in medical specialty certification. *Applied Measurement in Education, 8,* 187–197.

Drake, L., Rudner, L., & Pierce, J. (1995). *Assessment and evaluation on the Internet.* Washington, DC: ERIC Clearinghouse on Assessment and Evaluation, Catholic University of America.

Dudycha, A. L., & Dudycha, L. W. (1972). Behavioral statistics: An historical perspective. In R. E. Kirk (Ed.), *Statistical issues: A reader for the behavioral sciences.* Monterey, CA: Brooks/Cole.

Dunbar, D. A., Float, B., & Lyman, F. J. (1980). *Report card revision steering committee final report.* Mount Lebanon, PA: Mt. Lebanon School District, November.

Dunbar, S. B., Koretz, D., & Hoover, H. D. (1991). Quality control in the development and use of performance assessments. *Applied Measurement in Education, 4*(4), 289–303.

Duran, R. P. (1989). Testing of linguistic minorities. In R. L. Linn (Ed.), *Educational measurement* (3rd ed., pp. 573–587). Englewood Cliffs, NJ: Merrill/Prentice Hall.

Duschl, R. A., & Gitomer, D. H. (1991). Epistemological perspectives on conceptual change: Implications for educational practice. *Journal of Research in Science Teaching, 28,* 839–858.

Ebel, R. L. (1951). Writing the test item. In E. F. Lindquist (Ed.), *Educational measurement.* Washington, DC: American Council on Education.

Ebel, R. L. (1965). *Measuring educational achievement.* Englewood Cliffs, NJ: Prentice-Hall.

Ebel, R. L. (1972). *Essentials of educational measurement* (2nd ed.). Englewood Cliffs, NJ: Prentice Hall.

Ebel, R. L. (1979). *Essentials of educational measurement* (3rd ed.). Englewood Cliffs, NJ: Prentice Hall.

Ebel, R. L., & Frisbie, D. A. (1991). *Essentials of educational measurement* (5th ed.). Englewood Cliffs, NJ: Prentice Hall.

Ebel, R. L., & Stuit, D. B. (1954). *Technical Bulletin No. 8.* Iowa City: University Examinations Service, State University of Iowa.

Educational Testing Service. (1986). *Test collection catalogue, Volume I: Achievement tests and measurement devices.* Phoenix: Oryx Press.

Educational Testing Service. (1987). *Test collection catalogue, Volume II: Vocational tests and measurement devices.* Phoenix: Oryx Press.

Egawa, K., & Azwell, T. (1995). Telling the story: Narrative reports. In T. Azwell and E. Schmar (Eds.), *Report on report cards: Alternatives to consider.* Portsmouth, NH: Heinemann.

Einhorn, H. J., & Bass, A. R. (1971). Methodological considerations relevant to discrimination in employment testing. *Psychological Bulletin, 75,* 261–269.

Ennis, R. H. (1985). Goals for a critical thinking curriculum. In A. Costa (Ed.), *Developing minds: A resource book for teaching thinking.* Alexandria, VA: Association for Supervision and Curriculum Development.

Equal Employment Opportunity Commission, Civil Service Commission, Department of Justice, Department of Labor, & Department of the Treasury. (1979). Adoption of questions and answers to clarify and provide a common interpretation of the uniform guidelines on employee section procedures. *Federal Register, 44* (Publication Number: 11996–12006).

Equal Employment Opportunity Commission, Civil Service Commission, Department of Labor, & Department of Justice (1978, August 25). Uniform guidelines on employee selection procedures. *Federal Register, 43* (Publication Number: 38290–38315).

Evaluation Center. (1995). *An independent evaluation of the Kentucky Instructional Results Information System (KIRIS).* Frankfort, KY: Kentucky Institute for Education Research.

Excelsior Software, Inc. (1991). *Excelsior 2 grade for Windows: Self-paced learning modules.* Greeley, CO: Author.

Feister, W. J., & Whitney, D. R. (1968). An interview with D. E. F. Linquist. *Epsilon Bulletin, 42,* 17–28.

Feldt, L. S. (1967). A note on the use of confidence bands to evaluate the reliability of a difference between two scores. *American Educational Research Journal, 4,* 139–145.

Feldt, L. S. (1976, December). *New uses of Iowa Tests of Educational Development as an instrument for evaluation.* Paper presented at the Sixty-first Annual Education Conference, Evaluation in the Schools, Iowa City.

Feldt, L. S., & Brennan, R. L. (1989). Reliability. In R. L. Linn (Ed.), *Educational measurement* (3rd ed.). Englewood Cliffs, NJ: Merrill/Prentice Hall.

Ferguson, R. L. (1970). A model for computer-assisted criterion-referenced measurement. *Education, 81,* 25–31.

Fillenbaum, S., & Rapoport, A. (1971). *Structures in the subjective lexicon.* New York: Academic Press.

Finley, C. J. (1977). *Errors in reporting data in Iowa.* Unpublished memorandums to Technical Assistance Center Directors, October 24, 1977.

Fischer, R. J. (1994). The Americans with Disabilities Act: Implications for measurement. *Educational Measurement: Issues and Practice, 13*(4), 17–26, 37.

Fisher, T. H. (1980). The courts and your minimum competency testing program—A guide to survival. *NCME Measurement in Education, 11*(1), 1–12.

Flanagan, J. C. (1967). Functional education for the seventies. *Phi Delta Kappan, 49,* 27–32.

Flanagan, J. C. (1969). Program for learning in accordance with needs. *Psychology in the Schools, 6,* 133–136.

Flaugher, R. L. (1978). The many definitions of test bias. *American Psychologist, 33,* 671–679.

Flavell, J. H. (1976). Metacognitive aspects of problem solving. In L. B. Resnick (Ed.), *The nature of intelligence* (pp. 231–235). Hillsdale, NJ: Erlbaum.

Fleming, M., & Chambers, B. (1983). Teacher-made tests: Windows on the classroom. *New Directions for Testing and Measurement, 19,* 29–38.

Forsyth, R. A. (1976, March). *Describing what Johnny can do.* (Iowa Testing Program, Occasional Paper, No. 17). Iowa City: University of Iowa.

Frank, L. K. (1939). Projective methods for the study of personality. *Journal of Psychology, 8,* 389–413.

Frederiksen, N. (1984). Implications of cognitive theory for instruction in problem-solving. *Review of Educational Research, 54,* 363–407.

Freeman, D. J., Kuhs, T. M., Knappen, L. B., & Porter, A. C. (1982). A closer look at standardized tests. *Arithmetic Teacher, 29*(7), 50–54.

Frisbie, D. A. (1992). The multiple true-false format: A status review. *Educational Measurement: Issues and Practice, 11*(4), 21–26.

Frisbie, D. A., & Becker, D. F. (1990). An analysis of textbook advice about true-false tests. *Applied Measurement in Education, 4,* 67–83.

Frisbie, D. A., & Waltman, K. K. (1992). Developing a personal grading plan. *Educational Measurement: Issues and Practice, 11*(3), 35–42.

Gaffney, R. F., & Maguire, T. O. (1971). Use of optically scored test answer sheets with young children. *Journal of Educational Measurement, 8,* 103–106.

Gagné, R. M. (1962). The acquisition of knowledge. *Psychological Review, 69,* 355–365.

Gagné, R. M. (1968). Learning hierarchies. *Educational Psychologist, 6,* 1–9.

Gagné, R. M. (1970). Instructional variables and learning outcomes. In M. C. Wittrock & F. Wiley (Eds.), *Evaluation of instruction.* New York: Holt, Rinehart & Winston.

Gagné, R. M., & Briggs, L. J. (1979). *Principles of instructional design* (2nd ed.). New York: Holt, Rinehart & Winston.

Gagné, R. M., Briggs, L. J., & Wagner, W. W. (1988). *Principles of instructional design* (3rd ed.). New York: Holt, Rinehart & Winston.

Gagné, R. M., Major, J. R., Garstens, H. L., & Paradise, N. E. (1962). Factors in acquiring knowledge of a mathematical task. *Psychological Monographs, 76* (7, whole No. 526).

Gagné, R. M., & Paradise, N. E. (1961). Abilities and learning sets in knowledge acquisition. *Psychological Monographs, 75* (14, whole No. 518).

Gardner, H. (1983). *Frames of mind: The theory of multiple intelligences.* New York: Basic Books.

Gardner, H. (1991). *The unschooled mind: How children think and how schools should teach.* New York: Basic Books.

Gardner, H. (1993). Educating for understanding. *American School Board Journal, 180,* 20–24.

Gick, M. L. (1986). Problem-solving strategies. *Educational Psychologist, 21,* 99–120.

Glaser, R. (1963). Instructional technology and the measurement of learning outcomes. *American Psychologist, 18,* 519–521.

Glaser, R. (1968). Adapting the elementary school curriculum to individual performances. *Proceedings of the 1967 Invitational Conference on Testing Problems,* 3–36. Princeton, NJ: Educational Testing Service.

Glaser, R. (1977) *Adaptive education: Individual diversity and learning.* New York: Holt, Rinehart & Winston.

Glaser, R. (1982). Instructional psychology: Past, present, and future. *American Psychologist, 37,* 292–305.

Glaser, R. (1984). Education and thinking: The role of knowledge. *American Psychologist, 39,* 93–104.

Glaser, R., Lesgold, A., & Lajoie, S. (1985). Toward a cognitive theory for the measurement of achievement. In R. R. Ronning, J. Gloveer, J. C. Conoley, & J. C. Witt (Ed.), *The influence of cognitive psychology on testing and measurement* (pp. 41–85). Hillsdale, NJ: Erlbaum.

Glaser, R., & Nitko, A. J. (1971). Measurement in learning and instruction. In R. L. Thorndike (Ed.), *Educational measurement* (2nd ed., pp. 625–670). Washington, DC: American Council on Education.

Gong, B., Venezky, R., & Mioduser, D. (1992). Instructional assessments: Level for systemic change in science education classrooms. *Journal of Science Education and Technology, 1,* 157–175.

Goodwin, D. L. (1966). *Training teachers in reinforcement techniques to increase student task-oriented behavior: An experimental evaluation.* Unpublished doctoral dissertation, Stanford University. (Cited in L. J. Cronbach, G. C. Gleser, H. Nanda & N. Rajaratnam, (1972). *The dependability of behavioral measurements: Theory of generalizability of scores and profiles.* New York: John Wiley.)

Gow, D. T. (Ed.). (1976). *Design and development of curricular materials: Instructional design articles* (Vol. 2). Pittsburgh: University Center for International Studies, University of Pittsburgh.

Green, K. (1984). Effects of item characteristics on multiple-choice item difficulty. *Educational and Psychological Measurement, 44,* 551–561.

Greene, H. A., Jorgensen, A. N., & Gerberich, J. R. (1942). *Measurement and evaluation in the elementary school.* New York: Longmans, Green.

Greene, H. A., Jorgensen, A. N., & Gerberich, J. R. (1943). *Measurement and evaluation in the secondary school.* New York: Longmans, Green.

Greeno, J. G. (1976). Cognitive objectives of instruction: Theory of knowledge for solving problems and answering questions. In D. Klahr (Ed.), *Cognition and instruction.* Hillsdale, NJ: Lawrence Erlbaum.

Greeno, J. G. (1978). Nature of problem-solving abilities. In W. K. Estes (Ed.), *Handbook of learning and cognitive processes: Vol. 5.* Hillsdale, NJ: Lawrence Erlbaum.

Gronlund, N. E. (1973). *Preparing criterion-referenced tests for classroom instruction.* New York: Macmillan.

Gronlund, N. E. (1976). *Measurement and evaluation in teaching* (3rd ed.). Englewood Cliffs, NJ: Merrill/Prentice Hall.

Gross, A. L., & Su, W. (1975). Defining a "fair" or "unbiased" selection model: A question of utilities. *Journal of Applied Psychology, 60,* 345–351.

Grossman, H. J. (1983). *Classification in mental retardation.* Washington, DC: American Association on Mental Deficiency.

Gulliksen, H. (1950). *Theory of mental tests.* New York: John Wiley & Sons.

Gulliksen, H. (1986). Perspective on educational measurement. *Applied Psychological Measurement, 10,* 109–132.

Haertel, E., & Calfee, R. (1983). School achievement: Thinking about what to test. *Journal of Educational Measurement, 20,* 119–131.

Hakstain, A. R. (1969, February). *The effects of type of examination anticipated on student test preparation and performance.* Paper presented at the annual meeting of the American Educational Research Association, Washington, DC.

Haladyna, T. M., & Downing, S. M. (1989a). A taxonomy of multiple-choice item-writing rules. *Applied Measurement in Education, 2,* 37–50.

Haladyna, T. M., & Downing, S. M. (1989b). Validity of a taxonomy of multiple-choice item-writing rules. *Applied Measurement in Education, 2,* 51–78.

Hambleton, R. K., & Murphy, E. (1992). A psychometric perspective on authentic measurement. *Applied Measurement in Education, 5,* 1–16.

Hambleton, R. K., & Sheehan, D. S. (1977). On the evaluation of higher-order science instructional objectives. *Science Education, 61,* 307–315.

Hardy, R. A. (1984). Measuring instructional validity: A report of an instrumental validity study for the Alabama High School Graduation Examination. *Journal of Educational Measurement, 21,* 291–301.

Harmin, M. (1994). *Inspiring active learning: A handbook for teachers.* Alexandria, VA: Association for Supervision and Curriculum Development.

Harris, W. S. (1973). Agreement among NCME members on selected issues in educational measurement. *Journal of Educational Measurement, 10*, 63–70.

Harrow, A. J. (1972). *A taxonomy of the psychomotor domain: A guide for developing behavioral objectives.* White Plains, NY: Longman.

Hawkes, H. E., Lindquist, E. F., & Mann, C. R. (Eds.) (1936). *The construction and use of achievement examinations: A manual for secondary school teachers.* Boston: Houghton Mifflin.

Helmke, A. (1988). The role of classroom context factors for the achievement-impairing effects of test anxiety. *Anxiety Research, 1*, 37–52.

Hembree, R. (1988). Correlates, causes, effects and treatment of test anxiety. *Review of Educational Research, 58*, 47–77.

Henrysson, S. (1971). Gathering, analyzing, and using data on test items. In R. L. Thorndike (Ed.), *Educational measurement* (2nd ed.). Washington, DC: American Council on Education.

Herman, J. L., Aschbacher, P. R., & Winters, L. (1992). *A practical guide to alternative assessment.* Alexandria, VA: Association for Supervision and Curriculum Development.

Herman, W. E. (1990). Fear of failure as a distinctive personality trait measure of test anxiety. *Journal of Research and Development in Education, 23*, 180–185.

Herndon, E. B. (1980). *Your child and testing.* Washington, DC: National Institute of Education, U.S. Department of Education.

Hewson, M. G. A. B., & Hamlyn, D. (1984). The influence of intellectual environment on conceptions of heat. *European Journal of Science Education, 6*, 245–262.

Hieronymus, A. N. (1976, December). *Uses of Iowa tests of basic skills in evaluation.* Paper presented at the 61st Annual Education Conferences, Iowa City, IA.

Hieronymus, A. N., & Lindquist, E. F. (1971). *Iowa tests of basic skills: Teacher's guide to administration, interpretation, and use* (Levels Edition, Form 6). Iowa City: Riverside Publishing.

Hieronymus, A. N., & Lindquist, E. F. (1974a) *Iowa tests of basic skills: Manual for administrators, supervisors, and counselors* (Levels edition, Forms 5 and 6). Iowa City: Riverside Publishing.

Hieronymus, A. N., & Lindquist, E. F. (1974b). *Iowa tests of basic skills: Teacher's guide for administration, interpretation, and use* (Forms 5 and 6). Iowa City: Riverside Publishing.

Highland, R. W. (1955). *A guide for use in performance testing in Air Force technical schools* (ASPRL-TM-55-1). Lowry Air Force Base, CO: Armament Systems Performance Personnel Research Laboratory.

Hills, J. R. (1976). *Exercises in classroom measurement.* Englewood Cliffs, NJ: Merrill/Prentice Hall.

Hills, J. R. (1990). Response to two letters: Grading practices and improving standardized test scores. *Educational Measurement: Issues and Practice, 9*(3), 33.

Hirsch, E. D., Jr. (1977). *The philosophy of composition.* Chicago: University of Chicago Press.

Holland, J. L. (1973). *Making vocational choices: A theory of careers.* Englewood Cliffs, NJ: Prentice Hall.

Holland, J. L. (1975). The use and evaluation of interest inventories. In E. E. Diamond (Ed.), *Issues of sex bias and sex fairness in career interest measurement.* Washington, DC: Career Education Program, National Institute of Education, Department of Health, Education, and Welfare.

Hoover, H. D., Hieronymus, A. N., Frisbie, D. A., & Dunbar, S. B. (1993a). *Directions for administration: Iowa Tests of Basic Skills, Levels 9–14, Forms K and L.* Chicago: Riverside Publishing.

Hoover, H. D., Hieronymus, A. N., Frisbie, D. A., & Dunbar, S. (1993b). *Interpretive guide for teachers and counselors: Iowa Tests of Basic Skills, Levels 9–14, Forms K and L.* Chicago: Riverside Publishing.

Hoover, H. D., Hieronymus, A. N., Frisbie, D. A., & Dunbar, S. B. (1993c). *Iowa Tests of Basic Skills: Norms and score conversions, complete and core batteries, Form K.* Chicago: Riverside Publishing.

Hoover, H. D., Hieronymus, A. N., Frisbie, D. A., & Dunbar, S. B. (1993d). *Iowa Tests of Basic Skills: Score conversions, complete and core batteries, Form K.* Chicago: Riverside Publishing.

Hopkins, K. D., Stanley, J. C., & Hopkins, B. R. (1990). *Educational and psychological measurement and evaluation* (7th ed.). Englewood Cliffs, NJ: Prentice Hall.

Horvath, F. G. (1991). *Assessment in Alberta: Dimensions of authenticity.* Paper presented at the annual meeting of the National Association of Test Directors and the National Council on Measurement in Education, Chicago, IL.

Huynh, H. (1976). On the reliability of decisions in domain-referenced testing. *Journal of Educational Measurement, 13*, 253–264.

Ismail, M. (1994). *Development and validation of a multicomponent diagnostic test of arithmetic word problem solving ability for sixth-grade students in Malaysia.* Unpublished doctoral dissertation, Pittsburgh, PA: University of Pittsburgh.

Iwanicki, E. F. (1980). A new generation of standardized achievement test batteries: A profile of their major features. *Journal of Educational Measurement, 17*, 155–162.

Jaeger, R. M. (1973). The national test-equating study in reading: Pre-Anchor Test Study. *NCME Measurement in Education, 4*, 1–8.

Jaeger, R. M. (1989). Certification of student competence. In R. L. Linn (Ed.), *Educational measurement* (3rd ed., pp. 485–514). Englewood Cliffs, NJ: Merrill/Prentice Hall.

Jakwerth, P. R., Stancavage, F. B., & Reed, E. D. (1999). *An investigation of why students do not respond to questions.* (NAEP validity studies). Palo Alto, CA: American Institutes for Research.

Jenkins, J. R., & Deno, S. J. (1971). Assessing knowledge of concepts and principles. *Journal of Educational Measurement, 8*(1), 95–101.

Johnson, H. M. (1928). Some fallacies underlying the use of psychological tests. *Psychological Review, 35*, 328–337. Reprinted in T. Engen & N. Levy (Eds.), *Selected readings in the history of mental measurement* (1955). Providence, RI: Brown University.

Johnson, H. M. (1936). Pseudo-mathematics in the mental and social sciences. *American Journal of Psychology, 48*, 342–351. Reprinted in T. Engen & N. Levy (Eds.), *Selected readings in the history of mental measurement* (1955). Providence, RI: Brown University.

Johnson, P. E. (1967). Some psychological aspects of subject-matter structure. *Journal of Educational Psychology, 58*, 75–85.

Johnson, R. T., & Thomas, W. P. (1979, April). *User experiences in implementing the RMC Title I evaluation modes.* Paper presented at the annual meeting of the American Educational Research Association, San Francisco.

Joint Advisory Committee on Testing Practices. (1993). *Principles for fair assessment practices for education in Canada.* Edmonton, Alberta: Author.

Joint Committee on Standards for Educational Evaluation. (1988). *The personnel evaluation standards: How to assess systems for evaluating educators.* Newbury Park, CA: Sage.

Joint Committee on Standards for Educational Evaluation. (1994). *Standards for evaluations of educational programs.* Washington, DC: Author.

Joint Committee on Standards for Educational Evaluation. (1994). *The program evaluation standards: How to assess evaluations of educational programs.* Thousand Oaks, CA: Sage.

Joint Committee on Testing Practices. (1988). *Code of fair testing practices in education.* Washington, DC: American Psychological Association.

Jones, L. V. (1971). The nature of measurement. In R. L. Thorndike (Ed.), *Educational measurement* (2nd ed.). Washington, DC: American Council on Education.

Jones, R. W. (1994). *Performance and alternative assessment techniques: Meeting the challenges of alternative evaluation strategies.* Paper presented at the Second International Conference on Educational Evaluation and Assessment, Pretoria, Republic of South Africa.

Ju, T-P. (1989). *The development of a microcomputer-assisted measurement tool to display a person's knowledge structure.* Unpublished doctoral dissertation. Pittsburgh, PA: University of Pittsburgh.

Kane, M. (1992). An argument-based approach to validity. *Psychological Bulletin, 112*, 527–535.

Karweit, N. L., & Wasik, B. A. (1992). *A review of the effects of extra-year kindergarten programs and transitional first grades.* (CDS Report 41). Baltimore: Center for Research on Effective Schooling for Disadvantaged Students, Johns Hopkins University.

Kaufman, A. S., & Kaufman, N. L. (1995). *Interpretive manual for the Kaufman Assessment Battery for Children.* Circle Pines, MN: American Guidance Service.

Keller, F. S. (1968). Goodbye teacher. *Journal of Applied Behavior Analysis, 1*, 79–89.

Keller, F. S., & Sherman, J. G. (1974). *PSI: The Keller Plan handbook.* Menlo Park, CA: Benjamin-Cummings.

Kelly, T. L. (1939). The selection of upper and lower groups for the validation of test items. *Journal of Educational Psychology, 30*, 17–24.

Kentucky Department of Education (1993a). *KIRIS Assessment Portfolio: Mathematics, Grade 4, 1993–1994*. Frankfort, KY: Office of Assessment and Accountability.

Kentucky Department of Education (1993b). *Portfolios and you*. Frankfort, KY: Office of Assessment and Accountability.

Kentucky Department of Education (1993c). *Teacher's guide: Kentucky mathematics portfolio*. Frankfort, KY: Office of Assessment and Accountability.

Kentucky Department of Education (1994). *KIRIS Mathematics Portfolio Assessment, Grade 8: Scoring Training Manual, 1992–93, Addenda 1994*. Frankfort, KY: Office of Assessment and Accountability, Author.

Khattri, N., Reeve, A.L., & Adamson, R.J. (1997). *Studies of education reform: Assessment of student performance*. Washington, DC: Office of Educational Research and Improvement.

King, W. L., & Janow, J. E. (1990). *Testing accommodations for students with disabilities*. Washington, DC: Association on Handicapped Student Services in Postsecondary Education.

Kintsch, W. (1974). *The prepresentation of meaning in memory*. Hillsdale, NJ: Lawrence Erlbaum.

Klaus, C. H., Lloyd-Jones, R., Brown, R., Littlefair, W., Mullis, I., Miller, D., & Verity, D. (1979). *Composing childhood experience: An approach to writing and learning in the elementary grades* (Experimental version). St. Louis: CEMREL.

Klausmeier, H. J. (1975). An alternative form of schooling. In K. Talmage (Ed.), *Systems of individual education*. Berkeley, CA: McCutchan.

Klopfer, L. E. (1969). *An operational definition of "understand."* Unpublished manuscript, Learning Research and Development Center, University of Pittsburgh.

Klopfer, L. E. (1971). Evaluation of learning in science. In B. S. Bloom, J. T. Hastings, & G. F. Madaus (Eds.), *Handbook on formative and summative evaluation of student learning*. New York: McGraw-Hill.

Koretz, D., Stecher, B., Klein, S., & McCaffrey, D. (1994). The Vermont portfolio assessment program: Findings and implications. *Educational Measurement: Issues and Practice, 13*(3), 5–16.

Kracke, E. A. (1953). *Civil service in early Sung China: 960–1067*. Cambridge, MA: Harvard University Press.

Krathwohl, D. R., Bloom, B. S., & Masia, B. B. (1964). *Taxonomy of educational objectives: Book 2: Affective domain*. White Plains, NY: Longman.

Kryspin, W. J., & Feldhusen, J. F. (1974). *Developing classroom tests*. Minneapolis, MN: Burgess.

Kuder, G. F., & Richardson, M. W. (1937). The theory of the estimation of test reliability. *Psychometrika, 2*, 151–160.

Kuhn, D. (1999). A developmental model of critical thinking. *Educational Researcher, 28*(2), 16–25, 46.

Kunder, L. H., & Porwoll, P. J. (1977). *Reporting student progress: Policies, procedures, and systems*. Arlington, VA: Educational Research Service.

Landau, D., & Lazarsfeld, P. F. (1968). Quetelet, Adolphe. *International encyclopedia of the social sciences, 13*, 247–257.

Lane, S. (1992). The conceptual framework for the development of a mathematics performance assessment instrument. *Educational Measurement: Issues and Practice, 12*(2), 16–23.

Lane, S., Parke, C., & Moskal, B. (1992). *Principles for developing performance assessments*. Paper presented at the annual meeting of the American Educational Research Association, San Francisco.

Langenfeld, T. E., & Crocker, L. M. (1994). The evaluation of validity theory: Public school testing, the courts, and incompatible interpretations. *Educational Assessment, 2*, 149–165.

Lawshe, C. H., & Balma, M. J. (1966). *Principles of personnel testing* (2nd ed.). New York: McGraw-Hill.

Liebert, R. M., & Morris, L. W. (1967). Cognitive and emotional components of test anxiety: A distinction and some initial data. *Psychological Reports, 20*, 975–978.

Lindquist, E. F. (1936). The theory of test construction. In H. E. Hawkes, E. F. Lindquist, & C. R. Mann (Eds.), *The construction and use of achievement examinations: A manual for secondary school teachers*. Boston: Houghton Mifflin.

Lindquist, E. F. (1951). Preliminary considerations in objective test construction. In E. F. Lindquist (Ed.), *Educational measurement*. Washington, DC: American Council on Education.

Lindquist, E. F., & Mann, C. R. (1936). The construction of tests. In H. E. Hawkes, E. F. Lindquist, & C. R. Mann (Eds.), *The construction and use of achievement examinations: A manual for secondary school teachers*. Boston: Houghton Mifflin.

Lindvall, C. M. (1964). Introduction. In C. M. Lindvall (Ed.), *Defining educational objectives: A report of the Regional Commission on Educational Coordination and the Learning Research and Development Center*. Pittsburgh: University of Pittsburgh Press.

Lindvall, C. M. (1967). *Measuring pupil achievement and aptitude*. New York: Harcourt, Brace and World.

Lindvall, C. M. (1976). Criteria for stating IPI objectives. In D. T. Gow (Ed.), *Design and development of curricular materials: Instructional design articles* (Vol. 2). Pittsburgh, PA: University Center for International Studies, University of Pittsburgh.

Lindvall, C. M., & Bolvin, J. O. (1967). Programmed instruction in the schools: An application of programming principles in "Individually Prescribed Instruction." In P. Lange (Ed.), *Programmed instruction: 66th Yearbook, Part II* (pp. 217–254). Chicago: National Society for the Study of Education.

Lindvall, C. M., & Cox, R. C. (1970). Evaluation as a tool in curriculum development: The IPI evaluation program. *AERA Monograph Series on Curriculum Evaluation* (Publication No. 5). Chicago: Rand McNally.

Lindvall, C. M., & Nitko, A. J. (1975). *Measuring pupil achievement and aptitude* (2nd ed.). New York: Harcourt Brace Jovanovich.

Linn, R. L. (1973). Fair test use in selection. *Review of Educational Research, 43*, 139–161.

Linn, R. L. (1993). Educational assessment: Expanded expectations and challenges. *Educational Evaluation and Policy Analysis, 15*, 1–16.

Linn, R. L. (1994). Performance assessment: Policy, promises, and technical measurement standards. *Educational Researcher, 23*(4), 4–14.

Linn, R. L., & Baker, E. (1997). CRESST conceptual model for assessment. *Evaluation Comment, 7*(1), 1–22, Summer.

Linn, R. L., Baker, E. L., & Dunbar, S. B. (1991). Complex, performance-based assessment: Expectations and validation criteria. *Educational Researcher, 20*(8), 5–21.

Linn, R. L., & Burton, D. (1994). Performance-based assessment: Implications of task specificity. *Educational Measurement: Issues and Practice, 13*(1), 5, 8, 15.

Linn, R. L., & Gronlund, N. E. (1995). *Measurement and assessment in teaching* (7th ed.). Englewood Cliffs, NJ: Prentice Hall.

Loevinger, J., Wessler, R., & Redmore, C. (1970). *Measuring ego development. Vol. 1: Construction and use of a sentence completion test; Vol. 2: Scoring manual for women and girls*. San Francisco: Jossey-Bass.

Lohnes, P. R., & Cooley, W. W. (1968). *Introduction to statistical procedures: With computer exercises*. NY: John Wiley & Sons.

Lord, F. M. (1953). The relation of test scores to the trait underlying the test. *Educational and Psychological Measurement, 13*, 517–549.

Lord, F. M. (1977). A study of item bias using item characteristic curve theory. In Y. H. Poortinga (Ed.), *Basic problems in cross-cultural psychology*. Amsterdam: Swets and Vitlinger.

Lord, F. M., & Novick, M. R. (1968). *Statistical theories of mental test scores*. Reading, MA: Addison-Wesley.

Lyman, H. B. (1998). *Test scores and what they mean* (6th ed.). Boston: Allyn & Bacon.

Mandler, G., & Sarason, S. B. (1952). A study of anxiety and learning. *Journal of Abnormal and Social Psychology, 47*, 166–173.

Marshall, J. C. (1967). Composition errors and essay examinations grades reexamined. *American Educational Research Journal, 4*, 375–385.

Marshall, J. C., & Powers, J. M. (1969). Writing neatness, composition errors, and essay grades. *Journal of Educational Measurement, 6*, 97–101.

Marshall, S. P. (1990). Generating good items for diagnostic tests. In N. Frederiksen, R. Glaser, A. Lesgold, & M. G. Shafto (Eds.), *Diagnostic monitoring of skill and knowledge acquisition* (pp. 433–452). Hillsdale, NJ: Lawrence Erlbaum.

Marshall, S. P., Pribe, C. A., & Smith, J. D. (1987). *Schema knowledge structure for representing and understanding arithmetic story problems*. (Report No. SE 047 910). San Diego: San Diego State University, Center for Research in Mathematics and Science Education. (ERIC Document Reproduction Service No. ED 281 716).

Marzano, R. J., Brandt, R. S., Hughes, C. S., Jones, B. F., Presseisan, B. Z., Rankin,

S. C., & Suhor, C. (1988). *Dimensions of thinking: A framework for curriculum and instruction*. Alexandria, VA: Association for Supervision and Curriculum Development.

Marzano, R. J., Pickering, D. J., Arredondo, D. E., Blackburn, G. J., Brandt, R. S., & Moffett, C. A. (1992). *Dimensions of Learning Teacher's Manual*. Alexandria, VA: Association for Supervision and Curriculum Development.

Marzano, R. J., Pickering, D., & McTighe, J. (1993). *Assessing student outcomes: Performance assessment using the Dimensions of Learning Model*. Alexandria, VA: Association for Supervision and Curriculum Development.

Matter, K. K. (1989). Putting test scores in perspective: Communicating a complete report card for your schools. In L. M. Rudner, J. C. Conoley, and B. S. Plake (Eds.), *Understanding achievement tests: A guide for school administrators* (pp. 121–129). Washington, DC: ERIC Clearinghouse on Tests, Measurements, and Evaluation.

Mayer, R. E., Larkin, J. H., & Kadane, J. B. (1984). A cognitive analysis of mathematical problem-solving ability. In R. J. Sternberg (Ed.), *Advances in the psychology of human intelligence*. Hillsdale, NJ: Lawrence Erlbaum.

McConney, A., & Ayres, R. R. (1998). Assessing student teachers' assessments. *Journal of Teacher Education, 49*, 140–150.

McCormick, R. A. (1974). Proxy consent in the experimental situation. *Perspectives in Biology and Medicine, 18*, 2–20.

McDonnell, L. (1997). *The politics of state testing: Implementing new student assessments*. CSE Technical Report 424. Los Angeles: National Center for Research on Evaluation, Standards, and Student Testing, UCLA.

McGregor, D. M. (1935). Scientific measurement and psychology. *Psychological Review, 24*, 246–266.

McKachie, W. J., Pollie, D., & Spiesman, J. (1985). Relieving anxiety in classroom examinations. *Journal of Abnormal and Social Psychology, 50*, 93–98.

Mealey, D. L., & Host, T. R. (1992). Coping with test anxiety. *College Teaching, 40*, 147–150.

Mehrens, W. A. (1991). Facts about samples, fantasies about domains. *Educational Measurement: Issues and Practice, 10*(2), 23–25.

Mehrens, W. A., & Kaminski, J. (1989). Methods for improving standardized test scores: Fruitful, fruitless, or fraudulent? *Educational Measurement: Issues and Practice, 8*(1), 14–22.

Mehrens, W. A., & Lehmann, I. J. (1991). *Measurement and evaluation in education and psychology* (4th ed.). Chicago: Holt, Rinehart, & Winston.

Mehrens, W. A., & Popham, W. J. (1992). How to evaluate the legal defensibility of high-stakes tests. *Applied Measurement in Education, 5*, 265–283.

Mercer, J. R. (1973). *Labeling the mentally retarded*. Berkeley, CA: University of California Press.

Merwin, J. C., & Womer, F. B. (1969). Evaluation in assessing the progress of education to provide bases of public understanding and public policy. In R. W. Tyler (Ed.), *Sixty-eighth yearbook of the National Society for the Study of Education (Part II): Educational evaluation. New roles. New means.* Chicago: University of Chicago Press.

Messick, S. (1989b). Validity. In R. L. Linn (Ed.), *Educational measurement* (3rd ed., pp. 13–103). Englewood Cliffs, NJ: Prentice Hall.

Messick, S. (1994a). The interplay of evidence and consequences in the validation of performance assessments. *Educational Researcher, 23*(2), 13–23.

Messick, S. (1994b, June). *Validity of psychological assessment: Validation of inferences from persons' responses and performances as scientific inquiry into score meaning*. Keynote address at the Conference on Contemporary Psychological Assessment, Stockholm, Sweden.

Meyer, G. (1939). The choice of questions on essay examinations. *Journal of Educational Psychology, 30*, 161–171.

Miller, M. D., & Seraphine, A. E. (1993). Can test scores remain authentic when teaching to the test? *Educational Assessment, 1*, 119–129.

Millman, J. (1961). *Multiple-choice test item construction rules*. Ithaca, NY: Cornell University Press (mimeographed). (Cited by J. C. Stanley & K. D. Hopkins (1972), *Educational and psychological measurement and evaluation* (5th ed.). Englewood Cliffs, NJ: Prentice Hall.

Millman, J., Bishop, C. H., & Ebel, R. L. (1965). An analysis of test-wiseness. *Educational and Psychological Measurement, 25*, 707–726.

Millman, J., & Green, J. (1989). The specification and development of tests of achievement and ability. (pp. 335–366) In R. L. Linn (Eds.), *Educational measurement* (3rd ed.). Phoenix, AZ: Oryx Press.

Minstrell, J., & Stimpson, V. C. (1990, April). *A teaching system for diagnosing student conceptions and prescribing relevant instruction*. Paper presented at the annual meeting of the American Educational Research Association, Boston.

Monroe, W. S., & Carter, R. E. (1923). The use of different types of thought questions in secondary schools and their relative difficulty for students. *University of Illinois Bulletin, 20*. (Bulletin N. 14).

Moss, P. A. (1992). Shifting conceptions of validity in educational measurement: Implications for performance assessment. *Review of Educational Research, 62*, 229–258.

Moss, P. A., Beck, J. S., Ebbs, C., Matson, B., Muchmore, J., Steele, D., Taylor, C., & Herter, R. (1992). Portfolios, accountability, and an interpretive approach to validity. *Educational Measurement: Issues and Practice, 11*, 12–21.

Moss, P. A., Cole, N. S., & Trent, E. R. (1979, October 24–26). *A comparison of multiple-choice answer formats in early elementary grades*. Paper presented at the Annual Meeting of the Northeast Educational Research Association, Mt. Pocono, PA.

Moyer, K. L. (1979, April). *Observed school district errors in the Title I evaluation and reporting system*. Harrisburg, PA: Division of Research, Pennsylvania Department of Education.

Muller, D., Calhoun, E., & Orling, R. (1972). Test reliability as a function of answer sheet mode. *Journal of Educational Measurement, 9*, 321–324.

Mullis, I. V. S. (1991). *The NAEP guide*. Princeton, NJ: National Assessment of Educational Progress, Educational Testing Service.

Murphy, L. B. (1956). *Methods for the study of personality in young children*. New York: Basic Books.

Murphy, L. L., Conoley, J. C., & Impara, J. C. (1998). *Tests in print V*. Lincoln, NE: University of Nebraska Press, Buros Institute of Mental Measurements.

Murray, H. A. (1938). *Explorations in personality*. New York: Oxford University Press.

National Assessment Governing Board. (1992). *Reading framework for the 1992 National Assessment of Educational Progress*. Washington, DC: U.S. Government Printing Office (Publication No. 316499/60006).

National Association of College Admission Counselors. (1988). *Statement of principles of good practices*. Alexandria, VA: Author.

National Board for Professional Teaching Standards. (1991, December 31). *Report to the U.S. Senate Committee on Labor and Human Relations and the U.S. House of Representative Committee on Education and Labor*. Detroit: Author.

National Council of Teachers of Mathematics (NCTM) (1989). *Curriculum and evaluation standards for school mathematics*. Reston, VA: Author.

National Council on Measurement in Education (NCME). (1995). *Code of professional responsibilities in educational measurement (CPR)*. Washington, DC: Author.

Naveh-Benjamin, M., McKeachie, W. J., & Lin, Y. G. (1987). Two types of test-anxious students: Support for an information processing model. *Journal of Educational Psychology, 79*, 131–136.

Naveh-Benjamin, M., McKeachie, W. J., Lin, Y. G., & Tucker, D. G. (1986). Inferring students' cognitive structures and their development using the "Ordered Tree Technique." *Journal of Educational Psychology, 78*(2), 130–140.

Nitko, A. J. (1980). Distinguishing the many varieties of criterion-referenced tests. *Review of Educational Research, 50*, 461–485.

Nitko, A. J. (1983). *Educational tests and measurement: An introduction*. San Diego: Harcourt Brace Jovanovich.

Nitko, A. J. (1984). Defining "criterion-referenced test." In R. A. Berk (Ed.), *A guide to criterion-referenced test construction* (pp. 8–28). Baltimore, MD: Johns Hopkins University Press.

Nitko, A. J. (1989). Designing tests that are integrated with instruction. In R. L. Linn (Ed.), *Educational measurement* (3rd ed., pp. 447–474). New York: Macmillan.

Nitko, A. J. (1995). Curriculum-based continuous assessment: A framework for concepts, politics, and procedures. *Assessment in Education: Principles, Policy, and Practice, 2*.

Nitko, A. J. (1996). *Educational assessment of students* (2nd ed.). Englewood, NJ: Prentice Hall/Merrill Education.

Nitko, A. J., Al-Sarimi, A., Amedahe, F. K., Wang, S., & Wingert, M. (1998, April).

How well are the Kentucky Academic Expectations matched to the KIRIS assessments, the CTBS, and the CAT? Paper presented at the annual meeting of the American Educational Research Association, San Diego (ED420677).

Nitko, A. J., & Hsu, T-C. (1974). Using domain-referenced tests for student placement, diagnosis, and attainment in a system of adaptive, individualized instruction. In W. Hively (Ed.), *Domain-referenced testing.* Englewood Cliffs, NJ: Educational Technology Publications.

Nitko, A. J., & Hsu, T-C. (1987). *Teacher's guide to better classroom testing: A judgmental approach.* Pittsburgh, PA: Institute for Practice and Research in Education, School of Education, University of Pittsburgh.

Nitko, V. V. (1995). Personal communication, March.

Niyogi, N. S. (1995). *Capturing the power of classroom assessment.* (Focus 28). Princeton, NJ: Educational Testing Service.

Norris, S. P., & Ennis, R. H. (1989). Evaluating critical thinking. Pacific Grove, CA: Midwest Publications, Critical Thinking Press.

Northwest Regional Educational Laboratory (1998). *Improving classroom assessment: A toolkit for professional developers* (2nd ed.). Portland, OR: Author.

Novick, M. R., & Peterson, N. S. (1976). Towards equalizing educational and employment opportunity. *Journal of Educational Measurement, 13,* 77–88.

Nunnally, J. C. (1967). *Psychometric theory.* New York: McGraw-Hill.

Nurss, J. (1994). *Metropolitan performance assessment.* San Antonio: Psychological Corporation.

Odell, C. W. (1928). *Traditional examinations and new-type tests.* New York: Century Co.

O'Donnell, T. J. (1974). Informed consent. *Journal of the American Medical Association, 227,* 73.

Oosterhof, A. (1994). *Classroom applications of educational measurement.* (2nd ed.). Englewood Cliffs, NJ: Merrill/Prentice Hall.

Oosterhof, A. & Glasnap, D. (1974). Comparative reliabilities and difficulties of the multiple-choice and true-false formats. *Journal of Experimental Education, 42*(3), 62–64.

Otis, A. S., & Lennon, R. T. (1990). *Technical manual: Otis-Lennon School Ability Test.* San Antonio: Psychological Corporation.

Paulson, F. L., Paulson, P. R., & Meyer, C. A. (1991). What makes a portfolio a portfolio? *Educational Leadership, 49*(5), 60–63.

Pearson, K. (1924). Historical note on the origin of the normal curve of errors. *Biometrika, 16,* 402–404.

Performance Assessment Laboratory. (1992, Winter). Proposed assessment system. *ADL Review, 2*(1), 2–3.

Perkins, D. N., & Salomon, G. (1989). Are cognitive skills context-bound? *Educational Researcher, 18,* 16–25.

Peterson, N. S., Kolen, M. J., & Hoover, H. D. (1989). Scaling, norming, and equating. In R. L. Linn (Ed.), *Educational measurement* (3rd ed., pp. 221–262). Phoenix: Oryx Press.

Pfanzagl, J. (1968). *Theory of measurement.* New York: Wiley.

Phillips, B. N., & Weathers, G. (1958). Analysis of errors made in scoring standardized tests. *Educational and Psychological Measurement, 18,* 563–567.

Phillips, S. E. (1994). High-stakes testing accommodations: Validity versus disabled rights. *Applied Measurement in Education, 7,* 93–120.

Pike, L. A. (1978). *Short-term instruction, test-wiseness, and the Scholastic Aptitude Test: A literature review with research recommendations.* (College Entrance Examination Board Research and Development Report 77–78, No. 2 and *Educational Testing Service Research Bulletin,* No. 78–2). Princeton, NJ: Educational Testing Service.

Plake, B. S., Impara, J. C., & Fager, J. J. (1993). Assessment competencies of teachers: A national survey. *Educational Measurement: Issues and Practice, 12*(4), 10–12, 39.

Popham, W. J. (1991). Appropriateness of teacher's test-preparation practices. *Educational Measurement: Issues and Practice, 10*(4), 12–15.

Portland House (1989). *Webster's encyclopedic unabridged dictionary of the English language.* New York: Author.

Preece, P. F. W. (1976). Mapping cognitive structure: A comparison of methods. *Journal of Educational Psychology, 68,* 1–8.

Prescott, G. A., Balow, I. H., Hogan, T. P., & Farr, R. C. (1978). *Metropolitan achievement tests (Complete Survey Battery, Intermediate, Form JS).* New York: Harcourt Brace Jovanovich.

Prichert, J. W., & Anderson, R. C. (1977). Taking different perspectives on a story. *Journal of Educational Psychology, 69,* 309–315.

Psychological Corporation. (1985). *Stanford diagnostic mathematics test* (3rd ed.), *Red Level, Form H.* Monterey, CA: Author.

Psychological Corporation. (1993). *Practice test: Otis-Lennon School Ability Test (OSLAT) Level D* (7th ed.). San Antonio: Author.

Psychological Corporation. (1990). *Resources for measuring educational performance.* San Antonio: Author.

Psychological Corporation. (1990). *Technical manual: Otis-Lennon School Ability Test* (6th ed.). San Antonio: Author.

Psychological Corporation. (1991). *The differential aptitude tests* (5th ed.): *Fall norms booklet.* San Antonio: Author.

Psychological Corporation. (1992a). *Focus on: Enhanced multiple-choice questions.* San Antonio: Author.

Psychological Corporation. (1992b). *Task 981 Clean Water Integrated Assessment System: Directions for Administering.* San Antonio: Author.

Psychological Corporation. (1993a). *Metropolitan Achievement Test* (7th ed.) *Forms S/T, fall.* San Antonio: Author.

Psychological Corporation. (1993b). *Technical manual: Metropolitan Achievement Test* (7th ed.) *Spring data.* San Antonio: Author.

Psychological Corporation. (1994). *Resources for measuring educational performance.* San Antonio: Author.

Public Law 94–142. (1975). Education for All Handicapped Children Act of 1975. *U.S. Code,* vol. 28 (section 1401 et seq.).

Purves, A. (1971). Evaluation of Learning in Literature. In B. S. Bloom, J. T. Hastings,

& G. F. Madaus (Eds.), *Handbook on formative and summative evaluation of student learning* (pp. 697–766). New York: McGraw-Hill.

Quellmalz, E. S. (1991). Developing criteria for performance assessments: The missing link. *Applied Measurement in Education, 4,* 319–331.

Ramseyer, G. C., & Cashen, V. M. (1971). The effects of practice sessions on the use of separate answer sheets by first and second graders. *Journal of Educational Measurement, 8,* 177–181.

Ravelo, N. E., & Nitko, A. J. (1988). Selection bias according to a new model and four previous models using admission data from a Latin American University. *Applied Measurement in Education, 20,* 105–119.

Reitman, J. S., & Rueter, H. H. (1980). Organization revealed by recall orders and confirmed by pauses. *Cognitive Psychology, 12,* 554–581.

Reschly, D. J. (1993). Consequences and incentives: Implications for inclusion/exclusion decisions regarding students with disabilities in state and national assessment programs. In J. E. Ysseldyke & M. L. Thurlow (Eds.), *Views on inclusion and testing accommodations for students with disabilities* (pp. 35–46). Minneapolis: National Center on Educational Outcomes, University of Minnesota.

Resnick, L. B. (1975). *The science and art of curriculum design* (Publication No. 1975/9). Pittsburgh: University of Pittsburgh, Learning Research and Development Center.

Resnick, L. B. (1976). Task analysis in instructional design: Some cases from mathematics. In D. Klahr (Ed.), *Cognition and instruction.* Hillsdale, NJ: Lawrence Erlbaum.

Resnick. L. B. (1989). *Tests as standards of achievement in schools.* Paper presented at the ETS Invitational Conference: The Uses of Standardized Tests in American Education, New York.

Resnick, L. B., Wang, M. C., & Kaplan, J. (1973). Task analysis in curriculum design: A hierarchically sequenced introductory mathematics curriculum. *Journal of Applied Behavior Analysis, 6,* 679–710.

Roberts, M. (1994, October). Testing accommodations for students with disabilities. *Teaching Times,* 7–8.

Robertson, G. J. (1990). A practical model for test development. In C. R. Reynolds and R. W. Kamphaus (Eds.), *Handbook of psychological and educational assessment of children: Intelligence and achievement* (pp. 62–85). New York: Guilford Press.

Royer, J. M., Cisero, C. A., & Carlo, M. S. (1993). Techniques and procedures for assessing cognitive skills. *Review of Educational Research, 63,* 201–243.

Rozeboom, W. W. (1966). Scaling theory and the nature of measurement. *Synthese, 16,* 170–233.

Rudner, L. M., & Boston, C. (1994). Performance assessment. *The ERIC Review, 3*(1), 2–12.

Rudner, L. M., Conoley, J. C., & Plake, B. S. (1989). *Understanding achievement tests: A guide for school administrators.* Washington, DC: The ERIC Clearinghouse on Tests, Measurements, and Evaluation.

Rulon, P. J. (1939). A simplified procedure for determining the reliability of a test by split halves. *Harvard Educational Review, 9,* 99–103.

Sanders, J. R. (1989). Joint Committee for Standard for Teacher Competence in Educational Assessment of Students. *Educational Measurement: Issues and Practice, 8*(2), 25–30.

Sanders, N. M. (1966). *Classroom questions: What kinds?* New York: Harper & Row.

Sarason, I. G. (Ed.) (1980). *Test anxiety: Theory, research, and application.* Hillsdale, NJ: Lawrence Erlbaum.

Sarason, I. G. (1984). Stress, anxiety, and cognitive interference: Reactions to tests. *Journal of Personality and Social Psychology, 46,* 929–938.

Sarnacki, R. E. (1979). An examination of test-wiseness in the cognitive test domain. *Review of Educational Research, 49,* 252–279.

Sattler, J. M. (1992). *Assessment of children* (3rd ed.). San Diego: Author.

Sattler, J. M. (1992). *Assessment of children: WSC-III and WPPSI-R supplement.* San Diego: Author.

Sax, G. (1974). *Principles of educational measurement and evaluation.* Belmont, CA: Wadsworth.

Sax, G. (1980). *Study guide for principles of educational measurement and evaluation* (2nd ed.). Belmont, CA: Wadsworth.

Sax, G. (1989). *Principles of educational and psychological measurement and evaluation.* Belmont, CA: Wadsworth.

Scannell, D. P., & Marshall, J. C. (1966). The effects of selected composition errors on the grades assigned to essay examinations. *American Educational Research Journal, 3,* 125–130.

Schafer, W. D. (1991). Essential assessment skills in professional education of teachers. *Educational Measurement: Issues and Practice, 10*(1), 3–6.

Schmeiser, C. B. (1992). Ethical codes in the professions. *Educational Measurement: Issues and Practice, 11*(4), 5–11.

Schmidt, W. H. (1983). Content bias in achievement tests. *Journal of Educational Measurement, 20,* 165–178.

Scriven, M. (1967). *The methodology of evaluation. AERA monograph series on curriculum evaluation* (Publication No. 1). Chicago: Rand McNally.

Shalaway, L. (1993). Perfecting parent conferences. *Instructor, 103*(1), 58–66, 64.

Shalaway, L. (1998). *Learning to teach . . . Not just for beginners.* New York: Scholastic Professional Books.

Shank, R. C., & Ableson, R. (1977). *Scripts, plans, goals and understanding.* Hillsdale, NJ: Lawrence Erlbaum.

Shannon, G. A. (1973). *The construction of matching tests: An empirical statement.* Master's thesis, University of Pittsburgh.

Shavelson, R. J. (1985). Schemata and teaching routines: A historical perspective. Paper presented at the annual meeting of the American Educational Research Association, Chicago.

Shavelson, R. J., & Baxter, G. P. (1991). Performance assessment in science. *Applied measurement in Education, 4,* 347–362.

Shavelson, R. J., & Stanton, G. C. (1975). Construct validation: Methodology and application to three measures of cognitive structure. *Journal of Education Measurement, 12,* 67–85.

Shavelson, R. J., & Stern, P. (1981). Research on teacher's pedagogical thoughts, judgments, decisions, and behavior. *Review of Educational Research, 51,* 455–498.

Shepard, L. A. (1990). Inflated test score gains: Is the problem old norms or teaching the test? *Educational Measurement: Issues and Practice, 9*(3), 15–22.

Shepard, L. A. (1991). Interview on assessment issues with Lorrie Shepard. *Educational Researcher, 20*(3), 21–23.

Shepard, L. A. (1993). Evaluating test validity. *Review of Research in Education, 19,* 405–450.

Shuell, T. J. (1990). Phrases of meaning learning. *Review of Educational Psychology, 60,* 531–548.

Silver, E. A., Smith, M. S., & Nelson, B. S. (1995). The QUAAR Project: Equity concerns meet mathematics education reform in middle school. In W. Secada, E. Fennema, & L. Byrd (Ed.), *New directions for equity in mathematics education.* New York: Cambridge University Press.

Silver, H., Strong, R., & Perini, M. (1997). Integrating learning styles and multiple intelligences. *Educational Leadership, 55*(1), 22–27.

Simon, H. A. (1973). The structure of ill-structured problems. *Artificial Intelligence, 4,* 181–201.

Slakter, M. J., Koehler, R. A., & Hampton, S. H. (1970). Grade level, sex, and selected aspects of test-wiseness. *Journal of Educational Measurement, 7,* 119–122.

Slavin, R. E. (1988). Cooperative learning and student achievement. *Educational Leadership, 46*(2), 31–33.

Smith, M. L. (1997). *Reforming schools by reforming assessment: Consequences of the Arizona Student Assessment Program (ASAP): Equity and teacher capacity building.* CSE Technical Report 425, Los Angeles: National Cancer for Research on Evaluation, Standards, and Student Testing, UCLA.

Smith, M. L., & Rottenberg, C. (1991). Unintended consequences of external testing in elementary schools. *Educational Measurement: Issues and Practice, 10*(4), 7–11.

Snow, R. E. (1980). Aptitudes and achievement. In W. B. Schrader (Ed.), *Measuring achievement: Progress over a decade.* Proceedings of the 1979 ETS Invitational Conference. New Directions for Testing and Measurement (No. 5). San Francisco: Jossey-Bass.

Spandel, V., & Stiggins, R. J. (1990). *Creating writers: Linking assessment and writing instruction.* New York: Longman.

Sparrow, S. S., Balla, D., & Cicchetti, D. V. (1984). *Vineland adaptive behavior scales: Expanded form.* Circle Pines, MN: American Guidance Service.

Spearman, C. (1910). Correlation calculated from faulty data. *British Journal of Psychology, 3,* 271–295.

Stalnaker, J. M. (1936). A study of optional questions in examinations. *School and Society, 44,* 829–832.

Stalnaker, J. M. (1951). The essay type of examination. In E. F. Lindquist (Ed.), *Educational measurement.* Washington, DC: American Council on Education.

Stanley, J. C. (1971). Reliability. In R. L. Thorndike (Ed.), *Educational measurement* (2nd ed.). Washington, DC: American Council on Education.

Stanley, J. C., & Hopkins, K. D. (1972). *Educational and psychological measurement* (5th ed.). Englewood Cliffs, NJ: Prentice Hall.

Sternberg, R. J. (1984). Preface. In R. J. Sternberg (Ed.), *Mechanisms of cognitive development.* San Francisco: W. H. Freeman.

Stevens, S. S. (1951). Mathematics, measurement, and psychophysics. In S. S. Stevens (Ed.), *Handbook of experimental psychology.* New York: Wiley.

Stiggins, R. J. (1987). Design and development of performance assessments: An NCME instructional module. *Educational Measurement: Issues and Practice, 6*(3), 33–42.

Stiggins, R. J. (1991). Relevant classroom assessment training for teachers. *Educational Measurement: Issues and Practice, 10*(1), 7–12.

Stiggins, R. J. (1994). *Student-centered classroom assessment.* Englewood Cliffs, NJ: Merrill/Prentice Hall.

Stiggins, R. J., Conklin, N. F., & Associates. (1992). *In teachers' hands: Investigating the practice of classroom assessment.* Albany, NY: SUNY Press.

Stiggins, R. J., Frisbie, D. A., & Griswold, P. A. (1989). Inside high school grading practices: Building a research agenda. *Educational Measurement: Issues and Practice, 8*(2), 5–14.

Stiggins, R. J., Rubel, E., & Quellmalz, E. (1986). *Measuring thinking skills in the classroom.* Washington, DC: National Educational Association.

Stodola, Q. (1961). *Making the classroom test: A guide for teacher* (No. 4. Evaluation and Advisory Services). Princeton, NH: Educational Service.

Strang, H. R. (1977). The effects of technical and unfamiliar options upon guessing on multiple-choice test items. *Journal of Educational Measurement, 14,* 253–260.

Subkoviak, M. J. (1976). Estimating reliability from a single administration of a criterion-referenced test. *Journal of Educational Measurement, 13,* 265–276.

Subkoviak, M. J. (1980). Decision consistency approaches. In R. A. Berk (Ed.), *Criterion-referenced measurement: The state of the art.* Baltimore: Johns Hopkins University Press.

Super, D. E. (1947). Vocational interest and vocational choice. *Educational and Psychological Measurement, 7,* 375–384.

Super, D. E. (1949). *Appraising vocational fitness.* New York: Harper & Row.

Suppes, P. (1974). A survey of cognition in handicapped children. *Review of Educational Research, 44,* 145–176.

Suppes, P., & Zinnes, J. L. (1963). Basic measurement theory. In R. D. Luce, R. R. Bush, & E. Galanter (Eds.), *Handbook of mathematical psychology* (vol. 1). New York: Wiley.

Surber, J. R. (1984). Mapping as a testing and diagnostic device. In C. D. Holley & D. F. Dansereau, *Spatial learning strategies: Tech-*

niques, applications, and related issues. Orlando: Academic Press, pp. 213–233.

Surber, J. R., & Smith, P. L. (1981). Testing for misunderstanding. *Educational Psychologist, 16*, 165–174.

Swaminathan, H., Hambleton, R. K., & Algina, J. (1974). Reliability of criterion-referenced tests: A decision-theoretic formulation. *Journal of Educational Measurement, 11*, 263–267.

Sweetland, R. C., & Keyser, D. J. (1985–1987). *Test critiques: Volumes I to VI*. Kansas City, MO: Test Corporation of America.

Sweetland, R. C., & Keyser, D. J. (1986). *Tests: A comprehensive reference for assessments in psychology, education, and business* (2nd ed.). Kansas City, MO: Test Corporation of America.

Tallmadge, G. K. (1973, March). *An analysis of the relationship between reading and mathematics achievement gains and per pupil expenditures in California Title I projects: Fiscal year 1972* (AIR-35100-3/73-FR). Palo Alto, CA: American Institutes for Research.

Tallmadge, G. K., & Horst, D. (1974). *A procedural guide for validating achievement gains in educational projects* (rev.) (RMC Report UR-240). Los Altos, CA: RMC Research Corporation.

Tallmadge, G. K., & Wood, C. T. (1976). *User's guide (ESEA Title I Evaluation and Reporting System)*. Mountain View, CA: RMC Research Corporation.

Taylor, C. S. (1998). An investigation of scoring methods for mathematics performance-based assessments. *Educational Assessment, 5*, 195–224.

Taylor, E. D., & Nuttall, D. L. (1974). Question choice in examinations: An experiment in geography and science. *Educational Research, 16*, 143–150.

Terry, P. W. (1933). How students review for objective and essay tests. *Elementary School Journal, 33*, 592–603.

Terwilliger, J. S. (1971). *Assigning grades to students*. Glenview, IL: Scott, Foresman.

Terwilliger, J. S. (1989). Classroom standard-setting and grading practices. *Educational Measurement: Issues and Practice, 8*, 15–19.

Test Takers' Rights Working Group. (1994). *Draft statement of test takers' rights*. Washington, DC: American Psychological Association, Joint Committee on Testing Practices.

Thorndike, E. L. (1910). Handwriting. *Teacher's College Record, 11*, 1–93.

Thorndike, R. L. (1949). *Personal selection: Test and measurement technique*. New York: John Wiley & Sons.

Thorndike, R. L. (1951). Reliability. In E. F. Lindquist (Ed.), *Educational measurement*. Washington, DC: American Council on Education.

Thorndike, R. L. (1971). Concepts of culture fairness. *Journal of Educational Measurement, 8*, 63–70.

Thorndike, R. L., & Hagen, E. P. (1977). *Measurement and evaluation in psychology and education* (4th ed.). New York: John Wiley & Sons.

Thorndike, R. M., Cunningham, G. K., Thorndike, R. L., & Hagen, E. P. (1991). *Measurement and evaluation in psychology and education.* (5th Ed.) New York: Macmillan.

Tippets, E., & Benson, J. (1989). The effect of item arrangement on test anxiety. *Applied Measurement in Education, 2*, 289–296.

Tittle, C. K. (1989). Validity: Whose construct is it in the teaching and learning context? *Educational Measurement: Issues and Practice, 8*(1), 5–13, 34.

Tittle, C. K., Hecht, D., & Moore, P. (1993). Assessment theory and research for classrooms: From taxonomies to constructing meaning in context. *Educational Measurement: Issues and Practice, 12*(4), 13–19.

Tobias, S. (1992). The impact of test anxiety on cognition in school learning. (pp. 18–31). In K. A. Hagtvet and T. Baker Johnson (Eds.), *Advances in test anxiety research*. Amsterdam: Swets and Zeitlinger.

Touchstone Applied Science Associates. (1995a). *Degrees of reading power and degrees of word meaning: An overview*. Brewster, NY: Author.

Touchstone Applied Science Associates. (1995b). *DPR catalog*. Brewster, NY: Author.

Tryon, G. S. (1980). The measurement and treatment of test anxiety. *Review of Educational Research, 50*, 343–372.

Tuckman, B. W. (1988). *Testing for teachers* (2nd ed.). San Diego: Harcourt Brace Jovanovich.

Tuinman, J. J., Farr, R., & Blanton, B. E. (1972). Increases in test scores as a function of material rewards. *Journal of Educational Measurement, 9*, 215–223.

Tyler, F. T., & Chalmers, T. M. (1943). The effect on scores of warning junior high school pupils of coming tests. *Journal of Educational Research, 37*, 290–296.

Tyler, R. W. (1930). A test of skill in using a microscope. *Educational Research Bulletin, 9*, 493–496.

Tyler, R. W. (1934). *Constructing achievement tests*. Columbus, OH: Ohio State University.

Tyler, R. W. (1966). The objectives and plans for a National Assessment of Educational Progress. *Journal of Educational Measurement, 3*, 1–4.

United States Supreme Court. (1971). *Griggs et al., Petitioners vs. Duke Power Company* (Publication No. 125, 401 U.S. 424, decided March 8, 1971).

Urevbu, A. O. (1984). School science curriculum and innovation: An African perspective. *European Journal of Science Education, 6*, 217–225.

Valencia, S. W., & Place, N. A. (1994). Literacy portfolios for teaching, learning, and accountability: The Bellevue Literacy Assessment Project. In S. W. Valencia, E. H. Hiebert, & P. P. Afferbach (Eds.), *Authentic reading assessment: Practices and possibilities*. Newark, DE: International Reading Association.

Vallance, T. R. (1947). Comparison of essay and objective examinations as learning experiences. *Journal of Educational Research, 41*, 279–288.

Vernon, P. E. (1962). The determinants of reading comprehension. *Educational and Psychological Measurement, 22*, 269–286.

Viadero, D. (1995). New assessments have little effect on contract, study finds. *Education Week, 14*(40), 6.

Wagner, R. K., & Sternberg, R. J. (1984). Alternate conceptions of intelligence and their implications for education. *Review of Educational Research, 54*, 179–223.

Wang, M. C. (1980). Adaptive instruction: Building on diversity. *Theory into Practice, 19*, 122–128. (Reprinted as Reports to Educators 5. Pittsburgh: University of Pittsburgh, Learning Research and Development Center.)

Wang, M. C., Gennari, P., & Waxman, H. C. (1983). *The adaptive learning environments model: An innovative variation on a recurrent theme*. Pittsburgh: University of Pittsburgh, Learning Research and Development Center.

Wang, M. C., & Resnick, L. B. (1978). *The primary education program: Manuals 1–8*. Johnstown, PA: Mafex Associates.

Wang, X-b. Wainer, H., & Thissen, D. (1995). On the viability of some untestable assumptions in equating exams that allow examinee choice. *Applied Measurement in Education, 8*, 211–225.

Waples, D., & Tyler, R. W. (1930). *Research methods and teacher problems*. New York: Macmillan.

Watkins, R. W. (1962). *Addenda to report of recommendations to the Testing Operations Board on the use of formula and rights scores*. Princeton, NJ: Educational Testing Service. (Unpublished report cited in R. L. Ebel, Essentials of educational measurement. Englewood Cliffs, NJ: Prentice Hall, 1972.)

Watman, K. K., & Frisbie, D. A. (1994). Parents' understanding of their children's report cards. *Applied Measurement in Education, 7*, 223–240.

Wechsler, D. (1939). *The measurement of adult intelligence*. Baltimore: Williams & Wilkins.

Weidemann, C. C. (1926). How to construct the true-false examination. *Teachers College, Columbia University. Contributions to Education* (No. 225). New York: Bureau of Publications, Teachers College, Columbia University.

Wesley, E. B., & Wronski, S. P. (1958). *Teaching social studies in high schools* (4th ed.). Boston: D.C. Heath.

Wesman, A. G. (1971). Writing the test item. In R. L. Thorndike (Ed.), *Educational measurement* (2nd ed.). Washington, DC: American Council on Education.

Whitney, D. R., & Sabers, D. L. (1970, May). *Improving essay examinations III: Use of item analysis*. (Technical Bulletin No. 11) Iowa City: University Evaluation and Examination Service, The University of Iowa.

Wick, J. W. and others. (1989). *School attitude measure* (2nd ed.). Iowa City, IA: American Techtronics.

Wiggins, G. (1990). *The case for authentic assessment*. (EDD-TM-9010). Washington, DC: ERIC Clearinghouse on Tests, Measurement, and Evaluation, American Institutes for Research.

Williams, R. L. (1975). THE BITCH-100: A culture-specific test. *Journal of Afro-American Issues, 3*, 103–116.

Wilson, J. A. (1976). Question choice in A-Level Physics. *Curriculum Studies, 8*, 71–78.

Wine, J. (1971). Test anxiety and direction of attention. *Psychological Bulletin, 76*, 92–104.

Wiser, B., & Lenke, J. M. (1987, April). *The stability of achievement test norms over time.* Paper presented at the Annual Meeting of the National Council on Measurement in Education, Washington, DC.

Wolf, D. P. (1989). Portfolio assessment: Sampling student work. *Educational Leadership, 46(2),* 4–10.

Wood, R. (1977). Multiple choice: A state of the art report. *Evaluation in Education: International Progress, 1,* 191–280.

Woolfolk, A. E. (1995). *Educational Psychology* (6th ed.). Boston: Allyn & Bacon.

Young, M. J. (1993). *Quantitative measures for the assessment of declarative knowledge structure characteristics.* Unpublished doctoral dissertation, University of Pittsburgh, Pittsburgh, PA.

Zoref, L., & Williams, P. (1980). A look at content bias in IQ tests. *Journal of Educational Measurement, 17,* 313–322.

Zuckerman, M., & Spielberger, C. D. (Eds.). (1976). *Emotion and anxiety: New concepts, methods, and applications.* New York: Lawrence Erlbaum.

AUTHOR INDEX

SUBJECT INDEX